International and Cultural Psychology

Series Editor: Anthony J. Marsella, Ph.D.

For further volumes:
http://www.springer.com/series/6089

Gideon Arulmani • Anuradha J. Bakshi •
Frederick T.L. Leong • A.G. Watts
Editors

Handbook of Career Development

International Perspectives

 Springer

Editors
Gideon Arulmani
The Promise Foundation
Bangalore
India

Frederick T.L. Leong
Michigan State University
East Lansing
MI, USA

Anuradha J. Bakshi
Department of Human Development
Nirmala Niketan College of Home Science,
     University of Mumbai
Mumbai
India

A.G. Watts
National Institute for Careers
     Education and Counselling
Cambridge
United Kingdom

ISSN 1574-0455
ISBN 978-1-4614-9459-1   ISBN 978-1-4614-9460-7 (eBook)
DOI 10.1007/978-1-4614-9460-7
Springer New York Heidelberg Dordrecht London

Library of Congress Control Number: 2013957934

This handbook is dedicated to all those who work towards the realization of human potential among individuals and communities across the world.

Preface

This handbook has been compiled in response to calls to broaden the knowledge base which informs the disciplines and services that pertain to career and workforce development. Accusing the West of being overbearing has become repetitive and these arguments have not gone much beyond vehement rhetoric. It is also being increasingly recognized that traditional bodies of knowledge offer epistemologies that can guide the generation of hypotheses, the formulation of research designs, and the creation of methods and techniques for practical applications. The time is ripe for us to draw from the wisdom and experiences of different cultures to consider both universal and specific principles for guidance and counseling that are socially and economically relevant to the contemporary situation.

A first step towards addressing these issues was taken by organizing an international conference on work and career under the aegis of International Association for Educational and Vocational Guidance (IAEVG) and The Promise Foundation (an Indian nongovernmental organization) in Bangalore, India, in October 2010. A careful process was followed in the conference through which a team of international scholars interacted with those who submitted papers to the conference, and helped them to develop papers that addressed the concerns raised above (for details see www.jivacareer.org). This conference forms the primary knowledge base for this handbook. Many of the chapters have been adapted from papers presented at the conference by researchers, practitioners, academics, and policymakers. Other scholars have been invited to address themes that were not covered at the conference.

This handbook also responds to calls for the discipline of career guidance and counseling to be informed by interdisciplinary dialogues. Therefore, in addition to career psychologists and sociologists, the handbook has writers from the fields of human development, economics, development studies, educational planning, environment and ecology, special needs, business and commerce, tribal studies, philosophy, and history. Stimulating the development of a literature in contexts where a field of activity is in its infancy requires close collaborations between scholars established in the field and fresh contributors. Many of the chapters in this book are the result of such collaborations, and several chapters carry data and constructs that have not appeared before in the literature.

Keeping the overall objectives of the book in mind, another feature is an attempt to maintain vertical and horizontal thematic consistency. Hence two sections are common to all chapters. These are multiple frames of reference for career guidance practitioners—sensitivity to the universal and the particular; and new concepts and viewpoints—charting new directions. This handbook rests upon the matrix of culture: a matter that has grown to acquire vital significance in a globalizing world of work. We invite the reader to look for the cultural thread that runs through the handbook.

Against this background, the handbook is designed as an academically sound teaching and reference book to be used for senior classes/advanced educational levels, as well as a practical resource book for practitioners. Many of our authors have generously provided original research instruments, questionnaires, checklists, and worksheets as part of their contributions.

An enterprise such as this depends upon a wide range of contributions. Other than us, this book is the work of 50 participating authors from different parts of the world. For their complete immersion in this project, for their forbearance with our many editorial requests, and of course for their stellar contributions, we are grateful. We thank our international team of reviewers who gave of their time generously and responded without hesitation to our short deadlines. The voluntary assistance provided by the staff at The Promise Foundation (Sajma Aravind, Kala B., and Robert D'Souza) at every stage of development of the project, from corresponding with authors, to proofreading, reference checking, developing the indexes, copyediting, and creating the graphics, often went well beyond the call of duty. For their unstinting and efficient support, we owe a debt of gratitude. We are deeply thankful to the Jacobs Foundation, for supporting this project with a generous grant. We are also grateful to the Nirmala Niketan College of Home Science, University of Mumbai, India, for their support. Tony Marsella, the editor of this series, saw the value of a work such as this and we thank him for his encouragement and endorsement. We are grateful to our editors at Springer, Sharon Panulla and Sylvana Ruggirello, who have been a constant source of motivation and have kept us on track. We are also thankful to our families for their invaluable support, and to our students. Finally, we thank in anticipation all those of you who will read this book and perhaps use it in your teaching, learning, research, and practice. We hope it will match your expectations, open new dimensions, and contribute in some way to the very important work you are doing. We look forward to your comments and feedback.

Bangalore, India   Gideon Arulmani
Mumbai, India   Anuradha J. Bakshi
East Lansing, MI, USA   Frederick T.L. Leong
Cambridge, UK   A.G. Watts
August 2013

Author Biography

Heidi Agbenyo is Senior Manager, Stakeholder Communications at the City and Guilds Centre for Skills Development (CSD). Heidi has an honors degree from St John's College, University of Cambridge, UK. She has managed a number of research projects on behalf of CSD, including a project that explored young people's experiences of careers advice and guidance in India, and careers advice and guidance for disadvantaged adults in the UK. *email*: heidi.agbenyo@skillsdevelopment.org

Sandra Albert, a former professor of dermatology, now works in public health at the Indian Institute of Public Health, Shillong, India. Her research interests include indigenous knowledge and indigenous health systems. Currently she is a Wellcome Trust Research Fellow at the London School of Hygiene & Tropical Medicine and the Public Health Foundation of India (PHFI). She was supported by a Wellcome Trust Capacity Strengthening Strategic Award to the PHFI and a consortium of UK universities. *email*: sandrashillong@gmail.com

Nirmala Almeida, Ph.D., Associate Professor, Department of Human Development, Nirmala Niketan, College of Home Science, Mumbai, has 35 years of teaching experience and has guided doctoral students. She has made numerous presentations at conferences, won awards, and has several publications. She is an invited special resource person on the Board of Studies at Universities and a consultant to NGOs. Counselling and Health Psychology are her special interest areas. *email*: nirmala.almeida@gmail.com

Nancy Arthur, Ph.D., is a Professor and Canada Research Chair in Professional Education, Educational Studies in Counselling Psychology, Werklund School of Education, University of Calgary, Calgary, Alberta, Canada. Dr. Arthur's research and teaching interests include professional education for cultural diversity and social justice, international transitions, and career development. She has developed curriculum on career development theory and counseling for classroom and distributed learning formats. She authored the book, Counseling International Students: Clients from Around the World. Her co-edited and coauthored book, Culture-Infused Counselling, received the Canadian Counselling Association Book Award. Her co-edited book, Case Incidents in Counselling for International Transitions, involved collaboration with authors from 12 countries. Dr. Arthur has published extensively about professional education and practice issues regarding career development and multicultural counseling. Dr. Arthur currently serves on the Board of Governors for the Canadian Career Development Foundation and the International Association for Educational and Vocational Guidance. Dr. Arthur is a registered psychologist. *email*: narthur@ucalgary.ca

Gideon Arulmani, Ph.D., is a clinical psychologist with an M.Phil. in Medical and Social Psychology from the National Institute of Mental Health and Neurosciences (NIMHANS), and a doctoral degree in Career Psychology from the University of Portsmouth, UK. He is the Founder and Managing Trustee of The Promise Foundation, Bangalore, India. His interests lie in the interdisciplinary understanding of the human potential. He has developed the Cultural Preparation Process Model of Career Development and formulated comprehensive culture-resonant systems of career counseling for India and other countries. He has also developed curricula for capacity building at the certificate, master's, and doctoral levels. He is the President of the Indian Association for Career and Livelihood Planning; a member of the Executive Board of International Association for Educational and Vocational Guidance; an International Fellow of the Consortium for Multicultural Psychology Research, USA; an International Fellow of the National Institute for Education and Counselling, Cambridge, UK; Visiting Senior Lecturer at the University of Canterbury Christ Church, UK; Visiting Professor at the Martin Luther Christian University, Meghalaya; and international consultant to a number of multilateral agencies. He is a reviewer and associate editor for a wide range of journals of psychology and counseling. His other interests include documentary film making, photography, folklore, historical fiction, craft, jewelry design, and wine making. *email*: garulmani@t-p-f.org

Anuradha J. Bakshi, Ph.D., is an Associate Professor and Head of the Human Development Specialization at the Nirmala Niketan College of Home Science, University of Mumbai, India. She is teaching in the B.S., M.S., and doctoral programs in Human Development. She has been teaching at the university level for over 20 years, and has taught at multiple colleges and universities. She also has extensive research experience, including coordination of national- and international-funded projects as well as research work with graduate students.

She is the Vice President of the Indian Association for Career and Livelihood Planning, and a Managing Editor of the *Indian Journal of Career and Livelihood Planning*. She is also an Associate Editor of the *Research Reach: Journal of Home Science*. She has been a Guest Editor of a special issue of the *International Journal for Educational and Vocational Guidance*. She has been appointed to one of the Board of Studies at the University of Mumbai, and curriculum development is one of her special strengths. Her specialty areas in teaching include research methods and statistics, and theories and models of human development. She is especially drawn to the convergence and divergence between Western psychological and Indian philosophical and spiritual literatures. She has been researching varied areas with her students, including spirituality, positive psychology, education, youth services, and career development. Her recent publications are in the area of career development. With higher educational qualifications from both India and the USA, she is particularly sensitive to cultural differences, and not just between two or more countries but also within a country. As a resident of Mumbai, she is encouraged by the overall indomitable spirit of enterprise and agency in Mumbai. *email*: anustra@gmail.com

Barbara Bassot, Ph.D., is a Senior Lecturer at the Centre for Career and Personal Development at Canterbury Christ Church University, UK. She teaches Reflective Practice in a range of programs at undergraduate and postgraduate levels. She is the Course Director for the Certificate in Careers Education and Guidance and the Certificate in Career Guidance and Development. Her research interests are in social constructivist approaches to career learning and development, and reflective practice. *email*: barbara.bassot@canterbury.ac.uk

Jenny Bimrose, Ph.D., is Deputy Director of the Institute for Employment Research, University of Warwick. Previously, she was Head of Centre for Training in Careers Guidance at the University of East London. With over 30 years' experience in higher education, researching, and teaching at the postgraduate level, Jenny is a Fellow of the Institute for Career Guidance, a Fellow of the Higher Education Academy, a Research Associate at the Nelson Mandela Metropolitan University, South Africa, and Coeditor for the *British Journal for Guidance and Counselling*. Many of her recent research projects have focused on the policy, theory, and practice of career counseling and guidance. An area of special interest is gender, especially older women. Other ongoing research interests include career adaptability, decision-making styles, career trajectories of mid-career workers in Europe, and the use of ICT and labor market information in career guidance. *email*: Jenny.Bimrose@warwick.ac.uk

William Borgen, Ph.D., has conducted research and has developed programs in the area of life transitions and career development for several years. His work has been adapted for use in Bhutan, Denmark, Finland, Hungary, and Sweden. In 2005, he was awarded an honorary doctorate from the University of Umea in Sweden, and was the President of the International Association for Counselling from 1998 to 2006. He was elected to the Board of Directors of the International Association for Educational and Vocational Guidance in 2011. *email*: william.borgen@ubc.ca

Alan Brown, Ph.D., is a Professorial Fellow at the Institute for Employment Research at the University of Warwick. His current research, which has a strong international orientation, focuses mainly upon changing occupational identities; workplace learning; vocational education and training; skill formation; organizational performance; and networks and supporting knowledge sharing, learning, and development in professional communities of practice. He was involved in the development of the UK's National Guidance Research Forum, a knowledge-sharing site that has considerable material on research and practice in career guidance, and research on lifelong learning and work-related learning. *email*: Alan.Brown@warwick.ac.uk

Stelina Chatzichristou, an economist by training has specialized in policy analysis. Stelina holds a B.A. in political science and economics and an M. Sc. in accounting and finance. She has significant experience in policy analysis and research, focusing primarily on education and training, labor market, and entrepreneurship. *email*: cstelina@gmail.com

Kathleen Collett is Senior Manager for Research and Economics at the City and Guilds Centre for Skills Development (CSD). Kathleen has an honors degree in the economics of education from Stellenbosch University, South Africa, where she wrote her thesis on the differential impact of education funding on different community groups. She also has a master's in Politics from Oxford University, and has authored several papers on community involvement in vocational training. Kathleen coauthored CSD's 2010 report Training for Rural Development. *email*: kathleen.collett@skillsdevelopment. org

V. R. Devika, Ph.D., founder and managing trustee of The Aseema Trust, a nonprofit organization for linking traditional performing arts and education and Mahatma Gandhi and education, is a cultural activist who has a passion for performing arts and education. She has received many awards for her contribution to arts and education. Devika was awarded a Ph.D., by the Department of Philosophy, University of Madras, for her work on "Gandhian communication for transformation: Philosophical issues and dimensions." She conducts regular workshops on charka-spinning, peace education, and communication skills for students and teachers. She is a freelance art critic contributing to leading publications, gives illustrated lectures on arts and culture of India, and has travelled extensively around the world. *email*: vrdevika@gmail.com

Rènette du Toit, Ph.D., is Research Manager at EE Research Focus, South Africa. *email*: renette@researchfocus.co.za

Simon Easton is a Chartered Clinical Psychologist, and lectures in clinical and counseling psychology in the Psychology Department of the University of Portsmouth, UK. Simon has worked for many years with various UK private and public sector organizations as consultant and clinician. Alongside his work to tackle stress and distress both within and without the workplace, Simon worked with Dr. Darren Van Laar to offer surveys and management support and consultancy using psychometrically sound questionnaires. That work has led to the development of the Work Related Quality of Life measure, which has to date been used in many countries and cultures and translated into several languages. *email*: simon.easton@port.ac.uk

Lea Ferrari, Ph.D., is an assistant professor in the Department of Developmental Psychology and Socialization, University of Padua, Italy. Her research is in the area of school-career counseling. She is a member of professors of the postgraduate master's course in School-Career Counseling. She is also a member of the Career Adaptability International Collaborative Group, SIO (Italian Society for Vocational Guidance), AIP (Italian Association of Psychology), and an international member of the Society of

Counseling Psychology (Division 17 of the American Psychological Association). She is one of the Italian representatives in the European project University Network for Innovation in Guidance—Lifelong Learning Programme. She is the author or coauthor of over 50 publications in the field of vocational psychology. *email*: lea.ferrari@unipd.it

Patricia Flederman has served in management and consultancy positions in the areas of career development, education reform, adult learning, organizational development, and equity in mainly low- and middle-income countries. As a consultant to the South African Qualifications Authority (SAQA) from 2008, she has contributed to South Africa's national career development helpline from its inception, with her research that recommended the helpline and her later roles in mentoring, training, and management capacities. She has an M.Sc. (Educational Studies) in youth development and an M.A. in Human and Organizational Systems. The positions she has held include Director of the Careers Research and Information Centre in South Africa, Project Director of a USAID-funded project in Malawi to increase girls' educational attainment, and Guidance Consultant to Liberia's Ministry of Education. Over many years she has also addressed systemic barriers to career development as a diversity facilitator and trainer in the USA, South Africa, Liberia, Zimbabwe, and five EU countries. *email*: patricia.flederman@gmail.com

Maria Cristina Ginevra, Ph.D., collaborates with La.R.I.O.S. Institute (Laboratory of Research and Intervention in Vocational Guidance), University of Padua, Italy. Her research is in the area of school-career counseling. She is a member of the Italian Society for Vocational Guidance and of AIP (Italian Association of Psychology). She is the coauthor of 16 national and international publications in the field of psychology of vocational guidance.

Radha Gopalan, Ph.D., has specialized in Environmental Science and Engineering from the Indian Institute of Technology, Bombay. After practicing as an Environmental Consultant for over 15 years in India, the USA, and the Middle East, Radha is currently based at the Rishi Valley Education Centre where she works with the surrounding rural community to enhance and sustain livelihoods through a responsible assertion of the community's rights to natural resources. This engagement with the community serves as the basis for the teaching of Environmental Science to high school students at the Rishi Valley School. *email*: radha.gopalan@gmail.com

Bryan Hiebert, Ph.D., has been a counselor educator for over 30 years. He served the International Association for Educational and Vocational Guidance from 1999 to 2011 as Vice President and President. In 2005, he was granted Honorary Life Membership in the Alberta Guidance Council and in 2007 he was awarded the Stu Conger Gold Medal and Diamond Pin for Leadership in Career Development. He has published more than 180 papers and 8 books dealing with career guidance, stress control, and counselor education. *email*: hiebert@ucalgary.ca

Archana Jain holds a master's degree in Human Development from the Nirmala Niketan College of Home Science, University of Mumbai, Mumbai, India. She is presently an Assistant Professor at the S V T College of Home Science, SNDT University, Mumbai, India. She has been working in the field for the last 17 years and her areas of research interest are developmental issues related to adulthood. She has carried out research on topics related to the impact of globalization on work conditions and its impact on individual and family life and the nature and challenges of caring for the elderly in the Indian family context. *email*: jainarchanas@yahoo.co.in

Jahnvee Joshi is a doctoral student in Human Development at the Nirmala Niketan College of Home Science, University of Mumbai, India. As part of her doctoral research, she is designing and evaluating career guidance interventions for rural disadvantaged youth in India. Jahnvee is also working as a Program Consultant for the Aga Khan Youth and Sports Board for India (AKYSBI), a faith-based youth-serving organization. At AKYSBI, Jahnvee is involved in designing and evaluating youth programs, conducting researches, and training volunteers to work with the youth. Jahnvee has also worked as a Visiting Lecturer at multiple colleges in Mumbai. *email*: jahnvee.joshi@gmail.com

Kartik Kalyanram is an alumnus of Rishi Valley School and graduated with a Bachelor's Degree (M.B.B.S.) in Medicine from the Armed Forces Medical College, Pune, India, and subsequently did his postgraduation (M.D.) in Aerospace Medicine from the Institute of Aerospace Medicine, Indian Air Force, Bangalore. He served in the Indian Air Force (IAF) for 17 years. In 1999, he opted for early retirement to set up, and now coordinate the Rishi Valley Rural Health Centre, which provides comprehensive primary level health care to below poverty line rural families in the Northern parts of Chitoor District, Andhra Pradesh, India. *email*: kartik.kalyanram@gmail.com

Kamakshi Kartik is a graduate of Madras Medical College, Chennai, and an M.D. in Pathology from the Armed Forces Medical College, Pune. She has served as a pathologist in a number of hospitals in India. She also did a 5-year stint as Medical Officer in the Indian Air Force. Since 2001, she has been working at the Rishi Valley Rural Health Centre as well as heading Laboratory Services at a small mission hospital in Madanapalle, Andhra Pradesh, India. *email*: kamakshi.kartik@gmail.com

Glenn. C. Kharkongor received his medical degree from Christian Medical College, Vellore, India, and his training in pediatrics at Loma Linda University, USA. He was a professor of pediatrics at Manipal University, India, before becoming vice chancellor and professor of health sciences at Martin Luther Christian University in Shillong, the capital of the state of Meghalaya in Northeast India. He is a Khasi who has recently delved into research in indigenous pedagogy and traditional knowledge. *email*: glenchristo@yahoo.com

Sachin Kumar holds a master's degree in Geography, an M.Phil. in Counseling Psychology specializing in Career Counseling and Livelihood Planning, and a Postgraduate Diploma in Training and Development. Earlier associated with The Promise Foundation, Bangalore, as a core team member and Master Career Counsellor Trainer of the Jiva Project, he is currently working as an Assistant Professor in a Government College in the Chamba district of Himachal Pradesh. One of the founder members of the Indian Association for Career and Livelihood Planning (IACLP) and a life member of Indian Society of Training and Development (ISTD) and National Association of Geographers, India (NAGI), he is also a part of Young Leaders Think Tank (YLTT), a group of young professionals brought together by Friedrich Ebert Stiftung, India, in order to deliberate on issues related to social democracy in the country. He also is a consultant for a number of educational institutions, civil society organizations, government departments, and corporate houses working with young people in the areas related to education and career development. His other interests include reading Hindi and Urdu poetry and engaging with issues related to preservation of the cultural heritage of the Himalayan region. *email*: samparksachin@gmail.com

Bill Law, Ph.D., a qualified teacher and guidance counselor, has, for approaching 40 years, worked on research and development in career management, and since 1992 as an independent freelancer. He is the founding Senior Fellow at the National Institute for Careers Education and Counseling, UK, and holds visiting roles in a number of research and development institutes in the UK and worldwide. His publications range from student and client learning material to academic books, chapters, and journal articles. Much of his current work is available online. That work includes an EU-funded project to further develop the narrative-based "three-scene storyboarding," a technique enabling career management. Bill is currently engaged in developing bases for the professional management of independent careers-work programs. All of the resulting material is open access from the home page of the career-leaning cafe, at http://www.hihohiho.com. The website is accessed widely and frequently from across the globe. Daily updates and alerts are posted at https://twitter.com/billaw

Frederick T.L. Leong, Ph.D., is Professor of Psychology and Psychiatry at Michigan State University. He is also Director of the Consortium for Multicultural Psychology Research in the Department of Psychology. He has authored or coauthored over 150 articles in various psychology journals, 100 book chapters, and also edited or co-edited 14 books. He is Editor-in-Chief of the Encyclopedia of Counseling (Sage Publications, 2008) and the APA Handbook for Multicultural Psychology (APA Books, 2013). Dr. Leong is a Fellow of the American Psychological Association (Divisions 1, 2, 5, 12, 17, 29, 45, 52), Association for Psychological Science, Asian American Psychological Association, and the International Academy for Intercultural Research. His major research interests center around culture and mental health, cross-cultural psychotherapy, and cultural and personality factors related to career choice and work adjustment. *email*: fleong@msu.edu

Aziel Marques, holds a master's degree in Human Development from Nirmala Niketan College of Home Science, University of Mumbai. She is currently a curriculum developer at Anandilal and Ganesh Podar Society, Mumbai, India. She is keenly interested in and has undertaken research in the area of career guidance. Education and counseling are her special interest areas.

Marina Mayer is Executive Director of the Economic Development Unit of the City of Johannesburg, South Africa. *email*: marina@joburg.org.za

Mary McMahon, Ph.D., is a Senior Lecturer in the School of Education at the University of Queensland, Australia, where she teaches career development and career counseling at postgraduate and undergraduate levels. She researches and publishes in child and adolescent career development, narrative career counseling, and qualitative career assessment; and her work is focused on developing systemic and narrative approaches for use by adolescents, parents, and practitioners. Mary is particularly interested in qualitative career research and how the stories of participants may be used to inform the development of theory, practice, and policy. *email*: marylmcmahon@uq.edu.au

Walter Müller, Ph.D., is Professor Emeritus for Sociology at the University of Mannheim and was co-founder and director of the Mannheim Centre for European Social Research. Besides various other topics, he has extensively published on the role of education for social inequality and patterns of social mobility in modern societies. *email*: wmueller@sowi.uni-mannheim.de

Srinivasa Murthy is former Professor of Psychiatry of National Institute of Mental Health and Neurosciences, Bangalore, India. Besides being a mental health researcher, teacher, and service provider, he has worked extensively in a number of developing countries. His area of interest is community mental health. He has edited five books and authored a number of manuals of mental health care for nonspecialist personnel. Currently he is developing interventions to empower the families of the persons with intellectual disability. *email*: smurthy030@gmail.com

Sonali Nag, Ph.D., is a Clinical Psychologist working with the Indian charity, The Promise Foundation. She is also the recipient of the prestigious Newton International Fellowship and is currently associated with the Department of Experimental Psychology, University of Oxford, UK. Sonali runs a Special Needs Center in Bangalore (India), supporting students in their school-to-career and other post-school transitions. A special interest is to understand how social cognitive environments in developing countries influence the coping and resilience of individuals with special needs. *email*: sonalinag@t-p-f.org

Roberta Neault, C.C.C., C.C.D.P., G.C.D.F., is a Canadian counselor and counselor educator, author, and keynote speaker with over three decades of experience. She is the recipient of the National Employment Counseling Association's Professional Development Award, the Canadian Career Development Foundation's Stu Conger Award for Leadership in Career

Counselling and Career Development in Canada, and the Gold Medal and Diamond Pin for Leadership in Career Development. Founding president of Life Strategies Ltd., a project-based organization with international contracts, co-creator of the fully online Career Management Professional Program, and past editor of the *Journal of Employment Counseling*, Roberta currently serves on the executive of the Career Counsellors Chapter of the Canadian Counselling and Psychotherapy Association. Through extensive travel in 60+ countries, teaching in international management programs, and supporting people from diverse cultures, educational levels, and employment experiences, Roberta has gained a unique understanding of the complexity of international/global careers. *email*: Roberta@lifestrategies.ca

Spencer G. Niles, Ph.D., is the Dean and Professor of the School of Education at the College of William & Mary, Williamsburg, USA. Prior to joining the faculty at the William & Mary College, he served on the faculty at the Pennsylvania State University (Distinguished Professor and the Department Head for Educational Psychology, Counseling, and Special Education) and on the faculty at the University of Virginia. Professor Niles is the recipient of the National Career Development Association's (NCDA) Eminent Career Award, American Counseling Association's (ACA) Thomas Sweeney Visionary Leadership and Advocacy Award, President's Award, David Brooks Distinguished Mentor Award, the ACA Extended Research Award, ACA's Visionary Leader and Advocate Award, and the University of British Columbia Noted Scholar Award. He is also an NCDA Fellow and an ACA Fellow. He has served as President for the NCDA and Editor for The Career Development Quarterly. Currently, he is the Editor of the *Journal of Counseling & Development* and serves on numerous journal editorial boards. He has authored or coauthored approximately 120 publications and delivered over 125 presentations on career development theory and practice. He has lectured in over 15 countries and is an Honorary Member of the Japanese Career Development Association, Honorary Member of the Italian Association for Educational and Vocational Guidance, and a Lifetime Honorary Member of the Ohio Career Development Association. *email*: sgn3@psu.edu

Laura Nota, Ph.D., is an associate professor in the Department of Developmental Psychology and Socialization, University of Padua, Italy. She conducts researches in the area of school-career counseling. She is the Director of the postgraduate master's course in Vocational Guidance and Career Counseling, and the Director of the La.R.I.O.S. Laboratory (Laboratory of Research and Intervention in Vocational Guidance). She is a member of the Executive Board of the SIO (Italian Society for Vocational Guidance); she is also a member of the Counseling Psychology Division in the International Association of Applied Psychology, the Life Design International Research Group, and the Career Adaptability International Collaborative Group. She is the IAEVG National Correspondent for Italy, and one of the Italian representatives in the European project University Network for Innovation in Guidance—Lifelong Learning Programme. She is the author of over 100 publications, more than 10 books, and many international and national articles related to the psychology of vocational guidance. *email*: laura.nota@unipd.it

Sarah Nunes (née Flynn) has completed her doctoral studies in counseling psychology at the University of Calgary. She is a registered psychologist and works at the University of Alberta Mental Health Centre. Sarah has experience in counseling international students both in the psychological and vocational realms. Her research interests include international student transition, acculturative stress, career decision-making, and stress and coping. Her dissertation research explored how Chinese international students use meaning-focused coping strategies to manage acculturative stress. Sarah has worked as a research assistant on projects related to counselor education and social justice, and evaluation tools for inter-professional collaboration. She has taught university courses on counselor communication skills and career management.

Lester Oakes is the current President of the International Association for Educational and Vocational Guidance and Deputy Chair of the International Centre for Career Development and Public Policy. His 29 years of experience in the career guidance field began as a practitioner in the government-owned Careers New Zealand before moving into management roles within the organization. He was Chief Executive of Careers New Zealand from 1998 to 2010, during which it became acknowledged internationally as a world leader in career guidance delivery and outcome measurement. *email*: oakes@paradise.net.nz

Wendy Patton, Ph.D., is Executive Dean, Faculty of Education at Queensland University of Technology, Brisbane, Australia. She has taught and researched in the areas of career development and counseling for more than 20 years. She has coauthored and co-edited a number of books, and is currently Series Editor of the Career Development Series with Sense Publishers. She has published widely with more than 100 refereed journal articles and book chapters. She serves on a number of national and international journal editorial boards. *email*: w.patton@qut.edu.au

Marina Pearce is a doctoral student of Organizational Psychology at Michigan State University. She received her master's degree in Organizational Psychology from Michigan State University in 2012. Her research and applied work spans multiple content areas, including teamwork and team dynamics, performance assessment and management, employee motivation, and career decision-making. *email*: marina@msu.edu

Pundy Pillay, Ph.D., is professor in Economics and Public Finance at the School of Public and Development Management, University of the Witwatersrand. *email*: pundy.pillay@wits.ac.za

Peter Plant, Ph.D., has worked in the field of career education and counseling since 1974 in schools, higher education institutions, and in the employment service in Denmark. He has worked as a researcher in many European projects on guidance and in various guidance-related capacities or as a Visiting Professor in the UK, Ireland, the Netherlands, Germany, Norway, Finland, Sweden, Iceland, Latvia, Slovenia, Bulgaria, Canada, Australia, and the USA. Currently, he is a Professor at the Danish School of Education, DPU, Aarhus University, Copenhagen, Denmark. He is also a consultant to the European Guidance Policy Network (ELGPN). He and his wife run an ecological farm, and a small booktown for second-hand books. *email*: pepl@dpu.dk

Kamini Ramachandran is a master storyteller with enormous stage presence and respect for the oral narrative tradition. She has been instrumental in the revival of the art of storytelling in Singapore as co-founder of MoonShadow Stories, Singapore's first storytelling partnership focusing on adult audiences. Drawing on her extensive knowledge of stories and the storytelling craft, Kamini has provided customized storytelling consultancy services for a variety of museums, educational institutions, organizations, and festivals. She has been commissioned to research and create storytelling content for animation projects, folklore publications, as well as curated museum exhibitions. She has gained an international presence with invitations to storytelling festivals to present keynotes, conduct workshops and master classes, as well as perform in public. Kamini is a founding member of the Storytelling Association (Singapore) having served four terms as President from 2008 to 2012. She is also the Artistic Director for the Singapore International Storytelling Festival. She teaches "The Storytelling Intensive" at college level for performing arts students. *email*: kamini@moonshadowstories.com

Anita Ratnam holds a Master of Arts degree in Development Studies from the University of East Anglia, UK, and has specialized in Rural Management, from the Institute of Rural Management, Anand, India. She is a specialist in Institution Leadership, Development and Governance, Training Design, Curriculum Development, and Facilitation. *Samvada*, the organization she founded, works with college students and youth to sensitize them to issues relating to caste, communalism, gender, environment, and poverty. It links them with social movements in the country and encourages them to work in the fields of alternative media, education, energy, and health. *email*: ratnam.anita@gmail.com

Hazel Reid, Ph.D., is Reader in Career Guidance and Counselling and Director of the Centre for Career and Personal Development at Canterbury Christ Church University, UK. She teaches in the areas of career and guidance theory and research methods. She also supervises students undertaking doctoral research and coordinates an auto/biography and narrative research group. Hazel is a Fellow of the Institute of Career Guidance, a NICEC Fellow (National Institute of Careers Education & Counselling), and coedits the *NICEC Journal*. She has published widely and is involved in European projects related to the work of career counseling. Her previous research was concerned with the meanings given to the function of supervision within guidance and youth support work. Currently she is exploring the development of constructivist approaches for career counseling. Hazel is a Fellow of the Academy of Higher Education and a founding member of the European Society for Vocational Designing and Career Counselling. *email*: hazel.reid@canterbury.ac.uk

Karen Schober is a sociologist who worked for 25 years in labor market, vocational education, and career research in the German Federal Employment Institute, and subsequently for 13 years as Head of the Department for Vocational Guidance and Counseling for the Federal Employment Agency, responsible for the management of guidance services. She participated in the OECD/EU Reviews on Career Guidance Policy, the Lifelong Guidance Expert Group of the European Commission, and the European Lifelong Guidance Policy Network (2007–ongoing). Since 2006, she is President of the German National Guidance Forum and since 2007, Vice President of the International Association for Educational and Vocational Guidance. *email*: karen@schober-brinkmann.de

Salvatore Soresi, Ph.D., is a full professor in the Department of Philosophy, Sociology, Education and Applied Psychology, University of Padua, Italy. He has conducted extensive research in the field of career counseling. He is the Editor of the Giornale Italiano di Psicologia dell'Orientamento (*Italian Journal of Vocational Psychology*) and the Director of the series Percorsi di Orientamento (Vocational Guidance Pathways) (Giunti-OS, Firenze). He is a member of the Life Design International Research Group of the Career Adaptability International Collaborative Group, and is one of the Italian representatives in the European project University Network for Innovation in Guidance—Lifelong Learning Programme. He is the author of about 250 publications, more than 20 books, and a number of important assessment instruments. In 2008, he received an award for his "Distinguished Contribution to the International Advancement of the Counseling Profession" from the Society of Counseling Psychology (Division 17 of the American Psychological Association). *email*: salvatore.soresi@unipd.it

Ronald G. Sultana, Ph.D., studied career guidance at the Universities of Reading (UK), Waikato (New Zealand), and Stanford (USA), where he was a Fulbright Fellow. He is professor of sociology and comparative education at the University of Malta, where he directs the Euro-Mediterranean Centre for Educational Research. He has participated as a consulting expert in several international reviews of career guidance, including those led by the OECD and the European Union. His most recent work includes comparative analyses of career guidance across Europe, and in the Middle East and North Africa region. Professor Sultana is a Fellow of the National Institute for Career Education and Counselling (NICEC-UK), and contributes concept papers to the European Lifelong Guidance Policy Network. He has served on the editorial board of the *British Journal of Guidance and Counselling* and the *Journal of Education and Work*. A list of his publications is available at: http://www.um.edu.mt/emcer. *email*: ronald.sultana@um.edu.mt

Darren Van Laar, Ph.D., is a Reader in Applied Psychology in the Department of Psychology, University of Portsmouth, where he is also the Director of the university's Graduate School. Darren has a B.Sc. in Psychology from Manchester Polytechnic, an M.Sc. in Information Processing from York University, and a Ph.D. in the use of color in computer displays from Imperial College, London. Darren's main teaching duties are in the area of research methods and he has taught units on survey methods, SPSS, and statistics units for undergraduate, postgraduate, and Ph.D. level courses. He has worked on many surveys for public organizations and been involved in all aspects of questionnaire design and analysis. Darren's non-teaching University work is focused at the interface between research and application. Darren's research covers three areas, the quality of working life of employees, the design of complex information displays, and the career destinations and aspirations of psychology students in the UK. *email*: darren.van.laar@port.ac.uk

Mark Watson, Ph.D., is a Distinguished Professor in the Psychology Department of the Nelson Mandela Metropolitan University in South Africa. He specializes, researches, and practices in child and adolescent career development, narrative career counseling, and qualitative career assessment. Mark has published extensively in international journals and has contributed chapters to international career texts. He is on the editorial advisory board of several international career journals and is a coeditor of the International *Journal for Educational and Vocational Guidance*. In addition, Mark has co-edited a book on career psychology in the South African context. Mark is an Honorary Professor at The University of Queensland, Australia, and a Research Associate at the Institute for Employment Research at the University of Warwick. He is particularly interested in the development of culturally appropriate approaches to career guidance and counseling. *email*: mark.watson@nmmu.ac.za

A. G. Watts is an international policy consultant on career guidance and career development, based in Cambridge, England. He is a Founding Fellow and Life President of the National Institute for Career Education and Counselling (NICEC), Visiting Professor of Career Development at the University of Derby, and Visiting Professor at Canterbury Christ Church University. In addition to his extensive publications, Tony Watts has lectured in over 60 countries, and has carried out a number of comparative international studies of career guidance systems. He has been a consultant to international organizations including the Council of Europe, the European Commission, OECD, UNESCO, and the World Bank. In 2001/2 he worked at OECD on a 14-country Career Guidance Policy Review, subsequently extended through other bodies to cover 55 countries. He is a consultant to the European Commission's European Lifelong Guidance Policy Network, and a member of the Board of the International Centre for Career Development and Public Policy. He was awarded an OBE in the 1994 Queen's Birthday Honours List for his services to education. His passions include his family, cricket, and early music. *email*: tony.watts@zen.co.uk

Linden West, Ph.D., F.R.S.A., is Professor and Director of Research Development in Education, Canterbury Christ Church University, UK, and Visiting Professor at the University of Paris Ouest. His books include Beyond Fragments (Taylor and Francis), Doctors on the Edge (FABooks), and Using Life History and Biographical Approaches in the Study of Adult and Lifelong Learning (Peter Lang). He is coauthor of Using Biographical

Methods in Social Research (Sage, 2009) and coeditor of Psychoanalysis and Education (Karnac, 2012). He has written widely on processes of managing change, careers, and transition; on learning in families, communities, and professional contexts; and in using auto/biography and psychosocial perspectives in building a better understanding of such processes. His writing has been translated into many languages, including French, Italian, Spanish, Chinese, and Polish. Linden co-coordinates a European Biographical Research Network and is also a qualified psychoanalytical psychotherapist. *email*: linden.west@canterbury.ac.uk

Helmut Zelloth, an Austrian, is a Senior Specialist in Vocational Education and Training (VET) Policies and Systems at the European Training Foundation (ETF), an agency of the European Union (EU). He has gained international experience in VET and career guidance in more than 50 countries in the world. He has coordinated major cross-country policy reviews, provided policy advice, and authored policy papers on career guidance for several governments (e.g., Turkey, Serbia, Kosovo, Jordan, and Egypt). *email*: Helmut.Zelloth@etf.europa.eu

Reviewers

Sajma Aravind holds a master's degree in Clinical and Counseling Psychology from the Mangalore University, India, and is presently engaged in doctoral studies related to career counseling for those with special needs. She is an experienced career counselor and counselor trainer, and leads career guidance services at The Promise Foundation, Bangalore. Sajma was also the editorial assistant for this handbook.

Gideon Arulmani, Ph.D., is a clinical psychologist with an M.Phil. in Medical and Social Psychology and a doctoral degree in Career Psychology from the University of Portsmouth, UK. He is the Founder and Managing Trustee of The Promise Foundation, Bangalore, India. He is the President of the Indian Association for Career and Livelihood Planning; a member of the Executive Board of International Association for Educational and Vocational Guidance; an International Fellow of the Consortium for Multicultural Psychology Research, USA; an International Fellow of the National Institute for Education and Counselling, Cambridge, UK; Visiting Senior Lecturer at the University of Canterbury Christ Church, UK; Visiting Professor at the Martin Luther Christian University, Meghalaya; and international consultant to a number of multilateral agencies.

Anuradha J. Bakshi, Ph.D., is an Associate Professor and Head of the Human Development Specialization at the Nirmala Niketan College of Home Science, University of Mumbai, India. She is teaching in the B.S., M.S., and doctoral programs in Human Development. She has been teaching at the university level for over 20 years and has taught at multiple colleges and universities. She also has extensive research experience, including coordination of national- and international-funded projects as well as research work with graduate students. She is the Vice President of the Indian Association for Career and Livelihood Planning and a Managing Editor of the *Indian Journal of Career and Livelihood Planning*.

Seth C.W. Hayden, Ph.D., N.C.C., is the Program Director of Career Advising, Counseling, and Programming at the Florida State University Career Center. Dr. Hayden has provided career and personal counseling in community agencies, secondary school, and university settings. He has provided individual and group counseling to people from various age groups and backgrounds. Dr. Hayden has focused on the issues of military service members and their families in both his research and practice. Dr. Hayden has extensive experience in providing career counseling to military personnel and veterans suffering from traumatic brain injury.

Ian King, Ph.D., is a portfolio educator advising on teaching, research, and assessment assignments in higher education and corporate business. Following a vocational realignment, he engaged with occupational research in the areas of career transition and organizational learning and completed his doctoral research with a study into the third-age career experience and aspiration of professional business workers in the knowledge economy. In an earlier occupational life, he held senior appointments as an organizational learning and development specialist in professional assurance and consulting organizations. As a business and management educator, he designed and facilitated a range of leadership, management, personal skills, and quality systems development programs to enhance individual and organizational effectiveness.

Roger Kjærgård, Ph.D., is an Associate Professor at the Department of Teacher Education, Buskerud University College, Norway. He is working as a researcher and teacher within the field of career guidance with special interest on lifelong guidance and the position of guidance being both a political tool and an individual service.

Bill Law, Ph.D., is the founding Senior Fellow at the UK National Institute for Careers Education and Counseling, holds visiting roles in a number of research and development institutes, and accepts commissions from the UK and worldwide. His publications range from student and client learning material to academic books, chapters, and journal articles.

Ashok Malla, M.B.B.S., F.R.C.P.C., M.R.C.Psych., D.P.M., is a Professor of Psychiatry, an Adjunct Professor in Epidemiology, and a Canada Research Chair in Early Psychosis at McGill University, and Director of Prevention and Early intervention Program for Psychoses at the Douglas Institute. He has conducted extensive neurobiological and psychosocial clinical research in psychotic disorders, especially on early phase. He has published over 200 peer-reviewed articles, held many peer-reviewed research grants, and been an advisor on program development and research in early intervention in psychotic disorders.

Meenakshi Parameshwaran, DPhil, is a sociologist at the University of Oxford and the University of Manchester. Her work investigates ethnic and educational inequality, with a particular focus on the structural, social, and cultural integration of the children of immigrants in the UK and Western European countries.

Wendy Patton, Ph.D., is Executive Dean, Faculty of Education at Queensland University of Technology, Brisbane, Australia. She has taught and researched in the areas of career development and counseling for more than 20 years. She has coauthored and co-edited a number of books, and is currently Series Editor of the Career Development Series with Sense Publishers. She has published widely with more than 150 refereed journal articles and book chapters. She serves on a number of national and international journal editorial boards.

Jérôme Rossier, Ph.D., is currently full Professor of vocational and counseling psychology at the Institute of Psychology of the University of Lausanne. He is editor of the International *Journal for Educational and Vocational Guidance* and member of several editorial boards. His teaching areas and research interests include counseling, personality, psychological assessment, and cross-cultural psychology.

Alok Sarin, M.B.B.S., M.D. (Psychiatry), is a practicing clinical psychiatrist in New Delhi, with an active interest in medicine, psychiatry, ethics, society, history, and literature. He has been in active clinical practice since 1985, and is currently attached as an honorary consultant to the Sitaram Bhartia Institute, New Delhi. He has been active in various nongovernmental organizations, and is presently a member of the Task Force on Mental Health Policy, set up by the Government of India. He was awarded the Senior Fellowship by the Nehru Memorial Museum and Library for research on the mental health aspects of history in 2009.

Jyoti Savla, Ph.D., is an Associate Professor in the Department of Human Development and a Research Methodologist at the Center for Gerontology at Virginia Tech, USA. Her research investigates the impact of everyday life stress and daily hassles on a combination of emotional, social, and physiological processes in middle-aged and older adults. She also serves as an investigator and a biostatistician on several state and federal grants.

Donna Jacobs Sife is a singer, storyteller, educator, and published writer, who uses her talents to enlighten and enhance tolerance and understanding within the people whose lives she touches. Well-known in the Sydney community, she has travelled throughout Australia, Israel and Palestine, the UK, and the USA and is internationally acclaimed in telling and teaching about story and bridging communities. A regular lecturer at Sydney University on interfaith and intercultural understanding, she is currently the School Programs Director of Together for Humanity, a diversity education organization.

S. Swaminathan was born in Pudukottai, Tamil Nadu (1940). He retired as Professor of Mechanical Engineering from Indian Institute of Technology, New Delhi. He is a co-founder of Tamil Heritage group and gives illustrated lectures on social and cultural subjects. Among other subjects, he is keenly interested in the story of Mahatma Gandhi.

Darren Van Laar, Ph.D., is a Reader in Applied Psychology at the University of Portsmouth, UK. He has taught a wide range of research methods including psychometric testing and multivariate statistics. Darren's research covers many areas of applied psychology including careers destinations, employee well-being, and even the design of color displays in command and control rooms.

Contents

1 The Manifestation of Career: Introduction and Overview . . .   1
Gideon Arulmani, Anuradha J. Bakshi, Frederick T.L. Leong,
and A.G. Watts

**Part I New Directions in Theoretical Perspectives for Career
Development and Guidance**

2 New Trends in Theory Development in Career Psychology . . .   13
Mary McMahon

3 Context-Resonant Systems Perspectives in Career Theory . . .   29
Mary McMahon, Mark Watson, and Wendy Patton

4 Life Span Theory and Career Theories: Rapprochement or
Estrangement?   43
Anuradha J. Bakshi

5 Indigenous Models of Career Development and Vocational
Psychology   67
Frederick T.L. Leong and Marina Pearce

6 The Cultural Preparation Process Model and Career
Development   81
Gideon Arulmani

7 Mahatma Gandhi's Ideas for Work, Career, and Life 105
V.R. Devika and Gideon Arulmani

Part II The Person in Contexts Across the Life Span

8 Personality and Self: Multiple Frames of Reference
for Career Service Professionals 121
Anuradha J. Bakshi

9 Parental Influences on Youth's Career Construction 149
Salvatore Soresi, Laura Nota, Lea Ferrari,
and Maria Cristina Ginevra

**10   The Interface between Positive Youth Development and
      Youth Career Development: New Avenues for Career
      Guidance Practice**   173
      Anuradha J. Bakshi and Jahnvee Joshi

**11   Mid-Career Progression and Development: The Role for
      Career Guidance and Counseling**   203
      Jenny Bimrose and Alan Brown

**Part III   Boom, Bust, and Suitability: Effective Career
             Preparation in a Volatile Labor Market**

**12   Understanding the Labor Market: Implications for Career
      Counseling**   225
      Sachin Kumar and Gideon Arulmani

**13   Labor Market and Career Development in the
      21st Century**   241
      Stelina Chatzichristou and Gideon Arulmani

**14   Career Advice and Guidance in a World Where Vocational
      Skills Matter**   255
      Heidi Agbenyo and Kathleen Collett

**15   Technical and Vocational Education and Training (TVET)
      and Career Guidance: The Interface**   271
      Helmut Zelloth

16   Second Career: An Eventual Need in Today's World   291
      Archana Jain

**Part IV   Making Our Careers Green: Work, Environmental
            Sustainability, and Social Justice**

17   Green Guidance   309
      Peter Plant

18   Career Guidance for Social Justice in Neoliberal Times   317
      Ronald G. Sultana

**19   Educational Inequality and Social Justice: Challenges for
      Career Guidance**   335
      Walter Müller

**20   Career Guidance and Counseling in the Context of
      Unemployment and Vulnerability: A Case Study of
      South Africa**   357
      Pundy Pillay, Rènette du Toit, and Marina Mayer

21   Tensions in Livelihoods: A Rural Perspective   377
      Kartik Kalyanram, Radha Gopalan, and Kamakshi Kartik

22 Traditional Occupations in a Modern World: Career Guidance, Livelihood Planning, and Crafts in the Context of Globalization 397
Anita Ratnam

Part V Career Services: New Directions for Practice

23 Telling Tales: Do Narrative Approaches for Career Counseling Count? 413
Hazel Reid and Linden West

24 Mind the Twist in the Tale: The Story as a Channel for Culture-Resonant Career Counseling 431
Kamini Ramachandran and Gideon Arulmani

25 Enabling Culturally Sensitive Career Counseling through Critically Reflective Practice: The Role of Reflective Diaries in Personal and Professional Development 453
Barbara Bassot

26 Online Careers Work: Colonist or Inhabitant? 465
Bill Law

27 Career Helplines: A Resource for Career Development 481
Patricia Flederman and A.G. Watts

Part VI Innovations in Career Counseling: Services for Special Groups

28 Special Educational Needs, Social Cognitive Environments, and Preparing for the World of Work 497
Sonali Nag

29 "I Don't Want to Make Candles!" Supporting the Career Development Needs of Those Recovering from Mental Illnesses 513
Gideon Arulmani and Srinivasa Murthy

30 Career Counseling among Indigenous Peoples 539
Glenn C. Kharkongor and Sandra Albert

31 Older Women's Retrospective Narratives of Their Work and Learning Pathways 555
Jenny Bimrose, Mary McMahon, and Mark Watson

32 The Immigrant, Expatriate, and Repatriate Experience: How Career Professionals Can Smooth the Way? 571
Roberta A. Neault

33 Should I Stay or Should I Go Home? Career Guidance with International Students 587
Nancy Arthur and Sarah Nunes

Part VII   Career Services: New Directions for Assessment and Evaluation

34   Assessment of Interest and Aptitude: A Methodologically Integrated Approach 609
Gideon Arulmani

35   Making Meaning of Quantitative Assessment in Career Counseling through a Storytelling Approach 631
Mark Watson and Mary McMahon

36   The Assessment of Quality of Working Life in Career Guidance and Counseling 645
Simon Easton and Darren Van Laar

37   Evaluation of the Quality of Career Guidance Centers 659
Nirmala Almeida, Aziel Marques, and Gideon Arulmani

38   Demonstrating the Impact of Career Guidance 671
Bryan Hiebert, Karen Schober, and Lester Oakes

Part VIII   Career Services: New Directions for Counselor Training, Competencies, and Standards

39   Career Counselor Competencies and Standards: Differences and Similarities across Countries 689
Bryan Hiebert and Roberta Neault

40   Orienting Educators to Contemporary Ideas for Career Counseling: An Illustrative Example 709
William Borgen and Bryan Hiebert

41   Training Career Practitioners: Opportunities and Challenges 727
Spencer G. Niles

Author Index 741

Subject Index 759

Contributors

Heidi Agbenyo Stakeholder Communications, City and Guilds Centre for Skills Development, London, UK

Sandra Albert Indian Institute of Public Health, Shillong, India

London School of Hygiene & Tropical Medicine, London, UK

Nirmala Almeida Department of Human Development, Nirmala Niketan College of Home Science, University of Mumbai, Mumbai, India

Nancy Arthur Canada Research Chair in Professional Education, Educational Studies in Counselling Psychology, Werklund School of Education, University of Calgary, Calgary, Canada

Gideon Arulmani The Promise Foundation, Bangalore, India

Anuradha J. Bakshi Department of Human Development, Nirmala Niketan College of Home Science, University of Mumbai, Mumbai, India

Barbara Bassot Centre for Career and Personal Development, Canterbury Christ Church University, Canterbury, UK

Jenny Bimrose Institute for Employment Research, University of Warwick, Coventry, UK

William Borgen Department of Educational and Counselling Psychology, and Special Education, University of British Columbia, Vancouver, Canada

Alan Brown Institute for Employment Research, University of Warwick, Coventry, UK

Stelina Chatzichristou Economist and specialist in Policy Analysis, Brussels, Belgium

Kathleen Collett Research and Economics at the City and Guilds Centre for Skills Development, London, UK

V. R. Devika Aseema Trust, Chennai, India

Simon Easton Department of Psychology, University of Portsmouth, Portsmouth, UK

Lea Ferrari Department of Developmental Psychology and Socialization, University of Padua, Padua, Italy

Patricia Flederman Claremont Consulting Incorporated, Western Cape, South Africa

Maria Cristina Ginevra University of Milan-Bicocca, Milan, Italy

Radha Gopalan Rishi Valley Education Centre, Madanapalle, India

Bryan Hiebert University of Calgary, Calgary, Canada

Archana Jain S V T College of Home Science, SNDT University, Mumbai, India

Jahnvee Joshi Nirmala Niketan College of Home Science, University of Mumbai, Mumbai, India

Aga Khan Youth and Sports Board for India, Mumbai, India

Kartik Kalyanram Rishi Valley Rural Health Centre, Madanapalle, India

Kamakshi Kartik Rishi Valley Rural Health Centre, Madanapalle, India

Glenn. C. Kharkongor Martin Luther Christian University, Shillong, India

Sachin Kumar Himachal Pradesh University, Himachal Pradesh, India

Darren Van Laar Department of Psychology, University of Portsmouth, Portsmouth, UK

Bill Law National Institute for Careers Education and Counseling, Cambridge, UK

Frederick T. L. Leong Michigan State University, East Lansing, MI, USA

Aziel Marques Anandilal and Ganesh Podar Society, Mumbai, India

Marina Mayer Economic Development Unit of the City of Johannesburg, Johannesburg, South Africa

Mary McMahon School of Education, University of Queensland, Brisbane, Australia

Walter Müller University of Mannheim, Mannheim, Germany

Srinivasa Murthy National Institute of Mental Health and Neurosciences, Bangalore, India

Sonali Nag The Promise Foundation, Bangalore, India

Roberta Neault Life Strategies Ltd, Aldergrove, BC, Canada

Spencer G. Niles School of Education, The College of William & Mary, Williamsburg, VA, USA

Laura Nota Department of Developmental Psychology and Socialization, University of Padua, Padua, Italy

Sarah Nunes (née Flynn) University of Alberta Mental Health Centre, Alberta, Canada

Lester Oakes International Association for Educational and Vocational Guidance, Wellington, New Zealand

Wendy Patton Faculty of Education, Queensland University of Technology, Brisbane, Australia

Marina Pearce Michigan State University, East Lansing, MI, USA

Pundy Pillay School of Public and Development Management, University of the Witwatersrand, Johannesburg, South Africa

Peter Plant Danish School of Education, Aarhus University, Copenhagen, Denmark

Kamini Ramachandran MoonShadow Stories, Singapore

Anita Ratnam Samvada, Bangalore, India

Hazel Reid Centre for Career and Personal Development, Canterbury Christ Church University, Canterbury, UK

Karen Schober German National Guidance Forum, Berlin, Germany

Salvatore Soresi Department of Philosophy, Sociology, Education and Applied Psychology, University of Padua, Padua, Italy

Ronald G. Sultana University of Malta, Msida, Malta

Rènette du Toit EE Research Focus, Gauteng, South Africa

Mark Watson Department of Psychology, Nelson Mandela Metropolitan University, Port Elizabeth, South Africa

A. G. Watts University of Derby, Derby, UK

Canterbury Christ Church University, Canterbury, UK

Linden West Research Development in Education, Canterbury Christ Church University, Canterbury, UK

Helmut Zelloth European Training Foundation, Turin, Italy

The Manifestation of Career: Introduction and Overview

Gideon Arulmani, Anuradha J. Bakshi, Frederick T.L. Leong, and A.G. Watts

Conceptual Location

This handbook is focused on work, occupation, and career development: themes that are fundamental to a wide range of human activities and relevant in some way across all cultures. Our focus in this writing is not "a" career, but "career" as a form of work. The manner in which career manifests itself is a complex phenomenon, influenced by a wide variety of factors. Therefore, we attempt at the outset to describe its conceptual location and do so by pointing to the nature and quality of transformations that have occurred in the evolution of work and career.

All through its evolution, large-scale factors operating at the macro level—such as industrialization, modernization, colonization, Westernization and, today, globalization—have shaped and formed human orientations to work. There are very few cultures and contexts (perhaps none) that have not been influenced by these forces in some way. An important milestone in the evolution of work in Western society was the Industrial Revolution. Coupled with the Protestant Reformation, a new work atmosphere was created wherein traditional practices of occupational role allocation were no longer as applicable as in earlier times when work role allocation was mainly based on one's social class. During those times, occupations and trades ran in families/close-knit groups, and expertise related to professions was transmitted from the adult to the young within the family or through guilds of professionals. In economies that came under the influence of the Industrial Revolution and the Reformation, the nature of work was no longer typified by a specific set of activities that one engaged in for a lifetime, in order to earn a living. Work now presented prospects for change and advancement. People began to approach work as a means for achieving growth and personal development, as also for changing their class or position in society. Thus was born the concept of career, which tends in a Western context to be described as a personal engagement with the world of work characterized by the exercise of volition and the identification of personal suitability, requiring preparation and specialization for ongoing, lifelong development.

As new occupations emerged, the issue of matching people to jobs surfaced as a question that needed an urgent answer. On the one hand, industry demanded workers with certain combinations of qualities, abilities and skills; on the other, the would-be worker needed guidance toward jobs for which he or she was most capable. It was at this point in the evolution of work that vocational guidance emerged as a method to support the new industrial work order. Accordingly, systems were developed whereby people could be matched for jobs on the basis of their traits, abilities, and talents. This systematization of methods to support and

G. Arulmani (✉)
The Promise Foundation, Bangalore, India
e-mail: garulmani@t-p-f.org

G. Arulmani et al. (eds.), *Handbook of Career Development*, International and Cultural Psychology,
DOI 10.1007/978-1-4614-9460-7_1, © Springer Science+Business Media, LLC 2014

facilitate career choice and decision making marks a notable landmark in the history of work. During earlier times when the allocation of work roles was led by social and cultural norms, there was possibly little or no need for career counseling and guidance. Today, in some cultures and economies, the individual has before him/her a wide assortment of occupational possibilities and prospects. In these cultures, individuals (based of course, on their qualifications and education) are relatively more free to select and follow the career of their choice. It is in the interface between the burgeoning of opportunities and the freedom of choice that career guidance and counseling finds its relevance. And since its inception more than a century ago, the field has grown and prospered, addressing, supporting, and facilitating individuals' engagement with the world of work.

But not all cultures and economies came *directly* under the influences of the Industrial Revolution and the Protestant Reformation. In other societies, human engagement with work progressed as it had for centuries earlier. Even today, all one has to do is to step a few miles outside the cities of economically developing countries to enter a world of work that is characterized by preindustrial features, where work is linked to the marshaling of resources to secure basic necessities such as food, clothing, and shelter. Career as it has been described earlier in this writing barely exists in these cultures and economies. Nonetheless, global forces have had and continue to have an impact on work behavior in almost all contexts. In virtually all societies, work has changed from being simply linked to survival needs to something far more complex, requiring increasing amounts of specialization and training. Accordingly, the notion of a personal career has made its appearance in many more parts of the world.

Although historically the notion of career was born in a Western, individualistic, industrialized context, and was nurtured by a work ethic that promoted freedom of choice, global forces over the years have transported it also to many other cultural and economic locations. It seems, therefore, that the manifestation of career can be seen in two broad contexts: contexts to which career is indigenous and contexts where it is, in many respects, culturally alien. In the former, the manifestation of career would be spontaneous and culturally congruent; in the latter, its manifestation could be the result of exigency induced by global transformations. It could thus be hypothesized that the delineation of career from work lies along a continuum. At one end is "career" in its fully developed form, as it has been described above; at the other end is a complete absence of this notion of career; and along the continuum are various manifestations of the idea of career. We further propose that this manifestation is strongly influenced by local social, cultural, economic, and psychological factors. Hence, the meaning of career for a middle-class, urban Indian might be very different from his/her middle-class German counterpart: the German, for example, may be relatively more accepting of a vocationally oriented, blue collar career, while to the middle-class Indian, given prevailing culturally mediated occupational prestige attributions, blue collar professions may not even be considered as a potential career path. At another level, a work day in the life of an illiterate paddy farmer with a small holding would be dictated by multiple requirements that range from weeding and pest management to harvesting and finding the best buyer for his crop: the topic of selecting an occupation for his children based on their interests and talents would be almost alien for him. The point we are making is that the notion of career is becoming more and more universal, as is the necessity of having to develop systems that would optimize individuals' engagement with career development. However, what it means, how it is manifested, and how the individual engages with career can vary from one context to another. In one setting, the focus of career guidance may be to help an individual discover whether he/she should take up law, business studies, or product design. In another, it may be to help an individual gain contemporary skills to manage his/her traditional, rural occupation more efficiently.

An examination of the literature pertaining to career development, counseling, and guidance that has developed over the last 60 years reveals the following:

- Theorizing and model building have been largely dominated by Western epistemologies. This is quite as might have been expected because the conception of career emerged in these contexts. The development of the field in Western contexts has been robust and has led to the advancement of a wide range of theories and methods for practice. The emergence of controversies, debates, and calls for improvement and expansion are signs of the good health of the discipline of career guidance in these contexts. This began perhaps with the quantitatively oriented trait-and-factor approaches and today the qualitatively oriented constructivist approaches are illustrative of new paradigms and conceptualizations of people's work lives.
- Some of the largest workforces in the world lie in the developing world—a world to which the notion of career is not indigenous. At the same time, career guidance is rapidly emerging as a strongly felt need in these contexts. Yet, very little attention has been directed toward understanding orientations to work and the manifestation of career in these environments. Instead, career guidance in these contexts is driven by definitions of career that have been transposed upon these cultures. As a result, those involved in workforce and career development in these contexts learn about constructs and ideas that do not equip them to effectively address felt needs.

It seems, therefore, that two pathways open up in relation to the advancement of career guidance research, theory, and practice. One leads toward the addressing of issues linked to *already established* forms of career development as it occurs in contexts to which career is indigenous. But given the reality that career now exists outside the setting in which it was born, the other pathway requires the breaking of *new ground*. The latter pathway is a less trodden one. For contexts in which career is not indigenous this may have to begin even with a redefinition of what career means in these environments.

This handbook is conceptually located in the dynamic and reciprocal interactions that constantly occur between universal trends and particular realities in relation to work and career. Some of the key targets at which this book aims are to:

- Extend existing theory, models, and methods into wider contexts
- Document hitherto undescribed orientations to work, livelihood, and career
- Discuss new directions that have relevance across cultural boundaries
- Exemplify sensitivity to culture
- Present ideas pertaining to less explored aspects of career guidance
- Be relevant to the wide range of newly emerging career counseling contexts around the world

An Overview of the Handbook

The handbook addresses eight themes which are now briefly summarized.

New Directions in Theoretical Perspectives for Career Development and Guidance

In this handbook we take the position that theory and practice are reciprocally connected and that one without the other would only partially address felt needs. In the first chapter, McMahon points out that critics have questioned whether the existing theory base within the discipline of career guidance and counseling is relevant for the current times. Reviewing longstanding ideas and constructs in career psychology, she identifies questions facing the field, contextualizes new trends, and discusses their possible future directions.

Presenting context-resonant systems perspectives in career theory, McMahon, Watson, and Patton highlight that taking account of contexts and their realities has today become an imperative. They call for the translation of these perspectives into methods and approaches that are respectful of diversity.

Keeping in view the interdisciplinary framework of this book, Bakshi explores the utility of one contemporary theory of human development, namely life span theory, for career theory, research, and practice. In order to identify new directions, she examines the extent of rapprochement between selected career theories and life span theory.

Leong and Pearce highlight the problems of cultural validity facing current psychological models: an integrative model of cross-cultural psychology is reviewed and suggested as an alternative. Of particular importance is their discussion of the relevance of indigenous psychological methods to the advancement of vocational psychology.

Based on constructs drawn from a wide range of disciplines, Arulmani formulates five interlinked propositions that together describe his cultural preparation process model, which he illustrates using constructs from Asian thought. He argues that career itself is a culture-bound concept and emphasizes the importance of developing frameworks that would allow the context to define career development.

The section is concluded by drawing upon the ideas of one of the most well-known figures of world history: Mahatma Gandhi. His ideas of work as a medium of learning are explored by V. R. Devika and Arulmani. They extract principles from the provocative ideas in Gandhi's writings on education and work that could point to a Gandhian form of career counseling.

The Person in Contexts Across the Life Span

The *person* is centrally important: It is the person's career development that we are committed to promoting. In this section, career development processes are described for persons who are located in traditionally important life periods such as adolescence and early adulthood, as well as for those who are negotiating challenges later in adulthood. There is clearly an emphasis on the contexts that define lifelong development.

Bakshi opens this section by reminding us that the person is central to all forms of career guidance activity. She discusses two constructs of focal interest to career guidance and counseling—personality and self—and describes the key dialogues in the indigenous Western literature as well as indigenous Indian literature. Of particular value is her exposition of *Advaita* philosophy to introduce indigenous Indian conceptualizations of personality and self. In presenting multiple frames of reference, she invites career service professionals to reexamine their orientations to the person whose welfare is their responsibility; in particular, their orientations to change and positive development across the life span.

Soresi, Nota, Ferrari, and Ginevra take up a discussion of one of the most critical influences on the young person's career construction: parents. They discuss the impact of structural and process family variables on adolescents' career development. Drawing upon data pertaining to socioeconomic status (SES) and social class across cultural groups, they make suggestions on how parental support of their children's career development could be strengthened.

Bakshi and Joshi continue the discussion on young people and present an in-depth analysis of positive youth development (PYD)—a framework that describes how youth development can be scaffolded through the planned changes located in the youth's own ecologies (e.g., school, community) which allow youth to thrive rather than only be problem-free. They provide a powerful case study that illustrates the role of community services in supporting the career development of youth.

Moving later into the life span, Brown and Bimrose discuss the role of career guidance and counseling in relation to mid-career progression.

Key findings are presented from their survey about the forms of learning and career development of 1,157 mid-career workers in 10 European countries. They introduce the idea that engaging with challenging work is a powerful form of learning and when coupled with other forms of learning may make positive contributions to employees' career development. A salient point they make is that career guidance practitioners need to recognize the complementarity of different forms of learning through which adult workers can optimize for their career development.

Boom, Bust, and Suitability

This theme focuses on the volatility and vagaries of the labor market and covers the issues that surround the relevance of career guidance given unstable and uncertain employment conditions. Addressing the practitioner, Kumar and Arulmani explain the concept of the labor market, list its key components, articulate significant trends, and discuss the meaning and role of labor market information (LMI) in career guidance. Ideas for application and practice are presented.

Continuing this discussion, Chatzichristou and Arulmani examine some of the factors that are expected to influence global labor markets in the 21st century and discuss these trends from the point of view of career guidance and counseling. They explain the implications of economic growth and slow down, outsourcing of jobs to emerging economies, immigration inflows within as well as across countries, and changes in the demographic compositions. They highlight the role that career guidance can play to ensure that the individual is not reduced to an undistinguished figment of human capital in a market-driven economic environment.

Agbenyo and Collett shift the discussion to a much debated topic: vocational skill training. Occupational prestige hierarchies in certain cultures typically place vocationally oriented careers at lower levels of preference although vocationally training is more likely to lead to early and fruitful employment. They explore the role of career guidance for vocational education

drawing on international evidence from studies conducted in nine different countries and argue that all those who are involved in career services have an important role to play in challenging perceptions of vocational education and training.

Zelloth deepens this argument by examining the relationship between career guidance and Technical and Vocational Education and Training (TVET) and shows that in reality, the interface between the two is not so clear and on occasion, may even be distorted. He discusses the barriers and stereotypes regarding TVET careers and develops a strong argument for the provision of career guidance services within and in relation to TVET.

Echoing a thread that runs through this section of the book, Jain's chapter discusses a relatively new but increasingly necessary aspect of career development in the contemporary context: the second career. She discusses that choosing the "one right career" and working for it may no longer be viable in today's world. This may be because of changing economic trends. But as Jain puts it, person-centered career guidance and counseling would recognize the significance of attending to individuals' developmental needs much before addressing the demands of their jobs and occupations. The final point she makes offers a fitting conclusion to this section of the handbook: If career guidance is to be relevant, it must also prepare the young person with skills to be able to anticipate and make smooth career transitions all through their lives.

Making Our Careers Green: Work, Environmental Sustainability, and Social Justice

From the rough and tumble of turbulent labor market dynamics, the handbook moves to another area that has been poorly addressed: the impact that career development has on the environment, issues related to sustainability, and matters pertaining to social justice.

We open this section with Plant's formulation of "green guidance." Linking environmental depredation to the individualistically mediated, exploitative and consumption-oriented predilections of career development as it is known today, Plant asks us to become aware of the environmental impact of many modern career paths. In this chapter, new directions are charted that point to the role that guidance and counseling can play to create a balanced, just, and peaceful society. Drawing upon the ancient Indian *ashrama* system's exhortation for service orientation across the life span and citing powerful examples from Inuit values, Plant describes how career guidance and counseling can envisage a shift toward a greener future.

Against this backdrop, Sultana's chapter explores alternative conceptions of social justice and reminds us that if individuals construct their own history, they do so in circumstances not of their own making. Drawing on recent theories of social justice, Sultana's chapter disturbs the comfortable, white, middle-class status quo that many forms of career guidance sustain and challenges us to imagine the ways career guidance can be of the greatest benefit to the least advantaged.

Müller continues this discussion by bringing attention to bear on educational inequality and social justice, and the challenges this presents for career guidance. An interesting tension emerges across chapters with regard to vocational education. Unlike the advocacy for vocational education in earlier chapters in this section, Müller's arguments favor the encouragement of higher educational aspirations to mitigate educational inequalities. He summarizes crucial findings on the materialization of inequality in educational opportunities from various countries and discusses the role that career guidance can play in reducing these inequalities.

Pillay, du Toit, and Mayer address the career development issues that surround unemployment, vulnerability, and economic disempowerment, focusing on youth in South Africa. They point to a critical economic indicator of the miscarriage of social justice: divergence between a country's relatively high economic status (as measured, for example, by GDP per capita) and its relatively low development status (measured, for example, by UNDP's Human Development Index) which indicates an inequitable distribution of the benefits of economic growth. Their case study of the South African situation highlights the critical role that career guidance and counseling can play within the context of socioeconomic/sociopolitical challenges.

Commenting on a similar theme from the Indian perspective, Kalyanram, Gopalan, and Kartik draw our attention to the phenomenon of rural–urban migration. They contrast the notion of livelihood with career, drawing upon the views of J. Krishnamurti, a provocative Indian educationist-philosopher, and consider the notion of a "right" livelihood. They highlight the allure that urban life has for the rural young person. They then consider what the career counselor ought to do in this situation: encourage rural young people to migrate to the city or encourage them to stay in their rural homes. Their case example of a livelihood planning exercise in South India asks the discipline of career guidance to include in its purview, a form of guidance and counseling that supports livelihood planning. Within such a scheme would be a *livelihood counselor*: a career counselor who is skilled in facilitating the process of career choice and discovery, as well as in understanding and optimizing rural/traditional occupational structures.

This section culminates with Ratnam's analysis of the challenges that neoliberal capitalism poses. She raises questions about the goals, techniques, ethics, and conceptual frameworks that currently guide the practice of career guidance. She draws our attention to the manner in which prevailing growth paradigms have ushered in new forms of social and economic exclusion, worker alienation, and the precarization of the livelihoods of marginalized groups. Using craft-oriented occupations as an example, she argues that traditional occupations can be repositioned as a career or livelihood option that mitigates social exclusion, disorientation, and the insecurities emanating from a volatile labor market.

New Directions for Practice

We stated earlier that theory and practice have a reciprocal relationship. This fifth theme of the handbook considers the practical dimensions of career guidance and counseling.

Reid and West begin this section by pointing to career counselors' concern about the inadequacy of quick-fix and reductionist methods in career guidance. They use information from a research project conducted in two phases in England to demonstrate the power of narrative approaches to help clients construct ideas about self and career futures in ways that are more meaningful, including in multicultural contexts.

Ramachandran and Arulmani present a traditional and ancient form of counseling—the story—as a channel for culture-resonant career counseling. Examples from a wide range of cultures are used to demonstrate how traditional counselors use the story as a tool for learning and teaching. They suggest that the modern career counselor can learn from these time-honored methods and create channels between pertinent, well-recognized stories and the person such that he or she could find answers by drawing upon the collective wisdom of the community. Three practical techniques that could be adopted for culture-resonant career counseling are described.

Bassot describes critically reflective practice and the role that reflective diaries could play in personal and professional development. The author uses her own reflective diary that she kept during her time in India as a case study to illustrate the theoretical models discussed in the chapter.

Information and communication technologies (ICT) have dramatically changed the ways in which we interact and engage both with ourselves and others. Law introduces the career counselor to online careers work. He makes a very useful distinction between natives of the Internet (those who use it so habitually that they can be said to inhabit it) and visitors (those who use it on an as-and-when basis). Discussing how the Internet can become a resource for career workers, he makes the very important observation that while online websites provide the content, and technology the tools, it is critical thinking that provides the process.

Responding to the realities of the global situation that call for distance career services, Flederman and Watts review the development of career development helplines across nine countries. Distance career services may use one or more of the following: SMS, telephone, VOIP, email, and social media. They demonstrate how these advances in technology can mitigate the constraints of geography, time, travel costs, physical disability, and social isolation, and thereby achieve the goals of social equity.

Services for Special Groups

Theme six responds to calls that have been repeatedly made for career guidance to bring into its purview those who are outside the mainstream. Nag begins this section by addressing the needs of individuals with learning disorders such as Dyslexia, Specific Learning Difficulties (SLD), and Specific Language Impairment (SLI). She points out that while special educational needs have been studied extensively from the remedial program point of view, not much is known about how these individuals can be supported for a smooth and secure entry into the world of work. Using narratives from interviews with 12 individuals with learning disorders, she describes multiple layers of influence that are relevant for the interface between education and work in the life of an individual with special needs. She highlights the skills that career counselors must develop in order to work with individuals with learning disorders, which includes ensuring a fine balance between supporting and making space for self-determination.

Arulmani and Murthy focus on another special group: those recovering from mental illnesses. They point out that although psychological disorders contribute to 13 % of the global burden of disease, exceeding both cardiovascular disease and cancer, very little has been done for the reintegration of this group into the workforce.

Addressing the career practitioner, they provide an overview of the signs and symptoms of mental illness and discuss the debilitating influence of stigma on the recovery of those who have been affected. Taking a functional rather than disabilities approach, they present the International Classification of Functioning, Disability, and Health (ICF) as a conceptual framework for the career counseling of those recovering from mental illness.

In the next chapter, Kharkongor and Albert speak to us about career counseling among indigenous peoples, also known as tribals, first peoples/nations, aboriginals, or minority ethnic groups. They point out that being close to nature and community is integral to the indigenous worldview and that influences from dominant societies, globalization, and indigenous peoples' own continuing evolution, place them at various points in the continuum between the traditional ways of life and the modern. Writing from Meghalaya, a predominantly tribal state in northeast India, they present an exploratory survey based on focus group discussions with 10 indigenous career counselors. Methods suited to the culture of indigenous young people are discussed against the background of culture-bound tests and standardized approaches. They recommend an approach to career counseling that could achieve better outcomes with indigenous youth and expand the effectiveness of career counseling as a discipline.

Bimrose, McMahon, and Watson draw our attention to the needs of another group: older women and their work and learning pathways. They emphasize the multiple disadvantages that affect individuals' engagement with the labor market, such as those associated with age and gender. They review the broad context of women's position in labor markets internationally and describe a qualitative study of the labor market transitions of older women (aged 45–65) in Australia, England, and South Africa. They present three key themes from their findings, and in the light of these findings, consider the relevance of existing career theory, practice, research, and policy for women.

Continuing the discussion on special groups, the topic shifts to the needs of immigrants: those who for various reasons leave their homes and have to make a new home away from home. Neault underscores the increasingly mobile nature of the global workforce and reminds us that not all migration experiences are positive ones. She reviews the literature and discusses the career development challenges encountered by immigrants, expatriates, repatriates, and global careerists. Career guidance must address, for example, culture shock, transitions, credential recognition, language competency, relocation, and settlement.

Taking this discussion forward, Arthur and Nunes focus specifically on international students. Highlighting the diversity among international student populations, they discuss the important question of whether students who complete their education in institutions away from their country should stay or return to their home countries. An illustration from their study of the higher-education-to-work transition experiences of a group of international students who studied in Canada is provided. Best practices for career guidance with international students are discussed.

New Directions for Assessment and Evaluation

Assessment and evaluation have perhaps elicited the most controversy within the discipline of career guidance and counseling. In this section, these controversies are addressed and innovations that could move the field further forward are examined.

Arulmani examines two constructs central to career assessment: vocational interests and aptitudes. The influence of collectivist social organization and the impact of socioeconomic change such as improvements in the availability of employment are presented as a matrix within which to understand, assess, and interpret vocational interests and aptitudes. The relative stability of these two constructs is discussed through two Indian studies of a methodologically integrated approach to career guidance and assessment. This data is used to introduce the notion of potential: a blend of interests and aptitudes, as a relatively more stable construct around which to develop career guidance services.

Watson and McMahon offer a response to the debates in this field by integrating traditional career assessment approaches with narrative career counseling. Using two case studies, they describe the use of an Integrative Structured Interview (ISI) process within a storytelling approach in conjunction with two internationally applied quantitative career assessment instruments (i.e.,—Holland's Self-Directed Search interest questionnaire and Super's Work Values Inventory-Revised) to demonstrate the complementarity of quantitative career assessment and storytelling.

Easton and Van Laar remind us of the interactions between economic growth, employment, and quality of working life. They describe quality of working life as the broader experience of employment and observe that there have been few valid and reliable measures of this important aspect of a person's engagement with work. They present an overview of the development of the Work-Related Quality of Life Scale (WRQoL) along with the psychometric properties of its six subscales. They recommend the use of a WRQoL scale for evaluating career guidance services.

Almeida, Marques, and Arulmani explore concepts and constructs related to the quality of career guidance centers through a study conducted in Mumbai (India) that used a multi-agent, multi-method, evaluative research design. From their data, they present seven thematic heads that could form a conceptual framework for the evaluation of career guidance centers. An illustration is presented for the conversion of these constructs and concepts into items for questionnaires, semi-structured interviews, and checklists.

Hiebert, Schober, and Oakes underscore a prominent theme emerging from contemporary discussions on career development and public policy: "prove it works." Emphasizing accountability, they describe outcome-focused, evidence-based approaches to practice that have been created in North America and many European countries.

New Directions for Counselor Training, Competencies, and Standards

Effective counselor training lies at the heart of successful career guidance service delivery. Along with counselor training come the issues of competencies and standards.

Turning to the issues that surround counselor training, Hiebert and Neault point out that raising the profile of career guidance involves developing ways of identifying and acknowledging the competencies required to deliver quality career services. They provide a comprehensive background for understanding different approaches for developing competency systems. The importance of adopting mechanisms for acknowledging and validating practitioners who possess the competencies needed to deliver quality career guidance services is discussed: The Global Career Development Facilitator (GCDF) and the Educational and Vocational Guidance Practitioner (EVGP) credentialing systems are presented as examples.

Responding to the radically altered context in which career decision-making is occurring today, Borgen and Hiebert provide a summary of emerging needs that young people face when trying to navigate the contemporary labor market. Underlining the importance of preparing professionals to provide the types of services that young people require, they provide an example of an initial step in professional development and describe a method for demonstrating the impact of that training on the participants involved.

Continuing with the theme of training and competency formation, Niles argues that if career practitioners wish to make a mark, they must be cognizant of the importance of demonstrating the efficacy of their work. For this to become a reality, the quality of career practitioner training must be of the highest level. This would mean equipping trainees not only with skills for service delivery but also for gathering and disseminating data to validate the efficacy of their work, and for engaging in advocacy to effectively communicate the value of career services to stakeholders.

Conclusion

A tendency when extending ideas into new contexts is to begin with the ideas of the dominant, more powerful group and suggest ways of adapting these ideas to the recipient context. Adaptations can be useful. However, unveiling what has been crusted over and neglected may be more relevant and effective. While this book highlights the relevance of traditional systems to local, particular contexts, it also attempts to demonstrate their potential for wider applicability. Therefore, this handbook attempts not only to adapt familiar theories and methods but also to introduce other epistemologies and worldviews so that the existing knowledge base can be broadened and enriched. If more relevant models are to be developed, frameworks from other cultures and economies must be acknowledged as providing different understandings of career development. This book rests on the understanding that all cultures have time-tested traditions of engaging with the world of work, some of which are thousands of years old. Career guidance and counseling is at a new threshold. The opportunity that presents itself is not for the creation of an Eastern as opposed to a Western form of career guidance and counseling. The task before us is to learn to draw from these different traditions with the objective of being more relevant in a complex and changing world. In keeping with this spirit of partnership, we conclude this introductory chapter with a *śloka* (verse) from one of the most ancient texts of human civilization: the *Rig Veda*. The first part is a transliteration from the original Sanskrit and this followed by an English translation:

Om saṃgacchadhwaṃ saṃvadadhwaṃ
saṃ vo manāṃsi jānatām
devā bhāgaṃ yathā pūrve
sañjānānā upāsate

May we move in harmony, our minds in agreement,
May we work together toward a common goal.
May we follow the example of our ancestors,
Who achieved a higher purpose by virtue of being open-minded,
May we share our thoughts for integrated wisdom (Rig Veda, ||10|191|2).

Part I

New Directions in Theoretical Perspectives for Career Development and Guidance

Overview

The first theme in this handbook explores new directions in theoretical perspectives that can underpin and guide contemporary career psychology. Chapters in this section provide comprehensive reviews of existing concepts and constructs and point to important trends in theory development. Career theory is considered in relation to a complex and diverse career decision-making environment and the imperative to take account of the contexts in which individuals construct careers is discussed. Indigenous models of psychology are increasing in their popularity as an approach for understanding behavior in specific cultures. Other chapters in this section discuss the relevance of such models to vocational psychology research and practice with culturally diverse populations. Problems facing current psychological models and methods of improving cultural validity are discussed. An integrative model of cross-cultural psychology is reviewed and the relevance of indigenous psychological methods for the advancement of vocational psychology are explained. Cultural preparedness is presented as a conceptual framework that could guide the development of culture-resonant interventions. Traditional knowledge is highlighted as an important resource for constructing career guidance programs to address the needs of clients from different cultural heritages. This section also draws upon viewpoints from other related disciplines such as theoretical perspectives in human development, economics, sociology, and anthropology along with ideas and concepts from non-Western (mainly Asian) thought and philosophy. Life span theory is examined for its relevance to career development and guidance. An interesting feature of this section is a detailed consideration of Mahatma Gandhi's views of work and education and their potential relevance to contemporary careers work. An attempt is made to interpret Gandhian thought into the career counseling framework.

In summary, this section reviews existing theoretical standpoints and interprets them for future applications, introduces concepts from other disciplines as potential building blocks for new theorizing, and finally, presents ideas with which to break new ground.

New Trends in Theory Development in Career Psychology

Mary McMahon

Introduction

By way of background to this chapter, I begin by considering the question: *What is a theory?* A simple explanation is offered by Krumboltz (1994) who has explained that "a theory is a way of explaining what we observe. It is a way of making sense of our experiences. It is a way of summarizing a large number of facts and observations into a few general principles" (p. 9). Thus, a theory may be regarded as a guide, a model, an explanation, or a hypothesis that helps us to explain or understand particular phenomena (Brown, 2002a; Krumboltz, 1994; Solmonson, Mullener, & Eckstein, 2009).

Good theory, however, is well founded on research-based evidence. Brown (2002a) has presented criteria for judging a theory. He suggests that well-developed theories have clearly defined constructs and are parsimonious. He contends that good theories are comprehensive in their ability to account for the career development of diverse populations throughout the world and concludes that many theories fail this criterion. Further, Brown suggests that good theory explains what happens and why, assists our understanding of past, present, and future events, and may be applied in practice. Brown

concluded that no career theory meets all of his criteria.

Brown's (2002a) criteria, however, that theory should account for diverse populations is also open to question in view of recent critiques of career theory and discussion about globalization, internationalization, and indigenization of career theory and practice (e.g., Arulmani, 2010; Leong & Pearce, 2011; Leung & Yuen, 2012; McMahon & Yuen, 2010; Mkhize, 2012; Watson, McMahon, Mkhize, Schweitzer, & Mpofu, 2011). For example, Leung and Yuen (2012) have cited four limitations of career development theory, specifically its focus on: (a) personal variables rather than contextual and cultural variables, (b) self-actualization and job-satisfaction as goals of career choice, (c) high levels of free choice and opportunities to make several decisions over time, and (d) developing practices and resources that are culture based and cannot easily be transported to other contexts. In this regard, Arulmani (2011) has explained that "a given culture has been already prepared in a certain way to engage with work, occupation and career" (p. 92) and has urged career guidance and counseling practitioners to learn from other cultures in order to move closer to delivering context resonant interventions. Thus, consideration must be given to the cultural base of the theoretical trends presented in this chapter and this will be revisited later in the chapter.

At first glance, the theory base of career psychology may be confusing because "the domain of career psychology . . . is characterized

M. McMahon (✉)
School of Education, The University of Queensland, Brisbane, QLD, Australia
e-mail: marylmcmahon@uq.edu.au

G. Arulmani et al. (eds.), *Handbook of Career Development*, International and Cultural Psychology,
DOI 10.1007/978-1-4614-9460-7_2, © Springer Science+Business Media, LLC 2014

by a plethora of theories, philosophical positions, and research camps" (Savickas & Lent, 1994, p. 1). Two decades since this observation was made, the position of career psychology could be similarly described although the plethora of theories has widened as new theories have emerged.

In approaching the topic of *new trends in theory development in career psychology*, I became intrigued about what actually constitutes a *trend*, and in particular, what constitutes a *new trend*. Dictionary definitions told me that a trend is a general course, a general direction, or a style or fashion (e.g., Butler, 2009). Further dictionary definitions described *fashion* as a prevailing custom or conventional usage (Butler, 2009) and *style* as "a particular, distinctive, or characteristic mode or form of construction or execution in any art or work" (Butler, 2009, p. 1254). Against this background, I then wondered what duration or lead-in time is needed before a general direction or general course or a trend is recognized. I then wondered at what point is a new theory development regarded as a new trend.

With these thoughts in mind, I considered the diverse theory base of career psychology and how I would select the new trends in theory development for inclusion in this chapter. While possible options may have been to identify theories developed within a particular timeframe or theories which have amassed substantial evidence bases comparatively recently, I chose to identify the new trends according to the philosophical positions underlying the extant body of career theory. From when the first career theory was proposed in the early 1900s (Porfeli, 2009) to the present time, the dominant philosophical position underlying it has been logical positivism which emphasizes the importance of logical proof, objective measurement, and linear progression (Brown, 2002a). Thus, for the purposes of this chapter, because of the longstanding and pervasive influence of logical positivism, I consider the theory base informed by it as a pervasive trend in theory in career psychology.

More recently, however, theories informed by the philosophical positions of constructivism and social constructionism have become more influential since being first recognized as a new trend by Savickas in 1989. Such was the influence of this new trend that Young and Collin (2004a) coedited a special issue of the Journal of Vocational Behavior that focused specifically on constructivism, social constructionism, and career. Theories informed by these philosophical positions emphasize narrative discourse, subjectivity, personal agency, meaning making, and connectedness between individuals and their broader contexts. In this regard, Mkhize (2012) has suggested that worldview is important in counseling African, indigenous, and other non-Western clients because of the value they place on connectedness and interdependence; this is reflected in the African construct of *Ubuntu* which refers to "our common humanity, our interconnectedness, and our spiritual connectedness" (Watson et al., 2011, p. 282). Watson et al. (2011) have indicated that approaches informed by constructivism and social constructionism and social justice may have some potential to accommodate non-Western cultural considerations. This is, however, yet to be tested. In this chapter, I consider theories informed by constructivism and social constructionism as new trends in theory development in career psychology.

The intention in this chapter is not to debate the merits of, or to advocate for, either philosophical position or particular theories. All have a place in career psychology and offer different and valuable contributions. Rather, the intention of this chapter is to focus on new trends in theory development in career psychology.

I begin this chapter by overviewing longstanding and pervasive trends in career psychology to provide necessary background for contextualizing the chapter's focus on new trends in theory development in the field. Subsequently, I discuss new trends in theory development and briefly introduce four theory developments, specifically, contextual action theory (Young et al., 2011; Young & Valach, 2008), the chaos theory of careers (CTC) (Bright & Pryor, 2005; Pryor & Bright, 2011), career construction theory (Savickas, 2005), and the Systems Theory Framework (STF) (McMahon & Patton, 1995; Patton & McMahon, 1999,

2006) of career development. I have also included the relational theory of working (Blustein, 2001, 2006, 2011a) as an emerging theory underpinned by propositions that, if adopted, could have a profound influence on career psychology. I then consider the possible futures of the new trends and influences from the field of career psychology that may contribute to these possible futures.

Pervasive Trends in Career Psychology

Parsons (1909) pioneering work in assisting people with their career decision-making gave rise to career theory. Essentially, Parsons believed that self-understanding in combination with knowledge of the world of work would result in sound career decision-making. He applied his tripartite model to assisting young, poor, and disadvantaged people find employment in cities at the beginning of the 20th century. Subsequently, Münsterberg developed the first vocational theory using Parsons' tripartite model as a foundation (Porfeli, 2009). Parsons' collaboration with Münsterberg also established vocational guidance, as it was then known, in the field of applied psychology (Porfeli, 2009) and in the traditions of logical positivism (McMahon & Watson, 2006). Thus, Parsons' early work spawned the trait and factor approach, predicated on assessment and its interpretation by career practitioners, which remains deeply entrenched in career psychology to the present day (Savickas, 2008).

Parsons (1909) work gave rise to two distinct and pervasive trends in the field of career psychology. The first and most significant pervasive trend is that of a discipline underpinned by a logical positivist philosophy. Career assessment is a distinct feature of theories informed by logical positivism and to this end a myriad of assessment instruments has been developed. Many of these instruments serve the dual purposes of facilitating research that provides an evidence base for its parent theory and also providing practitioners with a means of assessing clients. Indeed, the use of career assessment instruments has been foundational to career development practice for much of its history. Criticism has, however, been leveled at many of these instruments in relation to their Western orientation and their application to diverse and non-Western populations within their own Western countries of origin and internationally (e.g., Leong & Pearce, 2011).

The second pervasive trend in career psychology that emerged out of the work of Parsons was the emergence of a discipline underpinned by social justice values. Yet, since the days of Parsons, career psychology has paid little attention to this underlying core value and has been criticized for its middle-class focus (Blustein, 2006, 2011b).

A further pervasive trend is also evident in the critique of career psychology where many calls have been made for the field to revise itself to remain relevant (e.g., Blustein, 2011b; Savickas, 2001, 2011; Savickas & Lent, 1994; Walsh, 2011). For over two decades, theorists have considered the future of the field. For example, in 1994, a group of researchers and theorists convened to discuss the diversity of the theory base and the issue of convergence (Savickas & Lent, 1994). In 2001, in a special issue of the Journal of Vocational Behavior, Savickas proposed a mission and objectives for vocational psychology. A decade on, Walsh (2011) edited a special issue of the Journal of Career Assessment that considered "big questions facing vocational psychology."

Across these three milestone publications in career psychology, the themes considered were similar, have remained largely unchanged for decades, and are reflected in Savickas's (2001) mission for vocational psychology:

> Vocational psychology, a specialty within applied psychology, conducts research on vocational behavior among all groups of workers, at each life stage, in order to advance knowledge, improve career interventions, and inform social policy. It is characterized by innovative theorizing to comprehend the diversity of human experience and the changing world of work; the use of diverse epistemologies and research strategies; an emphasis on programmatic and longitudinal studies; and the translation of research findings into models,

methods, and materials for career education and intervention. (p. 286)

Pervasive themes in the critique of career psychology include: lack of consensus with regard to key terms and their definitions; the Western and increasingly middle-class focus that has seen the field lose touch with its core value of social justice; the changing nature of society, globalization, and the internationalization of career psychology; the need for more diverse research methodologies; and the disciplinary isolation of career psychology from other fields that also share an interest in work and employment such as sociology, developmental psychology, and management and organizational psychology. Each of these themes warrants brief consideration to contextualize the new trends in theory development which will be discussed next in this chapter.

Lack of Consensus with Regard to Key Terms and Their Definitions

The lack of consensus with regard to key terms and their definitions has long been an issue for career psychology. For example, terms such as career development, career psychology, vocational psychology, career development, career guidance, and vocational guidance are widely used. Internationally, the terms career development, career psychology and vocational psychology have tended to be more widely applied in the American context and the term career guidance has tended to be more widely applied in the European and British contexts. In 1994, when convergence in career theory was debated, the term career psychology was used (Savickas & Lent, 1994). In 2001, Savickas proposed a mission and objectives for vocational psychology, and more recently a special issue of the Journal of Career Assessment (Walsh, 2011) also used the term vocational psychology. Of interest, many of the same researchers and theorists have contributed to all of these debates. Does this lack of consensus with regard to key terms and definitions matter? When we use the terms *career psychology*, *vocational psychology*, or *career guidance*, are we referring to the same discipline?

Are there nuanced differences in meaning between these terms that should be taken into account? This lack of consensus regarding terminology remains unresolved in the field and thus, remains a point of confusion within the field and more broadly with key stakeholders and clients.

Western Middle-Class Focus and Social Justice

Since Parsons (1909) emphasis on vocation, the field has moved increasingly toward the use of the term career in response to changes in the world of work and corresponding changes in theory and practice. Richardson (1993, 1996, 2000) has however, been critical of the use of the term career for its perceived middle-class bias. She has advocated use of the term *work* as a more inclusive term that can take account of paid, unpaid, volunteer, and caring work. Similarly, Blustein (2001, 2006, 2011a, 2011b) believes that work is a more inclusive term and has advocated a psychology of working which addresses the limitations of our field in relation to the way in which gender, social class, family background, and cultural characteristics impact on individuals' career development. In this regard, Blustein (2011b) has urged the field to broaden its base to consider unemployment and poverty.

As evidenced in the thoughts of Richardson (1993, 1996, 2000) and Blustein (2001, 2006, 2011a, 2011b), although social justice underpinned Parsons (1909) work, it has been marginalized over time. A pervasive trend in critiques of career psychology relates to a perception that it is a Western white middle-class discipline that does not cater well to women and minority groups and may not translate well across countries and cultures (Blustein; Richardson). In this regard, Stead and Perry (2012) have contended that "career psychology needs to focus less on its largely individualist, reductionist, and positivist focus toward research and practice and address inequities in communities through ethically-based social justice and community work." (p. 68).

Similarly, Watson and McMahon (2012) have observed that "the pendulum of career development has swung to and remained too long at the privileged end of the continuum" and that the field has "moved radically away from the roots of the discipline at the start of the last century" (p. 152). They have strongly advocated "revisiting that end of the continuum" in order to meet the challenges of career psychology in a globalized society (p. 152). In this regard, the development of theoretical accounts that are contextually and culturally sensitive to non-Western and indigenous people are still urgently needed in the field. While several non-Western authors have made important contributions to the field (e.g., Arulmani, 2007, 2010, 2011; Leong & Pearce, 2011; Mkhize, 2012) that can inform theory and practice, no major theoretical position has yet been offered although Arulmani's (2011) cultural preparedness approach offers potential in this regard.

Changing Society, Globalization, and Internationalization

In many ways globalization and internationalization of career psychology have magnified the challenges presently facing career psychology. Globalization has resulted in more diverse client groups within both the traditional Western home of career psychology and internationally as the discipline is increasingly internationalized. Internationalization, however, has largely seen a one-way flow of theory and practice from Western countries, predominantly the United States of America, to other countries and cultures. Further, by their nature and origin, the discipline of career psychology is "anchored in a Western cultural context" (Leung & Yuen, 2012, p. 76) and its translation beyond Western cultures remains uncertain. In reflecting on this issue in the South African context, Watson and Stead (2006) asked "What should our theory base be? Are our theories sufficiently sensitized to local cultural, socioeconomic, and social conditions? What should our role be and who are the clients? What values should be promoted?" (p. 8).

Indigenization of career theory has been proposed as a possible solution (e.g., Leong & Pearce, 2011). Hou and Zhang (2007), however, have expressed concerns about the "voicelessness" (p. 47) of authors who are less proficient in the English language in disseminating their research to a wide international audience. Thus, a challenge remains in achieving a "multidirectional flow of philosophy, theory, practice, and research" (McMahon & Yuen, 2010, p. 103).

Diversifying Research Methodologies

In keeping with the dominant logical positivist philosophy, research in career psychology has been conducted primarily using quantitative methodologies. Qualitative methodologies have had a very limited profile in career psychology. Stead et al. (2012) who conducted a content analysis of articles published in 11 key journals between 1990 and 2009 found that only 6.3 % of the 3,279 articles they analyzed used qualitative research methods. Importantly, these authors also highlighted the need for greater academic rigor in qualitative research. Looking through the lens of systems theory, McMahon and Watson (2007) have offered some insight into the complexity of this issue in terms of the history of career psychology, the dominant voices evident in training new entrants to the field, and publication.

Disciplinary Isolation

A further theme in critiques of career psychology concerns the need for interdisciplinary collaboration with other fields who also share an interest in work and employment such as sociology, developmental psychology, management, organizational psychology, and education. In this regard, discussion about interdisciplinary collaboration (e.g., Collin & Patton, 2009; McCash, 2010) and multidisciplinary collaboration (Leung & Yuen, 2012) has begun. Arthur (2008) has perceived "an urgent need for interdisciplinary careers research in the emerging global knowledge economy" (p. 163) and the term *career studies* has been proposed as a way of overcoming boundaries between disciplines (Arthur, 2010; Collin, 2010; Gunz & Peiperl, 2007). Indeed, Gunz and Peiperl (2007) published the first text focusing on career studies. The tenet behind the move to greater interdisciplinary collaboration is that a more unified discipline may have greater capacity to address issues that have not been traditionally well attended to within more narrowly defined disciplines.

While the issues presented in this section have been discussed as pervasive themes in critiques of career psychology, they could also be viewed as potential trends should they be addressed.

New Trends in Theory Development in Career Psychology

It is against this background that new trends in theory development in career psychology are now considered. New trends in theory development in career psychology could, to some extent, be regarded as responses to the questions generated by critiques of career psychology and massive changes in society as a result of globalization and dramatic changes in technology. In many disciplines, responses to societal change have been informed by constructivism and social constructionism which have greater capacity to accommodate the complex and dynamic processes of a rapidly changing society than theories underpinned by the logical positivist worldview which offer narrow but detailed accounts of particular phenomena.

The new trend towards theories informed by constructivism and social constructionism was largely driven by trends in practice (Young & Collin, 2004b) as career practitioners sought ways to respond to complex client needs and issues. There are more similarities than differences between constructivism and social constructionism with the most commonly agreed difference being whether construction is understood as a cognitive process or as a social process (Young & Collin, 2004b). *Constructivism* is sometimes used as a generic term and Raskin (2002) adopted its plural form, *constructivisms*.

Emanating out of the growing influence of constructivism and social constructionism and trends in practice, a number of theory developments in career psychology have emerged including contextual action theory (Young et al., 2011; Young & Valach, 2008), the CTC (Bright & Pryor, 2005; Pryor & Bright, 2011), career construction theory (Savickas, 2005), and the STF (McMahon & Patton, 1995; Patton & McMahon, 1999, 2006) of career development. The relational theory of working (Blustein, 2001, 2006, 2011a) is also included as an emerging trend. Each of these new and emerging trends could be regarded as responses to identified issues in the field of career psychology. Each of these new trends in theory development will now be briefly introduced. A detailed account of each theory is not possible within the scope of this chapter and is available in references to the theories cited in this chapter.

Contextual Action Theory

Contextual action theory (Young et al., 2011; Young & Valach, 2008; Young, Valach, & Collin, 2002) is focused on explaining the career process. With a history of over two decades, it has amassed a substantial evidence base focused on supporting adolescents in the complex transition to adulthood. Essential to this theory is an understanding of behavior as goal-directed action. Intentional goal-directed behavior of individuals is regarded as action. Goal-directedness is also regarded as intentionality. Action may be cognitively directed and regulated and is also subject to social influence. Action comprises manifest behavior (e.g., making notes, reading a textbook), internal processes (e.g., worrying, identifying a task to do), and social meaning (e.g., training to win a competition, achieving good results) (Young et al., 2002). Contextual action theory stresses a recursive relationship between career behavior and context.

The main constructs of action theory are action systems, perspectives on action, and levels of action organization. Action systems include action, joint action, project, and career, each of which may be viewed from the perspective of manifest behavior, internal processes, and social meaning and defined as goals, functional steps, and elements. In attempting to understand action more fully, Young et al. (2002) adopted the constructs of *joint action* to understand action with others, *project* to understand action over time, and *career* to understand action containing goals. Where groups of actions have common goals, they are regarded as projects. In general, actions are short-term and projects operate over a mid-term timeframe. When projects come together over a longer period of time they are referred to as career.

Joint action is essentially co-constructed between two or more people and necessarily involves communication. In contextual action theory, the focus is on the action rather than interaction. Joint action recognizes the shared transition to adulthood and takes account of individual agency as well as the social and cultural influences of families. For example, adolescents may discuss and plan for their future with their parents. Action occurs over time during which contingencies and life circumstances may intervene, resulting in the need to define and redefine goals and actions. Project is a broader construct than action but it also has social meaning (Young et al., 2002). For example, adolescents and their parents may construct a project by deciding what information they need to make their decisions, and determining that they will go to a career fair together and that the adolescent will make an appointment to see a career counselor. Career extends over a longer time span than project and may encompass more actions. Thus, career becomes a complex interaction of goal-directed behaviors, social meaning, and internal processes.

Chaos Theory of Careers

The CTC (Bright & Pryor, 2005, 2011; Pryor & Bright, 2011) represents an application of chaos theory to the field of career development. It views individuals as "complex, dynamical, nonlinear, unique, emergent, purposeful open systems, interacting with an environment comprising systems with similar characteristics" (Pryor & Bright, 2003, p. 123). Thus the process, rather than the content, of career development is central to CTC especially in relation to unpredictable and chance events. Pryor and Bright contend that chance events occur more frequently than individuals imagine.

Bright and Pryor (2011) regard complexity, change, chance, and construction as the cornerstone constructs of the CTC. Complexity recognizes the multiplicity of influences on the lives of individuals which are interconnected and may interact in unpredictable ways. In this regard, CTC argues that "people and environments cannot be reduced to static three- or four-letter codes, nor can they be slotted into programmatic stages and cycles" (Bright & Pryor, 2011, p. 163). CTC is a dynamic theory that emphasizes continual change and the need for individuals to continually adapt as they, their contexts, and society changes. Particularly noteworthy in this theory is its incorporation of chance as a pivotal element. To date, chance has not been widely incorporated into career theory with the notable exception of Krumboltz and his colleagues (Krumboltz & Levin, 2004; Mitchell, Levin, & Krumboltz, 1999) who considered the concept of planned happenstance, that is, the decisions individuals make in response to chance events.

CTC stresses that individuals are complex systems subject to a complex array of contextual influences. Pryor and Bright (2011) have argued that individuals are well placed to actively create their futures because of the unpredictability of such complex personal and contextually embedded systems. Within complex systems, there are limitations, termed *attractors* in chaos theory. Attractors tend to constrain functioning in some way by influencing behavior towards particular directions. Behavior may focus on goals (point attractors), move between two points (pendulum attractors), progress through a series of habitual steps (torus attractors), or demonstrate stability over time but also the possibility of change (strange attractors). Over time, patterns emerge within systems. As individuals interact within these complex systems, their career behavior is characterized by fractal patterns, that is, ways of behaving that are similar. For example, a young person who is captain of his football team, chairperson of a student committee at his school, and a team leader in his part-time job in a fast-food outlet may reflect a pattern of behavior that demonstrates high levels of ability in communication, leadership, and organization. Constructivism proposes that individuals look for patterns in their lives. In CTC, looking for patterns of behavior in complex systems is termed emergence which in turn facilitates meaning making. CTC has been applied in career counseling and, similar to other theoretical developments described in this chapter, relies on the use of narrative.

Career Construction Theory

Career construction theory is essentially an "expanded and updated version of Super's theory of vocational development" (Savickas, 2002, p. 154) underpinned by personal constructivism and social constructionism (Savickas, 2005). Critical to this theory is the notion that careers do not simply unfold but rather, they are constructed by individuals by "imposing meaning on their vocational behavior and occupational experiences" (Savickas, 2005, p. 43). Described by Sharf (2010) as a metatheory, career construction theory is founded on three key components, specifically, vocational personality, career adaptability, and life themes (Savickas, 2005). The metatheoretical capacity of career construction theory is evident in the relationships between: vocational personality and vocational traits and their relationship to person–environment fit theory; life themes and Super's notions about vocational preferences and occupational choice being the implementation of self-concept; and career adaptability as a psychosocial activity focusing on the process rather than the content of person–environment fit theory as individuals seek to implement their self-concept.

Vocational personality is defined as "an individual's career-related abilities, needs, values, and interests" (Savickas, 2005, p. 47). This component of career construction theory draws on Holland's (1997) RIASEC typology of interests. Career construction theory, however, views interests as relational and socially constructed and as a dynamic process rather than as stable traits. In practice, career construction theory suggests that assessment scores be used to generate possibilities rather than be used in traditional predictive ways.

Career adaptability is described as "the coping processes through which individuals connect to their communities and construct their careers" (Savickas, 2005, p. 48). Thus, vocational personality refers to the *what* of career construction whereas career adaptability refers to the *how*. Central to career adaptability are the developmental tasks of the stages described by Super (1990), specifically growth, exploration, establishment, management, and disengagement (Savickas, 2002). The stages represent a structural account of career adaptability. Response readiness and coping resources are central to career adaptability (Savickas, 2005) and are conceptualized along the four dimensions of concern, control, curiosity, and confidence. Concern relates to having a future orientation and contemplating a vocational future. Control relates to *owning a career* and taking responsibility for constructing it. Curiosity relates to being inquisitive, wanting to learn, and exploring options and possibilities. Confidence relates to being able to face and overcome difficulties and problems. In this regard, an employee may become aware that staying in the same organization is not a long-term option for her because she is becoming increasingly unhappy as a result of the restructuring that has occurred in her workplace (concern). She begins to talk to friends from her network about her hopes to find a new job and to look through advertised positions (control). She identifies possible employers and investigates information from their websites (curiosity). She becomes increasingly more certain about the work she would like to do and the employers she would like to work for (confidence).

Life themes are described as the narrative component of career construction theory which "focuses on the why of vocational behavior" (Savickas, 2005, p. 57). This component imbues career construction with meaning and recognizes the dynamic process of career development. Career stories offer accounts of the decisions made by individuals and facilitate a coherence between past, present, and future. Further, they contextualize individuals in a way that is not possible through the constructs of vocational personality or career adaptability. In essence, life themes are the patterns that are present in the stories told by individuals. For instance, a life theme of the employee in the previous example, may concern helping people and be reflected in the stories she tells about caring for aged parents, volunteer work on weekends in a homeless shelter, and her employment as a social worker. Narration and life themes constitute essential elements of the career theme interview ([Savickas, 2002]; more commonly referred to as the career style interview [Savickas, 2005]) and life design counseling that is a practical application of career construction theory (Savickas et al., 2011).

Systems Theory Framework of Career Development

The STF (McMahon & Patton, 1995; Patton & McMahon, 1999, 2006) of career development was proposed in response to the convergence debate of the early 1990s. Unlike other theory developments in career psychology, the STF is a metatheoretical framework rather than a theory. It is the first such framework proposed in career psychology. Calls for a systems view of career development have been evident for over two decades (e.g., Osipow, 1983) and more recently there has been greater acknowledgement of systems theory in career development (e.g., McMahon & Patton, 1995; Patton & McMahon, 1999, 2006; Pryor & Bright, 2011; Young et al., 2011). While theories such as chaos theory and contextual action theory also assume systems perspectives, the STF is the only theoretical

development based solely on systems theory. Moreover, as an overarching framework, the STF values the contribution of other theories as they provide detailed accounts of constructs it depicts.

The STF (Patton & McMahon, 2006) is depicted as a series of interconnected circles, each representing a system of influence on the career development of individuals. At the center of the STF, the individual is located as the *individual system*. Within this system a range of intrapersonal influences are included such as values, personality, interests, disability, and sexual orientation. In career psychology, detailed accounts of many of the extant influences are provided by theories informed by the logical positivist philosophy. For example, Brown (2002b) has offered a detailed account of values whereas Holland (1997) has offered a detailed account of personality. Other constructs, however, such as disability and sexual orientation have not been well attended to in career psychology. From an STF perspective, such influences may be accounted for by subjective narrative accounts told by the individual themselves and by drawing on theory and research from other disciplines.

Surrounding the individual system of influences is the *social system* including family, peers, and schools and the broader *environmental–societal system* that includes influences such as globalization, socioeconomic circumstances, and geographic location. Influences contained in the social system and the environmental–societal systems have not been adequately researched or theorized in career psychology. Importantly, the metatheoretical orientation of the STF (Patton & McMahon, 2006) accommodates detailed accounts of such influences drawn from other disciplines. For example, Roberts (2005, 2012) from the field of sociology, has provided considerable insight into the influence of socioeconomic disadvantage on career development. The discipline of economics offers insight into labor market trends and organizational psychology may provide insight into the relationship between individuals and work organizations.

The STF (Patton & McMahon, 2006) acknowledges the dynamic nature of career development through the inclusion of three process influences. *Recursiveness* is the process of inter-action within and between influences. More specifically, recursiveness is about connectedness within and between all elements of the system and also between systems. Thus, it accommodates the individualism more evident in Western cultures and the collectivism more evident in non-Western cultures. *Change over time* at the macro level is the process by which the past influences the present, and the past and present influence the future. At the micro level, change over time relates to processes such as career decision-making. The third of the process influences is *chance*, the random occurrences that may irreversibly change the life and career of an individual.

At the macro level, the influences depicted in the STF (Patton & McMahon, 2006) apply to most people. At the micro level, the STF recognizes the personal and subjective nature of career development. Thus it is applied in practice through a storytelling approach (McMahon & Watson, 2010) which encourages individuals to identify and tell stories about their personal influences and to recognize themes that pervade these stories. Through storytelling, individuals position themselves in relation to their culture, families, and communities. Thus, an important contribution of the STF is its comprehensiveness and its application in diverse settings and with diverse populations. In this regard, Mkhize (2012) believes McCormick and Amundson's (1997) career-life planning model for first nations people echoes the STF approach. For example, the model offers a communal process that recognizes connectedness, especially with family and community; and balance, needs, and roles. Importantly, the model integrates culturally relevant practices that have been found beneficial to first nation's youth (Neumann, McCormick, Amundson, & McLean, 2000).

Relational Theory of Working

In 2001, Blustein urged the field to move towards a more inclusive and integrative psychology of working based on work in all its forms which he subsequently published as a major text (Blustein, 2006). Derived from the psychology of working, Blustein (2011a) proposed his relational theory of working which focuses on the neglect of populations with limited choice and how career theory may also be inclusive of them as well as of those who do have choice. His particular concern was to propose a theory "relevant to those who work with little or no volition in their choice of market-based work" (Blustein, 2011a, p. 9). The relational theory of working, as the first theory to be proposed from the psychology of working, advocates a more inclusive notion of work.

The relational theory of working challenges career psychology in its present form. While Blustein (2011a) has commended the field of career psychology for its contribution to understanding people who have some degree of choice in their working lives, he also contends that for many people, self-determined choice about work is not possible. Thus, the relational theory of working is about "the lives of people with less than optimal choice in their educational and occupational lives as well as those with more choices" and stresses "the common element for all people who work—the relational context" with a view to creating "an integrative theoretical perspective that addresses working people across the spectrum of work-based privilege and volition" (Blustein, 2011a, p. 2).

Central to this theory is Blustein's (2011a) focus on how relationships are the basis of all life experience including work experience. Building on a social constructionist base, the relational theory of working assumes that individuals learn about themselves through their relationships with others and their environments. Further, work and relationships are considered central to the lives of most people around the world and are conceptualized as recursively influential. His theory is founded on seven propositions, specifically:

1. The centrality of work and relationships and their recursive relationships on our internal worlds and lived experiences
2. The internalization processes that influence emotions, cognitions, perceptions, and work experiences

3. The contextual location of work and relationships (e.g., in the market place and in caregiving)
4. The influence of relationships on work decisions, transitions, exploration, and training options
5. The relational nature of the formation of interests and values, and of meaning making
6. The influence of relational discourse on the meaning of work to individuals
7. The importance of culture in relationships and working

Blustein (2011b) believes that career psychology is at a "fork in the road" where it can maintain the status quo or "take the road less travelled" (p. 216). Specifically, Blustein claims that the options facing the field are to maintain its middle-class focus or to expand its focus to include the poor and unemployed. Essentially, Blustein is urging the field to reflect on its social justice origins and embrace a new direction. Importantly, the psychology of working is the only new trend in career psychology to focus specifically on the social justice origins of career psychology.

Relevance for Multiple Cultures: Sensitivity to the Universal and the Particular

Prior to considering the possible futures of the new trends in theory developments, I will briefly overview their similarities and differences and possible contributions to the field. In particular, their relevance to multiple cultures will be considered. Each of the theory developments has a capacity to accommodate complexity in people's lives and in society because they take holistic, contextual perspectives of career development. Thus, all are concerned with the contextually embedded nature of career development and also the process of career development. Moreover, in practice, all value the notion of subjective careers (Collin, 1986) or personal experiences of career as well as the observable, objective career. In addition to subjectivity, other less tangible influences on individuals' careers such as spirituality may be accommodated.

While career development theory itself has paid little attention to spirituality, more broadly in the field of career development, several authors have considered spirituality in relation to careers and work (e.g., Bloch & Richmond, 1997; Hansen, 1997). A capacity to consider intangible influences such as spirituality in career theory and practice may increase relevance to non-Western cultures. In practice, the subjective career is critical to the narrative practices emanating out of these theory developments. The features of the new trends in theory development set these theories apart from many extant career theories. It is not helpful to the field of career psychology, however, to polarize theories informed by different philosophical positions. Rather, it is more helpful to value the contribution of all theories (Sampson, 2009).

Taking Brown's (2002a) criteria for good theory into account, it seems that none of these new trends yet fits his criteria. What is evident, however, is the focus of these newer theoretical positions on practical application and that the evidence bases being developed in regard to these theories are related to their practical applications. Thus, these new trends in theory development are responsive to Brown's claim that good theory should apply in practice. However, taking the concerns about Brown's criteria that were discussed earlier in this chapter into account, it remains to be seen whether these new trends will address issues of cultural relevance and appropriateness and be sensitive to the universal and also to the particular. Indeed, Stead and Perry (2012) have recommended that career psychology should be a "cultural enterprise" (p. 59). To this end, Arulmani (2011b) has proposed a cultural preparedness approach that contextualizes career interventions for local contexts.

In the special issue on big questions in vocational psychology (Walsh, 2011), Reardon, Lenz, Sampson, and Peterson (2011) posed three questions that warrant consideration in terms of the new trends in theory development in career psychology: "Where should new knowledge for vocational psychology come from? How do career theories and research find their way into practice? What is the nature of career development and vocational choice in a global economy?" (p. 241). It is interesting that in this special issue, an invitation was extended to leaders in the field of career psychology yet there was little international representation. While not to diminish the contribution of these eminent researchers and theorists, it is curious that at a time when the global discipline of career psychology is faced with questions that concern its sustainability and relevance globally, input was sought primarily from one section of the globe. In this regard, three of the new trends presented in this chapter emanate from countries other than the United States of America and two (i.e., CTC and STF) have drawn their theoretical bases from other disciplines. Of these new trends, the STF has had its application tested to some extent in a non-Western culture (e.g., McMahon, Patton, & Watson, 2005; McMahon, Watson, Foxcroft, & Dullabh, 2008). Further, career construction theory (Savickas, 2005) has stimulated investigation into the international application of its Career Adapt-Abilities Scale (Savickas & Porfeli, 2012) in a process reminiscent of Leong's cultural accommodation model (Leong & Pearce, 2011).

Thus, the future of the new trends in theory development in career psychology needs to be considered in view of influences present in career psychology. For example, the voices of the new trends are very small in comparison to the voices of the pervasive trends which dominate psychology training, research methodology, publication in the field, and practice (McMahon & Watson, 2007). Further, the voices proposing these new theoretical trends remain Western and despite the potential capacity of these theories to be more culturally sensitive, there remains an urgent need to encourage and privilege voices from non-Western cultures.

New Concepts and Viewpoints: Charting New Directions

In the dynamic world of work of the 21st century where globalization is resulting in more diverse communities, career development services have much to offer. However, "theory, research and practice conceived in the 20th century have served career development well but they are not sufficient to strategically position career development in a global world and ensure a sustainable and relevant future" (McMahon & Watson, 2012, p. 7). Thus, it is hoped that the new trends in theory development towards more holistic and inclusive accounts of career development and closer links between theory, research, and practice may, in combination with the pervasive trends of the dominant theory base, contribute toward the construction of a richer and more sustainable discipline of career psychology that is culturally relevant in contexts beyond its traditional Western base. Further, it is hoped that new trends in theory development will emerge from non-Western contexts that may contribute to enhanced understanding of culturally relevant approaches.

Major commentary on career psychology seems to occur approximately every decade. How will such future commentary judge the contribution of these new trends in theory development in career psychology? What is the future of these new trends in career psychology and how will they coexist with the pervasive trends that have long been dominant? Will these new trends address issues that have been evident in the field for many years? Will history ultimately view them as enduring trends or as *fads*, "temporary, usually irrational pursuit, by numbers of people, of some action that excites attention and has prestige" (Butler, 2009, p. 437). Only time will tell therefore, whether the new trends of theory development in career psychology become general trends or whether in fact, they were only fads; and only time will tell what the contribution of the new trends of theory development in career psychology will actually be and whether they address longstanding concerns about cultural relevance.

References

Arthur, M. B. (2008). Examining contemporary careers: A call for interdisciplinary inquiry. *Human Relations, 61*, 163–186.

Arthur, M. B. (2010). Promoting career studies in theory and practice. *Career Research and Development, 23*, 4–8.

Arulmani, G. (2007). *Pride and prejudice: How do they matter to career development?* Derby, UK: Centre for Guidance Studies, University of Derby.

Arulmani, G. (2010). The internationalization of career counselling: Bridging cultural processes and labour market demands in India. *Asian Journal of Counselling, 16*, 149–170.

Arulmani, G. (2011). Striking the right note: The cultural preparedness approach to developing resonant career guidance programmes. *International Journal for Educational and Vocational Guidance, 11*, 79–93.

Bloch, D. P., & Richmond, L. J. (Eds.). (1997). *Connections between spirit & work in career development*. Palo Alto, CA: Davies-Black.

Blustein, D. L. (2001). Extending the reach of vocational psychology: Toward an inclusive and integrative psychology of working. *Journal of Vocational Behavior, 59*, 171–182.

Blustein, D. L. (2006). *The psychology of working*. Mahwah, NJ: Lawrence Erlbaum.

Blustein, D. L. (2011a). A relational theory of working. *Journal of Vocational Behavior, 79*, 1–17.

Blustein, D. L. (2011b). Vocational psychology at the fork in the road: Staying the course or taking the road less travelled. *Journal of Career Assessment, 19*, 316–322.

Bright, J. E. H., & Pryor, R. G. L. (2005). The chaos theory of careers: A user's guide. *Career Development Quarterly, 53*, 291–305.

Bright, J. E. H., & Pryor, R. G. L. (2011). The chaos theory of careers. *Journal of Employment Counseling, 48*, 163–166.

Brown, D. (2002a). Introduction to theories of career choice and development. In D. Brown & Associates (Ed.), *Career choice and development* (4th ed., pp. 3–23). San Francisco, CA: Jossey Bass.

Brown, D. (2002b). The role of work values and cultural values in occupational choice, satisfaction, and success: A theoretical statement. In D. Brown & Associates (Ed.), *Career choice and development* (4th ed., pp. 465–509). San Francisco, CA: Jossey Bass.

Butler, S. (2009). *Macquarie concise dictionary*. Sydney, NSW, Australia: Macquarie Dictionary.

Collin, A. (1986). Career development: The significance of the subjective career. *Personnel Review, 15*(2), 22–28.

Collin, A. (2010). The challenge of career studies. *Career Research and Development, 23*, 12–14.

Collin, A., & Patton, W. (Eds.). (2009). *Vocational psychological and organisational perspectives on career: Towards a multidisciplinary dialogue*. Rotterdam, The Netherlands: Sense Publishers.

Gunz, H., & Peiperl, M. (Eds.). (2007). *Handbook of career studies*. Thousand Oaks, CA: Sage.

Hansen, L. S. (1997). *Integrative life planning*. San Francisco, CA: Jossey-Bass.

Holland, J. L. (1997). *Making vocational choices: A theory of vocational personalities and work environments* (3rd ed.). Odessa, FL: Consulting Psychologists Press.

Hou, Z., & Zhang, N. (2007). Counseling psychology in China. *Applied Psychology: An International Review, 56*, 33–50.

Krumboltz, J. D. (1994). Improving career development theory from a social learning perspective. In M. L. Savickas & R. W. Lent (Eds.), *Convergence in career development theories* (pp. 9–31). Palo Alto, CA: CPP Press.

Krumboltz, J. D., & Levin, A. S. (2004). *Luck is no accident: Making the most of happenstance in your life and career*. Atascadero, CA: Impact.

Leong, F. T. L., & Pearce, M. (2011). Desiderata: Towards indigenous models of vocational psychology. *International Journal for Educational and Vocational Guidance, 11*, 65–77.

Leung, S.-M. A., & Yuen, M. (2012). The globalization of an ethnocentric career theory and practice. In M. Watson & M. McMahon (Eds.), *Career development: Global issues and challenges* (pp. 75–91). New York, NY: Nova Science.

McCash, P. (2010). Editorial. *Career Research and Development, 23*, 3.

McCormick, R. M., & Amundson, N. E. (1997). A career-life planning model for first nations people. *Journal of Employment Counseling, 26*(1), 49–60.

McMahon, M., & Patton, W. (1995). Development of a systems theory framework of career development. *Australian Journal of Career Development, 4*, 15–20.

McMahon, M., Patton, W., & Watson, M. (2005). *The my system of career influences (MSCI): Reflecting on my career decisions*. Camberwell, VIC, Australia: ACER Press.

McMahon, M., & Watson, M. (2006). Career research in a post-modern era. *Australian Journal of Career Development, 15*(2), 26–31.

McMahon, M., & Watson, M. (2007). An analytical framework for career research in the postmodern era. *International Journal for Educational and Vocational Guidance, 7*, 169–179.

McMahon, M., & Watson, M. (2010). Story telling: Moving from thin stories to thick and rich stories. In K. Maree (Ed.), *Career counselling: Methods that work* (pp. 53–63). Cape Town, South Africa: Juta.

McMahon, M., & Watson, M. (2012). Career development: 21st century global issues and challenges. In M. Watson & M. McMahon (Eds.), *Career development: Global issues and challenges* (pp. 1–11). New York, NY: Nova Science.

McMahon, M., Watson, M., Foxcroft, C., & Dullabh, A. (2008). South African adolescents' career development through the lens of the systems theory framework: An exploratory study. *Journal of Psychology in Africa, 18*(4), 531–538.

McMahon, M., & Yuen, M. (2010). Career counselling and internationalization. *Asian Journal of Counselling, 16*, 91–111.

Mitchell, K. E., Levin, A. S., & Krumboltz, J. D. (1999). Planned happenstance: Constructing unexpected career opportunities. *Journal of Counseling and Development, 77*(2), 115–124.

Mkhize, N. (2012). Career counselling and indigenous populations: Implications of worldviews. In M. Watson & M. McMahon (Eds.), *Career development: Global issues and challenges* (pp. 125–142). New York, NY: Nova Science.

Neumann, H., McCormick, R. M., Amundson, N. E., & McLean, H. B. (2000). Counselling first nations youth: Applying the first nations career-life planning model. *Canadian Journal of Counselling, 34*(3), 172–185.

Osipow, S. H. (1983). *Theories of career development* (3rd ed.). Englewood Cliffs, NJ: Prentice-Hall.

Parsons, F. (1909). *Choosing a vocation*. Boston, MA: Houghton-Mifflin.

Patton, W., & McMahon, M. (1999). *Career development and systems theory: A new relationship*. Pacific Grove, CA: Brooks/Cole.

Patton, W., & McMahon, M. (2006). *Career development and systems theory: Connecting theory and practice*. Rotterdam, The Netherlands: Sense.

Porfeli, E. J. (2009). Hugo Münsterberg and the origins of vocational guidance. *Career Development Quarterly, 57*, 225.

Pryor, R. G. L., & Bright, J. E. H. (2003). Order and chaos: A twenty-first century formulation of careers. *Australian Journal of Psychology, 55*(2), 121–128.

Pryor, R. G. L., & Bright, J. E. H. (2011). *The chaos theory of careers: A new perspective on working in the twenty-first century*. New York, NY: Routledge.

Raskin, J. D. (2002). Constructivism in psychology: Personal construct psychology, radical constructivism, and social constructionism. In J. D. Raskin & S. K. Bridges (Eds.), *Studies in meaning: Exploring constructivist psychology* (pp. 1–26). New York, NY: Pace University Press.

Reardon, R. C., Lenz, J. G., Sampson, J. P., Jr., & Peterson, G. W. (2011). Big questions facing vocational psychology: A cognitive information processing perspective. *Journal of Career Assessment, 19*, 240–250.

Richardson, M. S. (1993). Work in people's lives: A location for counseling psychologists. *Journal of Counseling Psychology, 40*, 425–433.

Richardson, M. S. (1996). From career counseling to counseling/psychotherapy and work, jobs, and career. In M. L. Savickas & W. B. Walsh (Eds.), *Handbook of career counseling theory and practice* (pp. 347–360). Palo Alto, CA: Davies-Black.

Richardson, M. S. (2000). A new perspective for counsellors: From career ideologies to empowerment through work and relationship practices. In A. Collin & R. A. Young (Eds.), *The future of career* (pp. 197–211). Cambridge, UK: Cambridge University Press.

Roberts, K. (2005). Social class, opportunity structures and career guidance. In B. Irving & B. Malik (Eds.), *Critical reflections on career education and guidance* (pp. 130–142). London, UK: Routledge Falmer.

Roberts, K. (2012). Career development among the lower socioeconomic strata in developed countries. In M. Watson & M. McMahon (Eds.), *Career development: Global issues and challenges* (pp. 29–44). New York, NY: Nova Science.

Sampson, J. P., Jr. (2009). Modern and postmodern career theories: The unnecessary divorce. *Career Development Quarterly, 58*, 91–96.

Savickas, M. L. (1989). Annual review: Practice and research in career counseling and development, 1988. *Career Development Quarterly, 38*, 100–134.

Savickas, M. L. (2001). The next decade in vocational psychology: Mission and objectives. *Journal of Vocational Behavior, 59*, 284–290.

Savickas, M. L. (2002). Career construction: A developmental theory of vocational behavior. In D. Brown & Associates (Ed.), *Career choice and development* (4th ed., pp. 149–205). San Francisco, CA: Jossey Bass.

Savickas, M. L. (2005). The theory and practice of career construction. In S. D. Brown & R. W. Lent (Eds.), *Career development and counseling: Putting theory and research to work* (pp. 42–70). Hoboken, NJ: Wiley.

Savickas, M. L. (2008). Helping people choose jobs: A history of the guidance profession. In J. A. Athanasou & R. van Esbroeck (Eds.), *International handbook of career guidance* (pp. 97–114). Dordrecht, The Netherlands: Springer.

Savickas, M. L. (2011). New questions for vocational psychology: Premises, paradigms, and practices. *Journal of Career Assessment, 19*, 251–258.

Savickas, M. L., & Lent, R. W. (1994). Introduction. A convergence project for career psychology. In M. L. Savickas & R. W. Lent (Eds.), *Convergence in career development theories* (pp. 1–6). Palo Alto, CA: CPP Press.

Savickas, M. L., Nota, L., Rossier, J., Dauwalder, J.- P., Duarte, M. E., Guichard, J., … van Vianen, A. E. M. (2011). Life designing: A paradigm for career construction in the 21st century. *Journal of Vocational Behavior, 75*, 239–250.

Savickas, M. L., & Porfeli, E. J. (2012). Career adaptabilities scale: Construction, reliability, and measurement equivalence across 13 countries. *Journal of Vocational Behavior, 80*, 661–673.

Sharf, R. S. (2010). *Applying career development theory to counseling* (5th ed.). Belmont, CA: Brooks/Cole.

Solmonson, L. L., Mullener, W., & Eckstein, D. G. (2009). *A thematic perspective to lifespan development*. El Cajon, CA: National Social Science Press.

Stead, G. B., & Perry, J. C. (2012). Practice trends, social justice and ethics. In M. Watson & M. McMahon (Eds.), *Career development: Global issues and challenges* (pp. 59–71). New York, NY: Nova Science.

Stead, G. B., Perry, J. C., Munka, L. M., Bonnett, H. R., Shiban, A. P., & Care, E. (2012). Qualitative research in career development: Content analysis from 1990–2009. *International Journal for Educational and Vocational Guidance, 12*, 105–122.

Super, D. E. (1990). A life-span, life-space approach to career development. In D. Brown & L. Brooks (Eds.),

Career choice and development: Applying contemporary theories to practice (2nd ed., pp. 197–261). San Francisco, CA: Jossey-Bass.

Walsh, W. B. (Ed.). (2011). The next big questions in vocational psychology and assessment [Special issue]. *Journal of Career Assessment, 19*(3), 235–236.

Watson, M., & McMahon, M. (2012). Globalisation and career development: A challenging future. In M. Watson & M. McMahon (Eds.), *Career development: Global issues and challenges* (pp. 143–152). New York, NY: Nova Science.

Watson, M., McMahon, M., Mkhize, N., Schweitzer, R., & Mpofu, E. (2011). Career counselling people of African ancestry. In E. Mpofu & L. Blokland (Eds.), *Counselling people of African ancestry* (pp. 281–293). Cambridge, UK: Cambridge University Press.

Watson, M. B., & Stead, G. B. (2006). An overview of career theory. In G. B. Stead & M. B. Watson (Eds.), *Career psychology in the South Africa context* (2nd ed., pp. 13–34). Pretoria, South Africa: Van Schaik.

Young, R. A., & Collin, A. (2004a). Constructivism, social constructionism and career [Special issue]. *Journal of Vocational Behavior, 64*(3), 373–534.

Young, R. A., & Collin, A. (2004b). Introduction: Constructivism and social constructionism in the career field. *Journal of Vocational Behavior, 64*, 373–388.

Young, R. A., Marshall, S. K., Valach, L., Domene, J. F., Graham, M. D., & Zaidman-Zait, A. (2011). *Transition to adulthood: Action, projects, and counseling.* New York, NY: Springer.

Young, R. A., & Valach, L. (2008). Action theory: An integrative paradigm for research and evaluation in career. In J. Athanasou & R. van Esbroeck (Eds.), *International handbook of career guidance* (see Savickas 2008, 1st ed., pp. 643–657). Dordrecht, The Netherlands: Springer.

Young, R. A., Valach, L., & Collin, A. (2002). A contextualist explanation of career. In D. Brown & Associates (Ed.), *Career choice and development* (4th ed., pp. 206–252). San Francisco, CA: Jossey Bass.

Mary McMahon, Mark Watson, and Wendy Patton

Introduction

A feature of career theory development over the last century has been its segmented nature. This is possibly because career theory evolved in order to meet the changing work contexts in which it developed. There have been several challenges to the development of career theory over its relatively brief history. One has been its slow evolvement, indeed with theory often lagging behind the changing nature of the world of work. Thus, trait-and-factor career theory held sway from its inception at the start of the last century until the middle of that century before career theory evolved to include more developmental perspectives. Since then, the assumptions of this earliest career theory remain embedded in a wide range of theories presently in practice (e.g., career construction theory; Savickas, 2005). While this testifies to the lasting contribution of trait-and-factor theory to the field, a need for more holistic and contextually based theories is also now widely recognized.

The slower evolvement of career theory has meant that theory often fails to accurately reflect the realities of individual career development; in this sense, career theory is mostly decontextualized for the times it is presented in. This mismatch between much of established career theory and the realities of the world of work has been exacerbated throughout recent decades by the rapidity of change and the lack of external stability in the world of work.

A related challenge to the development of career theory has been the increasingly diverse contexts from which career clients come. Traditional career theory was formulated in a world (and a world of work) in which there was a greater degree of homogeneity. Indeed, the criticism of established career theory has been its limited target population—usually middle-to-upper class, Caucasian, and, particularly for much of the first half of the last century, male (Patton & McMahon, 2006). The cultural/contextual heterogeneity of populations that career theory now needs to address has challenged the relevance of extant career theory which assumes an orderly, logical, and linear career developmental progression that is increasingly becoming the exception rather than the rule. These challenges have led to the more recent development of career theories which have either emphasized the notion of chance (e.g., the Systems Theory Framework (STF), Patton & McMahon, 1999, 2006) or exclusively focused on chaos and chance (e.g., chaos theory, Bright & Pryor, 2005; Pryor & Bright, 2011), thus shifting career theory development to the other end of the continuum from its stable, predictable roots. For example, the STF incorporates chance as one of a multiplicity of factors that may influence the process of career development. The chaos theory of careers locates

M. McMahon (✉)
School of Education, The University of Queensland, Brisbane, QLD, Australia
e-mail: marylmcmahon@uq.edu.au

G. Arulmani et al. (eds.), *Handbook of Career Development*, International and Cultural Psychology, DOI 10.1007/978-1-4614-9460-7_3, © Springer Science+Business Media, LLC 2014

chance and unpredictability more centrally as cornerstone constructs.

There is a need to address the persistent criticism that career theories are largely decontextualized and thus increasingly less valid and relevant (McMahon & Yuen, 2010; see Stead and Watson (2006) and Watson (2010) in reference to the South African context). At the same time, there is a need for some stability in career theory development. We should be introducing career theories that can accommodate change rather than changing career theories every time significant change occurs in the world of work. Change is a constant that we must live with and stable (but not rigid) career theoretical perspectives are needed that provide us with a way of understanding and adapting to such change. We also need career theories that are inclusive of the broader contextual influences on an individual's career development but which, at the same time, do not lose sight of the traditional focus on the individual. Thus career theories are needed that move from the present focus on decontextualized individuals to a focus on contextualized individuals.

Further on in this chapter, there is a discussion of more recent theoretical movement towards constructivism and towards systemic approaches to career development. Such theoretical developments maintain the focus on the individual, a focus that has been central to career development since career theory was first formulated over a century ago (Parsons, 1909). However, where they differ from previous theories is in their emphasis on internalizing the locus of control of career development to within the individual and in their recognition of the uniqueness of individuals' external contextual factors that impact their career development. A systems theory approach also emphasizes that individuals, as open systems, interact with their contexts and that the impact of contextual factors is a multifaceted recursive process. All this places individuals in the middle of their contextual worlds and the process of career counseling becomes a process of empowering individuals to identify, understand, and adapt to the systemic influences on their career development.

In this chapter, we consider context-resonant systems perspectives in career theory. First, systems theory will be introduced followed by an overview of career theory that includes the philosophical underpinnings of career theory. Next, there is an introduction to the assumptions of systems theories and the role of systems theories in career development is considered. This will be followed by an account of the STF of career development (Patton & McMahon, 1999, 2006), the first and most comprehensive application of systems theory in career development, and its practical applications. The chapter is concluded with a brief summary of the contribution of systemic thinking in career development.

Introducing Systems Theory

Career development is fundamentally about individuals. It is clearly evident, however, that the world in which individuals make decisions about learning and work has become more complex. Correspondingly, the work of career development practitioners has also become more complex and the relevance of career development theory has sometimes been questioned. In response, career development practitioners have sought methods and approaches that enable them to take account of greater complexity in their work with clients. Conceptualizing the complexity of career development may be facilitated by systemic thinking which is evident in recent approaches to career counseling that view clients holistically in the context of their lives (e.g., Amundson's (2009) active engagement; Cochran's (1997) narrative career counseling; McMahon and Watson's (2010) story telling; Peavy's (1998) sociodynamic approach; Savickas et al.'s (2009) life designing). Essentially, these approaches are narrative in orientation and encourage clients to tell their career stories and make meaning of their experiences. Systemic thinking, derived from systems theory, takes an *individual in context* view of clients that considers complexity and avoids oversimplification of career decision-making and career development. Indeed, systems thinking dates back to the time of Aristotle who claimed that the whole is more than the sum of its parts.

First proposed by Ludwig von Bertalanffy and described comprehensively in his seminal text, "General System Theory," in 1968, general systems theory had its origins in biology and offered a new way of viewing organisms by considering them as a whole of interacting parts rather than as parts functioning in isolation from other parts. As early as 1928, von Bertalanffy recognized that investigating "single parts and processes cannot provide a complete picture of the vital phenomena" (von Bertalanffy, 1934, p. 64). Since that time, general systems theory has been applied in mathematics, technology, and philosophy. In the social sciences, systems theory has been applied in a number of fields including counseling, family therapy, and career development. Von Bertalanffy (1968) regarded a system as a "complex of elements standing in interaction" (p. 33). Thus, in practice, systems thinking necessitates thinking in terms of the whole rather than parts; in career development, systems thinking necessitates viewing individuals in the context of their lives.

In this regard, a consistent criticism of career theory is that it has emanated out of a Western, primarily American, context and its application beyond that context and even to all people within that context is uncertain. For example, its application to the career development of women has been criticized (Bimrose, 2008; Cook, Heppner, & O'Brien, 2002a) and its application in other countries and cultures has been questioned (e.g., McMahon & Yuen, 2010; Stead & Watson, 2006; Watson, 2010). Increasingly there have been calls for "new perspectives for a new era" (Coutinho, Dam, & Blustein, 2008, p. 5) in the context of an increasingly global and diverse society (Blustein, 2006; Savickas et al., 2009; Van Esbroeck, 2008).

Systems theory has long been considered as a possible unifying framework in career theory. For example, Osipow (1983) suggested that systems theory had the potential to enhance understanding of individuals by applying concepts from all theories. More recently, counseling approaches informed by systems theory have shown promise in their capacity to be applied in diverse cultures (e.g., McMahon & Watson, 2008; Watson & McMahon, 2009). To date, however, there remains a disconnect between theory and practice in relation to the level of attention they pay to context and the application of systems theory.

Career Theory

Changes in the contexts of career and the broadening of the concept of career development have far outpaced the development of theory to account for it (Amundson, 2005; Brown & Associates, 2002; Patton & McMahon, 2006). Traditional career theories have been challenged as being too narrow, although the more narrow theories have attempted to acknowledge the influence of elements of the broader system in their revised formulations (see Patton & McMahon, 2006). For example, while Super's early work (Super, 1953, 1957) focused on individual development, his later work introduces a greater focus on environmental influences on career (Super, 1992). Theoretical frameworks have been proposed to encompass elements of the social system (e.g., family and friends) and the environmental--societal system (e.g., geographic location, globalization, and socioeconomic circumstances), and the potential for integration and convergence of theories has been explored (Chen, 2003; Patton & McMahon, 1999, 2006; Savickas, 2005; Savickas & Lent, 1994).

Proponents of moves towards convergence in career theory (Chen, 2003; Patton & McMahon, 1999, 2006; Savickas & Lent, 1994) have emphasized the importance of viewing career behaviors as a whole, and also the relationship between all relevant elements in the career decision-making process to each other and to the whole. For example, Patton and McMahon (2006) described the example of a rural adolescent considering postcompulsory schooling which would necessitate a long bus trip morning and night to and from a neighboring city or boarding in that city. Despite achieving well at school and wanting to continue his education, his family felt that because of his age and their socioeconomic circumstances, boarding was not an option and supported their son to accept a secure job in their town and complete further study by correspondence. It is therefore important that contributions from all theories are considered in exploring an individual's career decision-making processes. Amundson (2005) has asserted that recent advances in constructivism, systems theory, action theory, and paradoxical theory have emerged to assist individuals and counselors in constructing personal development in a world of rapid and unprecedented change.

This section of the present chapter will focus on how systems theory has been applied in the career theory field. It is in connecting these two literatures of constructivism and integration that the major contribution of systems theories can be specified. A brief overview of philosophical underpinnings of career theory will be discussed first, followed by a brief description of the major assumptions of systems theories. Finally, an explication of specific systems theories and their contribution will be offered.

Philosophical Underpinnings of Career Theory

For most of its history, career development theory has been influenced by the logical positivist worldview which emphasizes rationality based on objective, value-free knowledge, objectivity over subjectivity, and facts over feelings. Core assumptions of logical positivism include the notion that individual behavior is observable, measurable, and linear, that individuals can be studied separately from their environments, and that the contexts within which individuals live and work are of less importance than their actions (Brown, 2002a). The trait-and-factor theories are illustrative of the assumptions of logical positivism. Specifically, by assessing the traits of an individual (e.g., personality or interests), predictions through a linear matching process may be made about possible occupational options.

More recently, there has been a rise in the influence of the constructivist worldview. Constructivists argue against the possibility of absolute truth, asserting that an individual's construction of reality is constructed *from the inside out* through the individual's own thinking and processing. These constructions are based on individual cognitions in interaction with perspectives formed from person–environment interactions. Constructivism is closely aligned with the philosophical underpinnings of systems theory; both view the person as an open system, constantly interacting with the environment, seeking stability through ongoing change.

Systems theory emphasizes that individuals are self-organizing and that all learning and knowing comprises complex dynamic processes through which the self organizes and reorganizes to achieve equilibrium. The human system is viewed as purposive, ever-evolving, and self-perpetuating. The process is interactive, and the human system operates interdependently with other systems (e.g., family, workforce). Thus, as Granvold (1996) explains, "Life is an ongoing recursion of perturbation and adaptation, disorganization and distress, and emerging complexity and differentiation" (pp. 346–347). The following description by Ford and Ford (1987) illustrates the systems theory contribution to this aspect of constructivism, as well as the integration of a range of interconnected theories in understanding human behavior:

> The Living Systems Framework (LSF) is designed to represent all aspects of being human, not merely a particular facet of behavior or personality.... It describes how the various "pieces" of the person—goals, emotions, thoughts, actions, and biological processes—function both semi-autonomously as a part of a larger unit (the person) in coherent "chunks" of context-specific, goal directed activity (behavior episodes). It also describes how these specific experiences "add up" to produce a unique, self-constructed history and personality (i.e., through the construction, differentiation, and elaboration of behavior episode schemata), and how various processes of change (self-organization, self-construction, and disorganization-reorganization) help maintain both stability and developmental flexibility in the organized patterns that result (steady states). Thus the LSF cannot be easily characterized in terms of traditional

theoretical categories. Rather, it is a way of trying to understand persons in all their complexly organized humanness. (pp. 1–2)

The underpinnings of both constructivism and systems theory represent an epistemological position that emphasizes self-organizing and proactive knowing. Both perspectives assert that individuals actively construct their own reality, and are able to actively construct a meaningful position within the work context.

Assumptions of Systems Theories

Patton and McMahon (1999, 2006) identified a number of key features of systems theory that were influential in their formulation of the STF. These included:

1. Wholes and parts, a concept which emphasizes that each element of a system or subsystem is interdependent upon other elements and that these elements should not be considered in isolation. Hence, a systems approach is holistic.
2. Patterns and rules, emphasizing that relationships exist within and between elements of a system which emerge as patterns within the system. Rules are special types of patterns formed by human systems and vary across different systems.
3. Acausality, emphasizing the multiplicity of relationships between elements, and thus the inherent difficulty in reducing and isolating simplistic causal linear relationships.
4. Recursiveness, a concept which describes nonlinear, multidirectional feedback amongst all elements of a system. It implies a dynamic, fluctuating process within the system as each element communicates with others in an ongoing manner.
5. Discontinuous change, emphasizing that a system is always in flux, albeit balanced by internal homeostatic processes. The term *discontinuous* acknowledges the unpredictability or suddenness of internal or external changes.
6. Open and closed systems, in which a closed system has no relationship to the environment

in which it is positioned, whereas an open system communicates with its environment. Its openness to its context is necessary for its regeneration.
7. Abduction, a concept which stresses the importance of abductive reasoning which is concerned with the emergence of patterns and relationships, and lateral thinking. Deductive and inductive reasoning are linear and therefore limited as processes.
8. Story, through which the whole accounts of relationships and patterns within systems are recounted.

Constructivism and Theory Integration: The Role of Systems Theories

As discussed previously, constructivism and integration of theories are key themes in the current career theory literature. It is within both these fields that we can see a major contribution of systems theory approaches to career. The emphasis on individual meaning-making shifts the focus from the theory to the individual for understanding the complexity of career behavior. It is within the individual that the theories make sense and where construction of meaning around the multiple influences which are relevant to career development occurs—constructivism and integration are key to understandings of career within this framework.

Patton and McMahon (1999, 2006) presented an extensive review of the theoretical journey towards integration, and identified the range of efforts theorists have made to integrate a variety of theoretical perspectives. Attempts at integration of career theory constructs have been located from as early as the 1950s (e.g., Super, 1992; Vondracek, Lerner, & Schulenberg, 1986). For example, Vondracek et al. (1986) integrated constructs from developmental psychology and vocational psychology, and emphasized the importance of integrating sociocultural, economic, and historical constructs into a conceptual model of career development (see Patton (2008) for a full discussion of integration examples). In addition to individual theorists working to develop an integration and comprehensiveness in theories, the literature on convergence has also focused on broad theoretical areas which may serve as bridging theories, or provide structures for an overarching framework. Of the six bridging frameworks identified by Savickas (1995), two are developmental systems theory (DST) and systems theory. Patton and McMahon (2006) added social cognitive theory, action theory, and Savickas' (2005) use of social constructionism as a metatheory. This section of the chapter will pay particular attention to the systems theory examples of frameworks for convergence.

Developmental Systems Theory and Motivational Systems Theory

DST (Ford & Lerner, 1992) was specifically developed to extend developmental-contextualism, the theoretical framework of Vondracek et al. (1986). DST represents a synthesis between developmental-contextualism and the living systems framework (LSF) of Ford and Ford (1987). In integrating a systems approach to developmental-contextualism, DST aims to include an understanding of all systems relevant to understanding an individual's behavior.

Motivational systems theory (MST) (Ford, 1992) was developed to provide a theoretical framework to integrate motivational and behavioral theories (e.g., social learning theory, attribution theory, self-efficacy theory). Its aim is very similar to that which underpinned the development of the STF (Patton & McMahon, 1999, 2006): "The primary theoretical rationale for MST is the urgent need for a conceptual framework that addresses the consensus, cohesion and integration in the field of motivation" (Ford, 1992, p. 244). Vondracek and Kawasaki (1995) have specifically used MST in the career theory literature. They have tried to integrate the centrality of motivational factors in an individual's career development and incorporate the interrelationship of motivational factors with both individual and contextual factors. For example, they have acknowledged that an individual's career decisions are related to motivations which are intricately connected to individual factors as well as contextual (such as socioeconomic, ethnicity) factors. Vondracek and Kawasaki illustrated the value of both DST (Ford & Lerner, 1992) and MST (Ford, 1992) to furthering our understanding of adult career development in particular. They have not yet incorporated the principles of these theoretical frameworks into a comprehensive overarching theoretical framework for career theories.

Systems Theory as a Convergence Framework

Both Blustein (2001) and Bordin (1994) acknowledged the value of systems theory as a basis for a convergence framework. Similarly, Krumboltz and Nichols (1990) applied the LSF to provide an inclusive *map* for specific career decision-making frameworks, its value being in its ability to integrate all of the determinants of human development, and specifically career choice and career development. Krumboltz and Nichols commented that the LSF expands the conceptual areas that have traditionally been considered in current theories of career behavior. While Krumboltz and Nichols believed that existing career theories could be embedded within the overall LSF, there has been no further development of this work by them.

The STF (McMahon & Patton, 1995; Patton & McMahon, 1997, 1999, 2006) was the first attempt to comprehensively present a framework of career development using systems theory. The STF is not a theory of career development; rather it represents a metatheoretical account of career development that accommodates career theories derived out of the logical positivist worldview with their emphasis on objective data and logical, rational processes, and also of the constructivist worldview with its emphasis on holism, personal meaning, subjectivity, and recursiveness between influences. Indeed, one of the advantages of the STF is that it values the contribution of all theories. This framework will be discussed in more detail in the next section of this chapter.

Other systems theory approaches which have attempted to integrate the complex array of career development influences and processes include the ecological approaches of Szymanski and Hershenson (1997) who sought to develop a more inclusive understanding of career and to represent people with disabilities, and Cook et al.'s (2002a) and Cook, Heppner, and O'Brien's (2002b) ecological model of women's career development that represented their multiple life roles and responsibilities and considered the relational and collective nature of women's careers.

The major contribution of systems theory to career theory is in connecting constructivist and convergence agendas and, as outlined by Patton and McMahon (2006), a focus on individuals making meaning of their own careers will continue to encourage a holistic understanding of career and an ongoing drawing on theoretical constructs by individuals as they are relevant to the construction of their career.

Systems Theory Framework of Career Development

Described by Blustein (2006) as an "excellent synthesis of the systems perspective of career development" (p. 94), the STF (see Fig. 3.1; Patton & McMahon, 2006) may be viewed as an integrative *person-in-context* model of career development that serves three primary purposes. First, as a metatheoretical framework, it embraces the diverse range of constructs that are relevant to career development some of which (e.g., interests and values) underpin extant theories and some of which (e.g., disability and socioeconomic circumstances) have traditionally been neglected. Thus, in accommodating extant theories, the development of the STF offered a response to the convergence debate of the early 1990s (Patton & McMahon, 2006). Second, the STF depicts the complexity of the systems within which individuals make decisions related to work and learning. Related to this second purpose, a

critical strength of the STF is evident, specifically its practical utility and relative ease of application in practices such as career counseling and career programs. Third, and related to the complexity of systems, the STF takes account of both the content and the process of career development through its emphasis on interaction and interrelationships and thus addresses criticisms about the static nature of some career theories. This section of the chapter will first describe the STF and subsequently outline its potential applications.

In common with other integrative frameworks (e.g., Bronfenbrenner's (1979) ecological systems theory; Vondracek et al.'s (1986) developmental contextual model), the STF positions the individual as central to a complex dynamic system of intrapersonal and contextual influences. The term *influence* was intentionally chosen by the STF's developers as a nonjudgmental term that does not presuppose, for example, advantage or disadvantage, inhibitor or facilitator. Rather, it is the relationship or interaction between the individual and the influence, and the meaning ascribed to the influence by the individual that are important. As a dynamic system, the STF incorporates both content influences and process influences.

The content influences are represented as interconnected systems, specifically the individual system and the contextual system; the latter comprises the social system and the environmental–societal system (Patton & McMahon, 2006). The individual, social, and environmental–societal systems are depicted within the broader context of time, that is, past, present, and future. In addition to the content influences, the STF incorporates three process influences. Recursiveness is the first of the process influences and may be described as the interaction within and between influences and within and between systems. Change over time is the second of the process influences. The third process influence is depicted by lightning flashes in Fig. 3.1 and represents the unpredictable but sometimes life-changing influence of chance. The subsystems and influences of the STF will now be described beginning with the content influences.

Fig. 3.1 The systems theory framework

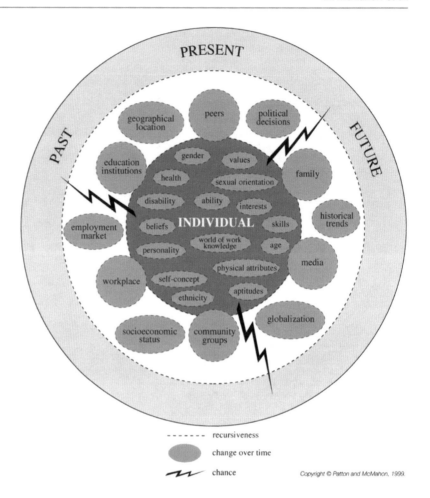

The central location of the individual system of influences in the STF purposefully illustrates the *individual in context* perspective of this metatheoretical framework (Patton & McMahon, 2006). The individual system comprises a range of intrapersonal content influences which are widely known as traits in career theory. Understanding the self has long been one of the primary tenets of career development practice (e.g., Parsons, 1909) and throughout the history of career development emphasis has been placed on particular intrapersonal influences (traits) such as personality, interests, values, and beliefs which have been described in detail in career theory (e.g., Holland (1997) offered a detailed account of personality and Brown (2002b) offered a detailed account of values) and have become subject to the development of an extensive range of career assessment instruments.

Indeed such instruments have resulted in a perception of career counseling as a reductionist *test and tell* process in which occupational predictions are made on the basis of assessment results.

In relation to the emphasis on the individual system evident in career theory to date, a number of points warrant further consideration in terms of the context-resonant nature of systems theory. First, the considerable influence of *test and tell* approaches has pervaded practice to the present time and has been widely criticized for its narrowness and limited emphasis on context. Second, knowing test results is far removed from fully understanding the meaning an individual ascribes to them or to a particular influence. Third, understanding individuals' perceptions of intrapersonal influences (e.g., sexual orientation and disability) that has been neglected in career theory is essential to assisting clients to achieve satisfying careers. Fourth, the cultural background of many individuals is such that an emphasis on individuals and personal traits may not be appropriate as there is a corresponding assumption that decision-making rests with individuals. Rather, in many cultures decision-making resides in families and so considering the individual system in isolation from the contextual system may render career practice inappropriate or ineffective.

The social system represents the social contexts in which individuals live. Few of the social system content influences have been well addressed in career theory to date. Of these influences, family has received most attention. Through interaction with social system influences, individuals construct values, beliefs, and attitudes which influence career decisions. Of the social influences depicted in the STF, media has received the least attention. However, society's increasing reliance on technology and the pervasive influence of media in all its forms suggests that this is an area in need of some attention by career theory.

The environmental–societal system has received little attention in career development although it has received considerable attention in other disciplines such as sociology. For example, socioeconomic status may have profound effects on an individual's learning and work options (Roberts, 2005) yet it has been largely ignored in career theory. More recently Blustein (2006) has raised awareness of this issue in career development. A possible explanation for the lack of attention to environmental–societal influences in career development theory could be that these influences are perceived as distal or indirect. Regardless, these influences cannot be ignored because of their potential influence on individuals. Further, consideration of environmental–societal influences may offer alternative possible accounts of client problems such as unemployment which could be systemically embedded rather than the "fault" of clients.

The process influences of recursiveness, change over time, and chance are significant inclusions in the STF and represent the dynamic nature of career development. Importantly, *recursiveness* represents the multiple and multidirectional interactions between individuals and their systems of influence, and within and between influences. Depicted by dotted lines in Fig. 3.1, recursiveness emphasizes the permeability of influences within and between systems and the nonlinear nature of career development, and minimizes the use of causal explanations. *Change over time* takes account of the widely accepted concept of lifespan career development. It considers both decision-making processes and evolution over time. A circular depiction is used in Fig. 3.1 to illustrate the nonlinear nature of career development and to accommodate the varied career paths possible. It also emphasizes the recursive influence between the past and the present; and between the past, the present, and the future. Possibly because of its random and unpredictable nature, *chance* has received little attention in the career literature until comparatively recently, most notably in the chaos theory of careers (Pryor & Bright, 2011). Chance, however, warrants inclusion because it is unlikely that career development will always be predictable. Chance events in any part of the system of influences may impact the career development of the individual.

The STF does not pretend to incorporate every possible influence. Rather, in recognizing the role of individuals in their career development, the STF may be personalized in practice and individuals may include influences of their own choosing. For example, the complex nature of important influences such as culture and spirituality and their potential location in the STF in more than one system or across influences and systems has resulted in their notable absence from the STF diagram. In practice, however, they are critical influences to explore with clients.

In its acknowledgement of process and individuals' relationship with their systems of influence, the STF is cognizant of the concept of subjective careers (Collin, 1986). Career has traditionally been viewed objectively, that is, the observable progress of an individual's career. The subjective career, by contrast, takes account of individuals' perceptions of their career and other life experiences. In practice, the concept of the subjective career underpins practices that encourage clients to tell stories and make meaning of their experiences.

Practical Application of the STF

A strength of the STF is its practical application. It has been applied in career assessment and career counseling, in settings as diverse as schools, higher education institutions, and large organizations, and in countries such as Australia, South Africa, England, Iceland, and Hong Kong. In the tradition of career theory, the STF has stimulated the development of a qualitative career assessment instrument, My System of Career Influences (MSCI) (McMahon, Patton, & Watson, 2005a, 2005b).

The MSCI is a booklet of 12 pages which begins with a reflection of individuals' career situation that is guided by a series of open-ended questions to which they write their responses. Subsequently, individuals work through a four-page section of the booklet in which they think about the influences on their career sequentially beginning by thinking about themselves (the individual system); the people around them (their social system); the society and environment around them (environmental—societal system); and past, present, and future influences. For each of these systemic reflections, a set of instructions is provided as well as examples on an STF diagram. Individuals may select from the examples or choose their own examples to add to the diagram. By the end of this process, individuals have identified a broad range of influences on their careers depicted on the previous pages. The next step in the process is to combine all of their influences into one systems of influences diagram on a further page of the booklet. On completion of this diagram, the MSCI diagram, individuals then complete a guided reflection based on 10 questions contained on the next page of the booklet where they write their responses. The conclusion to the guided reflection is to prepare an action plan in response to five questions that are listed on a further page of the booklet. A strength of the booklet is that its concluding page provides an opportunity for individuals, after a period of time has elapsed, to complete a second reflection process and draw another system of career influences diagram in order to see how their career influences have changed over time.

Unlike most career assessment instruments that are quantitative in nature, the MSCI offers a qualitative reflective process that may be used with adolescents in career counseling or in career education settings. For example, in Australia the MSCI has been used in career education classes with rural and urban adolescents who were making decisions related to their transition from secondary schooling. Subsequently, the students participated in one-on-one career counseling interviews that were based on their MSCI diagrams. In South Africa, the MSCI has been used with urban middle-class adolescents and with disadvantaged Black adolescents from rural and urban areas. A particular strength of the MSCI is its successful application in disadvantaged settings in South Africa (e.g., Nyoni, 2010). In Hong Kong, the MSCI has been used to explore the career construction stories of three high ability Chinese female college students (Yuen, 2011). The students were interviewed once and then again 1 year after the first interview to discuss their influences, concerns, and career management strategies.

An adult version of the MSCI (McMahon, Watson, & Patton, 2013a, 2013b) has also been developed and trialed successfully in one-on-one career counseling and in corporate and large public sector organizations in South Africa, Australia, and England with individuals as diverse as blue collar workers and executives. Further, in South Africa, it has been used in a university counseling service to assist young women from disadvantaged backgrounds (McMahon, Watson, Chetty, & Hoelson, 2012a, 2012b).

Fundamental to systems theory is the use of story, and the STF has stimulated the development of a story telling approach to career counseling (McMahon, 2005; McMahon &

Watson, 2008; Watson & McMahon, 2009) for which an evidence base is beginning to be built, attesting to its applicability across cultures (McMahon et al., 2012a, 2012b; see Watson & McMahon, 2014, Chap. 35). Story telling is a narrative approach to career counseling. Consistent with other narrative career counseling approaches, the story telling approach identifies connectedness, meaning making, and agency as core constructs. Unlike other narrative approaches, the story telling approach explicitly identifies reflection and learning as core constructs. In the story telling approach, career counselors are positioned as learners and as facilitators who enter the lifespaces of clients to assist them to tell their career stories and construct meaningful futures. Thinking systemically enables individuals to understand the complex systems in which their careers are being constructed (Ryan & Tomlin, 2010).

In relation to multicultural career counseling, Arthur and McMahon (2005) considered the possibility of interventions at different levels of the system (e.g., within families, workplaces, or organizations) other than at the individual level in order to achieve satisfying outcomes for clients. For example, a career adviser may suggest to an adolescent student that it may be worthwhile to include a parent in their discussion of postschool career options. Employee assistance advisors may advocate to management in a workplace on behalf of workers whose needs are not being met. Similarly, a career counselor could negotiate with an employer about the workplace accommodations required by a person with a disability to adequately perform his/her work role.

Relevance for Multiple Cultures: Sensitivity to the Universal and the Particular

As evidenced in the previous section, the MSCI and the story telling approach have been applied in Western cultural settings, as well as in African and Asian cultural settings. The flexibility of the MSCI enables individuals to complete it in culturally sensitive ways. For example, they may begin by reflecting on their intrapersonal influences or by reflecting on influences from their social systems. The example of the MSCI as an application of a context-resonant systems perspective suggests relevance in different cultures. Allowing individuals to construct and tell their own stories gives voice to *their* experience of *their* particular situations from *their* perspectives rather than imposing a more "universal" perspective on them.

New Concepts and Viewpoints: Charting New Directions

As evidenced by the STF and its applications, systems theory and the resultant systems thinking that informs practice has an important contribution to offer career development. For example, context-resonant systems perspectives challenge reductionist, "parts in isolation," and narrowly focused theories and practices to become more holistic and take greater account of context. Second, systems thinking, in its recognition of content and process, encourages career development to be understood from the subjective perspective of clients. Third, the importance of relationship and process necessitates a strong emphasis on collaborative relationships with clients and a reduced emphasis on expert-driven processes. One of the most significant possibilities offered by the application of systemic thinking in practice is its accommodation of the subjective career and thus its capacity to take greater account of context. In so doing, practices informed by systems theory may facilitate relevance to a more diverse client group in more diverse settings. In a world that has become increasingly global and diverse, it seems that context-resonant systems perspectives in career theory are essential to ensure the future of career development.

References

Amundson, N. (2005). The potential impact of global changes in work for career theory and practice.

International Journal of Educational and Vocational Guidance, 5, 91–99.

Amundson, N. E. (2009). *Active engagement* (3rd ed.). Richmond, BC, Canada: Ergon Communications.

Arthur, N., & McMahon, M. (2005). Multicultural career counseling: Theoretical applications of the systems theory framework. *Career Development Quarterly, 53*, 208–222.

Bimrose, J. (2008). Guidance with women. In J. Athanasou & R. van Esbroeck (Eds.), *International handbook of career guidance* (1st ed., pp. 375–404). Dordrecht, The Netherlands: Springer.

Blustein, D. L. (2001). Extending the reach of vocational psychology: Toward an inclusive and integrative psychology of working. *Journal of Vocational Behavior, 59*, 171–182.

Blustein, D. L. (2006). *The psychology of working.* Mahwah, NJ: Lawrence Erlbaum.

Bordin, E. S. (1994). Intrinsic motivation and the active self: Convergence from a psychodynamic perspective. In M. L. Savickas & R. W. Lent (Eds.), *Convergence in career development theories* (pp. 53–62). Palo Alto, CA: CPP Books.

Bright, J. E. H., & Pryor, R. G. L. (2005). The chaos theory of careers: A user's guide. *Career Development Quarterly, 53*(4), 291–305.

Bronfenbrenner, U. (1979). *The ecology of human development.* Cambridge, MA: Harvard University Press.

Brown, D. (2002a). Introduction to theories of career development and choice. Origins, evolution, and current efforts. In D. Brown & Associates (Ed.), *Career choice and development* (4th ed., pp. 3–23). San Francisco, CA: Jossey Bass.

Brown, D. (2002b). The role of work values and cultural values in occupational choice, satisfaction, and success: A theoretical statement. In D. Brown & Associates (Ed.), *Career choice and development* (4th ed., pp. 465–509). San Francisco, CA: Jossey Bass.

Brown, D., & Associates. (2002). *Career choice and development* (4th ed.). San Francisco, CA: Jossey-Bass.

Chen, C. P. (2003). Integrating perspectives in career development theory and practice. *Career Development Quarterly, 51*, 203–216.

Cochran, L. (1997). *Career counseling: A narrative approach.* Thousand Oaks, CA: Sage.

Collin, A. (1986). Career development: The significance of the subjective career. *Personnel Review, 15*(2), 22–28.

Cook, E. P., Heppner, M. J., & O'Brien, K. M. (2002a). Feminism and women's career development: An ecological perspective. In S. G. Niles (Ed.), *Adult career development: Concepts, issues and practices* (3rd ed., pp. 168–189). Alexandria, VA: National Career Development Association.

Cook, E. P., Heppner, M. J., & O'Brien, K. M. (2002b). Career development of women of color and white women: Assumptions, conceptualization, and

interventions from an ecological perspective. *Career Development Quarterly, 50*, 291–305.

Coutinho, M. T., Dam, U. C., & Blustein, D. L. (2008). The psychology of working and globalisation: A new perspective for a new era. *International Journal for Educational and Vocational Guidance, 8*, 5–18.

Ford, M. E. (1992). *Motivating humans: Goals, emotions, and personal agency beliefs.* Newbury Park, CA: Sage.

Ford, M. E., & Ford, D. H. (Eds.). (1987). *Humans as self-constructing living systems: Putting the framework to work.* Hillsdale, NJ: Lawrence Erlbaum.

Ford, D. H., & Lerner, R. M. (1992). *Developmental systems theory: An integrative approach.* Newbury Park, CA: Sage.

Granvold, D. K. (1996). Constructivist psychotherapy. *Families in Society: The Journal of Contemporary Human Services, 77*, 345–359.

Holland, J. L. (1997). *Making vocational choices: A theory of vocational personalities and work environments* (3rd ed.). Odessa, FL: Consulting Psychologists Press.

Krumboltz, J. D., & Nichols, C. W. (1990). Integrating the social learning theory of career decision making. In W. B. Walsh & S. H. Osipow (Eds.), *Career counseling: Contemporary topics in vocational psychology* (pp. 159–192). Hillsdale, NJ: Erlbaum.

McMahon, M. (2005). Career counseling: Applying the Systems Theory Framework of career development. *Journal of Employment Counseling, 42*(1), 29–38.

McMahon, M., & Patton, W. (1995). Development of a systems theory of career development. *Australian Journal of Career Development, 4*, 15–20.

McMahon, M., Patton, W., & Watson, M. (2005a). *The My System of Career Influences (MSCI) facilitators' guide.* Camberwell, Australia: ACER Press.

McMahon, M., Patton, W., & Watson, M. (2005b). *The My System of Career Influences (MSCI): Reflecting on my career decisions.* Camberwell, Australia: ACER Press.

McMahon, M., & Watson, M. (2008). Systemic influences on career development: Assisting clients to tell their career stories. *Career Development Quarterly, 56*, 280–288.

McMahon, M., & Watson, M. (2010). Story telling: Moving from thin stories to thick and rich stories. In K. Maree (Ed.), *Career counselling: Methods that work* (pp. 53–63). Cape Town, South Africa: Juta.

McMahon, M., Watson, M., Chetty, C., & Hoelson, C. (2012a). Examining process constructs of narrative career counselling: An exploratory case study. *British Journal of Guidance and Counselling, 40*, 127–141.

McMahon, M., Watson, M., Chetty, C., & Hoelson, C. (2012b). Story telling, career assessment and career counselling: A higher education case study. *South African Journal of Higher Education, 26*(4), 729–741.

McMahon, M., Watson, M., & Patton, W. (2013a). *The My System of Career Influences Adult Version (MSCI Adult): A reflection process. Facilitators' Guide* Brisbane, Australia: Australian Academic Press.

McMahon, M., Watson, M., & Patton, W. (2013b). *The My System of Career Influences Adult Version (MSCI Adult): A reflection process.* Brisbane, Australia: Australian Academic Press.

McMahon, M., & Yuen, M. (2010). Internationalisation and career counselling. *Asian Journal of Counselling, 16*(2), 91–112.

Nyoni, A. (2010). *Systemic influences in the career development of low socio-economic status black South African adolescents* (Unpublished B. Psych treatise). Nelson Mandela Metropolitan University, South Africa.

Osipow, S. H. (1983). *Theories of career development* (2nd ed.). Englewood Cliffs, NJ: Prentice-Hall.

Parsons, F. (1909). *Choosing a vocation.* Boston, MA: Houghton Mifflin.

Patton, W. (2008). Recent developments in career theories: The influences of constructivism and convergence. In J. Athanasou & R. Van Esbroeck (Eds.), *International handbook of career guidance* (pp. 133–156). Dordrecht, The Netherlands: Springer.

Patton, W., & McMahon, M. (1997). *Career development in practice: A systems theory perspective.* Sydney, NSW, Australia: New Hobsons Press.

Patton, W., & McMahon, M. (1999). *Career development and systems theory: A new relationship.* Pacific Grove, CA: Brooks/Cole.

Patton, W., & McMahon, M. (2006). *Career development and systems theory: Connecting theory and practice.* Rotterdam, The Netherlands: Sense Publishers.

Peavy, R. V. (1998). *Sociodynamic counselling: A constructivist perspective.* Victoria, BC, Canada: Trafford.

Pryor, R. G. L., & Bright, J. E. H. (2011). *The chaos theory of careers: A new perspective on working in the twenty-first century.* New York, NY: Routledge.

Roberts, K. (2005). Social class, opportunity structures and career guidance. In B. Irving & B. Malik (Eds.), *Critical reflections on career education and guidance* (pp. 130–142). London, UK: Routledge.

Ryan, C. W., & Tomlin, J. H. (2010). Infusing systems thinking into career counseling. *Journal of Employment Counseling, 47,* 79–85.

Savickas, M. L. (1995). Current theoretical issues in vocational psychology: Convergence, divergence, and schism. In W. B. Walsh & S. H. Osipow (Eds.), *Handbook of vocational psychology* (pp. 1–34). Mahwah, NJ: Erlbaum.

Savickas, M. L. (2005). The theory and practice of career construction. In S. D. Brown & R. W. Lent (Eds.), *Career development and counseling: Putting theory and research to work* (pp. 42–70). Hoboken, NJ: Wiley.

Savickas, M. L., & Lent, R. W. (Eds.). (1994). *Convergence in career development theories: Implications for science and practice.* Palo Alto, CA: CPP Books.

Savickas, M. L., Nota, L., Rossier, J., Dauwalder, J.-P., Duarte, M. E., Guichard, J., . . . van Vianen, A. E. M. (2009). Life designing: A paradigm for career construction in the 21st century. *Journal of Vocational Behavior, 75,* 239–250.

Stead, G. B., & Watson, M. B. (Eds.). (2006). *Career psychology in the South Africa context* (2nd ed., pp. 13–34). Pretoria, South Africa: Van Schaik.

Super, D. E. (1953). A theory of vocational development. *American Psychologist, 8,* 185–190.

Super, D. E. (1957). *The psychology of careers.* New York, NY: Harper and Row.

Super, D. E. (1992). Toward a comprehensive theory of career development. In D. H. Montross & C. J. Shinkman (Eds.), *Career development: Theory and practice* (pp. 35–64). Springfield, IL: Charles Thomas.

Szymanski, E. M., & Hershenson, D. B. (1997). Career development of people with disabilities: An ecological model. In R. M. Parker & E. M. Szymanski (Eds.), *Rehabilitation counseling: Basics and beyond* (3rd ed., pp. 327–378). Austin, TX: Pro-Ed.

Van Esbroeck, R. (2008). Career guidance in a global world. In J. A. Athanasou & R. Van Esbroeck (Eds.), *International handbook of career guidance* (pp. 23–44). Dordrecht, The Netherlands: Springer.

von Bertalanffy, L. (1934). *Modern theories of development.* UK: Oxford University Press. (German original: von Bertalanffy, L. (1928). *Kritische Theorie der Formbildung.* Berlin: Borntraeger.)

von Bertalanffy, L. (1968). *General system theory.* New York, NY: George Braziller.

Vondracek, F. W., & Kawasaki, T. (1995). Toward a comprehensive framework for adult career development theory and intervention. In W. B. Walsh & S. H. Osipow (Eds.), *Handbook of vocational psychology* (2nd ed., pp. 111–141). Mahwah, NJ: Erlbaum.

Vondracek, F. W., Lerner, R. M., & Schulenberg, J. E. (1986). *Career development: A life-span developmental approach.* Hillsdale, NJ: Erlbaum.

Watson, M. (2010). Transitioning contexts of career psychology in South Africa. *Asian Journal of Counselling, 16*(2), 133–148.

Watson, M., & McMahon, M. (2009). Career counseling in South African higher education: Moving forward systemically and qualitatively. *South African Journal of Higher Education, 23*(3), 470–481.

Watson, M., & McMahon, M. (2014). Making meaning of quantitative assessment in career counseling through a story telling approach. In G. Arulmani, A. J. Bakshi, F. T. L. Leong, & A. G. Watts (Eds.), *Handbook of career development.* New York, NY: Springer.

Yuen, M. (2011). *Understanding Chinese female college students' career construction: The use of My System of Career Influences (MSCI) in Hong Kong.* (Unpublished manuscript).

Life Span Theory and Career Theories: Rapprochement or Estrangement?

Anuradha J. Bakshi

Introduction

Why do we need theories? I would like to answer this question using Kuhnian notions (see Kuhn, 1970). Theories provide important lenses or frames of reference to those committed to a field, that is, to academicians, researchers, and practitioners. Theories, within a field of study, are selective about the phenomena they address and thus by implication those phenomena are judged worthy for inclusion in research and practice. They provide a construal of the phenomena and the interrelationships between phenomena; they construct the world of such phenomena. In effect, theories guide us in constructing and viewing the phenomena in our discipline. They not only inform us about "what to see," but also "what it is" and "how to see it." Interpretive filters, (at least while in prominence) theories help us in making meaning, in making sense of the complexities that otherwise characterize the phenomena in our discipline. As explanatory frameworks, theories have the right balance of certainty and uncertainty, that which is thought to be known and that which needs exploration. Because of such balance, theories do not promote mere complacency but invite continuing work in extending the boundaries of the known and the

useful. Theories permit prediction. Human beings, including scientists, are not satisfied with describing what they think *is* happening under x, y, z conditions; they like to think of what *will* happen given particular circumstances. In short, theories enable selection, construction, description, explanation, and prediction of phenomena and the pattern of relationships between phenomena.

Why do we need new theories? Once again, I have answered this question drawing on Kuhn's (1970) ideas. This chapter is predicated on the assumption that we do need theories and as is quintessential of human culture, once we have a product, we have set ourselves to ongoing innovation—the product of yesterday always has benefits and shortcomings. When fresh, the benefits eclipse and obscure the shortcomings. When we come to take the product more for granted, the shortcomings become increasingly visible until they are glaringly obvious and impel redesigning. Kuhn has indicated that the shortcomings had existed all along; they do. At the same time, changing times and changing relevance may also bring particular shortcomings to the fore.

Unlike products of human culture such as a mobile phone or a car, a theory is a set of (partially verified) beliefs. When a particular model of a phone or a car is launched in the market, already replacement models with improved features are being designed in the research and development departments of respective industries. Such fast-paced deliberate innovation

A.J. Bakshi (✉)
Department of Human Development, Nirmala Niketan College of Home Science, University of Mumbai, Mumbai, India
e-mail: anustra@gmail.com

G. Arulmani et al. (eds.), *Handbook of Career Development*, International and Cultural Psychology,
DOI 10.1007/978-1-4614-9460-7_4, © Springer Science+Business Media, LLC 2014

does not characterize theoretical advancements in a field. Human beings when committed to a set of beliefs are likely to resist change (Kuhn, 1970). In the end, however, the theory is also a product of human culture and cannot escape innovation. As Kuhn has clarified (albeit with the use of the word *paradigm*), for a person with reduced commitment to the set of beliefs that comprise a theory (e.g., a new entrant to the field, who could have crossed over from another discipline), the shortcomings are visible, insupportable or at least unnecessary, and require an alternative construal and viewing. Such a person or group of persons may propose an alternative set of beliefs. When the force of arguments of this person or group coincides with escalating discomfort with and diminished confidence in the beliefs and benefits of an existing theory (or paradigm), allegiance is transferred; commitment to a new set of beliefs gives rise to a new theory/paradigm (see Kuhn, 1970).

An existing theory provides a useful box or frame; a new theory requires us to step outside this box (even though into a new box). In so doing, a new theory provokes fresh thinking and renews the field. It redirects the efforts of professionals and redoubles benefits for the field and those for whom (or for which) the field's professionals strive. Therefore, the second assumption in this chapter is that we need *new* theories.

A third assumption is that cross-fertilization across (allied) disciplines is profitable. Innovations and advancements in allied fields can be tapped gainfully. A new theory can be sought from an allied field, and applied to the field of one's interest. A fourth assumption, which brings us closer to the purpose of this chapter, is that human development is an allied field which has exceptional salience for professionals in the careers field (i.e., researchers or practitioners). Career development, logically, is subsumed under human development and subject to principles of development formulated both generally as well as specifically. It follows that theoretical advancements in the study of human development can have a bearing on our understanding of career development and

thereby the practice of career guidance and counseling.

Of the many recent theoretical developments in human development, one that stands out is life span theory. The utility of life span theory is evident in its overarching framework, comprehensiveness, inclusion of multiple levels of generality/specificity, and clear applicability to emerging concerns. Therefore in this chapter, I have selected life span theory as one contemporary human development theory and advocated its usefulness for the careers field. In order to clarify the extent to which life span theory opens new perspectives or reiterates extant perspectives, I have examined whether and in what ways there is a meeting ground between life span theory in human development on the one hand, and career theories on the other. Thus, first I have outlined and discussed some of the key ideas of life span theory. Next, I have examined career theories for the extent of their rapprochement with life span theory. This exercise yields new directions as well as reinforces existing foci in career theory, research, and practice.

Life Span Theory

The chief protagonist of life span theory (or life span developmental psychology) is Paul B. Baltes (1939–2006). There are many current proponents including Ulman Lindenberger and Ursula Staudinger. In this section, I first present an overview of key ideas of life span theory. Following which, in the remaining subsections I discuss the key ideas one-by-one.

Overview of Key Ideas

Several of the key ideas of life span theory, largely adapted from Baltes, Lindenberger, and Staudinger (2006), are listed in Box 4.1. Also using Baltes et al. (2006), I have explained the interdependence between these key ideas in this subsection.

Box 4.1: Selected Key Ideas from Life Span Theory (Adapted from Baltes et al., 2006)

- Lifelong processes in development
- Change as a pivotal concept; more importance to change than in previous theories of development
- Reformulation of the concept of developmental change
- Development as a gain-loss dynamic
- Development as a process of selective adaptation
- Culture as compensation
- Development as a process of biocultural co-construction
- Incomplete architecture of human development

The foundational idea in life span theory is that there are lifelong processes in development (Baltes et al., 2006). The acknowledgement of lifelong developmental processes makes *change* the cornerstone of human development. After all, we cannot say that (ontogenetic) development is ongoing across the span of a human lifetime and concomitantly expect no change during a substantial part of this lifetime, or rather for the majority of the lifetime. Yet, change cannot be integrated into characterizations of the entire life span without invalidating conventional notions of change. The recognition that change occurs past adolescence and stretches across adulthood simultaneously requires a reformulation of the concept of change. Developmental change can no longer be confined to a unidirectional progressive process (Baltes et al., 2006). In the grand theories of human development (e.g., Freud's theory of psychosexual development, Piaget's theory of cognitive development), change was defined as universal gains until adolescence; those studying adulthood typically stressed losses across adulthood. In contrast, change in life span theory is conceptualized as multidirectional: instead of gains until adolescence/young adulthood and gradually increasing losses thereafter, development at each point or period in the life span is thought to be constituted

of both gains and losses (Baltes et al., 2006). Of course, the proportion of gains versus losses may shift across the span of one's life (Baltes et al., 2006). The gain-loss dynamic idea dovetails with the core idea of development as a process of selective adaptation. Each selection (specialization) followed by selective optimization entails "not only advances in adaptive capacity but also losses in adaptivity for alternative pathways" (Baltes et al., 2006, p. 581).

Three other interrelated set of ideas deserve mention. Physically, the human being is deficient in most respects in comparison to other species (Baltes et al., 2006). Without the products of human culture, our survival would be severely threatened. For instance, there are many species that can literally outrun us; we do not qualify as the fastest runners in a cross-species comparison. Yet, as a consequence of human knowledge and technology, we have diverse vehicles and transport systems many of which allow travel at speeds much faster than that of any other species, with far greater adaptability, over or under land/water and in the air/outer space. In fact, one of the speed cars (a product of human culture) is named after just such a species that otherwise can outpace us with ease—jaguar. Therefore, in this set, the first idea is that human cultural products compensate the biology of human beings (Baltes et al., 2006). The next idea is a clear corollary: Development is a process of biocultural co-construction (Baltes et al., 2006). Processes and products of human culture compensate human biology and extend the functional capacities of human beings. Development, then, is the outcome of these changed functional capacities. Moreover, since human cultural innovations are ongoing, biocultural co-construction is likewise evolving (Baltes et al., 2006). Newer cultural processes and products will enable novel functional capacities or enhance existing functional capacities, which in turn can lead to heretofore unknown or less known developmental outcomes. To the extent that human culture continues to produce new processes and products, to that extent biocultural co-construction will also yield novelties, and the architecture of human development will continue to change (Baltes et al., 2006).

Lifelong Processes in Development

Principal Idea

As reflected in the title of the theory, life span theory is founded on the acknowledgement of lifelong adaptational processes (Baltes, 1987). Developmental processes are conceptualized as occurring across the entire age spectrum from conception into old age (Baltes et al., 2006). Despite sounding self-evident, this is in sharp contrast to the grand theories of human development (e.g., those of Sigmund Freud and Jean Piaget), which locate the terminal stage (representing the highest developmental achievement) in adolescence or at best early adulthood. The stage conceptualizations of Freud and Piaget imply that there are no (notable) developmental achievements after adolescence. Given the new and changing challenges, roles, and settings in and across adulthood (e.g., worker roles and settings; family roles such as those of a parent, grandparent, aunt, uncle, and other significant kinship roles), it is perplexing why an end-stage in development would be located at the onset of adulthood. In my view, it is quite like fairytales which end prematurely and unsatisfyingly with "and they lived happily ever after."

Historically, we have swung from disregarding early years (see Cairns & Cairns, 2006) to revering/elevating the role of early years (ignoring developmental opportunities that come later), and life span theory counters the assumption that adult years are not important for development. As specified by Baltes, Staudinger, and Lindenberger (1999), the core assumption of life span theory is that development is not concluded on reaching adulthood; instead developmental processes regulate the entire life course such that "from conception onward lifelong adaptive processes of acquisition, maintenance, transformation, and attrition in psychological structures and functions are involved" (p. 472). No one period in individual development is privileged over another, except in regard to a temporal order (Baltes et al., 2006). Temporal priority of earlier years or periods in the life span does not diminish or undermine the unique developmental agenda of later years. The point is not to "disproportionately emphasize adulthood rather than childhood" (Baltes, 1987, p. 623) but to "expect each age period of the life span (e.g., infancy, childhood, adolescence, adulthood, old age) to have its own developmental agenda and to make some unique contribution to the organization of the past, present, and future in ontogenetic development" (Baltes et al., 2006, pp. 569–570). Even an infancy researcher can espouse a life span orientation; for example, in examining the interaction patterns between infants and caregivers, it is relevant to recognize that "adults are not fixed personages but that they are themselves subject to developmental goals and challenges" (Baltes et al., 2006, p. 571).

A consensus about the importance of the entire life course is a substantial achievement in Western thought. In Eastern thought, when linear time frames are chosen, developmental processes are considered as occurring before, during, and after any single lifetime: conception and death are not the boundary markers.

Historical Background/Impetus

Baltes et al. (e.g., 1999, 2006) have pointed out that it is in American psychology that life span thinking (or a consensus about the necessity of a life span orientation) has a short history; in contrast in Germany, developmental psychology has always had a life span orientation, starting from the influential work of Johann Nikolaus Tetens in 1777. Although Freud's stage conceptualization appears to be an exception, Baltes et al. (2006) have asserted that in the German intellectual heritage, human development has not been identified with physical growth such that one would expect developmental achievements to be attained at adolescence/early adulthood; instead, it is the roles of socialization, education, and culture that have been favored in the study of human development. In contrast, developmental psychology in North America and England emerged within an intellectual context dominated by genetics and theories of biological evolution in the early 1900s (Baltes et al., 1999). "From biology, with its maturation-based concept of growth, may have sprung the dominant American emphasis in developmental psychology on child psychology and child development" (Baltes et al., 1999, p. 473). The study of human development in the North American tradition, therefore, is less unified and is strongly characterized by age specializations (e.g., child development, gerontology) also reflected in divisive Divisions of the American Psychological Association (APA): Adult Development and Aging is an independent division (Division 20), not part of Developmental Psychology (Division 7) (Baltes et al., 1999, 2006). Baltes et al. (1999, 2006) have attributed the more recent consensus about a life span approach in American psychology to three events: the greying of populations, the emergence of the field of gerontology, and the follow-up of child participants of longitudinal studies into adult years, including later adult years. In an intellectual context like that in the United States, partnership among age specialists is crucial but may fall short unless the essentially integrative character of a life span orientation is recognized and lived (Baltes et al., 2006).

Plasticity as Pivotal

The declaration of lifelong processes in development necessitates an increased attention to developmental change (Baltes, 1987). It obliges us to be open to the possibility of (intraindividual) changes in structural and functional capacities beyond the threshold of adulthood, and to direct efforts to identify and optimize developmental changes especially in later sections of the life span. Unsurprisingly, therefore, is Baltes's observation that plasticity (i.e., intraindividual modifiability or malleability) "is the concept most emphasized by life span researchers" (Baltes et al., 2006, p. 584), or his assertion that life span researchers have a "strong belief" in the "sizeable plasticity" of humans (Baltes, 1987, p. 618). Of course, Baltes et al. (2006) have specified that the construct of plasticity rather than implying "complete or arbitrary malleability of behavior," indicates that "behavior is always open

and constrained at the same time" (p. 584). They endorse Brim and Kagan's statement that

> ... humans have a capacity for change across the life span from birth to death ... [and that] the consequences of the events of early childhood are continually transformed by later experiences, making the course of human development more open than many have believed. (as cited in Baltes et al., 2006, p. 584)

The notion of plasticity is antithetical to developmental fixities or "a highly constrained" developmental course (Baltes et al., 2006). Moreover, plasticity and optimal human development go hand-in-hand: "Because of its investability into many activities, generating a high level of general plasticity is the perhaps most significant target for successful development" (Baltes et al., 2006, p. 593).

Development as a Gain-Loss Dynamic

Shortcomings of the Traditional Formulation of Developmental Change

Life span scholars were struck by the shortcomings of traditional formulations of developmental change. Many stage conceptualizations of development were not only faulty in their omission of a large chunk of the life span. Any stage conceptualization (regardless of the extent of its coverage of the life span) by implication promotes the following questionable ideas about development:

- Development as constituted of unidirectional changes (Baltes et al., 2006).
- Development as characterized by (only) growth or progression; akin to physical maturation (Baltes et al., 2006).
- Development as comprising stepwise universal gains: That is, from one step to another there is an expectation of a system-wide change. In other words, this change is an overall, pervasive gain and one that is applicable to a person by virtue of age regardless of who the person is. The notion of a system-wide change fails to take into account:

– Multidimensionality and multifunctionality (Baltes, 1997).
– Uneven rates of development/achievement
  across multiple functional domains;
  differences in age-onsets and age-offsets
  of particular developmental trajectories
  (Baltes et al., 2006).
– Adaptive specificities (Baltes et al., 2006).
– Multidirectional developmental changes:
  developmental changes are not always
  incremental, they do not always yield an
  increase in functional efficacy; development at no age can be expressed as pure
  gain (Baltes, 1987, 1997; Baltes et al.,
  2006).
– Discontinuities in prediction (Baltes et al.,
  2006, p. 581); asequential aspects in development (Flavell, as cited in Kagan, 1980).
– Developmental changes that are not
  associated with chronological age (Baltes
  et al., 2006).
– The role of agency; individual differences
  in rates of development; intraindividual
  plasticity (Baltes et al., 2006).
– The roles of culture, history (Baltes, 1987),
  gender, poverty.
– Plurality, dynamism, and openness in
  development (Baltes, 1987, 1997; Baltes
  et al., 2006).

Kagan (1980), in a similar vein, observed that
most developmental psychologists appear to be
mechanistic (i.e., they view development as
constituted of linear chains of derivatives) and
romantic (i.e., they view development as an inex-
orable advancement towards a desired end-state).
In applying the concept of development to the
entire life span, life span scholars were clear that
they had to "go beyond the traditional conception
of development as growth and open the concept
of development to a larger framework of
changes" (Baltes et al., 2006, p. 582). Conversely, the period through adulthood and especially in late adulthood was traditionally
conceptualized as characterized by only decline
(i.e., by losses) (Baltes, 1987; Uttal & Perlmutter,
1989). Life span scholars, therefore, have also
had to deconstruct the "decline view of aging"
and integrate aging into a framework of development (Baltes, 1987, p. 616).

Dynamics of Gains and Losses

How can the concept of development embrace a
"larger framework of changes" that is relevant
across the life span? Clearly, it became essential
to define development as "*any* change in the
adaptive capacity of an organism, whether positive or negative" (Baltes, 1987, p. 616). One may
still argue that all that is accomplished is that
now aging is also recognized as development;
thus, in the early periods of the life span, there
are positive changes in the adaptive capacity of
humans, and later there are negative changes.
However, the expansion of the concept of development has one other crucial feature: simultane-
ity of gains and losses at each point along the life
span. Replacing the either-or notion (i.e., developmental periods characterized by either gains or
losses), across the life span, development is
conceptualized as always constituted of "the
joint occurrence of gains and losses, both within
and across domains of functioning" (Baltes et al.,
2006, p. 583). In other words, "there is no development (ontogenetic change) without a loss, just
as there is no loss without a gain" (Baltes et al.,
2006, p. 570). Development is "an ongoing,
changing, and interacting system of gains and
losses in adaptive capacity" (Baltes et al., 2006,
p. 583); that is, development is characterized by
the "dynamics of gains and losses" (p. 574).

Life Span View

At the same time, the dynamics of simultaneous
gains and losses do not overrule the occurrence
of overall trends in growth or decline across the
life span (Baltes et al., 2006). That is, gains and
losses do not occur in equal proportions throughout life (Baltes, 1987). In proposing a life span
view of the dynamics of gains and losses, Baltes
et al. (2006) have described *three* developmental
functions:

• Growth, which involves behaviors targeted
  at achieving enhanced levels of adaptive
  capacity/functioning.
• Maintenance and resilience, which involve
  behaviors targeted at maintaining (when a
  challenge is encountered) or recovering
  (when a loss has occurred) levels of adaptive
  capacity/functioning. Given that maintenance

requires efforts, it is not quite a "no change" phenomenon (see Valsiner, 2006).

- Regulation of loss, which involves behaviors that are targeted at organizing satisfactory functioning at levels lower than previous levels because of biological or social/material (and other environmental) losses.

Resources are largely allocated to growth during childhood and early adulthood; whereas, resources are allocated increasingly to maintenance and resilience during adulthood. In late adulthood, resources are allocated increasingly to management of loss. Nonetheless, in old age "some targets for positive change continue to be realistic, such as advances in emotional and spiritual regulation or wisdom" (Baltes et al., 2006, p. 579).

Universal and Particular

The gain-loss dynamic principle of development replaces the notion of universal gains (i.e., gains that are pervasively applicable across domains, individuals, cultures, and historical times). What remains universal is that there is a gain-loss dynamic at all points in development for everyone; also that successful development entails the maximization of gains and the minimization of losses (Baltes et al., 2006). Very importantly, the gain-loss dynamic principle is especially respectful of the particular. Baltes et al. (2006) have stressed that a gain in ontogenetic development or a loss "defies an absolutist definition" (p. 570). In considering what is a gain and what is a loss, and also thereby to identify and promote successful development, it is critical to take into account the person, age, culture, and historical time (Baltes et al., 2006).

Development as Selection and Selective Adaptation

Life span researchers reject the perspective that development is largely governed by a process of unfolding of characteristics. Instead, they assert that in ontogenesis, development is the outcome of "selection from a pool of more or less constrained potentialities and the subsequent selective optimization of the entered pathways including the construction of novel pathways that were not part of the original system" (Baltes et al., 2006, p. 582). Adaptive capacities are created or strengthened in selected and optimized areas; in other areas there is reduction in adaptive capacities. The principle of development as a process of selective adaptation interlocks with the principle of gain-loss dynamics in development. Each principle is a corollary of the other.

Selective Optimization with Compensation

Selective optimization with compensation (SOC) theory is an "overall theory of successful life span development" (Baltes et al., 2006, p. 574). Baltes et al. (e.g., 2006) promote the theory as *one* example of an all-purpose or widely relevant life span developmental theory. The principal tenet of this theory is that successful development requires "the specification and coordinated orchestration of three processes: Selection, optimization, and compensation" (Baltes et al., 2006, p. 574). At any given point in development, an individual selects from multiple possible developmental trajectories which provides a focus in development and allows advanced levels of functioning; furthermore, for such selection to effect successful development (i.e., maximizing gains and minimizing losses), selection needs to be synchronized with optimization and compensation (Baltes et al., 2006). It is not necessary that selection, optimization, and compensation always entail conscious and active processes; in fact, these processes could be conscious or unconscious, internal or external, active or passive (Baltes et al., 2006).

There are six additional postulates that provide a clearer perspective on SOC (Baltes et al., 2006):

- SOC is a broadly applicable system of proactive development; SOC can enhance functioning in any domain of functioning.
- Selection, optimization, and compensation constitute universal processes beneficial to development.

- The particular expressions of selection, optimization, and compensation are specific to the person and the context(s).
- SOC has a developmental path. Peak usage is in adulthood.
- There can be contexts wherein SOC is not adaptive.
- A behavior is not fixed in whether it is only indicative of selection, optimization, or compensation. A behavior, which in one context was part of compensation, can in another context become part of optimization.

Selection

Baltes (1997) has reminded us that selection is a necessary process in development: Development occurs within conditions that include limited time and resources; development is always oriented towards specific goals. Baltes et al. (2006) have described two types of selection. Elective selection entails an active agent who takes initiative and chooses a focus and directionality that (s)he desires in his/her development. Loss-based selection refers to the choices that a person is forced to make in order to accommodate to losses (e.g., loss in functioning in old age). This may include reorganizing one's goal-related priorities, decreasing the number of goals through reduced aspirations, and formulating new potential goals that can be met with the limited resources. In my view, the notions of elective selection and loss-based selection have an even more general relevance than that elucidated in Baltes's writings. For example, an important question to ask is whether in conditions of poverty, or family dominance, loss-based selection is higher than elective selection regardless of developmental stage.

Optimization

Selection although necessary to development is not sufficient by itself (Baltes et al., 2006). Just by choosing goals, a person cannot attain desired developmental outcomes. Relevant means/methods/resources have to be acquired, refined, and coordinated such that goals can be achieved (Baltes et al., 2006). Thus the processes involved in the "procedural mechanisms of goal-attainment" are referred to as optimization (Baltes et al., 2006, p. 593). The more complex the goals, the more likely it is that optimization requires reciprocal enhancement and organization among multiple means or methods. Baltes et al. add that optimization can be specific to a particular domain and to a particular goal; alternatively, optimization can also include the means or methods that promote the achievement of successful development across domains and across goals. As already mentioned, generation of high levels of general plasticity is a domain-general means of achieving successful development. Also, once again I would like to ask a context-specific question: Are the methods or means for optimization fewer for those in poverty?

Compensation

Under conditions of loss of means, the process of compensation helps in maintaining functioning by substituting or replacing means (Baltes et al., 2006). Baltes et al., specify the two types of conditions requiring activation of compensation: (a) Selection and optimization themselves require compensation in nontargeted or nonfocal domains. When particular goals are selected and optimized, there is reduced time and means for attaining other goals. This is a reiteration of the gain-loss dynamic principle in development. For example, Howard Gardner's selection of the goal of becoming a psychologist and not a concert pianist led him to extensively diminish time and resources allocated to playing the piano and refining his technique. Moreover, optimization in one domain sometimes has a negative transfer to another skill-set which then necessitates the use of compensation. (b) Compensation is also required when the person experiences negative changes in available resources biologically, socially, or environmentally; of which, Baltes et al. have particularly focused on the decrease in resources due to aging. As before, the context-specific question that could be asked is whether those in poverty are more likely to engage in the process of compensation rather than optimization?

Research Support

Baltes et al. (2006) have reported substantial support for SOC theory (in samples drawn from Germany or the United States). For example, individuals have been found to engage in behaviors that are congruent with SOC premise. Moreover, the use of SOC processes is associated with increased levels of functioning. Developmentally, the peak usage (as mentioned) is in adulthood whereas in childhood/adolescence and in late adulthood, the SOC processes are not completely acquired, or put to use, managed, and synchronized.

SOC processes have been studied with regard to careers as well. In a study conducted in Germany (Schmitt, Zacher, & Frese, 2012), the interrelationships between problem solving demands at work, SOC strategy use, fatigue, and job satisfaction were examined in employed adults. It was found that problem solving demands were positively correlated with fatigue but uncorrelated with job satisfaction; in comparison, SOC strategy was positively correlated with job satisfaction and uncorrelated with fatigue. Zacher and Frese (2011) in another study in Germany examined the interrelationship between age, complexity of job, use of SOC strategies, and a focus on opportunities. Older employees who were more successful in maintaining a focus on opportunities were either engaged in a high-complexity job or were making a greater use of SOC strategies in a low-complexity job. In contrast, older employees engaged in low-complexity jobs who used SOC strategies less frequently were not as successful in focusing on opportunities at work. Weise, Freund, and Baltes (2000) studied employed young German adults and found that SOC in the occupational domain was positively correlated with three indicators of work-related well-being (i.e., emotional balance in the work domain, job satisfaction, and subjective success in the work domain).

Development as a Process of Biocultural Co-construction

Definition of Culture

Baltes et al. (1999) have defined culture as comprising all "psychological, social, material, and symbolic (knowledge-based) resources" developed by humans across history, transferred from one generation to another, and responsible (in large part) for human development. Included among these resources are "cognitive skills, motivational dispositions, socialization strategies, physical structures, the world of economics as well that of medical and physical technology" (p. 475). Moreover, culture is dynamic; new cultural products and processes are being fashioned in all areas of human endeavor.

Culture as Compensation

The notion of "culture as compensation" means that culture has evolved to redress the biological frailties and deficits of human beings (Baltes et al., 1999, p. 478). In other words, the deficits themselves have impelled innovation and thereby led to progress (Baltes et al., 1999). Cultural resources are available in an astounding variety (and are continually innovated) to compensate for human deficits with regard to innumerable functions (e.g., thermoregulation, gripping strength, cutting, night vision, low frequency hearing, speed in locomotion, communication across distance, flying, breathing underwater, physical endurance). Prolonged parenting, purposeful teaching, communal life, complex social interdependencies, medicine, and counseling (to name a few) are also examples of cultural resources that have evolved to offset vulnerabilities associated with human survival and wellness (e.g., Bogin, 1990). I would say that culture, which is indispensable to human development (ontogenetically and phylogenetically [Baltes, 1997; Bogin, 1990; Scarr & Kidd, 1983]), is an outcome of human biology in *two* ways: (a) through the "deficits-breed-growth" idea advanced by Baltes et al. (e.g., 1999, p. 478) in several of their writings and (b) through the facility of the sophisticated human brain (also part of human biology). It is in the conjunction of the two that culture is innovated (i.e., new cultural products and processes are devised).

Coevolution of Biology and Culture and Biocultural Co-construction

The process of innovating (e.g., writing a book/composing music) and the process of using the innovation (e.g., reading the book/dancing to the music) both can optimize the experience-dependent plasticity of the human brain. Cognitive adaptive capacities are extended through such plasticity; adaptive capacities in the user are also enriched in one or more of the specific areas addressed by the innovation (e.g., language fluency/artistry in body movements), and by due reciprocities in other areas (e.g., teaching competence/emotional well-being). The process of using one innovation can lead to another innovation (e.g., a new academic program/new dance steps or even a new dance form).

A major developmental principle of life span theory (Baltes et al., 2006) is that development is a process of biocultural co-construction. The adaptive capacities of humans are co-constructed and enhanced through the interplay of biology and culture. As humans engage in cultural processes and use cultural products, their adaptive or functional capacities are enhanced—crucially beyond what would be possible without the benefit of cultural processes and products.

> Thus, human development the way we know it in the modern world is essentially and necessarily tied to the evolution of culture and its impact on genetic evolution and the kind of life environments individuals transact with as they develop during ontogenesis. (Baltes et al., 2006, p. 577)

In human ontogenesis, progressively higher levels of functioning and longer lifetimes have required "a conjoint evolutionary increase in the richness and dissemination of culture" (Baltes et al., 2006, p. 577). Baltes et al. draw our attention to the dramatic increases in life expectancy and literacy rates in industrialized countries in the last century—changes in the life span and in human functional capacities that quite evidently must be attributed to altered quality of human culture and not to altered genomes.

Incomplete Architecture of Human Development

As the life stages and the functional capacities of humans are co-constructed and extended in the context of evolving/enhanced cultural resources and access to these resources, Baltes et al. (2006) have urged us to recognize "that the future is not fixed either, but includes features of an open system" (p. 575). Moreover, they point out that this incompleteness in the architecture of human development is most characteristic of the second or latter part of the life span and old age.

Extent of Rapprochement Between Life Span Theory and Career Theories

In this section, some of the major career theories have been selected. Each of these career theories has been briefly described. Importantly, as a reflexive exercise I have evaluated each career theory for its rapprochement or estrangement with the key ideas of life span theory.

Theory of Work Adjustment

The theory of work adjustment (TWA) was developed as a theoretical framework to address a 20-year research project in the United States (i.e., the University of Minnesota's Work Adjustment Project in the 1960s and 1970s) (Dawis, 2005; Dawis & Lofquist, 1984). Typical of career theories, TWA is a Person-Environment (P-E) theory or more specifically a Person-Work Environment theory. Congruent with a P-E theoretical approach, TWA explains outcomes (e.g., job stability or tenure) using P-E combinations rather than P or E variables by themselves. Two types of P-E combinations are central to TWA: P-E fit and P-E interaction (Dawis, 2005). An example of a P-E fit is the match between P's work skills and E's requirements for such skills. P-E interaction adds *coresponsiveness* to correspondence; instead of a static congruence between P and E, the P-E interaction model recognizes adjustment behaviors of P and E towards each other that can possibly improve the congruence (Dawis, 2005).

First of all, complementary, paired sets of P and E variables have been identified. Each of P and E has requirements that have to be met; P and E together form a (potentially) mutually beneficial arrangement, meeting (at least some of) each other's requirements. Fulfillment of P's requirements by E leads to P's *satisfaction* with E; complementarily, when P meets E's requirements, E finds P *satisfactory* (Dawis, 2005). When satisfaction and satisfactory concur, maintenance behaviors are expected. Other pairings (i.e., satisfied with unsatisfactory, dissatisfied with satisfactory, and dissatisfied with unsatisfactory) predict adjustment behaviors aimed at changing the situation, and in the extreme case, can lead to termination of tenure (leaving or losing the job) (Dawis, 2005). TWA has many other examples of complementary P and E variables: P's skills or abilities (response capabilities) versus E's skill or ability requirements (response requirements); P's needs or values (reinforcer requirements such as pay and prestige) versus E's reinforcers (reinforcement capabilities) (Dawis, 2005).

Of the 17 postulates in TWA, Dawis (2005; Dawis & Lofquist, 1984) has confirmed strong support for 6, in research in the United States. These six postulates, adapted from Dawis (2005, pp. 20–21), are listed as follows:

- At any given point, concurrent levels of P Satisfaction and P Satisfactoriness explain work adjustment.
- P Satisfaction is predicted from correspondence between P Values and E Reinforcers, provided that there is correspondence between P Abilities and E Ability Requirements.
- P Satisfactoriness is predicted from correspondence between P Abilities and E Ability Requirements, provided that there is correspondence between E Reinforcers and P Values.
- The higher is the level of P Satisfaction, the lower is the probability that P will quit E.
- The higher is the level of P Satisfactoriness, the lower is the probability that E will fire P.
- P Tenure is an outcome of P Satisfaction and P Satisfactoriness.

Examining TWA Using a Life Span Theoretical Lens

The constructs and proposed interrelationships in TWA partly approximate some of the key principles of life span theory. Dawis (2005) has outlined TWA-related developmental agenda for children and youth. This includes the roles of teachers and counselors in scaffolding children's learning about self and Es, and in coping with salient Es. Children must learn about their own needs, values, skills, abilities, and adjustment styles; they must learn about E skill requirements and E reinforcement capabilities. Satisfaction and satisfactoriness, he suggests, can be framed as relevant constructs within the school E; also, children experience varying levels of P-E correspondence in their school, family, and other contexts. Next, he has described the relevance of TWA in choosing a career, and in the three steps of implementing a career choice: career preparation, identifying a beginning position, and "working up the career ladder" (p. 19). For example, in career progression he recommends that a person prepare for new skill and style requirements (instead of focusing largely on anticipated elevation in reinforcers). A new position as a manager may require complex decision-making skills and a style of working at an intense-yet-erratic pace/rhythm. Career progression and work adjustment are the main features during adult years. The goal is P-E correspondence that yields high levels of P Satisfaction and P Satisfactoriness. The correspondence can be adjusted by P acting on E to alter E's reinforcers and/or skill requirements, or by P altering his/her own needs and values and/or skill set (Dawis, 2005). Dawis and Lofquist (1984) have extended TWA to late adulthood by addressing adjustment to retirement. They suggest that successful retirement will require maintaining acceptable levels of P-E correspondence in nonwork contexts (e.g., volunteering or other consultative/honorary positions in the community). Barriers such as reduced finance and health, and lack of organized data on nonwork Es have to be overcome (Dawis & Lofquist, 1984).

Much of the TWA theory and research is to do with the working adult years; this itself is compatible with life span theory which remedies the neglect of adult years in developmental psychology. Yet, if the focus was only on adult years, TWA could not be considered life span in orientation. In this regard, to the credit of Dawis and his associates, the relevance of TWA constructs and relationships has been extended to both younger and older periods in the life span. Of course, these extensions appear to be more promissory rather than established in research.

What about plasticity, a key construct in life span theory? Both traits (stable characteristics) and states (fluctuating characteristics) are included in TWA; thus, P Satisfaction and P Satisfactoriness are conceptualized as states whereas P Values (operationalized as six factors, namely safety, comfort, status, autonomy, achievement, and altruism) are couched as traits. Personality style and adjustment style variables are also construed as traits. However, the inclusion of process constructs in TWA mitigates the substantial dependence on stabilized traits. Thus, TWA admits scope for plasticity at both P and E levels. "Workers and work environments are not static, unchanging entities, but rather, they can and do change" (Dawis, 2005, p. 4). Most importantly, P skills and E skill requirements are viewed as adaptable and changeable. "Though basic skills may reach relative stability (typically in adulthood), P continues to acquire new skills (such as work skills) developed from basic skills all through life" (p. 5). Also as already mentioned, the P-E interaction model includes two modes of adjustment (potentially activated when P-E correspondence is low): P acting to alter E or P reacting by altering self. "For example, P could use skills better or acquire new skills to do a better job to convince E to improve P's compensation" (p. 9). P-E correspondence is an ongoing goal rather than a once-for-all end-state and is "achieved, maintained, and reachieved, if necessary" (p. 8).

TWA could benefit from integrating simultaneous gain-loss dynamics in work adjustment.

Also missing in TWA is the *development* of adaptive capacities (in this case work skill sets) through selection of a particular work E followed by optimization within this E. Workers must apprehend the concurrent and projected gains and losses (in P Values and skills) through selection of a particular E, and optimization therein. Development/enhancement of skills need not be conceptualized only as an outcome of *discorrespondence* and the use of a conforming, reactive mode of adjustment. Selection of and optimization within specific work environments are processes that result in development/enhancement of certain skill sets and loss of other skill sets.

TWA also omits addressing historical embeddedness of developmental processes. In fact, the propositions advanced using data from the 1960s and 1970s may not capture current relevancies. Decisions to lay off workers are not only based on P-E correspondence. More and more, such decisions may not be made at an individual level at all; in the current historical context of economic volatility, decisions to hire, retain, or terminate jobs may be made at (and for) a group or organization level.

Holland's Theory of Vocational Personalities in Work Environments

Also a Person-Work Environment fit theory, John L. Holland's theory (1959, 1997) is particularly famed for its classificatory scheme. This theory is located within the extensive body of work in the United States on stable individual differences and corresponding classificatory schemes. By way of novelty, the thrust in Holland's theory and related research is on classifying individuals into types and subtypes that reflect liking or leaning for particular kinds of work; also as it is a P-E fit theory, the types and subtypes have analogues in education and work settings. Holland's theory and the considerable research it has produced are founded on the following assumptions:

- Vocational[1] interests reflect the personality.
- Therefore, there is an overlap between vocational interests and personality such that we can talk of "vocational personalities."
- The vocational personality is formed before adulthood (i.e., by the end of adolescence).
- Vocational interests are stable; in other words, vocational personalities are stable.
- There are a limited number of types of vocational interests or vocational personalities: Realistic, Investigative, Artistic, Social, Enterprising, and Conventional (RIASEC).
- Most individuals can be successfully classified into one of these six types.
- Finer distinctions are obtained by classifying an individual into a subtype that reflects a priority sequence of the six vocational interests (or of the three most dominant ones), which Holland called "hierarchy of adjustive orientations" (Spokane, Luchetta, & Richwine, 2002, p. 375).
- Likewise, work environments and occupations also can be successfully classified into (a) types and (b) subtypes.

Based on research in the United States, for each of the six types, Holland's theory identifies associated "behavioral repertoires, patterns of likes and dislikes, specific values, and unique self-descriptions" (Spokane & Cruza-Guet, 2005, p. 25). For example, the self-ratings of the Realistic type include mechanical, scientific, quiet, and reserved; whereas, those of the Artistic type include idealistic, imaginative, intellectual, introspective, intuitive, and original (Spokane et al., 2002). Similarly, the potential of a Realistic type is outlined as best expressed in the area of Mechanics, that of an Investigative type in Science, Artistic type in the Arts, Social type in Human Relations, Enterprising type in Leadership, and Conventional type in Business

(Spokane et al., 2002). At the same time, Holland's theory clarifies that "many people resemble more than one, and in most cases all, of the types to a degree" (Spokane et al., 2002, p. 380). Thus, a subtype indicates the degree to which each of the six types is reflected in an individual's personality, summarized in letter codes (representing types) that are sequenced from highest to lowest dominance. The convention in designating a subtype, generally, is to consider the three most ascendant types represented in a person's profile (e.g., IAS which implies that Investigative was the most dominant followed by Artistic and Social); the first letter code, of course, identifies the type. Those of a subtype have common vocational preferences as also common occupational settings in which they are expected to thrive (Spokane & Cruza-Guet, 2005).

There is mathematical support for arranging the RIASEC in a clockwork fashion into a hexagon (or circle) such that R and S, I and E, and A and C are counter-opposed; in contrast, R shares some attributes with I (e.g., mechanical) as also with C (e.g., dogmatic), A shares some attributes with I (e.g., open) and with S (e.g., feminine), and so on (Spokane & Cruza-Guet, 2005; Spokane et al., 2002). This hexagon forms part of a diagnostic system which, along with (the following) four diagnostic indicators, can be used in vocational choice-making and career counseling (Spokane & Cruza-Guet, 2005; Spokane et al., 2002):

- *Congruence* refers to the extent of fit between an individual's subtype and his/her (current or anticipated) work-setting subtype. The higher the match between the individual and the setting subtypes, the higher the congruence; best is if the letter code sequences are matched perfectly. Congruence is posited as determining vocational choice and vocational satisfaction.
- *Consistency* refers to the coherence or harmony of the combination of types within a subtype. As is clear in the hexagonal arrangement, certain types are opposites whereas others share attributes. If opposite types co-occur in a subtype (especially in the first two

---

[1] The term *vocational* as used in the career theories reported in this chapter refers to that which is work-related, or career-related, or to do with an occupation. It does not refer to technical education or training. For example, Savickas (2005) defined *vocational personality* as "an individual's career-related abilities, needs, values, and interests" (p. 47).

letter codes), consistency is low. The higher the proximity of the first two letter codes on the hexagon, the higher the harmony or consistency of the subtype. Individuals whose interest types are consistent are thought to experience greater ease in relating to their own personality and in making vocational choices.

• *Differentiation* refers to a clear pattern of dominance of one or few types over others in the subtype. It ranges from only one type as dominant (highest differentiation) to identical or near-identical scores across all six types (lowest differentiation). It is expected that the higher the differentiation, the easier it is to make vocational choices.

• *Identity* refers to the extent to which a person identifies with or has clarity about his/her particular combination of interests, strengths, and thereby, goals. Identity is hypothesized as facilitated through consistency and differentiation.

Holland has postulated that (by and large) an individual who is congruent, consistent, and differentiated will have a clearer vocational identity, and will be competent and satisfied at work; moreover, work settings also differ in the extent to which they are consistent, differentiated, and have a clear identity (Spokane & Cruza-Guet, 2005).

Of the many instruments generated in this theory, the Self-Directed Search (SDS; www.self-directed-search.com) is the "most representative of the theory" (Spokane & Cruza-Guet, 2005, p. 29). Holland's theory has also yielded the greatest research output among career theories (Spokane & Cruza-Guet, 2005). Empirical support for the theory can be stated as encouraging rather than unequivocal. Thus, Spokane and Cruza-Guet (2005) have concluded that:

> A surprising amount (though certainly not all) of this research has been supportive of the existence of a limited set of types, the underlying circular (or hexagonal) structure of those types, the validity of the instruments to measure types, though not to the same degree for the instruments designed to measure environments, and, to a lesser extent, the interactive proposition of the theory. (p. 30)

In Holland's theory, the term *interaction* refers to the P-E fit or congruence and the behaviors that result from the fit. Interestingly, despite being a P-E fit theory, it is the congruence aspect of the theory that is found to be least fit. Spokane et al. (2002) have cited Tinsley as stating that studies of P-E fit models are complicated by fit indices that are unfit, and that the lack of commensurability of P and E variables has compromised Holland's P-E fit propositions. Spokane and Cruza-Guet (2005) have reported that congruence is adequate but not essential for vocational satisfaction, and factors such as anxiety or the desire to identify with a particular group may override the need for congruence while making decisions about vocational choice. Further research will undoubtedly clarify whether measurement issues or unaccounted for factors explain the lack of fit.

There are two other concerns; the first relates to gender differences. In the United States, women's scores on the SDS are consistently higher on Social and Artistic and lower on Realistic and Investigative than that of men (Spokane & Cruza-Guet, 2005). Moreover, these gender differences are also reflected in career choice and development. Betz (2008) has reported that in the United States, "women remain seriously underrepresented in scientific and technical careers and in high-level positions in business, government, education, and the military" (p. 721). The second concern relates to the applicability of Holland's theory to cultures outside the United States, especially in Asia. Farh, Leong, and Law (1998) tested both etic and emic hypotheses in a sample of college students in Hong Kong: they found reasonable support for the presence of six types of vocational interests in the college students, and partial support for congruence with future career plans; conversely, they found less support for the structural arrangement hypotheses. Whereas, the circumplex hypotheses were unsupported, students low on (Chinese) traditionality fit the circular model hypothesis better than did students high on traditionality. In another study, Leong, Austin, Sekaran, and Komarraju (1998) once again found support for the existence of the typology in a sample of employed adults (22–63 years) in urban India; however, no support for the usefulness of the typology was found. In other words, congruence, consistency, and differentiation did not predict job satisfaction. Leong et al. suggest that it is not necessary for vocational interests to determine vocational choices in all cultures.

Examining Holland's Theory Using a Life Span Theoretical Lens

For the most part, Holland's theory provides a poor fit with the constructs in life span theory. The central tenets of Holland's theory are out of alignment with those of life span theory. It is the typology and the "prediction of person-occupation fit" (Ackerman & Beier, 2003, p. 211) that receive focal attention in Holland's theory. Thereby unsurprisingly, the key propositions do not include lifelong developmental processes that help create, nurture, maintain, enhance, or atrophy interests. In sum, lifelong adaptational processes are not postulated as characterizing interests. Instead, by late adolescence the interest type/subtype is considered (largely) formed and thereafter characterized by stability. In adulthood, it is expected that clarity about an already-existing stable structure of vocational personality/interests will enable an individual to seek matched work environments and thereby experience satisfaction; in counseling, the person is to be facilitated in establishing or increasing congruence between own and work-setting subtypes. Gains and losses in interests and related strengths, through selection-optimization-compensation at multiple points across the life course, appear antithetical to the current framework of Holland's theory.

Methodologically, the typology approach as opposed to a trait continua approach (see Ackerman & Beier, 2003) also obstructs the examination of gains and losses in interests (based on particular selection of jobs and work settings, and the opportunities that these provide for optimization). Interests when measured using continuous scores rather than categorization into types and subtypes may permit a better assay of gains and losses.

Hansen (2005) has claimed that "(c)onstruct stability is an important prerequisite for any variable incorporated into decision-making exercises such as those used in career counseling"; and that "(i)f interests are not stable (in other words, if interests are a state rather than a trait), interest inventories have no chance of predicting occupational or educational choices even over short time spans" (p. 284). However, I would like to point out that the utility of the construct of interests does not have to lie in its inflexibility. It is useful to facilitate a person's career decision-making and say, for example, "Based on your *current* interests, you may find these types of work settings and positions more likable and fulfilling."

Hansen (2005) has stated that "interests may be the most stable of all psychological constructs" (p. 284) with stability coefficients for a sample in the range of 0.70 and 0.80 between ages 18 and 22, or 18 and 32, or 33 and 45. Note of course, that the r^2 (i.e., shared variance[2]) would then be in the range of 49–64 %[3] which still leaves scope for alteration of interests—or rather it indicates that some individuals in the group did not have the same interests at Time 2. This is confirmed as well through examining intraperson stability. The intraperson correlation coefficients range from $-.20$s to $.90$s, with approximately 50 % of individuals displaying fairly similar interest profiles across time (Hansen, 2005). It is clear that when interests are being touted as stable, the conclusion is based on half the sample, and that "stable" does not preclude either the evidence of change or the possibility of change. For that matter, even if one person does not show stability, the evidence and the possibility of change both exist. We must remember that in mathematics, one exception is enough to nullify

---

[2] In a bivariate correlation coefficient, this refers to how much of the variance in one variable is explained by the variance in the other variable. In this case, for example, how much of the variability in Time 2 is explained by the variability at Time 1. The square of a correlation coefficient (r^2) is also called the Coefficient of Determination.

[3] Technically, this refers to the Percent of Shared Variance ($r^2 \times 100$).

a theorem (or more generally to invalidate an assertion).

Betz's (2005, 2008) work also draws attention to the utility of acknowledging the plasticity of interests. Consistent gender differences in interest profiles can only be linked to gender-discriminatory socialization; moreover, surely it is possible to undo any "harm" from unfair socialization and to prevent it with appropriate advocacy/intervention. This is compatible with the conclusions that Betz (2008) has made:

> There is strong evidence that these interest differences are in part due to stereotypic gender socialization, because boys are exposed to different types of learning opportunities growing up than are girls. Educational and career options are thus restricted because of restricted interest development. (p. 728)

Neither is absence of discrimination good enough because neutral environments may also not remedy gender-limited interest development. Interests may fail to expand or be enhanced in a "null environment" which "neither encourages nor discourages individuals—it simply ignores them" Betz (2008, p. 731). In Betz's view, the failure to act is tantamount to passive discrimination. She recommends that in counseling, women be viewed "as work in progress" rather than as "a finished product," such that new opportunities can be set up to facilitate interest *development* (p. 742).

Hansen (2005) has outlined a life span usage of self-knowledge of stable interests (which can be facilitated through career counseling): for educational decisions, career entry/first job decisions, subsequent job or career decisions (for career progression/search for more challenging positions), during job losses, and while planning for retirement. In her framework, career counseling using interest profiles is useful because it enables prediction. The question we must ask is whether prediction, with shades of fortune-telling, is more important than optimizing development? Which goal is more worthwhile? Sometimes it may be optimal to sustain already existing interests (e.g., given environmental exposure and encouragement to develop any from a wide variety of interests).

Sometimes it may be necessary to expand interests (e.g., given gender-discriminatory or otherwise limited environmental exposure and encouragement, or given a null environment).

Super's Life-Span, Life-Space Approach to Career Development

Donald Super defined a career as "a sequence of positions occupied by a person during the course of a lifetime" and as "a series of life stages in which differing constellations of developmental tasks are encountered and dealt with" (1980, p. 283). On the other hand, he felt that career theorists (e.g., Holland) have "dealt with occupational choice rather than with career development" (p. 282), focusing on predicting preferences, for example. His life span, life-space approach to career development exemplified a step towards moving the career field towards more developmental and contextual approaches (Brown & Lent, 2013; Savickas, 1997).

Across a lifetime and for both genders, Super (1980) viewed the *life space* as constituted of nine major roles (e.g., student, worker, spouse, parent) and four main theaters (i.e., home, community, school, workplace). Every person, he conceded, need not experience all nine roles and/or all four main theaters (e.g., a person who does not get married, or a homemaker who is not engaged in paid work). He proposed that generally there was an order in the experience of these roles and theaters across the life course; nonetheless this order permitted both overlapping and individual variations. Further, each role was characteristically played in a designated theater (e.g., worker in a workplace) with spillover into a secondary theater (e.g., home) which could cause role conflict as well as be a source of enrichment of the other theater (e.g., provide children exposure to the parent's world of work). A role he conceptualized as constituted of: (a) own expectations, (b) others' expectations, (c) satisfying and satisfactory performance (i.e., in enactment of the role), and (d) shaping (e.g., the actor redefines own and others' expectations and shapes the role as it develops). A role was not fixed but changed over time. The worker role (or an individual's career) may be characterized by multiple "sequences and simultaneities" (Super, 1980, p. 286) within or across occupations. He described four kinds of career patterns: conventional, stable, multiple trial, and unstable (Savickas, 2001).

Proliferation of roles (within and across theaters) may cause role conflict or lead to self-actualization. For example, he hypothesized that "the more a person's abilities and interests find ready and temporally compatible outlets in the full range of the activities engaged in, the more successful and satisfied that person will be" (Super, 1980, p. 287). He acknowledged that a person played multiple roles simultaneously in many theaters and that these different roles influenced each other. Sensitive to "the constellation of all life roles" (Savickas, 1997, p. 248), Super (1990) specified constructs such as role salience. Brown and Lent (2013) have interpreted the role salience construct as liberating: it frees us to form more holistic as opposed to work-centric views of people and their lives.

Super posited linkages in developmental outcomes across time as well as admitted that intervening variables could diminish the impact of earlier periods. For example, he proposed that self-perception and other perception of satisfactoriness in pre-occupational roles (e.g., student) increases the likelihood of satisfaction and achievement in the worker role. Yet, vocational development at 18 years is better correlated with satisfaction and achievement as a worker at 25 years than at 36 years because as the time gap increases intervening circumstances that attenuate linkages also increase.

Super (1980, 1990) structured the *life span* into a "maxicycle" of life stages with approximate age periods for each stage: growth (4–13 years), exploration (14–24 years), establishment (25–44 years), maintenance (45–64 years), and decline/disengagement (65+ years). Super (1980) located the worker role in the exploration, establishment, and maintenance stages of the life span, followed by the role of the pensioner in the last stage. Along with the maxicycle, he also outlined the numerous decision points within each role across the life span, which could be decisions dependent on or independent of other life roles. "Decision points occur before and at the time of taking on a new role, of giving up an old role, and of making significant changes in the nature of an existing role" (Super, 1980, p. 291). Each decision point he distinguished as a period of "anticipation, planning, action, and adaptation" (p. 292); also, within each stage, a person may have a mini experience of one or more of the five stages ranging from growth to disengagement—in effect *recycling* through the stages. Super (1990) termed this a minicycle.

At each of the life stages, Super (e.g., 1990) provided examples of relevant vocational developmental tasks. Super extended his conceptualization of adolescent career maturity (i.e., the adolescent's "readiness to make educational and vocational choices" [Savickas, 1997, p. 250]) and proposed it as a construct to capture the extent to which a person meets the developmental task requirements of each stage; however, Super and Knasel (1981) also suggested that *career adaptability* (i.e., the "readiness to cope with changing work and working conditions" [p. 195]) rather than career maturity may be more relevant in adulthood.

Super (1990) conceptualized career determinants as an archway: personal and situational determinants each formed one pillar of this archway; the two pillars were joined by an arch in which the central position was accorded to the self, flanked by role self-concepts and the developmental stage. In other words, the self both connects and is based on personal and situational characteristics; also, the self is most proximally influenced by role self-concepts and the developmental stage. Super's (1980, p. 295) perspicacious list of immediate personal determinants included situational awareness, self-awareness, attitudes, interests, values, needs, academic achievement, specific aptitudes, and intelligence; and biological heritage as a remote personal determinant. As immediate situational determinants, he included family, community, school, and employment; moreover, he discerningly listed socioeconomic organizations, historical change, and social structure and economic conditions as remote situational determinants.

In career development, Super (e.g., 1990) clearly allocated the central position to the self/self-concepts. Super reversed the idea that a self-concept is an outcome of vocational choice; instead his assertion was that a self-concept is implemented in career choice and development (Savickas, 1997). This entails objective and subjective processes. The person uses objective data (e.g., about his/her interests and abilities, employment) and subjectively makes meaning of this data; the person then evaluates work roles vis-à-vis the self-concepts that have been constructed using such complementary processes, and works towards choosing and experiencing situations/opportunities that cohere with and actualize the mental representations about the self (Hartung, 2013).

Examining Super's Theory Using a Life Span Theoretical Lens

Donald Super is credited with introducing and promoting a developmental perspective in career theory and research, over and above a focus on individual differences or differential psychology (Hartung, 2013; Savickas, 1997, 2001). Brown and Lent (2013) have called Super "the dean of the developmental career theorists" (p. 10). Super's maxicycle does cover the life span. Although, the life stages in this maxicycle are prototypical of conventional notions of developmental change, Super's inclusion of minicycles is more aligned with the idea that developmental changes are simultaneously multidirectional. In other words, even in the maxicycle stage of disengagement, it is possible for a person to have one or more short cycles of growth, exploration, maintenance, and establishment.

Other key constructs in his theory fare slightly less favorably when juxtaposed with Baltes's life span theory. A prime example is Super's focus on the development and *implementation* of a person's self-concept in career development; that a career provides an outlet for one's self-concept (Hartung, 2013). It is important to reflect

on whether such a conceptualization respects plasticity in development. Actions in adulthood are not just expressive of one's self and earlier development; they are *constitutive* or *formative* of development. It is a machine that has to be completed before it can function. On the contrary, in an organism there is a bidirectionality between structure and function: nascent structure allows (early) function, which enhances structure and thus allows more complex function—which again advances structure and in turn function; of course after a point, in the absence of novel function, structure is altered to appear "maintained"; and a reduction in function or abusive function can deteriorate structure. Both structure and function contribute to and evolve from each other. Super was right in contending that a self-concept is implemented in career development. However, he positioned this as overwriting the idea that vocational choice implemented a self-concept. Neither one-way process is apt (by itself). Developmental processes are two-way. Moreover, in life span theory (e.g., Baltes et al., 2006) the optimization of particular structures and functions is always at the cost of alternative structures and functions. Thus, self-development is selectively enhanced through realization of particular career opportunities (e.g., strengths developed in certain areas coupled with reduced competencies in other areas).

Once again to Super's credit, his ideas appear to have leaned towards such life span developmental processes, although not explicitly or adequately. For example, that work may provide the means "to *become* the person one imagines" (Brown & Lent, 2013, p. 3, emphasis added). These ideas are discussed more in the next subsection, that is, in relation to Savickas's career construction theory.

Theory of Career Construction

Mark Savickas's (2002, 2005) career construction theory draws its principal inspiration from Super's life-space, life span theory. In fact, it is an elaborated, adapted, and updated version of

Super's theory. The 16 propositions of career construction theory reflect an amalgamation of multiple perspectives, namely constructivist, life course, contextual, differential psychological, P-E fit, developmental, and phenomenological. Core notions addressed in the theory include the development and implementation of vocational self-concepts and the role of career adaptability in career construction. The theory is labeled using the constructivist approach, the essence of which is captured in the statement: "Careers do not unfold; they are constructed" (Savickas, 2002, p. 154). The theory is based on the epistemological constructivist premise that *representations* of reality are constructed as opposed to the ontological constructivist premise that reality itself is constructed.

Illustrative of an explicit unifying approach, four propositions (4–7) of career construction theory uphold the individual differences perspective and the corresponding notion of P-E fit in vocational psychology. However, detailed attention in career construction theory is directed at the "individual development view of careers" rather than the "individual differences view of occupations" (Savickas, 2002, p. 149). Respectful of Super's elucidation of the life-space within which life span development occurs, Savickas has elaborated the contextual perspective in his theory, tying together life-course (i.e., sociological) and developmental-contextual (i.e., psychological) paradigms. Individuals construct their careers in relation to the opportunities and constraints of each of their multiple ecologies (e.g., physical environment, family, neighborhood, school, racial and ethnic group, socioeconomic level, culture, and historical period) (Savickas, 2002). Compatible with Super's theory, the first proposition in Savickas's theory starts with: "A society and its institutions structure an individual's life course through social roles" (p. 154); differences in role salience are linked to social practices (e.g., those that are gender discriminatory) and concomitant inequities in social positions. A person's decisions and actions (including those relating to his/her career) can be interpreted through the configuration of core and peripheral roles called

life structure (Savickas, 2002). Thus, a central premise in career construction theory and counseling practice is that "(t)o understand an individual's career, it is important to know and appreciate the web of life roles that connects the individual to society" (Savickas, 2002, p. 159).

Savickas has retained most of Super's life span theorizations, including the maxicyle of life span stages and the occurrence of minicycles. One change that he has made is to rename the fourth stage, calling it the *career management* stage (instead of maintenance). This change, he explains, represents current historical relevancies better. Instead of maintaining and preserving stable careers, many individuals have to resiliently construct and manage their "protean" (e.g., Hall, 2004) and "boundaryless" (e.g., Arthur, Khapova, & Wilderom, 2005) careers given shifting economies, unstable job markets, and changing job trends (Savickas, 2002). Also, Savickas (2005) has asserted that "the grand narrative of career" has changed "from stability to mobility" in postindustrial society, with the result that the experience of minicycles is on the rise (p. 50).

Importantly, Savickas (2002) has continued Super's project of merging self-concept theory into a life span maxicycle and minicycles. During the childhood years of *career growth*, the vocational self-concept is formed. During adolescence and *career exploration*, the vocational self-concept has to become publicly visible in a vocational identity: this entails "translating private vocational self-concepts into public occupational roles" (Savickas, 2002, p. 175) with the subtasks of crystallizing, specifying, and actualizing an occupational choice. During young adulthood and approaching middle adulthood, *career establishment* consists of implementing the self-concept in an occupational role. Subtasks include "stabilizing in an occupational position that allows self-expression," consolidation by refining the self-concept, and progression to novel responsibilities that permit enhanced self-expression (p. 178). In the context of instability of economies, labor markets, and jobs, the middle adulthood years are devoted to *career management*. Lastly, in late adulthood *career disengagement* entails the subtasks of reorienting and disengaging, along with a life-review of the vocational self-concept.

Super and Knasel's (1981) notion of career adaptability is extended and positioned as a pivotal construct in Savickas's theory, in place of vocational maturity. Savickas (2005) has defined career adaptability as "an individual's readiness and resources for coping with current and imminent vocational development tasks, occupational transitions, and personal traumas" (p. 51). Savickas clarifies that vocational personality has to do with *what* (or which) career is constructed (i.e., career content), whereas career adaptability has to do with *how* the career is constructed (i.e., career processes). Career adaptability, which allows individuals to successfully "implement their self-concepts in occupational roles" (p. 51), has four dimensions: concern (vs. career indifference), control (vs. career indecision), curiosity (vs. career unrealism), and confidence (vs. career inhibition) (Savickas, 2005).

Savickas (2005) has addressed the *why* of career construction by integrating a narrative approach: individuals' *career stories* reflect their ideographic *life themes*. In counseling, individuals are supported in using the medium of career stories to recognize how they are making meaning and how their life projects matter to themselves and others.

Examining Career Construction Theory Using a Life Span Theoretical Lens

To the extent that career construction theory advances Super's conceptualization of a maxicycle and minicycles, it does incorporate life span processes. To Savickas's credit, he has noted an increase in the experience of minicycles at transition points between maxicycle life stages as well as within a life stage: this reflects a (more) open, pluralistic, and multidirectional framework of developmental changes. Switching from maintenance to management in describing career development in middle adulthood, especially in response to changing historical times is likewise creditable. However, statements like the following would perhaps need to be reconsidered if (greater) compatibility with life span approaches is desired: "The developmental

tasks of retirement living, such as life review, are best addressed in gerontology textbooks, not books that tell the story of careers" (Savickas, 2002, p. 182). After all, successful aging requires retention of meaningful roles in old age; this may include translating earlier work experiences into a different yet valuable form in old age. Life expectancy is increasing as is the possibility of a healthy old age (or has increased—depending on the country/region). It is in late adulthood that the incomplete architecture of human development is most evident and for which the most concerted professional efforts are needed (Baltes et al., 2006). Moreover, it is possible (although not universal) that in old age a person can successfully contribute to his/her professional or other community using means such as advanced expertise and wisdom (Baltes et al., 2006).

The other constructs in Savickas's theory vary in their extent of rapprochement with life span constructs. For example, consistent with the apparent consensus in the career literature, vocational self-concept and vocational personality are fixed early in life (albeit with a qualifier that these can change). On the other hand, career adaptability is posited as malleable. Plasticity is somewhat implicit in the life themes, especially in Savickas's (2005) description that tensions and preoccupations are turned into occupations (e.g., "the shy child who becomes an actor"): "Career construction revolves around turning a personal problem into a public strength and then even a social contribution" (p. 59).

Social Cognitive Career Theory

Social Cognitive Career Theory (SCCT) advanced by Lent, Brown, and Hackett (1994) is also an integrative approach to career theorization. For example, SCCT is not positioned to contradict but to complement trait-factor approaches (e.g., Holland's theory) (Lent, 2005).

As is evident in the name, SCCT is an application of Bandura's (1986) social cognitive theory to career development. The focus is on models that explain the development of vocational interests, making and remaking of vocational choices, and vocational performance (Lent, 2005). In drawing its principal inspiration from Bandura's work, human agency and the pathways through which agency can be curtailed or enhanced receive crucial attention in SCCT (e.g., gender-role socialization). Agency (amplified or diminished) is operationalized in SCCT primarily using self-efficacy beliefs and outcome expectations regarding each of varied performance areas and activities. A pivotal conjecture in SCCT is that self-efficacy beliefs (e.g., "I can do this" or "I cannot do this") and outcome expectations (e.g., "If I do this, I will be rewarded" or "I will not be rewarded if I take this option") influence the development of academic and career interests (Lent, Brown, & Hackett, 2002). Realistic and positive self-efficacy beliefs and outcome expectations are likely to facilitate the development of career-related interests; interests in turn lead to goals (i.e., selection of a performance domain and the level of desired performance in that domain), which lead to "activity selection and practice" (Lent, 2005, p. 106). Of course, other pathways are also specified in the model. Supplementary pathways (e.g., direct paths from self-efficacy beliefs and outcome expectations to goals and actions) have been formulated to better capture the constraints (e.g., financial, familial) that sever or reduce the linkage between interests and goals/actions (Lent et al., 2002). Experiences in the past and aptitudes are posited as influencing interests through self-efficacy beliefs and outcome expectations (Lent et al., 2002). Contextual influences are presented as playing both a distal and mediated role as well as a proximal and moderating role on choice goals, choice actions, and performance (see Lent et al., 2002).

SCCT is backed by extensive research in the United States (Lent et al., 2002). Therefore, there is research support for key ideas such as the relationships between interests and self-efficacy beliefs and outcome expectations; and for a partial mediation model explaining the influence of self-efficacy beliefs and outcome expectations on career choice (Lent et al., 2002).

Examining SCCT Using a Life Span Theoretical Lens

SCCT's interest, choice, and performance models are not articulated using lifelong adaptational processes. A few statements in their theory (see Lent et al., 2002) address life span ideas (even if inadequately); for example, that efficacy-enhancing interventions are beneficial all through life but are most useful during or before early adolescence. Importantly, the vocational interest and choice models include notions that seem compatible with selection and optimization processes in development. Also, the use of a balance sheet in counseling, to examine and overcome potential barriers to successful educational and career decision-making and action, appears to bear a faint resemblance to gain-loss dynamics in development.

To what extent does SCCT focus on plasticity? By selecting modifiable constructs such as self-efficacy and outcome expectations and by positioning these as central to the theory, Lent et al. (2002) appear to be inclined towards plasticity. However, they limit modifiability to some extent by their dependence on the stability of other constructs such as abilities. Therefore, it is largely in the context of a discrepancy between ability measurement and interest measurement (i.e., the ability related to an educational or career choice is high but the interest is low) that they see a need to "expand" vocational interests. Expanding interests then means that in counseling the person is facilitated in bringing interests in line with abilities. Gender discriminatory socialization, for example, could be remedied through such an approach if and when ability measurements yield a positive picture (which is not guaranteed). Nevertheless, a more open view of plasticity would require less dependence on *stable* abilities. In their favor is their clarification that "self-efficacy beliefs may facilitate attainment in a given academic or career domain as long as an individual possesses at least minimal levels of requisite ability in that domain" (Lent et al., 2002, p. 291).

Conclusion

There is some rapprochement between life span theory in human development and career theories. However, this rapprochement is inconsistent and, at present, less than adequate. There is at best some recognition of the need for a life span orientation and variable acknowledgement of the value of plasticity.

New Concepts and Viewpoints: Charting New Directions

Baltes's life span theory offers a fresh lens for viewing career development, and thereby new directions for career research, theory, and practice. Examples of possible new directions include the following:

- Greater attention to lifelong processes in career development.
- Valuing plasticity in career development.
- Viewing career development as constituted of gains and losses in adaptive capacities or functions through selection and selective optimization at multiple points in the life span.
- Assisting individuals and groups in identifying the specific adaptive capacities or functions that they would like to strengthen and the careers or types of jobs that provide the means to do so.
- Facilitating successful career development by promoting (a) general plasticity, and (b) assisting individuals and groups in maximizing gains and minimizing losses.
- Acknowledging and supporting career development as a biocultural co-construction.
- Recognizing that the limits of human development are unknown because these limits are continually extended through biocultural coevolution. Therefore, the conclusions about career development can be only based partly (and not wholly) on the past. Moreover, "the future is not something we simply enter but also something that we help create" (Baltes et al., 2006, p. 575).

Relevance for Multiple Cultures: Sensitivity to the Universal and Particular

Baltes's life span theory is especially sensitive to both the universal and the particular. Key principles such as lifelong processes, plasticity, dynamics of gains and losses, adaptive specificities, SOC, biocultural co-construction, and incomplete architecture of human development are universally relevant. Simultaneously, these notions are relativistic as well. The theory has been especially formulated to incorporate cultural, historical, and ideographic influences on human development. For example, although gain-loss dynamics in development are universal, what constitutes a gain and what is considered a loss is relative to the person, culture, and historical time. In career counseling, for example, this would mean that the career counselor refrains from imposing own definitions of gains and losses. Instead, the counselor must assist the person in identifying personal meanings of gains and losses. In respecting more collectivist orientations, next the career counselor could support the person in viewing gains and losses from multiple perspectives. Finally, in encouraging successful development, the person can be assisted in maximizing gains and minimizing losses after considering multiple perspectives and how these tie with own definitions of gains and losses.

References

Ackerman, P. L., & Beier, M. E. (2003). Intelligence, personality, and interests in the career choice process. *Journal of Career Assessment, 11*(2), 205–218.

Arthur, M. B., Khapova, S. N., & Wilderom, C. P. M. (2005). Career success in a boundaryless career world. *Journal of Organizational Behavior, 26*, 177–202.

Baltes, P. B. (1987). Theoretical propositions of life-span developmental psychology: On the dynamics between growth and decline. *Developmental Psychology, 23*(5), 611–626.

Baltes, P. B. (1997). On the incomplete architecture of human ontogeny: Selection, optimization, and compensation as foundation of developmental theory. *American Psychologist, 52*(4), 366–380.

Baltes, P. B., Lindenberger, U., & Staudinger, U. M. (2006). Life span theory in developmental psychology. In W. Damon & R. M. Lerner (Series Eds.), & R. M. Lerner (Vol. Ed.), *Handbook of child psychology, Vol. 1. Theoretical models of human development* (pp. 569–664). Hoboken, NJ: Wiley.

Baltes, P. B., Staudinger, U. M., & Lindenberger, U. (1999). Lifespan psychology: Theory and application to intellectual functioning. *Annual Review of Psychology, 50*, 471–507.

Bandura, A. (1986). *Social foundations of thought and action: A social cognitive theory*. Englewood Cliffs, NJ: Prentice-Hall.

Betz, N. E. (2005). Women's career development. In S. D. Brown & R. W. Lent (Eds.), *Career development and counseling: Putting theory and research to work* (pp. 253–277). Hoboken, NJ: Wiley.

Betz, N. E. (2008). Women's career development. In F. L. Denmark & M. A. Paludi (Eds.), *Psychology of women: A handbook of issues and theories* (pp. 717–752). Westport, CT: Praeger.

Bogin, B. (1990). The evolution of human childhood. *BioScience, 40*, 16–25.

Brown, S. D., & Lent, R. W. (2013). Understanding and facilitating career development in the 21st century. In S. D. Brown & R. W. Lent (Eds.), *Career development and counseling: Putting theory and research to work* (pp. 1–28). Hoboken, NJ: Wiley.

Cairns, R. B., & Cairns, B. D. (2006). The making of developmental psychology. In W. Damon & R. M. Lerner (Series Eds.), & R. M. Lerner (Vol. Ed.), *Handbook of child psychology, Vol. 1. Theoretical models of human development* (pp. 89–165). Hoboken, NJ: Wiley.

Dawis, R. V. (2005). The Minnesota theory of work adjustment. In S. D. Brown & R. W. Lent (Eds.), *Career development and counseling: Putting theory and research to work* (pp. 3–23). Hoboken, NJ: Wiley.

Dawis, R. V., & Lofquist, L. H. (1984). *A psychological theory of work adjustment: An individual-differences model and its applications*. Minneapolis, MN: University of Minnesota Press.

Farh, J.-L., Leong, F. T. L., & Law, K. S. (1998). Cross-cultural validity of Holland's model in Hong Kong. *Journal of Vocational Behavior, 52*, 425–440.

Hall, D. T. (2004). The protean career: A quarter-century journey. *Journal of Vocational Behavior, 65*, 1–13.

Hansen, J.-I. C. (2005). Assessment of interests. In S. D. Brown & R. W. Lent (Eds.), *Career development and counseling: Putting theory and research to work* (pp. 281–304). Hoboken, NJ: Wiley.

Hartung, P. J. (2013). The life-span, life-space theory of careers. In S. D. Brown & R. W. Lent (Eds.), *Career development and counseling: Putting theory and research to work* (pp. 83–114). Hoboken, NJ: Wiley.

Holland, J. L. (1959). A theory of vocational choice. *Journal of Counseling Psychology, 6*, 35–45.

Holland, J. L. (1997). *Making vocational choices: A theory of vocational personalities and work environments*. Odessa, FL: Psychological Assessment Resources.

Kagan, J. (1980). Perspectives on continuity. In O. G. Brim Jr. & J. Kagan (Eds.), *Constancy and change across the life span* (pp. 26–74). Cambridge, MA: Harvard University Press.

Kuhn, T. S. (1970). *The structure of scientific revolutions*. Chicago, IL: University of Chicago Press.

Lent, R. W. (2005). A social cognitive view of career development and counseling. In S. D. Brown & R. W. Lent (Eds.), *Career development and counseling: Putting theory and research to work* (pp. 101–127). Hoboken, NJ: Wiley.

Lent, R. B., Brown, S. D., & Hackett, G. (1994). Toward a unifying social cognitive theory of career and academic interest, choice, and performance. *Journal of Vocational Behavior, 45*(1), 79–122.

Lent, R. W., Brown, S. D., & Hackett, G. (2002). Social cognitive career theory. In D. Brown et al. (Eds.), *Career choice and development* (pp. 255–311). San Francisco, CA: Jossey-Bass.

Leong, F. T. L., Austin, J. T., Sekaran, U., & Komarraju, M. (1998). An evaluation of the cross-cultural validity of Holland's theory: Career choices by workers in India. *Journal of Vocational Behavior, 52*, 441–455.

Savickas, M. L. (1997). Career adaptability: An integrative construct for life-span, life-space theory. *The Career Development Quarterly, 45*, 247–259.

Savickas, M. L. (2001). A developmental perspective on vocational behaviour: Career patterns, salience, and themes. *International Journal for Educational and Vocational Guidance, 1*, 49–57.

Savickas, M. L. (2002). Career construction: A developmental theory of vocational behavior. In D. Brown et al. (Eds.), *Career choice and development* (pp. 149–205). San Francisco, CA: Jossey-Bass.

Savickas, M. L. (2005). The theory and practice of career construction. In S. D. Brown & R. W. Lent (Eds.), *Career development and counseling: Putting theory and research to work* (pp. 42–70). Hoboken, NJ: Wiley.

Scarr, S., & Kidd, K. K. (1983). Developmental behavior genetics. In P. H. Mussen (Series Ed.), & M. M. Haith & J. J. Campos (Vol. Eds.), *Handbook of child psychology, Vol. 2. Infancy and developmental psychobiology* (pp. 345–434). Hoboken, NJ: Wiley.

Schmitt, A., Zacher, H., & Frese, M. (2012). The buffering effect of selection, optimization, and compensation strategy use on the relationship between problem solving demands and occupational well-being: A daily diary study. *Journal of Occupational Health Psychology, 17*(2), 139–149.

Spokane, A. R., & Cruza-Guet, M. C. (2005). Holland's theory of vocational personalities in work environments. In S. D. Brown & R. W. Lent (Eds.), *Career development and counseling: Putting theory and research to work* (pp. 24–41). Hoboken, NJ: Wiley.

Spokane, A. R., Luchetta, E. J., & Richwine, M. H. (2002). Holland's theory of personalities in work environments. In D. Brown et al. (Eds.), *Career choice and development* (pp. 373–426). San Francisco, CA: Jossey-Bass.

Super, D. E. (1980). A life-span, life-space approach to career development. *Journal of Vocational Behavior, 16*, 282–298.

Super, D. E. (1990). A life-span, life-space approach to career development. In D. Brown & L. Brooks (Eds.), *Career choice and development* (pp. 197–261). San Francisco, CA: Jossey-Bass.

Super, D. E., & Knasel, E. G. (1981). Career development in adulthood: Some theoretical problems. *British Journal of Guidance and Counselling, 9*, 194–201.

Uttal, D. H., & Perlmutter, M. (1989). Towards a broader conceptualization of development: The role of gains and losses across the life span. *Developmental Review, 9*, 101–132.

Valsiner, J. (2006). Developmental epistemology and implications for methodology. In W. Damon & R. M. Lerner (Series Eds.), & R. M. Lerner (Vol. Ed.), *Handbook of child psychology, Vol. 1. Theoretical models of human development* (pp. 166–209). Hoboken, NJ: Wiley.

Weise, B. S., Freund, A. M., & Baltes, P. B. (2000). Selection, optimization, and compensation: An action-related approach to work and partnership. *Journal of Vocational Behavior, 57*, 273–300.

Zacher, H., & Frese, M. (2011). Maintaining a focus on opportunities at work: The interplay between age, job complexity, and the use of selection, optimization, and compensation strategies. *Journal of Organizational Behavior, Special Issue: Contemporary empirical advancements in the study of aging in the workplace, 32*(2), 291–318.

Indigenous Models of Career Development and Vocational Psychology

Frederick T.L. Leong and Marina Pearce

The current era of globalization is continuing to influence theoretical developments in psychology in general and vocational psychology in particular. For example, Leong, Pickren, Leach, and Marsella (2012) recently published a volume to promote the internationalization of the psychology curriculum in the United States. Consistent with this internationalization movement, the purpose of this chapter is to discuss the recent developments in indigenous psychologies and how these indigenous models can help advance the field of vocational psychology. These indigenous models attempt to explain psychological phenomena in their native cultural contexts. To provide context for the need for such indigenous models, we will address the reasons why current models of psychology (both in general and with regard to vocational psychology in particular) lack cultural validity and relevancy. We will also discuss the positive and negative forces influencing the general cultural movement in psychology. Integrative and culturally accommodating models will be introduced and reviewed to highlight the importance of considering culture in vocational psychology models. In addition, we will discuss the advantages of indigenous models of psychology with particular attention to their use in vocational psychology. Finally, we will discuss the steps required to create indigenous models of vocational psychology, as well as examples of ones published in the recent literature.

Three Approaches to the Study of Culture in Psychology

There are three major approaches to the study of culture in psychology: (a) cross-cultural psychology, (b) cultural psychology, and (c) indigenous psychologies. Each approach has its own intellectual ancestry and traditions and a unique history of development. Of the three, cross-cultural psychology is by far the most prominent. As a subdiscipline of mainstream psychology, cross-cultural psychology was institutionalized during the 1960s as a means of testing Western-originated theories in other cultures. It has been defined as "the study of similarities and differences in individual psychological functioning in various cultural and ethnic groups; of the relationship between psychological variables and sociocultural, ecological, and biological variables; and of current changes in these variables" (Berry, Poortinga, Segall, & Dasen, 1992, p. 2).

From this and other definitions, three related goals for cross-cultural psychology have been identified: (a) testing the generality of existing psychological knowledge and theories in other cultures, (b) exploring other cultures in order to discover psychological variations that are not covered in existing knowledge and theories, and

F.T.L. Leong (✉)
Michigan State University, East Lansing, MI, USA
e-mail: fleong@msu.edu

G. Arulmani et al. (eds.), *Handbook of Career Development*, International and Cultural Psychology,
DOI 10.1007/978-1-4614-9460-7_5, © Springer Science+Business Media, LLC 2014

(c) generating a universal psychology by assembling and integrating the results obtained from the first two goals (Berry & Dasen, as cited in Berry et al., 1992). As a subdiscipline of mainstream psychology, cross-cultural psychology adopts natural science as its theoretical and methodological inspiration. The main purpose of cross-cultural psychology is to search for universal laws of psychological functioning applicable to people in diverse societies through the use of a scientific, positivistic paradigm similar to the one used in the natural sciences.

Following a different course, cultural psychology has grown not only out of dissatisfaction with cross-cultural psychology but also out of anthropologists' desire to understand the person in context. A basic premise of this approach to culture is the integration of psychology and anthropology and their different methodologies. Cultural psychology is still far from being a unitary theoretical system. Various cultural psychologists have conceptualized their discipline by emphasizing different aspects of their theoretical and methodological endeavors. Richard Shweder is the cultural psychologist who has been most enthusiastic about producing definitions for this renewed field. He has defined cultural psychology as "the study of the way cultural traditions and social practices regulate, express, transform, and permute the human psyche, resulting less in psychic unity for humankind than in ethnic divergences in mind, self, and emotion" (Shweder, 1990, p. 1). Other theorists have given definitions quite different from Shweder's. Berry (1994) considered cultural psychology to be "the attempt to understand individual psychological functioning in the cultural context in which it developed" (p. 120).

Cultural psychologists generally reject natural science as their theoretical and methodological model in favor of a human or cultural science requiring sympathetic understanding. Although cultural psychologists do not deny the assumption of psychic unity or the possibility of identifying universal or pan-human characteristics, they do tend to question whether a focus on such universals is theoretically fruitful or productive. Without an enthusiasm in the search for universals like cross-cultural psychologists, cultural psychologists prefer to set the development of culture-bound knowledge systems across specific cultures as the primary goal for their field.

Indigenous psychology—the third approach to the study of culture in psychology—is relatively new. Enriquez (1989, 1990), Kim and Berry (1993), Sinha (1993, 1997), and Yang (1993, 1999) have pointed out that indigenization of psychological research has become an academic movement in several developing and developed societies—especially non-Western ones. This indigenization movement, which reflects a worldwide concern for making psychological knowledge culturally appropriate (Sinha, 1997), is a counterposition to the time-honored domination of Western (especially American) mainstream psychology and of Western-oriented cross-cultural psychology as applied to non-Western societies.

Theorists have defined indigenous psychology in a variety of ways. Enriquez (1990) regarded indigenous psychology as a system of psychological thought and practice rooted in a particular cultural tradition. Kim and Berry (1993) defined indigenous psychology as "the scientific study of human behavior (or mind) that is native, that is not transported from other regions, and that is designed for its people" (p. 2). For Berry et al. (1992), it is "a behavioral science that matches the sociocultural realities of one's own society" (p. 381). Ho (1998) viewed indigenous psychology as "the study of human behavior and mental processes within a cultural context that relies on values, concepts, belief systems, methodologies, and other resources indigenous to the specific ethnic or cultural group under investigation" (p. 93).

Yang (1993, 1997) defined it as an evolving system of psychological knowledge based on scientific research that is sufficiently compatible with the studied phenomena and their ecological, economic, social, cultural, and historical contexts. No matter how these psychologists define indigenous psychology, the definitions all express the same basic goal of developing a scientific knowledge system that effectively reflects, describes, explains, or understands the psychological activities in their native contexts in terms of culturally relevant frames of reference and culturally derived categories and theories.

The primary goal of indigenous approaches is to construct a specific indigenous psychology for each society with a given population or a distinctive culture. After that, the specific knowledge system and its various research findings may be used to develop the indigenous psychologies of progressively larger populations defined in terms of regional, national, ethnic, linguistic, religious, or geographical considerations. Finally, the highest indigenous psychology, a universal, or more properly a global, psychology for all human beings on the earth will be formed by integrating lower-level indigenous psychologies (Yang, 1993, 1997).

Kim and Berry (1993) have pointed out that the indigenous approach is not opposed to scientific (including experimental) methods and that it does not preclude the use of any particular method. They have also asserted that the indigenous approach does not assume the inherent superiority of one particular theoretical perspective over another on a priori grounds. Yang (1993, 1999) has recommended that the principle of multiple paradigms be adopted. Under this principle, indigenous psychologists in the same society may be encouraged to apply different or even conflicting paradigms to their own research. This rule has been actually practiced among indigenous psychologists in Chinese societies (Taiwan, Hong Kong, and mainland China) for some years. In this chapter, we will draw upon the unique advantages of the indigenous approach in the study of culture as a means to help advance the field of vocational psychology.

Cultural Validity of Psychological Models

In vocational psychology, a series of different frameworks have been used to predict career choice and work adjustment. These frameworks include personality models (e.g., employee selection), environmental models (e.g., organizational culture), and—most popular of all—person-by-environment models (e.g., fit) (Leong & Pearce, 2011). The

application of person-by-environment models involves identifying the degree of match between an applicant or employee and his or her work environment. The more a person matches his or her work environment, the higher his or her job satisfaction or job performance is expected to be. While this model is the dominant conceptualization, it may be inadequate because the culture of the person and the culture associated with the environment (or the people within the environment) are ignored (Leong, 2002). For this reason, Leong and Pearce (2011) argued that the relationship between employees and important work outcomes (e.g., job satisfaction) would be better understood by accounting for the cultural influences associated with individuals and their environments. As one example:

> …while it is currently assumed that vocational choice is a function of a person's general interests, abilities, and values, the decision could be more completely described by including factors specific to the person's culture (i.e., factors specific to the person's race, ethnicity, or nationality, such as collectivism in Asian populations), rather than assuming that all important predictors are global. (Leong & Pearce, 2011, p. 67)

This lack of attention paid to culture may also be associated with the client "uniformity myth" (e.g., Kiesler, 1966), which applies when one ignores important individual (and cultural) characteristics that significantly differentiate clients and their responses to psychological interventions.

The validity and specificity of an assessment are critically reduced when culture is neglected (Leong & Pearce, 2011). Whether or not motivated by a mistaken "color blindness" (Neville, Lilly, Duran, Lee, & Browne, 2000) or a belief that culture is a nuisance variable in science, it is a serious problem that underlies major cultural gaps in psychological theory and research. Leong and Brown (1995) have clarified that *cultural validity* (etic) has to do with the appropriateness of scientific models *across* cultural groups, and *cultural specificity* (emic) involves a question of whether scientific models are appropriate *within* a particular cultural group. Without considering cultural validity and specificity, a culture-specific assumption may be inappropriately applied to one or more other cultures (i.e., an *imposed etic* model). The inappropriateness of imposed etic models stems from potential issues concerning cultural sensitivity and may be avoided by carefully considering the cultural validity and specificity of an intervention before implementing it in a new cultural setting (Benet-Martinez, 2007; Leong & Brown, 1995).

In their review of the literature, Leong and Pearce (2011) recommended several methods for addressing these problems by extending the concepts of cultural validity and cultural specificity for vocational psychology research and theory building. First, they pointed to the need for vocational psychologists to take into account the dual influence of culture-general and culture-specific factors in career choice and work adjustment when initially building scientific models. Second, they called for culture-relevant data (e.g., ethnicity) to be collected consistently and for such diversity constructs to be formally operationalized as significant moderators of existing models in vocational psychology research. Such consistency is needed in order to promote the systematic development of our knowledge-base and would also facilitate future meta-analyses and systematic reviews of the literature. Third, they asked that researchers consider the cultural validity of Western models for non-Western contexts as well as the cultural specificity of variables that might provide incremental utility when predicting key vocational outcomes.

Finally, Leong and Pearce (2011) indicated that efforts should be made to educate research scientists about etic, emic, and imposed etic models in order to decrease the implementation of the lattermost approach. Just as psychologists are now recognizing the value of the dialectical use of mixed-methods research approaches (integrating quantitative and qualitative methods), they should also be made aware of the dual importance of culture-general and culture-specific factors in vocational choices and adaptation. Indigenous or culture-specific variables can no longer be classified as error or nuisance variance in our research programs. Cheung, van de Vijver, and Leong's (2011) recent

article calling for a combined etic–emic approach to the study of personality illustrates the importance of such integrative approaches.

Current Models of Vocational Psychology and the Multicultural Movement

Given the importance of ensuring cultural validity and cultural specificity in research, extant models of vocational psychology fall short for a number of reasons. Later in this chapter, we will explain the importance of the indigenous psychology approach for research with culturally diverse populations. Before doing so, we will first discuss why new or different models of vocational psychology seem necessary. Most researchers use a homogenous sample—namely Western populations consisting mostly of majority (White, middle-class) individuals—to develop their models, without attending to how the model may apply differently to minorities or persons from other cultures (Leong & Brown, 1995; Leong & Pearce, 2011). They also tend to use cultural terms like *race*, *ethnicity*, and *minority* interchangeably, which makes it difficult for practitioners to appropriately apply—and for other researchers to test—their models in different populations. Because of issues like these, there is a need to create and apply new culturally valid models of vocational psychology. These and other limitations have resulted in a lack of culturally valid research as well as the dismissal of current psychological models as irrelevant for culturally diverse populations (or requests to change the models to make them more relevant).

Leong's Prevailing and Countervailing Forces Influencing the Multicultural Movements

Over the past decade or so, there has been a clear push toward multiculturalism in psychology—still, progress has been slow. In an effort to illustrate why, Leong (2002) developed a theory of prevailing and countervailing forces influencing the movement based on Lewin's (1938, 1975) classic theory of driving and restraining forces, as well as his widely popular idea that individuals behave based on their own personal inclinations as well as the environmental context in which they operate (also see Leong & Santiago-Rivera, 1999). While *prevailing forces* push (positive) change forward, *countervailing forces* inhibit that change. Leong (2002) extended this framework to apply to broader social movements like the trend toward multiculturalism in psychology. In doing so, he warned against using Western models in non-Western environments.

While prevailing forces like globalization, migration, online information-sharing, and culturally based political events might prompt researchers to consider multicultural issues when developing and implementing scientific models, countervailing forces like ethnocentrism, the false consensus effect, psychological reactance, and the attraction–selection–attrition cycle impede the likelihood of such considerations (Leong, 2002). *Ethnocentrism* is the tendency, often cited as a source of prejudice and racism, to use one's own culture as the standard for understanding the thoughts and behaviors of persons from other cultures. *The false consensus effect* involves humans' propensity to assume that one's own thoughts and behaviors are normal and, consequently, to assume that persons from other cultures should think and behave in similar ways. *Psychological reactance* describes a person's drive to regain his past (lost) freedoms and to oppose people or things that threaten to reduce his current freedoms. Because multiculturalism requires a new basic framework for thinking about thoughts and behaviors, people may perceive it as a threat to one's familiar ways (i.e., monoculturalism). *The attraction–selection–attrition cycle* is the title given to a phenomenon that occurs in many organizations (and, by extension, geographical regions or social groups) during which a particular type of employee (e.g., with regard to personality or demographics) is *attracted* to an entity and is *selected* to join it, while other types of employees simultaneously *attrite* from it. This process ultimately leads to homogeneity within whatever grouping of persons is the entity of interest, potentially making it difficult for new changes (e.g., multiculturalism) to gain momentum.

Considering these potential concerns is worthwhile because whether or not indigenous models of psychology become popular likely depends on the (im)balance of prevailing and countervailing forces in psychology.

The Integrative and Cultural Accommodation Models of Cross-Cultural Psychology

Half a century ago, Kluckhohn and Murray (1950) introduced the idea that, "Every man is in certain respects: (a) like all other men, (b) like some other men, and (c) like no other man" (p. 35). Termed the "tripartite" framework, this idea has served as inspiration for a variety of cross-cultural psychologists. In a stream of research and theory spanning over a decade, Leong and his colleagues (Leong & Brown, 1995; Leong & Huang, 2008; Leong & Lee, 2006; Leong & Ow, 2003) have developed a culturally valid model for counseling and psychotherapy based on Kluckhohn and Murray's original tripartite theory. Leong's *integrative model* asserts that each person can be conceptualized as belonging to three dimensions or levels simultaneously: the Universal (like all other men), the Group (like some other men), and the Individual (like no other man). He suggested that psychologists need to pay attention to all three dimensions or levels in order to appropriately understand and aid clients.

While most models used in cross-cultural psychology and career counseling focus on only the Individual without regard for the social and cultural groups he or she belongs to, Leong's integrative model provides a framework for more comprehensively attending to client issues. During its development, Leong noted that all three dimensions or levels exist within clients as well as psychotherapists, and that all people can shift their focus from any given dimension to the next depending on the situation and the stage of the client–psychotherapist relationship. What does this mean for vocational psychology in particular? In vocational psychology, using the integrative model might entail considering an employee as an individual, as part of one or more work teams and departments, and as part of the organization as a whole. With regard to which dimension is most salient at any given time, an employee might focus most on the Individual dimension when receiving performance feedback but also on the Group dimension by comparing himself with other employees in his department and on the Universal dimension by thinking about how his personal efforts contribute to whether the company ultimately performs more favorably than its competitors.

More recently, Leong introduced the cultural accommodation model for cross-cultural psychology and career counseling. Rather than providing a framework for conceptualizing the needs, thoughts, and behaviors of individuals with regard to their culture—as did the integrative model—the goal of the cultural accommodation model was to outline means for identifying culture-specific variables that can be assessed to enhance the effectiveness and cultural validity of psychological interventions. Because of the widespread, often inappropriate, application of Western models to non-Western populations, the cultural accommodation model asserts that psychologists must investigate whether any given intervention, practice, or framework can be appropriately applied to a different cultural population than the one it was used for originally (Leong & Brown, 1995). This method is carried out to determine the cultural validity of any given model and to highlight any gaps or concerns associated with its use for persons from a different cultural population.

Because most models are originally developed using members from dominant (i.e., Western) cultures, it is imperative to understand whether they are applicable to other cultures and how they might be updated if not. For example, it is often possible to identify gaps that are missing from original models that, if filled, would allow them to be appropriately applied to members of a new cultural population. Thus, the cultural

accommodation model involves three steps. First, the psychologist must examine the existing theory to determine its cultural validity as well as any "blind spots" that might cause difficulties when applying it to a new cultural population. Second, the psychologist must figure out which culturally specific variables might help decrease the likelihood of these difficulties. At this point, it is pertinent to discuss how one might go about finding these valuable culturally specific variables that will enhance the model's applicability to the new population.

Leong and Pearce (2011) have suggested an evidence-based practice approach for this purpose. Evidence-based practice entails using results available from scientific literatures to guide one's real-world interventions and methods (Cochrane, 1979). With regard to the selection of culturally specific variables discussed above, the cultural accommodation model requires that a psychologist reviews scientific outlets to discover which culturally specific variables are deemed critical influencers of people's thoughts, feelings, reactions, and behaviors in the cultural population of interest. Consider, for example, a situation where a psychologist wishes to apply a Western model of career planning—which was originally developed using dominant majority individuals as its basis—to an Asian-American population. Because he or she is concerned that Asian-Americans' motivations and preferences with regard to career planning might be different than those of White/majority individuals, he or she examines the scientific literature and considers assessing and controlling for variables like identity, communication style, conflict avoidance, or propensity to conform. Which variables he or she ultimately decides to use will depend on how likely each is to explain the differences in career planning processes of Asian-American versus White/majority individuals.

The third and final step of the cultural accommodation model involves an empirical test of the incremental value of the culturally accommodating version of the theory, intervention, practice, framework, model, and so on, above and beyond its original (non-culturally accommodating) version. If its incremental value is significant, then the new version is worthy of further research and adoption. Taken together, these steps essentially involve investigating and assessing whether the cultural-generalized aspects of Western models should and can be supplemented by including additional culture-specific information. These same steps can be taken to apply the cultural accommodation model for use in indigenous psychology, by identifying, measuring, and "accommodating" for variables specific to particular cultural populations.

The Importance of and Trends Toward Indigenous Models of Psychology

The main goals of these models are to explore phenomena in different cultures and to understand the underlying causes of observed differences (Berry et al., 1992). Note that this approach entails searching for effects *across* cultures. Alternatively, indigenous psychologists develop models regarding effects *within* a culture (Triandis, 2000). They often use bottom-up and culture-specific methods that are typically developed using a particular non-Western cultural population. In doing so, indigenous psychologists focus on culture-specific phenomena and tend to assume that Western theories and models are not culturally valid in a given non-Western cultural population of interest.

What drives indigenous psychologists to create culture-specific models in this way? As noted by Leong and Pearce (2011), Sinha's (1993) account of the importation of Western models to Indian psychology provides one adequate rationale: The desire to understand phenomena in a particular culture more deeply than it occurs in general (i.e., across cultures) or in Western-majority individuals.

> When modern scientific psychology, based on the empirical, mechanistic, and materialistic orientations of the West, was imported into India as part of the general transfer knowledge, it came in as a readymade intellectual package in the first decade of the century. It tended to sweep away the traditional psychology, at least among those who had been involved in modern Western education. In fact, this transfer in a way constituted an

element of the political domination of the West over the third world countries in the general process of modernization and Westernization. The domination was so great that for almost three decades until about the time India achieved independence in 1947, psychology remained tied to the apron strings of the West and did not show any signs of maturing. ... Very little originality was displayed, Indian research added hardly anything to psychological theory or knowledge, and was seldom related to problems of the country. Research conducted was by and large repetitive and replicative in character, the object being to supplement studies done in the West by further experimentation or to examine some of their aspects from a new angle. Thus, the discipline remained at best a pale copy of Western psychology, rightly designated as a Euro-American product with very little concern with social reality as it prevailed in India. (Sinha, 1993, p. 31)

As described in this quotation and in earlier sections of this chapter, Western models have often been applied to different cultural populations without acknowledging that the models may not be culturally valid or incrementally informative. In addition, indigenous psychologists believe that the study and application of psychology is entirely specific to a given cultural population and, consequently, that each culture must develop its own methods for psychological research and practice. Thus, it is considered inappropriate to use models from other cultures because they cannot explain phenomena as optimally as can models developed from within one's own culture.

Indigenous psychologies have become widely popular in academia, especially for scholars working in developing and non-Western developed regions (Kim & Berry, 1993; Sinha, 1997; Yang, 1999). Sinha (1997) suggested that the trend toward indigenization reflects a growing concern among psychologists that Western models are not applicable to other cultural populations. Similarly, Triandis (1997) and Yang (2000) have noted that the world's psychological science is almost entirely comprising *one* indigenous psychology— which was developed in and specifically for Western/majority individuals.

Before moving on to discuss recommendations for those interested in applying indigenous psychologists' approach to theory and practice, we will define and describe the science in greater detail. As with many other scientific labels and domains, a number of definitions exist for indigenous psychology (Enriquez, 1990; Ho, 1998; Kim & Berry, 1993; Yang, 1999, 2000). Nonetheless, as Yang (2000) has noted, these definitions all similarly incorporate indigenous psychologists' goal of "developing a scientific knowledge system that effectively reflects, describes, explains, and/or understands the psychological and behavioral activities in their native contexts in terms of culturally relevant frames of reference and culturally derived categories and theories" (Yang, 2000, pp. 245–246).

In other words, indigenous psychologists seek to first create a culture-specific psychological science using individuals from a particular cultural population (e.g., individuals associated with any given region, nation, ethnicity, language, religion) in order to most comprehensively understand a phenomenon of interest *in that culture specifically*. Knowledge garnered from one indigenous psychology can later be broadened by studying larger populations or can be combined with knowledge from other indigenous psychologies. Note that this bottom-up approach requires culture-specific indigenous psychologists to create and then broaden a theory or model along with others; it would be inappropriate to first create one broad psychology and then apply it to different cultures within or outside of it. In addition, it should be noted that indigenous psychologists are encouraged to use many different scientific methods, theories, interventions, etc. to study culture-specific phenomena—no one method or theory is regarded as superior to another and, often times, multiple different or conflicting paradigms are to be utilized for the same purpose (Kim & Berry, 1993; Yang, 1999, 2000).

Steps for Developing and Using Models of Indigenous Psychology

Leong and Pearce (2011) described the movement toward indigenous psychologies as requiring several steps. First, we should question and challenge the cultural validity and specificity of the (likely Western) models that we currently use. Kuhn (1962), in his discussion of the nature of scientific revolutions, had referred to this stage as the emergence of unexplained phenomena at the edges of dominant paradigms. As these new developments gather momentum, eventually proponents of the dominant paradigm can no longer ignore them and instead try to account for them by expanding their own models. Similarly, we begin to examine the cultural validity of our current vocational models just as we begin to explore the role of culture-specific elements and their influence on the career behaviors of our clients (e.g., by using the cultural accommodation approach). As we recognize the value and incremental validity of these culturally specific constructs, we must also consider whether indigenous constructs could enrich our models as well as their validity and utility. Finally, as enough scientists begin to explore these indigenous models of psychology in an effort to collectively improve our field, we will witness the beginnings of a paradigm shift.

Having provided a theoretical rationale for the value of indigenous approaches to vocational psychology, we will follow Leong and Pearce (2011) by next providing some guidance about how to conduct indigenous psychological research by highlighting several studies that have been published recently and that identify culturally specific variables and their incremental value in vocational psychology research. The first example is that of Hardin, Leong, and Osipow (2001) who challenged the universality of the concept of career maturity and suggested that there exists cultural relativism in the conceptualization and measurement of career constructs. Specifically, they claimed that the finding that career maturity is lower in Asian-Americans than in European Americans is due to a Western-European bias in constructs and measures. In extant theory, there is a biased assumption that cultural differences in independence explain the lower career maturity in Asian-Americans (i.e., Asian-Americans make less mature career choices because they lack independence in decision-making unlike European

Americans). Believing that many career constructs are promoted as universal when in fact they are Eurocentric (i.e., an imposed etic), Hardin et al. (2001) sought to demonstrate the cultural relativity of the concept and measurement of career maturity. Using a sample of racially diverse students, their findings supported their argument regarding possible cultural relativism in measurement of career maturity. Specifically, they found that career maturity does not differ between low-interdependent Asian-Americans and European Americans. In other words, if interdependence (which otherwise is a valued cultural attitude and behavior) is low, then an Asian-American's career maturity will be as high as that of a European American. While previous research endeavors had pointed to the importance of *in*dependence as a cultural differentiator of career maturity—this newer work suggests that *inter*dependence, a separate construct from independence, may underlie commonly recognized cultural differences in career maturity. Leong and Pearce (2011) noted that results like these are important because they demonstrate the value in considering how and why cultural differences might influence interrelationships among variables, rather than assuming generalizability. Relevant to our current discussions, testing culturally specific or indigenous constructs as moderators and mediators is critical for the advancement of authentic evidence-based vocational psychology. The use of a culturally relative approach helps us guard against ethnocentricism in our science and the imposition of a pseudo etic (i.e., assuming that what works for us will automatically work for those in other cultures).

In a second study illustrating the value of using indigenous constructs, Pek and Leong (2003) studied the relationships between sexist values and Traditionality–Modernity in the Chinese population in Singapore. In the United States, cultural identity and its influence on human behavior is usually studied via the acculturation paradigm whereby immigrants choose the degree and amount of adoption of the cultural values, norms, and beliefs of their host culture over time as a result of contact. In addition to selecting the

host cultural elements to adopt, immigrants, refugees, and other sojourners need to make parallel choices regarding how much of their own traditional culture will be kept or discarded. The combined outcome of these two sets of choices produces their level of acculturation according to Berry's (1980) model of acculturation. The acculturation paradigm does not fit for nationals who remain in their own country because no extended contact with a host culture is involved. Instead, cultural identity for these nationals is usually conceived of from the perspective of Traditionality–Modernity (Yang, 1996) where the individual's identity varies along a continuum of traditional versus modern values and beliefs. For example, in Chinese culture, those with Traditional cultural identity maintain very conservative and patriarchal gender roles.

Using the Traditionality–Modernity (Yang, 1996) approach with a sample of employees in Singapore, Pek and Leong (2003) investigated the nature of general ambivalent sexism and workplace-specific sexism in this particular culture. Consistent with previous research, they found that participant sex (male), low femininity, and high authoritarianism predicted sexist attitudes toward women. In addition, (indigenous) Chinese values incrementally predicted general and workplace-specific sexism. This study demonstrated the value in studying culture-related differences in variables such as Traditionality–Modernity in relation to Western constructs such as benevolent sexism, particularly with regard to the incremental explanation of effects they provide.

Chang, Arkin, Leong, Chan, and Leung (2004) provide a third example of the indigenous psychology approach. They investigated whether (subjective) overachievement is experienced similarly or differently between Chinese college students enrolled at the Chinese University of Hong Kong and the National University of Singapore and (Caucasian) American college students enrolled at the Ohio State University (the United States). This subjective overachievement construct—termed *kiasu* in Singapore— serves as a powerful but negative motivating force among many Chinese students. When cultural differences in self-construal (independence and interdependence) were controlled for in the study, Chinese participants' experiences differed in meaningful ways versus their American counterparts: Chinese students were less concerned with their performance, more likely to doubt themselves, and more prone to modesty when overworked. Chang et al. suggested that differences in beliefs may underlie these results: For example, the American belief that "failure may not always be a bad thing" (p. 166) is in direct contrast with the Chinese norm that failure is indeed always a bad thing, especially in competitive situations. Once again, this operationalization of the indigenous concept "kiasu" resulted in the finding that there are indeed important culturally specific moderators that deserve recognition in psychology, particularly for researchers planning to examine Western constructs (e.g., achievement motivation) in non-Western contexts.

The fourth and final example of the indigenous approach to psychological investigations is illustrated by the research program of Cheung, Cheung, Leung, Ward, and Leong (2003). These researchers were interested in learning whether the Chinese Personality Assessment Inventory (CPAI) could be translated for application with English-speaking populations, and whether it might also be more informative than the very commonly used five-factor model (FFM). When administered to an English-speaking (Singaporean) Chinese sample as well as an English-speaking (Caucasian) American sample, similar factor structures held across both (and both structures were similar to the original Chinese CPAI structure). The authors discovered that the FFM does not tap Interpersonal Relatedness, a key personality factor in Chinese culture, and that the CPAI does not tap Openness, a key personality factor in American culture. This research provides support for our current argument regarding the need to consider cultural dissimilarities when taking a measure developed in one setting and implementing it in another; a measure's meaning, value, and essential elements may differ meaningfully when applied to a new cultural group.

Recommendations for Research and Practice: Sensitivity to the Universal and the Particular

One of the three approaches (i.e., cross-cultural psychology, cultural psychology, and indigenous psychologies) is typically used to investigate the role of cultural context in human psychological and behavioral phenomena (Yang, 2000). Our main focus in the current chapter was on describing the unique value of the approach used by indigenous psychologists, who examine peoples' thoughts, feelings, and behaviors in their native cultural contexts in order to cultivate a targeted—and therefore exceptionally appropriate—understanding of any given phenomenon of interest. Currently, cross-cultural and cultural approaches still dominate the field of vocational psychology. In fact, a review of empirical articles published in four of the domain's more popular journals (i.e., *Journal of Vocational Behavior*, *Journal of Career Assessment*, *Career Development Quarterly*, and *Journal of Career Development*) revealed eight culture-focused research endeavors conducted in 2011—four of which incorporated a cross-cultural approach, three a cultural approach, and one an indigenous approach.

Just as there are barriers in the movement from mainstream to cross-cultural psychology, there are barriers to our movement from cross-cultural psychology to indigenous psychologies. Leong and Santiago-Rivera (1999) have recommended that a critical step in these movements is to recognize and counter our own ethnocentricism. A quotation from Triandis (1994) has provided a working definition in his textbook *Culture and Social Behavior*:

> We are all ethnocentric, some of us more than others, especially if we have not tasted another culture. How could it be otherwise? Most of us know only our own culture, and it is natural that we will consider it as the standard against which to judge others.
>
> The more another culture is like our own, the "better" it is. That is the essence of ethnocentrism. (p. 249)

Hence, ethnocentrism is a natural human tendency and it consists of using our own culture as a standard for evaluating others. We propose that vocational psychologists, like other psychologists, are not immune to this natural tendency. However, ethnocentrism in our science and practice, if not examined and minimized, will result in the development of theories and models that will not only be inadequate for culturally diverse populations but in fact may be iatrogenic. Triandis (1994) proposed that:

> Ethnocentrism and cultural distance work together to create perceived dissimilarity. Dissimilarity results in conflict, and conflict results in negative stereotypes. As a result, people make non-isomorphic attributions and experience the relationship as one in which they have no control. They feel culture shock, and they feel hostility toward the other group. (p. 249)

The end result of ethnocentrism is increased cultural distance and cultural stereotypes and misunderstandings. Furthermore, Brislin (1993) has pointed out that:

> When people make ethnocentric judgments about culturally diverse others, they are imposing the standards with which they are familiar given their own socialization… Ethnocentric judgments, then, are based on feelings that one's own group is the center of what is reasonable and proper in life. Further, the term implies that others can be judged according to one, central set of standards. An implication of the judgments is that one group is clearly better, even superior, than the other since its members practice proper and correct behaviors. As might be expected, the group considered better or superior is the one to which the person making the ethnocentric judgments belongs. (p. 38)

One way to view the three approaches to culture is in terms of Bogardus' (1959) concept of social distance. This concept reflects the degree of prejudice (and therefore maintained social distance) between the dominant White Anglo-Saxon Protestant majority and immigrants of different race and ethnicity. The three approaches also reflect a similar cultural distance between investigators and subjects. In a way, *cross-cultural psychology* is a top-down approach with the greatest cultural distance between investigator and subjects. These researchers arrive with fully formed models and theories to be tested on passive subjects. On the other hand, *cultural psychology* is an attempt to reduce the cultural distance and advocate a more bottom-up approach where the subjects or participants are active members with cultural knowledge to share with the investigators. However, this approach still suffers from the cultural encapsulation of investigators who are primarily Westerners studying non-Western cultures. *Indigenous psychologies* involve not only a bottom-up approach like cultural psychology but its investigators are members of the culture under study and have the advantage of native phenomenology and "insider knowledge." As vocational psychologists, we may not have the advantage of being native to the cultures we are studying but we can certainly try to immerse ourselves in that culture, collaborate with psychologists from that culture, and include cultural informants from that culture (Brislin, Lonner, & Thorndike, 1973; Rogler, 1989).

As vocational psychologists, we need to explore and research the many ways in which ethnocentricism may be inhibiting our progress. To expand our understanding of cultural influence, we need to collaborate with others and consider indigenous perspectives as much as possible. Understanding each culture, as well as the differences across cultures, can only be achieved by exerting effort toward learning the various culturally unique ways of being human. In line with this perspective, we suggest that the incorporation of indigenous psychologies in vocational research will enhance the cultural validity and specificity of already-used, as well as entirely new, psychological assessments and interventions.

New Concepts and Viewpoints: Charting New Directions

The major new direction which we have offered in this chapter is for vocational psychologists to begin to develop and apply indigenous models in their work. We have described the problems created when Western models have often been applied to different cultural populations without acknowledging that these models may not be culturally valid or incrementally informative. We also argue that indigenous psychology, as the study and application of psychology specific to a given cultural population, will enrich the methods for vocational psychological research and practice. Our advocating for the development and application of indigenous approaches is predicated on the findings that it is often inappropriate to use models from other cultures because they cannot explain phenomena as optimally as those models developed from within one's own culture.

A second new direction which we have offered to counter the ethnocentricism in our science and practice is to apply Leong's (Leong & Huang, 2008; Leong & Lee, 2006; Leong & Ow, 2003) cultural accommodation model for cross-cultural psychology and career counseling. As indicated earlier, the goal of the cultural accommodation model is to identify culturally specific variables that can be assessed to enhance the effectiveness and cultural validity of our psychological interventions. To counter the widespread, often inappropriate, application of Western models to non-Western populations, the cultural accommodation model argues that we must investigate whether any given intervention, practice, or framework can be appropriately applied to a different cultural population than the one it was used for originally (Leong & Brown, 1995). In many ways, the cultural accommodation model is a flexible framework for promoting cross-cultural psychology, cultural psychology, and indigenous psychologies in the pursuit of cultural validity.

References

Benet-Martinez, V. (2007). Cross-cultural personality research. In R. W. Robins, R. C. Fraley, & R. F. Krueger (Eds.), *Research methods in personality*

psychology (pp. 170–189). New York, NY: The Guilford Press.

Berry, J. W. (1980). Acculturation as varieties of adaptation. In A. Padilla (Ed.), *Acculturation: Theories, models and some new findings* (pp. 9–25). Boulder, CO: Westview Press.

Berry, J. W. (1994). An ecological perspective on cultural and ethnic psychology. In E. J. Trickett, R. J. Watts, & D. Birman (Eds.), *Human diversity: Perspectives on people in context* (pp. 115–141). San Francisco, CA: Jossey-Bass.

Berry, J. W., Poortinga, Y. H., Segall, M. H., & Dasen, P. R. (1992). *Cross-cultural psychology: Research and applications* (2nd ed.). New York, NY: Cambridge University Press.

Bogardus, E. S. (1959). *Social distance*. Los Angeles, CA: University of Southern California Press.

Brislin, R. (1993). *Understanding culture's influence on behavior*. New York, NY: Harcourt Brace.

Brislin, R. W., Lonner, W. J., & Thorndike, R. M. (1973). *Cross cultural research methods*. New York, NY: Wiley.

Chang, L. C., Arkin, R. M., Leong, F. T. L., Chan, D., & Leung, K. (2004). Subjective overachievement in American and Chinese college students. *Journal of Cross-Cultural Psychology, 35*, 152–173.

Cheung, F. M., Cheung, S. F., Leung, K., Ward, C., & Leong, F. (2003). The English version of the Chinese personality assessment inventory. *Journal of Cross-Cultural Psychology, 34*, 433–452.

Cheung, F. M., van de Vijver, F. J. R., & Leong, F. T. L. (2011). Toward a new approach to the study of personality in culture. *American Psychologist, 66*, 593–603.

Cochrane, A. L. (1979). 1931–1971: A critical review with particular reference to the medical profession. In *Medicines for the year 2000* (pp. 1–11). London, UK: Office of Health Economics. Retrieved from http://www.cochrane.org/about-us/history/archie-cochrane

Enriquez, V. G. (1989). *Indigenous psychology and national consciousness*. Tokyo, Japan: Institute for the Study of Languages and Cultures of Asia and Africa.

Enriquez, V. G. (Ed.). (1990). *Indigenous psychologies*. Quezon City, Philippines: Psychology Research & Training House.

Hardin, E. E., Leong, F. T. L., & Osipow, S. H. (2001). Cultural relativity in the conceptualization of career maturity. *Journal of Vocational Behavior, 58*, 1–17.

Ho, Y. F. (1998). Indigenous psychologies: Asian perspectives. *Journal of Cross-Cultural Psychology, 29*, 88–103.

Kiesler, D. J. (1966). Some myths of psychotherapy research and the search for a paradigm. *Psychological Bulletin, 65*, 110–136.

Kim, U., & Berry, J. W. (1993). *Indigenous psychologies: Research and experience in cultural context*. Newbury Park, CA: Sage.

Kluckhohn, C., & Murray, H. A. (1950). Personality formation: The determinants. In C. Kluckhohn & H. A. Murray (Eds.), *Personality in nature, society, and culture* (pp. 35–48). New York, NY: Knopf.

Kuhn, T. S. (1962). *The structure of scientific revolutions* (1st ed.). Chicago, IL: University of Chicago Press.

Leong, F. T. L. (2002). Challenges for career counseling in Asia: Variations in cultural accommodation. *Career Development Quarterly, 50*, 277–284.

Leong, F. T. L., & Brown, M. T. (1995). Theoretical issues in cross-cultural career development: Cultural validity and cultural specificity. In W. B. Walsh & S. H. Osipow (Eds.), *Handbook of vocational psychology* (pp. 143–180). Hillsdale, NJ: Lawrence Erlbaum.

Leong, F. T. L., & Huang, J. L. (2008). Applying the cultural accommodation model to diversity consulting in organizations. *Consulting Psychology Journal, 60*, 17–185.

Leong, F. T. L., & Lee, S.-H. (2006). A cultural accommodation model of psychotherapy: Illustrated with the case of Asian-Americans. *Psychotherapy: Theory, Research, Practice, and Training, 43*, 410–423.

Leong, F. T. L., & Ow, R. (2003). Towards a cultural accommodation model for effective cross-counseling in Asia. *Asia Pacific Journal of Social Work, 13*, 1–21.

Leong, F. T. L., & Pearce, M. (2011). Desiderata: Towards indigenous models of career development and vocational psychology. *International Journal for Educational and Vocational Guidance, 11*, 65–77.

Leong, F. T. L., Pickren, W., Leach, M. M., & Marsella, A. J. (2012). *Internationalizing the psychology curriculum in the United States*. New York, NY: Springer.

Leong, F. T. L., & Santiago-Rivera, A. (1999). Climbing the multiculturalism summit: Challenges and pitfalls. In P. Pedersen (Ed.), *Multiculturalism as a fourth force* (pp. 61–72). Philadelphia, PA: Brunner/Mazel.

Lewin, K. (1938). *The conceptual representation and the measurement of psychological forces*. Durham, NC: Duke University Press.

Lewin, K. (1975). *Field theory in social science: Selected theoretical papers*. Westport, CT: Greenwood Press.

Neville, H. A., Lilly, R. L., Duran, G., Lee, R., & Browne, L. (2000). Construction and initial validation of the color-blind racial attitudes scale (CoBRAS). *Journal of Counseling Psychology, 47*, 59–70.

Pek, J. C. X., & Leong, F. T. L. (2003). Sex-related self-concepts, cognitive styles, and cultural values of traditionality-modernity as predictors of general and domain-specific sexism. *Asian Journal of Social Psychology, 6*, 31–49.

Rogler, L. H. (1989). The meaning of culturally sensitive research in mental health. *American Journal of Psychiatry, 146*, 296–303.

Shweder, R. A. (1990). Cultural psychology: What is it? In J. Stigler, R. A. Shweder, & G. Herdt (Eds.), *Cultural psychology: Essays on comparative human development*. New York, NY: Cambridge University Press.

Sinha, D. (1993). Indigenization of psychology in India and its relevance. In U. Kim & J. W. Berry (Eds.), *Indigenous psychologies: Research and experience in cultural context* (pp. 30–43). Newbury Park, CA: Sage.

Sinha, D. (1997). Indigenizing psychology. In J. W. Berry, Y. H. Poortinga, & J. Pandey (Eds.), *Handbook of cross-cultural psychology* (2nd ed., Vol. 1, pp. 129–169). Boston, MA: Allyn & Bacon.

Triandis, H. C. (1994). *Culture and social behavior*. New York, NY: McGraw-Hill.

Triandis, H. C. (1997). Cross-cultural perspectives on personality. In R. Hogan, J. Johnson, & S. Briggs (Eds.), *Handbook of personality psychology* (pp. 439–464). San Diego, CA: Academic.

Triandis, H. C. (2000). Dialectics between cultural and cross-cultural psychology. *Asian Journal of Social Psychology, 3*, 185–195.

Yang, K. S. (1993). Why do we need to develop an indigenous Chinese psychology? *Indigenous Psychological Research in Chinese Societies, 1*, 6–88 (In Chinese).

Yang, K. S. (1996). The psychological transformation of the Chinese people as a result of societal modernization. In M. H. Bond (Ed.), *Oxford handbook of Chinese psychology*. Hong Kong, China: Oxford University Press.

Yang, K. S. (1997). Indigenizing Westernized Chinese psychology. In M. H. Bond (Ed.), *Working at the interface of cultures: Eighteen lives in social science* (pp. 62–76). London, UK: Routledge.

Yang, K. S. (1999). Towards an indigenous Chinese psychology: A selective review of methodological, theoretical, and empirical accomplishments. *Chinese Journal of Psychology, 41*, 181–211.

Yang, K. S. (2000). Monocultural and cross-cultural indigenous approaches: The royal road to the development of a balanced global psychology. *Asian Journal of Social Psychology, 3*, 241–263.

The Cultural Preparation Process Model and Career Development

Gideon Arulmani

Introduction

David Greybeard settled down to another work day. He set himself up at his workstation and prepared and meticulously checked his work tools. Once all was ready, he carefully began a complex activity. Eyebrows knitted in concentration and hands steady, he deftly but slowly manipulated his work tool. Holding steady for a while, manipulating occasionally, and sometimes even jiggling the instrument, he exerted skilled and concentrated effort. After a while he very gently retracted his tool and grunted with satisfaction. His efforts were rewarded. His grass-stalk tool was teeming with the termites he so loved. Popping them into his mouth and glancing at Goliath, his associate who was performing a similar operation nearby with a leaf-tool, Greybeard resumed "termite fishing" once again. David Greybeard and Goliath are chimpanzees from the anthropologist Jane Goodall's Kasakela community inhabiting the Gombe National Park near Lake Tanganyika in Tanzania (Goodall, 1986). Chimpanzees were using tools at least 4,300 years ago which included tool kits, as well as compound tools having two or more working components (McGrew, 2010). Do Greybeard and Goliath's endeavors and the similar efforts of these phylogenetic neighbors of ours qualify as "work?" What *is* work? And how does it characterize the human being?

I attempt to address these questions by focusing on two objectives. The first is to articulate the dynamics of a culturally mediated model to propose that the manner in which individuals and groups are prepared by their cultures (cultural preparedness) explains their engagement with work and career development. The second is to apply the model to understand concepts and constructs from Asian epistemologies.

Cultural Learning

Humankind has given itself the name *Homo sapiens* implying that we as a species are capable of actions that transcend a merely need-based engagement with the surroundings. In fact, by calling ourselves sapient we refer to ourselves as being wise, endowed with the ability to discern. It is this wisdom and intelligence that qualifies human beings' ongoing encounter with the environment. The human being is capable of directing effort, both intellectual and physical, toward constructions and fabrications, both material and nonmaterial, that can endure for durations of time beyond the phase of fabrication and construction. This is the human activity called work. Hannah Arendt (1958) names *Homo sapiens* in this garb, as *Homo faber*— human as a maker, the working human.

G. Arulmani (✉)
The Promise Foundation, Bangalore, India
e-mail: garulmani@t-p-f.org

G. Arulmani et al. (eds.), *Handbook of Career Development*, International and Cultural Psychology,
DOI 10.1007/978-1-4614-9460-7_6, © Springer Science+Business Media, LLC 2014

Human work began in a world that was wild, untamed, and perhaps hostile. Survival was likely the prime concern. Small bands of early humans would have secured ongoing safety and survival through generic work activities such as building shelters against the elements, hunting, and gathering food. These groups tended to be wanderers, following herds of animals and other sources of food and sustenance, and at the same time making discoveries that improved the quality of their lives as they trudged along. It is quite probable that during the initial stages in the evolution of work, work tasks were linked to the *identification* and *adaptation* of sources of security and sustenance (Marlowe, 2005). It also seems that at that time work was a group activity (Gowdy, 1998). It is probable that individual members of the group had to learn to provide for and support the group's needs as quickly as possible. It also seems clear that work was not considered separate from daily life. Work was integral to existence (Barnard, 2004).

Developmental psychologists and anthropologists have pointed to two key differences between nonhuman primates such as Greybeard and Goliath and the human being which ultimately have an impact on orientations and definitions of work. The first difference is the distinction seen between human and nonhuman *learning*. Tomasello (1999) has referred to the kind of learning found among nonhuman primates as *emulation learning*, which "focuses on the environmental events involved—results or changes of state in the environment—rather than on the actions that produced those results" (p. 510). By contrast, Tomasello has described human learning to be *imitative learning*, which means "reproducing an instrumental act understood intentionally." Through the capacity for *joint engagement*, human infants are able to use adults as reference points and thus "act on objects in the way adults are acting on them" (Tomasello, 1999, p. 513). The human infant is, therefore, able to identify others as "intentional agents... who have goals and make active choices among behavioral means for attaining those goals" (Moore & Dunham, 1995, p. 76).

This capacity for imitative learning brings us to the second distinction between the nonhuman primates and human beings, which is the ability to represent experiences *symbolically*. This enabled the human being to not only invent but also preserve learnings for others to learn from. It is this feature of the human being that lays the foundations for *cultural learning*. This is a distinctive process whereby the learner is not only learning about things from other persons but also learning things through them and at the same time becoming a vehicle for the transmission of these learnings to others (Tomasello, 1999). It is this capacity for cultural learning that transforms the human being's engagement with work into a manifestation of culture. It is this unique and distinguishing quality of human learning that underlies the *cultural preparation process model of career development* that is described in this chapter.

Work as Culture

A significant milestone in the evolution of work was perhaps triggered by the Neolithic Revolution—circa 10,000–5,000 BCE (Scarre, 2005). Humankind gradually decreased its itinerant search for food and began to domesticate plants and animals. Hunter-gatherers, on different parts of earth, began to make the transition to agriculture and to establishing themselves in a specific location (Scarre, 2005). This transition perhaps presaged the imbuing of work with cultural overtones.

Anthropologists describe culture as human phenomena that cannot be attributed to genetic or biological inheritance, but reflective of a cohesive and assimilated system of learned behavior patterns which characterize the members of a social group (Hoebel, 1966). Other features of culture include the symbolic representation of experiences and the distinct ways in which groups of people classify and represent their collective experience (Geertz, 1973; Liu & Sibley, 2009). By Neolithic times, humanity had evolved three distinctive features: (a) the ability to create and use symbols including linguistic symbols and their derivatives, such as written language and mathematical codes; (b) the ability to create tools and instrumental technologies to meet the requirements of specific tasks; and (c) the ability to create and participate in complex social organizations and institutions (Tomasello, 1999). Since it was a fundamental and dominant activity, it is likely that work began to be characterized by each of these features.

In this regard, the impact of the Neolithic Revolution on work was profound. It led to a tremendous diversification of work skills. The development of agriculture led to a number of cultural innovations and shifts in social dynamics (Pringle, 1998). The settling down of groups in specific locations led to the gradual transformation of human beings from nomadic groups into sedentary societies. Villages were established which grew into towns and later into cities. By this time, people had developed the ability to wrest the land from the wild, tame it, and make it arable. Given the massive investment of effort and the highly satisfactory returns on this investment, people became attached to certain locations and land increased in its value. Property ownership became increasingly important and acquired the status of being a highly valued possession (Scarre, 2005). If identification and adaptation of sources of security and sustenance were key work tasks of the nomadic period, the importance of *organizing*, *preserving*, and instituting *order* and *continuity* became important now (Scarre, 2005). With the passage of time, a complex of other occupations began to evolve which included trade and business, construction and architecture, administration and management, law and governance, protection and security, health and medicine, and industry and technology. It is possible that systems emerged to classify workers according to ability and status. Specializations began to evolve and thus emerged occupational categories such as fishermen, farmers, cattle breeders, weavers, healers, and traders—a list that will continue to grow for as long as human needs exist.

The point being made here is that, from the Neolithic times, work was slowly transformed from a raw and primal engagement with the surroundings, to an activity that was characterized by the codification of experiences through symbols, the organization and classification of work activities into occupations that were governed by hierarchies, and the transmission of these learnings to others through the process of cultural learning. Work began to be characterized by customs, laws, value attributions, social standards, religious beliefs, and traditions (Scarre, 2005). It has also been observed that populations that were able to organize work around a central principle (for example, principles emanating from religion) were more prosperous (e.g., Bellwood, 2004; Childe, 1936; Pringle, 1998). Hence, work as a human activity became deeply embedded in human culture.

Work and Global Transformations

As we have just seen, a reciprocal relationship seems to exist between the nature of work and co-occurring cultural and economic transformations. Molded by ideologies, shaped by the tenets of a variety of philosophies, and transformed by revolutions, the meaning and purpose of work has undergone significant changes over time. With a view to illustrating the link between global trends and work culture, three significant aspects of the history of work, namely the Protestant Reformation, the Industrial Revolution, and globalization, are now briefly discussed.

The Protestant Reformation

Discontent with the Church, its creeds, and unreasonable doctrines led to massive political upheaval in Europe during the 16th century. This protest movement that aimed at reforming the church was later called the Protestant Reformation. Martin Luther's reformatory theology went against the prevailing feudal social order—priest, noble, king, and peasant—and declared that all were equal in the eyes of God. The Reformists emphasized that work was a "calling" and Luther preached that work was a channel of service to God. Luther confronted the prevalent dogma that one form of work was superior to another and proclaimed the usefulness of all professions. The Reformists encouraged the creation of wealth through hard, honest labor. This fundamental divergence from accepted beliefs created new understandings that redefined attitudes toward work which later came to be called the protestant work ethic (Weber, 1905/2002). Doing one's best, persisting toward work goals, postponement of need gratification, working hard with sincerity, involvement, and passion, achieving financial and economic success were all linked to social acceptance and ultimately to salvation. This new work ethic which gave moral approval to making a profit by working hard, rational calculation, and planning spread all over Europe and England and was later carried to America (Yankelovich & Immerwahr, 1984). Today, Western work behavior continues to be significantly influenced by these social cognitions.

The Industrial Revolution

The Industrial Revolution which occurred almost in parallel with the Reformation is another important milestone in the evolution of work in the West. Until now, production was small scale and much of it was undertaken through direct, skilled, physical effort. The Industrial Revolution transformed the concept of production. New inventions such as the flying shuttle, the spinning jenny, and the steam engine facilitated the application of power-driven machinery to manufacturing. Goods could now be produced at greater speed, in larger quantities, and at significantly lower costs. By the beginning of the 18th century, the use of machines in manufacturing became widespread across England and Europe. Until the Industrial Revolution, most of Europe's population was rural, and work behavior was governed by feudal systems. However, by the mid-19th century, people broke away from this social order and lived in cities as independent workers. An immediate outcome of this change in production methodology was that the skilled artisans of the older order gradually found themselves to be redundant as machines began to mass produce the products they formerly handcrafted. This pattern of emergent methods rendering older methods "redundant" is seen all through the history of work.

Globalization

The human being's sojourn on this planet began as a nomad who moved from one place to another seeking greater security, food, and comfort. This tendency continued and the history of human beings travelling from one location to another for the exchange of goods, services, and ideas is an ancient one. Advances in modes of transport and communication have hastened the pace and quality of these exchanges, and today we refer to this international exchange/transfer of resources and ways of living as globalization. Giddens (1991) defines globalization as "the intensification of worldwide social relations which link distant localities in such a way that local happenings are shaped by events occurring many miles away and vice versa" (p. 64). I now highlight three aspects of globalization that are related to work and cultural preparedness: international trade, the emergence of a global workforce, and the new international division of labor.

International Trade

The practice of trading goods and services across international borders is also an ancient one. The Silk Route is an example of a network of trade routes that stretched for nearly 4,000 miles linking China, the Afro-Eurasian landmass, and Asia to Europe. While traditional trade focused on the buying and selling of goods that were not available locally, a key distinguishing feature of contemporary, globalized, international trade is the seeking of trading opportunities that have a cost advantage. In the globalized world, therefore, the exchange of goods and services can occur not merely because they are not available locally, but because it is cheaper to procure them from elsewhere. This has had a profound impact on local workforces, leading to loss of jobs at some locations and an unprecedented increase in job opportunities at other locations.

Global Workforce

One of the outcomes of the globalization of trade is the emergence of a global workforce: the extensive, international pool of workers employed mainly by multinational companies connected across nations to a global network of job tasks and work functions. As of 2005, the global labor pool of those employed by multinational companies consisted of almost three billion workers (Freeman, 2008). A key qualifying feature of this workforce is its skill for using communication technologies to interact with professional colleagues in other global locations.

The New International Division of Labor

This feature of globalization emerges when manufacturing and production are no longer restricted to local economies. With an eye on lowering costs of production and increasing profits, companies relocate production processes and outsource them to locations that offer cost advantages. While this division of labor benefits the outsourcing company, it does not benefit the individual worker in such companies who is laid off or retrenched. For example, between the years 2000 and 2007, a total of 3.2 million manufacturing jobs were lost in the USA due to outsourcing (Crutsinger, 2007). On the other side of outsourcing pipeline is the recipient country—usually a developing country offering cheap labor—where a massive increase in jobs is seen. A significant proportion of the recently seen economic growth and increase in gross domestic product (GDP) seen in these countries is related to this new international division of labor (ILO, 2013).

The Impact of Globalization on Work Behavior

These processes impact the interface between culture and work behavior in many ways. This form of globalized trade requires cultural realignments and usually it is the recipient (developing) country that is required to realign. Let us take the example of the business process

outsourcing industry (call centers) in India as an example. This is an industry that has created millions of jobs and is described as an engine of economic development for this country. Seen from another perspective, working in a call center requires the worker to undergo an acculturation process (discussed in a later section), that could include change of name, alteration of English accent, and imbibing and developing fluency with cultural phenomena (e.g., ways of greeting, language usage, festivals) to suit the client country (Upadhya & Vasavi, 2006). Most of these jobs require the worker to also rearrange sleep–wake patterns to suit the availability of clients in other time zones. Further analysis of this phenomenon points to the creation of a cultural dissonance within the individual. An Indian call center, for example, is structured to mimic the culture of the client country: Accents, identities, and lifestyles all are molded to resemble those in the client country. But in reality, the culture of these workers is completely different and sometimes contradictory to the client country (Nadeem, 2009). The psychological fallout of this kind of forced acculturation has been observed and ranges from psychosomatic illnesses and loss of self-esteem to strained friendships and marital discord (e.g., Arulmani, 2005; Upadhya & Vasavi, 2006).

Work as Socialization

A key construct in theories of psychology and sociology, socialization, has been defined and described from multiple viewpoints. In summary, socialization refers to the lifelong process whereby a society, directly or indirectly, formally or informally, transmits to its members the norms and customs by which it characterizes itself and through the processes of cultural learning forms and shapes individual members to conform to its conventions (Durkheim, 1893/ 1984; van de Walle, 2008). The global trends and transformations described in effect underlie a global socialization process. Embedded within the construct of socialization are two constructs: *enculturation* and *acculturation*, which are of relevance to the idea of cultural preparedness being developed in this chapter.

Enculturation

The process by which a person adapts to and assimilates the culture in which he or she lives has been described to be enculturation (Grusec & Hastings, 2007). Enculturation is the anthropological description of the processes of socialization. This term has been adapted for the purposes of this writing: While socialization is the broader construct aimed at "socializing" the individual to conform, enculturation is used here to describe socialization with reference to more specific and circumscribed phenomena. Within the cultural preparedness model described later in the chapter, enculturation is depicted as the process by which people learn the obligations of the culture that enfolds them, assimilate the values of that culture, and acquire the behaviors that are suitable and obligatory in that culture—for specific practices. Therefore, for example, while the practice of greeting another person is an aspect of socialization, greeting a younger person, a peer, and an elder in differing ways would be an aspect of enculturation. Hence, enculturation in this description has greater specificity to particular groups and to particular practices.

An Illustration

From the work behavior point of view, understanding that one day, one will become a worker and preparing for this role could be an aspect of socialization. Enculturation on the other hand would be seen in the transmission of beliefs pertaining to preparing and qualifying for work. Arulmani (2010b) reported, for example, that Indian young people from lower socioeconomic status (SES) homes, in comparison to their peers from higher SES backgrounds, tend to lay a lower emphasis on qualifying for work. In this illustration, enculturation has differentially socialized lower and higher SES youth in the value they learn to place on formal preparation and qualifications to become a worker.

Keeping the central point of this chapter in mind, namely cultural preparedness, it is underscored that the forces of enculturation prepare the members of a culture to engage with each other, their surroundings, and other communities, and to global trends in a unique and distinctive manner.

Acculturation

If enculturation describes endogenous processes that influence culture and cultural preparedness, acculturation describes how cultures are influenced by exogenous processes when societies come into contact with each other, which in turn influences cultural preparedness. One of the earliest and most widely used definitions of acculturation has been articulated by Redfield, Linton, and Herskovits (1936), when they described acculturation as "those phenomena which result when groups of individuals having different cultures come into continuous first-hand contact, with subsequent changes in the original cultural patterns of either or both groups" (p. 150). Usually, acculturation occurs such that it is the minority/submissive group that is required to espouse the living patterns of the dominant group. But by definition it is possible that acculturation can be reciprocal, whereby the dominant group imbibes the behavior and values of the minority group.

As with globalization, the notion of acculturation is perhaps as old as humankind's ability to voyage and travel and thereby meet and engage with other cultures. Ancient Sumerian inscriptions from nearly 4,000 years ago show that, with a view to protecting traditional ways of life and cultural practices, rules pertaining to trade and contact with foreigners were formed to mitigate the forces of acculturation (e.g., Gadd, 1971). The ancient Greeks also do not seem to have favored acculturation and Plato himself expressed the concern that acculturation would lead to social disorder (Rudmin, 2003). The overall pattern seems to be that while some cultures made significant efforts to protect themselves against the effects of acculturation, others sought to engage and gain from reciprocation.

Hence, voyaging with the intention of conquest and colonization began to characterize the intentions of certain civilizations (e.g., Britain, Spain, and Portugal). Gradually, acculturation became a forced requirement of the victims of conquest. Moving to another aspect of cultural contact in the contemporary context, the issues that surround migration (both as a result of distress and upheaval, and for professional and other reasons) have brought the dynamics of acculturation into even sharper focus (this is discussed in greater detail in a later section). It is also clarified that the position taken in this chapter is that acculturation can occur without actual physical contact between members of a culture. Globalization coupled with advances in information and communication technologies (ICT) has brought the values and ways of life of Western cultures to the doorstep of groups in other parts of the world. It has, for many reasons (economic incentives being salient here), become necessary for these other groups to accept Western values. The notion of career itself is an example. It originated in a Western, industrialized culture but has today become a reality in many other cultures around the world.

Numerous theories of acculturation have been propounded. In summary, acculturation has been described to be manifested as *integration* (retaining heritage culture and identifying with the host culture), *assimilation* (orientation toward the host culture and away from the heritage culture), *separation* (orientation toward the heritage culture and away from the host culture), or *marginalization* (affiliating to neither culture) (Sam & Berry, 2010).

Acculturation as Cultural Imperialism

The nature of acculturation could be visualized as lying along a continuum characterized by the nature of influence exerted by one culture on the other. At one end, acculturation could be entirely reciprocal whereby both cultures mutually influence each other. At the other end, driven by motivations such as *cultural imperialism* and *ethnocentric* orientations, acculturation could be deliberately designed such that the dominant culture unidirectionally transfers its values and

norms to a less dominant one. Cultural imperialism is defined as the "creation and maintenance of unequal relationships between civilizations favoring the more powerful civilization" (Tomlinson, 1991, p. 44). Cultural imperialism is a hegemony that can manifest itself in several ways, such as an attitude, a formal policy, or even military action (Sarmela, 1977; Xue, 2008).

The point being made here is that acculturation has a critical influence on cultural preparedness. As will be discussed in greater detail in the following sections, if enculturation creates a certain status or quality of cultural preparedness, the necessity for acculturation causes shifts in cultural preparedness, which may or may not be beneficial to the culture that is required to acculturate.

Work as Career

The purpose behind performing a set of activities defines whether an activity is work or career. Arulmani and Nag-Arulmani (2004) provide an example that illustrates the difference between work and career. Shanthi and Sukumar plant a garden. Both these persons expend energy and effort in caring for their gardens and making them fruitful. However, these two people are quite different in their motivations for gardening. Shanthi has not studied agricultural science but has inherited a large piece of land and loves plants. She planted a garden with a view to earning from the produce of her garden. She has been able to successfully sell her mangoes and carrots and greens to make a profit. If her garden does not do well, her income would be affected. Sukumar on the other hand loves plants and watching things grow. He too devotes every spare moment to his garden and directs a great deal of effort toward his plants. "Every spare moment" is the phrase that distinguishes these two ardent gardeners from each other. Sukumar is a stockbroker. His garden is his hobby. Unlike Shanthi, he does not require his garden to be financially viable. In fact, he proudly gives his fruits and vegetables away as gifts! In physiological terms, both Shanthi and Sukumar are at work, expending effort, in their gardens. But in psychological terms, gardening is *work* for Shanthi but a *leisure time pursuit* for Sukumar.

Career is an artifact that has emerged within the broader framework of the human activity called work. Work is as old as the history of mankind. Career, on the other hand, is a relatively newer construct whose emergence coincides with changes in the evolution of work. These changes throw up work roles that require specialization in a particular skill-set and the commitment to meet the demands of these specialized work roles. The modern concepts of specialization and the focused development of specific work roles distinguish career from work. To illustrate, Ravi is introduced into the gardening example. Ravi has just completed a degree in agricultural science and chose to specialize in organic farming and agricultural management. He does not have his own land and is looking for opportunities to offer his services as a consultant. Shanthi's garden in the meanwhile has flourished and she now wishes to retain the services of a professional to take her initial work to a more productive level. Shanthi interviewed Ravi, assessed his skills, and employed him to manage her garden. Gardening to Shanthi is work and perhaps in the broadest sense it is also her career. Ravi's approach to gardening, however, would be characteristically different. He brings schooled skills and professionalism, into this area of work. As a professional he will expect his work roles to grow, he will specialize further, aim for promotions, and set higher career aspirations. He is free to choose to continue to work for Shanthi or seek other avenues to maximize what he gains from his career as a gardener. Ravi is a "career gardener."

All careers are forms of work, but the reverse may not be always true. As an area of human activity, work is more universal in what it encompasses. Career, therefore, is work imbued with certain characteristics: the exercise of volition, suitability, preparation, and ongoing development (Arulmani & Nag-Arulmani, 2004). Career is a mechanism whereby society draws upon the services of its members to contribute to its well-being, progress, and development. An individual's career, therefore, has its being in the dynamic interaction between the accumulation of personal benefits and the services he or she provides to society at large. Career development would suffer or even grind to a halt if this delicate equilibrium is upset. Drawing these points together, Arulmani and Nag-Arulmani (2004) defined career by distinguishing it from work as follows:

> A career is characterized by the volitional direction of energy and specialized effort, toward meeting societal needs through a specific area of work, for which one gains not only material reward but also the opportunity for the realization of personal potentials. (p. 29)

Summary and Consolidation: Part One

This writing has until now spanned a wide range of disciplines including biological and cultural anthropology, sociology, and labor economics and discussed the following key themes and constructs:

1. Work as culture
2. The impact of global trends on work with specific emphasis on globalization
3. Enculturation and acculturation as specific aspects of socialization
4. Career as a feature of the broader construct of work
5. The human capacity for cultural learning as a mediating influence across each of these factors

In the next section I will develop the notion of cultural preparedness. Three constructs: the individualism–collectivism continuum; value attributions, work ethic, and career beliefs; and the processes of role allocation will be used to understand how cultural preparedness is formed and shaped.

Work, Career, and Cultural Preparedness

As already proposed, the forces of enculturation and acculturation work together to create a quality of cultural preparedness whereby the members of a culture are primed to engage with life in a particular manner. The learning that occurs between an individual and his or her culture is not only the result of interfaces with present members of that culture but is derived from a deep repository of experience that has accrued and matured over the ages. This interface creates a cultural preparedness *status* which is influenced by the following processes.

Social Organization: The Individualism–Collectivism Continuum

One of the important influences on cultural preparedness is the manner in which a social group is organized along the individualism–collectivism continuum. Hofstede (1991) defined individualism as "pertaining to societies in which the ties between individuals are loose: Everyone is expected to look after himself or herself and his or her immediate family" and collectivism as pertaining to "societies in which people from birth onwards are integrated into strong, cohesive in-groups, which throughout people's lifetime continue to protect them in exchange for unquestioning loyalty" (p. 51). The description of preagricultural societies at the beginning of this chapter pointed to the strong possibility that social delineations such as division of labor were minimal and conceptions of separate and unified selfhood were more or less absent (Westen, 1985). It was much later in human history when religions became more firmly systematized that human-divine and individual–environment distinctions began to emerge, leading for the first time to a clearly structured conception of the self (Bellah, 1964). In the West, it was perhaps the Protestant Reformation and the resulting development of the protestant work ethic (Weber, 1905/2002) that heralded the priority of the individual over the collective becoming a dominating Western doctrine (Allik & Realo, 2003). In contemporary, individualistic, secularized societies, the individual is seen as an indivisible, autonomous human being to whom a supreme value is attached and each individual is seen to represent the whole

of mankind (Allik & Realo, 2003). A further point of relevance is the apparent link between affluence and individualism. Hofstede (1980), in his study of 40 different cultural groups, made the observation that, with industrialization, urbanization, and growing affluence, societies tend to become increasingly individualistic, while traditional, less affluent, and rural societies tend to remain collectivistic. Summarizing the literature, the central features of individualism have been described to be a belief in personal uniqueness and independence while interdependence, duty to the in-group, and maintaining harmony are the main characteristics of collectivism (Oyserman, Coon, & Kemmelmeier, 2002).

Social Organization and Cultural Preparedness

For the cultural preparedness understanding of orientations to work and career, the individualism–collectivism description of social organization is significant. The protestant work ethic brought the individual and his or her productivity onto center stage in the West. The emphasis was and continues to be on the individual and his or her desires and attitudes. Although economic forces may not allow a full and free exercise of this value, freedom of choice and self-determination are deeply cherished by the Western worker. Conversely, work behavior in many collectivistic societies requires that the role of the individual be subordinated to the collective. Just as kinship influences had an effect on work behavior in the West during feudal, preindustrial times, ties with the community have continued to play a powerful role in the individual's orientation to work in collectivistic environments.

Drawing upon our earlier descriptions of imitative and cultural learning, the point emerges here that individualistic/collectivistic cultural environments could differentially shape the individual's conception of work, occupation, and career. If independent decision-making is not directly nurtured in collectivistic societies (as is probable), then it is also likely that the individual would have been enculturated to view self-assertion as being selfish, and divergence from family and parental directions as the equivalent of disobedience. The possible difference between collectivistic and individualistic societies being highlighted here is that in collectivistic societies, it is more likely that decisions are made at the family/society level rather than at the individual level. A concrete example of this form of enculturation would be seen in the individual's expression of vocational interests, which is a central construct in career counseling. In a collectivistic context, the individual's articulation of vocational interests might in fact be an extension of the values and beliefs of the collective. In an individualistic situation, however, it is more likely that the individual has greater freedom to express personal, rather than community-approved, preferences.

Value Attributions, Work Ethic, and Career Beliefs

The manner in which phenomena are bestowed with worth, importance, or significance within a certain cultural group is another key influence on cultural preparedness. Philosophies tend to create mindsets and attitudes, which in turn could mold behavior. Mindsets engendered by social and moral frames of reference could give a particular coloring and interpretation to the meaning and purpose of work. We have used the term *social cognitive environment* to describe the milieu within which attitudes toward work, livelihood, and career are forged (Arulmani & Nag-Arulmani, 2004). Within these environments, positive or negative values could be attributed to work in general, toward occupational clusters, or even to the process of career development.

Social cognitive environments foster the evolution of a *work ethic*: a set of social norms that describe a particular approach to work. For example, a certain work ethic may place a positive, morally endorsed value on hard work, based on the belief that work has innate value and must be pursued for its own sake. Another social cognitive environment may promote a work ethic whereby some forms of work may be attributed with a higher level of prestige than others. In other words, a work ethic is the result of a

collection of social cognitions about work, which is transmitted within the group through the processes of enculturation and cultural learning.

Social cognitions could guide and influence people's work behaviors and their orientation to career development. We have referred to these cognitions as *career beliefs*: "a conglomerate of culturally mediated attitudes, opinions, convictions and notions, which cohere together to create mindsets that underlie and influence people's orientation to the idea of a career and to their engagement with career development" (Arulmani & Nag-Arulmani, 2004, p. 107). Career beliefs in fact reflect career stereotypes. Some examples of common career beliefs are "Boys are better at mathematics and science than girls," or "It is the government's responsibility to give me a job," or "Immigrants are at a disadvantage in the job market." These beliefs affect the meaning and value attributed to work by an individual or a group. Krumboltz (1994) in his early work on career beliefs indicated that regardless of their accuracy, career beliefs exercise facilitative or inhibitive influences on individuals' decisions and actions as they attempt to develop and implement career goals. A further point to be noted is that patterns of beliefs may be internalized not only within the minds of individuals but also in the community as a whole and transmitted to the young in that community through a process of cultural learning (Arbib & Hesse, 1986). Career beliefs influence value attributions and their impact on the career development process can be marked and critical. Field experience and research has consistently demonstrated that the effects of career counseling are often insignificant when career beliefs are not accounted for (e.g., Arulmani & Abdulla, 2007; Arulmani & Nag-Arulmani, 2005). Research has further indicated that "types" of career beliefs exist and the content of career beliefs can be thematically classified (e.g., Arulmani, 2010b; Arulmani & Nag, 2006; Sidiropoulou-Dimakakou, Argyropoulou, Drosos, & Terzaki, 2012). Some of the most common belief themes that have emerged during the course of our investigations in different cultural contexts are briefly described in Box 6.1.

Box 6.1: Career Belief Themes

Proficiency Beliefs

These beliefs describe the willingness to submit to the rigors of a formal training program and spend resources (time, effort, and finances) to achieve the distinction of being formally qualified as per the norms of a given educational system. An example of a common proficiency belief we have documented among Asian young people from lower SES backgrounds is that "going to school is a waste of time, since this does not lead to a job anyway."

Control and Self-Direction Beliefs

These beliefs reflect the individual's sense of control over his or her life situation and the orientation to directing his or her life. Mindsets in this category are linked to the career aspirant's belief that he or she can deal with the exigencies presented by life situations. An example of a common belief among Asian girls from less privileged homes is reflected in this statement: "I have many responsibilities at home and I cannot say what will be expected of me. So I cannot make a plan for my career."

Common Practice

Common practice and unwritten norms shape the career preparation behavior of a community in a certain way. In middle-class India, for example, it is expected that a "bright" student would take up either medicine or engineering as a career. Young people strive to fit into this expectation. The following statement made by a 17-year-old boy reflects this belief theme: "It is expected in my family that I take up the sciences and study engineering. Boys are expected to take up engineering."

Self-Worth

This theme is related to one's belief in personal ability for career preparation. A section of high school students in India commonly say, "I keep on failing in Mathematics and Science. I am not talented enough to get a good job." This statement reflects the career chooser's self-belief in relation to academic performance and career preparation.

Persistence Beliefs

All careers are punctuated by barriers and difficulties. This belief theme reflects the willingness to stay at a task and attempt to overcome hurdles that mark progress toward the completion of that task. The content of persistence beliefs reflects a sense of purposefulness and resolve to strive for positive outcomes in the future. The following statement is an example reflecting low persistence: "I joined a course in basic computer skills for beginners. The course is so hard. I find it boring. I feel this course is not suitable for me and I want to stop."

Fatalism

The content of these beliefs portrays a sense of resignation and a passive acceptance of one's life situation. Fatalistic beliefs are colored by pessimism, a sense that nothing can be changed, and that matters are preordained by more powerful forces. The following statement displays fatalistic content: "Life situations are such that one cannot 'choose' a career. We are just given something. Then fate takes its course."

Note: Adapted from "The Career Belief Patterns Scale: Version 2 [Monograph]," by G. Arulmani, and S. Nag, 2006. Copyright 2006 by The Promise Foundation, Bangalore, India.

Value Attribution and Cultural Preparedness

The dynamics between the attribution of dignity to labor versus occupational prestige hierarchies permits us to understand value attribution and cultural preparedness. In the preindustrial period, work in the West was equated with toil and drudgery. Those who worked were relegated to the lowest classes of the social order (Tilgher, 1930/1977). As we have seen, the reformed work ethic drastically changed this attitude. Work regained dignity and was imbued with worth. As a result, the value of labor both in economic and social terms increased. The dignity and inherent value of labor is an attitude that continues to strongly influence Western orientations to work. A concrete manifestation of this work ethic is seen in the equanimity with which vocationally oriented careers are accepted by certain cultures and accorded low levels of prestige by others. In India, the attribution of value to occupations has an interesting history. Initially, the person-centered *varna* system accorded the same level of dignity to all work roles. However, with the passage of time this system was gradually replaced by the caste system. Caste is linked to the migrations of a wide variety of cultural groups into the Indian geographical area and can be explained as an attempt to diminish the impact of acculturation and thereby maintain social power hierarchies to justify the subjugation of some groups by others. Each group that arrived in India with its occupational specialization was placed in a separate subcaste and thereby given a place and a position in the larger caste structure (Thapar, 1966). Over the centuries, the caste system grew into a vast network of subcastes based on which a wide spectrum of occupational roles were classified. This complex of subcastes based on occupational characteristics and work specializations began to control the social order. The perpetuation of the caste system was ensured when it was made mandatory to inherit one's caste. Caste was determined by birth. Membership in a particular caste could not be assumed in any other manner. This division of people along caste lines into watertight compartments led to a high level of rigidity in occupational mobility. Movement across occupations was prohibited. The roots of caste run deep in the Indian psyche and have become intertwined with personal and occupational identity. A study that tested Holland's Vocational Preference Inventory (VPI) on an Indian sample provides an interesting insight into the impact of caste on occupational orientations (Leong, Austin, Sekaran, & Komarraju, 1998). The findings indicated that congruence, consistency, and differentiation did not predict job satisfaction. Furthermore, the cultural frameworks, within which the Holland instruments had been developed, did not allow for an easy fit into Indian ways of thinking. Leong et al. (1998) found, for example, that they could not use the VPI "as is," because it included occupations that would be considered too low in the caste and prestige hierarchy for some members of their sample to even consider. Although the overt influence of the caste system has begun to fade, this class- and prestige-based approach to work roles continues to have a subtle but strong influence on work behavior in the Indian situation.

The observation that can be made here is that the processes of enculturation and cultural learning could influence the manner in which members of different social groups approach or avoid aspects of work and career development based on the value and prestige attribution tenets and beliefs of their culture. The young in a culture would be enculturated through a process of cultural learning to view work and career along a hierarchy of prestige, status, and social acceptability.

Processes of Role Allocation

Roles define the individual's relationship with a social group. They delineate obligations and describe expectations. The acting out of a role is controlled by a reciprocal give–receive dynamic between the individual and society and is characterized by culturally defined norms, rules, and behaviors. A role may be ascribed, achieved, or assumed. An ascribed role is a set of obligations that are assigned to the individual by the group. This may or may not be on the basis of merit or justification and could even be forced upon a person (Biddle, 1986; Merton, 1957). A male, for example, may be ascribed the psychological role of mother on the death of the family's biological mother. An achieved role is voluntarily assumed by the person. It could reflect the person's effort, recognition of skills, manifestation of interests, and expression of abilities (Biddle, 1986; Merton, 1957). Becoming the company's head of human resources is an example of an achieved role. Roles could also be arbitrarily assumed by a person, as is the case when an individual forces his or her leadership upon a group. Roles could vary in their permanence. The role of father, for example, is relatively more permanent than the role of birthday party organizer. Roles are in effect social positions and hence carry status valuations. The position of manager carries a lower status than that of the company director. Roles could also become interrelated through role sets that emerge from the status associated with the primary role (Merton, 1957). The community priest, for example, by dint of his status could also be the community's adjudicator and counselor. Many roles require qualifications. These may be culturally defined. For example, in certain cultures it is only the son who can light a family member's funeral pyre. Qualifications may reflect more formal stipulations. A doctor, for example, must study and be licensed to practice medicine in order to achieve the role of being a healer.

Role Allocation and Cultural Preparedness

The process by which people are assigned, achieve, or assume occupational roles offers a pertinent platform to further describe cultural preparedness. Across civilizations, the initial approaches to the division of labor seemed to be governed by the principle that a systematic division of work into categories based upon the person's natural tendencies would contribute to order and progress in society (Tilgher, 1930/1977). While subtle variations

could be described from one culture to another, the allocation of work roles seems to have been characterized across civilizations by a high degree of *automaticity*. Skills and trades ran in families or within groups, and expertise related to a particular profession was transmitted from the adult to the young within the family or by apprenticeships offered through guilds of professionals (Thapar, 1966). With the passage of time, person-centered methods for the division of labor were overcome by a variety of social, moral, and religious philosophies that defined the framework for occupational role allocation. In the West, during the middle ages, for example, the dogma that the individual's social position was determined by a divine, natural categorizing of all people characterized the social order. Common people were not expected to pursue work activities that would take them beyond their social class (Braude, 1975). This changed dramatically after the Protestant Reformation and the Industrial Revolution. Mobility across occupations became more of a function of the individual's effort and talents. On the other side of the world, the system of varnas in India also allowed for occupational classification on the basis of the individual's nature. Within certain limits, people could move between varnas according to the quality and type of work they performed. The caste system, however, drastically changed this orientation and the work one was expected to perform was determined by the caste one was born into.

The following observation can be made with regard to the link between role allocation and cultural preparedness. The philosophic and cultural persuasions of a group could influence its orientation to occupational role allocation. The processes of enculturation and cultural learning could foster the freedom with which an individual is allowed to make occupational choices. In certain cultures, occupational roles may be ascribed and the individual may be expected by the larger group first to conform to the requirements of ascribed roles. It may also be expected that the achievement of a role is to be subsumed and accommodated under the ascribed role. The mediation of gender with occupational role allocation provides a stark example. In certain cultures, the primary female role ascribed upon the female is that of wife and mother. The firm, cultural expectation is that any career role she wishes to achieve is subsumed under the primary ascribed role.

Summary and Consolidation: Part Two

I have now laid out the various constructs related to the cultural preparation process model. In summary, these constructs can be classified into three broad themes:

1. Cultural and economic factors related to the evolution of work: work as culture, the impact of global trends on work, and career as a feature of the broader construct of work.
2. The socialization of work: enculturation and acculturation.
3. Three constructs that influence cultural preparation status: the individualism–collectivism continuum, value attribution, and the processes of role allocation.

Cultural learning has been presented as a mediating influence across each of these factors. I will now compose these constructs into a model that describes cultural preparedness.

The Cultural Preparation Process Model of Career Development

The constructs described until now will be drawn together and presented as propositions that together describe the cultural preparation process model.

Proposition 1: Global Trends and Transformations

Global conditions, trends, and transformations form the backdrop against which human engagement with work and career occurs. These are major external factors that affect the individual/group but over which the individual/group has little or no control. These factors could include social philosophies, economic trends, political changes, technological advances, and natural phenomena.

Proposition 2: Influences on Preparedness

At the level of the individual/group, preparedness for career development is influenced by three key factors: patterns of social organization along the individualism–collectivism continuum, patterns of value attribution, and the processes of role allocation. These factors are in continuous and dynamic interaction with each other.

Proposition 3: The Mediation of Cultural Learning

The human ability for cultural learning through the processes of enculturation and acculturation mediates the interaction between global trends and influences operating on preparedness.

Proposition 4: Enculturation and the Emergence of Equilibrium

The socializing forces of enculturation interact continuously and dynamically with global trends and the three factors that influence preparedness. This interaction could occur individually or severally between these constructs. This interaction places the individual/group in a unique state of equilibrium to engage with career development. Career beliefs are an outcome of this interaction and contribute to the maintenance of this equilibrium. This may be referred to as the individual/group's cultural preparation status equilibrium in relation to career development.

Proposition 5: Acculturation and the Alteration of Equilibrium

The socializing forces of acculturation interact continuously and dynamically with global trends and the three factors that influence preparedness. This interaction could occur individually or severally between these constructs. Acculturative forces could be consonant or dissonant with the individual/group's cultural preparation status. Consonance would mean that the acculturation supports, enhances, or further stabilizes the existing career preparation status equilibrium. Dissonance would mean that the forces of acculturation disturb the existing career preparation status equilibrium. An illustration of the model is provided in Box 6.2 in the form of a case study.

Box 6.2: The Cultural Preparation Process Model as a Framework for Observing Career Development: An Illustration

Shama was an 18-year-old Indian girl from a traditional Hindu middle-class, urban family. She was in Class 12, the final year of her higher secondary education. She had the option of taking up the sciences, humanities, or business studies streams of specialization. She did visit a career counselor (the author) who recommended the humanities for her.[4,6] But her family[1] preferred that she take up the sciences since they wanted her to become a medical doctor.[3] Her brother had already taken up a course in engineering as per the family wishes.[5,6] This is also what Shama's grandparents[1] wished for her,[5,6] since medicine would give her respectability in society.[2,8] Also, her family felt that since she was a girl,[3] medicine was a suitable career for her.[5,6,8] Shama obtained 85 % in her higher secondary exams.[7] Her performance on the entrance exam to medical school was also similar. She and her family were disappointed since a much higher score is required for entrance into medical school. They visited the career counselor again and were advised once again that Shama switches to humanities and aims for careers in social work or psychology.[4,6] Shama wanted to make the switch but her parents and extended family[1] were of the opinion that the humanities did not lead to prestigious careers.[2] Also, careers based in the humanities required long-term study which in the opinion of the family was not suitable for a girl[3] since she must get married[3] at a suitable age.[8] Further, a degree in medicine would make her more attractive in the marriage market.[3] Since Shama did not make it to the merit list,[7] her family took up the option of negotiating a "management seat" for her which meant paying the college a large sum of money.[7] Finally a seat was secured for Shama in a second-grade medical school and Shama joined the course. Five years later she completed the course and passed with a second class. Her family was overjoyed. Their son was an engineer and their daughter was a medical doctor! Now she was ready to be married.[3] A suitable match was found and soon Shama was a married woman! She was lucky because her husband, who was a mechanical engineer working in the computer industry, was willing to allow Shama to continue with her career.[3] Shama tried to find a job but with only a bachelor's degree in medicine she couldn't find a suitable job.[7] The kind of positions that her family wanted for her required a master's degree. Shama was not interested in studying further. A sudden turn of events led to her husband's company having to downsize.[7] His job was threatened since the business process industry of which he was a part was starting to move away from India, to cheaper markets.[7] This confronted the family with a financial crisis because they had taken a number of loans to finance the apartments they had bought, their car, their insurance schemes, and many other investments.[7] Shama and her husband had planned to start a family but since his job was no longer secure, they had to postpone their

(continued)

Box 6.2 (continued)

plans.[4] Shama decided to find a job, any job that would avert the financial crisis that loomed before them.[4] Shama's grandfather was upset that she was not starting a family,[1] but there was no choice. Shama took up medical transcription, a job that required her to convert voice-recorded reports dictated by medical doctors in the USA into text[4,7] through the internet. She was sad that she couldn't practice medicine although she was a fully qualified medical doctor. But at least she had a job, a well-paid one, and one that could be adapted to the demands of the new opportunity.[4]

Note: Adapted from "Unpublished Clinical Records (2000–2006)," by G. Arulmani, 2006, The Promise Foundation, Bangalore, India.

Aspects of this illustration that carry apparently sexist and other stereotypes are intentionally retained with a view to providing an example of underlying cultural processes.

[1]Collectivist orientations; [2]value attribution; [3]role allocation; [4]acculturation; [5]enculturation; [6]cultural learning; [7]global trends and transformations; [8]career beliefs

Relevance for Multiple Cultures: Sensitivity to the Universal and the Particular

This writing is located in the Indian/Asian context. However, the model that has been described has the potential to be used across other cultures. Also, an impression that may have emerged is that this writing juxtaposes Western and Eastern cultures. This is not the intention. It is well known, for example, that even within Western countries, subcultures exist that are strongly collectivistic in their orientation (Vandello & Cohen, 1999). I will now discuss a few specific ways in which the cultural preparation process model could be used across multiple cultures.

Addressing Felt Needs

The notion of career emerged at a time in history when ideas pertaining to work in the West had been transformed by highly influential developments such as the Protestant Reformation and the Industrial Revolution. It is important to note that this idea of choosing a personal career was not intrinsic to the cultural and economic environment that prevailed at that time in parts of the world that did not experience such transformation in orientations to work and career. In contexts where one's occupation was determined by birth and one's occupation was almost certainly going to be the family trade or industry, choice was not likely to have been a matter for deep consideration. So different was the Indian work milieu, for example, that one wonders if the idea of a career would have developed at all, had this cultural setting not come under the influences of colonization. The more recent forces of globalization have led to internationalizing the notion of career, and today work more strongly carries connotations related to gender, SES, prestige, and self-actualization in many more parts of the world. Formal vocational guidance services have been described to be a part of economic development, where the division of labor that follows industrialization eventually extends to a point where traditional mechanisms of role allocation start to break down and formal guidance services are required to supplement them (Watts, 1996). Career guidance and career counseling in developing world contexts are currently at this stage of development. However, a closer examination of orientations to work and career in developing world contexts reveals several paradoxes. At one level within developing world contexts—mainly urbanized locations, that have come under the influence of modernization—the personal career, as it has been described in this writing, has indeed become a reality. At another level—mainly rural locations where traditional cultures still thrive—work continues to remain linked to survival, carrying connotations of earning a livelihood to take care of one's basic needs for food, clothing, and shelter and the notion of a personal career has not emerged. Guidance and counseling that can facilitate effective career development, therefore, assumes special characteristics, since as described in this chapter, undergirding these variations is culture and the attending processes of enculturation, acculturation, and cultural learning. While guidance pertaining to work, occupation, and career may be a universal requirement spanning all cultural groups, the idea of career itself may need to be (re)defined keeping the notion of cultural preparation status in mind. For example, it may be that for cultures that engage with work from a livelihood perspective, career guidance ought to focus on *livelihood planning* (Arulmani, 2010a). The cultural preparation status model aims at providing a frame within which to identify felt needs in relation to career development.

The Practice of Career Guidance and Counseling

Methods of counseling that were formulated in the West were fashioned by members of a particular culture in response to needs that emerged from that culture. These approaches were created by a people, and for a people, with specific cultural orientations. One of the reasons for the success of these approaches could be that both the creators of the service and the recipients of the service are culturally prepared in a closely similar manner to offer and partake of the service (Arulmani, 2009). They share a comparable language of values and cherish a particular approach to life. Hence, conditions could be created and counseling techniques developed that were necessary and sufficient for that context (Arulmani, 2011a). Against the background of the arguments presented in this chapter, a critical question emerges here: Would the

same conditions be necessary or sufficient for a people from a different cultural heritage? An individualistically oriented counseling paradigm that celebrates the individual and his or her desires may not be effective with a collectivistic client group whose culture has prepared them over the ages, through a process of cultural learning, to view and interpret their life situation through an entirely different framework of value attribution. An important point to be noted is that Western ideas continue to dominate research in other parts of the world (Leong & Pearce, 2011). Observers of the Indian situation have pointed out that the empirical, mechanistic, and materialistic orientations of the West were imported into India as part of the general transfer knowledge "which in a way constituted an element of the political domination of the West over the third world countries in the general process of modernization and Westernization" (Sinha, 1993, p. 31). As a result, traditional, indigenous frameworks tended to be ignored and discredited and fell into disuse. This trend has also been seen in other Asian countries where modernization is often perceived as the wholesale adoption of Western models of science (Leong & Pearce, 2011). Having said this, accusing the West of being overbearing has become repetitive and these contentions have not really led to fruitful change. There is a deeper issue that must be addressed. The logical and empirical approach that characterizes the West fits well into a culture that is itself founded on materialistic individualism. The question is: Would the same approach "take" in a different soil? A purely empirical method may not suit collectivistic cultures that are rooted in intuitive and experiential approaches. Indeed, what is customary in one context may be experienced as contrary in another context (Arulmani, 2009).

Research into the impact and outcome of developmental initiatives has shown that interventions that are based upon worldviews that are dissimilar to the worldview of the group that the intervention is intended to serve have insignificant community participation which affects sustainability and program effectiveness in the long run (Reese & Vera, 2007). The applicability of an intervention seems to be affected when "universal" principles are applied without adapting them to the "particular" characteristics of a specific setting (Griffin & Miller, 2007). The effectiveness of an intervention could be higher when the ideas and concepts that lie behind an intervention cohere with the history, values, and beliefs of a particular community (Arulmani, 2011a; Arulmani & Abdulla, 2007). Successful outcomes are not achieved merely by "respecting" others' points of view. It rests also upon the inclination to enable a reciprocity of learning between the counselor and the counselee (Arulmani, 2011a). It is here, perhaps, that the notion of cultural preparedness could have relevance to planning and developing career counseling programs that are culturally resonant.

New Concepts and Viewpoints: Charting New Directions

The importance of accepting the methods and approaches of non-Western epistemologies has been increasingly recognized. Pointing to traditional knowledge systems, the International Union of the History and Philosophy of Science (IUHPS) (2001) in its position paper asserted that these epistemologies represent time-tested methods and systems which could guide the generation of hypotheses, the formulation of research designs, and the creation of methods and systems for practice. More importantly, not only has the relevance of these systems to local, particular contexts been highlighted, their potential for wider applicability has been underlined. Keeping this in mind, I draw upon non-Western epistemologies and discuss constructs that have relevance to an alternative formulation of career development. The objective of this final exercise is twofold. The first is to use some of these non-Western constructs to illustrate the application of the cultural preparation process model and the second is to introduce ideas and interpretations into the career

guidance and counseling literature that could be further studied and investigated.

A Nonlinear Approach to Career Development: Career Development as a Spiral

This principle is drawn from the cultural constructs of *samsara and karma* described in Asian thought to symbolize the circularity of life (Arulmani, 2011a). From a Western, objective position circularity may be perceived to be fatalistic, evoking a sense of inevitability. However, if the counselor pauses to understand samsara and karma from the cultural preparedness view point, their empowering of the individual to shape the future through actions executed thoughtfully and willfully in the present would become visible. In this view, it is unusual for development to have a linear and sequential growth pattern. The application of the cultural preparedness model would reveal that these constructs point to an understanding of development that is nonlinear. Over time, one returns to where one started, but in a qualitatively different manner: One has learned from the wide range of incidents, encounters, and events that have occurred in one's life. Hence, development follows a *spiral* pattern whereby the individual moves to another plane in his or her development. The cultural preparedness understanding of these non-Western concepts yields a valuable principle for career development. The contemporary career development requirement of having to make career shifts could be viewed from the spiral perspective: One moves from the path that one was a part of, onto a related, but different, path drawing upon the multiplicity of earlier experiences. These movements may not necessarily always point in the forward direction. The retrenched modern worker, for example, must have the ability to return to earlier learnings, let go of former (cherished) positions, and begin anew—on a different plane of development. Hence, in the Eastern formulation, career development is portrayed "not only as achieving mastery over age-specific developmental tasks but as overlapping movements whereby the individual's engagement with work is a continuous elaboration and construction, characterized by adaptation, discovery and renewal" (Arulmani, 2011a, p. 84). This could be seen as the interplay between enculturation and acculturation, mediated by cultural learning against the background of global trends and transformations.

Dispassionate Decision-Making: Managing Emotions

At its depths, one's career is deeply entwined with one's feelings and emotions. Career successes bring joy and fulfillment while failures could bring despair and disillusionment. The notion of dispassionate decision-making is drawn from the *karmic* concept of *nishkama* which encourages the individual to practice detachment in the face of emotional arousal. The Eastern view would say that career success is related to dispassionate involvement. The principle focuses on restraint, flexibility, and self-mediation and could be applied to a feature of the contemporary economic situation: growth without development. A large number of jobs that are lost in one economy (e.g., the UK, the USA) migrate to other economies (e.g., Cambodia, India, Malaysia, Philippines, Vietnam). This has led to an unprecedented increase in job opportunities in countries to which jobs migrate. Many economies that are the recipients of outsourced jobs were previously deficient of opportunities. As a result, career choosers rush to grasp new opportunities merely because they exist, placing a "good job" at the center of their decision rather than personal satisfaction (Arulmani, 2011a). A common trend in India, for example, is for young people to drop out of education to take up one of these outsourced jobs because of the high levels of remuneration that are on offer. However, it is often not acknowledged that job offerings such as these are in effect a function of the short-term interests of employers, where "growth" becomes a double-edged sword—benefiting a few by exploiting many others (Arulmani, 2011b). We

are today seeing the fallout (psychological distress, loss of interest, dropout) of people taking up jobs for which they have a low suitability. The cultural preparedness approach would respond to this paradox by developing career guidance systems that foster the career development skill of dispassion: weighing up pros and cons and then accepting or perhaps even *rejecting* a possibility. Similarly, in contexts characterized by job loss, this principle would lead the counselor to help the individual to not only deal with the negative emotions resulting from job loss but also view the future with a sense of equanimity rather than eager anticipation or rising dread.

Career Development and Environmental Sustainability: Sensitivity to the Other

Collectivism is one of the key constructs in the cultural preparedness model. This form of social organization is rooted in the concept of *dharma* which sets a code of behavior for "right living." Central to the principles of dharma is the requirement that the individual is deeply sensitive to the "other." Other here means other human beings as well as all manifestations of the animate and inanimate universe. Today, aspects related to environmental protection, such as global warming, renewable energy, waste management, and transportation alternatives, impact the practice and development of all careers. At the same time, economic growth is firmly linked to consumption-oriented economic policies although it is clear that we are living on increasingly shaky ecological credit and rapidly depleting reserves of natural capital (Bissell, 2010). Included under this theme are the matters related to social justice and traditional ways of living. Our consumption patterns are such that we consume more than 25 % of what the planet can replace, although more than one-third of the world lives below the poverty line (Chen & Ravallion, 2004). The manner in which we engage with our career development has a direct effect on environmental sustainability and social justice. Culturally grounded career counseling can do much to address these issues if it orients itself to cultural preparedness. A further point that is relevant here is that today, traditional occupations vetted by age-old ways of working in harmony with the environment are no longer accorded prestige or status. These ways of life are increasingly deemed to be unconnected to the industrialized, market economy. Underlying a market-driven definition of career is a singular promotion of the self, increase in consumption, and an unsustainable exploitation of natural resources. An application of the cultural preparedness model would help the individual to define the purpose and outcomes of his or her engagement with work. The integration of the principle of dharma into career would view career development as a process whereby the realization of an individual's potential would support rather than exploit the environment.

Coping with Unpredictability: The Changing and the Unchanged

Constructs in Eastern thought describe the cosmos as a paradox of change and constancy and explain that while appearances and external forms may change, the essence remains unchanged. This principle would apply to the reciprocal interaction between global trends and culture described by the cultural preparation model. The recent past has been witness to enormous changes in the world of work and the labor market. The traditional "9 to 5 job" is rapidly being pushed out of existence and the contemporary worker must perhaps consider 5 to 9 jobs in one lifetime! The de-linearization and desynchronization of time and space in conjunction with developments in ICT depict the creation of virtual workspaces (Tractenberg, Streumer, & van Zolingen, 2002). Indeed today, "geography has become history" resulting in the migration of jobs rather than people. A participant in the contemporary labor market, particularly in economically developed countries, must develop the career management skills of handling uncertainty and unpredictability. The cultural preparedness model presents the notion of cultural preparation status

equilibrium and describes how the forces of acculturation could be consonant or dissonant with this equilibrium. The application of this principle would mean sensitizing the worker and career chooser to the importance of finding the balance between what changes and what does not change. A very specific phenomenon that could illustrate this point is that of retrenchment which has become common place in a number of economically developed countries. The gloom and disappointment that could follow in the wake of being laid off are profound. It is important to note that the requalification requirements that follow retrenchment could be culturally mediated. It is possible that requalification requires the individual to consider career options that do not fit into his or her cultural paradigm. A retrenched worker or someone who has been made redundant could initially hold the hope that he or she could easily obtain a similar job once again. Within an economic environment characterized by jobless growth (Arulmani, 2011a), the career counselor's role would be to help the individual assess the viability of such a hope. Perhaps, in such a situation, the instilling of hope may be related to widening the individual's horizons and addressing the necessity of a career shift. Such requirements could have strong cultural colorings. For example, a middle-aged worker who is attempting to retrain and build a new career would be at high risk to repeatedly experience despair when confronted by younger colleagues and new learning methods. A career guidance target here would be to help the career chooser identify aspects of his or her self that are stable and use that as the anchor to re-chart a career path. The career counselor's role here would be to understand the processes that affect the individual's cultural preparation status equilibrium in order to help the person fruitfully re-engage with the world of work (Arulmani, 2011c).

Conclusion

Greybeard and his friend Goliath gave this chapter its start and raised the question of whether the work habits of these chimpanzees are any different from human work. The key difference that has been drawn out is the human being's capacity for and reliance on cultural learning. Indeed, this human characteristic is central to the cultural preparation process model described in this writing. The cultural preparedness paradigm asks researchers and practitioners regardless of their cultural backgrounds to appreciate that culture through a complex and enduring process prepares individuals and groups to engage with work, occupation, and career in a certain manner. The model proposed in this writing juxtaposes broad global changes and trends against cultural processes and uses cultural learning to describe the resulting transformations. This is not a new concept and indeed the evolution of work has been characterized all through its history by the reciprocity of interactions between broader external processes and cultural practices. What could be comparatively new is the introduction of cultural learning into understanding career development. As we have seen, career itself is a culture-bound concept with specific historical and economic connotations. Yet cultural definitions of career are vague or mere adaptations of existing definitions. Outside the context in which the notion of career emerged, the question what *is* career remains poorly addressed. This has led to the imposition of a definition of career onto contexts where such a definition may be culturally alien. The cultural preparedness model offers a framework that would allow the context to define career development.

References

Allik, J., & Realo, A. (2003). Individualism-collectivism and social capital. *Journal of Cross-Cultural Psychology, 35*(1), 29–49.

Arbib, M. A., & Hesse, M. B. (1986). *The construction of reality*. London, UK: Cambridge University Press.

Arendt, H. (1958). *The human condition*. Chicago, IL: University of Chicago Press.

Arulmani, G. (2005). *The psychological fall out of the call center industry*. Bangalore, India: The Promise Foundation.

Arulmani, G. (2006). *Unpublished clinical records (2000 to 2006)*. Bangalore, India: The Promise Foundation.

Arulmani, G. (2009). Tradition and modernity: The cultural preparedness framework for counselling in India. In L. H. Gerstein, P. P. Heppner, S. Aegisdottir, S. A. Leung, & K. L. Norsworthy (Eds.), *International handbook of cross-cultural counselling: Cultural assumptions and practices worldwide* (pp. 251–262). Thousand Oaks, CA: Sage.

Arulmani, G. (2010a). *The Jiva approach to career guidance and counselling: An Indian model* (Project Report). Bangalore, India: The Promise Foundation.

Arulmani, G. (2010b). Enough for my mealie-meal: The cultural preparedness approach to the delivery of careers services. In K. Maree (Ed.), *Career counselling: Methods that work* (pp. 1–15). Johannesburg, South Africa: Juta Academic.

Arulmani, G. (2011a). Striking the right note: The cultural preparedness approach to developing resonant career guidance programmes. *International Journal for Educational and Vocational Guidance, 11*(2), 79–93.

Arulmani, G. (2011b). Receive in order to give: Eastern cultural values and their relevance to contemporary career counselling contexts. In H. L. Reid (Ed.), *Vocation, vocation, vocation: Placing meaning in the foreground of career decision-making* (pp. 16–22). Canterbury, UK: Centre for Career and Personal Development, Canterbury Christ Church University (Occasional Paper).

Arulmani, G. (2011c). Instilling hope: Meanings and realities for career guidance. *VejlederForum: Danish Professional Career Guidance Journal, 14*(3). Retrieved from http://www.vejlederforum.dk/

Arulmani, G., & Abdulla, A. (2007). Capturing the ripples: Addressing the sustainability of the impact of social marketing. *Social Marketing Quarterly, 13*(4), 84–107.

Arulmani, G., & Nag, S. (2006). *The career belief patterns scale: Version 2 (monograph)*. Bangalore, India: The Promise Foundation.

Arulmani, G., & Nag-Arulmani, S. (2004). *Career counselling: A handbook*. New Delhi, India: Tata McGraw-Hill.

Arulmani, G., & Nag-Arulmani, S. (2005). *Work awareness and responses to career choices: Indian regional survey (WORCC-IRS)*. Bangalore, India: The Promise Foundation.

Barnard, A. J. (2004). *Hunter-gatherers in history, archaeology and anthropology*. Oxford, UK: Berg.

Bellah, R. N. (1964). Religious evolution. *American Sociological Review, 29*, 358–374.

Bellwood, P. (2004). *First farmers: The origins of agricultural societies*. Hoboken, NJ: Blackwell.

Biddle, B. J. (1986). Recent developments in role theory. *Annual Review of Sociology, 12*, 67–92.

Bissell, W. N. (2010). *Making India work*. New Delhi, India: Penguin.

Braude, L. (1975). *Work and workers*. New York, NY: Praeger.

Chen, S., & Ravallion, M. (2004). *How have the world's poorest fared since the early 1980s?* (Policy research

Working Paper No. 3341). Washington, DC: World Bank.

Childe, G. (1936). *Man makes himself.* Oxford, UK: Oxford University Press.

Crutsinger, M. (2007, April). Factory jobs: 3 million lost since 2000. *USA Today.* Retrieved from http://usatoday30.usatoday.com/money/economy/2007-04-20-4155011268_x.htm

Durkheim, E. (1984). *The division of labor in society.* London, UK: MacMillan (Original work published 1893).

Freeman, R. B. (2008). The new global labor market. *Focus, 26*(1), 1–6.

Gadd, C. J. (1971). Code of Hammurabi. In W. E. Preece (Ed.), *Encyclopaedia Britannica* (Vol. 11, pp. 41–43). Chicago, IL: William Benton.

Geertz, C. (1973). *The interpretation of cultures.* New York, NY: Basic Books.

Giddens, A. (1991). *The consequences of modernity.* Cambridge, UK: Polity Press.

Goodall, J. (1986). *The chimpanzees of Gombe: Patterns of behavior.* Cambridge, MA: The Belknap Press of Harvard University Press.

Gowdy, J. M. (1998). *Limited wants, unlimited means: A reader on hunter-gatherer economics and the environment.* St. Louis, MO: Island Press.

Griffin, J. P., & Miller, E. (2007). A research practitioner's perspective on culturally relevant prevention: Scientific and practical considerations for community-based programs. *The Counseling Psychologist, 35*(6), 850–859.

Grusec, J. E., & Hastings, P. D. (2007). *Handbook of socialization: Theory and research.* New York, NY: Guilford Press.

Hoebel, E. A. (1966). *Anthropology: The study of man.* New York, NY: McGraw-Hill.

Hofstede, G. (1980). *Culture's consequences: International differences in work-related values.* Beverly Hills, CA: Sage.

Hofstede, G. (1991). *Cultures and organizations: Software of the mind.* London, UK: McGraw-Hill.

ILO. (2013). *Global employment trends for youth 2013: A generation at risk.* Geneva, Switzerland: Author.

IUHPS (International Union of the History and Philosophy of Science). (2001). *Position paper on science and indigenous knowledge.* Retrieved from http://www7.nationalacademies.org/usnciuhps/Indigenous_Knowledge.html

Krumboltz, J. D. (1994). The career beliefs inventory. *Journal of Counseling and Development, 72*(4), 424–428.

Leong, F. T. L., Austin, J. T., Sekaran, U., & Komarraju, M. (1998). An evaluation of the cross-cultural validity of Holland's theory: Career choice by workers in India. *Journal of Vocational Behavior, 52*(3), 441–455.

Leong, F. T. L., & Pearce, M. (2011). Desiderata: Towards indigenous models of vocational psychology.

International Journal for Educational and Vocational Guidance, 11(2), 65–77.

Liu, J. H., & Sibley, C. G. (2009). Culture, social representations, and peacemaking: A symbolic theory of history and identity. In C. J. Montiel & N. M. Noor (Eds.), *Peace psychology in Asia.* New York, NY: Springer Science + Business Media.

Marlowe, F. W. (2005). Hunter-gatherers and human evolution. *Evolutionary Anthropology: Issues, News, and Reviews, 14*(2), 54–67.

McGrew, W. C. (2010). Chimpanzee technology. *Science, 328*(5978), 579–580.

Merton, R. K. (1957). The role-set: Problems in sociological theory. *British Journal of Sociology, 8,* 106–120.

Moore, C., & Dunham, P. (1995). *Joint attention: Its origins and role in development.* Hillsdale, NJ: Erlbaum Press.

Nadeem, S. (2009). Macaulay's (cyber) children: The cultural politics of outsourcing in India. *Cultural Sociology, 3,* 102–122.

Oyserman, D., Coon, H. M., & Kemmelmeier, M. (2002). Rethinking individualism and collectivism: Evaluation of theoretical assumptions and meta-analyses. *Psychological Bulletin, 128,* 3–72.

Pringle, H. (1998). The slow birth of agriculture. *Science, 282*(5393), 1446.

Redfield, R., Linton, R., & Herskovits, M. J. (1936). Memorandum for the study of acculturation. *American Anthropologist, 38,* 149–152.

Reese, L. E., & Vera, E. M. (2007). Culturally relevant prevention: The scientific and practical considerations of community-based programs. *The Counseling Psychologist, 35*(6), 763–778.

Rudmin, F. W. (2003). Critical history of the acculturation psychology of assimilation, separation, integration, and marginalization. *Review of General Psychology, 7*(1), 3–37.

Sam, D. L., & Berry, J. W. (2010). Acculturation: When individuals and groups of different cultural backgrounds meet. *Perspectives on Psychological Science, 5*(4), 472–481.

Sarmela, M. (1977). What is cultural imperialism? In C. Sandbacka (Ed.), *Cultural imperialism and cultural identity* (pp. 13–36). Helsinki, Finland: Transactions of the Finnish Anthropological Society.

Scarre, C. (2005). *The human past: World prehistory and the development of human societies.* London, UK: Thames & Hudson.

Sidiropoulou-Dimakakou, D., Argyropoulou, K., Drosos, N., & Terzaki, M. (2012). Career beliefs of Greek and Non-Greek vocational education students. *Creative Education, 3*(7), 1241–1250.

Sinha, D. (1993). Indigenization of psychology in India and its relevance. In U. Kim & J. W. Berry (Eds.), *Indigenous psychologies: Research and experience in cultural context* (pp. 30–43). Newbury Park, CA: Sage.

Thapar, R. (1966). *A history of India* (Vol. 1). New Delhi, India: Penguin.

Tilgher, A. (1977). *Homo faber: Work through the ages*. In D. C. Fisher (Trans.). New York, NY: Harcourt Brace (Original work published 1930).

Tomasello, M. (1999). The human adaptation for culture. *Annual Review of Anthropology, 28*, 509–529.

Tomlinson, J. (1991). *Cultural imperialism: A critical introduction*. London, UK: Printer.

Tractenberg, L., Streumer, J., & van Zolingen, S. (2002). Career counselling in the emerging post-industrial society. *International Journal for Educational and Vocational Guidance, 2*, 85–99.

Upadhya, C., & Vasavi, A. R. (2006). *Work, culture, and sociality in the Indian IT industry: A sociological study*. Bangalore, India: School of Social Sciences, National Institute of Advanced Studies.

van de Walle, G. (2008). Durkheim and socialization. *Durkheimian Studies, 14*(1), 35–58.

Vandello, J. A., & Cohen, D. (1999). Patterns of individualism and collectivism across the United States. *Journal of Personality and Social Psychology, 77*(2), 279–292.

Watts, A. G. (1996). Toward a policy for lifelong career development: A transatlantic perspective. *The Career Development Quarterly, 45*(1), 41–53.

Weber, M. (2002). *The protestant ethic and the spirit of capitalism*. In P. Baehr & G. C. Wells (Trans.). New York, NY: Penguin Books (Original work published 1905).

Westen, D. (1985). *Self and society: Narcissism, collectivism, and the development of morals*. Cambridge, UK: Cambridge University Press.

Xue, C. (2008). A review of Tomlinson's views on cultural globalization. *Asian Social Science, 4*(6), 112–114.

Yankelovich, D., & Immerwahr, J. (1984). Putting the work ethic to work. *Society, 21*(2), 58–77.

Mahatma Gandhi's Ideas for Work, Career, and Life

V.R. Devika and Gideon Arulmani

Introduction

Sa vidya ya vimukthaye: What liberates is education (Vishnu Purana 1.19.41).

Mahatma Gandhi is a name that is recognized not only by every Indian but also by millions of others in most parts of the world. Gandhi was the face of the Indian struggle for independence against more than 200 years of British colonization and he is known as the Father of the Nation. At another deeper level, Mohandas Karamchand Gandhi was one of our civilization's foremost proponents of active and applied spirituality. At the heart of Gandhi's philosophy lies the notion of *satyagraha*, a term that he coined bringing two Sanskrit words together: *sathya* (truth) and *agraha* (insistence). Satyagraha therefore means *insistence on truth*. Behind the legendary freedom movement that he led and won with nonviolence, he was a man who experimented with sathya and that is what he called his autobiography: *The Story of My Experiments with Truth* (Gandhi, 1927). It is these experiments and this practical spirituality that underlie Gandhi's grappling with the evils of the caste system and untouchability, his work for the upliftment of women, his definition of civil rights, and his devising of methods of nonviolent protest such as non-cooperation and civil disobedience. Indeed, it is this spirituality that won him the title *mahatma* or great soul.

The purpose of this chapter is to examine the discipline of career guidance through principles drawn from Gandhi's educational ideas. It must be stated at the outset that the Gandhian position rejects the tenets of modern civilization. Indeed so vehement was this rejection that Gandhi describes modern civilization as the *Kingdom of Satan* (Gandhi, 1909). He wrote this 30,000 word book while on a journey on board the ship, Kildonen Castle, returning to South Africa from London where he had gone to plead for the repeal of certain draconian acts against Indians and for equality for all British subjects. He had meetings with many people and decided that India must find an alternative way of development more in tune with its culture, geography, and vast numbers of poor citizens—an ideology based on truth and nonviolence. He published these ideas in the Gujarathi language as *Sarvodaya*. Industrialization, machine-based production, parliamentary government—the mainstays of modernization and considered to be vehicles of growth, advancement, and development are all rejected in the Gandhian position. In its place Gandhi proposed the ways of ancient Indian civilization as carrying the answers to well-being in the contemporary context. It is against this background that what is presented in the rest of this chapter must be interpreted. While Gandhi commented

V.R. Devika (✉)
The Aseema Trust, Chennai, India
e-mail: vrdevika@gmail.com

G. Arulmani et al. (eds.), *Handbook of Career Development*, International and Cultural Psychology, DOI 10.1007/978-1-4614-9460-7_7, © Springer Science+Business Media, LLC 2014

on almost all aspects of life, his position with regard to work, economic development, and education are of pertinence to this chapter.

His deep commitment to the empowerment of the weak and downtrodden yielded an economic philosophy based on self-reliance that celebrates human effort and skill as capital. This pedagogy of prosperity blended education and economics with ethics. In his view, economic activity that hurt or exploited the worker was immoral. Gandhi's economics places the worker rather than production at the center. Industry, from the Gandhian view point, ought to be concerned not only with dividends but also with the creation of an environment for work that promotes the worker's physical, mental, social, and spiritual well-being. His ideas of economic growth take a diametrically opposite position to what it is upheld today. He emphasized the development of small, locally managed cooperatives at the village level and was against large-scale industrialization and corporatization. Gandhi emphasized *plain living*, which is in contrast to the consumerist and market-driven tendencies of today. He made a distinction between standard of living and standard of life where the former is related to material benefits while the latter is related to spiritual, social, cultural, mental, and economic well-being.

Another aspect of the Gandhian position that is of particular relevance is his description of work and education. Gandhi conceived the idea of *Nai Talim* (Basic Education) as an integral part of his vision of society. Here again, there is a blending of spirituality with pedagogy. This view does not separate knowledge and learning from work and effort. Gandhi saw education that was introduced by the British into India to be exclusionary in character and the result of an artificially instituted dichotomy between work and knowledge. He observed that those who worked with their hands and produced wealth were denied access to formal education while those who had access to formal education not only denigrated productive manual work but also lacked the necessary skills for it. The Gandhian approach calls for a pedagogical linking such that engagement with work becomes the medium of

knowledge acquisition, development of values, and skill formation. This approach identified productive work as the antidote as it were, to bookish and information-oriented education.

In this chapter we will discuss career development in the modern context from the point of view of Gandhian spirituality, economics, and pedagogy.

Glimpses into the Life of M. K. Gandhi

Mohandas Karamchand Gandhi, born in 1869, obtained his education in Gujarat, a state in the Western part of India, and then studied law in London. When Gandhi left for England to study, he had promised his pious mother that he would not touch wine, women, and meat. He did give in to temptations initially, but soon realized that he had to keep his promise to his mother and understand his own culture. He read the *Bhagawad Geeta* (an important part of the Indian scriptures, from an epic called the *Mahabharatha*) and began to search for answers to questions he had about his own religion. He also read the writings of other major religions like Buddhism, Jainism, Christianity, and Islam and concluded that all religions preached the same thing and that all religions were far from perfect. After he graduated in law, he returned from London and tried to find employment in India. He subsequently went to South Africa in pursuit of a career in law. Gandhi's experience of social discrimination and his confrontation of it in South Africa are well known. These experiences affected him deeply and transformed him. He returned to India to lead millions of illiterate Indians into the Indian freedom movement. He brought in a new element of introspection and self-criticism into the freedom movement that hitherto had been dominated by the English-educated elite of India. He quickly became the most important political and ideological leader of India during the Indian independence movement.

Assuming leadership of the Indian National Congress in 1921, Gandhi led nationwide campaigns for ending untouchability, promoting religious and ethnic amity, easing poverty, expanding women's rights, increasing economic self-reliance, but above all for achieving *swaraj*— the independence of India from foreign domination through the building of self-confidence which he felt, could only come about by becoming self-sufficient (Gandhi, 1927). Gandhi devised many original methods to counter the might of the British Empire. Central to his philosophy was his emphasis on fearlessness and individual freedom from dogmas and dependency. He believed that these qualities would make it possible for nonviolence to be a weapon in the hands of millions of people with astonishing diversity in language, cultural practices, and economic status. This commitment to *sathya* (truth) led to the emergence of *satyagraha*, a nonviolent movement for persuasion and transformation. He advocated civil disobedience and resistance to violence as strategies for the freedom movement. Gandhi led India to freedom and also inspired many freedom movements around the world through nonviolent means. His birthday, October 2, is commemorated in India as *Gandhi Jayanthi*, a national holiday. On June 15, 2007, the United Nations General Assembly unanimously adopted a resolution declaring his birthday to be the International Day of Nonviolence.

Key Constructs from Indian Spirituality

As indicated in the introduction to this chapter, Gandhi's philosophy was deeply influenced by Indian spirituality. We begin, therefore, by providing a brief overview of the important constructs from Indian spirituality that have a bearing on the Gandhian perspective.

Belief in spiritual power is a recurrent theme in Indian tradition. It is believed that one can acquire a substantial measure of divine power by undertaking the requisite spiritual training and penance. Indian philosophy may be classified into three schools of thought with regard to the relationship they describe between the creator and the created. *Advaita* takes the monistic position and accordingly the supreme creator is believed to be manifest in all beings. *Dvaita*

philosophies are dualistic and believe that the creator and the created are separate and different from each other. *Vishishtadvaita* is a qualified monism which acknowledges individuality but at the same time points out that individuality is subsumed under a fundamental unity. Despite these differences, each of these philosophies point to *moksha*, the returning of the individual to godhood as the ultimate aim. While Gandhi's spirituality was not otherworldly, he considered every individual to be a child of god, whose life on earth ought to be reflective of that divinity.

According to the Indian view, in order to attain moksha, an individual has to do the *karma* (action or duty) assigned to his or her *dharma* (placement in the social order) with complete engagement and sincerity. Karma which represents work and action is a word that dominates Indian thought, and work and action are considered to be routes to salvation. It is believed that the discharging of one's duties to the best of one's ability ensures salvation. This intimate connection between work and spirituality portrayed in Indian thought is strongly reflected in Gandhi's philosophy as well. For him, work and effort were sacred.

Ashrama is another Indian concept that is closely relevant to the function and purpose of work. Ashramas are the stages in a life cycle through which the individual moves from infancy and studentship to worker, householder, and finally to spiritual pursuits. It is believed that a person who performs all that is expected of him or her at every stage in life comes closer to attaining moksha.

Varnashrama refers to a person's placing in society. There are four *varnas* (colors) that the ancient scriptures talked about. The *brahmin's* duty is to be the teacher and adviser and to formulate the rules of conduct. This varna is placed above the others since it is this group that formulates rules and codes of conduct. Then comes the *kshatriya* varna which is of the ruling class. Members of this group are the protectors. They wage wars and govern the people. They are advised by the brahmin on auspicious times to start campaigns or conduct rituals as per the movement of the stars and the planets in the firmament. The third varna is that of the trader or *vaishya*, the merchant class. This group conducts trade and manages wealth. Then comes the labor class called *sudras*. The role of this class is to serve the other classes. Each of the four varnas has several subgroups, each determined by the work and duties to be performed by that group. The point to be noted here is that the original idea that lay behind varna was in fact related to the allocation of occupational roles and was aimed at bringing about order in work (Arulmani & Nag-Arulmani, 2004). Of course, this later deteriorated into the evil of caste. But the initial purpose was closely related to work and the duties that surround work. Caste-based discrimination is an aspect of the Indian way of life to which Gandhi was vehemently opposed. In fact, he renamed the lowest castes who were placed even lower than the sudras and called them *harijan* (child of god).

The key point that emerges from these introductory observations is that work and spirituality are closely intertwined in Indian ways of thinking. Work is portrayed not merely as an activity through which a livelihood is gleaned. Hard work is considered to be a duty, a responsibility, and ultimately a means of attaining moksha. Gandhi was a deeply spiritual person. At the same time, his spirituality was action-oriented. He absorbed and then revived these constructs and brought them into the mainstream of daily life.

Gandhi's Engagement with Contemporary Indian Philosophers

Before we begin to trace Gandhi's conceptions of work and learning, it is important to note that his views were deeply debated and respected by two other contemporary Indian philosophers: Rabindranath Tagore (1861–1941) and Aurobindo Ghoshe (1872–1950). All three had been educated in the English language and had studied abroad. All three laid stress on the spiritual yet all three thought beyond religion. All three felt that the spiritual was embedded in work and work-based learning was basic learning.

Rabindranath Tagore was a Bengali polymath who reshaped the literature and music of his region. He is the author of the famous *Gitanjali* which won him the Nobel prize for literature, making him the first non-European Nobel laureate in 1913 and his poetry was viewed as spiritual and mercurial. As a champion of the Bengal Renaissance, he created paintings, texts, and a new music genre now known as *Rabindra Sangeet*, and founded the *Visva Bharati* University. Tagore envisioned an education that was deeply rooted in one's immediate surroundings but connected to the cultures of the wider world, predicated upon joyful learning, and individualized to the personality of the child. Gandhi had already conducted his experiments on communal living and work as learning in South Africa by the time he came to India. Tagore and Gandhi were in close communication. It appears that they vigorously discussed the ideas of work being the basis for learning and that work done with sincerity was its own reward.

Aurobindo Ghoshe synthesized Eastern and Western philosophy, religion, literature, and psychology in his writings. Ghoshe formulated a pedagogy which is referred to as Integral Education. The first principle of education for him was that the teacher is not an instructor or taskmaster. He or she is a helper and a guide. A principle of Integral Education is to work from the near to the far, from that which is to that which shall be. These ideas influenced Gandhi's philosophy of education. The key debate between Ghoshe and Gandhi was how to assimilate Western values, science, and knowledge into an Indian educational framework.

Extensive dialog took place between Tagore, Ghoshe, and Gandhi on the interface between spirituality, work, and learning. While Gandhi stressed the importance of productive work and skilled work as a basis for learning, Tagore looked at engaging with works of art and beauty as the foundation of learning. Ghoshe emphasized the integration of mind and body as necessary to carry work forward. What is clear here is that for all three, work and spiritual pursuit were one and the same.

Gandhi's Philosophy of Work and Learning

To Live, Man Must Work

Of particular relevance to this writing is Gandhi's assertion that to live, man must work. This first came home to him upon reading Tolstoy's description of *bread labour* in his book *The Kingdom of God Is Within You* (Tolstoy, 1894). The same principle, Gandhi said, has been set forth in the third chapter of the *Bhagawad Geetha* where it is explained that he who eats without offering sacrifice eats stolen food. Gandhi (1908) interpreted sacrifice to mean bread labor when he said:

> The economics of bread labor are the living way of life. It means that every man has to labor with his body for his food and clothing. If I can convince the people of the value and the necessity of bread labor, there never will be any want of bread and cloth. (p. 171)

According to Gandhi, if all worked for their bread, distinctions of rank would be obliterated. The rich would still be there, but they would deem themselves only trustees of their property, and would use it mainly in the public interest. Gandhi emphasized that the idea that we work for others is only an illusion, when he pointed out that we always work for ourselves and that we attain deliverance only if we work exclusively for our higher self (Gandhi, 1948).

The manner in which Gandhi highlighted the purpose of work in our lives has relevance to the notion of career development. Work has been human beings' constant companion. For some, work maybe associated with getting ahead, reaching the top, a means of gaining social acceptance and prestige. In Gandhi's (1933) formulation, work could be a means of self-realization:

> If everybody thinks about the work he is doing, and so works intelligently, he would get the best education, would find his work interesting, develop his intellect, enlarge and purify his heart, acquire efficiency in his work and make inventions and improvements which would benefit the world. As the work becomes more interesting, it gives him

joy; he feels no fatigue in doing it and the work becomes artistic, whether it is cleaning lavatories or roads, writing accounts or something else. (p. 296)

Work and Skill as Capital

Gandhi strongly advocated that work and skill were also powerful, and that work and skill were not subordinate to capital. "If capital is power, so is work. Either power can be used destructively or creatively. Immediately, the worker realizes his strength, he is in a position to become a co-sharer with the capitalist instead of becoming his slave" (Gandhi, 1933, p. 296).

Ruskin's (1862) writings had a deeply formative influence on Gandhi's ideas of economics and education when he first read them in 1903 on a train journey from Johannesburg to Durban. He summarized his learning from the book into three points (Gandhi, 1956). First, Ruskin asserts that the good of the individual is contained in the good of all. This was already a part of Gandhi's thinking. Secondly, Gandhi's commitment to the dignity of labor was also highlighted by Ruskin when he says that a lawyer's work had the same value as the barber's, as all had the same right to earn a livelihood. The third point was Ruskin's assertion that a life of labor, that is, the life of the tiller of the soil and the handicraftsman is a life worth living. This influenced Gandhi's view of work profoundly.

For Gandhi, a seeker of truth through action, the worth of an idea could be proven only by putting it into practice. So he set up farms (Phoenix Settlement in 1904 and the Tolstoy Farm in 1910, in South Africa) which gave him the opportunity to experiment with the ideas of work and skill as capital. The settlements consisted of men, women, and children, who were Hindus, Muslims, Christians, or Parsees, white or Indians, people who spoke one or more languages from among Gujarati, Hindi, Tamil, and English. As an extension of Gandhi's assertion that labor and skills were capital, produce was shared by the inmates and education was offered during the course of manual labor. This form of education, in Gandhi's view, prepared the child and young person for the mother economy wherein producers themselves became consumers. Gandhi ran these settlements drawing from the primary idea that self-realization was the individual's final objective. He believed that self-realization could come from a self-mediated search for truth during the process of manual work. Of interest here is the relativity with which Gandhi viewed truth when he highlighted that an individual must determine what truth meant for him or her and practice it with single-mindedness.

Gandhi's interpretation of effort, work, and skills as economic capital therefore had deeply spiritual overtones. Against this background, he rejected Western (capitalist) notions of development which, according to him, described well-being and happiness to be primarily related to physical well-being and economic prosperity. He asserted that the pursuit of happiness by a majority does not allow the sacrificing of the happiness of a minority and goes on to point out that the pursuit of happiness does not sanction the breaking of the laws of morality. "Our work should be neither exclusively physical nor exclusively mental, nor such as ministers merely to the pleasure of the moment" (Gandhi, 1921, p. 121). His radically different position is discussed in the next section.

A principle of career development that emerges here is related to occupational prestige. It is well known that across most cultures, blue collar professions are usually evaluated as less prestigious than white collar jobs. When asked, 88 % of an Indian sample of more than 8,000 adolescents and young adults studied by Arulmani and Nag-Arulmani (2004) described vocationally oriented occupations as being dirty and of low value because they were associated with manual work. The respondents in this study felt that they would not be respected if they opted for vocationally oriented careers. Similar findings have been reported by studies from other parts of the world (see Agbenyo & Collett, 2014, Chap. 14; Zelloth, 2014, Chap. 15). By imbuing work with spiritual meanings, Gandhi highlighted the economic value of effort and skill irrespective of the occupation that these skills relate to.

Spinning as a Philosophy of Work

The *charkha* or spinning wheel is closely associated with Gandhi. Invented between 500 and 1,000 AD, the spinning wheel has a simple design with two wheels of unequal sizes wherein the larger wheel turns a smaller wheel. The spindle at the center of the smaller wheel is fed a sliver of cotton, which is caught on the spindle, and twisted. Additional bits of material are fed to the end of the twisted yarn, making it longer, and they in turn are twisted together. Gradually the mass of fluffy material is spun out into a long thread, suitable for weaving into cloth. When Gandhi saw the spinning wheel, he sensed that it could be a powerful symbol to represent his ideas. He used the spinning wheel as an emblem of liberation and a tool for development. Gandhi's introduction of the spinning wheel and what it stood for, was one of the most significant unifying elements of the nationalist movement in India. Spinning was seen as an economic and political activity that could bring together the diverse population of the country, and allow the formerly elite nationalist movement to connect to the broader Indian population.

The philosophy of work that underlies spinning is that Gandhi portrayed it to be an instrument of service. The symbolism of spinning cotton on the spinning wheel demonstrated the individual's self-dependence for the most basic of needs, namely clothing. The charkha brought focus to bear on work as a way to liberation, both economic and spiritual. Gandhi believed that if all Indians would spin their own cotton to make *khadi* (cloth) instead of buying British-made cloth, they could become self-sufficient. Spinning promoted a respect for work just as the notion of bread labor highlighted the dignity of labor that Gandhi propagated.

The key career development point related to Gandhian economics to be noted is that the spinning wheel became such an important symbol of freedom, not because it was big and powerful but because it was small and could come alive as a sign of resistance and creativity in the smallest of huts and poorest of families. In smallness lay its power. Embedded in Gandhi's ideas of bread labor, trusteeship, and spinning is a philosophy of work that questions the mindless competitiveness of our contemporary market-driven economies. The charkha was to become the central point in Gandhi's pedagogy as well, since Gandhi felt that true learning was only possible when learning emerged from doing. The charkha provided that connectivity to learning by doing.

Nai Talim: Gandhi's Philosophy of Education

Contemporary Indian thinkers have pointed out that no one rejected colonial education as sharply and as completely as Gandhi did, nor did anyone else put forward an alternative as radical as the one he proposed (e.g., Kumar, 1994). In Gandhi's view, the prevailing British educational system had the negative effect of alienating Indian children from the mainstream of Indian society, it promoted a disdain for manual work, and fostered the development of a new elite class. He felt that all work must be treated equal. He says, "All useful work ranks the same. If I could bring people round to my view, the literate and the illiterate, the teacher and the scavenger, would be paid the same remuneration for their work" (Gandhi, 1931, p. 422). According to him, the more one was educated, the more the person tended to move away from real life since this form of education was based on developing abstract intellect that was out of touch with the realities of daily life. It contributed to the increasing problems of industrialization and urbanization and bore no relation to the actual conditions of life in India (Gandhi, 1931). Based on these observations of Western models of education, Gandhi became convinced that India needed an entirely different path, a path that looked inwards into its own culture for the education of its children. He emphasized that education ought to shape lives and answer the wants of people and as he said, "It is no education if it fails to make a farmer's son a better farmer" (Gandhi, 1931, p. 54). He wanted productive work to be a tool of education right from childhood. This was pathbreaking and had a direct reformative impact on a culture in which occupational role allocations were based on a deeply entrenched caste system. It was through this redefinition of work that Gandhi attempted to deconstruct caste and remove untouchability.

Work as Education

Gandhi did not separate work and education. His educational philosophy rests on the central principle that all learning would be located around work. He called this approach *Nai Talim*: *nai* means new and *talim* in the Urdu language means education. Nai Talim represents basic education for all. The genesis of the idea for Nai Talim goes back to Gandhi's encounter with Ruskin's essays. The teachings of Ruskin not only reflected Gandhi's own deep convictions but in its exaltation of labor and of work with one's hands, they seemed to provide a ready answer for self-sufficiency. Gandhi's Nai Talim reflects a spiritual principle which states that knowledge and work are not separate. This pedagogy rests on three pillars. The first is that education is a lifelong process. The second is that education has a social dimension. The third is that education ought to address the holistic development of the individual. Box 7.1 presents the key tenets of Nai Talim as summarized by Solanki (1958).

A common objective of career guidance is to guide the individual toward educational pathways that lead to the career that he or she wishes to pursue. Such an approach views education as a separate activity from work and rests on the understanding that one completes education and then enters a profession. Over the recent past however, the importance of lifelong learning has become obvious. This can, in fact, be linked to Gandhian concepts whereby education and work are deeply intertwined, one drawing upon the other and thereby infusing deeper meaning into education as well as work. At a practical level, of course, the individual for whom work is education, would be a better worker.

Redefinition of Learning and Teaching

Nai Talim expanded and redefined the role of the teacher. The Nai Talim teacher was not merely a person trained in pedagogy and skilled in delivering the content of an academic curriculum. This teacher was one who would be able to establish rapport with the student such that teaching and learning could be effected through dialog. As Gandhi (1942) pointed out:

> A teacher who establishes rapport with the taught, becomes one with them, learns more from them than he teaches them. He who learns nothing from his disciples is, in my opinion, worthless. A true teacher regards himself as a student of his students. If you will teach your pupils with this attitude, you will benefit much from them. (p. 123)

Nai Talim aimed at removing distinctions between the teacher and the taught, and between knowledge and work. An important point emerges here that has relevance to the process of career guidance and counseling. The settings in which counseling must be delivered are becoming more and more multicultural. The beliefs and motivations of counselor and client might differ considerably. The Nai Talim approach here would be for the counselor to create an environment wherein the interaction is a teaching–learning experience *both* for the client and for the counselor. At the deepest level, this is an attitude: An attitude that allows the counselor to also be a learner. An attitude that allows the counselor to receive in order to give (Arulmani, 2011).

Productive Work, Education of the Hand, and Self-Reliance

Gandhi's Nai Talim reflected his vision that the individual's realization of personal potential was closely connected with his or her contribution to the rest of society. Gandhi's belief was that education was much broader than schooling and comprised development of attitudes and outlooks that matched with the actual happenings in the community. Contrasting *word*-based education with *work*-based education, he (1935) provocatively said:

> It is a superstition to think that the fullest development of man is impossible without a knowledge of the art of reading and writing. That knowledge undoubtedly adds grace to life, but it is in no way indispensable for man's moral, physical, or material growth. (p. 121)

Gandhi believed that teaching children a useful vocation could be a means of cultivating their mental, physical, and spiritual faculties. He asserted that literary education should follow the education of the hand and that the outcomes of education should be of relevance to daily life. He highlighted that education was not derived exclusively from books and theoretical pursuits and that instead of regarding crafts and industry as different from education, the crafts and industry must be regarded as the media for achieving education. Nai Talim places productive work at the center of the teaching–learning process, as a powerful corrective to the bookish and information-oriented character of academic, school education. Gandhi's firm belief was that education should ultimately provide the individual the means to become self-supporting. It must enable a person to earn a living and cut at the root of unemployment. Education must also be related to the student's surroundings and the culture. Gandhi believed that education meant character building such that the individual developed a deep knowledge of duty and responsibility to self and to others. Gandhi's concept of education included harmonious development of all aspects of the human personality. That a sound body required physical labor and physical labor sharpened the mind was a tenet he espoused. Gandhi held that, since the largest part of everyone's time is devoted to labor to earn bread, children must from their infancy be taught the dignity of such labor. For Gandhi, self-reliance emerged when education inculcated an attitude of dignity toward manual labor and handicraft. He asserted that self-reliance would be promoted in an educational system wherein skill of the hands became the basis for the development of the intellect.

It is important for the career counselor to note the emphasis that Gandhi places on manual labor and work being a vehicle for education. A practical career guidance point that could be drawn here is the importance of *skill literacy* (Arulmani, 1998). It is not uncommon for young people today to experience a career development lag—a delay between qualifying for a career and actually entering a career. One of the factors that seem to be associated with this lag is the nature of the career aspirant's career preparation: the longest lag periods are associated with career aspirants' low levels of skill literacy (Arulmani & Nag-Arulmani, 2004). A student who has moved from one degree course to a higher one without the actual development of skills (education of the hand) is an unattractive prospect in the employment marketplace. Career counseling could address this by drawing the student's attention to the importance of developing skills for the practice and application of the theoretical concepts that he or she is studying. This would improve skill literacy and make the individual more attractive to potential employers. In many ways this is what Nai Talim represents.

Handicraft as an Instrument of Education

This section must be prefaced, first of all, with a note about Gandhi's views regarding industrialization. In keeping with his rejection of most aspects of modern civilization, he was vehemently opposed to modern machinery. This was because in his view, automation and the use of technology stole work from the hands of the worker and thereby cut away the individual's sense of self-reliance. Taking the example of the textile industry, he pointed out that in places such as Bengal, where the production of cloth was not industrialized, the original occupation of hand-weaving was flourishing. In contrast where cloth mills had been introduced, he observed that workers had lost their identities and had become slaves. Gandhi's (1935) position regarding industrialization is very clear in the following:

> What did India do before machine made goods were introduced? As long as we cannot make pins without machinery, so long will we do

without them. The tinsel splendour of glassware we will have nothing to do with, and we will make wicks, as of old, with home-grown cotton and use hand-made earthen saucers or lamps. (p. 136)

It is against this background that his positioning of handicraft as an instrument of education must be understood. In Gandhi's pedagogy, students ought to be the true representatives of the culture of their nation. He felt that education could be best imparted when theory and practice are combined in craft-centered, productive work that connects the learning of the student to the environment. Gandhi recommended craft-centered education since India is an agricultural country and over 60 % of the population depends on manual agricultural work (these figures have not changed significantly since Gandhi's times). It may appear that such ideas do not fit into economic life as it is today, but behind Gandhi's proposal of making handicraft a tool for education lay his vision of radically restructuring the social organization of the India of his times. The abstract text-based learning of the time had become elitist and the domain of the upper castes. Gandhi (1935) defined literacy differently:

> Literacy is not the end of education or even the beginning. It is only one of the means by which man and woman can be educated. Literacy in itself is no education. I would therefore begin the child's education by teaching it a useful handicraft and enabling it to produce from the moment it begins its training…literacies of the lower castes such as spinning, weaving, leatherwork, pottery, metalwork, basket-making and book-binding must be made central. (p. 48)

Gandhi believed in craft-based education because it also inculcated sensitivity to the environment. Learning a craft was seen as a means for a better understanding of nature and the environment such that the individual developed love for nature. Much before the world had sensed and become aware of greenhouse emissions and the impact of environmental degradation, Gandhi warned about the dangers of unplanned and reckless industrialization. In Gandhian education, the aim is to learn to practice voluntary simplicity in life; it is expected that this in turn would lead to a way of living that is less consumerist in its orientation. The Nai Talim approach teaches children how to recycle materials and be energy efficient, linking them intimately with nature. Self-reliance, self-help, decentralization, labor-intensive engagement with work, localized and small-scale work organizations were all to be included in education.

A further reason for Gandhi's emphasis on handicraft emerged from his views on the dialectic between the human being and the machine or technology. As discussed, Gandhi rejected the machine in favor of manual, effort-based work. In his view, technology and industrialization contributed to the dehumanization of the worker. In contrast, he believed that handcraft epitomized *swaraj* (self-sufficiency) and *swadeshi* (indigenous production).

Box 7.1. The Key Tenets of Gandhi's Nai Talim: Basic Education for All

- The first stage of education must be up to the age of 8 in which children are not taught reading or writing. They are to be taught mainly by manual training under the supervision of an educationist. At this stage, education ought to seem like playing
- The second stage is from the age of 9 until the age of 16. This is primary education or basic education. Gandhi laid great emphasis on this stage. This stage covered all the subjects up to matriculation, including the teaching of a vocation. During this stage, education may become self-supporting by marketing the goods made by the students
- The third stage lasts 9 years after primary education. During this stage every young person ought to get an opportunity to study according to his/her interests and circumstances

Note. Adapted from "The Technique of Correlation in Basic Education," by Solanki, 1958. Ahmedabad, India: Navajivan.

Gandhi and Career Development: Relevance for Multiple Cultures

Gandhi's views point in quite the opposite direction to what education and career development are understood to be today. At a superficial level, Gandhi's ideas may seem to be romantic ideals that are no longer relevant in an industrialized and globalized world. At a deeper level, there are

important values that could inform career guidance and counseling across cultures and at multiple levels. First of all, Gandhi's views provoke the career counselor to consider the meaning of economic development. Should the career counselor endorse a model of development that is based on increasing consumption and competition and one where growth is measured by the volumes of production? Then comes the question of opportunity-based career decision-making. Career choice is often swayed by labor market cycles, pushing personhood to the background. The Gandhian principle for career guidance would be to counsel the career chooser to not choose a career path only for the remuneration it offers but make decisions instead which are based on the realization of personal potential and personal satisfaction. Another career development principle relates to sensitivity to the environment. The Gandhian position here would be for the career counselor to counsel the career chooser to reject or at least question the validity of jobs that harm the environment. Furthermore, the forces of globalization and economic development are pushing traditional occupations and livelihoods to the background. As predicted by Gandhi, crafts which were originally linked to ways of living are today neglected and considered irrelevant in an industrialized, market economy. Craft represents work-cultures and the Gandhian career counselor would strive to sensitize career choosers to the value of careers in these fields. What appear, therefore, to be impractical and romanticized ideas about work are in fact prophetic and have deep relevance to a philosophy of career guidance in the contemporary context.

New Concepts and Viewpoints: A Gandhian Approach to Career Counseling?

In this chapter, we have gone over some of the ideas that Gandhi expressed with regard to prosperity, work, education, and the role of the individual within the larger society. They are radical no doubt and a question that surfaces is, can the notion of *career* be reconciled with the Gandhian description of work. Indeed, his own disdain for the term career comes starkly through when Tendulkar (1960) described Gandhi as discarding all forms of education whereby "career-based thinking would become dominant" (p. 56). The answer to this question would be a straightforward *no* if career is associated with the promotion of self, with economic growth that bypasses the well-being of the whole of society, and the denigration of human effort. On the other hand, there is much to be learned from the Gandhian position if career is understood to be a lifelong process of self-realization, characterized by a deep respect for the other, undergirded by the firm conviction that all forms of useful work are equal.

The Gandhian concept of swaraj serves well to draw links between career development and the many points discussed above. From a political point of view, swaraj is interpreted as self-rule and also as self-reliance. If we were to develop a Gandhian form of career counseling, swaraj could be interpreted to mean self-mediation and self-assessment. Self-mediated career development would ensure that it is the individual who is in charge and not merely the dictates of a labor market. Assessment of aptitudes, interests, and other such personal attributes by a trained counselor are central to career guidance and counseling. If career counseling were to take a self-assessment perspective, it would immediately shift the point of focus to the individual and he or she would be encouraged to seek the truth about oneself and one's capacities and whether they are commensurate with one's desires.

Decision making is integral to career choice. Gandhi measured all decisions against truth. Career selection when based on the Gandhian principle of truth would move the chooser toward careers that are not exploitative and draw him or her into the circle of justice and equity. Gandhi spoke about means and ends and this has direct relevance to career choice. A critical message that comes from Gandhi both to the counselor and career chooser is that the means of arriving at an end must be as honorable as the end. Career counseling based on the Gandhian principle of truth would help the career chooser define his or her "no compromise" position. At the same time,

maintaining a personal policy of refusal to compromise does not mean a dogmatic commitment to a single path. Gandhi urged the individual to be open to different paths and being open is not compromise. This requires a courage of conviction as preached and practiced by Gandhi. Gandhi believed in following pragmatic approaches and in maintaining a balance with traditional systems of education, occupation, and family. Gandhi's fervent belief was that true freedom lay in the thorough practice of one's chosen occupation and in giving equal opportunity to every citizen to practice, perform, and progress. Young people could look at career as social innovation as they experiment with new technologies, new services, and new methodologies in career development. Extending Gandhi to the notion of career implies defining it as a vehicle of service. The service attitude in the person would imbue career with a sense of responsibility, moral value, and spiritual insight as contrasted with a mindless and selfish promotion of the self at the expense of others.

We began this chapter by stating that Gandhi rejected modernization and all that it stood for. Looking back at his position it seems that many of his predictions have come true. The manner in which work has been deployed has brought us today to a point where our world is tottering under environmental, political, economic, and social turmoil. The call for alternatives from all quarters is strident. This chapter has pointed to various aspects of the Gandhian position that could offer these alternatives. Of interest here are seven deadly sins against which he cautioned us (Gandhi, n.d.): wealth without work, politics without principle, pleasure without conscience, knowledge without character, science without humanity, worship without sacrifice, and commerce without ethics. Each of these points has relevance to career guidance and counseling, which is focused on the central Gandhian principles of responsibility to self and sensitivity to the other. In highlighting these principles, Gandhi was referring to the age-old human predilection of exploiting others for personal benefit. Gandhi made a distinction between an honest day's hard work and extracting profit for self from others' labor.

Perhaps this writing has piqued your interest and made you wonder about the principles that undergird your own practice of career guidance and counseling. Box 7.2 provides a set of guidelines you could use to assess how Gandhian is your approach to career guidance and counseling.

Box 7.2. How Gandhian Is My Approach to Career Guidance and Counseling?

1	I make it a point to highlight to my clients that career can be a means of self-realization
2	I ensure that my clients are aware of the manner in which perceptions of occupational prestige are affecting their career decisions
3	I make it a point to highlight to my clients that all careers are equal in their value
4	I highlight to my clients the manner in which the mindless competitiveness of our contemporary market-driven economies influences career decisions
5	I encourage my clients to understand that lifestyles and career paths can be changed according to the values dear to them
6	I discuss with my clients that the means of reaching a goal is as important as the end and that clean practices ensure a clean track record
7	I use the principles of nonviolence to point out to my clients when the practice of a career degrades the environment or exploits others, it is a form of violence
8	I ask my clients to consider how selflessness links with positive career development
9	I make it a point to highlight to my clients that approach to work and career would be rewarding if it is born out of courage
10	I discuss with my clients that the net payoff of a career ought to be joy of service

---

Conclusion

The cornerstone on which the edifice of Gandhi's life stood was a deep and irrevocable commitment to truth. This was the searchlight he unflinchingly turned upon himself. Although Gandhi derived his ideas from Indian antiquity, he gave his own interpretation to tradition and sought to make it compatible with the modern ideas of individual freedom of choice and economic freedom. So even though we learn from the past, like Gandhi, we can never be wedded to it. Gandhi sought to question age-old practices in the religion he practiced and firmly believed in reforming and improving them. Similarly, the career counselor too could constantly renew his or her practice, examining it for relevance and striving always to make career development a vehicle for self-realization and service. A final point that must be highlighted in conclusion is the way Gandhi lived his own life. He carved an original path for himself and stayed on that path with courage and integrity. He epitomizes for us the deep career guidance principle that ultimately, the joy of work is its own reward.

References

Agbenyo, H., & Collett, K. (2014). Career advice and guidance in a world where vocational skills matter. In G. Arulmani, A. J. Bakshi, F. T. L. Leong, & A. G. Watts (Eds.), *International and cultural psychology.* New York, NY: Springer.

Arulmani, G. (1998). Developing skill literacy: Ideas for interventions against unemployment. *Voices for Change, 2*(1), 14–20.

Arulmani, G. (2011). Striking the right note: The cultural preparedness approach to developing resonant career guidance programmes. *International Journal for Educational and Vocational Guidance, 11*(2), 79–93.

Arulmani, G., & Nag-Arulmani, S. (2004). *Career counselling: A handbook.* New Delhi, India: Tata McGraw-Hill.

Gandhi, M. K. (1908). *Indian opinion* (p. 171). Phoenix Farm, South Africa: Author.

Gandhi, M. K. (1909). *Hind Swaraj.* South Africa: Author.

Gandhi, M. K. (1921). *A guide to health.* Ahmedabad, India: Navajivan.

Gandhi, M. K. (1927). *The story of my experiments with truth.* Ahmedabad, India: Navajivan.

Gandhi, M. K. (1931). *Collected works of Mahatma Gandhi.* New Delhi, India: Publications Division, Government of India.

Gandhi, M. K. (1933). *Harijan* (p. 296). Sewagram, India: Author.

Gandhi, M. K. (1935). *The selected works of Gandhi.* Ahmedabad, India: Navajivan.

Gandhi, M. K. (1942). Talk to Khadi Vidyalaya students, Sevagram. *Sevak, 75*(26).

Gandhi, M. K. (1948). *Delhi diary: Speeches from 10-9-47 to 30-1-48*. Ahmedabad, India: Navajivan.

Gandhi, M. K. (1956). *Unto this last: A paraphrase*. Ahmedabad, India: Navajivan.

Gandhi, A. (n.d.). *The seven deadly social sins: Explained by Arun Gandhi, grandson of Mohandas Gandhi*. Retrieved from http://www.jpcarter.com/Spirituality/PDF/SevenDeadlySinsExplained.pdf

Kumar, K. (1994). Mohandas Karamchand Gandhi. In Z. Morsy (Ed.), *Thinkers on education* (Vol. 2, pp. 47–65). Paris, France: UNESCO.

Ruskin, J. (1862). *Unto this last*. London, UK: Author.

Solanki, A. B. (1958). *The technique of correlation in basic education*. Ahmedabad, India: Navajivan.

Tendulkar, D. G. (1960). *Mahatma: 1869–1920*. New Delhi, India: Publications Division, Government of India.

Tolstoy, L. (1894). *The kingdom of God is within you*. Retrieved from http://www.gutenberg.org/cache/epub/4602/pg4602.html

Zelloth, H. (2014). Technical and vocational education and training (TVET) and career guidance: The interface. In G. Arulmani, A. J. Bakshi, F. T. L. Leong, & A. G. Watts (Eds.), *International and cultural psychology*. New York, NY: Springer.

Part II

The Person in Contexts Across the Life Span

Overview

This section elaborates the theme that optimally career paths must arise out of an evolving personhood across the lifespan. Chapters in this section discuss personhood embedded and expressed in social relationships, and in groups such as families, schools, and communities. Constructs central to career guidance and counseling such as personality and self are comprehensively discussed from the perspectives of Western and Eastern epistemologies. Traditionally, career psychologists have used the personality literature for understanding personhood. This literature is contrasted with the extensive literature on self-systems, opening possibilities for the exploration of new concepts pertaining to personhood in career psychology. In many cultures, decisions that impact career choices are influenced by parents, and other factors such as socioeconomic status and gender. Family relationships have long been considered a strong influences on people's school/career development. Parents' role in their children's career construction is discussed as being the result not only of intra-personal processes, but also of contextually-built and shared intra-family and social processes. Hence, vocational guidance activities for parents are also important. Personhood in context also includes the location and participation of the individual within a community. Communities provide resources and settings for youth engagement and participation which can contribute to their career development. Community youth services are reviewed to ascertain the role of a community in providing resources, settings, roles, and activities. This is examined within the theoretical framework of positive youth development with particular reference to young people's career development. Career experiences are changing and people often go through multiple transitions. The evolution of individuals' careers over time and mid-career changes as facilitated by a combination of learning, working, and reframing perspectives are discussed.

In summary, this section discusses career development as encompassing lifelong processes which are constructed in reciprocity with the dynamics of the context. Career development is discussed as an ongoing process not related merely to early adulthood: a becoming that has no neat beginnings or endings.

Personality and Self: Multiple Frames of Reference for Career Service Professionals

Anuradha J. Bakshi

Introduction

Those who, in one or the other professional capacity, work towards promoting career development of individuals can be termed career service professionals. Career services, a heterogeneous field, attracts, and benefits from the committed participation of professionals from psychology, sociology, education, public policy, development studies, and other disciplines. Regardless of their educational origins, those who work in the area of career services have in common—the person. In whichever role a career service professional is engaged (e.g., debating or formulating career guidance policy, providing individual career counseling, supporting a person on a career helpline, conducting a career-related workshop for parents of youth)—the person remains central.

We are living in times characterized by startlingly high levels of change (e.g., Global Trends 2030, 2012; Kotler & Caslione, 2009). Prominent features include raised or lowered expectations, aspirations, and quality of life; urbanization and globalization; physical and/or virtual migration of people and jobs; generational shifts in occupations; changing occupational structure and related educational/competence requirements;

instability and uncertainty in the local, national, and global labor markets and economies; shifting balance of power amongst nations; altered demographic trends and workforce composition; factionalism or separatism and conflict/violence; accelerated advancements in knowledge and technology; and, increasing experience of cultural diversity. Our societies are in flux; occupations and careers are in flux. Who is the person, amidst all of this? How oriented is the person to change? How oriented can the person be to positive development?

It is time to *revisit* key dialogues about the person in the Western literature. Given the increasing interface between cultures and the call for indigenization of psychology (or more generally knowledge) (Leong & Pearce, 2011; Yang, 2012), it is the most pressing time to *visit* key dialogues about the person in the Eastern literature. Accordingly, this chapter presents an overview of key dialogues with regard to (a) personality in Western psychology, (b) self in Western psychology, and (c) personality and self in Indian literature drawn from philosophy and spirituality. In each case, the intention is to represent indigenous perspectives. Therefore, although of value, cross-cultural psychological perspectives (i.e., Western psychologists' efforts to test and extend Western theories in other cultures) are not included. Instead, for this chapter, I have chosen Western psychological perspectives on personality and self, drawn from research and theory in the West, because these amount to indigenous

A.J. Bakshi (✉)
Department of Human Development, Nirmala Niketan College of Home Science, University of Mumbai, Mumbai, India
e-mail: anustra@gmail.com

G. Arulmani et al. (eds.), *Handbook of Career Development*, International and Cultural Psychology, DOI 10.1007/978-1-4614-9460-7_8, © Springer Science+Business Media, LLC 2014

Western psychology. Likewise, it is indigenous Eastern thought about the person that I have chosen to represent, regardless of whether this forces me to use philosophical rather than scientific psychology.

My aim is to present the multiple frames of reference, both within indigenous Western psychology, and also vis-à-vis indigenous Eastern thought. Confronting these varying frames of reference may help dislodge complacency (if any) about beliefs relating to the personality and the self. No special effort at all is made to include career-related literature: This is because my premise is that each career professional has to be oriented to the *person* whose career development is to be supported, and thereby it is important for each career professional to bring to mind what his or her beliefs are about the person. This chapter will assist career professionals to clarify and possibly widen their perspectives about the person.

Reflections across the multiple frames of reference pivot around the articulation of an orientation to change in describing the person. In later sections of the chapter, conclusions are made for career service professionals and new directions for the field are indicated. The methodological style is qualitative; therefore, insofar as possible, a theorist's words are illustrated verbatim.

Personality in Indigenous Western Psychology

In Western Psychology, the study of the personality has attracted extensive effort. The literature generated is vast, characterized with ample variability. Rather than a clear overriding consensus, there are larger or smaller pockets of consensus. Some of this varied literature has been *sampled* in this section. A comprehensive coverage of the literature is beyond both the aim and scope of the chapter. Given the aim of presenting multiple frames of reference, it is the key contradictions, oppositions, and agreements with regard to the personality in indigenous Western Psychology that have been illustrated. Also in line with this aim, points for reflection

have been drawn keeping in mind Eastern perspectives.

Five Different Personality Paradigms

Wiggins (2003) has identified five different paradigms, each of which, he stated, has provided its own answer to "what is the personality?" and to the "what and how of personality assessment." These include the psychodynamic (Freud—focus: drives), the interpersonal (Sullivan—focus: interpersonal relations), the personological (Murray—focus: life history), the multivariate (Cattell—focus: structure of traits), and the empirical (Hathaway—focus: psychiatric diagnosis) (Wiggins, 2003). Further, he has described each of these paradigms as explained in this subsection.

The Psychodynamic Paradigm

For Freud, the founding theorist of the psychodynamic paradigm, personality was the outcome of the intrapsychic conflict between unconscious drives and societal restrictions, expressed through the interplay of the id, ego, and superego. Adult personality was founded on early experiences, with psychological processes displaying "a relatively slow rate of change" and "permanence of organization and function" (Rapaport as cited in Wiggins, 2003, p. 29). Later developments in this paradigm include ego psychology and object relations theory (e.g., attachment theory); for example, Bowlby's concept of "internal working models" (i.e., unconscious representations of self and others based on interactions in the early years). Personality types in this paradigm represent what has gone *wrong*: Examples in classical psychoanalysis include Freud's description of an "anal character," Reich's description of "passive–feminine," "paranoid–aggressive," etc.; in ego psychology, Shapiro's description of obsessive-compulsive, hysterical, paranoid styles, etc. Traditionally, projective tests have been used to measure personality in the psychodynamic paradigm (e.g., the various versions of the Rorschach Inkblot Test, the Thematic Apperception Test [TAT]).

The Interpersonal Paradigm

Instead of viewing *an individual* (and his/her personality), Sullivan was struck by the matrix of (innumerable) interrelationships *between individuals*; accordingly, we become who we are only through interpersonal processes. Thus for Sullivan, the personality grew out of (culturally embedded) interpersonal processes and was visible in repeated patterns in relating to others. "Interpersonal force fields" is an illustrative term in this paradigm used by Sullivan and others; for example, Kiesler (1996) talked of a force field emanating from each person which impels others to react in complementary ways, resulting in the validation of the person's notions of who-I-am: "In the process of emitting distinctive 'force fields' we attempt to influence others into reactions that confirm our definition of self and others" (p. 5). The interpersonal paradigm has been operationalized using circumplex models with two chief antipodes: one to do with control (or instrumentality, agency), and the other with affiliation (or nurturance, communion), together yielding eight (or 16) dimensions. Each of these eight dimensions is graphically depicted as one sector of a circle (i.e., an octant). Wiggins's Interpersonal Adjective Scales (IAS) is an example of a test developed using the circumplex model; examples of octants are assured-dominant which is next to arrogant-calculating but diametrically opposite to unassured-submissive. A person's personality profile is assessed vis-à-vis the extent of ascendency of each octant; typology is determined through the most elevated octant. Thus, a person can be a "warm-agreeable" type.

The Personological Paradigm

Case studies, life histories, and psychobiographies typical of the personological paradigm have yielded quite varied conclusions about the personality. For instance, Allport and his associates remarked on the "extraordinary continuity and sameness in the individual personality" (as cited in Wiggins, 2003, p. 96). On the other hand, Erikson (1963) was convinced of notable transformations in the personality right through the life span, with strengths (e.g., trust, initiative,

intimacy, integrity) and virtues (e.g., hope, purpose, love, wisdom) gained with positive development at each stage. Using Erikson's theory as a backdrop, McAdams (1993, 2006) shifted attention to self-constructions: Through the life span (especially from adolescence onward), each of us is creating and refining/refashioning a mythic life story which interweaves what we remember of our past, perceive of our present, and expect of our future; culture provides the menu of plots and themes for these "self-defining life narratives." His interview methods entailed asking the person to imagine their life as a story in a book, with each chapter being a part of their life, creating a table of contents, identifying key events and people, the overall life theme, etc.

The Multivariate Paradigm

In the multivariate paradigm, the personality is viewed as a person's relative standing on various traits capturing individual differences which are "moderately heritable" and "relatively stable over the adult life span" (Wiggins, 2003, p. 10). Adjectives (e.g., organized, worrying, outgoing) are garbed as traits as they are assumed to reflect a lexical source of personality attributes; families of traits have been identified through factor analysis of self-ratings on adjectives. Thus, this paradigm is founded on a two-step tradition in personality theory and research: lexical (yielding *surface* traits) followed by structural (yielding *source* traits or higher-order traits). The Big Five model or the Five-Factor Model (FFM) has emerged from such lexical and statistical efforts and its popularity in personality psychology is well established. The five families of traits or five factors (i.e., higher-order traits) are: Openness, Conscientiousness, Extraversion, Agreeableness, and Neuroticism (e.g., McCrae & Costa, 1987). An individual's personality (i.e., relative position on each of the five factors) is typically measured using a self-report personality inventory such as the Revised NEO Personality Inventory (NEO PI-R Form S) (Costa & McCrae, 2008).

The Empirical Paradigm

In the empirical paradigm, the focus is on identifying personality abnormalities, and the

Minnesota Multiphasic Personality Inventory (i.e., the MMPI and its revisions—the MMPI-2 for adults and the MMPI-A for adolescents) has been the principal measurement aid. In fact, Wiggins has called this paradigm *empirical* not because it is the only paradigm based on substantial research but rather to acknowledge that the MMPI has "the *largest* empirical literature associated with any existing personality test" (Wiggins, 2003, p. 179; emphasis added). The 567 self-reported but clinically administered true-false items cohere into an impressive range of scales and subscales (see the product description of the MMPI-2 at http://psychcorp. pearsonassessments.com): The MMPI-2 has 8 Validity Scales, 10 Clinical Scales (e.g., Depression [D], Psychopathic Deviate [Pd]) along with many Clinical Subscales (e.g., Familial Discord [Pd1]), 15 Content Scales (e.g., Type A [TPA], Low Self-Esteem [LSE], Work Interference [WRK]), 27 Component Content Scales (e.g., Competitive Drive [TPA2]), and numerous Supplementary Scales. Currently the MMPI-2 has ample versatility. Not only does it allow (clinical) typological categorization of personality using the scales on which a person's scores are most elevated but it also measures continuously distributed individual differences on trait dimensions.

Notion of Trait, Role of Consistency, and Other Key Dialogues

Notwithstanding Wiggins's discerning and fairly comprehensive work in identifying and portraying five personality paradigms, there are key dialogues in the study of personality in indigenous Western Psychology that warrant inclusion. In relation to these dialogues the following set of questions is relevant:

- To what extent does the notion of a trait rest on consistency or stability?
- What are the *limits* of this consistency? Alternatively, how *far-reaching* is this consistency?
- In other words, how *flexible* are traits across time, across situations? Alternatively, how

pervasive are traits across time, across situations?
- Where does a trait come from, where can it go if at all?
- If traits are modifiable, what is the explanation for this modifiability?
- Until when are traits in their formative state, and when do they become "set-for-life" or at least resistant to change?

In order to be tenable, the construct of personality requires more than a modicum of stability. If there were no (relatively) typical ways in which a person's behaviors were distinguishable from another's, we could not talk of a personality. Nonetheless, such stability could still be within bounds for adaptive purposes. Therefore, these questions enable reflection over the degree of adaptiveness of the personality as construed in the indigenous Western literature. Given the increasing need for adaptability and flexibility in career development, undoubtedly these questions are particularly salient for career service professionals.

Gordon W. Allport's Position

Allport's overriding conclusions were in clear favor of traits as consistent, as stable. For instance, note his conclusion on the sameness of personality cited in the previous subsection. This, of course, does not mean that he conferred robotic rigidity to trait expressions in human beings. Zuroff (1986) has highlighted the different ways in which Allport admitted to variability in expression of traits (albeit limitedly in my view): (a) Cross-situational inconsistency as error variance: A person may be inconsistent across situations because of a temporary psychological state, a temporary change in a setting, or in order to defensively dissemble underlying traits. (b) Cross-situational inconsistency as researcher error: This is when the researcher has misidentified behavior as reflecting a comprehensive trait when instead the behavior is explained by two separate specific traits. The example given is about a child who steals but does not lie; instead of a trait of honesty which would mean that the child was inconsistent, Allport has claimed that the behavior is explained by two specific traits (one to do with stealing, the other with mendacity). (c) Coexistence of contradictory traits: "Conquering and yielding, extraverted and introverted, saintly and sinful dispositions may reside within one breast" (Allport as cited in Zuroff, 1986, p. 994). Allport illustrated how a person could be submissive towards those with authority or high prestige and be dictatorial and offensive with all others; how a teacher was careful with own possessions and not so with others' possessions. He concluded that "traits are often aroused in one type of situation and not in another; not all stimuli are equivalent in effectiveness" (as cited in Zuroff, 1986, p. 994).

Allport's first two depictions of cross-situational inconsistencies are actually arguments in favor of consistency (Zuroff, 1986). Zuroff considered the third explanation to be an acknowledgment of authentic cross-situational variability. Further, he felt that this explanation clarified the extent of cross-situational consistency or stability of personality traits: not pervasive (i.e., across all situations) but limited to the same type of situations.

My view is more moderate. I would say that the third explanation is more accepting of cross-situational differences in a person's behavior. Yes, it does set some limits to the pervasiveness of trait *expressions*. Largely because Allport, it appears, had conceded to a trait-situation fit. Nevertheless, this explanation falls short with regard to the possibility of modifiability of traits. For the underlying traits remain the same; which ones are provoked or elicited at which point depends upon the qualities of the situation or the context. That is, it is the (external) expression of traits that may change from one type of context to another but the (internal) trait structure remains the same. Therefore, the focus on sameness remains somewhat formidable: congruent behaviors across the same types of contexts, and an unchanging internal structure. To add to this, Allport differentiated between cardinal, central, and specific traits; some people he claimed possessed an all-pervasive cardinal trait, although most possessed central and specific traits with reduced generality (Zuroff, 1986).

Allport represents the *realist* position in personality psychology (Caspi & Shiner, 2006; Zuroff, 1986). This position is also called the *explanatory* position (Caspi & Shiner, 2006) because for Allport traits were causal entities, his "analysis of the causes of behavior relied entirely on the trait concept" (Zuroff, 1986, p. 995). Thus Allport fenced himself within the limits of more or less direct causation (internal structure to behavior) without seeing the benefits of a process theory; his only concessions in this regard were his recognition that situations could "arouse" particular traits, and that people selected the very situations in which they could freely express their traits (e.g., a garrulous person will look out for and create situations in which he/she can talk fairly uninterruptedly) (Zuroff, 1986).[1]

Zuroff has attempted but failed to recast Allport as a clear interactionist or process theorist. Amongst other things, this would also have required Allport to grant formative or transformational power to the environment. In striking contrast, Allport was a continuity theorist, unconvinced that the environment could alter the personality (Zuroff, 1986).

Walter Mischel's Position

Allportian notions have most commonly been pitted against those of Walter Mischel. Mischel's 1968 monograph was misunderstood as venerating the situation over the person and decrying the need to study personality (Mischel, 2004). Regardless of seemingly disparate positions at earlier points (see Zuroff, 1986), Mischel's current position is congruent with Allport's in a *few* respects. One meeting point between them is Mischel's conviction (as well) that the personality is invariant, in spite of evidence of cross-situational inconsistency (see Mischel, 2004). How has Mischel resolved the paradox of an invariant personality generating

---

[1] The latter is compatible with literature on active gene-environment correlations (e.g., Plomin, DeFries, & Loehlin, 1977). This idea is also part of Mischel's theory (cf. Mischel & Shoda, 1995).

cross-situational inconsistency? The first part of the answer to the "personality paradox" (Mischel, 2004) brings us (as Zuroff [1986]) precociously noted), to the second meeting point between Allport and Mischel: the idea that the consistency is to be located in the same types of situations (i.e., situations which are functionally equivalent for the individual). Compatible with Allport's third explanation of cross-situational variability, is Mischel's observation that: "(B)ehaviors are stable within each type of situation but varied from one type to another...A person may be less agreeable than others in one type of situation, but more agreeable than others in another type" (Mischel, 2004, p. 6) or (depending on the type of situation) "both hurtful and kind, caring and uncaring, violent and gentle" (Mischel & Shoda, 1995, p. 258).

Unlike Allport who did not explicate the processes through which the functional equivalence of a subset of situations could be established (Zuroff, 1986), Mischel has centered his theory and research on the processes that explain "invariance—in the variability" (Mischel, 2004, p. 2). Neither a realist nor supportive of the structural approach, his stand is that personality psychology need not only refer to "the study of differences between individuals in their global trait descriptions on trait adjective ratings" (i.e., the lexical and structural approaches); instead it can also pertain to "the study of the distinctiveness and stability that characterize the individual's social cognitive and emotional processes as they play out in the social world" (Mischel, 2004, p. 5). His work is mainly classified as a *process* approach. The term "processing structures" (Mischel & Shoda, 1995) is preferred over traits in his theory—a temperate position which stands in sharp contrast to the Allportian construal of traits as inherent, real-yet-inferred causal entities.

Keeping in mind the cognitive paradigm in psychology, he has accorded the person with meaning-making and discriminative judgment in regard to situations and corresponding response tendencies. At the same time, he has contended that there are repeated patterns in such sense-making and response tendencies, which he

has termed *behavioral signatures*. A behavioral signature of personality can also be defined as a unique pattern of *if-then* relationships that explain a person's psychological invariance despite variability ("if" = psychological aspects of a situation; "then" = the cognitions and affects that are activated by these psychological features) (Mischel, 2004; Mischel, Shoda, & Mendoza-Denton, 2002). Therefore, for the same type of situations, there is temporal stability even though concurrent consistency across different types of situations may remain low. Methodologically he has preferred to use in vivo observations to identify *stable patterns* of intrapersonal behavioral variability in personality research as opposed to using lexically sourced ratings or aggregated conclusions across observed situations.

As an illustration, Mischel and Shoda (1995) have developed a model: the Cognitive-Affective Processing System (CAPS). This model integrates a systems view, theory/research from the cognitive paradigm, and the study of social and emotional competence; it also appears allied to attachment theory (e.g., Bowlby) and action perspectives. In this model, the personality system holds mental representations in the form of varied cognitive-affective units (CAUs). These CAUs are "the person's construal and representations of the self, people, and situations, enduring goals, expectations-beliefs, and feeling states, as well as memories of people and past events" (Mischel, 2004, p. 11); they reflect the person's genetic endowment, biological history, culture/subculture, and social learning history (Mischel et al., 2002, p. 53). True to a system, the CAUs are interconnected and mutually influential. However, the extent of influence and accessibility of CAUs may vary. Thus, there can be individual differences in the content/quality of CAUs, their interconnections, and their accessibility. CAUs mediate situation–behavior relationships (through conscious and unconscious processes). CAUs explain the manner in which "individuals interact with, select, and change their personal social world" (Mischel & Shoda, 1995, p. 259). The central premise is that the CAUs are differentially yet characteristically activated in various situations, resulting in a behavioral signature. This behavioral signature, the original identifier of the personality, is given flesh and bone only through patterned relationships between CAUs and situations. Consider their example of two boys with the same (aggregated) overall level of aggression: one was more aggressive than other children when the situation involved an adult, and less aggressive when it involved a peer; the reverse was the case with the second boy. Despite the same overall level of a behavioral disposition, there was a different pattern in their cross-situational variability—their behavioral signatures were unique.

The CAPS model also potentially yields personality types based on similarity in the personality system; for example, if people share the same kind of CAUs and their inter-coordinations, and hence have the same if-then pattern such as the rejection-sensitivity type (Mischel, 2004; Mischel & Shoda, 1995). A person who is the rejection-sensitive type, for instance, may interpret an otherwise innocuous behavior of a friend turning away to talk to another as a deliberate attempt to insult and may express inappropriate anger that may well lead to rejection. A particularly ingenuous feature of this theory is the postulation that like the CAPS which distinguishes a person, there can be a CAPS which distinguishes a dyad (e.g., a married couple).

Although the use of the verb "activate" (or trigger) in if-then relationships appears to denote a mechanical or at best a chemical reactive mode, Mischel (2004) has not foreclosed other avenues of *action* (see for example, Brandtstädter, 2006). If a person is credited with meaning-making and discriminative judgment, it follows that the person need not only use these to perpetuate patterns of response tendencies in relation to particular types of situations. It also awards agency such that a person could use revised judgment to refashion meanings and affects and alter past patterns or behavioral signatures. And here is where there is a definite breach in the theories of Allport and Mischel. Mischel and Shoda's CAPS model lends coherence and continuity to the personality but not as a closed system impervious to change: "the cognitive-affective system

theory of personality assumes that the organization of relations within the person's mediating network, the structure of the personality system, remains relatively stable and invariant across situations *unless* new learning, development, or biochemical changes occur" (Mischel & Shoda, 1995, p. 256; emphasis added). Despite the oft-repeated claim of an invariant personality, Mischel allows human agency and its corollary: that is, modifiability of the personality system (see Mischel, 2004). In line with action perspectives (i.e., intentional self-development), he recognizes the principal role of self-regulation in accounting for either possibility in (personality) development—continuity *or change*. In Allport's theory, the constituents of the personality have always been set-for-life; in contrast, in Mischel and Shoda's model, the personality remains an open system throughout (although genes and early experiences are given temporal priority). The dynamic personality system in Mischel and Shoda's model can well be maintained as stable but holds possibilities for positive change. "That also increases the hope that ultimately people do not have to be the victims of either their predispositions or their biographies" (Mischel, 2004, p. 18).

Additional Examples

In portraying additional examples of agreements and disagreements in the personality literature in Western Psychology, I have included the work of Block (e.g., 2002), Caspi and Shiner (2006), Mroczek (e.g., Mroczek, Spiro, & Almeida, 2003), and Holland (1959, 1997).

Block

From 1968, resistance to Mischelian ideas has been evident in personality psychology, particularly illustrated by the person–situation debate that had ensued in personality psychology (cf. Mischel, 2004). Over 40 years later, a sizable group of personality psychologists continue to oppose newer Mischelian ideas. Block (2002), for example, disparaged the CAPS model as underdeveloped (e.g., the CAUs are broadly rather than specifically explicated), overly ideographic, and focused on idiosyncrasies.

Block (e.g., 2002) proposed a nomothetic process theory, distinguishable in his view from structural approaches such as those of Costa and McCrae which he considered essentially atheoretical (i.e., lacking a deductive system), and from ideographic process approaches (i.e., Mischel and Schoda's CAPS model[2]). His theory is exclusively focused on one (albeit important) self-regulative function: optimizing the balance between overcontrol and undercontrol (i.e., context-sensitive "adaptive modulation"). The foundational notion is that "the human goal is to be as undercontrolled as possible and as overcontrolled as necessary" (Block & Kremen, 1996, p. 351). In an interesting parallel to CAUs, Block's personality system includes interrelated "ego-functioning structures" which are mental representations (or relational rules, scripts). These are involved in self-regulation of impulse, and (ideally) entail assessing the context to judge whether delay of gratification or spontaneity is justified, whether it is best to exercise caution or to be playful. Self-regulation of impulse is also useful for holding aggression in check. The developmental progression is from undercontrol to overcontrol and lastly to optimization of control (i.e., "resilience" or ego-resiliency), credited not to genes but to Freudian (e.g., reality principle) and ego-psychological explanations (e.g., internal working model). Not everyone makes it to the third step; therefore, Block's typology contrasts ego-resilients with ego-brittles (Block & Kremen, 1996). Ego-brittles are either "more undercontrolled than is adaptively effective" (i.e., undercontrollers) or "more overcontrolled than is adaptively required" (overcontrollers) (Block & Kremen, 1996, p. 351; Caspi & Shiner, 2006). Moreover by adulthood, ego-resiliency or ego-brittleness becomes a relatively enduring characterological quality of the person.

Caspi and Shiner

Caspi and Shiner (2006) represent the neo-Allportian position which is favored by many personality psychologists. Continuing in the Allportian tradition, they consider traits as real entities located in an internal structure which cause and thereby explain stable individual differences (i.e., the realist or explanatory position in personality psychology). The Big Five provides the taxonomy of individual differences in personality in adulthood; they cite evidence of its utility in mapping individual differences in personality during childhood and adolescence as well.

In response to the criticism that "(t)rait models are often caricatured as static, nondevelopmental conceptions of personality" (Caspi & Shiner, 2006, p. 302), they offer multiple unidirectional hypotheses and supporting research findings. They start by couching personality traits as organizational constructs which impact the manner in which a person organizes behavior in relation to environmental or developmental challenges. They select the word "elaboration" (of available structure) to capture developmental processes. Six processes are listed through which the early temperament/personality ("part of each individual's genetic heritage" [p. 326]) *shapes* later personality,[3] or is *elaborated* into later personality: learning processes, environmental elicitation, environmental construal, social/temporal comparisons and self-construal, environmental selection, and, environmental manipulation (p. 326). They illustrate these processes clearly: a child high on openness may engage in complex and challenging learning tasks (learning processes); a child high on extraversion may convincingly push others into accepting him/her as the group leader (environmental manipulation). They also posit the personality as a unidirectional influence on multiple developmental domains as follows: (a) how personality *shapes*

---

[2] Block (2002) was also in disagreement with Mischel's (e.g., 2004) stance on the "cooling" benefits of delayed gratification. Block who lauded contextually-relevant undercontrol, was opposed to a unidimensional view of impulse modulation.

---

[3] Also compatible with the evocative/reactive and active gene-environment correlation model (e.g., Plomin et al., 1977).

relationships, (b) how personality *shapes* school and work performance, and (c) how personality *shapes* health, including risk or resilience with regard to psychopathology. All developmental processes elucidated are to do with strengthening and widening of the influence of personality. Further, Caspi and Shiner (2006) have (conspicuously) omitted Glen Elder's (e.g., Elder & Shanahan, 2006) work on turning points, included in an earlier writing (i.e., in Caspi, 1998), and thus appear to have ruled out the possibility of qualitative transformation of the personality.

Mroczek

Overall, Mroczek's work promotes a more open understanding of personality stability and change, especially across adulthood. In adopting an explicitly developmental view, he is helping to loosen the rather deeply established notions in Western thought about the (relative) invariance of the personality. Mroczek et al. (2003), for example, have identified multiple types of differences with regard to the personality: (a) between-person variability (e.g., individual differences in typical levels of neuroticism); (b) within-person change over time (i.e., trends in the personality trajectory over time such as an overall increase or decrease in extraversion); and (c) within-person fluctuation or variation in response to situations or to daily rhythms (i.e., differences in neuroticism during a project presentation at work versus a lower-stress time, differences in neuroticism in the morning versus evening). Mroczek and Spiro (2003) have argued in favor of yet another type of difference: Between-person variability in within-person change over time. Thus, they state that it is not a question of personality "stability versus change" (p. 153); that is, one does not have to select one position, that of stability or that of change. The personality can be stable over time or change over time; both occur but across different individuals. The "concept of interindividual differences in intraindividual change" (p. 153) indicates that people differ in whether they change or remain stable.

Holland

In the career literature, Holland's theory of vocational personalities and work environments has made a definite mark (Leung, 2008). Based on extensive research in the United States, Holland (1959, 1997) has formulated a typology of vocational personalities, namely *R*ealistic, *I*nvestigative, *A*rtistic, *S*ocial, *E*nterprising, and *C*onventional (RIASEC). A person's vocational personality type (e.g., artistic) or subtype (i.e., the three most ascendant types represented in the person's profile such as RIC) reflects suitability and affinity for congruent kinds of work and work environments. By the end of adolescence, a relatively stable vocational personality is formed and it is expected, for example, that an artistic person's vocational satisfaction and competence will be higher when the work environment is artistic.

Conclusion and Reflections

In personality psychology, Block (2002) wryly observed, "rather different cartographies of the field have been offered up as guides to the terrain" and "the place-names or routes accorded by one mapmaker arouse anathema in other assayers." He added that "it also has become increasingly clear that large congruencies exist, or seem to exist" (p. xi). It is these multiple frames of reference (along with some overlaps) that I have attempted to illustrate in this section. The personality literature, of course, extends well beyond the samples presented here.

There are many points of reflection that can be raised using the personality literature in this section. These points can allow a career service professional to examine his or her own orientation to the *person*.

A Moot Point About Traits and Their Modifiability

Is the trait an entity? Is it an underlying structure that a person possesses? Does a person possess fixed quantities of various qualities? Do these qualities unidirectionally influence various developmental outcomes? It is unclear how the Allportian or neo-Allportian position can be reconciled with notions of development otherwise in Western Psychology (cf. Gottlieb, Wahlsten, & Lickliter, 2006; Thelen & Smith, 2006) of (for example) probabilistic rather than deterministic influences, feed-forward and feed-backward coactions (multidirectionality of influences), and experience-dependent plasticity. It is one thing to say that something is quite stable or rather can be quite stable (and specify the conditions under which stability is actively maintained in a dynamic system); it is another thing to exclude the possibility of modifiability. That is tantamount to denying hope (cf. Mischel, 2004) and declaring the irredeemable inequality of individuals.

A related point for reflection is whether the worthiness of a phenomenon depends upon its continued presence. If we include plasticity (i.e., modifiability or mutability) does the phenomenon become weak or less worthy? Perhaps, the reverse is the case. Note Lerner's (2006) statement that "the potential for plasticity at both individual and contextual levels constitutes a fundamental strength of all human development" (p. 3). Perhaps, as Mroczek and Spiro (2003) have noted, "It is time for our notions of personality stability to change" (p. 163).

What Is the Goal of Personality Development?

In some perspectives or positions, there is no explication of a goal in personality development. This is not surprising because goals require movement. Only a theorist who is ready to allow change or some progression towards a desired point will include goals.

A person may have a particular personality structure, mapped using the Big Five. Perhaps the person is low on conscientiousness. We know from research that the trait conscientiousness is helpful for success in one's career (e.g., Barrick & Mount, 1991), but what of it? How does this research finding benefit those who are low on conscientiousness? Such research is taxonomically useful for researchers but a dead-end for individuals if movement towards higher levels

of conscientiousness is precluded. On the other hand, once again note Lerner's (2006) impelling orientation: "The potential for and instantiations of plasticity legitimate an optimistic and proactive search for characteristics of individuals and of their ecologies that, together, can be arrayed to promote positive human development across life" (p. 3).

Block's (2002) theory identifies an optimum goal (although by adulthood movement becomes restricted). Whenever personality theorists are simultaneously psychotherapists, movement towards optimum points (wellbeing) is always predicated (e.g., Freud, 2002; Kiesler, 1996). Mischel (2004) has also allowed the possibility of movement towards more adaptive states.

Other interrelated reflective points are to do with agency, the roles ascribed to the person, and those to the context.

Self in Indigenous Western Psychology

In reviewing their orientation to the *person* (whose career development is to be supported), career service professionals need to also (re) examine the substantial body of literature on the self. Overall, self theorists do not quite see eye-to-eye with personality theorists. However, there are also some crossovers or overlaps: that is, personality theorists whose suppositions include self-construals. The work of these scholars will be discussed first, followed by the legacy positions of William James and Charles Cooley, and offshoots such as Susan Harter's (2006) contemporary theory and Hubert Hermans' (e.g., 2001) dialogical self theory.

Overlaps: Personality and Self

Examples of personality scholars (cited in the previous section) whose work includes self-construals are McAdams (1993), Kiesler (1996), and Mischel (e.g., 2004). Let us consider Kiesler's work. He has described the conjoint transaction between persons each of whom uses a "who-I-am template" or a self-schema and self-other schema (credited to genes and childhood experiences); these schemas produce selective patterns of attention, recall, participation, and reaction. Self-fulfilling prophecy and interpersonal complementarity are key constructs in his theory. Interactants use their self- and self-other schemas conjointly to express complementary reactions that confirm and preserve their respective self-schemas. At the same time, such transactional patterns need not remain intractable. Human fulfillment requires that we transcend stubborn and automatic reactions, and experience moments with others in which we conjointly create unscripted and reciprocally joyful outcomes: possible, for example, through contemporary interpersonal psychotherapy (Kiesler, 1996, p. x).

William James's Theory

Hierarchy and Multiplicity of the "Me Self"

William James (1890/2007) saw the self as clearly multidimensional. A multi-tiered aggregate constitutes the "empirical self" (observed/experienced self) commonly understood as "me" or the "me self." The bottom tier of the "me" he identified as the "material self," the next tier as the "social self," and third as the "spiritual self": an arrangement also, one may say, from concrete to abstract. He posited multiplicity within the tiers as well. Thus the material self includes identifications first with the body, next with clothes (more generally, adornment), the home, products of our labor, possessions, and other material wealth. The material self may be aggrandized through satisfaction of bodily appetites, acquisitiveness, etc.; self-evaluation of the material self may result, for example, in vanity (or modesty) with regard to one's appearance, and pride with regard to one's possessions (or fear of privation).

"(A) *man has as many social selves as there are individuals who recognize him* and carry an image of him in their mind" (James, 1890/2007, p. 294). For practical purposes, however, he reduced this to "as many different social selves

as there are distinct *groups* of persons about whose opinion he cares"; moreover, a person, by and large, "shows a different side of himself to each of these different groups" (p. 294). Individuals differ in how harmoniously their multiple social selves coexist. The social selves are aggrandized through sociability, ambition, and love; self-evaluation of the social selves, for example, may result in pride (or humility) with regard to one's family or social achievements.

The word "spiritual" in relation to the spiritual self is to be understood broadly rather than narrowly. More generally the spiritual self refers to self-identification with thought; more specifically it refers to self-definitions based on our intellectual faculties, moral sensitivities, or religious orientations. These "psychic dispositions" are a far greater source of fulfillment than the constituents of the lower-tiered selves such as material possessions. They "are the most enduring and intimate part of the self, that which we most verily seem to be" (p. 296). The spiritual self can be aggrandized through heeding one's conscience, through intellectual or moral aspirations; self-evaluation of the spiritual self may result, for example, in a sense of moral superiority (or inferiority).

Selectiveness, Salience, and Self-Esteem

There are multiple possible selves, "(b)ut to make any one of them actual, the rest must more or less be suppressed" and having picked out one, "(a)ll other selves thereupon become unreal": this is a cogent example of the "selective industry of the mind" (James, 1890/2007, p. 310). Successes and failures of the chosen self are experienced as real and are accompanied with strong emotions (e.g., joy or shame); the person, conversely, is not concerned about failure or inadequacy in relation to other (i.e., discarded) possible selves. Our evaluative self-feeling is largely contingent on our selection of what to be and do. Therefore, "Self-esteem = Success/Pretensions"; logically, "(s)uch a fraction may be increased as well by diminishing the denominator as by increasing the numerator" (pp. 310–311). Each addition of what one wants to be or do is both a potential source of esteem as also a burden. James saw the person as the agent of these additions and subtractions, and concluded that self-esteem was in our power. (At another point, he also recognized the influence of another on the self-feeling associated with a social self.)

The "I-Self" as the Creator of the "Me-Selves"

Where does this aggregate or collective comprising the "me" come from? The answer to this question brings us to the "I-me" distinction. "I" is the knower, the observer, the evaluator (i.e., thought rather than a soul); "me" is the known, the observed, and the evaluated. James has also called the "I" the owner of the me-collective or the thinker that construes and coordinates the collective of me-selves.

What About Continuity of the Self?

"I" (constituted of thoughts) is the "proprietor" of the selves; the "I" renders continuity and sameness by linking to the present, selected features of the past. The "I" observes, remembers, judges, identifies, collects, owns, or appropriates some of the past, disowns other past, and creates a unity. The vantage point is the present feeling, "(w)hatever remembered-past-feelings *resemble* this present feeling are deemed to belong to the same *me* with it" (James, 1890/2007, p. 400). Each new thought becomes the fresh past with its appropriated history of thoughts and is selectively appropriated into the next thought. At the same time, James asserted that "this generic unity coexists with generic differences just as real as the unity" (p. 335).

Charles H. Cooley's Theory

James's influence on Cooley is readily evident as some of Cooley's (1902) key ideas are extensions of James (1890/2007); however, Cooley's emphasis, principal orientation, and conclusions are original.

Emphasis on the Social Self

The I-me distinction and the three-tiered hierarchy of me-selves are missing from Cooley's theory. For Cooley (1902) the empirical or observed self was social. He did not believe that there existed a self that was not social; accordingly, his theory centers around the social self.

The self is essentially social because it is appropriative of physical (e.g., toys in childhood, house in adulthood), social (e.g., relationships), and mental (e.g., ideas, opinions) objects as "my/mine" and distinct from those of others. Without these others, there would be no need for appropriation, no need for distinguishing and asserting what was mine or not (whether a theory, a friend, or a cell phone), and therefore no basis or need for defining the self. To put it simply, there is no self, if there is no other. It is in this regard that Cooley (1902) called the "I" a "militant social tendency, working to hold and enlarge its place" (p. 149) in a world shared with other persons.

"I," "my/mine," and appropriation begin in the early years (credited to observation and a hereditary instinct) and are accompanied with an "emotional animus." Self-assertion however, is balanced by impressibility, framed as the looking-glass self.

The Social Self as the Looking-Glass Self

The looking-glass self is an extension of James's observation that we apprehend and are susceptible to the "images of me in the minds of other men" (James, 1890/2007, p. 321). Like we look into a mirror and see ourselves and judge ourselves depending on what we would like to see, "so in imagination we perceive in another's mind some thought of our appearance, manners, aims, deeds, character, friends, and so on, and are variously affected by it" (Cooley, 1902, p. 152). The self is therefore composed of three chief aspects: (a) how we imagine we appear to the other person, (b) how we imagine the person judges how (we think) we appear to him/her, and (c) the affect that accompanies our imagination of that person's judgment.

Multiplicity

The multiplicity of selves is implied because the content of these three aspects may vary depending on who the other person is. Cooley (1902) acknowledged that the personality takes form based on imaginations of our self in other minds; and that we learn "to be different things to different people" (p. 165).

Renewal and Plasticity

A current project or purpose may animate and define the self; on completion or failure, however, the self must cut loose, "renewing its skin like the snake"; the self's "rigidity must be broken up by growth and renewal," "it must be more or less decisively 'born again'"—thus a "healthy self must be both vigorous and plastic" (Cooley, 1902, p. 157). Cooley recommended that (some) impressibility and receptivity be retained in a character, making it open to learning and growth. "In character, as in every phase of life, health requires a just union of stability with plasticity" (p. 176). In fact, it is a proud man who "is not *immediately* dependent upon what others think" (p. 201); such pride could be considered a strength but in the long term "stunts a man's growth by closing his mind to progressive influences" (p. 202).

Larger Conception of Self

A larger conception of the self is one that is liberated from the "passions of the lower self" such as "sensual needs and worldly ambitions" and is "joyful, boundless, and without remorse" (Cooley, 1902, p. 227).

Susan Harter's Theory

Self as a Cognitive and Social Construction

The legacies of James and Cooley have survived into Harter's (e.g., 2006) contemporary theory which incorporates key elements from their perspectives. Therefore, the pivotal tenet of her theory is that the self is both a cognitive and a social construction. The word "construction"

implies agency and allows the possibility of modifiability. The qualifier "cognitive" brings to the fore the role of the I-self as the architect of the me-selves; the qualifier "social" recognizes the substantial contributory role of (significant) others in our self-representations. Harter, (also) using cognitive-developmental and neo-Piagetian perspectives, has described how the person's theory of self reflects the strengths and limitations of a particular cognitive-developmental stage/mini-stage. Across childhood and adolescence, there is an increase in differentiation (e.g., multiplicity) and integration of the self (e.g., coming to meaningful terms with contradictory selves). Likewise, using symbolic interaction theory (which includes Cooley's looking-glass self) and attachment theory, she has explained the role of parents, teachers, and peers in influencing the content and favorability of self-representations.

Attributes as a Construction, Role of Others, and Variability

Harter (2006) has drawn attention to the salience of attributes[4] like extrovert, talkative, cheerful, irresponsible, worrying, intelligent, and so on in the self-portrayals of adolescents. Given that the self is a construction, we may deduce that these and other attributes are a *construction*. Contradictions/variability and the role of others are also readily apparent in these self-representations. For example, she has illustrated how an adolescent described herself as cheerful when with friends (who she thought saw her as awesome), and mad and sad when around parents (who had told her that she was lazy and irresponsible). In line with James's theory (from early adolescence), there is a "proliferation of selves that vary as a function of the social context" (Harter, 2006, p. 531). The construction of multiple selves varying across different roles and relationships is a critical developmental task in adolescence, aided by cognitive *and* social processes. Harter has reported a 25–30 % overlap in self-attributes across different social contexts

---

[4] Called traits in personality research.

in early adolescence which drops to 10 % in late adolescence.

Self-Descriptions and Self-Evaluations

Continuing in James's tradition (i.e., self as multidimensional), self-representations include both self-descriptions and self-evaluations (Harter, 2006). There are two types of self-evaluations: (a) domain-specific (i.e., the self-concept) and (b) global (i.e., the self-esteem). The domains of self-evaluation change as well as increase in number from childhood to adulthood. For example, Harter (2012) has identified domains of self-evaluation for early childhood, middle-to-late childhood, adolescence, college years, early/middle adulthood, and late adulthood. Examples of the five domains in middle-to-late childhood include scholastic competence, physical appearance, and social competence. Examples of the 13 domains in late adulthood include cognitive abilities, job competence, family relationships, health status, life satisfaction, and reminiscence. The self-evaluations are weighted by the salience of particular domains to the person.

Global self-evaluation (i.e., the self-esteem or self-worth) is the overall judgment of one's worth: in Harter's conceptualization, this is not an average across specific domains of self-evaluation. In respecting that from middle school years onward, individuals report experiencing different levels of overall self-worth in regard to different relational contexts, Harter has also proposed relational self-esteem as a construct. My overall liking for myself can thus vary depending on the relational context (e.g., parents, friends at work, friends in the neighborhood).

Mutability of the Self

Using research investigating the stability or malleability of self-esteem, Harter has clarified her stance that self-esteem itself is neither a trait nor a state. In relation to their self-esteem, some individuals behave in a trait-like manner (i.e., show stability); others behave in a state-like manner (i.e., show contextual and temporal lability). She has concluded that "trait and state

attributions lie in individuals, not in the constructs themselves" (Harter, 2006, p. 554).

Hubert Hermans' Dialogical Self Theory

Decentralized Multiple I-Positions, Each with its Own Voice

The central premise of Hubert Hermans' dialogical self theory is that the self is constructed and represented through multivoiced, internal and external dialogues (e.g., Hermans, 2001). In other words, the internal dialogue is constituted of multiple voices because there are many autonomous "I-selves" or rather "I-positions" (e.g., I as a writer, I as a daughter, I as a learner), each with dominion over its multiple me-selves. Likewise, the external dialogue also comprises multiple voices because we live in a society populated by many others (e.g., my workmates, my sister). Hermans (a Netherlander) draws his inspiration from the American psychologist, William James (e.g., the "I-me" distinction); and the Russian literary scholar, Bakhtin (e.g., polyphony in literature). In integrating Bakhtin's notion of multivoicedness into a theory of I-self and me-selves, the outcome is a self characterized by "a decentralized plurality of characters" (Hermans, 2001, p. 248). That is, the central, coordinating, "authoritarian" "I-self" is replaced by a multiplicity of varied, even contradictory "I-positions," each with its own voice.

> The voices function like interacting characters in a story, involved in a process of question and answer, agreement and disagreement. Each of them has a story to tell about his or her own experiences from his or her own stance. As different voices, these characters exchange information about their respective *Me's*, resulting in a complex, narratively structured self. (Hermans, 2001, p. 248)

Continuity and Discontinuity

Hermans (2001) has uniquely combined continuity and discontinuity in the dialogical self. From the Jamesian perspective, the continuity of experience of *my* mother, *my* employer, and *my* friends emerges out of the common "my and mine"; in comparison, from a Bakhtian-derived perspective, my *mother*, my *employer*, and my *friends* reflect varied and possibly contrasting voices in the self-space which draw attention to discontinuity (Hermans, 2001). "In this conception the existence of unity in the self, as closely related to continuity, does not contradict the existence of multiplicity, as closely related to discontinuity" (Hermans, 2001, p. 248).

Positioning in Time and Space

Unlike the Cartesian rationalistic self *Cogito, ergo sum* ("I think, therefore I am") (Hermans & Kempen, 1993, p. 1), "the dialogical self is always tied to a particular position in space and time" (Hermans, 2001, p. 249). "The *I* in the one position, moreover, can agree, disagree, understand, misunderstand, oppose, contradict, question, challenge and even ridicule the *I* in another position" (Hermans, 2001, p. 249). These I-positions are social because another person (whether real, imaginary, or a combination) is incorporated into a position which allows an alternative perspective on who one is (Hermans, 2001). In this regard, it is important to consider Hermans' distinction between internal I-positions (experienced as part of myself) and external I-positions (experienced as part of the environment). Each derives its relevance from the other: for example, the internal position of "I as a teacher" is relevant because of the external positions of "my students"; likewise, "my students" are important to "I as a teacher." Moreover, "internal and external positions meet in processes of negotiation, cooperation, opposition, conflict, agreement and disagreement" (p. 153) both intrapersonally (internal dialogue) and interpersonally (external dialogue).

McIlveen and Patton (2007) have indicated the usefulness of dialogical self theory for the career development literature. They recommend that the life themes component of Savickas's career construction theory can especially benefit from the application of dialogical self theory.

Conclusion and Reflections

The literature on the self is quite prolific; the samples presented here are illustrative. Among the many other examples, career service professionals may be familiar with Donald Super's (e.g., 1990) early interest in role self-concepts and the more recent narrative, constructivist movement in career counseling (McIlveen & Patton, 2007; Savickas, 2002; Watson & McMahon, 2014, Chap. 35). The multiple indigenous Western views on the self, presented in this section, offer career service professionals novel points for reflection, especially when these views are juxtaposed with perspectives on the personality presented in the earlier section.

Same Person, Different Conclusions

Whether we consider the personality or the self, ultimately we are talking of the same person. Yet depending on our frame of reference, we appear to reach somewhat different conclusions about the same person. It seems that self theorists especially draw attention to the plurality of who the person is, and (interrelatedly) are more open to the possibility of change. This is an overall slant that one can perceive; it does not indicate that there is unanimity in the self literature. For example, even Swann, whose self-verification theory explains stability of self-views (e.g., Swann & Pelham, 2002), does not rule out the possibility of change. In light of the finding that those with negative self-views have a reduced quality of life, he presses for the need to develop strategic ways to improve negative self-views (e.g., Swann, Chang-Schneider, & McClarty, 2007). He has also recently advanced the notion of the self as "functional fiction" (Swann & Buhrmester, 2012). The adjective *functional* serves to remind us that the coherent, stable presence of a made-up self facilitates the pragmatics of daily living; the noun *fiction* (as I see it) quashes the finality with which some scholars may be inclined to view the person.

The Importance of a Theory

No doubt a scientific theory is important. It provides direction to the field—influencing the type of questions to be asked, the methods to be used, the manner of interpretation, and the orientation in the conclusions (Kuhn, 1970). Theory-building is not restricted to scientists; and if a scientific theory can direct the activities of scientists and the outcomes thereof, so will a person's (explicit or implicit) theory about their self direct their activities and outcomes. Whether a person experiences change or not, then depends on that person's (albeit implicit) theory of self. Carol Dweck's work in this area is particularly noteworthy. People hold either an "entity theory" (fixed attributes—a structure that one possesses which one can do nothing about) or an "incremental theory" (malleable attributes—that can be bettered through efforts) about one or more of their personal qualities (e.g., intelligence, math ability, verbal ability, personality) which has "profound consequences" (p. 124) for quality of self-regulation, actions, and outcomes (Dweck & Molden, 2005). Failure can be interpreted as indicating inherent inadequacy leading to a withdrawal of effort and poor outcomes (entity theorists); or failure can be understood as reflecting insufficient or inefficient efforts, making it more likely that efforts are pumped up, leading to enhanced outcomes (incremental theorists) (Dweck & Molden, 2005). Children and adults holding an entity theory versus an incremental theory have been found to be equally well-represented in research in the United States. As for whether an incremental theory is right or wrong, there are two things to note: (a) Accuracy of cognitions or metacognitions used in self-regulation is not quite the issue so long as these enhance rather than debilitate performance (e.g., Ferrari & Sternberg, 1998; Swann & Buhrmester, 2012); and (b) "evidence increasingly suggests that important parts of many abilities can be acquired" (Dweck & Molden, 2005, p. 123).

Personality and Self: Indigenous Eastern Perspectives Drawn from Philosophical Psychology

Psychology in modern India has been largely based on Western theory and research and

cannot be used (yet) to illustrate Eastern thought. Yang (2012) has adapted Wallerstein's world-system theory to propose that akin to a Western-hegemonized world-economy, there is a Western-hegemonized world-system for (academic) psychology such that "local psychologists in almost all major non-Western societies have developed the same kind of artificially transplanted psychology" (p. 9); that is, they have copied Western Indigenous Psychology (i.e., an imposed-etic psychology) despite being situated in culturally distinct non-Western contexts.

Therefore, in this section, Indian philosophy and spirituality (i.e., Vedic scripture-based literature) are used to illustrate Eastern perspectives. This fits with Yang's (2012) notion of *philosophical* psychology (which he has distinguished from *folk* psychology and *scientific* psychology). He has defined philosophical psychology as "the formal systems of psychological thought proposed by a society's philosophers" (p. 3) comprising a cultural group's knowledge-heritage.

Selection of *Advaita* Philosophy

There are six main orthodox schools of philosophical thought in India of which the Vedānta is one (Paranjpe, 1988). The literature selected for this section (e.g., Nisargadatta Maharaj, and the Bhagwad Geeta) represents the nondualist (*Advaita*) position in Vedānta. Whereas, the origin of these ideas is traced to approximately 2000–600 BC and the influential reinterpretations of Śaṅkara (or Śaṅkarācārya) in the 8th/9th century AD (Paranjpe, 1988), the interpretive lens used in this chapter is that of contemporary Indian scholars/philosophers (i.e., of the 20th century). Paranjpe's assertion that the Vedānta satisfies the criteria for a formal theory of personality (i.e., it is explicit, comprehensive, organized, thorough, open to experiential verification/empirical testing, and both abstract and applied) lends further credibility to the selection of resources for this section.

Introduction

In Advaita philosophy, there are explicit and carefully articulated notions of the self and personality (as also of emotional competence). The aim, however, is not to merely describe nor to only classify. Unlike the realist personality psychologists, the aim is neither to explain behavior as a representation of a stable internal structure nor to predict behavior based on indirect assessments of this supposed internal structure. In fact, there are many points of departure between Western psychology and Indian philosophy/spirituality with regard to notions of self, personality, and emotional competence. The distinguishing features of Indian thought (drawn from selected Indian philosophical psychology) are:

- Spiritual or a metaphysical/incorporeal orientation
- Fundamental difference in answering the question of "Who am I?"
- Transcendence as a key theme
- Malleability
- Complex notions of agency
- Hierarchically ordered classification allowing movement on a spiritual path
- Doctrine of oneness

Moreover, these features are necessarily overlapped and circular. Logically interconnected, one premise leads to the next. Therefore, in more ways than one, the approach is holistic. In the subsections that follow, indigenous Indian thought on self and personality is illustrated. Career service professionals can make an attempt to consider the many differences between indigenous Western and Eastern perspectives.

Position Articulated in J. Krishnamurti's Discourses

To know oneself, be an observer in the present and not a recorder replaying images of the past. "So the mind must be in a constant state of learning, therefore always in the active present, always fresh; not stale with the accumulated knowledge of yesterday" (Krishnamurti, 1972,

p. 15). If one looks at oneself (or for that matter at another) with "I know," the images of the past overlay and obstruct any viewing of the self (or another) in the ever-evolving present. "To learn about myself there must be freedom to look and this freedom to look is denied when I look through the knowledge of yesterday" (Krishnamurti, 1972, p. 15). In fact, Bierman's (1990) research with rejected children in the United States supports such a claim: rejected children continued to be viewed negatively by their peers despite improvements in their behaviors. And so Krishnamurti's (1972) radical statement: "I know merely the images; a living thing I cannot know—dead images are what I know" (p. 32).

Implicit in Krishnamurti's notions of the self is transcendence of the past; the idea of the self in the here-and-now is explicit. Relating to oneself with vitality, relating to others (and more generally life) with vitality, are founded in awareness in the present. Liberating the present from the past and locating the self in the here-and-now are repeated motifs in Eastern thought (e.g., Thich Nhat Hanh's "Miracle of Mindfulness" [1999]).

Position Articulated in Nisargadatta Maharaj's Discourses

Nisargadatta Maharaj's emphatic and provocative statements once again illustrate the Indian (philosophical/spiritual) position on the self and personality. "How does personality come into being? By memory. By identifying the present with the past and projecting it into the future. Think of yourself as momentary, without past and future and your personality dissolves." (Nisargadatta, 1973/1997, p. 206) Overdependence on space and time along with the facility of memory allows for a stable or enduring imagination of self. However, he has reminded us that space and time "are modes of perception, but they are not the only ones" (p. 205).

In notions of the self, he has contrasted personal with impersonal, particular with universal, experiencing with being, "*what* I am" with "*who* I am," "I am this" with "I am." Personality is a result of identifying the self with the personal and the particular, with experiencing, with "*what* I am," and concluding "I am this." But that is not all that self is. An alternative is to recognize the self as impersonal, universal, located in "to be" and therefore in "I am"—an "I am" complete in and of itself without any need for qualifying further.

In fact, in his view all intrapsychic conflict is an outcome of identifying the self with time and space, with the mind and the body. "You have enclosed yourself in space and time, squeezed yourself into the span of a lifetime and the volume of a body and thus created innumerable conflicts" (Nisargadatta, 1973/1997, p. 204). "All your problems arise because you have defined and therefore limited yourself. When you do not think yourself to be this or that, all conflict ceases." (p. 204)

Which is real, which is illusory? The transcendental, unlimited being is real; the person with limitations is illusory. "The 'I am' is certain. The 'I am this' is not." (Nisargadatta, 1973/1997, p. 70) "The impersonal is real, the personal appears and disappears. 'I am' is the impersonal Being. 'I am this' is the person. The person is relative and the pure Being—fundamental." (p. 71) Using an analogy, he has clarified, "(t)he person merely appears to be, like the space within the pot appears to have the shape and volume and smell of the pot" (p. 204). Audaciously, he has declared: "Fight with all the strength at your disposal against the idea that you are nameable and describable. You are not. Refuse to think of yourself in terms of this or that" (p. 204).

Transcendence is a key theme in Nisargadatta's discourses on the self. To go beyond "I am this or that" is not to move towards vagueness, the apathetically inarticulate, or the lazily undifferentiated. Instead, the boundaries through which we define ourselves have to be surrendered to pure awareness, an awareness that yields oneness and a powerful love-of-all.

> Stop imagining yourself being or doing this or that and the realization that you are the source and heart of all will dawn upon you. With this will come great love which is not choice or predilection, nor attachment, but a power which makes all things

love-worthy and lovable. (Nisargadatta, 1973/ 1997, p. 3)

General Position Articulated in the *Bhagawad Geeta*

In the Bhagawad Geeta (considered as much a philosophical treatise as a religious text), in understanding the self, attention is drawn to the metaphysical or incorporeal Self[5]; therefore, reflection on "who am I?" yields spiritually oriented expansive answers. Further, it is clear that one has a choice. A person can identify with his/ her limiting attachments, which include notions of self as the particular (Chinmayananda, 2011). The optimal goal, on the other hand, is to transcend limited views of the self through contemplation and realize that one's nature is Pure Being (Chinmayananda, 2011). Clearly, when the vocabulary goes beyond the self to include the Self, transcendence becomes a necessary corollary.

In articulating such transcendence, the doctrine of oneness is unequivocally presented in the Bhagawad Geeta:

- "With the mind harmonised. . .he sees the Self abiding in all beings, and all beings in the Self; he sees the same everywhere." (VI/29,[6] p. 451)

Moreover, this Self is simultaneously the one God. Therefore, the Bhagawad Geeta, written as a dialogue between Lord Krishna and Arjuna, a mighty warrior king, is a philosophical discourse urging engagement in the battlefield of life through realization of the supreme Self. Lord Krishna in the Geeta has stated:

- "He who see Me everywhere, and sees everything in Me, he never gets separated from Me, nor do I get separated from him." (VI/30, p. 452)

---

[5] The capitalization of "Self" is deliberate and communicates the distinction between the personal self and the impersonal Self.

[6] Chapter number and verse number; verse translated from Sanskrit. Page numbers are from Chinmayananda (2011).

- "I am the Self…seated in the hearts of all beings; I am the Beginning, the Middle and also the End of all beings." (X/20, p. 702)

Specific Position Articulated in the Bhagawad Geeta: The Theory of the *Gunas*

More specifically, the position in the Bhagawad Geeta with regard to the self and personality is clarified through the theory of the gunas. The gunas yield a typology: there are three types of gunas, namely *sattvic*, *rajasic*, and *tamasic*. Therefore, on the face of it, we can talk of three types of individuals or three types of personalities (see Table 8.1).

So far, one may wonder whether the gunas merely produce another interesting classification of individuals; if so, what value do they add? After all, there are many such classifications available already in the Western literature. However, there are many differences between gunas and personality typologies in the Western literature.

Hierarchy

As is clear from Table 8.1, the three personality types are in a hierarchical relationship with each other: at the lower level is the Tamasic person whose orientation to life is characterized by indolence, ignorance, and carelessness. At the middle level is the Rajasic person whose over-ardent egotistical actions create a restless, not-yet-satisfied, agitated, and fatiguing orientation. At the higher level is the Sattvic person who exemplifies temperance. Engaged in balanced activity without expectation of reward or reciprocity, rational, and discriminative, such a person achieves both happiness and knowledge.

Mutability

A pivotal distinction between Western and Eastern thought on personality is that mutability of personality is fundamental in Eastern thought and at best debated in Western thought. In order to understand the mutability of gunas, it is

essential to ask: What are gunas? The Sanskrit word "guna" can mean the property, quality, virtue, or distinguishing feature of an object. Swami Chinmayananda (2011) has explained the use of "guna" in the Geeta in various ways. A person's psychological being can take on a Tamasic quality, for example. However, a guna is not an ordained quality of a person. It is not a fixed or inherent property of a person. Depending upon the person's attitudes and actions, a guna can become predominant in a person and therefore, for the duration of that prominence, define the person's qualities or virtues. In other words, the person is not a victim of his/her prominent guna; the person is responsible for cultivating a particular guna. When a person continues to foster a particular guna, his/her psychological being becomes enthralled by that guna. For instance, repeated inaction, living life without thought to consequence, without defining a deeper purpose in life, invite a Tamasic orientation to one's psychological being. Therefore, Chinmayananda has described a guna as an attitude cultivated by a person—an attitude reflected in the manner in which a person's mind functions. Each of the three gunas is akin, he has explained, to one of "three different climatic conditions" (p. 941) that can prevail in our psychological being. The differences in climatic conditions arise from and strengthen a particular orientation to life.

Moreover, no person is exempt from any of the three gunas. All three gunas are present in each person; individuality is manifest through the varying proportions of each of the three gunas. So also, is the personality defined. Thus, Chinmayananda (2011) has stated, "hence the distinct aroma in the character, conduct and behaviour of each individual" (p. 941). By now the mutability of the guna-made personality must be self-evident. As a guna is harbored and not predetermined or preformed, it is vulnerable to change. The stability of a guna-made personality is a function of what mental climate a person continues to harbor. Of course, in Indian thought, such a mental climate and therefore the personality can extend through a lifetime and even beyond a lifetime: on rebirth, a person can continue to be stuck in the same psychological

Table 8.1 Personality typology using the three gunas

	The Sattvic person: the pure	The Rajasic person: the passionate	The Tamasic person: the lethargic, ignorant
Characterized by	Purity and health; balanced joy	Passion and agitations	Inertia; sloth; absence of awareness (therefore, darkness); ignorance
Level of activity	Balanced activity	Over activity	Inactivity/under-activity; lethargy; indolence
		Over-fervent activities; feverish and ambitious activities	Tendency to avoid responsibilities; perceived incapacity in practicing initiative; unenthusiastic; non-achieving
Intelligence	Rational and discriminative	Creates mental agitations which make the intellect unsteady	Veils, distorts, and dishonors intelligence; reduced intelligence; makes it impossible to distinguish between right and wrong; misguided; destructive of discriminative judgment
	Ability to observe, analyze, comprehend, be aware of, and discern the outer world with accuracy		Miscalculates the world around him/her, misinterprets own potential, inaccurate in relating to the world. Perverted and false view of the world
Attachment to	Happiness and knowledge	Action	Lower nature through heedlessness, indolence, and lack of awareness
Brings to the forefront	"(D)ynamic quietude" (p. 974) Learning and knowledge	Greed, undertaking of numerous actions, restlessness, longing/ insatiable desires; absence of quietude	Absence of awareness, sloth, carelessness, ignorance, and delusion
Nature of actions	Action without expectation of reciprocity or reward	Egotistical actions, expectation of reciprocity or reward	Careless, uncontrolled, irresponsible actions
In relation to own divinity	Of the three, "the most divine mental attitude, still it binds us and acts as a limitation on our divine nature" (p. 955)	Middle ground	Oblivious to higher calls within self; heedless of the more noble and divine life purposes

Note: This table has been created using Chinmayananda (2011)

conditions. Simultaneously, the facility of change is ever-available. All it takes is a change of mind, a new orientation.

The preeminent guna has a decided influence on intelligence. Consistency in rational and discriminative thinking and accurate discernment of the outer world is the outcome when the Sattvic guna is prominent. Agitations and inconsistency in quality of mental functioning are the result when the Rajasic guna overwhelms the other two gunas. Preponderance of the Tamasic guna results in reduced intelligence, and false, perverted, and misguided perceptions. Clearly, therefore, in Indian thought intelligence is not fixed either. Intelligence is also mutable. It is a result of the quality of attitudes we nurture. In changing the quality of our attitudes, we can modify our intelligence.

Progression Within the Gunas

In order to achieve a better quality of life (and afterlife), a person is expected to exercise prudence and progress from cultivating predominantly lower to higher gunas. That is, if a person has been harboring a Tamasic orientation, it is considered best that he/she works to alter the Tamasic orientation to Rajasic; similarly, a Rajasic orientation to Sattvic. Within the play of the three gunas, the ideal is the Sattvic orientation. This ideal, importantly, is not foreclosed to those who may not be living their lives currently through such an orientation. The Sattvic orientation is not the privilege of a few. Within the gunas, it is considered an optimal state that any and all *can* and *must* strive for. Thus, it is not just that the gunas are mutable. Transcendence of lower gunas is anticipated and valued.

Beyond the Gunas: Beyond the Mind, Beyond the Personality

Transcendence from lower to higher gunas is not the end of the story, so to speak. The exhortation is to transcend *all* gunas, including the Sattvic guna. This is reasonable given the ultimate goal, which is to transcend the mind, transcend the personality. Chinmayananda (2011) has explained, for example:

> When anger conquers my mind, I experience and behave as an angry man; but when anger has receded and my mind is calmed, I can no longer continue to behave as a bad-tempered man. The tricks of the mind consist in projecting a world-of-Creation, thought by thought, and in feeling oneself irredeemably conditioned by one's imaginations. As long as one is drowned in the mind, ...storms... must necessarily toss one about. On transcending the mind, we realise the Self and its Infinite Nature. (p. 947)
>
> He who has understood that he is not "the reflection in his own mind" but...something other than the mind and therefore something higher than the *gunas*—he is the one who has escaped forever the shackles of all limitations... (p. 981)

In explaining why one needs to unshackle oneself from the gunas and therefore from a particular personality, Lord Krishna in the Bhagawad Geeta has described the universe and its evolution. "...(T)he universe is evolved by the union between spirit and matter—Spirit enveloped in Matter is the pluralistic expression of Existence in the world" (Chinmayananda, 2011, p. 948). The gunas can also be likened to chords that bind Spirit to matter and entangle the Spirit in matter. Through the play of the gunas, a person is "bound to the limitations and finitude of matter" (p. 954) and lives using dreamlike "projections of a delusory world-of-matter" (p. 953). Each of the gunas represents attachment to matter; the Indian ideal (as upheld in the Geeta) is to go beyond attachment.

A person with a Tamasic orientation is attached to the material world through heedlessness, indolence, and absence of awareness. He or she remains chained to the imaginations/delusions of the material world through slothful carelessness. A person with a predominantly Rajasic orientation is attached to the material world through action. Lost in doingness, and the arrogance of "I am the doer" (p. 959), such a person loses sight of a higher calling.

What may come as a surprise to some is that even a Sattvic orientation is to be transcended. This is because Sattwa also exemplifies identification with matter. A person with a Sattvic orientation is attached to the material world through attachment to happiness and knowledge. A person can be lost in the pleasures of goodness and therefore remain attached to matter: "A gold-chain, if sufficiently strong can also bind as any iron-chain. 'Goodness', though it gives us the freedom from all vulgarities, can also shackle us within its own limitations!" (Chinmayananda, 2011, pp. 955–956).

The gunas "bind us down to the lower plane of matter identifications, and therefore, to the ego-sense" (Chinmayananda, 2011, p. 946). Self-realization is the outcome of the transcendence of the three gunas. "When once we get away from the *gunas*..., we get redeemed from our limited sense of individuality, and instantaneously, we shall experience our Absolute Universal Nature" (p. 946). Thus, the Self-realized man/woman recognizes and acknowledges oneness: "He who has transcended the three *gunas* comes to experience the very plurality in the world as the play of the One Infinite (p. 1188)."

It is unmistakably lucid thus far that mutability and transcendence of self/personality/mind are condiciones sine quibus non; they are indispensable to Indian notions of "Who am I?" The whole scheme collapses unless there exist mutability and transcendence.

Complex Notions of Agency: Choice and Surrender

Notions of agency are unremittingly complex in Indian thought. On the one hand, "I-ness," "my-ness," and "I am the doer" have to be set aside or surrendered to the realization that the one Supreme Self is the agent. Simultaneously, this realization itself is a choice that the person must exercise. To reiterate, it is up to the person to exercise agency in moving from a Tamasic orientation to a Rajasic orientation or to move beyond the gunas altogether. Yet the seeker is still lost to the material world unless he/she confronts, acknowledges, and surrenders agency to the one Self.

Note the following verse from the Geeta: "Thus, the 'Wisdom' which is a greater secret than all secrets, has been declared to you by Me; having reflected upon it fully, you now act as you choose" (XVIII/63, p. 1236).

Stated Utility of Knowledge of Gunas: Why Should One Know About Gunas?

The knowledge of gunas is provided so that it can be used as a self-monitoring aid as one journeys through life, or in Indian thought (if necessary) through lifetimes. Chinmayananda (2011) used an analogy of a person who were to drive a car (i.e., body and mind) on a long journey (i.e., life path): Knowledge of the engine (i.e., the gunas) can allow a person to make adjustments even when there is a breakdown and have a successful journey. He has clarified that knowledge of the gunas helps a person anticipate, comprehend, and manage "the possible mischiefs of the mind" (p. 944). Understanding the nature of the gunas and their tyranny—that is, the manner in which they can rule the mind—is prerequisite to gaining wisdom. "But in order to conquer the mind, a seeker must know very clearly the tricks by which the mind generally hoodwinks him...a thorough knowledge of the *gunas* will be helpful to everyone trying to master his own mind" (p. 947). Knowledge of the gunas, he has stated, provides us with "a charter of freedom, a scheme

for getting ourselves freed from the tentacles of our own imaginations" (p. 954).

That such knowledge is to be used solely for self-management and self-regulation, guiding self-development, has been clarified strongly: "Remember, and I repeat, REMEMBER, these classifications are given NOT TO CLASSIFY OTHERS but to provide us with a ready-reckoner to help us in our constant and daily self-analysis and self-discipline" (p. 1187; emphasis in original). Paranjpe (1988) has called it "a self-help program for those who aspire to higher levels of fulfillment" (p. 205).

Conclusions

It is not whether one agrees that there are gunas, or agrees about their assigned qualities. The point to take to heart is that our qualities, good or bad, serviceable or dysfunctional, are harbored choices. No one is more privileged than another with regard to personal qualities; no one is left out of the fold. Anyone can attain good qualities; anyone can attain the Self. There is no (unjust) Maker or genetic blueprint inflexibly bestowing more on one and less on the other.

Repeated Motifs

The Self as real and the need to return awareness to this *one* Self are repeated motifs throughout Advaita philosophy. Selected verses from Ādi Śaṅkarācārya's *Aparokṣānubhuti* (8th–9th century AD/2011) serve as additional examples:

- "I am not this body, the bundle of elements, nor am I the senses, I am something other than this." (Verse 13, p. 12)
- "A heap of timber is considered as a house; a piece of steel is understood to be a sword, so too the Ātman[7] is mistaken to be the body by the ignorant." (Verse 74, p. 67)
- "Just as all things of large dimension and magnitude appear to be very small and

---

[7] Ātman is the Supreme self, Pure Awareness or Consciousness.

insignificant due to great distances, so too does a person, on account of his spiritual ignorance, perceive the Ātman as the body." (Verse 80, p. 70)

- "Thus when the Self is not known, the idea that I am the body, persists, when the Self is known, the same will dissolve in the Supreme Self." (Verse 87, p. 75)

From a deeper level of transcognitive awareness, the phenomenal (or material) world (including limited notions of "I am this" or "I am that") is considered illusory or arising from ignorance (i.e., in Sanskrit: *māyā*, *avidyā*) (Chinmayananda, 2011; Paranjpe, 1988; Śaṅkarācārya, 8th–9th century AD/2011). The plurality within and across objects/persons is part of the nature of the material world, also not characteristic of ultimate reality which is One. Consider the following, also from the Aparokṣānūbhuti: "At the very instant of the ignorance of the rope, it appears as a snake, so too, the pure and Changeless Consciousness Itself appears as the world of plurality because of ignorance" (Verse 44, p. 43). Of course, for all *ordinary* purposes, the phenomenal world is construed as real (Paranjpe, 1988); exclusive or even primary belief and attachment to the phenomenal or material world is in Indian thought always a misconstrual.

Further, the One or the Supreme Self is frequently referred to as *Brahman*, constituted of *Sat-Cit-Ānanda*, that is, Pure Being (without qualification)–Pure Awareness–Pure Bliss (Śaṅkarācārya, 8th–9th century AD/2012). Attachment and misconstrued beliefs in the material world explain human suffering; in contrast, bliss is the core of each being, experienced through Self-realization (Nisargadatta, 1973/1997; Paranjpe, 1988).

The three gunas are binding forces, attaching the unlimited being to the limitations of the world-of-matter. The gunas account for individual differences; albeit changeable differences (Chinmayananda, 2011; Paranjpe, 1988). Shifting one's focus towards Brahman or the One Supreme Self or the single cosmic energy expressed as Being-Awareness-Bliss, requires surrendering the variegated, multi-faceted individual self (Śaṅkarācārya, 8th–9th century AD/2012). Then, one is back to square One—or more appropriately, one circles back to One.

Points of Departure from Western Personality Theory

It is clear that in indigenous Indian thought (as illustrated in the selected resources used in this chapter), personality theory has been integrated with a metaphysical purpose in life, a larger purpose in life, or with spiritual goals in life. In such writing, it appears that life *is* about spiritual goals: all else is lack of awareness, a lack of wakefulness to one's spirit. When spiritual goals are seen as the fulcrum of life and self-regulation, notions of self and personality can take on a different hue. Therefore the idea that in movement on a spiritual path, a personality may obstruct, or facilitate; but in either case, needs to be transcended.

Why does the personality need to be transcended? Caspi and Shiner (2006) have started their chapter on *Personality Development* with the following statement: "This chapter focuses on individual differences in personality, because differences among individuals are the most remarkable feature of human nature" (p. 300). Personality is essentially about individuality or individual differences. In Indian thought individuality is counter-opposed to Self-realization. In other words, the attainment of spiritual goals, the raison d'être of life, requires the relinquishing of false notions of individuality. The one Self and thus the doctrine of oneness, logically requires both a personality that can be changed *and* transcended. If we are all one, or are sourced from One, and I appear stressed at work today, I can change that and be calm tomorrow (or in the next instant). Also, as I grow in awareness and wakefulness, I realize my (one) Self. In this case, all apparent differences are as substantial or insubstantial as are shadows. Or in the words of Nisargadatta (1973/1997): "Just as each flower has its own colour, but all colours are caused by the same light" (p. 3).

In Indian thought, there are complex layers of being. The personality is integral to some but not all layers. And very importantly, a recurrent theme is that the personality or one's psychological being is the outcome of the mental climate that is cultivated. Choice and surrender are paradoxically coupled in resolving and evolving the unity of the Self from seeming plural differences.

Multiple Frames of Reference for Career Service Professionals: Sensitivity to the Universal and the Particular

So, who is the person? In this chapter, career service professionals were invited to examine their personal and professional orientations to the person, whose career development is their prime interest. It is possible that in the course of facilitating self-awareness, career exploration, career choice, or career transitions, a career service professional may operate from relatively fixed ideas about who is a person, and how open is the person's developmental trajectory. For example, the professional may believe in early formulations of the vocational personality with naught else thereafter, or at least no noteworthy novelties in later development (see Bakshi, 2014, Chap. 4). The overview of indigenous Western perspectives on the personality and those on the self, as well as the radically different indigenous Indian perspective, must convince career service professionals that there are multiple answers to the question, "Who is the person?"

The second point of reflection, given the volatility of lives, careers, and contexts, is to consider whether construals of the person favor adaptability. Thus it is relevant to ask: What are the varying points of view in the Western personality and self literatures with regard to the adaptability of the person; are the construals of the person angled towards positive development? What is the point of view in the Advaita position in Indian philosophical psychology? The Western personality literature is divided on its stance on modifiability of individuals, the Western self literature leans towards including modifiability,

and the Advaita position unequivocally is in support of modifiability or mutability. In fact, the Advaita position *rests on* modifiability or mutability. Explication of optimal goals in development and movement towards fulfillment are at times part of theoretical formulation about the person in Western personality or self literatures. In the Advaita position, they constitute the exclusive focal point: all efforts are centripetally (urged to be) directed towards this center. In turbulent times (e.g., Kotler & Caslione, 2009), which worldviews may enable resilience and positive development? At the level of the individual and that of a professional community, we have to reflect on our orientation to change/adaptability and the outcomes of such an orientation.

In presenting varied views on personality and self in this chapter, the intention has been to offer opportunities for reflection on contrasts and meeting-points within and across domains, within and across cultures. When there is knowledge of multiple points of view, one potential advantage is that one may be less likely to be bound only to one view, if not for one's own way-of-being, at least in relating to others whom we come across both personally and professionally. With globalization, internationalization, and cultural-diversification of most societies in the world, it is imperative that each of us broaden our outlook and hold plural frames of reference.

In the same vein, it is also timely to decolonize our minds. The economic and political colonization of regions of the world (e.g., India by the British) has been dismantled. Yet, in the dependence largely or solely on Western theory and research in academia and professional practice, the colonization of the mind and intellect has pervasively continued. It is time to liberate the mind and intellect from such hegemony. This is needed for both the Western and Eastern minds—for either to flourish. Diversity (as opposed to monopolization), after all, is not just a valued feature in an economy or in an ecosystem.

Exploration of ideas from multiple cultures promotes sensitivity to the particular, and sensitivity to the other. It helps us to become aware of and to deconstruct ethnocentrisms (see Leong & Pearce, 2014, Chap. 5). Simultaneously, despite the challenge of cultural relativism (in a cross-cultural dialogue) and the risks "of pleasing neither the traditionalist nor the modernist—neither the easterner nor the westerner," such explorations are worthwhile "because, if successful, we may find something of truly panhuman and transhistorical significance" (Paranjpe, 1988, p. 186).

New Concepts and Viewpoints: Charting New Directions

In relation to the person, notions of permanence, transience, finality, transcendence, mutability, agency, individuality, and oneness (for example) have been redefined in this chapter using an Eastern lens. In the Eastern or Advaita view, the personality (or the construal of self as personal) is serviceable and tenable up to a certain point on a path defined (exclusively) by spiritual goals. Personality, self, and intelligence—central constructs in Western psychology—have been presented in a new light that is simultaneously age-old. It is hoped that the diversity represented in this chapter vitalizes new developments in the career services field. The disenchantment with "test and tell" approaches in career guidance (Zelloth, 2014, Chap. 15); the growing attention to systems and narrative approaches respectful of both human agency and contextual influences (e.g., McMahon, Watson, & Patton, 2014, Chap. 3; Watson & McMahon, 2014, Chap. 35); the gathering impetus in favor of indigenization of psychology (Leong & Pearce, 2014, Chap. 5); the reentry of spirituality into Western psychology (e.g., Oser, Scarlett, & Bucher, 2006); and amplified interest in positive psychology, positive development, and thereby notions such as generosity, contribution, transcendence (e.g., Lerner, Roeser, & Phelps, 2008; Proyer, Sidler, Weber, & Ruch, 2012) are a few examples of related new directions already palpable in the Western literature.

One of the recommendations ensuing from this chapter is to use multicultural teams: a confident person from a non-Western background may bring in frames of reference that are not easily apprehensible to a Western researcher, theorist, or practitioner. Novelties and qualitative shifts that move a field ahead are brought about by those less tied to a paradigm or an ingrained way of thinking (Kuhn, 1970). Otherwise, anomalies may be invisible. Belief in the paradigm helps make it invulnerable to a precocious ending; at the same time, overly stable invulnerability chokes growth. There are times when it is best to move on, to break new ground. Now may be such a time.

References

Bakshi, A. J. (2014). Life span theory and career theories: Rapprochement or estrangement? In G. Arulmani, A. J. Bakshi, F. T. L. Leong, & A. G. Watts (Eds.), *Handbook of career development: International perspectives*. New York, NY: Springer.

Barrick, M. R., & Mount, M. K. (1991). The Big Five personality dimensions and job performance: A meta-analysis. *Personnel Psychology, 44*(1), 1–26.

Bierman, K. (1990). Improving the peer relations of rejected children. In B. B. Lahey & A. E. Kazdin (Eds.), *Advances in clinical child psychology* (pp. 131–149). New York, NY: Plenum Press.

Block, J. (2002). *Personality as an affect-processing system. Toward an integrative theory*. Mahwah, NJ: Lawrence Erlbaum.

Block, J., & Kremen, A. M. (1996). IQ and ego-resiliency: Conceptual and empirical connections and separateness. *Journal of Personality and Social Psychology, 70*(2), 349–361.

Brandtstädter, J. (2006). Action perspectives on human development. In W. Damon & R. M. Lerner (Series Eds.) & R. M. Lerner (Vol. Ed.), *Handbook of child psychology, Vol. 1: Theoretical models of human development* (pp. 516–568). Hoboken, NJ: Wiley.

Caspi, A. (1998). Personality development across the life course. In W. Damon (Series Ed.) & N. Eisenberg (Vol. Ed.), *Handbook of child psychology: Vol. 3. Social, emotional and personality development* (pp. 311–388). New York: Wiley.

Caspi, A., & Shiner, R. L. (2006). Personality development. In W. Damon & R. M. Lerner (Series Eds.) & N. Eisenberg (Vol. Ed.), *Handbook of child psychology, Vol. 3: Social, emotional, and personality development* (6th ed., pp. 300–365). Hoboken, NJ: Wiley.

Chinmayananda. (2011). *The holy Geeta. Commentary by Swami Chinmayananda*. Mumbai, India: Central Chinmaya Mission Trust.

Cooley, C. H. (1902). *Human nature and the social order*. New York: Charles Scribner. Retrieved from http://www.archive.org/details/humannaturesocia00cooluoft

Costa, P. T., Jr., & McCrae, R. R. (2008). The revised NEO Personality Inventory (NEO-PI-R). In G. J. Boyle, G. Mathews, & D. H. Saklofske (Eds.), *The SAGE handbook of personality theory and assessment, Vol. 2: Personality measurement and testing* (pp. 179–198). London, UK: Sage.

Dweck, C. S., & Molden, D. C. (2005). Self-theories: Their impact on competence motivation and acquisition. In A. J. Elliot & C. S. Dweck (Eds.), *Handbook of competence and motivation* (pp. 122–140). New York, NY: Guilford Press.

Elder, G. H., Jr., & Shanahan, M. J. (2006). The life course and human development. In W. Damon & R. M. Lerner (Series Eds.) & R. M. Lerner (Vol. Ed.), *Handbook of child psychology, Vol. 1: Theoretical models of human development* (pp. 665–715). Hoboken, NJ: Wiley.

Erikson, E. H. (1963). *Childhood and society* (2nd ed.). New York, NY: W.W. Norton.

Ferrari, M., & Sternberg, R. J. (1998). The development of mental abilities and styles. In W. Damon (Series Ed.) & D. Kuhn & R. Siegler (Vol. Eds.), *Handbook of child psychology* (Vol. 3, pp. 899–946). New York, NY: Wiley.

Freud, S. (2002). *The 'wolfman' and other cases*. New Delhi, India: Penguin.

Global Trends 2030. (2012). Retrieved from www.dni.gov/nic/globaltrends

Gottlieb, G., Wahlsten, D., & Lickliter, R. (2006). The significance of biology for human development: A developmental psychobiological systems view. In W. Damon & R. M. Lerner (Series Eds.) & R. M. Lerner (Vol. Ed.), *Handbook of child psychology, Vol. 1: Theoretical models of human development* (pp. 210–257). Hoboken, NJ: Wiley.

Hanh, T. N. (1999). *The miracle of mindfulness: An introduction to the practice of meditation*. Boston, MA: Beacon.

Harter, S. (2006). The self. In W. Damon & R. M. Lerner (Series Eds.) & N. Eisenberg (Vol. Ed.), *Handbook of child psychology, Vol. 3: Social, emotional, and personality development* (6th ed., pp. 505–570). Hoboken, NJ: Wiley.

Harter, S. (2012). *The construction of the self: Developmental and socio-cultural foundations*. New York, NY: Guilford Press.

Hermans, H. J. M. (2001). The dialogical self: Toward a theory of personal and cultural positioning. *Culture Psychology, 7*(3), 243–281.

Hermans, H. J. M., & Kempen, H. J. G. (1993). *The dialogical self: Meaning as movement*. San Diego, CA: Academic.

Holland, J. L. (1959). A theory of vocational choice. *Journal of Counseling Psychology, 6*, 35–45.

Holland, J. L. (1997). *Making vocational choices: A theory of vocational personalities and work environments*. Odessa, FL: Psychological Assessment Resources.

James, W. (1890/2007). *The principles of psychology* (Vol. 1). New York, NY: Cosimo Classics.

Kiesler, D. J. (1996). *Contemporary interpersonal theory and research: Personality, psychopathology, and psychotherapy*. New York, NY: Wiley.

Kotler, P., & Caslione, J. A. (2009). *Chaotics: The business of managing and marketing in the age of turbulence*. New York, NY: AMACOM.

Krishnamurti, J. (1972). *You are the world*. London, UK: Krishnamurti Foundation Trust.

Kuhn, T. S. (1970). *The structure of scientific revolutions*. Chicago, IL: University of Chicago Press.

Leong, F. T. L., & Pearce, M. (2011). Desiderata: Towards indigenous models of vocational psychology. *International Journal of Educational and Vocational Guidance, 11*(2), 65–77.

Leong, F. T. L., & Pearce, M. (2014). Indigenous models of career development and vocational psychology. In G. Arulmani, A. J. Bakshi, F. T. L. Leong, & A. G. Watts (Eds.), *Handbook of career development: International perspectives*. New York, NY: Springer.

Lerner, R. M. (2006). Developmental science, developmental systems, and contemporary theories of human development. In W. Damon & R. M. Lerner (Series Eds.) & R. M. Lerner (Vol. Ed.), *Handbook of child psychology, Vol. 1: Theoretical models of human development* (pp. 1–17). Hoboken, NJ: Wiley.

Lerner, R. M., Roeser, R. W., & Phelps, E. (2008). Positive development, spirituality, and generosity in youth. An introduction to the issues. In R. M. Lerner, R. W. Roeser, & E. Phelps (Eds.), *Positive youth development and spirituality: From theory to research* (pp. 1–24). Conshohocken, PA: Templeton Foundation Pres.

Leung, S. A. (2008). The Big Five career theories. In J. A. Athanasou & R. Van Esbroeck (Eds.), *International handbook of career guidance* (pp. 115–132). Berlin, Germany: Springer.

McAdams, D. P. (1993). *The stories we live by: Personal myths and the making of the self*. New York, NY: The Guilford Press.

McAdams, D. P. (2006, October). Moral personality, generativity, and the redemptive self. In J. Lies (Chair), *Notre Dame symposium on personality and moral character*. Symposium hosted by the Center for Ethical Education, University of Notre Dame, Indiana.

McCrae, R. R., & Costa, P. T., Jr. (1987). Validation of the Five-Factor Model of personality across instruments and observers. *Journal of Personality and Social Psychology, 52*(1), 81–90.

McIlveen, P., & Patton, W. (2007). Dialogical self: Author and narrator of career life themes. *International Journal for Educational and Vocational Guidance, 7*, 67–80.

McMahon, M., Watson, M., & Patton, W. (2014). Context-resonant systems perspectives in career theory. In G. Arulmani, A. J. Bakshi, F. T. L. Leong, & A. G. Watts (Eds.), *Handbook of career development: International perspectives*. New York, NY: Springer.

Mischel, W. (2004). Toward an integrative science of the person (Prefatory Chapter). *Annual Review of Psychology, 55*, 1–22.

Mischel, W., & Shoda, Y. (1995). A cognitive-affective system theory of personality: Reconceptualizing situations, dispositions, dynamics, and invariance in personality structure. *Psychological Review, 102*(2), 246–268.

Mischel, W., Shoda, Y., & Mendoza-Denton, R. (2002). Situation-behavior profiles as a locus of consistency in personality. *Current Directions in Psychological Science, 11*(2), 50–54.

Mroczek, D. K., & Spiro, A., III. (2003). Modeling intraindividual change in personality traits: Findings from the Normative Aging Study. *Journal of Gerontology: Psychological Sciences, 58B*(3), 153–165.

Mroczek, D. K., Spiro, A., III, & Almeida, D. M. (2003). Between- and within-person variation in affect and personality over days and years: How basic and applied approaches can inform one another. *Ageing International, 28*(3), 260–278.

Nisargadatta. (1973/1997). *I am that. Talks with Sri Nisargadatta Maharaj.* Mumbai, India: Chetana.

Oser, F. K., Scarlett, W. G., & Bucher, A. (2006). Religious and spiritual development throughout the life span. In W. Damon & R. M. Lerner (Eds.), *Handbook of child psychology, Volume I, Theoretical models of human development* (6th ed., pp. 942–998). Hoboken, NJ: Wiley.

Paranjpe, A. C. (1988). Personality theory according to Vedānta. In A. C. Paranjpe, D. Y. F. Ho, & R. W. Rieber (Eds.), *Asian contributions to psychology* (pp. 185–212). New York, NY: Praeger.

Plomin, R., DeFries, J. C., & Loehlin, J. C. (1977). Genotype–environment interaction and correlation in the analysis of human behavior. *Psychological Bulletin, 84*, 309–322.

Proyer, R. T., Sidler, N., Weber, M., & Ruch, W. (2012). A multi-method approach to studying the relationship between character strengths and vocational interests in adolescents. *International Journal of Educational and Vocational Guidance, 12*(2), 141–157.

Śaṅkarācārya, Ā. (2011). *Aparokṣānubhuti. Intimate experience of the reality. Commentary by Swami Chinmayananda.* Mumbai, India: Central Chinmaya Mission Trust (Original work published 8th/9th century AD).

Śaṅkarācārya, Ā. (2012). *Ātmabodha. Commentary by Swami Chinmayananda.* Mumbai, India: Central Chinmaya Mission Trust (Original work published 8th/9th century AD).

Savickas, M. L. (2002). Career construction: A developmental theory of vocational behavior. In D. Brown et al. (Eds.), *Career choice and development* (pp. 149–205). San Francisco, CA: Jossey-Bass.

Super, D. E. (1990). A life-span, life-space approach to career development. In D. Brown & L. Brooks (Eds.), *Career choice and development* (pp. 197–261). San Francisco, CA: Jossey-Bass.

Swann, W. B., Jr., & Buhrmester, M. D. (2012). Self as functional fiction. *Social Cognition, 30*(4), 415–430.

Swann, W. B., Jr., Chang-Schneider, C., & McClarty, K. L. (2007). Do people's self-views matter? Self-concept and self-esteem in everyday life. *American Psychologist, 62*(2), 84–94.

Swann, W. B., Jr., & Pelham, B. (2002). Who wants out when the going gets good? Psychological investment and preference for self-verifying college roommates. *Journal of Self and Identity, 1*, 219–233.

Thelen, E., & Smith, L. B. (2006). Dynamic systems theories. In W. Damon & R. M. Lerner (Series Eds.) & R. M. Lerner (Vol. Ed.), *Handbook of child psychology, Vol. 1: Theoretical models of human development* (pp. 258–312). Hoboken, NJ: Wiley.

Watson, M., & McMahon, M. (2014). Making meaning of quantitative assessment in career counseling through a story telling approach. In G. Arulmani, A. J. Bakshi, F. T. L. Leong, & A. G. Watts (Eds.), *Handbook of career development: International perspectives.* New York, NY: Springer.

Wiggins, J. S. (2003). *Paradigms of personality assessment.* New York, NY: The Guildford Press.

Yang, K.-S. (2012). Indigenous psychology, Westernized psychology, and indigenized psychology: A non-Western psychologist's view. *Chang Gung Journal of Humanities and Social Sciences, 5*(1), 1–32.

Zelloth, H. (2014). Technical and Vocational Education and Training (TVET) and career guidance: The interface. In G. Arulmani, A. J. Bakshi, F. T. L. Leong, & A. G. Watts (Eds.), *Handbook of career development: International perspectives.* New York, NY: Springer.

Zuroff, D. C. (1986). Was Gordon Allport a trait theorist? *Journal of Personality and Social Psychology, 51*(5), 993–1000.

Parental Influences on Youth's Career Construction

9

Salvatore Soresi, Laura Nota, Lea Ferrari,
and Maria Cristina Ginevra

Introduction

Numerous research studies have focused on the complex set of influences between parents and children; this includes the quality and quantity of experiences, including social experiences, which parents allow children to have right from early childhood. Researchers have highlighted that adequate learning styles, lack of exposure to deviant behaviors or traumas, and having the early opportunity to create positive social experiences, besides favoring children's cognitive development, allow for the development and strengthening of relational abilities necessary for social integration (e.g., Kowal, Kramer, Krull, & Crick, 2002; McDowell, Parke, & Spitzer, 2002). In this context, over the last 10 years an increasing number of career development scholars have recommended that the role of social relationships, especially those between parents and children, in the career development of children should be addressed more deeply (Blustein, 2001; Phillips, Carlson, Christopher-Sisk, & Gravino, 2001; Schultheiss, 2000, 2003; Schultheiss, Kress, Manzi, & Glasscock, 2001).

Some recent models and theoretical approaches (e.g., contextual action theory, social cognitive model, and the life design approach)

recognize the need to carefully consider the role that parents play in their children's career development.

1. Contextual action theory explicitly considers children's career development plans as part of the family and growth processes; in other words, a set of goals and actions identified by parents and their adolescent children to favor the latter's career development. Young et al. (2001) believe that the activities that adolescents carry out to the advantage of their career development are not independent but rather part of a complex hierarchy of family projects and goals.

2. The social cognitive model pivots around the self-efficacy construct, which is assumed to play a crucial role also as regards choice. People tend to develop interests, also professional ones, in activities they believe they are good at (self-efficacy) and that will allow them to achieve positive results (outcome expectations). On the other hand, people tend to avoid or not like activities they feel incompetent at and in which they think they will achieve negative results. Together with self-efficacy and outcome expectations, interests contribute to the choice of activities to be carried out (e.g., university majors or professional courses), which, in turn, can support a person to achieve his or her goals. Objectives and actions can be affected by contextual influences that may either facilitate or hinder achievement of one's own goals (Lent, 2007). In all of this, parents have a

S. Soresi (✉)
Department of Philosophy, Sociology, Education and Applied Psychology, University of Padua, Padua, Italy
e-mail: salvatore.soresi@unipd.it

G. Arulmani et al. (eds.), *Handbook of Career Development*, International and Cultural Psychology,
DOI 10.1007/978-1-4614-9460-7_9, © Springer Science+Business Media, LLC 2014

significant role, as they (a) favor exposure to certain experiences in childhood and adolescence; (b) facilitate the acquisition of abilities and knowledge and the development of specific self-efficacy beliefs, through performance accomplishments, vicarious experience, and verbal persuasion; (c) provide supports or create barriers, economic or interpersonal, which can influence the range of interests their children have (Bandura, 1997, 2012; Lent, Brown, & Hackett, 2000; Soresi & Nota, 2000).

3. The life design approach (Savickas et al., 2009) also emphasizes the parents' role, given that career construction is considered the result not only of intrapersonal but also of contextually built processes, and the family context is certainly one of the most significant for adolescents. Past and present family environments, interaction of the individual with these environments, and the way such environments have been observed and interpreted by the person are important. So, for instance, we have to take into account how often all the family members witness behaviors and aspects associated with work, from morning, when people get ready to go to work, until evening, when they return home and talk about what they and their colleagues have done at work, about their income and how adequate/inadequate it is, and about their working conditions, the loyalty of colleagues and employers, and so on.

These approaches value interactions between children and other family members, reciprocity and interdependence within the family, and also underline that children's development is influenced by parents' attitudes and behaviors. Further, as they consider their children's career achievements as one of their objectives in life, parents experience positive or negative feelings in relation to the development of adolescents' and young adults' career co-construction and, given the socioeconomic uncertainty people around the world are living with, they share feelings of worry and discomfort with their children. The emphasis on co-construction of career

is in line with the approaches that consider the family as a social system in which parent–child, marital, and sibling subsystems interact and influence the process of children's socialization (Parke & Buriel, 2006). These interactions are assumed to be influenced by many factors among which we can find family forms, cultural and practice beliefs, ethnicity, organization, lifestyle, etc.

In this chapter, taking into consideration the family as a system which includes multiple interrelated influences, the main focus is on one set of these influences, namely, parent influences. We will first overview literature from Western countries as well as examine some studies from non-Western countries that focus on the obstacles and challenges that parents have to cope with in this new century to adequately support their children's planning for the future. Next, we will present some research data that we have collected on parental influences in the Italian context. In the final part of the chapter, we will make some suggestions that might be useful in the implementation of career interventions led by parents, that is, which envisage their active involvement.

Challenges in Parenting in the New Century: Parents' Role in Their Children's Professional Development at a Time of Socioeconomic Crisis

Unlike those of past generations, today's parents find themselves playing their support role in their children's career development within much more complex societies and at a time of widespread socioeconomic crisis. Prospects of economic growth and development have decreased dramatically in many Western countries (e.g., Greece, Italy, Spain, the United States, Ireland), such that "the future is no longer what it once was" (Paul Valéry, as cited in Soresi, 2011). We are going toward a threatening future. We are transitioning from the first modernity, built on security, certainty, defined spaces for the individual and the community, to the second modernity characterized by insecurity, uncertainty, and the fall of all frontiers (Beck, 2000). We are going toward a *global-risk society*, in which we will have to deal with environmental crises, international terrorism, economic and health threats, new inequalities, increasing poverty, unemployment, precariousness, and underemployment even in the richest countries (Adam, 1998). Also, Zygmunt Bauman (2011), the sociologist of the so-called liquid society, has recently stated that unemployment and poverty are multiplying in such a way across the globe that the world will be in trouble if politics cannot determine a substantial change in course by exerting its control on the whims of markets and finance.

Poverty is expanding. In Western countries, between 1979 and 2005, the top 5 % of families saw their real incomes increase 81 %, whereas the bottom 20 % experienced a 1 % decline (Broda, Leibtag, & Weinstein, 2009). Globally today, the income of the 225 richest people equals that of the poorest 40 %—that is, 2.7 billion people (Glenn & Gordon, 2007). Increasing inequality creates enormous human immiseration and growing global instability, and indeed more and more families are finding themselves in such a situation.

Some parents may find it hard to plan for the future, particularly those who are experiencing underemployment, unemployment, and chronic illnesses. These experiences may cause them focus on the present rather than on the future. Thus, they do not encourage their children and do not start interactions centered on the future with them. Parents with low socioeconomic status (SES) reflect to their children the sense of hopelessness they feel about their own lives. When asked about their children's future, they rather talk about their own life, about the difficulties they themselves have encountered all along. Even if they are concerned that their children should not repeat their own mistakes, they do not say what their children should do to avoid them (Usinger, 2005). Sometimes, because of the work conditions they have experienced, parents confess very limited, low, or vague hopes for the future. Many merely say they want their children to "be happy" or to have a "good job."

Sometimes they may inadvertently exclude some occupational options for their children because of their own limited education and inadequate employment experiences. Such low aspirations may limit their children's career options and interests (Lindstrom, Doren, Metheny, Johnson, & Zane, 2007).

Higher levels of self-sufficiency are a primary developmental task for adolescents as they approach adulthood (Arnett, 2000). Favoring this transition is important to parents; it is a task they see as essential and to which they have committed themselves almost all through while taking care of their children. So much so that middle-aged parents often report that their own happiness is closely connected with the happiness of their adult children (Ryff, Schmutte, & Lee, 1996). Yet in crisis-ridden times, parental support in moving toward self-sufficiency is not guaranteed. This is especially pronounced for economic and career-related self-sufficiency. For example, in the United States and Singapore given the economic crisis and the few employment opportunities currently available, parents and adolescents are generally equally pessimistic in their overall perception of the economy, and personal economic pressure is generally related to self-reported anxiety and depression (Lim & Loo, 2003; Stein et al., 2011).

Challenges in Parenting in the New Century: Culturally Complex Societies and Immigrant Families

Parents who are experiencing compounded difficulties in today's culturally complex societies include those who are immigrants. In Western communities, there are a growing number of immigrant parents who have experienced dramatic cultural changes and now find themselves in a reality which is very different from what they had expected and hoped for. *Immigration* is a phenomenon in continuous evolution which today concerns almost all the countries in the world and impacts every sector of society. And more and more are the social occasions, from school to workplace, in which we all come into contact with people who come from cultures different from our own. Migration is an extremely stressful experience that negatively affects the well-being and functioning of immigrants and of refugees. Rumbaut (1991) stated that "*migration* can produce profound *psychological distress* among the most motivated and well prepared individuals and even in the most receptive circumstances" (p. 56).

For immigrant parents, job placement is often a strong challenge (Yakushko, 2006). Even if many immigrants choose to migrate to other countries to do any job just to help their families, most of them really wish to find a good job or a job that may allow them professional development (Diemer & Ali, 2009; Fouad & Fitzpatrick, 2009). However, they are soon disappointed and experience frustration with regard to their career aspirations (Berger, 2004; Yakushko, 2006). Adult immigrants, also with a family to keep, find themselves unemployed, underpaid, and unable to make use of the professional competencies they had acquired in their country of origin (Ali, Lewis, & Sandil, 2006; Berger, 2004). Also, they very seldom find a job in line with what they did in their country and with their abilities, and are often forced to work at the bottom of the professional ladder (Yakushko, 2006). Immigrants, moreover, often find only jobs that require physical work and in workplaces where the risk of accidents is higher (Center for Workforce Success, 2007; Pransky et al., 2002). Their earnings are usually low (Larsen, 2004) and frequently sent to the family they have left behind (Mehta et al., 2000). The children of these immigrants who live in our contexts often experience more barriers than nonimmigrant youth do, their potential can go unrealized, and their dreams may not be actualized (Teranishi, Suarez-Orozco, & Suarez-Orozco, 2011).

In addition to this, the culture of the host country could represent a barrier to family life and children's career development. *Acculturation* is the term used to describe the change that occurs when at least two different cultural groups interact. There tends to be an acculturation gap between parents and children due to differences in the rates of their interactions with the new culture; this could lead to parent–child conflict and negatively impact child outcomes (Phinney, Ong, & Madden, 2000). In various researches it has been found that in Indian, Latino, Russian, and Jewish families with a higher acculturation gap, the parent–child relationship is more problematic (Birman, 2006; Farver, Narang, & Bhadha, 2002; Martinez, 2006). In partial confirmation, Schofield, Parke, Kim, and Coltrane (2008), in their study with Mexican Americans, found the acculturation gap to exist only in relation to fathers. Further, the quality of the father–child relationship mediated the relationship between acculturation gap and father–child conflict. In other words, the stress due to the acculturation gap was lower when the father and child enjoyed a positive relationship. They also found that the quality of the father–child relationship mediated the relationship between acculturation gap and child outcomes: When children did not have positive relationships with their parents, the acculturation gap was associated with children's problem behaviors. Such findings underscore how important the quality of the parent–children relationship is for children's development.

Thus parents, who may have to cope with cultural challenges and/or have to face underemployment or unemployment in a precarious and perilous work market that jeopardizes their children's secure job placement, could experience difficulties in parent–child interactions and in investing in their children's education and training. All this can strongly affect their ability to facilitate youth's professional constructions. Clearly, this strongly highlights the need for career services that can assist parents as primary agents of socialization and primary supporters of their children's career life designing.

Socioeconomic Status and Children's Professional Development

In everyday life, parents can affect their children's professional development in many ways. Whiston and Keller (2004) have identified two interdependent contextual family factors that are important for adolescent career development: (a) structural family variables (e.g., parents' training and occupation, parents' SES and social class) and (b) process family variables (e.g., parents' aspirations, supplied supports, family interactions). As regards structural variables, we will examine socioeconomic background and social class.

Socioeconomic Background and School–Career Opportunities

Youth from low-income families seem to have more limited opportunities for career development and find it more difficult to access educational and social opportunities. High SES families offer greater possibilities for professional development, better education, traveling and study holidays, and a large number of advantageous social contacts. Schoon and Parsons (2002) observed that British youth from low-income families have reduced possibilities for professional development, lower access to educational and social opportunities, and nurture lower career aspirations than their peers from higher-income families. Also, British and the US adolescents from lower-SES families have lower career expectations than their peers from higher-SES families (Blustein et al., 2002; Rojewski & Kim, 2003; Schoon & Parsons, 2002). Wu (2009) conducted a study on 1,510 undergraduate students in Taiwan and concluded that a large proportion of students who attend prestigious universities come from middle and high socioeconomic groups. On the contrary, a large number of students who attend non-prestigious universities come from low SES communities, have parents without college preparation, and have to spend several hours a week in paid jobs. These disparities differentially influence students' college experiences, their career choices, and work opportunities; in fact, these remain at a lower level for poor students. Arulmani, Van Laar, and Easton (2003), who studied 1,366 Indian final-year high-school students, found that lower-SES adolescents

showed higher levels of negative career beliefs. Using the social learning theory of career decision-making (Mitchell, Jones, & Krumboltz, 1979), they concluded that negative career beliefs could contribute to the intergenerational perpetuation of poverty, because negative beliefs prevent individuals from grasping or persistently working toward better life chances. Also in Latino students, low SES has been found to thwart career development. Aguayo, Herman, Ojeda, and Flores (2011), in their study of a group of Mexican Americans, have reported that SES was a significant predictor of college self-efficacy and performance. College students with higher SES level showed higher self-efficacy in their college performance and better academic performance than students who had fewer financial resources.

Across cultures, parents from lower socioeconomic strata appear to have more difficulty in guiding their children's career development (Blustein et al., 2002; Bryant, Zvonkovic, & Reynolds, 2006). For example, in a study of highly talented US middle-school children from low-income families, Jordan and Plank (2000) found that lack of parental guidance in acquiring career information was the main reason why these adolescents did not attend college. In addition, Cinamon and Dan (2010) highlighted that low SES and uneducated Israeli Jewish parents demonstrated more negative attitudes toward the implementation of preschool career education programs that introduced children to their adult lives and their future work roles, and, moreover, specified that they never talked about occupations with their children. We believe such negative attitudes stem from the parents' own occupational and financial difficulties, and worries about the future.

However, also in families with low SES, higher parental support to children can positively affect children's development. In this regard, some researches (Raikes & Thompson, 2006, 2008) have revealed that when low-income parents show positive individual (e.g., high self-efficacy, no maternal depression) and socio-relational characteristics (e.g., high social support, secure attachment with their children, conducive family emotional climate), their relationships with children are more supportive; this, in turn, could help enhance children's development in multiple areas such as social, emotional, and cognitive. Regarding career development, Ali, McWhirter, and Chronister (2005) reported that social support may play a significant (buffering) role in lower-SES adolescents' career development. They studied a group of ninth-grade students in the United States and observed that social support was a significant predictor of educational and career self-efficacy expectations among lower-SES youth.

Social Class

Social class is a more difficult structural variable to define than SES. It has been analyzed mainly from three different perspectives (Ali, 2009): sociological, socioeconomic, and psychological. The sociological perspective considers macro-level forces and socio-structural constructs rather than internal traits and focuses on how access to external resources related to career issues (e.g., quality of neighborhood and schools, career role models, significant others' expectations) which vary by social class (as well as race/ethnicity) can affect career development and career attainment. The SES tradition, typically measured through educational/career achievement, income, and/or occupational prestige, is a quantitative approach which downplays the psychological impact of social class. A more psychological and phenomenological approach emphasizes how individuals understand their social class, how class shapes a person's view of the world, and how others view an individual because of his or her perceived social class. In line with this third perspective, Storck (1997) defined social class as:

> A person's level of education and type of occupation, combined with behaviors, thoughts and feelings that include expectations and value systems with which a person manages everyday life and his or her relationships with others, in local groups or larger communities and societies. (p. 334)

Liu, Soleck, Hopps, Dunston, and Pickett (2004) have devised the social class worldview model (SCWM), which considers how individuals behave within self-identified and self-constructed economic cultures. The model considers the influence of the following five components:

1. Consciousness, attitudes, and salience: These three interrelated constructs define the capacity to understand the importance of own social class. Specifically, consciousness is to do with the awareness of how social class characterizes one's life; attitudes include beliefs, feelings, values, and behaviors related to own social class; and salience refers to the significance and relevance of social class.
2. Referent groups comprise the people who influence the way the individual thinks of social class.
3. Property relationship means the role of materialism in a person's life.
4. Lifestyle is the way individuals organize their time and their resources to be consistent with the social class they think they belong to.
5. Behaviors entail resorting to purposeful and instrumental actions that reinforce an individual's social class worldview.

The SCWM provides a framework to understand how the economic culture and social class worldviews (also) in the family context can inform perceptions of working and class-based stereotypes. There are illustrative examples from research conducted in the United States. For example, Blustein et al. (2002) found that lower social class youth tended to view work as a means of survival or making ends meet, whereas upper social class youth tended to view work as a means of identity, life satisfaction, or upward mobility. Lapour and Heppner's (2009) findings endorse the view that privileged adolescents' career aspirations are upwardly mobile. They examined the perceived career options of ten girls who experienced social class privilege in their family. Their qualitative interviews showed that the adolescents tended to seek maintenance of their privileges by identifying occupations that could guarantee such maintenance. Those jobs that were not deemed in line with their social class, which if carried out, would lower their social status, were excluded from the range of options the adolescents considered potentially worthwhile. Owens (1992) highlighted that individuals from the higher classes have greater chances to attend university, while those from the lower classes directly enter the world of work or join the armed forces. Clearly, social class privilege helps create opportunities.

Social class is thus characterized as a cultural, psychological, and subjective factor internalized by the individual which goes beyond income, upbringing, and education, and would in any case shape the construction of the self (Blustein, Coutinho, Murphy, Backus, & Catraio, 2011). Career practitioners should then be urged to carefully consider the increasing poverty level reported in a number of Western societies. Poverty becomes manifest in a complex set of deprivations that impact communitarian and personal lives of individuals. Among those we can find public policy that reduces the investment in education, as is now happening in Europe; environments that do not promote the use and development of cognitive and noncognitive resources; and fewer parental and neighborhood social networks (Anand & Lea, 2011; Lin, 2001).

Parental Support, Family Interactions, and Children's Professional Development

Some scholars (Felsman & Blustein, 1999; Lindstrom et al., 2007) have explained that children invest in the school–career choice process in the context of parental support, positive family interactions, and parents' propensity to optimism. For example, youth from poor disadvantaged classes who live in the suburbs of North American cities and have experienced many discriminations such as racism and economic disparity seem to expect a career breakdown and predict their own failure even before they start a job (Barling, 1991). Such youth may find an important source of support in their family. In multiple ethnic groups (i.e., African-Americans,

Latino, Chinese-American), parental support and positive parent–adolescent relationships have been identified as protective factors against disengagement, guaranteeing better school and career adjustment and a more satisfactory quality of life (Brewster & Bowen, 2004; Juang & Alvarez, 2010; Kenny, Blustein, Chaves, Grossman, & Gallagher, 2003; Sirin & Rogers-Sirin, 2004).

In accordance with systemic approaches, researchers have clarified that the quality of the parent–child relationship is subject to multiple influences including family form and ethnicity, which impact child outcomes. In this regard, Leidy et al. (2011) studied 393 Mexican-American and European-American adolescents and their parents in order to examine whether fathering behaviors were associated with preadolescent adjustment. They found that in stepfamilies the quality of parenting was lower than in intact families and could be considered an index of lower involvement, monitoring, and acceptance. Moreover, both Mexican-American and European-American adolescents in stepfather families showed a higher risk of maladjustment than their peers in intact families, probably due to a high level of perceived stress.

Support, Context Exploration, and Decidedness

Adolescents in the United States who perceive greater support are more engaged in designing their school–career future than those who perceive lower parent support (Blustein, Walbridge, Friedlander, & Palladino, 1991; Felsman & Blustein, 1999; Ketterson & Blustein, 1997; Lindstrom et al., 2007). Vignoli, Croity-Belz, Chapeland, de Fillipis, and Garcia (2005) in a study with final-year high-school students found that the more French adolescents show secure attachment to parents, the more they explore their educational and career environments. Vignoli et al. maintain that the quality of the relationship between parents and adolescents provides emotional support, which buffers the threatening effects of school–career transition and facilitates environmental and vocational exploration regarding occupations, jobs, organizations, and educational pathways through visiting career counseling centers, requesting information, reading brochures, and even seeking out information not linked to career plans.

Some career research has been focused on the impact of parental support on career decision/indecision. Career indecision could be defined as an inability to make a decision about the vocation one wishes to pursue (Guay, Senécal, Gauthier, & Fernet, 2003). Career decision involves a commitment to career choice and exploration and could be considered a measure of career development (Guerra & Braungart-Rieker, 1999). The more one takes care of the future and tries to prepare for one's career future, choosing and assuming both responsibilities and risks, the more one can cope with career tasks (Savickas & Porfeli, 2012). In this regard, Guerra and Braungart-Rieker (1999) have argued that the perception of positive and supportive relationships with parents is also associated with higher levels of decision regardless of the student's age. Adolescents who perceive their mother as favoring and supporting their own autonomy and independence show less indecision than those who perceive their mother as too protective. Guay et al. (2003) studied French-Canadian college students and observed that when parents supported their career-choice autonomy by providing information, feedback, and involvement, students showed higher career self-efficacy beliefs and career decision-making autonomy, and perceived that they were able to make decisions about the future of their careers. Nota, Ferrari, Solberg, and Soresi (2007) have reported similar findings; although in their research, the relationships between family support, self-efficacy beliefs, and career decisions were different for boys and girls. Using a sample of 253 Italian high-school students, they found a partial-mediation model supported for boys. In contrast, a full-mediation model was found supported for girls. In other words, parental support predicted career indecision in boys both directly and indirectly (i.e., mediated through career search self-efficacy). Contrary to

expectations, for girls there was no direct relationship between perceived parental support and career indecision; the role of parental support as a predictor of adolescent girls' career indecision was fully mediated through career search self-efficacy. These results are consistent with the social cognitive career theory with its premise that family support plays a role in career decision-making through career search self-efficacy (Lent, 2007).

Vignoli (2009) also found that parental support was important for adolescents' career development in a group of French adolescents. Adopting the attachment paradigm, she observed that the more girls felt attached to their mother and boys felt attached to their father, the easier it was for them to make career decisions. She also found that this relation was mediated by self-esteem in both genders. This suggests that secure attachment provides a base from which one can explore with self-confidence; it also helps adolescents make decisions about their career choices and encourages them to take the risk associated with the decisional process.

The support provided within the family can be related to the cultural context, in particular, individualistic versus collectivistic orientations. For instance, Howard, Ferrari, Nota, Solberg, and Soresi (2009) examined the role of supportive relationships established by family, teachers, and peers, and sense of agency (e.g., self-efficacy, motivation, and goal-setting orientation) on three outcomes: academic grades, distress, and career decidedness. Multi-group comparison and a subsequent test of mediation using data from 588 middle-school youth from Northern ($n = 322$) and Southern ($n = 266$) Italy showed that the role of supportive relationships differs across gender and region (see Figs. 9.1 and 9.2). The role of family support emerged both in the Northern and Southern Italy and indicates that parents have a positive role in the career development of their children.

Nevertheless some differences were obtained between the two regions: Family support was directly related to career decidedness for youth from Northern but not Southern Italy. This regional difference may be due to how different

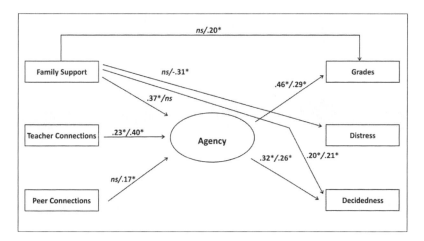

Fig. 9.1 Model for adolescents from Northern Italy (boys/girls). *Note*: For ease of interpretation only paths that were significant for at least one group are shown. Path coefficients are presented in pairs: Coefficients for male adolescents are presented first and those for female adolescents are presented second (adapted from Howard et al., 2009). *Asterisks* denote a significant path coefficient at the .05 level

economic conditions impact the perceived need for making early career decisions. The industrial economy of Northern Italy creates many occupational opportunities and selecting a high school will often rule out many occupations due to the specialization of studies that are offered. For this reason, families in Northern Italy more strongly emphasize the importance of early career exploration. These economic differences could interact with cultural differences and also explain gender differences across region. Communities in the North of Italy are more inclined toward individualistic values and have a modern idea of family and education. Communities in the South of Italy are considered more inclined toward collectivistic values and have a traditional and more Catholic idea of family and education. It is possible that boys in Southern Italy are often expected to continue their fathers' professions and girls in Southern Italy are often expected to work in the home and only part-time outside the home. In contrast, boys in the North are expected to be autonomous in their career decision-making and are required to achieve career success outside the family context, whereas girls in the North are expected to make their career-related decisions and have a career but at the same time maintain some strong connectedness with their family of origin. Surprisingly, teacher

connections had a negative influence on grades in the boys of Southern Italy. It could be speculated that for these boys friendliness with teachers meant that there was a reduced need to obtain approval and therefore they could relax their standards with regard to school achievement.

Congruent with systemic approaches, research emphasizes the relevant role of family interactional processes in facilitating career exploration. When parents are open about discussing issues, share new information in a friendly manner, try to understand their children's desires and developments, and promote autonomous thinking and actions, adolescents are more involved in career exploration and construction (Vondracek & Hartung, 2002). Adopting such an educational style could contribute to creating the conditions for supporting engagement with lifelong learning (i.e., learning during different phases of career construction across life) (Savickas et al., 2009).

Support, Self-Efficacy Beliefs, and Career Adaptability

When focusing on the role of parental behaviors in facilitating adolescents' career development, some studies have addressed general aspects of

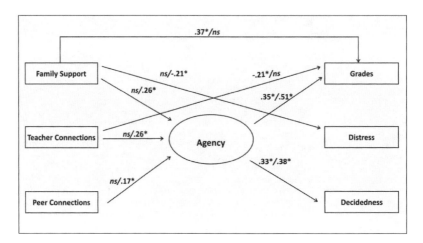

Fig. 9.2 Model for adolescents from Southern Italy (boys/girls). *Note*: For ease of interpretation only paths that were significant for at least one group are shown. Path coefficients are presented in pairs: Coefficients for male adolescents are presented first and those for female adolescents are presented second (adapted from Howard et al., 2009). *Asterisks* denote a significant path coefficient at the .05 level

the parent–adolescent relationship as predictors of career self-efficacy (Guay et al., 2003; Lim & Loo, 2003; O'Brien, Friedman, Tipton, & Linn, 2000; Ryan, Brown, & Solberg, 1996). Whiston (1996), for instance, has found that both US boys' and girls' career decision-making self-efficacy is positively correlated with the degree to which the family encourages and supports independence and autonomy in a wide range of activities. Restubog, Florentino, and Garcia (2010) have examined the relationship between parental support, number of career counseling sessions received, self-efficacy, level of decidedness, and academic persistence in a group of students enrolled in a nursing program in the Philippines. They found that, consistent with their hypotheses, parental support in addition to the number of career counseling sessions received can be useful in sustaining career-related self-efficacy beliefs by providing positive reinforcements in the form of verbal encouragement, informational advice, and practical support. In turn, high career self-efficacy increases a person's career decidedness, which then leads to greater persistence in academic programs.

With regard to self-efficacy beliefs in mathematics and science, Ferry, Fouad, and Smith (2000), using a sample drawn from two US universities, have found that parental encouragement is directly related to self-efficacy beliefs, outcome expectations, and interest in mathematical–scientific occupations among undergraduate students aged 17–23 years. Turner, Steward, and Lapan (2004) and Fouad and Smith (1996) have found that the US middle-school students' self-efficacy beliefs in mathematics are positively related to their outcome expectations and interest in mathematical–scientific occupations. Turner et al. (2004) have underlined the fundamental role of maternal support as an influence on outcome expectations in mathematics. Maternal support in exploring mathematical occupations and in finding connections between studying mathematical–scientific disciplines and possible occupations was found to be especially important in developing children's positive expectations. Turner and Lapan (2002), focusing on middle-school students in the United States, have found that perceived parental support with regard to Holland's six occupational categories (realistic, investigative, social, artistic, enterprising, and conventional) predicts level of self-efficacy across Holland themes, which in turn influences interest in the six professional areas. These results suggest that there is an association between perceived parental support in pursuing different professional paths and adolescents' self-confidence with regard to potential success in these professions; this can strongly impact the school–career choices that young adolescents have to make.

Ginevra, Nota, and Ferrari (2011) in a study involving 100 Italian adolescents ($M_{age} = 16.9$ years; SD = 0.77 years) and 200 parents (100 fathers and 100 mothers) administered the following questionnaires to adolescents: Career Decision Self-Efficacy Scale—Short-Form (Betz, Klein, & Taylor, 1996; Nota, Pace, & Ferrari, 2008), to assess adolescents' degree of confidence in their career decision-making abilities; and Thoughts about the Future (Nota, Ferrari, & Soresi, 2007), to identify possible irrational ideas and dysfunctional thoughts associated with one's future. Irrational ideas are maladaptive beliefs regarding self, world, decisional processes, and conditions for career satisfaction (Krumboltz, 1991). These beliefs include generalizations, illogical thinking, and distortions of reality which tend to lower career confidence, career flexibility, openmindedness, and willingness in making efforts to obtain work. They might hinder systematic and organized thinking about the future and behaviors fostering career adaptability and advantageous decision-making (Saunders, Peterson, Sampson, & Reardon, 2000; Savickas, 2005). At the same time, parents were asked to fill out the questionnaire The Children's Future (Nota, Ginevra, Ferrari, & Soresi, 2012), which assesses parental support for school–career choices. Specifically, it is a unidimensional scale that focuses on parents' tendency to give support and encouragement to their children about the future and their propensity to encourage professional exploration. In line with literature (Restubog et al., 2010; Whiston, 1996), parental support that aided children's reflection on the future and professional exploration predicted somewhat higher self-efficacy beliefs in decision-making about the future among adolescents ($\beta = .176$; $p < .05$). In addition, Ginevra et al. (2011) observed that parental support modestly predicted less irrational ideas in the adolescents ($\beta = -.153$; $p < .05$). These irrational ideas are internalized from familial or

societal messages (Roll & Arthur, 2002), and those shown by children are considered the outcome of interactions with parents (Krumboltz, 2009). Therefore, parents may play a significant role in fostering openmindedness, flexibility, curiosity about the world, and positive perceptions of the possibilities in the future. Parents can support their children to create, recognize, and facilitate positive chance events in their life designing and help them to anticipate opportunities, thus favoring the development of career adaptability (Krumboltz, 2009).

Personal initiative and career adaptability have become key career development factors (Savickas et al., 2009). Career adaptability is conceptualized as a "psychosocial construct that denotes an individual's resources for coping with current and anticipated tasks, transitions, traumas in their occupational roles that, to some degree large or small, alter their social integration" (Savickas & Porfeli, 2012, p. 662). It includes the tendency to become concerned about the career future (concern), take control of trying to prepare for one's career future (control), reveal curiosity by exploring possible selves and future scenarios (curiosity), and strengthen the confidence to pursue one's aspirations (confidence) (Savickas & Porfeli, 2012).

Recent studies focus on the relevance of social and parental supports for facilitating career adaptability. Hirschi (2009), for example, considered the perception of social support; in a sample of 330 Swiss eighth-grade students, supportive social context beliefs (i.e., the informative, emotional, and concrete support perceived from parents, teachers, friends, and significant others) significantly predicted career adaptability. Using a sample of 322 US ninth graders, Kenny and Bledsoe (2005) showed that adolescents who perceived more emotional parental support, and also teacher and close friend support, reported higher levels of career adaptability. Also, Nota and Soresi (2012) have reported similar results. In their study, involving 94 Italian high-school students and both their parents, parental support, assessed by The Children's Future (Nota et al., 2012), was a significant predictor of adolescents' career adaptability, assessed by the Italian Form of Career Adapt-Abilities Inventory (Soresi, Nota, & Ferrari, 2012). In addition, they observed that higher level of career adaptability in parents was associated with higher levels of hope, optimism, career aspirations, and career adaptability in their children.

Career adaptability is considered a key requisite that people across different life stages have to demonstrate in order to cope with the uncertainty and rapid changes that characterize the actual world of work. Optimally, its development should start from infancy and should be fostered across the life-span (Hartung, Porfeli, & Vondracek, 2008). In this regard, parents can play a crucial role and career counselors can help them to facilitate the development of career adaptability in their children through engagement in specific activities.

Interactions with Parents and Ideas About Professional Life

It is in the family that children begin to give meaning to the world of work, to study, and to leisure, by observing family members and listening to them recount their work experiences (Galambos & Sears, 1998). From these discussions, young people construct their idea of education and work and of their career lives, even before their formal education begins (Bryant et al., 2006; Soresi & Nota, 2009).

In the family, children learn that their parents, and maybe their brothers and sisters, go to work and this is one of the early sources of knowledge on occupations. The higher the mother's command of the language, the more detailed the descriptions that children give of occupations (Jordan & Pope, 2001). Although some children base their knowledge of adult work on direct observations of their parents at work, most children's knowledge of adult work comes about indirectly or incidentally by overhearing conversations about work (Galinsky, 2000). However, the messages that children extract from these conversations appear to provide a biased impression of adult work and incomplete

knowledge of how parents feel about their jobs. Galinsky found that 61 % of fathers and 69 % of mothers reported that they liked their work "a lot" but only 41 % of children thought that their parents liked their work. He also found that children were more aware of the financial rather than the psychological rewards of their parents' work, that children perceived their parents' attitudes toward work more negatively than was actually the case, and that children had little direct knowledge of their parents' work.

Ginevra and Nota (2010) conducted a semi-structured interview with a group of 80 Italian adolescents and their parents with the aim of examining their concepts of work, study, and leisure. They involved parents from low (27.5 %), middle (52 %), and high SES (20.5 %). The parents' age ranged from 36 to 65 years ($M_{age} = 46.6$ years; SD = 5.04 years). Using qualitative methods, they found that both parents and adolescents tended to consider work first as a means to obtain financial advantages and second as a means to achieve personal satisfaction. In addition, both parents' and adolescents' answers outlined the idea that study is an instrument for personal growth that can impact professional development and that can incite positive (a sense of pleasure and enjoyment) and negative (boredom and sense of fatigue) feelings. As regards leisure, they observed that the concept of leisure was seen as an opportunity to rest, do pleasant activities, be socially committed, express oneself, and achieve realization. In addition, using quantitative (log-linear) analyses (see Table 9.1) they observed significant two-way interactions between participant type (parents vs. children) and mentioned versus not mentioned category. Specifically, children mentioned more frequently than their parents that work was a means to earn money, the negative aspects of study, and the idea that leisure was a time that allows one to rest and relax and was a time other than work or study. However, these significant differences were observed for only 4 out of the 16 categories. Accordingly, this seems to indicate that parents and adolescents have overlapped or shared perceptions of work, study, and leisure.

Table 9.1 Log-linear parameter estimates, values, and goodness-of-fit index

Domain	Subcategory	λ	Z	p
Definition of work	Economic advantages	−.161	−2.38	<.01
Definition of study	Negative aspects	−.345	−3.13	<.01
Definition of leisure	Participating in relaxing activities	−.133	−2.36	<.01
Definition of leisure	Time other than work or study	−.175	−2.33	<.01

As regards perceptions about work, research conducted in diverse countries shows that parents who have unfavorable work experiences (e.g., perceive their work to be a barrier to their family responsibilities, have inflexible and extended work schedules, and/or have insecure jobs that demand simple and repetitive tasks) tend to have children with lower academic achievement, less prestigious career aspirations, and decreased confidence in their future (Barling & Mendelson, 1999; Cinamon, 2001; Galinsky, 1999). Porfeli, Wang, and Hartung (2008) studied 100 US children aged about 11 and found that their expectations about the emotions and experiences they presumed they would have in future at work were correlated with the perceived positive or adverse emotions and experiences their parents were perceived to have at work, and both impacted children's motivation to engage in their school and future work settings. Porfeli and Ferrari (2011) reconfirmed these findings in a research involving 326 Italian families with children aged 8–11 years. Specifically, they found that the relationship between fathers' work valence (favorable and unfavorable work experiences and emotions) and boys' work valence was mediated by boys' perceptions of their fathers' work valence, and that the relationship between mothers' work valence and girls' work valence was mediated by girls' perceptions of their mothers' work valence. This pattern of relationship did not emerge for the opposite gender alignment of girls–fathers and boys–mothers.

Propensity to Optimism

In times of crisis and uncertainty like those characterizing many countries currently, the optimism existing in the parent–child relationship can play an important role. Dispositional optimism is the positive expectation of beneficial results by the individual when handling major problems or deep stress (Carver & Scheier, 2002; Scheier & Carver, 1985). Personal optimism has been found to be associated with greater adaptation and adjustment (Ben-Zur, 2003; Chang & Sanna, 2003; Soresi, Nota, Ferrari, & Sgaramella, in press). The experience of effective, supportive, and optimistic parenting in one's childhood fosters the growth of an optimistic view of the world in the child and then later in the adult that he or she becomes. The mediational role of optimism has also been endorsed in research in many cultures. Lemola et al. (2010) found that Finnish parents' reports of their children's optimism and pessimism were connected with their own optimism and pessimism, and that children who showed more optimism also showed higher levels of self-esteem, social competence, extraversion, effortful control, and lower negative affectivity and behavior problems. As regards Asian collectivistic culture, Chong, Huan, Yeo, and Ang (2006) studied 519 middle-school students in Singapore and found that adolescents who perceived positive support from their family, peers, and school displayed greater optimism and that positive support was associated with higher psychological adjustment and school satisfaction. This is also in line with Ben-Zur's (2003) results. He found dispositional optimism to play a significant role in Israeli adolescents' well-being and showed that positive relationships with parents were related to adolescents' greater mastery and optimism. Similar data have been found in the Italian context: In a research involving 130 high-school students and their parents, it was found that parents' optimism and hope predicted their children's optimism (Coppola, 2011).

However, daily interactions at home about the working experiences of adult family members and their more or less optimistic attitude toward work also seem to play an important role in forming career knowledge networks, and impact the way children and adolescents think of work and of their future opportunities. In any case, as concerns professional planning, propensity to optimism facilitates greater professional exploration, higher investment in setting goals, and more responsibility about one's future (Patton, Bartrum, & Creed, 2004). It also encourages preparedness because it makes people more aware of the career tasks and occupational transitions they have to face and the choices that need to be made in the near and distant future (Savickas, 2005; Savickas & Porfeli, 2012).

Preventive Career Education and the Involvement of Parents

From an application point of view, helping parents adequately support the realization of their children's professional projects represents a key strategy for achieving preventive goals in career education. The life design approach maintains that:

> Vocational guidance can no longer confine itself to intervening at transition times and making predictions or proposing suggestions on the basis of present stocktaking. It should also include a markedly preventive role. It is necessary to act on settings, looking for early preventive alliances and collaborations (Savickas et al., 2009, p. 245).

Parents should be involved in activities in order to ensure that children can benefit from opportunities that are more equitable; this can help reduce social and economic disadvantages and the early experience of discrimination (McLeroy & Wendel, 2011).

Caplan (1964) has grouped prevention programs into three large categories: (a) primary prevention programs entail preventing or altering the predictors of future difficulties; for example, creating supportive networks that facilitate the conditions for a positive career development; (b) secondary prevention programs are aimed at inhibiting the onset of future difficulties as much as possible by means of early assessment and intervention; (c) tertiary prevention programs are aimed at giving support in situations that are already presenting difficulties and discomfort. The first category includes programs for teachers and parents aimed at increasing their abilities to facilitate the professional development of students and adolescent children.

If parents were adequately trained and supported with regard to issues of career development, they could become our strong allies, given that: (a) Generally, parents are more interested in their children's future than other supporters such as peers, teachers, and career counselors. (b) Parents who activate supportive relationships with their children encourage context exploration, support learning in diverse settings, and contribute to the development of self-efficacy beliefs and positive outcome expectations in their children (Paa & McWhirter, 2000; Ryan et al., 1996; Wolfe & Betz, 2004). (c) Parents are privileged witnesses of their children's interests and abilities and those who have a more positive relationship with their children could facilitate their career development, expanding the range of activities the children engage in and giving them positive feedback. Moreover, in accordance with the recent life design approach, parents are a relevant source for fostering their children's career adaptability and helping them sustain a positive life design. (d) Parents can contribute to spreading an educational and preventive conception of career education not only within their own family but also with other parents. They can advertise the importance of assisting children in developing abilities considered crucial in a number of career models (e.g., self-efficacy, self-determination, problem-solving skills) (Nota, 2007; Soresi, Nota, & Ferrari, 2006).

Examples of Practice Interventions

We believe that career services should do a lot more to implement career education projects "in favor of sons and daughters." In addition to promoting mass media debates and reports on the importance of career education and of parents' roles, they should make publications expressly directed to parents more readily available. As examples, we will describe two parent training programs.

The first is titled *The Partners Program*. Based on a developmental framework, it is a structured program for parents, designed to promote career planning and development of their adolescent children (Whiston & Keller, 2004). It can be conducted in group or self-administered format. When self-administered, the parent is required to study the manual before helping his/her child to complete the workbook. The program follows the stages of the career counseling: self-awareness, through exercises that help in matching self with occupations; career awareness, useful in identifying career options and translating individual motives into career goals; reflection and decision; and lastly, planning, that is, making a plan for one or more occupations. Therefore, it comprises the use of a manual that highlights the role of parents in their children's career development, and three workbooks. These include a self-exploration workbook (Activity Self-Exploration Workbook, Cochran & Amundson, 1985) that facilitates the identification of interests, values, and strengths through the analysis of past and current activities; a Career Grid Workbook (Cochran, 1985a) that focuses on exploration of career values and occupations and on a systematic evaluation of career options; and a Planning Workbook (Cochran, 1985b) that assists parents and their children in career planning for one or more occupations. This workbook also includes three scenarios to help make a planning vocabulary. The efficacy of the program has been tested in two studies with Canadian parents and their high-school adolescents. Palmer and Cochran (1988) found that adolescents reported higher career orientation and a strengthening of bonding with parents. Kush and Cochran (1993) found that the experimental group reported less career indecision and greater career confidence and motivation at posttest (effect size of .27).

The second is the *Career Education for Children* (Soresi & Nota, 2009; Soresi, Nota, & Ferrari, 2007a). It is a parent training program that invites participation from parents either before or parallel to the career education interventions planned for their children in order to facilitate the use of the same language and stimulate a similar way of conceiving career construction. The content of this parent program includes dimensions that are useful in achieving personal and satisfactory career projects. For example, we looked at the most important things that are examined with an undecided or insecure individual during career counseling and what could be done by parents with their children in similar situations. Table 9.2 presents the *didactic units* that could be directed to parents. Each didactic unit could lead to an in-depth study of a specific issue and involve parents for a 2-hour session.

The training was administered to a group of 20 parents, 12 mothers (M_{age} 42.34 years; SD = 4.12 years), and 8 fathers ($M_{age} = 44.5$ years; SD = 3.51 years) of high-school adolescents who were on the verge of school-to-school or school-to-work transitions. The parents lived in a largely rural underprivileged economy in Northern Italy (the Rovigo province). Two of the parents had a college degree, eight had a high-school diploma, and ten had a middle-school certificate.

The questionnaire How much confidence do I have in myself? (Soresi, Nota, & Ferrari, 2007b) that measures the self-efficacy beliefs in one's own educational abilities and the questionnaire My life as a Parent (Soresi et al., 2007b) that measures the satisfaction with quality of life in different domains were administered at pre- and posttest. Quantitative tests included repeated measures ANOVA. Parents on completion of the parent program had higher self-efficacy beliefs in their ability to support their children ($F[1,19] = 28.86$; $p = .01$; Cohen's $d = .78$), higher levels of satisfaction with relationships with their children ($F[1,19] = 21.99$; $p = .01$; Cohen's $d = .66$), and higher levels of satisfaction with self-determination opportunities for

Table 9.2 The didactic units of the parent training "Career Education for Children"

Career Education for Children—an early involvement program for parents (Soresi et al., 2007a)
1. *Overview of the course*: After a brief description of the course, we presented data on adolescents' perceived insecurity about the future, on the importance parents attribute to future career projection, and on the difficulties parents often report, and encouraged discussion on these issues
2. *Interests*: After defining interests, we discussed with parents that they can "urge" their children to do several things and support them when having novel experiences (Savickas, 2005) to favor a wide range of interests, which in turn increases choice opportunities (Lent et al., 2000)
3. *Self-efficacy beliefs*: After defining and explaining about self-efficacy beliefs, we presented the sources of self-efficacy beliefs and started a discussion on the role of parents, especially with regard to "self-efficacy beliefs in mathematics and decisions about the future." Self-efficacy beliefs in mathematics are considered relevant for career development because they seem to assure a wider range of career choices (Fouad et al., 2010)
4. *Irrational ideas and openmindedness*: After examining the definition of irrational ideas and analyzing some examples, a discussion was started on the consequences of having irrational ideas
5. *How and when to speak of career education in the family*: We facilitated their ability to start a dialog about school–career choices, to express intentions, to keep an "open" attitude, and try to check their understanding of other people's viewpoint in a calm way, and to resort to reiteration
6. *How to help one's children focus on their career goals with creativity*: Parents were encouraged to reflect on strategies they could use to foster their children's creativity in exploring additional career options and were steered toward considering the idea of goals and planning the future by connecting the past and present
7. *How to help one's child to get information on career options*: Parents were invited to encourage their children to think of several career options by putting together their ideas and reflections on careers and the world of work and to stimulate novel exploration through interviews and direct observation
8. *How to help one's child choose among options*: Adaptive and maladaptive decisional styles were discussed. Parents were invited to analyze with their children the career options of the latter
9. *Transitions and the journey "toward" the future*: Parents were encouraged to consider the transitions that their children were going to face and were invited to discuss ways to support them
10. *How to support self-determination in one's child*: Parents were encouraged to consider some data on the relation between self-determination, time perspective, creativity, and optimism among youth, and discuss the importance of supporting their children's self-determination

their children $(F[1,19] = 10,83;$ $p = .004;$ Cohen's $d = .59$).

We also used qualitative procedures. Drawing on McAdams's (1995) and Rehfuss's (2009) work, we asked parents at the beginning and at the end of the intervention to write answers to the following:

1. Could you please write down a few lines or a brief paragraph about what you hope for your son's/daughter's future?
2. Could you please complete the following statement: "I think Career Education is..."

Before the intervention, the following issues emerged in answers to the first question:

1. Choice: (a) making a conscious choice (e.g., Parent No. 3: "I would like him to make a conscious career choice when he leaves school"); and (b) making a choice in line with interests and aspirations (e.g., Parent No. 7: "I hope my daughter will make a choice based on her interests").

2. Career possibilities: (a) chances of job placement (e.g., Parent No. 16: "I would like him to find a job, given the crunch we are experiencing these days"); and (b) economic security (e.g., Parent No. 18: "I hope she can find a job that will enable her to make a living").

As regards the second question, the following issues emerged before the intervention: (a) career education understood as proper advice (e.g., Parent No. 1: "A good piece of advice for my child"); (b) career education understood as a means to support youth in decision-making (e.g., Parent No. 5: "It is above all a way to help youth make a decision"); and (c) career education understood as the action of experts (e.g., Parent No. 13: "It is a difficult issue that should be left up to counselors or teachers"). What can be especially observed are fuzzy hopes and an idea of career education based on advice and on the role that career counselors could have in promoting career development.

At the end of the training, parents' narrations still partly contained issues similar to those mentioned at the pretest, but they were more organic and detailed and they also included new issues. This shows that in-depth thinking and reappraisal had taken place and that some issues had been better mastered and more greatly reflected on. In response to the first question, the following issues emerged:

1. Choice: (a) making a conscious choice following exploration of several possibilities and options (e.g., Parent No. 14: "I would like my son to make a decision about the future after wholly understanding what it means to do different jobs"); and (b) youth making a choice in line with their interests and aspirations by getting rid of irrational career beliefs (e.g., Parent No. 2: "I hope my daughter will reason about her future and take full advantage of her abilities because, even if she is a woman, she will have to get along by herself").

2. Career possibilities: (a) job satisfaction (e.g., Parent No. 20: "I would like my daughter to find a job that will enable her to grow and find satisfaction in her work as a person, and also to pursue her career goals"); and (b) ability to cope with transitions (e.g., Parent No. 17: "I hope he will be able to exploit the opportunities that will come his way and also be satisfied").

3. Relationships: having a family life and developing abilities to play different roles (e.g., Parent No. 11: "I wouldn't like it if he was appreciated only for the way he does his job . . . I would like him to be also a good husband and father").

As to the second question the following issues emerged after the training:

1. Career education concerns the ability to plan one's own future (e.g., Parent No. 6: "Career education doesn't mean giving advice on this or that profession. It means learning to see the different aspects of this or that profession and set one's own professional goals").

2. Career education is a constructive dialog between parents and children, which must be properly supported (e.g., Parent No. 10: "As a parent, I think it means to reason with my children at a time when they ask for support and to help them realize their dreams"). Attention seems to have been given to the "process," to "how to do." Very importantly parents appeared to acknowledge and value co-construction and their own role in explicitly supporting their child's career development (Nota & Soresi, 2010).

New Concepts and Viewpoints: Charting New Directions

These two programs we have presented could inspire "original" national and local editions when modified or adapted to suit particular cultures and socioeconomic circumstances. Also, one can design interactive online programs specifically directed to parents. These programs could become part of broader community programs that aim to increase family health and well-being and also prevent poverty in more disadvantaged areas. Adaptations could be done, for example, in order to teach parents how they can increase their social networks in order to find support or where and how they can find financial support for their children's career development.

We believe it is also important to involve parents in the conduction of career education courses, as it will be difficult for career designing experts and career counselors to reach out to all at-risk groups and respond to all those who need assistance in a community. From this perspective, we think it is right to encourage practitioners who believe they fulfill preventive goals by transferring their competencies to others, as far as it is possible, in order to increase the number of those who could "multiply" career education interventions, at the same time limiting the costs involved in the execution of these types of interventions. In any case, in planning and implementing the interventions to support parents in scaffolding their children's career development, the following should not be forgotten:

1. Many parents are genuinely concerned about their children's future and the consequences that this might have on the family as a whole.

2. Many parents understand the complexity of their child's career construction and have an idea of the risks associated with inadequate choices. However, they wish neither to give up to their supportive role nor to totally delegate responsibilities and initiatives to others, nor to be wholly substituted by them.

3. Many parents are aware that their children's career trajectories depend on the quality of their support, on their own commitment to their children's educational process, and all that is an integral part of the family project regardless of the socioeconomic levels of their family.

4. Many parents wish to take an active role in the process of their children's career development and are, therefore, interested in career education, even if sometimes, albeit in good faith, the quality of their support and action may hinder their children's self-determination and the optimization of their child's potential.

Working with parents in different contexts to address the issue of career construction requires, in our opinion, a complex set of professional skills. Career counselors should be able to carry out preventive interventions and reduce social, economic, and political barriers by helping their clients to cope with these barriers as also through working directly with policy (Nota & Ferrari, 2011). We believe that university-based career training programs should guarantee that career counselors, besides possessing the competences necessary to supply help and support to the single individual, should also be able to carry out interventions in small group settings, where participants can learn from each other. A crucial challenge for career counseling experts today is to achieve the benefits of individual counseling in group counseling (Bernard et al., 2008), with the aim of making guidance and counseling available on a broader scale and concurrently contain its costs.

At the same time, reduced funding compels career counselors to develop effective and inexpensive intervention programs that can be implemented on a larger scale, for broader sections of the population, especially for at-risk citizens. This new view, therefore, implies the need to work with large groups. There is research evidence in support of group methods: These represent an ideal economical approach for counselors attempting to meet the career developments needs of middle-to-low-income individuals (Niles & Harris-Bowlsbey, 2005) and to demonstrate their commitment to social justice (Vera & Speight, 2003).

In this regard, the use of information communication technologies could represent a highly promising career planning approach that can overcome numerous obstacles for many people, such as problems of disability and/or marginalization and, therefore, assist people who traditionally have not had easy access to career guidance and counseling services (Bandura, 2002; Harris-Bowlsbey & Sampson, 2005).

Relevance for Multiple Cultures: Sensitivity to the Universal and the Particular

As regards a universal point of view, our analyses of literature show that parents represent an important source of support for children's career construction across cultures. Generally speaking, both structural family variables (e.g., parents' SES and social class) and process family variables (e.g., parents' aspirations, supplied supports, family interactions) appear to be factors that have a cross-cultural valence. At the same time, the complexity with which these factors influence the quality of the parent–child relationship and their impact on life designing and career construction require scholars and career counselors to take into consideration the specificity of family culture and practice and other impactful features of the context while planning their researches and devising their interventions. Adopting an approach that focuses on the specific without forgetting the universal could be a key strategy in carrying out researches and interventions that are more responsive to the needs of diverse families.

References

Adam, S. (1998, May). *Competences and other factors affecting the small enterprise sector in Ibadan, Nigeria.* Paper presented at the conference Enterprise in Africa: Between poverty and growth, Edinburgh.

Aguayo, D., Herman, K., Ojeda, L., & Flores, L. Y. (2011). Culture predicts Mexican Americans' college self-efficacy and college performance. *Journal of Diversity in Higher Education, 4*(2), 79–89.

Ali, S. R. (2009). Review of psychology and economics injustice: Personal, professional, and political intersection. *Psychology of Women Quarterly, 33*(1), 145–146.

Ali, S. R., Lewis, S. Z., & Sandil, R. (2006). Career counseling for Asian women. In W. B. Walsh & M. J. Heppner (Eds.), *Handbook of career counseling for women* (2nd ed., pp. 241–270). Mahwah, NJ: Lawrence Erlbaum.

Ali, S. R., McWhirter, E. H., & Chronister, K. M. (2005). Self-efficacy and vocational outcome expectations for adolescents of lower socioeconomic status: A pilot study. *Journal of Career Assessment, 13*, 40–58.

Anand, P., & Lea, S. (2011). The psychology and behavioral economics of poverty. *Journal of Economic Psychology, 32*(2), 284–293.

Arnett, J. J. (2000). Emerging adulthood: A theory of development from the late teens through the twenties. *American Psychologist, 55*(5), 469–480.

Arulmani, G., Van Laar, D., & Easton, S. (2003). The influence of career beliefs and socioeconomic status on the career decision-making of high school students in India. *International Journal for Educational and Vocational Guidance, 3*, 193–204.

Bandura, A. (1997). *Self-efficacy: The exercise of control.* New York, NY: Freeman.

Bandura, A. (2002). Growing primacy of human agency in adaptation and change in the electronic era. *European Psychologist, 7*(1), 2–16.

Bandura, A. (2012). On the functional properties of perceived self-efficacy revisited. *Journal of Management, 38*(1), 9–44.

Barling, J. (1991). Fathers' employment: A neglected influence on children. In J. V. Lerner & N. L. Galambos (Eds.), *Employed mothers and their children* (pp. 181–209). New York, NY: Garland.

Barling, J., & Mendelson, M. B. (1999). Parents' job insecurity affects children's grade performance through the indirect effects of beliefs in an unjust world and negative mood. *Journal of Occupational Health Psychology, 4*(4), 347–355.

Bauman, Z. (2011). *Collateral damage: Social inequalities in a global age.* Cambridge, MA: Polity.

Beck, U. (2000). *The brave new world of work.* Cambridge, MA: Polity.

Ben-Zur, H. (2003). Happy adolescents: The link between subjective well-being, internal resources, and parental factors. *Journal of Youth and Adolescence, 32*, 67–79.

Berger, R. (2004). *Immigrant women tell their stories.* New York, NY: Haworth Press.

Bernard, H., Burlingame, G., Flores, P., Greene, L., Joyce, A., Kobos, J. C., …Feirman, D. (2008). Clinical practice guidelines for group psychotherapy. *International Journal of Group Psychotherapy, 58*, 456–542.

Betz, N. E., Klein, K. L., & Taylor, K. M. (1996). Evaluation of a short form of the Career Decision-Making Self-Efficacy Scale. *Journal of Career Assessment, 4*(1), 47–57.

Birman, D. (2006). Acculturation gap and family adjustment: Findings with Soviet Jewish Refugees in the United States and implications for measurement. *Journal of Cross-Cultural Psychology, 37*(5), 568–589.

Blustein, D. L. (2001). Extending the reach of vocational psychology: Toward an inclusive and integrative psychology of working. *Journal of Vocational Behavior, 59*, 171–182.

Blustein, D. L., Chaves, A. P., Diemer, M. A., Gallagher, L. A., Marshall, K. G., Sirin, S., et al. (2002). Voices of the forgotten half: The role of social class in the school-to-work transition. *Journal of Counseling Psychology, 49*, 311–324.

Blustein, D. L., Coutinho, M. T. N., Murphy, K. A., Backus, F., & Catraio, C. (2011). Self and social class in career theory and practice. In P. J. Hartung & L. M. Subich (Eds.), *Developing self in work and career: Concepts, cases, and contexts* (pp. 213–229). Washington, DC: American Psychological Association.

Blustein, D. L., Walbridge, M. M., Friedlander, M. L., & Palladino, D. E. (1991). Contributions of psychological separation and parental attachment to the career development process. *Journal of Counseling Psychology, 38*(1), 39–50.

Brewster, A. B., & Bowen, G. L. (2004). Teacher support and the school engagement of Latino middle and high school students at risk of school failure. *Child & Adolescent Social Work Journal, 21*(1), 47–67.

Broda, C., Leibtag, E., & Weinstein, D. E. (2009). The role of prices in measuring the poor's living standards. *Journal of Economic Perspectives, 23*, 77–97.

Bryant, B. K., Zvonkovic, A. M., & Reynolds, P. (2006). Parenting in relation to child and adolescent vocational development. *Journal of Vocational Behavior, 69*(1), 149–175.

Caplan, G. (1964). *Principles of preventive psychiatry.* Oxford, England: Basic Books.

Carver, C. S., & Scheier, M. F. (2002). Optimism. In C. R. Snyder & S. J. Lopez (Eds.), *Handbook of positive psychology* (pp. 231–243). New York, NY: Oxford University Press.

Center for Workforce Success. (2007). *Improving workplace opportunities for limited English speaking workers. National Association of Manufacturers.* Retrieved from http://www.kidscount.org/news/May2008/PDFs/ImprovWplaceELL.pdf

Chang, E. C., & Sanna, L. J. (2003). Optimism, accumulated life stress, and psychological and physical adjustment: Is it always adaptive to expect the best? *Journal of Social and Clinical Psychology, 22,* 97–115.

Chong, W. H., Huan, V. S., Yeo, L. S., & Ang, R. P. (2006). Asian adolescents' perceptions of parent, peer, and school support and psychological adjustment: The mediating role of dispositional optimism. *Current Psychology, 25,* 212–228.

Cinamon, R. G. (2001). Father's unemployment and career related variables of his adolescent child. *International Journal for the Advancement of Counseling, 23,* 295–309.

Cinamon, R. G., & Dan, O. (2010). Parental attitudes toward preschoolers' career education: A mixed-method study. *Journal of Career Development, 37*(2), 519–540.

Cochran, L. (1985a). *Career grid workbook.* Richmond, BC: Buchanan-Kells.

Cochran, L. (1985b). *Planning workbook.* Richmond, BC: Buchanan-Kells.

Cochran, L., & Amundson, N. (1985). *Activity self-exploration workbook.* Richmond, BC: Buchanan-Kells.

Coppola, M. (2011). *Credenze stereotipate sulle professioni e abilità sociali in un gruppo di adolescenti di scuola media superiore* [Stereotypical belief about professions and social skills in a group of high school students] (Unpublished master's thesis). Padua: University of Padua.

Diemer, M. A., & Ali, S. R. (2009). Integrating social class into vocational psychology: Theory and practice implications. *Journal of Career Assessment, 17*(3), 247–265.

Farver, J. A. M., Narang, S. K., & Bhadha, B. R. (2002). East meets West: Ethnic identity, acculturation, and conflict in Asian Indian families. *Journal of Family Psychology, 16*(3), 338–350.

Felsman, D. E., & Blustein, D. L. (1999). The role of peer relatedness in late adolescent career development. *Journal of Vocational Behavior, 54*(2), 279–295.

Ferry, T. R., Fouad, N. A., & Smith, P. L. (2000). The role of family context in social-cognitive model for career related choice behaviour: A math and science perspective. *Journal of Vocational Behavior, 57,* 348–364.

Fouad, N. A., & Fitzpatrick, M. E. (2009). Social class and work-related decisions: Measurement, theory, and social mobility. *Journal of Career Assessment, 17*(3), 266–270.

Fouad, N. A., Hackett, G., Smith, P. L., Kantamneni, N., Fitzpatrick, M., Haag, S., et al. (2010). Barriers and supports for continuing in mathematics and science: Gender and educational level differences. *Journal of Vocational Behavior, 77,* 361–373.

Fouad, N. A., & Smith, P. L. (1996). A test of a social cognitive model for middle school students: Math and science. *Journal of Counseling Psychology, 43*(3), 338–346.

Galambos, N. L., & Sears, H. A. (1998). Adolescents' perceptions of parents' work and adolescents' work values in two-earner families. *Journal of Early Adolescence, 18,* 397–420.

Galinsky, E. (1999). *Ask the children: What America's children really think about working parents.* New York, NY: William Morrow.

Galinsky, E. (2000). Findings from ask the children with implications for early childhood professionals. *Young Children, 55*(3), 64–68.

Ginevra, M. C., & Nota, L. (2010, October). *Conception of work, school and leisure in parents and their children.* Poster session presented at the 5th ESFR Congress, Milan.

Ginevra, M. C., Nota, L., & Ferrari, L. (2011, September). *Supporto genitoriale, indecisione, credenze di efficacia e pensieri circa il futuro di un gruppo di adolescenti* [Parental support, career indecision, self-efficacy beliefs and thoughts about the future in a group of adolescents]. Poster session presented at the XXIV National Congress of Italian Psychological Association, University of Genova, Genova.

Glenn, J. C., & Gordon, T. J. (2007). *2007 State of the future.* Washington, DC: World Federation of United Nations Associations and American Council for the United Nations University.

Guay, F., Senécal, C., Gauthier, L., & Fernet, C. (2003). Predicting career indecision: A self-determination theory perspective. *Journal of Counseling Psychology, 50,* 165–177.

Guerra, A. L., & Braungart-Rieker, J. M. (1999). Predicting career indecision in college students: The role of identity formation and parental relationship factors. *Career Development Quarterly, 47,* 255–266.

Harris-Bowlsbey, J., & Sampson, J. P., Jr. (2005). Use of technology in delivering career services worldwide. *Career Development Quarterly, 54*(1), 48–56.

Hartung, P. J., Porfeli, E. J., & Vondracek, F. W. (2008). Career adaptability in childhood. *Career Development Quarterly, 57,* 63–74.

Hirschi, A. (2009). Career adaptability development in adolescence: Multiple predictors and effect on sense of power and life satisfaction. *Journal of Vocational Behavior, 74*(2), 145–155.

Howard, K. A. S., Ferrari, L., Nota, L., Solberg, V. S. H., & Soresi, S. (2009). The relation of cultural context and social relationships to career development in middle school. *Journal of Vocational Behavior, 75*(2), 100–108.

Jordan, W. J., & Plank, S. B. (2000). Talent loss among high-achieving poor students. In M. G. Sanders (Ed.), *Schooling students placed at risk: Research, policy, and practice in the education of poor and minority adolescents* (pp. 83–108). Mahwah, NJ: Lawrence Erlbaum.

Jordan, T. E., & Pope, M. L. (2001). Developmental antecedents to adolescents' occupational knowledge: A 17-year prospective study. *Journal of Vocational Behavior, 58*(2), 279–292.

Juang, L. P., & Alvarez, A. A. (2010). Discrimination and adjustment among Chinese American adolescents:

Family conflict and family cohesion as vulnerability and protective factors. *American Journal of Public Health, 100*(12), 2403–2409.

Kenny, M. E., & Bledsoe, M. (2005). Contributions of the relational context to career adaptability among urban adolescents. *Journal of Vocational Behavior, 66*(2), 257–272.

Kenny, M. E., Blustein, D. L., Chaves, A., Grossman, J. M., & Gallagher, L. A. (2003). The role of perceived barriers and relational support in the educational and vocational lives of urban high school students. *Journal of Counseling Psychology, 50*(2), 142–155.

Ketterson, T. U., & Blustein, D. L. (1997). Attachment relationships and the career exploration process. *Career Development Quarterly, 46*, 167–178.

Kowal, A., Kramer, L., Krull, J. L., & Crick, N. R. (2002). Children's perceptions of the fairness of parental preferential treatment and their socioemotional well-being. *Journal of Family Psychology, 16*(3), 297–306.

Krumboltz, J. D. (1991). *Manual for the Career Beliefs Inventory*. Palo Alto, CA: Consulting Psychologists Press.

Krumboltz, J. D. (2009). The happenstance learning theory. *Journal of Career Assessment, 17*(2), 135–154.

Kush, K., & Cochran, L. (1993). Enhancing a sense of agency through career planning. *Journal of Counseling Psychology, 40*(4), 434–439.

Lapour, A. S., & Heppner, M. J. (2009). Social class privilege and adolescent women's perceived career options. *Journal of Counseling Psychology, 56*(4), 477–494.

Larsen, L. J. (2004). *The foreign-born population in the United States: 2003. Current population reports*. Washington, DC: U.S. Census Bureau.

Leidy, M. S., Schofield, T. J., Miller, M. A., Parke, R. D., Coltrane, S., Braver, S., . . . Adams, M. (2011). Fathering and adolescent adjustment: Variations by family structure and ethnic background. *Fathering, 9*, 44–68.

Lemola, S., Raikkonen, K., Matthews, K. A., Scheier, M. F., Heinonen, K., Pesonene, A.-K., . . . Lahti, J. (2010). A new measure of dispositional optimism and pessimism in young children. *European Journal of Personality, 24*, 71–84.

Lent, R. W. (2007). La teoria sociocognitiva centrata sulla scelta professionale: le sue applicazioni nella ricerca internazione [Social cognitive career theory: Its application in the international research]. In S. Soresi (Ed.), *Orientamento alle scelte*. Firenze: Giunti-Organizzazioni Speciali.

Lent, R. W., Brown, S. D., & Hackett, G. (2000). Contextual supports and barriers to career choice: A social cognitive analysis. *Journal of Counseling Psychology, 47*, 36–49.

Lim, V. K. G., & Loo, G. L. (2003). Effects of parental job insecurity and parenting behaviors on youth's self-efficacy and work attitudes. *Journal of Vocational Behavior, 63*, 86–98.

Lin, C. A. (2001). Audience attributes, media supplementation, and likely online service adoption. *Mass Communication & Society, 4*(1), 19–38.

Lindstrom, L., Doren, B., Metheny, J., Johnson, P., & Zane, C. (2007). Transition to employment: Role of the family in career development. *Council for Exceptional Children, 73*(3), 348–366.

Liu, W. M., Soleck, G., Hopps, J., Dunston, K., & Pickett, T. (2004). A new framework to understand social class in counseling: The social class worldview and modern classism theory. *Journal of Multicultural Counseling and Development, 32*, 95–122.

Martinez, C. R. (2006). Effects of differential family acculturation on Latino adolescent substance use. *Family Relations, 55*, 306–317.

McAdams, D. P. (1995). What do we know when we know a person? *Journal of Personality, 63*(3), 365–396.

McDowell, D. J., Parke, R. D., & Spitzer, S. (2002). Parent and child cognitive representations of social situations and children's social competence. *Social Development, 11*(4), 469–486.

McLeroy, K. R., & Wendel, M. L. (2011). Health equity or iniquity? *The Journal of Primary Prevention, 32*(1), 1–2.

Mehta, K., Gabbard, S. M., Barrat, V., Lewis, M., Carroll, D., & Mines, R. (2000). *Findings from the National Agricultural Workers Survey (NAWS), 1997–1998: A demographic and employment profile of United States farmworkers* (Report No. ED 446887). Washington, DC: Department of Labor. Retrieved from http://eric.ed.gov/ERICDocs/data/ericdocs2/content_storage_01/0000000b/80/23/86

Mitchell, A. M., Jones, G. B., & Krumboltz, J. D. (1979). *Social learning theory of career guidance*. Cranston, RI: Carroll Press.

Niles, S. G., & Harris-Bowlsbey, J. (2005). *Career development interventions in the 21st century* (2nd ed.). Upper Saddle River, NJ: Merrill Prentice Hall.

Nota, L. (2007). Indicatori di efficacia di un progetto di formazione per insegnanti referenti per l'orientamento [Efficacy indicators of a training program for guidance referent teachers]. In S. Soresi (Ed.), *Orientamento alle scelte: rassegne, ricerche, strumenti ed applicazioni* [Vocational guidance: Reviews, research, instruments and practice] (pp. 250–262). Firenze: Giunti-Organizzazioni Speciali.

Nota, L., & Ferrari, L. (2011, May). *Italian network university training in vocational guidance*. Paper session presented at the NICE Conference, Heidelberg.

Nota, L., Ferrari, L., Solberg, V. S. H., & Soresi, S. (2007). Career search self-efficacy, family support, and career indecision with Italian youth. *Journal of Career Assessment, 15*(2), 181–193.

Nota, L., Ferrari, L., & Soresi, S. (2007). Pensieri sul futuro [Thoughts about the future]. In S. Soresi & L. Nota (Eds.), *ASTRID Portfolio per l'assessment, il trattamento e l'integrazione delle disabilità—ORIENTAMENTO* [ASTRID Portfolio for assessment, intervention and inclusion of disability—vocational guidance]. Firenze: Giunti-Organizzazioni Speciali.

Nota, L., Ginevra, M. C., Ferrari, L., & Soresi, S. (2012). Il Futuro dei Figli: Uno strumento per misurare il supporto fornito dai genitori ai processi di scelta e progettazione del futuro sclastico-professionale dei figli [The children's future: A questionnaire to evaluate parents' support to their children's school-career choices and future planning]. *Gipo—Giornale Italiano di Psicologia dell'Orientamento, 12*(1), 3–17.

Nota, L., Pace, F., & Ferrari, L. (2008). Career Decision Self-Efficacy Scale—Short form: Uno studio per l'adattamento Italiano [Career Decision Self-Efficacy Scale—Short Form: A study for the Italian adaptation]. *Gipo—Giornale Italiano di Psicologia dell'Orientamento, 9*(2), 23–35.

Nota, L., & Soresi, S. (2010, July). *Training practitioners for life designing.* Paper presented at the 27th International Congress of Applied Psychology, Melbourne, Australia.

Nota, L., & Soresi, S. (2012, September). *Parental support and optimism in youth's career construction and optimism.* Paper presented at the 6th Congress of the European Society on Family Relations (ESFR), Lillehammer, Norway.

O'Brien, K. M., Friedman, S. M., Tipton, L. C., & Linn, S. G. (2000). Attachment, separation, and women's vocational development: A longitudinal analysis. *Journal of Counseling Psychology, 47*(3), 301–315.

Owens, T. J. (1992). Where do we go from here? Post-high school choices of American men. *Youth & Society, 23*, 452–477.

Paa, H. K., & McWhirter, E. H. (2000). Perceived influences on high school students' current career expectations. *Career Development Quarterly, 49*(1), 29–44.

Palmer, S., & Cochran, L. (1988). Parents as agents of career development. *Journal of Counseling Psychology, 35*(1), 71–76.

Parke, R. D., & Buriel, R. (2006). Socialization in the family: Ethnic and ecological perspectives. In W. Damon & R. M. Lerner (Series Eds.) & N. Eisenberg (Vol. Ed.), *Handbook of child psychology, Vol. 3: Social, emotional, and personality development* (pp. 429–504). Hoboken, NJ: Wiley.

Patton, W., Bartrum, D. A., & Creed, P. A. (2004). Gender differences for optimism, self-esteem, expectations and goals in predicting career planning and exploration in adolescents. *International Journal for Educational and Vocational Guidance, 4*(2–3), 193–209.

Phillips, S. D., Carlson, C., Christopher-Sisk, E. K., & Gravino, K. L. (2001). Treating clients with decision-making problems: A developmental-relational model. In L. VandeCreek & T. Jackson (Eds.), *Innovations in clinical practice: A source book* (pp. 129–140). Sarasota, FL: Professional Resource Press/Professional Resource Exchange.

Phinney, J. S., Ong, A., & Madden, T. (2000). Cultural values and intergenerational value discrepancies in immigrant and non-immigrant families. *Child Development, 71*(2), 528–539.

Porfeli, E. J., & Ferrari, L. (2011, September). *The role of parents in shaping children's' views about work.* Poster presented at the International Conference Career Counseling and Vocational Designing: Challenges and New Horizons, Padua, Italy.

Porfeli, E. J., Wang, C., & Hartung, P. J. (2008, July). *The intergenerational transmission of work affectivity and experiences.* Poster presented at XXIX International Congress of Psychology, Berlin, Germany.

Pransky, G., Moshenberg, D., Benjamin, K., Portillo, S., Thackrey, J. L., & Hill-Fotouhi, C. (2002). Occupational risks and injuries in nonagricultural immigrant Latino workers. *American Journal of Industrial Medicine, 42*, 117–123.

Raikes, H. A., & Thompson, R. A. (2006). Family emotional climate, attachment security and young children's emotion knowledge in a high risk sample. *British Journal of Developmental Psychology, 24*(1), 89–104.

Raikes, H. A., & Thompson, R. A. (2008). Conversations about emotion in high-risk dyads. *Attachment & Human Development, 10*(4), 359–377.

Rehfuss, M. C. (2009). The future career autobiography: A narrative measure of career intervention effectiveness. *Career Development Quarterly, 58*(1), 82–90.

Restubog, S. L. D., Florentino, A. R., & Garcia, P. R. J. M. (2010). The mediating roles of career self-efficacy and career decidedness in the relationship between contextual support and persistence. *Journal of Vocational Behavior, 77*(2), 186–195.

Rojewski, J. W., & Kim, H. (2003). Career choice patterns and behavior of work-bound youth during early adolescence. *Journal of Career Development, 30*(2), 89–108.

Roll, T., & Arthur, N. (2002). *Beliefs in career counselling.* Retrieved from http://contactpoint.ca/wp-content/uploads/2013/01/pdf-02-03.pdf

Rumbaut, R. G. (1991). The agony of exile: A study of the migration and adaptation of Indochinese refugee adults and children. In F. L. Ahearn & J. L. Athey (Eds.), *Refugee children: Theory, research, and services* (pp. 53–91). Baltimore, MD: Johns Hopkins University Press.

Ryan, N. E., Brown, S. D., & Solberg, V. S. H. (1996). Family dysfunction, parental attachment, and career search self-efficacy among community college students. *Journal of Counseling Psychology, 43*, 84–89.

Ryff, C. D., Schmutte, P. S., & Lee, Y. H. (1996). How children turn out: Implications for parental self-evaluation. In C. D. Ryff & M. M. Seltzer (Eds.), *The parental experience in midlife* (pp. 383–422). Chicago, IL: University of Chicago Press.

Saunders, D. E., Peterson, G. W., Sampson, J. P., Jr., & Reardon, R. C. (2000). Relation of depression and dysfunctional career thinking to career indecision. *Journal of Vocational Behavior, 56*(2), 288–298.

Savickas, M. L. (2005). The theory and practice of career construction. In S. D. Brown & R. W. Lent (Eds.), *Career development and counseling. Putting theory and research to work* (pp. 42–70). Hoboken, NJ: Wiley.

Savickas, M. L., Nota, L., Rossier, J., Dauwalder, J.-P., Duarte, M. E., Guichard, J., . . . van Vianen, A. E. M. (2009). Life designing: A paradigm for career construction in the 21st century. *Journal of Vocational Behavior, 75*, 239–250.

Savickas, M. L., & Porfeli, E. J. (2012). The Career Adapt-Abilities Scale: Construction, reliability, and measurement equivalence across 13 countries. *Journal of Vocational Behavior, 80*, 661–673.

Scheier, M. F., & Carver, C. S. (1985). Optimism, coping, and health: Assessment and implications of generalized outcome expectancies. *Health Psychology, 4*, 219–247.

Schofield, T. J., Parke, R. D., Kim, Y., & Coltrane, S. (2008). Bridging the acculturation gap: Parent–child relationship quality as a moderator in Mexican American families. *Developmental Psychology, 44*(4), 1190–1194.

Schoon, I., & Parsons, P. (2002). Teenage aspirations for future careers and occupational outcomes. *Journal of Vocational Behavior, 60*(2), 262–288.

Schultheiss, D. E. P. (2000). Emotional-social issues in the provision of career counseling. In D. A. Luzzo (Ed.), *Career counseling of college students: An empirical guide to strategies that work* (pp. 43–62). Washington, DC: American Psychological Association.

Schultheiss, D. E. P. (2003). A relational approach to career counseling: Theoretical integration and practical application. *Journal of Counseling & Development, 81*(3), 301–310.

Schultheiss, D. E. P., Kress, H., Manzi, A. J., & Glasscock, J. (2001). Relational influences in career development: A qualitative inquiry. *The Counseling Psychologist, 29*, 214–239.

Sirin, S. R., & Rogers-Sirin, L. (2004). Exploring school engagement of middle-class African American adolescents. *Youth & Society, 35*(3), 323–340.

Soresi, S. (2011, September). *Vocational designing and career counseling: Challenges and new horizons.* Paper presented at International Conference Vocational Designing and Career Counseling: Challenges and New Horizons, University of Padua, Padua.

Soresi, S., & Nota, L. (2000). *Interessi e scelte* [Interests and choices]. Firenze: Giunti-Organizzazioni Speciali.

Soresi, S., & Nota, L. (2009). Career counseling in Italy: From placement to vocational realization. In P. Heppner, L. Gerstein, S. Ægisdótti, A. Leung, & K. Norsworthy (Eds.), *Handbook of cross-cultural counseling: Cultural assumptions and practices worldwide* (pp. 291–300). Thousand Oaks, CA: Sage.

Soresi, S., Nota, L., & Ferrari, L. (2006). Family setting in Down syndrome. In J. A. Rondal & J. Perera (Eds.), *Down syndrome, neurobehavioral specificity* (pp. 191–211). Chichester: Wiley.

Soresi, S., Nota, L., & Ferrari, L. (2007a). Considerations on supports that can increase the quality of life of parents of children with disabilities. *Journal of Policy and Practice in Intellectual Disabilities, 4*(4), 248–251.

Soresi, S., Nota, L., & Ferrari, L. (2007b). Qualità della vita di operatori e genitori [Quality of life of social service providers and parents]. In S. Soresi & L. Nota (Eds.), *ASTRID Portfolio per l'assessment, il trattamento e l'integrazione delle disabilità* [ASTRID Portfolio for assessment, intervention and inclusion of disability] (Vol. 1, pp. 219–285). Firenze: Giunti-Organizzazioni Speciali.

Soresi, S., Nota, L., & Ferrari, L. (2012). Career Adapt-Abilities Scale-Italian Form: Psychometric properties and relationships to breadth of interests, quality of life, and perceived barriers. *Journal of Vocational Behavior, 80*(3), 705–711.

Soresi, S., Nota, L., Ferrari, L., & Sgaramella, T. M. (in press). Career development and career thoughts. In M. L. Wehmeyer (Ed.), *The Oxford handbook of positive psychology and disability.* New York: Oxford University Press.

Stein, C. H., Abraham, K. M., Bonar, E. E., Leith, J. E., Kraus, S. W., Hamill, A. C., . . . Fogo, W. R. (2011). Family ties in tough times: How young adults and their parents view the U.S. economic crisis. *Journal of Family Psychology, 25*(3), 449–454.

Storck, E. (1997). Cultural psychotherapy: A consideration of psychosocial class and cultural differences in group treatment. *Group, 21*(4), 331–349.

Teranishi, R. T., Suarez-Orozco, C., & Suarez-Orozco, M. (2011). Immigrants in community colleges. *Immigrant Children, 21*(1), 153–169.

Turner, S., & Lapan, R. T. (2002). Career self-efficacy and perceptions of parent support in adolescent career development. *Career Development Quarterly, 51*, 44–55.

Turner, S., Steward, J. C., & Lapan, R. T. (2004). Family factors associated with sixth-grade adolescents' math and science career interests. *Career Development Quarterly, 53*, 41–52.

Usinger, J. (2005). Parent/guardian visualization of career and academic future of seventh graders enrolled in low-achieving schools. *Career Development Quarterly, 53*(3), 234–245.

Vera, E. M., & Speight, S. L. (2003). Multicultural competence, social justice, and counseling psychology: Expanding our roles. *The Counseling Psychologist, 31*(3), 253–272.

Vignoli, E. (2009). Inter-relationships among attachment to mother and father, self-esteem, and career indecision. *Journal of Vocational Behavior, 75*, 91–99.

Vignoli, E., Croity-Belz, S., Chapeland, V., de Fillipis, A., & Garcia, M. (2005). Career exploration in adolescence: The role of anxiety, attachment and parenting style. *Journal of Vocational Behavior, 67*, 153–168.

Vondracek, F. W., & Hartung, P. J. (2002). Introduction: Innovating career development using advances in life course and life-span theory. *Journal of Vocational Behavior, 61*, 375–380.

Whiston, S. C. (1996). The relationship among family interaction patterns and career indecision and career decision-making self-efficacy. *Journal of Career Development, 23*, 137–149.

Whiston, S. C., & Keller, B. K. (2004). The influences of the family of origin on career development: A review and analysis. *The Counseling Psychologist, 32*, 493–568.

Wolfe, J. B., & Betz, N. E. (2004). The relationship of attachment variables to career decision-making self-efficacy and fear of commitment. *Career Development Quarterly, 52*(4), 363–369.

Wu, C. C. (2009). Higher education expansion and low-income students in Taiwan. *International Journal of Educational Development, 29*, 399–405.

Yakushko, O. (2006). Career development of immigrant women. In W. B. Walsh & M. J. Heppner (Eds.), *Handbook of career counseling of women* (2nd ed., pp. 387–426). Hillsdale, NJ: Lawrence Erlbaum.

Young, R. A., Valach, L., Ball, J., Paseluikho, M., Wong, Y., DeVries, R., . . .Turkel, H. (2001). Career development in adolescence as a family project. *Journal of Counseling Psychology, 48*, 190–202.

The Interface between Positive Youth Development and Youth Career Development: New Avenues for Career Guidance Practice

10

Anuradha J. Bakshi and Jahnvee Joshi

Introduction

I am 18, and for many years till now, I did not know what I was good at. When I got the opportunity to organize a program for our community youth, I became aware of my own strengths. I discovered that I was good at planning, organizing, and managing. I developed a sense of responsibility. In fact, now I have moved to the city to pursue a course in Event Management. I am enjoying the course, and am doing well. I learnt to overcome challenges and work hard, and I believe that just do your work and results will be good. (18-year-old male youth from rural India)

This example is illustrative of the main ideas that underpin this chapter. Youth form an integral part of the community. When they participate in community-based youth services, they and the community experience multiple benefits (Perkins, Borden, Keith, Hoppe-Rooney, & Villarruel, 2003). Such participation strengthens ties among youth, between youth and adults, and between youth and the community as a whole. Youth experience firsthand that they matter to the community; likewise, the community begins to matter more to youth. Youth develop a range of competencies useful for their own development and the community's development in the present as well as in the future (Huebner, 2003).

The central thesis of this chapter is that the benefits of youth participation in (high quality) community-based youth services extend to youth *career* development. The 18-year-old youth's example represents the developmental pathways of many beneficiaries of youth services. When youth participate in youth services, they are better able to identify and build on strengths, overcome limitations, add interests, develop interpersonal competencies required for success in a career, and form responsible work habits. The premise is that participation in well-designed and well-executed community-based youth services enables youth to have access to pragmatic and concrete self-knowledge and the tools for developing the broad and specific competencies that aid their career development. Youth are able to expand their notions of who they are, who they can be, and who would they like to be, and set forth on the challenging task of navigating adulthood and (more specifically) their careers.

This signifies that there are new settings and new roles for career practitioners—a movement away (a) from an individual focus *to* a group focus and (b) from a guidance setting in which youth come to a service provider *to* a community setting in which the service provider goes to youth. All in all, the recommendation is that career practitioners recognize the community as a powerful context for youth development (including youth career development) and join hands with other youth professionals in augmenting (quality) structured opportunities for youth that are situated in the youth's ecology.

A.J. Bakshi (✉)
Department of Human Development, Nirmala Niketan
College of Home Science, University of Mumbai,
Mumbai, India
e-mail: anustra@gmail.com

G. Arulmani et al. (eds.), *Handbook of Career Development*, International and Cultural Psychology, 173
DOI 10.1007/978-1-4614-9460-7_10, © Springer Science+Business Media, LLC 2014

In this chapter, first relevant terms/constructs are reviewed. Key notions regarding youth development versus positive youth development (PYD), community youth development, and youth career development are clarified; examples are provided of relevant Western research. The linkages between youth career development, on the one hand, and PYD and community youth development, on the other hand, are explored. Next, these linkages are substantiated through an example of a faith-based/religious community's youth services in India. This simultaneously is a step toward righting the balance between scientific knowledge sourced from (and representing) the East versus the West (see Yang, 2012). In the closing sections of the chapter, implications for career practitioners, relevance for multiple cultures, and new directions for the field are outlined.

Reviewing Relevant Constructs and Exploring Linkages

Youth

Rationale
Youth is an applied construct. The use of *youth* in this chapter is justified because this chapter represents what Lerner and Steinberg (2009) have identified as the third phase in the scientific study of adolescent development (1990 onward); in their judgment, a phase distinctively characterized by (p. 4):
• Applied developmental science
• Research ↔ application syntheses
• Applications to youth programs and policies
• Positive youth development (PYD)

Definitional Issues
Governments of various countries and international organizations such as the United Nations (UN) have defined youth for the purposes of demographic profiling as also for earmarking target age groups for policymaking, deployment of funds, and strategic intervention. The UN has defined youth as "a period of transition from the dependence of childhood to adulthood's independence and awareness of our interdependence as members of a community" (UNESCO, n.d.). The UN states that youth, thus, refers to those who are in the in-between stage of being old enough to exit compulsory education but who have not yet started (full-time) paid work. With entry into "adult" careers appearing to be the marker for closing the youth category, the UN recognizes that there is fluidity (across time and country) rather than fixity in the age categorization of youth, and has both universal (applicable across countries) and particular (for a particular country or Member State) age definitions of youth. All UN youth statistics are based on an age definition of youth as those between 15 and 24 years of age; whereas for interventions within a country, the age definition of the country (i.e., Member State) is adopted. India, for example, has defined youth as those in the age category of 13–35 years; the draft National Youth Policy (Ministry of Youth Affairs and Sports, Government of India [n.d.]) proposes to reduce this age bracket to 16–30 years. The African Youth Charter (n.d.), endorsed in 2006, defines youth as those between the ages of 15 and 35 years. The Commonwealth defines youth as those who are 15–29 years old (The Commonwealth, n.d.).

The International Labour Office (ILO, 2010) has clarified that "the statistical definition of 15–24 years may no longer be valid, given that today more and more young people postpone their entry into labour markets to well beyond the age of 25"; in contrast, particularly in developing countries "the typical age of entry into the labour market may be below that of 15 years," blurring the distinction between child and youth labor (p. 1). Differences in age of entry into the labor market can be observed within and across cultures, within and across generations. For developing countries like India, precocious entry can be linked to financial disadvantage and class, compounded with rural residence; in contrast, in developed countries such as the United States, youth from disadvantaged families have a lower likelihood of being engaged in paid work than youth from advantaged families (Greene & Staff, 2012). The UN has noted that delay in entry is linked to precarious availability of jobs and high rates of unemployment (UNESCO, n.d.). Among the privileged, and across generations, delay in assuming adult responsibilities of a job/career may not just be because of unemployment but also because of an increasing investment in education and the length of tertiary educational paths for highly specialized occupations (see ILO, 2010).

Youth in this chapter refers to those in the formative period of dependency after childhood, inclusive of adolescence and early adulthood. In congruence with Paul Baltes's (e.g., Baltes, Lindenberger, & Staudinger, 2006) postulation of an incomplete and thereby *evolving* architecture of human development, it is assumed that as cultures become more and more knowledge and technology dependent, educational attainment will culminate from increasingly prolonged educational paths, and the formative dependency of the young will be extended—therefore, it is best to keep broader rather than narrower age brackets for operationalizing youth. In addition, even if the problem of age differentials did not exist, entry into the labor market is not a clear upper limit for defining youth because entry does not imply a stable presence in the job market. Career trajectories are not smooth, and youth may have to make multiple attempts to find a foothold in the labor market. Their first or first few forays may well serve to reconnoiter rather than to establish them firmly on a career path. Our conceptualization of youth matches Eccles and Gootman's (2002) statement that "the length of adolescence has extended to the mid- to late twenties, and the pathways to adulthood have become less clear and more numerous" (p. 2).

Positive Youth Development

Youth development is similar to terms such as child development or adult development and refers to the developmental processes and outcomes pertaining to youth. An important point to note is that in the absence of planned interventions, developmental outcomes can be positive or negative. That is, there is no guarantee that a youth's developmental path will be positive. On the other hand, *positive* youth development or PYD is a specific approach/orientation within youth development aimed at (working toward) ensuring that youth choose and thrive on a positive developmental trajectory. It can variously be identified as a theory, philosophy, framework, or a consensus that (in the United States) has both arisen from and been applied to youth programs, community initiatives, researches, and policies with the express aim of optimizing youth development (Benson, Scales, Hamilton, & Sesma, 2006a; Lerner, 2011; Silbereisen & Lerner, 2007).

Applied, Interdisciplinary, and Integrative

PYD is an applied, multidisciplinary, interdisciplinary, and integrative endeavor (Benson et al., 2006a). In the United States, PYD represents an exemplary confluence of theory and research with advocacy, policy, and practice (Lerner & Steinberg, 2009). Professionals from a number of disciplines (e.g., developmental psychology, social work, sociology, education, public health, and prevention) have committed themselves to supporting PYD (Benson et al., 2006a). It follows that there is no single theorist, researcher, or practitioner who can be credited with the PYD model. Instead, PYD theory and practice is the (ongoing) result of integrating the notable achievements of many US scholars (Lerner, 2011), some of whom are cited in this section (e.g., [the late] Peter Benson from the Search Institute, William Damon, Richard Lerner, Jacquelynne Eccles).

Asset Rather than Deficit Model

Damon (2004) has argued that the PYD approach has emerged as a contraposition to the negative view of youth that prevailed in psychology, criminal justice, and media. In youth work (in the United States), a reliance on mental health and/or criminal justice models had led to a sustained focus on youth *problems* and *deficits* (e.g., substance abuse, delinquency) (Damon, 2004). Instead, the PYD approach "has introduced a more affirmative and welcome vision of young people," which "emphasizes the manifest potentialities rather than the supposed incapacities of young people" (Damon, 2004, p. 15). It is grounded in the belief that youth are "resources to be developed rather than problems to be managed" (Roth & Brooks-Gunn, 2003, p. 172). It reflects a shift in paradigms from "deterrence to development" (Pittman, Irby, & Ferber, 2000, p. 18), from "prevention science to promotion science" (Benson, 2007, p. 49), from an eclipsing focus on "deficit and risk reduction" (Benson & Saito, 2000, p. 135) to the inclusion of a strength-based conception (Benson, 2007; Lerner, Almerigi, Theokas, & Lerner 2005) dedicated to "understanding what can go right in the development of young people" (Lerner, Almerigi, et al., 2005, p. 13).

In fact, Lerner (2005) has pointed out that "for about the first 85 years of the scientific study of adolescent development, the field was framed almost exclusively by a deficit perspective" (p. 4), starting with Hall's notion of adolescence as a period of "storm and stress." Before the 1990s, he states positive development was construed explicitly or implicitly as the absence of damaging, high-risk, or health-compromising behaviors. Thus, a youth on a positive trajectory was one who avoided substance abuse, unsafe sexual behaviors, or violence, for example. However, in the United States from the 1990s, a consensus has grown that transitioning successfully to adulthood entails more than avoiding high-risk or negative behaviors (Catalano, Berglund, Ryan, Lonczak, & Hawkins, 2004). Problems and competencies are (relatively) independent dimensions such that the absence of problems does not automatically mean presence of competencies that aid successful development (e.g., Achenbach, 1991a, 1991b). Therefore, preventing risk is not the same as promoting positive development (Benson, 2007; Lerner, 2003); as a matter of fact, promoting positive development can have a dual benefit of (a) reducing risk and negative outcomes as well as (b) facilitating developmental strengths and positive outcomes (Benson, Scales, Hamilton, & Sesma, 2006b). Accordingly, there are two complementary constructs of developmental success: reduction of damaging behaviors and the promotion of thriving (Benson et al., 2006b, p. 2).

Pooled Perspectives from Multiple Theories

PYD theory is constructed using perspectives from multiple theories such as developmental systems theory (e.g., Lerner, 2006), ecological systems theory (e.g., Bronfenbrenner, 1979), dynamic systems theory (e.g., Thelen & Smith, 2006), action theory (e.g., Brandtstädter, 2006), and life span theory (e.g., Baltes et al., 2006).

PYD scholars (e.g., Benson, 2007; Lerner, 2005) have acknowledged the influential role of developmental systems theory. Lerner's central premises in applying developmental systems theory to PYD are as follows: There are bidirectional influences between youth and their contexts; youth's developmental trajectories reflect the impact of these bidirectional influences; both youth and their contexts/ecologies have the potential for plasticity; therefore, the development of both youth and their contexts/ecologies can be optimized; and the efforts of developmental scientists (whose primary work is with youth) must be directed at promoting PYD.

Benson (e.g., 2007) integrated the following into PYD theory from Bronfenbrenner's (1979) ecological theory: a determined focus on the developmental ecologies in a youth's life; a concern for the quality of developmental opportunities in these ecologies (e.g., formation of caring relationships); the need to have beneficial interconnections between multiple ecologies; and instead of being preoccupied with describing the status quo, to imagine and experiment with new social forms which can help optimize human potential.

Brandtstädter's (e.g., 2006) action theory has also been knit into the PYD framework—for instance, the notion of youth as deliberate actors and coproducers of their own development (Benson et al., 2006a). Self-regulation from action theory (Brandtstädter, 2006), self-organization from dynamic systems theory (Thelen & Smith, 2006), and the key processes of selection and optimization from Baltes's (e.g., Baltes et al., 2006) life span theory also feature in PYD theory. With regard to the latter, Benson et al. (2006a) have explained that youth make a selection (e.g., of interests) from the opportunities and supports available in their developmental ecologies, and optimization may follow selection. Youth workers and researchers must ask about the extent to which youth's ecological settings provide youth with constructive choices that can be optimized into empowering strengths or make it possible for youth to create such choices for themselves (Benson et al., 2006a). Richard Lerner (e.g., Gestsdóttir & Lerner, 2007; Lerner & Lerner, 2012) has adapted Baltes's selection, optimization, and compensation (SOC) theory in operationalizing PYD: A young person on a positive developmental trajectory is one who is able to select positive life goals, optimize opportunities and actions to achieve these goals, and compensate for obstacles that could stall the achievement of goals.

All Youth

In deficit reduction approaches, only a subset of youth—those at risk—are targeted (Benson, 2007). Resiliency research, which preceded the PYD movement, differed from deficit approaches because it "put a number of important positive youth attributes squarely on the psychological map" (Damon, 2004, p. 16) (chief among them being resilience—that is, successful adaptation despite experience of adversity). Yet, resiliency research fell short of a PYD approach because it implied that the development of personal strengths required a context of high stress/adversity rather than a context of normative developmental challenges (Damon, 2004). PYD, on the contrary, is restricted neither to those at risk (deficit approaches) nor to those who have successfully resolved risk (resiliency research). PYD offers a universal model of youth development (Damon, 2004): *All* youth can be supported in developing personal and community resources (Benson, 2007). Targeting all youth in a community is also aligned with the systems view that is embraced by PYD scholars.

Developmental Assets

When will a youth be likely to thrive on a positive life trajectory? When is it likely for PYD to occur? In the language of Benson

and his colleagues at the Search Institute (Minneapolis, USA), a youth is likely to thrive when the youth is asset rich (as opposed to asset depleted) *and* when the youth's ecologies are asset rich (e.g., Benson, 2007). Of course, these assets are not part of a financial portfolio; they are a part of the psychological portfolio of a person (e.g., interpersonal competence) as also of a setting/developmental ecology (e.g., caring school climate). These psychological assets clarify: How developmentally advantageous are the person's qualities and behaviors? Similarly, what is the extent to which the ecological setting is pro-development or facilitative of positive development of its members? Further, the word *asset* brings to mind an advantage that can be gained or collected. Benson (2007) contended that youth can "proactively procure" (p. 40) developmental assets; likewise, it is within the capacity of communities to acquire developmental assets. In other words, assets are malleable; and enrichment of assets is a key strategy for optimizing development—youth's personal developmental assets can be enriched, and concomitantly youth's developmental ecologies can be enriched with assets (Benson, 2007). As developmental assets create/build positive development, they have also been termed developmental nutrients; other synonymously used terms include developmental strengths, developmental resources, and developmental supports (e.g., Benson, 2007; Silbereisen & Lerner, 2007).

From the vantage point of youth, the building blocks of positive development are internal and external developmental assets (Benson, 2007). "Internal" is not to be confused with inherent; "internal" is used to distinguish the youth's own developmental assets from assets that are located in one or more of the youth's developmental ecologies (i.e., relating to the person versus relating to the person's setting/context). Internal developmental assets are also called individual-level assets (Benson, 2007) or personal assets (Eccles & Gootman, 2002); likewise, external developmental assets are also called ecological assets (Benson, 2007) or social assets (Eccles & Gootman, 2002). As "part of the intent of the developmental assets construct has been to provide a theoretically grounded understanding of the bidirectional interplay of context and person in propelling youth toward developmental success" (Benson, 2007, p. 47), equal weightage has been assigned to individual-level and ecological assets in the developmental-asset framework advanced by the Search Institute. The 20 individual-level assets are grouped into four categories: (a) commitment to learning (e.g., youth has high achievement motivation, youth does at least 1 hour of homework every school day, youth reads for pleasure for at least 3 hours/week), (b) positive values (e.g., youth is caring and likes helping other people; youth values sexual and physical health and practices restraint with regard to sex, drugs, alcohol, etc.), (c) social competencies (e.g., youth is competent in planning and decision-making, youth has interpersonal skills, youth is culturally competent and is comfortable with people from different cultures or communities), and (d) positive identity (e.g., youth has high self-esteem, youth has developed a life purpose and is optimistic about his or her future) (Benson, 2007). The 20 ecological assets (facilitative of PYD) are also grouped into four categories: (a) support (e.g., supportive relationships in the family, supportive relationships with at least three nonparent adults), (b) empowerment (e.g., availability of useful roles for youth in the community), (c) boundaries and expectations (e.g., parents and teachers have high expectations from youth), and (d) constructive use of time (e.g., availability and utilization of youth programs in the community) (Benson, 2007).

The 40 developmental assets (each with equal weightage) have been put together at the Search Institute using resilience, prevention, and adolescent development literatures along with research conducted on more than two million youth (6th- to 12th-grade students from 3,000 communities) in the United States (Scales & Leffert, 2004). Criteria for selection of developmental assets were (a) empirical evidence of a two-pronged outcome, namely, prevention of high-risk behaviors and promotion of thriving; (b) evidence of cross-community generalizability; (c) permitting of balance between internal and external assets; and (d) acquisitional quality of the asset at either individual or ecological level (Benson, 2007). In an aggregated US sample of 217,277 school-going youth, the mean number of assets documented is 19.3 (theoretical range: 0–40); most commonly youth report having have 11–20 assets (41 %), and only 9 % report having 31–40 assets. Such findings further authenticate the all-youth focus in PYD work (Benson, 2007).

Applying principles of developmental systems, Benson (2007, p. 38) asserted that, "Positive development... occurs in the fusion of an active, engaged, and competent person with receptive, supportive, and nurturing ecologies. In our terms, this is the fusion of external (i.e., ecological) assets and internal assets." Likewise, Silbereisen and Lerner (2007) have talked about the need to align the developmental strengths of the youth with the resources in his/her ecologies. Of the many evidence-based hypotheses relating to developmental assets, a central one is "the more, the better" hypothesis: "developmental success is dynamically related to the presence of a full complement of both external and internal assets," and as assets increase, both concurrent and longer-term well-being are enhanced (Benson, 2007, p. 38; Eccles & Gootman, 2002). Asset-building youth in asset-building and asset-favoring communities are expected to experience a *vertical pileup* (increase in assets in the same sector—e.g., family) and *horizontal stacking* (increase in assets in multiple sectors—e.g., family, school, neighborhood) (Benson, 2007).

Theokas et al. (2005) have factor-analyzed Search Institute youth data to reduce the 40 developmental assets into 14 crucial strengths: 6 each at the individual (e.g., social conscience, activity participation) and ecological levels (e.g., adult mentors, contextual safety) and 2 cross-specified assets (i.e., *positive identity* which conceptually is at the individual level but which mathematically hung together with the ecological assets and *rules and boundaries* which hung together with individual assets). The cross-specification of positive identity with ecological assets and that of rules and boundaries with individual assets, in their view, is a prime example of fusion of levels in developmental systems. Their conclusion: "There can be no pure discrimination between internal and external settings in a youth who is actively engaging and is engaged by the context" (p. 137). Such a principle of indivisibility is reflected in approaches characterized by probabilistic epigenesis (see Gottlieb, Wahlsten, & Lickliter, 2006).

Five Cs

Bidirectional relations between individual-level and ecological assets result in the five Cs (Lerner, 2011). In Richard Lerner's PYD model, the mutuality between assets at multiple levels (e.g., individual, community, society) leads to PYD as indicated by the five Cs, and PYD in turn predicts concurrent and future developmental outcomes (see Lerner, 2011). The five Cs—competence, confidence, connection, character, and caring—offer a fairly popular means of representing or operationalizing PYD; Lerner and others have consistently used the five Cs in their PYD researches (e.g., Lerner & Lerner, 2012; Roth & Brooks-Gunn, 2003). Most of the Cs are credited in idea to Rick Little (Lerner, 2011), and for theoretical and empirical support, all Cs can largely be credited to Richard Lerner.

Roth and Brooks-Gunn (2003) have detailed each of the five Cs. In their operationalization, there are four different types of *competence*: social competence (e.g., communication, assertiveness, conflict resolution skills), cognitive competence (e.g., problem solving, goal setting), academic competence (e.g., regularity in attendance, satisfactory or high academic performance), and vocational competence (e.g., career choice explorations). *Confidence* has to do with youth's empowering notions of self in the now and future: Roth and Brooks-Gunn include identity, self-efficacy, self-esteem, self-concept, and a belief in the future. They describe *connections* as strong relationships of youth with peers, adults, and institutions (preferably in multiple settings or sectors). Under *character* they cover, for example, restraint, respect, morality, and

spirituality. *Caring and compassion* are defined as youths' empathetic orientation to others.

In our view, the theoretical integration of developmental assets with the five Cs needs more attention. Lerner (e.g., 2011) has presented a longitudinal model in which the mutually impactful individual and ecological assets (step 1) lead to the five Cs as PYD (step 2), which next lead to (further) desirable developmental outcomes (step 3). Despite appreciating the time element in the three steps, in a developmental system it is unlikely that the progression from one step to another is one way; for example, the presence of five Cs surely strengthens individual and ecological assets and their fused interplay. Feed-forward *and* feed-backward coactions characterize multiple levels of developmental systems (Gottlieb et al., 2006). Moreover, individual assets (prerequisites of PYD) and the five Cs (indicators of PYD) appear to be conceptually overlapped. Silbereisen and Lerner (2007) on their end have clarified that internal assets "often represent outcomes rather than antecedents or may be partially confounded with outcomes" (p. 13). Similarly, Theokas et al. (2005) have stated that "work needs to be done to differentiate individual assets, as a setting condition for PYD, from measurement of individual thriving behaviors" (p. 140).

Development of Initiative

Reed Larson (e.g., 2000) has drawn attention to the malaise of "boredom, alienation, and disconnection from meaningful challenge" (p. 170) afflicting American adolescents and argued that development of initiative is a core requirement for PYD in the United States:

> In the emerging heterogeneous global society where job demands and basic life course and lifestyle decisions are not preconfigured, adolescents will need to acquire the motivation and skills to create order, meaning, and action out of a field of ill-structured choices. Individuals will need the capacity to exert cumulative effort over time to reinvent themselves, reshape their environments, and engage in other planful undertakings. A generation of bored and challenge-avoidant young adults is not going to be prepared to deal with the mounting complexity of life and take on the emerging challenges of the 21st century. (p. 171)

Initiative is increasingly critical for occupational and other success in adulthood, yet the imminence of adulthood does not appear to push youth into developing initiative. Neither does the prospect of adult careers pull youth into exercising initiative; youth, he adds, are not necessarily attracted by images of possible adult careers especially because "the path into adult occupations is opaque to young people" (p. 172).

Larson (2000) has identified three features of initiative: intrinsic motivation, concerted engagement, and a temporal arc of goal-directed effort that is sustained past start-up. In his research with American youth, he has found that youth participation in (adult- or youth-organized) structured voluntary activities (e.g., performing arts, youth groups) meets the criteria for development of initiative; in contrast, structured compulsory activities (e.g., school-work) and unstructured voluntary activities (e.g., watching TV or hanging out with friends) do not meet all the three requirements for development of initiative.

Development of Purpose

Damon is a strong advocate for the central role of purpose in PYD. Drawing on Viktor Frankl's *Man's Search for Meaning* and the importance of "high-level belief systems," he views purpose "as a motivator of good deeds and galvanizer of character growth" (Damon, Menon, & Bronk, 2003, p. 119). Damon et al. (2003) have defined purpose as a high-level goal or intention which (a) is more enduring and influential than low-level goals such as to buy an ice cream or choose the right dress to wear to a get-together, (b) represents a person's "intention to accomplish something that is at once meaningful to the self and of consequence to the world beyond the self" (p. 121), and (c) allows self-regulated movement toward a desired and desirable endpoint. In the words of a ninth-grade student in Mumbai who had participated in a counselor-initiated program for developing a positive purpose in life, "When we have a purpose, we have an aim in life and we get to know what we want and where we are

going" (Valles, 2012, p. 38). Adaptive and widely beneficial life trajectories (are expected to) ensue when youth are supported in developing a positive and preferably noble purpose; in contrast, the absence of such a purpose may mean that the youth is a soft target for being co-opted into others' misconceived negative or even ignoble intentions and plans, including extremism, violence, and terrorism (Damon et al., 2003). Damon et al. (2003) have reviewed the numerous studies in the United States that confirm that a purpose in life is related to a lower incidence of maladaptive behaviors (e.g., psychopathology, drug use, alcoholism) and to a higher incidence of adaptive behaviors (e.g., commitment to social action).

Promotion of the Common Good

The focus is not just on promoting individual well-being (i.e., youth development) but also on promoting the common good (e.g., community development) (Benson et al., 2006a). Youth's positive development is a vehicle for benefiting the community—through youth who are energized, empowered, and engaged with the community. Rick Little and Richard Lerner have indicated that the outcome of the five Cs is a sixth C, contribution (Lerner et al., 2005). Lerner et al. obtained unitemporal empirical evidence that "a young person enacts behaviors indicative of the Five Cs by contributing positively to self, family, community, and, ultimately, civil society" (Lerner, Lerner et al., 2005, p. 23). More recently, Lerner and Lerner (e.g., 2012) have also reported longitudinal (or cross-temporal) evidence that the presence of the five Cs (e.g., at Time A) predicts youth contribution (e.g., at Times B or E); at the same time, as contribution is high at Time A for youth high on the five Cs, it is unclear, in our opinion, whether the sixth C is only an outcome of the five Cs or whether all six Cs co-occur in mutually influential ways.

In fact, Benson et al. (2006a, 2006b) have posited that contribution is necessary to and formative of PYD. Thus, they state that when youth are supported in taking the initiative to improve their communities, multiple (and possibly escalating) benefits accrue: It enhances the competencies of the youth actors themselves and (given that their efforts are successful) makes the context more favorable for these youth as well as for others in the same context; further, youth actors are more likely to engage again with the community, and nonacting youth may follow their example.

Intentional Change

The bidirectional interconnections between person and context that are indispensable to PYD theory and practice form only part of the story. What lies at the core of the theory is the "possibility of creating change": Thus, PYD theory, research, practice, and policy are "incomplete without incorporating the concept of intentional change" (Benson et al., 2006a, p. 910). Benson et al. add that intentional change is the fulcrum that distinguishes PYD theory from a theory of adolescent development. Both the person and the context are seen as amenable to change; because of bidirectionality of influences, change in one influences change in the other. Change is not left to chance such that it manifests in either positive or negative ways; positive changes at individual and community levels are planned and executed with the support of relevant (and integrative) theory, research, available best practice models, and policy.

For example, an evidence-based key PYD hypothesis is the *contextual change* hypothesis which reads as follows: (a) "contexts can be intentionally altered to enhance developmental success" and (b) "changes in these contexts change the person" (Benson et al., 2006a, p. 916). Or the following which is part of the *youth action* hypothesis: "Processes for strengthening youth impact on context and self—youth participation and leadership—can be designed and implemented" (Benson et al., 2006a, p. 917). In sum, Benson et al. (2006b) have reiterated that the emphasis is on "transforming environments, not just 'fixing' kids"; simultaneously, youth are "key actors in their own development" and can be supported such that their positive "actions also change their environment" (p. 4).

Community Youth Development

Definition of Community

Benson and Saito (2000) have identified four ascending (subsuming) levels of settings within which they state (positive) youth development occurs: programs (semi-structured processes), organizations (place-based activities and relationships), socializing systems (e.g., the family), and the community. They define the community as including "not only the geographic place within which programs, organizations and systems intersect, but also the social norms, resources, relationships and informal settings that can dramatically inform human development, both directly and indirectly" (p. 127).

Relationship of Community Youth Development to PYD

The constructs of *positive youth development* and *community youth development* are substantially overlapped although there is no clear agreement over the exact manner in which they are interrelated. Small and Memmo (2004), for example, have distinguished three main approaches in the field of youth development—prevention, resilience, and PYD—and have classified community youth development under the umbrella of PYD, albeit "a variant." On the other hand, Perkins, Borden, and Villarruel (2001) regard PYD as a precursor and community youth development as a later development. In their perspective, PYD forms the base, and community youth development adds to this base. Principles of development across the two constructs are shared: Some have the same emphasis, and others receive singularly focal attention in community youth development.

Community Youth Development and PYD: Common Principles with the Same Emphasis

Community youth development also avows a shift in foci from (a) youth problems to youth competencies, (b) at-risk youth to all youth, and (c) youth as individuals to reciprocal youth-context relationships (Perkins et al., 2003). For example, Perkins et al. (2003) in defining community youth development start out with "As with positive youth development, a community youth development orientation involves a shift away from concentrating on problems toward concentrating on strengths, competencies" (p. 5), or "community youth development framework shifts the focus from the individual to the interaction of the individual with the multiple levels of his or her environment" (p. 6). Other principles/constructs that are embraced from PYD into community youth development with the same emphasis are developmental assets, the five Cs, and planned (positive) change.

Community Youth Development and PYD: Common Principles with an Increased Emphasis

The centrality of the community context, and youth contribution and action, is further amplified in community youth development. Of course, each of these is also crucial in PYD (e.g., Benson et al.'s youth action hypothesis). Yet, if we go with the idea that the community youth development approach can be distinguished from PYD, we must say that in community youth development, the reciprocity between community and youth receives almost exclusive attention: that is, the reciprocal relationship between adults and community engaged with youth, and youth engaged with adults and community (Perkins et al., 2003).

Youth Participation and Youth Engagement

In the 1990s, the paradigm shift to PYD was compellingly framed in Pittman's statement, "Problem free is not fully prepared"; community youth development goes one step further, framed in another of Pittman's statements, "Fully prepared isn't fully participating" (as cited in Perkins et al., 2003, p. 3). The word "prepared" connotes having got ready for something in the future, in this case, for successful adulthood (Perkins et al., 2003). However, it is (also) the "participation in the now" that interests community youth development scholars and practitioners. Moreover, what guise does participation take?

In the community youth development approach, youth participate as partners, simultaneously contributing to their own and community development. Thus, "(c)ommunity youth development shifts the emphasis from a dual focus of youth being problem-free and fully prepared, to a triadic focus for youth being problem-free, fully prepared, and engaged partners" (Perkins et al., 2001, p. 43).

Youth participation, also called youth voice, youth decision-making, youth empowerment, or youth engagement (O'Donoghue, Kirshner, & McLaughlin, 2002), is pivotal to community youth development. It has been defined "as a constellation of activities that empower adolescents to take part in and influence decision-making that affects their lives and to take action on issues they care about" (O'Donoghue et al., 2002, p. 16). Youth participation is a challenge to adults to "take youth seriously, not just as potential future actors but as actors now" (Kirshner, O'Donoghue, & McLaughlin, 2002, p. 5). In a Youth Engaged in Leadership and Learning (YELL) resource book (2007, p. 290), the key features of a community development approach are listed as follows:

- Embraces youth as authentic partners in the task of community development
- Promotes programs and practices that support youth leadership and impact the community
- Encourages collaboration and shared responsibility for youth outcomes

Fusion of Youth Development and Community Development

To state the obvious, community youth development integrates youth development and community development (Perkins et al., 2003), or in Huebner's (2003) words, there is "recognition of community development and youth development as intertwined endeavors" (p. 351). Youth participation is considered indispensable in accomplishing "the goal of making communities better places for young people to grow up" (Perkins et al., 2003, p. 7).

Youth design and implement different ways of serving their community. For instance, Zoroastrian youth who organized and participated in a large-scale money/staple food collection drive from well-to-do Zoroastrian families in Mumbai, followed by redistribution to disadvantaged Zoroastrian families in Gujarat, shared that they were surprised at how joyful and satisfying the service event had been for them, that their intention to serve the community had been strengthened as also their own sense of usefulness (Mazkoory, Irani, & Bakshi, 2010). Zoroastrian youth volunteering as youth facilitators in Zoroastrian Youth for the Next Generation (ZYNG) shared, for example:

- "The events organized are not for the Zoroastrian youth to just get together, it is also for the youth to get a sense of belonging, to do something, to give back to their own community. This actually is beneficial for them."
- "We have to change from takers to givers."

PYD/Community Youth Development Programs

Youth development programs are organized, structured activities for youth beneficiaries that are more than one-time efforts, are offered during nonschool hours, and have well-defined goals (Perkins & Borden, 2003); PYD programs are designed for development of competencies in all youth. Examples in the United States "include, but are not limited to, sports programs, before- and after-school clubs, service clubs, faith-based organizations, 4-H Youth Development programs, Boys and Girls Clubs, Boy Scouts and Girl Scouts, YMCA, and those sponsored by other community and/or youth-serving organizations" (Perkins & Borden, 2003, p. 328).

Characteristics of High-Quality PYD/Community Youth Development Programs

Catalano et al. (2004) identified the characteristics of effective PYD programs in the United States. They found that effective PYD programs promote at least five PYD constructs such as competence (i.e., social, behavioral, emotional, cognitive, and/or moral competencies), self-efficacy, bonding, belief in the future, and positive identity. Importantly, effective PYD programs measure

outcomes: optimally both problem behaviors and positive outcomes. Effective programs are more likely to have a structured curriculum and high fidelity in program delivery. Effective programs were also found to offer a 9-month or longer program of activities with high periodicity.

Roth and Brooks-Gunn (2003) have recommended three defining characteristics of PYD programs. First, the *program goals* must be directed to PYD (e.g., the five Cs). Second, the *program atmosphere* must be caring and supportive and facilitate high-quality relationships with adults and peers. The program must provide sustained engagement in a physically and psychologically safe environment, help create belongingness and commitment, have clearly stated rules/responsibilities, and have expectations and positive recognition for youth success. Third, the *program activities* must be participatory; engage youth in authentic activities; include opportunities to develop and exercise leadership, build interests, learn new skills, and broaden horizons; and increase the quality of other developmental contexts (e.g., family, community).

Perkins and Borden's (2003) list of characteristics of high-quality youth programs also includes, for example, the following: High-quality youth programs engage youth as partners at every step, have youth participate in organized community service, proactively recruit and work with youth from diverse backgrounds, collaborate with other youth-serving organizations, and have well-trained staff. Perkins et al. (2003) reiterated that community youth development programs are "done with and by youth" and (despite being valuable) are not "done to or for youth" (p. 8).

Efficacy of PYD Programs

Roth and Brooks-Gunn (2003) observed that although the number of PYD programs was substantially high (in the United States), most programs had not been evaluated using experimental or quasi-experimental research designs. In the literature they found 48 rigorously evaluated youth programs that had successfully led to positive outcomes for participating youth; of these they identified 21 as PYD programs (i.e., aiming to and succeeding in promoting positive outcomes relating to three or more Cs) and 27 as youth programs (i.e., programs aiming to and succeeding in developing fewer than three Cs). Similarly, Catalano et al. (2004) were able to locate 25 PYD programs (in the United States) that met stringent conceptual (i.e., use of PYD constructs), methodological (e.g., availability of a control/comparison group), and outcome (i.e., significant effects) criteria.

Youth Career Development

Youth career development is one rather salient aspect of youth development focused on helping youth prepare for successful integration into the (adult) world of work. In the PYD perspective, "(o)ne aspect of life for which they must be fully prepared is the world of work" (Ferrari, 2003, p. 202).

Importance of Youth Career Development

The necessity of directing increasing attention to youth career development is cogently presented in the *Global Employment Trends for Youth 2010* (ILO, 2010). We must remind ourselves that:

> Young men and women today build the foundations for the economies and societies of today and tomorrow. They bring energy, talent and creativity to economies and make important contributions as productive workers, entrepreneurs, consumers, agents of change and as members of civil society. (p. 2)

In regard to labor market entry, the youth represent "a group with serious vulnerabilities even at the best of times" (p. 2); and "the global economic crisis has further exposed the fragility of youth in the labour market" (p. 1). Many youth, across the world, are experiencing mounting levels of insecurity about transitioning (successfully) into the labor market (ILO, 2010). In 2010, the youth labor force participation rate was 50.9 % (i.e., one out of every two young persons was active in the labor market). Although this figure reflects a positive trend of a growing number of youth extending their stay in education, it also includes youth who are neither in education nor employment (NEET). Some of these NEET

youth are "discouraged workers," that is, youth who have given up hope and disengaged from the labor market. Among the employed youth, especially in developing regions, "decent work deficits" (e.g., working under suboptimal conditions which include low wages, generally in the informal economy) are increasing the proportion of the working poor. "A lack of decent work, if experienced at an early age, threatens to compromise a person's future employment prospects and frequently leads to unsuitable labour behaviour patterns that last a lifetime" (p. 6). Moreover, the ILO notes that youth's labor market knowledge, job search skills, social networks, self-promotion skills, and prior work experience are frequently less than adequate, especially in comparison to older workers. Unsurprisingly therefore, youth have to face a labor market bias such that they are the first to be laid off during downsizing and the last to be hired when there is a shortage of jobs in the labor market (i.e., "first out/last in") (ILO, 2010).

Building Career Readiness of Youth

Career development, of course, is a lifelong process. There are several aspects to consider while supporting youth who are yet to enter the labor market.

Facilitating Youth in Self-Exploration and Self-Development

Especially in cultures/subcultures in which gender gaps in education and employment have diminished, a paid career/occupation is a prominent means of self-definition and self-construction for both young men and women. Considering or thinking about selecting various occupations/careers is simultaneously an exercise in self-exploration. An evolving personhood hinges on this process. Who have I been? Who would I like to be? Who could I be? What do I like doing? What would I like to learn? Halpern (2012, p. 87) has also suggested questions such as the following: How personally important is work for me? What do I want to get out of my work? What kind of work will fit my sense of who I want to become? What or who do I want to become?

Box 10.1 Self-exploration versus self-development

Exploring the self	Extending or developing the self
• Identifying potential and current strengths and limitations	• Identifying and following up on new areas of learning
	• Building on potential strengths
	• Working on current limitations
• Exploring interests (Hynes, 2012), confirming or disconfirming emerging interests (Halpern, 2012)	• Following up on emerging interests; creating new interests
• Identifying hopes and fears (e.g., some youth have hopes of moving out of poverty, others fear moving into poverty [ILO, 2010])	• Selecting actions that increase hope and diminish fears/concerns about educational and career success
• Identifying gender stereotypes/barriers	• Transcending gender stereotypes/barriers
• Identifying own values and examining overlap/ distinction with family or community values	• Respecting roots, yet able to begin work toward (upward) social class mobility/occupational mobility
	• Selecting (career-related) values that promote the common goodness (e.g., practicing a sustainable career [Arulmani, 2011])
• Recognizing the role of social-cognitive environments, collective self-efficacy beliefs, and (negative or dysfunctional) career beliefs (Arulmani & Nag-Arulmani, 2004; Bandura, 2002; Naylor & Krumboltz, 1994)	• Reconsidering and refashioning career beliefs (Arulmani & Bakshi, 2012; Krumboltz, 2009)
• Making realistic life goals and plans	• Making life goals and plans which are feasible in small steps, yet are personally challenging, inspiring, and allow reaching for the extraordinary

These questions and their possible beneficial outcomes may be constrained by gender stereotypes/barriers, social class stereotypes/ barriers, negative career beliefs, and concerns about access to financial, social, and educational resources. For the less privileged, these questions may be colored or even overshadowed by fears about making it; survival for some may be more important than examining the self or envisioning ideal selves. The self-exploration of youth especially in more collectivistic cultures may also involve the following: Who would my parents/ teachers like me to be? What do my parents want me to do? How important are my parents' or community's preferences for me?

In assisting youth in meaningful self-exploration, it is important to acknowledge that self-processes are multiple and ongoing rather than predetermined or fixed (e.g., Harter, 2006). There are past and current selves; there are possible and future selves. The focus must not only be on exploring the self but also on extending the boundaries of "who I am" and "who I can be" (see Box 10.1). Krumboltz and Worthington (1999) have asserted that youth need to *expand* their interests and capabilities instead of basing career choice and other decisions only on existing characteristics.

Moreover, although the self is an agentic construct, the self also reflects (conscious or unconscious) social influences (Cooley, 1902; Harter, 2006). In career guidance, parents can be involved in youth's self-exploration (see Salvatore, Nota, Ferrari, & Ginevra, 2014, Chap. 9); the goal is to promote agency within a collaborative context of the family (also, school and community). Especially in cultures with a more collectivist orientation, youth may benefit from assistance in consensus generation with co-constructors and coproducers of their life goals and plans (mainly parents, elders, and— when married—spouse and in-laws). In formulating positive vocational identities, all youth will benefit from supportive processes that acknowledge their contexts and the extent to which these contexts favor their vocational inclinations (Porfeli & Lee, 2012). Advocacy and mobilization of resources/support for youth in the community may be crucial for facilitating youth in extending "who they can be."

Facilitating Youth Exposure to the World of Work

Youth can only select an occupation from the range of occupations they know about. Their self-exploration and self-development in relation to future careers is enhanced or limited depending on the range of occupations to which they are exposed. Supporting youth in this regard entails providing:

- Exposure to a wide range of career options (Ferrari, 2003), exposure to sustainable careers (see Arulmani, 2011), and in-breadth and in-depth exploration of careers vis-à-vis the self (Porfeli & Lee, 2012)
- Exposure to career role models, followed by opportunities to reflect and discuss (Ferrari, 2003) and opportunities to interact with different adults and older/experienced peers who talk about/demonstrate their specialized knowledge, attitudes, and skills (Hamilton & Hamilton, 2012)
- Exposure to male and female leaders who can help youth overcome gender stereotypes (Denner & Griffin, 2003)
- Access to actual working environments (Mekinda, 2012) such that youth can observe the differences in vocations and vocational cultures; day-in and day-out experiences at work; the variety of roles in a work setting; and the "rhythms, distinct pleasures, and difficulties of work" (Halpern, 2012, p. 98)

The methods/means of promoting the mutuality between self-exploration/self-development and career exploration/career development among the youth are many. Some examples are:

- Opportunities for project-based or experiential learning (Mekinda, 2012, p. 45)
- Supervised work experiences (Hynes & Hirsch, 2012)

- Partnerships with local/regional employers and businesses (or not-for-profit institutions) who can offer part-time jobs, job shadowing, internships, and mentoring (Klein, 2012; Mekinda, 2012)
- Apprenticeships in a wide range of professions/occupations (Mekinda, 2012)
- Community volunteering (Alexander & Hirsch, 2012)
- Youth enterprise and youth entrepreneurship (Hamilton & Hamilton, 2012)

Such experiences are essential for developing a more "concrete sense of possible occupational choices" (Halpern, 2012, p. 96).

Helping Youth Build a Network of Caring Adults and Peers Who Can Mentor

In facilitating the social capital of youth, Hamilton and Hamilton's (2012) strategy of bonding (i.e., strengthening relationships within existing social networks) and bridging (i.e., creating new connections with those outside existing social networks) can be used. Social networks in which youth have opportunities to be coached and mentored are invaluable for self- and career exploration and related decision-making (Hamilton & Hamilton, 2012; Mekinda, 2012). "Adult mentors …serve as exemplars, modeling the practice, general behavior, and affective commitment of one with that particular identity" (Halpern, 2012, p. 95). Mentors can help make education and career paths transparent; they are sources of new social connections and can "teach the small things critical to socialization into particular work settings" (Halpern, 2012, p. 98; Hamilton & Hamilton, 2012). The salience of adult mentors may make their depiction of particular career paths (e.g., through conversations, role modeling) more alive and appealing (than say, descriptions of an occupation on websites); youth may be persuaded to embark on and/or persist in trajectories that are daunting in the hard work required but have the clear advantage of helping youth attain desirable career goals. Other advantages of social networks include support for job search, placement, and retention (ILO, 2010).

Supporting Youth in Negotiating a Dynamic World of Work

"A life's work in a single occupation is no longer a likely prospect for youth" (Hamilton & Hamilton, 2012, p. 73). Youth must prepare for career trajectories that will possibly have multiple beginnings and endings, crossroads, and changes in routes and destinations. Accordingly, Porfeli and Lee (2012) have recommended that youth learn how to formulate and *revise* vocational identities. They outline three intertwined processes: career exploration, career commitment, and career reconsideration.

- Career exploration—youth must be facilitated in developing skills in assaying the changing world of work in conjunction (in our view) with their own evolving personhood. Youth must understand that such career exploration is a lifelong goal.
- Career commitment—youth can be supported in selecting a career and connecting their identity to this career after due exploration. Timing is dependent on the individual; what is important is that the decision must not be premature or precipitate such that necessary self-processes are foreclosed.
- Career reconsideration—youth must be assisted in reflecting over career commitments and comparing these to other available options; the outcome of such a reflective process is either a strengthening/further specification of a career commitment or a change in career. Career reconsideration is a needed process in current times, especially when it represents required adaptability and flexibility rather than self-doubt.

To reiterate, not only must youth be assisted in engaging in each of these processes, they must also be taught how to engage in these processes time and again such that they remain responsive and perhaps even proactive to changes in the world of work as well as in their own selves.

At a narrower yet crucial level, youth have to be assisted in learning how to search for, procure, and retain a job (Greene & Staff, 2012). This too is needing to be a lifelong set of skills because it is far less likely that a person will have the same job across their (paid) working life or even across large segments of it. For example, youth can be taught interviewee skills (e.g., self-presentation and self-promotion) (Alexander & Hirsch, 2012). Moreover, given that the availability, quality, or longevity of jobs cannot be guaranteed, entrepreneurship education is also exceedingly important for youth career development today (Hamilton & Hamilton, 2012).

Supporting Youth in Learning Transferable Skills and Substantive Skills

Variously called transferable skills, 21st century skills, soft skills, or skills sought by employers, the following are useful in many work environments and remain relevant regardless of a change in job or occupation (Alexander & Hirsch, 2012; Greene & Staff, 2012; Hynes, 2012; Hynes & Hirsch, 2012; Perry & Wallace, 2012; SCANS, 1991):

- Professionalism, dependability, regularity, punctuality, accountability, and self-management
- Teamwork, collaboration, and sociability
- Good oral and written communication
- Skills in selecting and utilizing information to solve problems
- Learning, evaluation, and reasoning skills
- Information and communication technology (ICT) skills
- Initiative and creative thinking
- Project management (steps in completing a project from start to finish; meeting project deadlines); sustaining goal-oriented activity over a short or long period

Another important transferable skill is prioritizing and balancing multiple demands and responsibilities across contexts of participation (e.g., one's work versus family and friends). Youth can also be supported in strengthening personal qualities that are transferable across work settings such as self-esteem, self-efficacy, integrity, and optimism (SCANS, 1991; Silbereisen & Lerner, 2007).

Other than a set of transferable skills and qualities, youth also need to be supported in beginning to learn occupation-specific skills (Greene & Staff, 2012). Success in the world of work is contingent on developing substantive expertise as well (Hynes, 2012). In this regard, youth can be offered opportunities to build technical/vocational skills and even obtain vocational certifications (Halpern, 2012; Mekinda, 2012).

Assisting Youth in Persisting in Education

Given job trends, in supporting youth career development the focus must also be on assisting youth to continue (higher) education and succeed in (higher) education (Hynes & Hirsch, 2012). Openness to formal and informal learning is indispensable to career development at every stage (see Bimrose & Brown, 2014, Chap. 11). Mentors can explain and model the process and benefits of such learning.

"Linking Youth to the Next Step"

Hynes (2012) has stressed the need to "link youth to the next step" (p. 109). Likewise, Ferrari (2003) has observed that the focus generally is on the "what" rather than the "how" of career development (i.e., what to become rather than how to go about making that career choice a reality). Knowledge about and facilitated access to the next steps are essential in youth career development. The next steps could be (a) planning for and enrolling in the educational paths leading to the desired career goal(s) or (b) transitioning from education to full-time paid work (Ferrari, 2003; Greene & Staff, 2012; Mekinda, 2012).

Youth Career Development Programs

A related construct in the American literature is *career programming*. Hynes and Hirsch (2012) have defined it as follows:

> Career programming refers to any systematic effort to expose youth to the world of work and teach them the skills and knowledge they need to be successful. It can include career exploration, job search and job readiness skills, supervised work experiences, and technical education. Career programming can be the main focus of a program, or career exploration and skill building can be integrated into a host of content-specific programming in areas such as sports, music, science, and technology. (pp. 1–2)

Characteristics of High-Quality Youth Career Development Programs

The content of high-quality youth career development programs must include the features discussed in the subsection on building career readiness of youth. Similar to the characteristics of high-quality PYD programs, the methods of high-quality youth career development programs include experiential learning methods; adequate duration, intensity, and frequency; and trained adult facilitators (Ferrari, 2003). Moreover, the content and methods should invite and sustain youth engagement (Hynes & Hirsch, 2012).

Efficacy of Youth Career Development Programs

One outstanding example of a youth career development program in the United States is *After School Matters* (ASM), which serves students (mainly low income and minority) in 45 public high schools in Chicago, offering more than 5,500 apprenticeships each term under the direction of community experts from a wide range of occupations/career fields (Mekinda, 2012). The positives in this program include sustained engagement (90 hours across 10 weeks), experiential learning, and access to mentors; the negatives include inadequate access to real work environments (school based) and a (greater) focus on occupations that are not priorities in the job market (e.g., those relating to the fine and performing arts) (Mekinda, 2012). Mekinda has described the rigorous evaluation conducted by Hirsch and colleagues in which ASM youth showed significant positive effects in comparison to control youth (participants in other after-school activities) on two out of several outcome measures: increased self-regulation and reduced problem behaviors. Alexander and Hirsch (2012) found no significant mean difference between mock hire rates of ASM youth versus control youth; however, ASM youth in particular apprenticeships were up to 47 % more likely to be hired than control youth. They found that the "best-hire" ASM apprenticeships had instructors who used positive communication (e.g., encouragement, correcting), whereas the "worst-hire" ASM apprenticeship instructors frequently used negative communication (e.g., unconstructive criticism); the best-hire apprenticeships were also characterized by greater professionalism (e.g., regularity, expectation of initiative and creativity from youth, sustained goal-oriented activity). Similarly, evaluation studies have been conducted with other youth career development programs in the United States such as Job Corps (see Mekinda, 2012).

Exploring Linkages

To what extent is career development part of the framework of PYD? Roth and Brooks-Gunn (2003) in defining the first C of PYD programs—competence—include vocational competence along with social, academic, and cognitive competencies. Likewise, Huebner's (2003) list of types of competence fostered through PYD programs includes employability; the other types of competence that she has listed are also directly relevant for career development (e.g., intellectual competence, social competence, cultural competence), as are those included by Roth and Brooks-Gunn.

The linkages between PYD/community youth development programs and youth career development can be specified as answers to two questions: (a) To what extent *does* PYD address youth career development? (b) To what extent *can* PYD address youth career development? In other words, what are the connections that exist, and what are the connections that can be developed. Of the multiple aspects necessary for promoting career readiness in youth, the following are well addressed in PYD/community youth development programs: (a) self-exploration and self-development, (b) access to mentors/positive role models/caring adults and supportive peers, (c) learning of transferable or soft skills, and (d) broadening of horizons. Developmental assets (internal and external), the six Cs, initiative, and a life purpose are all constructs which are overlapped in yielding benefit for broader

developmental goals as well as more specific goals such as career development.

In comparison, the following aspects relating to building career readiness of youth need more explicit attention and may or may not feature in a PYD/community youth development program: (a) extensive exposure to the world of work; (b) skills in revising vocational identities; (c) learning occupation-specific skills; and (d) linking youth to the next steps in education, job search, job procurement, and job retention.

Further, we strongly argue that it is vital to strengthen the connection between PYD and youth career development: That youth career development can be optimized through the use of a PYD approach. Key principles of PYD (e.g., augmenting developmental ecologies of youth, meeting youth needs within their ecologies, enhancing positive reciprocities between youth and their ecologies, youth action, youth contribution) make interventions particularly impactful both in the short run as well as the longer run.

Case Example from India: PYD Programs of the Shia Ismaili Muslim Community

Introduction

India has the largest youth population in the world (550 million); 70 % of the population is below 35 years (Ministry of Youth Affairs and Sports, 2011). Youth work in India is carried out through government-supported programs (e.g., National Cadet Corps [NCC], National Service Scheme [NSS], guides and scouts), nongovernmental organization (NGO) initiatives, school-based and college-based programs (e.g., community service/volunteering programs), faith-based/religious community initiatives, youth wings of clubs such as Rotary Club and Lions Club, and youth wings of spiritual movements such as Swadhyay or Art of Living.

There are many faith-based organizations in India who offer activities and programs for (positive) youth development. Many of these youth-serving organizations limit their outreach to youth from the same religious faith. For example, Zoroastrians, Kutchi Jains, Catholics, and Ismailis have faith-based youth-serving organizations for youth of their own faith. A few youth-serving organizations, although grounded in one faith, have youth missions which cover youth from any faith (e.g., the Chinmaya Mission Trust and the Don Bosco Youth Services); a few of the activities and programs of such organizations are specifically directed to youth of the same faith. Because of their prominence in youth work in India, we have decided to use a faith-based organization's youth development programs as an illustration in this chapter. Further, we selected the youth programs of the Shia Ismaili Muslim community in India. The methods used were interviews with functionaries holding key positions and with youth beneficiaries, examination of evaluation data, and participant observations of the second author.

The Aga Khan Youth and Sports Board for India

The Shia Ismaili Muslim community, popularly known as the Aga Khan community, is the second largest Shia community, located in more than 20 countries (http://www.akdn.org/about_imamat.asp). Services to community members are provided through the Aga Khan Development Network (AKDN); youth development in AKDN is the responsibility of the Aga Khan Youth and Sports Board for India (AKYSBI).[1]

The AKYSBI conducts extensive developmental programs for youth of the community (supported by internal evaluation studies). These programs are designed using the Search Institute's developmental assets framework. Individual-level developmental assets such as

personal power, *self-esteem*, *responsibility*, and *sense of purpose* have been selected as targets.

Organizational Structure

The AKYSBI has distributed its functions across three types of boards (i.e., national, 6 regional, and 30 local). For example, the national board, constituted of experts appointed from the community,[2] is responsible for identifying youth needs, conceptualizing/designing programs, building capacity among youth and older volunteers[3] for the meaningful execution of designed programs, and executing the national-level programs.

Beneficiaries

Various programs are designed for Ismaili youth in the age group of 8–25 years from varied socio-economic backgrounds. The other beneficiaries include parents of youth (through parenting programs) and youth volunteers who participate in detailing, organizing, and conducting the programs. Each year AKYSBI reaches out to over 14,000 Ismaili youth in India.

Range of Youth Development Programs

The programs are classified using the following: (a) age groups (i.e., 8–11, 12–15, 16–19, 20–25 years) and (b) urban-versus-rural residence and privilege (i.e., urban privileged, urban underprivileged, and rural). The range of programs/services include self-development programs, sports, fitness activities, youth awards for excellence, and parenting workshops. The key features of programs/services conducted at the national and local levels are listed in Tables 10.1 and 10.2, respectively. The content in these tables has been organized such that the extent to which a program addresses career development

---

[1] Another relevant AKDN organization is the Aga Khan Education Service India (AKESI) which provides career guidance among other services.

[2] The AKYSBI employs a few professionals from the fields of human development/psychology to assist the national board members in their work.

[3] Youth volunteers are mostly in the age group of 18–25 years; older volunteers are mostly in the age group of 25–45 years, a few are older.

Table 10.1 AKYSBI youth programs conducted at the national level

Program	Age group (year)	Sector	Explicit career development activity	Activities also supportive of career development	Other activities	Duration and periodicity
The National Rural Youth Project, *Aashayein* (Hopes, Aspirations)	• 12–15 • 16–25	Rural	• Personal growth activities (e.g., self-awareness, teamwork, leadership) • Developing/expanding a sense of purpose in life • Career guidance and counseling • Exposure visits • Interactions with inspirational role models • English and computer classes • Tracking and follow-up to assess progress made and further assistance required	• Outdoor adventure • Theater workshop	• Sports • Fitness • Sessions on anti-tobacco use • Advocacy drive against substance abuse organized by youth • Recreational nights organized by youth	Multiple segments of 7–10 day residential camps; total duration 40 days; one such 40-day program/year benefitting 120–125 Ismaili youth
Laqsh (Goal) (Follow-up of the *Aashayein* program)	• 12–15 • 16–25	Rural	• Career guidance and counseling • Entrepreneurship education workshops (how to start/expand a business) • Information on courses offered by Industrial Training Institutes (ITI) • Information on loans and scholarships for further education • Beautician course in the city (for women) • Job placements in the city • City skills for those moving to urban areas for education or job	—	—	2-day follow-up event organized between 1 and 3 years of completion of the *Aashayein* program

(continued)

Table 10.1 (continued)

Program	Age group (year)	Sector	Explicit career development activity	Activities also supportive of career development	Other activities	Duration and periodicity
Hum Honge Kamyaab (We Shall Succeed)	• 12–15	Rural	• Personal growth activities (e.g., self-awareness, teamwork, leadership) • Exposure visit • Goal-setting and creating a roadmap • Interactions with inspirational role models	• Outdoor adventure • Theater workshop	• Sessions on anti-tobacco use	7-day residential camp; 1–2 camps/year targeting different groups of youth Each camp size: 90 youth
The Heroes Project	• 12–15 • 16–19	Semi-urban	• Personal growth activities (e.g., self-awareness, value clarification) • Goal-setting and creating a roadmap • Interactions with inspirational role models	• Activities to build life skills such as critical thinking (e.g., analyzing influence of media), assertiveness training	• Sessions on anti-tobacco use • Advocacy drive against substance abuse and other risky behaviors organized by youth	5-day residential camp; 2–3 camps/year targeting different groups of youth Each camp size: 90 youth
Youth Camp	• 16–22	All India	• Activities on self-development (e.g., value clarification) • Leadership and team-building activities	• High-level adventure activities • Intellectually-challenging activities like Mock UN, mock Crime Scene Investigations • Youth-led committees (e.g., bloggers team, video shooters, camp news reporters) • Community service projects	–	5-day residential camp; one camp/year Camp size: 90 youth
Youth Awards for Excellence (An event for youth; not a program)	• 8–25	All India	–	• Awards for excellence in varied fields such as sports, literature, fine arts, performing arts, crafts, leadership, social service	–	Once in 2–3 years

can be quickly noted. Of these, selected programs are described in detail.

1. The National Rural Youth Project, *Aashayein* (see Table 10.1): This program was started in 2008 after surveying Ismaili youth needs through focus group discussions with youth and interviews with parents and other adults from rural areas. The major findings were that rural youth lacked inspirational role models and had low aspirations, low self-confidence, and difficulties with English language and computer skills. Also, tobacco usage was noted as high among boys (AKYSBI, 2005). Those who wanted to pursue further education did not have anyone to guide them. There was limited career information and no formal educational and vocational guidance. Some youth were not motivated, and others prioritized family responsibilities and/or felt restricted by their socioeconomic conditions. For example, a 16-year-old boy stated:

I want to go out (to the city) for further education. But there is no one else who can look after my family. I am responsible for my mother and sister, and I have to earn for the family.

The varied activities that comprise the Aashayein youth program are listed in Table 10.1 and include many that directly promote the career readiness of youth. The follow-up of participants of Aashayein has yielded a mixed picture of the impact of this program. Some youth have reported positive outcomes related to career development such as realizing the importance of education and a good career and getting wider information about possible careers. To illustrate:

Earlier I had no idea of what I want to become. Now at least, I have thought of being a business-man. (15-year-old boy)
    In the past due to certain reasons, I gave up education. But now I feel that it is important to get good education and career to meet my responsi-bilities towards my family. (17-year-old boy)
    I would like to resume education. I had left my studies because I failed in Grade 8, but I realize that was just a failure and I can succeed if I try really hard. (15-year-old girl)

Aashayein also appears to potentially support career development through the promotion of self-development. Youth have reported experiencing personal power, developing a sense of purpose, having higher ambitions, taking ownership for own development, and enhancing skills such as critical thinking and decision-making. Even theater workshops and outdoor adventure activities appear to have relevance for the career development of participating youth:

If I can climb 10 meters on a rock, I can do anything in life. (18-year-old male youth)
    I used to think that others are better, but now I think that I am also good. (15-year-old boy after participating in the theater workshop)

On the downside, the follow-up research indicates that there have been many youth who nonetheless have not taken any further action toward their career goals. Many rural youths' career paths have remained stalled. The focus on urban careers in career guidance could be one reason for this finding. Also, many youth's increased interest in education has translated into a desire to pursue short-term (and not longer-term) courses such that they can start earning sooner. Such a finding is common in a culture of disadvantage: Bakshi (2011) found that the less privileged in Mumbai had engaged in paid work sooner than the more privileged; similarly, Arulmani, Van Laar, and Easton (2003) found that a larger proportion of youth from lower SES groups in India discontinued their education early in order to start earning an income. Youth who have been interested in studying further have faced barriers such as poor academic scores, difficulties with English language, financial constraints, and lack of family support.

2. *Laqsh* (see Table 10.1): The follow-up program of Aashayein is known as *Laqsh*, meaning *a goal*. This intervention was designed to address the issues identified in the impact evaluation of Aashayein.

The Laqsh program explicitly targets youth career development through a range of activities which are listed in Table 10.1. The Laqsh intervention has been helpful to some youth. For example, a few youth have reported benefits with regard to their business skills. Some girls have moved to cities to pursue their careers as beauticians. A handful of boys have accepted the city jobs that were offered through Laqsh. Youth have also reported benefits such as a change in how they spend their time. In the words of these youth:

I had opened my shop about four years back, but Aashayein (Laqsh) has helped me to work hard, to handle it more efficiently, and so my business has increased. (25-year-old participant)

I got inspired when I attended the Aashayein (Laqsh) program. I have come to Mumbai to learn to be a beautician. City skills that we learn during Laqsh program are helping me a lot. (21-year-old female youth)

Earlier I watched television for long hours, but now I have developed a habit of reading books too. (14-year-old boy)

Other Laqsh participants appear to not have been benefitted in the ways that were conceptualized in the program design. For example, training opportunities in multiple work sectors in the city were made available. No rural youth accepted these training opportunities, which entailed a move to the city and required the youth to arrange for own accommodation and finances. The job offers from businesspersons in the city were accepted by few and refused by many. In explaining their decision to not accept city jobs, some youth said that they were happy with their current income (which was less than half of what was being offered), while others said that they did not want jobs in towns/cities as it would mean moving to urban areas, away from their families:

I make Rs. 5000/month (USD 92) from my shop. I am happy. I don't want to go anywhere for a better job. (22-year-old male youth)

I would like to take the job so that I can earn better; but I have to look after my family here. I can't go (to the city) leaving behind my mother and sister. (20-year-old male youth)

The findings across the Aashayein and Laqsh programs indicate that over the years,

19 % (124 out of 647) youth have moved to urban areas to pursue better quality education or jobs. Of these 124 youth, most are older boys ($n = 71$, 57 %), followed by older girls ($n = 33$, 27 %), younger boys ($n = 16$, 13 %), and then younger girls ($n = 4$, 3 %). The reasons for migrating were better education ($n = 64$, 52 %), job ($n = 51$, 41 %), and participation in courses enabling one to work, for example, as a beautician or a computer hardware technical assistant ($n = 9$, 7 %).

3. The Heroes Project (see Table 10.1): This camp, designed for youth in the ages 12–15 and 16–19 years from semi-urban areas, is based on a needs assessment exercise in which lack of purpose and direction, high tobacco consumption, and a strong negative influence of media were identified as the major challenges for this group. Thus, the camp has been positioned as a "Heroes" camp that invites youth to be real heroes—productive members of society who can restrain from tobacco and other harmful substances and live a life of meaning and purpose.

During the five-day camp, trained volunteers (including older youth) conduct small-group activities that are aimed at promoting the personal growth of youth. Youth are assisted in identifying personal qualities that make a person a hero and in analyzing their own lives—aspects that they are happy about and those that they would like to address. Here, many participants have identified education- and career-related aspects as those that they would like to improve. Next, youth create their road maps, with facilitators helping them to identify the broad steps (e.g., gathering information about courses and institutions) that youth need to undertake to achieve their goals.

Participants of this program are tracked to determine their progress with regard to life goals and health habits; the follow-up is currently in process. Findings from the end-of-camp evaluation indicated that many youth would like career guidance to be provided in the refresher camps. Youth participants have shared what they have learnt:

I will be successful in life. I didn't know before that I can be a hero. Previously I didn't have a hero, but now I am my own hero. (17-year-old girl)

I have got confidence, learnt to say no to bad habits like drinking and smoking, and be active in studies and enjoy life. (14-year-old boy)

After my HSC (Grade 12), I will take the stream which I wish and not the stream which my friends tell me. (16-year-old girl)

Along with youth participants, youth volunteers have also reported benefits. A youth facilitator shared:

I have been a participant of local programs, and now a volunteer (for national programs). It feels good to see yourself affecting change. It has taken me from being powerless to achieving a sense of power. By virtue of being a volunteer, I have developed my own personality. I have learnt to overcome challenges and to thrive. (22-year-old female youth)

4. *Café YSB* (see Table 10.2): Café YSB is a youth-led, local-level program. This program provides youth with opportunities to identify and work on personal strengths/limitations, build teamwork and management skills, and have exposure to and interaction time with inspirational role models. Examples of youth participants' perception of their achievements through Café YSB include:

I was in two teams: stage decoration and anchoring. I was never proud of myself. When I started, I was not willing to do the program. But now, I feel proud that we organized such a brilliant program. I was a 'never-ready' person, but now I am an 'always-ready' person. (17-year-old girl)

I am 16, and at this young age, I headed a committee (Catering Committee). I learnt how to lead and manage a team, how to deal with people and work in a group. (16-year-old girl)

I was highly inspired by the guests and now I know how high should I aim. (14-year-old boy from the audience)

Conclusion

This case example serves to illustrate a faith-based community's efforts to reach out and bolster the positive development of its youth. That these efforts simultaneously subsume programs

and activities to promote youth career development is also readily apparent. Attention has also been drawn to the potential linkages and mutuality between self-development, community development, and career development. It appears, for example, that participation in such community programs is helpful in the development of the much needed transferable skills or soft skills (e. g., teamwork and collaboration); also these programs may be beneficial with regard to the development of personal qualities such as confidence which are part of the PYD framework as well as important for career success (see Lerner, 2005; Savickas, 2005). Opportunities to build some substantive expertise or occupation-specific skills, exposure to positive peer and adult role models, and assistance with defining a life purpose are other strengths of the AKYSBI programs.

At least some youth have benefited from these multiple opportunities. At the same time, there are clear areas that need strengthening. Some recommendations are:

- To alter the episodic nature of the programs such that youth have sustained engagement in the same program for at least a year with sufficient periodicity through the year (e.g., at least once a week). This will also enable sustained relationships between youth and adult or older peer mentors.
- To focus more attention on "linking youth to the next steps" (Hynes, 2012, p. 109).
- To build higher levels of youth action (e.g., involve youth in conceptualization and designing of youth programs).
- To work toward expanding career opportunities (i.e., training, jobs, and entrepreneurship) in rural settings and identifying higher aspirations that can be met in rural areas instead of largely creating higher aspirations that require migration/urbanization. In fact, if higher aspirations are put into action in rural areas, it logically will lead to rural development which in turn will contribute to rural youth development.
- To build an interface with youth and youth programs from other communities and to provide structured opportunities for Ismaili youth

Table 10.2 AKYSBI youth programs conducted at the local level

Program	Age group (year)	Description of the program: activities supportive of, but not explicitly designed for career development	Duration and periodicity
Holiday Club	• 8–11 • 12–15	• Theme-based activities (e.g., pottery, film-making) • Opportunity for constructive use of free time • Trained volunteers, many of whom are youth, conduct the activities for younger children • Culminates in a youth-led finale	5 days; 1–2/year at different local centers
Theatre Workshop	• 8–11 • 12–15 • 16–19	• *Theater*—used as a medium for self-expression, self-development • Youth identify own talents and build upon them • Conducted by professional faculty • Culminates in a youth-led finale	5 days; 0–2/year at different local centers
Design for Change (DFC)	• 12–15 • 16–19	• "The program challenges youth to identify problems that bother them and the society they live in; think of solutions and implement them; and lastly, share their stories with others" (www.dfcworld.in) • A platform to exercise agency; youth work in groups • Examples of projects executed: installation of dustbins in housing societies, gathering funds for social causes	7–21 days; 0–2/year at different local centers
Café YSB	• 16–19	• Youth-led program: Youth form and work in various committees to organize a coffee talk with an inspirational guest • Beneficiaries: audience youth, and most importantly, youth from the organizing committees (e.g., research team, hosts, marketing team, ambiance team, finance team) • Event followed by guided reflection on learning and insights gained through participation	7–14 days; 0–2/year at different local centers
Touch the Sky	• 12–15	• Aims to facilitate young people to overcome own limitations, enhance self-esteem, increase emotional wellbeing, and to strengthen a positive view of personal future • Workshop-based program; conducted by professional faculty	1 day; 0–1/year at few local centers
Excellence Aspirations	• 16–19 • 20–25	• The aim is to encourage young people to aspire for excellence • Workshop-based program; conducted by trained faculty from the community	2 days; 0–1/year at few local centers
Mentoring	• 16–19 • 20–25	• A recent initiative to promote the personal development of both mentor and mentee • Mentor helps mentee to feel good about oneself, set desirable goals, use free time constructively, develop solutions to the challenges faced by mentee, and enhance various life skills	6 months interaction; recently launched at few local centers
Sports	• Open age group	• Provision of sports facilities (e.g., table tennis equipment) • Tie-ups with coaching agencies • Sports tournaments at local, regional, and national levels	Round the year
Fitness	• Open age group	• Marathon training • Fitness walks • Yoga	Round the year
Parenting Programs	• Open age group	• Organized for parents of youth in the ages 8–25 years • Conducted by certified volunteers	2 days; 1–2/year at different local centers

to collaborate with youth from other faiths. For success in the world of work, youth need to successfully integrate into culturally diverse, multi-faith contexts (SCANS, 1991).

• To increase the partnership between community experts and professionals.

• To use multiple types of evaluation research designs (e.g., a quasi-experimental design with a control group, youth-led evaluation).

Implications for Career Guidance: New Avenues for Career Guidance Practice

The interface between PYD and youth career development offers new avenues for career guidance practice. In this regard, we have the following recommendations:

• To maximize developmental achievements, we need "bridges between individuals and the contexts in which they live" (Perkins et al., 2003, p. 16). Career guidance practitioners must shift directions and invest effort in helping the youth and the community forge stronger bridges with each other such that both holistic and career-related developmental goals are promoted.

• Therefore, instead of the traditional focus on the individual, career guidance practitioners must expand their focus to work with communities. Their work must be founded in the belief that bolstering the developmental ecologies of youth is a powerful means to supporting youth career development. Benson et al. (2006b) have proposed that "the largest improvements in PYD will occur more in response to interventions/initiatives that are aimed at the community level than those aimed at individuals" (p. 8). Moreover, although Benson (2007) observed that in the United States an increase in professionalization of services has been accompanied with civic disengagement, we are contending that well-trained professionals can facilitate and empower civic engagement.

• Career guidance practice needs to be specially adapted for work with rural communities especially so in developing economies with a large rural population.

• Professional training of career guidance practitioners must (also) specifically address the skills needed for working with communities, including rural communities.

• Although PYD programs are aimed at enabling successful transitions to adulthood, Roth and Brooks-Gunn (2003) found that only 21 % of the effective programs that they located (in the United States) included vocational competence as a program goal. Benson et al. (2006a) in their list of disciplines working in the PYD field have not mentioned career psychologists or allied career guidance practice fields. It is clear that specific aspects of career development goals are underrepresented in PYD programs as are the career guidance practitioners themselves. It is time to remedy these gaps.

• The critical importance of youth participation/youth engagement is heavily underlined in community youth development approaches. Career guidance practitioners must integrate this principle in the interventions they design. At the community level, they can elicit partnership of youth and design youth events and programs, and build youth leadership.

• The community can benefit from the expertise of career guidance practitioners in designing and executing experiences that allow for self- and career exploration and self- and career development. For example, youth's part-time or internship placement in a real work environment without requisite (occupation-specific) skills may misinform the youth about the match between self and occupation. Such experiences have to be carefully scaffolded and include exposure to different worker's roles in that setting, the layered competencies that these roles required, demonstration of how these may be developed, and training along with work.

• Thus, by reducing the time spent in testing (e.g., aptitudes), career guidance practitioners can reallocate their time and (also) spend time augmenting structured community-based opportunities for youth career development and (for example) organize youth and business collaborations and facilitate youth exposure to a variety of work environments and role models such that youth move beyond gender or community stereotypes and other limiting notions. This will also shift foci from (a) appraisal-focused, diagnostic, and prescriptive career guidance practice in which the youth is a recipient who is expected to adjust or crudely compromise with test results to (b) an ecology-respecting career guidance practice in which an active co-constructing youth is supported in self-exploration in the (scaffolded yet) real world. Such a youth recognizes what *is*, and more so what *can be*—the multiple possibilities that can emerge by building on one's strengths.

- Career guidance practitioners can also engage in community capacity building through designing and providing training to youth and adult volunteers in community-based youth-serving organizations.
- In countries such as the United States, the number of PYD programs far exceeds the number of researches examining the outcomes of these programs (especially using rigorous quantitative or mixed methods research designs). In other types of countries such as India, community-based youth programs (which include explicit components relating to career development) are subjected to even less scrutiny. We would say, therefore, that the researcher role is also available in community settings.
- Also, the developmental assets framework and the five Cs are useful constructs to explore in career guidance research and practice. For example, the relationship between the PYD Cs and Savickas's (2005) career adaptability Cs could be examined.

Relevance for Multiple Cultures: Sensitivity to the Universal and Particular

Youth in countries across the world include those who are reciprocally engaged in contexts characterized by warmth, connection, and expectations, as well as those alienated from a context of caring. Healthy development, including successful career development, requires strengthened connections to positive contexts. In the absence of efforts to promote such connections, we incur double losses: We lose out because positive life trajectories are preempted; we also incur harm from the negative life trajectories that are then created. Without positive connections, life trajectories may be characterized by apathy, disengagement from meaningful work, and, in extreme instances, grievously harmful actions such as those of the juvenile boy in the much-publicized heinous gang rape incident that took place in Delhi in December 2012. Youth work does not reach out to each youth. Youth work needs to be accelerated; in youth-populous countries like India, this goal requires more effort.

Furthermore, it is very important to acknowledge and consider the heterogeneity of youth within and across cultures. Whereas, in this chapter the discussion of youth career development centers around building career readiness for youth who are yet to enter the job market, it is important to note that close to 90 % of the youth live in developing economies and underprivileged youth in these economies enter the job market early or begin their careers in childhood as support labor in family occupations (Bakshi, 2011; ILO, 2010). Approaches described in this chapter need to be adapted for bolstering the career success of these youth.

New Concepts and Viewpoints: Charting New Directions

"Community as an analytical and applied construct holds high promise," and community-based approaches to human development are becoming increasingly relevant (Benson & Saito, 2000, p. 132). The benefits of the confluence of community-based, systemic, and asset-based approaches in studying and scaffolding human development are being realized in PYD theory and practice. It is time for career guidance practitioners to capitalize on the opportunities and advantages that PYD theory and practice offer.

We too stand to thrive as we integrate our services more fully into the developmental ecologies of youth and adults.

References

Achenbach, T. M. (1991a). *Manual for the child behavior checklist/4-18 and 1991 profile*. Burlington, VT: Department of Psychiatry, University of Vermont.

Achenbach, T. M. (1991b). *Manual for the youth self-report and 1991 profile*. Burlington, VT: Department of Psychiatry, University of Vermont.

African Youth Charter (n.d.). Retrieved from http://africa-youth.org/sites/default/files/AFRICAN_YOUTH_CHARTER.pdf

Aga Khan Youth and Sports Board for India (AKYSBI). (2005). *Addressing the needs of rural youth*. Unpublished report.

Alexander, K. P., & Hirsch, B. J. (2012). Marketable job skills for high school students: What we learned from an evaluation of After School Matters. *New Directions for Youth Development, 134*, 55–63.

Arulmani, G. (2011). Striking the right note: The cultural preparedness approach to developing resonant career guidance programmes. *International Journal for Educational and Vocational Guidance, 11*(2), 79–93.

Arulmani, G., & Bakshi, A. J. (2012, October). *Career belief patterns: A framework to understand orientations to career development across cultures and socioeconomic status groups*. Paper presented at the IAEVG international conference, Mannheim, Germany.

Arulmani, G., & Nag-Arulmani, S. (2004). *Career counselling: A handbook*. New Delhi, India: Tata McGraw-Hill.

Arulmani, G., Van Laar, D., & Easton, S. (2003). The influence of career beliefs and socio-economic status on the career decision-making of high school students in India. *International Journal for Educational and Vocational Guidance, 3*, 193–204.

Bakshi, A. J. (2011). Past adolescence, into and across adulthood: Career crises and major decisions. *International Journal for Educational and Vocational Guidance, 11*(2), 139–153.

Baltes, P. B., Lindenberger, U., & Staudinger, U. M. (2006). Life span theory in developmental psychology. In W. Damon & R. M. Lerner (Series Eds.), & R. M. Lerner (Vol. Ed.), *Handbook of child psychology, Vol. 1: Theoretical models of human development* (pp. 569–664). Hoboken, NJ: Wiley.

Bandura, A. (2002). Social cognitive theory in cultural context. *Applied Psychology: An International Review, 51*(2), 269–290.

Benson, P. L. (2007). Developmental assets: An overview of theory, research, and practice. In R. K. Silbereisen

& R. M. Lerner (Eds.), *Approaches to positive youth development* (pp. 33–58). London, UK: Sage.

Benson, P. L., & Saito, R. N. (2000). The scientific foundations of youth development. In *Youth development: Issues, challenges and directions* (pp. 125–148). Philadelphia, PA: Public/Private Ventures.

Benson, P. L., Scales, P. C., Hamilton, S. F., & Sesma, A., Jr. (2006a). Positive youth development: Theory, research, and applications. In W. Damon & R. M. Lerner (Series Eds.), & R. M. Lerner (Vol. Ed.), *Handbook of child psychology, Vol. 1: Theoretical models of human development* (pp. 894–941). Hoboken, NJ: Wiley.

Benson, P. L., Scales, P. C., Hamilton, S. F., & Sesma, A., Jr. (with Hong, K. L., & Roehlkepartain, E. C.). (2006b). Positive youth development so far: Core hypotheses and their implications for policy and practice. *Search Institute Insights & Evidence: Promoting Healthy Children, Youth, and Communities, 3*(1), 1–13.

Bimrose, J., & Brown, A. (2014). Mid-career progression and development: The role for career guidance and counseling. In G. Arulmani, A. J. Bakshi, F. T. L. Leong, & A. G. Watts (Eds.), *Handbook of career development: International perspectives*. New York, NY: Springer.

Brandtstädter, J. (2006). Action perspectives on human development. In W. Damon and R. M. Lerner (Series Eds.), & R. M. Lerner (Vol. Ed.), *Handbook of child psychology, Vol. 1: Theoretical models of human development* (pp. 516–568). Hoboken, NJ: Wiley.

Bronfenbrenner, U. (1979). *The ecology of human development*. Cambridge, MA: Harvard University Press.

Catalano, R. F., Berglund, M. L., Ryan, J. A. M., Lonczak, H. S., & Hawkins, J. D. (2004). Positive youth development in the United States: Research findings on evaluations of positive youth development programs. *The Annals of the American Academy of Political and Social Science, 591*, 98–124.

Cooley, C. H. (1902). *Human nature and the social order*. New York, NY: Charles Scribner. Retrieved from http://www.archive.org/details/humannaturesocia00cooluoft

Damon, W. (2004). What is positive youth development? *The Annals of the American Academy of Political and Social Science, 591*, 13–24.

Damon, W., Menon, J., & Bronk, K. C. (2003). The development of purpose during adolescence. *Applied Developmental Science, 7*(3), 119–128.

Denner, J., & Griffin, A. (2003). The role of gender in enhancing program strategies for healthy youth development. In F. A. Villarruel, D. F. Perkins, L. M. Borden, & J. G. Keith (Eds.), *Community youth development: Programs, policies, and practices* (pp. 118–145). Thousand Oaks, CA: Sage.

Eccles, J., & Gootman, J. A. (Eds.). (2002). *Community programs to promote youth development (Committee on Community-Level Programs for Youth. Board on Children, Youth, and Families, Division of Behavioral and Social Sciences and Education. National*

Research Council/Institute of Medicine). Washington, DC: National Academy Press.

Ferrari, T. M. (2003). Working hand in hand: Community youth development and career development. In F. A. Villarruel, D. F. Perkins, L. M. Borden, & J. G. Keith (Eds.), *Community youth development: Programs, policies, and practices* (pp. 201–223). Thousand Oaks, CA: Sage.

Gestsdóttir, S., & Lerner, R. M. (2007). Intentional self-regulation and positive youth development in early adolescence: Findings from the 4-H study of positive youth development. *Developmental Psychology, 43*(2), 508–521.

Gottlieb, G., Wahlsten, D., & Lickliter, R. (2006). The significance of biology for human development: A developmental psychobiological systems view. In W. Damon & R. M. Lerner (Series Eds.), & R. M. Lerner (Vol. Ed.), *Handbook of child psychology, Vol. 1: Theoretical models of human development* (pp. 210–257). Hoboken, NJ: Wiley.

Greene, K. M., & Staff, J. (2012). Teenage employment and career readiness. *New Directions for Youth Development, 134*, 23–31.

Halpern, R. (2012). Supporting vocationally oriented learning in the high school years: Rationale, tasks, challenges. *New Directions for Youth Development, 134*, 85–106.

Hamilton, S. F., & Hamilton, M. A. (2012). Development in youth enterprises. *New Directions for Youth Development, 134*, 65–75.

Harter, S. (2006). The self. In W. Damon and R. M. Lerner (Series Eds.), & N. Eisenberg (Vol. Ed.), *Handbook of child psychology, Vol. 3: Social, emotional, and personality development* (6th ed., pp. 505–570). Hoboken, NJ: Wiley.

Huebner, A. J. (2003). Positive youth development: The role of competence. In F. A. Villarruel, D. F. Perkins, L. M. Borden, & J. G. Keith (Eds.), *Community youth development: Programs, policies, and practices* (pp. 341–357). Thousand Oaks, CA: Sage.

Hynes, K. (2012). Next steps for research and practice in career programming. *New Directions for Youth Development, 134*, 107–114.

Hynes, K., & Hirsch, B. J. (2012). Issue editors' notes. *New Directions for Youth Development, 134*, 1–6.

International Labour Office (ILO). (2010). *Global employment trends for youth August 2010. Special issue on the impact of the global economic crisis on youth*. Geneva, Switzerland: Author.

Kirshner, B., O'Donoghue, J. L., & McLaughlin, M. (2002). Issue editors' notes. *New Directions for Youth Development, 96*, 5–7.

Klein, D. (2012). Building business-community partnerships to support youth development. *New Directions for Youth Development, 134*, 77–84.

Krumboltz, J. D. (2009). The happenstance learning theory. *Journal of Career Assessment, 17*(2), 135–154.

Krumboltz, J. D., & Worthington, R. L. (1999). The school-to-work transition from a learning theory perspective. *Career Development Quarterly, 47*(4), 312–325.

Larson, R. W. (2000). Toward a psychology of positive youth development. *American Psychologist, 55*(1), 170–183.

Lerner, R. M. (2003). Developmental assets and asset-building communities: A view of the issues. In R. M. Lerner & P. L. Benson (Eds.), *Developmental assets and asset-building communities: Implications for research, policy, and practice* (pp. 3–18). New York, NY: Kluwer Academic/Plenum.

Lerner, R. M. (2005, September). *Promoting positive youth development: Theoretical and empirical bases*. White paper prepared for the Workshop on the Science of Adolescent Health and Development, National Research Council/Institute of Medicine. Washington, DC: National Academies of Science.

Lerner, R. M. (2006). Developmental science, developmental systems, and contemporary theories of human development. In W. Damon & R. M. Lerner (Series Eds.), & R. M. Lerner (Vol. Ed.), *Handbook of child psychology, Vol. 1: Theoretical models of human development* (pp. 1–17). Hoboken, NJ: Wiley.

Lerner, R. M. (2011, October). *Positive youth development: Processes, philosophies, programs, and prospects*. Keynote address at the Youth-Nex inaugural conference entitled "Forward thinking: Preparing our youth for the coming world". Curry School of Education, University of Virginia, Charlottesville, VA.

Lerner, R. M., Almerigi, J. B., Theokas, C., & Lerner, J. V. (2005). Positive youth development: A view of the issues. *Journal of Early Adolescence, 25*(1), 10–16.

Lerner, R. M., & Lerner, J. V. (2012). *The positive development of youth. Report of the findings from the first eight years of the 4-H Study of Positive Youth Development*. Chevy Chase, MD: National 4-H Council.

Lerner, R. M., Lerner, J. V., Almerigi, J. B., Theokas, C., Phelps, E., Gestsdottir, S., ... von Eye, A. (2005). Positive youth development, participation in community youth development programs, and community contributions of fifth-grade adolescents: Findings from the first wave of the 4-H study of positive youth development. *Journal of Early Adolescence, 25*(1), 17–71.

Lerner, R. M., & Steinberg, L. (2009). The scientific study of adolescent development: Historical and contemporary perspectives. In R. M. Lerner & L. Steinberg (Eds.), *Handbook of adolescent psychology, Vol. 1: Individual bases of adolescent development* (3rd ed., pp. 3–14). Hoboken, NJ: Wiley.

Mazkoory, P., Irani, B., & Bakshi, A. (2010, October). *Youth services in the Zoroastrian community: Critical evaluation with regard to career guidance*. Poster presented at the International Association for Educational and Vocational Guidance IAEVG-Jiva conference, Bangalore, India.

Mekinda, M. A. (2012). Support for career development in youth: Program models and evaluations. *New Directions for Youth Development, 134*, 45–54.

Ministry of Youth Affairs and Sports. (2011). *Report of Working Group on Adolescent and Youth Development, Department of Youth Affairs, Ministry of Youth Affairs and Sports for formulation of 12th five year plan (2012–17)*. New Delhi, India: Government of India.

Ministry of Youth Affairs and Sports, Government of India (n.d.). Exposure draft National Youth Policy 2012. Retrieved from http://www.yas.nic.in/writereaddata/mainlinkfile/File1039.pdf

Naylor, F. D., & Krumboltz, J. D. (1994). The independence of aptitudes, interests, and career beliefs. *Career Development Quarterly, 43*(2), 152–160.

O'Donoghue, J. L., Kirshner, B., & McLaughlin, M. (2002). Introduction: Moving youth participation forward. *New Directions for Youth Development, 96*, 15–26.

Perkins, D. F., & Borden, L. M. (2003). Key elements of community youth development programs. In F. A. Villarruel, D. F. Perkins, L. M. Borden, & J. G. Keith (Eds.), *Community youth development: Programs, policies, and practices* (pp. 327–340). Thousand Oaks, CA: Sage.

Perkins, D. F., Borden, L. M., Keith, J. G., Hoppe-Rooney, T. L., & Villarruel, F. A. (2003). Community youth development: Partnership creating a positive world. In F. A. Villarruel, D. F. Perkins, L. M. Borden, & J. G. Keith (Eds.), *Community youth development: Programs, policies, and practices* (pp. 1–24). Thousand Oaks, CA: Sage.

Perkins, D. F., Borden, L. M., & Villarruel, F. A. (2001). Community youth development: A partnership for action. *The School Community Journal, 11*(2), 39–56.

Perry, J. C., & Wallace, E. W. (2012). What schools are doing around career development: Implications for policy and practice. *New Directions for Youth Development, 134*, 33–44.

Pittman, K., Irby, M., & Ferber, T. (2000). Unfinished business: Further reflections on a decade of promoting youth development. In *Youth development: Issues, challenges and directions* (pp. 17–64). Philadelphia, PA: Public/Private Ventures.

Porfeli, E. J., & Lee, B. (2012). Career development during childhood and adolescence. *New Directions for Youth Development, 134*, 11–22.

Roth, J. L., & Brooks-Gunn, J. (2003). Youth development programs: Risk, prevention and policy. *Journal of Adolescent Health, 32*(3), 170–182.

Salvatore, S., Nota, L., Ferrari, L., & Ginevra, M. C. (2014). Parental influences on youth's career construction. In G. Arulmani, A. J. Bakshi, F. T. L. Leong, &

A. G. Watts (Eds.), *Handbook of career development: International perspectives*. New York, NY: Springer.

Savickas, M. L. (2005). The theory and practice of career construction. In S. D. Brown & R. W. Lent (Eds.), *Career development and counseling: Putting theory and research to work* (pp. 42–70). Hoboken, NJ: Wiley.

Scales, P. C., & Leffert, N. (2004). *Developmental assets: A synthesis of the scientific research on adolescent development*. Minneapolis, MN: Search Institute.

Secretary's Commission on Achieving Necessary Skills (SCANS). (1991). *What work requires of schools: A SCANS report for America 2000*. Washington, DC: U.S. Department of Labor.

Silbereisen, R. K., & Lerner, R. M. (2007). Approaches to positive youth development: A view of the issues. In R. K. Silbereisen & R. M. Lerner (Eds.), *Approaches to positive youth development* (pp. 3–30). London, UK: Sage.

Small, S., & Memmo, M. (2004). Contemporary models of youth development and problem prevention: Toward an integration of terms, concepts, and models. *Family Relations, 53*(1), 3–11.

The Commonwealth. (n.d.). *Young people*. Retrieved from http://www.thecommonwealth.org/Internal/180392/

Thelen, E., & Smith, L. B. (2006). Dynamic systems theories. In W. Damon & R. M. Lerner (Series Eds.), & R. M. Lerner (Vol. Ed.), *Handbook of child psychology, Vol. 1: Theoretical models of human development* (pp. 258–312). Hoboken, NJ: Wiley.

Theokas, C., Almerigi, J. B., Lerner, R. M., Dowling, E. M., Benson, P. L., Scales, P. C., & von Eye, A. (2005). Conceptualizing and modeling individual and ecological asset components of thriving in early adolescence. *Journal of Early Adolescence, 25*(1), 113–143.

United Nations Educational, Scientific, and Cultural Organization (UNESCO). (n.d.). *What do we mean by youth?* Retrieved from http://www.unesco.org/new/en/social-and-human-sciences/themes/youth/youth-definition/

Valles, R. (2012). Creating awareness among students aged 13–15 years towards the development of a purpose in life. *Indian Journal of Career and Livelihood Planning, 1*(1), 36–43.

Yang, K.-S. (2012). Indigenous psychology, Westernized psychology, and indigenized psychology: A non-Western psychologist's view. *Chang Gung Journal of Humanities and Social Sciences, 5*(1), 1–32.

Youth Engaged in Leadership and Learning (YELL). (2007). *A handbook for supporting community youth researchers*. Stanford, CA: John W. Gardner Center.

Mid-Career Progression and Development: The Role for Career Guidance and Counseling

Jenny Bimrose and Alan Brown

Introduction

The changing patterns of work-related learning and career development of mid-career workers in Europe are the focus of this chapter, which draws on evidence from a major comparative study involving workers from 10 European countries (Brown, Bimrose et al., 2010a). In tracing the strategic learning and career biographies of these mid-career workers, we found that the careers of many workers demonstrated the value of learning while working as this helped them keep their skills, knowledge, and competences up-to-date and maintain a positive disposition towards learning. Many workers were agentic and also supported in their learning in different ways, leading to career progression. At the same time, we contend that career guidance for mid-career workers could play a key role in facilitating successful transitions involving upskilling, reskilling, and/or career change, thereby increasing the likelihood that workers remain active in the labor market for longer. With changing expectations of how long many people will work, and aging of the workforce, there are challenges in supporting the continuing development of mid-career workers who may need to maintain a set of work-related

competences and manage effective work transitions for much longer than has been customary in the past. In such circumstances, there could be cost-benefit advantages in offering mid-career workers career guidance which could extend the length and quality of their careers. Accordingly, in each section that describes a prominent theme related to mid-career progression and development of European workers, we discuss what role career guidance and counseling could play. Moreover, implications for relevant career guidance policy and practice are summarized in the latter sections of the chapter.

The aim of the study was to develop an understanding of the different ways in which individual careers are constructed over time, as learning and working interact across the life-course and impact adaptability and mobility in the labor market. Data were collected using an online survey from which aspects of the career histories of 1,157 respondents drawn from 10 European countries (France, Germany, Italy, the Netherlands, Norway, Poland, Portugal, Romania, Turkey, and the United Kingdom) were obtained; 902 respondents also gave personal data. In the total sample (i.e., $N = 1,157$), 74 % were in full-time permanent employment; 57 % were male; 83 % were in their mid-career (aged 30–55 years); 83 % had achieved skilled worker and/or degree qualifications; and 80 % were working in engineering, ICT, health, or in related sectors such as education or manufacturing. The sample included a small

J. Bimrose (✉)
Institute for Employment Research, The University of Warwick, Coventry, UK
e-mail: Jenny.Bimrose@warwick.ac.uk

G. Arulmani et al. (eds.), *Handbook of Career Development*, International and Cultural Psychology, DOI 10.1007/978-1-4614-9460-7_11, © Springer Science+Business Media, LLC 2014

Table 11.1 Respondents by country, occupational sector, and qualification level

		Occupational sector				Qualification level			
Country	N	Health care	Metal/ engineering	ICT	Other	High	Intermediate	Low	Not specified
France	141	35	36	60	10	78	38	24	1
Norway	150	26	49	26	49	55	60	20	15
Germany	142	17	75	34	16	58	68	14	2
Italy	100	30	38	32	0	35	50	15	0
UK	147	53	8	29	56	109	29	5	4
Portugal	115	37	36	32	10	54	35	19	7
Romania	117	16	40	33	28	84	24	7	2
Poland	109	34	33	38	4	53	24	28	4
Turkey	71	3	6	21	40	18	36	14	3
Netherlands	65	31	6	15	13	49	7	3	6

subset of participants with few qualifications and/or who worked in jobs requiring few qualifications. Details of the workers in relation to their country, occupational sector, and qualification level are given in Table 11.1.

Changing Understandings of Career Development

Osipow and Fitzgerald (1996) have distinguished between career choice as a point-in-time *event* versus a developmental *process* over a longer period of time (p. 54), while others have emphasized career as "the evolving sequence of a person's work experiences over time" (Arthur, Hall, & Lawrence, 1989, p. 8). Young and Collin (2000) have argued that "overall, career can be seen as an overarching construct that gives meaning to the individual's life" (p. 5).

The nature of career development has changed and continues to change. One key change has been that individuals are expected to be much more self-directed in relation to navigating their way through a more complex labor market, but policymakers in particular should try to ensure that "individuals are not expected to assume greater individual responsibility without being offered appropriate support" (Sultana, 2011, p. 183). Ball (1996) has recognized that individuals are able to take responsibility for their own career choices and

decisions and in order to achieve this effectively, individuals' abilities to review and reflect upon their career transitions need to be developed. Through a process of self-reflection and evaluation, individuals become: more comfortable and confident in their decisions (Gati & Saka, 2001); aware of their particular skills (Boyatzis, Goleman, & Rhee, 2000; Gati & Saka, 2001); and are able to identify preferred outcomes and goals (Boyatzis et al., 2000).

The process of self-reflective evaluation (sometimes prolonged) that is characteristic of this evaluative career decision-making style is closely linked to the development of greater levels of self-awareness and self-knowledge, with individuals using this as the basis for future action and decisions (Bimrose & Barnes, 2007). Yet, individuals who have taken opportunities that have presented themselves, however unexpected, and have tried (often successfully) to turn them to their advantage could be described as engaged in a process of opportunistic career decision-making. These individuals exploit opportunities rather than make active choices about work (Banks et al., 1992; Bimrose, Barnes, & Hughes, 2008). Clients' career plans could seem vague, undecided, and uncertain. This readiness to respond rather than plan, however, resonates with the concept of *planned happenstance* that encourages receptiveness to randomly occurring opportunities that could be critical in shaping careers (Mitchell, Levin, &

Table 11.2 Ways in which the knowledge and skills required to perform in the current or last job were acquired

Knowledge and skills required to perform in current or last job acquired through	Total (%)	Female (%)	Male (%)
Studies (higher education) or initial training (e.g., apprenticeship)	74.1	77.3	71.7
Learning through work by carrying out challenging tasks	60.1	62.8	58.1
Self-initiated (directed) learning, inside or outside the workplace	57.1	56.3	57.8
Learning from others at work*	53.4	59.1	49.2
Additional training in current work*	54.6	59.9	50.6
Learning through life experiences (other than work and education)	47.8	49.7	46.3
Learning from networks, working with clients	32.0	34.6	30.0
Other	5.8	4.7	6.6
Total number of respondents (N)	900	384	516

Note: *Statistically significant gender difference at the 0.05 level (chi-square test)
Multiple responses possible from checklist

Krumboltz, 1999) and the need for practitioners to place greater importance on context (Bright, Pryor, Wilkenfeld, & Earl, 2005).

The importance of personal agency is emphasized in more planful approaches to career development such as the integrative process model which explains mechanisms through which intrinsic motivation can influence career self-management and subsequent career success (Quigley & Tymon, 2006). Another relevant concept is career-related continuous learning (CRCL). A key assumption here is that individual and organizational learning are intertwined. Individuals learn as members of organizations, pursue their own interests, and expect a personal benefit from engaging in learning activities. The concept of CRCL relates to a process of individual, self-initiated, discretionary, planned, and proactive pattern of activities that are sustained over time for the purpose of career development (London & Smither, 1999; Rowold & Schilling, 2006). This approach draws attention to how these different types of learning interact across the life-course and how they may facilitate mobility in the labor market.

Overall then, it is clear that career development is enabled by individuals adopting different approaches to career-related learning, underpinned by a variety of distinct career decision-making styles (Bimrose & Barnes, 2007). In the next section, we provide more detail on the actual contexts in which career decisions are made through a closer examination of the changing patterns of work-related learning and career development of mid-career workers in Europe.

Learning and Development Associated with Career Transitions

From an analysis of their current occupations and short description of their work duties, it was clear that about three quarters of the participants of the European study were in (highly) skilled employment, such as managers, professionals, associate professionals, technicians, and skilled nonmanual and manual workers. They had a wide range of formal qualifications and 83 % had completed a degree and/or initial vocational training such as an apprenticeship (see Table 11.1). However, the most striking results were the breadth and depth of forms of learning they had undertaken in order to acquire the skills and knowledge necessary to perform their current work (see Table 11.2). More than 50 % of the workers had acquired knowledge and skills needed for job performance through each of: initial education/training, engagement in challenging tasks, self-directed learning, learning from others at work, and additional training. Moreover, there were significant gender differences with regard to two ways of learning: women reported making greater use of (a) additional training and (b) learning from others at work in acquiring the knowledge and skills necessary to perform their current or last job (see Table 11.2). Women were also more likely to regard their formal qualifications as being very useful in their current job (63 %) compared to men (53 %) (Brown, Bimrose et al., 2010b).

For over 70 % of workers, *initial education or training* provided a continuing underpinning for their current work. This was self-evident for those engineers, health professionals, and skilled workers for whom initial education and training de facto or de jure functioned as a license to practice. However, many workers who had made a significant career shift away from their initial occupation still emphasized the value of their initial training: For example, an engineer who had become a civil servant highlighted how in her new job her systematic approach to problem-solving and team-working was still highly relevant. Highly skilled workers working in areas other than those for which initially trained often have to engage with a (new) substantive knowledge base that undergirds their work practice, but learning to master a knowledge base can itself be a transferable skill (Brown, 2009). That is, when initial education and training has involved an induction into the inner logic of the subject, discipline, or occupation and its ways of thinking and practising, it can facilitate the process of mastering ways of thinking and practicing appropriate to a new area of work. Additionally, those workers who had developed their careers well beyond their initial training or reoriented their careers in ways that distanced them from their original training also emphasized the importance of *learning through engaging with new work processes.* Another engineer, on switching from working on aircraft design to project management in the health service, highlighted how she had to learn to adapt to very different organizational cultures and ways of working in the two contexts: Indeed, the desire for a change from a very "macho culture" in aerospace had been one of the drivers in her decision to change careers.

Overall, over 60 % of workers saw *learning through work by carrying out challenging tasks* as important for acquiring the knowledge and skills necessary to perform their current job. Such learning was important when taking on

new roles (involving upskilling or reskilling) linked to promotion or other forms of career progression. For example, one worker highlighted how on being promoted to a Practice Development Adviser, he learned much in his new role which required the development of a system of care planning for patients in order to improve quality of care and clinical governance. His learning was a consequence of engaging in the following challenging activities: deputizing for and supporting the ward manager in day-to-day management of the ward; promoting and developing clinical leadership by acting as a positive role model with good delegation and supervisory abilities; taking on the duty of Senior Nurse/bleep holder role as required; acting as unit co-coordinator and the point of contact for all external bodies providing advice/liaison; acting as a role model in demonstrating the ability to work collaboratively with other professionals; initiating, leading, and maintaining positive change within own and other areas; taking a lead role in the unit wide teaching and learning program; actively addressing own developmental needs through personal development reviews/plans; actively participating in training and educational activities promoting the development of others; providing structured support (preceptorship), mentorship, and supervision for staff, students, and junior members of staff; ensuring staff demonstrate commitment to equal opportunities for all and are sensitive to individual needs; facilitating junior staff's knowledge on various clinical excellence guidelines, policies, and procedures; identifying clinical needs and prioritizing resources; actively participating in Clinical Governance and audits; and implementing and promoting evidence-based practice. Such a substantive list emphasizes the importance of continuing learning through challenging tasks for many people engaged in (highly) skilled work.

Learning through self-directed or self-initiated learning, inside or outside the workplace, was another important theme characterizing 55 % of the workers. This acknowledges the role of personal agency in responding to learning opportunities at work and/or in seeking to supplement learning at work in order to pursue personal learning goals. An example of self-directed learning was where an employee upon promotion asked to visit the headquarters of the engineering company in another country for two weeks so that she could place what she was expected to do in her new role in the wider context of the company as a whole. Another example was where someone working in a care home sought to learn more about cultural diversity on her own in order to deal more effectively with a range of patients.

That over 50 % of workers acknowledged that *additional training at work* was important for the acquisition of skills and knowledge relevant to current performance, showed that formal continuing vocational training could play an important role in professional development and that many people undertook a mix of formal and more informal methods of skill development. Additional training was often associated with new ways of working, undertaking a new role, or the introduction of new equipment. Interestingly, in some hospital contexts, one person undertook most of the formal training associated with working with new equipment—they then cascaded the new way of working to all the other members of the department. These other members were learning from other colleagues rather than through formal additional training, even though the end result was the same. This may have been one of the reasons why *learning from others at work* was also popular: 53 % of the mid-career workers had acquired valuable work-related knowledge and skills in this way.

Work-related learning and development also occurred *through the use of networks and/or engagement with clients* for over 30 % of workers. For those workers employed in the ICT sector, learning through networks (including personal networks) was almost universal, and in an exceptional case, one worker complained that one key element of his dissatisfaction with his work which lacked challenge was that it did not allow opportunities to learn through networking. For those working in engineering, learning through interaction was more likely to be team-based, but could also involve learning through

interaction with clients, professional and personal networks or in performance improvement teams where members are drawn from different disciplines, departments, hierarchical levels, and organizations (Brown, Bimrose et al., 2010a).

In summary, acquisition of valued work-related skills and knowledge often came through interactions at work. At the same time, however, 47 % of the workers also shared that *learning through life experiences* had helped them acquire some skills and knowledge necessary to perform their current (or last) job. Some workers emphasized the value of having lived in a number of different countries in helping them develop their communication skills, while others pointed to how certain life changes, including taking on caring responsibilities, moving to a more rural location, and so on had increased their reflexivity as they reexamined their skill sets and reconsidered how their careers might develop. Overall, the relationship between career development and learning while working highlights how learning while working is an established form of learning at work in many contexts (especially for the highly skilled) and how continuing vocational learning, when coupled with career progression, increases the extent of engagement in ongoing learning (Brown, Bimrose et al., 2010a).

The Importance of Personal Agency

To reiterate, many cases demonstrated the value of learning while working. Access to opportunities for learning and development was crucially important with some workplaces providing what Fuller and Unwin (2004) identify as much more "expansive learning environments" than others. For example, one French worker completed a Master's level qualification in communication and media studies as a mature student while on paid sabbatical leave from her company. This was part of the French *Congé Individual de Formation* scheme whereby employers contribute to a training fund and are then reimbursed the cost of an employee's salary while he or she is absent on training. Access to

Table 11.3 Recent forms of learning or training activities in which workers had engaged (in the last five years)

Recent forms of learning or training activities	%
Learning through work by carrying out challenging tasks	65.0
Learning through life experience	59.6
Seminars, conferences	59.6
Learning from others at work	58.2
Self-directed learning inside or outside the workplace	55.3
On-the-job training	53.5
Learning from networks, working with clients	50.2
Course provided by a training center/organization/institution at workplace	42.9
Course provided by training center/organization/institution outside workplace	42.5
Off-the job training	38.0
Additional training in current work	35.9
Group training in workplace provided by employer	33.4
Individual training at workplace provided by mentor/tutor/colleague	30.6
Training that leads to further qualifications	25.5
Correspondence course	7.4
Other	2.3
Total number of respondents (N) = 895	

Note: No statistically significant gender differences
Multiple responses possible from checklist

such rich learning opportunities was very varied. However, some individuals were also much more proactive than others in seeking learning opportunities relevant to their work, even if there were only limited opportunities at their workplaces. For example, a research manager with specialist expertise in web development developed his technical skills away from work but these gradually became central to how he did his work. From a career guidance perspective, it was interesting to examine the dynamic interplay of personal agency with opportunity structures in the working lives of the respondents and the role of guidance in sometimes mediating the two. Career guidance practitioners often seek to help clients develop a sense of personal agency in order to help them navigate their way through an uncertain labor market in a changing career development landscape.

The participants were generally well-qualified with 83 % having achieved skilled worker and/or degree qualifications, and they had opportunities for learning and development associated with their jobs, but even so, the extent of their positive actions and attitudes towards learning was striking. While Table 11.2 has helped in

demonstrating how individuals had learned the skills necessary to perform their current job, Table 11.3 presents findings related to patterns of learning and training in the past five years (i.e., the five years previous to data collection). Most workers' answers demonstrated very positive actions and attitudes towards learning in a wide variety of forms, many of which were also described in Table 11.2. These included learning through work by carrying out challenging tasks, learning through life experience, learning through participating in seminars and conferences, learning from others at work, self-directed learning, on-the-job training, and learning from networks and working with clients (see Table 11.3).

Interestingly, the reasons they took part in training and learning activities were primarily related to skill development and personal development. Many individuals were driving their own development; they liked learning new things related to their job and enjoyed new challenges at work because these offered opportunities for learning (see Table 11.4). The mid-career workers largely remained committed to learning, training, and development in the future too

Table 11.4 Reasons for taking part in training/learning activities

Reasons for taking part in training/learning activities	%
I wanted to develop a broader range of skills and/or knowledge	77.9
I wanted to develop more specialist skills and/or knowledge	67.6
I took part for my own personal development	60.6
I wanted to perform new tasks or more demanding tasks in my current job	45.0
I thought it would improve my job prospects (i.e., find new job, advance my career, get a promotion, earn better money)	43.1
The successful completion of training activities is required for my occupation	36.2
I wanted to change my career options	29.2
I wanted to prepare myself for a new job or new career	26.8
My employer requested/required me to do so	26.7
Because of rights to training granted by my employer or legislation	13.6
Because of threat of restructuring/redundancies in my area of work	4.4
I wanted to obtain unemployment benefits that depend on training attendance	0.4
Other	1.5
Total number of respondents (N) = 895	

Note: No statistically significant gender differences
Multiple responses possible from checklist

Table 11.5 Reasons for intending to undertake more training or learning activities in the next five years

Reasons for intending to undertake more training or learning activities in the next five years	%
I want to develop a broader range of skills and/or knowledge	79.8
I want to develop more specialist skills and/or knowledge	65.1
Training will be part of my own personal development	55.5
I want to improve my job prospects (i.e., find new job, advance my career, get a promotion, earn better money)	45.9
I need to perform new tasks or more demanding tasks in my current job	36.9
I will have more opportunities to change my career in the future	34.5
The successful completion of training activities is required for my occupation	30.5
I want to change my career options	26.6
I need to prepare myself for a new job or new career	20.8
Because my employer offers training	11.7
Because of rights to training granted by my employer or legislation	11.1
My employer requires me to do so	10.2
Because of threat of restructuring/redundancies in my area of work	5.4
I want to obtain unemployment benefits that depend on training attendance	0.6
Other	2.7
Total number of respondents (N) = 830 (answers from respondents who planned to undertake further training)	

Note: No statistically significant gender differences
Multiple responses possible from checklist

(see Table 11.5). They were also prepared to be proactive in terms of their own learning and development, with most workers strongly agreeing that they liked learning new things which were required for their jobs and that they enjoyed new challenges as they offered opportunities for learning (see Table 11.6).

The workers, however, had had varying degrees of success in the labor market over their life-course and relatively few had had completely untroubled career histories. Their learning and work trajectories resonated with the structural contexts in which they operated. For example, in Romania and Poland, mid-career

Table 11.6 Ratings of experience of training or learning activities

Experience of training or learning activities	Mean rating
I like learning new things for my job	3.7
My job requires that I keep learning new things	3.6
I enjoy new challenges as they offer opportunities for learning	3.5
I take the initiative in finding new things to learn	3.3
I am serious about career development	3.2
I think my career is important	3.2
I learn new things for my job as it is a requirement	2.9
My employer supports my career development/learning activities	2.8
My opportunities for advancement are good	2.6
My employer does not support/offer any training	1.9
There are few opportunities for me to learn	1.7
I am too old to learn	1.3
I don't like learning new things	1.3
Total number of respondents (N) = 971	

Note: No statistically significant gender differences
Rating scale used, ranging from "1 = strongly disagree" to "4 = strongly agree"

workers had had to negotiate major shifts in societal and organizational structures and demonstrate the ability to function effectively in very different situations, as organizations had operated very differently in the communist era in comparison to the transition regimes of the 1990s, or more recently as part of the European Union. Another participant, a Spanish woman working in the UK, was even more explicit about how opportunity structures constrained personal agency:

> Employment opportunities in the public sector across Europe are very dependent on the different selection processes (e.g., in Spain you need to sit an exam to get a general post in the health service). Also, a non-medical consultant in public health in the UK couldn't get a job at that level in Spain. This is restricted for medical doctors. So career development in this area is pretty much exclusive to the UK, as far as I know.

Personal agency is clearly an important driver of individual work and learning trajectories, but for many mid-career workers their working lives had become more complex.

Additionally, it was found that there was an increased role for reflection on action and behavior; in particular, reflexivity in thinking about reasons and motivations for actions while shaping one's work trajectory, especially since choices and possibilities have expanded, and

structural, organizational, and technological changes have added complexity. For example, one participant shared how there were, partly as a consequence of changes in work organization and technology, major differences in the skillsets of people working in technical-based industry and in the public sector and policy communities, and that it was necessary to adapt your behavior and ways of thinking and practicing as you moved between communities. Another participant pointed out how as she operated within (self-imposed) constraints over where she was willing to work geographically, she had to reflect carefully on her options and think strategically about how best to represent her skills to be as attractive as possible to a wide range of possible employers: she looked to create opportunities for herself and had a very proactive mindset.

For most (highly) skilled workers, experience developed through engagement with challenging work is the main vehicle for professional growth, but this needs to be supplemented in a variety of ways and individuals have choices in the combination of learning activities (formal, nonformal, and informal) with which they engage. Participants were reflexive about how different forms of learning had contributed to the manner in which their careers were developing:

I spent 10 years getting my qualifications as an adult and worked part time in the education sector whilst I did it. On graduating, I was looking for full time work and found a training position in the National Health Service. Since then I have changed departments three times on different secondment opportunities and now do Project Management and IT.

When I left university with my qualifications I didn't have a set career in mind. Over the years I have acquired experience by working in different sectors and with different people. All of this has developed my transferable skills and I take forward learning experiences from one work place to the next. I am now in a set career path and believe that the experiences along the way have helped to bring me here.

Individuals seek a degree of personal autonomy in how their careers develop (and the meaning attached to career) but, in parallel, they also seek opportunities to engage with peers, colleagues, and experts to support their career development (Brown, Bimrose et al., 2010a). Union learning representatives have proved to be effective in this respect, operating as "trusted intermediaries" who are "able to engage 'hard-to-reach' employees and help stimulate and meet their demand for learning and skills opportunities, particularly opened up through government intervention. Their activities encompass giving information and advice, arranging courses and conducting learning needs assessment" (Clough, 2010, p. 22). One of the workers was a lorry driver who had switched to part-time work in order to study for a degree. He had then worked as a union project officer helping recruit and develop union learning representatives, taking further short courses in coaching, mentoring, supporting dyslexic workers, identifying learning, working with employers, and facilitating access to higher education. Such findings substantiate the idea that individuals are responsible actors in creating their own career pathways through learning and development using opportunities in education, training, employment, and other contexts. However, at the same time, there is an urgent need to support individuals in navigating their way through increasingly complex work and life contexts and, in particular, helping individuals become more reflective at the individual level

through provision of career guidance and counseling as a key component of a lifelong learning strategy. In corroboration, Biesta (2008) in describing the learning biographies of 120 adults in the UK has emphasized that while informal support was ubiquitous, in a number of instances professional support was *very valuable*, particularly where it was linked to a major personal change or crisis.

Even within generally successful careers, anxieties were expressed about the risks connected to overall dynamics and change associated with career development and with organizational changes and structural constraints—people recognized that navigating a career path could be fraught with difficulties, circumstances in which professional support could have played an important role, as the following examples demonstrate:

My career history has been largely determined by living in very rural areas. I became a careers adviser 'by accident' because the employer happened to be based near-by and had a reputation as a good employer. I wanted to work 'with people' but for anything else I would have had to move. I have since moved to even more rural areas and this has meant I have haphazardly taken opportunities whenever they have arisen. This has led me to build up a wide range of skills and I think keeps me highly employable but doesn't necessarily mean that I am specialising in one area of my career. Because of my rural location senior jobs and ones where I might use my skills more fully are much less possible to progress into.

I went to university in Canada as a mature student and single mother. I lived in a remote community but was unable to move to follow my preferred career or training. In 2004, I moved to Holland to live with my Dutch husband; my Canadian job did not transfer well, and I have been having problems learning Dutch. In addition, my age has been a barrier to employment, and, along with my non-EU passport, has made retraining too expensive.

My career development has been chequered, mainly because of part time working when my daughter was small. I was a single parent also, from another country. Now being in a senior position and on reflection I would say I was actively discriminated against in terms of opportunities for promotion, etc. because of being part time and also by nationality. I feel that because I had a very good education I was able to make progress despite the barriers. I was also determined to succeed! I think I have proved that to my satisfaction … [and] I feel I have contributed hugely to this organisation and the public in my 40 years [of work].

Personal agency (proactivity and responding to opportunities) is important but there is also value in helping individuals develop their own career story of where they have been and where they are going. Many individuals are actively shaping their personal work biographies (and even then they may value help in doing this), while others feel they would like to develop a clear sense of career direction but are struggling to do so without support:

> I don't feel like my career has been very well planned and I don't have a clear plan for how it will develop in the future, which means that it's difficult for me to choose training or learning (particularly long-term or big commitments) to develop my career.

Career options and choices are limited by context, but individuals can use career self-management to negotiate their own position within these constraints. It has been suggested that individuals utilize three types of career self-management behavior as adaptive responses to career development tasks: positioning through strategic choice of mobility opportunities, strategic investment in human capital, active network development, and job content innovation; influence, including self-promotion; and boundary management of work and nonwork domains through boundary maintenance and role transition (King, 2004). All these strategies are intended to reduce external constraints that would otherwise prevent people from achieving their desired outcomes.

Sometimes, however, personal agency leads away from developing a progressive career. One well-qualified respondent recounted how in the last eight years she had worked as a training officer, a clerk, a receptionist, a checkout operator at a supermarket, a library assistant, a part-time dance teacher, and a part-time lecturer "teaching fiction writing to adult students at a university." It is only the last role which gives any purchase on understanding her job history: "All of the paid employment I have done has

been purely to pay my bills. My real career ambitions have always lain outside of my working life. It is something I can only pursue on my own time and under my own steam. Everything else is just supporting my mortgage, kids, food, pets, clothes, etc. I have no real interest in any kind of work but my one lifelong ambition is to become a published fiction author." The career decision-making style of this individual is aspirational, her apparently chaotic career understandable only in terms of working towards her long-term goal (Bimrose et al., 2008).

Structural Constraints on Personal Agency

In transition economies such as Poland and Romania, the shift towards personal responsibility for career development was a major turning point for workers brought up under centrally planned economies. In Romania, one legacy of the earlier system was a feeling that school-based training resulting in formal certification was the most "powerful" form of training. On the other hand, the emergent economy was making use of different types of jobs, skills, companies, forms of work organization, and career patterns. In such circumstances older low-skilled workers could be part of a "fatalistic" culture in which they viewed themselves as out-of-step with the way the economy was evolving, with immobility being linked to age, and getting employment depending on luck and contacts rather than individual merit. Two respondents in their 40s exemplified how if they were in employment they were determined to hang on to their current jobs and saw no prospects of doing anything else. The first person had worked in a large factory for 15 years but, following restructuring, was made redundant and then, after a spell of unemployment, retrained as a tram driver:

> I am satisfied with my job because it is well paid and I can support my family, although it is difficult and stressful. I don't have the formal qualifications to think of a better position in the company. I am fed up with training and courses.

Table 11.7 Matching of skills with duties in current or last job

Matching of skills with duties in current or last job	%
My duties correspond well with my present skills	40.9
I have the skills to cope with more demanding duties	37.0
I need further training to cope well with my duties	17.0
I am new to the job so I need some further training to learn new aspects of my duties	5.1
Total	100.0

Total number of respondents (N) = 1,115

Note: No statistically significant gender differences
Mutually exclusive categories provided

The second person was working as a chef:

> I have no formal qualification. I learned cooking from my mother and I also learned a lot from my colleagues. I think it is a good job in that I can support my children growing up without any other support. The new colleagues that come have certificates but they still ask for my help. For the future, I am waiting for my pension time only.

Similarly, seeking to make a labor market transition at a time of high unemployment could be constraining. A Library and Information Services Manager in Health Care recalled how initially:

> My career was blighted by the recession of the early 1980s. I could not find work after university for four months, and I found the experience of unemployment (and unsuccessful job interviews) very traumatic. Once I had found work (in the book trade) I stayed in that sector for too long, fearful of unemployment again, although I was not happy; it was 11 years before I found my present career as a librarian, in which I am much happier.

Some qualified workers had made successful transitions or exhibited greater resilience in overcoming periods of unemployment, but even when they were in stable employment over a third of participants believed they had the skills to cope with more demanding duties (see Table 11.7). Now, in some contexts, this over-qualification compared to the jobs available could be due to the lack of opportunities available as in the examples provided, but it could also be because individual skill development was being driven by broader considerations than just those directly related to the labor market. Indeed a number of workers emphasized how for them learning was primarily about

personal development. The most striking example of learning not being portrayed in instrumental terms was by a worker who stated, "I love learning—for the pure enjoyment of learning something new."

Indeed, where there are high unemployment rates and a chronic lack of "good jobs," as had occurred in a number of the countries during our participants' careers, focusing upon employability could be a less effective tool than using the oft-expressed interest in learning as a driver of personal development; this then could act as a less direct but nonetheless powerful tool for career progression. It may be that the policy messages that promote learning through a strong emphasis on employability are less effective than those which place emphasis on personal development, establishing social networks, meeting a wider range of people together with increasing the likelihood of getting employment. That is, messages should also emphasize some of the more intrinsic benefits from being a learner rather than judging learning primarily by where it might lead.

From an individual perspective, handling the interplay between opportunity structures (Roberts, 2009) and personal agency (proactivity) is not easy to achieve on your own. Being able to discuss such issues with a career guidance practitioner could be useful any time an individual is considering a major transition (Biesta, 2008). However, an interesting manner in which guidance could be valuable for mid-career individuals is through helping them make sense of their existing career narrative, and aiding them in projecting their career story into the future (Savickas, 2005).

Intensive Periods of (Significant) Learning Across the Life-Course

One striking finding of the research was that learning which results in significant changes in values, attitudes, or behavior for individuals tends to be episodic across the life-course (Brown, Bimrose et al., 2010a). In emphasizing significant learning, it is necessary to distinguish it as learning which entails substantial personal development or transformation—quite different from other learning which involves adaptation to minor changes in context, organization, practices, and processes of work, where basic values, attitudes, and behaviors remain largely unchanged. Significant learning which is episodic fits with a more general pattern of increasing engagement by people in lifelong learning (Field, 2000). Nearly all the (highly) skilled workers in the study engaged with formal post-compulsory education and training at some point in their life, with many having a number of bouts of intensive periods of significant learning across the life-course. These intensive periods of significant learning, following initial vocational education and training or higher education (HE) studies, were typically concerned with either upskilling within recognized career pathways or reskilling associated with a significant career change. The upskilling or reskilling could comprise a formal educational program, continuing vocational training, learning while working, or a mixture of two or more of these components.

The career trajectory of one worker illustrated how an intensive period of part-time formal learning (educational upskilling), followed later by a period of formal training coupled with engagement in more challenging work lead to another round of development, upskilling, and reskilling. In 1989, Bella (a pseudonym) started doing routine administrative work on benefit claims right after completing high school. While working, Bella completed a range of part-time qualifications culminating in a technician level qualification, which facilitated her entry into university. She completed a degree in professional learning and development in 2000 and this helped

Bella refocus her career as a trainer. While working in a variety of training and management roles over the next decade, Bella took further qualifications in training, coaching, and performance improvement to underpin her subsequent switches from regional trainer to operations manager before taking a job in a new sector (health) as a manager with responsibilities for business change based upon IT systemic change.

How learning at work is coupled with career progression influences how individuals engage in continuing learning which is significant. For example, in some contexts, after initial recruitment, promotion is almost wholly dependent upon performance at work, which is itself linked to learning through challenging work, interactions, and work-related networks. In other cases, some form of formal continuing professional development would be expected, such as taking *Meister* qualifications in Germany, as a prelude to promotion. Another participant provides an example of upskilling through initial hospital-based (sub-degree HE equivalent) vocational training coupled with completion of two intensive mid-career postgraduate diploma programs as well as learning while working and through career progression. Karen qualified as a radiographer in 1984; in 1991 she completed a Diploma in Management Studies and in 2004 a Postgraduate Diploma in Advanced Practice (Imaging) as she progressed through linked progression pathways as an advanced practitioner, clinical tutor, and then a Research Radiographer from 2004.

Rather than engaging in continuous life-altering learning at an even pace year-after-year, people are likely to have periods of more and less intensive learning. Many respondents to the survey identified that the learning and development had played a key role in making significant work-related transitions; periods of intensive learning were often seen as decisive in bringing about changes in individuals' career direction. Most people with successful careers display episodic learning: periods of intensive learning interspersed with ostensibly quieter times (which nevertheless can involve less intensive learning through challenging work, etc.).

This finding is really important in planning career guidance support for mid-career workers. It helps counter the view that "I am not a lifelong learner—it is a long time since I engaged in substantive learning associated with education and training or learning a new role at work, etc." Almost everyone across their life-course engages in episodic learning—at some periods making a conscious effort at learning compared to other times when other aspects of their lives may take priority. Acknowledgement of such a rhythm in learning would seem much more empowering. This line of argument was often used by "women returners": "Now it is my turn." It is not a deficit model but rather a positive one: In a lifetime there will be a number of times when a person makes learning a priority—would now be a good time to do so?

Skill Development for Workers in Low-Skilled Work by Changing Jobs

Brynin and Ramioul (2007) in their findings from a major European project on work organization reported on individual-level change using panel data and found that both "dissatisfaction with work and skill mismatches are widespread, and while tending to be overcome through career switches, thereby contribute to the overall prevalence of work flexibility" (p. 7). So, job mobility can be viewed as positive for individuals where it leads to progression, greater satisfaction, and personal development, or negative if it is considered forced, unrewarding, and involves a "sense of loss" rather than development.

Interestingly, in nearly all European countries the most common way for people in low-skilled employment to update their skills was by changing their jobs (Brynin & Ramioul, 2007). This finding is important in two respects. First, it means that public policy should encourage people to find more challenging work if they are in undemanding work—guidance and counseling could play a key role in this respect. Second, it resonates with a number of case histories of our respondents whereby their personal development took off when after a

period of low-skilled employment they switched to other work which opened up opportunities for learning and development through training and/ or more challenging work. For example, in Portugal and Poland, a number of people worked in assistant or junior positions before finding more challenging work in the same sector or in a different field altogether (after transferring, for example, from work in hotel and catering). In some cases *a shift between different forms of low-skilled work* could facilitate development within work, enhancing adaptability, and the ability to apply skills, knowledge, and understanding in different contexts. For example, one woman recounted how she had moved through a range of relatively low-skilled jobs such as preparing and serving food, issuing tickets for picking lines in a warehouse, performing low-level general administrative tasks, working as a sales assistant, etc. She found she could adapt to many different types of work, so that, following the birth of her first child, when she did want "to turn my life around from the boring, mundane and low-paid work I was doing" by taking a part-time degree, she already had an impressive soft skill set in terms of ability to communicate, work in teams, etc. Upon completing her degree, she then worked as a careers coordinator in a school and emphasized how "I now have a great career that I love with excellent prospects and a reasonable work-life balance (I have 2 children now so this is very important)."

Another worker described how he had started out over 40 years ago without any formal qualifications as an apprentice painter and decorator and then moved through a number of low-level jobs in construction and retail and progressed to managing a mobile shop, then a small travel agency, before becoming self-employed as a grocery shop owner. Apart from some training and minor qualifications related to work in a travel agency, what propelled development was always self-directed learning, inside or outside the workplace.

Being able to apply your skills, knowledge, and understanding in a number of contexts can itself act as a considerable spur to development. Again, this has profound implications for the career guidance of mid-career workers. Career guidance practitioners need to be sensitive to the possibility that individuals in their early 40s have made considerable progress with their skill development since entry into employment and now need a slightly different approach to enable them to make a career transition. It is at this point that they would value support (i.e., in making that transition). For a number of our respondents, career possibilities had broadened since their first entry into the labor market because they had been developing their work-related skills, knowledge, and understanding over time and now had greater experience and more to offer a prospective employer. Such transitions often appear to reenergize work and learning trajectories, as seen in the example of another woman whose career really took off when she went back to work after a period at home exercising primary care responsibility for her young children. Initially she began her career by working as a pharmacy assistant for five years after completing initial vocational training and then worked as a sales representative for another five years. Subsequently, she had at least ten career changes, and reflected that:

> Over the years I have acquired experience by working in different sectors and with different people. All of this has developed my transferable skills and I take forward learning experiences from one work place to the next. I am now in a set career path and believe that the experiences along the way have helped to bring me here.

As employees in low-skilled work may upskill by changing jobs, public policy could promote career guidance to encourage people in undemanding work to find more challenging employment (CEDEFOP, 2010), although some employees engaged in low-skilled work already have skill sets which are highly valued in the labor market and are just "passing through" such work: for example, graduates moving on to career-related employment (Purcell, Elias, & Wilton, 2004). However, other employees need to develop their skills further in order to find longer-term career-related employment, and career guidance can play a role in helping them articulate both the types of skills and knowledge which they may

wish to develop and the education, training, or employment contexts in which such skills and knowledge may be developed. For example, practical or psychomotor skills could be developed through a combination of work and training, while cognitive skills could be developed partly in context at work but also in formal education within integrated programs such as adult apprenticeships. Such apprenticeships also engage with issues linked to identity development and the affective domain that help in developing ways of thinking and practicing appropriate for a skilled worker. Guidance may also help those workers in low-skilled work, who might be interested in career progression, reflect upon the nature of their skill sets, their attitude towards learning, and help them become more proactive in their own career development. Other workers in low-skilled employment might, however, wish to remain in their current jobs because it is congruent with their life goals.

Problematizing Some Mid-Career Workers' Stable Careers

While many mid-career workers were engaged in active career development, a few had decided that they were not going to engage any further in significant learning and development and would just do the minimum required in their current job. One worker represented this as "coasting": just doing enough in their current job to get by but without wishing to engage more fully nor wanting to go further in their career. In some cases this had been associated with waiting for early retirement, although in many countries this option was now being withdrawn. In other cases this was seen as a psychological response to the dangers of burnout: one worker recognized this as an adaptive response to over-commitment, involving working very long hours, earlier in her career. From a policy perspective, such workers are seldom recognized as at risk. One worker did recognize that there were dangers associated with coasting in that employability becomes dependent almost solely upon the current job. This attitude was sometimes also linked with a lack of reflexivity of individuals in thinking about their own skills, a reluctance to think in terms of skill sets—rather there was a tendency to rely upon an attachment to an occupational/organizational identity that may be vulnerable to change. In this context, coupled with the demographic shift towards an aging workforce, it is clear that there could be real cost-benefit advantages in offering mid-career workers guidance which could extend the length and quality of their careers. One benefit could come from an increased willingness to continue working after a career shift for some, while others could also value the guidance process for affirming them in their current path (Bimrose et al., 2008).

Evidence from the survey highlighted the importance of job mobility for individuals in a range of contexts to promote upskilling, reskilling, employability, and integration of workers for longer in the labor market (Brown, Bimrose et al., 2010a). Individuals often valued support in making career decisions (Bimrose & Barnes, 2007), which could help them develop resilience in coping with change (CEDEFOP, 2008). This support could take various forms: access to career advice and guidance services for adults at times of transition appears crucial in facilitating positive outcomes both for the individual and for the smooth functioning of the labor market (Biesta, 2008).

Implications for Career Development Support for Mid-Career Workers

The European research discussed in this chapter highlighted how personal agency is an important driver of individual work and learning trajectories, while scrutiny of individual cases showed how many people have reflexively constructed strong career narratives. These narratives helped individuals make sense of how their careers had developed and where they might go in the future. However, around a quarter of the workers related career stories of how earlier in their careers they sometimes had found it hard to establish a clear sense of direction in the labor market. The reasons for these struggles could have been structural, when unemployment was high and/or they lived in a rural location; or attitudinal, as, for example, when people had had their confidence shaken by being made redundant or due to the trauma of an earlier spell of unemployment. Such individuals could be supported in navigating their way through and being reflective upon their increasingly complex work and life contexts through provision of career guidance as a key component of a lifelong learning strategy (Biesta, 2008), which also promotes reflective strategies in organizations (in support of individual empowerment and organizational development). Savickas (2005) has contended that there is value in helping individuals develop a coherent career narrative: where they have been, where they are, and where they are going. Bimrose and Barnes (2007) meanwhile have identified that while some individuals adopt a career decision-making style whereby they readily respond to career opportunities, others may be much slower to adapt and would welcome more formal guidance support.

While career guidance services for adults at times of transition can have positive outcomes for individuals and the labor market, issues of access to such provisions remain a challenge (Brown, Bimrose et al., 2010a). Indications from this research are that individuals would welcome guidance support when they see themselves in transition rather than when they are defined as such by the system. That is, guidance is often made available after an individual has become unemployed, whereas individuals who see themselves as engaged in transition, in that they are looking for a change in career direction, while still in apparently stable employment do not qualify for support, even though it is much easier to get another job if you are currently in a job rather than unemployed. In this sense, a career service which is driven by individual needs may be a more cost-effective way of ensuring that the career development support of individuals is appropriate or relevant to particular phases and stages of their career trajectories. For example, workers in undemanding jobs (low-skilled employment), those wishing to change sectors, or seeking to change intensity of work because of changed responsibilities, and older workers seeking a career change, are all groups that could benefit from improved access to career guidance. Additionally, policy could give greater emphasis to the value of career guidance in helping individuals articulate and possibly align goals, expectations, development strategies, and outcomes in relation to learning and career development.

Many mid-career workers in the sample were committed to learning and development, so it is clear that a lack of engagement with learning is not a function of age per se. It is partly about access to opportunities to learn and partly about motivation, so for those who have not engaged in learning for some time, involving them in identifying the type of learning with which they want to engage is critical (Brown, Bimrose et al., 2010a).

Policymakers and practitioners should consider the following points of leverage in trying to engage more mid-career workers in learning and development in order to keep them in the labor market for a longer period. It is important to recognize the importance of the personal dimension in generating commitment to continuing learning, consider the idea of using key transition points to help target provision, and to acknowledge the significance of networks in supporting skill development at work. These points could be aligned with broader goals such as supporting the development of career management skills, promoting career adaptability, and improving access to adult guidance services at times most helpful for clients.

Research findings from this more highly skilled segment of mid-career workers can contribute ideas about constructing a model of how to support effective learning and development for mid-career workers more generally. Career guidance practitioners and others supporting learning and development could consider the following characteristics in developing or evaluating appropriate provision:

• Individual engagement: Is it personally meaningful for individuals in relation to development in their current occupation or career progression and/or is it personally rewarding, for example, resulting in an increase in self-esteem, confidence as a learner, or self-efficacy? Does it resonate with an individual's motivation, where the individual feels a clear drive for achievement and development? Does it require active engagement of participants—is it sufficiently demanding (for example, does it challenge or extend current ideas, assumptions, attitudes, constructs, knowledge, and understanding)? Does it require engagement with particular ways of thinking and practicing (including how individuals are connected to particular knowledge cultures)? This might include development of particular approaches to critical analysis, evaluation, problem-solving, etc.

• Personal development: Does it provide opportunities for a significant shift in personal perspective (whether this is value-based or interest-based)? Does provision help individuals develop greater opportunity awareness, especially because much continuing vocational learning is at least partly dependent upon an individual being aware of and then taking advantage of opportunities for learning and development? Does it help individuals develop judgment, for example, in the ability to make choices in relation to values, goals, plans, and aspirations; make decisions; self-motivate; and display resilience? Does it use reflection upon experience (including reflections on prior learning) as a driver of further learning?

• Collaboration: Does it encourage collaboration between learners: for example, are learners engaged in a collective enterprise (for example, in relation to performance improvement activities, or as a member of group engaged in a formal program of study)? Or even if the learning activity is predominantly an individual activity, does it draw on the support of others at the workplace, for example, in order to help them reflect upon and consolidate their learning?

- Progression: Is it relevant for vocational progression (either as part of an established progression pathway or through establishing an enhanced personal base from which to seek further career development—for example, through the completion of a substantive further qualification)?
- Career orientation: Is provision linked to a clear career orientation? In other words, is it linked to an individual's career goals directly or else is helpful in developing skills facilitative of career management and does it fit with an individual's clear career narrative about "becoming"?

The research findings provide a strong endorsement for the complementarity of learning through engaging with challenging work and institutionalized learning which enables individuals to look beyond their immediate context (Brown, Bimrose et al., 2010a). Such complementary learning has underpinned many apprenticeship systems, sandwich degrees, and much professional training. Corroboratively, in the European research reported in this chapter there were many examples from the strategic learning and career biographies of mid-career workers where individuals had applied such modes of alternance learning across the life-course, that is, where learning was predominantly work-based but with periods of institutionalized learning interspersed. Learning through challenging work alone may be insufficient and other forms of learning may be necessary to help the employee make a quantum leap in their broader understanding of a particular field. Career guidance practitioners need to recognize the complementarity of different forms of learning in promoting skill development.

Additionally, it is also important to recognize that the quality of work remains a key factor in determining the extent of continuing vocational learning and skill development. Where individuals are engaged in challenging work, they are likely to have opportunities for development in significant ways from learning while

working. However, a company's field of operation, future horizons, product market strategy, and organization of work may all place constraints on the extent to which workplaces offer expansive learning environments (Fuller & Unwin, 2004). Where a company offers only limited opportunities for substantive learning while working, efforts to encourage employers to offer additional training have had only limited success, not least because employers may think employees would then be more likely to leave. Public policy should, therefore, perhaps focus upon giving workers entitlements to career guidance and further learning opportunities.

Promoting continuing vocational training development and access to career guidance could also be linked to Sen's notion (1999) of the importance of developing individual capabilities in a broader sense. In applying this idea to skill development, the ultimate goal is to increase the freedom for individuals to exercise greater control over their own lives (in relation to what they value being or doing). This greater control for individuals would require that at both societal level and within communities there are political commitments to expanding opportunities for individuals to access knowledge, undertake meaningful work, engage in significant relationships, and exercise self-direction (Sen, 1999).

New Concepts and Viewpoints: Charting New Directions

The greater entitlements to career guidance should be informed by paying attention to the following factors:

- Reflection and guidance support: This would involve helping individuals become more reflective at the individual level through provision of career guidance and counseling as a key component of a lifelong learning strategy, coupled with introducing reflective strategies in organizations (in support of both individual empowerment and organizational development).

- Support for those with successful careers: This could comprise support for individuals with apparently stable careers who may be experiencing career anxieties, associated with changes (e.g., in the labor market, organization of work, technology) or with structural constraints in the opportunities available to them, or else who may wish to initiate a career change. Even people with successful careers recognize that navigating a career path can be fraught with difficulties and might welcome support.
- Personal agency and career narratives: Proactivity and responding to opportunities is important but there is also value in helping individuals develop a coherent career narrative of where they have been, where they are currently, and where they are going. Many individuals are actively shaping their personal work biographies but they also value help to do this.
- Engagement with continuing learning opportunities: A proactive approach to career development, self-management behavior, and positive experiences of learning influence engagement and persistence with continuing learning. People can reinforce their satisfaction (and in some cases even overcome dissatisfaction) with work by engaging in continuing vocational training or other forms of learning (which people often believe has value in itself—even when not strictly necessary for current or likely future job performance).
- Active career management: Much continuing vocational learning is influenced by motivational factors (such as willingness to make the most of learning affordances and opportunities at work). By engaging with continuing learning, many individuals have learnt how to actively manage their careers and progress their future plans (this could be either through self-directed learning or where formal continuing learning opens up other potential career pathways). One key factor in continued career success for mid-career workers in changing contexts is a positive disposition towards learning and development.

- Space for career development: A proactive approach to career development is associated with employees being given encouragement, time, and space to engage in self-directed learning and critical reflection; learning from others and through networks; organizations that emphasize breadth of competence development; timely and appropriate feedback and support for development of employees' learner identities (Brown, Bimrose et al., 2010a).

Relevance for Multiple Cultures: Sensitivity to the Universal and the Particular

The focus of this chapter was upon the implications for career guidance of changing patterns of work-related learning and career development of (highly) skilled workers in their mid-career in Europe. At one level, the globalization of the market for high skills makes this chapter relevant to segments of the populations of all countries (Brown, Lauder, & Ashton, 2008). The key question is the size of the segment of workers engaged in high-skilled work in the economy and the relationship to the numbers of such people being produced by the national education and training systems, although international mobility means that the two do not necessarily have to be in close correspondence. Indeed Brown, Lauder, and Ashton (2010) have argued that the competition for good, middle-class jobs is now a worldwide competition. They see this competition as a global auction for talent fuelled by an explosion of education and training, but especially higher education, across the world and the emergence of huge demand for highly skilled labor in economies such as China and India. The implications of this change will be that globally higher-skilled workers will be less well paid than currently or in the past. Fighting for a dwindling supply of good jobs will compel the middle classes to devote more time, money, and effort to set themselves apart in a competition that will leave many disappointed in multiple economies across the globe (Brown, Lauder et al., 2010). In this chapter, the focus has been upon the career development of those who successfully made the transition into good jobs and how they have continued to build their careers—for these "winners" in the global economy then much of what has been written here is of relevance in whichever society they live. The global changes just mentioned, however, raise much wider questions about the kinds of society we want to live in, social mobility, and how to shape the global economy so that the benefits do not accrue just to the winners in the "global auction" for good jobs, while condemning millions in emerging economies to a continuing life of poverty.

In this chapter, attention has also been paid to how employees in low-skilled work could upgrade their work-related skills, knowledge, and understanding through changing jobs (Brynin & Ramioul, 2007). Public policy should therefore promote guidance to encourage people in undemanding work to find more challenging employment (CEDEFOP, 2010). Even switching between forms of low-skilled employment may build confidence in individuals that they are able to apply their skills in different contexts and this can act as a spur to further development. Career guidance may also help workers reflect upon the nature of their skill sets and whether switching between low-skilled work contexts could nevertheless help them develop their adaptability or employability. Guidance can also help employees change their perspective towards aspects of learning, training, and working, so that they become more proactive in their own personal development, even if their opportunities for further career development are constrained. In all stages of life, career guidance can help workers in low-skilled employment consider the most effective ways they can deploy and develop their skills, knowledge, and understanding through a range of employment, education, and training contexts.

However, depending upon their national context, workers engaged in low-skilled work may still face barriers to accessing such provision, despite attempts in many countries to develop a greater range of services to cater to the information, counseling, and learning needs of more hard-to-reach groups (CEDEFOP, 2010). Access to career guidance provision has been widened in some contexts through a combination of web-based and telephone provision to go alongside more traditional face-to-face guidance which is generally much harder for those in employment to access. However, the development of web-based information sources, made available by a wide variety of providers, has far outstripped provision of impartial labor market information and purely guidance-oriented online services to such an extent that quality assurance of guidance has itself become a priority (CEDEFOP, 2010). So meeting the challenges of securing progression from low-skilled work and gaining access to appropriate guidance to facilitate career development continue to require a combination of individual action and appropriate structural support.

Overall then, this chapter has focused upon issues which have universal relevance for the role career guidance may play in supporting people in their mid-career in different societies in two contrasting situations. First, it can help address the issue of how the highly skilled continue to develop their skills within an increasingly global market for such skills. Secondly, it can play a role in meeting the pressing challenge of how to support those in low-skilled work in continuing to build their skill sets in ways which make them more adaptable in increasingly dynamic labor markets.

References

Arthur, M. B., Hall, D. T., & Lawrence, B. S. (1989). *Handbook of career theory*. Cambridge, UK: Cambridge University Press.

Ball, B. (1996). *Assessing your career: Time for a change?* Leicester, UK: British Psychological Society.

Banks, M., Bates, I., Breakwell, G., Bynner, J., Elmer, N., & Jamieson, L. (1992). *Careers and identities*. Buckingham, UK: Open University Press.

Biesta, G. (2008). *Strategies for improving learning through the life-course*. London, UK: TLRP.

Bimrose, J., & Barnes, S.-A. (2007). *Navigating the labour market: Career decision making and the role of guidance*. Coventry: Warwick Institute for Employment Research and Department for Education and Skills. Retrieved from http://www2.warwick.ac.uk/fac/soc/ier/publications/2008/2007/egreport08.pdf

Bimrose, J., Barnes, S.-A., & Hughes, D. (2008). *Adult career progression and advancement: A five year study of the effectiveness of guidance*. Coventry: Warwick Institute for Employment Research and the Department for Innovation, Universities and Skills. Retrieved from http://www2.warwick.ac.uk/fac/soc/ier/publications/2008/eg_report_4_years_on_final.pdf

Boyatzis, R., Goleman, D., & Rhee, K. (2000). Clustering competence in emotional intelligence: Insights from the emotional competence inventory. In R. B.-O. J. Parker (Ed.), *Handbook of emotional intelligence* (pp. 343–362). San Francisco, CA: Jossey-Bass.

Bright, J. E. H., Pryor, R. G. L., Wilkenfeld, S. H., & Earl, J. (2005). The role of social context and serendipitous events in career decision making. *International Journal for Educational and Vocational Guidance, 5*(1), 19–36.

Brown, A. (2009). *Higher skills development at work: A commentary by the teaching and learning research programme*. London, UK: ESRC.

Brown, A., Bimrose, J., Barnes, S.-A., Kirpal, S., Grønning, T., & Dæhlen, M. (2010a). *Changing patterns of work, learning and career development across Europe* (Final Report EACEA/2007/07). Brussels: Education, Audiovisual & Culture Executive Agency. Retrieved from http://ec.europa.eu/education/more-information/doc/2010/warwick_en.pdf

Brown, A., Bimrose, J., Barnes, S.-A., Kirpal, S., Grønning, T., & Dæhlen, M. (2010b). *Follow-up of the Copenhagen process: Research into forms of individual career development and continuing vocational training. Technical report on development, implementation and results of the survey*. Brussels: Education, Audiovisual & Culture Executive Agency.

Brown, P., Lauder, H., & Ashton, D. (2008). Education, globalisation and the future of the knowledge economy. *European Educational Research Journal, 7*(2), 131–156.

Brown, P., Lauder, H., & Ashton, D. (2010). *The global auction: The broken promises of education, jobs and rewards*. New York, NY: Oxford University Press.

Brynin, M., & Ramioul, M. (2007). The transformation of work? A quantitative evaluation of the shape of employment in Europe. An introduction to the research reports from the quantitative research of WORKS. In N. Greenan, E. Kalugina, & E. Walkowiak (Eds.), *The transformation of work?* CEE, France: WORKS Project.

CEDEFOP. (2008). *Career development at work: A review of career guidance to support people in employment*. Thessaloniki, Greece: Author.

CEDEFOP. (2010). *Access to success: Lifelong guidance for better learning and working in Europe*. Luxembourg, Luxembourg: Publications Office of the European Union.

Clough, B. (2010). *The origins, role and impact of union learning representatives in the UK and other countries* (Working paper 1). London, UK: Unionlearn.

Field, J. (2000). *Lifelong learning and the new educational order*. Stoke-on-Trent, UK: Trentham Books.

Fuller, A., & Unwin, L. (2004). Expansive learning environments: Integrating personal and organisational development. In H. Rainbird, A. Fuller, & A. Munro (Eds.), *Workplace learning in context*. London, UK: Routledge.

Gati, I., & Saka, N. (2001). High school students' career-related decision-making difficulties. *Journal of Counseling and Development, 79*(3), 331–340.

King, Z. (2004). Career self-management: Its nature, causes and consequences. *Journal of Vocational Behavior, 65*(1), 112–133.

London, M., & Smither, J. W. (1999). Career-related continuous learning: Defining the construct and mapping the process. In G. E. Ferris (Ed.), *Research in personnel and human resources management* (pp. 81–122). Oxford, UK: Elsevier.

Mitchell, K. E., Levin, A. S., & Krumboltz, J. D. (1999). Planned happenstance: Constructing unexpected career opportunities. *Journal of Counseling and Development, 77*(2), 115–124.

Osipow, S. H., & Fitzgerald, L. F. (1996). *Theories of career development* (4th ed.). Needham Heights, MA: Allyn & Bacon.

Purcell, K., Elias, P., & Wilton, N. (2004). *Higher education, skills and employment: Careers and jobs in the graduate labour market*. Coventry, UK: Warwick IER.

Quigley, N. R., & Tymon, W. G. (2006). Toward an integrated model of intrinsic motivation and career self-management. *Career Development International, 11*(6), 522–543.

Roberts, K. (2009). Opportunity structures then and now. *Journal of Education and Work, 22*(5), 355–368.

Rowold, J., & Schilling, J. (2006). Career-related continuous learning: Longitudinal predictive power of employees' job and career attitudes. *Career Development International, 11*(6), 489–503.

Savickas, M. L. (2005). The theory and practice of career construction. In S. D. Brown & R. W. Lent (Eds.), *Career development and counseling: Putting theory and research to work*. New Jersey, NJ: Wiley.

Sen, A. (1999). *Development as freedom*. New York, NY: Knopf.

Sultana, R. G. (2011). Lifelong guidance, citizen rights and the state: Reclaiming the social contract. *British Journal of Guidance and Counselling, 39*(2), 179–186.

Young, R. A., & Collin, A. (2000). Introduction: Framing the future of career. In A. Collin & R. A. Young (Eds.), *The future of career*. Cambridge, UK: Cambridge University Press.

Boom, Bust, and Suitability: Effective Career Preparation in a Volatile Labor Market

Overview

Trends in the labor market are a powerful influence on career development. The nature of economic development today has caused the emergence of new occupational opportunities in some economies and job loss and retrenchment in others. Chapters in this section introduce the concept and key components of labor market and labor market information, and their interface with guidance and counseling. Expected future influences on global labor markets are projected and the implications for career guidance and counseling are delineated. Key skills associated with the effective use of labor market information in the process of career guidance are articulated. That the world is changing is stated so often that it is written off as a cliché. But, this is more true now than ever before. The shift of the centers of economic and political power away from those of the 20th century, climate change, longer life spans, and the scramble for security are all considerations shaping the labor markets of today. Chapters in this section discuss how these influences affect new entrants to the global labor markets of the future. Labor markets today require skilled workers to push up production. Vocationalization has been presented as the answer to the "skilling-up" of workforces. A question that has not been adequately addressed, however, is whether vocationalization that is driven by labor market dynamics optimizes or obstructs the realization of a person's potentials in the world of work. Writers in this section explore career guidance for vocational education from the perspective of young people, their parents, and prospective employers. Career counseling optimally is a service to empower the individual to find a happy blend between personal potentials and the labor market, as well as a mechanism to sensitize representatives of the labor market to move beyond considering the worker merely as a factor of production. This section discusses in depth the interface between career guidance and Technical and Vocational Education and Training and provides a framework within which this interaction can be optimized. The notion of career shifts is discussed against the background of today's excessively competitive and ever-changing work environment. The importance of a proactive and preventive approach that would help individuals actualize multiple career interests is discussed.

In summary, this section provides information that would help the career service professional understand the labor market better. It juxtaposes the individual's personal wellbeing and labor market demands and demonstrates how career guidance and counseling could be a bridge between the two.

Understanding the Labor Market: Implications for Career Counseling

12

Sachin Kumar and Gideon Arulmani

Introduction

Accurate, easily accessible, and regularly updated labor market information (LMI) is central to any career guidance system. The need for information varies across individuals according to the stage and the conditions within which their career development is occurring. Given below are statements that illustrate this variability in the type of LMI that career choosers express.

> What is the scope of Biotechnology in Himachal Pradesh? What would be the salary for beginners? *20-year-old science graduate in Himachal Pradesh, India.*
>
> I have been retrenched. I do see lists of job advertisements. But how do I figure out what kind of job I should be looking for? Does getting another job mean I have to go back to study? *42-year-old man in York, England.*
>
> I have a postgraduate degree in marketing. I've just come back to work after a five year break. I want to know if there are projects or work I can do and how I can get an exciting job again. And I am also a mum now! *44-year-old woman in Singapore.*
>
> I am a farmer. I want my son to go the city to study. But I want him to come back to our village and work here and expand our farming business. Is there any special government scheme for this? *59-year-old man in a village in South India.*

LMI has been viewed as vital throughout the history of career development practice. Parsons (1909) described it as "a knowledge of the requirements and conditions of success, advantages and disadvantages, compensation, opportunities, and prospects in different lines of work" (p. 5). Since then, providing information remains one of the dominant approaches that career guidance and counseling services has taken (Grubb, 2002). The need for information is constant, because the world of work changes and people make career-related decisions regularly (Savard & Michaud, 2005). This is perhaps why most major competency frameworks for career practitioners have included skills related to understanding labor market and information management as key competencies. For example, the framework designed by the International Association for Educational and Vocational Guidance (IAEVG, 2003), underlines familiarity with information on educational, training, employment trends, labor market, and social issues as one of the 11 core competencies which a career practitioner is expected to demonstrate. Information management has been listed as one of the specialized competencies and this includes collecting, organizing, maintaining, and disseminating information pertinent to education, training, occupations, and employment opportunities and coaching clients in its effective use. However, LMI competencies related to understanding the world of education, training, and work have not been emphasized sufficiently in most countries. The emphasis on acquiring competencies related to understanding education and employment sectors is inadequate and

S. Kumar (✉)
Government College, Chowari, Chamba,
Himachal Pradesh, India
e-mail: samparksachin@gmail.com

G. Arulmani et al. (eds.), *Handbook of Career Development*, International and Cultural Psychology,
DOI 10.1007/978-1-4614-9460-7_12, © Springer Science+Business Media, LLC 2014

225

teaching–learning material for it is almost non-existent in a number of countries. A similar trend seems evident in relation to international research pertaining to LMI and career guidance. We conducted a review to gauge the frequency with which scholarly articles related to LMI were published in leading journals in the field of career development during last decade. The proportion of articles with *labor market* or *LMI* or *occupational/career information* in the title of the article was low in relation to other topics of career guidance. It seems possible therefore, that LMI and analysis do not seem to adequately inform the practice of career guidance and counseling. One of the possible reasons has been described to be the lack of skills necessary to engage effectively with the information (Bimrose, Marris, Barnes, & Mason, 2006).

In this chapter we describe the concept of the labor market and LMI, their key components, and their interface with guidance and counseling. We then articulate key competencies and implications for application and practice for the effective use of LMI.

Understanding the Labor Market and its Trends

The Labor Market: Concept, Components, and Changes

Effective career decision-making entails an awareness of the environment within which occupations and jobs become available, the qualifications required, tasks expected to be performed, working conditions, remuneration, the benefits offered by the job, and so on. Seen from the career guidance side, this environment is often referred to as the *world of work*. Seen from the side of the economists, it is described as the *labor market* (Kumar, 2009). Hence, in the labor market those who need labor (employers or buyers) interact with those who supply labor (employees or sellers) and come to a mutual agreement with regard to the price of this engagement. It is a mechanism where *supply* comprises the entire pool of available workers

of all types, possessing various levels of skills and abilities. The *demand* refers to the requirement for these workers at a given point in time. Therefore, we could say that the labor market is composed of:

- Workers in various industries or in the government.
- Employers including private and government organizations.
- Self-employed- or partially employed persons.
- Those who are currently unemployed.
- Those who are in the process of entering the labor market.

Another useful framework within which to understand the labor market is to consider it from the point of view of *industrial sectors*, *occupations*, and *geographies* (DfES, 2004). An understanding of the status, needs, and changes across and within these artificial boundaries would aid the effective delivery of career guidance services. Career choosers or job choosers would find it useful to know how their skills relate to other occupations, to other industrial sectors, and even to another geographical area. A critical concept related to the dynamics of the labor market is *sectoral change*. This refers to the change in the relative share taken by the primary, secondary, and tertiary sectors, in a particular economy. For example, in India, there has been a noticeable change from the primary to tertiary sector. This has a number of labor market implications in terms of jobs available and skills required. For example, retail firms that used to employ anyone with a basic education as a salesperson now demand qualified retailing professionals. *Geographical change* refers to the movement of jobs from one area to another. Initially, people used to migrate to work (Chanda, 2007) but now jobs migrate to people (Upadhya & Vasavi, 2006). This relocation of jobs from one geographical area to another—job migration—can occur because of changes in one or many of the following: supply and demand for products and services, business conditions, government policies, competition, environmental conditions, local business costs, or technological obsolescence. Understanding the labor market requires a thorough insight into these changes and the ability to deal with these changes effectively (Kumar, 2009).

Understanding Key Trends in the Labor Market

Accelerated Change

Like other markets, labor markets also change at all scales and in all geographies. However, in recent times, the pace, magnitude, complexities, and dimensions of these changes have accelerated and intensified largely due to macro processes such as an upsurge in globalization, advances in technology, greater access to information, as well as industrial and demographic shifts (e.g., Coutinho, Dam, & Blustein, 2008; Schell, Follero-Pugh, & Lloyd, 2010). These processes have altered the labor market by changing the number and types of jobs available in different geographies. Working conditions have been altered, and today virtual workspaces, with slick, paperless offices are exceedingly common.

Nonstandard Work

A further interesting development is the emergence of nonstandard work. As Presser (2003) points out, more and more workers today are engaged in part-time work, contract work, temporary, and on-call work. The worker of today is free to work for more than one employer or be self-employed. This form of work is executed in nonstandard hours rather than during fixed-day schedules. Agency work is another example of changes in conceptions of work. Here, a company may contract with another agency for the supply of labor. Hence, the worker could work for a company, but be employed by a different organization. Nonstandard work also includes freelancers, independent consultants, who may not even work on the premises of the firm for which they are delivering a service. Such an approach to work has also changed the manner in which work is executed. Today, joint ventures, work alliances, subcontracting, outsourcing, and offshoring are in common practice. An important point to be noted is that these changes have redefined the employer–employee relationship. A person following the nonstandard approach to work is no longer under the complete control of an employer. The nonstandard worker of today can choose the kind of work to take up as well as how much work to take up.

New Possibilities and Precarization of Work

The recent phase of globalization has given rise to a new set of careers which were not present earlier (Friedman, 2006). Easy access to a range of new ideas, technologies, information, resources, and markets has empowered people to find and even create new opportunities. However, it must be noted that, on the other hand, opportunities for employment and career development are rapidly declining in some contexts. This is because of a number of reasons including the flight of capital to low-wage locations (Arulmani, 2011; Friedman, 2006), replacement of domestically produced goods with goods produced abroad, mechanization, and increase in automation leading to a reduced dependence on human labor. Traditional occupations are the worst hit, rendering these populations jobless and forcing them to migrate (ILO, 2004; Scrase, 2003). Rural migrants end up working in exploitative conditions where minimum wage laws, overtime pay laws, and legal working hours are often ignored (Sehgal, 2005). Coined from the word *precarious*, labor market analysts today refer to the *precarization* of work to describe the manner in which work, for some sections of the labor force, has become unsure, precarious, and uncertain, where the worker is expected to work without guarantees. As van der Hoeven (2010) has noted, trends such as "declining employment-to-population ratio, growing informalization, the declining wage share and increasing income inequality, have enhanced precarization for many workers and their families" (p. 5). Therefore, on the one hand, the global labor market is becoming increasingly integrated for the highly skilled, who form a "global professional elite" (UNDP, 1999, p. 13), offering them high mobility and enhanced wages. On the other hand, the labor market is becoming precarious for increasingly large numbers. As stated in the 1999 Human Development Report (UNDP, 1999): "Collapse of time, space and borders may be creating a global village but not everyone can be a citizen" (p. 31).

Economic Shifts

The structure of an economy, as we know, is made up of sectors. Economic forces often lead to changes in the economic structure whereby the primary engagement of a labor force shifts from one sector to another. Such shifts in economies also change labor markets in significant ways. Today, for example, as countries restructure their economies, a definite trend seen is a shift from the manufacturing to the service sectors in most countries undergoing economic shifts (OECD, 2000) and from agricultural to service economies in other countries (Banga, 2005). There is also a growing inclination to move towards becoming a knowledge economy (OECD, 2001; World Bank, 2003) and a green economy (UNDP, 2011a; UNEP, 2010, 2011). Each of these shifts is bringing about concomitant changes in the labor market largely in terms of the number and types of jobs available and the skills profile required.

Demographic Shifts

Economies are also experiencing changes in their demographic profiles, which are referred to as *demographic shifts*. These shifts result from a change in the balance between birth and mortality rates within a population. Changed demographics can affect the labor market by altering the composition of the labor force. The fact that the global population is aging rapidly, albeit at different rates both in developed and developing world contexts (UN, 2009), has significant implications for careers and employment. Changes in the demography of the country can affect the occupations required and the occupational opportunities available. It may also alter the demand for a particular job or occupation.

Employer–Employee Relations

As mentioned above, another noteworthy trend can be seen in changes in the manner in which employers and employees relate to each other. With fewer trade barriers, less market protection, intense competition, and diminishing union pressure, job security has been weakening (Solomon & Scuderi, 2002). Earlier, the psychological contract between workers and employers used to be all about job security and steady advancement within the firm. In the present day, the focus is on competency development, continuous training, and work/life balance (Heerwagen, Kelly, & Kampschroer, 2010). This phenomenon coupled with performance-linked salaries and incentives have led to the individualization of the workplace with reduced scope for collective bargaining (Upadhya & Vasavi, 2006). In this context, the individual is expected to steer his/her working life independently across jobs and careers. Terms such as protean career (Hall, 2004), boundaryless career (Briscoe, Hall, & Frautschy DeMuth, 2006), and portfolio career (Templer & Cawsey, 1999) are being increasingly used to describe current forms of engagement with the world of work.

On reviewing relevant research, Bimrose (2006) concluded that grand visions of labor market change may be true in a limited sense only and point out that "there are significant deviations and extensive variations" and "a highly complex picture, with multiple strands emerges" (p. 2). It is evident that while a worker is finding numerous new opportunities in the current labor market, he/she is simultaneously presented with newer challenges.

Skills for Success in the Labor Market: Contemporary Observations

There appear to be some universal ways in which one may succeed in the labor market today. This section will extrapolate from these observations to deduce career guidance messages that have specific relevance to the contemporary worker.

Be Untouchable and Remain Employed

Put forward by Friedman (2006), what this means is that one needs to be in one of those jobs that cannot be automated, digitized, or outsourced! These jobs include those which need *specialized* skills that have global marketability, those which are *anchored* or localized, and need some indigenous knowledge or face-to-face interaction with customers, and those which are *adaptable*. From this perspective, people who are likely to remain safe in a volatile labor market include those who can collaborate, synthesize, explain, leverage the power of information technology, and develop fresh skills in a short time. It refers to those who can adapt to changing situations, deliver services with a personal touch, and take advantage of global facilities to serve local communities.

Skills for Learning How to Learn

Toffler (1971), quoting an informal conversation he had with psychologist Herbert Gerjuoy said, "Tomorrow's illiterate will not be the man who can't read; he will be the man who has not learned how to learn" (p. 375). Lifelong learning has been repeatedly pointed to as being vital for success in the current labor market characterized by increasing skill redundancy (OECD, 2004a; Torres, 2011; World Bank, 2003). Workers today are required to continually enhance their skills in order to remain employable. In addition to job-specific skills, a set of generic skills also known as employability skills, key competencies, or foundational skills are considered essential for positive career development in today's labor market. Employability skills have been defined as transferable core skill groups that represent functional knowledge, skills, and attitudes necessary for career success at all levels of employment and for all levels of education (Overtoom, 2000). Various organizations have operationalized this idea in different ways. In Australia, the Department of Education, Science and Training (DEST, 2006) has identified a set of 13 personal attributes contributing to employability. Some examples are loyalty, commitment, sense of humor, reliability, motivation, and adaptability. DEST has also described a set of eight generic skills that include communication, teamwork, problem solving, self-management, planning and organizing, fluency with technology, lifelong learning, and initiative

and enterprise. In its report, the U.S. Secretary of Labor's Commission on Achieving Necessary Skills (SCANS, 1992) described a three-part foundation skill set for success in the 21st century workplace. The list included basic skills (reading, writing, arithmetic/mathematics, listening, and speaking), thinking skills (creative thinking, decision making, problem solving, seeing things in the mind's eye, knowing how to learn, and reasoning), and personal qualities (responsibility, self-esteem, sociability, self-management, integrity/honesty).

Labor Market Information

LMI: The Concept

There are a number of varied, but related views on the concept of Labor Market Information. Some definitions are given below:

> Statistical and non-statistical information concerning labor market actors and their environment, as well as information concerning labor market institutions, policies and regulations that serves the needs of users and has been collected through the application of accepted methodologies and practice to the largest possible extent. (Sparreboom, 1999, p. 3)
>
> Any quantitative or qualitative information and intelligence on the labor market that can assist labor market agents in making informed plans, choices, and decisions related to business requirements, career planning and preparation, education and training offerings, job search, hiring, and governmental policy and workforce investment strategies. (Woods & O'Leary, 2006, p. 14)
>
> . . . knowledge, facts, data, and relevant institutional information on the supply and demand of the various different types of labor services (employment), including prices such as wages and other forms of compensation as well as quantities, both at the detailed and aggregate levels, that is used for analysis and decision-making. (Drummond, Beale, Kolby, Loiselle, & Miner, 2009, p. 4)

The following can be deduced from these definitions:

- LMI may include a number of data types. As Murray (2010) has summarized, LMI consists of information about:

– Labor market trends (including projected future trends), both at the aggregate level and by region, sector, industry, and occupation
– Specific job openings
– The skills and other characteristics of individual workers

• A distinction exists between *information* and *intelligence*. The former constitutes raw units of discrete data. The latter is a result of processing and interpreting this data such that it is relevant to a particular context and offers a platform upon which decision-making can occur.

• Information could be available in the form of either quantitative or qualitative data which could be related to historical, current, or projected circumstances.

• What constitutes LMI is ultimately defined by the user/s of the information.

• The process and method of data collection are crucial for sound, timely, and error-free LMI.

However, in the context of career guidance, the term LMI has been used loosely for any information used during the process of career choice and development, which may include information related to occupations, jobs, careers, employers, educational and training opportunities, and employment trends (Bimrose et al., 2006). This means that information which apparently does not seem to be LMI from the point of view of economics (such as boarding available at the place of work or training, transportation facilities, information related to scholarships and grants for further studies) may be considered LMI from the point of view of career guidance.

LMI: Components

Demand, supply, and price have been described as components of LMI (Drummond et al., 2009). On the supply side, LMI covers: the availability of workers by region, occupation, industry, and firm; hours supplied; the skill and educational level of workers that comprise the economy's human capital; other characteristics of workers including age, sex, disabilities, group (e.g., aboriginal people, minorities), and immigrant status; demographic projections of the labor force showing young people entering the labor force, older people retiring, immigrants arriving from abroad; graduates from educational institutions and training programs; and investments in human capital. On the demand side, it includes: employment by region, occupation, industry, and firm; hours demanded; the skill, educational qualifications, and credential requirements of various jobs; job vacancies or unfilled jobs also by region, occupation, industry, and firm; and occupational projections. The price side of the LMI includes wages, salaries, earnings, wage settlements, total compensation including fringe benefits like time off, pension plans, and various forms of insurance and working conditions, which can also be considered part of total compensation. All the three components may be broken down by occupation, industry, and region.

LMI and Career Guidance

An overall analysis of LMI usage and career guidance indicates that except in a few countries, LMI is not available in an organized manner. More often than not, vital information at the local level is not available. There is also a lack of clarity about the information that is available. Even if high quality data is available, the practitioner may not be trained enough to make meaning of it and use it effectively in a career guidance interaction. In this section we discuss some of the key points pertaining to the interface between LMI and career guidance.

LMI for Career Guidance: Does it Matter?

Research on the impact of using LMI during career guidance clearly indicates the importance of using LMI. Borhans, De Grip, and Haijke (1996) found that labor market forecasts were crucial in assisting appropriate student choice in the Netherlands. Bimrose, Barnes, Hughes, and Orton (2004) found that LMI is highly valued by guidance clients in the UK who reported that the manner in which LMI was provided changed their views regarding the opportunities available to them. In a comprehensive literature review of the impact of LMI on the career decision-making process, Savard and Michaud (2005) found that LMI has an impact on career development, but that it is virtually of no significance unless transmitted through a counselor. Murray (2010), in another literature review, also found that individuals and employers consider it useful and do use LMI in decision-making pertaining to investment in education and training.

LMI for Career Guidance: Identifying What is Useful

LMI areas that are known to be useful from the client's career decision-making perspective have been listed as follows: "the competition faced, entry routes, the rewards available, the availability of jobs within certain travel-to-work areas, the prospects of securing employment in particular jobs, and the value of particular qualifications, experience, or training" (Bimrose et al., 2006, p. 93). Offer (2001) indicated that there could be six types of LMI that are useful from the practitioner's point of view: "the demand for labor (how easy is it to get a job in this occupation, industry, role?); progression routes, career structure, and earnings (what are the prospects?); geographical availability (how available is this in my travel-to-work area?); overall trends (is employment on the increase in this occupation or industry?); transferability (will I be able to transfer the competences and skills developed in this industry should job opportunities decrease?); recruitment and selection methods (where and how do people get jobs in this industry?)" (p. 78).

LMI and Career Guidance: Target Groups

It is also important to note that clients need different types of information at different stages of their career development (Bimrose et al., 2006). For example, a student who is about to complete high school in the Indian context, may require a general awareness of broad occupational families, general eligibility criteria, and educational milestones because the key career development task for this young person is to decide which stream to choose further: Humanities, Science, Commerce, or vocational pathways. A student who is about to complete higher secondary education needs information to decide whether to go for a professional Bachelor's course, a nonprofessional Bachelor's course, a vocational course, or look for a job. On the other hand, a student who is completing his/her Bachelor's or Master's degree would have more specific queries related to the labor market. The one who has completed studies and needs an internship position, the one who has been laid off and needs another job in the same sector, the one who is an immigrant, the one who is planning a career shift, and yet another one who is looking for a post-retirement engagement, all require different kinds of LMI. It follows that LMI needs to be tailored to the client's requirement and that the closer the person is to actually entering the labor market, the more specific would be the LMI requirements.

When Should LMI be Provided?

Which is the ideal stage in the guidance process to provide the client with LMI? Generally a client is encouraged to engage in career exploration after completing self-exploration which has yielded an understanding of interests, values, abilities, and preferences. Our experience in India has informed us that most clients come with LMI-related queries. However, our experience has further indicated that when LMI is delivered prematurely and independently of opportunities for self-exploration, clients usually report a higher level of confusion with regard to career decision-making (Arulmani & Nag-Arulmani, 2006). Hence, it would be good practice to begin with activities related to self-understanding (e.g., exploring personal interests and aptitudes) and simultaneously expose clients to broad labor market information. Career guidance could then follow a process whereby information about self is blended with LMI to finally help the client identify career alternatives. Our outcome studies have indicated that this approach has higher acceptability as well as greater effectiveness (Arulmani & Abdulla, 2007; Arulmani & Nag-Arulmani, 2004).

Application and Practice: Ideas for the Effective Delivery of LMI

We now translate what we have discussed in earlier sections into ideas for application and practice.

Researching LMI

This is a competency related to the career guidance practitioner's ability not only to find LMI but also to process and transform it such that it is relevant to the career chooser. Ours is often described as the Information Age. Yet, the required information is often hard to find or sometimes not available at all. Even the countries with the best of LMI systems such as Canada, have reported a number of information gaps (Drummond et al., 2009). Therefore, career guidance practitioners must become fluent at researching LMI and develop the skill of identifying primary and secondary sources of LMI. Box 12.1 provides a list of sources and pointers to locate LMI.

Using Locally Available Sources to Extract LMI

LMI is available all around us. It goes without saying, therefore, that along with the skill of researching these sources to collate information, organizing information into meaningful formats is another key competency for the effective use

Box 12.1: Sources of LMI
Tuning into Global LMI Trends
     The following sources provide reliable and regular information pertaining to global LMI trends:
- World of Work reports and Magazines published by the International Labor Organization (ILO, 1996–2012a, 1996–2012b).
- Global Employment Trends series (ILO, 1996–2012c).
- Employment Outlook published by the Organization for Economic Cooperation and Development (OECD, n.d.).
- Human Development Reports (UNDP, 2011b).
- World Development Reports (World Bank, 2011).

Tuning into LMI at National and Local Levels
     Centralized LMI is quite often not available at the national and local level. Information may be scattered and available through different organizations. In such contexts, sources of LMI could include the following:
- If the country or province has an LMI portal, the careers practitioner should be familiar with it and be able to navigate through it.
- National Census data (e.g., information regarding demographic and occupational profiles).
- Statistics published by departments/ministries of labor.
- Study reports by various professional bodies.
- Industry-specific data bases.
- Job portals.
- Education portals.
- Prospectuses of educational and training institutions give vital and specific information about courses and programs.
- Speaking with professionals from different fields would give an insider's view of the profession.
- Reports by consulting firms who specialize in LMI such as wage surveys, business activity surveys, and employment trends.

of LMI. It is up to the interested user to gather LMI from a wide variety of sources. The daily newspaper is a ready and immediate source of labor market information. This includes supplements on career and job information as well as education pages. News reports about policy changes, new investments, new occupational possibilities, all add up to becoming useful, locally relevant LMI (Kumar, 2009). Box 12.2 presents an exercise on using newspaper articles to extract LMI.

Box 12.2: Converting Newspaper Articles into LMI—An Exercise

The daily newspaper serves as a readily available source of LMI. Scan your local newspaper and identify articles that carry LMI. Examples of criteria you can use to identify articles that have implications for your career guidance practice are given below:

- Announcement of a change in an existing government policy related to education or labor or any industrial sector.
- Any new provision or amendment in existing provisions for education, training, or employment sector.
- Information about vacancies in organizations.
- Any notification or news in changes in eligibility or qualification or entrance scheme for entry into any educational institute or a firm.
- Important dates for different entrance procedures.

Having selected an article convert the information in the article into LMI by asking yourself the following questions:

- What is the implication of this news for the career aspirant?
- Does the news give generic trends, or specific nuggets of information?
- What type of LMI is contained in this piece? Does it contain one or more

(continued)

aspects of the following: increase or decrease in opportunity; change in eligibility, working conditions, remuneration, and/or training opportunities?
- What kind of client is likely to be benefited most by this information: a career chooser at High School, Higher Secondary or a College graduate; one who is switching careers and moving from one job to another; one who is looking for financial assistance; one who is looking for a post-retirement engagement?

Assessing LMI

The National Guidance Research Forum (NGRF) describes this competency as the ability to assess and validate the accuracy and applicability of LMI (NGRF, n.d.). It is also linked to assessing a unit of LMI for its appropriateness to meet the particular information needs of clients. Assessment of LMI, therefore, could occur at two levels: assessment of the reliability and validity of the information, and assessment of the relevance of LMI to the needs of the client. Box 12.3 provides a few simple pointers to assess the validity of LMI.

Presenting LMI

LMI may sometimes be too technical for a young career chooser to make sense of it. The career counselor, therefore, needs to develop the ability to present LMI such that it is easy to understand and comprehend (NGRF, n.d.). In situations where labor market data is only available as information and not as intelligence, it may not be suitable to be presented directly to the client. It is important to tailor the information as per the needs of the individual/group. Thus, for example, LMI may be presented in visual form such as bar graphs or pie graphs. Other clients may prefer looking at tables or reading an explanatory note.

Box 12.3: Assessing Labor Market Information

Don't accept information just because it is printed! Check the following:

- Who commissioned and funded the study? How reliable is the source of the information?
- What could be the possible objectives behind the report: both stated and ulterior?
- How was the LMI collected? Who asked what types of questions, of whom, and to how many?
- Are the conclusions reliable and reasonable?
- When was the study carried out and when was it published?
- Are you aware of any significant event which might have taken place between these two dates which have a bearing on the report made by the study?
- Are the findings corroborated by other sources of information?
- Is the information useful and relevant to your local context or the client's context?

It is important also to use jargon-free, succinct, and clear language.

Visiting Opportunity Providers

This competency reflects the career guidance practitioner's ability to arrange and conduct a worthwhile visit to an opportunity provider (e.g., employer/college/placement provider) to glean LMI (NGRF, n.d.). Employers are key resources for providing LMI. Visiting opportunity providers with specific objectives can give useful information related to jobs available, skills required, working conditions, compensation, and similar information. It is important that the practitioner chooses the appropriate organization, approaches

it in a professional manner, and meticulously plans the meeting. These meetings also provide the valuable opportunity to clarify misunderstandings, misinformation, or misconceptions about an occupation. Box 12.4 provides a set of guidelines on how such visits could be optimized.

Box 12.4: Optimizing Visits to Opportunity Providers

- Identify employers/training providers in your locality through multiple sources including newspapers, websites, and your own network of friends and clients.
- Be clear about what you want to know/ clarify during your visit.
- Approach the organization and brief them about your purpose and possible mutual benefits much before you intend to visit.
- It is a good idea to bring your colleague along. Brief your partner beforehand to ensure that he or she covers what you may miss during your conversation.
- Other than collecting requisite information using a pre-prepared checklist, it is important that you are able to discuss any prevalent misconceptions related to the occupational sector/s that the organization represents.

Note: Adapted from "Career Counselling: A Handbook," G. Arulmani, and S. Nag-Arulmani, 2004. New Delhi, India: Tata McGraw Hill.

Equal Opportunities and LMI

Over the recent past, there has been a call to include the social justice agenda into career counseling (e.g., Arthur, 2005; Hansen, 2003). Therefore, this competency is linked to the skill of being up-to-date with relevant equal opportunities legislations and having the confidence to translate this knowledge into practice

(NGRF, n.d.). Governments across the world have passed equal opportunity legislations that institute provisions for marginalized communities. It is important that the practitioner is aware of such provisions and is able to translate this knowledge into practice. Quite often, the marginalized and the disadvantaged are not aware of the many schemes and privileges that have been made available for them and these resources remain unutilized. A critical aspect of career guidance is to link this clientele with what is relevant to their situation. We provide a case illustration in Box 12.5.

This information was collated into a Career Information Resource Handbook (The Promise Foundation, 2010) which counselors around the country today use in their work with this client group. This experience has also been used to train practitioners from other states to develop similar LMI resources.

Promoting Self-Access of LMI

In most contexts, the client-to-counselor ratio does not allow the counselor to devote sufficient time to each client. Also, LMI is constantly changing and reaching the latest information to a client may not be possible. It is necessary, therefore, for the client to take responsibility to avail LMI. This competency, therefore, is related to helping clients learn skills to access, assess, and interpret LMI on their own (Arulmani & Nag-Arulmani, 2006). In certain economies LMI becomes obsolete very quickly. Hence it is important that workers are able to deepen their understanding of the labor market in an independent manner. We provide illustrations of methods to achieve this target in Box 12.6.

Box 12.5: Collating Career Development Resources for the Disadvantaged—A Case Study from India

Thanks to equal opportunity legislations and related provisions, a number of opportunities are available in India for the marginalized and disadvantaged in terms of education/training/work experience opportunities as well as in terms of financial support such as scholarships and loans. Most of the available LMI caters to the people from middle- and upper-middle backgrounds (Kumar, 2009). The Jiva Project executed by The Promise Foundation in Bangalore, India, experimented with a collation of LMI for disadvantaged high school students in the province of Karnataka (Arulmani, 2010). An exhaustive review of all relevant government schemes for the marginalized was conducted. It was found that the Department of Social Welfare and Department of Employment and Training along with a number of other allied departments, offered schemes and programs for the career development of the marginalized. This included groups such as scheduled castes, scheduled tribes, religious minorities, women, and persons with special needs. Examples of these schemes are free training programs, scholarships, loans, hostel facilities, reservations, eligibility waivers, travel allowances, and exemptions.

Box 12.6: Preparing Clients to Take Charge of Their Learning: A Worksheet

The result of a career talk can have the outcome of it having merely been a "nice" experience; a visit to a workplace can remain just an "excursion." Actual learning may not take place. The worksheet given below provides the young career chooser a template to ask questions and record information. After attending the career talk or completing an industry visit, students could use their worksheets to make a presentation to the rest of the class, thus reinforcing the learning that accrued during the experience.

(continued)   (continued)

Box 12.6 (continued)

A set of questions that could be developed into a worksheet is provided below:

- What is the name of this career?
- Which are the various departments/jobs linked to this career?
- What are the activities and tasks I would perform if I took up this career?
- What working conditions would I experience if I were to practice this career (hours, location, environment)?
- Would I be working mostly alone or within a group? Are jobs within this career mostly indoors or outdoors?
- Would I mostly be working with people or machines?
- What are the occupational hazards or risks that I need to be prepared for?
- What is the salary and perquisites I can expect at the start up level and as I progress through this career?
- What is the highest position in this career? What are the steps to reach there?
- What are the primary talents required for success in this career?
- What is the entry route into this career (educational and other qualifications; whether the course type is university-based or vocational; entrance tests; age limits; other requirements)?
- Will I obtain a degree, certificate, or diploma if I take up courses related to this career? Which type of qualification offers me the best prospects within this career?
- What is the first qualification to enter this career? What is the further education required? Up to what level should I study before I can start working and how long will it be before I qualify for a job?
- Which are the most well-known training institutes where I can study to qualify for this career?

(continued)

- What is the cost of training? Are there scholarships/stipends available during training?
- What are the future prospects of this career?
- What are the points I must keep in mind as I prepare to enter courses for this career?

Note: Adapted from "Career and Livelihood Planning: Training Manual," G. Arulmani & S. Kumar, 2009. Bangalore, India: The Promise Foundation.

Using LMI: The Necessity for Discretion

This competency requires the career guidance practitioner to exercise caution in the manner in which LMI is used (Arulmani & Nag-Arulmani, 2006). This is particularly true in economies where the labor market plays a powerful role in influencing career decisions. A newspaper article, for example, may announce that the government is going to recruit certain kinds of professionals in large numbers. Recruiters from a strong industry may make attractive presentations that pass off as career guidance, where in fact, the information presented has the underlying purpose of recruitment rather than guidance. Employment-oriented messages from the labor market could influence young career choosers to take up courses leading to these qualifications, not mindful of their suitability for a career in this field. In such cases, career choice could be over-influenced by labor market cycles and the question of finding a good fit between self and occupation could be left unanswered. In such situations, the possibility of career development being a mechanism for learning, personal growth, and potential realization is pushed to the background (Arulmani & Nag-Arulmani, 2006). Although labor market trends are a powerful influence on career development, career guidance is not chained to economic cycles and it ought to be the personhood of the worker that lies at the heart of the process (Arulmani & Nag-Arulmani, 2006). Being equipped both with attitudes and skills to strike this essential balance is the hallmark of effective career counseling. The key function of LMI is to inform and not determine the career development process (Kumar, 2009). Career counseling could in effect be the bridge between education and the labor market, rather than merely being the handmaiden of the labor market (Arulmani & Nag-Arulmani, 2006).

Conclusion

Relevance for Multiple Cultures: Sensitivity to the Universal and the Particular

As pointed out earlier in the chapter, some trends in the labor market are universal, having relevance to a wide range of economies. Other trends are more circumscribed and are relevant to smaller groups of economies. Generally, career choosers come with specific queries related to the labor market and allied sectors of education and training. It is important that the career guidance practitioner is prepared to answer questions related to a particular client group in a particular geography. However, a thorough understanding of general labor market trends is essential. Firstly, this is because general/global trends are likely to affect, shape, and sometimes even determine trends at the local level. Secondly, the contemporary worker, who is aware of universal trends in the labor market, would be better equipped to ensure that his or her career is maturing effectively. Therefore, the task before contemporary career guidance practitioners is not only to prepare to deliver specific LMI but also acquire the skills for spotting and delivering universal labor market messages. Hence, catering to *specific* requirements keeping *universal* trends in mind is one of the key competencies expected from a careers practitioner in the contemporary labor markets.

New Concepts and Viewpoints: Charting New Directions

Effective transitions into and navigation through the labor market is crucial for maximizing the human potential and ensuring economic prosperity. Perhaps, that is why, career information, guidance, and counseling services have been described to be a public as well as a private good (OECD, 2004b). The timely availability of quality information remains crucial for the effective delivery of these services (Grubb, 2002).

While it is the government's role to make a robust labor market information system (LMIS) available, career guidance practitioners are expected to convert this *data* into *information* and customize it for their clients. In the current era of information overload, the skill to find, validate, and interpret information becomes vital. Further, career guidance professionals working with disadvantaged groups may find that LMI specifically related to this group is not readily available or accessible. Specialists for this client group need to source and collate information particularly relevant to this group. Developing fluency with LMI, therefore, is a skill that is integrally connected with successful career guidance. The time is ripe for curricula to be designed that prepare careers professionals and arm them with competencies related to the effective use of labor market information.

References

Arthur, N. (2005). Building from cultural diversity to social justice competencies in international standards for career development practitioners. *International Journal for Educational and Vocational Guidance, 5*(2), 137–149.

Arulmani, G. (2010). *The Jiva approach to career guidance and counselling: An Indian model* (Project Report). Bangalore, India: The Promise Foundation.

Arulmani, G. (2011, December). *Political, economic and social changes and the changing role of career guidance and career guidance policies: Synthesis report.* Presented at the Sixth International Symposium on Career Development and Public Policy, Budapest, Hungary.

Arulmani, G., & Abdulla, A. (2007). Capturing the ripples: Addressing the sustainability of the impact of social marketing. *Social Marketing Quarterly, 13*, 84–107.

Arulmani, G., & Nag-Arulmani, S. (2004). *Career counselling: A handbook.* New Delhi, India: Tata McGraw Hill.

Arulmani, G., & Nag-Arulmani, S. (2006). *Work orientation and responses to career choices: Indian regional survey* (Draft Report). Bangalore, India: The Promise Foundation.

Arulmani, G., & Kumar, S. (2009). *Career and livelihood planning: Training manual.* Bangalore, India: Jiva Project, The Promise Foundation.

Banga, R. (2005). *Critical issues in India's service led growth* (Working Paper No. 171). New Delhi, India: Indian Council for Research on International Economic Relations.

Bimrose, J., Barnes, S.-A., Hughes, D., & Orton, M. (2004). *What is effective guidance? Evidence from longitudinal case studies in England.* Coventry, UK: Department for Education and Skills, Warwick Institute for Employment Research.

Bimrose, J. (2006). *The changing context of career practice: Guidance, counselling or coaching?* Derby, England: Centre for Guidance Studies, University of Derby.

Bimrose, J., Marris, L., Barnes, S.-A., & Mason, A. (2006). Labour market information: Broadening horizons and connecting practitioners. In H. Reid & J. Bimrose (Eds.), *Constructing the future IV: Transforming career guidance* (pp. 89–102). Stourbridge, UK: Institute of Career Guidance.

Borhans, L., De Grip, A., & Haijke, H. (1996). Labour market information and the choice of vocational specialism. *Economics of Education Review, 15*(1), 59–74.

Briscoe, J. P., Hall, D. T., & Frautschy DeMuth, R. L. (2006). Protean and boundaryless careers: An empirical examination. *Journal of Vocational Behavior, 69*, 30–47.

Chanda, N. (2007). *Bound together: How traders, preachers, adventurers and warriors shaped globalization.* New Delhi, India: Penguin/Viking.

Coutinho, M. T., Dam, U. C., & Blustein, D. L. (2008). The psychology of working and globalisation: A new perspective for a new era. *International Journal for Educational and Vocational Guidance, 8*(1), 5–18.

Department of Education, Science and Training (DEST). (2006). *Employability skills for the future.* Melbourne, Australia: Author.

DfES. (2004). *LMI matters! Understanding labour market information.* Nottingham, UK: Author.

Drummond, D., Beale, E., Kolby, K., Loiselle, M., & Miner, R. (2009). *Working together to build a better labour market information system for Canada.* Toronto, Canada: Advisory Panel on Labour Market Information.

Friedman, T. L. (2006). *The world is flat: A brief history of the twenty-first century* (Expanded edition). New York, NY: Farrar, Straus & Giroux.

Grubb, W. N. (2002). *Who am I? The inadequacy of career information in the information age.* Paris, France: Organisation for Economic Co-operation and Development.

Hall, D. T. (2004). The protean career: A quarter-century journey. *Journal of Vocational Behavior, 65*, 1–13.

Hansen, L. S. (2003). Career counsellors as advocates and change agents for equality. *Career Development Quarterly, 52*(1), 43–53.

Heerwagen, J., Kelly, K., & Kampschroer, K. (2010). *Changing nature of organization, work and workplace.* Retrieved from http://www.wbdg.org/resources/chngorgwork.php

IAEVG. (2003). *International competencies for educational and vocational guidance practitioners.* Bern, Switzerland: IAEVG. Retrieved from http://www.iaevg.org/iaevg/nav.cfm?lang=2&menu=1&submenu=5

ILO. (1996–2012a). *World of work magazines.* Geneva: International Labour Office. Retrieved from http://www.ilo.org/global/publications/magazines-and-journals/world-of-work-magazine/issues/lang–en/index.htm

ILO. (1996–2012b). *World of work report 2011.* Geneva: International Labour Office. Retrieved from http://www.ilo.org/global/publications/ilo-bookstore/order-online/books/WCMS_166021/lang–en/index.htm

ILO. (1996–2012c). *Global employment trends.* Geneva: International Labour Office. Retrieved from http://www.ilo.org/global/publications/books/global-employment-trends/lang–en/index.htm

ILO. (2004). *A fair globalization: Creating opportunities for all.* Geneva, Switzerland: International Labour Office.

Kumar, S. (2009). *Socioeconomic status and career development* (Unpublished M.Phil. dissertation). Martin Luther Christian University, Shillong, India.

Murray, A. (2010). *The state of knowledge and impact of labour market information: A survey of the Canadian evidence.* Ottawa, Canada: Centre for the Study of Living Standards.

NGRF (National Guidance Research Forum. (n.d.). *How skilled am I? Competency checklist.* Retrieved from http://www.guidance-research.org/lmi-learning/lmi_competence_check

Organisation for Economic Cooperation and Development. (n.d.) *OECD employment outlook.* Retrieved from http://www.oecd.org/els/emp/oecdemployment outlook.htm

OECD. (2000). The service economy. In *Business and industry policy forum series.* Paris, France: Author.

OECD. (2001). Competencies for the knowledge economy. *Education policy analysis.* Paris, France: Centre for Educational Research and Innovation.

OECD. (2004a). *Lifelong learning: OECD policy review.* Paris, France: OECD.

OECD. (2004b). *Career guidance and public policy: Bridging the gap.* Paris, France: OECD.

Offer, M. (2001). The discourse of the labour market. In B. Gothard, P. Mignot, M. Offer, & M. Ruff (Eds.), *Careers guidance in context* (p. 76). London, UK: Sage.

Overtoom, C. (2000). *Employability skills: An update.* Columbus, OH: ERIC Clearinghouse on Adult, Career and Vocational Education. Retrieved from http://www.ericdigests.org/2001-2/skills.html

Parsons, F. (1909). *Choosing a vocation.* Boston, MA: Houghton Mifflin.

Presser, H. B. (2003). Race-ethnic and gender differences in nonstandard work shifts. *Work and Occupations, 30*(4), 412–439.

Savard, R., & Michaud, G. (2005). *The impact of LMI on the career decision-making process: Literature review*. Sherbrooke, Canada: Forum of Labour Market Ministers.

Schell, D., Follero-Pugh, F., & Lloyd, D. (2010). *Making career sense of labour market information*. Ottawa, Canada: Canadian Career Development Foundation.

Scrase, T. J. (2003). Precarious production: Globalization and artisan labour in the Third World. *Third World Quarterly, 24*(3), 449–461.

Secretary's Commission on Achieving Necessary Skills (SCANS). (1992). *Learning a living: A blueprint for high performance*. Washington, DC: U.S. Government Printing Office.

Sehgal, R. (2005). Social reproduction of third world labour in the era of globalisation: State, market and the household. *Economic and Political Weekly, 40*(22–23), 2286–2294.

Solomon, B., & Scuderi, L. (2002). *Youth guide to globalization*. Surry Hills, Australia: OXFAM Community Aid Abroad.

Sparreboom, T. (1999). *Improving labour market information in Southern Africa* (ILO/SAMAT Policy Paper No.10). Harare, Zimbabwe: ILO, Southern Africa Multidisciplinary Advisory Team.

Templer, A. J., & Cawsey, T. F. (1999). Rethinking career development in an era of portfolio careers. *Career Development International, 4*(2), 70–76.

The Promise Foundation (2010). *Career resource handbook*. Bangalore, India: Jiva Project, The Promise Foundation.

Toffler, A. (1971). *Future shock*. London, UK: Pan.

Torres, R. M. (2011). Lifelong learning: Moving beyond education for all (EFA). In J. Yang & R. Valdes-Cotera (Eds.), *Conceptual evolution and policy developments in lifelong learning* (pp. 40–50). Hamburg, Germany: UNESCO Institute for Lifelong Learning.

UN. (2009). *World population ageing 2009*. New York, NY: Department of Economic and Social Affairs, United Nations.

UNDP. (1999). *Globalization with a human face* (Human Development Report). New York, NY: Author.

UNDP. (2011a). *Sustainability and equity: A better future for all* (Human Development Report). New York, NY: Author.

UNDP. (2011b). *21 years of Human Development Reports*. Retrieved from http://hdr.undp.org/en/reports/

UNEP. (2010). *Green economy: Developing countries success stories*. Nairobi, Kenya: Author.

UNEP. (2011). *Towards a green economy: Pathways to sustainable development and poverty eradication*. Nairobi, Kenya: Author.

Upadhya, C., & Vasavi, A. R. (2006). *Work, culture and sociality in the Indian IT industry: A sociological study*. Bangalore, India: National Institute for advanced studies.

van der Hoeven, R. (2010). *Labour market trends, financial globalization and the current crisis in developing countries* (DESA Working Paper No. 99). New York, NY: United Nations Department of Economic and Social Affairs.

Woods, J. F., & O'Leary, C. J. (2006). *Conceptual framework for an optimal labour market information system: Final report* (Upjohn Institute Technical Report No. 07–022). Kalamazoo, MI: W.E. Upjohn Institute for Employment Research.

World Bank. (2003). *Lifelong learning in the global knowledge economy: Challenges for developing countries*. Washington, DC: Author.

World Bank. (2011). *World development reports*. Washington, DC: Author.

Labor Market and Career Development in the 21st Century

13

Stelina Chatzichristou and Gideon Arulmani

Introduction

One of the central goals of career counseling is to prepare young people for employment and simultaneously enhance their self-development. The world today is globalized as never before and the careers of new entrants into the labor markets may be influenced by developments in distant countries or regions. In this chapter we describe some of the factors that already shape or are expected to affect labor markets across the globe and discuss the challenges this could bring to career counseling. Although these factors vary in magnitude across countries or regions, our analysis attempts to uncover interrelationships among them, with a view to forging stronger links between the labor market of the 21st century and the process of career guidance and counseling.

Emerging Economies: The Eastward Shift of Influence

The 21st century signaled the advent of the "emerging economies." These are low-income

S. Chatzichristou
Economist and specialist in Policy Analysis, Brussels, Belgium
e-mail: cstelina@gmail.com

G. Arulmani (✉)
The Promise Foundation, Bangalore, India
e-mail: garulmani@t-p-f.org

yet rapidly growing countries, stimulated by industrialization and economic liberalization (Hoskisson, Eden, Lau, & Wright, 2000). Changes in the economic growth patterns of these economies, coupled with stagnation in the West, have led to a rebalancing of the global economy in favor of Asia, Latin America, and Eastern Europe, as well as portions of the Middle East, North, and sub-Saharan Africa (Bisson, Kirkland, & Stephenson, 2010). These shifts and changes raise new and special challenges for the discipline of career guidance and counseling, given the increased participation of non-Western, nonwhite individuals in the global arena (Coutinho, Dam, & Blustein, 2008). Some of the specific characteristics of emerging economies that have particular relevance to guidance and counseling are discussed in this section.

Economic Growth: New Options for Employment

Economic growth refers to the annual percentage change in the quantum of marketable goods and services or gross domestic product (GDP) that a country registers. Supported by policies that have allowed economic reform, economies that were referred to as developing economies have been able to significantly increase their GDP and have shown high rates of economic growth over the last 2 decades. It is this dramatic change in the rate of economic growth that has led to these economies being described as emerging economies.

G. Arulmani et al. (eds.), *Handbook of Career Development*, International and Cultural Psychology, DOI 10.1007/978-1-4614-9460-7_13, © Springer Science+Business Media, LLC 2014

Economic growth tends to bring with it new and better paid avenues for employment. The economic growth of these countries is substantially linked to their ability to produce goods and services at lower costs, hence allowing the export of their products at highly competitive prices in global markets. Emerging economies are today able to offer their workers higher salaries and emoluments leading to a rise in per capita incomes. Very quickly, however, this ongoing increase in salaries affects the ability of these economies to continue to produce goods and services at lower costs. Indeed, this is a phenomenon noticed in India, particularly in the Business Process Outsourcing (BPO) industry where local salaries have gradually risen to a point where outsourcing to India may no longer have a sufficient cost advantage (Bissell, 2010). This is a tension that must be noted by the career counselor.

Nevertheless, the increase in disposable incomes (at least in the short run) has enhanced the capacity of larger numbers of people within these economies to spend more. Along with economic growth there is a more recent phenomenon, namely, the increase in the size and capacity of domestic markets. Goods and services that were once almost exclusively meant for export are today finding increasing numbers of domestic buyers. The forces driving economic growth are expected to shift the balance from "made in China" to "consumed in China"; that is, domestic markets in emerging economies are also growing and demonstrating an increasing capacity for higher spending and consumption.

At the heart of this economic ferment is employment. Job opportunities are expected to see a marked increase in such countries, especially in China, India, and Latin America. Increases are expected and are already evident in traditional sectors such as construction, transportation, housing, safety, health, and education (Sankh et al., 2010). In addition, new sectors have also opened up and examples are entertainment, information technology, communication, hospitality, and advertising (Asian Development Bank, 2012). Members of the workforce in emerging economies are today presented with an array of employment possibilities. A question that emerges against this background is related to the importance given by the career chooser to these possibilities and it is here that career guidance has the potential to play a critical role.

Outsourcing: Influence on Sustained Career Development

A company can choose to carry out the manufacture of its products domestically and manage all its operations directly. It can also assemble its products overseas by engaging in foreign direct investment (FDI) and setting up subsidiaries in other countries. Alternatively, it can disaggregate production and choose to outsource an input from another location or another country (Antràs & Helpman, 2003). Goods we use every day, such as computer or even a pair of shoes, involve the production of innumerable elements and parts, all of which need to be produced separately before the final assembly. Box 13.1 presents examples of how the production of Barbie dolls, Nike shoes, American cars, and microchips have been fragmented and spread all over the world.

These decisions are largely influenced by factors related to cost and the skill-levels of labor forces. Emerging economies with their large workforces and significantly lower cost of labor have over the recent past become attractive outsourcing destinations. In fact, the employment boom in emerging economies is strongly connected with jobs that have been outsourced to these locations. The rationale used by companies for outsourcing has important implications for guidance and counseling with reference to emerging economies. It has been argued that:

> Production stages vary considerably in the relative intensity with which they use labor of different skill types, which creates a rationale for moving non-skill intensive activities abroad. Product design and development require workers with at least a college education and the production of components may require skilled technicians. Product assembly, on the other hand, generally requires workers with only rudimentary skills. (Feenstra & Hanson, 1996, p. 4)

Box 13.1: Outsourcing and Offshoring

Barbie Doll products are designed in the USA, production is managed from Hong Kong, raw material is sourced and supplied by China, and Barbie is finally assembled in bits, in India, China, and Malaysia.

Nike Shoes subcontracts most of its manufacturing to independent producers in Thailand, Indonesia, Cambodia, and Vietnam.

Intel Microchips are assembled by wholly owned subsidiaries in China, Costa Rica, Malaysia, and the Philippines.

American car manufacturers retain about 37 % of production in the USA most of which is the high-end design component. The rest of the car is made in Japan, Germany, Taiwan, Singapore, the United Kingdom, Ireland, and Barbados.

Note: Adapted from "Globalisation, Outsourcing and Wage Inequality (Working Paper No. 5424)," by C. R. Feenstra and H. G. Hanson, 1996, Cambridge, Massachusetts: National Bureau of Economic Research.

Outsourcing has increased job opportunities in emerging economies and has provided a foothold for individuals to attain higher income levels. However, the argument that underlies outsourcing raises important questions that have long-term implications. Most importantly, the low-skill and low-cost rationale for outsourcing could lead to a situation where workforce development in emerging economies is tied to the economic policies of advanced economies, in ways which carry the potential to delay or even harm the long-term economic development of emerging economies. If it is true that workers in emerging economies demonstrate lower skills levels, then the objective ought to be to focus on their education and on enhancing their skill literacy rather than exploiting this lower-skill level for economic benefits (Arulmani, 2009). The deployment of an emerging economy's workforce to engage with low-skill jobs could

hinder the holistic and comprehensive occupational development of the workforce. It may be true in the short run that endlessly sewing buttons on to garments, soldering circuit points, or answering telephone enquiries in call centers increase the worker's income. But in the long term, no transferable skill or knowledge development has occurred (Scrase, 2003). Yet, the desire to augment income causes large numbers of workers in emerging economies to abandon education and their current occupations to take up outsourced, low-skill jobs, which appear gilt-edged in the here and now but which in reality do not offer sound prospects for sustained career development. Examples of such outcomes abound in emerging economies. Box 13.2 provides an illustration from the Indian call center industry. A further issue associated with the long-term implications of outsourced jobs is that these jobs can quickly migrate to another location where labor is cheaper and production conditions have cost advantages for the outsourcing company. Helping the worker, particularly young people, find the balance between quick earning and sustained career development is an increasingly salient challenge for career guidance and counseling in emerging economies.

Box 13.2: Call Centers in India: An Abbreviated Case Illustration

This is an excerpt from case notes of a counseling session with a 25-year-old male, holding a Bachelor's Degree in Mechanical Engineering and working for the last 18 months as a Call Center Agent in one of the most well-known call centers in Bangalore, South India. He self-referred himself for counseling with the presenting complaints of disillusionment with his job, confusion about the future, and the inability to build on the work experience gained from the present job.

(continued)

Box 13.2 (continued)

Client:

I took up this job only for the money. I have earned well. But now my future is not moving. This job has given me work experience but it is of no use. According to my plan, I wanted to work here for about 2 years and then carry on with my real career. I have been applying for jobs since the last 2 weeks. I went for three interviews. But I was shocked when I was told in the interview that they could offer me a job only as a trainee. I told them I have work experience. But they all told me that working in the call center industry is not counted as work experience.

Counselor:

Did you ask them why?

Client:

They told me that when they have taken call center employees they have had problems. They demand a high salary. It seems they also demotivate the others in the firm.

Counselor:

Do you think that is true?

Client:

I never realized this before. But now I think it is true. Even I would feel that I am getting a low salary. I was offered less than half of what I am getting now.

Counselor:

Do you think this is justified?

Client:

Now I think that the call center business is a big bubble. We live in a strange world. We are paid more than what any other Indian earns. The job interviews I went for are the real jobs. You can grow in these jobs.

Counselor:

Do you think the bubble will burst?

Client:

For me it has burst already! My career can't go up in the call centers. I should just take a real job even if I have to start at the bottom. Then I can slowly come up.

Note: Excerpt from "Unpublished Clinical Records (2004 to 2005)," G. Arulmani, 2006. Bangalore, India: The Promise Foundation.

Going to the City: A New Beginning or a Final Destination?

As already noted, the increase in opportunities for employment is an economic feature that characterizes emerging economies. But there is another side to this coin which also falls under the purview of career guidance and counseling. The largely urban-centric nature of economic development in emerging economies has led to a massive wave of internal migration. It is estimated that one-and-a-half-million people in these economies each week leave their rural homes and arrive in cities in search of work (Bisson, Kirkland et al., 2010) and it must be noted that particularly in Africa and Asia, it is commonly the entire household that migrates, not just the individual (Dick & Schmidt-Kallert, 2008). The effects of urbanization are manifold, but there are some outcomes that call for the attention of the contemporary career counselor. This unprecedented scale of urbanization causes an expansion in the size of cities and today we speak of megacities. More often than not, the infrastructural development required to absorb the continuous and massive inflow of people lags far behind. This typically leads to a growing number of unplanned low-income urban settlements. Economic growth is likely to stall, slow down, or even go into decline if the development of infrastructure does not rise up to meet the needs of a growing population (Asian Development Bank, 2012). A further issue is that much of the workforce from rural areas does not have the skills that are required for the occupations that have emerged in the cities. A large section of them are from agricultural backgrounds or those who practiced traditional occupations. Hence, these migrants are often used in the cities as cheap, unskilled labor. This could widen the gap among social classes and create dissatisfaction and frustration, which in

(continued)

turn affects occupational development (Rode et al., 2009).

Implications for Career Guidance and Counseling

The role of the career counselor becomes vital in an economic environment where job opportunities are unprecedented in type and scale. Career counselors are called upon to provide their services to ensure that these new job opportunities are filled by suitable individuals. The concomitant development of economic sectors requires the career counselor to be alert to and informed about new employment trends, and to actively collaborate with employment authorities, education institutions, and employers in this respect (also see Kumar & Arulmani, 2014, Chap. 12).

Career Guidance Services and Emerging Economies

An important concern is that models for career guidance that are suited to the culture and economic processes of emerging economies are at best in the early stages of their development. It is, therefore, common for their young and vibrant workforce to enter the labor market without being adequately guided/coached about how to navigate through the labor market (e.g., Arulmani & Abdulla, 2007). It is urgent and important that greater resources are directed toward conducting research to understand the dynamics between the young person and the labor market in emerging economies. Moreover, it is essential that models that are culturally and economically relevant to these contexts are developed along with services that can be implemented on a mass scale.

Foundations for Dreams

People migrating from their village homes are in search of a "better life." However, it is likely that there is no demand for their traditional skills in a city (e.g., pottery making or skills for agriculture) or that they lack the contacts and/or the skills to market their products or talents. It is also likely that their skills for the kinds of occupations available in urban areas are not adequately developed. It is important for the career counselor to be aware that a common trend is for rural young people to take up low-skilled occupations and work as casual laborers, which in turn denies them the opportunity to become skill-literate for city jobs. Given the resultant absence of skill development for city jobs, they could in the long term lose their traditional skills and remain poorly paid, teetering on the edge between underemployment and unemployment.

Other groups of rural young people moving into the city are those who may have completed basic education in a village school and are now seeking higher or further education in the city. One of the factors closely associated with their poor performance is their lower level of proficiency in the English language which is an almost essential qualification for a city job in many countries. A further observation is that the numbers of young people returning to their villages after further education in the city tend to be insignificant. Yet, the very same economic forces discussed above have also created occupational possibilities in the rural sector, as the booming agriculture-based industries in emerging economies prove (e.g., agricultural engineering, agricultural machinery maintenance, agricultural marketing, organic farming, food processing and packaging). However, information gleaned from those who have left their villages for a life in the city indicates that low levels of prestige are often attributed to these career options (e.g., Arulmani & Nag-Arulmani, 2006) and the preference to go to or stay in the city remains high.

Clearly, there is a pressing need for career counseling services that are designed for rural areas. One objective of such a service could be to offer career preparation skills to those who are planning to leave their rural homes to seek employment in the city. Another crucial objective would be to sensitize rural young people to careers that could be built within the rural setting after completion of education in the city. Career counselors could play a vital role in making rural occupations more attractive. One aspect could be to refocus on the traditional occupations that globalization and economic development tend to push to the background. Reestablishing the position and value that traditional occupations once had could be an important target for career guidance. Indeed, by doing this the career counselor would contribute to expanding the scope of the labor market that is otherwise largely focused on urban occupations.

Demographic Changes and Career Development

Demographic composition is closely linked to a country's economy, growth potential, and culture. The labor market of the 21st century is expected to be significantly impacted by its demographic profiles. Longer life-spans and varying population growth rates have a direct effect on the size and composition of the working population among countries. Career development needs that emerge as a result require skilled handling by career counselors.

Demographic Transitions: Differential Changes in Age Structures

The world population is expected to increase, but not homogenously. While some countries (e.g., Japan and Russia) are expected to decrease in population, the greatest population growth rates are expected in already populous countries (e.g., India, Nigeria, the USA, the Democratic Republic of Congo) (United Nations Department of Economic and Social Affairs, 2011b). In most countries, life expectancy has risen during the 20th century, as a direct outcome of ameliorated living conditions. This creates both opportunities and challenges. Longevity implies the need for readjustment of all major institutions, including education, health, and social security systems and policies. At the same time, older citizens constitute a distinctive, growing consumer group that requires special treatment and approach

techniques from companies (Leventhal, 1997). Since the frailty of old age has not diminished, extended life-spans mean a longer need for support. This further implies that more young employees need to enter the workforce.

Declining Fertility Rates

Fertility rates (the number of children per woman) have declined globally (United Nations Department of Economic & Social Affairs, 2011a) but especially in the countries with the highest rates of aging populations. Consequently, there are numerous countries whose populations are growing old. Interestingly enough, this trend concerns the more economically developed countries. In such countries, the population aged over 60 years is expected to rise by at least 50 % in the next 40 years. In sharp contrast, populations in many developing countries are considered young, with 33 % on an average being under 15 years of age and 18 % falling in the 15–24 age group (United Nations Department of Economic and Social Affairs, 2011b).

Shrinking Workforce

Population aging means that the proportion of older people increases, while that of younger persons decreases (United Nations Department of Economic and Social Affairs, 2011b). This leads to high dependency ratios: that is, more active-aged employees are needed to support retirees and children within a population. This is a major issue for a number of countries, such as Germany, Japan, Italy, Russia, and South Korea (Buhler, 2011). In other words, some of the world's strongest economies seem to lack young professionals and their population is expected to start shrinking in the next 2 or 3 decades. China is a very distinct case. Given the one-child policy, the country is not only "going gray" fast, but is believed to have reached "a late stage of demographic transition at a relatively early stage in its economic development" (Fang, 2011). Thus, its competitive advantage in labor-intensive industries is expected to decline over time.

Population aging brings about another challenge: the number of pensioners. The immediate effect on labor policies, at least until retirement age limits change, is the increase in flexible work arrangements by retired people, as a means to ease the burden on younger employees and pension funds. While this may enhance the productivity of the economy somewhat, it also shifts boundaries in the work–life balance equation (Bisson, Stephenson, & Viguerie, 2010).

Emergence of a New Middle Class

The soaring increase in population, along with increasing per capita incomes fuelled by economic growth, has led to the rise of a new middle class. According to Court and Narasimhan (2010), the middle class in emerging countries is estimated at almost two billion people. It is anticipated that this group will spend almost $7 trillion per year, which is projected to reach $20 trillion by 2020. This is as much as the USA consumed in 2010. Consequently, multinational corporations have begun to focus on this cohort of people, given the relative economic stagnation of the developed countries. It is anticipated that this new middle class would be able to afford a wider range of goods and services, a fact that is expected to stimulate job creation across sectors (Saxena, 2010).

Issues of Immigrants

Another significant implication stemming from demographic changes is the need for more developed countries to find ways to enhance their productivity, given the fact that they will have fewer workers. One can presume that immigration flows from countries with large, young populations to the aging, more developed countries will intensify. However, international migration mostly concerns mobility within the global South, rather than from South to the global North (Munck, 2008), due to certain limitations of migration, such as immigration policy restrictions in developed countries (Vargas-Silva, 2011). In both cases, the role of career counseling is of paramount importance.

Implications for Career Guidance and Counseling

Longer Working Lives: Career Guidance for Older Workers

Rapid aging and the simultaneous growth in the number of retirees reveal fresh opportunities and challenges for career counseling (Vaupel & Schwentker, 2011). Extending retirement age to address the new reality stresses the need for targeted career counseling. Older workers will undoubtedly need effective career coaching, so as to successfully cope with their new role in the local labor market and overcome possible skill obsolescence (Cedefop, 2010, 2011).

The Silver Economy

Older citizens are expected to have a significant impact on local economies as consumers too. Described today as the silver economy (Eizmendi, 2008), widespread opportunities are linked to the satisfaction of the needs of this group. The silver economy encompasses all the products and services pertinent to older citizens. Therefore, segments of the population over the age of 65 can also contribute to economic growth, especially in sectors such as health care, food, medicine, and tourism. All this, of course, ushers in new careers and occupational possibilities which must come into the purview of career guidance.

Career Guidance for a Young Workforce

The increasing youth population in certain countries presents fresh challenges for the career counselor. The millions of youth that enter the labor force each year need to be adequately educated/trained and of course, counseled, so that they can access job opportunities that can help them build satisfying careers. A critical issue that career counselors could keep in mind is that young people need to be equipped to become "viable employees" (Saxena, 2010, p. 4). When new opportunities flood into an economy, existing educational systems may not be equipped to prepare young people to manage these opportunities. An oft-heard complaint from employers is that educational curricula are not in synchrony with the actual demands of professions (Krishna, 2013). A further complaint from employers is that fresh entrants into the workforce have not been adequately prepared with soft skills such as communication skills, work ethic, basic computer literacy, and interpersonal skills (Arulmani & Nag-Arulmani, 2006). Hence, this young workforce may be unprepared and unskilled to meet the new demands of the labor market. This is a challenge that could be addressed by career guidance services that target young workforces in emerging economies.

Career Guidance and the New Middle Class

A critical point to be noted by the career counselor is that the wealth which typical middle class families in emerging economies have created is not sufficient to preclude the necessity of children from these families having to become independent earners. These families have enough but there are no surpluses. The middle classes in emerging economies are at the same time challenged by the risk of slipping back to lower levels of social status, contrasted with the real opportunity of ascending the social status continuum. Indeed it is this group that "has everything to lose and everything to gain" (Arulmani & Nag-Arulmani, 2004, p. 56). The career success of their children is the foremost mechanism available to these families to ensure that they keep rising up the socioeconomic status ladder. Driven as they are by high aspirations and the desire to reach higher pinnacles of success, the middle classes are at high risk of pushing their children toward what the career offers rather than grounding career choice in the personhood of the career chooser. For example, a firm belief among emerging middle classes is

that their children must have a college education. It may be that a particular child from a middle class home is practically oriented and is likely to do well at vocational courses. It is highly likely in this situation that the firmly held belief that vocational courses do not lead to "respectable" jobs would override the young person's talent profile and that he or she would be pushed toward a college degree. Gender is also known to have a significant influence on career decision-making behavior among middle class families. Making a career choice and pursuing independent earning for girls is likely to be secondary to responsibilities associated with marriage and raising a family (Arulmani & Nag-Arulmani, 2004). Therefore, career should aim at ensuring that such beliefs do not adversely affect the career development of these groups.

Immigration Inflows

Career counselors should be prepared to handle the changing demographic profile resulting from immigrants entering new countries. Both the immigrants and their new countries could benefit from such flows, provided that culturally relevant career counseling programs are developed. Issues related to the relevance, suitability, and appropriateness of Western counseling frameworks to a labor force that has grown up in non-Western cultural contexts would need to be addressed. Preparing a workforce to contribute effectively in a labor market for which it is not culturally prepared would be a specific challenge that the career counselor would face. Moreover, the notion of work and career may significantly differ between the home and host country. The challenge enlarges if the home country is characterized by different social values and cultural norms that shape the individual's self-evaluation (Brown, 2002).

Environmental Changes and Career Development

As with all aspects of human life, employment and labor markets are also affected by the physical environment. The increase of average temperatures and the subsequent rise in sea levels, the scarcity of rain in some regions that coexist with unexpected extremes in rainfall and other weather events, are considered, among others, as shaping factors of the future world of work. Drought, flood, and high temperatures cause significant damage to local and regional economies, disrupt the course of life, and affect local populations. According to the International Labour Organisation (ILO, 2011a), it is the poorest populations in the developing countries that suffer most from environmental change and weather events.

Environmental Immigrants

Sudden or long-term changes in the local environment force people to abandon their homes and seek refuge and subsequently employment in other areas within their country or abroad. These groups of people are referred to as environmental migrants and climate refugees (Biermann & Boas, 2010; Dun & Gemenne, 2008; International Organization for Migration, 2007). Environmental immigrants may have been forced to flee their place of residence due to extreme weather events (e.g., a tsunami) or accumulating changes in their local natural environment, such as land degradation, rising sea levels, or impoverished access to freshwater, among others (Reuveny, 2007). The forced abandonment of homes and traditional occupations has major implications for career and livelihood planning.

Climate Changes Redefine Sector Dynamics

The productivity and consequently the employment prospects within some sectors, especially those prone to environmental shocks (e.g., agriculture and tourism), are severely impacted by climate change. In developing countries, where prosperity heavily relies on agriculture, such impacts could be disastrous. Additionally, climate change or sudden and violent weather events may force businesses to relocate, leaving an employment gap in their previous base. Such decisions can ripple out to the rest of the economy, causing higher unemployment (Harsdorff, Lieuw-Kie-Song, & Tsukamoto, 2011).

Resource Constraints

The economic, technological, and social progress of the 20th century was marked by the lack of prudence, particularly regarding the use of fossil fuels and the consequent carbon dioxide emissions (Intergovernmental Panel on Climate Change, 2007). More such challenges lie ahead in the future. The rapid economic and demographic development of Asian and Latin American countries, and the rise of millions of people to middle class consumption positions, along with massive urbanization, are resulting in a soaring demand for products that rely on resource consumption from resource-intense sectors (Dobbs, Oppenheim, & Thompson, 2012). Water management has also risen to the top of the global agenda, given the reckless use of water bodies, pollution, and unsustainable modes of irrigation. Meeting future demands for energy, both from traditional and renewable sources, water and agricultural products will require investment in capital, research, dissemination of new products and mechanisms that will address the effects of global warming. Most importantly, this will require changes in approaches to work and career which are explored in greater detail below.

New Skills, New Occupations, and a New Mentality

The adverse effects of climate change call for an urgent reshaping of consumption and production. The green economy has emerged as a novel, more sustainable approach to human development. A green economy implies a more sustainable mode of development that can simultaneously boost employment. Channeling public resources into green investments has been found to produce more job positions than investments in private consumption or traditional industries (Pollin, Garrett-Peltier, Heintz, & Scharber, 2008). Moreover, the technologies, and the structural and regulatory changes required for the shift to a more sustainable living, create a platform for new occupations (ILO-Cedefop, 2011).

Green jobs refer to all economic sectors. According to the International Labour Organisation (2011c), "Jobs are green when they help reduce negative environmental impact and ultimately lead to environmentally, economically and socially sustainable enterprises and economies" (p. 8). Renewable energy, energy-efficient technologies, green buildings and transportation, biological agriculture, waste management are just a few of the possible avenues for sustainable growth. It is evident, however, that besides completely new sectors or radical transformation in existing sectors, re-skilling is needed for almost all types of professions, aptly referred to as "greening of existing jobs" (ILO-Cedefop, 2011, p. 36). This process marks another stream of employment, given that specialized trainers, career counselors, and human resources professionals are needed to (re)train and guide employees. This is time-consuming but can be expected to have broad positive effects on workers and communities both in the short- and the long term.

Implications for Career Guidance and Counseling

The survival of our planet is directly linked to the manner in which careers are practiced. From the analysis presented above, the interface between environmental issues, the labor market, and career guidance could be delineated under the following themes.

Sharpen Sensitivity

An emerging aspect of career guidance is to use the counseling interaction to sharpen the sensitivities of young entrants into the labor market, as well as established workers, toward the environment. Green Guidance according to Plant (Plant, 2008; also see Plant, 2014, Chap. 17), should be proactive, questioning, probing, reflexive, and client-centered. The career chooser today could opt for careers that are *directly* related to environmental issues. Since the effects of weather events (either chance or chronic) can have such severe impacts, new professions that directly address environmental issues have emerged and possibilities of existing career routes have been extended. Careers related to the application of technology that can anticipate weather events and predict their long-term effects are beginning to flourish. Flood management, water resource management, waste management, pollution control, evacuation experts, and sustainable urban planners are some examples of careers that would allow a direct engagement with environment-oriented careers. In this respect, a career counselor needs to be fully aware of the choices available on a local, regional, or even global scale.

However, career counseling and guidance has a broader role to play and that is to underline that, as with every human action, career choice and development could have an *indirect* impact on supporting the environment. In this sense, all careers could become environment-friendly. The career counseling role here is to sharpen the career chooser's awareness to crucial issues related to the environment such as global warming, dwindling biodiversity, conservation of water and energy, waste management, transportation alternatives, and environmental health. The objective is to bring to the career chooser's awareness the fact that the manner in which we practice our careers, whatever that career may be, has an impact on the environment.

A third level of awareness building is related to the impact certain kinds of careers have upon the environment, a kind of *environmental work ethic*. The labor market is a place where jobs and careers are on offer. The question to be raised in the career counseling interaction is whether one would accept a labor market offering, if that offering were to be environmentally toxic. Would one accept a lucrative job even if it meant that the tasks of that job directly affected the environment?

Environmental Immigrants and Career Counseling

In addition to general issues relating to career guidance for immigrants as analyzed earlier, environmental immigrants present special requirements. Given that they have been forced to flee their residences, environmental immigrants have been found to face a variety of unique career development challenges. Career counselors need to be sensitive to their pre-migration stressors (e.g., trauma, loss of family, job, and possessions) and factors that could affect their progress in the post-migration period (e.g., culture shock, language barriers) (Chung, Bemak, & Grabosky, 2011).

A Globalizing World: The Case of the Global Financial Crisis of 2008

The most severe financial crisis that the global economy faced after World War II broke out in September 2008. The crisis resulted from inadequately controlled financial markets, which led to the development of risky financial products. The deployment of these products skewed financial flows and created unsustainable global imbalances (te Velde, 2009). The severity of the crisis and the speed of its spread throughout the world underlined the side-effects of the interdependency of economies and the vulnerability of workers to external, global shocks. Given that employment is one of the first factors to be affected by recession, labor markets around the globe were strongly impacted.

Impact on Unemployment

Unemployment soared in Europe and the USA, especially among the young. According to the European Commission (2011) in 2011, the labor market conditions of young people (15–24 years of age) severely deteriorated in many European

Union (EU) countries. Moreover, the combination of recession and lasting uncertainty made firms conservative in hiring, thus stalling the recovery of employment. Therefore, many firms turned to flexible employment arrangements (temporary and part-time jobs), that accounted for a significant proportion of employment recovery in the West.

Emerging economies were not left unhurt by the crisis, mainly due to their high dependency on exports to developed countries. High unemployment in developed economies led to less consumption, decrease in investments, and, therefore, a slowing of growth rates in the developing world. This in turn led again to conservative hiring and personnel shrinkage (ILO, 2011b). This vicious cycle went around the global economy, demonstrating the interconnectedness of labor markets across regions. Moreover, Asian countries faced high inflation in the cost of food that extended the impact of the crisis to the poor (ILO, 2009). The Overseas Development Institute (te Velde, 2009) in their research found that poor countries were hit harsher than originally expected. A number of developing countries, such as Kenya and Cambodia, saw significant downturns to their, till then, strong economic growth. Decrease or withdrawal of FDI in these countries led to loss of jobs. Restricted spending in overseas markets affected exports. Industries that relied on international clientele, such as tourism, were badly hit. All this led to a dramatic increase in the number of households falling below the poverty line.

Impact on Youth Unemployment

Scarpetta, Sonnet, and Manfredi (2010) noted that the financial crisis brought about not only high youth unemployment but also low-quality jobs and labor market exclusion for those aged 15–24 years, notably in the EU, where only temporary jobs increased. Simultaneously, most of the available jobs had low-skill expectations. It has also been found that young employees/job seekers were disproportionately affected in Asia

(ILO, 2009). To illustrate, FDI-based employment in Ghana fell by 30 % between 2007 and 2008; a 35 % decrease in horticultural exports in Kenya led to a massive rise in unemployment in this sector; close to 25 % of workers in the mining industry in Zambia were laid off; and 63,000 jobs in the garments manufacturing sector were lost in Cambodia. In the post-crisis period, jobs that have become available have low-skill expectations. The scarcity of quality (or of any) jobs for a long period of time fosters sentiments of discouragement, dissatisfaction, poor health, and social unrest (Andersen, 2009). Many unemployed in the EU; reportedly left the labor market and shifted to the long-term unemployed cohort. This group of unemployed is expected to face severe difficulties in finding satisfying jobs in the near future (ILO, 2011b).

Implications for Career Guidance and Counseling

One of the career guidance points that emerges from this discussion is that a large segment of populations in certain economies will have to work post (current)-retirement age. Also, it seems that a large number of experienced workers have suffered unemployment as a result of the global economic crisis. Given that their experience can bring significant added value to their economies, career counseling can become a bridge between these individuals and the labor market. Hence, coaching the unemployed and the retraining of experienced workers to reenter and cope with fragile labor markets should rise to the top of the career counseling agenda. Additionally, unemployment at a progressed stage of career development can be particularly debilitating. Taking into consideration the individual's needs and talents, prior experience, and ultimate professional goals, career counseling can boost the individual's self-esteem and self-efficacy, which can in turn function as the elevating wheel for the individual's reactivation.

The financial crisis of 2008 exposed the volatility of the global business and financial environment and, therefore, the vulnerability of employment. One side of the coin may be

uncertainty, but the other should be agility. Employees, new entrants or established ones, must be encouraged and helped to be flexible and capable of embracing change. By this it is not implied that workers must passively accept labor market demands, abandoning the possibilities for collective action and resistance. On the other hand, employment is now synonymous with a continuous learning path within fluid labor market conditions. To be effective, career counseling must sensitize people to new skills, next steps, and relevant adjustments.

It is also possible that information and communication technologies and overall technological advancement will make some professions obsolete in the coming years. Making a career shift may be the only option for those who have lost their employment in countries that have been severely hit by the crisis. Super has reiterated that "multiple-trial careers and midcareer crises are not only normal but psychologically advantageous in a climate of rapid social change" (as cited in Smart & Peterson, 1997, p. 360). Career counseling can play a vital role in the transition period, by cultivating a mentality of openness toward career change among students and workers.

Conclusion

Relevance Across Multiple Contexts

Among the diverse and varied effects of globalization some of the transformations described in this chapter with reference to the labor market are unprecedented. Around the world, workers and young workers-to-be face a new horizon, the contours of which are still being formed. Given the universal nature of some of the requirements of today's labor market, we are today seeing a simultaneous convergence in career preparation requirements around the world, as well as specific, locally defined labor market dynamics that call for context-specific handling. From the descriptions provided above, it is clear that a wide network of interconnected factors operate at various scales and intensities to influence labor markets. The financial crisis of 2008 underlined the vulnerability of jobs to economic phenomena that occur far away from where one's job is located. Immigration resulting from a variety of factors, the emergence of new sectors and obsolescence of others, the pervasiveness of technology, and new age structures within work environments meld together to characterize the labor market of our times.

Viewpoints for Charting New Directions

A critical skill that contemporary career guidance needs to foster in the worker is the skill of agility. Unanticipated yet significant changes may occur in one's work environment, calling for multiple career transitions during one's work life (also see Jain, 2014, Chap. 16). The employee of the 21st century should be able to reassess his/her priorities and options and continuously readjust to changing trends in the labor market. The 21st century has seen human capital being recognized as the most significant asset of a country, a region, or a company. We conclude this chapter by raising for the reader's consideration the fact that behind human capital is the human being. The dynamics of today's labor market are such that the "human" in human capital could be missed and reduced to a mere factor of production. Effective career counseling can equip the individual to mediate the labor market of the 21st century with the same cleverness of our forefathers who successfully mediated their unchartered environments, rather than be naively buffeted by its vagaries.

References

Andersen, S. H. (2009). Unemployment and subjective well-being: A question of class? *Work and Occupations, 36*(1), 3–25.

Antràs, P., & Helpman, E. (2003). *Global sourcing* (Working Paper No. 10082). Cambridge, MA: National Bureau of Economic Research.

Arulmani, G. (2006). *Unpublished clinical records (2000 to 2006)*. Bangalore, India: The Promise Foundation.

Arulmani, G. (2009). Career counselling: A mechanism to address the accumulation of disadvantage. *Australian Journal of Career Development, 19*(1), 7–12.

Arulmani, G., & Abdulla, A. (2007). Capturing the ripples: Addressing the sustainability of the impact of social marketing. *Social Marketing Quarterly, 13*(4), 84–107.

Arulmani, G., & Nag-Arulmani, S. (2004). *Career counselling: A handbook*. New Delhi, India: McGraw Hill.

Arulmani, G., & Nag-Arulmani, S. (2006). *Work orientations and responses to career choices: Indian regional survey (WORCC-IRS)*. Bangalore, India: The Promise Foundation.

Asian Development Bank. (2012). *Asian development outlook*. Manila, Philippines: Author.

Biermann, F., & Boas, I. (2010). Preparing for a warmer world: Towards a global governance system to protect climate refugees. *Global Environmental Politics, 10*(1), 60–88.

Bissell, W. N. (2010). *Making India work*. New Delhi, India: Penguin.

Bisson, P., Kirkland, R., & Stephenson, E. (2010, June). The great rebalancing. *McKinsey Quarterly*, 1–7.

Bisson, P., Stephenson, E., & Viguerie, S. P. (2010, June). The productivity imperative. *The McKinsey Quarterly*, 19–27.

Brown, D. (2002). The role of work and cultural values in occupational choice, satisfaction, and success: A theoretical statement. *Journal of Counseling and Development, 80*, 48–56.

Buhler, P. (2011, December 19). The shrinking North. *Project Syndicate*. Retrieved from http://www.proj ect-syndicate.org/commentary/buhler4/English

Cedefop. (2010). *The right skills for silver workers: An empirical analysis*. Luxembourg: Publications Office of the European Union.

Cedefop. (2011). *Working and ageing: Guidance and counseling for mature learners*. Luxembourg: Publications Office of the European Union.

Chung, R. C.-Y., Bemak, F., & Grabosky, T. K. (2011). Multicultural-social justice leadership strategies: Counseling and advocacy with immigrants. *Journal for Social Action in Counseling and Psychology, 3*(1), 57–69.

Court, D., & Narasimhan, L. (2010, July). Capturing the world's emerging middle class. *The McKinsey Quarterly*, 14–19.

Coutinho, M. T., Dam, U. C., & Blustein, D. L. (2008). The psychology of working and globalisation: A new perspective for a new era. *International Journal for Educational and Vocational Guidance, 8*(1), 5–18.

Dick, E., & Schmidt-Kallert, E. (2008). Relevant rural-urban interplay. In *World development report*. Washington, DC: World Bank.

Dobbs, R., Oppenheim, J., & Thompson, F. (2012, January). Mobilizing for a resource revolution. *The McKinsey Quarterly*, 18–23.

Dun, O., & Gemenne, F. (2008, September). Defining environmental migration. *Forced Migration Review*. Retrieved from http://www.fmreview.org/FMRpdfs/FMR31/10-11.pdf

Eizmendi, G. (2008). Ageing economy: From social responsibility to new business opportunities. *Gerontechnology, 7*(2), 252.

European Commission, & Directorate General Economic and Financial Affairs. (2011). *European economic forecast: Autumn 2011*. Luxembourg: European Union.

Fang, C. (2011, December 19). Aging before affluence in China. *Project Syndicate*. Retrieved from http://www.project-syndicate.org/commentary/fcai1/English

Feenstra, C. R., & Hanson, H. G. (1996). *Globalisation, outsourcing and wage inequality* (Working Paper No. 5424). Cambridge, MA: National Bureau of Economic Research.

Harsdorff, M., Lieuw-Kie-Song, M., & Tsukamoto, M. (2011). *Towards an ILO approach to climate change adaptation*. Geneva, Switzerland: International Labour Office, Employment Sector, Employment Intensive Investment Programme.

Hoskisson, R. E., Eden, L., Lau, C. M., & Wright, M. (2000). Strategy in emerging economies. *Academy of Management Journal, 43*(3), 249–267.

ILO-Cedefop. (2011). *Skills for green jobs: A global view*. Geneva, Switzerland: ILO.

Intergovernmental Panel on Climate Change. (2007). Climate change 2007: Synthesis report. In R. K. Pachauri & A. Reisinger (Eds.), *Contribution of working groups I, II and III to the fourth assessment report of the intergovernmental panel on climate change* (p. 104). Geneva, Switzerland: Author.

International Labour Organisation. (2011). *Green jobs becoming a reality. Progress and outlook*. Geneva, Switzerland: International Labour Office.

International Labour Organization. (2009). *The fallout in Asia: Assessing labour market impacts and national policy responses to the global financial crisis*. Bangkok, Thailand: Author.

International Labour Organization. (2011a). *Towards a green economy: Pathways to sustainable development and poverty eradication*. Geneva, Switzerland: ILO/UNEP.

International Labour Organization. (2011b). *World of work report 2011: Making markets work for jobs*. Geneva, Switzerland: Institute for Labour Studies.

International Organization for Migration. (2007). *Discussion note: Migration and the environment*. Geneva, Switzerland: Author.

Jain, A. (2014). Second career: An eventual need in today's world. In G. Arulmani, A. J. Bakshi, F. T. L. Leong, & A. G. Watts (Eds.), *Handbook of career development*. New York, NY: Springer.

Krishna, S. (2013, January 26). The great number fetish. *The Hindu*, p. 11.

Kumar, S., & Arulmani, G. (2014). Understanding the labor market: Implications for career counseling. In G. Arulmani, A. J. Bakshi, F. T. L. Leong, & A. G. Watts (Eds.), *Handbook of career development*. New York, NY: Springer.

Leventhal, C. R. (1997). Aging consumers and their effects on the marketplace. *Journal of Consumer Marketing, 14*(4), 276–281.

Munck, R. (2008). Globalisation, governance and migration: An introduction. *Third World Quarterly, 29*(7), 1227–1246.

Plant, P. (2008). Green guidance. *Career Edge, 19*, 4–6.

Plant, P. (2014). Green guidance. In G. Arulmani, A. J. Bakshi, F. T. L. Leong, & A. G. Watts (Eds.), *Handbook of career development*. New York, NY: Springer.

Pollin, R., Garrett-Peltier, H., Heintz, J., & Scharber, H. (2008). *Green recovery: A program to create jobs and start building a low-carbon economy*. Amherst, MA: Department of Economics and Political Economy Research Institute, University of Massachusetts-Amherst and Center for American Progress.

Reuveny, R. (2007). Climate change induced migration and violent conflict. *Political Geography, 26*, 656–673.

Rode, P., Burdett, R., Brown, R., Ramos, F., Kitazawa, K., Paccoud, A., et al. (2009). *Cities and social equity: Inequality, territory and urban form*. London, UK: Urban Age Programme, London School of Economics.

Sankh, S., Vittal, I., Dobbs, R., Mohan, A., Gulati, A., Ablett, J., et al. (2010). *India's urban awakening: Building inclusive cities, sustaining economic growth*. Boston, MA: McKinsey Global Institute.

Saxena, R. (2010). *The middle class in India*. Frankfurt, Germany: Deutsche Bank Research.

Scarpetta, S., Sonnet, A., & Manfredi, T. (2010). *Rising youth unemployment during the crisis: How to prevent negative long-term consequences on a generation* (OECD Social, Employment and Migration Working Papers No. 106). Paris, France: OECD.

Scrase, T. J. (2003). Precarious production: Globalisation and artisan labour in the Third World. *Third World Quarterly, 24*(3), 449–461.

Smart, R., & Peterson, C. (1997). Super's career stages and the decision to change careers. *Journal of Vocational Behavior, 51*, 358–374.

te Velde, D. W. (2009). *The global financial crisis and developing countries: Taking stock, taking action* (Overseas Development Institute Briefing Paper 54). London, UK: Overseas Development Institute.

United Nations Department of Economic and Social Affairs, Population Division. (2011a). *World fertility report 2009* (ST/ESA/SER.A/304). Retrieved from http://www.un.org/en/development/desa/publications/world-fertility-report-2009.html

United Nations Department of Economic and Social Affairs, Population Division. (2011b). *World population prospects*: The 2010 revision (Volume II: Demographic Profiles, ST/ESA/SER.A/317). Retrieved from http://esa.un.org/wpp/Other-Information/faq.htm

Vargas-Silva, C. (2011). Policy primer: Migration and development. *The Migration Observatory. London, UK: Oxford*. Retrieved from http://www.migrationobservatory.ox.ac.uk/sites/files/migobs/Migration%20and%20Development%20Policy%20Primer.pdf

Vaupel, J. W., & Schwentker, B. (2011, October 19). Managing longer lives. *Project Syndicate*. Retrieved from http://www.project-syndicate.org/commentary/vaupel1/English

Career Advice and Guidance in a World Where Vocational Skills Matter

Heidi Agbenyo and Kathleen Collett

Introduction

Effective career advice and guidance has a dual role to play. It needs to help fill skills gaps in the economy by providing information about what kinds of jobs are available and the skills that are needed for them. It also needs to help young people invest their educational efforts wisely to prepare for work that suits their interests and abilities. Ensuring that the work-related skills demanded by employers are broadly matched with the skills that the workforce is able to provide is often seen as one of the key challenges for national education and training systems in both developing and developed country contexts. Despite the variations in employment opportunities that countries experience during economic slump periods, there are likely to always be skill shortages in many sectors, in both developing and developed countries (e.g., Büning, Cantrell, Marshall, & Smith, 2011; Schwalje, 2011). In addition to skill shortages with respect to the current needs of economies, skills may also be short in relation to the industrial ambitions of a country. In other words, there may not be enough skilled workers to support the development of strategic industrial development (Kahyarra, 2007).

Arguments in Favor of Vocational Education and Training

Developing countries need to improve productivity throughout the economy if they are to compete successfully in a global economy which is increasingly characterized by rapid technological change. This requires not only investment but also a workforce which has the flexibility to acquire new skills for new jobs as structures of economies and occupations change. The skills development literature has developed arguments that "limited skills are the key to understanding poor performance in African countries, particularly in their manufacturing sectors".

The mismatch between skills supply and demand internationally is, in part, a result of changes in the structure of the global economy. Changes in the global division of labor have meant that countries have had to adjust to changing demands from industry on their workforces. According to many authors (e.g., Dunning & Lundan, 2008), technological change, particularly the mechanization of standard processes, has meant that there may now be a lesser need for routine workers at all levels and, hence, a greater need for individuals who are trained to undertake nonroutine tasks. As Brown, Hesketh, and Williams (2003) point out ". . .the changes in skill requirements not only reflect an increase in technological complexity but changes in models of organizational efficiency, leading to greater

H. Agbenyo (✉)
City and Guilds Centre for Skills Development, London, UK
e-mail: heidi.agbenyo@skillsdevelopment.org

G. Arulmani et al. (eds.), *Handbook of Career Development*, International and Cultural Psychology, DOI 10.1007/978-1-4614-9460-7_14, © Springer Science+Business Media, LLC 2014

emphasis on problem-solving, communication, teamwork and self-management skills" (p. 23).

As well as the demand for new sets of skills created by these changes, there continues to be a shortage of people trained in traditional vocational occupations (e.g., Department of Labour, 2011; Karmel & Mlotkowski, 2010; Wegner, 2008). According to a nine-country survey by the City & Guilds Centre for Skills Development (CSD) where employers were asked to consider the extent to which they believed there was a shortfall in the supply of appropriately skilled labor, the average response was 4.93 on a scale ranging from 1 (*no shortfall at all*) to 10 (*a great shortfall*) (City & Guilds Centre for Skills Development, 2008). When they were asked specifically about the supply of job-specific technical skills, they indicated that this was higher, at an average of 5.10 on the same scale. These skill shortages represent an opportunity for young people to improve their chances in the labor market by gaining specific job-related skills through education and training.

The changes in the organization of economies internationally may also pose a threat. Young people who enter the labor market without appropriate skills find it increasingly difficult to find sustained employment which offers progression opportunities in many countries and may struggle to find a job at all (e.g., Bell & Blanchflower, 2010; Gregory, 2010; Oesch, 2010). The notion that labor markets are polarizing, with high-paid, high-skill jobs, alongside large numbers of jobs which are low-paid and low-skill (Brown, Green, & Lauder, 2001), has gained currency, in both developed and developing countries. On the other hand, recent research by the Organisation for Economic Co-operation and Development (OECD) finds that "countries with strong initial vocational education and training (VET) systems have been relatively successful in tackling youth unemployment, even during the recent economic crisis" (OECD, 2010, p. 10). This suggests that access to high-quality VET, which is developed with reference to the needs of the labor market, can help young people at risk of unemployment enter the labor market successfully. West (1999) defined VET as formal, post-compulsory education that develops knowledge, skills, and

attributes linked to certain forms of employment. According to West three types of VET exist:

- Initial VET: occurring from 15 to 16 years of age and after compulsory school, but prior to work. It is typically provided by a local college or training institute.
- Continuing VET: for adults in the labor market, leading to personal, flexible, or vocational competence.
- VET for the unemployed: aimed at people who are out of work.

As Keep (2009) pointed out, much employment remains in vocational occupations, and vocational educational routes of high quality continue to be an important part of education and training systems. At the same time, these jobs and the labor market as a whole are changing, and learners need to know where they should best direct their efforts to get a reward in the labor market. Arulmani and Nag-Arulmani (2005) commenting on career guidance in India also emphasized that economic change creates new types of work: "The relevance of career counseling to the Indian context becomes sharper against the backdrop of economic reforms...An obvious corollary to economic development is the widening of occupational possibilities. New occupational opportunities are constantly emerging" (p. 12). The OECD (2010) highlighted the increasing importance of career advice and guidance in the context of changing economies:

> As careers diversify, career guidance is becoming both more important and more challenging...More complex careers, with more options in both work and learning, are opening up new opportunities for many people. But they are also making decisions harder as young people face a sequence of complex choices over a lifetime of learning and work. (p. 6)

Good career advice and guidance play an important role in preparing all young people for the workplace. But it may be more difficult for young people to get appropriate career development support for vocational routes that could benefit them. Keep (2009) pointed out that the academic route from school to higher education tends to be well resourced, and progression paths into work are often relatively clear (graduate programs are one example of this). On the other hand, those who are not able to, or choose not to, take this route face a challenging and uncertain path through education and training. In this chapter, we discuss the particular challenges of providing career advice and guidance that adequately covers vocational options, analyze the influences on young people as they make vocational choices, and outline the implications for career guidance.

Evidence of the Outcomes of VET

There are limited international studies on the economic returns to VET and the results of existing studies are mixed. This is in part due to significant variations in socioeconomic contexts. Furthermore, there are mixed views among researchers on how best to measure returns. Some studies focus on the returns to individuals, while others focus on company returns in an attempt to "translate individual benefits into national economic growth; the effects of educational investment have to appear at the level of firms and economic sectors" (Cedefop, 2011, p. 12). The results of a meta-analysis of the impact of training investments undertaken by Cedefop in 2011 led to the conclusion that VET does have a positive impact on company performance across a range of performance indicators, including productivity, innovation, and quality. Cedefop stated: "This finding confirms the role attributed to investment in skills in national strategies for growth" (Cedefop, 2011, p. 69). However, the report also indicated that the evidence available to quantify the effects in a comparable way across studies is unclear (Cedefop, 2011, p. 69). Cedefop also found that studies that focus on costs and profitability for the firm demonstrate nonsignificant findings.

On the other hand, Hoeckel (2008) explored the cost and benefits in VET for individuals and found that benefits arise at different points in time. For example, in the short term, individuals can expect improved employment chances, increased earnings, and work satisfaction. Hoeckel also has drawn our attention to the fact that studies show that individuals with VET qualifications receive higher wages than those without post-school qualifications. In the long term, individuals can experience increased mobility (OECD, 2009, p. 4). Meer (2007) confirmed that there are benefits to the individual by pointing out that the evidence illustrates that the demand for blue-collar workers, that is, VET graduates, is high and salaries are on the rise. However, Meer also points out that individual returns from VET are dependent on the individual students as well as their abilities and background—as well as labor market demand.

Decision-Making: An Overview of Key Theories

What influences young people when they are making decisions about their education, training, and future careers? The existing theories about how young people make career decisions can be grouped into three main sets.

Instrumental Rationality

This group of theories emphasize and see young people as active decision-makers who gather relevant information and then weigh up the costs and benefits of alternative courses of action, to arrive at a decision which maximizes the benefits to them (Paton, 2007; Payne, 2003). These theories assume that young people try to maximize the benefits to themselves over their lifetime when they make career choices, their choices are basically self-interested, they decide only after they have collected enough relevant information to make a fully informed choice, and when they make a choice, they compare alternative courses of action in an entirely rational way (Paton, 2007, p. 4).

One example of this type of decision-making at play is when an individual forms an estimate of the expected earnings from each education, training, and employment option and selects the option which offers the greatest return. Young people who make choices in an instrumentally rational way would place a lot of value on what they could expect to earn on graduation when making decisions about what to study. However, this approach has several limitations. The returns to training usually take time to accrue and short-term benefits (e.g., my friends are doing it) can significantly influence young people's considerations. Reliable and realistic information about the expected returns to different types of education and training might not be easy to find or interpret, and returns might change significantly over time in a changing economy, making it difficult for young people to accurately assess the benefits of different choices. The assumption of instrumental rationality has also been criticized for not capturing "the complexity of human motivation and the role of social class, gender, and ethnicity in decision-making processes" (Paton, 2007, p. 5; see also Johnston, 2007).

Pragmatic Rationality

These theories assert that young people make neither rational nor nonrational choices about work. Instead, they are limited by or enabled by their horizons for action (Hodkinson & Sparkes, 1997). These authors suggest that there are three main aspects to decision-making within this framework. Decision-making is part of a wider choice of lifestyle, influenced by social context and culture, and part of an ongoing life course and evolves through interactions with others. Hence, decisions are the outcomes of negotiations between people's social networks of friends, family members, and others.

Structuralist Theories

These are theories that emphasize the extent to which career choices are a result of the institutional, economic, or cultural environment in which young people find themselves, rather than free choice (Bandura, Barbaranelli, Caprara, & Pastorelli, 2001). According to these theories, factors such as class, gender, ethnicity, the education system, and economic conditions structure the opportunities available to young

people to such an extent that it makes more sense to say that people "take what is available" (Paton, 2007, p. 7) rather than saying that they choose their occupation. These approaches emphasize the influence of teachers, parents, and others on the decision-making process and see decisions as driven primarily by emotional and psychological factors rather than a rational assessment of the options.

Hybrid Models

These approaches acknowledge that career choice involves reasoned decision-making in the light of the information about jobs and wage but also acknowledge that this reasoning is influenced by "external job and educational opportunities and personal perceptions of what is possible, desirable and appropriate" (Paton, 2007, p. 7). These personal perceptions, in turn, are influenced by cultural factors, and individuals' own personal life experience. Hodkinson, Sparkes, and Hodkinson (1996) suggested that there are three main aspects of career decision-making by young people: They undertake pragmatically rational evaluation of the options available, given their perception of their opportunities; they are influenced by people in their social field, including those that they identify with, those whose opinions they particularly care about, and those who are making similar decisions at the same time as them; and they make decisions in the real world and are influenced by "the partly unpredictable pattern of turning-points and routines that make up the life course" (Hodkinson & Sparkes, 1997, p. 29).

Keep (2009) presented what could be seen as an alternative form of the hybrid model. He maintains the assumption that young people are fundamentally choosers who are responding rationally to incentives, but argues that their incentives have not been well understood and have been defined too narrowly. According to Keep, when young people make choices about whether and how to invest in learning, they are responding to incentives which include (but are not limited to) opportunities to learn about something which interests them, to gain through paid employment, and to achieve career progression and promotion opportunities. At the same time, he also emphasizes that social and cultural expectations create an incentive to comply with educational norms for the group within which the young person is situated. He also posits that expectations and rewards within the education system itself create incentives to engage with different types of learning for different lengths of time. These incentives may reinforce or counteract one another. For example, learners receive more praise, recognition, and financial support for some types of learning than others. The result of this is that individuals from different social backgrounds, with different economic starting points and enrolled in different types of schools, may in fact be responding to very different sets of incentives to undertake training after school.

What is the role of career advice and guidance, if hybrid model theories are accepted? Ideally, good career advice and guidance provisions give learners more and more accurate and nuanced information about the returns they might expect when undertaking particular forms of learning. It should also broaden their perceptions of the options that are open to them, and it makes them aware of the routes into various careers. Importantly, it must also help them understand the social and cultural influences on them and give them tools to mediate this influence. The purpose here is not to remove these influences but to help young people understand themselves within a wider context and make decisions accordingly. To be effective, career guidance must also recognize that decision-making even in more individualistic cultures is (at least partly) collaborative and dependent on influences of others, especially parents. Moreover, the influence of parents and the community would be more pronounced in collectivistic cultures.

The theories detailed above clearly place the individual at the heart of the decision-making process and, ultimately, assume that individuals are driven by self-interest. These values are commonly associated with the Western values of an individualistic culture. Markus and Kitayama (1991) argued that although these theories may fit developed country contexts, they are not always applicable to developing country contexts. They argue that in collectivist cultures of Asia, Africa, and South America, the view of the community of which the individual is a part influences the decision-making process. The direct influence of the family is a prime factor in influencing decision-making. In such cultures, they claim decisions are formed around family views and cultural values and these values can have an impact on self-efficacy.

The outcomes of a study (City & Guilds Centre for Skills Development, 2008) which examined the understanding of the local labor market and vocational training opportunities of school leavers from Hyderabad (an Indian city) support this assertion. Here is the response of one of the participants, which typified the responses of these youth. The questions asked were: "What are your aspirations for the future? What type of job would you like to have and how did you make that decision?" The response of this 12-year-old male participant in the study indicated that he had decided to become a doctor and that his parents had influenced his decision. There is also evidence that the need to help others and to support the development of the region and, ultimately, the country heavily influenced the decision-making process. A 12-year-old girl stated, "There are many poor people in Hyderabad. I want to stay in Hyderabad and treat them." Responses such as these support the assertion that in collectivistic cultures, decisions are made for the young person and independent decision-making may not be directly nurtured. This finding is supported by Arulmani and Nag-Arulmani (2005) who also highlighted the influence of socioeconomic status (SES). In their study of participants' perceptions of their parents' support, approval, and endorsement of career options across a sample of high school, higher secondary school, and vocational course students, they found that for all three groups decisions appear to have been made for them by their parents or at least had required parental approval. A high interest for full-time further studies after school completion was exhibited across all groups who took part in the study. However, the biggest barrier to pursuing these ambitions among low-SES groups appeared to be related to financial difficulties and family responsibility. They also found that there is a "markedly lower level of perceived parental approval for career paths other than full time study amongst middle and upper SES groups" (p. 42).

It may appear that the influence of parents is stronger in collectivistic cultures. However as will be argued in a later section, it must be noted that irrespective of cultural background, parents emerge as a powerful influence on career decision-making.

Career Guidance for Vocational Education

While career guidance is particularly important for young people for whom vocational routes might be an appropriate option, it is at the same time, less oriented towards helping these young people with effectiveness. In this section, we explore this argument by considering the various factors that drive young people's choices and by drawing upon research conducted by the City & Guilds Centre of Skills Development (CSD).

Interests and Aptitudes

From young people's perspectives, their own interest in and aptitude for particular subjects or career areas is one of the most important factors in determining what they choose to study. In a recent study of a broadly representative sample of learners in the United Kingdom (UK) aged 16–18 years, the top reasons for the selection of subjects or qualifications were:

- "I chose the subjects I'm most interested in": 74 % indicated that this was an important factor.
- "I chose the subjects I'm good at": 59 % indicated that this was an important factor.

Young people's top three responses to the question of how they had decided which career to take, likewise, emphasized interest and aptitude: 80 % said that they had made the choice based on what they were most interested in; 57 % said that their skills and qualifications were an important consideration, and 49 % said they had made the choice based on what would be most satisfying and worthwhile to them (Batterham & Levesley, 2011). These UK findings are echoed in the international literature (e.g., Ackerman & Beier, 2003; Byars-Winston, Estrada, Howard, Davis, & Zalapa, 2010).

A significant proportion of young people find that vocational pathways into work suit their interests and aptitudes. There are multiple qualitative studies which suggest that some young people prefer to learn in a practical way and that this type of VET learning engages them in a way that academic study does not. Stokes, Wierenga, and Wyn (2003), for example, found that Australian vocational learners gained confidence with respect to their learning and also with respect to their ability to work and that a majority of students found that vocational subjects improved their attitudes to other learning and to education in general. Research in England, South Africa, and the Netherlands (City & Guilds Centre for Skills Development, 2008) also found that young learners aged 16–18 years were positive about their experience of VET. They enjoyed "learning by doing," felt their courses were "right for them," and felt motivated to face the challenge.

At the same time, in non-Western contexts, the evidence suggests other orientations. Reporting a study from the Republic of Maldives, Arulmani and Abdulla (2007) observed that factors such as prestige, job availability, community interests, and salary could push the individual's interest and aptitude into the background. Arulmani and Nag-Arulmani (2005) based on their survey of attitudes in India stated that "mindsets that place occupations on a prestige hierarchy quite often prevent young career aspirants from actualizing their talents for emerging careers" (p. 7). The forces of collectivism and individualism differentially influence young people's preferences for vocationally oriented courses and professions, and career advice and guidance needs to take this into account in order to be effective.

Perceptions of Vocational Education and Training

Since young people are influenced by their parents, peers, and those with whom they interact socially, widely held perceptions of the relative value of different education and training routes also influence their decision-making about learning and career pathways. VET has often been described as the "poor cousin" of the education system and seen as a route for those who have not flourished in academic settings. The regard in which vocational education is held can be a deterrent for many young people (and those advising them) when making career choices. CSD conducted an international survey with employers, trainers, policymakers, and others with a stake in skill development to explore attitudes and perceptions around vocational training. Respondents were asked to rate, on a scale of 1–10 (1 being *low* and 10 being *high*), how VET is regarded in their country. The findings showed an average perceived regard for VET of 6.6. Figure 14.1 shows that esteem varies significantly across the nine countries surveyed with Germany rating it at 7.79 and Hungary at 5.2. German employers were satisfied with the quality of their employees' training in job-specific skills. Furthermore, they believed that they get an adequate return on their investment with 98 % of employers in agreement. Similarly, practitioners in Germany had high regard for VET. This is in part due to the long-standing history of apprenticeship in Germany. VET is viewed as an artisan craft and people train over a long period of time to earn their qualifications. Historically, apprentices in Germany have been held in high social regard. In Hungary, by comparison, a high proportion of employers did not invest in training. Vocational education is negatively perceived with VET being commonly described as a pathway for the less academically gifted that fails to lead to decent pay (City & Guilds Centre for Skills Development, 2008, p. 10). This outlook may also be because of cultural differences which lead to a pattern of negative thinking.

Furthermore, the research showed strong agreement from all countries with the statement, "Vocational education and training is viewed as being a pathway for the less academically gifted" (City & Guilds Centre for Skills Development, 2008). In Ghana, the picture is similar with a "widely held perception... that only people who are academically weak undertake technical and vocational education" (Bortei-Doku, Doh, & Andoh, 2011). The availability of money was cited as another factor influencing decisions as to whether to continue with academic education or go into vocational training. A 17-year-old female participant in the study stated, for example, "My parents could not afford to send me to school so they asked me to learn a vocation ... there is no money at home for further education." Views such as the one from this young woman in the UK can be found echoed around the world: "This may sound ridiculous, but where I'm from originally, vocational courses were sort of 'frowned upon', so I just grew up with thinking it's either university or nothing" (Batterham & Levesley, 2011, p. 22). In Australia, Dalley-Trim, Alloway, and Walker (2008) found that students generally perceive VET as "a road to nowhere" or that "those who can't, do VET."

These widely held perceptions about the value of VET affect the way that vocational options are presented to young people at school. In South Africa, for example, it has been observed that "schools appear either to ignore the option of study at Further Education and Training (FET) colleges or actively to downplay it" (Needham & Papier, 2011, p. 53). This situation can also be exacerbated, as it has in the UK, by funding mechanisms and league tables that have the unintended consequences of disincentivizing the promotion of vocational options by schools. City & Guilds Centre for Skills Development (2008) showed that there is a global trend for schools to actively encourage the academic routes at the expense of vocational options. Figure 14.2 shows the extent to which employers and practitioners agreed with the statement, "Schools encourage children towards academic pathways."

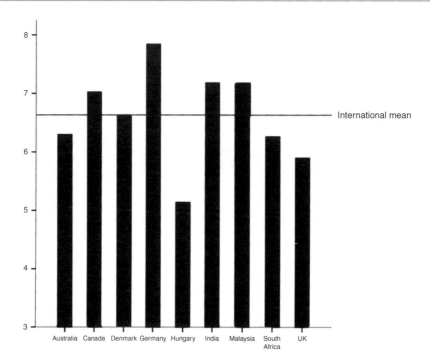

Fig. 14.1 Employers, trainers, and policymakers' attitudes and perceptions about vocational training: findings from a CSD survey (2008). Respondents were asked to rate, on a scale of 1–10 (1 being low and 10 being high), how vocational education and training is regarded in their country

Parental Influence

For many young people, their parents will be the single biggest influence in the decisions they make about their study options and career choices. In South Africa, Needham and Papier (2011) found that for young people "career choices were overwhelmingly influenced by family members, particularly their parents, and parental careers were often cited as the school students' career choice" (p. 23). In the UK, parents are the most widely accessed source of information with 68 % of young people turning to them for advice. This places parents ahead of career guidance professionals, teachers, and tutors as the preferred source of advice for young people. Overall, young people said parental advice is the most frequently sought and useful source for making job, career, and course decisions (Batterham & Levesley, 2011). Bortei-Doku et al. (2011) found that guidance and counseling among VET trainees in Ghana was primarily derived from informal family advice. There was no indication from any of the

respondents of any formal provision to assist young people to make informed choices about the pathways they chose. One trainee, a 19-year-old male participant in the study stated, "My father has a basis of technical education. He has the knowledge in it so he advises me. He told me that welding is at the heart of industries. That every industry in Ghana will need a welder. So he encouraged me." Arulmani and Nag-Arulmani (2005) report that 45 % of their national sample in India indicated that parents played the most significant role in their career decisions, followed by friends and teachers. Meijers, Kuijpers, and Winters (2010) in their review of the literature on career advice in the Netherlands found that parents have a greater influence on learner choice than student counselors and/or teachers. They found that parents either take an active role in helping their child to assess the information available to them and support a reasoned decision-making process or they are perceived to offer more of a nudge in the direction of particular options. In some cases, the nudge is more of an obligation. Research

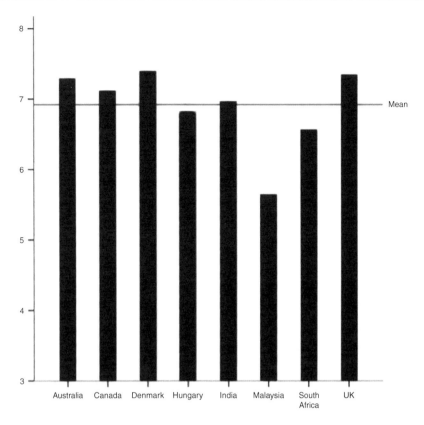

Fig. 14.2   Findings from a CSD survey (2008). School preferences for academic pathways: extent to which employers and practitioners agreed with the statement "Schools encourage children towards academic pathways"

in the UK has shown that parents with higher levels of educational attainment feel more confident and better able to give advice and guidance to their children (Batterham & Levesley, 2011). It has also been found that the educational attainment of parents is closely correlated with SES, and those from poorer backgrounds are statistically more likely to enter vocational routes (Bowers-Brown, 2006). In other words, many of the young people who are more likely to go into vocational routes do so, following their parents' footsteps rather than sound career guidance. When this is considered alongside the fact that one in four young people in the UK claim to have not received any form of career advice and guidance (Batterham & Levesley, 2011), it is easy to see how young people struggle to access good information on the vocational options available to them.

Career advice and guidance, thus, has an important role to play in making young people

who might benefit from vocational routes, aware of options their parents may not have considered, or about which they have outdated and inaccurate perceptions. Programs aimed at broadening young people's awareness of their career options also need to consider how they inform parents about pathways with which they may not be familiar, and, in some cases, respectfully challenge assumptions about the type of education that is appropriate for their children.

Class and Socioeconomic Status

The influence of parents over their children's career choices is closely related to the way that class affects career choice. Both parents' attitudes and the prevailing perceptions of the social group in which young people move affect how young people see themselves and the range of choices open to them. Much has been written about class barriers to higher education, but perceptions that vocational pathways are for those of a different class are also, in some cases, major barriers for young people who might wish to explore these options. In Ghana, there is strong social stigma attached to sectors such as hair and beauty and automotive repair which has meant that in spite of considerable demand for workers and the opportunity for significant financial remuneration, many jobs remained vacant (Bortei-Doku et al., 2011). The prejudice and societal stigma attached to vocational routes is compounded by a lack of progression routes into formal sector employment (Monk, Sandefur, & Teal, 2008). This lack of progression is not so much a reflection of the abilities of young learners as it is indicative of societal perceptions of them as undeserving of further investment in education and incapable of progressing into formal sector employment.

The rural–urban divide is also a key element, as illustrated by Ghanaian discussions on equity. Ensuring that training in rural areas meets the needs of local communities can help to mitigate rural–urban migration, which is causing high levels of unemployment in cities (Mureithi, 2009). In the UK, "differences in perception between those choosing more academic courses (e.g., engineering) and those in more practical courses (e.g., hair and beauty) could be linked to social and class-based status" (Atkins, Flint, & Oldfield, 2011, p. 34). The notion of class is deeply embedded in Britain and the effects of this are felt heavily in vocational education which has been shown to be accessed largely by people from lower socioeconomic groups (Colley, James, Tedder, & Diment, 2003; Macrae, Maguire, & Ball, 1997). In South Africa, the government has stated a clear intention to bring about race, gender, and employment equality. The FET colleges are seen as instrumental in creating opportunities for historically disadvantaged people to "access education to improve their prospects of gaining employment and to redress historical inequalities" (Needham & Papier, 2011, p. 23). At the time of this writing, they are struggling with this task, as VET appears to maintain the class, gender, and race divisions. This poses a significant challenge for a balanced and informed career advice and guidance system. Arulmani and Nag-Arulmani (2005) also recommended that career guidance services must vary across differing social groups since each group could experience different needs and pressures driving the decision-making process. They argued that a sensitive career guidance program would take privilege and disadvantage into account.

Gender

Gender stereotypes strongly influence young people's concept of themselves and can often be viewed by young people as natural and universal. There is clear evidence that gender significantly influences career choices and poses a very real challenge to any career advice and guidance provision. Fuller and Unwin (2003) found that in the UK, the take up of apprenticeships was significantly gendered in certain sectors. In England, one can clearly see a heavy gender bias. For example, childcare groups are almost exclusively female and the engineering sector is male dominated even when the qualification and socioeconomic levels of the young people entering the fields are equivalent.

Rather than merely influencing the nature of the work undertaken, gender identities also give rise to differences in the criteria by which potential vocations are appraised. In another study, Beck, Fuller, and Unwin (2006) found that female students sought job satisfaction more than their male counterparts, who sought financial security. This is linked in part to perceived gender roles where the male feels the need to be the primary source of income. These gender divisions are replicated across the globe and the divisions are maintained by the limits placed upon individuals by their own gendered self-concept as well as the limits placed upon them by their communities. Drawing again upon the example from Ghana, women have less access to training and their lack of access is compounded by low literacy rates, family responsibilities, limited female autonomy, gender stereotypes within educational curricula, and a lack of awareness about training opportunities (Botchie & Ahadzie, 2004). The Ghanaian Ministry of Education, nevertheless, aims to secure 50 % female enrolment in TVET by 2015 (Ministry of Education, 2010). This example illustrates the role that balanced career advice and guidance needs to play, alongside other educational interventions, in enabling women to contribute to and benefit from economic development. An effective career advice and guidance system needs to understand the story behind these figures and ensure that if the information being provided is found to be at fault, the advice given can be adapted to reduce rather than reinforce gender divisions.

The questions we must ask are: Are these perceptions of VET accurate? Is parental demand for academic education justified? One way of assessing their efficacy and the value of VET is by understanding the rate of return to VET. There are limited studies on this subject in both developed and developing country contexts and any evidence that does exist is mixed. Bennell (1996) reported a higher rate of return to vocational education in developing countries and argued against an assumption that academic education has a higher return than vocational education. A review of the literature between 1970 and 1990 found 12 studies on returns to VET in developing countries. While some of these studies report lower returns, the trend in these studies point to a higher return in investments to education implying that the individual who invests in VET gains in the long term.

Evidence from parents, policymakers, and in some instances trainees and VET graduates in Ghana suggests that VET is perceived to have a poor rate of return. Parents believe there are limited employment opportunities for those who undergo technical education and that income is not stable. In their study of the returns from vocational schooling in Tanzania, Kahyarra (2007) found that returns are dependent on the level of training/education at which they are measured. Key factors included the actual entry point and size of the firm. Very importantly, Kahyarra points out that any return was also dependent on matching skills to employment opportunities and understanding the nature of demand for skills in the labor market. This makes a strong case for integrating career guidance with VET.

Relevance for Multiple Cultures: Sensitivity to the Universal and the Particular

In this chapter, we have argued that vocational training has close relevance to the worker's viability in the contemporary labor market in most parts of the world. This is perhaps a universal phenomenon, given the nature of occupational opportunities available the world over. However, there are two important factors pertaining to the implementation of VET when universal and particular issues are considered. Firstly, skill-based courses and careers are related to the individual's interests and aptitudes. It is possible that an individual's interest–aptitude profile is such that VET is *not* a suitable option for this person. It is also possible that individuals who are not suitable for VET take up this path given economic pressures and the urgency to earn quickly. If the realization of the person's potentials is to lie at the heart of career guidance, then it is important that the career counselor acknowledges the possibility that VET may not be a universal solution to the issues that surround occupational viability. A relevant career counseling program would address the question of transition into the world of work in a person-centered manner. For some this may mean college education; for others it may mean vocational education. Effective counseling would enhance the individual's employability by preparing him or her to enter the world of work from a position of strength rather than disadvantage. Secondly, as we have pointed out, cultural factors mediate the manner in which vocational courses and careers are viewed. In certain countries (e.g., Germany, Austria), vocational courses are the preferred option. In other (mostly Asian) countries, vocational courses are placed at a lower level of prestige. The enduring belief that vocational courses are only for the poor is an example of a commonly held worldview generalization in these cultures (Arulmani & Nag-Arulmani, 2005). It is also known that when VET is introduced into cultures that afford them low prestige, these programs struggle to thrive (e.g., Arulmani & Abdulla, 2007). It is vital, therefore, that cultural factors are taken into account when VET initiatives are planned. As Arulmani and Nag-Arulmani (2005) have recommended, it is vital to note that it is *not* the objective of career counseling to "convince" young people that they ought to take up a degree or study the arts or go for vocational training. Instead, a fundamental concern of career counseling would be to help the young make choices based on personal potentials and personal satisfaction. Further, they have highlighted that the longest lag periods between qualifying for a career and actually entering a career seem to be closely linked to the nature of the career aspirant's career preparation. Notion of skill literacy is of particular relevance here, and it has been noted that the longest delays are associated with the lack of *skill literacy* in the career aspirant. *Skill* in this sense is not limited to the dexterity with which a person handles equipment and tools—ideas associated with vocational careers. Skill literacy is the fluency that a person develops for the practice and application of the theoretical concepts that comprise a body of knowledge. Even a highly theoretical field of study and the occupations it qualifies a person for require a set of skills without which the job tasks of those occupations cannot be successfully executed. A historian, for example, requires skills for referencing and research, just as a mechanical engineer needs to be skilled at understanding how machines work or a psychologist needs skills to listen with empathy. The most urgent need presented by the world of work is for *skilled* manpower. For Asian countries, against the background of the apparent failure of vocational training to evoke adequate interest, the development of courses that blend the curricular objectives of university-based (degree) programs with vocational courses (diplomas, certificates) could offer an effective solution.

Charting New Directions: Implications for the Provision of Effective Career Advice and Guidance

The numerous, complex factors affecting the decisions being made by young people with respect to their study and career options present a major challenge for the design of effective career advice and guidance systems. This is especially true when it comes to supporting young learners who may want to follow vocational routes. VET systems have frequently been tasked with supporting economic development and also with helping to redress imbalances in gender, race, and class. The converse, however, has not always been true: Vocational options have not been well served by existing systems. In order to engage the range of young people who could benefit, many existing prejudices and misconceptions that currently surround VET have to be overturned.

The hybrid model of decision-making that has formed the framework for this chapter shows that helping equip young learners with the tools to challenge prejudices and understand the social factors shaping their own self-concept is a sensitive and demanding task. Developing a career advice and guidance system is, therefore, about much more than simply training career counselors. If gaps in our workforces are to be filled and the advantages of newly emerging occupations are to be optimized, responsibility stretches from government and employers right down to the individual in order to ensure that young people can make informed choices that fulfill their needs, interests, and aptitudes.

The Policy Level

As discussed, the perception that vocational routes have limited progression opportunities is one reason that learners are often discouraged from undertaking training which they might otherwise choose. To ensure that vocational training opens up career opportunities for learners and does not limit their prospects, policymakers must support a framework that improves transferability between different learning pathways. Career advice and guidance is needed that emphasizes the transferability of skills and knowledge gained through vocational qualifications and the routes they open up for further study.

Policymakers could also promote a more balanced approach to career advice and guidance in schools by requiring them to provide information on vocational options. Funding, or otherwise supporting the training and development of career advice and guidance counselors in both formal and informal training systems, and equipping teachers with knowledge about both academic and vocational routes would also help. Teachers should be encouraged to provide information on where these routes may lead and employers' workplace expectations, informed by a reasonable picture of the supply and demand of skills in the economy. Policymakers must consider how they can address the challenge of ensuring that improved labor market information is collected, which can give an accurate picture of the demand at national, regional, and local levels, and how to make this easily accessible to those imparting advice. Policymakers should also be doing more to encourage employers to make work placements available to enable young learners to experience trades and occupations before they begin training.

Employer Engagement in Career Advice and Guidance

Engagement with employers can have a significant impact on young people's awareness of their career options and the demands that different careers make. Giving young people the opportunity to experience a vocation through well-structured work experience programs can help them make more informed choices and make their transition into the labor market easier (Harvey, 2003). As Shamash and Shoesmith (2011) found, the experience and insights gained by learners during work placements cannot be underestimated as a means of career advice and guidance. These need to be offered before young

people have to make important decisions about learning routes. In terms of encouraging employers to participate, there is also evidence to suggest that work experience programs can form part of effective recruitment, talent development, and community engagement strategies for the businesses themselves (Shamash & Shoesmith, 2011).

Another way in which employers can contribute to better career advice and guidance is to work with the local schools and training providers to ensure accurate information about the skills and aptitudes needed by their employees is communicated to young learners. This could give young learners a clearer picture of what is expected of them, and it would also help to ensure young learners enter the workplace with the skills the employers need. Employers can play a valuable role in showing the career pathways that are open to young people choosing to learn a particular skill. By doing so, employers can ensure they have engaged and motivated young learners entering the workplace.

If employers want to attract the best young learners to their place of work, they must play their part in raising the profile of VET and celebrating excellence in VET. Career fairs and skill competitions are a way to showcase the skills required for vocational occupations and give young learners a chance to "taste" a trade, engage with employers, and understand the levels of excellence and the opportunities vocational training can offer. This form of career experience may help young people make informed decisions, and this sort of hands-on experience is likely to be more engaging for young people who want to find out about vocational routes than traditional face-to-face discussions. Skill competitions also represent an opportunity for employers to see some of the best young talent they could be recruiting.

Practitioners: Counselors and Teachers

Those who are tasked with delivering career advice and guidance are usually very familiar with the complexity of issues and challenges outlined in this section. One of the challenges they face is engaging constructively with other players that influence the decisions of the young people they work with. For example, because of the influence parents have, it is important for schools, colleges, and other training providers to acknowledge them and do their part to involve and educate them about all the options— vocational as well as academic—open to their children. In the same way we have seen advertising aimed at children trying to develop "pester power" (Spungin, 2004), career guidance could be furnishing young learners with the information that will help alleviate concerns and challenge misplaced prejudices held by their parents.

Career advisors, counselors, and teachers need to also challenge the prejudices and misconceptions held by young learners. The influence of society and family attitudes is significant, and a good career counselor needs to be able to help young learners look at the factors that have shaped their self-concept and encourage them to take up routes and opportunities that they may have ruled out without much thought. Career guidance counselors need, with the help of all those with a stake in skills development, to ensure they can access up-to-date and reliable information on a broad range of educational routes and career options. This will ensure they can give young learners a comprehensive guide to the options available to them.

Research has shown that young learners seek advice from people they trust and that this is one reason why parents are still the preferred source of information for them in the UK (Batterham & Levesley, 2011). Career guidance counselors need to be given the time to get to know the individuals they are working with, to understand their interests and aptitudes, and to work collaboratively with the individual and his/her family to ensure they arrive at the best possible study or career option.

Conclusion

It is important to remember that study options and career choices are made at various stages throughout our lives and the number of decision points is rapidly increasing and changing in the world of work today. An effective career advice and guidance provision should not simply help learners arrive at a decision but needs to equip them with the skills and tools to evaluate options and continue to make informed choices throughout their lives. Such a service requires all those with a stake in education to play their part. A critical point that has emerged in this writing is that VET must not be dismissed out of hand or downplayed for reasons of perceived low prestige or poor occupational outcomes. At the same time, neither is it to be promoted regardless of the individual's suitability especially among the less advantaged—perpetuating class differences. Done well, a comprehensive and balanced approach has the potential to help redress the mismatch between supply and demand, improve the quality of learners entering the workplace, develop a more motivated workforce, offer multiple pathways to success and, at the same time, support ongoing economic development around the world.

References

Ackerman, P. L., & Beier, M. E. (2003). Intelligence, personality, and interests in the career choice process. *Journal of Career Assessment, 11*(2), 205–218.

Arulmani, G., & Abdulla, A. (2007). Capturing the ripples: Addressing the sustainability of the impact of social marketing. *Social Marketing Quarterly, 13* (4), 84–107.

Arulmani, G., & Nag-Arulmani, S. (2005). *Work orientations and responses to career choices: Indian regional survey*. Bangalore, India: The Promise Foundation.

Atkins, L., Flint, K., & Oldfield, B. (2011). *Practical matters: What young people think about vocational education in England*. London, England: City & Guilds Centre for Skills Development.

Bandura, A., Barbaranelli, C., Caprara, G., & Pastorelli, C. (2001). Self-efficacy beliefs as shapers of children's aspirations and career trajectories. *Child Development, 72*(1), 197–206.

Batterham, J., & Levesley, T. (2011). *New directions: Young people's and parent's views of vocational education and careers guidance*. London, England: City & Guilds Centre for Skills Development.

Beck, V., Fuller, A., & Unwin, L. (2006). Safety in stereotypes? The impact of gender and race on young people's perceptions of their post-compulsory education and labour market opportunities. *British Educational Research Journal, 32*(5), 667–686.

Bell, D., & Blanchflower, D. (2010). Youth unemployment: Déjà Vu?. *Stirling Economics Discussion Paper 2010-04*. Scotland: University of Stirling.

Bennell, P. (1996). Rates of return to education: Does the conventional pattern prevail in sub-Saharan Africa? *World Development, 24*(1), 183–199.

Bortei-Doku, E., Doh, D., & Andoh, P. (2011). *From prejudice to prestige: Vocational education and training in Ghana*. London, England: City & Guilds Centre for Skills Development.

Botchie, G., & Ahadzie, W. (2004). *Poverty reduction efforts in Ghana: The skill development option*. Accra, Ghana: University of Legon.

Bowers-Brown, T. (2006). Widening participation in higher education amongst students from disadvantaged socio-economic groups. *Tertiary Education and Management, 12*(1), 59–74.

Brown, P., Green, A., & Lauder, H. (2001). *Globalisation, competitiveness and skill formation*. Oxford, England: Oxford University Press.

Brown, P., Hesketh, A., & Williams, S. (2003). Employability in a knowledge-driven economy. *Journal of Education and Work, 16*(2), 107–126.

Büning, N., Cantrell, S., Marshall, B., & Smith, D. (2011). Solving the skills crisis. *Outlook: The Journal of High-Performance Business, 3*, 1–12.

Byars-Winston, A., Estrada, Y., Howard, C., Davis, D., & Zalapa, J. (2010). Influence of social cognitive and ethnic variables on academic goals of underrepresented students in science and engineering: A multiple-groups analysis. *Journal of Counselling Psychology, 57*(2), 205–218.

Cedefop. (2011). *The impact of vocational education and training on company performance*. Thessaloniki, Greece: Author.

City & Guilds Centre for Skills Development. (2008). *Skills development: Attitudes and perceptions*. London, England: Author.

Colley, H., James, D., Tedder, M., & Diment, K. (2003). Learning as becoming in vocational education and training: Class, gender and the role of vocational habitus. *Journal of Vocational Education and Training, 55*(4), 471–497.

Dalley-Trim, L., Alloway, N., & Walker, K. (2008). Secondary school students' perceptions of and the factors influencing their decision-making in relation to VET in schools. *The Australian Educational Researcher, 35*(2), 55–69.

Department of Labour. (2011). *Skills challenges report: New Zealand's skills challenges over the next 10 years*. Wellington, New Zealand: Author.

Dunning, J., & Lundan, S. (2008). *Multinational enterprises and the global economy*. Cheltenham, England: Edward Elgar Publishing.

Fuller, A., & Unwin, L. (2003). Creating a 'modern apprenticeship': A critique of the UK's multi-sector,

social inclusion approach. *Journal of Education and Work, 16*(1), 5–25.

Gregory, R. (2010). *Dark corners in a bright economy: The lack of jobs for unskilled men*. Tokyo, Japan: Institute of Economic Research, Hitotsubashi University.

Harvey, L. (2003). *Transitions from higher education to work*. Sheffield, England: Centre for Research and Evaluation, Sheffield Hallam University.

Hodkinson, P., & Sparkes, A. C. (1997). Careership: A sociological theory of career decision-making. *British Journal of Sociology of Education, 10*(1), 23–35.

Hodkinson, P., Sparkes, A. C., & Hodkinson, H. (1996). *Triumphs and tears: Young people, markets and the transition from school to work*. London, England: David Fulton.

Hoeckel, K. (2008). *Costs and benefits in vocational education and training*. Paris, France: OECD.

Johnston, B. (2007). *Methodological review: Mapping the literature in relation to the challenges for the non-participation project*. Southampton, England: University of Southampton.

Kahyarra, G. (2007). *The returns to vocational and academic education: Evidence from Tanzania*. Oxford, England: Centre for Studies of African Economies.

Karmel, T., & Mlotkowski, P. (2010). *Tradespeople for the resources sector: Projections 2010–2020* (Paper prepared for the National Resources Sector Employment Taskforce). Adelaide, Australia: NCVER.

Keep, E. (2009). *Internal and external incentives to engage in education and training: A framework for analysing the forces acting on individuals* (Monograph No. 12). Cardiff, UK: Cardiff University, SKOPE.

Macrae, S., Maguire, M., & Ball, S. (1997). Whose 'learning' society? A tentative deconstruction. *Journal of Education Policy, 12*(6), 499–509.

Markus, H. R., & Kitayama, S. (1991). Culture and the self: Implications for cognition, emotion, and motivation. *Psychological Review, 98*(2), 224–253.

Meer, J. (2007). Evidence on the returns to secondary vocational education. *Economics of Education Review, 26*, 559–573.

Meijers, F., Kuijpers, M., & Winters, A. (2010). *Leren kiezen/kiezen leren—een literatuurstudie*. 's-Hertogenbosch, The Netherlands: Ecbo.

Ministry of Education. (2010). *Monitoring and evaluation plan 2010–2013*. Accra, Ghana: Author.

Monk, C., Sandefur, J., & Teal, F. (2008). *Does doing an apprenticeship pay off? Evidence from Ghana* (p. 288). Oxford, England: The Centre for the Study of African Economies.

Mureithi, G. (2009). *Technical, vocational education and training in Africa: Has it lost its significance?* Eldoret, Kenya: Moi University.

Needham, S., & Papier, J. (2011). *Practical matters: What young people think about vocational education in South Africa*. London, England: City & Guilds Centre for Skills Development.

OECD. (2009). *Education at a glance 2009: OECD indicators*. Paris, France: Author.

OECD. (2010). *OECD reviews of vocational education and training: Learning for jobs*. Paris, France: Author.

Oesch, D. (2010). What explains high unemployment among low-skilled workers? Evidence from 21 OECD countries. *European Journal of Industrial Relations, 16*(1), 39–55.

Paton, K. (2007). *Models of educational decision-making* (Working Paper 6). England: University of Southampton.

Payne, J. (2003). *Choice at the end of compulsory schooling: A research review* (Research Report RR414). London, England: Department for Education and Skills.

Schwalje, W. (2011). *The prevalence and impact of skills gaps on Latin America and the Caribbean* (MPRA Paper 30247). Germany: University Library of Munich.

Shamash, J., & Shoesmith, K. (2011). *Transforming work experience into work inspiration—The business benefits*. London, England: City & Guilds Centre for Skills Development.

Spungin, P. (2004). Parent power, not pester power. *Young Consumers, 5*(3), 37–40.

Stokes, H., Wierenga, A., & Wyn, J. (2003). *Preparing for the future and living today: Young people's perceptions of career education, VET, enterprise education and part-time work*. Canberra, ACT, Australia: Department of Education, Science and Training, Australian Government.

Wegner, L. (2008). Investing in Africa's youth. *Policy Insights* (No. 62). Paris, France: OECD Development Centre.

West, A. (1999). *Vocational education and training indicators*. Thessaloniki, Greece: European Centre for the Development of Vocational Training (Cedefop).

Helmut Zelloth

Introduction: The Two Sides of a Coin

Setting the Technical and Vocational Education and Training (TVET) Scene

The priority task of all Technical and Vocational Education and Training (TVET) policies and systems, distinctively and in contrast to general education, is to prepare individuals for specific occupations and for the world of work. Boundaries between general education and TVET are becoming more blurred, and increasingly TVET is associated with having a broader scope including personal, general, and entrepreneurial skills which can help individuals in their lifelong learning, improve their employability, and facilitate overall involvement in society. At its core, however, TVET remains concerned with those aspects of the educational process, in addition to general education, which involve the study of technologies and related sciences and the acquisition of practical skills, attitudes, understanding, and knowledge relating to occupations in various sectors of economic life (UNESCO, 2001). Such a view of TVET is not always shared by the academic community, since postsecondary and university education also prepares students for the world of work and often for specific occupational fields. It is not

the preparation for work which sets TVET apart from higher education, Bosch and Charest (2010) have argued; instead, the main difference between TVET and higher education is that a TVET learner specializes for an occupational field earlier or precociously and TVET has lower social status.

Another distinctive feature compared to general education is that TVET, by definition, has a practice-oriented component or work-based learning aspect involved. The principle of *dualism*, of theoretical and practical learning (i.e., learning in the work process), is an indispensable and fundamental principle of TVET which supports the development of professional competence. It can even be reasoned that ultimately any occupation must be learned on the job, regardless of whether it is an academic profession or a nonacademic occupation (Rauner & Smith, 2009).

Moreover, unlike general education, the area of TVET is rather complex and not as homogenous as one would suppose. TVET provision may differ from country to country and even within countries. Target groups and age cohorts may be quite diverse, and learning and training may take place in a very wide variety of formal, informal, and nonformal arrangements. Apart from schools, TVET involves different actors and may be provided by different types of public or private institutions, including enterprises or nongovernmental organizations (NGOs). As documented by the National Centre for Vocational Education Research (NCVER, 2009),

H. Zelloth (✉)
European Training Foundation, Turin, Italy
e-mail: Helmut.Zelloth@etf.europa.eu

some countries (e.g., Canada, the UK) co-opt or integrate industry partners in their TVET system to a lesser degree, others do better in this respect (e.g., Australia), while others have an even higher level of employer involvement in TVET provision and governance (e.g., Germany, Sweden). Policy responsibility in TVET is often shared by the Ministry of Education (or a separate Ministry of TVET) with other Ministries (e.g., Labor, Manpower, Industry, Agriculture, Higher Education), and governance of the TVET system can be highly fragmented (e.g., Egypt). It can vary from fragmented, input-oriented governance (e.g., Germany) to coordinated, output-oriented governance (e.g., Denmark, Switzerland) (Rauner, 2009).

TVET takes place along the entire lifelong learning spectrum, spanning prevocational education (or prevocational literacy), initial and secondary TVET, postsecondary, and further or continuing VET. The functions of TVET are manifold. Gasskov (2000) has identified six different dimensions in the mandate of TVET: (a) The ultimate economic objective of TVET is basic improved personal and social productivity (efficiency argument); (b) TVET is often an instrument for structural change such that if jobs are no longer in demand, new jobs are created or old jobs are performed in new ways with different technologies; (c) TVET can equalize the opportunities that people have to earn their living through the acquisition of skills (equity argument), though the outcome of training may still remain unequal; (d) TVET can be a tool for achieving national economic and social objectives (i.e., supporting priority industrial sectors, attracting foreign investment); (e) in addition to economic benefits, TVET can generate massive social benefits (externalities) and can be seen as an important avenue for the socialization of young people; and (f) TVET can have benefits not directly connected with employment as vocational skills can be also used to reduce the cost of living.

A number of these characteristics, principles, and functions of TVET are closely related to career guidance and will be further elaborated and analyzed in the next section of the paper. In principle, TVET and career guidance necessarily need each other and both entities could gain important benefits from cooperating. Career guidance cannot neglect TVET as an option in its advice, given that it exists. And, there are good reasons to assume that career guidance can make TVET more efficient and also help to increase the attractiveness of TVET pathways. This chapter covers mainly the initial and secondary TVET levels, with some reference also to postsecondary TVET.

Quo Vadis Career Guidance?

The new paradigm of career guidance (European Union Council, 2004, 2008; OECD, 2004a; Sultana, 2004; Watts & Fretwell, 2004) on which this chapter relies created new dimensions of potential interface between TVET and career guidance. It started to shift the mode of delivery from the traditional psychological model to a more pedagogical or hybrid model. This means a gradual move from an approach of psychological *testing* the individual to *tasting* the world of work and an increase in emphasis on career information (Jarvis, 2003) and contextual labor market realities. Furthermore, the new paradigm aims at reducing the reliance on external expert support in favor of the empowerment of the individual through career self-management skills. It also moves from career guidance provision at only key points in life to a lifelong guidance perspective (ELGPN, 2012). In this chapter, therefore, the international state-of-the-art definition of career guidance is adopted, that is, services (career information, career education, guidance and counseling) intended to assist people of any age and at any point in their lives; to make education, training, and occupational choices; and to manage their careers (OECD, 2004a).

For the sake of analysis, it is important to distinguish career guidance from other related concepts and processes, which are different although partly overlapped. Sultana and Watts (2007) have described these distinguishing features as follows: (a) promotion (attempting to persuade individuals to make particular choices, e.g., TVET, at the expense of others), (b) induction (supporting entrants in managing their transition into a new learning or work environment), (c) selection (somebody else making decisions about individuals), and (d) placement (matching individuals to specific jobs). While some overlap exists, these concepts are primarily designed to serve the interests of opportunity providers (i.e., education institutions, TVET providers, and employers). However, it is important to note that career guidance integrally addresses the interests of individuals within their social context. It is concerned with helping individuals to choose from a full range of available opportunities, to optimally utilize their abilities, and to address their interests and values, thereby leading to better performance and greater fulfillment.

Though the focus of career guidance is on the individual, it is not only a *private* good but also a *public* good. The reasons why governments invest in career guidance are usually connected with the expected outcomes of guidance, namely, the ability to contribute to public policy goals in education, training, employment, and equity. Ultimately, career guidance is supposed to increase the efficiency of education, training, and labor market systems. It is widely agreed, even common sense, that ill-informed and ill-thought-through initial education and occupational choices can result not only in individual dissatisfaction and low learning and work productivity but also in high public and private costs. This could be seen in terms of people dropping out from education and training, choosing another field of study or work, postponing transition from school to work, or increasing skill gaps (Sweet, 2006).

Interface or Strange Relationship?

If we compare the functions and objectives of career guidance in the new paradigm with those of TVET mentioned before, a great deal of interface, communalities, and even a certain convergence between the two areas can be observed. Thus, good arguments for strengthening career

guidance in relation to TVET can be made. This concerns career guidance both *prior to* and *within* TVET: a helpful distinction introduced by Watts (2009). Career guidance could not only serve as an *eye-opener* to stimulate TVET demand but also as a *change agent* to improve current TVET supply. Provision of career guidance prior to TVET is in a way vital for TVET as it lays the foundations and can influence choices and access to TVET. Career guidance within TVET can help to improve the internal and external efficiency of TVET, for example, in terms of better matching to specializations and smoother transition to work.

Career guidance can have at least a triple role vis-à-vis TVET (Zelloth, 2010a): (a) a *turning point* role prior to TVET, when it comes to choosing TVET as a pathway, as opposed to opting for general and academic education; (b) a *supporting* role within TVET, in choosing or changing a specialization or preventing dropout; and (c) an *empowerment* role to manage various transitions and to become or remain employable throughout life. The empowerment function concerns guidance provision both along and beyond TVET (within but also prior and post-TVET). Under certain conditions, career guidance could also contribute in raising the social attractiveness of TVET.

At the same time, some features of career guidance such as its inherent duality and ambiguity with regard to private-public good or the principle of impartiality versus potential external demand for promotion constitute a kind of dilemma in which career guidance seems to be "trapped" vis-à-vis TVET. For example, can career guidance deliberately support TVET options in case public policy pushes it to do so, or would it lose its impartiality, neutrality, innocence, and credibility by taking such an approach? On the other hand, can it be taken for granted that career guidance practice always is impartial, and that it always takes into account the full range of opportunities (or at least a wide range) and all information that exists when assisting individuals? Can users of career guidance be sure that services and/or practitioners are not biased towards certain opportunities that are mainstream thinking or trendy in society, that is, general and academic education instead of TVET, white collar instead of blue collar jobs, or desk work instead of manual work?

These and other questions raise concerns and also show that the relationship between TVET and career guidance is quite complex and even runs the risk of becoming distorted. Certainly the interface between TVET and career guidance has various dimensions. A few of these will be further explored.

Methodology

This chapter draws on my longstanding and privileged experience of working as a policy analyst and adviser on both TVET and career guidance in an international context at the European Training Foundation (ETF), an agency of the European Union (EU). The institutional learning provided by this context has engendered valuable insights which have allowed certain conclusions to be drawn using data and experiences from many different countries around the world. The topics in this chapter are not analyzed using an academic perspective. Rather, the analysis is based on engagement with the constant interplay between knowledge, experience, practice, and policy. Experience gained through working in the geographical contexts of former transition countries such as the new member states of the EU and low- and middle-income countries neighboring the EU (North Africa, the Middle East, the former Soviet Union, Central Asia, Eastern Europe, and the Western Balkans) has been especially relevant. Numerous field visits and interviews with practitioners and policymakers in TVET and/or in career guidance in more than 20 countries have contributed to this analysis. In addition, involvement in the preparation of policy papers on career guidance for several governments, including those of Turkey, Serbia, Kosovo (this designation is without prejudice to positions on status and in line with UNSCR 1244 and the ICJ Opinion on the Kosovo declaration of independence: hereinafter "Kosovo"), Jordan, and

Egypt (Akkok & Zelloth, 2009; National Task Force, 2010; Zelloth, 2008, 2010b, 2011b), have led to the insights presented in this chapter.

The chapter additionally draws on specific but limited literature related to the issue of TVET and career guidance (UNESCO, 2002; Watts, 2009, 2011); on information and analysis provided by OECD (2004a), World Bank (Watts & Fretwell, 2004), and ETF (Sultana, 2003; Sultana & Watts, 2007; Sweet, 2006) country reviews and comparative analyses of career guidance policies (Zelloth, 2009); and TVET systems (ETF, 2011; Zelloth, 2010a, 2011c) in different geographical contexts.

Dimensions of the Interface

While it is safe to say that TVET systems are present in most countries, or at least in the vast majority of them, it can be also said that with regard to career guidance services, the opposite is the case. Many countries across the globe either do not have such services at all or they lack a critical mass or have limited service capacity. The stage of provision and development in many countries is such that services hardly reach potential users and the impact is often unknown. And if such services are in place, they tend not to take place in TVET or to be linked with it. This a priori "TVET-blindness" within career guidance forfeits a possible relationship.

A Neglected Interface and Relationship

There are different reasons why in many countries students from TVET pathways receive significantly less career development assistance than students in general education pathways. One of them could be that it is not considered as a priority or as needed. The OECD (2004a) has clarified that it has to do with the assumption that upper-secondary students (and in particular TVET students) have made specific educational and career choices and that they do not need further support. This argument is probably the most typical to be found and it may be coupled with an image of TVET as a rather rigid system that does not allow for much flexibility or choice. These assumptions completely overlook the fact that the labor market is much more diverse and complex than TVET pathways and that TVET students, for example, even if they had made a "right choice" before, will have to face an unavoidable transition either to the labor market or to postsecondary and tertiary TVET. It also ignores the possibility that often young people do not have the choice but are rather being "streamed" into TVET pathways. This may occur as a result of inadequate examination and allocation systems at the end of compulsory education which allow only the "better performers" to continue in the academic streams and, in many instances, may have little to do with real talents or interests of individuals.

Another reason for the relative absence of career guidance in TVET could be a possible "color blindness" of career guidance providers. Career guidance staff often spend substantial time in preparing students to choose and compete for tertiary education places (OECD, 2004a), which as a result can crowd out potential activities for TVET. If this is true, it would also put in question the impartiality of certain career guidance practices and may impute to career guidance the tendency of a bias that favors general and academic education. In case overall career guidance services in a given country were dominated by *educational guidance* and by guidance staff with a rather academic than TVET or labor market background, this suspicion would become even more plausible, as the link to the labor market and job or careers would be naturally weaker.

By contrast, however, there are a few examples of countries and projects where either career guidance services include TVET, usually in a context of well-developed guidance systems (e.g., Finland, Australia, the Netherlands, Austria, Germany), or governments or donors put deliberate attention on career guidance development within the TVET sector. Examples of such strategies in Jordan and Serbia, of career consultants in TVET Centers in Georgia, of career centers in TVET schools in the former

Yugoslav Republic of Macedonia, described later in the chapter. This newly emerging pattern may be the result of a national policy priority to promote TVET for various reasons coupled with the desire for career guidance to facilitate this process. Sometimes it can be explained due to donor-supported or donor-driven initiatives.

An Underexplored Interface

The potential and nature of the interface between career guidance and TVET remain underexplored to date. Though a comprehensive international literature review (Hughes & Gration, 2009) on the impact of career guidance reveals positive effects on generic issues like decision-making skills, participation in informal learning, reduced course-switching, and work attitudes, it lacks specific reference to TVET. Also the OECD (2004b) in its *Career Guidance: A Handbook for Policy Makers* does not elaborate on TVET and tends to generalize issues that apply to all levels of schooling. It misses the opportunity to draw policy options for TVET apart from indicating that it must be ensured that career guidance is an integral part of adult learning programs in publicly funded education and training institutions. This also applies to other international reviews of career guidance (e.g., ILO, 2006; Watts & Fretwell, 2004). The UNESCO, however, has occasionally addressed the issue of TVET in relation to career guidance, stressing that career guidance in the 21st century will be more necessary than ever before in schools and technical colleges (Hoxte, 2002; UNESCO, 2002). The omission of the impact of TVET-related career guidance in research may mirror the negligence of TVET in career guidance policy and practice, but at the same time it also reveals a blind spot in current global research and analysis and the possibility of institutional bias. Some of the limited work done in this area includes Sultana (2006) who developed a practical resource entitled *Guidebook for Vocational School Directors* to support TVET students in their transition to work and Watts (2009, 2011) who examined the relationship of career guidance to (postsecondary) TVET as part of a recent OECD (2010) review. Nonetheless, different interfaces between TVET and career guidance exist, among them the linguistic notion described below.

The Linguistic Notion of the Interface

One similarity between the terms *TVET* and *career guidance* is that neither can claim exclusivity in their respective areas. The term *TVET* itself is by far not the only one used to describe TVET. Many countries as well as international organizations prefer the term *vocational education and training* (VET), to describe the same phenomenon, or just *vocational training* (VT). While these terms can be used interchangeably, TVET lays a strong emphasis on the *technical* dimension and VT on the notion of *training* as opposed to educational aspects. The USA, for example, used TVET until a few years ago when it was changed to *career and technical education* (CTE) because it was believed to convey a better image.

The use of the terms *career* and *career guidance*, emerging from the Anglo-Saxon context, has been on the rise globally over the past 20 years, in the literature and in policy language. However, in several countries a shift can be observed towards the term *career development* (e.g., Canada, the USA, Australia, New Zealand, the UK). In many postcommunist countries, especially in Eastern Europe, there are still negative connotations and mental barriers associated with the term *career*. This is due to the historical legacy of a dualistic pattern of state (reliance/obedience) versus individual (empowerment) which emphasized the former rather than the latter. In these contexts, the individualistic connotations of the term *career* led to it being perceived as a social vice. In the Arabic world too, the term *career* is more problematic to translate whereas counseling and guidance translate easily. There is no single Arabic word that comprehensively reflects the word *career* or the term *career guidance* (Badawi, 2006). Others consider that

perhaps a new word or term must be introduced which indicates that the concept has some fluidity within this region (Sultana & Watts, 2007).

However, while career guidance embraces both educational/academic guidance and vocational guidance, terms that were employed earlier continue to coexist or are even predominant in day-to-day practice or official documents. This is the case in quite a number of countries around the world. Probably the most common term is *vocational guidance* followed by *professional orientation*, used, for example, in South Europe and in former Soviet Union countries. Widely used is also *guidance and counseling*, which may or may not assume a wider concept that goes beyond career guidance.

Such terminological pluralism has led to terminological confusion in certain instances. Vocational education occasionally has become mixed up with vocational guidance and career education (TVET in the USA) with career guidance. Paradoxically, this confirms the strong linguistic interface between the two areas. The common semantic denominator in both TVET and career guidance (vocational guidance) is the word *vocational*. The meaning of it leads us to the next dimension of the interface.

The Vocational or Occupational Interface

Ultimately, the scope of any career guidance and any TVET is related to the future occupation(s) of an individual and, more broadly, their life path. Occupations and vocational development are, therefore, at the heart of both, and career or occupational choices are among life's most important decisions for every individual. TVET pathways and qualifications can lead to many but not all occupations, while career guidance is supposed to be able to provide advice on all occupations and related qualifications. Though not all individuals have access to certain types of occupations and in extreme cases can even be excluded from a large number of occupations (e.g., Palestinian refugees in Lebanon remain still excluded by law from more than 30 occupations). The waste of human capital and talent caused by wrong or forced choices is huge but avoidable. As individuals are increasingly expected to make multiple occupational and career changes throughout their lives and to continually upgrade their skills, both career guidance and TVET are ever more in demand but also challenged by these developments. Qualification frameworks with portable credits designed to make TVET and education systems more transparent and flexible are emerging in many countries across the globe, thus further enhancing the opportunities for TVET learners and increasing the scope for career guidance (Sultana & Watts, 2008). The importance of vocational development has been stressed by Super's *Psychology of Careers* (1957) in its analysis of the nature of work and occupational life spans. One dimension of vocational development and the occupational interface is represented by self-employment and entrepreneurship as a career choice. It constitutes the other side of the coin to classical employment. It may or may not require the same vocational competences as in traditional craft occupations (e.g., technical skills), but it calls for a specific set of skills and talents (e.g., creativity, initiative, risk taking). Entrepreneurship has become particularly important for TVET because self-employment and establishing one's own business is a very realistic aspiration and sometimes the option with the greatest opportunities for a number of TVET learners (e.g., hairdressers, plumbers, or electricians). Though entrepreneurship is increasingly being promoted by national policies in many countries, students are often not aware or sufficiently prepared for entrepreneurship career options and prefer more traditional employment positions. In principle, career guidance can also play a role in helping students to build a foundation for entrepreneurship (i.e., sense of initiative, *can-do* attitude) or even to prepare for it more specifically. However, its role could become limited if guidance professionals tend to have limited contacts with the business world and real entrepreneurs (Cedefop, 2011).

The Labor Market and World-of-Work Interface

The ultimate orientation of both TVET and career guidance is related to the labor market and the world of work. TVET is constantly challenged to meet ever-changing labor market demands and is criticized for not sufficiently achieving its main objective, namely, preparing individuals for the world of work. This is not new and is the case in almost all countries where TVET exists. At the same time, career guidance can provide an essential link between education, TVET, and the labor market, as well as between school and society. In playing its part in contributing to a better and dynamic match between the individual and the labor market, career guidance has to deal with moving targets and is required to achieve a difficult balance: helping individuals to find the optimal mix in their choices between interests, dreams and values, talents and competences, on the one hand, and career options and available jobs in the formal and informal labor markets, on the other. With a view to the latter, the important role of career information (based on sound labor market information) is increasingly recognized: career information + career management skills = keys to a great career and a great life (Jarvis, 2003). The new paradigm of career guidance has added a further dimension to this arithmetical metaphor: experiencing the world of work as part of career guidance. Since the new *pedagogical* paradigm by its nature has a higher affinity to the world of work than the previous *psychological* paradigm ever had, it is in a way potentially moving closer to the world of TVET. It, therefore, may be able to support a change in perceptions which in turn could increase the attractiveness of TVET such that the likelihood of it being chosen as an option is enhanced. Empirical and longitudinal studies confirm that work experience not only helps young people clarify their career aspirations and thereby become less likely to be labeled as NEET (not in employment, education and training) at 16+ but also helps them get a job after education (Mann, 2012a). Other UK and US research shows that even a certain frequency of employer contacts at school (i.e., career talks, work experience) can make a difference to employment prospects of 14–19-year-olds and strengthen confidence towards career goals (Mann, 2012b). The level of young people's career exploration skills seems another key factor for successful transitions at age 16 (Hughes & Gration, 2009). Opportunities for real-life *immersion* (like work experience), however, depend on the strength and quality of the overall education/TVET-business relation and cooperation in a given context. The weaker this relation is, the less career guidance can develop its full potential to develop this key interface.

The Status, Class, and Choice Interface

It is widely known that TVET as opposed to academic or general education suffers a low status and negative image problem in many countries in the world. TVET is often only a second-best option for learners in initial education and training, and even within TVET vertical segmentation may occur as work-based forms of TVET rank the lowest in some countries in terms of image and qualifications (Sweet & Zelloth, 2009). By vertical segmentation we mean that even within TVET there is sometimes segmentation by status, and, for example, work-based forms of TVET may rank lower than school-based forms, industrial tracks higher than commercial or agriculture tracks, and so on. The relative low status of TVET is due to several reasons. Among those are the academic drift in education and society overall, structural supply and quality challenges of TVET itself, and inappropriate allocation

mechanisms for progression in education systems, including channeling of lowest performers to TVET tracks. TVET programs are also often aimed at attracting students from lower socioeconomic status backgrounds. Further, the unrealistic career aspirations of large numbers of individuals and the lack of information and proper career guidance to support more rational choices can be attributed to this phenomenon. On the other hand, career guidance is facing problems related to relevance and growth rather than status and prestige. This, along with an absence of strong policies in support of career guidance, affects the necessary scaling up of decent services. On relevance, Sultana (2006) has argued that career guidance as a *language* or form of socially constructed interaction is a fundamentally white and middle-class practice which might need to be reconceptualized if it is to be at all meaningful in TVET settings.

Overall, there is a risk that career guidance might be negatively affected by the low status image of TVET, and, therefore, perhaps there is a conscious or unconscious attempt to avoid identifying with it too closely. The negative image of TVET and the preference for academic career paths in society complement each other; both are deep-rooted and not supportive of TVET options. In a study on the image of TVET in Jordan, it was found that parents discourage their children from even considering TVET opportunities despite the fact that TVET-based career development opportunities are improving (Prisma, 2010). Career guidance also faces restrictions due to limited choices or rigid and sometimes even forced allocation of students to TVET (e.g., Egypt and Jordan) and related specializations based on academic achievement measured solely by their final grades in school; in other words, no choice, therefore, no guidance (Zelloth, 2011a, 2012). Such an approach perpetuates the negative image of TVET as a destination largely for low achievers and low performers. It also enhances the probability and risk that career guidance reproduces this mainstream thinking and that career guidance tends to avoid or does not do enough to tackle wrong perceptions on TVET.

The Policy Interface

Both TVET and career guidance have in common a certain isolated policy rhetoric on their respective importance and relevance. Both topics are moving up the policy agenda and are also expanding in a number of countries. Achtenhagen and Grubb (2001) have noted a renewed interest around the globe in the economic purpose of education which has sent "policymakers scurrying after more overtly vocational forms of education" (p. 605). Meanwhile numerous efforts at national, supranational, and international levels are being made to improve the status and attractiveness of TVET and align TVET to the framework of lifelong learning so that its potential to substantially contribute to developing a *knowledge-based economy* could be more fully exploited. Some 10 years ago, the 27 EU countries started a joint process to foster TVET at national and European levels: the Copenhagen Process. Recently, the ETF has launched a parallel initiative in TVET: the Torino Process, covering almost 30 low- and middle-income countries neighboring the EU. The UNESCO has adopted a new TVET Strategy in 2010 and aims to implement it with the support of international agencies (UNESCO, 2010).

A trend that career guidance is also moving up the policy agenda and developing or expanding services can be noted in particular in Europe. Strong impetus came through the first ever European Union Council Resolutions (2004, 2008) adopted on lifelong guidance as well as the latest EU policy on TVET (European Commission, 2010). The latter stresses that career guidance should equip young people with career-management skills and provide them with an opportunity to get acquainted with different vocational trades and career possibilities. It furthermore recommends that career guidance needs to be redirected from a testing to a (work) tasting approach and special attention be paid to the issues of transitions, learning, and gender equality in TVET.

Policy frameworks for career guidance with some links to TVET are emerging also in low- and middle-income countries neighboring the EU, although the level of policy profile varies by country. There are strong examples for these trends, for example, in the Mediterranean region (i.e., Egypt, Jordan, Morocco), in countries in the Western Balkans (i.e., Serbia, Montenegro, Kosovo), as well as in some countries of the former Soviet Union (i.e., Ukraine, Georgia). The reasons for this trend are manifold and can be largely explained by economic and labor market developments, as a result of ongoing education and training reforms, and by other policy-induced drivers (Zelloth, 2009, 2012). Although implementation challenges remain, the policy interface between TVET and career guidance shows clear signs of increasing interrelation.

Obstacles Affecting the Strengthening of the Interface

Despite the development of interfaces and commonalities, and even a certain convergence between TVET and career guidance, certain challenges and obstacles continue to obstruct the strengthening of their interface.

Insufficient Mutual Interest, Access, and Capacities

This includes the earlier-mentioned belief that TVET may not need career guidance as individuals have already made their choices before entering the TVET system and these choices are fixed thereafter. The problems arising from such a belief are compounded by an awareness of a low status attributed to TVET, and the limited capacity of TVET systems to reach out to decision-making points to pre-TVET and post-TVET. It also points to the possibility that TVET often lacks *transition responsibility* in terms of offering the support necessary to foster the employability and employment of their students. Career guidance systems may have similar perceptions and thus not attach enough attention or priority to potential and current TVET learners. In contexts where policies to foster career guidance in TVET are in place, they often face various obstacles on the road from policy to implementation (e.g., capacity bottlenecks). If comprehensive services are lacking or if critical mass has not been achieved for career guidance service delivery, access levels and impact on choices of TVET learners are low or negligible. It has also been noted in many low- and middle-income countries (i.e., the Asia-Pacific region) that the lack of reliable labor market information constitutes a significant obstacle, leaving career guidance practitioners inadequately prepared and confused in their efforts to cater to TVET needs (National Institute for Educational Policy Research, 2007).

The Old and the New Paradigms

The earlier TVET paradigms that prepared learners for the single and lifelong jobs through narrow specializations with dead-end routes had much less scope and space for career guidance. Newer paradigms emphasize broader occupational profiles, recognition of prior learning, lifelong learning, employability, flexibility, and occupational as well as geographical mobility. These TVET models offer great room for career guidance to be effective. However, all TVET systems in reform have not yet reached this stage and maturity. In similar vein, the traditional but still prevailing *psychological* paradigm of career guidance is less connected to TVET or even disadvantaged TVET as a potential option in the past. The new *pedagogical or hybrid* paradigm has the potential to better understand and consider TVET as it places more emphasis on the labor market and on exploring the world of work. Instead of testing the individual, the preferred mode is for the individual to taste the world of work. This new paradigm promises to provide more relevant and powerful career information, particularly in relation to TVET. But in many countries there is still a long way to go to make this new paradigm a reality. At the point where both new paradigms

will meet, career guidance could make an important contribution to TVET.

The Practitioner Dilemma and Bias

Delivery agents in TVET can be divided into four different categories according to their background and focus: (a) teachers in general education subjects, (b) teachers in vocational education subjects, (c) vocational teachers and external trainers in practical learning in schools/institutions, and (d) in-company trainers. In career guidance, delivery agents are either specialists with often a psychological or counseling background or semi-specialists (i.e., any kind of teacher or other staff) who undergo some specific retraining in career guidance. The different backgrounds of TVET staff and of career guidance staff can, therefore, be distinguished as being vocational versus academic. While in TVET institutions a career guidance practitioner is more likely to have a closer affinity to the world of work (i.e., being a vocational subject teacher), in the educational pathways prior to TVET, this is less likely the case. And the crucial decision to opt for TVET pathways or for general education and academic pathways, if such choices exist, does not take place within TVET but prior to TVET. Therefore, career guidance practitioners are vulnerable to being criticized or suspected as being potentially biased towards academic education at the expense of TVET. On the other hand, a risk of bias *towards* TVET and certain occupational areas also may exist in the case of, for example, a vocational subject teacher who delivers a few career guidance sessions to TVET students.

Findings from an OECD paper (Watts, 2009) support the above arguments. The academic background of guidance practitioners appears to translate into a tendency to favor academic over vocational options, despite the sacrosanct *impartiality* principle of career guidance. This issue is reiterated by the OECD (2010) viewpoint that recommends the development of a coherent career guidance profession, independent of psychological counseling and well informed by labor market information. This maybe particularly relevant since career guidance sometimes plays a subsidiary role to psychological counseling and staff are sometimes inadequately prepared for dealing with labor market issues.

Models of Career Guidance Delivery in TVET

The relevance and impact of career guidance in relation to TVET also depends on the models and modality of delivery. While there is no single, magical policy stance, a taxonomy of possible career guidance intervention models could serve as inspiration for policy options (see Table 15.1). Five different approaches of career guidance delivery can be distinguished that are applicable to TVET (both prior to TVET and within TVET): the curriculum model, the center model, the individual model (specialist or semi-specialist), and the virtual model. Each of these models can be provided in seven modalities (career information, career management, work tasting, testing, individual guidance, group guidance, and career counseling) though not each of the different models can offer these modalities to the same extent. For example, while the curriculum model is highly appropriate for delivering career-management skills, career information, or work tasting opportunities, it is not as well adapted for offering individual guidance or counseling. A checklist has been provided in Table 15.1 as a template for assessment of which model(s) and modalities a country relies upon and to identify gaps.

In low- and middle-income countries neighboring the EU, the most frequent models being adopted are the individual specialist model and the center model, located in educational and labor market settings (Zelloth, 2009). The curriculum model seems to be on the rise; however, virtual or semi-specialist approaches are uncommon in these countries, and their potential remains untapped despite offering cost-efficient approaches in contexts where resources are scarce. In reality, sometimes two or more models are combined and finding the right mix in a multitier approach, if affordable, would be the most promising solution in terms of effectiveness of career guidance services. Regarding the delivery methods, the psychological model appears to be still dominant, but the pedagogical or hybrid models are gaining ground (Sweet, 2006; Zelloth, 2009).

In a TVET context, guidance should in any case be embedded in the learning process to support the occupational choices of individuals and the acquisition of career-management and entrepreneurial skills, building on the foundations gained prior to TVET. The modalities of work tasting and career information are particularly relevant and can be offered throughout the TVET curriculum. Individual guidance or counseling may be offered on demand or at certain transition points prior and within TVET.

Emerging Examples of Policy and Practice in TVET: Relevance for Multiple Cultures

In the past, TVET and career guidance have been less mutually attentive, and clearly provision of career guidance within and in relation to TVET remains underrepresented even today. However, there are signs that the interface is improving both at policy and practice levels. Apart from the development trends at inter- and supranational levels (i.e., EU), mentioned earlier, some countries with well-developed guidance systems either already include career guidance in TVET or are fostering such inclusion (e.g., Finland, Austria, the Netherlands). More recently a similar trend of policies and practices in career guidance which aim to support students and learners in relation to TVET (both prior and within) can be observed also in a number of low- and middle-income countries which in general tend to have less developed guidance provision (e.g., Serbia, Jordan, Egypt).

Table 15.1 Taxonomy of possible career guidance intervention models in TVET

Model	Modality						
	Career information	Career management	Work-tasting	Testing	Individual guidance	Group guidance	Career counseling
Curriculum model							
Compulsory career education subject							
Compulsory part of (an)other subject(s)							
Compulsory curriculum principle (all or several subjects)							
Elective career education subject or similar							
Part of (an)other elective subject(s)							
Part of curricular activities							
Part of extracurricular activities							
Part of a vocational training module							
Center model							
Center inside TVET school/institution							
Specific center outside TVET school/institution							
National Employment Service center for the unemployed serving also TVET students							
Center for all citizens, in/out of education/labor market							
Specialist model							
School counselor (full time)							
School counselor (part time)							
School psychologist							
School pedagogue, sociologist, or social worker							
National Employment Service guidance specialist							
Semi-specialist model							
Class or head teacher in TVET school/institution							
Subject teacher (TVET or general)							
(Deputy) Director of TVET school/institution							
Training or employment counselor at National Employment Services							
Virtual model							
Website							
Web-based interactive service							
Email-based, SMS guidance							

Note: Adapted from "In demand: Career guidance in EU neighbouring countries," by H. Zelloth, 2009, Luxembourg: Office for Official Publications of the European Communities

Policy Framework and Governance

A strong framework for policy and governance forms the bedrock for creating systems such that career guidance and TVET can strengthen their interface. These trends are slowly beginning to emerge. This section provides two examples.

At policy level, a career guidance strategy targeting the TVET sector was adopted by the E-TVET Council in Jordan in 2011. It focuses on strengthening career guidance in community colleges, vocational training centers (VTC), and employment services. Pilot career centers in these settings include a TVET image campaign for teachers and parents, an electronic labor-market-information system, and a suite of career guidance workshops focusing on transition points through the establishment of a career guidance unit in the E-TVET Council and by building education-industry partnerships which promote active employer involvement. An Action Plan supports implementation of the strategy in the period 2011–2015 and is embedded in wider policy goals related to the National Agenda aiming to prepare Jordanians for lifelong learning and progressively in higher value-added occupations.

In Sri Lanka, the draft National Human Resources and Employment Policies (Government of Sri Lanka, 2011) has dedicated a separate chapter to Career Guidance and Counseling with strong linkages to TVET. In this document, it is clearly stated that there is a need for TVET programs to become *preferred options* for youth and that this would require effective career guidance programs. Further, the current career guidance services and capacities at schools are judged as insufficient and inadequate especially because school career guidance teachers are thought to lack contact and understanding of the world of work to be successful in guidance. The recommendation is to establish a National Career Guidance Council with a planning, development, and supervision function, supported by a network linking the Council with career guidance units in all TVET institutes.

Awareness-Raising Campaign and Career Guidance Plan

In Kyrgyzstan, as part of an Asian Development Bank (ADB) project on Vocational Education and Skills Development (ADB, 2010), a career guidance plan and an awareness-raising campaign among students and parents were developed. The initiative included an image campaign to make TVET more attractive, and it introduced measures to strengthen career guidance services prior, within, and post initial TVET. Some activities targeted students in eighth and ninth grade comprehensive schools, and others helped students choosing a specialty in the first and third year of TVET. It also supported retraining of TVET graduates, out-of-school youth, and unemployed youth through career information and guidance. Though results are yet to be seen, one of the recommendations of the project was that regular career guidance is needed to increase the prestige of vocational education (ADB, 2010).

Leadership by the TVET Sector

In Egypt, the major initiative to introduce career guidance services in the country has been led by the TVET sector in the Ministry of Education. A high-level interministerial National Task Force of Undersecretaries, General Directors, as well as stakeholders outside public administration, supported by the ETF, prepared a strategic document which was adopted by four ministries (education, higher education, manpower and migration, trade and industry) in 2010. Out of six priority areas and related target groups for career guidance in Egypt, four priorities are dedicated to TVET and respective transitions: from preparatory school to TVET, specialization in the second and third year of TVET, from TVET to higher education, and transition from TVET to work (National Task Force, 2010). However, this proposal has not yet reached the implementation stage due to the political upheavals in Egypt in 2011 and the subsequent instability in the country, as also the unrest and conflict in 2013.

Multitier and Multi-Stakeholder Approach

Among the countries with well-developed career guidance systems, the case of Germany shows a multitier and multi-stakeholder approach in career guidance provision related to TVET. Career education (including internships) is an integral part of the school curriculum and a common guidance activity of most secondary schools in Germany, though intensity of provision varies by region and type of secondary school (i.e., academically oriented *gymnasia* versus vocationally oriented secondary schools). It is complemented by extracurricular activities (often in collaboration with companies), the use of a *career choice passport*, and the involvement of career counselors from public employment services as they have more expertise in labor market issues and closer connections with training companies and employers. In addition, guidance practitioners from the chambers of commerce and crafts, industrial federations, and social partners also provide services for information and advice related to TVET, addressed to schools, universities, and enterprises. Specifically on questions related to apprenticeship, guidance practitioners in the chambers by legal obligation have to give advice to trainees, parents, companies, trainers, and teachers in TVET schools (Jenschke, Schober, & Fruebing, 2011). Young people in Germany who do not meet the requirements to enter TVET may continue with a year of vocational preparation in TVET schools or other vocational preparation courses by private training providers or NGOs. Participants receive career orientation and guidance, social pedagogical assistance, as well as work experience and practical training to help them acquire vocational skills and capabilities.

The Role of Economic Bodies

Similarly, in Austria a multilayer career guidance system is in place prior to TVET and within TVET. One specific layer has to do with the career information centers run by the Economic Chambers in nearly all provinces which provide a program of formally organized group visits that give school students access to both extensive career information (print and audiovisual materials) and a network of employer contacts. The service tends to concentrate on TVET careers (i.e., apprenticeship) rather than upon careers that follow completion of a tertiary qualification (OECD, 2002). A few years ago, a nationwide platform for lifelong guidance, including all relevant stakeholders for career guidance in Austria, was established. It is coordinated by the national government (Federal Ministry for Education) and the Styrian Association for Education and Economics as a nongovernmental body. Both in Germany and Austria, the high attention paid to career guidance in relation to TVET can be explained by their traditionally strong TVET systems (i.e., the choice of vocationally oriented secondary schools with a dual system of apprenticeships and school-based TVET) which are acknowledged to be one of the key factors explaining the success of their economies.

Career Guidance and Apprenticeships

Another example is the recent UK ambition to achieve a million new apprenticeships in the 2011–2012 and 2012–2013 academic years which has been boosted by massive promotional campaigns (i.e., City & Guilds' "Million Extra") and substantial public funding through incentives to employers and training providers. This has triggered the provision of enhanced career information about apprenticeships as well as debates on how to improve overall career guidance linked to apprenticeships. Interviewed apprentices believe that work tasting and access to information (also for parents) are key for embarking on this route but also that schools and colleges need to play a stronger role in career guidance (National Institute of Adult Continuing Education, 2012). A City and Guilds' poll showed that those on vocational courses (i.e., apprenticeships, vocational qualifications awarded by the Business and Technology

Education Council: BTECs, and General National Vocational Qualifications: GNVQs) were least likely to have been given guidance among all 15–19-year-olds surveyed (Shepherd, 2011). The relatively recent apprenticeship initiative is part of wider measures to tackle the longstanding productivity deficit in the UK economy compared to key European and OECD trading partners, recognized by successive governments (City & Guilds, 2012).

Compulsory Career Education in TVET

One of the reasons for strengthening career guidance in TVET in the Netherlands is the increasing flexibility and mobility within TVET to make it a more attractive option (Van Deursen & Jansen, 2006). Career education was made compulsory in prevocational education ("Orientation towards Learning and Working" as part of general subjects and "Orientation towards the Sector," included in all vocational subjects). In addition, work placement advisors and career advisors help students to choose an appropriate course or to find a suitable placement or profession. At secondary TVET level, every Regional Training Center (ROC) has a central student service center with career guidance specialists. Guidance is also done by teachers, and portfolio systems are used to enable students to record the development of their skills. Since 2012, in the context of tackling skill shortages in technical sectors, VET institutions receive additional support including career guidance measures.

Promotion of Career-Management Skills in TVET

In Finland, according to legislation a student attending TVET schools is entitled to receive personal and other necessary counseling during studies. Career guidance is part of the curriculum (separate classes and integration into other instruction) combined with study visits and learning at the workplace. Each TVET school has to allocate a sufficient amount of time and personnel to reach the guidance objectives (Onnismaa & Viljamaa, 1999). In particular, the acquisition of career-management skills is being promoted in TVET secondary level education in all vocational subjects (ELGPN, 2012). The qualifications of staff in charge of guidance are defined by national legislation. Some research and development projects advocate a multiprofessional approach in career guidance and stress the important role of regional/local guidance networks (Nykaenen, Karjalainen, & Poeylioe, 2007).

Donor-supported Initiatives in TVET

Many of the existing or emerging initiatives where governments or donors put deliberate attention on career guidance development in the TVET sector (either prior to or within TVET) are the result of a national skills agenda to improve and promote the TVET system, ultimately linking it to enhanced competitiveness and growth of the economy. In low- and middle-income countries, emerging initiatives in career guidance linked to TVET are often stimulated or coupled with support from international or bilateral donors. Whereas some examples are already described (e.g., Kyrgyzstan, Egypt), other such promising examples from Georgia, Chile, Serbia, Kosovo, and the former Yugoslav Republic of Macedonia are listed in Table 15.2.

While donor-funded projects are often the only way to innovate or introduce career guidance in a context of scarce resources in low- and middle-income countries, its implementation poses a number of challenges, particularly with regard to sustainability. Practice shows that local ownership, local capacities, and embeddedness in wider national strategies are integral to the survival of projects as well as for further systemic development of career guidance. In the end, an approach which fosters demand, rather than supply-driven career guidance provision, and a *homegrown* approach which aims to fit to the size and sociocultural circumstances of a country will be more likely to be successful both prior to TVET and within TVET.

Table 15.2 Examples of emerging career guidance initiatives in TVET settings in low- and middle-income countries

Career consultants in VET Centers. In Georgia, the Ministry of Education (MoE) decided to introduce a full-time career consultant in each of the VET Centers in the context of a rationalization process of VET schools. The MoE opted for a pragmatic approach by training a number of teachers and young professionals (psychologists) in cooperation with a Georgian NGO (Foundation for Development of Human Resources). In 2008, the first career consultants started to deliver a variety of services to VET students, including selection of students for their VET Centers, career information, and work experience placements. They are also supposed to provide professional diagnostic interventions and group and individual consultations as well as to establish partnerships with local enterprises and business (Zelloth, 2009)

Career centers in VET schools. In the former Yugoslav Republic of Macedonia, a USAID-funded project (2005–2007) established Career Centers in all 57 TVET schools (2005–2007). The center consists of a meeting room assigned for students for a few hours per day for the purpose of career development activities. It is equipped with printed and audio/video materials and run by the VET student organization in cooperation with a school teacher in his/her voluntary role as career coordinator. Instructional guides and manuals have been developed and training is provided in job-searching techniques, curriculum vitae (CV) and interview preparation, and public speaking (Zelloth, 2009)

Supervised occupational experience programs (SOE). Combined with the Career Center approach in the former Yugoslav Republic of Macedonia, one form of SOE, the Exploratory SOE, is designed primarily to help students to become aware of possible careers in specific clusters. Examples of exploratory SOE activities might include observing workers and becoming familiar with their tasks and responsibilities. Records are kept by the students. As another form of SOE, Real Firms were established in some VET schools that received a startup grant for equipment and machines in case their business plan was approved. Firms produce goods or services for the local market and students gain work-based learning and entrepreneurship experience within this school-based firm (Zelloth, 2009)

Networks of school counselors and Web-based career information system. The Califica program in Chile (2002–2005), supported by the World Bank, aimed to strengthen articulation between grades 11 and 12 of TVET secondary and postsecondary TVET, including their links with the labor market. It included components on career guidance to develop a new Web-based career information system and support for strengthening career guidance by school counselors and in employment offices. Networks of school counselors from schools and adult education centers were formed, and plans were developed on how to make the best use of the career information system being developed by the program (ILO, 2006)

Model for career guidance in TVET. In the framework of an EU-financed VET Reform Program in Serbia, a model for Career Guidance and Counseling in secondary vocational schools was developed in order to advance and promote TVET. Career guidance is seen as a systemic and institutional innovation within TVET which better connects schools and the world of work and involves social partners and local communities. The first pilots, started in 2005 in selected food processing and agricultural TVET schools, served as precursor of a TVET Career Guidance Center network (Zelloth, 2010b). Teachers who have gone through training on career guidance are now the basic resource for further development (Secibovic, 2005), and owing to these initiatives, there are an increasing number of expert associates from primary and secondary schools who engage in information provision and career guidance in an organized manner (Government of Serbia, 2010)

Girl's day. As a joint activity of the Ministry of Education, Science and Technology in Kosovo, the Ministry of Culture, Youth and Sports, and two donor projects assisted by GTZ (*Gesellschaft fuer Technische Zusammenarbeit*) from Germany, the first Girl's Day took place in 2008 (Renewal of the Vocational Education and Training in Kosovo, Empowerment and Development of Youth in Kosovo). The program aims at tackling gender stereotypes in choosing TVET fields or an occupation. Around 1,200 young girls from lower- and upper-secondary schools from 12 municipalities participated in this activity which offered visits and job shadowing in various producing companies as well as visits to workshops of TVET schools to get familiarized with technical professions untypical for women (Zelloth, 2008)

New Concepts and Viewpoints: Charting New Directions

The relationship between TVET and career guidance has been traditionally ambiguous and not very clear-cut. Career guidance services often remain underdeveloped in the TVET sector though the situation has seemed to improve over the recent past. Various barriers and stereotypes regarding TVET careers impact the educational and occupational choices of individuals in both developed and developing countries. This has also had an impact on career guidance provision itself. Career guidance has come under attack for having lost its impartiality and of being biased in favor of general and academic education pathways and careers. Some of the latest research on equality and diversity in career guidance confirms such a view. Hutchinson, Rolfe, Moore, Bysshe, and Bentley (2011) have highlighted, for example, that stereotypical information and guidance can limit young people's options and aspirations at an early age, and when career advice reinforces traditional choices, young people may be left with limited information on the advantages of nontraditional routes.

A major challenge for forging a relationship between TVET and career guidance will be for career guidance to cross its comfort zone and advise against societal mainstream options, perceptions, and stereotypes. This would mean becoming more TVET sensitive and TVET friendly and thereby providing more comprehensive information and advice regarding TVET opportunities. In fact, career guidance has to tackle a double bias risk: on the one hand, the negative societal perception of TVET, and on the other hand, the academic background of its own guidance practitioners. Another possibly beneficial strategy is the shift in career guidance practice from the old psychological paradigm of guidance to the new pedagogical or hybrid paradigm. As the new paradigm has a closer affinity to the world of work, career guidance is more likely to include TVET.

If these challenges are negotiated well, and assuming that a critical mass of quality career guidance provision is in place to achieve impact, career guidance can make important contributions to raise the social attractiveness of TVET (Zelloth, 2010c). In this context, Watts' (2009) distinction between career guidance *prior* to TVET and career guidance *within* TVET is useful, although career guidance *post*-TVET also needs to be considered. Certainly, the provision prior to TVET is crucially important as the foundations are laid and fundamental choices are being made during this stage of career development. If career guidance services prior to TVET are not sufficiently developed, the entry

into TVET is likely to be limited. If career guidance services within TVET are not developed or even missing, the risk is high that TVET is implemented less efficiently and that learning as well as mobility in TVET is inadequately supported. This can have a negative impact on both the quality of learning outcomes and the transition from TVET to work. The double role that career guidance can play as a change agent to improve current TVET supply and as an eye-opener to stimulate TVET demand is not to be underestimated.

However, healthy relationships are never one-way streets and always based on a proper dialogue. Mutual efforts are needed to improve the current situation. While career guidance needs to become more TVET sensitive, TVET systems need to better consider, involve, and integrate career guidance. Awareness needs to be raised among TVET actors on the vital functions career guidance can have to improve efficiency as well as the attractiveness of TVET. At the analytical level, for example, national or international reviews of TVET policies and systems need to include the career guidance dimension. Some of the latest examples are the UNESCO guidelines for TVET policy reviews and the ETF analytical framework of the Torino Process in TVET for EU-neighboring countries. Reports and documents such as these offer guidelines on how to integrate career guidance in TVET issues. In turn, future career guidance reviews, drawing on the earlier OECD (2002) questionnaire and its modified versions (Sultana & Watts, 2007; Watts & Fretwell, 2004), need to take into account TVET needs and strengthen links between career guidance and TVET. At the implementation level, one effective way is to integrate career guidance within wider reforms in TVET. For example, a TVET or apprenticeship reform project could include the development of a career information system and the training of teachers and in-company trainers with career guidance functions. Curriculum reform in TVET could go hand in hand with the piloting or introduction of career education or career-management skills (Zelloth, 2011b). In any case, TVET systems should choose the right mix among the possible career guidance models and intervention modalities (see Table 15.1).

Policymakers and policy designers in both TVET and career guidance are well advised to look at the manifold interfaces between the two areas and to pay special attention to the various key transitions related to TVET. Another recommendation is to ensure translation from policy into practice and to foster coordinated pilots and innovation to avoid the proliferation of fragmented initiatives.

Given the complexity of TVET systems, improved internal cooperation and networking is crucial. Experience shows that in many countries, existing services and initiatives in guidance are not well connected and even communication with each other is often lacking. This concerns services within and prior to TVET and within and post-TVET. Given the breadth of the topic and the many actors involved in TVET and career guidance, the issue of fostering national dialogue and cooperation to develop a shared vision, strategy, and action plan is essential for success. Viable platforms could also help to sustain donor-supported innovations once projects expire, and they could play a pivotal role in fostering homegrown career guidance development in TVET.

References

Achtenhagen, F., & Grubb, W. N. (2001). Vocational and occupational education: Pedagogical complexity, institutional diversity. In V. Richardson (Ed.), *Handbook of research in teaching* (4th ed., pp. 604–639). Washington, DC: American Educational Research Association.

Akkok, F., & Zelloth, H. (2009). *Lifelong guidance: A feasible policy option for Turkey* (Working document). Turin, Italy: European Training Foundation.

Asian Development Bank. (2010). *Plan on career guidance and awareness campaign among students and their parents* (Project document of the project vocational education and skills development in Kyrgyzstan). Bishkek, Kyrgyzstan: Author.

Badawi, A. A. (2006). *Career guidance in the MEDA region: Country report Egypt*. Turin, Italy: European Training Foundation.

Bosch, G., & Charest, J. (Eds.). (2010). *Vocational training: International perspectives* (pp. 1–26). New York, NY: Routledge.

Cedefop. (2011). *Guidance supporting Europe's aspiring entrepreneurs. Policy and practice to harness future potential* (Research Paper No. 14). Luxembourg, Luxembourg: Publications Office of the European Union.

City and Guilds. (2012). *The economic value of apprenticeships*. London, UK: Author.

ELGPN. (2012). *Lifelong guidance policy development: A European resource kit*. Jyvaskyla, Finland: Author.

European Commission. (2010). *A new impetus for European cooperation in vocational education and training to support the Europe 2020 strategy* (Communication from the Commission to the European Parliament, the Council, the European Economic and Social Committee and the Committee of Regions COM(2010) 296/3). Brussels, Belgium: Author.

European Training Foundation. (2011). *The Torino process. Evidence-based policy making for vocational education and training*. Turin, Italy: Author.

European Union Council. (2004). *Resolution of the council and of the representatives of the member states meeting within the council on strengthening policies, systems and practices in the field of guidance throughout life in Europe*. Brussels, Belgium: Council of the European Union.

European Union Council. (2008). *Council resolution on better integrating lifelong guidance into lifelong learning strategies*. Brussels, Belgium: Council of the European Union.

Gasskov, V. (2000). *Managing vocational training systems. A handbook for senior administrators*. Geneva, Switzerland: ILO.

Government of Sri Lanka. (2011). *National human resources and employment policies* (First Draft). Sri Lanka: Secretariat for Senior Ministers, Government of Sri Lanka.

Government of the Republic of Serbia. (2010). *Career guidance and counselling strategy for the Republic of Serbia*. Pursuant to Art. 45, Item 1 of the Law on Government (Official Journal of the Republic of Serbia, Belgrade), Nos. 55/05, 71/05-amendment, 101/07 and 65/08.

Hoxte, H. (2002). Introduction. Counselling and guidance: International perspectives. In *Technical and vocational education and training in the 21st century. New roles and challenges for guidance and counselling*. Paris: UNESCO.

Hughes, D., & Gration, G. (2009). *Literature review of research on the impact of careers and guidance-related interventions*. Berkshire, UK: DMH Associates and CfBT Education Trust.

Hutchinson, J., Rolfe, H., Moore, R., Bysshe, S., & Bentley, K. (2011). *All things being equal? Equality and diversity in careers education, information, advice and guidance* (Research Report No. 71). Manchester, UK: Equality and Human Rights Commission.

ILO. (2006). *Career guidance: A resource handbook for low and middle income countries*. Geneva, Switzerland: Author.

Jarvis, P. (2003). *Career information + career management skills. Keys to a great career, and a great life.* Ottawa, ON, Canada: National Life/Work Centre.

Jenschke, B., Schober, K., & Fruebing, J. (2011). *Career guidance in the life course: Structures and services in Germany.* Berlin, Germany: National Career Guidance Forum in Education, Career and Employment.

Mann, A. (2012a). *Work experience: Impact and delivery: Insights from the evidence.* London, UK: Education and Employers Task Force.

Mann, A. (2012b). *It's who you meet: Why employer contacts at school make a difference to the employment prospects of young adults.* London, UK: Education and Employers Task Force.

National Institute for Educational Policy Research. (2007). *From school to work: Contemporary TVET regional experiences* (Final Report). Tokyo, Japan: Author.

National Institute of Adult Continuing Education. (2012). *The apprentices' journey: Stories of nominees for the adult apprentice of the year award, adult learner's week.* Leicester, UK: Author.

National Task Force. (2010). *Proposal for introducing career guidance in Egypt. The need for a strategic and integrated approach to career guidance development.* Cairo, Egypt: National Task Force on Career Guidance in Egypt.

NCVER. (2009). *Governance and architecture of Australia's VET sector* (Report Prepared for Skills Australia). Australia: National Centre for Vocational Education Research (NCVER).

Nykaenen, S., Karjalainen, M., & Poeylioe, L. (2007). *The development of a guidance service system in vocational education and training.* Jyväskylä, Finland: Institute for Educational Research, University of Jyvaskyla.

OECD. (2002). *OECD review of career guidance policies. Country note, Austria.* Paris, France: Author.

OECD. (2004a). *Career guidance and public policy: Bridging the gap.* Paris, France: Author.

OECD. (2004b). *Career guidance: A handbook for policy makers.* Paris, France: Author.

OECD. (2010). *Learning for jobs* (Synthesis report of the OECD Reviews of Vocational Education and Training). Paris, France: Author.

Onnismaa, J., & Viljamaa, H. (Eds.). (1999). *Guidance and counselling in Finland: Best practices and current policy issues.* Helsinki, Finland: National Board of Education.

Prisma Marketing and Communication. (2010). *E-TVET public awareness campaign, secondary research study.* Amman, Jordan: E-TVET Council.

Rauner, F. (2009). Differences in the organisation of apprenticeship in Europe: Findings of a comparative evaluation study. In F. Rauner, E. Smith, U. Hauschildt, & H. Zelloth (Eds.), *Innovative apprenticeships. Promoting successful school-to-work-transitions* (pp. 233–237). Berlin, Germany: LIT Verlag.

Rauner, F., & Smith, E. (Eds.). (2009). Rediscovering apprenticeship. Research findings of the international network on innovative apprenticeship. In *UNESCO-UNEVOC Book Series: Vol. 11: Technical and vocational education and training.* New York, NY: Springer.

Secibovic, R. (2005). *A model of career guidance and counselling for vocational education and training in Serbia.* Belgrade, Serbia: Belgrade Open School.

Shepherd, J. (2011, September). One in four young people get no careers advice, survey shows. *The Guardian.* Retrieved from http://www.guardian.co.uk/education/2011/sep/20/careers-advice-survey

Sultana, R. G. (2003). *Review of career guidance policies in 11 acceding and candidate countries: A synthesis report.* Luxembourg, Luxembourg: European Training Foundation (ETF), Office for Official Publications of the European Communities.

Sultana, R. G. (2004). *Guidance policies in the knowledge society: Trends, challenges and responses across Europe: A synthesis report.* Luxembourg, Luxembourg: Cedefop, Office for Official Publications of the European Communities.

Sultana, R. G. (2006). *Educating students for labour market needs. A guidebook for vocational school directors.* Warsaw, Poland: ECORYS.

Sultana, R. G., & Watts, A. G. (2007). *Career guidance in the Mediterranean region.* Turin, Italy: European Training Foundation.

Sultana, R. G., & Watts, A. G. (2008). Career guidance in the Middle East and North Africa. *International Journal for Educational and Vocational Guidance, 8*(1), 19–34.

Super, D. E. (1957). *The psychology of careers. An introduction to vocational development.* New York, NY: Harper and Row.

Sweet, R. (2006). *Career guidance in the Western Balkans Region* (ETF working document). Turin, Italy: European Training Foundation.

Sweet, R., & Zelloth, H. (2009). We need them, they need us: Work-based learning programmes for young people in the Mediterranean region. In Rediscovering apprenticeship: Research findings of the international network on innovative apprenticeship. In *UNESCO-UNEVOC Book Series: Vol. 11. Technical and vocational education and training* (pp. 103–112). New York, NY: Springer.

UNESCO. (2001). Revised recommendation concerning technical and vocational education. In *Normative instruments concerning technical and vocational education* (p. 7). Paris: Author.

UNESCO. (2002). *Technical and vocational education and training in the 21st century. New roles and challenges for guidance and counselling.* Paris, France: Author.

UNESCO. (2010). *Guidelines for TVET policy review* (Draft). Paris, France: Author.

Van Deursen, P., & Jansen, M. (Eds.). (2006). *Career guidance in the Netherlands.* 's-Hertogenbosch, The Netherlands: Euroguidance Netherlands.

Watts, A. G. (2009). *The relationship of career guidance to VET* (Background document for the OECD reviews of vocational education and training). Paris, France: OECD.

Watts, A. G. (2011). *Career guidance and post-secondary vocational education and training* (A paper prepared for the OECD Review of Post-Secondary Vocational Education and Training, Skills Beyond School). Paris, France: OECD.

Watts, A. G., & Fretwell, D. (2004). *Public policies for career development. Case studies and emerging issues for designing career information and guidance systems in developing and transition economies.* Washington, DC: World Bank.

Zelloth, H. (2008). *Career guidance policy and practice in Kosovo. Review of progress and feasibility of future intervention* (ETF working document). Turin, Italy: European Training Foundation.

Zelloth, H. (2009). *In demand: Career guidance in EU neighbouring countries.* Luxembourg, Luxembourg: Office for Official Publications of the European Communities.

Zelloth, H. (2010a). *Preliminary mapping of apprenticeship supply in 29 EU neighboring countries* (Draft working document presented to a Delegation of EU Parliamentarians) Turin, Italy: European Training Foundation.

Zelloth, H. (2010b). *Career guidance development trends in Serbia* (ETF working document). Turin, Italy: European Training Foundation.

Zelloth, H. (2010c, November). *Career guidance and attractiveness of TVET.* Paper presented at the regional GTZ conference for Arab countries, Beirut, Lebanon.

Zelloth, H. (2011a). *The way forward in career guidance development in Jordan. A policy paper* (ETF working document prepared for the E-TVET Council and the National Human Resource Development Centre [NCHRD]). Amman, Jordan: E-TVET Council.

Zelloth, H. (2011b). Career guidance in ETF partner countries: A missing link in the transition from education to the labour market (ETF policy brief). *Inform, 6,* 2.

Zelloth, H. (2011c). *Vocational education and training (VET) policies and systems in the ENPI East Region: Cross-country analysis* (Torino Process Regional Report). Turin, Italy: European Training Foundation.

Zelloth, H. (2012). No choice—No guidance ? The rising demand for career guidance in EU neighbouring countries and its potential implications for apprenticeships. In L. Deitmar, U. Hauschildt, F. Rauner, & H. Zelloth (Eds.), *Technical and vocational education training: Issues, concerns and prospects series: Vol. 18. The architecture of innovative apprenticeship* (pp. 69–87). Dordrecht, The Netherlands: Springer.

Second Career: An Eventual Need in Today's World

16

Archana Jain

Introduction

The propensity to work is a natural human quality. Until recently, pursuing a career meant building one's career within the purview of a particular occupational area. Indeed for many, career development meant spending the better part of one's life working faithfully for a particular company. This has changed quite profoundly. Indeed the intransience of a career has been much challenged by the dramatic changes we see in the modern labor market. It is this aspect of career development, the *second career* that I set out to examine in this chapter. While I draw primarily upon examples and illustrations from career development in the Indian context, the concepts discussed have relevance to a wide range of other contexts.

Choosing the "right vocation" is one of the most important tasks faced by an individual during early and late adolescence. Most educational systems are designed such that they are broad-based during the early years, requiring students to study all subjects and begin to narrow at higher grades, and students *specialize* as their education progresses. In India, for example, students are expected to specialize by making choices of subject groups (science, humanities, commerce,

or vocational subjects) on the basis of their interest and aptitude. These choices are important decisions since they have implications for the future educational and career options available to the student. A student who has taken the commerce stream for higher secondary studies in India, for example, would not be able to later switch to biotechnology, since this is a career option that requires the student to have studied science, with biology at the higher secondary stage. A further issue to be noted is that the point at which these decisions are expected varies across systems. In most countries, it is around the age of 15–17 years.

The critical role that career guidance and counseling could play in the life of the young person is obvious. Yet, the extent to which students have access to information and guidance could vary depending on their socioeconomic status, place of residence, and culture. Professional career guidance services are not easily available, and when available, the extent to which they are accessed varies (e.g., Arulmani & Nag-Arulmani, 2004). In many cases, the services are not accessed at all (e.g., Bakshi, 2011), and vocational choices are solely based on parental aspirations or marks obtained by the students. For example, Binita (pseudonyms have been used to preserve confidentiality), an Indian adolescent girl had to choose her subject stream after her tenth grade examination results were declared. When she was asked what she was planning to do, she promptly replied that the decision would depend on her marks: if she got

A. Jain (✉)
SVT College of Home Science, SNDT Women's University, Mumbai, India
e-mail: jainarchanas@yahoo.co.in

more than 95 %, she would take up medicine; if between 90 and 95 %, then it would be engineering; and anything less than 90 % would leave her "no choice" other than commerce. Although Binita could have, she had not accessed professional career guidance support as she felt that what mattered were her marks and not her personal preferences. Awareness about the importance of professional career guidance services and the possible implications for the overall well-being of the individual are low both among students and their parents. Some parents and children consider career guidance services to be a one-time interaction needed just before the child needs to choose educational streams. Take the case of Vijay, a young boy aged 16 years from a middle-class family living in Chennai, a large city in south India, who used to participate in all the academic and extracurricular activities at school. He displayed exceptional talent for using space and color creatively. Vijay was also an expert in repairing gadgets; he could repair almost anything and spontaneously understood the functioning of most household appliances. Family members and well-wishers were divided in their opinion as to whether Vijay should take up interior designing or computer engineering. Vijay needed to choose his educational stream by the time he finished his tenth grade. Making this decision at the age of 16 years was a challenge for him. Was he ready for it? Was it really fair to force him to make such a momentous decision so early in his life? Moreover, what was the guarantee that the decision made would be the right one? The point that emerges is that educational systems and economic and social factors require the individual to commit to a certain career path, most often, at a stage in life when he or she is perhaps not mature or ready to make this life commitment. Furthermore, adolescence is a time for self-discovery, and individuals are likely to show changes in their interests and disposition as they mature and have varied experiences. Typically, the adolescent displays interest in pursuing many different activities and exploring aptitudes in more than one area. Biological factors and environmental influences work together, all across the life span, to undergird an

individual's development (e.g., McCrae & Costa, 2003). Of particular relevance to the argument being made in this chapter is the one made by Donald Super (Super 1990) when he revised his life stage model of career development and took the position that a person may recycle through life stages at transition points in the course of development. This implies that an individual may choose a career, work in it for some time, and at significant points in time such as middle adulthood, the person may explore a new career and seek to be established in this newly discovered area of work. The contemporary world of work is such that most individuals can expect to have to change careers during their work life. Bakshi (2011), in her research on adults in the age range of 18–75 years working in Mumbai (India), found that almost all of them had made major career-related decisions which included changing their careers, jobs, departments, or their type of business (i.e., entrepreneurial activity). This dispels the myth that there is only "one right" career choice (Lemme, 1999; Safaye, 2002). Going back to the example of Vijay, he could have chosen to pursue both his interests. He could have perhaps started with engineering as his primary career and continued to engage in interior designing as a serious hobby. Given his interest in design, he could have obtained the necessary qualification at a later stage and shifted to a career in design. The point being made here is that committing one's life to a single career and expecting that career to be the vehicle to realize one's aspirations is perhaps a characteristic of career development that is an artifact of the past. Today, career development by its very nature requires flexibility and adaptability to successfully negotiate a volatile and ever-changing labor market.

Based on these observations, the term *second careers* is taken in this writing to symbolize the willingness to change and switch adroitly from one pathway to another, both to realize the multiple facets of one's self as well as to actualize one's aspirations in an ongoing manner. Indeed, second career means openness to the multiple possibilities that are available to a participant in today's labor market. As described in the next

section, contemporary theories of human development highlight that possibilities for change,
engagement, and re-engagement are available
all through one's life.

Developmental View of Career Guidance and Counseling

Considering the fact that work plays a significant
role in identity formation, the need to focus on
the individual's development becomes imperative. Life-career development has been described
as self-development over the life span through
the integration of roles, settings, and events in a
person's life (Gysbers & Moore, 1987). The purpose of guidance is to help individuals identify
their needs, assess their potentials, and develop
and revise life goals that are individually
satisfying and socially desirable (Gupta, 2003).

Development is viewed as multidimensional
and lifelong (Baltes, 1987). The willingness to
examine change or flexibility beyond adolescence defines a life span approach (Baltes,
1987). An central concept of the life span perspective is *plasticity* (Baltes, Lindenberger &
Staudinger, 2006). In the developmental view,
there is acknowledgement that growth and
change in an individual is an ongoing process
and that needs alter over time. Career guidance
and counseling professionals with a developmental view recognize the importance of paying
more attention to the individual's developmental
needs as opposed to only job demands. Developmentally oriented career guidance and
counseling focuses on meeting not only the current needs of the individual but also the future
needs. Safaye (2002) has pointed out that it is
important to move away from a narrow preoccupation with employment and earning a living to
focusing on life goals. As individuals progress
into adulthood their aspirations from life undergo
changes. During young adulthood the focus may
be on achieving success. By middle adulthood
optimizing one's potential may gain significance,
and by late adulthood the goals may turn towards
serving others. Sharma (2005) has categorized
life goals in the following manner: achieving

personal satisfaction, self-realization, and
serving others. Achieving personal satisfaction
emphasizes meeting personal targets of success
or growth. Here, the individual would like to
have the freedom to maintain an occupation that
is suited to his or her needs as well as seek a
career transition if and when such a need arises.
For example, a sportsperson may not be satisfied
with being a leading player in his/her area of
sport at the state level but may continue to aspire
to the top position at the national or international
level. Self-realization involves becoming aware
of one's abilities and limitations, working on
one's weaknesses, and acquiring skills that lead
to better vocational opportunities. For some
workers, the career goal may be to enhance
their skills and self-actualize. For example, a
music composer's goal could be to make increasingly melodious compositions. Serving others
involves acquiring the skills of being able to
meet the needs of others. For such workers, the
joy would be in providing assistance or support
to others. For example, a lawyer may decide to
quit practicing law and start a nongovernmental
organization (NGO) for street children. Ebner,
Freund, and Baltes (2006) found that younger
adults showed, on an average, a stronger orientation towards growth than towards maintenance or
prevention of loss. Middle-aged adults showed
an increase in the orientation towards maintenance and prevention of loss but still reported a
primary focus on growth. Thus, shifts in the
manner in which career satisfies needs across
the life span must be acknowledged to ensure
overall well-being among adult workers throughout their life span.

Second Career: An Inevitable Need in Today's World

Gibson and Mitchell (1981) have stated that
"There is an increasing possibility that most
individuals will have several significant careers
over the life span of their life's work" (p. 213).
Such changes may be made out of choice or due
to necessity. The future of one's career need
not be predicted necessarily by one's present

occupation. This change in careers, termed as a second career in this chapter, has been theoretically associated with a career crisis during middle adulthood (e.g., Rice, 1986). However, the nature of the labor market today is such that career changes need not be the result of a crisis. In fact, unlike earlier times, the world of work today offers possibilities that allow for the expression of different aspects of oneself. Yet, when adults contemplate changing their career, they are usually discouraged by the larger society. They are instead encouraged and expected to show some stability in their decisions. Asha, a young girl aged 25 years from a middle-class family living in Mumbai (India), graduated in early childhood education with the idea of pursuing a career that focused on young children. After graduating in early childhood education, Asha worked for about 5 years as a nursery school teacher; however, she lost interest in her job and then chose to make a career shift and take up a job in a fashion boutique. Most of her teachers were upset and wondered how she could take up "such a job" when she was so good with children. Their general opinion was that Asha was wasting her time and talent. Asha's parents felt that she was confused and not serious about her career. As a result, Asha ended up feeling guilty for wanting to work in a field for which she had not originally planned or qualified. She also began to feel that probably something was wrong with her. Asha needed someone to reassure her that it was alright to make a change in her career choice. Sharma (2005) has stated that "Life goals develop slowly and may be revised from time to time. Its important elements begin to appear during adolescence, with the development of a philosophy of life" (p. 203). Communicating to the client that it is important to recognize a job as not an end in itself but merely a means to a larger and more important life goal becomes imperative. It is also vital as career guidance professionals that we help clients understand why and when such career shifts occur and how to prepare for them.

Rohit, a young man aged 30 years from a middle-class family living in Bangalore, a large city in South India known for its information technology infrastructure, graduated in computer engineering and mastered a highly specialized aspect of programming. He took up a job with a good salary in a leading information technology company. However, due to rapid changes in technology, the demand for these specialized skills declined. Rohit's knowledge and skills now became redundant, and he was at risk of losing his job. At that point it became very difficult for Rohit to cope with this crisis as he had spent nearly 10 years specializing in one field. The point to be noted is that he had been preparing for just one career and was unprepared for any change. Rohit lost his job and experienced extreme frustration. More and more members of the contemporary workforce are likely to experience similar career crises and would be required to consider career shifts, sometimes even in their early adulthood.

Second Career in Early Adulthood

Safaye (2002) has pointed out that "We are living in a highly complex and rapidly changing world of work. There are changing requirements in industrial jobs, and altered market conditions for professional manpower" (p. 12). Most adults may need to make adjustments and consider variations in their career plan in their early adulthood years. According to the US Bureau of Labor Statistics, the typical American worker's tenure with his or her current employer was 4.1 years in 2008 (Bialik, 2010). The world of work has many dimensions, and there are ongoing changes in one or more of these dimensions at any given time. There is a need to understand the changes in each of these dimensions and their implications for the individual worker, if the career guidance services provided are to be relevant to their needs. As career guidance professionals we need to know which aspects in the world of work are changing. Some of these changes are discussed as follows.

Changes in the Nature of Work

A variety of forces working together have led to dramatic changes in the nature of work requiring (sometimes forcing) individuals to shift careers from time to time, to match changing economic trends and emerging occupational opportunities. Individuals working in agriculture-based occupations could experience financial losses due to unpredictable climatic conditions and lack of resources. This scenario could be typical of developing countries whose economies are largely agrarian. Take the example of Thukaram, aged 33 years, from Devas, a village in Madhya Pradesh, India, who during his adolescent years worked as a farmer along with his father on their 4 acre farm. Thukaram's father borrowed a large sum of money to buy good quality seeds and advanced equipments to enhance their crop production. However, due to reversals in climatic conditions, the family faced heavy losses and could not repay the loans. He lost his traditional family occupation. Many other adults like him in his village also had to give up their traditional occupations such as cloth weaving and toy making due to stiff global competition. These conditions coupled with the lure of "better paying" jobs have induced many of them to give up their professions and to take up jobs in factories. Changes such as these have had a significant impact on the nature of work as the individuals move from working independently and engaging in traditional occupations to working in factories or industries. Loss of traditional occupations may also force many adults to migrate to urban areas in search of better occupations. However, many of these individuals are neither aware of nor prepared for urban occupations nor are they aware of how they could adapt their traditional occupations and make their living.

Until recently, an adult could afford to work in a small company to earn a living and yet enjoy adequate job security. Today, the forces of globalization and increasing technological advancements in the world of work are affecting the survival of such companies. Small-scale industries have to face stiff competition from multinationals, due to which many of them face difficulties in sustaining their competitiveness in the market (Suresh & Shashidhar, 2007). As a result, retrenchment and job loss in such organizations have become common. Multinational firms provide higher wages and better working conditions than their local counterparts (Brown, Deardorff, & Stern, 2003). Therefore, workers seek jobs in multinational firms. However, their lack of awareness of the nature of work and job demands in these firms lead to adjustment problems (e.g., Upadhya & Vasavi, 2006).

Economic changes have led, around the world, to a decrease in the manufacturing industry (e.g., Steindel, 2004) and an increase in the proportion of the population working in the service sector (e.g., Ganz, 2005). However, the service sector demands highly specialized training along with a continuous updating of skills. Lemme (1999) has stated that "Work is becoming increasingly cognitive and decreasingly physical" (p. 301). The kinds of jobs being created today require higher skill levels than before. Here is another example. Hemant, aged 30 years from a socioeconomically disadvantaged family living in Nasik, a small city in India, worked as a packer in a pharmaceutical company. He was at risk of being retrenched when the company imported new machinery to do the packing. He was offered a chance to save his job by shifting to another occupational area and taking up the responsibility of quality check and control. But for that, he needed to be computer literate, which he was not. Fortunately for Hemant, his company provided an in-service training facility to all its employees. Hemant underwent training in the use of computers for the operation of machinery and continued to work in the same company. All companies may not have such services, and reaching out to help people like Hemant is a difficult task. It is important for career guidance professionals to regularly update themselves about changes in market trends and career opportunities in order to effectively address the felt needs of the contemporary worker.

Changes in the Work Environment

The work environment is constantly changing and that too at a rapid pace. Vembu (2008) has stated that stress at the workplace can lead to attrition, and factors at the workplace such as long working hours, differences in the timings of work to suit international clients, demanding customers, and imposing bosses can lead to stress. Workers frequently experience changes in their work environment, which may not be conducive to their personal well-being, and they may thus develop the need to look for a second career. Decisions about which career to choose from available options and analyzing the stability and security of available careers can be a daunting task.

Additionally, job-related skills today require a greater use of interpersonal skills such as teamwork, listening, negotiating, reasoning, and nurturing: skills not necessarily honed by all (Mannering, 2002). Organizational restructuring and issues of hierarchy can create psychological stress and feelings of discontent among the workers. Most organizations remain more or less bureaucratic, ignoring human needs and values (Schultz & Sydney, 1994). The aim of providing personal guidance and counseling at most workplaces is to give the worker the motivation to stay and simultaneously get the maximum benefit from his or her abilities. In reality, workers are offered attractive pay packages, facilities, and perquisites as long as they serve the employer's needs. The worker in turn gets caught up with earning a living and satisfying the boss, and personal needs could be sidetracked.

Traditionally career development was pegged as a linear sequence of "education-work-retirement." Individuals got promoted on the basis of their seniority. Today, however, this simple linear arrangement has given way to the necessity of consciously fostering a reciprocal interaction between job tasks and skill acquisition. Lifelong learning has become essential for successful career development. Seniority-oriented promotion has almost entirely been replaced by performance-based advancement. A major shift required of the contemporary worker is the ability to recognize the importance of lifelong education and teamwork (Tractenberg, Streumer, & Zolingen, 2002). Traditional conceptions of work timings have also undergone dramatic changes. With the infusion of advanced information and communication technologies into the workplace, most adults today are working in a virtual world. Today in certain work

environments a worker may come on duty at midnight because his/her collaborators live in a different time zone and begin their work at 10 in the morning. As a result it is common today for workers from different parts of the globe to enter a virtual work space, interact with each other across time zones, and complete job tasks without ever meeting each other (Tractenberg et al., 2002). Communication across time and distance are a reality of today's work environment.

Career guidance professionals can play a very important role in helping adults prepare for impending challenges emerging from the constant changes in the work environment. Affiliating with employers and providing guidance services in the form of workshops, seminars, and talks is one of the ways of meeting the needs of the employer and employee.

Changes in the Individual's Needs

As the individual moves from one stage of life to another, his or her developmental tasks and needs change, causing changes in what he or she expects from work and career. Arulmani, Bakshi, Flederman, and Watts (2011) have stated that "Career development and related needs are shaped out of differences that characterize (a) the person; (b) the contexts, and very importantly; (c) the transactions of the person-in-contexts" (p. 64). When young adults take up their first job, they are often single, have fewer responsibilities, and they may have no difficulties with work involving a large amount of travelling and erratic schedules. At this stage, perhaps these work conditions are even welcomed by them and taken as an opportunity to see the world and have an exciting career. However, once commitments are made to a partner and/or to an elderly parent who needs caregiving, the need to be around the family and to have some amount of predictability regarding work schedules increases. Individuals may now be less motivated to engage in work tasks that require extensive travelling or working overtime. Women, after marriage, with the responsibilities of young children and running a home may want to work part time. With the passage of time and changing life roles, jobs that were earlier considered as attractive or satisfactory may be perceived by the individual as unfavorable. Individuals may need to make changes in their career to ensure that their needs are met.

At the beginning of a career, the individual may have certain expectations of the job that he or she has taken up. It is not unusual, however, that when the individual comes face-to-face with reality, he or she may experience disillusionment. Vrutika, a young girl aged 20 years from a middle-class family living in New Delhi, India, was very excited about taking up a job as an airhostess with an international airline. She thought she would get to roam the world, dress smartly, and meet lots of interesting people. In a few months, Vrutika grew tired of all the travelling. She had hardly seen any of the countries she had flown to and had barely been able to talk or get to know the travelers. She soon lost interest in her job and grew very unhappy with her work situation. Realizing she had made an unsuitable choice for herself, she quit the job and started working in a hotel as a front desk operator. The reason for a career change may vary from individual to individual, yet the reality is that the need for a career change is a common experience among adults today.

The Importance of Timely Intervention

Work is one of the most time consuming, significant, and identity-defining aspects of adult life (Bee, 1996). On an average, an individual spends about 8–10 hours per day at his or her workplace. Consequently, a major part of one's lifetime is spent at work, and any disturbance in it has an impact on one's life overall. Thus, if the world of work is constantly changing, there is an urgent need to offer career guidance and counseling to an adult after career entry as well. Along with the annual performance assessments, employers must make the services of career guidance professionals available on a regular basis for the benefit of their employees.

Work can mean a lot more than economic gain. For some, it is an entrance into the adult world and the gaining of adult social acceptance. For others, it is a source of self-esteem, self-respect, and personal well-being. At times it not only meets financial needs but also provides challenge, autonomy, and a sense of generativity. Identifying what an individual wants from work life and how far those needs are being met would be extremely important to ensure that satisfaction accrues from work. Moreover, it must be kept in mind that these needs may not remain the same and they may change from time to time. Recognizing when and how these needs change and preparing for these changes would be critical. Early identification of occupations which are at risk of becoming obsolete and of individuals experiencing discontentment would go a long way in preventing career crises.

Timely and appropriate handling of the anticipated changes in the nature of work, work environment, and the changing needs of the individual worker will help energize individuals to move on, grow, and self-actualize. While globalization has brought in a certain form of prosperity, it has also created a work environment that affects the worker. Canton (2007) highlighted, for example, that workers reported their personal lives to have been severely affected because of the demands of their workplaces. In a study of adult workers in the age range of 20–60 years in Mumbai, Jain and Koshy (2008) reported that work had taken a heavy toll on many aspects of adult workers' lives such as sleep, relationships, recreation, mental peace, time for self, social life, and health. Feelings of sadness, irritability, restlessness, and angry outbursts were reported in the above 40 age group as a result of work-related conditions. In such cases, excessive delay in making the relevant support available could lead to increased negativity, maladjustments, decreased sense of self-esteem, and feelings of disillusionment. Employers need to refer such workers for career guidance, provided such services are available and awareness of such services is created.

Preparing for Second Careers: The Role of Career Guidance Professionals

Individuals work in different circumstances and present differing needs. Hence career guidance professionals must also learn to work at different levels. Creating awareness regarding the importance and need to access these services, along with making them available is important. At the same time, the quality of these services must be fine tuned, to make them relevant to a wide range of workers such that more and more people access the services. Some of the aspects that need the attention of career guidance professionals are described as follows.

Plan and Prepare for Multiple Career Options

In today's times when second careers are inevitable, planning and preparing for more than one career from the early years becomes essential. Career guidance professionals, in their vocational guidance programs for children and adults at schools and in the community, must lay emphasis on the fact that all individuals have the ability to engage with more than one career if and when they desire to. Building a successful career is not about choosing one occupation and learning to be good at it. Arora (2004) has pointed out that most professionals face career blues 4 or 5 years into the job and start experiencing a lack of challenge and disillusionment. Hence individuals would do well, to explore their interests in more than one area. Career guidance professionals when consulted must identify more than one career option for each client. This would act as a safety net if their clients fail to enter or succeed in the career of their first choice. In the excessively competitive world of higher education and super-specialization, the possibility of students experiencing such disappointments is very high. Professional intervention may prevent cases of depression and suicide among the student population. Arulmani and Nag-Arulmani (2004) in their career discovery path model have emphasized the need for students to develop *career alternatives* and avoid the error of planning for just one career. When exploring multiple career options, career guidance professionals could advise their clients to work in one field as their primary area of work but continue to maintain other career possibilities as a hobby or possibly a part-time activity. These leisure activities would serve as a means for overall well-being, as well as serve as a backup support system if something were to go wrong with their first career choice. At any point in a lifetime an individual could plan a career shift by combining the use of existing skills and knowledge with further training through short-term courses and career transition support. Identification of personal strengths, polishing them, and converting them to professional opportunities is possible today. Entrepreneurs' success is based on knowing their skills, actualizing them, and marketing them successfully. An individual with good management skills, for example, could offer services ranging from delivering homemade food at the workplace to running a hotel. At times, hobbies and creative pursuits could prove to be more lucrative and satisfying than continuing to work in the original profession. Ria, a young woman aged 26 years from a middle-class family living in New Delhi, graduated in interior design and made a career in designing luxury homes for wealthy clients looking for exclusive and innovative décor. Along with her studies, she continued to polish her hobby of mural painting and making artifacts out of waste. Over the years, Ria was able to establish and further develop her career because of her ability to creatively use waste rather than just focusing on designing interiors. Not all individuals are as resourceful as Ria was. Hence, career guidance professionals must step in and create awareness about complementary courses to help clients learn to be flexible and creative in planning the progression of their careers.

Stay Updated

Rapid changes in technology and demand for highly specialized services create new career opportunities. The earlier these opportunities are identified and exploited, the speedier would be the client's career growth. Technology-driven jobs such as the use of laser in surgery and that of computer software programs in accountancy should be identified by career guidance professionals, and this information must be provided to clients to open fresh dimensions to their own careers. For example, providing daycare services for infants is well known. But there is a growing demand now for daycare centers for the elderly and caregiving for senior citizens. Homemade diet food for special populations, providing teachers services to create teaching aids, and creating jewelry from found objects are all examples of potential careers that one can craft from matching one's interests to new niches in the market.

Changes in economic cycles such as a recession lead to a sudden drop in job opportunities. It is important for career guidance professionals to be aware of these changes in the market place and make this information available to career choosers. Career guidance in such situations also involves providing information and skills training to prepare for and cope with these changes. Baskin and Guindon (1998) have recommended that career guidance professionals can help clients to regularly update their knowledge about career opportunities, market trends, and changes in the nature of workplaces. Career guidance professionals could stay abreast of changing career options by reading business- and work-related articles in journals, sharing and collecting resources on courses available, and attending conferences and workshops on career development. Richmond (2003) has suggested visiting corporate websites and employment sites and building a network of experts for guidance in different professions as an effective means of looking for job opportunities currently in demand.

Identify At-Risk Workers

Changes in the client's attitude towards work, behavior, and emotional disposition could be important indicators of a mismatch between the client's needs and the demands of the job. Career counselors could help employers identify employees who are at risk of experiencing discontentment at work. When the client continually refuses to talk about work, is critical of it, and views it negatively, there arises a need to explore the causes of these negative thoughts and feelings. Sometimes, the signs could be subtle ones such as the client being sluggish at work, appearing to be disconnected from work, and repeatedly making silly errors. It is important that the employers refer these clients to counselors. The most common career counseling objective here might be to get the client to accommodate and adapt to job demands. A more comprehensive approach on the other hand would deeply examine the necessity of a career shift, before the dissatisfaction becomes intolerable. Assessing what is really bothering the individual at the workplace, helping him or her consider and articulate the changes he or she wishes for, would help to throw light on whether a career shift is indicated. Excessive leave taking, being late for work, waiting for holidays, and Monday blues could all be treated as danger signals if they happen too often. Difficulties in maintaining relationships with colleagues, angry outbursts, and frequent spats could be stronger signs of a client at risk of having career development complications. Early identification of these at-risk workers must be followed by career counseling. Employers, organizational psychologists, researchers, social workers, and other such professionals need to collaborate to create awareness, increase accessibility, and use career guidance services for at-risk workers. This may help clients to identify changes in their needs and interests and continue to work on the development of their life goals. For example, the careers of professionals in the field of sports peak by the time they are around 25 years of age.

During this phase they may enjoy a lot of attention and success. But, their bodies also suffer a lot of physiological wear and tear, and they may be mentally exhausted with years of disciplined training. Further, post the age of 30 years, it may not be possible for many to continue with their sports career. Many of them fail to seek professional advice on planning their career. Helping such individuals plan for a second career is essential.

Certain occupational areas by their very nature cause stress, leading to employee attrition. Business process outsourcing (BPO) services could be considered as an example. The NIAS-IDPAD study (Upadhya & Vasavi, 2006) of Indians working in this field has reported that although software and BPO companies provide financially attractive job opportunities, there are several discouraging factors such as long working hours and spillover of work into the home leading to the blurring of boundaries between work and private life. Such working conditions lead to stress and burnout and have a debilitating effect on work-life balance. Preoccupied with earning, workers may not be aware of the impact of their work conditions on their current and future life. Some may not know how to cope with the demands of their work. Career guidance professionals could play a very important role here by helping individuals cope with career demands and plan for their future work life. Effective career guidance would help employees construct long-term professional goals. Services for the same could be made available for interested workers through workshops either at the workplace itself or privately.

Enhance Efficiency at Work

Survival in a competitive work environment necessitates appropriate retraining in skills along with provision of education. This is more so due to the shift in occupations from manufacturing and production to the service sectors. The ability to meet deadlines is an essential skill for career success today. Career guidance professionals could conduct or work along with specialists to organize workshops in time management and organizational skills. Managing deadlines would also require training in skills like self-discipline, stress management, and coping with burnout. In this age of information technology, the skills to use computers and other communication methodologies, like e-mailing and videoconferencing to name a few, would be essential for almost all types of occupations. Most professions would expect the individual to take full responsibility for work roles, thus making thinking skills such as reasoning and decision-making essential, along with the willingness to learn. Working in a team calls for good communication skills along with the ability to get along with others. Career guidance professionals could offer training for all types of workers to develop these skills, including those who are happy with their current career. Bakshi (2011) has recommended that such interventions be positioned as working towards enhancing workers' skills rather than overcoming deficiencies so that many participate and thereby are better prepared for their old or new careers across adulthood.

Preparing for Career Transitions: Relevance to Multiple Cultures

As reiterated in this chapter, the importance of flexibility with regard to career development has become a necessity irrespective of clients' cultural or economic background. Indeed, given the climate changes of today, even the farmer needs to be prepared for transitions and flexibility in methods of irrigation, planting, and cropping patterns. Hence, a goal of career counseling across multiple cultures and economic contexts would be "to develop transition skills, of developing one's competencies to face adversities and opportunities, obtain information on the transferability of one's skills to new opportunities and engage in continuous learning" (Tiwari, 2009, p. 205). Shifts in career are not always anticipated; sometimes they are sudden and barely give the individual time to get ready to capitalize on a new opportunity. Thus, being *prepared* for career transitions would help the individual deal with them more effectively as these have become a necessity in today's world. Keeping oneself updated by reading, by exploring career trends, and by advancing one's education and expertise in accordance with market demands should be emphasized as a part of effective career development practice for all workers. Education must be seen as an ongoing process. Qualifications could be obtained through formal, advanced education programs. Alternatively, shorter training programs, workshops, and seminars could be considered. Lifelong learning is a critical adaptive mechanism for adult workers (Muchinsky, 2001). For example, cardiac surgeons who progress from conducting bypass surgeries to endoscopic and laser surgeries would typically be the ones who have increased the longevity of their careers in medical practice.

Professionals who are new to the world of work must be encouraged to identify mentors, build their contacts, and network with professional associations for appropriate guidance. Mentors can educate newcomers on how to handle the complexity as well as the opportunities related to their profession (Mannering, 2002). Volunteering one's services is one of the ways suggested through which one could cultivate professional contacts and explore new opportunities (Dyer, 2005).

On getting a high-paying job, the individual may assume that all is now settled and so may reduce or cease to give attention to ongoing career planning and the monitoring of his or her personal growth. With the passage of time, this could ultimately lead the individual to a state of unpreparedness to handle a career shift. Moreover, it has been observed that young adult workers often experience financial crises at the time of a career transition. Career guidance professionals need to help clients become wary of sinking into a comfort zone. Instead, they could help clients make a conscious effort to stay updated. A seemingly small but vital and often neglected aspect of preparedness for a career transition is a continuous updating of one's resume. Trying to prepare one's resume at the 11th hour by just relying on one's memory could result in the omission of important achievements. It may also leave one without the relevant documents to support the declared achievements.

Identify the Need and Opportunities for a Career Transition

Recognizing the right time to make a career shift may not be an easy task for working adults, and this could vary across cultures and economic conditions. They are usually so engrossed in their work that they may fail to consider making a transition or a shift. Career transitions are often associated with changes in life. Events such as getting married, parenthood, increased demands of family at middle adulthood, and retirement are common examples. However, the need for a career transition can occur at any point, and appropriate guidance and counseling by career guidance professionals could help the individual recognize this. Tiwari (2009) lists the following learning outcomes of guidance that includes being prepared for transitions: self-awareness, opportunity awareness, decision-making, and transition skills. Self-awareness involves helping the client recognize changing needs, work values, motivations, and preference for work environments. Opportunity awareness entails helping clients become aware of better alternatives available to them when they wish to make a career transition. Decision-making involves helping individuals decide and then take steps in the direction of a career transition. Counselors provide assistance in choosing a new career and also help in overcoming clients' fears of the unknown and their feelings of insecurity. Finally, transition skills would focus on helping clients identify their strengths and weaknesses in relation to their chosen career and to work on the skills required for the new career.

Help Individuals Make Career Transitions

An unplanned career transition could be experienced as an overwhelming life-changing event, bringing about a sudden change in work responsibilities and work environment (Richmond, 2001). It is important to recognize that making a career transition is a process that involves an anticipation of the need for it, being prepared for it, and then finally making the transition. Richmond (2001) has described two components in every job. One component has to do with the job responsibilities, along with the duties and skills needed for it. The other component is the field of work or the industry in which the work is done. For example, being a secretary involves job responsibilities of filing papers and fixing appointments along with typing letters, but the secretary could be working in any field such as the hotel industry or an educational institution. Richmond (2001) has suggested that one can have smooth career transitions by keeping the same job responsibilities and just changing the field of work or by staying in the same field and gradually working towards changing one's work responsibilities. For example, one could continue to work as a secretary with the same responsibilities and change the field from an educational institution to the hotel industry. The other option would be to continue to work in the same field but update one's skills and move to other job tasks and thereby advance one's career prospects. Higher levels of career growth would be experienced by making changes in job responsibilities, but this calls for the readiness to learn, to update one's skills, and to face challenges. At times, the need to make a change in the field would be necessitated by changes in market trends or by redundancy of a given field. The closure of many companies producing photo films due to the advent of digital photography is one illustration of redundancy.

The need for support from career guidance professionals would continue to be essential for some time after the transition is made. At times, the client may feel dejected and defeated and say things like, "Life is so unfair, I feel so miserable and hopeless," "I will never get another job, no point trying," or "My new colleagues would never accept me." Here it becomes important to counsel the client and to help him or her develop a more positive outlook. In situations where job satisfaction is low, clients may start to get restless and wish for things to be hurried up. They may say, for instance, "I can't wait anymore, I will take any job other than my current one even if I don't get paid enough" or "Why am I not getting called for job interviews even though I am usually the first one to apply?" Occasionally, they may worry, "I am constantly asking for help from others, when will I become independent again?" It is important for career guidance professionals to recognize the stressors that clients may be experiencing and help them develop proactive coping skills to deal with this time of uncertainty in their lives. Sometimes clients may make a half-hearted attempt to look for jobs and say, "I have submitted applications at four places already, what more can I do?" or "I just don't have the time to update my resume; if I am destined to get the job I shall get it." Some begin to get philosophical. "After working for so many years in the field, I am not going to take up new courses or apply for jobs. If I am good enough, the companies will approach me." Helping clients overcome their reticence and to make efforts to find a new job becomes a challenging task for career guidance professionals. Updating one's skill, looking out for jobs, applying for them, and appearing for interviews can be a fulltime job for the client (Arulmani & Nag-Arulmani, 2004). At times, a client may experience financial difficulties or emotional turmoil during the transition process. Bakshi (2011) found that "Common sources of support for career-related crises and major decisions were friends and spouse, followed by seniors at workplace, parents, siblings, and other family members. Professional career guidance services did not feature as a support for either career crises or major career decisions" (p. 149). This is a sad commentary on the effectiveness and relevance of career guidance services in people's lives. At the same time, professionals could turn such a finding into a strength for their profession if they increase their collaboration with the family and community (see Bakshi & Joshi, 2014, Chap. 10).

New Concepts and Viewpoints

Second careers or even third or fourth careers are becoming inevitable in today's world, and most people have to make these transitions, whether in early adulthood (Bakshi, 2011) or later. Hence, preparation for second careers must start in adolescence or sooner. In the rapidly changing world of work, the role of career guidance professionals in assisting individuals through this process is crucial. Even as the process of career guidance begins, it would be imperative to advise each individual to maintain multiple career options. At any given point in life, there may arise a need for making a career shift, and individuals must be prepared for it. The process of learning and getting an education does not stop when adulthood is attained. It is, in fact, a continuous process of lifelong learning that has become essential for succeeding in the contemporary world of work. Such a proactive and preventive approach to career guidance would go a long way in minimizing the underutilization of the human potential and at the same time maintaining psychological well-being among workers. When helping someone make a career shift, career guidance professionals encounter differing needs ranging from choosing career options, enhancing the worker's skills and abilities to perform more effectively, preparing for, and finally making the transition. The changing labor market demands that career guidance professionals constantly update themselves about the career opportunities and thereby enhance the quality of the services they offer. Career guidance services need to be provided across an individual's life span. Reaching out to adult workers through workshops, seminars, special programs at their workplace (Bakshi, 2011) and utilizing the media to address career

development concerns are some of the means through which use of career guidance services could be increased. The nature of services required from career guidance professionals is also likely to undergo change. Thus, career guidance professionals also need to engage in lifelong learning and networking.

Conclusion

I conclude this chapter with the pertinent example of Priya, a young woman aged 20 years from a middle-class family living in Mumbai, who completed her graduation in the field of special education and who was also interested in animation design. On graduating from college, she took up a part-time job as a special educator and simultaneously enrolled for a course in computer-based animation design. Priya was aware that at this stage in her life, her financial needs were not very high. She was also well aware of the fact that in the near future she would need to earn more. Keeping this in mind, Priya further developed her interests in both career possibilities. She focused on improving her skills for animation design and continued with a part-time job as a remedial teacher for children. Although this gave her parents the impression that she was confused, as both areas of work were of interest to Priya, in actuality she was happy with the way her career was growing. Soon Priya became good enough at design software and began taking up assignments to prepare posters and visiting cards. Her plans are to work in the field of animation design and continue with her remedial work as a part-time occupation. In effect, Priya is keeping both her options open, and she plans to pick her options as per the changing needs of her life. She may move from one option to another during significant transition points in her life such as marriage, child bearing, changing financial needs, and the availability of options. The thought of preparing software programs for special children is the kind of assignment that excites Priya and for which she aspires. There is no single correct choice.

Whatever Priya takes up as a profession, would be a win-win situation for her. Individuals planning their career with such flexibility are more likely to be satisfied with their work life.

References

Arora, S. (2004, August). Combating mid-career blues. *Express Computer Business Weekly Magazine*. Retrieved from http://www.expresscomputeronline. com/20040823/

Arulmani, G., Bakshi, A. J., Flederman, P., & Watts, A. G. (2011). Editorial: East and west: Exploring new concepts for career guidance (special issue). *International Journal for Educational and Vocational Guidance, 11*(2), 61–64.

Arulmani, G., & Nag-Arulmani, S. (2004). *Career counselling: A handbook*. New Delhi, India: Tata McGraw Hill.

Bakshi, A. J. (2011). Past adolescence, into and across adulthood: Career crises and major decisions. *International Journal of Educational and Vocational Guidance, 11*(2), 139–153.

Bakshi, A. J., & Joshi, J. (2014). The interface between positive youth development and youth career development: New avenues for career guidance practice. In G. Arulmani, A. J. Bakshi, F. T. L. Leong, & A. G. Watts (Eds.), *Handbook of career development*. New York, NY: Springer.

Baltes, P. B. (1987). Theoretical propositions of life-span developmental psychology: On the dynamics between growth and decline. *Developmental Psychology, 23*(5), 611–626.

Baltes, P. B., Lindenberger, U., & Staudinger, U. M. (2006). Life span theory in developmental psychology. In W. Damon & R. M. Lerner (Series Eds.), & R. M. Lerner (Vol. Ed.), *Handbook of child psychology, Vol. 1: Theoretical models of human development* (pp. 569–664). Hoboken, USA: Wiley.

Baskin, B., & Guindon, M. (1998, August). Considering the services of a career counselor. Part I. *Selfhelp Magazine*. Retrieved from http://www.selfhelpmagazine. com/article/node/793

Bee, H. (1996). *The journey of adulthood* (3rd ed.). Englewood Cliffs, NJ: Prentice Hall.

Bialik, C. (2010, September). Seven careers in a lifetime? Think twice, researchers say. *The Wall Street Journal*. Retrieved from http://online.wsj.com/article/SB1000 1424052748704206804575468162805887799.html

Brown, D. K., Deardorff, A., & Stern, R. (2003). *The effects of multinational production on wages and working conditions in developing countries*. Cambridge, UK: National Bureau of Economic Research (Working paper series 9669). Retrieved from http://www.nber.org/chapters/c9541.pdf

Canton, N. (2007, August 5). City execs head for burnout. *Hindustan Times*, p. 1.

Dyer, F. (2005, July). From volunteer to new career. *E-Volunteerism, 5*(4). Retrieved from http://www. e-volunteerism.com/quarterly/05jul/05jul-dyer

Ebner, C., Freund, A. M., & Baltes, A. (2006). Developmental changes in personal goal orientation from young to late adulthood: From striving for gains to maintenance and prevention of losses. *Psychology and Aging, 21*(4), 664–678.

Ganz, W. (2005). *Research in services sector*. Stuttgart, Germany: Fraunhofer Institut fur arbeitswirtschaft und organisation. Retrieved from ftp://ftp.cordis.europa. eu/pub/foresight/docs/kte_services.pdf

Gibson, R., & Mitchell, M. (1981). *Introduction to guidance*. New York, NY: Macmillan.

Gupta, M. (2003). *Effective guidance and counselling*. Jaipur, India: Mangal Deep.

Gysbers, N., & Moore, E. (1987). *Career counseling: Skills and techniques for practitioners*. Englewood Cliffs, NJ: Prentice Hall.

Jain, A., & Koshy, S. (2008). Globalization: Work conditions and its impact on individual and family life. In A. Bakshi & P. Maheshwari (Eds.), *Proceedings of the national conference on human development research: Commitment to processes of change* (pp. 113–121). Mumbai, India: Mahavir.

Lemme, B. (1999). *Development in adulthood* (2nd ed.). London, UK: Allyn & Bacon.

Mannering, K. (2002). *Staying ahead at work*. Mumbai, India: Jaico.

McCrae, R. R., & Costa, P. T., Jr. (2003). *Personality in adulthood: A five factor theory perspective* (2nd ed.). New York, USA: Guilford Press.

Muchinsky, P. (2001). *Psychology applied to world* (6th ed.). Belmont, CA: Wadsworth.

Rice, P. (1986). *Adult development and aging*. London, UK: Allyn & Bacon.

Richmond, A. (2001, March). Making a smoother career transition. *Career Intelligence, 2*(6). Retrieved from http://www.career-intelligence.com/transition/ ChangingPlaces.asp

Richmond, A. (2003, June). Creating a strategic job search plan is the key to success. *Career Intelligence, 4*(12). Retrieved from http://www.career-intelligence. com/transition/WhereTheJobsAre.asp

Safaye, B. N. (2002). *Guidance and counselling*. Chandigarh, India: Abhishek.

Schultz, D., & Sydney, E. (1994). *Psychology and work today: An introduction to industrial and organizational psychology* (6th ed.). New York, USA: Macmillan.

Sharma, S. (2005). *Career guidance and counselling: Principles and techniques*. New Delhi, India: Kanishka.

Steindel, C. (2004). The relationship between manufacturing production and goods output. *Current Issues in Economics and Finance, 10*(9). Retrieved from http://www.newyorkfed.org/research/current_ issues/ci10-9.pdf

Super, D. E. (1990). A life-span, life-space approach to career development. In D. Brown & L. Brooks (Eds.), *Career choice and development* (pp. 197–261). San Francisco, CA: Jossey-Bass.

Suresh, V., & Shashidhar, P. (2007, May). *Competitiveness in small scale industries in India.* Paper presented at the Indian Institute of Management Conference on Global Competition and Competitiveness of Indian Corporate, Bangalore, India. Retrieved from http://dspace.iimk.ac.in/bitstream/2259/501/1/439-453.pdf

Tiwari, R. (2009). *Guidance and counselling.* Delhi, India: Kunal Books.

Tractenberg, L., Streumer, J., & Zolingen, S. (2002). Career counselling in the emerging post-industrial society. *International Journal for Educational and Vocational Guidance, 2,* 5–99.

Upadhya, C., & Vasavi, A. R. (2006). *Work, culture, and sociality in the Indian IT industry: A sociological study.* Bangalore, India: School of Social Sciences, National Institute of Advanced Studies.

Vembu, R. (2008). *Can workplace stress lead to attrition?* Retrieved from http://www.expresspharmaonline.com/20080315/pharmalife01.shtml

Making Our Careers Green: Work, Environmental Sustainability, and Social Justice

---

Overview

The survival of our planet is directly linked to the manner in which we practice our careers. Chapters in this section address the impact that career development has on the issues that surround environmental degradation and sustainability. Indeed, career counseling encourages individuals to "reach for the sky." But the time is well-nigh to also consider the question: "When we reach for the sky, are we also turning the earth brown?" Furthermore, the forces of globalization and economic development impact social equity and social justice. Writers in this section address the impact of the meritocratic redistribution of material resources and life chances on social equity. Social disparities in the acquisition of education and the manner in which career guidance can help to reduce such inequalities are discussed. The critical role played by systemic factors such as public policy is explained. This section also highlights the issues related to rural–urban migration. The need for upward mobility is common to all youth. Rural young people's strong aspirations to leave their village homes to seek the bright lights of the city and implications for career guidance in non-urban contexts are discussed. Every culture has had its own ways of inducting its young into the workforce. The value of this wisdom has been eroded. Age-old ways of working in harmony with the environment are placed at a low level of prestige and status. Crafts which were originally linked to ways of living are neglected and considered irrelevant in an industrialized, market economy that is driven by the forces of globalization. Crafts represent work cultures and there is much to be learned from them. Drawing on current debates on sustainable development and inclusive growth, writers in this section examine the challenges in re-inventing traditional occupations into viable production systems with the potential to promote equitable work spaces, economic and social inclusion, esthetics, and ecological sustainability. These discussions probe historical paradigms of production, sociology of work, and frameworks of consumption, which affect the survival of these occupations.

In summary, this section throws light upon the links between career services, environment and sustainability, livelihoods and careers, and tradition and modernity. The fulfillment of personal aspiration and individual mobility, as well as social and ecological justice as potential action points for contemporary career counseling services are discussed.

Green Guidance

Peter Plant

Introduction

A number of well-known career development theories are focused on the individual's career. Examples of this include Super's life-span theory (Super, 1957), illustrated later by the career rainbow which goes up and down on an individual basis (Super, 1980). Holland (1997) used the metaphor of the hexagon to illustrate his highly influential person-environment fit theory: another individualistic approach. Gottfredson (2002), in her theory of circumscription and compromise, also focused on the individual career. So did Gelatt (1989) in introducing the concept positive uncertainty and Krumboltz, Levin, and Mitchell (1999) and Krumboltz and Levin (2004) with their equally bipolar and dialogical ideas of planned happenstance. What these North American mainly middle-class-based theories have in common is that they reflect a mainstream, individualistic culture, a Westernized culture. Even constructivist approaches have this bias when addressing moral and ethical issues in career development: "Every worry and trouble, big and small, that a person can experience has an ethical-moral dimension. To ask: what kind of career is best and possible for me is to ask: How should I live my life?" (Peavy, 2002, p. 12).

P. Plant (✉)
Danish School of Education, Aarhus University,
Copenhagen, Denmark
e-mail: pepl@dpu.dk

Likewise, in introducing the boundaryless career (Arthur & Rousseau, 1996), the mental boundary remains the same: The focus is on the individual career. Thus, it is no wonder that career guidance practitioners mostly have an individual focus: They deal mainly with individuals and they are supported by deeply rooted ideas of client-centered approaches (e.g., Rogers, 1951). In addition, Max Weber (1958), who coined the concept of the protestant work ethic and analyzed Westernized individualistic work values, has linked prosperity, economic growth, protestant work ethic, and capitalism, thus pointing to the complex linkages between culture, religion, and economic philosophy. Such concepts and values are reflected in current (Westernized) guidance and counseling practices and theories. In addition, the European Union has issued a number of important policy papers, such as the European Union Resolution on Lifelong Guidance in which the emphasis is also on individual careers as the main focal point, and stresses "the preventive role of guidance services in encouraging school completion and the contribution [of these services] to the empowerment of individuals to manage their own learning and careers" (European Commission, 2004, p. 7).

Influential models that capture learning aspects of guidance also build on such individualistic approaches such as the DOTS model which has been used in formulating learning goals for guidance (Law & Watts, 1977, p. 8): D, decision learning; O, opportunity awareness; T, transition learning; and S, self-awareness.

G. Arulmani et al. (eds.), *Handbook of Career Development*, International and Cultural Psychology,
DOI 10.1007/978-1-4614-9460-7_17, © Springer Science+Business Media, LLC 2014

Even in these broad terms, O for opportunity awareness is associated with individual progress:

> We mean opportunity awareness also to refer to the exploration of the different paths and strategies which are open (or closed) to particular individuals for gaining entry to those opportunities. And at the level of the individual we take it to refer to the combination of demands, offers and strategies which match (or at least do not mismatch) a particular individual's characteristics. (Law & Watts, 1977, p. 8)

In short, there seems to be a blind spot here. Some of the main roots of individualistic thinking stem from market-oriented thinking, which implies that individual decisions, ego-centered as they may be, sum up to a collective good, steered by the market's "invisible hand," as so famously phrased by Adam Smith (1776). It has been argued that:

> Career development could be viewed (not only by economic liberals) as a classic case of Adam Smith's famous dictum that individuals encouraged to pursue their own interests are led by an "invisible hand" to promote an end that is no part of their intention—the public interest—and to do so more effectually than when they intend to promote it. In this sense, career development services could represent Smith's 'invisible hand' made flesh. (Watts, 2003, p. 12)

Inconvenient Truths

The values behind Adam Smith's thinking represented answers to societal questions of his time, no doubt. But it seems fair to observe that Smith, and his economic followers, may not be the final answer to the problems of (post) modern times, as the present worldwide financial and environmental crises show. Perhaps, the pursuit of one's own interests in a narrow sense does not promote the public interest, after all. In his film, An Inconvenient Truth, Gore (2006) stated that:

> Humanity is sitting on a ticking time bomb. We have just ten years to avert a major catastrophe that could send our entire planet into a tail-spin of epic destruction involving extreme weather, floods, droughts, epidemics and killer heat waves beyond anything we have ever experienced. (p. 146)

Gore's persuasive argument is that we can no longer afford to view global warming as a political issue; rather, it is the biggest moral challenge facing our global civilization. Gore is not alone: Other influential policymakers have raised these issues. The influential French commentator Hulot (2006), for example, has introduced five concrete proposals on environmental issues and policies, including CO_2 taxation, sustainable agriculture, and eco-education. Stern (2006), speaking from the UK, in his important report, linked economic growth issues with climate change, by pointing out that production processes that are not sensitive to the environment create waste and produce emissions which cause climate changes. US-based commentator Rifkin (2010) has claimed, even more radically, that transition to "biosphere consciousness" has already begun: A younger generation is beginning to realize that one's daily consumption of energy and other resources ultimately affects the lives of every other human being and every other creature that inhabits the Earth. And in a forecast for the next 40 years, Randers (2012) has predicted that there will be an increasing focus on human well-being rather than on per capita income growth.

Still, the present role of career guidance remains pointed toward the promotion of economic growth that is powered by individualistic aspirations. For example, in policy documents such as the European Union Resolution on Lifelong Guidance (European Commission, 2004), mentioned earlier, guidance is a vehicle for economic growth in a global race for better competitiveness, the irony being that much of this growth is what has been labeled "jobless growth" and with a notable absence of any concern for the environmental impact of this particular approach. Surely, economic growth without an ecological impact is possible, but we have not seen much of this yet. The Global Green Growth Institute headquartered in Seoul, Korea, for instance, was founded on the belief that:

> (E)conomic growth and environmental sustainability are not merely compatible objectives; their integration is essential for the future of humankind... [it] is dedicated to

pioneering and diffusing a new model of economic growth, known as "green growth", that simultaneously targets key aspects of economic performance, such as poverty reduction, job creation and social inclusion, and those of environmental sustainability, such as mitigation of climate change and biodiversity loss and security of access to clean energy and water. (Global Green Growth Institute, n.d.)

The European Union (EU), in its goals for 2020, now has realized a need for refining its thinking on these issues. Growth in itself is no longer the answer to future challenges: Smart, sustainable, and inclusive growth is the future lead concept (European Commission, 2011). Even if such a concept relies heavily on traditional one-dimensional growth thinking, it represents steps toward a greener and more wide-ranging direction. This will have an impact on the societal goals of guidance, which, so far, in many countries have been preoccupied with individual paths, exemplified by goals such as reduced educational dropout and increased employability, international competitiveness, or full employment. All are commendable goals, but driven by narrow individualistic and economic growth concepts, even if disguised as social inclusion goals.

Interestingly, the well-established yardstick for prosperity, economic growth seen as GNP (Gross National Product), is now being questioned, even by the Organisation for Economic Co-operation and Development (OECD), which, so far, has had a narrow focus on economic growth. Now the OECD (2011) has introduced the *Better Life Initiative* which aims to measure well-being and progress. The index allows citizens to compare lives across 34 countries, based on 11 dimensions: housing, income, jobs, community, education, environment, governance, health, life satisfaction, safety, and work-life balance. Career guidance is not (yet) on the list. In the EU, the French commissioned the Stiglitz Report (Stiglitz, Sen, & Fitoussi, 2009) which scrutinized the concept of GNP in relation to social progress and produced a number of recommendations to supplement current GNP concepts. Other organizations, such as the German Wuppertal

Institute for Climate, Environment and Energy, aim at developing strategies to support sustainable development. For example, the focus of this institute is on analyzing and supporting technological and social innovations that decouple prosperity based on economic growth from the use of natural resources, using the complete life-cycle model to illustrate the ecological footprints of particular products. Finally, on a global basis, the United Nations Development Programme (UNDP) has issued a number of *Human Development Reports*. The first report in 1990 opened with the simple premise that has guided all subsequent reports: "People are the real wealth of a nation." Featuring a Human Development Index, a recent report (UNDP, 2011) has outlined the potential for positive synergies in the quest for greater equality and sustainability. The 2011 report has further emphasized the human right to a healthy environment, the importance of integrating social equity into environmental policies, and the critical importance of public participation and official accountability. UNDP calls for bold new approaches to global development financing and environmental controls, arguing that these measures are both essential and feasible. One of these new, bold approaches could be green guidance, which is not (yet) on the UNDP agenda.

Non-Western Inspiration

Interestingly, a number of inspirational points come from non-Western cultures, as a counterbalance to the concepts and values that underpin current individualistic career development theories which were mentioned above. This is not to say that the individual in a non-Western perspective does not have a will of his/her own. But the balance and perspectives are different. "Career" within such epistemologies is viewed from a wider perspective. Inspiration can be found, for instance, in ancient Indian approaches to career development. Life and career are intertwined and seen as playing out over four stages (ashramas). Not all these stages focus merely on the individual. Arulmani and Nag-Arulmani (2004, p. 9) interpreted the duties prescribed for these stages of life into the framework of career development as follows:

- *Brahmacharya* ashrama is the first stage and is a period of learning. Learning is accomplished not only through didactic teaching but also by serving and working for the *guru* (teacher).
- *Grihastha* ashrama is the stage of life devoted to living the life of a householder, starting and caring for a family and building a career. Career is expected to be practiced as an integral part of the community as a whole.
- *Vanaprastha* ashrama is the next stage and is a time of life when career development continues but not for personal gain. The individual is urged to imbue the purpose of work with a service orientation whereby he or she supports the career development of younger members of society.
- *Sannyasa* ashrama represents the final stage of life and is devoted to spiritual pursuits. The individual voluntarily gives up physical comforts and here again it is expected that life is characterized by service to others. It is also expected that younger members of society care for those in this stage. The giving of alms to a *sannyasi*, for example, is considered to be a sacred duty.

"Serving humanity" hardly figures in traditional Westernized career paths. Without entering into the philosophy of the ashrama system, it seems fair to observe that in this conception, cultural factors come to the forefront when economic and social policy goals are expressed. In contrast, Westernized models such as Super's Career Rainbow include growth, exploration, establishment, maintenance, and end with "decline" from the age of 60 (Super, 1980).

Another example comes to us from the far North, where green considerations are prominent. Finn Lynge, an indigenous Inuit politician from Greenland (which is part of the Danish Commonwealth), focused on Inuit values in his address to the 1998 General Assembly of the Inuit Circumpolar Conference (Lynge, 1998, pp. 2–3). His points included:

- *Nunamut ataqqinninneq*, that is, pride of this marvelous land, feeling it in our bones, knowing its whales and caribou, its endless plains and mountains, its light and dark, both unparalleled anywhere in the world, its hardness and its beauty.
- *Akisussaassuseq*, that is, responsibility toward the land and everything that lives here. We harvest what we need, but Inuit take no pride in needless killing. The fish, the seals and the whales, the caribou and the musk oxen, and the birds of the sea and of the land, they are all given in our hands for sensible stewardship. Those living in the small settlements know this better than many others.
- *Tukkussuseq*, that is, generosity and hospitality, those are Inuit values. They have their roots in the close ties of our extended families, and they have always been guarded and cultivated in the small places where considerations over money do not dictate the agenda of the day.

Such values are far from most Westernized considerations. They point toward stewardship and mutual responsibility, on a sustainable basis. Moving to the East again, Bhutan, for example, has introduced the concept of the Gross National Happiness (GNH), which builds on four pillars of development: (a) sustainable and equitable socioeconomic development, (b) conservation of the environment, (c) preservation and promotion of cultural heritage, and (d) good governance (Gross National Happiness, n.d.; Plant, 2007a). Thirty-three indicators provide a framework for indexing the GNH approach, grouped in the overarching domains of psychological well-being, health, education, culture, time use, good governance, community vitality, ecological diversity, and resilience. Even from this short list of factors, it is clear that green issues are brought into focus rather than left in oblivion unlike GNP approaches, where all kinds of economic factors are bundled together, with no view to their environmental impact.

Along similar lines, the concept of *Sufficient Economy* is pivotal to understanding the main economic and social policy goals in Thailand. The sufficient economy focuses on the middle path approach as a mode of conduct to achieve moderation in life. The main point is to live together in peace and harmony with nature and the environment. *Yuyen Bhensuk*, happy and healthy living, is the policy driver here.

Approaches such as these have huge implications for career guidance policies which in this light will not seek, for example, to advance economic growth at the expense of sustainability. Individual career choices, in this perspective, have a wider scope than just the pursuit of narrow individual goals. Guidance will have to take a stand when faced by such challenges. The point being made here is that career guidance serves as a link between the aim of economic growth at the expense of other, perhaps more important, goals and the essentially individualistic values which have underpinned much career development theory over the last few generations in Westernized cultures. This is not to say that the individual can no longer pursue personal fulfillment and happiness through personal career development. But green guidance will be a pivotal component in the already disputed concept of careers (Barham & Hall, 1996; NCGE, 2009; Plant, 1996, 1999, 2003, 2007b, 2008). Career choices, individual as they may be, have implications beyond the individual, especially when linked to the wider societal goals of social justice, as pointed out by Irving and Malik (2005). It is high time these issues are acknowledged.

Green Guidance: Economy and Ecology

A new approach is on its way, and it is green. As a reaction against the often one-dimensional economic thinking and its market-driven principles, a new wave, concerned with ecological issues, is in view. It simply does not pay to think only of short-term economic goals. Clearly, the analysis of cost-benefit ratios, for example, falls far behind a number of important issues in terms of environmental concerns. Large companies, such as General Electric, have recognized this and coined the strategy of Ecomagination, that is,

producing with less energy and pollution. Other major companies such as Wal-Mart Stores, Tesco PLC, and the Virgin Group have seen the writing on the wall and introduced CR, that is, Corporate Responsibility, and banks are into what they label as Conscious Banking. Green accounting also includes factors other than mere economic performance aspects, such as carbon emission, waste handling, and such environmental footprint indicators (Schaltegger & Burritt, 2000).

The International Association for Educational and Vocational Guidance (IAEVG), already in 1995, adopted a statement on global ethical standards, which included recognition of the tensions between economic growth and environmental issues, that is, ecology. Back in 1995, the text was followed by a question mark: How should educational and vocational guidance services ethically respond to the global tensions between economic and environmental issues in the working lives and workplaces of clients? (IAEVG, 1995). Now it would more likely be followed by an exclamation mark! In short, new concepts are under way to challenge current paradigms of blind growth. Green guidance is a part of this trend. What would this indicate?

Green guidance would define guidance, and especially career choice, in terms of ecology rather than just economy. Environmental concern will be put to the forefront of many daily activities, including guidance, and guidance workers will have the difficult task of transforming this concept into daily practice, still keeping global perspectives in view. It does matter now, perhaps more than ever, what people do with their working lives: Whether they produce lethal weapons or design new systems of rain harvesting. The need to make such choices is globally evident: pollution, overconsumption in some areas and fundamental unmet needs in others, the pressure on scarce water resources, overfishing, global warming, and ozone holes; the list is endless. At the recent meeting (December 2011) of the United Nations Framework Convention on Climate Change (UNFCCC) held in Durban, South Africa (known as COP 17),

Nnimmo Bassey, Chair of Friends of the Earth International, referred to apartheid when declaring:

> Delaying real action until 2020 is a crime of global proportions. An increase in global temperatures of four degrees Celsius, permitted under this plan, is a death sentence for Africa, Small Island States, and the poor and vulnerable worldwide. This summit has amplified climate apartheid, whereby the richest 1 % of the world have decided that it is acceptable to sacrifice the 99 %. (COP 17, 2011)

Some economists and some politicians are aware of the clash between senseless economic growth and environmental concern. Wars are already being fought over oil and the next wars will be fought over water resources, no doubt. Whereas economic growth used to be the solution, it now seems to create as many problems. Jobless growth and a deterioration of the natural resources: These are some of the present predicaments. In this situation guidance must become part of the solution rather than the problem.

New Viewpoints and Relevance Across Cultures

A new approach, a mental U-turn (Scharmer, 2007), is needed based on a number of principles for green guidance:

- Guidance should take into account and create awareness of the environmental impact of vocational choices.
- Guidance should play an active role in establishing training and education opportunities with a positive contribution in environmental terms.
- Informational materials on career options should include environmental aspects.
- Guidance should be measured, not only by an economic yardstick, but also by green accounting (i.e., by integrating environmental goals in guidance activities).
- Guidance theories and practices should address common career development issues in addition to individualistic approaches, with a focus on environmental impacts of career choices.

- On a much smaller scale, guidance workers themselves should inspect their own practice: How green are my routines of recycling waste and cutting down on power consumption? How is ICT used to cut down on travelling, for example?

This is not an exhaustive list and it should be read along with an inspirational list of green jobs and activities such as:
- Green activist working with neighborhood ecological gardening
- Green greenkeeper working with a no-pesticide approach to maintenance of sports grounds
- Green lawyer working with environmental cases
- Green transport engineer working with nonpollutant means of traffic and transport
- Green farmer working with ecological practice in fields and stables
- Green painters using nontoxic and degradable paints
- Green builders using natural insulation materials
- Green hairdressers

In short, most careers could be seen as potentially green.

Conclusion

Some guidance workers, no doubt, will find the outlined approach dangerously directive. It may indeed question some current guidance practices and perhaps even the traditional Rogerian client-centered approach itself. But then, all new approaches would threaten older ones, and new philosophies take some time to break through. Even Parsons (1909), the well-known guidance revolutionary who is considered the father of modern career guidance and counseling, had visions which reached far beyond guidance and counseling itself. His vision was for a balanced, just, and peaceful society. He saw the link between career development and a society which made the best use of its human resources though career counseling, to the benefit of all.

In his days, economic growth and social justice went hand in hand. Based on "brotherly love," he named his societal vision *mutualism* (Parsons, 1894) and, surely, today he would have added a green guidance dimension to his thinking. He was a prophet and a practical utopian (Gummere, 1988). Now, we need new utopians, the green ones.

At its best, green guidance could be proactive, questioning, probing, reflexive, and client-centered in the real sense: It leaves the decisions to the client but, perhaps, on a higher note of commitment. Moreover, especially in relation to globalization, it puts guidance into a central position: Environmental issues and concerns know no boundaries (Monbiot, 2006). This is why it is so urgent that guidance workers make their contribution toward green changes. With this kind of approach, the individual career fades into the background, and common goals come into focus. This is green guidance.

References

Arthur, M. B., & Rousseau, D. M. (1996). *The boundaryless career: A new employment principle for a new organizational era*. New York, NY: Oxford University Press.

Arulmani, G., & Nag-Arulmani, S. (2004). *Career counselling. A handbook*. New Delhi, India: Tata McGraw-Hill.

Barham, L., & Hall, R. (1996). Global guidance goes green. *Career Guidance Today, 4*(1), 26–27.

COP 17. (2011). *Climate change talks in Durban*. Retrieved from http://cop17insouthafrica.wordpress.com/

European Commission. (2004). *Resolution on lifelong guidance*. Bruxelles, Belgium: Author. Retrieved from http://ec.europa.eu/education/policies/2010/doc/resolution2004_en.pdf

European Commission. (2011). *EU's 2020 growth strategy*. Bruxelles, Belgium: Author. Retrieved from http://ec.europa.eu/europe2020/index_en.htm

Gelatt, H. B. (1989). Positive uncertainty: A new decision-making framework for counseling. *Journal of Counseling Psychology, 36*, 252–256.

Global Green Growth Institute. (n.d.). *Overview*. Retrieved from http://www.gggi.org/about/overview

Gore, A. (2006). *An inconvenient truth: The planetary emergency of global warming and what we can do about it*. New York, NY: Bloomsbury.

Gottfredson, L. S. (2002). Gottfredson's theory of circumscription, compromise and self-creation. In D. Brown (Ed.), *Career choice and development* (4th ed., pp. 85–148). San Francisco, CA: Jossey-Bass.

Gross National Happiness. (n.d.). *A short guide to gross national happiness*. Retrieved from http://www.grossnationalhappiness.com/

Gummere, R. M. (1988). The counselor as prophet: Frank Parsons, 1854–1908. *Journal of Counseling and Development, 66*(9), 402–405.

Holland, J. L. (1997). *Making vocational choices: A theory of vocational personalities and work environments* (3rd ed.). Odessa, TX: PAR.

Hulot, N. (2006). *Pour un Pacte écologique*. Paris, France: Éditions Calman-Lévy.

IAEVG. (1995). *IAEVG ethical standards*. Retrieved from http://www.iaevg.org/iaevg/nav.cfm?lang=2&menu=1&submenu=2

Irving, B. A., & Malik, B. (Eds.). (2005). *Critical reflections on career education and guidance: Justice within a global economy*. London, England: Routledge Falmer.

Krumboltz, J. D., & Levin, A. S. (2004). *Luck is no accident: Making the most of happenstance in your life and career*. New York, NY: Impact.

Krumboltz, J. D., Levin, A. S., & Mitchell, K. E. (1999). Planned happenstance: Constructing unexpected career opportunities. *Journal of Counselling & Development, 77*, 115–124.

Law, B., & Watts, A. G. (1977). *Schools, careers and community. A study of some approaches to careers education in schools*. London, England: Church Information Office.

Lynge, F. (1998, July). *Subsistence values and ethics*. Paper presented at the 1998 General Assembly of the Inuit Circumpolar Conference, Nuuk, Greenland. Retrieved from http://arcticcircle.uconn.edu/HistoryCulture/icc_lynge.htm

Monbiot, G. (2006). *Heat: How to stop the planet burning*. London, England: Penguin.

NCGE. (2009). *Creative guidance in challenging times*. Dublin, Ireland: National Centre for Guidance in Education. Retrieved from http://www.ncge.ie/reports/Creative%20Guidance%20FINAL.pdf

OECD. (2011). *Better life initiative: Measuring well-being and progress*. Paris, France: Author.

Parsons, F. (1894). *The philosophy of mutualism*. Philadelphia, PA: Bureau of Nationalist Literature.

Parsons, F. (1909). *Choosing a vocation*. Boston, MA: Houghton Mifflin.

Peavy, R. V. (2002). *Wisdom-based helping practice*. Victoria, Canada: Human Science Research.

Plant, P. (1996, May). *Economy & ecology: Towards a change of paradigms in careers guidance*. Paper presented at the IRTAC/BCSCA/CGCA International Conference on Counselling: Enhancing Personal Issues in the Global Community, Vancouver, Canada.

Plant, P. (1999). Fringe focus: Informal economy and green career development. *Journal of Employment Counseling, 36*(3), 131–139.

Plant, P. (2003). Green guidance: Fringe focus. In E. Kalinowska (Ed.), *Counsellor: Profession, passion, calling?* Wroclaw, Poland: Dolnoslaska Szkola Wyzsza Edukacji.

Plant, P. (2007a). *When is enough enough? Economic and social goals in career guidance.* Copenhagen, Denmark: Gratisartikler. Retrieved from http://www.gratisartikler.com/articledetail.php?artid=241&catid=381&title=When+is+enough+enough?+Economic+and+social+goals+in+career+guidance

Plant, P. (2007b, May). An inconvenient truth: Green guidance. *IAEVG Newsletter,* 1–3. Retrieved from http://www.iaevg.org/crc/files/newsletters/Newlet58en.doc

Plant, P. (2008). Green guidance. *Career Edge,* 4–6.

Randers, J. (2012). *2052: A global forecast for the next forty years* (A report to the club of Rome commemorating the 40th anniversary of The Limits to Growth). New York, NY: Chelsea Green.

Rifkin, J. (2010). *The empathic civilisation: The race to global consciousness in a world in crisis.* New York, NY: Tarcher/Penguin.

Rogers, C. (1951). *Client-centered therapy.* Boston, MA: Houghton Mifflin.

Schaltegger, S., & Burritt, R. (2000). *Contemporary environmental accounting: Issues, concept and practice.* Sheffield, England: Greenleaf.

Scharmer, C. O. (2007). *Theory U: Leading from the future as it emerges.* Cambridge, MA: Society for Organizational Learning.

Smith, A. (1776). *An inquiry into the nature and causes of the wealth of nations.* Edinburgh, England: Nelson.

Stern, N. (2006). *The economics of climate change: The Stern review.* London, England: H.M. Treasury.

Stiglitz, J. E., Sen, A., & Fitoussi, J. P. (2009). *Report by the commission on the measurement of economic performance and social progress.* Paris, France. Retrieved from www.stiglitz-sen-fitoussi.fr

Super, D. E. (1957). *The psychology of careers: An introduction to vocational development.* New York, NY: Harper.

Super, D. E. (1980). A life-span, life-space approach to career development. *Journal of Vocational Behavior, 16*(3), 282–298.

UNDP. (2011). *Sustainability and equity: A better future for all.* New York, NY: Author.

Watts, A. G. (2003, November). *Working connections: OECD observations.* Presented at Working Connections: A Pan-Canadian Symposium on Career Development, Lifelong Learning and Workforce Development, Toronto, Canada. Retrieved from http://www.iaevg.org/crc/files/Watts-Toronto_Canada_2003719_2.pdf

Weber, M. (1958). *The protestant ethic and the spirit of capitalism.* New York, NY: Charles Scribner's Sons.

Career Guidance for Social Justice in Neoliberal Times

Ronald G. Sultana

Introduction

In much of the work on career guidance that has appeared over the past decade, particularly that triggered by the set of overlapping reviews carried out internationally (by the OECD [2004], the European Union [Sultana, 2003, 2004, 2008; Sultana & Watts, 2006a, 2006b], and the World Bank [Watts & Fretwell, 2004]), it has been claimed that guidance can contribute to both private and public goals. Explicitly or implicitly, the argument has been made that career guidance can enhance social justice by mobilizing knowledge and information resources as well as a panoply of services on behalf of citizens, and especially of vulnerable groups, easing their transition to economic independence and dignified living, thus facilitating a foundational principle—many would say myth—of modern democracies, meritocracy. It has also been claimed that guidance can increase prosperity and can support sustainable employment through, for instance, ensuring a better match between the supply and demand of skills, by socializing and preparing citizens for flexible engagement with the world of work (including geographic and occupational mobility), and striking a balance between fulfilling personal aspirations and contributing to broader economic goals. Additionally, career guidance is often assumed to help reduce social costs, in the form of lost wages, lost taxes, and social unrest, so that at the end of the day, "governmental provision of career services will pay for itself by helping clients obtain better jobs, better salaries, return higher taxes" (Herr, 2008, p. 14), and so on. While it is important not to overestimate the role that career guidance can play, it is reasonable to argue that it *can* make a positive difference in the lives of citizens, possibly contributing to equalizing life chances, particularly during an economic downturn (Hughes & Borbély-Pecze, 2012), and not merely serve to reproduce social class destinies (Willis, 1977).

As a contributor to several of the international reviews referred to above, I have worked with and effectively endorsed what one could refer to as a "progressive" (as opposed to a radical, conservative, or liberal stance [Watts, 2002]) understanding of the link between career guidance and social justice (see Table 18.1). The public policy orientation of the reviews, while leaving ample space for critique, tends to lead to a focus on what can be done *within* the prevailing system, so that the adage that "politics is the art of the possible" applies equally well here. Working within the system, however, does not preclude working *against* aspects of it. The international reviews, together with the efforts of think tanks and professional associations such as the European Lifelong Guidance Policy Network and the International Association for Educational and Vocational Guidance (IAEVG), have not only helped to put guidance on the public policy

R.G. Sultana (✉)
University of Malta, Msida, Malta
e-mail: ronald.sultana@um.edu.mt

G. Arulmani et al. (eds.), *Handbook of Career Development*, International and Cultural Psychology,
DOI 10.1007/978-1-4614-9460-7_18, © Springer Science+Business Media, LLC 2014

Table 18.1 Career guidance and socio-political ideologies

	Core focus on society	Core focus on individual
Change	Radical (social change)	Progressive (individual change)
Status quo	Conservative (social change)	Liberal (nondirective)

Source: Watts, A. G. (2002). Socio-political ideologies in guidance. In A. G. Watts, B. Law, J. Killeen, J. M. Kidd, & R. Hawthorn (Eds.), *Rethinking careers education and guidance: Theory, policy and practice* (pp. 351–365). London, UK: Routledge

agenda; they have also generated a space where critical discourses have flourished, underpinned by a firm conviction that all citizens, and particularly the most vulnerable, have a *right* to quality services that support their career planning and career management, especially at a time when economic circumstances are particularly grim.

Indeed, in promoting career guidance not only in economically developed countries but also in the Middle East and North Africa region (Sultana & Watts, 2007, 2008) and beyond, my work with policymakers, practitioners, and researchers is informed by the hope that our efforts have a beneficial effect on individuals and the economy alike. The key argument here is that career guidance, as a discourse and as a practice, can claim its lineage within that historic arch of Enlightenment social dreaming that we now refer to as *modernity*, where individuals are encouraged to carve out dignified and fulfilling lives for themselves, irrespective of social origin, gender, ethnicity, and other hitherto ascriptive factors. Within such a discourse, social justice has particular connotations, relating to the meritocratic distribution of material resources and life chances in ways that reward ability, effort, and achievement. Needless to say, having to think this through for such contrasting contexts as post-conflict Kosovo, beleaguered Palestine, impenetrably complex Egypt, and a range of other, very distinct countries and regions have both tempered my claims and obliged me to recognize that theories can never really capture the vibrant "messiness" of real life (Law, 2004).

Counting What Counts Most

Some have bravely attempted the technically difficult if not near-impossible task of measuring the impact of career guidance on both individual and public well-being—a goal that could be commended given that governments often require evidence that its use of public money is contributing to the public good. As for myself, I tend to agree with anti-positivists who state that in life, what counts most often cannot be counted (and not everything that can be counted counts). I also have a healthy skepticism of the insistence of some on "evidence-based policy," when what we often see is "policy-based evidence," with evidence being generated a posteriori in order to legitimize policies that have already been decided a priori. Research, thus, becomes a tool for compensatory legitimation rather than an honest guide to good governance, in support of upright policies that promote social justice.

While, I am sure, our guidance community welcomes evidence that buttresses claims that we *do* have a positive effect on individuals and societies alike, many of us in the field are driven by other sorts of evidence, which might not move governments to open their purse but which fills us with hope that our professional lives are well spent, that we *do* give service, and that we *do* work to make our world more socially just. For those of us who are or who have been practitioners, we know only too well that sound career guidance *can* make an enormous difference in the lives of others. Such a claim is certainly sustainable at the micro- and meso-levels. We all can narrate stories of students who suddenly come alive and blossom in front of our eyes when they finally find the education pathway that corresponds to who they are and who they are striving to become; or stories of youths who find work and purpose in life after months of anguished job search that eats away at their confidence in themselves and in the society that has filled their hearts with dreams but fails to deliver when and where it matters most; of stories of citizens who, with our help, fight exclusion from the labor market due to disability or prejudice linked to class, gender, ethnicity, belief, or sexual orientation; of adults with families to feed whom we help find jobs when their company makes them "redundant"—superfluous, unneeded, of no further use—at particularly critical junctures in their lives; or stories of senior citizens whom we support in finding meaning and value in living and in giving, after society pensions them off, forgetting that the "gospel" of lifelong learning and self-development that it preaches cannot and should not lead to the travesty that automatically seems to equate seniority with senility.

Levels of Engagement with Social Justice Agendas

The preoccupation of the guidance field with social justice issues, therefore, has a long history, not least because career guidance often brings practitioners face to face with individuals and groups on the receiving end of social *in*justice. Practitioner efforts in furthering social justice have tended to be criticized for operating at the interactive level, leaving us with little hope in terms of the transformation of the social structures that create inequality. Such efforts, which at best impact at the micro- and meso-levels, that is, at the level of everyday individual lives, performed within institutional structures that are human-made—and, therefore, susceptible to change by human minds, hands, and heart—are nevertheless vitally important and should be celebrated. They represent genuine efforts to do the best one can on Monday morning, under the prevailing historical and economic circumstances, which are far larger than us. I am a bit tired of facile critiques and guidance bashing by left-wing scholars like myself, where we have been too often prone to scoff, somewhat self-indulgently from the height of our ivory towers, at career guidance practitioners for trying to tackle unemployment by teaching youths self-presentation skills, how to sit for an interview, or how to write up a seductive curriculum vitae. Of course, such so-called "career management skills" will not create jobs, and yes, it is true that what they ultimately do is shuffle the deck of cards, bringing the lucky few

to the head of the queue, since 100 applicants into one vacancy will not go. But for that individual concerned, the care and attention that go along with these programs, the effort to revive confidence in oneself, and the networks and resources that are mobilized on his or her behalf can make a difference between despondency and despair on the one hand and the recovery of determination and drive that can indeed lead to a breakthrough on the other. To deride career guidance practitioners for doing what, at the one-to-one interactive level, *can* be done is as ungracious and as perverse as putting down ambulance workers who attend to the wounded, criticizing them for not stopping the war.

At another linked level—the meso or institutional one—career guidance practitioners can make a difference by adopting a stronger advocacy role, working with and on behalf of the citizens they serve in order to lobby for the transformation of social structures, and institutional practices that reproduce and reinforce injustice. In our guidance community, we have some particularly outstanding role models to emulate: I am here thinking of people like Tony Watts in the UK (2011), Edwin Herr in the USA (2008), and Gideon Arulmani (2010) and The Promise Foundation in India—among several others— who have advocated change that serves the interests of citizens generally, and especially those most in need, through their skillful interventions in a range of public policy forums. But I am also thinking of more modest efforts, such as of a career adviser in a school who not only develops programs to reach out to "dropouts" but lobbies hard to change school curricular, pedagogical, and organizational practices that serve to "push out" vulnerable youths, thus combating a blame-the-victim approach. Working with citizens, young and adult, in encouraging their *capacity to aspire* (Appadurai, 2004), to move beyond their *bounded rationality* (Simon, 1991) and their *adaptive preferences* (Biggeri, 2010; Nussbaum, 2001), and to contest the seductive imperative of *realism* and *realistic choices* (Colley, 2000) is a major achievement— perhaps not so much for children who come from privileged families and whose "horizons for action" (Hodkinson, Sparkes, & Hodkinson,

1996, p. 123), therefore, stretch far, thanks to their parents' economic, social, and cultural capital, but certainly for those on the margins of society, for whom the task of transcending notions they have developed about the self, gaining knowledge of the opportunities their environment provides, and overcoming perceptions from their life histories as to what they thought was achievable is as challenging as it is vital from the perspective of social justice. Our advocacy is even more likely to be effective when it takes the form of a collective response, whether as part of a commitment by the whole institution, by a professional association, or as part of an alliance with broader social movements. The meso-, micro-, and macro-levels of course connect and interconnect in myriad ways, with choices and aspirations being "deformed in and through the tiny and big details" (Walker, 2003, p. 169) of individuals' everyday lives in such social spaces as families, schools, labor offices, shopping malls, and so on.

Without, therefore, wanting to make any grand claims about the effectiveness of career guidance practice in furthering social justice, I would nevertheless like to claim that, with all our faults and within the limitations of the possible, we do "good," or at least we try to, to the best of our ability and within the structural constraints of the economic and political systems that we live in. It is to this structural dimension, the macro-level, that I wish to focus most of my attention on in the rest of this chapter, not because I believe that career guidance can do much in transforming social structures into ones that respect social justice more but because I am deeply convinced that *we need to have a profound understanding of the complex world we live in if we are to develop socially just practices at the levels where we are likely to have most impact.*

From a "Pessimism of the Intellect" to an "Optimism of the Will"

Roberts (2005) has put class at the heart of an analysis of social injustice—though of course economic inequality has complex intersections

with forms of injustice linked to, among others, gender and ethnic identity. Provocatively, he has also stated that:

> Challenging the powerful is not a realistic agenda for early twenty-first century career guidance. How can guidance hope to succeed when trade unions and political parties of the left have failed? Maybe class inequalities need to be challenged . . . but the crucial point remains; career guidance is simply not an appropriate weapon. (p. 141)

In some ways, this is a damning conclusion, relegating our profession's impact to the micro- and meso-levels referred to earlier. But such a conclusion also seems reasonable, confirmed by common sense and everyday evidence.

This, however, is where the Italian political philosopher Gramsci (1971) provides us with pragmatic guidance, thanks to his pithy aphorism exhorting those who would struggle for a more socially just world to, yes, indeed, embrace a "pessimism of the intellect" but to counter that with "an optimism of the will." What Gramsci is reminding us of, with reference to his own brand of emancipatory politics, is that engagement with the world as it is, in order to imagine and bring about a world as it could and should be, requires us all to work in that uncomfortable zone where—*despite* the structural constraints that we intellectually apperceive and indeed analytically understand as daunting and which, from our position in space and time, actually seem to be quite intractable—we nevertheless continue the struggle, refusing to be overwhelmed, but rather persevere, almost, as it were, against reason.

That such a political and ontological stance is not unreasonable can be deduced from what is at stake, as I will soon argue. Suffice it to say that here we are also in the realm of history, for what is history but the record of humanity's efforts to rise above the constraints imposed by nature and by tyrants, constraints that, for those caught in the nitty-gritty of the everyday struggle called life, seemed to be quite insurmountable? And yet slavery and serfdom, as dominant forms of life, *have* been overcome, and while there is nothing that is necessarily or comfortably linear and progressive in history, the emancipatory project of humanity remains a constant, with the Arab Spring being just one other reminder that the striving for social justice blossoms when and where we least expect it to—and not always with the hoped for results, one might add. The remarkable thing about the Arab Spring is that none of the most notable and expert commentators on the Middle East and North Africa region had predicted the rise of the masses and least of all that the spark would come from an unemployed graduate who would rather immolate himself than suffer further indignities.

Indeed, the Tunisian Mohamed Bouazizi is the latest of a series of individuals who, throughout history, have succeeded in galvanizing a *Politics of Indignation* (Mayo, 2012): It is these *Indignados*, whether in the squares of Madrid or Rome, Aleppo or Athens, or Wall Street or London City, who we need to keep in mind when we talk about "social justice," lest we fall into the typical middle-class trap of thinking of social justice in the abstract and become a latter-day example of that character from one of Dostoevsky's novels, who weeps over the misfortunes of the down-and-out in a tragic opera she is enjoying in Moscow while keeping her cabby driver waiting in the freezing night outside. It is quite significant, at this point, to consider what Gonthier's (2005) analysis of the representations and theories of social justice held by citizens across Europe has to tell us. Drawing on the European Values Survey data, Gonthier concluded that Europeans "tend to privilege an idealistic conception of social justice" and are quicker on the draw when declaring "what kinds of goods *a* society should provide" rather than when considering "how they would have to react if the society they belong to was to provide certain kinds of goods" and whether, therefore, collective welfare would take precedence over personal comfort. In Weberian terms, therefore, Europeans seem to conform to "an ethic of conviction" rather than to "an ethic of responsibility."

The optimism of the will that I am recommending is not based on a blind sanguinity that would see *la vie en rose* at all costs. Rather, it is first of all based on how we perceive social justice. The realistically pessimistic position that Roberts (2005), like many others, adopts in

relation to the ability of career guidance to promote economic social justice tends to take what Sen (2008) has referred to as a "transcendental approach," which is common to practically all the classical and modern theories of social justice. Now Sen, a Nobel laureate Indian economist, is actually quite important to any consideration of social justice, given that his celebrated "capabilities approach" helps us focus on the possible, on "what people are actually able to do and to be," and how, as Nussbaum has stated (2000), one can create the conditions for enacting "a life that is worthy of the dignity of the human being" (p. 5). Sen has reasonably argued that there is value in achieving greater justice, and he steers clear of an all-or-nothing approach which can ultimately be paralyzing (Sen, 2008). My reading of Sen's position is that social justice is not a *state* that can be reached—not only because this is too politically optimistic, given the inevitable imbalance of power between different groups and the ultimately perennial victory of self-interest against that of the collective, but also because even if such a state were ever to be reached, it would necessarily be temporary, as the sweep of history brings in new situations and new opportunities for one group to lord it over the other—again, the Winter following the Arab Spring in many countries in the region is a timely reminder of this. The Poles have much to teach us here, and their historical experience with tyranny has led them to wryly coin a proverb that says: "When you pull down the statue of the tyrant, make sure you leave the pedestal." Furthermore, as Fraser (1997) has argued, the attempt to achieve certain dimensions of social justice inevitably leads to disregarding or even giving up on others. Trying to address economic injustice, for instance, through the redistribution of social wealth, is likely to clash with demands for cultural justice, that is, for the recognition of rights to enact certain lifestyles. In short, there are no blueprints out there, and "any meaningful discussion of what counts as justice needs to engage with concrete, practical dilemmas and not merely abstract conceptualisations" (Gewirtz, 2006, p. 70).

In my view, therefore, social justice is a *stance* rather than a state. It is an unquenchable thirst that keeps us ever on the alert and always on the quest for more equal, more equitable, more just, more fair social relations, helping us find a balance between what Bauman (2006) considered the perennial concerns of humanity: freedom and security. That quest and thirst permeates all our human activities and the structures, practices, rituals, and routines that we develop—in other words, the forms of life that we co-create, including this "thing" called *career guidance.*

A Thirst for Social Justice

What, then, is this context-bound social justice that we should have an unquenchable thirst for, and how does it relate to prosperity and well-being? Furthermore, what would career guidance practices that promote social justice look like? And is a socially just career guidance at all possible in the neoliberal times that we live in? These are some of the fundamental questions that career guidance practitioners and researchers need to address—questions that constitute a research agenda and an action program for the whole field, assuming that we truly aspire to put social justice at the heart of our community of inquiry and our community of practice.

First, however, we need to arrive at some shared, context-relevant understanding of social justice in relation to career guidance. Like many, I often find myself slipping in the phrase *social justice* in my professional work, generally with a feeling that this is certainly something good to do, and to encourage myself and others to achieve. But, as others before me have noted, the term *social justice* is so frequently bandied about by politicians, governments, and all sorts of organizations that it has practically lost its meaning (Irving, 2010; North, 2006), and most importantly, it seems to have lost its punch. It is therefore vital to decipher some of the different meanings of this slippery term, this "floating signifier" social justice, since different ways of understanding it have important implications for

the way we understand and practice career guidance. We must not imagine, for a single moment, that here we are pioneering a new field. Social and political science, legal studies, philosophy, economics, sociology, theology, and anthropology: most, if not all, the disciplines and their subfields of knowledge have paid a great deal of attention to the issue of how one might enact socially just forms of life—not least because, as I have just argued, social justice is a never-ending process that needs constantly to be striven for and constantly to be reinvented. Is social justice best served by giving free reign to the market in the belief that a fair equilibrium is eventually reached, or is human life too precious to be trusted to invisible forces that are ultimately driven by self-interest? And what view of human nature do we have? Are humans irredeemably self-centered and driven by what one of the founders of political philosophy, the English Thomas Hobbes (1651), called "a perpetual and restless desire of power after power," or are we more akin to the beings represented in John Rawls' (1971) political philosophy, where we are depicted as capable of reason, with a capacity for genuine toleration and mutual respect? Will "the poor always be with us," as prophesized by a Palestinian preacher two millennia ago, or are we truly capable of bringing about utopia, despite the fact that so many societal blueprints have given birth to nothing but dystopias and suffering of all kinds?

For the time being, and to set the stage for what follows, let us go back to that simple but hopefully not simplistic declaration that I made earlier: "we do good" or at least we are trying to, to the best of our ability, and within the structural constraints of the economic and political systems that we live in. To "be good," to "do good," and to "act virtuously in relation to others" might sound trite and even childish, but this is the foundation on which, in my view, the best philosophical traditions, whether western or otherwise, were built and on which I wish to anchor my understanding of social justice. The Brazilian educator Paolo Freire (1970) reminded us, through his powerful writings, including that symphony of a manifesto to social justice,

Pedagogy of the Oppressed, that we can still be intellectually profound when we use such seemingly and disarmingly simple terms as *love*, *humility*, *trust*, and *hope*. We are of course not naive enough to think that by wishing to "do good" or to "do the right thing," we are actually doing so. "Hell," as the English say, unwittingly synthesizing the theology of Bernard of Clairvaux, "is paved with good intentions." My point is, however, that social justice is intimately related to "being good" and to "doing good"—in other words, *to being and acting virtuously*, not only in the privacy of myself with my "self" but also in my relations to others and, indeed, to all sentient beings. While many of us might be hardpressed to come up with a philosophically or politically sound definition of social justice, most if not all of us would recognize social justice when we experienced it—or the lack of it—and indeed, even very young children will shout out spontaneously, "It ain't fair" when they are on the receiving end of an injustice (Krebs, 2008).

New Concepts, Viewpoints, and Directions: Career Guidance and Approaches to Social Justice

What social justice is, whether career guidance can actually help make our world a more socially just place, or whether we are merely the oil that lubricates the machine are questions that are increasingly troubling our own community of inquiry and of practice—and this is an excellent sign, as career guidance emancipates itself from its sole anchorage in personal psychology, neoliberal economics, and human capital theory to adopt more critical perspectives enriched by a dialogue with the social sciences. Here, the work of Blustein, McWhirter, and Perry (2005) and their articulate plea for emancipatory communitarianism to temper the reproductive tenor of mainstream vocational psychology immediately comes to mind, as do the important insights from critical sociology in the work of Colley (2000), Hodkinson, Sparkes, and Hodkinson (1996), and Hodkinson and Sparkes (1997),

among others. We should draw sustenance from the work that already exists and build upon it. Some from our international community have been inspired by frameworks and typologies proposed by Young (1990) and by Fraser (1997, 2009), usefully distinguishing between *retributive*, *distributive*, and *recognitive* justice, thus highlighting approaches to social justice that are based on everybody getting his or her "just deserts" (hence, retributive justice); on ensuring that there is a level playing field in the access to the "goodies" of life, whether economic or otherwise (hence distributive justice); and on acknowledging that society is made up of different groups, whose diverse identities and cultures render them susceptible to different forms of oppression, including cultural domination, nonrecognition, and disrespect (hence, recognitive justice).

Irving (2010) from New Zealand has used such frameworks to good effect, and in a volume co-edited with Malik (2004), engaged a number of colleagues from around the world tasking them to consider the ways in which career education and guidance can act as a vehicle for promoting social justice within a global economy. Others, like Berthet and his colleagues (Berthet, 2010; Berthet, Dechézelles, Fouin, & Simon, 2009) at the Sciences Po in Bordeaux, have tried to explore how Sen's capabilities approach, as well as Nussbaum's (2000) contributions to that political economic tradition, can inform our understanding of career guidance as a practice that promotes social justice through facilitating the conversion of personal resources into actual capabilities. Yet others, such as Sampson, McClain, Musch, and Reardon (2011) at Florida State University, for instance, have highlighted the fact that equitable access to career guidance services is a social justice issue, particularly at a time when a "perfect storm" is brewing, given that public funding for career services is decreasing just when the demand and need for such services is increasing, with detrimental consequences, especially for the least well-off members of the society. Career guidance associations, including the IAEVG, and the Society for Vocational Psychology (whose tenth Biennial Conference, held in Boston, Massachusetts, on November 6, 2011, was dedicated to *Forging Career Policy for the Greater Good*) have not kept back from dedicating annual conferences to social justice, and we have also seen special issues of journals being published, focusing on how guidance can promote social inclusion (e.g., *Australian Journal of Career Development*, Volume 19, No. 1, 2010; *International Journal for Educational and Vocational Guidance*, Volume 14, No. 1, 2014).

Such work helps us further unpack what we mean by social justice in relation to concrete, practical dilemmas that the career guidance professional community has to deal with. Other typologies are also helpful in thinking through the many possible relations between career guidance and social justice, thus increasing an understanding of both the bright side and the dark side of this relationship. Especially useful in this context is the work of the Scottish philosopher Alisdair MacIntyre (1984, 1988). In his efforts to decode our complex times, MacIntyre has drawn creatively from Aristotle's classic *Nicomachean Ethics*, which had distinguished between four types of justice, namely, distributive (relating to how organization resources are allocated), commutative (relating to the restoration of justice by means of exchange or payment), corrective (remedying unfair distribution), and procedural (relating to the process leading up to an outcome) justice. He then argued that if one had to review and synthesize the main currents of Western philosophy, four rival philosophical traditions would become evident (Ruitenberg & Vokey, 2011). Some—such as Socrates and Plato—have conceptualized social justice as any action that contributes to *social harmony*. Inspired by this tradition, career guidance would stress the value of each citizen, discovering his or her talents and putting them at the service of the community. Other political and philosophical traditions—such as those represented by Kant, for instance—have made *equality* the litmus test of social justice. This tradition resonates with efforts by the career guidance community to level the playing field for decision-making and to infuse forms of

rationality in a process that is often based on factors that are not always a guide for good action.

In the view of yet another tradition—best represented by the American political philosopher John Rawls—*equity* is superior to equality in that there is an acknowledgement of the fact that treating unequal people equally reproduces and reinforces social inequality and social injustice. This approach raises tricky questions for career guidance, particularly in relation to "accident of birth": Is it fair to reward individuals for talents that they were born with, and is it just to withhold social rewards—in terms of remuneration and status—from individuals to whom nature and fortune have either given no particular gift or whose talents are not particularly valued, recognized, or required within a given society? Here, as Durkheim has perceptively pointed out (see Green, 1989, for a discussion), social justice seems to be dependent on fortunes of birth and of place, rather than anything else, which is why Rawls' proposal of allocating resources and opportunities for well-being on the basis of a "veil of ignorance"—whereby individuals formulate a standard of justice while unaware of their place in or value to their society—is important and has particular relevance to our field.

The fourth philosophical tradition breaks with the ontological assumptions made by these three traditions and, by conceptualizing social justice in terms of *difference*, gives pride of place to ethics, arguing that "we cannot think about what it means to be human without thinking about what it means to be ethically bound by our relations with others" (Ruitenberg & Vokey, 2011, p. 408), with the "other" being seen in terms of an absolute "alterity." The Kaunas-born philosopher Emmanuel Levinas (1989) as well as his Franco-Algerian contemporary Jacques Derrida (1991) are key exponents of this important strand of thought. These are less interested by classical "justice-as-fairness" approaches, which ultimately avoid dealing with the absolutely central issue of human dignity and of human suffering. Ethical and socially just behavior would impel me to respond to the singular "other," who "calls me into responsibility and who remains ungraspably 'other' to me" (Ruitenberg & Vokey, 2011, p. 408). The self gains its identity from the ethical demands made upon it in relationship to the other: "the self is itself when and only when it is for-the-other" (Cohen, 2002, p. 57). This, then, entails a different logic to the one that we operate within the current form of life we inhabit, where the self is defined without reference to others (Goodman, Walling, & Ghali, 2010): It is a logic that "trembles" and "vibrates" at the transcendence of the call of the other for dignity and respect, who is treated as an end, not as a means to an end. Levinas has asserted that that "justice in a society is significantly tied to its inherent definitions of the self. He argued that a society which employed self-interested depictions of the self could not cultivate the interhuman responsibility necessary for justice and love to thrive" (Goodman et al., 2010, p. 589). This is not, either, a logic about persons "deserving" social rewards—think here of the "illegal" immigrants in many of our Public Employment Services—persons are worthy of respect *qua* human beings, irrespective of the rhetoric of political institutions whose language speaks of "merit" rather than "hospitality." For Derrida, for instance, "there is always necessarily violence at the borders" (Lawlor, 2011), and all social institutions operate through establishing boundaries, which some of us—employment and career advisers included—are paid to guard and patrol.

Relevance for Multiple Cultures: Sensitivity to the Universal and the Particular

This is a hurried sketch of how the four main Western philosophical approaches to social justice could relate to specific ways of understanding and enacting career guidance. This is not the place to paint a detailed canvas, which would also require a critical appraisal of how the various strategies and tools that we use in our profession hearken back to one or more of these philosophical traditions. There is much work that still needs to be done in this regard, and here we have not even started considering how

other non-Western philosophical approaches to social justice would impact our understanding of career guidance. Needless to say, what we have in front of us is nothing less than a lifetime project. Within the limits of this chapter, however, I would like to make three points that I feel could provide us with some kind of conceptual map or compass. In making these three points, the main focus will be on the first of the four traditions—namely, social justice as social harmony—and work on that in order to illustrate some of the benefits and insights that can emerge from engaging in such an exercise. I will refer to the three other traditions briefly, *en passant*.

Ethical Traditions as Templates for Action

First, the four different approaches to social justice that in MacIntyre's view represent the key traditions in Western philosophy, consciously or unconsciously *constitute the template through which we act as moral and ethical human beings*, and therefore how we practice "socially just career guidance." In other words, the distinctive, rival approaches to social justice—and whether we privilege *social harmony*, *equality*, *equity*, or *difference* as our way of reading the world and acting on it as human beings and workers—are critically important if we are to be reflexive about the career theories we subscribe to, the tools and strategies we use, and the goals and ends we aspire to. I am not excluding the possibility that we are able to operate with two or more of these traditions, despite the tensions that this may give rise to and which were briefly referred to earlier when discussing Fraser's work. Indeed, so-called "plural conceptions of social justice" (Honneth, 2004) have become quite common, with social justice being viewed as having a variety of facets, including being able to simultaneously address "the distribution of material goods and resources on the one hand and the valorization of a range of social collectivities and cultural identities on the other" (Gewirtz & Cribb, 2002, p. 499). However, it is important that we recognize the value of identifying these four traditions not merely for heuristic purposes, as a guide to our reflection on a complex and thorny matter, but also to alert us to the different conceptualizations of the social that each entails.

Career guidance advisers who, consciously or unconsciously, work with a theory of justice that puts a premium on social harmony will tend to value the abilities and talents of every individual and consider that virtue lies in discovering what these might be and how they might contribute to the good of society overall. Socrates and Plato subscribed to this view, and it might come as a surprise to some that in the 4th century BCE, the notion of career guidance—like so many other notions that we erroneously consider modern—was already in gestation. For Socrates, and in Plato's *Republic*, the exercise on the part of a citizen of an occupation was intimately linked to the notions of social justice. In Socrates' ontology, every person has an *arete* or excellence, and it is by being the best that one can be, through putting one's talent at the service of the community, that one attains virtue. Indeed, a foundational principle for Plato's *Republic* is that "everyone ought to perform the one function in the community for which his nature best suited him." (Here I use the masculine pronoun advisedly, given the inherent gender inequality underpinning the classical philosophers of ancient Greece.) The author then goes on to claim that "that principle, or some form of it, is justice" (*The Republic*, Cornford, trans., IV, sec 432). From this perspective, then, our career guidance programs, strategies, and methodologies are socially just, and contribute to social justice, if and when they help the individual find and build his or her *arete*, or "excellence," and to be the best that she or he can be, with a view to best serving the community's interests and needs.

The Importance of the "Larger Picture"

Second, whichever theory or approach to social justice we embrace, *the implications that that has for our career guidance practice need to be considered in terms of the larger picture that we operate in.* In other words, the convictions we

hold about socially just career guidance need to be examined in the light of the structural constraints of the economic and political systems that we live in. I would like to refer to a little-known essay penned in Latin in August 1835 by a youthful Karl Marx and titled "Reflections of a Young Man on the Choice of a Profession." Here, indeed, we already see the aspiration to transcend personal interests and to commit oneself to the interests of humanity. Noting that the choice of occupation "is a great privilege of man over the rest of creation," (p. 1), Marx also reflected that the possibility of choice is, at the same time, "an act which can destroy his whole life, frustrate all plans, and make him unhappy" (p. 1) (apologies, yet again, for the ubiquitous masculine pronoun). Marx, therefore, in what may very well be the first pitch for career guidance in modern Europe, cautioned against choosing an occupation for the wrong reasons, arguing that choices motivated by mere ambition, or an overactive imagination, or opportunism could lead to unhappiness, self-contempt, self-deception, and ultimately the betrayal of the self. Instead, heed should be given to the advice and guidance of experienced elders, giving due consideration to one's talents and physical constitution. Marx concluded by practically echoing the classics, stating that "the chief guide which must direct us in the choice of a profession is the welfare of mankind and our own perfection" (p. 3).

Such views of one's arete, or talent, and how social justice is served by virtuously placing one's talents and labor at the service of the common good, acquire meaning in some contexts across time and space but are simply alien to most of our contemporary conceptions of career guidance, which, in most cases, have hollowed out the social. Marx, like Plato and Socrates, saw no contradiction between individual and social interests: "On the contrary," he claimed, "man's nature is so constituted that he can attain his own perfection only by working for the perfection, for the good, of his fellow men" (Marx, 1835, p. 3). The very act, therefore, of choosing a profession, and of helping individuals choose that profession, contributes to social justice because the exercise of that task, however humble, contributes to the greater good.

This is where Socrates and Marx meet, two contemporary thinkers whose work is of enormous importance to the career guidance field: Sennett and the social theorist already referred to earlier, Bauman. Both employ a language of justice that speaks to the heart as much as to the mind, performing the role of "public sociologists" who strive to "enlighten" us—in terms of both "throwing light" on difficult and complex areas of our lives and also "lighting us up" with the urge to translate reflection into action. Sennett (1998, 2006) has shown us how the very notion of *career*, in its etymological meaning of a consistent direction and a path, has been lost, with the best that one can hope for being a sequence of jobs, that ultimately alienates us not only from ourselves but from the community—corroding our very humanity. In a similar vein, Bauman (2001) has noted that from the ethical perspective, in the past, no kind of work "could be seriously argued to be deprived of value and demeaning; all work added to human dignity and all work equally served the cause of moral propriety and spiritual redemption" (p. 323). Bauman has argued, however, that under the conditions of contemporary capitalism, the work ethic point of view and its salvific qualities have been replaced by "the aesthetics of consumption." Like a consumer good, work that is "rich in gratifying experience, work as self-fulfillment, work as the meaning of life, work as the core or the axis of everything that counts, as the source of pride, self-esteem, honor, and deference or notoriety, in short, work as vocation, has become the privilege of a few; a distinctive mark of the elite" (p. 325). It is, in short, "a way of life the rest may watch in awe, admire and contemplate at a distance but only experience vicariously through pulp fiction and the virtual reality of televised docu-drama. That rest is given no chance of living-through their jobs in a way the vocations are lived" (p. 325).

Sennett and Bauman, in their respective but overlapping analyses of *liquid modernity*, trouble us further: Not only is it difficult to see how career guidance can engage socially just practice when, for many, the jobs available are too small

for their spirits (Terkel, 1974); moreover, most people have been uprooted from their social anchorage. In such a situation, how does one go about supporting individuals in their efforts to weave, in Sennett's words, "a sustaining life narrative" (2006, p. 5) when, given the culture of the new capitalism, it is flexibility that is given pride of place over security? As Bauman has noted:

> The 'flexible labour market' neither offers nor permits commitment and dedication to any currently performed occupation. Getting attached to the job in hand, falling in love with what the job requires its holder to do, identifying one's place in the world with the work performed or the skills deployed, means becoming hostage to fate; it is neither very likely nor to be recommended, given the short-lived nature of any employment and the 'until further notice' clause entailed in any contract. (Bauman, 2001, p. 325)

"For the majority of people other than the chosen few," concluded Bauman, "in the present-day flexible labour market, embracing one's work as a vocation carries enormous risks and is a recipe for psychological and emotional disaster" (p. 325). Many of us might find it difficult to imagine just how deadening many jobs are, and the extent to which, for several classes of people, the notion of self-fulfillment through work, which is at the heart of career guidance, is simply too ludicrous to even imagine. Indeed, it might do the guidance community a great deal of good to experience the existential angst that Ehrenreich (2001) bravely and dramatically captured in her undercover journalistic work *Nickel and Dimed*, as she divested herself of links with middle-class comforts to sample life as a waitress, hotel maid, house cleaner, nursing-home aide, and Wal-Mart salesperson. Her odyssey in the low-waged sector of America puts paid to so many career guidance theories we all tend too merrily to work with, in the comfortable assumption that most people live for jobs and not for the weekend.

All this, it goes without saying, is deeply troubling for our involvement in career guidance and career education. If social justice is to be achieved by mobilizing the best of oneself to put it at the service of the community, and where, as Socrates as well as the young Marx claimed, individual interests are best served when he or she serves the interests of the "common good," what does this mean to our contemporary understanding and practice of career guidance, given that it is so starkly and brazenly focused on the individual, often with the total exclusion of the social? And how can we claim the social justice banner if Sennett and Bauman are right in their depiction of the contemporary world of work, which, in so many ways, and despite the rhetoric of "choice," "freedom," "lifelong learning," "portfolio" careers, and the like, ultimately isolates individuals, setting them "adrift" (Sennett, 2006, p. 27) in an insecure world where, curiously and ironically, we admonish them to develop "life projects," to construct "life narratives," and to engage with "personal action planning"—when the only constant is change. And this change is of course neither natural nor ordained by the gods; it is neither normal nor inevitable. Rather, it is the result of the choices that we have made based on particular understandings of what counts as wealth, how to create such wealth, how much of this wealth is needed, and what to do with it, and how to distribute it once we have it. The forms of life that we experience in the mad rush of everyday existence, where the clocks tick ever faster and the incitement "to have" overshadows the moral imperative "to be," are fuelled by impatient capital's rush for profits, no matter what, so that the very notion of "sustainable employment" is anathema to the logic of capital, which depends on flexibility and the intensification of insecurity in order to reach its ends.

At this level, then, how are we, as mediators between individuals and societies, to act ethically and how can we be socially just, in our effort to support the search for meaningful social being, when public troubles are experienced as private tragedies, and the culture of competitive capitalism, where the winner takes all, leaves individuals so damaged and crippled with self-hatred that the Socratic ideal of discovering and mobilizing one's arete in the service of the common good is barely conceivable, let alone realizable?

Locating Practice Within the Bigger Picture

This brings me to the third point I would like to address in this chapter. If, indeed, rival philosophical approaches to social justice are in tension with one another, and if we can only understand what is at stake when subscribing to one or other of these four approaches by seriously taking context into account, then *we need to be equally serious about how we think of our practices at the levels where we are most likely to have an impact in terms of furthering the social justice agenda*—that is, what was earlier on referred to as the micro- and meso-levels. I am thinking specifically of our actions, as career guidance professionals, in one-to-one and group interventions, in career learning programs, and in all the advocacy work that we do in order to change institutions and structures in educational, Public Employment Service, work and community settings. What I see happening in our field is what might, at first blush, appear to be quite innocuous and even progressive: We see the development of approaches and tools and strategies that privilege the individual, the strengthening of the individual's decision-making capacity, and the promotion of skills to manage one's own careers and to design one's own life in order to enhance personal fulfillment (Savickas et al., 2009). This "constructivist" and even "existentialist" if not "spiritualist" and "philosophical" (Hansen & Amundson, 2009) turn needs to be considered within the context of an overarching and globalized neoliberal regime that gives short shrift to social justice in whichever way this is defined, rendering the social subservient to the market (Bassot, 2012; Colley, 2007). By focusing on the individual at the expense of the social, we play into the hands of capital and the state with which it has made a historical pact, whereby we end up abetting a "politics of responsibilization" (Sultana, 2011; see also Watts & Knasel, 1985).

To explain further—within the neoliberal world—social justice is defined not as an inalienable right of every citizen but is rather, like everything else, circumscribed and captured within the economy. Neoliberalism thus "normalizes the logic of individualism and entrepreneurialism, equating individual freedom with self-interested choices, making individuals responsible for their own well-being" (Leitner, Shepphard, Sziarto, & Maringanti, 2007, as cited in Hursh & Henderson, 2011, p. 178). Citizens are "reconfigured as productive economic entrepreneurs of their own lives," and the welfare state is "reconstituted as an economically and socially costly obstacle to the economic performance upon which survival depends" (Davies & Bansel, 2007, p. 248), and it is the moral duty of the upright citizen to be the active entrepreneur of the self:

> This is not simply a reactivation of liberal values of self-reliance, autonomy and independence as the necessary conditions for self-respect, self-esteem, self-worth and self-advancement but rather an emphasis on enterprise and the capitalization of existence itself through calculated acts and investments combined with the shrugging off of collective responsibility for the vulnerable and the marginalized. (Davies & Bansel, 2007, p. 252)

This imperative of "freedom" is lived as "ambivalence, confusion, doubt, fear, failure and anxiety, as the individualized, competitive, responsibilized subjects of neoliberalism attempt to live out their freedoms in such a way as to maximize individual potential and thence their competitive advantage" (Davies & Bansel, 2007, p. 255). Career guidance approaches that eschew the social may very well end up reinforcing these broader trends, which is why the bigger picture cannot be forgotten, even as we struggle to live up to the demand of social justice in the face-to-face encounter with the "other."

Indeed, my claim is that within the current historical conjuncture, career guidance risks becoming entrapped within the master discourse of neoliberalism and that it has become absolutely vital to recognize this and to come up with alternative ways of reimagining what a socially just career guidance practice could and should be like. Earlier I referred to our, and children's, innate sense of justice that impels us to cry out against unfairness. But as Kohlberg,

Piaget, and Gilligan, among others, have taught us, our sense of justice is "innate" not in the sense that it is grounded in some kind of essentialist, species-specific quality—a sixth sense, as it were—but it is rather, at least in large part, the result of socialization. How, then, has our generation been socialized into which sense of social justice? How has the ideological matrix of neoliberalism shaped our thoughts and our deepest feelings about what constitutes a socially just world, in ways that also shape our actions not only as fathers, mothers, husbands, wives, sons, and daughters but also as workers and professionals in the career guidance field? For neoliberal discourses are not merely outside of us, they are not just an external force. Rather, neoliberal discourses are also internalized. They "colonize us—gifting us with our existence and shaping our desires, our beliefs in what is right" (Davies, 2005, p. 1). It is a subjectivity, "manifested in our talk about ourselves and our experiences" (Davies & Bansel, 2007, p. 248).

And lest we are tempted to take the easy way out, by pointing out that these economic, political, and cultural movements, for which we use the shorthand terms of neoliberalism and globalization, are too powerful and too gargantuan for us to dent, let alone overcome, let us trouble ourselves further by recalling Bauman's analysis of totalitarianism and domination which, he has claimed, in modernity was achieved through processes of *adiaphorization* (Bauman, 1989), that is, "the emptying of actions of moral content and consideration and the mediating of acting through chains of command and technological means making no one responsible" (Jacobsen & Marshman, 2008, p. 9). As Arthur (2005) has so well argued, career guidance workers committed to social justice cannot see themselves as technicians who merely employ professional competences skillfully. Indeed, that is the whole problem with competences narrowly defined (Sultana, 2009). Rather, while certainly acknowledging that we are not politicians, we are nevertheless inexorably enmeshed in the sphere of politics, and our actions, albeit practiced at micro- and meso-levels of human interaction within institutions, nevertheless inescapably resonate with, and feed into, the larger social issues that a consideration of social justice entails. In short, to enact social justice at the micro- and meso-levels, we need to have a bigger theory of justice. As Walker (2003) has put it, we need:

> A theory or principles of justice which enable us to adjudicate between our actions so that we can say with some confidence this action is more just than that. Patchwork actions, the individual pieces of cloth, however bright and lively, are just that, bits of cloth. Only when we stitch the pieces (our actions) together to make a quilt do the patterns emerge and transform the pieces into something new; we need to know what we are trying to make and to be able to judge whether we have made it well. (p. 169)

Not a "Conclusion"

In films, novels, and other genres of literary work, we speak of "tropes," or styles of representation, that signal to the audience or reader that this is the start of the climax, the denouement, or the conclusion of a "story." The trope, which is culturally embedded in ways that make it recognizable, is signaled by music, pace, tone, light, and so on, leaving the reader or viewer with a sense of satisfaction, not unlike the "they lived happily ever after" trope of children's fairytales. A chapter is, in some ways, also a performance with its own tropes. As we move towards *the* conclusion, I would like to stress that this reflective piece was not meant to provide a pleasing conclusion in the form of answers but rather to trouble the reader—as much as the author—by asking questions even if, in doing so, one finds the beginnings of ways of addressing the challenges identified. These are, for many citizens, desperate times. However, despite the pessimism that the current economic and social climate generates as we see, despite our best efforts, a whole generation of young people frustrated and going to waste, it is important to hold fast to our principles of making a difference where a difference can be made. I have frequently made reference to the classical philosophers in this chapter in an effort to displace our understanding of words and their referents, taking us back to a time when

reflection on virtuous living within the social mattered—even if the delights of philosophy were savored on the back of slaves and of women relegated to catering for the pots and pan(t)s. Let me, despite that, again refer to the classics by conjuring up the term *phronesis*, which does justice to the ideal of active citizenry where the identities of scholar, professional, and citizen merge together. This classical Greek term reminds us that "understanding" carries with it a responsibility *to be* and the challenge *to act* in accordance with what we now see to be the best—in terms of the most virtuous course of action. For career guidance has, since its ancient beginnings, been associated with the search for the "good life," a life worth living in accordance with principles that connect with and promote the common good.

This is all the more important given the spirit underpinning this chapter: It would be most unfortunate if these reflections were taken to be a "critique from above," as if scholarly analysis was an abstract exercise "distinct and distant from the realm of practice" (Gewirtz & Cribb, 2002, p. 500). Critique is not without value, as critical reflection, if it has to retain its utopic element, cannot and should not always be reducible to the empirical. Nevertheless, constantly harping on the social, economic, and political contexts that shape or constrain the work of practitioners or on "the mechanisms of social reproduction to which [practitioners] are often presented as contributing" (Gewirtz & Cribb, 2002, p. 500) can demoralize and extinguish hope. While our community of reflective practitioners should mobilize all the available resources to develop a deeper understanding of the facets that trouble the relationship between career guidance and social justice, it is also necessary to carefully consider the ways in which practitioners, driven by that unquenchable thirst for social justice referred to earlier, try to implement socially just practices and the way they deal, resolve, and accommodate the practical difficulties they face in doing so, particularly within the hostile context of neoliberalism. Here, too, there are already examples of good practice to build on, for example, the case studies that feature in Barham's and Irving's co-edited volume titled *Constructing the Future: Diversity, Inclusion, and Social Justice* (Barham & Irving, 2011) as well as the explorative studies carried out by McMahon, Arthur, and Collins (2008) in Queensland, Australia, and Arthur, Collins, McMahon, and Marshall (2009) in Calgary, Canada—where we see what Watson (2010), with an eye on social justice issues in South Africa, called a shift from an attention on addressing social justice issues to redressing them and from denunciation of what is wrong to annunciation of how wrongs are righted.

This, then, is the agenda that I would argue our profession needs to *collectively* take up, thus ensuring that the optimism of the will translates into a more grounded understanding of the possibilities of enacting social justice and not serve as a mere rhetorical flourish.

References

Appadurai, A. (2004). The capacity to aspire: Culture and the terms of recognition. In V. Rao & M. Walton (Eds.), *Culture and public action* (pp. 59–84). Palo Alto, CA: Stanford University Press.

Arthur, N. (2005). Building from diversity to social justice competencies in international standards for career development practitioners. *International Journal for Educational and Vocational Guidance, 5*, 137–148.

Arthur, N., Collins, S., McMahon, M., & Marshall, C. (2009). Career practioners' views of social justice and barriers to practice. *Canadian Journal of Career Development, 8*(1), 22–31.

Arulmani, G. (2010). Career counselling: A mechanism to address the accumulation of disadvantage. *Australian Journal of Career Development, 19*(1), 7–13.

Barham, L., & Irving, B. A. (2011). *Constructing the future: Diversity, inclusion, and social justice.* Stourbridge, UK: Institute of Career Guidance.

Bassot, B. (2012). Upholding equality and social justice: a social constructivist perspective on emancipatory career guidance practice. *Australian Journal of Career Development, 21*(2), 3–13.

Bauman, Z. (1989). *Modernity and the holocaust.* Cambridge, UK: Polity Press.

Bauman, Z. (2001). Globalization and the new poor. In P. Beilharz (Ed.), *The Bauman reader* (pp. 298–333). Oxford, UK: Blackwell.

Bauman, Z. (2006). *Liquid life: Living in an age of uncertainty.* Cambridge, UK: Polity Press.

Berthet, T. (2010). *Capability approach, policy analysis and school based guidance policies in France.*

Collaborative Project WorkAble, Deliverable 2.2 Final Report (mimeo).

Berthet, T., Dechézelles, S., Fouin, R., & Simon, V. (2009, September). *Toward a 'capability' analytical model of public policy? Lessons from academic guidance issues.* In 9e Congrès: Asociaciòn Española de Ciencia Politica: "Repensar la democracia: inclusion y diversidad", Atelier 6 "Politicas públicas": 6.1: "Modelos, enfoques y perspectivas analíticas actuales en el análisis de politicas publicas", Malaga, Spain.

Biggeri, M. (2010). Children's valued capabilities. In M. Walker & E. Unterhalter (Eds.), *Amartya Sen's capability approach and social justice in education* (pp. 197–214). Basingstoke, UK: Palgrave Macmillan.

Blustein, D. L., McWhirter, E. H., & Perry, J. C. (2005). An emancipatory communitarian approach to vocational development theory, research, and practice. *The Counseling Psychologist, 33*(2), 141–179.

Cohen, R. (2002). Maternal psyche. In E. Gantt & R. Williams (Eds.), *Psychology for the other: Levinas, ethics and the practice of psychology* (pp. 32–64). Pittsburgh, PA: Duquesne University Press.

Colley, H. (2000). Deconstructing 'realism' in career planning: How globalisation impacts on vocational guidance. In *Career guidance: Constructing the future: A global perspective.* Stourbridge, UK: Institute of Career Guidance.

Colley, H. (2007). Career counselling: Constructivist approaches, by M. McMahon & W. Patton (Eds.). *British Journal of Guidance and Counselling, 35*(4), 480–482.

Davies, B. (2005). The (im)possibility of intellectual work in neoliberal regimes. *Discourse: Studies in the Cultural Politics of Education, 26*(1), 1–14.

Davies, B., & Bansel, P. (2007). Neoliberalism and education. *International Journal of Qualitative Studies in Education, 20*(3), 247–259.

Derrida, J. (1991). In P. Kamuf (Ed.), *A Derrida reader: Between the blinds.* New York, NY: Columbia University Press.

Ehrenreich, B. (2001). *Nickel and dimed: On (not) getting by in America.* New York, NY: Metropolitan Books.

Fraser, N. (1997). *Justice interruptus. Critical reflections on the 'postsocialist condition'.* New York, NY: Routledge.

Fraser, N. (2009). *Scales of justice: Reimagining political space in a globalizing world.* New York, NY: Columbia University Press.

Freire, P. (1970). *Pedagogy of the oppressed.* New York, NY: Continuum.

Gewirtz, S. (2006). Towards a contextualized analysis of social justice in education. *Educational Philosophy and Theory, 38*(1), 69–81.

Gewirtz, S., & Cribb, A. (2002). Plural conceptions of social justice: Implications for policy sociology. *Journal of Education Policy, 17*(5), 499–509.

Gonthier, F. (2005, September). *Representations and theories of social justice in Europe.* Paper presented at the Seventh Conference of the European

Sociological Association "Rethinking Inequalities", Torun, Poland.

Goodman, D. M., Walling, S., & Ghali, A. A. (2010). Psychology in pursuit of justice: The lives and works of Emmanuel Levinas and Ignacio Martín-Baró. *Pastoral Psychology, 59*, 585–602.

Gramsci, A. (1971). *Selections from the prison notebooks.* New York, NY: International.

Green, S. J. D. (1989). Emile Durkheim on human talents and two traditions of social justice. *British Journal of Sociology, 40*(1), 97–115.

Hansen, T., & Amundson, N. (2009). Residing in silence and wonder: Career counselling from the perspective of 'being'. *International Journal of Educational and Vocational Guidance, 9*, 31–43.

Herr, E. L. (2008, July). *The importance of career development for an uncertain world: Public policy, legislation and professional advocacy.* Keynote speech presented at the National Career Development Association Global Conference, Washington, DC.

Hobbes, T. (1651). *Leviathan: Chapter 11.* Retrieved from http://courses.washington.edu/hsteu302/Hobbes%20selections%202010.htm

Hodkinson, P., & Sparkes, A. C. (1997). Careership: A sociological theory of career decision making. *British Journal of Sociology of Education, 18*(1), 29–44.

Hodkinson, P., Sparkes, A. C., & Hodkinson, H. (1996). *Triumphs and tears: Young people, markets and the transition from school to work.* London, UK: David Fulton.

Honneth, A. (2004). Recognition and justice: Outline of a plural theory of justice. *Acta Sociologica, 47*(4), 351–364.

Hughes, D., & Borbély-Pecze, T. B. (2012). *Youth unemployment: A crisis in our midst—The role of lifelong guidance policies in addressing labour supply and demand* (Concept note commissioned by ELGPN). Jyväskylä, Finland: Kariteam.

Hursh, D. W., & Henderson, J. A. (2011). Contesting global neoliberalism and creating alternative futures. *Discourse: Studies in the Cultural Politics of Education, 32*(2), 171–185.

Irving, B. A. (2010). (Re)constructing career education as a socially just practice: An antipodean reflection. *International Journal of Educational and Vocational Guidance, 10*, 49–63.

Irving, B. A., & Malik, B. (Eds.). (2004). *Critical reflections on career education and guidance: Promoting social justice within a global economy.* London, UK: Routledge.

Jacobsen, M., & Marshman, S. (2008). The four faces of human suffering in the sociology of Zygmunt Bauman—Continuity and change. *Polish Sociological Review, 1*(161), 3–24.

Krebs, D. L. (2008). The evolution of a sense of justice. In J. Duntley & T. K. Shackelford (Eds.), *Evolutionary forensic psychology.* Oxford, UK: Oxford University Press.

Law, J. (2004). *After method—Mess in social science research.* Oxon, UK: Routledge.

Lawlor, L. (2011). Jacques Derrida. In N. Zalta (Ed.), *The Stanford encyclopaedia of philosophy* (Fall 2011 ed.). Retrieved from http://plato.stanford.edu/archives/fall2011/entries/derrida/

Leitner, H., Shepphard, E. S., Sziarto, K., & Maringanti, A. (2007). Contesting urban futures: Decentring neoliberalism. In H. Leitner, E. S. Sheppard, & J. Peck (Eds.), *Contesting neoliberalism: Urban frontiers* (pp. 1–25). New York, NY: Guildford Press.

Levinas, E. (1989). In S. Hand (Ed.), *The Levinas reader.* Cambridge, MA: Blackwell.

MacIntyre, A. (1984). *After virtue* (Vol. 211). Notre Dame, IN: University of Notre Dame Press.

MacIntyre, A. (1988). *Whose justice? Whose rationality?* Notre Dame, IN: University of Notre Dame Press.

Marx, K. (1835). Reflections of a young man on the choice of a profession. In *Marx and Engels Collected Works* (Vol. 1). First published in Archiv für die Geschischte de Sozialismus und der Arebiterbewegung, 1925. Retrieved from http://www.marxists.org/archive/marx/works/cw/volume01/preface.htm

Mayo, P. (2012). *Politics of indignation: Imperialism, postcolonial disruptions and social change.* Hants, UK: Zero Books, John Hunt.

McMahon, M., Arthur, N., & Collins, S. (2008). Justice and career development: Views and experiences of Australian career development practitioners. *Australian Journal of Career Development, 17*(3), 15–25.

North, C. E. (2006). More than words? Delving into the substantive meanings of 'social justice' in education. *Review of Educational Research, 76*(4), 507–535.

Nussbaum, M. (2000). *Women and human development. The capabilities approach.* Cambridge, MA: Cambridge University Press.

Nussbaum, M. (2001). Adaptive preferences and women's options. *Economics and Philosophy, 17*, 67–88.

Organisation for Economic Co-operation and Development (OECD). (2004). *Career guidance and public policy: Bridging the gap.* Paris, France: Author.

Rawls, J. (1971). *A theory of justice.* Cambridge, MA: Harvard University Press.

Roberts, K. (2005). Social class, opportunity structures and career guidance. In B. A. Irving & B. Malik (Eds.), *Critical reflections on career education and guidance* (pp. 130–142). London, UK: RoutledgeFalmer.

Ruitenberg, C., & Vokey, D. (2011). Equality and justice. In *The Sage handbook of philosophy of education, 2010.* Retrieved from http://www.sage-ereference.com/hdbk_philosophyeducation/Article_n27.html

Sampson, J. P., Jr., McClain, M. C., Musch, E., & Reardon, R. C. (2011, November). *The supply and demand for career interventions as a social justice issue.* Plenary Presentation, 10th Biennial Conference of the Society for Vocational Psychology: Forging Career Policy for the Greater Good, Boston, Massachusetts.

Savickas, M. L., Nota, L., Rossier, J., Dauwalder, J. -P., Duarte, M. E., Guichard, J., . . . van Vianen, A. E. M. (2009). Life designing: A paradigm for career construction in the 21st century. *Journal of Vocational Behaviour, 75*(3), 239–250.

Sen, A. (2008). The idea of justice. *Journal of Human Development, 9*(3), 331–342.

Sennett, R. (1998). *The corrosion of character: The personal consequences of work in the new capitalism.* New York, NY: Norton.

Sennett, R. (2006). *The culture of the new capitalism.* New Haven, CT: Yale University Press.

Simon, H. (1991). Bounded rationality and organizational learning. *Organization Science, 2*(1), 125–134.

Sultana, R. G. (2003). *Career guidance policies in 11 acceding and candidate countries.* Turin, Italy: European Training Foundation.

Sultana, R. G. (2004). *Guidance policies in the learning society: Trends, challenges and responses across Europe.* Thessaloniki, Greece: CEDEFOP.

Sultana, R. G. (2008). *From policy to practice: A systemic change to lifelong guidance in Europe.* Thessaloniki, Greece: CEDEFOP.

Sultana, R. G. (2009). 'Competence' and 'competence frameworks' in career guidance: Complex and contested concepts. *International Journal for Educational and Vocational Guidance, 9*(4), 15–30.

Sultana, R. G. (2011). Lifelong guidance, citizen rights, and the state: Reclaiming the social contract. *British Journal of Guidance and Counselling, 39*(2), 179–186.

Sultana, R. G., & Watts, A. G. (2006a). *Career guidance in Europe's Public Employment Services: Trends and challenges.* Brussels, Belgium: DG Employment, Social Affairs and Equal Opportunities.

Sultana, R. G., & Watts, A. G. (2006b). Career guidance in Public Employment Services across Europe.

International Journal for Educational and Vocational Guidance, 6(1), 29–46.

Sultana, R. G., & Watts, A. G. (2007). *Career guidance in the Mediterranean region.* Turin, Italy: European Training Foundation.

Sultana, R. G., & Watts, A. G. (2008). Career guidance in the Middle East and North Africa. *International Journal for Educational and Vocational Guidance, 8*(1), 19–34.

Terkel, S. (1974). *Working: People talk about what they do all day and how they feel about what they do.* New York, NY: Pantheon Books.

Walker, M. (2003). Framing social justice in education: What does the 'capabilities' approach offer? *British Journal of Educational Studies, 51*(2), 168–187.

Watson, M. (2010). Career psychology in South Africa: Addressing and redressing social justice. *Australian Journal of Career Development, 19*(1), 24–29.

Watts, A. G. (2002). Socio-political ideologies in guidance. In A. G. Watts, B. Law, J. Killeen, J. M. Kidd, & R. Hawthorn (Eds.), *Rethinking careers education and guidance: Theory, policy and practice* (pp. 351–365). London, UK: Routledge.

Watts, A. G. (2011, January 21) Broken futures and a step back in time: Career guidance is at risk of being cut to shreds. *The Times Educational Supplement* www.tes.co.uk/article.aspx?storycode=6068032.

Watts, A. G., & Fretwell, D. H. (2004). *Public policies for career development: Policy strategies for designing career information and guidance systems in middle-income and transition economies.* Washington, DC: The World Bank.

Watts, A. G., & Knasel, E. G. (1985). *Adult unemployment and the curriculum: A manual for practitioners.* London, UK: Further Education Unit.

Willis, P. (1977). *Learning to labour: How working class kids get working class jobs.* Farnborough, UK: Saxon House.

Young, I. M. (1990). *Justice and the politics of difference.* Princeton, NJ: Princeton University Press.

Educational Inequality and Social Justice: Challenges for Career Guidance

Walter Müller

In this chapter, I shall be discussing career guidance in terms of the potential contribution it can make to promoting social justice. The example I focus on is that of social inequalities in the acquisition of education, discussing them in connection with notions of social justice and inquiring how career guidance can help to reduce inequalities. My perspective on justice is neither that of a philosopher nor that of an expert on career guidance. It is the perspective of a sociologist and an empirically oriented education researcher. Accordingly, the focus in the chapter will be on recent findings in education research on the genesis of inequalities, moving on from there to attempt a link-up with the other two disciplines (i.e., social justice and career guidance). In what sense does educational inequality have a bearing on the problem of social justice? In the light of specific notions of social justice, what are particularly relevant aspects of educational inequality? At what point in the process in which educational inequality materializes can career guidance be helpful, and what form must it take to get closer to the objective of ensuring greater equality in educational opportunity? My aim will be to indicate, with reference to the specific societal problem of educational inequality, how career guidance can profit from the research done in other disciplines.

What can empirically oriented research contribute to the subject of educational equity? One thing it can do is to identify the different notions of social justice that exist in a society, and inquire how these different notions have come about, and how they are tied to the social status of individuals, their interests, value systems, and so on. Secondly, empirical research can indicate the forms and degrees of inequality that exist. It can help elucidate the individual and societal conditions and processes that create results that either conform with or violate concrete notions of social justice. Lastly, empirically oriented research can indicate what can be done to more nearly approximate the notions that we find appropriate. The chapter begins with some conceptual thoughts on the relationship between educational inequality and social justice. Then a number of crucial findings on the materialization of inequality in educational opportunities are summarized and illustrated with reference to selected research findings from various countries. After that I discuss what we can learn from these findings with a view to reducing inequality of educational opportunities and defining the specific role career guidance can play in this. Finally, the chapter is concluded with some reflections about the intercultural validity of claims made along with an outlook on the future.

W. Müller (✉)
Mannheim University, Mannheim, Germany
e-mail: wmueller@sowi.uni-mannheim.de

G. Arulmani et al. (eds.), *Handbook of Career Development*, International and Cultural Psychology, DOI 10.1007/978-1-4614-9460-7_19, © Springer Science+Business Media, LLC 2014

Social Justice and Inequality of Educational Opportunities

In the modern world, education is one of the most important individual and societal resources. For individuals, hardly anything else has such a strong influence on later job, profession, career, and income opportunities as the level and nature of the educational qualifications they have achieved (Kogan, Noelke, & Gebel, 2011; Müller & Shavit, 1998; Treiman & Yip, 1989). As the Organisation for Economic Co-operation and Development (OECD, 2012) has established for many countries, educational qualifications also have a high degree of impact on other aspects of individual quality of life, such as lifestyle, personal participation in cultural practices and goods, the ability to identify and assert personal rights and interests, the potential for societal participation and active involvement in political life, social relations, and not least health and life expectancy. In all these areas, good education improves the quality of life, while poor education is associated with a number of disadvantages. At the societal level, education is also of crucial importance. Many economists (Card, 1999; Hanushek & Wößmann, 2007; Heckman, Stixrud, & Urzua, 2006; Lange & Topel, 2006) have emphasized that education—especially high-quality education—enhances economic productivity, strengthens a country's competitive status in the global context, lowers crime, and increases prosperity. Inadequate education impairs social and political participation and thus violates elementary features of democratic political order. In addition, unequal educational opportunities contradict essential notions of justice and modern societies' ideals of equality. The violation of such elementary values weakens many people's willingness to concede to the social order and impairs societal cohesion and solidarity.

Though ideals of equality enjoy a high status in the discourse on justice in modern society (Parsons, 1970), the actual notions advanced on the subject vary widely and are highly controversial. At best there is a high degree of consent that educational justice is not about giving everyone precisely the same education and ensuring the same educational outcomes. The point at issue is rather the social distribution of the opportunities/risks of receiving more/less of this advantageous good and achieving more/less advantageous educational results. This aspect needs to be distinguished from another fundamental aspect of inequality, the so-called distributional inequality which refers to the issue of how a good of which one can possess more or less is distributed among the members of a society. An initial central gauge for determining distributional inequality is the range between the lowest and the highest instance of the value of the good in question. For example, if we measure the extent of education by the number of years of participation in education, the wider is the gap between the shortest and the longest duration of education that different people go through, the higher is the distributional inequality. In other words, it increases with the proportion of individuals displaying education durations that lie far apart.

Instead of distributional (in)equality, this chapter is based on the notion of *equal opportunities* as a central element in social justice, exemplified in Rawls' (1971) and Sen's (1973) theories of justice. Achieving such a state of social justice does not require the same results for all but merely that all individuals have the same opportunities for achieving certain results.

In public discourse and the political rhetoric and programmatic statements of political parties and interest groups, the insistence on equal educational opportunities is also widespread. But this general formula tells us nothing about what equality of opportunity actually means, or when it can be said to have been achieved. Ideas on the matter vary widely. Neither in philosophy nor in public discussion are there unanimous notions of what the distribution of opportunities and risks should look like; what criteria and procedures should be operative in distributing education; and how much inequality of what kind is unavoidable, acceptable, or intolerable in that process. Different conceptions of equal opportunities derive eventually from (a) the conditions and factors one considers to be legitimate determinants of unequal results, and (b) those one rejects as unjustified. From a social justice point of view, it is the latter that requires mitigation or amelioration. One important voice in the growing and variegated discussion of this matter, above all in economics, is that of the Yale economist Roemer (1998) in his book *equality of opportunity*.

In his bid to systematize the issue, Roemer (1998) has called the non-legitimate factors, *circumstances* (i.e., things beyond people's control), and the legitimate factors, *effort* (i.e., what a person invests in order to achieve a certain result). For the postulate *equality of opportunity* to be fulfilled, circumstances beyond the control of individuals must not lead to unequal results. Or, as Rawls (1971, p. 63) has it, individuals investing the same degree of effort should have the same prospects of success, irrespective of (say) the place in society that they were born into. Results may legitimately differ, but only to the extent that they are based on different degrees of effort. As a third factor, Roemer concedes that luck may also be a reason for different outcomes. But this does not affect the central role of circumstances and effort in our interpretation of the legitimate and non-legitimate factors determining outcomes (for a discussion on luck, see also Lefranc, Pistolesi, & Trannoy, 2009).

Unless there are special measures, circumstances in real societies will inevitably also affect outcomes. To achieve equality of opportunity, potential outcome differences resulting from circumstances beyond the control of an individual should be avoided by making use of appropriate societal resources. In the case of education, this can be achieved by such things as extra-learning support or selective public subsidizing of costs involved in the acquisition of education.

An operationalization of equality of opportunity clearly depends on which factors leading to unequal outcomes are counted as *effort* and which as *circumstances*. Ultimately, this cannot be determined academically but only at a socio-political level. Some authors, Roemer included,

proceed on the assumption that everything for which one is not personally responsible must be considered circumstance (Arneson, 1989; Cohen, 1989; Roemer, 1998). This is not quite as simple as it sounds. Anyhow, let us note that there is wide acceptance of the fact that different social, cultural, economic, and other conditions characterizing the parents' home cannot be considered the child's responsibility, so societal resources should be drawn upon and measures taken to offset the differences deriving from them.

But how are we to judge differences in the cognitive, emotional, or motivational resources of individuals that lead to different outcomes, for example, intelligence? Roemer's (1998) view is that there are good reasons for seeing even genetic endowments as circumstances, because they are beyond the control of their owners and individuals have no way of influencing the properties they are blessed with at birth. Others take a different line and contend that properties such as intelligence are part of a person's entirely individual "equipment" and that it cannot be the task of society to iron out any inequalities resulting from them (Dworkin, 1981).

There are three arguments supporting Roemer's (1998) contention that personal properties like intelligence should also be compensated for. First, intelligence is known not to be a mere matter of genetic equipment. It is also affected by familial and societal conditions of the environment in which a person grows up and the degree of encouragement he/she receives (e.g., Scarr & Weinberg, 1976). Second, there are other areas of society where it is widely accepted that resources should be activated to offset individual handicaps such as disabilities or the treatment of illnesses that may not only be very costly to deal with but also derive from the individual's own lifestyle. Why should this not also apply to the compensation of differences in intellectual gifts, which in addition might strengthen productive forces or reduce costs of a different kind? The third argument is a response to those decrying the compensatory use of resources to prevent learning impairments, because they believe society stands to lose from the increased use of resources for inefficient learners. It would gain more by placing those resources at the disposal of more efficient learners (concerning discussions of the equality–efficiency tradeoff, see Fehr & Schmidt, 2004; Okun, 1975; Vallentyne, 2000). For Roemer this objection lies on a different level. Efficiency considerations have to do with the economics of the general increase of prosperity. And that implies deliberating on what is to be given higher priority in the value system, equality of opportunity or greater prosperity. There then still remains the question of how we are to measure greater prosperity. Greater prosperity for everyone, for individual groups, or for people in highly disadvantaged positions? And is prosperity to be measured in terms of gross domestic product (GDP) alone or with the inclusion of many other aspects that come under the heading *quality of life* and to which education makes a major contribution? In public and political debate, the equal opportunities issue is frequently subjected to a narrow species of efficiency-mindedness, rather than addressing fundamental questions of this kind. Support for measures improving equality of opportunity and educational equity is most likely to be enlisted with arguments suggesting that greater equality of opportunity and more systematic exploitation of talent reserves will create resources for the increase of economic prosperity and enhance international competitiveness.

Hardly less controversial is the more precise definition of effort. Here Roemer's (1998) take on the matter is relative. The different conditions individuals are exposed to are categorized into types that are more or less favorable for the attainment of educational success. If in absolute terms different types show evidence of different levels of effort, this should not lead to advantages for those belonging to a type that on an average exhibits higher effort; nor disadvantages for those belonging to a type that by-and-large exhibits lower effort (from a social justice point of view). This is a charitable view that assumes that differences in the average amount of effort expended result from the specific circumstances of the respective type. For instance, what fault is it

of children from poorly educated families who frequently skip school if their parents attach little importance to regular attendance or decent homework and hence hardly ever check up on these things? Accordingly, social work or school homework supervision would have to kick in to ensure at least an average degree of participation. Within the different types there will still be individuals displaying above- or below-average willingness to make an effort. Such differences can indeed lead to different outcomes, but they do not contradict the idea of equal opportunities because they result from differences in *relative* effort.

In due course, greater equality of opportunity as envisaged by Roemer (1998) would also bring about greater distributional equality because this would improve the opportunities of individuals laboring under unfavorable circumstances and accordingly narrow the range of outcomes. These ideas may appear abstract and unrealistic. But they can perhaps help to systematize the different facets of an issue that frequently suffers from a lack of conceptual clarity. Also, they imply formidable challenges both for sociopolitical debate and for the more practical side of things, as exemplified by the following questions: What conditions do we classify as circumstances? Which of these circumstances generally lead to disadvantage but—from a social justice point of view—should not be allowed to do so? Which of these circumstances can and should we attempt to offset? As of when is a person responsible for his/her actions and learning behaviors? What is our position on the charitable interpretation of effort?

These are normative, sociopolitical questions. Empirical research cannot provide a direct answer, but it can establish what different notions on these points exist in society and how such differing notions come about. It can also help elucidate which circumstances and attitudes toward effort lead to inequality of opportunity, the extent to which they do so, and the reasons why they do so. Finally, it can suggest how conditions and circumstances that generate inequality can best be remedied or mitigated.

Inequality of Educational Opportunity: Materialization and Development

In what follows I go along with a widely shared, relatively straightforward definition of inequality of opportunity as systematic disparities in educational attainment caused by conditions of social origin and a number of other features for which a child cannot be held responsible (e.g., sex or a migration background). In this specific understanding of inequality of opportunity, what is measured is the size of differences in educational attainment related to social backgrounds. As available data frequently do not contain convincing (e.g., longitudinal) measurements of individual conditions, the focus remains on the degree to which background determines (educational) futures. Educational attainment is understood here as the highest educational qualification a person has achieved at the end of his/her educational career (and not the competencies acquired at a given point in the school career—as for example in the PISA studies). After all, for labor-market and income opportunities, the qualifications ultimately achieved and certified play a considerable role.

Though such disparities in educational attainment run counter to the normative notions adhered to in modern societies, we still find them everywhere, whatever be the nature of societal conditions and educational institutions. Various mechanisms operative in all modern societies contribute to these disparities. The effects of these mechanisms are so pervasive that it is not easy to offset and reduce inequalities of opportunity in educational systems. The question that poses itself is whether they are in fact susceptible to change at all.

Shavit and Blossfeld (1993) in their major comparative study concluded that despite educational reforms and expansion in the last decades, inequality of educational opportunities had in almost all countries not changed at all. This thesis, long accepted as an established fact in the literature, is contested by more recent research which shows that in the course of the 20th century, inequalities in educational opportunities have indeed lessened in many countries. Figure 19.1 depicts a seven-country comparative summary analysis of changes in disparities in the educational attainment of women and men from different social classes across multiple birth cohorts (Breen, Luijkx, Müller, & Pollak, 2009, 2010; Breen et al. 2012). In the graph of each country the zero-line indicates the educational attainment of the children from the most-privileged (service-class) backgrounds in each of the five observed birth cohorts. The other lines show the extent to which sons and daughters from less-privileged backgrounds lag behind that reference in achieving advantageous educational qualifications and how this inequality changed in the sequence of the birth cohorts in the course of the 20th century.[1] In all the countries investigated, inequalities related to social origins decreased in the course of time for both sexes.[2] One remarkable feature is the similarity in the inequality of educational opportunities for men and women in each given country and also the similarity in the way this inequality has dwindled in the course of time for both men and women.[3] In addition to what Fig. 19.1 demonstrates, women have made good their former gender-based disadvantages in educational participation in these countries. This phenomenon of women catching up on men is also especially noteworthy (see Becker & Müller,

---

[1] The scores are also weighted in accordance with the proportions of children in the individual cohorts that have grown up in background situations with a certain degree of disadvantage in connection with educational opportunity. This weighting slightly reinforces the trend toward regressive inequality because in the sequence of cohorts the proportions of children growing up in background situations disadvantageous for the acquisition of education progressively decreased.

[2] Shavit and Blossfeld's (1993) conclusions were different probably because the sample sizes they used were too small for reliable observation of changes in inequalities over time. Much the same is true of Pfeffer (2008).

[3] Only in Poland woman lag behind men to a statistically significant extent; and this appears to result from especially disadvantaged educational opportunities of daughters in farmers' families in the cohorts studied (Breen et al., 2010).

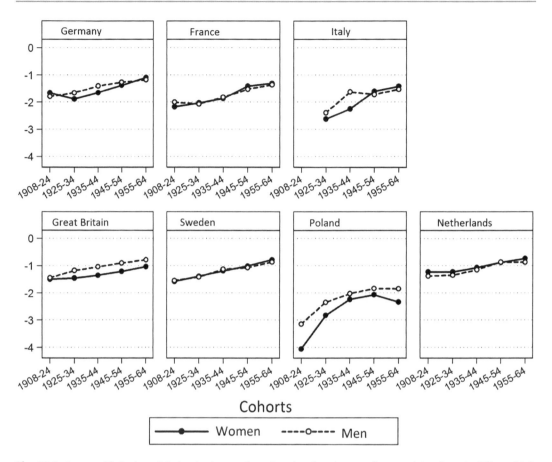

Fig. 19.1 Impact of father's social-class background on educational attainment of sons and daughters in different birth years: Weighted median values from ordinal logistic regressions. Source: Breen, Luijkx, Müller, and Pollak (2012), p. 359

2011; Breen et al., 2010). All in all, recent research findings indicate that inequality of educational opportunity is by no means inalterable and that measures designed to reduce it even further can be successful, although the change takes place slowly and a reduction of inequalities is by no means easy to achieve.

A more concrete idea of the still extensive degree of inequality underlying the curves in Fig. 19.1 is supplied by Fig. 19.2, which is restricted to Germany. This figure also indicates how one partial aspect of educational inequality has developed up to the present, in years subsequent to the birth cohorts drawn upon for Fig. 19.1—the prospect of obtaining the qualifications for embarking on a course of higher education. The point at issue here is the

probability of passing the final examination called *Abitur* (school-leaving examinations) at the end of general upper-secondary education, which makes students eligible for university education. Investigations of birth years that have completed their educational careers show that in Germany inequality in the eligibility for university education is a good predictive indicator of inequality after completion of the entire educational career. For younger age-groups, this indicator can thus be used for accurate estimates of the probable degree of inequality of educational opportunities (Klein, Schindler, Pollak, & Müller, 2009; Schindler, 2012).

The graphs in Fig. 19.2 compare the chances for the sons and daughters of parents with at best low-, intermediate-, and at least high-level

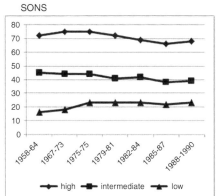
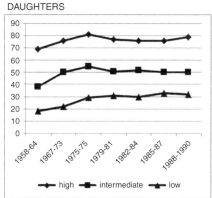

Fig. 19.2 Expected proportions* of sons and daughters attaining university education eligibility in different birth cohorts according to level of secondary education of parents in West Germany. *For operationalization see Klein et al. (2009); data source: German Microcensus Scientific Use Files 1976–2008

secondary education to attain university education eligibility. As we can see, the children's prospects correlate to a high degree with the parents' education. But here again we observe in the course of time a reduction of the inequality related to educational background. For men, the inequality span between the two extreme educational background groups (higher secondary education certificate at least vs. low-level secondary education certificate at best) drops from 56 to 45, for women from 51 to 47 % points. Here the reduction of inequality seems less marked for women than for men. However, when social class is also taken as an indicator of family background, inequalities for women decline more than for men (Klein et al., 2009, not shown in Fig. 19.2). Thus, for both men and women, inequalities have declined, yet for different aspects of social origin conditions. Accordingly, though inequalities in educational opportunity related to social background are still high, they appear to have declined somewhat in the recent past as well (at least in Germany).

The descriptive findings displayed in Figs. 19.1 and 19.2 do not indicate precisely what factors are at the bottom of the inequality reduction. For most of the period of observation there are no data with which corresponding hypotheses for the different countries could be tested. But recent research has come up with temporally more restricted data that are richer

in substance and provide potential insights into the factors and mechanisms that cause inequalities in educational attainment to become manifest. Following the lead of Mare (1980), the attempt is made to (ideally) depict the entire stepwise process in which individuals make their way through the various institutions and stages of an education system, finally acquiring an education certificate with which they leave that system. At various points on the education pathway, there are junctions at which individuals have to decide which of the available options they intend to avail themselves of in order to continue on their educational route, or whether they intend to terminate their education and exit the system. For understanding what goes on in this process and how disparities and inequalities in educational attainment materialize, it has proved useful to draw upon the distinction between the so-called primary and secondary factors/mechanisms (Boudon, 1974; Erikson & Jonsson, 1996) and (accordingly) primary and secondary disparities or inequalities.[4]

---

[4] This distinction is advantageous not only for the explanation of inequalities conditioned by social background but also for the explanation of inequalities between sexes, ethnic groups, indigenous populations and various migration groups, or other characteristics of individuals or social groups.

The *primary* factors and mechanisms lead to differences in learning performances in school (e.g., high or low), and these have an influence on the further course of the education path. They are based in the fact that from earliest infancy and depending on their family and social background, children (a) profit less or more from cultural, social, and economic resources for the development of their cognitive skills and other abilities significant for learning, and (b) receive differing degrees of support and motivation for learning in school. By contrast, the term *secondary* factors and mechanisms is used for disparities and inequalities that come about by virtue of the fact that even though learning performance is the same, students will still choose education paths that differ in terms of the demands these paths make and the openings they provide. In spite of similar performance, students thus leave the education systems with different attainments and achieve different qualifications and certificates. Rational choice theory is widely used to explain such different decisions. Here *rational* means that the decision-makers weigh up the existing alternatives and then opt for the alternative that appears most advantageous to them, given their respective social situation and the resources at their disposal. Essential factors taken into consideration in this weighing-up process are:

- The extent to which it is expected that a particular education pathway can be coped with successfully.
- How easily the attendant costs can be paid for.
- The extent to which, after comparison with the costs, the alternative appears to be profitable in terms of future returns.

In the assessment of returns, the so-called status-maintenance motive plays a crucial role.[5] Families want their children to attain in later life at least as high a status as the parents have

themselves. They are eager to avoid social decline. As a consequence, middle- and upper-class families attach greater importance to their children achieving a high degree of educational attainment than working-class families. For the former, high-level educational attainment is a strategic instrument assuring status maintenance, while for the working classes such qualifications are not required for status maintenance (Breen & Goldthorpe, 1997; Erikson & Jonsson, 1996).

Many studies (e.g., Becker, 2003; Breen & Goldthorpe, 2001; Goldthorpe, 1996; Schindler, 2012; Stocké, 2007) indicate that all these elements contribute toward prompting children from families with limited resources and no experience of high-level education to decide in favor of less demanding and (in the long term) less advantageous educational pathways than children from families with better resources, although they may be just as good at school.

Table 19.1 illustrates the emergence of primary and secondary disparities connected with a specific educational option in the German education system (Müller et al. 2009). It shows what proportion of students entitled to go to university studies as a result of passing the Abitur school-leaving examinations actually embark on such a course, and how this depends (a) on their performance at the Abitur exams (expressed by the grades achieved) and (b) on their social background. The difference to 100 % in each cell of the table are those who (in Germany) mainly obtain a vocational qualification and do not take up university studies. Their later job returns and incomes are substantially inferior to those available to the university graduates. Less than half of the males from working-class backgrounds opt for higher education if they belong to the group with the weakest Abitur results (lowest quintile). Even in the group with the best grades, only 71 % of these graduates embark on university studies. By contrast, school-leavers from the service class with the same grades are 15–20 % more likely to opt for higher education. Of these young people, approximately as many of those in the group with the weakest Abitur grades will go to university as the working-class school graduates with the best grades. Given equal performance, the differences

---

[5] This motive has to do with the psychologically well-known fact that on average the experience of loss has a greater (negative) effect than the (positive) satisfaction afforded by a correspondingly substantial gain (Keller & Zavalloni, 1964).

Table 19.1 Expected percentages[a] of West German male and female Abitur graduates entering university education by parental class and education and grades obtained at Abitur examination

| | Low class and education | | High class and education | |
	Abitur grades lowest 20 %	Abitur grades best 20 %	Abitur grades lowest 20 %	Abitur grades best 20 %
Men	48	71	69	86
Women	37	62	61	81

[a]Percentages expected from logistic regression model
Source: Müller, Pollak, Reimer, and Schindler (2009), Table 7)

in deciding for university in the two background groups are a direct gauge of secondary disparities. In the present case, these differences in university attendance between equally performing children of different social backgrounds are similar in size to the differences within the two background groups between those who did best and those who did worst in their school-leaving examinations. As the differences in performance also affect the likelihood of opting for university education, primary (background-related) disparities in university attendance will emerge to the extent the background groups differ in performance.

Among the women, the differences between the performance and social-background groups are similarly large as among men. But in each performance and social-background group, women (particularly if their social background is low) are somewhat less likely than men to go to university. The differences between men and women from the same backgrounds who did equally well (or badly) in their school-leaving exams might be regarded as secondary *gender* disparities.

In light of the distinction between circumstances and effort discussed earlier, the differences in university attendance between same-performance social-background groups (and gender) quite definitely qualify as circumstances and hence appear to pose a particular problem in connection with equal opportunities. In contrast, the differences between the performance groups cannot be unambiguously ascribed to different degrees of effort, as defined by Roemer (1998). Depending on whether one assesses the reasons for the emergence of performance gaps more or less

charitably, the part attributed to different degrees of effort will vary, and a larger or smaller part will be seen as conditioned by circumstances.

Leaving aside the example we have been using for illustrative purposes, what do we know in more general terms about the significance of primary and secondary disparities in educational careers? And how do the German findings fit in with the situation observed for other countries? All education systems are stratified (to a higher or lesser degree), and in the course of education, career decisions have to be made at various junctures. Numerous studies in different countries have repeatedly confirmed the following findings:

• Primary and secondary background-related disparities are to be found in almost all educational decisions and transitions.

• In general, their incidence is usually particularly high at the earlier junctures of an educational career and diminishes progressively in transitions at higher levels of education. This is true especially of primary disparities. At higher levels, student populations are more homogeneous as a result of selection processes at lower levels. Normally, students have to satisfy certain minimal performance requirements if they want to participate in courses requiring a higher degree of proficiency. Because of primary factors, students of families from the lower classes perform less well on average. As a consequence, fewer of them make it to the higher levels, but among those who do make it, performance differences over and against children from more advantageous backgrounds are less marked, which in its turn means correspondingly lower primary background-related disparities at higher-level transitions(Mare, 1980, 1981). In the example of the German Abitur school-leaving examination discussed earlier, there was little difference in performance between the background-related groups, and the primary disparities at this educational transition were appreciably lower than the secondary disparities (Neugebauer & Schindler, 2012). The reason is that at earlier transitions only very bright working-class children have survived. At the Abitur level they represent a highly positively selected group.

- While as a rule, primary disparities are particularly strong at early transitions, secondary disparities can also be substantial at higher levels of education. Outside the limits imposed by compulsory education, shorter and less costly education options may be more attractive than a lengthy period of study for people with limited resources. Expense can become a burden not only because of the costs directly incurred in connection with studying but also because the possibility of earning an income instead of continuing with one's education raises the opportunity costs. Finally, at higher levels the status-maintenance motive becomes relevant, largely for children from privileged backgrounds. Children from less-privileged strata of society can normally achieve a status equivalent to that of their parents with less investment in education.

- Normally, boys and girls display little difference in performance at school. Boys may be a little better in mathematical subjects; girls tend to excel in languages. On average, girls appear to perform slightly better than boys in the early years of schooling. Therefore, the overall disparities between the sexes conditioned by primary factors and mechanisms tend to be slight. If there are disparities between the sexes in educational acquisition, they are grounded largely in secondary factors and mechanisms. The highly marked tendency for women to be disadvantaged in education vis-à-vis men, which existed formerly in many societies (and still exists in some), was (is) due not to differences in performance at school but to a different assessment of the benefit of education for men and women leading to different decisions on the nature and duration of participation in education for men and women. The attendant secondary gender disparities have been quick to change or indeed turn into their opposite as the new understanding of the role of women in society has made higher participation in education just as important for them as for men, if not more so (Becker & Müller, 2011; Buchmann, DiPrete, & McDaniel, 2008; DiPrete & Buchmann, 2006). In most countries, the preferences evinced for different fields of study by men and women still make for marked differences in educational acquisition. These are essentially conditioned by secondary factors.

- If educational reforms or other factors lead to a substantial increase in educational participation at the lower levels, there may be a partial shift in the generation of disparities from lower- to higher-level transitions (for Germany, see, for example, Müller & Pollak, 2004; Schindler, 2012; for France, see Selz & Vallet, 2006).

- In almost all cases, secondary influences are operative at every juncture and every transition in the education system, so the sum of secondary effects will increase with the number of ramification points (and hence decision situations) that a system has from one end of an educational career to the other. The more complex, variegated, and ramified an education system is, the greater the size of probable secondary disparities.

The shift of (self-)selection from a lower to a higher educational transition can be illustrated particularly well for the German case with Schindler's (2012) findings. In Germany, as in many other countries over the past few decades, the aim of increasing the number of university graduates and reducing the social disparities has led to the establishment of new routes for acquiring the entitlement to go to university. Alongside the traditional secondary schools (*gymnasia*) preparing students for higher education with a general, academically oriented curriculum, vocationally oriented pathways with a stronger emphasis on learning for jobs have been installed. Success here also opens the door to higher education, albeit in some cases only for selected subjects or for universities of applied sciences and not for traditional (comprehensive) universities. Some of these pathways also provide vocational qualifications for direct entry into jobs with a medium qualification level. More and more young people have taken advantage of these alternative routes to higher education. They have been selected mostly by working-class children because these routes square with their interest in carving out a path into the labor market via the acquisition of vocational skills and competencies. This development has led to a clear reduction of social disparities in acquiring the entitlement to embark on higher-education courses.

However, as indicated in Table 19.2, this growing group of students with higher-education entitlements from the vocationally oriented paths has been progressively reluctant to actually use the entitlement. At present, significantly less than half of all students from poorly educated backgrounds with an Abitur obtained from the vocationally oriented circuit actually embark on a course of study at university. As this abstinence has grown above all among school-leavers from the working classes, the equalization of opportunities created by these new pathways to the acquisition of higher-education entitlements has only to a limited extent actually paid off in terms of university degrees. While socially conditioned selection has indeed been curbed in terms of opportunities for the acquisition of higher-education entitlements, it now kicks in at the higher stage where decisions are made as to whether these young people actually want to go to university or not. Similar developments are also observable in other countries that have devised different, more or less difficult ways of attaining the credentials for higher education (see, for France, Selz & Vallet, 2006).

The findings of a study from France (Ichou & Vallet, 2013) are an eloquent reflection (a) of the cumulative inequality effect that may be related to the early segmentation of educational pathways and successive ramification points in the education system, and (b) of the way in which the reduction of ramifications can reduce inequality of opportunity. Up to 1975, children in France completing their 6 years of primary school were allocated to different kinds of education pathways in lower-secondary school depending on how they had performed up till then.[6] At the end of the lower-secondary stage came another ramification into the educational pathways of the upper-secondary stage. In both cases, academically oriented pathways primarily geared to later higher education were available alongside nonacademic pathways either leading directly to the labor market or having a vocational orientation. A reform dating from 1975 did away with the first ramification and introduced the so-called *collège unique* for the lower-secondary stage that all French children now attend together.

Table 19.3 shows the shift in the background-related primary and secondary disparities attendant upon these changes. The outcomes for the birth cohorts 1951 and 1984 correspond to the system before and after the reform, respectively. The numbers in the upper part of the table indicate the percentages by which the probability of entering the next-higher academically oriented branch of education is higher for children from the service classes than for children from a working-class background, divided in each case into the effects from primary and secondary mechanisms. In the 1951 birth cohort, secondary effects had a major impact at all transitions. Only at the first transition do we find significant primary disparities, resulting from performance differences at primary school. For the 1984 birth cohort (i.e., after the reform), we find that the situation changed appreciably. Now the student population only splits up

---

[6] This still happens equally early, if not earlier, in various other European countries (e.g., Germany, Switzerland, Austria, and the Netherlands).

Table 19.2 Percentage of general Abitur graduates attending university by parental education and class and secondary education path; West Germany 1976–2006

Type of secondary education path	Parents' education and class	1976–1978	1983	1992–1996	2002–2006
Vocational schools	High education and class	84	71	78	74
	Low education and class	78	62	62	46
Gymnasium	High education and class	91	86	87	88
	Low education and class	77	62	67	73

Source: Schindler (2012, Table C33)

Table 19.3 Percentage points primary and secondary disparities at educational transitions among 1951 and 1984 birth cohorts in France

I. Transitions		Birth cohort 1951		Birth cohort 1984	
From	To	Primary disparities	Secondary disparities	Primary disparities	Secondary disparities
Primary education	Lower-secondary academic	15	32		
Lower secondary	Upper-secondary academic	2	25	19	20
Baccalauréat	University	0	30	ns	ns
Baccalauréat	*Grandes Écoles*	3	38	11	12

II. Odds ratio comparing children with service-class vs. working-class backgrounds in		
Making it to upper-secondary academic	10.2	6.6
Making it to university or *Grandes Écoles*	12	4.3

Note. For each type of disparity, the numbers in part I indicate by how many percentage points the probability of transition to the next education level is higher for children of service-class origin than for children of working-class origin

Source: Adapted from Ichou and Vallet (2013). The figures for the primary and secondary disparities are calculated from the estimated factual total disparities (difference between the SS- and WW-cells) for each transition in Tables 5.2 and 5.3, using for the decomposition the corresponding results in Table 5.3 according to the Karlson, Holm and Breen (2012) method. The odds ratios are from a pre-print version of Ichou and Vallet (2013)

at the transition to the upper-secondary stage, so (understandably) performance differences also influence transition behavior, both at secondary level and at the higher-education level in connection with access to the elite universities (i.e., the *Grandes Écoles*). In the course of the reforms, the differentiation into types of *baccalauréat* (i.e., high school diplomas) with varying levels of content and difficulty was reinforced. Moreover, admission into the Grandes Écolesis is based on national-level competitive examinations unlike the public universities in France that accept all candidates with a high school diploma. Not surprisingly, therefore, primary effects now play a

significant role in access to the Grandes Écoles rather than the public universities. Also, what is especially striking is that the secondary disparities became appreciably smaller. The two bottom lines (the sum of primary and secondary disparities measured in terms of the odds ratio between service-class and working-class backgrounds) show the reduction in the inequality of opportunities for entering the upper-secondary stage or tertiary education. Comparing the older and the younger cohorts, inequality has plummeted at both junctures for the 1984 cohort. While these changes are probably not entirely attributable to the reform of the education system, the removal of the earlier selection hurdle certainly did have an effect. Erikson (1996) and Erikson and Rudolphi (2010) have corroborative findings on the removal of early selection hurdles and a longer period of joint education for all school students by corresponding school reforms in Sweden.

A new international comparative study of various European countries and the USA offers important insights into the differing role of primary and secondary disparities in transitions within the secondary stages and between the secondary stage and tertiary education (Jackson & Jonsson, 2013). Here the extent of primary disparities differs much less markedly between the various countries than the impact of secondary disparities. Consequently, the differences between the countries in terms of overall inequality rest mainly on differences in the impact of secondary disparities.

All countries display relatively high similarity in the role played by the children's cognitive and noncognitive skills in learning for school and the way in which this depends on conditions in the families they come from. Nor is there much difference between the countries in the ways in which learning and performance are evaluated in school. Thus, the differences in the extent of primary disparities between different countries are also limited. But things are different with the institutional conditions in different countries that are relevant for the structuring of educational pathways and for regulating access to different educational institutions and associated costs. Depending on the organization of the education system, families have different educational pathways to choose from. Their children are given access to these pathways on the basis of various criteria. Different systems give parents and children different degrees of influence and scope in making the educational decisions they are faced with at different ages of the children, at variously numerous and complex ramification points, with further continuation points that are more or less easy to navigate, and so on. All this can influence education decisions. Different regulations can have different impacts on decisions made by different social groups. As a result, it seems readily understandable that

differences in the extent of inequality between countries should be determined above all by secondary factors and mechanisms.

In the meantime, a great deal of research has been done on the factors and institutional regulations that (probably) reinforce secondary disparities. For example, secondary inequalities are normally larger if access to advantageous educational institutions is regulated not exclusively on the basis of performance credentials but on the basis of relatively free selection by parents and/or students (Dollmann, 2011; Jackson & Jonsson, 2013). If a system is complex, if its structure is difficult to fathom, and if it involves a large number of decisions, it will reinforce secondary inequality because practically every decision will come up with outcomes that vary in accordance with social background. Also, parents with a university degree will find it easier to navigate a complex or opaque system in the interests of their children. Many investigations suggest that inequalities are reinforced by high education costs and the absence of generous and socially equitable education funding by the public authorities. As we saw earlier, other studies testify to the inequality-reducing effect of the dismantling of early differentiation of students into segregated education pathways (e.g., Erikson, 1996; Ichou & Vallet, 2013). Probably this is especially the case where there is little or no permeability between different education pathways and little opportunity for remedying earlier decisions at later stages of education. Early division into education pathways that do not lead relatively directly to the highest qualifications is disadvantageous for poorly educated families because they are the ones that tend to find themselves on those pathways and because as a rule detours on the way to the top are less likely to be successfully navigated than direct routes (Schindler, 2012).

An eloquent example is provided by the education systems in Germany and a number of neighboring countries with similar educational traditions (i.e., Austria, Switzerland, Luxembourg, Denmark). At the secondary stage already, they have vocationally oriented education paths in which major sections of the student population are educated in the form of the so-called dual apprenticeships. At school, the students are instructed in the theoretical knowledge they require for a vocation, while in private enterprises they learn the practical basics of the job by way of participation in the production process. Such courses provide a good foundation for jobs at an intermediate qualification level and especially facilitate the transition from education to work without any major risk of youth unemployment. But with regard to equality of opportunity, they have the drawback that they may divert gifted students with lower social backgrounds from academically oriented education paths leading to later study at university level. The conviction that different people have different gifts has prompted educational systems to separate children into different tracks at an early stage. Some of these will almost certainly lead directly to vocational training. This option is attractive for families with limited economic resources because as trainees their children will earn an apprentice wage. Risk of failure in these courses is fairly slight, and they lead to relatively well-paid jobs relatively quickly and with little risk of unemployment. For this reason, and because in lower social classes courses like these suffice to maintain family status without studying, they are particularly attractive for those social classes.[7] Accordingly, young people from such backgrounds frequently opt for nonacademic vocational education and are less likely to embark on a course of higher education (that would ultimately be more advantageous in economic terms) than they would in systems that do not have the vocational education option. However beneficial an extensive and efficient vocational education system may be in providing many young people with qualifications and integrating them into the labor market, it leads overall to relatively low percentages of higher-education graduates and tends to reinforce rather than reduce educational inequality.

The Role of Career Guidance in Equalizing Educational Opportunity

What could be done to improve equality of opportunity (always assuming that the requisite political will to do so actually exists)? Obviously the point cannot be to enhance equality of opportunity by putting obstacles in the way of those families that do everything they can to further their children's educational success (provided, of course, that such backing is geared to performance criteria and does not seek to procure unjustified advantages for them). The essential thing is to find suitable ways of counteracting those primary and secondary mechanisms that mitigate educational success in children from lower classes or poorly educated family backgrounds. Of course, educational inequality comes about at many points, starting in earliest infancy and continuing in various ways throughout entire educational careers. Therefore, individual measures will always be restricted in their impact. This also means that if their ultimate success is to be appreciable, remedial measures of different types will need to be applied at many points.

Numerous suggestions have been made on how to offset primary mechanisms. Ultimately, they all aim at helping children to do better in squaring up to the expectations of the respective educational institutions in terms of performance. As the requisite abilities will develop differently depending on the stimuli the child receives from earliest infancy, it has quite convincingly been argued that corresponding support needs to set in at an early stage in the children's lives. Ground lost in the early stages can hardly be made up for later (Heckman et al., 2006). One concrete eventuality is high-quality professional support at the preschool stage to supplement family care, all the way up to measures in school designed to nip emergent performance disparities in the bud. I cannot go into this here in detail. Suffice it to say that the immense benefit of such support in the development of performance

---

[7] On the theoretical side of the issue, see Goldthorpe (1996) and Hillmert and Jacob (2003); for an empirical international comparison, see Shavit and Müller (2000); for the USA see Arum and Shavit (1995); for Sweden see Murray (1988); for Germany see Becker and Hecken (2009), Müller and Pollak (2004), and Schindler (2012).

potential is that its impact extends beyond school and can have an advantageous effect on the entire lives of individuals.

But we must not close our eyes to the difficulties involved. It is not easy to alleviate primary inequalities as to a large extent their causes are rooted in things that happen in the families' everyday lives (recurrently and over long periods). In addition, family autonomy is a precious asset and should not be interfered with lightly. Also, training extrafamilial teaching and care personnel for the requisite qualifications is a lengthy process.

Without any intention of arguing against measures for reducing primary disparities (such measures are indispensable), I shall concentrate in the following on the special benefits of interventions designed to prevent the emergence of secondary disparities. They are likely to be more efficient and quicker to take effect. Such measures will after all be angled at individuals whose good educational performance has proved their potential and their ability to learn. The main thing to ensure is that (a) they do not recoil from ongoing education at too early a stage, and (b) they are able to resume their educational careers if they have previously dropped out. In short, what can we do to dismantle the barriers to participation in higher levels of education that even good performers come up against?

Recent research findings (Becker, 2003; Becker & Hecken, 2009; Breen & Goldthorpe, 1997; Jackson, Erikson, Goldthorpe, & Yaish, 2007) suggest that there are three main conditions that prevent gifted children from poorly educated backgrounds and financially disadvantaged families from choosing educational pathways that lead to higher educational attainment:

1. Difficulty in paying for education and a restricted time frame within which costs are expected to be balanced by returns.
2. Uncertain and pessimistic assessment of the likelihood that their children will be successful in dealing with the demands of higher-level educational pathways.
3. The status-maintenance motive.

If it is the aim of education policy to improve this situation and equalize opportunity, then systematic measures will have to be taken to counter these conditions. Reducing the cost barrier would mean introducing generous financial support tailored to social conditions and convincingly propagated to ensure that the relevant families and children perceive this support as a clear and viable incentive.

Essential as they are in connection with education costs—information, counseling, and guidance are even more crucial in dealing with the other two conditions. Given that secondary disparities very largely come about as a result of circumstantially distorted perception and misprision, persuasive and forceful professional guidance (Jackson & Jonsson, 2013) for parents, schoolchildren, and potential university students is a crucial instrument that can (a) help students to draw upon their own potential and embark on an educational career in line with their abilities, and (b) thus reduce secondary disparities. To achieve this, we need suitable career-guidance models. Ideally, all families (and especially those from the poorly educated strata of society) should be convinced of the value of school-level guidance in establishing what is best for their children. To be as effective as it can, extrafamilial guidance needs to set in at as early a stage as possible, preferably in infancy. Families need support in finding suitable educational pathways, preferably routes that can take their children straight to the top of the educational hierarchy without any detours on the way. Some may think it a viable option to initially make for interim goals that are easier to achieve. But research has shown that on such indirect and sometimes circuitous routes, individual potential is in many cases not exploited to the utmost (Schindler, 2012).

Career guidance should make a consistent attempt to encourage educational aspirations and thus counterbalance the aspirational edge bestowed on upper-class families by the status-maintenance incentive. This is probably best achieved by providing a hands-on and realistic picture of the many concrete advantages associated with higher-level education. It is not an easy task, because unfavorable circumstances and a relative dearth of resources frequently engender perceptions, assessments, and preferences that are unlikely to make demanding and lengthy education look like the best option available.

Another beneficial contribution that career guidance can make lies in support for the formation of realistic expectations. As Erikson and Jonsson (1996) have rightly pointed out, parents who have been to university know that one does not need to be a genius to end up with a degree. The many children from the middle and upper classes who embark on, and complete, a course of study although they were no great shakes at school are the living proof of this. But without such knowledge, higher education can easily look like a formidable and risky undertaking. Career guidance should be there to provide realistic information and strengthen self-confidence.

A further potential strategy among the set of instruments available to impactful professional guidance is to organize cooperation between the various institutions involved in the education process. Such collaboration between institutions at different levels of education would enhance the effectiveness of active recruiting strategies by higher secondary schools and universities, enabling them to address talented students directly and gain their interest in what they have to offer.

Such measures for reducing secondary disparities can take effect without changing the system from the bottom up and can hence lead to relatively quick success. This does not of course mean that all secondary disparities would disappear overnight. Where institutional features of the education system favor the emergence of such disparities, reforms of the institutional structure of the system will be indispensable for equalization of opportunity. These reforms might include the integration of hitherto segregated education paths, the postponement of student separation to later stages in ongoing education, or greater ease of transition between different educational routes.

As we have seen, secondary disparities are frequently based on lack of information or on distortions of perception and misprision.

Accordingly, career guidance can play an important part in attempts to reduce inequalities of opportunity.

Relevance for Multiple Cultures: Sensitivity to the Universal and the Particular

Educational inequalities exist in practically every modern society and culture, and they affect the quality of life and the opportunities of individuals everywhere. There is also a substantial degree of commonality in the factors and mechanisms by which inequalities are generated. The distinction made in this chapter between primary and secondary factors and mechanisms is probably of universal relevance. Everywhere the educational attainment of individuals will partly depend on their performance in school and on educational decisions and choices between the various alternatives available. Yet there is variation between countries and cultures with regard to the extent of the resulting inequalities. In some countries, educational disparities are larger than in others. For a number of economically highly developed Western societies, we know from Jackson (2013) and the contributors to her volume that secondary factors and mechanisms are largely responsible for the inter-country differences in the extent of inequalities resulting at the end of the educational careers of individuals raised in families with different social backgrounds. As the various student assessment programs indicate,[8] factors and mechanisms leading to primary disparities also differ between countries, but apparently not as widely as the secondary ones.

What makes outcomes differ between different countries are the differences in macro-social conditions and educational institutions. The

---

[8] These programs assess student's performance in school subjects. Especially when these tests are taken in the early stages of the educational career, they mainly relate to the primary dimension in the process of educational attainment.

educational systems in different countries provide different educational options and pathways. With their particular characteristics, these are more or less attractive and feasible for individuals with different social backgrounds, even if they have similar performance records for learning tasks. The set-up of educational institutions also varies between countries in their links to other social areas such as the labor market (Müller & Gangl, 2003). Qualifications obtained on available educational paths can have a different bearing on later work careers in different countries, and this can also affect their attractiveness for different social groups. The macro-social conditions of a country provide the larger social context in which education operates. Depending, say, on the level of economic development, the nature of the economy, or the political organization of the society in question, the role played by education may differ substantially, both in general terms and with regard to social inequality.

This latter point is of course particularly apposite when we apply the findings and arguments in this chapter to economic, social, and cultural contexts that are very different from those obtaining in the economically advanced modern societies for which these findings and arguments have been developed. Of course, the overall approach may still be valuable. For instance, Arulmani, Van Laar, and Easton (2003) found for India that a greater proportion of youth from lower SES groups terminate their education early in order to immediately engage in paid work. On a similar line, Bakshi (2011) reported from a study in Mumbai that many more individuals in privileged than those in less-privileged conditions join a degree or certificate course after career entry to enhance career prospects. If we want to understand social inequalities in educational attainment, it will be helpful to study the factors which—under different social conditions—affect differential learning and performance plus those that have an impact on differential choices, as both together lead to disparities in outcomes. Yet it will be crucial to adequately account for (a) the resources available to actors and the constraints they are subject to, (b) the options and opportunities they

have under the given macrostructural and institutional conditions, and (c) the aims they may want and be able to pursue with their educational assets under the given economic, social, and cultural contexts. The social groups especially affected by inequalities are likely to be different in economically less-developed countries. Differences between urban and rural populations, say in China (Wu, 2007; Wu & Zhang, 2010), or between particular ethnic groups may interact with or dominate class or gender inequalities. As discussed in Buchmann and Hannum's (2001) review, family conditions such as lone mothers or large sibship sizes that typically lead to educational disadvantages in highly developed societies may in fact actively facilitate schooling in the social contexts we find in some African or South Asian societies, where the extended family is prepared to provide resources and support. In several East Asian countries, longstanding Confucian cultural traditions attach an exceptionally high value to education, and this may engender particular local and culture-specific conditions which to some extent may dilute the conditions for the emergence of educational disparities. These cultural traditions show up both in the alacrity with which parents are prepared to invest large parts of their resources in the education of their children (e.g., paying for shadow education and high student fees) and in the children's willingness to work hard, face extreme competition, and survive the "examination hell" (Byun & Kim, 2010; Marginson, 2011). Also the culture specific traditions in the socialization of self-regulation in the Confucian cultural contexts, notably behavioral control and emotion regulation, is found to foster academic achievement (Trommsdorff, 2009; Trommsdorff, in press). These instances may suffice to indicate how important it is to be sensitive at all times to the way in which particular conditions on the demand side interact with institutional features on the supply side of educational provision.

Charting New Directions

When it comes to the practical side of designing measures to counteract educational inequalities, it is especially crucial to know exactly how they are generated. The observations made in the previous section make it more than clear that much further research is needed to obtain this basic knowledge, especially in various parts of the developing world, where there are still many gaps in the pertinent knowledge base. The experience and knowledge gained in countries with longer traditions of research can be helpful for contexts where this kind of research is either nonexistent or needs to be substantially extended. Vice versa, research in more industrially/economically advanced parts of the world will profit from studies in less industrially/economically advanced societies, because these will indicate the limitations of existing theories and hopefully help either to develop theories of more general validity or to improve existing ones on this score.

At all events, even the distinction between the primary and secondary factors, mechanisms, and corresponding disparities on which much of the discussion in this chapter has been based displays critical gaps that need to be filled out. In practical research it is not easy to assess precisely the extent to which disparities are due to primary or secondary factors. Lower or higher investments in improving learning and performance at school may be due to educational aspirations and aims that are of an essentially secondary nature. In families with high educational aspirations, more may be invested in improving performance at school and in fulfilling the requirements for embarking on a promising educational path or attending a prestigious institution than in families with lower aspirations or fewer of the resources required to make such aspirations realistic. We need new longitudinal research in order to better understand and measure the complexities involved in these interdependent processes.

Future research would also profit from closer links between theories of justice and empirical investigation. Empirical findings may become more significant for normative and sociopolitical discussions if studies are more precisely attuned to capturing the core concepts figuring in the philosophical discourse on justice. Vice versa, philosophical discourse on the subject stands to gain from better knowledge of how the social world works in practical terms. Drawing upon realistic assumptions about this world and the human action taking place in it may help this discourse to achieve greater practical relevance.[9]

Suggestions have been made in this chapter about how career guidance might contribute to reducing social disparities in educational attainment. These suggestions are based on what we know currently about the generation of inequalities. From recent field experimental studies, for instance, we know that even information about programs like college financial aid and especially support of students in the application process or simplification of application procedures can help to enhance participation in higher education among students of disadvantaged social origin (Bettinger, Long, Oreopoulos, & Sanbonmatsu, 2012; Oreopoulos & Dunn, 2013). In many places, guidance-oriented intervention programs do exist.[10] But we do not really know how effective they are or which elements of the programs and of the support offered work best in achieving the aims of the intervention. To find this out, a major task for the future will be to systematically and rigorously evaluate interventions in terms of (a) the effects and side-effects they produce, and (b) the degree of social and financial efficiency that different programs display. Through the use of different procedures attuned to this aim (experimental or otherwise) we will not only learn how well various possible interventions work, they will also help us to improve our theoretical knowledge and in the long run to develop best-

---

[9] For promising attempts to gear the empirical study of inequality of educational opportunities and the distribution of income to Roemer's philosophical conception, see Björklund, Jäntti, and Roemer (2012) or Lefranc, Pistolesi, and Trannoy (2009).

[10] See for examples of various mentoring programs in Germany (http://www.studienkompass.de/; http://chancenwerk.de/home/startseite; http://www.arbeiterkind.de/). At the University of Trento, Italy, a project directed by Carlo Barone is currently in progress studying the subjective beliefs of students about costs, benefits, and chances of success of the investment in Higher Education and assessing the causal effect of these beliefs on social inequalities in higher education decisions.

practice guidance procedures that can help reduce to some extent the large social inequalities to be found in educational attainment.

Acknowledgments Earlier shorter versions of this chapter have been presented at the Kongress der Schweizerischen Gesellschaft für Bildungsforschung SBGF, Bern, July 2–4, 2012, and at the International Conference "Career Guidance for Social Justice, Prosperity and Sustainable Employment—Challenges for the twenty-first Century" HdBA, University of Applied Labour Studies, Mannheim, October 3–6, 2012. A shorter version has appeared under the title, Bildungsungleichheit und Gerechtigkeit—Gesellschaftliche Herausforderungen, in Rolf Becker, Patrick Bühler, und Thomas Bühler (Eds.), *Bildungsungleichheit und Gerechtigkeit—Wissenschaftliche und gesellschaftliche Herausforderungen* (pp. 27–51). Bern 2013: Haupt. The author thanks Anuradha Bakshi for helpful suggestions to improve the chapter.

References

Arneson, R. (1989). Equality and equal opportunity of welfare. *Philosophical Studies, 56*, 77–93.

Arulmani, G., Van Laar, D., & Easton, S. (2003). The influence of career beliefs and socio-economic status on the career decision-making of high school students in India. *International Journal for Educational and Vocational Guidance, 3*(3), 193–204.

Arum, R., & Shavit, Y. (1995). Secondary vocational education and the transition from school to work. *Sociology of Education, 68*, 187–204.

Bakshi, A. J. (2011). Past adolescence, into and across adulthood: Career crises and major decisions. *International Journal for Educational and Vocational Guidance, 11* (2), 139–153.

Becker, R. (2003). Educational expansion and persistent inequality of education. *European Sociological Review, 19*, 1–24.

Becker, R., & Hecken, A. E. (2009). Why are working-class children diverted from universities? An empirical assessment of the diversion thesis. *European Sociological Review, 25*(2), 233–250.

Becker, R., & Müller, W. (2011). Bildungsungleichheiten nach Geschlecht und Herkunft im Wandel. S. In A. Hadjar (Ed.), *Geschlechtsspezifische Bildungsungleichheiten* (pp. 55–75). Wiesbaden, Germany: VS Verlag für Sozialwissenschaften.

Bettinger, E. P., Long, B. T., Oreopoulos, P., & Sanbonmatsu, L. (2012). The role of application assistance and information in college decisions: Results from the H&R block fafsa experiment. *The Quarterly Journal of Economics, 127*(3), 1205–1242.

Björklund, A., Jäntti, M., & Roemer, J. E. (2012). Equality of opportunity and the distribution of long-run income in Swede. *Social Choice and Welfare, 39*, 675–696.

Boudon, R. (1974). *Education, opportunity, and social inequality: Changing prospects in Western society.* New York, NY: Wiley.

Breen, R., & Goldthorpe, J. H. (1997). Explaining educational differentials: Towards a formal rational action theory. *Rationality and Society, 9*, 275–305.

Breen, R., & Goldthorpe, J. H. (2001). Class, mobility and merit. The experience of two British cohorts. *European Sociological Review, 17*(2), 81–101.

Breen, R., Luijkx, R., Müller, W., & Pollak, R. (2009). Nonpersistent inequality in educational attainment: Evidence from eight European countries. *American Journal of Sociology, 114*(5), 1475–1521.

Breen, R., Luijkx, R., Müller, W., & Pollak, R. (2010). Long term-trends in educational inequality in Europe: Class inequalities and gender differences. *European Sociological Review, 26*(1), 31–48.

Breen, R., Luijkx, R., Müller, W., & Pollak, R. (2012). Bildungsdisparitäten nach sozialer Herkunft und Geschlecht im Wandel—Deutschland im internationalen Vergleich. In H. Solga & R. Becker (Eds.), *Kölner Zeitschrift für Soziologie und Sozialpsychologie Sonderhefte* (Soziologische Bildungsforschung, Vol. 52, pp. 346–373). Heidelberg, Germany: Springer.

Buchmann, C., DiPrete, T. A., & McDaniel, A. (2008). Gender inequalities in education. *Annual Review of Sociology, 34*, 319–337.

Buchmann, C., & Hannum, E. (2001). Education and stratification in developing countries: A review of theories and research. *Annual Review of Sociology, 27*, 77–102.

Byun, S.-Y., & Kim, K.-K. (2010). Educational inequality in South Korea: The widening socioeconomic gap in student achievement. In E. Hannum (Series Ed.), *Research in the sociology of education: Vol. 17.* E. Hannum, H. Park, & Y. G. Butler (Eds.), *Globalization, changing demographics, and educational challenges in East Asia* (pp. 155–182). London, UK: Emerald Group.

Card, D. (1999). The causal effect of education on earnings. In O. Ashenfelter & D. Card (Eds.), *Handbook of labor economics* (Vol. 3A, pp. 1801–1859). Amsterdam, Netherlands: Elsevier.

Cohen, G. A. (1989). On the currency of egalitarian justice. *Ethics, 99*(4), 906–944.

DiPrete, T. A., & Buchmann, C. (2006). Gender-specific trends in the value of education and the emerging gender gap in college completion. *Demography, 43*, 1–24.

Dollmann, J. (2011). Verbindliche und unverbindliche Grundschulempfehlungen und soziale Ungleichheiten am ersten Bildungsübergang. *Kölner Zeitschrift für Soziologie und Sozialpsychologie, 63*(4), 431–457.

Dworkin, R. (1981). What is equality? Part 2: Equality of resources. *Philosophy & Public Affairs, 10*(4), 283–345.

Erikson, R. (1996). Explaining change in educational inequality–Economic security and school reforms. In R. Erikson & J. O. Jonsson (Eds.), *Can education be equalized? The Swedish case in comparative perspective* (pp. 95–112). Boulder, CO: Westview Press.

Erikson, R., & Jonsson, J. O. (1996). Introduction. Explaining class inequality in education: The Swedish test case. In R. Erikson & J. O. Jonsson (Eds.), *Can education be equalized? The Swedish case in comparative perspective* (pp. 1–64). Boulder, CO: Westview Press.

Erikson, R., & Rudolphi, F. (2010). Change in social selection to upper secondary school—Primary and secondary effects in Sweden. *European Sociological Review, 26*(3), 291–305.

Fehr, E., & Schmidt, K. (2004). The role of equality, efficiency, and Rawlsian Motives in social preferences: A reply to Engelmann and Strobel (Working Paper No. 179). Zürich: Institute for Empirical Research in Economics, University of Zürich.

Goldthorpe, J. H. (1996). Class analysis and the reorientation of class theory: The case of persisting differentials in educational attainment. *British Journal of Sociology, 47*(3), 481–505.

Hanushek, E. A., & Wößmann, L. (2007). *Education quality and economic growth.* Washington, DC: The World Bank.

Heckman, J. J., Stixrud, J., & Urzua, S. (2006). The effects of cognitive and noncognitive abilities on labor market outcomes and social behavior. *Journal of Labor Economics, 24*, 411–482.

Hillmert, S., & Jacob, M. (2003). Social inequality in higher education: Is vocational training a pathway leading to or away from university? *European Sociological Review, 19*(3), 319–334.

Ichou, M., & Vallet, L.-A. (2013). The relative importance of academic achievement, tracking decisions, and their relative contribution to educational inequalities: Change over four decades in France. In M. Jackson (Ed.), *Determined to succeed? Performance versus choice in educational attainment* (pp. 116–148). London, UK: Stanford University Press.

Jackson, M. (Ed.). (2013). *Determined to succeed? Performance versus choice in educational attainment.* London, UK: Stanford University Press.

Jackson, M., Erikson, R., Goldthorpe, J. H., & Yaish, M. (2007). Primary and secondary effects in class differentials in educational attainment the transition to A-level courses in England and Wales. *Acta Sociologica, 50*(3), 211–229.

Jackson, M., & Jonsson, J. O. (2013). Why does inequality of opportunity vary across countries? Primary and secondary effects in comparative context. In M. Jackson (Ed.), *Determined to succeed? Performance versus choice in educational attainment* (pp. 306–348). London, UK: Stanford University Press.

Karlson, K. B., Holm, A., & Breen, R. (2012). Comparing regression coefficients between same-sample nested models using logit and probit: A new method. *Sociological Methodology, 42*(1), 286–313.

Keller, S., & Zavalloni, M. (1964). Ambition and social class. A respecification. *Social Forces, 45*, 58–70.

Klein, M., Schindler, S., Pollak, R., & Müller, W. (2009). Soziale Disparitäten in der Sekundarstufe und ihre langfristige Entwicklung. In J. Baumert, K. Maaz, & U. Trautwein (Eds.), *Bildungsentscheidungen in differenzierten Schulsystemen.Zeitschrift für Erziehungswissenschaften* (Vol. 12, pp. 47–73). Wiesbaden, Germany: Verlag für Sozialwissenschaften.

Kogan, I., Noelke, C., & Gebel, M. (Eds.). (2011). *Making the transition: Education and labor market entry in Central and Eastern Europe.* Stanford, CA: Stanford University Press.

Lange, F., & Topel, R. (2006). The social value of education and human capital. In E. Hanushek & F. Welch (Eds.), *Handbook of the economics of education* (pp. 459–509). Amsterdam, Netherlands: Elsevier.

Lefranc, A., Pistolesi, N., & Trannoy, A. (2009). Equality of opportunity and luck: Definitions and testable conditions, with an application to income in France. *Journal of Public Economics, 93*(11), 1189–1207.

Mare, R. D. (1980). Social background and school continuation decisions. *Journal of the American Statistical Association, 75*, 295–305.

Mare, R. D. (1981). Change and stability in educational stratification. *American Sociological Review, 46*, 72–87.

Marginson, S. (2011). Higher education in East Asia and Singapore: Rise of the Confucian model. *Higher Education, 61*(5), 587–611.

Müller, W., & Gangl, M. (Eds.). (2003). *Transitions from education to work in Europe. The integration of youth into EU labour markets.* Oxford, UK: Oxford University Press.

Müller, W., & Pollak, R. (2004). Weshalb gibt es so wenige Arbeiterkinder in Deutschlands Universitäten? In R. Becker & W. Lauterbach (Eds.), *Bildung als Privileg? Erklärungen und Befunde zu den Ursachen der Bildungsungleichheit* (pp. 311–352). Wiesbaden, Germany: VS Verlag für Sozialwissenschaften.

Müller, W., Pollak, R., Reimer, D., & Schindler, S. (2009). Hochschulbildung und soziale Ungleichheit. In R. Becker & A. Hadjar (Eds.), *Lehrbuch der Bildungssoziologie* (pp. 281–320). Wiesbaden, Germany: VS Verlag für Sozialwissenschaften.

Müller, W., & Shavit, Y. (1998). The institutional embeddedness of the stratification process: A comparative study of qualifications and occupations in thirteen countries. In W. Müller & Y. Shavit (Eds.), *From school to work: A comparative study of educational qualifications and occupational destinations* (pp. 1–48). Oxford, UK: Oxford University Press.

Murray, M. (1988). Educational expansion, policies of diversion and equality: The case of Sweden, 1933–1985. *European Journal of Education, 23*(1/2), 141–149.

Neugebauer, M., & Schindler, S. (2012). Early transitions and tertiary enrolment: The cumulative impact of primary and secondary effects on entering university in Germany. *Acta Sociologica, 55*, 19–36.

Okun, A. M. (1975). *Equality and efficiency: The big tradeoff.* Washington, DC: Brookings Institution Press.

Oreopoulos, P., & Dunn, R. (2013). Information and college access: Evidence from a randomized field experiment. *The Scandinavian Journal of Economics, 115*(1), 3–26.

Organisation for Economic Co-operation and Development (OECD). (2012). *Education at a glance.* Paris, France: Author.

Parsons, T. (1970). Equality and inequality in modern society, or social stratification revisited. In E. O. Lauman (Ed.), *Social stratification: Research and theory for the 1970s.* New York, NY: Bobbs Merill.

Pfeffer, F. (2008). Persistent inequality in educational attainment and its institutional context. *European Sociological Review, 24,* 543–565.

Rawls, J. (1971). *A theory of justice.* Cambridge, MA: Harvard University Press.

Roemer, J. E. (1998). *Equality of opportunity.* Cambridge, MA: Harvard University Press.

Scarr, S., & Weinberg, R. A. (1976). IQ test performance of black children adopted by white families. *American Psychologist, 31*(10), 726.

Schindler, S. (2012). *Wege zur Studienberechtigung—Wege ins Studium? Eine Untersuchung sozialer Inklusions- und Ablenkungsprozesse* (Doctoral Dissertation). Universität Mannheim, Fakultät für Sozialwissenschaften.

Selz, M., & Vallet, L.-A. (2006). *La démocratisation de l'enseignement et son paradoxe apparent.* Paris, France: INSEE.

Sen, A. (1973). *On economic inequality.* Oxford, UK: Clarendon.

Shavit, Y., & Blossfeld, H.-P. (Eds.). (1993). *Persistent inequality. Changing educational attainment in thirteen countries.* Boulder, CO: Westview.

Shavit, Y., & Müller, W. (2000). Vocational secondary education, tracking and social stratification. In M. T. Hallinan (Ed.), *Handbook of sociology of education* (pp. 437–452). New York, NY: Plenum.

Stocké, V. (2007). Explaining educational decision and effects of families' social class position. *European Sociological Review, 23,* 505–519.

Treiman, D. J., & Yip, K. B. (1989). Educational and occupational attainment in 21 countries. In M. L. Kohn (Ed.), *Cross-national research in sociology* (pp. 373–394). Newbury Park, CA: Sage.

Trommsdorff, G. (2009). Culture and development of self-regulation. *Social and Personality Psychology Compass, 3*(5), 687–701.

Trommsdorff, G. (in press). Socialization of self regulation for achievement in cultural context. A developmental-psychological perspective on the Asian miracle. In U. Kim & Y. S. Park (Eds.), *Asia's educational miracle: Psychological, social and cultural perspectives.* New York: Springer.

Vallentyne, P. (2000). Equality, efficiency, and the priority of the worse-off. *Economics and Philosophy, 16*(1), 1–19.

Wu, X. (2007). *Economic transition, school expansion, and educational inequality in China, 1990–2000* (Research Report No. 07-627). Ann Arbor, MI: University of Michigan Population Studies Center.

Wu, X., & Zhang, Z. (2010). Changes in educational inequality in China, 1990–2005: Evidence from the population census data. In *Research in the sociology of education Series: Vol. 17.* E. Hannum, H. Park, & Y. G. Butler (Eds.), *Globalization, changing demographics, and educational challenges in East Asia* (pp. 123–152). Bingley, UK: Emerald Group Publishing Limited.

Career Guidance and Counseling in the Context of Unemployment and Vulnerability: A Case Study of South Africa

20

Pundy Pillay, Rènette du Toit, and Marina Mayer

Introduction

South Africa currently faces a youth unemployment crisis of unprecedented proportions. The country's peaceful transition to democracy in 1994 was greeted with jubilation by the black majority and heralded as a miracle by the international community. Hope was high. So was the expectation that the grinding poverty experienced by the black majority would be eradicated. Some 20 years into democracy, poverty, inequality, and unemployment remain stubbornly high, despite economic growth, albeit at modest rates. The concentration of unemployment among young people, especially black youth, is increasingly becoming a socioeconomic and political risk.

Since 1994, the South African government has pursued a number of strategies aimed at better equipping young people to become economically independent. Despite this effort, in 2011 youth unemployment and marginalization remained disconcertingly high. While many more young people have access to education than the generation before them, this education is not equipping them to access the economy at the required scale. This new generation of young South Africans is facing precisely the same future that young people faced

at the end of apartheid—this time without the hope that a new political and policy environment will bring change.

We start the chapter with an overview of the development context by first comparing Sub-Saharan Africa (SSA) with other regions in terms of a set of international development indicators. Second, we highlight the challenge of youth unemployment on a global scale, at the same time drawing attention to the nature and scale of youth unemployment in SSA. Third, we analyze the nature, magnitude, and causes of youth unemployment in South Africa. In the subsequent sections, we spell out the role of career guidance in the South African context and outline the current state of career guidance services in the country, and introduce new developments. We close by suggesting what the new direction regarding career development services in South Africa may bring about.

The International Development Context

Tables 20.1 and 20.2 illustrate different aspects of the comparative development context. Table 20.1 provides data on gross national income (GNI) per capita by region in both US dollars and purchasing power parity (PPP) terms.

Table 20.1 shows average annual gross domestic product (GDP) growth rates (i.e., economic growth) by region for the period 2000–2010. In terms of income per capita, in both US dollars and

P. Pillay (✉)
School of Public and Development Management,
University of the Witwatersrand, Johannesburg,
South Africa
e-mail: pundy.pillay@wits.ac.za

G. Arulmani et al. (eds.), *Handbook of Career Development*, International and Cultural Psychology,
DOI 10.1007/978-1-4614-9460-7_20, © Springer Science+Business Media, LLC 2014

Table 20.1 Income per capita and economic growth by world region

Type of country/region	GNI per capita (US$) (2010)	GNI per capita (US$–PPP) (2010)	GDP growth: annual average rate (2000–2010)
Low income	510	1,246	5.5
Middle income	3,764	6,780	6.4
High income	38,658	37,183	1.8
Region			
East Asia and Pacific	3,691	6,623	9.4
Latin America and Caribbean	7,802	10,951	3.8
South Asia	1,213	3,208	7.4
Sub-Saharan Africa	1,165	2,108	5.0

Source: World Bank (2012a); PPP refers to "Purchasing Power Parity"—adjusting prices and exchange rate to reflect more accurately the purchasing power of local currencies relative to the dollar
Note. Low income countries: annual income per head less than $1,005; Middle income: $1,005–12,275; High income: greater than $12,275

PPP terms, it is evident that SSA fares poorly with respect to both middle- and high-income countries, and against such regions as East Asia and the Pacific, and Latin America and the Caribbean. SSA's average per capita income is close to that of South Asia (primarily made up of Bangladesh, India, and Pakistan). In terms of economic growth, the picture is more positive with SSA outperforming both high-income economies and the Latin America and Caribbean region. However, SSA's average growth rate for the decade 2000–2010 was below the average especially for middle-income countries, and East Asia and the Pacific, and South Asia regions. Moreover, the low income-per-capita figures for SSA (as also for South Asia) suggest that the benefits of economic growth are not permeating broadly across the population. In other words, growth does not appear to be pro-poor and inclusive.

Table 20.2 shows a set of noneconomic, development indicators for the same set of countries and regions as Table 20.1.

From Table 20.2 it is evident that SSA fares the worst of all regions on four of the indicators and shares a suboptimal profile with South Asia on three indicators. It fares better than South Asia on Internet users. On measures such as child mortality, maternal mortality, HIV prevalence, and incidence of tuberculosis, SSA lags far behind both industrialized and developing countries, including South Asia.

Next, we examine the United Nations Development Programme's (UNDP) Human Development Index (HDI) by type of HDI group and world region. The HDI is an extremely useful statistic because it combines social and economic indicators to provide a more holistic measure of development. Essentially, the HDI is a composite index based on measures of education and health, and economic development. In 2011, 47 countries were categorized as *very high human development* with Norway, Australia, and the Netherlands at ranks 1, 2, and 3, respectively, and Croatia and Barbados at the bottom end of this group. Examples of newly industrialized and developing countries in this group were South Korea (15), Singapore (26), and Chile (44). A further 48 countries were categorized into the next group as *high human development*. Included here were Cuba (51), Mexico (57), Malaysia (61), and Brazil (84). The only African countries with high HDI in 2011 were Mauritius (77) and Tunisia (94). The next category of *medium human development* comprised 47 countries including China (101), Egypt (114), Botswana (118), Namibia (120), South Africa (123), and India (134). In total, 12 African countries were in this group. Finally, the last group of *low human*

Table 20.2 Some indicators of development by world region

Type of country/region	Adult literacy 2005–2009	Universal primary education (UPE)	Child mortality	Maternal mortality	HIV prevalence	Incidence of tuberculosis	Access to improved sanitation	Internet users per 100 people
Low income	61	65	119	590	2.6	296	36	2.6
Middle income	83	92	52	210	0.7	139	56	20.7
High income	98	97	7	15	0.3	14	100	72.3
Region								
East Asia and Pacific	94	97	26	89	0.2	136	59	24.1
Latin America and Caribbean	91	102	23	86	0.5	45	79	31.5
South Asia	61	61	71	290	0.3	180	36	5.5
Sub-Saharan Africa	62	62	130	650	5.5	342	31	8.8

Source: World Bank (2012b)

Note. (1) Adult literacy—% aged 15 and older; (2) UPE—primary completion rate %; (3) Child mortality—under five mortality rate per 1,000; (4) HIV prevalence: % of the population aged 15–49; (5) Incidence of tuberculosis—per 100,000 of the population; (6) Access to improved sanitation facilities—% of the population

development countries comprised 46 countries of which 35 are African, in fact all in SSA. The bottom 14 countries are also all African. Prominent African countries in this group are Kenya (140), Angola (148), Tanzania (152), Nigeria (156), Uganda (161), Zimbabwe (173), Mozambique (184), and Democratic Republic of Congo (in position 187 as the bottommost).

The analysis of these development indicators particularly the HDI reveal the following about SSA: (a) Relatively high rates of economic growth are not translating into higher levels of development for the population as a whole. The evidence from international agencies such as the World Bank suggests that the growth rate for SSA for the last 5 years has surpassed the average of 5.5 % for the 2000–2010 period. Examples of African countries with high growth rates during the 2000–2010 period were Angola (12.9 % average per annum, HDI in 2011—148/187 countries); Mozambique (7.7 %, 184); Nigeria (6.7 %, 156); Rwanda (7.6 %, 166); and Uganda (7.7 %, 161) (World Bank, 2012b). These figures suggest that growth in SSA is not leading to greater inclusiveness in terms of increase in employment and significantly lower levels of poverty. (b) A further constraining factor on growth and development is income inequality. The evidence suggests that SSA is now the "inequality continent" usurping that dubious honor from Latin America. Some evidence for the high levels of inequality is available from UNDP's HDI (2011) report which allows for a comparison of a country's HDI with its income per capita measure. Table 20.3 shows a comparison of HDI and GNI per capita in terms of world rankings for six African countries, namely Botswana, Equatorial Guinea, Gabon, Namibia, South Africa, and Swaziland. This table shows the wide discrepancy between their (relatively high) economic status (GNI per capita) and their (relatively low) development status (HDI).

There is increasing recognition today within the economics discipline that income and other inequalities constrain economic growth in significant ways. Stiglitz (2012) has shown that one way in which this occurs is that increasing inequality (of income, for example) leads to

Table 20.3 Comparing GNI per capita and HDI in selected African countries, 2011

Country	GNI per capita ranking	HDI ranking
Botswana	62	118
Equatorial Guinea	45	136
Gabon	66	106
Namibia	99	120
South Africa	79	123
Swaziland	113	140

Source: UNDP, 2011

Table 20.4 Youth unemployment by world region: actual and projected percentages

Region	2012	2017
Global	12.7	12.9
Central and Eastern Europe	16.9	17.0
Developed economies	17.5	15.6
East Asia	9.5	10.4
Latin America and the Caribbean	14.6	14.7
Middle East	26.4	28.4
North Africa	27.5	26.7
South Asia	9.6	9.8
South East Asia and the Pacific	13.1	14.2
Sub-Saharan Africa	12.0	11.8

Source: ILO, 2012

diminishing equality of opportunity (for instance, in education and health).

Global Youth Unemployment

In 2007, there were an estimated 1.2 billion young people between 15 and 24 years in the world comprising just under 25 % of the world's working-age population (Coenjaerts, Ernst, Fortuny, Rei, & Pilgrim, 2009). Moreover, about 87 % of the youth are estimated to be living in developing countries. Between 1997 and 2007, the proportion of employed youth declined from 49.2 to 44.5 %, and the total number of unemployed youth increased from 63 to 71 million (Coenjaerts et al., 2009). In SSA, the number of unemployed youth increased from 8 to 10 million. More recently, the International Labour Organisation (ILO, 2012) has reported that the global youth unemployment rate reached 12.7 % in 2012, close to its "crisis peak" in 2009. It is estimated that nearly 75 million youth are unemployed around the world, an increase of 4 million since 2007.

Table 20.4 shows ILO youth unemployment rates for 2012 and projections for 2017 by region. From Table 20.4 it is evident that there are significant regional differences in youth unemployment rates, with the highest levels in the Middle East and North Africa.

Notwithstanding these differences, it is evident that all regions face major youth challenges in terms of absolute numbers of those unemployed. For SSA, the ILO ratios are relatively low in world terms but highly consequential in terms of the numbers of youth who remain unemployed.

Moreover, this ratio is masked by the high rates of vulnerable employment and working poverty in many developing regions, in particular SSA (ILO, 2012). According to the ILO (2012), the share of workers in vulnerable unemployment (characterized by inter alia, poor pay and working conditions, and lack of security) ranges from one in five in Central and South-Eastern Europe (non-EU) to more than three out of four workers in South Asia and SSA. Moreover, South Asia and SSA are the regions in which the youth labor force is growing. In SSA, an average of 2.1 million young people will be entering the labor market each year between 2011 and 2015, while in South Asia this figure is 465,000 (ILO, 2012).

General Unemployment in South Africa

In March 2011, South Africa's official unemployment rate stood at around 25 % or approximately 4.4 million people (Statistics South Africa, 2011). If "discouraged" workers (workers who are not looking for jobs anymore) are added, this ratio rises to close to 40 % or 6.6 million.

An important characteristic of South Africa's unemployment crisis is its concentration in the 15–34 age cohort. It is, therefore, substantially a problem of youth unemployment. In 2011, approximately 3.2 million or 72 % of the unemployed were in this cohort.

Table 20.5 Unemployment by race

Race	Proportion of the population	Number unemployed	%
African	79.2	3,743,825	85.7
Colored	8.9	435,554	10.0
Indian	2.5	64,070	1.5
White	9.4	127,582	2.9
Total	100.0	4,371,030	100.0

Sources: Statistics South Africa, Quarterly Labour Force Survey, March 2011; Statistics South Africa, Census, 2011

A second important characteristic is the racial nature of unemployment. In South Africa, the race groups are described as African, Colored, Indian, and White; *Black* is the terminology used for Africans, Coloreds, and Indians collectively. Of these, the African group constitutes the overwhelming majority of the South African population: approximately 80 % (Statistics South Africa, 2011). It is also this group that faced the greatest degree of discrimination in the apartheid era in terms of access to employment, education, health, and the urban areas of the country. The recently released Census 2011 data shows that 36 % of Africans, 22 % of Coloreds, 12 % of Indians, and 6 % of Whites in South Africa are unemployed (Statistics South Africa, 2011). Clearly, the unemployment rate among Blacks in South Africa is sixfold the rate among Whites, and exceeds one-third of the Black population. Table 20.5 displays the distribution of unemployment by race with Africans comprising almost 86 % of the unemployed and Coloreds, the next largest group at 10 %.

From Table 20.5, it is evident that there is a 6 % overrepresentation of Blacks among the unemployed (80 % representation in the population but 85.7 % representation among the unemployed).

A third characteristic of unemployment is that it is more heavily concentrated among women, especially African women. Among all unemployed, women comprised 51.3 % in 2011 (Statistics South Africa, 2011). However, unemployment is disproportionately concentrated among African women, and more so among those living outside the urban areas. From Table 20.6, the following conclusions can be drawn: African women constitute 86 % of all unemployed women, 52 % of African unemployment, and 44 % of total unemployment. With regard to the last statistic, it implies that more than two out of every five unemployed persons is a female African.

In summary, it is clear that race, age, and gender are key elements in explaining unemployment. There is moreover, a rather paradoxical situation in the South African labor market in that high unemployment coexists with a serious skills shortage.

Youth Unemployment in South Africa

In order to appreciate the pivotal role of career guidance and counseling in resolving South Africa's youth unemployment crisis, it is necessary to understand the socioeconomic context. South Africa is characterized as an upper-middle-income developing country in terms of GDP per capita. It is also ranked as one of the most unequal countries in the world. This incongruity (as illustrated in Table 20.3, for example) is the consequence of the apartheid regime whose aim was to create racial inequality by directing resources and opportunity to the white minority, while excluding the black majority. It is also the unintended consequence of inappropriate and/or poorly implemented economic and social policies in the democratic era. During the apartheid era, black South Africans were not only disenfranchised, but also excluded from the formal economy through discriminatory education, ownership, and labor mobility policies and practices.

During the democratic regime, South Africa's growth trajectory has been characterized by significant structural change and growth, alongside stubbornly high levels of poverty and growing inequality. These socioeconomic trends have been exacerbated by the impact of the global economic recession in 2008, which resulted in the economy contracting and one million jobs being lost in 2009 (Mayer, 2011). In terms of skill levels, most of the lost jobs are in unskilled and semiskilled occupations. Given their low education and skills levels in relation to the rest

Table 20.6 Unemployment by race and gender

	Male		Female		
	N	%	N	%	Total
African	1,806,394	41.3	1,937,431	44.3	3,743,825
Colored	226,695	5.2	208,859	4.8	435,554
Indian	34,228	0.8	29,842	0.7	64,070
White	62,394	1.4	65,188	1.5	127,582
	2,129,711	48.7	2,241,320	51.3	4,371,031

Source: Statistics South Africa, Quarterly Labour Force Survey, March 2011

Table 20.7 Characteristics of the youth labor market

Youth (15–34) characteristics		
Youth population	18,825,743	% Of Youth population
Employed	5,660,214	30.1
Unemployed	3,157,533	16.8
Unemployed 15–24 years	1,363,521	7.2
Unemployed 25–34 years	1,791,414	9.5
Discouraged jobseekers	1,407,895	7.5
Other not economically active	8,602,699	45.7

Source: Statistics South Africa, Quarterly Labour Force Survey, March 2010

of the population, black South Africans were the most affected by this employment crisis.

In short, the growth-employment-poverty-inequality dynamic has not resulted in inclusive growth, mainly because it has not been labor-absorbing. The lack of access to wage income is the main driver of poverty, and together with growing income differentials within and between racial groups, has driven up inequality. With a Gini-coefficient for income distribution at about 0.65, the country is one of most unequal in this regard. Furthermore, a disturbing feature of inequality is that democracy has not yet reversed this trend.

At least two aspects of exclusion from the labor market are evident: first, low participation rates (at around 60 %, regarded as low in a middle-income country context) which are largely the consequence of poverty and spatial segregation by race hampering job search; and, second, high unemployment rates, or exclusion from the formal labor market. The latter is concentrated among young people exiting education and training with aspirations of entering the labor market.

Table 20.7 presents some relevant characteristics of the youth labor market, namely the low levels of employment (about 30 % of the economically active population), the high levels of unemployment, and the high proportion of those who are not economically active (about 46 %).

Table 20.8 portrays unemployment by education level and race. In the previous subsection, we have already mentioned that 72 % of total unemployment is in the youth category (some 3.2 million out of a total of 4.4 million). Of this number, Africans comprised 87 % (from Table 20.9) or 2.7 million, and Coloreds, 9 % (294,089). Among African youth, 55 % of the unemployed had an education level of up to *incomplete secondary*, a further 39 % had completed secondary schooling, and almost 6 %, tertiary education. Furthermore, in all race groups other than Indian, the highest percentage of unemployed were in the category *secondary not completed*, followed by those in the category *secondary completed*. These findings are not significantly different from those for the total pool of the unemployed. In this latter group, 59 % had less than a *matriculation* (i.e., *matric*) or *school-leaving qualification*, 35 % had completed schooling, and 6 % had tertiary education (Statistics South Africa, 2011).

What is common across the pool of those unemployed is that schooling is not translating into appropriate skill acquisition and employment, especially for large numbers of African and Colored youth, in spite of high levels of public investment in education. This underscores the need to better prepare young people to enter

Table 20.8 Unemployment of the 15–34 age group by educational status and race

	African		Colored		Indian		White		
Educational status	N	%	N	%	N	%	N	%	Total
No schooling	14,297	0.5	0	0.0	0	0.0	0	0.0	14,297
Less than primary completed	114,152	4.2	8,626	2.9	1,008	1.8	1,711	2.3	125,497
Primary completed	83,551	3.1	18,376	6.2	0	0.0	913	1.2	102,840
Secondary not completed	1,291,744	47.2	157,146	53.4	13,561	24.8	27,095	36.2	1,489,546
Secondary completed	1,062,905	38.9	102,711	34.9	36,902	67.6	24,309	32.5	1,226,827
Tertiary	157,206	5.7	5,412	1.8	3,121	5.7	20,752	27.8	186,491
Other	10,217	0.4	1,818	0.6	0	0.0	0	0.0	12,035
Total	2,734,072	100.0	294,089	100.0	54,592	100.0	74,780	100.0	3,157,533

Source: Statistics South Africa, Quarterly Labour Force Survey, March 2010

Table 20.9 Duration of unemployment of the 15–34 age group by race

How long been trying to find work	African		Colored		Indian		White		
	N	%	N	%	N	%	N	%	Total
Less than 3 months	333,083	12.2	52,991	18.0	2,540	4.7	12,873	17.2	401,487
3 Months to less than 6 months	188,946	6.9	28,015	9.5	1,485	2.7	9,702	13.0	228,148
6 Months to less than 9 months	154,573	5.7	19,602	6.7	2,867	5.3	9,166	12.3	186,208
9 Months to less than 1 year	183,914	6.7	19,456	6.6	2,338	4.3	5,914	7.9	211,622
1 Year to less than 3 years	791,792	29.0	81,696	27.8	13,825	25.3	23,238	31.1	910,551
3 Years to 5 years	456,971	16.7	38,231	13.0	15,395	28.2	3,890	5.2	514,487
More than 5 years	622,423	22.8	53,731	18.3	16,142	29.6	9,998	13.4	702,294
Do not know	2,370	0.1	367	0.1	0	0.0	0	0.0	2,737
Total	2,734,072	100.0	294,089	100.0	54,592	100.0	74,781	100.0	3,157,534

Source: Statistics South Africa, Quarterly Labour Force Survey, March 2010

the labor market, both in terms of formal education and soft skills. In fact, an astounding 2.13 million young people aged 15–34 years remained unemployed for over a year, while about 1.03 million were unemployed for less than a year before entering the labor market (see Table 20.9). In relative terms, 63 % of new labor market entrants were unemployed for more than a year after exiting education and training and commencing a job search. Disaggregated by race, 83.1 % of unemployed Indians remained unemployed for a year or more; corresponding figures were 68.5 % for Africans, 59.1 % for Coloreds, and 49.7 % for Whites (see Table 20.9).

The labor market and the pathway into it (through education and training) are key

determinants of mobility out of poverty and exclusion from the formal economy and the fruits of its growth. Empirical analyses in developing countries (Pillay, 2011) show that initial inequalities in the distribution of physical capital (e.g., land) and human capital (e.g., education and health) represent obstacles to economic growth, with the effects being almost twice as great for the poor as for the population as a whole. In South Africa, the persistence of high income inequality, which is clearly inhibiting economic growth and poverty reduction, cannot be meaningfully disassociated from the limited and unequal access to human capital; they are inextricably linked (Pillay, 2006).

In order to redress poverty and inequality, the ultimate objective of the country's growth and development path for the next two decades should be to enable rapid social mobility, with the aim of creating a large middle class. There is substantial agreement that this will be achieved through the labor market, by forging a growth path that enables the poor to secure decent paying jobs. Any future growth path that is not labor-absorbing will exacerbate the challenges of poverty and inequality. The critical issue is the role that career guidance and counseling can play within the context of the socioeconomic challenges confronting South Africa.

The Education and Training System

Career guidance and counseling are embedded in a country's education and training institutions. Education, and the knowledge it generates, is a key factor in development—it is crucial for economic and social progress everywhere (Pillay, 2011). No country has managed to attain a high level of economic and social development without appropriate investments in good quality schooling and post-school education (PSE). Education and training impact economic development in many ways, through for example, their impact on labor productivity, poverty eradication, technology, and health. Investment in technical skills at both the schooling and post-schooling levels is critical for the optimal performance of various economic sectors (Pillay, 2011).

However, the current state of education and training in South Africa is not conducive to knowledge generation and the development of the appropriate technical skills necessary for growth in key sectors such as mining. The education and training challenge comprises both quantitative and qualitative dimensions. At the schooling level, significant progress has been made in terms of enrolment at primary and secondary levels. However, the quantitative challenges in education are at extreme ends of the system: in preprimary and early childhood education (identified as key for children's further development) and in the post-schooling sector, specifically in vocational and technical education. PSE in South Africa refers to tertiary education at

universities and universities of technology or further education and training (FET) at FET colleges. In both the subsectors of preprimary education and FET, enrolment levels are relatively low. Going beyond these enrolment deficiencies, the biggest systemic challenge in education and training relates to *efficiency* and *quality*. First, it should be noted that South Africa spends a large proportion of its national budget on education and training. In the fiscal year 2011/2012, expenditure on education and training accounted for 22 % of the budget and about 5.5 % of GDP (National Treasury, 2011). Both these figures are well above the average for both developing and middle-income countries. However, with regard to efficiency, outputs are not in line with the massive financial investments made in education and training, and are reflected, for example, in high repetition and dropout rates. Poor performance with regard to quality is visible in the glaringly low achievements of a large number of students in key subject areas such as reading, mathematics, and science.

Quality of Education

There is little doubt that improving the quality of education provision at all levels—including effective career guidance and counseling—represents one of the greatest challenges to policymakers and implementers in South Africa. The limited evidence on measurements of quality indicates that considerable efforts need to be made in this regard. At the current time, South Africa fares extremely poorly in both international and regional assessments of school performance in reading and mathematics. For example, the SACMEQ (Southern and Eastern Africa Consortium for Monitoring Educational Quality) tests on reading and mathematics scores for primary school children in the 15 SADC (Southern African Development Community) countries reveal that while South Africa is one of the three richest countries in the region in terms of GDP per capita (the other two being Botswana and Mauritius) and spends the most on education and training, it was surpassed by eight SADC countries in reading performance in 2005 and 2007, and by nine countries in 2005 and seven in 2007 in mathematics (SACMEQ, 2005, 2007).

One of the major challenges in the education system relates to mathematics and science education. A study by the Centre for Development and Enterprise (2007) argued that the South African schooling system continues to produce far fewer passes in mathematics and science than the country's economy requires. Many university degrees and professional and technical careers require grounding in math and/or science, and the critical shortfall in learners leaving the schooling system with these qualifications was identified as a significant constraint to economic growth. This lack of quality math and science was seen also as an impediment to the development of state capacity, and further undermined both public and private programs for black economic empowerment. It is also well-known that the major hurdle in math and science education is the inadequate number of properly qualified teachers. One report estimated that the teacher training system is producing only about a third of the country's requirement of about 25,000 new teachers a year (Centre for Development and Enterprise, 2007).

A feature of the schooling system post-1994 has been the rapid quantitative expansion. This is reflected in increasing enrolments at primary and secondary levels (the Gross Enrolment Ratios were 94 % and 86 %, respectively, in 2010—Department of Basic Education [DBE], 2011a); and rising pass rates in the matric or school leaving examinations, up from around the 50 % mark in 1994 to 70 % in 2011. However, there is substantial evidence that the quality of schooling has not kept up with rising enrolments and pass rates. The DBE no longer publishes information by race so it is not easy to determine how black students are performing. However, it is possible to use poverty as a proxy and the evidence suggests that schooling performance in both poor provinces and poor schools (both with an overwhelming majority of black students) is far below that of more affluent provinces and schools that are better-resourced. For example, in 2010, 23.5 % of matric candidates achieved a pass rate that enables them to study for Bachelor's degrees at university. In the more urban provinces, such as Gauteng and Western Cape, this rate was 34 % and 32 %, respectively. In the poorer rural provinces such as Eastern Cape, Limpopo, and Mpumalanga, the corresponding figure was approximately 16 % (DBE, 2012). A similar finding emerges in a comparison of Grade 6 learner performance in language and mathematics across schools ranked from *least poor* to *poorest*. In the poorest schools, the average percentage scores in language and mathematics were 21 % and 26 %, respectively, and in the least poor schools they were 47 % for both subjects (not a very encouraging sign on its own anyway!).

There is substantial inequity in access to quality education and success in education. What all this suggests is that the schooling system has a long way to go before it can claim to be producing matriculates with a skill base that adequately prepares them for tertiary education and/or the labor market.

Training

Training in South Africa takes places essentially at three sites: (a) at the level of the firm, (b) at the Sectoral Education and Training Authorities (SETAs)—there are 22 SETAs covering all economic sectors, and (c) FET colleges—there are 50 FET colleges spread across the country which provide formal vocational education training programs as well as training on behalf of firms and SETAs.

The national skills development strategy (NSDS-1) introduced by the Government of South Africa in 2001 is funded through an employee payroll tax. The rationale for the introduction of such a levy to fund training of the employed and unemployed was twofold. First, the new democratic government of 1994 inherited an education and training system characterized by a chronic shortage of skills necessary for stimulating economic growth and reducing unemployment. Second, the private business sector of the apartheid era seriously underinvested in workplace training initiatives mainly because of an undue emphasis on short-term profits and a tendency to see training as a cost rather than as an investment. For these reasons, the postapartheid government was compelled to develop and implement a tax-funded skill development strategy which was met at its commencement, by a high level of hostility by the private business sector (Gustafsson & Pillay, 2009). The NSDS was intended to "radically transform education and training in South Africa by improving both the quality and quantity of training to support increased competitiveness of industry and improved quality of life for all South Africans" (Department of Labour, 2005, p. 2).

The first NSDS (NSDS-1) was launched in February 2001 with targets to be achieved by March 2005. The strategy was underpinned by the Skills Development Act (SDA) of 1998 and the Skills Development Levies Act (SDLA) of 1999. This legislation provided the basis for the skills development system which was aimed at addressing the structural problems of the labor market inherited from the past, and at transforming the South African labor market "from one with a low skills base to one characterized by rising skills and a commitment to lifelong learning" (Department of Labour, 2001, p. 4). Twelve success indicators and three equity targets were associated with the following five objectives of the NSDS-1 (Department of Labour, 2001):

- Developing a culture of high quality lifelong learning.
- Fostering skills development in the formal economy for productivity and employment growth.
- Stimulating and supporting skills development in small businesses.
- Promoting skills development for employability and sustainable livelihoods through social development initiatives.
- Assisting new entrants into employment.

These objectives were met with varying degrees of success. A follow-up to NSDS-1 was introduced in 2005 (NSDS-2) for the period 2005–2010, and a third (NSDS-3) in February 2011.

A study commissioned by the Department of Labour (Peterson, McGrath, & Badroodien,

2003) to investigate skills development in the public sector identified the following challenges:

- Critical skill needs are not being adequately addressed in the areas of financial management, computer skills, project management, human resource management, customer care, communication skills, and Adult Basic Education and Training.
- Inadequate exposure of management to key skills such as financial management and computer skills.
- Slow progress on the implementation of learnerships—a learnership is a training program that combines theory delivered by a training provider with practical experience in the workplace and it is always linked to a qualification.
- Insufficient expertise in the collection of skill development information and reporting on training.
- Low attention paid to quality assurance of training.

Post-school Education

It is becoming increasingly evident to policymakers that PSE is critical for economic growth, technological absorption, and advancement towards a knowledge economy. The PSE sector in South Africa faces many challenges. The first challenge relates to access. Although South Africa has a relatively high gross enrolment ratio in universities (at around 17–18 %), this figure masks the fact that very few students are enrolled in the PSE vocational education subsector, namely in the FET colleges. In general, the main barrier to access is poor and inadequate schooling. For instance, large numbers of students leave the schooling system each year without having the necessary qualifications to enter the PSE sector. The second challenge relates to equity. There are usually three important determinants of inequity: gender, socioeconomic status, and region of origin. South Africa, in contrast to most African countries, does have a higher proportion of women in PSE. However, access to the higher quality higher education (HE) institutions is significantly determined by socioeconomic status, often because children from richer households attend better quality schools. Finally, participation in the better quality HE institutions is skewed in favor of students from urban and metropolitan areas.

The third challenge relates to quality. As with the schooling sector, the challenge of quality is pervasive in the higher education (HE) sector, with large numbers of students obtaining certification that does not appear to equip them with the requisite skills for gainful employment. The fourth challenge in South African higher education relates to the relative underproduction of graduates in the science and engineering disciplines. This is directly related to the poor standard of mathematics and science education prevailing in the schooling system.

The Role of Career Guidance

According to the World Bank (World Bank, 2012a), in many middle income and developed countries there is a move away from viewing career guidance in institutional and reactive terms—as a measure designed to lubricate the operation of the education system and its relationship to the labor market, and to combat such phenomena as unemployment or the mismatch between the demand for and supply of labor. There is, instead, a more dynamic and proactive view of the role of career guidance as an integral part of a human resource development (HRD) strategy designed to harness technological and economic change and enable a country to compete effectively in global markets.

South Africa has seen over the last decade a plethora of national, sectoral, and regional growth and development policies and strategies, most of which are aimed, among other things, at making the economy grow and creating employment. Most of these policies and strategies (discussed in the next section) emphasize the importance of HRD. Although none of these policy documents explains explicitly how career

guidance will support economic growth, it stands to reason that:

- Career guidance can encourage people, including youth and adults, to engage in career planning and learning throughout life, so that they can respond more flexibly to the opportunities offered by a dynamic labor market (World Bank, 2012a).
- Correct and timely information on the labor market can guide people in the direction of the greatest needs—in this way preventing the development of skill shortages. This means that the labor market signals that indicate demand-side trends and directions need to be monitored, translated into digestible form, and made available to the different users of career guidance and information. Skill shortages not only stifle growth and entrepreneurship; they also drive up labor costs and by so doing undermine the competitive advantage that a country or a region may have as an investment destination. The opposite is also true: An abundance of appropriately skilled labor available at a reasonable price enhances the attractiveness of a country or region as a destination for investment and the location of new industries.
- Career choices that fit people's interests and abilities can lead to greater productivity in employment.
- Conversely, the high cost of wrong career choices can be avoided. These costs include:
  - The costs associated with high dropout rates of first-year students at college and university.
  - The costs for employers of low morale, poor performance, and bad service levels of employees (which may be the result of wrong career choices).
  - The cost to employers when employees leave their jobs because of bad person-job-fits—for example, recruitment costs, training costs, and hidden costs resulting from the lack of continuity within the organization.
  - In the case of dismissal, the possibility of added costs arising from stringent labor laws.

The South African Policy and Legislative Context Relating to Career Guidance

There are numerous policies and legislation in South Africa relating to education, the labor market, job creation, and career guidance. The Human Resources Development Strategy of South Africa (HRDSA) is the axis of all these policies; it is the core strategy for HRD in South Africa. The key elements of the HRDSA are the following: (a) it recognizes both the demand and supply side of HRD issues; (b) it acknowledges that HRD spans several stages of human development from early childhood development through to labor market entry and participation; (c) it recognizes systemic challenges as impediments to successful HRD policy implementation; and (d) it locates HRD in the broader development context and takes into account the challenges posed by issues such as poverty, inequality, and high unemployment (Department of Higher Education and Training [DHET], 2010a). The reference to lifelong learning, education and training, skill development, employment and the labor market, social equity, and economic and general development in the HRDSA is of particular relevance to career guidance.

The national qualifications framework (NQF) was established in 2008 introducing a new qualification-framework for South Africa. The objectives of the NQF are the following: (a) creating an integrated national framework for learning achievements; (b) facilitating access to and mobility and progression within education, training, and career paths; (c) enhancing the quality of education and training; and (d) accelerating the redress of past unfair discrimination in education, training, and employment opportunities (NQF, 2012). In terms of career development or career guidance, the NQF is portrayed as a bridge to lifelong learning, facilitating access, mobility, and progression in relation to career pathways.

It was mentioned earlier that one of the strategies that South Africa has put in place to enhance skill development and address employability challenges is the NSDS. The country is already in the third phase of NSDS, that is, NSDS III. The premise of NSDS III is that individuals are to be guided before they enroll in any learning or training program to ensure their success in the labor market (DHET, 2010b). SETAs are seen as points where career- and labor market-related information about the different sectors of the economy are gathered and where support services can be generated. The NSDS III, therefore, emphasizes the need for such information to be synchronized centrally and made available nationally. To this effect SETAs are commissioned, under the NSDS III, to submit information in a standard format and to help expose learners to the work before they make their final career decisions. The standard formats for information will be developed by the skills planning unit of the DHET. The related success indicators for SETAs in terms of career guidance-related objectives are the following (DHET, 2010b):

- SETAs to submit a comprehensive occupational profile of their sector and a guide to employment opportunities in their sector in the format prepared by the DHET by March 2013. Such a profile and guide to be updated by March 2016.
- SETAs to provide information on the steps taken to expose prospective learners to work in their sector.

In terms of career information, guidance, and counseling at school level, the National Curriculum Statement Grades R to 12 (January 2012) and the Curriculum and Assessment Policy Statements for Life Orientation Grades 10–12 (January 2012) are relevant (DBE, 2011b). The National Curriculum Statement Grades R to 12 makes provision for a subject called Life Skills in the foundation, intermediate, and senior phases of school. The Curriculum and Assessment Policy Statement for Life Orientation Grades 10–12 provides the framework for career development during the last 3 years of school. Career development is one of the six topics (called careers and careers choices) in the subject called Life Orientation.

In order to regulate, enable, and transform PSE in South Africa in the recent Green Paper on PSE and Training (DHET, 2012b), the Minister of Higher Education and Training has made it clear that the focus of higher education in South Africa will shift from universities to FET colleges, positioning the vocational college system as the main platform for skills development training. The Green Paper indicates that the public FET colleges will expand in order to provide PIVOTAL programs especially to young post-school learners and adults at turning points in their careers. PIVOTAL programs are learning programs that meet critical needs for economic growth and social development. The Green Paper further states that career guidance and information will be critical for assisting potential entrants to choose the right study fields; "career guidance must become available to all young people as they choose their career paths" (DHET, 2012b, p.78). Currently the Framework for Student Support Services of the DHET is the guide that is used by the FET colleges to organize and provide support services for students (including career guidance) (DHET, 2007).

In terms of the higher education institutions (universities and universities of technology), the Higher Education Act, 1997 (Government of South Africa, 1997) under which the council on higher education (CHE) was established, states that the CHE may advise the Minister on any aspect of higher education at its own initiative. This could also include advice on student support services which could include career guidance. However, the reality is that the higher education institutions are functioning quite independently and many of the institutions established well-organized student counseling services outside of any legislative prescriptions. The overarching body that oversees the student counseling services at higher education institutions is called the Southern African Association for Counselling and Development in Higher Education (SAACDHE). SAACDHE is a voluntary body that sets standards for practice at the student counseling services units. A quality assurance framework for best practice is applied and all institutions are monitored against it.

In terms of employment (and unemployment) and the labor market, the Department of Labour (DoL) currently delivers employment services under the Skills Development Act, 1998 (Government of South Africa, 1998) while the Employment Services Bill (Government of South Africa, 2010) is still negotiated at the National Economic Development and Labour Council (Nedlac—a tripartite body comprising members from the private business sector, government, and the labor unions). The relevant sections in the Employment Services Bill refer to the provision of the following services to facilitate the matching of work seekers to employment opportunities: vocational and career counseling and labor market information; assessment of work seekers to determine suitability; and other related life skills to secure employment. Private employment agencies that render recruitment and placement services (some of them also provide career guidance-related services) fall under the Skills Development Act, 1998, and are required to register with the DoL.

Youth development with specific reference to entrepreneurial skills development is the mandate of the national youth development agency (NYDA). The NYDA derives its mandate from the National Youth Development Agency Act, No. 54 of 2008 and the National Youth Policy 2009–2014 (2009). According to the Act, the NYDA has the following functions: (a) national youth service and social cohesion; (b) economic participation; (c) policy, research, and development; (d) governance, training, and development; (e) youth advisory and information services; and (f) the National Youth Fund. The youth advisory and information services refer to career guidance.

In a context with such high unemployment, government's priority is not only to strengthen the education, skills, and human resource base, but also to promote economic growth and job creation. Policies and strategies for growth and job creation are necessary in order to ensure that newly educated and trained entrants into the labor market can get access to decent work opportunities and that current workers in the labor market can experience continuation of employment. The strategies and initiatives that promote growth and job creation are the national growth path (NGP), the Industrial Policy Action

Plan (IPAP2), and the Jobs Fund. The NGP of the Economic Development Department (EDD) is an economic framework with the objective of creating a better labor-absorbing growth path (EDD, 2010), the IPAP2 is an industrial policy plan to expand production in sectors with high employment and high possibility for growth (Department of Trade and Industry [dti], 2010), and the Jobs Fund (announced by the President during the State of the Nation Address on 10 February 2011) is a fund established to co-finance public- and private sector projects that will significantly contribute to job creation.

New Policy Initiative for Cooperation in the Provision of Career Development Services in South Africa

The policy and legislative context described thus far that relate to career guidance clearly shows that South Africa had a history of fragmentation in terms of thinking about, organizing, managing, and providing career-and labor market-related information, career guidance, and career counseling services. The history has shown that no single agency either at a national or at a provincial level ever had the exclusive or predominant responsibility for the management, coordination, and/or provision of career- and labor market-related information, career guidance, and counseling services. All of this has now changed. In 2012, the DHET in partnership with the South African Qualifications Authority (SAQA) took the lead and developed a policy framework for the management and coordination of the provision of career development (information, advice, and guidance) services in South Africa (SAQA, 2012). The framework was developed in collaboration with a wide range of stakeholders.

The key aim of the policy framework is to establish a national model of career guidance services and activities that could assist all South African citizens of any age and at any point in their lives, to make decisions about their education, training, and work. The framework also promotes that people should be resilient and should take responsibility for managing their own lifelong learning and work. The specific objectives of the framework are the following (DHET, 2012a):

• To obtain a common understanding of career guidance-related terminology in South Africa in order to build and enhance cooperation between stakeholders.

• To establish guidelines and a process for cooperation and collaboration at all levels of government as well as with nongovernmental organizations (NGOs) and the private sector.

• To propose the development and implementation of system-wide policies and practices.

• To assign stakeholders roles and responsibilities for different areas and aspects of career guidance services in the country.

• To propose standards for career guidance systems, services, and practitioners.

• To explore ways to ensure sufficient allocation of resources for a national service.

• To sensitize stakeholders about the role that evidence plays regarding the contribution of career guidance initiatives in reaching related national goals.

• To provide suggestions for the strengthening and continuity of leadership regarding career guidance services in South Africa.

• To serve as the basis and starting point for the development and implementation of career guidance policy in South Africa.

The process for the development and implementation of career guidance policy is currently underway under the leadership of DHET and SAQA. The process is consultative including most of the stakeholders involved in career guidance activities in South Africa.

Another important development in addition to the career development policy framework is the establishment of the South African Career Development Association (SACDA). The SACDA was established in 2012 as a non-profit organization (NPO) with the main aim of developing the professional status of career guidance practitioners in South Africa. One of the specific objectives is to promote the role, professional development, and education of career guidance practitioners.

Preliminary work has already been done by the SACDA in terms of listing the different categories of practice in the career guidance field. The model that is being investigated provides for different levels and categories of practitioner status linked to the environment a person works in and the training that practitioners need to be competent to fulfill their duties. The suggested levels and/or designations are: (a) career adviser, (b) career guidance practitioner, and (c) career counselor.

The Different Modes of Current Career Guidance Delivery in South Africa

The previous section showed that similar to many other countries, career guidance services in South Africa are distributed across various sectors under different ministries and jurisdictions. Career guidance services are offered at: (a) schools (general education and training [GET] and FET); (b) FET colleges; (c) higher education and training institutions (universities and universities of technology); (d) public employment services; (e) SETAs; (f) statutory bodies; (g) nongovernmental services; and (h) private services. For the purposes of this article, the different modes of delivery of career guidance were categorized. Five models or modes of delivery are distinguished: the curriculum-based model, the career center model, the industry-based model, the ICT or virtual-based model, and the career event model.

The curriculum-based model refers to career guidance as part of a curriculum, as curricular activities, and as a compulsory subject. In the South African context the career education model is applied in the school sector. A Life Orientation curriculum and school subjects are provided that partially cover career development and provide career guidance to learners. The main advantage of this model is that it can reach large numbers of school learners as they move through the education system. It is in the school phase where the foundation for career development is laid and the education model provides an opportunity for all citizens to develop the knowledge,

skills, and motivation to take responsibility for their own lifelong career development. The main limitation of this model is that Life Orientation as a subject competes with other subjects for time, teachers, and other resources such as computer and Internet access. In the subject of Life Orientation, career-related content competes with other components of the subject. This results in limited time allocation.

A career center model refers to a practice where a unit/center and/or space are established, and dedicated personnel are employed and trained to deliver career guidance and information-related services. Entities that apply this model are the student support units of FET colleges, the student counseling and career services centers at higher education institutions, the labor centers of the DoL, the offices of the NYDA, NGOs, and public libraries (although personnel may not be specifically trained to deliver career guidance). Private entities such as a consortium of psychologists or career practitioners may also apply this model. The scope and intensity of the services offered at these centers vary from center to center.

The industry-based model refers to the career-guidance-related activities of employers and private employment agencies. Employers and employment agencies usually use assessment for recruitment and selection purposes. The advice that is provided mainly relates to skills development opportunities, placement, and career pathing. SETAs mostly prepare career guides or booklets as required by the DHET. These guides are predominantly distributed to schools and education and training institutions.

The fourth model is the ICT or virtual model. This model offers services through the Internet, helplines (call centers), mobisites, social networking, and CDs and DVDs (see Flederman & Watts 2014, Chap. 27). The model can be used to reach all users and potentially has a very wide reach. It is also a very cost-effective way of making information available to large numbers of people. Some of these services may, however, be accessible only to people who have access to computers and phones and who are functionally and computer literate. The most recent examples of good use of this mode of delivery are the career advice service (CAS) of SAQA and the National Career Advice Portal (NCAP) that are currently under development—a DHET and SAQA initiative. The NCAP system is a web- and mobi-based system that will comprise four primary components. These are information on the learning pathways for occupations on the organising framework for occupations (OFO); a learning directory of all public education and training in South Africa (courses and providers); an e-portfolio function where users can build up their portfolios as they navigate through the system; and an occupational information center. The NCAP will be hosted on the DHET website, will be linked to the CAS website, and will become the primary national self-help service available to all the citizens of South Africa.

The career event model refers to career information offerings that are short in duration and that are offered by various role players. This model includes career exhibitions and career fairs. The once-a-year visits that the marketing divisions of educational institutions or NGOs pay to schools can also be categorized as career events. Career events provide opportunities to learners, students, and adults to interact with industry role players and with education and training providers in groups or one-on-one. They also provide opportunities for career-related information to be disseminated over a wide geographical area—if the events move from one location to another. Events like career exhibitions and career fairs can expose large numbers of users to a wide variety of careers, industries, and education and training opportunities.

The Challenges and the Gaps

Despite considerable progress since the advent of democracy, South Africa faces many challenges and gaps regarding the provision of career guidance and information services. Some of the major challenges are the following:

- The large numbers of people in need of career guidance services, making it impossible for institution-based services to meet all needs.

- The lack of resources (human resources, systems, and funding) in the provision of career guidance-related services at schools, FET colleges, higher education institutions, employment services of the DoL, NGOs, and private providers.
- The lack of comprehensive and centralized labor-market information.
- The weak linkages between industry and the career guidance and information delivery systems.
- The lack of all-inclusive coordination between all the role players that provide career guidance-related services—which will hopefully change now.

The school sector is the biggest in terms of the demand for services and encounters specific challenges that relate to the following:

- Systemic challenge—Life Orientation is not an externally examinable subject with the result that school principals, teachers, and learners all place less emphasis on the subject.
- Curriculum challenge—the design of the curriculum is based on an academic premise that all learners will study after school. This premise is incorrect, as around 40 % of youth between grades 9 and 12 drop out of school (DBE, 2012). Current curriculum interventions mostly focus on career choice. Many learners, however, simply need to find gainful employment and need assistance in this regard.
- The high turnover of Life Orientation teachers—frequently, Life Orientation teachers leave to go and teach other subjects. The crux of this challenge lies with school principals, who at the start of each academic year evaluate the learner-to-subject ratio and then allocate necessary educators to the subject. In the majority of cases, the very first educators to be allocated to demand-driven academic subjects are the Life Orientation teachers.
- The insufficient time provided for the subject Life Orientation on the school calendar.
- Learners' lack of accessibility at schools to electronic media that contains career-related information.

- The lack of evaluation studies of the curriculum content and career guidance-related activities in World of Work and Careers and Careers Choices parts of the Life Orientation subject to ensure that they are relevant and useable by learners.

The international literature clearly shows that South Africa's challenges regarding career guidance are not unique. An OECD study of 14 countries (OECD, 2004a) showed that the challenges regarding career education and guidance at schools in developed countries are similar to South Africa's. Although career guidance is covered in the curricula of many schools, the time allocated to teaching it is often not sufficient to meet the career development needs of the learners. Similar to the situation in South Africa, the main reasons are the lack of resources and the fact that the school teachers are not adequately trained. The study further showed that the emphasis in those countries is disproportionally on one-to-one services and that other delivery models are not utilized sufficiently.

In most parts of the world the demand for career services surpasses the supply and many people still do not have access to career services over a lifelong period. Furthermore, insufficient locations or sites are available to deliver career services. A theme that permeates the international literature is that not enough use is made of self-service models (which are usually less expensive and can reach the masses of people in need of services). The lack of comprehensive labor-market information in a format digestible in a career guidance environment is another common problem that is found throughout the world (ILO, 2006; OECD, 2004b).

The developing countries are confronted with another set of circumstances, which as discussed in earlier sections of this chapter also confront South Africa, and which exacerbate the burden on the career guidance and information system. These circumstances include high unemployment, high levels of poverty, huge informal economies, an over-supply of unskilled or semiskilled people, the lack of highly skilled people, and limited resources (World Bank, 2012b).

New Concepts and Viewpoints: Charting New Directions

We have showed that youth unemployment and marginalization remain disconcertingly high in South Africa. While many more young people have access to education than the generations before them, education is not translating into appropriate skill acquisition and employment, especially for large numbers of African youth. The critical issue is the role that career guidance and counseling can play within the context of the socioeconomic challenges confronting South Africa. However, such services cannot be put in place if HRD, education, and job creation strategies are not coordinated. Only then can career development services strive to motivate the youth to stay in school to receive quality and relevant education; to choose subjects and study fields that could lead them to learning pathways that will prepare them for occupations that are in demand; and to provide them with work readiness programs or other grounding opportunities to facilitate the transition from education to work.

The government's new career development initiative under the leadership of DHET endeavors to bring together all the relevant stakeholders necessary to drive an integrated and coordinated vision in terms of HRD, job creation strategies, and career development services; it is a new path for South Africa. The stakeholders that took part in the establishment of the career development framework are inter alia the following: the DBE that is responsible for education and career development services at school level; the FET colleges and the higher education institutions providing guidance to post-school learners in terms of learning pathways that will lead to occupations that the economy needs and which are in demand in the labor market; the DoL and NYDA providing career guidance services to vulnerable groups such as unemployed youth, also offering entrepreneurial, skills, and employability training; the dti and the EDD investing in job creation initiatives; the newly formed SACDA promoting the professionalization of career guidance practitioners; and

DHET and SAQA establishing the NCAP system that will be accessible to all citizens of South Africa.

This is the first time in the history of South Africa that a comprehensive service will be available to all citizens irrespective of race, gender, age, education, and employment status. The new initiative has created the platform for coordinated and collaborative thinking and planning regarding career development services in a difficult socioeconomic context. Moreover, the new initiative and thinking in this regard will promote the establishment of a culture of resilience and self-management of the career development of every South African.

The Youth Employment Accord signed on 18 April, 2013 is the new initiative that targets addressing the challenges of youth unemployment as part of the decent work agenda (EDD, 2013). The Accord signatories (government, organized labor, organized business, and community and youth formations) emphasize the importance of joint actions of all "accords" such as the following: (a) the Basic Education Accord—a framework for partnerships to strengthen basic education in order to provide foundational learning for training and accessing the labor market; (b) the National Skills Accord—whose aim is to develop targets and joint actions that will enable youth to get access to training and work placement opportunities; (c) the Local Procurement Accord—to reindustrialize South Africa and provide opportunities to young people; and (d) the Green Economy Accord—to establish new "green" jobs as an entry point for young people to the labor market. The main focus of the Youth Employment Accord is the agreement of all signatories to implement a coordinated youth employment strategy (YES) from 2013.

Relevance for Multiple Cultures: Sensitivity to the Universal and the Particular

South Africa shares the problem of distressingly high levels of youth unemployment with the rest of the world. Countries and regions may have both similar and unique ways of firstly addressing youth unemployment, and secondly, providing career development services to young people in this context. However, the recent initiatives in thinking about and planning future career development services in South Africa can serve as an example to many countries. The drive is to think and plan in a coordinated, collaborative, and inclusive way. The development of the Framework for Cooperation in the Provision of Career Development (Information, Advice, and Guidance) Services in South Africa is a case in point. In addition, the concurrent youth employment initiative, the Youth Employment Accord, and accompanying YES is a good example of a combined initiative of government, organized labor, organized business, and community and youth formations to tackle youth unemployment.

References

Centre for Development and Enterprise. (2007). *Doubling for growth: Addressing the maths and science challenge in South Africa's schools* (CDE Research Paper No. 15). Retrieved from www.cde.org.za/article

Coenjaerts, C., Ernst, C., Fortuny, M., Rei, D., & Pilgrim, M. (2009). Youth employment. In *Promoting pro-poor growth employment*. Paris, France: OECD.

Department of Basic Education (DBE). (2011a). *Curriculum and assessment policy statements Grades R -12*. Pretoria, South Africa: Author.

Department of Basic Education (DBE). (2011b). *Report on dropout and learner retention strategy to portfolio committee on education*. Pretoria, South Africa: Author.

Department of Basic Education (DBE). (2012). *Education statistics in South Africa 2010*. Pretoria, South Africa: Author.

Department of Higher Education and Training (DHET). (2007). *Student support services framework for further education and training colleges*. Pretoria, South Africa: Author.

Department of Higher Education and Training (DHET). (2010a). *Framework for the national skills development strategy*. Pretoria, South Africa: Author.

Department of Higher Education and Training (DHET). (2010b). *Human Resources Development South Africa (HRDSA), 2010–2030*. Pretoria, South Africa: Author.

Department of Higher Education and Training (DHET). (2012a). *Framework for cooperation in the provision of career development (information, advice and* guidance) services in South Africa. Pretoria, South Africa: Author.

Department of Higher Education and Training (DHET). (2012b). Green paper for post-school education and training. Pretoria, South Africa: Author.

Department of Labour, Republic of South Africa. (2001). The national skills development strategy. Pretoria, South Africa: Author.

Department of Labour, Republic of South Africa. (2005). National skills development strategy, 2005–2010. Pretoria, South Africa: Author.

Department of Trade and Industry (dti). (2010). Industrial Policy Action Plan (IPAP2). Pretoria, South Africa: Author.

Economic Development Department (EDD). (2010). The new growth path: The framework. Pretoria, South Africa: Author.

Economic Development Department (EDD). (2013). Youth employment accord. Pretoria, South Africa: Author.

Flederman, P. J., & Watts, A. G. (Forthcoming, 2014). Career helplines: A Resource for career development. In G. Arulmani, A. J. Bakshi, F. T. L. Leong, & A. G. Watts (Eds.), Handbook of career development. New York, NY: Springer.

Government of South Africa. (1997). Higher Education Act, 1997. Pretoria, South Africa: Author.

Government of South Africa. (1998). Skills Development Act, 1998. Pretoria, South Africa: Author.

Government of South Africa. (2010). Employment services bill. Pretoria, South Africa: Author.

Gustafsson, M., & Pillay, P. (2009). Financing vocational education and training in South Africa. In R. Maclean & D. Wilson (Eds.), International handbook of education for the changing world of work (pp. 1091–1106). Dordrecht, Netherlands: Springer.

International Labour Organisation (ILO). (2006). Career guidance: A resource handbook for low and middle-income countries. Geneva, Switzerland: Author.

International Labour Organization (ILO). (2012). Global employment trends for youth 2012. Geneva, Switzerland: Author.

Mayer, M. (2011). Towards a youth employment strategy for South Africa (Working Paper No. 28). Midrand, South Africa: Development Bank of Southern Africa.

National Qualifications Framework. (2012). What the NQF does. Retrieved from http://www.nqf.org.za/page/what-nqf-does/

National Treasury, Republic of South Africa. (2011). Budget review 2011. Pretoria, South Africa: Author.

Organisation for Economic Cooperation and Development (OECD). (2004a). Career guidance: A handbook for policymakers. Paris, France: Author.

Organisation for Economic Cooperation and Development (OECD). (2004b). Career guidance and public policy: Bridging the gap. Paris, France: Author.

Peterson, A., McGrath, S., & Badroodien, A. (2003). A national skills survey, 2003. Pretoria, South Africa: Human Science Research Council.

Pillay, P. (2006). Human capital development and growth: Improving access and equity in education and health services. Development Southern Africa, 23(1), 63–83.

Pillay, P. (2011). Higher education and economic development: A literature review. Cape Town, South Africa: Centre for Higher Education Transformation.

Presidency. (2009). National youth policy 2009–2014. Pretoria, South Africa: Author.

SAQA (South African Qualifications Authority). (2012). An environmental scan of career advice services in South Africa 2012. Pretoria, South Africa: Author.

Southern and Eastern Africa Consortium on Measuring Education Quality (SACMEQ). (2005). Report on the quality of education 2005. Gaberone, Botswana: Author.

Southern and Eastern Africa Consortium on Measuring Education Quality (SACMEQ). (2007). Report on the quality of education 2007. Gaberone, Botswana: Author.

Statistics South Africa. (2010). Quarterly labour force survey, March 2010. Pretoria, South Africa: Author.

Statistics South Africa. (2011). Quarterly labour force survey, March 2011. Pretoria, South Africa: Author.

Stiglitz, J. E. (2012). The price of inequality. New York, NY: Penguin.

The Treasury and Development Bank Southern Africa. (2011). The jobs fund. Pretoria, South Africa: Author.

United Nations Development Programme (UNDP). (2011). Human development report. New York, NY: Oxford University Press.

World Bank. (2012a). Knowledge and skills for the new economy. Retrieved from http://web.worldbank.org/wbsite/external/topics/exteducation

World Bank. (2012b). Selected world development indicators 2012. Washington, DC: Author.

Tensions in Livelihoods: A Rural Perspective

Kartik Kalyanram, Radha Gopalan, and Kamakshi Kartik

Introduction

Rural India, as is the case with rural areas of most emerging economies, has remained less affected than urban locations by the sweeping changes of modernization. If one looks at the lifestyle of a farmer, a potter, or a shepherd, in emerging economies, there is, usually, a set pattern to their lives closely linked to diurnal as well as seasonal cycles. It is unlikely that rural folk are even aware of the vagaries of the stock market, economic crises, national debt, and such other socioeconomic phenomena. Not many living in rural locations are in a position to consider pension schemes or make plans for long-term financial security. Daily living is dictated by the need to ensure that there is adequate food for the family and something put away for education and health concerns.

The winds of change are, however, sweeping the country side. Many of the families living in rural hamlets have become aware that there is a different, exciting world out there, far removed from their own experiences. Most feel the need to educate their children in English medium schools. Many feel that their children should move out of the family home/village to a city and get a job in an office. Today, the sight of rural young adults dressed in jeans, the ubiquitous messenger bag slung across the shoulder, plugged into cell phones, waiting for a bus heading to the nearest town, is becoming increasingly common. Underlying the desire to go the city/town is the hope of getting a job and thereby becoming a part of the economic boom that is surging across India and most other emerging economies.

At the same time, however, there are variations from one person to another. Box 21.1 gives illustrations of young Indian adults, who have chosen to tread their own paths although they have grown up in the same area. Two of these young persons have chosen not to move out of their rural homes. Our objective in this chapter is neither to encourage nor discourage rural–urban migration. It is instead to question whether the search for the better always involves a move to the city. Simultaneously, we do not intend to romanticize rural life but instead offer strategies to promote the career development of rural youth such that they have a choice to seek their own development within their rural communities or to move to the city. We do not imply that the individuals in the illustration who migrated to the city are less happy than the ones who chose to stay behind. Instead, we raise questions that have direct relevance to the practice of career guidance for rural young people. What made some of them stay and what made the others decide to move out? Indeed, what is it that motivates young people around the world to leave their village homes and move toward cities? And most importantly, what could be the stance

K. Kalyanram (✉)
Rishi Valley Rural Health Centre, Madanapalle, India
e-mail: kartik.kalyanram@gmail.com

G. Arulmani et al. (eds.), *Handbook of Career Development*, International and Cultural Psychology,
DOI 10.1007/978-1-4614-9460-7_21, © Springer Science+Business Media, LLC 2014

Box 21.1: Staying in Village Versus Going Away to the City: Illustrations from India

Uday is the only son of a fairly prosperous farming family. He has just graduated with a master's degree in business administration (MBA) in finance from a small institution. His aim is to work in a corporate, wearing a tie, blazer, and shoes. The authors of this chapter have seen him ploughing an absolutely straight furrow, tilling the soil, and looking after his fields with loving care. He enjoys his work as a farmer, yet has chosen to step into the unknown.

Kiran comes from a family of potters. He works the clay like a magician and his fingers produce wonderful pieces. He is articulate, full of ideas, and wants to make a different life for himself. He has also gone the MBA way and is now looking for a job, and one hopes that it will be one which will combine his talents, skill, and give him a good income.

Jayaprakash again comes from a farming family. His family has sufficient land to meet its needs. He trained as an electrician at a local industrial training institute and was selected for an ad hoc post of lineman in the government-owned electricity board. His life is now considered completely secure since this is a government job. However, to finally get the job he had to pay a bribe, which he did and is now an earning member of his family.

Suresh completed his fifth grade and the family decided that he should not continue in school. On what basis this decision was made is not clear. He now works as a farmhand and seems to be happy with what he is doing. He is the only one of the four boys in this illustration who did not and does not want to step out of the valley in which he has been brought up.

Vijaya, the daughter of a local farmer, is a motivated, bright, hardworking girl. She found great support and encouragement from her father. He ensured that her dreams were fulfilled and sent her to the city for her education. Armed with a bachelor's degree in biomedical engineering and an MBA, Vijaya works with a pharmaceutical firm in Hyderabad, a large city in South India.

Susheela, one of the daughters of a lorry fleet owner, was passionate about becoming a doctor. The impossibly high fees and cash donations required for a seat in a private medical college and the fact that she did not do well enough in the qualifying exams, coupled with her father's loss in business, were deterrents. She had to accept a government-aided (free) seat in a nearby engineering college. Neither the course nor the college was what she desired. Her unhappiness with the way her life had unfolded manifested as recurrent headaches, a somatic response to her stress.

Anuroopa having lost her mother at an early age knows the value of fighting for what she considers valuable. She worked as a construction helper during her vacations to pay for her education. Her hard work and aptitude saw her getting admission through a government-aided (free) seat for a master in computer applications (MCA) in Tirupati, a mid-sized town in South India. There is in her an intense need to be financially independent. She dreams of working in an office or an institution.

Malleswari schooled till fifth grade and was forced to work thereafter as her father died of a snake bite. Her mother took on various casual jobs to support the family. Malleswari was married off at the age of 16, and now 24, is the mother of two school-going boys. Her intention is to augment her domestic income, to educate her sons, and to save for a home they would like to purchase soon.

(continued)

taken by the career guidance professional in relation to this phenomenon? In the following sections, an attempt has been made to discuss the various factors that go into the making of such decisions.

Livelihood Versus Lifestyles

Livelihood

The standard dictionary definition of *livelihood* is "means of securing the necessities of life" (Concise Oxford English Dictionary, 2003). The word, however, derives from the root which means *a way of life* (life + course) from old English (Merriam-Webster's online dictionary, n.d.). Therefore, a livelihood is not just a means of earning money or activities related to being financially secure. It goes deeper into the question of living itself. From a development perspective, there has been an increasing thrust toward what is called *sustainable livelihoods* (e.g., Serrat, 2008). There are a number of models available, but all are variations of this basic theme:

> A livelihood comprises the capabilities, assets (including both material and social resources) and activities required for a means of living. A livelihood is sustainable when it can cope with and recover from stress and shocks and maintain or enhance its capabilities and assets both now and in the future, while not undermining the natural resource base. (Chambers & Conway, 1991)

The obvious question that arises then is: If it is just not earning the necessities, is there a "right" livelihood?

We refer here to the views of J. Krishnamurti, whose life and teachings spanned the greater part of the 20th century (see also Bakshi, 2014, Chap. 8). Krishnamurti's teachings are regarded by many as having had a profound impact on contemporary thought. A sage, philosopher, and thinker, he influenced the lives of millions the world over: intellectuals and laypersons, young and old alike. Breaking away from organized religion and denying his role as a guru, he spelt out his mission: *to set man absolutely and unconditionally free*. His thoughts have engendered a philosophy of education that has influenced ideas of work and livelihood. The points he raised about livelihoods and professions are deeply meaningful, albeit provocative. To quote:

> Now, as society exists at present, there is no choice between right livelihood and wrong livelihood. You take any job you can get, if you are lucky enough to get one at all. So, to the man who is pressed for an immediate job, there is no problem. He takes what he can get because he must eat. But to those of you who are not so immediately pressed, it should be a problem, and that is what we are discussing—what is the right means of livelihood in a society which is based on acquisition and class differences, on nationalism, greed, violence, and so on? Given these things, can there be right livelihood? Obviously not. And there are obviously wrong professions, wrong means of livelihood, such as the army, the lawyer, the police, and the government. Similarly, you cannot expect to find a right means of livelihood in the big corporations of business men who are amassing wealth, nor in the bureaucratic routine of government with its officials and red tape. (Krishnamurti, 1948a, para. 13)

There is something strangely prescient here. This was written in 1948, when the world had just come through the horrors of World War II and society was still coming to grips with man's savagery. Today's world is not much different. For many in emerging economies, the overwhelming tendency is to take the first job that one gets. For young adults, who are educated, the need to get a job, any job, is of paramount importance. Economic independence is, perhaps, the single-most important motivator. Only a very few at the time of first jobs make a conscious decision to look at the larger question of livelihood and what it entails. Here, again, Krishnamurti's points are thought provoking. With a view to bringing Krishnamurti closer to the reader, we interviewed Radhika Herzberger, a specialist in Indology and a longtime associate of Krishnamurti. Her comments are presented in Box 21.2.

Lifestyle

This is a word that is much in use these days. The dictionary defines it as "the way in which one lives" (Concise Oxford English Dictionary, 2003). While the question of livelihoods raises

Box 21.2: A Right Livelihood: The Views of J. Krishnamurti as Commented on by Radhika Herzberger

Krishnamurti weighed in on the problem of right livelihoods even before the debate about the future of the planet was part of public consciousness. His focused attention, as indicated in the quotations below, was on the destructive impulses that reside, as he put it, in the human heart.

> Some weeks ago I was in India, in a little valley, unknown, there are no tourists fortunately there, it is a quiet valley, beautiful, restful, full of ancient rocks, and two villagers were passing by, uneducated, illiterate, and they were quarrelling, ready to fight and destroy each other about a piece of earth. And this disorder seems to exist in every corner of our heart and our mind. Now if one is serious about it, how is order to come out of this?

Krishnamurti wove together the militarism built into the modern nationalist state, the competition between nations and livelihoods that denude nature: exploitation of the land, of the poor who occupy the land, and of the animal and insect life that share the planet with human beings. He urged his audiences and the students and teachers of his schools to examine the kind of social order they belonged to and within which are forced to choose their livelihoods.

> We must examine society as it is with its weaknesses, its foibles; and to examine it we must see directly our connection, our relationship with it, not through a supposedly intellectual or theoretical explanation.

While acknowledging that few have the luxury of choice, he wonders whether any kind of nonexploitative livelihoods is immediately available in modern societies.

> What is the right means of livelihood in a society which is based on acquisition and class differences, on nationalism, greed, violence, and so on? Given these things, can there be right livelihood?

Krishnamurti saw that even when individuals have no choice, they do depend on society for their basic needs and are inextricably linked to the social order.

> Seeing that, what is an earnest man to do? Is he to run away and bury himself in some village? Even there, he has to live somehow. He can beg, but the very food that is given to him comes indirectly from the lawyer, the policeman, the soldier, the government. And he cannot live in isolation because that again is impossible; to live in isolation is to die, both psychologically and physiologically.

These observations did not lead Krishnamurti to a pessimistic conclusion because he believes that society can "be transformed to form a right society in which there can be right livelihood. Such a revolution is not an impossible task. You and I have to do it."

> All that one can do, if one is earnest, if one is intelligent about this whole process, is to reject the present state of things and give to society all that one is capable of. That is, sir, you accept food, clothing, and shelter from society, and you must give something to society in return. But if you reject the things of society and accept only the essentials, you must give something in return. It is more important to find out what you are giving to society than to ask what is the right means of livelihood.

Rather than providing ready-made and general answers to the question what is a right livelihood to follow, Krishnamurti argued that individuals draw benefits from society and are required, therefore, to work for the good of society: not to adapt to the social order but to change it using intelligence and compassion. So, what is a right livelihood is a process of discovery for each individual, the result of an intelligent and informed awareness of oneself and the world we live in.

(continued)   (continued) philosophical questions, the issue of lifestyle seems to appeal to our more materialistic instincts. A lifestyle is taken to mean the way one dresses, the accouterments, where one lives, which car one drives, which mobile phone one uses, and such indicators of social status. The media has a field day in appealing to these instincts among us. Given the profusion of advertisements, television shows, and films which link these frills and trappings to wealth and success, there naturally is an attraction to this lifestyle. The powerful forces of marketing cut away our immunity to being seduced by these images. Let us for a moment put ourselves in the place of an Uday, Kiran, or Susheela (the young people presented in Box 21.1). For them the urban world is incredibly attractive and the question does pop up: Why should I spend the rest of my life following in my ancestors' footsteps, in this valley, where everything is so predictable, the rocks do not change, the sunrise and sunsets are the same, there is a sameness to the pattern in my life, the crops I plant, the sheep that I graze, the pots that I make? Why can I not partake in what the world has to offer? This other life could seem to these young people to be exciting, full of vigor, full of opportunities, changeable, and, most importantly, achievable. Foremost on the mind of the young adult from the village could be the desire to look for and probably jump at the first opportunity to escape the apparent drudgery of life in the village and change one's lifestyle.

Passion Versus Necessity

Passion is what drives us, the fire in us to do something with our lives, the need to excel, the job which we would love to be doing, and the job that gives us satisfaction. It is the feeling that drives one to achieve something by oneself. In the quest for a job, this is often forgotten, sidelined, or simply not acknowledged. The love of one's job, however mundane and routine it might be, is in itself a passion. Yet, when a different way of life beckons and the city lights flash invitingly, all this may feel like drudgery, particularly to the young person who is craving for freedom and the opportunity to determine his/her own destiny. Not many realize that in the quest for a different way of life, they may simply replace one form of drudgery with another.

Of course, rarely is it enough for just the passion to sustain one's family in the quest for a livelihood. Necessity is the cold water that douses these passions. For the farmer, when the rains fail or prices crash, there is a terrible feeling of loss and frustration. Stoicism and blaming it on fate are two common defense mechanisms that are employed. Such coping mechanisms can at best be a rationalization. The need to have some money to look after the family is of paramount importance. Debt drives thousands of rural families to look for alternate sources of income. And this is most easily available in the city with its profusion of construction work, cable laying, and ditch digging. This sort of work carries little meaning and does not lead to the same sense of fulfillment or happiness.

What would be the thoughts of a young adult growing up in a community which does not guarantee a regular income? A generation ago, opportunities to do something else were quite limited. Today, the young adult sees greater opportunities in cities as opposed to rural communities. These opportunities, for which a degree or a multiplicity of degrees is of paramount importance, may drive one to set aside one's talents and abilities and stretch beyond one's financial means. This urge could cloud the young person's judgment and he/she may not pause and think whether the choices made are best suited for him/her, as an individual, or for the family.

Rootedness Versus Mobility

For a young adult growing up in a village, there exists an entire community of which he/she is a part. This community, to a certain extent, is like a large extended family, at times intrusive, at times supportive, at times hostile, but at all times there is the feeling that one is not alone. The interactions between families could be dictated by socioeconomic status or family livelihood. Caste, race, or ethnicity could play a significant role in certain countries. In India, for example, there is a clear divide among the farmers and the shepherds, the landowners and the landless. However, the village and community do offer support systems, which maybe rough, practical, highly subjective, and oriented to the group rather than the individual. Many a time, the village elders could decide among themselves what is best and then expect that this decision is followed by the rest of the community. Similarly, the family, of which one is part, could exert its will on choices being exercised by the young person. Despite this, village life offers a sense of rootedness. Today, the penetration of the media is deep. Even a hamlet, be it of a few houses or a large village with a 100 households, has the ubiquitous satellite dish antenna sprouting from rooftops. Evenings are spent in watching television soaps or pirated DVDs of the latest movies, appropriately dubbed into the local language, rather than sitting together, following humanity's age-old ritual of just talking. This sharing, in a sense, was also the sharing of one's own ups and downs, somewhat like a large support group used in psychological therapy. However, the powerful impact of the mass media: radio, television, and cinema, has ensured that the young person in these communities has become aware of the different kind of life that could be led in a city. In such settings, it is but natural for young adults to become restless and feel a strong need to explore a different world, a different occupation, and a different way of life. Questions about the system, coupled with the feeling that one is stuck and tied down, all lead to the young seeking other environments and opportunities. The need for individual expression could also play a significant role. The need to be an individual could take precedence over the needs of the family or the community. This is more so in today's world of economic change and liberalization which have engendered the beliefs that change is possible, change is essential, change is for the better, and change is exciting. Also, questions reflecting a deeper need for individuation may arise: Why should I continue with the family profession? Why can I not make my own path in life? These are questions that any young adult in any environment could have, more so if the young adult perceives the community as being intrusive, restrictive of freedom, and constrictive in allowing personal space. A rural young person, visiting an urban area, would see people of the same age going around on motorbikes, dressed well, with money to flash around: only seen until now on television or in a movie. It, therefore, stands to reason that a rural young adult would possibly desire and seek what he/she perceives as a better lifestyle.

These seeds of discontent are sown in the process of obtaining an education, in the acquisition of technical skills and degrees, which in effect make one a misfit for the ways of life practiced in one's rural society and community. Education, as it is delivered in India today, frequently emphasizes rote learning, a blind adherence to a rigid syllabus, in which there is no scope for an individual becoming aware of his/her potentials. So also, the context in which many lessons are placed is alien to the rural child. An oft quoted example is "A for Apple," wherein a child in certain parts of rural India may not ever have tasted an apple! There is usually no provision for understanding and appreciating one's own land, culture, and way of life. From a career development point of view, most educational pathways lead the young person toward careers that are located in urban contexts. Very few point back to building a modern and contemporary career back in one's own village.

Education needs to be rooted in the local context and at the same time equip the learner with skills to understand and benefit from the modern, technology-driven world.

Nuclear Families Versus a Common Kitchen

Villages themselves are in a process of transition. The earlier concept of a common kitchen catering to an extended, joint family is slowly being done away with. A common practice in rural South India, for example, was that all the males, with their families, shared one building, with each having their own room. Income used to be pooled together and food cooked in a common kitchen. There was, thus, a sense of togetherness as well as individual spaces. This seems like an ideal situation, though there were family tensions to contend with. This shared sense of destiny or fate meant that one was never alone either in happiness or in time of need. Over the past few years, this system is slowly being replaced by nuclear families, with each adult male and his family preferring to have their own house and kitchen. This feeling, the need for individual space, the need to manifest one's own identity, now influences choices being made. As a result, the support system that one has grown up with, or taken for granted, is also being eroded. Now, when a young adult migrates to the city, he/she has no support, no family to bank on, no comfort zones in which to find respite. The young adult must struggle on his/her own until he/she becomes familiar with the workings of the city which are far removed from what he/she has been used to.

Regular Income Versus Seasonal Variations

In addition to the reasons already listed, one of the most important drivers of change is economic security. The typical economic cycle of a farmer is till the fields, borrow money to buy seeds, apply fertilizer and pesticide, take care of the crop, harvest, sell the produce, pay off debt, and hope that at the end of it all there is something left over for essentials. This extra money will have to see the family through the next 3–6 months till the next harvest is ready. Similarly for a shepherd: borrow money to buy lambs, nurture them, graze them for 1–3 years, then sell them, pay off debt, buy more sheep. Some money maybe left over for the family needs. However, if the rains fail, or the seed turns bad, disease afflicts the flock, or the prices crash, then there is no hope of ever recovering the cost. Given this precarious economic situation, it is not surprising that the young adult feels compelled to look for a job that will assure a regular income. It is taken for granted that the young adult, who migrates to a city, looks for and gets a job, will also carry the responsibility of sustaining the family back in the village. This young man and, on occasion, young woman will also be faced with the choice of either embracing the lifestyle that a city has to offer or skimp in order to ensure more money goes back home. There is a growing realization in the villages that at least one person in the household needs to be educated, and that this person must find a regular job, preferably in the city, since income levels are higher. What this also means is that the burden of responsibility is now transferred to this person, who as it is, is struggling to cope with the demands of a job and an alien culture in the city.

Working in an Urban Environment

It is unlikely that the young adult from a rural environment would have the necessary skills and the street-smart attitude necessary to work and survive in an urban environment. The rural young person has to learn, in most cases painfully, that for every one success story, there are possibly ten other young people who have fallen by the way side. Lack of support, the need to fend for oneself, the expectations from the family, a new vernacular dialect or even language, the inability to converse in English (the lingua franca of any white collar job in urban India), noise, pollution, traffic, attractions, and the glitz and glamour all tend to load the dice against the new entrant to the city. These young adults take up almost any job that comes their way, irrespective of their qualifications. This may range from hard labor on construction sites, road works, or landfills to the bottom rungs of white collar jobs. Some lucky ones (mainly in the white collar sector) may have supportive managers or organizations, who are able to look beyond their rural facade and nurture their career growth. However, the vast majority are often confined to an office space (if they are lucky), or end up as glorified salespersons in the malls and chain stores, or as office boys, peons, drivers, or such un-/low-skilled work. Most often, these jobs are not fixed to specific job roles. The driver, for example, is not just a person who drives the car but will be expected to carry other responsibilities: paying utility bills, buying groceries, and such extra chores. The other side of the coin is that back home, in their village, these young people are looked upon as those who have made it in the city. They are pointed to as examples worthy of emulation. Therefore, starting with a trickle, there is today a steady stream of young adults moving into the city to try and "make it."

A point emerges here that has direct relevance to career guidance and counseling. These so-called jobs are precarious and do not offer security (see also Kumar & Arulmani, 2014, Chap. 12). They are subject to the requirements of the employer, and the individual's services could be terminated at the employer's whim. Provided in Box 21.3 is an illustration from our grassroots interactions with rural youth of the impact that precarious city jobs can have on the trajectory of the rural young person's career development. What happens to those who do not make it is a different story altogether. Our experiences through the Rishi Valley Rural Health Centre (www.rishivalley.org/rural_health/overview.html) often confront us with young people, who have not been successful at their city jobs. We have had to deal with various levels of psychological trauma, including attempted suicides. Both counseling and medication have been used. But since these individuals no longer identify with the village in which they grew up (in many instances actually rejecting their roots), the support system offered by

> **Box 21.3: Impact of Precarious City Jobs: An Illustration**
>
> A few years ago, a cook, who had learned his trade in one of the hotels in a nearby town, paid money (much of it borrowed) to a recruiter, to get a job as a cook in the Middle East. He got a job and soon, substantial remittances started coming in. Two things happened almost simultaneously. Firstly, other boys started applying and getting jobs in the Middle East, and he also started encouraging other boys from the village to come and work with him. Secondly, he began to take loans to acquire what he desired. All went well for a year or so until the global financial crisis of 2007 began to take its toll. Many of these workers found themselves without a job and with debts to service. The jobs they had held at home were by now gone. It was exceedingly difficult for those who came back to readjust to a village life. Frustration, depression, breakdowns, denial, and hostility became common. Some of them then migrated out to other cities and towns, preferring to take their chances in a now familiar environment rather than attempting to make a life in the environment in which they had grown up.

their community does not suffice. It is left to (now aging) parents, who had spent money, sold land, taken loans from the local moneylender, to offer some sort of support, while at the same time coping with their own disappointments and loss.

The Young Village Girl/Woman

We see increasing trends among parents, wishing to educate their daughters as far as their finances permit. Mothers dream of their daughters' education as a passport to economic independence. Unlike themselves, they wish their daughters to have the freedom of choice and action in their lives. The education of girls is also witnessing an upheaval of life issues. Having qualified with a skill set, the young girl now looks at opportunities outside the village, either in nearby towns or cities. This attraction of an ever-expanding freedom brings changes in attire and attitude. Empowered by her education, the girl is now more assertive about satisfying her desires and needs. Conflict arises, when the time for marriage arrives, or even while living at home, in the village, with all its attendant restrictions. Earlier, conflict that could arise remained suppressed. This is changing and the girl is more assertive in opposing expectations to conform to the way of life dictated by the village ethos. A few do try and juggle to make a success of both the marriage and the dream job. Our observations have indicated that the success of this attempt is largely dependent on the husband, his attitudes, and encouragement. Education empowers the young rural girl with a sense of financial freedom, which probably is the cornerstone of her decision to move to a nuclear family. This move could set off another cycle of stress and coping which could tell on her at some stage. Our field observations have repeatedly indicated that the stress of running a house in an alien environment, the lack of support systems while managing the home, children, and a job, could manifest as psychosomatic ailments, endocrine dysfunctions, or just premature aging. In a sense, these women are pioneers, leading a quiet, unsung, unheralded revolution.

There is yet another set of rural girls, who are bright and dream big but are unable to follow their dreams because of financial constraints. This brings to the fore the urgent need to help these young people match their dreams to opportunities, within the framework of the constraints they face. We clearly see that education and academic qualifications for girls are driven partly by parental motivation and to a larger extent by the individual's own dreams and aspirations. There is no dearth of bright, young, educated women in rural India as would be the case in other countries. They, however, continue to have very little choice in making a

Box 21.4: Support for Career Preparation: An Example of Positive Outcomes

The Rishi Valley Rural Education Centre's educational philosophy is based on the multigrade, multilevel methodology (now called the RIVER methodology, developed at the Rishi Valley Rural Education Centre), which is rooted in the local context and ethos. This model has been replicated in over a 100,000 schools in India and abroad.

Shankaramma is a past student of the center. Circumstances common to many girls like her required her to quit her education at the second year of her Bachelor of Arts course, to get married to Chakrapani (also a student of the Rural Education Centre). In other similar instances, it is most likely that the girl would have withdrawn from education and career and her role relegated to that of a housewife. But the fruit of the education she and her husband received is in clear evidence. The couple joined hands and have turned their barren land to a green space. Together, they have learned and adopted practices of sustainable organic agriculture. She is also the leader of the Self Help Group (SHG) in her village. Leading by example, she straddles home and work with ease, pride, and satisfaction.

Note: Further details of this model are available at www.rishivalley.org and www.river.org

life for themselves, when financial constraints limit possibilities. There is a need for guidance to equip the young rural girl with skills to understand and make choices that will lead to an appropriate yet meaningful career/livelihood. Box 21.4 provides an example of the remarkable difference that can be made when such supports are provided. Cases such as that of Shankaramma (Box 21.4) can be used to motivate other girls to learn from her positive attitude to life and its vicissitudes. In fact, such real life stories could be used with boys to illustrate to them, their responsibilities to their spouses.

Livelihood Planning for Rural Young People

Background

Several institutions, including the United Nations Development Programme (UNDP) and Asian Development Bank (ADB), have attempted to develop frameworks to enhance livelihoods. In developing these frameworks, attempts have been made to define the term *livelihood*. The definition adopted by the UNDP as well as the Sustainability Livelihood Framework proposed by the ADB advocates an approach that is component/kit based with theoretical linkages being drawn between the various discrete elements such as natural capital, social capital, financial resources, and so on (e.g., Serrat, 2008; UNDP, 2010).

These frameworks, in their current forms, may be useful as starting points in the development of strategies or models of sustainable livelihoods. However, they need to be adapted to the local nuances of communities' natural resource dependencies, culture, and traditions. The absence of such adaptations can lead to engagements that poorly realize their objective of stabilizing livelihoods such that marginal existence is alleviated. In other cases, they can even be detrimental and destabilize well-functioning communities. The possibility of a negative outcome is further exacerbated when the definition of quality is driven by indicators determined by a skewed understanding of rural life and livelihoods and the expectation that poverty alleviation will fulfill the aspirations of rural communities. These general frameworks could be used as skeletal guidelines upon which the specifics of local contexts, influencing factors, and the dynamics between these factors could be integrated.

Typically, designing and implementing effective livelihood programs are driven from the outside so much so that even the vocabulary associated with livelihoods drives it in this direction (see Fig. 21.1). The drivers could be government, nongovernmental organizations (NGOs), multilateral funding agencies, and philanthropic individuals or institutions. Most often, livelihood interventions are planned with the intention of providing more job opportunities in rural areas to minimize migration, alleviate poverty, and improve quality of life be it through the National Rural Livelihood Mission in India or similar programs supported by donor agencies in other developing countries. Yet the word *intervention* itself connotes something coming in from the outside, and if they are to be effective, they must be open to understanding the aspirations, occupational hopes, and needs of rural communities. When this attuning does not occur, well-intended external interventions could unwittingly become one of the factors contributing to the tensions between the facilitating agencies and the communities.

The need for a bottom-up approach has been articulated in various schemes and programs from the public and private sector, as well as civil society. If improvement is to be significant and sustained, initiatives must be driven from within the community. However, what is not appreciated is that if development or livelihood enhancement is to be community driven, it takes time for results to accrue. Enabling conditions have to be created in order to lift the existing apathy among communities. This is a slow, time intensive process. There are several initiatives, albeit in pockets, all over the world where community-initiated livelihood development has been made possible (see also Bakshi & Joshi, 2014, Chap. 10). But by and large, livelihood enhancement is driven from the outside with targets to be achieved for every dollar or rupee provided as funding. Outcomes are measured, for example, by the number of households that have risen above the poverty line in a year, annual rise in rural income, increase in literacy levels, acreage brought under cultivation, number of children graduating high school, employment statistics among youth, or decrease in the number of school dropouts.

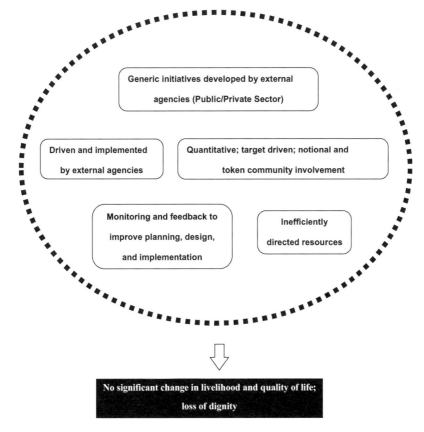

Fig. 21.1 Conventional model of livelihood enhancement: one size fits all

Yet it must be kept in mind that very few of these indicators can really show improvements in a few months or even a year.

Understanding the Basis of Rural Livelihoods

An apt illustration of the points just made emerges from the figures released by the National Sample Survey Office (NSSO) for the key indicators for employment and unemployment in India, generated from the data collected between July 2009 and June 2010 (NSSO, 2010). The overall employment situation in India does not appear to have changed much with (a) agriculture continuing to be the key employer in rural areas and (b) casual/informal employment remaining a major source of livelihood. The trend observed in rural areas, according to this survey, is that of a significant increase in self-employment. In the case of rural areas, 54.2 % are self-employed with the percentage of self-employed rural women being 56 % compared to 54 % in rural men. Based on this data, analyses have been presented regarding the policies that must be put in place to address livelihood enhancement issues. However, very few of these analyses have emphasized the single-most important point, and that is any planning or policy development must start from the hamlets and converge at the district, state, and central levels. This is because rural livelihoods are inextricably linked to and shaped by local resources. Therefore, any livelihood enhancement initiative must start from a sound understanding of (a) the local resource base, (b) natural cycles that influence usage patterns, (c) historic use patterns, (d) multiplicity of livelihoods and interlinkages between these livelihoods vis-a-vis resources, (e) changes in livelihood sources, (f) resilience of local communities, and (g) the social structure of the community. The most effective initiative would, therefore, be one that emerges from the community since the members of the community are best equipped to understand these dynamics. It is imperative, therefore, that resourceful people who can take the initiative are motivated to stay and work in the rural areas. This also means that the erosion of the resource base on which these livelihoods are based must be actively prevented and appropriate support systems put in place to afford a life of quality and dignity which allows aspirations to be met both for the young and the old.

The Role of Education

The difficult question to be answered then is: What are the enabling conditions that need to be put in place to give rural young people sufficient reason to not want to migrate to the cities? Given the uniqueness of resources in each rural location, there can be no universal solution to reverse or mitigate this migration. Education is often touted as the panacea to all problems particularly to stem youth migration to urban areas. The reality is that acquiring a degree seems to propel youth toward urban areas where, very often, they may barely earn enough and compromise significantly on their self-respect and dignity. What must, therefore, be emphasized is that it is not education per se but the type of education and its relevance to local lifestyles and challenges that can contribute to better and sustained livelihoods in rural areas. Then there is the issue of aspirations. A large segment of initiatives focuses on ensuring that rural youth stay back in their village to meet their aspirations. The career development and livelihood planning point that is missed is that certain kinds of aspirations can be met in villages while others are best pursued in cities. The same argument could be made for urban youth: they could be educated to meet their aspirations in the villages.

An essential gap that must be filled if rural livelihoods are to be sustained and strengthened is related to the utilization of nature and natural resources. It is very likely that rural livelihoods would vanish with the erosion and overexploitation of natural resources, and with it, the quality and dignity of rural life would be denigrated. This could in turn force migration to urban areas. This is not to advocate a Luddite form of protest, relegating rural populace to rural areas. It means proactively diffusing and disseminating appropriate techniques and technologies to meet the difficulties that rural workers encounter. This would include creating entrepreneurial opportunities for rural and urban youth through which they can be equipped to apply technology, business, and economics to improve their stewardship of nature and natural resources and thereby strengthen the quality of their lives. A prerequisite for all of this is access to a relevant form of education, not just academic but a skill-oriented education that would foster the interdependency between work, health, nutrition, environment, and quality life.

The Role of External Facilitators

Our primary experience has been with small and marginal farmers and pastoral communities in a resource-fragile rain-fed part of the Rayalaseema region of Andhra Pradesh state in South India (it may be noted that at the time of going to press, this region was split into two separate states as part of a political process). Andhra Pradesh has been a large agrarian state which has among the highest farmer suicide rates in India. We highlight here that in the project area where we are based, agriculture-linked farmer suicides have not occurred. This is because most of the farmers, albeit small and marginal, have *multiple* sources of income including agriculture, goat herding/ shepherding, and dairying. Our experiences have made it clear that issues and solutions can emerge from the community when suitable platforms and spaces are created. Examples include enabling peer-to-peer networking, experience sharing by facilitating community meetings through creation of *sanghas* or collectives, supporting exposure visits, enriching education programs both in local schools and among adults to make it relevant. The role of external facilitators, be they government, NGOs, educational institutions, or, indeed, career development professionals, is to create these enabling conditions and allow development to happen from within. Once the issues and solutions emerge, the appropriate resources (physical/labor, financial, technical) can be identified to implement the solution and monitor its effectiveness.

Improving Rural Livelihoods: The Rishi Valley Grassroots Action Model (RiVaGRAM) as a Case Study

It is clear that there is no universal solution to improving rural livelihoods. Livelihoods cannot be imposed. They must rather be based on community members' aspirations and perceptions of development. The wisdom that can be gleaned from these grassroots level perceptions could lay strong foundations for effective program implementation. Box 21.5 provides snippets from the conversations we and other NGOs have had with the local communities in the region about *manchi jeevitham* (good life) and how this can be maintained. The challenge is to enable a livelihood planning model that is appropriate and relevant to local geographical and climatic conditions, independent of constant external financial support. Such a model would be embedded in the cultural and spiritual context of the communities and their relationship with their natural resources. The rest of this chapter is devoted to extracting key principles from an attempt that has been made by the Rishi Valley grassroots action model (RiVaGRAM) to develop a model for rural livelihoods that can address some of these issues.

A recent compilation of studies on poverty in various developing countries (India, Bangladesh, and South Africa) called *Portfolios of the Poor* (Collins, Morduch, Rutherford, & Ruthven, 2009) emphasized the need to understand the link between livelihoods and poverty as the first step in alleviating it and, therefore, in mitigating

Box 21.5: Manchi Jeevitham (Good Life): Wisdom from the Grassroots

Manchi jeevitham means good life in Telugu, a South Indian language. A series of discussions facilitated by one of the authors is currently under way in several of the hamlets in the area to discuss what a good life means to people. This dialogue is being carried out to understand people's perceptions of what "real livelihoods" mean and how development can be made relevant and meaningful. The dialogue and its title were inspired by an elaborate and detailed effort undertaken by Yakshi, an organization that has been working with *adivasis* (indigenous people) in South India for over 25 years. The ongoing dialogue in the Rishi Valley area is with non-adivasi communities. Given below are snippets from our learnings (translated from Telugu and rephrased).

- Livelihood programs cannot only focus on income generation. While income allows for access to education and better living standards in terms of amenities, it does not guarantee good health. This wisdom was imparted by Redamma, a female resident of one of the hamlets. Redamma is a small and marginal farmer who has about two acres of land and 50 sheep. While her husband manages the sheep and practices subsistence farming largely for home consumption with half an acre dedicated to groundnut cultivation for the market, Redamma works at the Rishi Valley Education Centre as a laborer. Their life and livelihood strategy, thus, has a *portfolio* approach which provides stability to their lives through their multiple sources of income.

- Any efforts at making livelihoods more sustainable from an ecological perspective, for example, collective management of water, protection of commons,

(continued)

its consequences. The reality of rural livelihoods described by these authors has been borne out in the RiVaGRAM experience: flow of income is not steady and hence the concept of monthly income does not exist; there is a need for multiple sources of income to reduce risks. In this situation, how can livelihoods be made sustainable while simultaneously addressing aspirations?

The RiVaGRAM evolved from over 5 years of direct engagement on livelihood issues with rural communities in the Rishi Valley area which is located in a low rainfall region of Southern India. The existence of the Rishi Valley Education Centre (RVEC) (dedicated to implementing the vision of philosopher J. Krishnamurti's) for over 80 years and the institution's engagement with the community in the area of health and education laid the foundation for this more recent engagement in livelihoods.

The terrain of the Rishi Valley area is rocky, and the natural resources and livelihoods are shaped by a historic 10-year drought cycle. Vegetation varies from dry, mixed deciduous to thorny scrub with occasional patches of dry, evergreen growth. This is a predominantly small and marginal farmer-based community with agriculture and livestock being the main sources of livelihood. Rain-fed agriculture and a largely pastoralist type of livestock management have been replaced with the Green Revolution (see Swaminathan, 2006 for an overview)-based agriculture and dairying using resource-intensive exotic breeds of Holstein Friesian cattle. This has resulted in high levels of groundwater extraction

(the only source of water) and has changed the nature of the dependencies between the community and the natural resources which form the basis of their livelihoods. Landless farmers and tribal communities in the area continue to depend on minor forest produce as a source of livelihood. Sheep and goatherds continuing to practice pastoralism depend on the hills and surrounding forests for their fodder needs. A characteristic of the rural communities in this area is the existence of multiple sources of income: subsistence farming, dairying, sheep/goat rearing, and farm labor. These incomes may not be large but provide a safety net and enable a certain degree of resilience. This resilience is, however, increasingly under threat by external factors such as trade agreements and pressure from global retailers wanting to expand their markets to these emerging economies leading to the erosion of rural livelihoods. This is not unique to rural communities in India. Small and marginal communities in several South Asian countries such as Bangladesh and Sri Lanka and African countries such as South Africa, Rwanda, Kenya, and Nigeria, along with several Latin American countries, are all facing similar challenges of sustaining livelihoods.

In an attempt to provide an alternate way of thinking about livelihoods, a possible model/framework is suggested in this chapter to facilitate the enhancement of livelihoods and quality of life in rural areas. This model aims at providing a cohesive framework within which the fluidity between natural resources and livelihoods could be integrated. Keeping felt needs and ground realities in mind, we have moved from practice to theory rather than vice versa. Figure 21.2 provides a description of the RiVaGRAM, and the following section outlines the key steps suggested by our framework.

Step 1: Identification of a Pilot Community

The initial step is to identify specific hamlets or villages where an approach can be tested. In the early stages of our work, the size of the population was identified as a major determinant of selection. It was noted that in a low-populated community

Fig. 21.2 Rishi Valley grassroots action model: tailored to fit

there may be less of an impact, but the program could be implemented quickly. Conversely, in a highly populated community, there may be more of an impact, but complete program implementation would take more time. Subsequently, it was felt that rather than using population as a selection criterion, other more effective criteria had to be identified. The selected communities had several common characteristics: (a) there was a general interest in being proactive within the community, (b) community members were willing to share information with others, (c) several people displayed strong leadership qualities and acted as peer motivators, and (d) there was a sense of openness to change.

Step 2: Building Relationships

After identifying the community, the next step is to begin building relationships so as to best understand the specific enabling factors needed to improve the livelihoods of residents. Methodologies used were as follows.

Community Liaison
Here, access to a community was made possible by establishing and building a relationship with

an individual residing in the village who showed an interest. This person was then able to act as a peer leader and a liaison between an external agency (in this case, the RVEC) and the rest of the community.

Coalition Building
A second method of building relationships within a community was through the formation of a community coalition around a particular issue. Examples include farmers' clubs and pastoralist sanghas (collectives). Information- or knowledge-sharing was the responsibility of peer educators, and the group agenda, structure, and actions were decided by those involved. The goal of community coalitions was for the members of the group to take ownership of the issue and subsequent problem-solving strategies. An additional benefit of this method was increased communication between residents and the empowerment that comes from group support.

Step 3: Facilitating Access to Outside Resources

The primary role of a coordinator/coordinating agency should be to utilize outside networks to access additional resources including education, training, linkages to markets, and value addition which have the potential to enhance the livelihoods of the communities engaged in the initiative. The coordinating agency can tap into established relationships and connections, such as government agencies, that could further the initiative by directing the appropriate resources where and when needed. However, a balance must be maintained between the support of external resources and the control that the community has over the initiatives. The long-term goal of community-driven solutions should always be sustainability without external support.

Step 4: Withdrawal of the Coordinating Agency

The final step in this approach is for the coordinating agency to withdraw from the function of leading or directing the initiative. This makes the role/function of the coordinating agency transferable and replaceable. Prior to withdrawal, it is critical that the coordinating agency ensures that the process is well documented and local capacity has been built to mainstream the program. Initiatives should always begin as a directive of the community, and leadership should emerge from within.

This approach is under implementation in the Rishi Valley area. The enthusiasm, energy, and a feeling of empowerment particularly among the women and younger farmers have been encouraging. The pastoralists, through their collective, are asserting their customary rights to traditional grazing lands in the forest and are developing forest protection plans. They have adopted a degraded grazing ground with the goal of reviving pastures and, therefore, enhancing their livelihoods. At the time of writing, this effort has been under way for over 3 years. Farmers' groups have set up an organic animal feed enterprise which sources the raw material from other farmers in the area, thereby driving a change in the cropping patterns to low-input, rain-fed crops such as millets. One of the young farmers has returned from the city to help improve incomes from dairying. More recently, the RVEC has

taken its engagement with the community to the next level. The Rishi Valley School which is a part of the RVEC with close to 400 students and faculty from different parts of India has become a market for some of the community's livelihood products. For example, fresh, organic vegetables are purchased for the school's dining hall from some of the farmers; a part of the school's milk requirement is now being met by a sangha (collective) of dairy farmers in the area. This is a "win-win" situation for all concerned: healthy, safe, and quality produce for the school and an assured market for the community which allows them to practice their traditional livelihoods with sovereignty and dignity.

Influencing Rural Livelihoods and Lifestyles: The Role of Career Counseling

Relevance for Multiple Cultures: Sensitivity to the Universal and the Particular

It has been argued that if they are to take root, livelihood planning and career counseling interventions must merge and blend with the culture for which they are intended (Arulmani, 2011). Bissell (2010) has pointed out that over the years, the forces of colonization and globalization have influenced prevailing ways of living and corroded the value placed on age-old customs, skills, and knowledge bases of local cultures. While planning for livelihoods, it is essential that one understands the rural ethos, the culture, the hopes, and aspirations of these youth. It is clear that one size does not fit all. A model based on an understanding of youth in rural Andhra Pradesh (from where this chapter has been written) need not necessarily work in rice fields of Cambodia or in other countries, where presumably youth from farming and rural communities have similar aspirations. Having said this, we now attempt to extract themes from the points we have discussed that could have relevance to other settings.

Most important to note is that irrespective of where it is implemented, developing a livelihood planning system for the rural sector requires the aspirations of rural youth to be viewed in a balanced manner. Migration from rural to urban areas is an age-old phenomenon that has been brought into sharper focus against the background of the economic and social change induced by globalization. A key question that a career counselor needs to ask is: Is it good livelihood planning to put the brakes on a young person who wants to break free, and move away from the rural home that he/she experiences as financially insecure and personally restrictive? Helping rural youth throw a different light upon their hopes and wishes is an essential first step. In some ways, this first step would be to brush away the stardust from their eyes.

The bedrock on which career counseling must rest is the conviction that all approaches must be nondiscriminatory, focusing on the young person's strengths, weaknesses, and potential rather than whether that person is from a rural or urban background. All jobs and job locations must be portrayed as equal and worthy of dignity. We highlight this point because it is possible that "urban jobs" are considered to be more valuable than jobs that compose rural livelihoods. And, hence, the career counselor may feel compelled to advice the rural young person to move to the city. We take the position that all jobs are worthwhile. Such an approach would accept with equanimity the possibility that one young person may be more likely to succeed in farming rather than a city job, while another maybe better suited to move out and build a different life in the city. Such an approach would carefully examine the strengths of an individual, taking into account all the factors that have gone into making him/her the person he/she is and from there provide advice pertaining to suitable jobs and careers. Take the case of Uday, a 20-year-old farmer who mentioned to one of the authors of this chapter that it must be wonderful working in an office. So he was invited to help with the office work for a day. At the end of 2 hours, he said that sitting in an office and taking decisions involved

a lot of hard work. He became restless and wanted to go out for fresh air, although this office had large windows and was quite well ventilated! By lunchtime he was ready to call it quits. It was then explained to him that office work was as hard work as his work in the farm: one was mental and the other physical. Uday was then able to look at the attraction of an office in a different light. Interestingly, this experience did not prevent him from applying for and taking up a low-paying job in the city!

The point we are making is that the career counselor must be vigilant against foisting his/her views upon the client. The task instead is to create the conditions necessary for rational and well-informed career decision making. It is essential that the approach to livelihood planning for rural youth be multipronged. This ranges from governmental policies on agriculture, forest rights, and rural artisans, providing market access, storage facilities, and fair prices, to the way youth are educated and prepared for the contemporary world of work either in rural or in urban areas. The emphasis must rest not merely on the acquisition of technical skills and knowledge but also on helping the young person understand him/herself and one's role as a worker. Additionally, education should seek to address issues such as (a) understanding of the role played by rural occupations (e.g., agriculture, animal rearing) in economic growth and development, (b) the role of the commons and community-based management of resources, (c) equipping youth with skills for value addition (e.g., in rural occupations such as agriculture and animal rearing) and efficient models of farming, (d) helping them understand innovative practices which have been successful elsewhere, and (e) helping youth realize that being in a rural area makes one no less a human being than an equivalent urban youth.

A crucial career counseling point that has relevance across cultures is that, in a rural setting, it is important to create an environment wherein the youth have the *choice* to either stay back or migrate to a city to seek a different lifestyle. Career guidance should not in any way stymie the person's choices and must ensure that the individual is free to build his or her career wherever he or she pleases: in the city or at home in the village, or perhaps even work out a blend of the two. Career guidance should be a liberating activity rather than a shackling one. Keeping the long term in view, the discipline of career guidance would do well to keep in mind the necessity of contributing to the creation of strong systems to sustain rural livelihoods.

New Concepts and Viewpoints: Charting New Directions

Livelihood somehow carries connotations of rural, low-economic-status occupational activities linked to survival. Livelihood is also linked to engagement with traditional occupations. Career, on the other hand, carries overtones of urban, higher-economic-status occupational activities related to high incomes and opportunities for potential realization. It is perhaps this differentiation that fuels the deep desire to migrate to the city. Perhaps, the contemporary notion of career has obscured the deeper meaning of livelihood: a way of life. This phenomenon of *livelihood* versus *career* against the background of rural–urban migration requires further investigation. An important new dimension emerges for career guidance from our discussions in this writing: Career guidance could explore the inclusion in its purview, of a form of guidance and counseling that supports *livelihood* planning. Within such a scheme would be a *livelihood counselor*: a career counselor who is skilled in facilitating the process of career choice and discovery as well as in understanding and optimizing rural/traditional occupational structures. A livelihood's focus in guidance and counseling could pave the way for rural young people to also experience *career* development without losing their cultural identity. This points to new directions that could be charted by the discipline of career guidance.

Conclusion

There are as many bright, young, thinking minds in rural areas as there in urban areas. All they need is opportunity, but opportunity wherein the human being in them and their aspirations are recognized and not just the fact that they have some marketable skills. The *human capability* as Amartya Sen has articulated in his capability approach (Sen, 1985) must be allowed to be realized if livelihoods and lives are to be made sustainable. Young men and women, urban and rural, who have been provided opportunities by their communities, must also give back to the community which has nurtured them and to their family which has sacrificed to provide for them. This may sound altruistic in today's materialistic world, but this is as important as anything else. As Krishnamurti (1948a) has argued, finding out what one is giving to society is more important than asking what is the right means of livelihood. The *right livelihood* approach is, therefore, one that will enable and empo wer us to make the right choices so that we can forge the "right" relationship with each other, with nature, and ultimately with oneself (Krishnamurti, 1948b). It is to realize this ideal that all stakeholders: the youth, the educator, the industry, and the government, need to come together to facilitate the right choices. And, indeed, it is the livelihood counselor who is best equipped to optimize this facilitation.

References

Arulmani, G. (2011). Striking the right note: The cultural preparedness approach to developing resonant career guidance programmes. *International Journal for Educational and Vocational Guidance, 11*(2), 79–93.

Bakshi, A. J. (2014). Personality and self: Multiple frames of reference for career service professionals. In G. Arulmani, A. J. Bakshi, F. T. L. Leong, & A. G. Watts (Eds.), *Handbook of career development*. New York, NY: Springer.

Bakshi, A. J., & Joshi, J. (2014). The interface between positive youth development and youth career development: New avenues for career guidance practice. In G. Arulmani, A. J. Bakshi, F. T. L. Leong, & A. G. Watts (Eds.), *Handbook of career development*. New York, NY: Springer.

Bissell, W. N. (2010). *Making India work*. New Delhi, India: Penguin.

Chambers, R., & Conway, G. R. (1991). *Sustainable rural livelihoods: Practical concepts for the 21st century* (Institute of Development Studies, Discussion Paper 296). Brighton, UK: University of Sussex.

Collins, D., Morduch, J., Rutherford, S., & Ruthven, O. (2009). *Portfolios of the poor: How the world's poor live on $2 a day*. Princeton, NJ: Princeton University Press.

Krishnamurti, J. (1948a, October). *Right livelihood* (Eighth Talk in Poona). Retrieved from http://www.jkrishnamurti.org/krishnamurti-teachings/view-text.php?tid=296&chid=4626

Krishnamurti, J. (1948b). *The collected works of J. Krishnamurti:* Vol. 5. Choiceless awareness. Chennai, India: Krishnamurti Foundation.

Kumar, S., & Arulmani, G. (2014). Understanding the labor market: Implications for career counseling. In G. Arulmani, A. J. Bakshi, F. T. L. Leong, & A. G. Watts (Eds.), *Handbook of career development*. New York, NY: Springer.

Lifestyle. (2003). *The Concise Oxford English Dictionary* (10th ed.). Oxford, UK: Oxford University Press.

Livelihood. (2003). *The Concise Oxford English Dictionary* (10th ed.). Oxford, UK: Oxford University Press.

Livelihood. (n.d.). In *Merriam-Webster's online dictionary* (11th ed.). Retrieved from http://www.merriam-webster.com/dictionary/livelihood

National Sample Survey Organisation [NSSO]. (2010). *Key indicators of employment and unemployment in India, 2009–10*. New Delhi, India: Author.

Sen, A. (1985). *Commodities and capabilities*. Oxford, UK: Oxford University Press.

Serrat, O. (2008). *The sustainable livelihoods approach*. Manila, Philippines: Regional and Sustainable Development Department, Asian Development Bank.

Swaminathan, M. S. (2006). An evergreen revolution. *Crop Science, 46*, 2293–2303.

United Nations Development Programme [UNDP]. (2010). *The guidance note on recovery: Livelihood*. New York, NY: UNDP and International Recovery Platform.

Traditional Occupations in a Modern World: Career Guidance, Livelihood Planning, and Crafts in the Context of Globalization

Anita Ratnam

Introduction

As globalization continues to bring changes in the ways in which education, work, and life are organized across the world, new challenges for career guidance and livelihood planning are inevitable. Theoretical frameworks, pedagogies, approaches, models, methods, and tools that have evolved since the inception of career guidance as a profession are today being examined afresh. Drawing on disciplines like sociology, economics, culture studies, and philosophy, new lenses are being deployed to redefine the purpose, scope, span, techniques, and even ethics of career guidance and livelihood planning. World systems theory, sustainable development, gender justice, and social inclusion are today increasingly part of the career guidance and livelihood planning discourses where concerns of marginalized groups, politics of knowledge, and questions about the nature and consequences of neoliberal capitalism are being debated. A fresh look at traditional occupations like crafts could enrich these discussions by posing new questions, while also offering insights, possibilities, and solutions to existing dilemmas for career guidance and livelihood planning.

For the purpose of this discussion, career guidance refers "to services and activities intended to assist individuals, of any age and at any point throughout their lives, to make educational, training and occupational choices and to manage their careers" (Organisation for Economic Co-operation and Development (OECD), 2004, p. 19). Drawing from the Institute of Development Studies' (IDS) framework for sustainable livelihoods, livelihood planning has been approached as a complex and normative process of helping make livelihood decisions based on multiple capabilities, contested cultural contexts, and social as well as material resources (Scoones, 1998).

This chapter begins with an examination of the threats and opportunities that globalization has brought to crafts and craftspeople. In the second section, the ways in which career guidance and livelihood planning can contribute towards the repositioning of crafts as a modern career option are outlined. In the last section, attention is drawn to the challenges in providing relevant career guidance and livelihood planning services to young people from craft communities.

Crafts, Craftspeople, and Globalization

Prior to the industrial revolution, practically everything used by humans was made through the highly skilled use of simple tools on raw materials from nature. This artisanal way of production existed for centuries with textiles, clothes, furniture, jewelry, ships, carts and chariots,

A. Ratnam (✉)
Samvada, Bangalore, India
e-mail: ratnam.anita@gmail.com

G. Arulmani et al. (eds.), *Handbook of Career Development*, International and Cultural Psychology,
DOI 10.1007/978-1-4614-9460-7_22, © Springer Science+Business Media, LLC 2014

artifacts, and tools being made by craftspeople. Different artisans could pool their efforts to produce buildings of all shapes and sizes from humble dwellings to palaces, cathedrals, and temples. Means of transport too were "crafted" by the skilled use of tools and techniques and it is, therefore, not surprising that boats, ships, and airplanes are referred to as *craft* even today (Ratnam, 2011).

This chapter focuses on crafts primarily because crafts have continuously adapted to changes in social structures and institutional frameworks, trade systems and markets, and national policies and international agreements over centuries. With such a history, crafts could offer valuable insights relevant to career guidance practice in the contemporary context of globalization. The potential for entrepreneurship, scope for constant innovations, and the increasing demand for traditionally produced goods all suggest that crafts could belong to the future as well as the past. At the same time, the unique dilemmas of the artisan demand an enquiry into the place of traditional crafts in the world of modern careers and career guidance.

Resilience of Crafts in the Face of Mechanization

With the advent of the industrial revolution, the artisanal mode of production faced the threat of extinction. Viewed as overly slow when compared with mechanized mass production, crafts were relegated to the margins. As factory-based mass production took center-stage, the roles of capital, technology, and commerce have been repeatedly emphasized (Hobsbawm, 1996). That artisanal skills and knowledge made the industrial revolution itself possible remains largely unacknowledged (Green, 2002).

In spite of the marginalization of crafts, it is clear that crafts and craftspeople have endured. Artisans all over the world still work magic with their deft hands and simple tools to create an alluring variety of textiles, accessories, furnishing, furniture, fixtures, pottery, and crockery. Handcrafted goods, with their own market

niche, are prominently displayed in craft fairs, designer boutiques, and fashionable malls as they adapt their products to changing needs, tastes, fashions, and trends. The volume and market value of production, and the sheer number of people across the world who are engaged in crafts, all point to a sector that cannot be ignored. In countries like the UK where traditional as well as contemporary crafts exist, crafts make a £3 billion contribution to the economy (Crafts Council UK, 2009). With developing countries supplying 40 % of world demand for crafts, crafts can become drivers of economic growth and development. For example, it is estimated that India has 8.6 million artisans (Liebel & Roy, 2003). The Export Promotion Council for Handicrafts in India (EPCH) has projected exports of Indian handicrafts at 3.3 billion USD in 2012–2013. This sector's potential for growth is well established by the fact that Indian exports of handicrafts reached USD 454 million in the month of December 2012 which is 34 % higher than exports in December 2011 (EPCH, 2013). Surely, this rate of growth demonstrates the increasing appeal and buoyancy of crafts. In a world of volatility and rapid change, such resilience is significant. It demonstrates not only the human being's yearning to use handmade products and the artisan's ability to adapt to changing tastes and market systems, but also reveals the emergence of supply chains and business mechanisms to market and distribute what artisans produce in different corners of the world.

Policymakers and International Agencies Pay Increasing Attention to Crafts

Policymakers too are taking a fresh look at traditional crafts as the export and rural employment potential of crafts are being recognized. The need for decentralized, non-capital-intensive, rural off-farm employment has led the Planning Commission of India (2007) to refer to village industries as "engines of sustainable and inclusive growth," and to handlooms as "hope looms" (p. 108). Such state patronage and attention are crucial to promote crafts and to address the poverty of artisans. In the UK, the state recognizes three kinds of crafts—traditional craft, contemporary craft, and heritage crafts— and has established agencies and policies to promote each of these. The Crafts Council's mission is to make the UK "the best place to see and buy craft" and the Creative and Cultural Skills Council aims to "convert talent into skills and jobs" (Creative and Cultural Skills Council and Crafts Council, 2009, p. 2). The two councils worked together on the 2009 Craft Blueprint that spells out plans to build a diverse and skilled workforce for the crafts through creation of multiple entry points, career guidance, continued professional development, business support, and qualifications reform and agreements with the UK Commission for Employment and Skills.

International agencies too increasingly are recognizing the scope that crafts have in redressing problems of unemployment and migration, enabling sustainability, and building respect for cultural diversity. Notably, the United Nations Educational, Scientific and Cultural Organisation (UNESCO, 2006) has developed a 10-year plan for Cultural and Creative Industries. Moreover, international movements such as the Green Building Congress, World Crafts Council, and Craftmark promote crafts as sustainable livelihoods, as sources of employment for women, and as sources of supplementary income for those engaged in crafts on a part-time basis (Ratnam, 2011).

The Need to Position Craft as a Modern Career Option

Traditional crafts not only have a global market; there are skilled communities across the world who can meet that demand. Beyond this logic of mere supply and demand, through the use of crafts we can encourage decentralized production, and help create both economically and environmentally sustainable and inclusive development. Crafts, which meet varied needs of consumers (e.g., for natural health products), can also help make the world a more humane and democratic space. Most importantly, crafts have the potential to offer meaningful work that can lead to viable livelihoods and careers, social innovation, flexibility, individual creativity, social inclusion, as well as expressions of cultural diversity and aesthetic sensibilities.

Though contemporary crafts are well highlighted in career information services in countries like the UK through organizations like Creative Choices and Creative Capital, as well as in general career portals, in the developing countries where traditional crafts are practiced, crafts are not perceived as a modern career option and not positioned adequately as a worthwhile, green, and decent career option that can preserve heritage, and indigenous skills and knowledge systems. In emerging career information systems and policies in developing countries, the focus instead is on industrial labor markets, and on rapidly securing employment, rather than self-actualization of individuals (Watts & Fretwell, 2004). As 85 % of the world's 1.1 billion youth, between the ages of 15 and 24 years, live in developing countries where rural and socially/economically disadvantaged youth are a majority (World Bank, 2006), their employment continues to pose a serious challenge. The UN World Youth Report 2011 stated that 75.8 million youth were unemployed in 2009, with the global youth unemployment rate being 12.6 % in 2010, much higher than the adult unemployment rate of 4.8 % (UNWYR, 2011). Reaching out to these large numbers of disadvantaged and rural youth, especially in developing countries, with economically viable and culturally appropriate work options, remains one of the biggest challenges for career guidance and livelihood planning practitioners. These services are in their infancy in most parts of the developing world, are expensive, and available mainly in urban areas. Middle-class youth trying to get government, manufacturing, or service sector jobs and affluent youth seeking information about prospects in multinational corporations, education in foreign universities, and higher levels of bureaucracy have been the first to gain access to such services. Their interests, their parents' anxieties and priorities, which are significantly different from those of disadvantaged youth, have dominated the emerging practice and discourses of career guidance. Extending the reach of these services to rural and disadvantaged youth or to affluent youth disinterested in such mainstream corporatism, and being relevant to them, demands an expansion of the professional discourse itself. In the context of increasing demand for crafts and the potential for crafts to provide employment along with scope for innovation, positioning crafts as a significant career option within the careers discourse and guidance practice would be a step in that direction.

Need for Career Guidance and Livelihood Planning for Craftspeople

Young people from craft communities could belong to indigenous groups or to marginalized castes/groups that are faced with threats to their traditional occupations and habitats alongside limited avenues for entering the new knowledge economies as their presence in higher education is insignificant. The Crafts Council of India survey report stated that less than 5 % of the artisan population has completed 10 years of schooling (Rajagopalan, 2011). Their educational disadvantages are compounded by confusions about aspirations and identities, even as they are increasingly faced with loss of decent livelihood options, social uncertainty, and economic insecurity (Bennell, 2007). Though career guidance and livelihood planning are vital services they need at this critical juncture, these are simply not available in their schools and neighborhoods.

The task of providing them these services could, therefore, fall on state and civil society organizations that work with craft communities. However, these organizations have focused on the craft, and not on the individual artisan's needs or young people's aspirations and dilemmas related to livelihoods and career. State agencies and civil society organizations need to integrate goals of promoting the craft with providing career guidance and livelihood planning services to craftspeople.

How Can Career Guidance and Livelihood Planning Help Position Crafts as Modern Careers?

Positioning traditional crafts as modern careers which are fulfilling and enjoyable for individuals, as well as necessary for an inclusive and sustainable society, calls for developing a critique of the current growth paradigm and including collective and societal good as a goal. Acknowledging craft as meaningful work, blurring the lines between art and craft, and validating traditional knowledge of craft communities are also essential steps in this direction.

Developing a Critique of the Current Growth Paradigm

The social and ecological value of craft emerges from a recognition of some of the consequences of mass production and consumption. Increasing awareness about the alienation experienced by industrial workers and growing inequalities have prompted a cultural and economic critique of the industrial modernization paradigm. Deindustrialization and unemployment in the first world and sweatshops in the third world, amidst the overemphasis on transnational capital markets, impel a search for an alternate development paradigm. This has prompted the World Commission on Culture and Development (UNESCO, 1995) to define "development as culture." The World Commission on Environment and Development (1987) had earlier emphasized the need for "sustainable development" and the United Nations Development Project (UNDP) Human Development Reports have been repeatedly stressing the need to address extreme inequalities across countries and within national boundaries (UNDP, 2011). More recently, the Occupy Wall Street movement has drawn attention to the harsh inequalities that have emerged from capitalist development (DeGraw, 2011).

As industrialization and the emergence of labor markets led to the beginnings of guidance services, the focus traditionally has been on helping individuals adapt to labor markets, rather than on a questioning of the underlying development paradigm. However, policymakers and practitioners are today being confronted with questions about the outcomes of modernization and industrialization, and about paradigms of development and their social and ecological consequences (Guichard, 2003). In the light of such challenge, there is a need to also offer a critique of established notions of work and success, and help analyze the personal, social, and ecological costs of mainstream corporate careers, as well as of the paradigm in which they are embedded (Ratnam, 2011). Career guidance and livelihood planning need to go beyond individual psychology to integrate knowledge about the political economy of the labor market and how it continuously creates and erases identities as well as aspirations. Such an approach can help broaden aspirations of young people beyond the hegemony of industrialism, consumerism, and corporatism that have permeated career guidance theory and practice, and can help position crafts as a career option that contributes to social inclusion and sustainable development.

Recognizing Porosity Between Art and Craft and Between Tradition and Modernity

Can craft survive if there is a constant disparaging of craft and craftsperson as mindless, and glorification of art and artist as aesthetic and cerebral? Will young people be attracted to something that is portrayed as steeped in tradition or lacking in creative freedom? Although craft has been largely left out from the modern worlds of art and design, newer collaborations between designers/artists and artisans in creating and executing designs are beginning to make the lines between art, craft, and design less distinct. Examining journals like *Crafts* and newly emerging disciplines like craft history and craft theory, Lees-Maffei and Sandino (2004) have pointed to the changing loyalties, affinities, and tensions between the three and underscored the need to include crafts in the art/design discourse. They have indicated that there is a movement away from the simple idea of craft as an antidote to industrialism, towards a more complex construal of craft as integrating skills, expressions, and aesthetics which draw craft into the purview of art and design.

When mechanization and industrialism have resulted in standardization, mass production, mass employment, and a wide array of products to satisfy consumer needs and demands, is there really a need for crafts? Crafts despite their versatility cannot provide for all modern human requirements which include, for example, hospital equipment and communication devices. Does this imply that advocates for crafts are taking an anti-modernist and anti-industrialization stance? These questions can be countered by another question: Is it possible and desirable to have a world with multiple modes of production? Charles and Ray Eames, American designers and architects, encouraged a fusion between craft and machine-work in their designs of buildings and furniture. Their designs traversed and wove together the industrial, the uniform, and the mass-produced along with the preindustrial, the personal, and the handmade (Kirkham, 1998). This combination of modernism and humanism manifested in multiplicity, creative diversity, and a hybridism that celebrates human dexterity and touch, alongside the marvel of machines, is not merely an eclectic ideal. In fact this hybridism is a reality even today as in most parts of the developing world, homes are built and then filled with both manufactured and handcrafted items. Multiple modes of production are practiced and coexist while complementing each other.

A discourse on hybrid worlds, dialectic identities, and transmodernity through craft is emerging, with a clear emphasis on moving beyond dichotomies. Greenhalgh (2002) has argued that the next phase of modernity will be characterized by blurring of lines between arts, science, and eclecticism. He predicts that "every craft studio will be an effortless mélange of traditional tools and high technology" with a move towards "interdisciplinarity, relational rather than reductive visions, globality, cultural diversity and pan-technicality" (p. 2). Crafts have the potential to straddle both the past and the future while being rooted in the contemporary—what Habermas (1984) calls a contemporariness that "repeatedly gives birth to new and subjective pasts" in a search for the true "presence." Career guidance and livelihood planning could contribute substantially towards acknowledging the artistic, aesthetic, and cerebral elements of craft and can highlight the hybrid, interdisciplinary, global, culturally diverse, and pan-technical character of traditional crafts in today's world.

Acknowledging Crafts as Meaningful Work

The collapse of manufacturing and manual trades in many parts of the "first" world has led to a crisis of identity as those brought up by working-class parents are unable to access or adapt to "client servicing" jobs (Nixon, 2006). It is no surprise that in a country where the rootless postmodern worker is disoriented, Michael B. Crawford, the American philosopher and motorbike mechanic, makes a case for "working with your hands" (Crawford, 2010). In such a scenario, for the large numbers of young unemployed youth, crafts—either traditional or contemporary—could be an opportunity for decent work "with one's hands."

The "limits to flexibility" in a world where young working-class people are expected to have infinite pliability and ambition, without direction or passion, are staring us in the face (Morgan, 2008). Cohen (2006) has drawn attention to the fissures caused by the disjuncts between material conditions and cultural codes and reminds us that work is a "culturally coded" notion. The discord between parental models and today's world of work, between parents' culture and youth culture, has created questions and confusions

about the idea of work, as parent culture dominates the way work is understood by young people (Nayak, 2006) even though working conditions and opportunities have changed. The crisis of "displaced and redundant masculinities" in the postindustrial working class used to working with their bodies also needs cognizance (McDowell, 2003). While career guidance has been expected to fashion a new breed of workers who can create careers out of multiple disparate jobs without a single vocational identity, we are reminded that all communities do not accept such a calculative attitude for career building (Connell, 2001). Here again, crafts have much to offer working-class youth by addressing the need for work opportunities where such discord can be mitigated. Not only do crafts offer meaningful work, identity, and flexibility per se, crafts could also become a tool of social inclusion of those marginalized by the new knowledge society.

Validating Traditional Knowledge in Crafts

Traditional knowledge in crafts has been developed over several generations. This knowledge is rooted in local culture and passed down orally after repeated testing, experimentation, and innovation. It is, therefore, empirical rather than theoretical, and encompasses a deep understanding of natural materials artisans use—be it cotton, jute, clay, copper, brass, bell metal, bamboo, palm leaves, wood, reeds, shells, tree barks, stones, vegetable extracts, cow dung, leaves, mud, sand, feathers, gems, silver, or gold. Their knowledge base also includes complex weaving, molding, stitching, carving, painting, dyeing, tanning, building techniques, metallurgical technologies, and a host of physical as well as chemical processes. Artisans use this knowledge base to produce a delightful array of products including, for example, textiles, jewelry, furniture, furnishing, and artifacts (Rajagopalan, 2011).

Despite such a rich resource of systematically and rigorously generated knowledge, the impoverishment of craftspeople, alongside the extreme affluence of designers and marketing professionals, confronts us with the unpalatable reality that one set of knowledge is overvalued and another undervalued. Foucault (1972), in his critique of modernity, has reiterated that knowledge itself is a means of domination. The indigenous knowledge of tribes, castes, and communities has been disparaged and made invisible; the written word has in effect subjugated oral traditions, resulting in a skewed political economy of knowledge characterized by hegemony of Western science and technology (Ratnam, 2011).

Those in favor of traditional knowledge being codified and integrated into formal education stress that accredited courses in traditional crafts, with master craftspersons as mentors and as repositories of local knowledge, skills, wisdoms, and worldviews, will validate and give voice and visibility to these important bodies of knowledge (Sethi, 2010). Others advocate for formal modern education as a supplement to traditional knowledge in farming/crafts communities because they fear dilution, co-option, or even the misappropriation of indigenous knowledge (State Council of Educational Research and Training, 2005). Both arguments emphasize the need to validate traditional knowledge. Career guidance and livelihood planning can play a crucial mediation role in validating indigenous knowledge and in depicting crafts as entailing an ongoing process of innovation and knowledge-building.

Appreciating the Flexibility That Crafts Offer in the Context of Volatile Job Markets

With mobility of capital and elimination of trade barriers, jobs have migrated across borders, and countries are competing to maximize production with cost-efficiency and speed. Moreover, automation and Information and Communication Technologies (ICTs) have meant that jobs are increasingly done by machines and microchips instead of people. Another phenomenal change has been the deindustrialization of industrially advanced countries which refers to a radical decline in manufacturing employment in affluent democracies from 1960 to 2001 (Brady & Denniston, 2006). Deindustrialization of the industrialized countries and transfer of production to developing economies with cheap labor and lax environmental laws are now well-entrenched dimensions of globalization. Secondary and tertiary sector jobs in the countries of the North are either being outsourced using ICTs or reinvented so that they require less specialized skills. The knowledge-based society that is emerging demands a workforce that adapts to changing markets and is flexible enough to shift from one sector to another.

This poses several new challenges for career guidance professionals, livelihood planners, and policymakers. Instead of focusing on building a long-term occupational identity and facilitating the transition from school to work, the challenge is now to help people shift from one precarious job to another across their life-span, taking employment, unemployment, and re-schooling in their stride. Helping individuals handle and face risks caused by changing labor markets has to become an integral part of guidance. Careers can hardly be planned in a volatile employment scenario and therefore "planned happenstance" (Krumboltz & Levin, 2004) and "positive uncertainty" (Gelatt, 1989) need to be included in career planning to address the disorientation and displacement experienced through job/occupation changes and shifts. Gelatt (1989) and Krumboltz and Levin (2004) have asserted that skills in changing one's mind, keeping one's mind open, and turning unplanned encounters into opportunities are becoming increasingly crucial to success. Lifelong learning is the new buzzword as international bodies like UNESCO, the World Bank (WB), the European Union (EU), and the International Labour Organisation (ILO) advocate the need for career guidance in helping manage life and work, while continuously coping and adjusting to changes in the labor market (EU, 2000; Jenschke, 2004; Medel-Añonuevo, 2002).

Crafts offer a cushion against such volatility as they are not dependent on mobility of capital. Secondly, craftspeople can alter their product range and styles using similar raw materials and their same old tools or simple machines without heavy capital investments. Intermediate technologies and tools can be used with versatility and are amenable to experimentation with new raw materials and designs. This flexibility with crafts, even though it has limits, is valuable and is more promising than expecting human beings to shift trades, skills, locations, and even identities. Kalamkari artisans in India, who used to produce handprinted and painted temple cloths, are now producing fabrics for hi-fashion garments, accessories, and furnishings, and Lambani tribal women who used to make patchwork quilts and skirts are now producing cushion covers, picture frames, wall hangings, stoles, and lampshades using their traditional embroidery skills and adapting those to modern aesthetics. Lifelong learning, which has been acknowledged as the way to survive, is possible in crafts without the dislocations, displacement, disorientation, and shifting from one sector to another.

Portraying Crafts as Sustainable Livelihoods and Green Jobs

As traditional crafts are often described as livelihoods instead of careers, it is also appropriate for livelihood planning to position crafts within the sustainable livelihoods framework (Chambers & Conway, 1992): that is, as a system made up of people's capabilities, natural resources, material and social assets, subsistence strategies, sociocultural contexts, risks and vulnerabilities within which a livelihood is embedded. The low carbon footprint of crafts is an important feature of the artisanal mode of production. Craft production is not energy-intensive and, therefore, not polluting. Use of renewable natural resources as raw materials also means that crafts are not depleting scarce nonrenewable resources. This suggests that crafts can be positioned as *sustainable* livelihoods as they have the potential to "cope with and recover from stresses and shocks, maintain or enhance its capabilities and assets, while not undermining

the natural resource base" (Scoones, 1998, p. 5). The potential of crafts in increasing energy efficiency has been highlighted by the European Association of Craft, Small and Medium-Sized Enterprises (2007) and, therefore, crafts can also be positioned as "green jobs" according to the definitions by the American Bureau of Labor Statistics and the ILO (BLS, 2010; ILO, 2010).

Representing Crafts as Expressions of Cultural and Creative Industry

While crafts have always represented cultural and creative diversity, the new labels of "cultural industries" and "creative industries" that have emerged after the Creative Economy Report (United Nations Conference on Trade and Development, UNCTAD/UNDP, 2008) are a pointer that creativity and culture make commercial sense. The world exports of crafts in 2006 have been estimated at 186 billion USD using the UNESCO taxonomy (Friel, 2012). In an age of homogenization of tastes and practices, the erosion of cultural diversity is challenged by crafts, which not only represent, nurture, and preserve our varied and rich cultural heritage but also have succeeded in using international trade to draw market resources into particular cultural regions and enhance cross-cultural communication (Eversole, 2005).

Challenges in Addressing Needs of Craftspeople

Apart from the above measures that career guidance and livelihood planning can take to position traditional and contemporary crafts as a viable career option for anyone who has interest and potential, there is an urgent need to reach out to young people from traditional crafts communities. In this section, key challenges before career guidance and livelihood planning in addressing needs of such youth are outlined.

Career guidance and livelihood planning entail an analysis of choices, motivations, and potential outcomes with the aim of assisting individuals in making well-informed decisions best suited to his/her interests, aptitudes, heritage, and realities (Medel-Añonuevo, 2002). In applying such a perspective, craftspeople must be supported in making well-informed decisions that transcend the immediate push/pull compulsions and apparent attractiveness of formal sector jobs or corporate employment. Although career guidance practice is usually based upon the desirability of occupational mobility in modern society, we need to assist young people from craft communities assert their entitlements and to examine the quality of their motivations. In sum, promote the ability to separate a genuine affinity/desire to do something new from a rejection of the crafts because of derision or despair (Ratnam, 2011).

Guidance services for those in traditional occupations like crafts is an area that needs much attention as the richness of craft and profit from craft coexists with poverty of craftspeople. Since the industrial revolution, artisans the world over have been forced to abandon their traditional livelihoods and join the pool of agricultural or other labor. This process of deindustrialization continues today. According to the United Nations, by the 1990s the number of artisans in India had reduced by 30 % (Bouchart, 1993). Though craft families in India were earlier found to have incomes exceeding the national average (Pye, 1988), the situation of crafts households has been deteriorating since the 1990s (Scrase, 2003). The precariousness of their existence became glaringly evident when the sudden failure of state-run cooperatives led to suicides and exits by weavers, which was investigated by the 2008 Parliamentary Standing Committee on Labour (Galab & Revathi, 2009).

Critical Engagement with Aspirations of Youth

While working with disadvantaged or marginalized groups like traditional craft communities, there is a need to look beyond psychological dispositions of individuals to the role of material resources in shaping aspirations (Jencks, Crouse, & Mueser, 1983). The role of social structure, social and economic history, culture, narrative, and self-perception in shaping individual interests, aspirations, and potentials can be regrettably sidelined when essentialism about individuals is foregrounded. The scope to address the needs of youth from craft communities can be greatly enhanced if practitioners draw from indigenous models of vocational psychology (Leong & Pearce, 2011) and from knowledge areas beyond vocational psychology.

Secondly, there needs to be an acknowledgement that aspirations are cultivated through opportunities in childhood, parental educational attainment, and parental career orientations (Lareau, 2011). Gutman and Akerman (2008) as well as Arulmani (2009) drew attention to low aspirations of those from socially disadvantaged groups and to declining aspirations over time among those who face multiple barriers as a psychosocial impact of exclusion. The role of socialization and social structure in curtailing a young person's capabilities and dreams is especially significant—as lack of opportunities results in disadvantaged youth not being fully aware of their potentials or their rights. They often prioritize survival, security, dignity, meaning, economic mobility, and status over individual interests, affinities, job satisfaction, and room for intellectual growth. The impact of poverty, gender, race, and ethnicity on educational and work aspirations has been well established (e.g., Baars, 2010; Kao & Tienda, 1998; Walker, Scrine, & Shepherd, 2008). Alongside low aspirations, youth from marginalized groups can also harbor unrealistic "rags to riches" fantasies or develop identities based on imaginary reinvented cultures as demonstrated by the imaginations about migration of immobile youth in Soninke, Mali (Jóhnson, 2008).

Working with youth from craft communities, therefore, requires increasing attention to the role of social structure in providing differential advantages and disadvantages to individuals within and outside these communities. Career guidance and livelihood planning need to move beyond essentialist frameworks and psychological theory to integrate sociology, culture studies, political economics, and other social sciences, which draw attention to the ways individuals shape and are shaped by social structure. It is critical that we focus on self-awareness, reflection on choices, and building community leadership while locating a young person in his/her culture and community, as was done in the Native Indians' career guidance system formulated in Colorado (Arviso-One Feather & Whiteman, 1985).

Watts (2001) has argued that the goals of career guidance need to be redefined to include changing and raising aspirations, when working with disadvantaged groups. Such an approach will help orient career guidance towards optimizing individual and collective societal development and developing human potential for the collective good (Guichard, 2003).

Understanding Work Codes of Craft Communities

Crafts are based on traditional knowledge and technologies, subsistence economies, and production systems which have been followed by successive generations and are, therefore, rooted in culture, customs, and practices. Career guidance and livelihood planning need to develop relevant policy and practice for craft communities that is grounded in an understanding of their experiences as artisans and their approach to work, so that they become open to expanding options for the community, instead of merely promoting or preventing exits from traditional occupations.

With their increasing vulnerability, young people from craft households are faced with the option of either migrating to urban hubs in search of unreliable wage employment or reinventing themselves as modern artisans and entrepreneurs. Having grown up watching their parents struggle to eke out a living, they are tempted to quit their traditional occupations and to venture out into an unknown world fraught with risks and uncertainties. More than just

a physical relocation, the process of shifting from family-based employment and traditional occupations of their communities to urban industrial and postindustrial work, where they have to function as autonomous individuals, creates much discord. They are confronted with fissures between their material conditions and their cultural codes about work (Cohen, 2006). While their material conditions demand that they acquire new skills, people skills, identities, work culture, and ethics to survive and grow in a competitive and sometimes anonymous environment, these new ways of being and working are alien and intimidating. Their cultural codes are dominated by the way work was understood, practiced, and perceived by parents who were rooted in tradition and located in the community (Nayak, 2006). These young people do not easily inculcate the calculative attitude needed for career building in the new work environment (Connell, 2001). Guidance practitioners, therefore, need to understand how this alienation could manifest in the form of anger, despair. Not being able to fit and not being understood or recognized could easily translate into inferiority and anger with oneself or hostility and anger towards the external world. In addition, there is a need to encourage autonomy in decision-making, based on a critical awareness of self and society, own potentials and limitations, rights and responsibilities, cultural codes, and material realities.

Exploring Possibilities of Non-kinship-Based Apprenticeships

Traditionally, craft learning is a long-term process beginning in childhood, through observations of parents at work. This is normally followed by demonstration, oral instruction, and practice within a close mentoring relationship. Generally, there is an insistence on imitating elders before innovating or experimenting. Women's learning was home-bound. They could only learn from their family members and were not allowed to leave home or acquire certain skills that were reserved for men, despite often playing a significant role (Rajagopalan, 2011). The stranglehold of caste and patriarchy disallowed occupational mobility.

Non-kinship-based apprenticeships were initiated during the European Arts and Crafts movement (1880–1920) and have gradually grown. Les Compagnons du Devoir in France, and the Dry Stone Walling Association of Great Britain, and others have engaged craftspeople in architectural restoration from the 1960s, helping create new craftspeople who are equipped with traditional skills and modern managerial knowledge (Donkin, 2001). Documenting of traditional knowledge and its dissemination outside of heredity groups has been a two-edged sword. While descent-based artisan groups could feel threatened by the loss of their "intellectual property," this has scope to facilitate occupational mobility, and challenge the monopoly of specific groups over skills and knowledge. Non-kinship-based apprenticeships organized by market and design-savvy organizations have been able to help artisans cater to changing consumer demands. Recognizing the growing need and demand for traditional construction skills to build eco-friendly buildings with mud, Hunnarshala, an NGO in Bhuj (India), has been training traditional construction artisans to design and construct eco-resorts and homes.

Attempts to bring women into crafts and to change their position within craft communities have also been made. Sheffield Hallam University's strategies to draw women into building trades included orienting and motivating, training, and meeting childcare needs of the trainees (Eaton, Collins, Morton, & Parnham, 2006). Similarly, gender-sensitive interventions have been made resulting in an enhanced status for women, for example, in the Toe Hold collective in India (Issac, 2005) and the weaving project in Nigeria (Renne, 1997). Clearly career guidance could guide young people towards non-kinship-based apprenticeships so that apart from learning skills from their elders, they are also able to acquire entrepreneurial knowledge and to move beyond the feudal and patriarchal systems that have been an integral part of traditional occupations.

Modernization of the Artisan

The craftsperson has been portrayed as a symbol of tradition and cultural nationalism by policy-makers, historians, and researchers alike (Kawlra, 2001; Lipsey, 1977). Unfortunately artisans have also internalized this attitude. The world over, artisans from low castes and indigenous communities need to slough the stigma of caste/ethnicity and construe themselves as designers, artists, and skilled/creative workers. This is a crucial first step in the empowerment and modernization of the artisan. As a majority of artisans are less able to assert themselves in their interactions with those who have power and wealth, negotiate a just price, communicate their wisdom, and understand markets and consumers in other regions or parts of the world, they are relegated to the periphery and margins of capitalism. They resign themselves to middlemen's exploitation. City-bred designers and even NGOs are able to coerce them into mass production of inferior goods or usurp their techniques, designs, and products and sell them in high-priced international markets (Scrase, 2003). The modern artisan needs to build himself/herself as a rational small-scale producer and entrepreneur who cleverly combines the traditional and the modern in his/her knowledge, skills, and attitudes. It is important for the artisan to be functionally literate, and to be better-versed with the markets and the political economy of crafts, and with the skills in connecting modern and traditional techniques of production. More importantly, the modern artisan should be able to question and overcome oppressive forms of capitalism that are founded on feudal and patriarchal power structures (Ratnam, 2011). The challenge, therefore, lies in helping the young artisan to approach her/his livelihood with a sense of entitlement—as comfortable in his/her work shed as at a craftspeople's movement or collective meeting or in negotiations with craft export houses and corporations.

Conclusion

New Concepts and Viewpoints: Charting New Directions

Traditional craft, often perceived as legacies of the past, can be repositioned as a creative and cultural industry for the future. With increasing demand and high growth rates, crafts can be a career or livelihood option that addresses social inclusion, cushions against the disorientation and insecurity of a volatile labor market, blurs artificial lines between art and craft, promotes ecological sustainability, and celebrates human dexterity alongside cultural diversity. Crafts have the potential to address challenges of worker alienation and disorientation, resource depletion and pollution, hierarchies of knowledge and power, and the multiple inequalities embedded in the growth paradigm.

Relevance for Multiple Cultures: Sensitivity to the Universal and the Particular

The scope for universally accepted values, such as equity, freedom, dignity, and individual mobility through crafts, calls for prioritizing and repositioning of crafts and craftspeople as necessary for humanity and for the sustainability of the planet. In this context, career guidance and livelihood planning can make significant contributions towards translating crafts into meaningful careers for individuals, into sustainable livelihood systems for communities, and into engines of inclusive growth through creative and cultural industry for marginalized regions and peoples.

References

Arulmani, G. (2009). Career counselling: A mechanism to address the accumulation of disadvantage. *Australian Journal of Career Development, 19*(1), 7–12.

Arviso-One Feather, V., & Whiteman, H. (1985). *American Indian and Alaska native career development youth manual: Leaders guide*. Fort Collins, CO: Colorado State Co-operative Extension Service.

Baars, S. (2010). *Social class, aspirations and cultural capital: A case study of working class children's plans for the future and their parents' involvement in life beyond the school gate* (Institute for Social Change Working Paper 2010-05). Manchester, England: University of Manchester.

Bennell, P. (2007). *Promoting livelihood opportunities for rural youth: World development report*. Rome, Italy: International Fund for Agricultural Development.

Bouchart, D. (1993). *Preliminary study on the status of craftworkers*. Paris, France: UNESCO.

Brady, D., & Denniston, R. (2006). Economic globalization, industrialization and deindustrialization in affluent democracies. *Social Forces, 85*(1), 297–329.

Bureau of Labour Statistics. (2010). *Green jobs*. Retrieved from http://www.bls.gov/

Chambers, R., & Conway, G. R. (1992). *Sustainable rural livelihoods: Practical concepts for the 21st century* (IDS Discussion Paper No. 296, pp. 7–8). Brighton, England: IDS.

Cohen, P. (2006). Re-doing the knowledge: Labour, learning and life stories. *Journal of Education and Work, 19*(2), 109–120.

Connell, R. (2001). *The men and the boys*. Berkeley, CA: University of California Press.

Crawford, M. (2010). *The case for working with your hands: Why office work is bad for us and fixing things feels good*. London, England: Penguin.

Creative and Cultural Skills and Crafts Council UK. (2009). *The craft blueprint*. London, England: Author.

DeGraw, D. (2011). *The occupy Wall Street movement, report from the frontlines: Origins of the 99% movement*. Retrieved from http://www.globalresearch.ca/the-occupy-wall-street-movement/26864

Donkin, L. (2001). *Crafts and conservation—Synthesis report for ICCROM*. Rome, Italy: International Centre for Study of Restoration of Cultural Property.

Eaton, D., Collins, J., Morton, P., & Parnham, P. (2006). *Moving back the walls*. Retrieved from http://ctiweb.cf.ac.uk/news/events/beecon2006/pdf/P9_Pat_Morton.pdf

European Association of Craft, Small and Medium-Sized Enterprises. (2007). *UEAPME comments on the energy policy communication of the European Commission and the energy policy conclusions from the spring summit 2007*. Retrieved from http://www.ueapme.com/docs/pos_papers/2007/070424_Energy_Strategy_final_ECOFIS.pdf

European Union. (2000). *A memorandum on lifelong learning*. Brussels, Belgium: Commission of the European Communities.

Eversole, R. (2005). Challenging the creative class: Innovation, "creative regions" and community development. *Australasian Journal of Regional Studies, 11*(3), 353–362.

Export Promotion Commission for Handicrafts (EPCH). (2013). Retrieved from http://www.epch.in/index.php

Foucault, M. (1972). *Archaeology of knowledge*. London, England: Tavistock.

Friel, M. (2012). Crafts: A hidden heart of creative industries. *Tafter Journal, 44*, 1–5.

Galab, S., & Revathi, E. (2009). Understanding power-loom weavers' suicides in Sircilla. *Economic and Political Weekly, 44*(8), 12–15.

Gelatt, H. B. (1989). Positive uncertainty: A new decision-making framework for counselling. *Journal of Counseling Psychology, 36*(2), 252–256.

Green, K. (2002, October). *A rough trade: How artisan ironworkers mediated architectural modernism. A case study of early steel-framed architecture, the 1897 Wesleyan Church, Darwin*. Paper presented at the Additions to Architectural History, XIXth Conference of the Society of Architectural Historians, Australia and New Zealand.

Greenhalgh, P. (2002). *Craft and modernity*. Toronto, Canada: Coach House Books.

Guichard, J. (2003). Career counseling for human development—An international perspective. *The Career Development Quarterly, 51*, 306–321.

Gutman, L. M., & Akerman, R. (2008). *Determinants of aspiration*. London, England: Centre for Research on the Wider Benefits of Learning, Institute of Education. ISBN 978-0-9552810-7-5.

Habermas, J. (1984). *The philosophical discourse of modernity*. Cambridge, England: Polity.

Hobsbawm, E. (1996). *Age of revolution 1789–1848*. New York, NY: Vintage Books.

International Labour Organisation (ILO). (2010). *Global employment trends for youth*. Geneva, Switzerland: Author.

Issac, B. (2005). *Challenges facing crafts communities* (Unpublished monograph). Bangalore, India: Samvada.

Jencks, C., Crouse, J., & Mueser, P. (1983). The Wisconsin model of status attainment: A national replication with improved measures of ability and aspiration. *Sociology of Education, 56*(1), 3–19.

Jenschke, B. (2004). *Career guidance challenges for the new century under an international perspective* (Vol. 4). Buenos Aires, Argentina: Orientación y Sociedad.

Jóhnson, G. (2008). *Migration aspirations and immobility in a Malian Soninke village* (Working Paper 10). Oxford, England: International Migration Institute, University of Oxford.

Kao, G., & Tienda, M. (1998). Educational aspirations of minority youth. *American Journal of Education, 106*(3), 349–384.

Kawlra, A. (2001). The tradition in crafts. *Indian Folk Life, 1*(4), 6–7.

Kirkham, P. (1998). Humanizing modernism: The crafts, 'functioning decoration' and the Eameses source. *Journal of Design History, 11*(1), 15–29.

Krumboltz, J. D., & Levin, A. S. (2004). *Luck is no accident: Making the most of happenstance in your life and career*. Atascadero, CA: Impact.

Lareau, A. (2011). *Unequal childhoods: Class, race, and family life* (2nd ed.). Berkeley, CA: University of California Press.

Lees-Maffei, G., & Sandino, L. (2004). Dangerous liaisons: Relationships between design, craft and art. *Journal of Design History, 17*(3), 207–220.

Leong, F. T. L., & Pearce, M. (2011). Desiderata: Towards indigenous models of vocational psychology. *International Journal for Educational Vocational Guidance, 11*, 65–77.

Liebel, M., & Roy, T. (2003). Handmade in India: Preliminary analysis of crafts producers and crafts production. *Economic and Political Weekly, 38*(51/52), 5366–5376.

Lipsey, R. (1977). *Coomaraswamy* (Vol. 3, Bollingen Series LXXXIX). Princeton, NJ: Princeton University Press.

McDowell, L. (2003). *Redundant masculinities*. Malden, MA: Blackwell.

Medel-Añonuevo, C. (Ed.). (2002). *Integrating life long learning perspectives*. Hamburg, Germany: UNESCO Institute of Education.

Morgan, G. (2008, December). *The just in time self? Work aspirations and the limits of flexibility in the creative economies*. Paper presented at the TASA Annual Conference, Melbourne, Australia.

Nayak, A. (2006). Displaced masculinities: Chavs, youth and class in the post-industrial city. *Sociology, 40*(5), 813–881.

Nixon, D. (2006). "I just like working with my hands": Employment aspirations and the meaning of work for low-skilled unemployed men in Britain's service sector. *Journal of Education and Work, 19*(2), 201–217.

Organisation for Economic Co-operation and Development (OECD). (2004). *Career guidance and public policy: Bridging the gap*. Paris, France: OECD & European Commission.

Planning Commission of India. (2007). *11th five year plan, Chapter 5: Rural urban livelihoods*. New Delhi, India: Author.

Pye, E. (1988). *Artisans in economic development*. Ottawa, Canada: International Development Centre.

Rajagopalan, R. (2011). *Crafts economics and impact study*. Retrieved from http://www.craftscouncilofindia.org/research.html

Ratnam, A. (2011). Traditional occupations in a modern world: Implications for career guidance and livelihood planning. *International Journal for Educational and Vocational Guidance, 11*(2), 95–110.

Renne, E. P. (1997). Traditional modernity and the economics of hand-woven cloth production in Southwestern Nigeria. *Economic Development and Cultural Change, 45*(4), 773–792.

Scoones, I. (1998). *Sustainable rural livelihoods* (IDS Working Paper 72). Retrieved from http://www.ids.ac.uk/files/dmfile/Wp72.pdf

Scrase, T. J. (2003). Precarious production: Globalisation and artisan labour in the third world. *Third World Quarterly, 24*(3), 449–461.

Sethi, R. (2010). *Coming out of the shadow* (Unpublished manuscript). New Delhi, India: Craft Revival Trust.

State Council of Educational Research and Training (SCERT). (2005). *Fishing craft and gear technology: Teachers source book*. Kerala, India: Department of Education, Government of Kerala.

United Nations. (2011). *World youth report*. Retrieved from http://www.un.org/esa/socdev/unyin/documents/wyr11/

UNCTAD/UNDP. (2008). *Creative economy report 2008: The challenge of assessing the creative economy towards informed policy-making*. Geneva, Switzerland: Author.

United Nations Development Programme. (2011). *Human development report 2011*. Retrieved from http://hdr.undp.org/en/reports/global/hdr2011/

United Nations Educational, Scientific and Cultural Organization (UNESCO). (1995). *Our creative diversity: Report of the World Commission on Culture and Development*. Paris, France: Author.

United Nations Educational, Scientific and Cultural Organization (UNESCO). (2006). *Ten-year plan of action 1990–1999 for the development of crafts in the world*. Paris, France: Author.

Walker, R., Scrine, C., & Shepherd, C. (2008). *Job aspirations of young indigenous people in the East Kimberley: Making new tracks*. Perth, Australia: Kulunga Research Network, Telethon Institute for Child Health Research.

Watts, A. G. (2001). Career guidance and social exclusion: A cautionary tale. *British Journal of Guidance and Counselling, 29*(2), 157–176.

Watts, A. G., & Fretwell, D. H. (2004). *Public policies for career development: Case studies and emerging issues for designing career information and guidance systems in developing and transition economies*. Washington, DC: World Bank.

World Bank. (2006). *2007 World development report: The next generation*. Washington, DC: Author.

World Commission on Environment and Development. (1987). *Our common future* (Chap. 5, Annex to General Assembly document A/42/427). Retrieved from http://www.un-documents.net/wced-ocf.htm

Part V

Career Services: New Directions for Practice

Overview

This section examines innovations in career guidance models, strategies, services, programs, and interventions that have been developed in various parts of the world. Making career choices is often set within an ideological climate in which people are held individually responsible for their predicament. Many career counselors are deeply concerned about the inadequacy of "quick-fix" and "dated responses" to the complex requirements of clients. Writers in this section examine the power of narrative approaches to help clients construct ideas about self and career futures in ways that are more meaningful in multicultural contexts. Over the last few years, the importance of culture-resonant forms of counseling has begun to be discussed in the literature. In Eastern cultures, traditional counselors (the wise elder, the healer, the grand-parent, the uncle or the aunt) typically use illustrations from parables, stories from the holy books, and folk tales depicting gods and folk heroes whom the help-seeker is already culturally prepared to revere. Drawing attention to these traditional approaches, the story is presented as a tool for career counseling. The role of critically reflective practice in enabling client-centered, empathic, and nonjudgmental career counseling is described with particular focus on the development of reflective skills. The section then moves into an examination of the most contemporary form of communication: the internet. The world wide web provides both a wealth and minefield of career-related information. The task of career planning can be a complex one which can be helped or hindered by an overload of this information. Writers discuss current and future activity on the web and show how its potential can be objectively optimized for the provision of career services. A specific application of information and communication technologies, namely, career development helplines is presented. Helplines provide access via the telephone and related web-based services and represent an underused potential for technologically-mediated career services. The rationales for multi-channel helpline services and the issues they raise are discussed.

In summary, this section explores ancient and traditional as well as modern and contemporary forms of communication and presents them to be considered as new directions for the practice of career guidance and counseling. Innovation is not easy in practice. Hence, the difficulties of implementation are explored and concrete suggestions for application are made.

Telling Tales: Do Narrative Approaches for Career Counseling Count?

Hazel Reid and Linden West

Introduction

In what the sociologist Anthony Giddens (1999) has termed a frantic *runaway world*, many career counselors are anxious about the inadequacy of "quick fix," superficial, or overly directional responses to the complex requirements of clients. Making career choices, at least in some Anglo-Saxon countries, takes place within a context where, increasingly, people are viewed as personally responsible for their actions, choices, and predicaments. In highly individualized and increasingly economically fragile societies, the concern is related to channeling people into short-term training or forms of work that the State and its agencies may prescribe, but which might be unsuitable for the individuals concerned. The aim of this chapter is to illustrate the power of narrative approaches to help clients to construct and experiment with ideas about self and career futures, and to think about them, imaginatively as well as realistically. Innovation can be important yet may also be difficult in practice for practitioners, in the context of constrained working cultures, as well as, for many, uncertain, anxiety-provoking labor markets.

In writing this chapter, we draw upon in-depth research that explored the use of narrative career

counseling derived from the work of Mark Savickas (1997, 2005, 2009). The first phase of the research adapted the Savickas model which was then used by practitioners working with clients in a number of contexts in England. This was then systematically evaluated (Reid & West, 2011a). The second phase of the study focused on the perceptions of the practitioners who used the model and on the auto/biographical resonances that such an approach may have evoked (Reid & West, 2011b). In using the term *auto/biographical*, we mean the way in which our own lives may affect the way we interpret the lives of others, as well as vice versa (Stanley, 1992). The notion of auto/biography emphasizes the interplay of understanding our own lives—through autobiography—and understanding others' lives, via biography. We cannot make sense of the other without reflection on our own histories, social and cultural locations, as well as subjectivities and values. The concept encompasses the interplay of self/other, immediacy/memory, biography, and autobiography, in a range of settings, including research but also career counseling practice.

Auto/biographical narrative methods (Merrill & West, 2009) were applied to explore the impact, meaning, and constraints experienced by eight practitioners who collaborated with us in the work. We wanted to examine, through their eyes, the effects of engaging (or trying to engage) with a new approach, in depth; as well as to understand more from the perspectives of clients. We were interested in the potential of narrative career counseling, but wanted to consider how useful—how "telling"—it might be when working in diverse

H. Reid (✉)
Canterbury Christ Church University, Canterbury, UK
e-mail: hazel.reid@canterbury.ac.uk

G. Arulmani et al. (eds.), *Handbook of Career Development*, International and Cultural Psychology,
DOI 10.1007/978-1-4614-9460-7_23, © Springer Science+Business Media, LLC 2014

communities, in specific guidance or counseling settings, with many work pressures and "efficiency" expectations.

The story of our research is also crucially located within the context of career guidance and counseling in the West: We explore the particularity of this but also how general issues are raised for career counseling more widely. The aim has been to consider the potential of narrative career counseling to provide interventions that are personally, socially, and economically meaningful in the complicated contemporary world of work. For most people, managing a career biography has become more unpredictable and uncertain as well as a more individualistic exercise; especially the case in marginalized communities where traditional structures of work that provided continuities across generations may have unraveled, under the impact of globalization and neoliberal economics.

We suggest that narrative career counseling is one of many new approaches that may fit into an integrative framework (e.g., Egan, 2007), moving from a hitherto dominant Western, overly scientistic orientation—with its presumptions of measuring traits, using "objective" psychological testing and matching these to occupations—to a greater focus on meaning in which subjective understanding is taken seriously. Perhaps there is a link here across many cultural boundaries.

What's in a Name?

Savickas (2011) has offered a clear definition of three types of career services as they developed over the 20th century. He explains that *career guidance* began as a scientific and objective matching project where guidance fitted people's traits to job factors, based on the work of Parsons (1909), Holland (1997), and others. Career development arose from the recognition that people (and jobs) develop over time and that learning about self and opportunities—*career education*—is a subjective developmental task (Super, 1957). The third type, arising in the late 20th century, was concerned with *career counseling*: In other words, working with individuals to identify the meaningful life themes that can be taken into a career as biographical

trajectories (that is, a fixed sequence of school/work/retirement) became more problematic and employment markets, more unpredictable. Each of these three aspects of careers work may be important. However, as indicated above, there is a dominant Western ideology here, which requires interrogation. Moreover, within Western countries, use of the terms *career guidance*, or *career education* (development), and *career counseling* is not stable and this can create confusion. The term *counseling* is considered by many to relate to therapeutic work, for which people do not necessarily see themselves as qualified. This is a major issue, we suggest, because too rigid a boundary around what career counseling actually is may close down possibilities for the counselor and his/her client, while too loose a boundary may take both into inappropriate, overly explicit therapeutic territory. In this chapter, we use the terms *career guidance practitioner* and *career counseling*: The former reflects the title our practitioners actually use, while the latter is a closer reflection of the work they engaged in when using a narrative approach; and, arguably, it reflects more of what clients might need in an uncertain world.

We should add that much of the debate over titles is linked to professional identity within a particular country and also within the practice context or sector of that country. Within the UK, there is often a requirement to develop some form of systematic understanding of professionalism that incorporates standardized criteria, which can lead to measurable competencies. However, neither qualifications nor competency portfolios and codes of ethics guarantee a "professional" service, but "good enough" training and continuing professional development is required to build relevant, reflexive forms of practice, to meet the complex needs of clients. So, when we refer to the need for professionalism, this is not a wistful looking back to a time when a professional was viewed as the expert "who always knew best." Our use of the term refers to a necessity for professionals to work knowledgeably, empathically, reflexively, and creatively with diverse clients in multicultural as well as unpredictable contexts—often in circumstances where boundaries and requirements can be unclear. However, political influences and potentially constraining discourses have to be negotiated too. Career counseling does not take place in a neutral, apolitical environment. There are, for example, structural constraints at work: As Roberts (2005) has suggested, opportunity structures that surround young people can remain heavily class-dependent which will affect what career counselors can hope to achieve, and yet these are insufficiently recognized by policymakers.

We think it important, at this stage, to clarify our use of the term *multicultural*. Multiculturalism, as used in the chapter, should not be confused with a liberal assimilation project that aims to create "insiders" out of "outsiders," through integration. A critical interpretation takes issue with such a pluralist view if it suggests that "anyone can make it," given the right opportunities: This ignores or downplays the effects of years of oppression as well as structuring processes (Reid, 2011). A multicultural understanding includes an awareness of the potential impact of *any* social difference which may affect access to resources (e.g., age and career guidance, gender and job progression, social class and education, sexuality and involvement in state or religious ceremonies in some cultures, disability and public transport). In addition, such reflexive awareness recognizes that there can be *difference* on *both* sides of the careers' interaction: In other words, it is not only the client who is to be considered as "different." We are mindful, too, of the diverse contexts—in the UK but also in other "developed" countries, in which careers counselors, like other professionals, increasingly operate in contexts of many languages, cultural traditions, and expectations. Professional encounters become spaces for negotiating the meaning of experiences and the nature of problems, shaped by culturally derived expectations, rather than the application of fixed assumptions to assumed commonalities (West, 2001).

Furthermore, a difficulty in advocating any new approach to career counseling will always arise if there are attempts to impose what works in one culture onto another. That is not the intention. Savickas et al. (2009) have offered a *life designing* framework which is broad, but also premised on recognizing the possibilities and constraints within a particular context. The life designing paradigm sees career decision-making as a dynamic, nonlinear process; influenced by multiple perspectives and informed by personal belief patterns. In this framework (within which culturally relevant models may fit), an individual's identity is viewed as psychosocially constructed through relationship with others.

Telling Tales

We want, at this stage, to explain the phrase "telling tales," as used in our title. Stories can describe and shape, reflect, and/or constitute experience. Reality and representation are not easily separated. The stories we tell, in these terms, are important, but have to be thought about: We may simply reiterate narratives that reflect other people's priorities, including those of dominant interests in a given social order. The stories we tell about ourselves can count for something: They are, in that sense, "telling tales." In career terms, a teller is someone who counts or keeps a tally of money or goods. In a narrative career counseling relationship, the stories the teller *recounts* are meaningful to them, they have significance, and deserve to be heard. The individual's stories have value and need to be paid attention to, with respect, but also with an ear that listens for other voices that may be present in the tales. This is not a judgmental listening that will *discount* stories that may not resonate with the listener's view of the world, but is an attention that searches for the, often, unconscious influences that may be placing barriers on the individual's view of self and possibilities for the future. For example, when a client tells a story that is peppered with words like *should* or *must*—who is telling them they should or must? If a client has a fixed idea of what they can and cannot do, what is the basis of this claim? It may be a realistic assessment or it can be a limitation imposed by external influences—perhaps imposed by others who have the power to define a client in certain ways. The listener will use appropriate challenging skills to explore the teller's perception of the power of these influences. Undertaken tentatively, this can increase the level of reflection within the interaction and has the potential to enhance the teller's autonomy; both in the storytelling and in future decision-making.

Our stories may be very important to us but the phrase "telling tales" can indicate that stories may be considered suspect versions of the "truth," evoking the picture of a child being scolded for telling fibs or being a tell-tale. Within narrative career counseling, however, the aim is not to recall a factual report of a childhood memory, but to remember a story, or rather stories, that have meaning in the present and for a potential future, related to the issue a client is currently working on. In that sense, the tale is a *reinterpretation*. It is a reinterpretation—because in each telling, the story is told in the light of its present meaning.

Of course, we cannot have an immaculate memory of a past experience, as the past can only be viewed through the lens of the present as well as available narrative repertoires. If stories live on in the present, the teller is constructing a present reality shaped out of past events. Used within a career counseling context, the telling— *out loud*—recalls and develops a sense of self, while the stories can be a means for building reflexivity. This can be important, at turning points, where a decision made can relate to continuity within, or radical challenge to, a life theme. In West's work on adults in higher education, for instance, stories became an important source of reflexive work as well as a vehicle for negotiating and renegotiating selves and possible *careers*, in the broadest sense. Interestingly, and relevant for career counseling, the response of significant others, including researchers, can be important in nurturing processes of self-renegotiation and in thinking of the endeavor as worthwhile (West, 1996). It should be remembered that some people often come to career counseling not expecting their stories to be valued. Indeed, many clients will arrive with stories that have been projected on to them by powerful others who may define them as simply "problems" rather than having potentially crucial experiential and narrative resources to draw on (Winslade & Monk, 2007). This has been chronicled, for instance, among young single parents living in marginalized communities (West & Carlson, 2006). So, the aim of telling stories is to engage the person in a kind of reflexive play, to encourage creativity, in a search for more meaningful career narratives. The

capacity for play, as the psychoanalyst Donald Winnicott (1971) noted—to let go of conscious functioning and to absorb ourselves in the moment, including in developing our stories in new and experimental ways—may be considered to be an essential feature of psychological well-being; as is an associated capacity to think about the processes involved, and the stories we tell, and what might shape these, for better and worse.

In the recent narrative turn in North America and elsewhere, as well as in other communities of practice (such as psychotherapy, social work, and health care) (Merrill & West, 2009), more attention is being paid to interdisciplinary, holistic, and wider cultural forms of understanding in interpreting the stories people tell. This includes integrating sociological and more psychological levels of analysis, including using psychodynamic perspectives (Bainbridge & West, 2012; Clarke, Hahn, & Hoggett, 2008). We suggest, in career counseling, that more attention should be paid to the person's historical and sociocultural contexts as well as their psychology and how they make sense of their world in a dynamic interplay of inner and outer influences (Guichard, 2005). We term this *psychosocial understanding*. This could include more sociological frames of reference (unequal opportunity structures and the sociocultural contexts of individual lives), alongside the world of inner meaning and interpretation.

The Project

Moving on, during the academic year 2008–2009, diverse practitioners in a local guidance service for young people (Connexions) were contacted by email and invited to join the project. It was explained that a number of workshops would take place where we would consider new methods in career guidance, trial one approach with clients, record interviews and reflections on the use of the approach, and later collaborate on an in-depth evaluation. Eight practitioners volunteered and three meetings took place in the first phase of the project. This was followed in 2009–2010 by individual interviews with four practitioners in a second, auto/biographical phase. Along with other reasons, primarily an interest in trying something new, all the practitioners valued "a space to think about practice and reflect on methods used." The project, in fact, provided a safe space, away from the workplace, to engage in some critical reflection on practice and self: this, within a context, where professional identity seems, as the practitioners experienced it, to have become far more fragile, as a consequence of perpetual restructuring of services and modes of delivery (Reid & West, 2011a, 2011b). In fact, it appears that at the very time career counseling has become more complex, space to prepare for such work appears to have diminished, at least in the UK, with an obsessive focus on getting on with the job (Reid, 2007). Funding, to emphasize, can depend on meeting targets and achieving prescribed outcomes. Criticism of the consequences of this "technicizing" of career guidance is reflected in one extensive study of the impact of particular reforms on the career guidance profession in England (Lewin & Colley, 2011). Any professionalism worthy of the name is becoming fragile.

We should explain certain changes in England more fully. The UK Labour government, concerned about youth exclusion, launched the Connexions service in England (Department for Education and Employment, 2000), to increase inclusion for those viewed as *at risk* of not engaging in mainstream society. There was a need, according to the rhetoric, to increase employability skills, to reduce hardship, increase global competitiveness, and relieve an overtaxed benefit system. The focus of activity moved from a career service for all young people, to supporting those at risk. Connexions services took over from the work of career companies and career advisers working with young people in the statutory sector (i.e., schools). At this point, professional status became more insecure as, no longer allowed to call themselves career advisers (as the focus shifted), practitioners were renamed personal advisers. Thus, during the period of the project, the climate for Connexions services was one where practitioners concentrated their guidance work to prevent at-risk young people becoming, in the acronym of the times, NEET (Not in Education, Employment, or Training). Personal advisers worked with other youth support agencies, similarly focused on policies of inclusion. The rhetoric was one of "joined up services for young people" and the evidence suggests that this weakened professional identity (Watts, 2010).

The organization of and funding for youth support and career guidance in England changed again in 2005 (Department for Education and Skills, 2005) becoming integrated into local government services supporting young people. More recently, Connexions was viewed as a failure by the new Conservative/Liberal Democrat coalition government and further changes have taken place since our project was completed. In 2010/2011, extensive cuts to public services and funding for Connexions and youth support services have substantially curtailed the service offered, leading to redundancies, office closures in many areas of England, and increasing anxiety over funding for a new (all age) National Careers Service (Watts, 2011). This fragile, shifting context is important in making sense of individual practitioners and their stories. Such shifting contexts, related to an economic downturn, are not restricted to England or the UK, but are taking place in other North Atlantic countries. However, elsewhere where other economies are more stable or "developing," there may be little evidence of established career services with robust and dedicated funding sources and the context for career work can be, correspondingly, fragile.

A further contextual issue should be mentioned. The existing qualifications in career guidance in the UK are at varying academic and professional levels and have widely different intellectual expectations of participants. In particular, the move to more "competency-based" methods (National/Scottish Vocational Qualifications—N/SVQ) was, in many cases, not underpinned by developed theoretical understanding. Although the current government has in principle supported a reprofessionalization of the career service (Institute of Career Guidance, 2010), it remains to be seen how this will be achieved in current austere times. The perceived loss of professional status was central to the reasons our career practitioners gave for wanting to join the project, while the professional educational background of individual participants was important in how they were able to make use of the work. We return to this issue later in the chapter.

Of course, attaining a standardized approach to qualification level across nations is exceptionally difficult as career education, guidance, and counseling vary within and across different sectors and countries. There are wide and distinctive variations in the type and duration of training programs (where they exist) for career guidance practitioners, which may or may not lead to formal qualifications (Reid & Ford, 2008). In some countries, career guidance may not be viewed as a separate role, but may be a sub-specialization of another occupation (in education, for example, that of school counselor or, indeed, teacher). The discipline within which training is sited is highly influential in terms of both role identity and professional status. In many countries, psychology dominates the curriculum for those with university qualifications, including school counselors. Thus, the purpose of career education, guidance, and counseling, and the successful use of any career counseling model, will be dependent on the social, historical, cultural, and economic contexts in which it is applied.

Adaptation and Evaluation of the Narrative Career Counseling Interview

The project group decided to trial the use of the Savickas (2009) narrative career counseling model which we adapted for use within a broad three-stage model. Reid and Fielding's (2007) three-stage model draws on the work of Egan (2007) and a simplified form is outlined in Fig. 23.1.

In the workshops, practitioners engaged with readings, a DVD example, role-play, and recorded discussion. The task was to consider how a practitioner, working alongside the clients, might assist them to "tell their story," so that both could identify patterns and, potentially, life themes. Following this, they would agree on career possibilities and related action. It was recognized that when

individuals are encouraged to tell their story, they do not necessarily recount chronological tales; they talk about episodes and events. These events are related to the individuals' psychosocially constructed view of themselves in the world; and biographical patterns begin to emerge. Identifying patterns—what can be "seen" in a story—can be a starting point to identify broader life themes and career interests. While the practitioners may "see" themes in the stories told, the aim is for the clients to identify these for themselves. This is harder than it might seem, as it is difficult to see in ourselves (as the client) what others may identify with relative ease. One of the strengths of the narrative approach is that the process provides an opportunity for clients to hear the advice they give to themselves in the stories they tell (Savickas, 2011). This is achieved through the articulation of role models, characters in favorite stories, and early recollected stories. From our perspective, the process has also to do with containing anxiety and encouraging playfulness in storytelling, in a kind of transitional narrative space (Reid & West, 2011a). Figure 23.2 below shows our adapted use of the Savickas model (Reid & West, 2011a). Our adaptation of the Savickas narrative career counseling model is generally faithful to the original, as the adaptations we made reflect cultural differences in the use of language. Such adaptations would be appropriate in any context to ensure that the intended meaning translates and is culturally relevant. In Fig. 23.3 we have provided an illustrative case study, drawing on the research material to demonstrate the use of the model in practice. This is not a verbatim example from a client or practitioner's transcript, but is presented as reflections on an interview recalled by a practitioner and extended to provide illustration.

The Wild Child: A Practitioner Recounts a Narrative Career Counseling Interview

Practitioners used the approach in practice with diverse young people in different contexts. All

Fig. 23.1 The three-stage model (Reid & Fielding, 2007, p. 20)

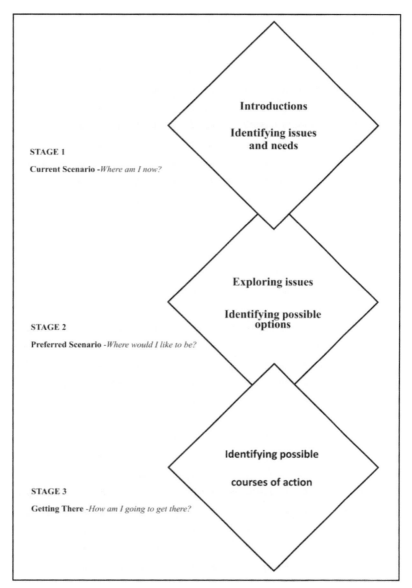

audio-recorded interviews were transcribed (and copies were given to clients) and practitioners made their own brief notes reflecting on their experience and use of the approach. At a further meeting, the practitioners and the two researchers listened to these first interviews and discussed the content. What the case study below demonstrates is that a particular question (in this case the motto or t-shirt message) can be a significant key that unlocks the life/career interest. With some clients, the questions alone can provide enough insight and there may be no need to explore stories from childhood. Our practitioners did not always use the entire model, which suggests a partial use, adapted to the particular context, is also useful.

The Analysis of Interviews with Young People

Ten interviews with young people were transcribed and analyzed, using a proforma developed in in-depth work with learners, professionals, and their clients (see Fig. 23.4). The proforma encourages a

[Stage 1] Beginnings—negotiating a contract
- Questioning: How can I be useful?
- Asking: Tell me why is this important now?
- Explaining: Format, number of meetings, note taking, and so on.
- Identifying: Topics and related issues.
- Agreeing: Aspects of confidentiality, how to proceed—an agenda.

[Stage 2] Middles—exploring the story
The task is to create a space where the person can *play* with ideas: to move beyond their expectations of what an interview should be. This can be both surprising and challenging for the individual, and the practitioner will need to be persistent and not give up too quickly. As always, genuineness and honesty are important; for example, "The reason I asked that question is :". or "What we could try here is... it may help us to think about... how would you feel about trying that?". It is at this second stage that Savickas' six favorite prompts are used, asking the client to talk about:
- Role models (3) when young (these can be a "real" person or a character from a book, TV show, cartoon).
- Magazines/TV shows (favorites, ones that are looked at regularly).
- Hobbies/interests (e.g., "What do you like to do in your free time?")
- Books—all-time favorites (could be films or other entertainment media).
- Favorite saying/motto (best describes an approach to life), could be a t-shirt message or a tag line.
- Favorite school subjects/and those disliked.

The exploration continues by visiting stories from childhood. Savickas has suggested that the stories selected reflect the current dilemma that brings a person to career counseling at this *turning point*—it reflects their *preoccupations* in both senses of the word (Savickas, 2005, 2006); past in present and present in the past. These are the *telling* stories, meaningful (rather than factual) at the present time. The stories *rehearse* the problem and can lead to insight and potential solutions. Questions focus on:
- Identifying the first significant story—what happened next (getting the detail)?
- Asking for two more stories—if the person is really stuck it *may* be helpful to prompt, for example, "How about when you were in primary school... when you moved up into secondary school?" It is also important that they know the story is not being judged; they do not *recount* a story to impress the listener.
- Summarizing the essence of the stories by turning them into headlines for a newspaper (the client does this).
- Listening for the first verb—the first things they say.
- Summarizing the stories—and feeding back actual words and working with the person to identify patterns and potential themes.
- Relating these to the presenting issue at the start of the conversation.
- Working at joint identification of the life interests.
- Relating these to future education, training and/or career goals.

[Stage 3] Endings—Having identified the goals, there is agreement on what action is required:
- Identifying potential action
- Evaluating potential action
- Clarifying the action steps
- Checking /asking—"So, what has been achieved today?" related to the initial "How can I be useful question?"

Savickas has stated that there needs to be a period of reflection after the meeting where the client has an opportunity to test the ideas. It is in the follow-up meeting (may not be face-to-face) that *reality checking* takes place—shaped by subsequent reflection and the experience of the action taken. Follow-up questions could include:
- What did we get wrong?
- What are your reflections on the discussion and the initial action?
- What are the goals now—are these the same or different?
- What further action is required?
- How will that be reviewed?
- What else needs to happen?

Fig. 23.2 The Savickas narrative career counseling model (adapted by Reid and West [2011a])

Anna turned up for her interview and I explained what I was doing and that it was a new approach to career guidance, and did she want to have a go and she said, "Yeah, that would be fine". Her role models were an older family friend who was very independent and did lots of travelling on her own and a character in a film that she described as being a risk taker, but "in a good way". She did not seem to have any favorite TV programs or books, although she said as a child she liked adventure stories, but couldn't name any particular ones. She told me stories from childhood and they were all about the outdoors, about collecting eggs with a friend and breaking them in their pockets, and about watching birds and playing on rope swings, and out and about on a farm. The stories were all with brothers and sisters or friends out in the open air, but the most telling response for me was the motto—"wildchild"! That was her response to my question about what she would have printed on a t-shirt that would sum her up. But then she retracted it and I said "but you can have wild child if you want to". At the end of the exploration bit, she got the stories, she got the headlines, which became pretty clear to me what it meant, and then I said, "So I wonder what all this means?" and she went back to, "I really don't know, don't know", and I think I said, "Well shall I explain what I see—here is someone who is outdoors all the time, in the environment—"wild". And she said yeah, and it began to dawn on her it really was a path that she could may be use in her life and develop this in a career. Interestingly she had come in talking about psychology, media studies or business studies as a university option, but she did not sound that enthusiastic. There was nothing about media in her stories, there was nothing about her staying in and watching television or reading books or anything, there wasn't psychology... but all the stories and the motto, in the narrative approach were about being outdoors—wild. It turned out that she thought business studies might be more secure long term—but when I reflected back her lack of enthusiasm she laughed. We thought about physical geography and she said "Well yeah, that sounds interesting", so we looked at how to research geography more effectively and she said she really liked Cornwall in the West of England, because she'd been there on holiday and loved the rocks and the outdoors and the environment. So we looked at doing geography at the University in Cornwall!

Fig. 23.3 An illustrative case study: the model in practice

focus on themes, processes, as well as auto/bio-graphical resonances (Merrill & West, 2009). The proformas were combined with practitioners' reflective notes: an approach that enabled us to identify those aspects of the model that worked well and areas that needed further thought. Practitioners were asked to note down their reflections, using the same headings that we used in the interview analysis proforma in Fig. 23.4. To be clear—the proforma was used to analyze the transcripts not to structure the interview (with either the clients or the practitioners).

In discussing what proved useful, practitioners liked the systematic structure that the Savickas model gives for interviewing. At the beginning of interviews, they sought permission to "try something different," which helped with the engagement of the young person. The most effective interviews were those where the practitioner explained what they were doing and why. This enhanced the collaborative process as both practitioner and young person were trying something new together. Using the opening line taken from Savickas—"How can I be useful today?"—was beneficial and differed from the more usual "How can I help you?" (the latter is, arguably, a more conventionally "expert" stance). Avoiding a checklist approach to structure was important to avoid superficial exploration: Although, a prompt sheet can be helpful when trying a new method and may be the basis for a document to give to clients at the end (Savickas, 2011, pp. 149–150, see Fig. 23.5). As mentioned previously, the language needs to be adapted for the particular context—this may mean reframing a question into one that is more culturally meaningful. For example, magazines and television could be replaced by other media and books, and movies by community stories and tales. To be effective, practitioners found there was a need to stay with the story, not to rush on to the next stage of the interview, but to ask follow-up questions, such as "tell me more about that" or "what did that feel like?" This opened up a reflexive opportunity for clients to

Fig. 23.4 Narrative and
Auto/Biographical
Interview Proforma, for
analysis of research
transcripts (Merrill &
West, 2009)

Narrative and Auto/Biographical Interview Proforma

The intention behind this proforma is to develop a way of recording key issues about interviews, in relation to a particular person, in a more standardized format (without jeopardizing the flexibility of the whole process; i.e., more open-ended forms of interviewing and bringing different and diverse interpretations into play, including our differing perceptions of material). And to explore, iteratively, themes, and any interpretative and conceptual issues raised, relevant literatures to consider [i.e., noting the academic texts that may be relevant for the insights that are emerging] and any autobiographical resonance. This would include issues that are not understood and need to be explored further. The point is to be inclusive and to use the document as an evolving text.

The Focus is on Four Main Aspects:
- *The themes*, which seem important, such as transitions and managing changing identities; the interplay of past and present; the interplay of the personal and the professional; role of significant others, transitional space etc. This section could include a summary of the themes to be explored further with the participant in the next cycle of interviews (where these take place).
- The second aspect has to do with *the process* of the interview and observations about the nature of the interaction, including issues of power etc. as well as the extent to which the process was more one of providing reports rather than stories. It is important to include any autobiographical resonance, and to document any thoughts and feelings as they arise, even from dream material or free associations.
- The third, thinking more ethnographically, is about the circumstances of the interview, including interruptions, and general impressions of the setting and what might have been happening around it.
- The fourth has to do with any sense of a Gestalt in the material: if there might be an overarching theme in building a career, shaping an identity and or in the management of change and transition. Or around the nature of the story being told. This can be done tentatively, more a play of interpretation as a basis for shared reflection.

(We seek, in effect, to identify the overall form, or Gestalt, of narrative material. The approach contrasts with conventional code and retrieve methods in computer-assisted qualitative data analysis, or even grounded theory, where data are disaggregated, often prematurely and then reaggregated with data from different cases, bringing the danger of losing the nuance, specificity and potential inter-connectedness of experience and meaning across individual lives).

From interview transcripts, cut and paste relevant (and brief) extracts into the proforma and add any thoughts on content, process, context and Gestalt. And, weave into the text, any quotations, readings or suggestions from the wider literature.

Participant's Name
Address, phone number and email
Interview 1 (date, time and place)
Name of interviewer(s)

Themes

Process

Ethnographics

Gestalt

Any other issues

Fig. 23.5 Career story interview form (Savickas, 2011)

[Opening question] How can I be useful to you as you construct your career?
1. Who did you admire when you were growing up? Tell me about him or her.
2. Do you read any magazines or watch any television shows regularly? Which ones? What do you like about these magazines or television shows?
3. What is your favorite book or movie? Tell me the story.
4. Tell me your favorite saying or motto.
5. What are your earliest recollections? I am interested in hearing three stories about things that you recall happening to you when you were 3-to-6-years-old, or as early as you can remember.

think at a deeper level, increased their confidence to tell a story, and enhanced rapport. In some cultures, this may enable the clients to be congruent with their answers, reflecting their personal interests rather than the interests that are culturally expected. Within the project, being listened to with respectful curiosity engaged shy, reluctant, or withdrawn young people and did lead to more meaningful engagement. It became clear that an over-reliance on structure, however, can result in a mechanistic approach. It was apparent that there were often two anxious people in the counseling session—the client and the practitioner—and that containing anxieties, for both, was important in how well the method worked. Too much anxiety could lead to an overly hasty and rigid approach and an associated inability to stay in a present moment to give space to new possibilities.

Our practitioners did modify some of Savickas' language to fit better with the client group; for example, Savickas uses the word *motto* which did not always work well, but a t-shirt message or tag did. Finding out about role models was achieved by asking questions such as, "Who did you admire when you were young—when you were growing up?" A real concern expressed at our first evaluation meeting was how to deal with any difficult stories that might emerge. This reflects the "we are not counselors" view of the work, alongside apprehension about relevance and boundary issues. In later discussions it was agreed that, as in any guidance interview, it is possible to listen and contain troubling stories while staying within the boundaries of career guidance (rather than therapeutic counseling) by being mindful about the role and not claiming more than can be offered. But this is problematic, as explored in other contexts such as teaching adults (Hunt &

West, 2006, 2009). Where the young person did speak about a sad or troubling event, the practitioners felt that this story was important to them—"telling"—and they, the clients, wanted the story to be heard. The practitioner concerned, in one instance, felt secure enough to listen and to contain her anxiety and to live, for the moment, in her own negative capability, or not knowing. She said, "The young person chose to tell me that story and I listened, until she was ready to move on." She did not grab after facts or certainties as a kind of defense.

Another concern was how to identify the themes. Training in the UK leads practitioners to avoid taking on a "directive" role. It is clear in the discussion of the model on the DVD (American Psychological Association, 2006) that the identification of the life themes arose from reflecting back particular words that the client used. The practitioner (on the DVD) notes down the client's words and uses them when they search together for patterns and themes. For example, the words the client uses to describe her role models and favorite books are expressed (by the client) with emphasis and repeated back to the client later; alongside similar words that emerge from the stories and the story headlines. In this way, patterns appear based around words such as independent, strong, in control, and curious.

Although some practitioners liked the very positive feel to the interview, others were concerned about the perceived level of intervention taken by the practitioner in the DVD example. This was expressed as not seeing themselves as "expert enough" to lead on the identification of the themes in such a way and (again) not viewing themselves as "counselors." However, Savickas is clear that it is the client's words and phrases that are fed-back and that an analysis is not the primary aim. However, these perceptions were meaningful to the practitioners involved and point to the importance of understanding the intersections between the theoretical, historical, cultural, and biographical traditions for career guidance and counseling in different contexts. Even where British and American practitioners may share a language, meanings (which are at the core of this work) can vary and models need to be adapted for particular cultural settings.

Savickas (2006) has stated with some emphasis that at the point when the client is asked to summarize the stories by providing headlines for a newspaper, the interview moves from storytelling to life theme identification. This is seen as the turning point when the clients encapsulate their life themes in the headlines and gain insight. At this point, practitioners pay close attention to language; again, they write down the words used and any emphasis. The method requires the clients to work in a different way to that which they might be expecting from a more conventional career guidance interview. For example, identifying role models (up to three) can involve using silence and giving the person space to think; knowing they are not being judged. It can be easy to impose the practitioner's knowledge of the role model if it/the role model is a known person or character. The practitioner then needs to wait and concentrate on what it is about the role model—their qualities—that the client finds admirable. Another point to emphasize in facilitating storytelling was to assure the client that this was not "tell me about your childhood," but "tell me about the first story that you think of": Otherwise the temptation, however unconscious, may be to search for a "good" story to please the listener.

So how did practitioners actually approach working with clients to recognize patterns and identify themes from the stories? One solution was to ask the client. As an approach, some practitioners felt this arose more from luck than design: one said, "I didn't know what to do next, so asked the young person what they thought!" Others used an explanatory introduction; for instance, "The theory goes that the stories that come to your mind are connected to the decisions that you are trying to make." This links to the concepts of exploring clients' *preoccupations* and *rehearsing the problem* in the interview (Savickas, 2011). In other words, our occupations (career choices) are related to the preoccupations that inform our career development as we grow up. The stories told in the narrative career counseling interview are not thought through before the interview, but are what come to mind when the questions are asked. They are stories that relate *at this point in time* to the career problem that the client is trying to solve. This can be seen in the sample story in Fig. 23.3. Following a summary, other examples used effectively were: "So, where has that discussion got us to?," "What is your thinking now?," and "What clues have emerged, do you think?"

The project was designed to be fundamentally collaborative: between researchers and practitioners, and practitioners and their clients. Building trust and rapport is essential in any intervention, but particularly when trying a different approach. Many of our practitioners work with young people whose answers to questions are likely to be "dunno," to coin a British colloquialism: They probably do know, but do not trust the practitioner enough to tell them. Used thoughtfully, the narrative career counseling interview demonstrates genuine interest in the person, alongside investing time in respectful listening. We should state at this point that while our practitioners all worked with young people, the approach is applicable to all ages—again, depending on the client's need.

The feedback from practitioners who recorded interviews and, importantly, from young people, has been positive. Practitioners thought that it provided a powerful way to get young people to think in deeper and unexpected ways, while getting to the heart of any indecision, as in the example provided. In turn, they believed this would lead to more positive outcomes. On the issue of painful stories, one practitioner stated, "Even when the childhood story was quite painful or negative, it worked well because they were in control—this is the story the young person had chosen to tell and they put their own interpretation on it." Young people made many positive statements, but one of the most powerful came from a young woman who said she had done computer tests before and they were "so in your face." By contrast, what emerged from the narrative interview, she said, while placing her hands on her heart, "all came from me!"

Impact and Constraints When Engaging with a Narrative Approach

In the second phase of the project we used, as indicated, auto/biographical narrative interviews to explore in more depth the impact and constraints experienced by the practitioners when engaging with the narrative approach adapted from Savickas (2009). Interviews were conducted with four practitioners. It is to be noted that the interviews were recorded, fully transcribed, and analyzed using protocols (as indicated earlier) developed in previous research. The transcriptions were shared with the participants (as were the transcriptions of the interviews with their clients in the first phase of the project). The analysis focused on theme identification, the quality of the process, the feelings and even fantasies of the practitioner, as well as any overall Gestalt or form in the material, to help illuminate some of the detail. All the analysis was eventually written up into case studies, which were shared with the practitioners, who then gave consent for publication (Reid & West, 2011b).

Good Enough Space

As within the first phase of the project, emphasis was given to taking time with the practitioners and to attentiveness and deeper forms of listening. The participating practitioners were given an initial checklist of points to be covered and an ethical code was carefully explained, including the right to say no as well as to be consulted in the use of the material. Within the analytical approach, there is a thorough immersion in recordings and transcripts, by each researcher separately. The completed proformas are then compared and contrasted. When thinking of the experiences of career guidance practitioners, but also of research, we use the

idea, as noted above, of transitional space (Winnicott, 1971). Winnicott (1971) regarded the capacity for play and creativity to lie at the core of positive human development. "Good enough" early relationships provide templates for more fulsome, less anxiety-ridden, and playful engagement with experience; for feeling contained and legitimate, as well as valued in the eyes of significant others, especially at times of transition. Such processes are not limited to childhood; they are seen as fundamental to development across a life. When times are difficult and we feel exposed, we can retreat into excessive concern for what others think, and even into fear as to how they might respond, rooted in our basic vulnerability. A need to appease or please can take over and a psychological split may develop. Thus, playfulness in professional life, with its imaginative and symbolic possibilities and its consequent satisfaction, can be lost. These processes may be reinforced in working contexts when space is overly colonized by others and their concerns.

New Concepts and Viewpoints: Charting New Directions

We want to summarize our analysis of the use of narrative career counseling as a new concept by identifying the significant themes located in the interview material. We will chart a number of themes and consider the issues involved. For example, how the project was experienced as liberating by two people; as also perplexing in relation to boundary issues; as bringing in its train reflections on the professional context and how problematic, even chaotic, these can be. And finally, there was an issue of supervision, or rather its absence, and the implications of the whole study for professional training more widely.

The practitioners said that they had achieved some success using the narrative approach, but this often involved struggle and difficulty; both professionally and personally. The results illuminated the difficulties of creating space for experimentation within particular environments, dominated by outcomes and targets. We now summarize the main themes from the practitioners' interviews:

above all, the need for creative space, in contexts where professionalism has diminished.

Liberation

There was a theme of liberation from two practitioners. John (all names are pseudonyms) talked of wanting to develop professionally at a time of difficulties and loss in his work. Of being stuck in a routine "week-in and week-out" and new opportunities had opened up via the project. Asking people to tell their story was both liberating and scary, he said: There was a fear about what might be unleashed and his capacity to handle this. But it was "liberating and enabled people to get back to basics" and think about what they wanted to do, why, and for whom. For John, it had even re-invigorated a career and reminded him of basic purpose: But, he insisted, narrative approaches could not be for everyone in a hard-pressed service; and there was concern about what might be unleashed. Zoe also felt liberated by the project and felt passionately about what she did and the need to experiment. Ticking boxes was the anti-thesis of professionalism, she insisted. The clients she worked with represent a mixed set of experiences: one enjoying the chance to talk and make connections back to primary school and parents; another referred to a history of violence and uncertainty, which Zoe found distressing. For both of them, the project represented a space to talk and experiment, including with us, as researchers, and to have serious professional conversations in a world of diminishing work satisfaction.

Context of Diminished Professionalism

The theme of a diminished professionalism was strong across all the material. Kelly yearned for some creative space and talked of the "rut that practice can become." She also complained of work intensification and the colonization of space to think. Yet, there was a tension at the heart of her narrative material, which she herself was trying to resolve: between the possibilities that narrative approaches opened up and "getting

in too deep." For one of her clients, the memory of a parents' divorce, although some time previously, was painful. But the client also moved forward in thinking about a career, and the client's mother liked it that her child had the space to talk about difficult issues.

The "real" world and practical constraints constantly intervened: the difficulty of finding a suit-able office for a narrative guidance interview, and some anxiety that people might hear, because walls were permeable. One practitioner tried a narrative approach with a broader group of guidance staff, in her training role. There was resistance and accusations of being overly intrusive. The practi-tioner concerned felt that it would have been easier to do this even a short time ago, but cuts and job insecurity made it difficult for staff to be open about thoughts and feelings. There was sadness and loss in some of the material, of worlds lost, and careers stymied.

The need to "get on with the job" (Reid, 2007) and ignore criticisms of the profession, it seems, really does inhibit reflexive and knowledgeable practice (Edwards, 1997). The requirement to meet targets and cut back on anything other than "essential" or frontline services may be presented as "common sense" in hard times, but such unquestioned thinking "shuts down the problem" (Britzman & Dippo, 2000, p. 32) and inhibits criticism. Our project provided space for some resistance, but time and other demands circumscribed further involvement of four of the eight practitioners in the research group.

Implications for Supervision and Training

All the practitioners, however, welcomed an opportunity to process complex thoughts and feelings and auto/biographical resonances. The narrative methods involved a loosening of space, for self as well as other. Difficult feelings could be engendered in working this way: For one practi-tioner, a narrative session had gone well, but then the client failed to return, which hurt and affected confidence. She, the practitioner, had thought she was engaging in something important but now felt knocked back. Another practitioner, Amy, with a more limited competency-based training felt out of her depth within the practitioner group, when engaging with ideas. She had read all the material before her interview with us and had got excited again. And yet reading the material felt like revisiting some kind of failure and inadequacy.

Clearly this study raises major questions about the role of supervision in career counseling (Reid, 2010) and the nature and form of professional training and continuing professional development. Supervision was, in the main, absent in these working lives in a country where career guidance is seen as "established"; and when there, it has often been mixed up with management. Working to schedules, or 12-point questionnaires, can be seen as a way of colonizing space and managing outcomes, while narrative-based methods open space, including for the unpredictable. Being sucked into therapy was a major anxiety and yet this potential is always there, whatever model is used. In some instances, the outcomes of greater openness and experiment were highly positive—for client and practitioner alike—while in other cases, the experience was more ambiguous.

Relevance for Multiple Cultures: Sensitivity to the Universal and Particular

We are arguing that there may be major implications here for the initial training, supervision, and the continuing professional development of career counselors in any context. Narrative methods require a whole repertoire of skills, understanding and self-awareness if they are to work more effectively. Attentive listening is clearly central to the process of meaning-making. Beyond a skill, this way of "being" in a relationship is viewed, increasingly—from diverse perspectives such as cultural anthropology and psychoanalytic object relations theory—to be crucial in engaging with another in ways that can be meaningful and agentic (West, 2009). It requires a level of openness to different ways of being and understanding by exploring the need for self-awareness as a prerequisite for awareness of others. This encompasses the auto/biographical resonance or counter-transference effect of an individual's story—its emotional as well as cognitive impact on the listener, as one life connects with another—which can offer potential insights for the practitioner. This is more than empathy or showing respect: It includes paying attention to the practitioner's own feelings and thoughts as one means to understand the other in processes of transference.

Also, it needs to be acknowledged that the perceived superiority of Western values and dominant beliefs (in much of the West) leads to a particular view of how career decisions are made which will be "foreign" in many countries. There are issues here related to the discursive power of Western assumptions in much of the literature: Any theoretical model which seeks to acknowledge and work with cultural difference needs to be built on social, cultural, historical, gendered, neocolonialist, and epistemological sensitivities and insights. Overly individualistic and perhaps rationalistic perceptions of decision-making may be at work, with neglect of any understanding of the individual in relationship to a wider community or of the spiritual dimensions of career choice. It is to be noted that many so-called psychological difficulties in the West can be considered to be more spiritual in their origins in other diverse cultures (West, 2001, 2013).

At the individual level, career counselors will be attracted to explanations that fit with their own view of the world; that uphold the beliefs and values they embody (Reid, 2011). However, any attempt to impose a model on another cultural context is unlikely to be successful. Adaptation and a willingness to recognize there may be other more appropriate models must be evident in the design of any training program. And, we also acknowledge here that in diverse situations clients may come to career counseling expecting an expert intervention. It may be the case that if they are not given advice—told what is the best thing to do—the "counseling" will not be valued.

With regard to this point, should career services match the profiles of their counselors to the profiles of their clients? For instance, by providing a black, Muslim counselor for a black, Muslim client or a match based on age or gender and so on? While this type of approach can help to balance an approach based on the mainstream values in a particular society, it is likely to be cost-prohibitive in most situations: But that ignores the greater effectiveness that can be derived from providing a diversity of provision. That said, a starting point in any career counseling relationship is to take account of difference on *both* sides of the relationship, as stated earlier, and be open about cultural issues at the start of the process. When we move from the general to the particular, what is important is to take account of the clients' views and work to their preferences, rather than making stereotypical decisions about what will work best for certain groups (Reid, 2011).

In terms of sensitivity in applying any model in a context of multiple cultures, we acknowledge that many of the approaches for career counseling assume a level of individual resourcefulness which may not be present. Experiences will be varied and an individual's capacity to effect change will be influenced by the social/cultural context within which they operate. Outside the cocoon of the career counseling space, a person's ability to make things happen in the larger context of his/her life will depend on his/her access to social and economic power.

At a practical level, demonstrating genuine sensitivity and reflexivity requires the practitioner to slow down, take time, to be in the moment—often difficult in "busy practice." Slowing down is more likely to achieve the cultural client-centeredness that career guidance practitioners often espouse. Giving a process time and living with uncertainty may well be a strength of career counseling in some Eastern traditions, drawing on particular spiritual frames of sense making (Arulmani, 2011).

At another level, the epistemological underpinnings of career counseling seem, as indicated, to require a different kind of psychology: one focused more on the semantics than the syntax of being human. Frosh (1989) has explained the gulf between syntactical and semantic levels of understanding in psychology. "Why did Jack hit Jill?" he asked, cannot be explained by reference to models of human behavior alone, but requires detailed psychosocial, biographical knowledge of a specific Jack and Jill. There is a fundamental problem in the psychological mainstream's neglect of the complexities of the particular and of ways to chronicle and theorize this (Bainbridge & West, 2012). Guidance practitioners need to understand some of the universals about human behavior (as in development stages) and also to engage with particular lives, as actually experienced, in nuanced ways. And they require a symbolic repertoire for doing so: such as narrative psychology and/or psychodynamics. Not forgetting of course, as already emphasized, in increasingly multicultural contexts, an understanding of the sociocultural and how this may intrude into meaning-making in many and diverse ways.

Conclusion: What Counts: For Clients, Practitioners, and Communities of Practice?

In conclusion, we are suggesting that narrative methods have universal applicability, but require new forms of psychosocial understanding, including personal as well as particular cultural awareness. Arulmani (2009) has suggested that there is a need to develop a *cultural preparedness* approach to interventions, attuned to the ways of thinking and being within a particular cultural context. The aspirations of people from minority communities are likely to reflect strongly held beliefs that are different from the dominant culture in any society or practice context. In the West, this point is worth bearing in mind for both newly arrived and second and third generation people from a number of minority groups. These were some of the people with whom practitioners like ours actually worked. But sensitivity to specifics and some knowledge of the internal world, and how and why particular people may tell the stories they do, perhaps in highly defended ways, is also a necessity.

In turbulent times, where stable careers are a thing of the past in many countries and the next job needs to be found, reflecting on core interests is crucial. There will be situations where a job—any job—has to be taken, but where choice is available, engaging in auto/biographical reasoning helps individuals to manage change, within transitions that are, for many, uncertain in current times. The narrative career counseling approach has the potential to help clients to "articulate their intentions" and it "clarifies the current choices to be made and enhances the ability to decide" (Savickas, 2011, p. 131). All assisted, ideally, by new forms of psychosocial and cultural sensibility. Our study provided a space to think and imagine career counseling in more holistic ways—ways that have potential for meaningful adaptation within multiple cultural settings.

References

American Psychological Association (Producer). (2006). *Career counseling* (Series II—Specific treatments for specific populations) [DVD].

Arulmani, G. (2009). A matter of culture. *Career Guidance Today, 17*(1).

Arulmani, G. (2011). Receive in order to give: Eastern cultural values and their relevance to contemporary career counselling contexts. In H. L. Reid (Ed.), *Vocation, vocation, vocation: Placing meaning in the foreground of career decision-making (Occasional Paper)* (pp. 16–22). Canterbury, England: Centre for Career and Personal Development, Canterbury Christ Church University.

Bainbridge, A., & West, L. (2012). *Psychoanalysis and education: Minding a gap*. London, England: Karnac.

Britzman, D., & Dippo, D. (2000). On the future of awful thoughts in teacher education. *Teaching Education, 11*(1), 31–37.

Clarke, S., Hahn, H., & Hoggett, P. (Eds.). (2008). *Object relations and social relations: The implications of the relational turn in psychoanalysis*. London, England: Karnac.

Department for Education and Employment. (2000). *Connexions: The best start in life for every young person*. London, England: Author.

Department for Education and Skills. (2005). *Youth matters*. Nottingham, UK: Author. Retrieved from http://pubications.everychildmatters.gov.uk/eOrdeing Download/CM5860.pdf

Edwards, R. (1997). *Changing places? Flexibility, lifelong learning and a learning society*. London, England: Routledge.

Egan, G. (2007). *The skilled helper: A problem-management and opportunity-development approach to helping* (8th ed.). Belmont, CA: Brooks/Cole.

Frosh, S. (1989). *Psychoanalysis and psychology: Minding the gap*. London, England: Macmillan.

Giddens, A. (1999). *Runaway world*. London, England: Profile Books.

Guichard, J. (2005). Life-long self-construction. *International Journal for Educational and Vocational Guidance, 5*, 111–124.

Holland, J. L. (1997). *Making vocational choices: A theory of vocational personalities and work environments* (3rd ed.). Odessa, FL: Psychological Assessment Resources.

Hunt, C., & West, L. (2006). Border country: Using psychodynamic perspectives in teaching and research. *Studies in the Education of Adults, 38*(2), 160–177.

Hunt, C., & West, L. (2009). Salvaging the self in adult learning. *Studies in the Education of Adults, 41*(1), 68–82.

Institute of Career Guidance. (2010). *New all-age careers service to launch in England in 2012*. Retrieved from http://www.icg-uk.org/article823.html

Lewin, C., & Colley, H. (2011). Professional capacity for 14–19 career guidance in England: Some baseline data. *British Journal of Guidance & Counselling, 39*(1), 1–24.

Merrill, R., & West, L. (2009). *Using biographical methods in social research*. London, England: Sage.

Parsons, F. (1909). *Choosing a vocation*. Boston, MA: Houghton-Mifflin.

Reid, H. L. (2007). The shaping of discourse positions in the development of support and supervision for personal advisers in England. *British Journal of Guidance & Counselling, 35*(1), 59–78.

Reid, H. L. (2010). Supervision to enhance educational and vocational guidance practice: A review. *International Journal for Vocational & Educational Guidance, 10*(3), 191–205.

Reid, H. L. (2011). Embedding multicultural principles and skills into counselling work with young people. In H. L. Reid & J. Westergaard (Eds.), *Effective counselling with young people* (pp. 59–75). Exeter, England: Learning Matters.

Reid, H. L., & Fielding, A. J. (2007). *Providing support to young people: A guide to interviewing in helping relationships*. London, England: Routledge Falmer.

Reid, H. L., & Ford, A. (2008). *Guide on the accreditation of careers guidance practitioners: Putting the EAS into practice (EU LdV project)*. Torino, Italy: COREP.

Reid, H. L., & West, L. (2011a). Telling tales: Using narrative in career guidance. *Journal of Vocational Behaviour, 78*, 174–183.

Reid, H. L., & West, L. (2011b). Struggling for space: Narrative methods and the crisis of professionalism in career guidance in England. *British Journal of Guidance & Counselling, 39*(5), 397–410.

Roberts, K. (2005). Social class, opportunity, structures and career guidance. In B. A. Irving & B. Malik (Eds.), *Critical reflections on career education and guidance: Promoting social justice within a global economy* (pp. 130–140). London, England: Routledge Falmer.

Savickas, M. L. (1997). Constructivist career counselling: Models and methods. *Advances in Personal Construct Psychology, 4*, 149–182.

Savickas, M. L. (2005). The theory and practice of career construction. In S. D. Brown & R. W. Lent (Eds.), *Career development and counseling: Putting theory and research to work* (pp. 42–69). Hoboken, NJ: Wiley.

Savickas, M. L. (2006). *Career counseling* (Series II—Specific treatments for specific populations) [DVD]. Washington, DC: American Psychological Association.

Savickas, M. L. (2009). Career-style counseling. In T. J. Sweeney (Ed.), *Adlerian counselling and psychotherapy: A practitioner's approach* (5th ed., pp. 183–207). New York, NY: Routledge.

Savickas, M. L. (2011). *Career counselling*. Washington, DC: American Psychological Association.

Savickas, M. L., Nota, L., Rossier, J., Dauwalder, J.-P., Eduarda Duarte, M., Guichard, J., ... van Vianen, A. E. M. (2009). Life designing: A paradigm for career construction in the 21st century. *Journal of Vocational Behavior, 75*(3), 239–250.

Stanley, L. (1992). *The auto/biographical I*. Manchester, England: University Press.

Super, D. E. (1957). *The psychology of careers*. New York, NY: Harper & Row.

Watts, A. G. (2010). National all-age career guidance services: Evidence and issues. *British Journal of Guidance & Counselling, 38*(1), 31–44.

Watts, A. G. (2011). The emerging policy model for career guidance in England: Some lessons from international examples. *Journal of the National Institute for Career Education and Counselling, 27*, 32–39.

West, L. (1996). *Beyond fragments*. London, England: Taylor and Francis.

West, L. (2001). *Doctors on the edge: Healing and learning in the inner-city*. London, England: FA Books.

West, L. (2009). Really reflexive practice: Auto/biographical research and struggles for a critical reflexivity. In H. Bradbury, N. Frost, S. Kilminster, & M. Zucas (Eds.), *Beyond reflective practice: New approaches to professional lifelong learning* (pp. 66–80). London, England: Routledge.

West, L. (2013). When Bourdieu met Winnicott and Honneth: Bodily matters in the experiences of non-traditional learners. In M. Horsdaly, L. Formenti, & L. West (Eds.), *Expanding connections: Learning, the body and the environment*. Odense, Denmark: University of Southern Denmark Press.

West, L., & Carlson, A. (2006). Claiming and sustaining space: Sure Start and the auto/biographical imagination. *Auto/Biography, 14*, 1–22.

Winnicott, D. (1971). *Playing and reality*. London, England: Routledge.

Winslade, J., & Monk, G. (2007). *Narrative counseling in schools: Powerful and brief* (2nd ed.). Thousand Oaks, CA: Corwin Press.

Mind the Twist in the Tale: The Story as a Channel for Culture-Resonant Career Counseling

Kamini Ramachandran and Gideon Arulmani

Introduction

The contemporary counselor applies the principles of the social and behavioral sciences to help people cope with or find solutions to the problems of daily life. It has been pointed out, however, that many (perhaps all) cultures have *traditional counselors* whose roles are endorsed by the consensus of the collective (e.g., Arulmani, 2009; Frazer, 2009). In Eastern cultures this could be the "elder" or the "wise person" of the village, who based on the collective wisdom of the community, personal experiences of life, and common sense, helps people with the problems they encounter. In a comprehensive survey by the Voluntary Health Association of India (VHAI) it was found, for example, that at some point in their lives more than 90 % of Indians turn to the succor offered by the priest, the faith healer, the soothsayer, the astrologer, the holy man/woman, the *guru*, and a wide range of others who are sanctioned representatives of culture, religion, or both, including practitioners of traditional methods of healing. Traditional counselors may also be a respected relative such as the grandparent, the uncle or the aunt, or a friend of the family (VHAI, 1991). Similar findings have been reported with regard to Native Americans (Smith, 2010), African and Caribbean communities (Wane & Sutherland, 2010) as well as indigenous communities in Northeast India (Albert & Kharkongor, 2010). "Whom do you first turn to when you or your family are in distress?" If this question were to be asked in non-Western cultures, it is most likely that an overwhelming proportion of responses would point toward members of the community upon whom culture and/or religion have bestowed the role of "healer" (Arulmani, 2009). The point we are trying to make at the beginning of this chapter is that while the objective study of human behavior has yielded various techniques for effective counseling, culturally grounded mechanisms that guide, support, and scaffold members of a society as they grapple with the tangles that life presents, have existed and continue to flourish in parallel with methods of counseling that are based on positivist epistemologies. Drawing a lesson from the fact that people spontaneously turn to these traditional and time-tested sources of comfort and guidance, this chapter focuses on a particular method that seems to characterize many forms of traditional counseling: the story.

A story has an almost irresistible allure. Embedded symbols reflect the human psyche. Characters carry features of the human personality. Situations mirror human predicaments. Plots portray wish fulfillment. And outcomes might be projections of deep yearning. Such features of the story offer the counselor a potentially powerful tool with which to engage the client. In this

K. Ramachandran (✉)
MoonShadow Stories, Singapore
e-mail: kamini@moonshadowstories.com

G. Arulmani et al. (eds.), *Handbook of Career Development*, International and Cultural Psychology,
DOI 10.1007/978-1-4614-9460-7_24, © Springer Science+Business Media, LLC 2014

chapter we explore how the story could become a culture-resonant tool for career counseling in the contemporary context.

We pause at the outset to outline the framework within which we will discuss the story and career counseling. There exist two well-developed bodies of knowledge related to the narrative form. On the one hand, is the narrative approach to career counseling (e.g., see Reid & West, 2014, Chap. 23). On the other, is the ancient practice of storytelling itself. This chapter was reviewed by experts from both these areas of specialization. Of interest are the key queries raised by both reviewers. The reviewer from the career counseling side pointed to the importance of creating space to listen to the stories of the client. The reviewer from the storytelling side wondered about teaching the career counselor the methods of storytelling. We clarify that this chapter does not deliberate on the narrative method nor does it concentrate on the techniques of storytelling. Our objective is to examine how the story, particularly well-established and well-known stories which are a part of the fabric of a community's culture, could become a tool for career counseling. We will describe how the career counselor could learn from the methods of traditional counselors to create channels between pertinent, well-recognized stories and the person such that he or she could find answers by drawing upon the collective wisdom of the community. Both reviewers placed this writing in the category of new trends in guidance practice! We attempt now to describe and operationalize ideas that do not as yet seem to have been examined in the career guidance and counseling literature.

What Is a Story?

There are many descriptions of the story. A definition provided by Sunwolf is particularly evocative. She defines story as a narrative, either true or fictitious; a way of knowing and remembering information; a shape or pattern into which information can be arranged and experiences preserved; an ancient, natural order of the mind; isolated and disconnected scraps of human experience, bound into a meaningful whole (Sunwolf, 2004).

Forms of Stories

Stories have been classified into types and genres. While it is true that genres overlap and watertight grouping is at best artificial, it is useful to know the broad classifications of stories.

Legends

These are stories that can refer to real people and tell of the feats, deeds, and achievements of historical, semi-historical, or mythical figures. Legends are usually told as if recounting an actual historical event. Legends often are elaborated, expanded, and sometimes embellished versions of an actual event. Legends are located in a specific place and usually, humans play important roles in these stories. Legends tend to evolve with time. Examples of legends include the Ramayana and the Mahabharata (India); Robin Hood; King Arthur and the Knights of the Round Table (England); Beowulf (Scandinavia); and Sun Wu Kong (China).

Folktales

These are tales that describe both the plausible and the implausible and usually have a lot to do with daily life. They usually involve animals and/or people in the plot. Typically, there are no known authors attributed to folktales and they are transmitted orally, passed down from generation to generation. Their origins tend to be unknown but universal themes that transcend physical and linguistic boundaries can be found in most folktales. Some well-known examples of folktales are, How Anansi got the Stories (African), Half a Blanket (Irish), Momotaro the Little Peach Boy (Japan), Nasruddin Hodja (Middle East), Stone Soup (European), Baba Yaga, Fire Bird and Vassilissa Stories (Russian), The Lost Horse (China), The Pied Piper (England), Three Billy Goats Gruff (Norway), Sang Kancil (Mousedeer) Tales

(Malaysia/Indonesia), and Tiger and the Persimmon (Korea).

Fables

A fable is usually populated by objects and animals with human characteristics and most often leads up to a moral. The fable is the most enduring form of oral literature and its transmission can be found in nearly all societies. Its purpose is most often to convey a lesson, a learning, or a compelling argument for a moral that is tagged at the end. Aesop's Fables (Greece, mid 6th century BCE) are well-known (e.g., Sour Grapes, The Ant and the Grasshopper, The Donkey in the Lion's Skin, The Boy who Cried Wolf, The Hare and the Tortoise). Jean de la Fontaine's fables (France, 1621–1695) are famous not only for their simplicity but for their multiple shades of meaning (e.g., The Crow and the Fox, Town Rat and Country Rat, The Fox and the Stork, The Oak and the Reed). Almost all Indian children grow up listening to the Panchatantra, an age-old collection of fables (e.g., The Crane and the Crab, The Indigo Jackal, The Monkey and the Crocodile, The Crow and the Snake, The Mongoose and the Farmer's Wife).

Parables

These are succinct and concise stories similar but different from the fable since they do not use animals or inanimate objects. Parables feature human characters. The parable is mainly used as an analogy to illustrate a principle. They are short stories that illustrate a universal truth. Parables tend to focus on a character facing a moral dilemma who makes a questionable decision and then has to face the consequences. They usually carry a prescription for leading life according to a certain value system. The parables of Jesus Christ (e.g., The Prodigal Son) are well known.

Fairy tales

These stories are based on fantasy. They involve invented creatures, enchantment, and magic and inevitably end with good triumphing over evil. Fairy tales tend to be a more conscious literary endeavor with a definite author attributed to them (e.g., Andersen, Grimms, Perrault). Grimms' fairy tales (Germany) are favorites all over the world and have even been made into highly sophisticated cartoon films (e.g., Rapunzel, Hansel and Gretel, Cinderella, Little Red Cap, Rumpelstiltskin). The fairy tales of Hans Christian Andersen (Denmark) have been told and retold at bedtimes across generations and shimmered on movie screens (e.g., Princess and the Pea, Thumbelina, Little Mermaid, Emperor's New Clothes, Ugly Duckling). Charles Perrault's (France) stories have captivated young and old alike (e.g., Sleeping Beauty, Little Red Riding Hood, Bluebeard, Puss In Boots, Tom Thumb).

Myths

This is another category of stories; it stands apart from other genres with its deep meanings and supernatural content. Myths seek to provide explanations of origins, extinctions, causes, and effects. They portray gods and demons, create heroes and heroines, and endow them with supernatural powers. They are usually entwined with religion, are metaphysical in nature, and offer descriptions of how natural and human worlds interact with each other. Sometimes classified as sacred stories, myths are usually endorsed by rulers and religious leaders. Many cultures have myths that are common to other cultures and contain archetypal themes and images. Examples of myths include stories about Thor, Odin, and Loki (Norse/Norwegian); and stories about the exploits of Odysseus, Zeus, Hercules, Athena, and Perseus (Greek/Roman). Stories about Chang Er and the Queen Mother of Heaven are Chinese myths; stories about Osiris and Ra are from ancient Egypt; and tales about the Sidhe, Chuchulainn, and Finn Mac Cool are from the traditions of Celtic mythology. Shiva and Parvathi, Lord Vishnu and The Churning of the Ocean, Ganesha, Ganga, Hanuman are examples of gods and goddesses in Hindu mythology which brims over with accounts of their benevolence, power, frailties, and sometimes indeed, their foolishness!

The most important point to be noted by the career counselor is that stories, whatever the form and genre, are in fact a repository of human history and experience. Bettelheim (1991), a child psychologist stated, "when you read a folk/fairy tale you enter a rich tradition that has been shaped not by one person, but by the consensus of many to what they view as universal human problems, and what they accept as desirable solutions" (p. 10). It must be noted also that the purpose of the story is not always to please. Stories can also be meant to disturb and intentionally mislead the listener (Law, n.d.). As we will see further ahead in this chapter, the story could become a platform upon which the individual can examine intentions and objectives, wishes and desires, in the light of his or her cultural heritage.

Why Do We Tell Stories?

The desire to make meaning out of experiences, to record the learnings that resulted from these experiences, and to pass them on to other generations has been a fundamental feature of human existence. Fisher (1987) has used the term *Homo narrans* to label this deep seated human tendency and points out that across time and in every culture, the human being has used the story to give order or structure to human experience and to share personal insights with others. What is special about story creation and storytelling is that learnings and experiences are skillfully embedded within the framework of entertainment and enjoyment. Stories transcend the limits of logic and rationality. They unleash imagination, create vivid images, present symbols, evoke laughter and tears, and thereby attract and hold the attention of the listener.

Stories Are Receptacles of Culture and Values

Our rituals, customs, practices, beliefs, indeed all aspects of our cultural lives are mirrored in our stories. Characters in stories depict human values

such as strength, honesty, persistence, and valor. At the same time, stories could also present the opposite of these values. Strength could be contrasted with weakness, honesty with deceit, persistence with transience, and courage with cowardice. Positive outcomes such as prosperity, well-being, success, and happiness are almost invariably linked to values that are positive within a certain culture. On the other hand, adverse outcomes are associated with values that are labeled as negative by a certain culture. An ancient Chinese legend offers a good example.

> The Phoenix and the Dragon were very dear and close friends. They discovered a flawless pearl and decided to care for the pearl. They spent time polishing and shining the pearl until its brilliance attracted the attention of the Queen Mother of the Heavens. Using stealth and cunning she arranged for the pearl to be stolen while the animals were asleep. She organized a celebration for her birthday and displayed the pearl to all her invited guests as her own treasure. Meanwhile, the phoenix and the dragon searched all day and all night for many days and nights, looking for their precious pearl. They did not give up and one day they saw the unmistakable brilliance coming from the heavens. The animals traveled upwards to heaven and arrived at the celebration. They asked for the pearl and the Queen Mother accused them of being liars. A terrible tussle ensued and the pearl fell down, down all the way down from heaven. The concerned animals flew downwards, towards Earth trying in vain to catch and save their pearl. But the pearl fell to the ground and created the Great West Lake of China. The animals were transformed into Jade Dragon Mountain and Golden Phoenix Mountain that flank either side of the lake, as a testament of their love and friendship.

Stories Create Connectedness

Stories are shared perceptions. Hence, they allow us to be connected to each other, to our forefathers as well as to future generations. Stories connect us to the natural world in which we live. Stories that are based on universal archetypes and common themes connect us to other cultures. Stories that have deeper mythical origins connect us to the cosmos and the universe. The folktale of the Sun and the Moon is an example from the Philippines.

The Sun and the Moon were married and their children were the stars of the firmament. But the sun was so hot that when he touched the stars, their children, he would burn them. So the moon warned her husband not to touch the stars. However, one day when she was collecting water from the spring, the sun touched and burnt some of the stars and they perished. The moon was so angry with him that she tried to beat him with a banana trunk and he tried to defend himself by throwing sand in her face. That is why until today the moon has dark marks on her face. That is why until today the sun chases the moon. Sometime he catches up with her and is very close to her, but she manages to escape and is once more far ahead of him.

Stories Offer Guidelines for Everyday Life

Stories describe situations that parallel everyday life. What the characters do in stories, their responses, and the outcomes of their actions offer guidelines for similar situations in our daily lives. Stories provide role models that could guide our daily behavior. Heroes and their valiant deeds could be emulated. Villains and their dastardly acts could be inspirations of what one's behavior must *not* be. Here is a German fairy tale that draws upon the universal human desires for wealth and a better life.

The story of the fisherman and his wife is a classic tale. The wife demands from her husband more fish so she can make more money selling them at the market. The poor fisherman, the husband, is satisfied with his simple abode, predictable routine, and quiet life. In order to please his wife he tries hard to catch more fish and finds an enormous, brilliantly shining fish in his net. The fish speaks to him and grants him three wishes if he spares its life. The fisherman asks for a better house and his wife is pleased with their improved circumstances. She forces him to ask for more elaborate and grand wishes from the magic fish and finally ends up asking to be the Queen of the Universe. The fish returns the couple to their original state and they both lose everything that was granted to them.

Stories Are Illuminative

At the deepest level, we tell stories to help us make sense of our world and our situation. Our existence is sometimes punctuated by questions that don't seem to have rational or verifiable answers. Where did we come from? Why are we here? What happens after we die? Why is there suffering? What is the purpose and meaning of life? Stories provide answers that go beyond the limits of logic and rationality. Made up of images and symbols, stories capture the essence of human experience in a way that historical accounts do not. The vital point to be noted is that these are descriptions of important truths. One of the key functions of myths is that they present deeper experiences in a language and form that is easily understandable. They are vehicles through which significant revelations are passed on from one generation to another. Stories are beyond the scope of reason and logic. Instead, they stimulate the imagination and touch feelings. They use the language of the common person. Therefore, they are easier to remember, understand, and identify with than complex philosophic discussions. Campbell (1972), a scholar of mythology, described the illuminative function of the symbolism of stories and myths when he said, "we see mythological characters who represent love, youth, death, wealth, virility, fear, evil, and other archetypal facets of life. As we read, we are viewing a dream-like fantasy which portrays the interaction of the elements of our own lives" (p. 56). An example is the well-known chapter in the world's longest epic the *Ramayana*, which describes the battle between the demon-king Ravana and Prince Rama's armies.

Ravana's army was made up of the best warriors and each battalion was led by his relatives and his son. Rama, however, only had a motley collection of monkeys, bears, and other enthusiastic animals. Ravana, due to his arrogance refused to go out and battle with mere mortals and monkeys and instead sent out to the battlefield, one by one, his twin nephews, his brother, and finally his own son. During one of these battles, Prince Lakshman (Rama's brother) was mortally wounded and Rama's army had dwindled to almost nothing. At this time Hanuman, the general of the monkey army was told to use his magical powers and retrieve the life-restoring herb, *sanjeevani* from the Himalayas. Hanuman grew large and flew fast to the mountains but once he was there he was unable to distinguish the herb from all the other greenery. So, Hanuman lifted the entire mountain in his palm and flew back to the battlefield. In this way, the correct healing herb was administered to Lakshman and the others and Ram's army was restored once more.

These are some of the edifying purposes that lie behind the reason for storytelling. However, it must also be kept in mind that values embedded in stories can be misdirected and can become a means of social control (Law, n.d.) Some of the bloodiest wars throughout history, for example, were inspired and sustained by myths that were deeply valued by those who engaged in such wars.

The Story as a Tool for Learning and Teaching

Across the ages, the story has been used as a tool for teaching and learning. Sunwolf (1999) identified certain stories as learning stories. She points out that the primary function of these stories is not to answer questions. Instead, learning stories stimulate questions and raise issues, rather than resolve them. Kirkwood (1992) described stories as concise, spoken narratives voiced with the intention to teach, guide, or influence listeners, rather than to entertain. It is also interesting to note that different cultures use the story as a teaching tool in different ways. We present some examples here.

Native American Lesson Stories

The custom of using the story as a vehicle for teaching and learning spans the culture and experiences of 400 different aboriginal people of North America with a great variety in their languages, history, and geography representing more than 2,000 cultures (Bruchac, 1997). In her analysis of the pedagogical and persuasive value of stories, Sunwolf (1999) observed that Native American tribes relied on their oral tradition and believed that teaching is most powerfully accomplished through the telling of stories. These stories were called "lesson stories." The telling of Native American stories rested on the deeply

held conviction that teaching is not instructing the child about what he or she "should" or "should not" do. An errant child would not be beaten, scolded, or treated harshly in the fear that it would break the child's spirit. Instead, the elder in the community would take the child aside and he or she would be told a story! The story, therefore, was used in this culture as a method of indirect pedagogy (More, 1987) and it was believed that a well-told tale would be remembered longer than saying either, "you should" or "you should not" (Bruchac, 1997). Native American stories are usually quite short, typically spanning events of the past and the present to comment on possibilities for the future. They may even be expressed as a joke, the purpose of which is not only to make people laugh but to get across, indirectly, but forcefully that the story carries a message directly applicable to the listener. A good example of a Native American lesson story goes like this.

> Only after the last tree has been cut down, only after the last river has been poisoned, only after the last fish has been caught, only then will you find that money cannot be eaten (Speake, 2009, p. 78).

This is a story that has recently become famous and is used all over the world as a slogan for environmental causes. And indeed it has a deep message for career development as well.

Sufi Wisdom Tales

Sufism is an aspect of Islam that follows a mystical pathway. Told and retold across hundreds of years, Sufi wisdom stories span a wide range of regions and include Persian, Arabic, and Turkish cultures. A particular character of Sufi tales is that they use psychological mechanisms to deliver their messages. Sufism believes that the mind functions at various levels and that a certain kind of mental activity can move the individual to what is termed as a *higher working of the mind*, the capacity for which is potentially present in all human beings (Shah, 1968). Within the Sufi understanding, rationality often becomes a filter, allowing as plausible only that which is logical. Yet, not all truth can be contained within the boundaries of logic and reason. Sufi wisdom stories are designed to get past the censoring effect of the rational mind to reach deeper levels within the individual. At a certain level, Sufi stories are told for their entertainment value. Their real purpose, however, is for students of Sufism to find the means to unlock internal dimensions, "without alarming psychic defences" (Shah, 1968, p. 67). The story is used as a tool to unlock the capacity for introspection and contemplation and thereby clear the pathway toward deeper insights. The telling of Sufi tales for the purposes of teaching rests on the premise that since they do not challenge the listener's values and beliefs, the rational mind does not censor or filter them out. The messages embedded within these tales slip through defense mechanisms and thereby influence socially conditioned perceptions and engrained thought habits. Sufi tales vary in length. But a characteristic feature of this type of teaching story is its succinctness. Here is a short Sufi teaching story.

> A seeker went up to a Sufi mullah (a cleric in the Islamic tradition) and told him that although he lived in a beautiful house and did not want for any pleasures, he always felt unsettled within. "How do I find the true light of Truth?" he asked. "What is your house like inside?" the mullah asked. "Very nice, oh mullah. I have all the comforts a home can give. But there is one problem with my house: There is no sunshine in it," the seeker replied. "Is there sunshine anywhere near your house?" asked the mullah. "Yes, my garden is always bathed in sunshine," the seeker said. Pat came the mullah's reply, "Then why don't you move the house into your garden?" (Shah, 1968, p. 30).

This is an example of how a Sufi wisdom tale jars conventional thinking and pushes the listener to view an issue from an altogether different perspective.

African Dilemma Tales

As with other cultures, African tales also include a wide variety of genres including folktales, fables, and myths. They reflect the universal desire to create order and reason out of chaos and accident (Courlander, 1975). Common across many parts of Africa, the dilemma tale fits into African cultures' preference for the indirect and courteous approach to an issue. The storyteller (an important and respected member of the community) would use the dilemma tale to proceed toward the purpose of the communication through a skillful use of digressions. A dilemma is a situation where a choice has to be made between two or possibly multiple options. The defining characteristic of the dilemma tale is that at the completion of its telling, the dilemma is outlined but no answers or solutions are given. Creating solutions or meaning is left to the listener. The characters in a typical dilemma tale all play their roles and it is the decision of the listener as to which of them deserves a reward, or should be punished, or win an argument or a case in court (Bascom, 1975). The storyteller's role is to tell of the adventure and detail the events and in the telling, stimulate the audience's interest and curiosity. Once the telling is done, the audience takes over and begins to debate and ponder over the questions that the story has raised. Hence, dilemma tales are described as unfinished tales (Berry, 1961) and tales which are open-ended rather than conclusive in their culmination (Bascom, 1975). A further objective of the dilemma tale is to demonstrate that in human affairs there are often no answers but only difficult choices. Hence, at the end of a telling, listeners would debate about what is fair and unfair, what is cowardly or courageous, or what is rational or unreasonable (Courlander, 1975). Here is a typical African dilemma tale collected and paraphrased by Bascom (1975).

> The drum asked the canoe of what use it was. The canoe replied, "I carry our master wherever he goes, I carry others who pay him for the ride, and because of me our master catches fish. Of what use are you?" The drum replied, "I am the mouth of our master and of the entire clan. I warn people when war comes, and I send messages when our master wants to speak with someone at a distance. During the dances, my voice speaks with joy and gives enthusiasm to the dancers. Am I not the most important of our master's servants?" They went to their master to settle the argument. He bent over to think but has not yet spoken. If you had to answer,

what would your reply be: which one, the drum or the canoe has the noblest work?

The question at the end of the tale is in fact an encouragement to contemplate and ponder and at the end draw one's own conclusions.

Cautionary Tales from the Malay Tradition

In Malay folklore, the fool stories that depict characters as foolhardy are cautionary tales masked in humor. The stories of Pak Pandir and his numerous adventures is an example from Malaysia. Here is an excerpt to illustrate this point (Knappert, 1980).

> The next day Pak Pandir's wife asked him to go and buy a bag of salt. While he was walking along the river with his bag, he felt the call of nature. Before squatting in the shallow water, as is the custom, he thought of a place to hide away his jute bag, full of salt, from the thieves. Of course! The best hiding place was . . .under water! He was much surprised later to find the bag empty as soon as all the water had run out!

Indian Story *Creators*

The tradition of storytelling in India is rich and of great variety. We present in this section not the story, but a brief glimpse into how the lives and deeds of traditional Indian counselors became stories that are told even today. Indian history is replete with examples of court-jesters, poets, wise advisors, and itinerant bards who drawing upon wit and wisdom communicated vital lessons. Avvaiyars, for example, were wise old women (there are three in recorded history who lived in the 1st, 2nd, and 13th centuries CE) who wandered around South Indian villages, advising commoners and kings alike through their stories and pithy aphorisms. Tenali Ramakrishna was a famous poet and court-jester of the 16th century CE who used humor and satire rooted in the cultural ethos of South India to advise his king. Raja Birbal was the Wazir-e-Azam (grand vizier) of the Mughal court in the 16th century CE. His stories reflect the culture of North India and offer simple but highly effective solutions to political crises and administrative tangles. One of the famous stories about Avvaiyar, for example, is the subtle way in which she prevented a war.

> Thondiaman a young king, eager to test his prowess declared war against the more seasoned veteran Adiyaman of the neighboring kingdom. Adiyaman had no choice other than to prepare his troops for war. Knowing the devastation that would ensue, the wise old Avvaiyar stepped into the political imbroglio and paid Thondiaman a visit. She was welcomed with all the respect she deserved. And then she asked to see the young king's armory. Nothing could have pleased the battle hungry king more! Proud of his arms he showed her around and displayed his weapons. "Hmmm," said the venerable old lady, "what an amazing collection of weapons. They are so new, so shiny, and so clean." Thondiaman glowed with pleasure. But the wise Avvai went on. "How different your weapons are from Adiyaman's weapons which are stained with blood and are marked by the ravages of so many wars. His soldiers are constantly repairing them." And that was when the penny dropped. The young king realized that Avvaiyar was indirectly letting him know that his chances were slim against a battle-hardened veteran. His juvenile lust for battle quickly subsided. Avvai took her leave with the words, "War is like plunging into a river with a grinding stone to help you float. The very rains pour for the sake of the man who prevents women from losing husbands and sons in senseless war" (Saletore, 1981, pp. 153–154).

This story is found even today in almost every primary school textbook in Tamil Nadu (South India) as are tales about the lives and actions of other traditional counselors.

Stories are part and parcel of everyday life and as described above, have been used with great effect as tools for teaching and learning. As we move ahead in this chapter, we will examine how the story could be used in today's world as a teaching and learning device for career counseling.

The Story and Meaning Making

The power of a story arises from the fact that it uses a metaphor. Stories use symbols, images, and comparisons to tangibly represent something that is not easy to grasp. The symbols embedded in stories are in fact representations of real life. For example, the coyote in Native American folklore is a symbol of a trickster, the fox in Western folklore is a symbol of cunning and elusiveness, the crane in Japanese mythology is a symbol of long life. In other traditions, a utensil or cooking pot may symbolize plentiful and an unending supply of food, a flower or fruit may symbolize fertility and result in the discovery of something that has been long awaited. Interpreting symbols and images and bringing out their relevance to daily life could help people understand their own thoughts, feelings, and actions.

Illogically Sound

When things go wrong and our well-being is low, it is difficult to maintain a clear view of self and of life. Our rational minds get clogged and all we can see is the problem. "Must" and "should," "do" and "don't," in such situations, can evoke a resistance in the person who hears these phrases. The story, on the other hand, is not judgmental of us. Since stories are not based on logic and reason, they enter our consciousness through other pathways: the pathways of wonder, of emotions and feelings. Stories allow for the imagination of alternative possibilities. In fact, when we daydream, we imagine what "could be." Stories open listeners' access to the resources available within themselves. Simms (2000) asserted that as the characters in a fairy tale cross thresholds into other realms, listeners are drawn inward, past the boundaries of their logical minds. She highlights that when the listener is able to engage with the story, storytelling allows the doors of his or her logical mind to "fall open inward," allowing the person to "dream awake" (p. 62), thereby creating the possibility for introspection that transcends the constraints of logic and reason. Indeed at the surface, in the Sufi tale described earlier, it seems illogical when the mullah says, "Why don't you move the house into your garden?" But if the seeker

were to consider more deeply, the question would take him beyond logic to the deeper principles that underlie the issues that surround the satiation of desire and the search for lasting peace.

The Larger Picture

Problems and difficulties tend to foreshorten our view. When we become preoccupied with ourselves and our discomforts we could lose touch with the larger world. Stories can take us out of ourselves and reorient us once again to the bigger world and the larger community of which we are a part. Daniel Taylor, who has analyzed the impact that stories have on human thought, has pointed out that stories can help the listener perceive his or her own position in the larger picture. A story can reveal to an individual that he or she is part of a world of other characters who are all under the influence of different kinds of forces. Helping people realize their roles in the broader story of life takes them out of a narrow focus on self, urging them toward a focus on their communities and the shared interwoven stories around them (Taylor, 1996). Let us go back to the Avvaiyar story summarized earlier. By drawing the younger king's attention to the fact that he was ranging his inexperienced army against a battle-hardened warlord, the wise old lady not only drew his attention to the futility of his efforts but to the deeper value of being a peacemaker rather than a warmonger.

The Story as a Tool for Career Counseling

The sections in the chapter so far have hinted at the many possibilities that the story offers for a culture-resonant form of career counseling. We will now draw these possibilities together to consider specific applications for the practice of career counseling.

Understanding Psychological Underpinnings

Using the story as a counseling tool requires us, first of all, to learn to analyze its behavioral/psychological structure and its inner dynamics. Let us consider four psychological constructs to understand what it is about the telling of a story that allows it to be used as a tool for career counseling.

Mindful Consideration

Listeners' responses to a story could vary. The same story may evoke different thoughts and emotions in different people. Some may be deeply touched, others may not understand the story, others may be disinterested, and still others may listen merely to be entertained. Our target when using the story as a counseling tool is to engage listeners' active cognitive and emotional involvement with the psychological elements of the story. If the story is to be used successfully, the first step is to engage the mindful consideration of the listener.

Themes and Motifs

At the heart of every story is a motif. This is the perceivable and salient recurring theme in a story. It is a repeated pattern that occurs through the story. Motifs may appear as word pictures, symbols, and linguistic images, in fragments and parts. But together they become a complete picture. The identification of these motifs would lead the listener to the meanings embedded within the story. The central motif of the Native American tale quoted earlier is the impact that human activities have on the environment: "...only then will you find that money cannot be eaten." In a career counseling session, this theme could be extended into a discussion to focus on the meaning of work, the impact of one's occupation upon the environment, or the questions that surround monetary gain and the importance of considering the larger issues related to the world that one inhabits.

Thoughts and Cognitions

Thoughts and cognitions are one aspect of the psychological content of a story. Thoughts are the result of the mental activity of thinking, deliberation, and reflection. Thoughts are related to concepts, opinions, and ideas. Cognition refers to the mental processes that underlie knowledge acquisition, understanding, and comprehension. This includes thinking, knowing, remembering, judging, and problem-solving. These are higher-order functions of the brain and are supported by language, imagination, reasoning, perception, and planning. Let's go back to the question at the end of the African dilemma tale quoted earlier: "Which one, the drum or the canoe, has the noblest work?" Finding an answer at the cognitive level would mean listing the different contributions made by the canoe versus the drum. For career counseling, a story such as this could be used to get the career chooser to begin thinking about attributes of careers and occupations and then debating the relative merits of each one. Keeping in tune with the dilemma tale's objective, a point that could be drawn out from a story like this is that a career by itself is neutral in its characteristics. What the drum offers and the canoe offers are in effect not comparable with each other. It is the actions of the practitioner of a career that matter in the end.

Emotions and Feelings

Stories carry emotions, moods, and sentiments. Emotions are subjective, conscious experiences, distinguished from mental phenomena such as reasoning, knowing, or comprehending. Love, joy, surprise, anger, sadness, and fear are said to be examples of primary emotions. Each primary emotion can be experienced at different levels of intensity. Love could be experienced as affection, fondness, adoration, lust, or longing. Joy could be associated with cheerfulness, amusement, gaiety, glee, jolliness, or ecstasy. Surprise could be related to amazement and astonishment. Anger could be linked to rage, irritation, and annoyance. Sadness could reflect hopelessness, gloom, grief, or sorrow. Fear could be seen as terror, panic, hysteria, nervousness, anxiety, and worry. Avvaiyar, in the South Indian story, approaches the young king's lust for war at the cognitive level. She presents him with a set of facts pertaining to his adversary's prowess: "They are stained with blood and are marked by the ravages of so many wars." But in effect, the thoughts that she triggered had an impact on emotions which ultimately doused the young king's desire for battle.

As the listener engages with a story, he or she becomes aware of the actions and the behaviors of the characters in the story. As the story plays out, the listener becomes mindful of the consequences, results, and outcomes of these actions and behaviors. The plot, content, and manner of the telling stimulate thoughts and emotions in the listener. These thoughts and emotions could in turn move the listener toward certain kinds of actions and behaviors. Keeping these basic psychological constructs in mind we will now consider three techniques that could be used to create channels between the story and the person for practice of culture-resonant career counseling.

Technique 1: Guided Deliberation

It has been pointed out earlier in the chapter that a story is not the result of a single person's conjecture. It has emerged from the distillation of human experience and rests upon the consensus of the members of the community (Bettelheim, 1991). It is these kinds of stories that the career counselor should search for, identify, and collect. Stories that are already accepted by a community as a part of its fabric would have a higher power of influence. A critical point to be noted is that it may not be the story itself that influences the person, but the thinking and feeling that results from the telling of the story and the ideas and arguments that emerge after exposure to a story (Sunwolf, 1999).

Listening to a story would generate thoughts and emotions within the listener. If unguided, the thoughts and emotions that arise would be random and arbitrary and dissipate after a while. However, when provided with a thematic frame of reference, thoughts and emotions that arise would be within that frame. This material could be garnered by the career counselor and used to promote deeper insights. Given here is an excerpt from an interaction with 39-year-old Indian female employee of a large information technology company, who was doing well at her career but was quite unhappy within herself. This person came from a Muslim background and hence the Sufi wisdom tale recounted above was used with her. She was asked to reflect upon the motifs of the "beautiful house" and "sunshine." Here is a brief glimpse into the interaction between the woman and the counselor (Arulmani, 2006). This is an abbreviated version of the interaction and only aspects that serve to illustrate the point being made in this section are reported.

Client: Yes! That's a story my father has often told me. It rings many bells. Ah! Such memories! But I never thought about it from the work angle.

Counselor: Use the images of the "beautiful house" and the image of "sunshine" to reflect upon the unhappiness you are experiencing with your work.

Client: I have been at this job for 12 years or so. I have done well. In fact I have been able to build my own beautiful house! But the story makes me think. My "career house" is not so beautiful. It has everything... money, position and all the perks. But the sunshine's not there.

Counselor: Let's talk some more about the sunshine. What are the thoughts that come into your mind and the feelings you experience when you think about sunshine?

Client: I came into information technology because it was the thing to do. In the beginning all seemed fine. But even then this job really wasn't me. I don't really like programming and as the days went on I found the people I worked with were also not my sort. My real desire was to be a jewelry designer. I do that on the side as a sort of hobby when my job gets too much! This story seems to tell me that jewelry designing is the sunshine in my garden! I want to move my house into the sunshine in my garden! But how will I make such a shift? Is there a way to do that?

Shortly after this, the counseling interactions moved on to the specifics of making a career shift. The point to be noted is that the telling of this story triggered old and pleasant memories and offered insights that were helpful to the client. It is also possible that stories trigger unpleasant memories. This too could be offered as material to promote insights.

Guided deliberation: counseling watchpoints. Here are some points to consider when using guided deliberation in career counseling:

- Select a story that has close resonance with the individual's situation and cultural background.
- Identify motifs in the story that can be linked to the client's situation.
- Outline a frame for deliberation within which the client could engage with the story. In the case of the woman from the information technology company, the client's unhappiness with her career was used as the frame for deliberation.
- Guide deliberation such that focus is brought to bear upon thoughts and emotions that emerge in relation to the identified motifs.
- Use the material that emerges from the deliberation to help the client move toward resolution.

Technique 2: Stories as Vicarious Learning

The term *vicarious* refers to imaginary experiences a person can have when exposed to the actions of another person. If one were to observe someone (a role model) similar to oneself succeed by consistent effort, this observation would raise that person's belief that he or she too can master similar activities (Bandura, 1995). In the same way, observations of others' failures despite strong efforts undermine observers' judgment of their own efficacy. The greater the real or assumed similarity of the model to the observer, the more powerful will be the impact of the model's success/failure on the observer

(Bandura, 1995). Stories break boundaries. Through stories we can walk beside gods and deities, heroes and heroines, as well as hold hands with people just like ourselves. When a character in a story suffers an injustice or struggles in a way similar to what we experience, we indirectly feel that somehow our own difficulties have meaning and personal pains and disappointments may become more bearable. Stories are powerful vehicles for the facilitation of vicarious learning experiences.

Thoughts-emotions-outcomes. Human behavior is the totality of responses or reactions made by a person or a group of persons in any situation. The cognitive-behavioral theories propounded by Aaron Beck (Beck, Rush, Shaw, & Emery, 1979) and Albert Ellis (1994), and their colleagues are based on the observation that underlying cognitive (thinking) patterns play a definitive role in influencing behavior. Thoughts, emotions, and outcomes (behavior) are described as interlocking variables. The origin of a behavior accordingly is traced to the kind of thought patterns that have become habitual in a person's mind. A requirement or situation in one's life triggers a thought pattern. The thought pattern leads to the experience of a certain type of emotion. This emotion triggers a particular action or behavioral response. Therefore, just behind a person's behavior are emotions and behind the emotions are thought patterns.

Cognitive-behavioral theorists further hold that inaccurate perceptions and distortions of reality lead to systematic biases in the interpretation of experiences causing errors in cognition (thinking). These cognitive errors are also called cognitive distortions (Beck et al., 1979). Cognitive distortions become automatic and the person is unaware of their operation. Behavior, according to this perspective, is the outcome of internally occurring, automatic, and habitual mindsets, thinking patterns, schema, and beliefs. Here is an illustration: A 17-year-old student who was completing higher secondary education in about 3 months requested to be seen individually, after she had participated in group career counseling workshops held routinely for her class. During the first session, she indicated that

Table 24.1 Extracts from a career beliefs diary

Date	Activity	Thought	Emotion	Outcomes
14 Jan 2010	Read about entrance examination to design school	Oh God! I have to prepare a portfolio	My work is not good to be shown to others	Stopped thinking about design as a career
15 Jan 2010	Completed Art Class record books for internal assessment	I will not get good marks	Felt so scared that I will fail	Didn't submit the book to teacher
16 Jan 2010	Have to go to principal for certificate to submit to design school	He will say he won't give a certificate	Everyone says I'm good, but I know I'm not...it's no use	Postponed going to principal

although a number of friends, teachers, and parents suggested that she selects careers in the field of design, she was still very confused. In keeping with the methods suggested by Cognitive Behavioral Therapy, she was asked to start a diary. Given in Table 24.1 is an extract of a few entries from her diary (Arulmani, 2010). The entries in the diary illustrate how thoughts can become habits. Quite often it is not events that upset us but our perception of these events. Our thoughts can be a filter through which we interpret and give meaning to events. Thought-emotion-action sequences that people are habituated to, can influence their belief in personal efficacy to manage life's demands which in turn affects psychological well-being, accomplishments, and the general direction their lives take.

Thoughts-emotions-outcomes in stories. Thoughts, emotions, and behaviors are the material with which the counselor works. At the heart of almost all stories are thoughts and beliefs, emotions and feelings which in turn reflect in behaviors and actions. Identifying the thought-emotion-action sequences in a story is a powerful means of creating insights into personal states of mind and behaviors. When a story is interpreted to a listener in this manner, he or she could learn more about the reasons behind his or her own actions. Let us now attempt to apply this idea at the level of practical career counseling.

The story we are using as an illustration is an episode from the Ramayana: how Rama (the crown prince) won the hand of the beautiful princess, Sita. Box 24.1 provides a worksheet that could be used for this exercise. In the worksheet in the example provided was completed by a 31-year-old Indian female employee of an advertising firm, who was doing well at some of her job requirements but not so well at other tasks. She came from a traditional Hindu background and hence, the Ramayana was used in the interaction with her. This is an abbreviated version of the interaction and only aspects that serve to illustrate the point being made in this section are reported (Arulmani, 2006). Text that has been italicized in the table represents material that the client had entered. In an unused worksheet, these parts of the table would be left blank for the client to fill in.

This was the first session with the client. The content of the interactions thereafter focused more closely on helping the client understand how her negative thinking affected her emotions and ultimately her performance at work. Other stories were used and the client was also encouraged to bring stories to the sessions that paralleled her situation.

Vicarious learning: counseling watch-points. Here are some points to consider when using vicarious experience as a technique in career counseling:

- Prepare a worksheet similar to the illustration in Box 24.1.
- Orient the client, with examples, to the manner in which thoughts, emotions, and actions reciprocally influence each other. It is important that this concept is clearly understood, if the method is to be effective. Hence, include this as a brief write-up in the worksheet (see Note to Counselor in Box 24.1).
- Give the background, set the context, and then tell the story.

Box 24.1: A Sample Worksheet Using Principles from Cognitive Behavioral Therapy

The Story Behind Your Actions!

Thoughts, Emotions, and Actions: What Are They and How Are They Related?
Note to counselor: As in the text of the chapter, provide information here on thoughts, emotions and actions, and their interactions.

Rama Wins Sita's Hand: An Episode from the Ramayana
Sage Vishwamitra (the most famous guru and teacher of the time) took Rama and Lakshmana (Rama's brother) to the City of Mithila to King Janaka's royal court. The King had an only daughter, Sita, and he was looking for a perfect husband for Sita. In the royal palace was an enormous bow belonging to Lord Shiva (one of the most powerful gods in the Hindu pantheon). Nobody had been able to lift the bow let alone string it. The man who could do so would win the hand of Sita. Bewitched by Sita's beauty, many, many princes, kings, emperors, and warriors had come to try and lift this bow, but they had all failed. When Rama arrived at Mithila Palace, he calmly walked up to the bow, lifted it easily, strung it, and broke it in two! The crowd was overjoyed and cheered Rama as he won Sita's hand in marriage. Their wedding was a wonderful celebration and Rama returned to Ayodhya, his kingdom, with his bride Sita by his side.

Thoughts-Emotions-Outcomes
Use the table below to look behind Rama's success. What do you think would have been the thoughts and emotions Rama experienced?

Requirement	Thoughts	Emotions	Outcome
Prove he is worthy of Sita's hand	*I can do this. It's easy. The gods are on my side!*	*Confident; focused; anti-cipating success*	Picked up the bow and broke it into two pieces

Consider the *successes* you are experiencing at work. Start with your actions and work backwards to trace the links with your emotions and thoughts.

Requirement	Thoughts	Emotions	Outcome
Train junior team members	*I'm good at this; I have always been a success*	*Confident; happy to do this task; motivated*	Successful at training juniors

Consider the *difficulties* you are experiencing at work. Start with your actions and work backwards to trace the links with your emotions and thoughts.

Requirement	Thoughts	Emotions	Outcome
Making presentations to clients	*My last presentation was bad! This is not my strength at all*	*Nervous; uncertain; not confident; low motivation*	Presen-tations not effective

How could you *change* your thinking in order to be successful?

Requirement	Thoughts	Emotions	Outcome
Making presentations to clients	*Let me prepare well. I must crack this like Lord Rama did!*	*Still a bit nervous; but more hopeful and motivated*	Better presentation

- As with the earlier example, select stories that have close resonance with the individual's situation and cultural background; identify motifs in the story that can be linked to the client's situation.
- Provide the client with a template to maintain a daily diary as shown in Table 24.1. Instruct the client to log daily experiences into the diary and to bring the diary to the counseling sessions. Discuss and interpret the material that the client has recorded.
- As counseling moves on, take care to draw the client's attention back to the character/s or aspects of the story that carry the main message. In this case, the client's attention was brought back to Rama's success: *I must crack this like Lord Rama did!*
- Be prepared with fresh stories to reinforce the client's learning.
- Encourage the client to search for stories that he/she feels are relevant to his/her situation and bring them to the counseling sessions for discussion.

Technique 3: Framing and Reframing

The story when used for entertainment only requires the listener to sit back and enjoy the telling. Our objective in using the story goes much beyond and aims at deeper issues such as attitude change, decision making, and helping the individual find solutions. The impact is likely to be stronger when the listener is not merely the passive recipient of a story. The active involvement of the listener is known to engender more lasting effects than if the teller of the tale supplies the correct reasoning and answer (Sunwolf, 1999). Framing and reframing a story is an exercise that requires the listener to play a more active and self-mediated role. This exercise will use a famous story from the Panchatantra (an ancient Indian compendium of animal fables): The Indigo Jackal. See Appendix for the complete story as retold by Ramachandran (2011).

Framing the story. The first step when using this method is for the counselor to clearly delineate the story's plot. A story plot describes a series of circumstances befalling a set of characters with a fairly clear sense of a beginning and an end, linked together by a cohesive narrative. The counselor is required to identify the central motif and theme of the story and establish its relevance to the issue. The next step is to frame the story. This means, reducing the story to its outline and its key points. Ideally, the reframed story should be condensed to 10–12 points. The first point should highlight the beginning and the last point should depict the final outcome of the story. Framing the story is an activity that the counselor completes before the interaction with the listener. Table 24.2 (column 1) illustrates the framing of the Indigo Jackal story. Having framed the story, the counselor tells the entire, unedited story to the whole group. It would be particularly effective if the listener (or one of the members of the group) told or read the story.

Table 24.2 A sample worksheet to illustrate the reframing technique

Original outline	What if?	How does it matter to me?
Dark cold night; no food	Dark cold night; no food	*Unhappy with studies; criticized by all for my poor performance*
Attacked by dogs; ran away	*Attacked but did not run away*	*Rather than withdraw, try to face the criticism*
Covered by indigo dye; discovered a suitable identity	*Used intelligence; apologized and argued his way out*	*Work out why I don't want to study this course*
Dogs ran away; other animals terrified	*Made friends*	*Write to my father and mother; meet and explain to them*
Became the king of the forest on pretenses	*No need to change; does not become king; won acceptance*	*Get details about the course I want to study and explain to my parents*
Comfortable; got everything he wanted	*Comfortable; because remained true to self*	*This way I will be able to satisfy my wishes; try not to offend family*
Desire to be a jackal; howled with the jackals	*Used his talents for self and others*	*Plug into what I am good at and like doing*
True identity revealed	*Identity grew stronger*	*I will be myself*
Torn to pieces; lost everything	Recognized for true qualities and therefore became king	*Be happy with my studies and my career development*

Reframing the story. One of the key objectives of using the story in counseling is to unveil new pathways and point to fresh perspectives. It is to achieve this objective that the technique of reframing is used. Once the listener has completely understood the story, the counselor is to draw the listener's attention to the story outline. This is the stage at which the listener's active participation begins. Reframing comprises changing the *outcome* of the story to a different conclusion, while no changes are made to the *beginning* of the story. As indicated by the non-italicized text in Table 24.2 (column 2), the counselor is to point out the situation at the beginning of the story: *dark cold night; no food* and the changed outcome at the end: *recognized for true qualities and therefore became king*. A discussion could be stimulated to highlight contrast between the conclusion in the original story outline and the changed outcome. In effect, the context and the circumstances remain the same, while the outcome is different. The exercise the listener is to engage in, is to ask the question "what if" (Table 24.2, column 2) and imagine events that could lead up to this new outcome. In other words, the listener applies his or her mind to reframe the story and propose changes in

behavior that could culminate in a new and different outcome.

Transpose to real life. Reframing is connected to the characters and plot of the original story. Still in the realm of fantasy and imagination, changes that are projected may be far removed from the client's real life situation. Reframing rests on the understanding that it is an intermediate stage in the counseling process before the client begins to become personally involved with the change process. Reframing is a simulation of real events and situations and helps the client project, create, and imagine the steps to a new and better outcome. We have found, when using stories for career counseling, that reframing is an effective way to help a career chooser learn about his or her thoughts, perceptions, and unexpressed feelings about matters related to career choice and development (Arulmani, 2006). Of particular importance is the fact that reframing offers a convenient psychological distance and prepares the individual to confront the difficulties that he or she is facing in real life (Arulmani, 2010). Once the client has become comfortable with the process, the counseling objective is to help the client use the images, symbols, and messages embedded in the story to resolve the issues he or she is facing. Career counseling, therefore, moves to the third step in the process: transposition of the story to real life. In effect, the client begins to ask himself/herself, "How does this matter to me?" As illustrated in Table 24.2 (column 3), the beginning of the story is recast to link more directly with the client's situation: *unhappy with studies*; *criticized by all for my poor performance*. The outcome is also recast to project what the client would like to happen in his or her life: *be happy with my studies and my career development*. The client and counselor then work collaboratively, against the backdrop of the story, to delineate the steps that could be taken to achieve the outcome desired by the client. These steps then become a guideline for the action to be taken by the client.

The example in Table 24.2 is a worksheet completed by a 21-year-old Indian male student in the first year of Bachelor's program in Engineering. He had taken up the course to please his parents and was deeply unhappy and uninterested in the course. Although he was doing poorly in the course, he was still trying to please his parents. But in real life, he had withdrawn from interacting with them. He was well acquainted with the Panchatantra and hence, the Indigo Jackal story was used with him (Arulmani, 2006). This is an abbreviated version of the interaction and only aspects that serve to illustrate the point being made in this section are reported. Text that has been italicized in the table represents material that the client recorded.

Reframing: counseling watch-points. Keep the following in mind when using reframing as a technique in career counseling:

- Select a story and prepare a worksheet similar to the illustration in Table 24.2.
- As with the earlier examples, it is essential that the story selected has close resonance with the individual's situation and cultural background.
- Frame the story in up to 10–12 steps and keep it ready.
- Give the background, set the context, and then tell the unedited story. Alternatively, the client could read and then tell the story.

- Now share the story outline with the client. Alternatively, the client and the counselor could work together to frame the story and develop the outline.
- Point out the situation at the beginning and the end (the outcome).
- In consultation with the client, change the outcome, keeping the beginning unchanged.
- Ask the client to reframe the story by working out the steps to reach the new outcome; discuss the steps that the client outlines.
- Move to transposing the images and messages in the story to the client's real life situation, by asking the client to reframe the beginning of the story to link more directly with his or her situation. Also, ask the client to redefine the outcome and to articulate what the client would like to happen in his or her life.
- Work collaboratively with the client to reframe the story and describe the actions that could be taken to achieve the outcome that the client has envisaged. The main task is to experiment with making modifications within the plot to alter the outcome of the client's story.
- Point out how these steps are the guideline for the action to be taken by the client.
- As counseling moves on, take care to draw the client's attention back to the character/s or aspects of the story that carry the main message.
- Follow up in further sessions as to how the client progresses with the guidelines developed from the story. Be prepared to make alterations in the guidelines. Support the client until the issue is resolved.

Stories could be used as a career counseling tool at the individual and group levels. The key difference between individual and group career counseling is that the group intervention is preplanned and based on the counselor's knowledge of a "common" need. Therefore, while at the individual level counseling is focused on personal, individualized scripts, at the group level, counseling is concentrated on socially shared cognitions, emotions, motives, and meanings. Each of the three techniques described in this chapter could be adapted for group workshops that target needs which are shared by a group of individuals.

Conclusion

Relevance for Multiple Cultures: Sensitivity to the Universal and the Particular

The learning that occurs between an individual and his or her culture is drawn from a storehouse of experience that has accumulated and grown over the ages. The story evolved within all human societies as the articulation of experiences and occurrences, incidents and encounters, imagination and inspiration, thoughts, ideas, and beliefs about what was, what is, and what is going to be. Only at the most superficial level is the story a medium of entertainment. Stories are in fact repositories of culture, describing ways of living. They are commentaries on social values defining codes of behavior. They are documents of history, recording the vagaries of humankind's journey. They are receptacles of collective human wisdom. Moreover, the commonalities of mythologies and folklore across cultures are intriguing. This has perhaps prompted psychologists to point out that a fundamental character of the story is that it is closely connected to deeper psychological forces (e.g., Jung, 1964). The story, therefore, could perhaps be described as a feature that characterizes human society as a whole. In this sense, the story spans all cultures demonstrating its universal nature. At the same time, every story has its culture-specific dimension, whereby meaning emerges from the manner in which a story is interpreted and this could vary from one context to another. A story with a theme that spans multiple cultures can be understood in a very personal way, just as the voices in a story with a specific theme can be amplified to be heard across multiple cultures. It must be noted that sometimes the values depicted in stories may not reflect current values. Many stories are gender-stereotyped or promote typically patriarchal ways. As illustrated in the technique of reframing,

these are opportunities to stimulate reflection and deliberately adopt a different set of values. Of relevance to career counseling is the fact that in today's multicultural societies, there is a high likelihood of counselor and counselee coming from differing cultural contexts, each influenced and guided by their own orientations to work and career. A characteristic of the story is that it does not demand acceptance and that it has the potential to connect the universal with the particular. Hence, stories could be a highly effective means of coming close to the psychological dynamics that are at play in the lives of our clients. We extend this point, to highlight the possibility that the story could in fact be a bridge between career counselor and client who each come from different cultural backgrounds. Indeed, by using the story we are drawing upon one of the oldest forms of counseling, one that offers the possibility of interpreting universal themes into local contexts and at the same time of extending culture-specific themes to broader contexts.

New Concepts and Viewpoints: Charting New Directions

We began this chapter began by pointing out that counseling, as it is most commonly practiced today, emerged within Western cultures and to that extent the methods and techniques of counseling are largely attuned to Western ways of life. Today, the relevance of these models and techniques to contexts outside which they were developed is being increasingly questioned (e.g., Reese & Vera, 2007). Hence, over the last few years, the importance of culture-resonant forms of counseling has begun to be increasingly discussed in the literature. The story has been used across the ages and across cultures as a teaching–learning tool as well as a form of counseling by traditional counselors. In Eastern cultures, the central function of storytelling is not amusement. Traditional counselors typically use illustrations from parables, stories from the holy books and folktales that depict the gods, folk heroes, and other characters whom the help-seeker is already culturally prepared to revere and respect. In these interactions, the attention of the help-seeker is drawn to how the characters in the stories deal with life's vicissitudes and the help-seeker is exhorted to emulate them. It is to this Eastern practice of directing the help seeker's attention to the collective wisdom of his or her community, that we draw the contemporary career counselor's attention. Traditional counselors use the story to lift the help-seeker above the strictures of logic, reason, and causality. Taking a leaf out of the traditional counselor's approach, we propose that creating a channel between the person and an appropriate traditional story has the potential to effectively touch the person, inform the person, and create an environment wherein the person does not merely identify solutions but constructs them within the fabric of his or her culture.

In this chapter we have demonstrated how the story can be used for contemporary career counseling. If the techniques presented above are to be effective, it is critical that the listener is able to identify with the stories being used. We, therefore, conclude by highlighting an obvious but essential point. To use the story as a part of his or her work, the career counselor must be committed to story collection! As is clear from this writing, individuals differ from each other with regard to their needs. These needs are further qualified by the culture of which the individual is a part. Hence, it is essential that the story telling career counselor has a wide collection of stories in his or her repertoire. While story collection is important, it is perhaps even more important that the counselor is fluent in the telling of the story. A story can have many themes. Being able to emphasize the motif that is appropriate to the situation is a fundamental skill that the career counselor must perfect! Indeed it is the skill of being able to *mind the twist in the tale* that lies at the heart of successful story telling for career counseling.

Appendix

The Indigo Jackal: A story from the Panchatantra adapted by: Kamini Ramachandran, MoonShadow Stories, Singapore.

Once, on a dark, cold winter's night, a jackal wandered into a village looking for food. The jackal was very hungry. The winter had been long and hard, and there was no food left in the forest. "Perhaps," said the jackal to himself, "I will find something to eat in the village." The jackal soon found a rubbish heap in the village. He began sniffing and scratching and rummaging about in the rubbish, looking for scraps to eat. Soon he was making such a noise that the village dogs heard him. Now, these dogs did not like jackals. They began barking and growling, and attacked the jackals from all sides. They scratched and bit the jackal with their sharp claws and big teeth. Terrified, the poor jackal ran from the dogs as fast as he could, through the dark deserted streets of the village. But the dogs did not give up. They ran after him, growling and snarling and barking even more loudly. The jackal did not know what to do. He did not dare to stop, and he knew he could not run for much longer. Suddenly he saw the wall of a courtyard before him. Without waiting to think he jumped over the wall, and straight into a large pot of indigo dye! The dye had been left there by a dyer, all ready to be used in the morning. The jackal was now dyed a rich indigo color! Meanwhile the dogs had stopped barking. They couldn't see or smell the jackal any more. They decided to wait near the courtyard wall, just in case he appeared again. But instead of the jackal, a strange blue creature came creeping out of the dyer's house! The dogs were terrified. They had never seen such an animal before. Much to the jackal's surprise, instead of attacking him, the dogs ran away yelping in fright.

A bit puzzled, but also very pleased with the dogs' fright, the jackal returned to the forest. Every forest creature that saw him also ran away, squealing in terror. The jackal soon realized it was his strange new color that was scaring all the animals away. They did not recognize him as a jackal any more. The cunning jackal now hatched a plan. He called all the animals to him. When they had gathered, trembling, before him, he said, "Dear animals, do not be afraid. I will not harm you. I have been sent by the gods themselves to look after you, to make sure you come to no harm. In return, you will have to make me your king, and do as I say. Otherwise the gods will be angry with you." The frightened animals agreed. They made him the king of the forest and did all that he asked. The jackal now had plenty to eat. He was never cold or hungry any more. Many months passed this way. One day, a pack of jackals came to live in the forest. Whenever the indigo jackal would see them, he would feel a strange desire to be with them, to be a jackal once again. One night, when the moon was full, the entire jackal pack lifted up their heads and howled. The indigo jackal could not stop himself. Forgetting his lies, he too lifted up his head and howled with the other jackals.

When the animals saw this, they realized they had been tricked. Their king was nothing but a common jackal! They were angry with themselves for having been fooled, and were furious with the jackal. When the jackal saw that the animals knew the truth, he tried to run away. But the furious animals chased him and caught and tore him to bits.

In the end, it wasn't a very good idea of the jackal to pretend to be someone he was not, was it?

References

Albert, S., & Kharkongor, G. C. (2010). Healing practices of the Khasi and Jaintia people of Northeast India. In R. Moodley & H. Yusuf (Eds.), *Building bridges for wellness through counselling and psychotherapy* (pp. 348–359). Toronto, Canada: Centre for Diversity in Counselling and Psychotherapy.

Arulmani, G. (2006). *Unpublished clinical records (2000 to 2006)*. Bangalore, India: The Promise Foundation.

Arulmani, G. (2009). Tradition and modernity: The cultural preparedness framework for counselling in India. In L. H. Gerstein, P. P. Heppner, S. Aegisdottir, S. M. A. Leung, & K. L. Norsworthy (Eds.), *International handbook of cross-cultural counselling: Cultural assumptions and practices worldwide* (pp. 251–262). California, CA: Sage.

Arulmani, G. (2010). Enough for my mealie-meal: The cultural preparedness approach to the delivery of careers services. In K. Maree (Ed.), *Career counselling: Methods that work* (pp. 1–15). Cape Town, South Africa: Juta Academic.

Bandura, A. (1995). *Self-efficacy in changing societies*. New York, NY: Cambridge University Press.

Bascom, W. R. (1975). *African dilemma tales*. Paris, France: Mouton.

Beck, A. T., Rush, A. J., Shaw, B. F., & Emery, G. (1979). *Cognitive therapy of depression*. New York, NY: The Guilford Press.

Berry, J. (1961). *Spoken art in West Africa*. London, England: University of London.

Bettelheim, B. (1991). *The uses of enchantment: The meaning and importance of fairy tales*. New York, NY: Knopf.

Bruchac, J. (1997). Storytelling and the sacred: On the uses of Native American stories. *Storytelling Magazine, 9*(5), 12–15.

Campbell, J. (1972). *Myths to live by*. New York, NY: Bantam Books.

Courlander, H. (1975). *A treasury of African folklore: The oral literature, traditions, myths, legends, epics, tales, recollections, wisdom, sayings, and humor of Africa*. New York, NY: Crown.

Ellis, A. (1994). *Reason and emotion in psychotherapy: A comprehensive method of treating human disturbances* (Revised and Updated). New York, NY: Citadel Press.

Fisher, W. R. (1987). *Human communication as a narration: Toward a philosophy of reason, value, and action*. Columbia, SC: University of South Carolina.

Frazer, J. G. (2009). *The golden bough: A study in magic and religion* (A new abridgement). England: Oxford World Classics, Oxford University Press.

Jung, C. G. (1964). *Man and his symbols*. New York, NY: Del.

Kirkwood, W. G. (1992). Narrative and the rhetoric of possibility. *Communication Monographs, 59*, 30–47.

Knappert, J. (1980). *Malay myths and legends*. Kuala Lumpur, Malaysia: Heinemann Educational Books (Asia).

Law, B. (n.d.). *The uses of narrative: Three-scene storyboarding*. Retrieved from http://www.hihohiho.com/storyboarding/sbL4L

More, A. J. (1987). Native Indian learning styles: A review for researchers and teachers. *American Indian Education, 27*, 17–29.

Ramachandran, K. (2011, September). *The indigo jackal*. Performance at the Singapore Story Telling Festival, Singapore.

Reese, L. E., & Vera, E. M. (2007). Culturally relevant prevention: The scientific and practical considerations of community-based programs. *The Counseling Psychologist, 35*(6), 763–778.

Reid, H., & West, L. (2014). Telling tales: Do narrative approaches for career counseling count? In G. Arulmani, A. J. Bakshi, F. T. L. Leong, & A. G. Watts (Eds.), *Handbook of career development*. New York, NY: Springer.

Saletore, R. N. (Ed.). (1981). *Encyclopaedia of Indian culture* (Vol. 1). New Delhi, India: Sterling.

Shah, I. (1968). *The way of the Sufi*. New York, NY: Penguin.

Simms, L. (2000). Crossing into the invisible. *Parabola, 25*, 62–68.

Smith, D. P. (2010). Native American, Sufi and Hindu spiritual therapeutics. In R. Moodley & H. Yusuf (Eds.), *Building bridges for wellness through counselling and psychotherapy* (pp. 319–334). Toronto, Canada: Centre for Diversity in Counselling and Psychotherapy.

Speake, J. (2009). *The Oxford dictionary of proverbs (Oxford paperback reference)*. Oxford, NY: Oxford University Press.

Sunwolf, J. D. (1999). The pedagogical and persuasive effects of Native American lesson stories, African dilemma tales, and Sufi wisdom tales. *Howard Journal of Communications, 10*, 47–71.

Sunwolf, J. D. (2004). Once upon a time for the soul: A review of the effects of storytelling in spiritual traditions. *Communication Research Trends, 23*(3), 3–19.

Taylor, D. (1996). *The healing power of stories: Creating yourself through the stories of your life*. New York, NY: Doubleday.

Voluntary Health Association of India. (1991). *India's health status*. New Delhi, India: Author.

Wane, N., & Sutherland, P. (2010). African and Caribbean traditional healing practices in therapy. In R. Moodley & H. Yusuf (Eds.), *Building bridges for wellness through counselling and psychotherapy* (pp. 335–347). Toronto, Canada: Centre for Diversity in Counselling and Psychotherapy.

Enabling Culturally Sensitive Career Counseling through Critically Reflective Practice: The Role of Reflective Diaries in Personal and Professional Development

Barbara Bassot

Introduction

In this chapter I examine the role of critically reflective practice in enabling client-centered, empathic, and nonjudgmental career counseling. For practitioners this means having a high level of self-awareness in relation to their attitudes and values, so as to be able to set them aside in order to practice in a nonjudgmental and culturally sensitive way. In particular, the chapter focuses on the role of diary writing in the development of reflective skills in counselors. To enable this process, I have included an analysis of, and extracts from, my own reflective diary kept during my visit to India. Here, my own experiences in India are used as a case study in order to discuss the theme of reflective practice and the diary extracts are used as a tool for analysis and as a means of illustrating a range of reflective practice theory.

In October 2010, I attended the Jiva conference, India's first International Association of Educational and Vocational Guidance (IAEVG) conference. My role at the conference was to lead a workshop on reflective practice, which included an evaluation of the use of reflective diaries with students undertaking an MA in career guidance in the UK. During the

B. Bassot (✉)
Centre for Career and Personal Development, Canterbury
Christ Church University, Canterbury, UK
e-mail: barbara.bassot@canterbury.ac.uk

conference and in the 2 weeks of holiday that followed, I kept a reflective diary in order to seek a deeper understanding of my time in India. The diary entries were later analyzed and some key themes in relation to my experience emerged. These themes included some assumptions I was making, some stark contrasts in aspects of life in India, alongside some clear constants and similarities. In this chapter, I discuss my thoughts on the process of diary writing and its place in professional learning and development.

From Reflective Practice to Critically Reflective Practice

I begin with an overview of some of the key concepts and constructs related to critically reflective practice. The word *reflection* has two particular meanings in relation to professional practice. First, it suggests a metaphor of looking in a mirror to see one's own reflection in order to gain a higher level of self-awareness. Second, the term denotes thinking and adopting a reflective approach in order to become a thoughtful practitioner. This process can facilitate change and in certain instances can mean that practitioners begin to think about things differently. Boyd and Fales's (1983) definition sums up both aspects effectively: "The process of internally examining and exploring an issue of concern, triggered by an experience, which creates and clarifies meaning in terms of self,

G. Arulmani et al. (eds.), *Handbook of Career Development*, International and Cultural Psychology,
DOI 10.1007/978-1-4614-9460-7_25, © Springer Science+Business Media, LLC 2014

and which results in a changed conceptual perspective" (p. 100).

Reflective practice has been taught in a range professional programs in the UK for a number of years, but only fairly recently has the adjective *critical* been added. In the past, reflective practice has been seen as an individual's way of evaluating his or her professional performance in order to seek to improve it. Many have advocated the use of learning cycles to enable the process. In particular, the work of Kolb (1984) has become seminal in this regard. This cycle enables us to understand the process of learning from experience and how professional practice can be improved over time. There are four steps in the cycle, which is depicted as a circle with clockwise arrows denoting its sequential nature. The first step is the *concrete experience* and this is often (but not always) where the cycle starts. Here an experience is selected for reflection and analysis. Some writers argue that professionals learn most from problematic experiences (Osterman & Kottkamp, 2004), so the concrete experience selected is likely to be a challenging one. Others argue that professionals also learn from positive experiences (Ghaye & Ghaye, 2011), emphasizing the need for professionals to remain in a positive frame of mind in relation to their practice and not to focus all their attention on problems in practice. The particular concrete experience selected is then analyzed in the second step of the cycle, *reflective observation*. This is then followed by the third step, *abstract conceptualization*, where knowledge gained from the experience is added to the professional's existing knowledge and new thoughts and ideas begin to emerge. This new knowledge is then tried out in the fourth step of the cycle, *active experimentation*, ready for the next relevant experience. All of this may happen in a matter of moments, or over days, weeks, or months, depending on the experience. Kolb argued that in order to learn most from experience, we need to complete all four phases of the cycle, although it is important to understand that this will not necessarily always happen.

Honey and Mumford (2000) have used Kolb's experiential learning cycle as the basis for their work on learning styles. They describe four styles and each is associated with one of the steps on Kolb's cycle as follows:

- Step 1—Concrete experience/activist: People with a strong preference for the activist style are doers and enjoy being involved in new experiences. They are open-minded and enthusiastic about new ideas. They enjoy getting on with things and can achieve a lot in a short space of time.
- Step 2—Reflective observation/reflector: These people are thinkers who like to stand back and look at a situation from different perspectives. They enjoy observation and collecting data. They think things through carefully before reaching any conclusions. They often observe others and listen to their views before offering their own. A strong reflector style would appear to be important for people who want to practice reflectively.
- Step 3—Abstract conceptualization/theorist: These are analytical people who enjoy integrating their observations into theories that have been tried and tested. They think problems through in a step-by-step way. They can be perfectionists who like to fit things into a rational scheme or model and also have an ability to see things in a detached and objective way.
- Step 4—Active experimentation/pragmatist: They are practical people who are keen to try out new ideas. They tend to favor concepts that can be applied easily in practice and enjoy problem-solving and decision-making.

If we accept Kolb's argument that in order to learn most from experience, the whole of the cycle needs to be completed, it would seem apparent that those who learn the most will have a good balance of all the styles associated with each of the steps on the cycle. Kolb's cycle can be described as single loop learning (Argyris & Schön, 1974).

Later writers on the subject of reflective practice (Boud, Keogh, & Walker, 1985; Gibbs, 1998) also encouraged us to think about our feelings in relation to professional practice. It is important to understand that as human beings we have an emotional response to the situations we face; Mullins (2010) argued that our emotional response comes first, and this is followed by a rational one. Boud et al. (1985) asserted that the feelings that emerge from our emotional response need to be processed, so they do not become a barrier to professional practice. For example, a practitioner may feel uncomfortable in relation to something that a client discloses. Unless these feelings are analyzed and evaluated, they may become a barrier to future effective communication with that client and others in similar situations. Critically reflective practice takes the process several steps further forward as practitioners are encouraged to examine their attitudes and values, in particular challenging any assumptions they may be making about their clients and their ways of working with them. In relation to career counseling, this could include assumptions regarding, for example, what someone might or might not be able to achieve because of their age, ability, or gender. Critically reflective practice asks us to question those things that we take for granted (Thompson & Thompson, 2008) and warns us against accepting things at face value. It encourages a deeper examination of issues via double loop learning (Argyris & Schön, 1974) and an openness to changing our ways of thinking. This is essential for client-centered practice, as it enables practitioners to gain greater empathy, focusing on the worldview of the client as far as possible. However, this does not mean that practitioners can be totally neutral. Corey, Corey, and Callanan (2007) pointed to the concept of reflexivity, which they describe as having a high level of self-awareness, where the counselors seek to prevent their values impinging on the client. This is an aim that counselors need to continually strive towards.

Argyris's (1982) Ladder of Inference provides a helpful explanation of how we make assumptions. The Ladder has the following seven steps:

- I experience a situation.
- I observe selectively; based on my past experiences, I see what I have seen before or what I expect to see.
- I make sense of what I see by adding meanings to my observations; these meanings are rooted in my past experiences, my personal views, and my cultural context.
- I make assumptions based on these meanings.
- I draw conclusions based on my assumptions.
- I adopt beliefs about the world and what I understand to be "true."
- I take action based on my beliefs.

Argyris (1982) argued that when we have similar experiences, we often jump to step two: observing selectively, which results in our assumptions being reinforced.

Mezirow (1978, 1981) described seven levels of reflectivity which help us to examine how we approach people and situations, in particular the assumptions we might make as a result of past experiences:

- Reflectivity involves a process of becoming aware of how we see things, how we think, and act. These are our habits that have developed over time.
- Affective reflectivity involves becoming aware of how we feel about our habitual ways of thinking and acting.
- Discriminant reflectivity encourages us to question whether or not our views of people and ourselves are accurate.
- Judgmental reflectivity means that we become aware of the value judgments we are making.
- Conceptual reflectivity means that we begin to question critically the way we view ourselves and others.
- Psychic reflectivity makes us recognize when we are quick to make judgments about people on the basis of limited information.
- Theoretical reflectivity recognizes that these quick judgments are based on our cultural and psychological assumptions.

Mezirow argued that the first four levels rest within our ordinary consciousness. In contrast, the last three levels lie within the realm of critical consciousness and can lead to perspective transformation, changing the way we think about people and situations.

Table 25.1 Some key distinctions between reflective and critically reflective practice

Reflective practice	Critically reflective practice
Reflection	Reflexivity
Single loop learning	Double loop learning
Action—focus on continuous improvement	Thinking—focus on perspective transformation
Focus on feelings	Focus on what feelings may show about counselor's attitudes and values
Less aware of assumptions and their impact on practice	More aware of assumptions and their impact on practice
Counselor neutrality not at the forefront	Towards counselor neutrality

Critically reflective practice leads to a much deeper understanding of professional practice and the importance of this in career guidance, particularly in relation to issues such as impartiality, stereotyping, and cultural sensitivity, where it is vital that the counselors are aware of any assumptions they may be making, cannot be overemphasized. Table 25.1 presents some key distinctions between reflective practice and critically reflective practice.

The Role of Writing in Reflection

Many writers emphasize the importance of writing as a reflective activity (Bolton, 2004; Moon, 2000) and many advocate the use of a reflective diary as an effective tool in the process of professional learning and development. Several reasons are given in relation to the purpose of diary writing. First, it is important to record experience; often we think we will remember things, but in our busy lives we do not, as there is simply too much happening. Writing helps us to examine our experiences in greater detail, fosters the development of critical thinking skills, and leads to a deeper understanding of practice; it also enhances skills of problem-solving. In a very significant way, writing helps us to slow down. This is particularly important when our daily lives seem constantly to demand that we work more quickly. Exercises such as *6 minutes of writing* (Bolton, 2004) can help people to get started and begin to write freely and reflectively.

In my own work, I also encourage students of career counseling to keep a reflective diary and many find this difficult, particularly in the early days of their professional training. To help them, I developed a diary for them to use and evaluated their experiences of using it through a series of questionnaires. Some sample questions are included in Box 25.1.

Box 25.1 Sample Questions for a Reflective Diary

1. Thinking back to the beginning, what were your first thoughts about the reflective diary?
2. If you use it, how does it help you in your development?
3. Consider the relationship of the diary to the following three areas.
   - Your knowledge, (things you know and understand).
   - Skills (things that you can do).
   - Attitudes (ways in which your thinking has been challenged).
4. What would you say are the main benefits of using the reflective diary?
5. How does keeping a reflective diary enable you to be impartial?
6. How does keeping a reflective diary enable you to be culturally sensitive?

In relation to question 1 (i.e., their first thoughts about the reflective diary), the students used the following terms to describe their varied early responses to the diary:

- "Something new to me, interesting, puzzling, looking at myself."
- "Excellent."
- "Writing about me—love it!"

Towards the end of the course when they were asked how they felt the diary had helped them in their learning, in response to questions 2 and 3 they said such things as:

- "It reinforced my learning."
- "Helped me improve my skills."
- "Brought to the surface half felt or maybe unconscious thoughts and feelings."
- "See myself moving forwards, enables me to think things through, think before I speak."

In relation to questions 4, 5 and 6 (especially to do with enabling impartiality and cultural sensitivity), students said:

- "Helped me to stand back and be more objective about myself, greater thought involved."
- "Brings into awareness biases, prejudices and other discriminatory ideas which inevitably everyone has."
- "Personal issues etc. can be logged and worked through, outside the professional setting. These can then be taken to supervision."

This shows how writing in a reflective diary can help some people to examine their practice in a deeper way, enabling them to move from reflective practice to critically reflective practice. However, one student began by saying, "Quite frightening, thought it wouldn't be helpful," and then said, "Don't feel it has helped me," showing that reflective diary writing will not suit everyone.

The Reflective Practice Workshop

Having presented an overview of reflective and critically reflective practice, I now move on to discussing these theoretical positions through a case study from my own experience which takes us back to the IAEVG-Jiva international conference I attended in Bangalore, India. The conference was organized around five key themes and the workshop I led was related to the theme *Give in Order to Get*. This theme focused on career counseling as a partnership where counselor and client learn from each other. As part of the learning process, the counselor is open to the client's background and way of life and seeks to practice in a culturally sensitive way. For me, one of the highlights of the conference was to learn more about the Jiva program being delivered to young people in schools in India (see Arulmani, 2011). *Jiva* in many Indian languages means *life* and this was prominent in all aspects of the conference, including its title: *Career: A Celebration of Life*. My own workshop was entitled: *Enabling Culturally Sensitive Career Counseling Through Reflective Practice: A Study of the Use of Reflective Diaries in the Development of Trainee Counselors in the UK*. The purpose was to show how writing in a reflective diary can help student counselors gain a deeper understanding of themselves and of their developing practice. This in turn can help them to stand back from their own attitudes and values, keeping the needs of the client at the center, and enable them to have a greater sensitivity to the culture and context of the client. Prior to the conference, I assumed that many of the people attending would have little or no knowledge of reflective practice; this was correct, but only in part.

Methodology

A Personal Reflective Diary

Before leaving for India I decided to keep a reflective diary while I was there in order to reflect on the experience of delivering a reflective practice workshop and to help me gain a deeper understanding of my time in a different cultural context (Bassot, 2010). As well as the three days at the conference, I also spent 2 weeks on holiday in Kerala (a South Indian state) and kept the diary throughout this time. I wrote in the diary each day during this period; sometimes this took the form of a log, where I noted down and described the things I had done, other days I also noted things I felt, assumptions I had made, and in particular things that stood out to me in relation to my emerging understandings of India. During this period, I also analyzed what I wrote and identified some key themes which emerged. In this way, the reflective diary became a research diary over a period of time. This methodology can be described as autoethnography; its purpose was to describe and analyze my own personal experience in order to seek to understand cultural experiences (Ellis, Adams, & Bochner, 2010). Following my return to the UK, I analyzed my diary entries and four groups of themes were identified: my assumptions, contrasts, constants, and similarities. These will now be explored.

My Assumptions

The visit to India was my first direct experience of a developing country. Clearly, no human being is a *tabula rasa* and my unexpected feelings of anxiety preceding the visit helped me to highlight some of the assumptions I was making. Before the trip, I found myself thinking about a good friend who was born in the UK but brought up in Bangladesh. She often spoke of her life there, in particular, her time at a boarding school and how much she loved the whole experience. This was very different from my own experience of being born in and attending school in the UK. At my own school, two of the girls in my class were from outside the UK; one was from Africa and the other from India. I had very limited exposure to people from other nationalities until I became a career counselor working in the south east of England. Here I met many young people from India and the Caribbean and began to learn about their ways of life and their culture, which was very different from my own. As the time for my trip to India drew nearer, I began to think about how I would cope with the challenges I would face. However, my feelings of anxiety became mixed with feelings of excitement once the flights and accommodation were in place.

So, what were the assumptions I was making about India? I knew that the climate would be hot and I assumed that I was likely to see people living in a depth of poverty that I would not have seen before. Bangalore (the city I was going to) is well known as the information

technology hub of India with all its call centers, so I also assumed I would also see familiar symbols and brands from the West. I expected to eat spicy food and took the necessary tablets with me, should my digestive system struggle to cope! My own desires to be culturally sensitive led to some anxieties about such things as "what not to wear" and "how to behave."

My Findings

Contrasts

When analyzing my diary entries, a range of areas which appeared to be full of stark contrasts emerged. These contrasts often seemed to exist side by side, sometimes even overlapping in a seamless way. Here are some examples.

Old and New, Present and Future

One of the Jiva conference themes was: *The Changing and the Unchanged* and conference participants were encouraged to reflect on the impact of globalization on life and labor markets and the need to preserve traditional occupations in India in order to protect livelihoods. At the conference this showed itself in an emphasis on crafts; the many traditional ways that Indian people make a living, through making things and growing things. This was concretized for all conference participants as we sat in the main auditorium decorated by handpicked locally grown flowers, ate locally sourced food at meal breaks, and (those of us who delivered sessions) received a gift presented in a handmade silk bag. Even the conference bag itself was locally produced and designed in such a way as to be convenient and reusable. The keynote session on crafts (Ratnam, 2011) was highlighted in the final plenary session as significant, particularly with its emphasis on the need to preserve traditional industries and their ways of working. However, social justice issues were also highlighted, in particular the need for goods to be sold at a fair price (particularly to the West) as an important element of enabling Indian workers to earn a good living and move their families out of poverty.

Alongside the emphasis on crafts, evidence of the impact of technology was everywhere, as you might expect in Bangalore, India's IT capital. The Wifi access in my hotel room via a fast broadband connection meant that using my netbook was easier than in most locations in the UK! The reception on my mobile phone was markedly better from Bangalore than it is from my own home. Once we were on holiday in Kerala, particularly in more rural parts, I wondered if this would still be the case and generally speaking it was. Analyzing my diary entries showed various examples of the ways in which traditional crafts and technology live seamlessly side by side in some aspects of Indian life. For example, one day we took a trip in a handmade boat into the backwaters of the Arabian Sea. The boat was punted and at various points in the trip the driver answered calls on his mobile phone; with his punt in one hand and mobile phone in the other! Women washing clothes by hand was a daily sight while every large community seemed to have an internet café, even if this consisted of one internet-linked desktop computer at the back of a small shop. Small homesteads in Kerala, some of which have been in existence for around a hundred years, contrasted sharply with large new hotels in major cities, showing some of the ways that India is changing. However, the trappings of temporary money were highlighted at the conference, for example, call centers closing in Bangalore as multinational corporations begin to get labor cheaper elsewhere (e.g., in Malaysia and Indonesia).

Noisy and Quiet, Fast and Slow

One of my first diary entries captures some of my initial impressions of Bangalore "fast pace, a bit chaotic, busy" (Bassot, 2010). Along with this was noise; whether it was the constant horns of the drivers of cars, taxis, autorickshaws, and buses or the more general buzz of city life with large numbers of people living and working alongside one another, noise was constant. This contrasted sharply with the quiet of the countryside in Kerala where two examples from my diary entry stand out. First, our overnight houseboat trip on the backwaters of Allepey (a smaller town in Kerala) can only be described as calm and serene: "Everywhere is so quiet and peaceful. There is a lovely cool breeze—no need for a fan. Sound of birds everywhere, kingfishers, terns etc. Plus the sound of the water lapping against the boat, cockerels crowing" (Bassot, 2010). Second, the 3-hour walk around the *Periyar* wildlife park, which I described in my diary, was "so peaceful and calm" (Bassot, 2010). The atmosphere in the whole of the park was quiet and our guide had to ask one member of our group to speak more quietly, so as not to scare away any nearby animals!

Wet and Dry, On and Off

Like any other city, Bangalore needs a regular and reliable supply of water. In my hotel room, I read the notices regarding the consumption of water carefully and complied with the requests made to shower, soap, and rinse, turning the water on and off during the process in order to save precious resources. Visiting Kerala shortly after the monsoon season I was struck by the numbers of large, fast flowing waterfalls by the side of the road; so many that we could not stop and admire all of them if we were to reach our next destination. A sign next to one particular waterfall saying "drinking water, please do not pollute" reminded me of the precious nature of clean water in India that living in the UK I take completely for granted. Power cuts were regular occurrences in Bangalore and elsewhere.

Strange and Familiar

I had expected to see different customs and practices during my time in India, and some of these were clearly evident from the beginning of the conference. My diary entry for the day of the opening ceremony is a case in point, where I noted that oil lamps were lit to symbolize the desire for our understandings to be enlightened, prayers were said by two young children, and we were given cards and wrote our own prayers and dreams on them. My diary entry finished with the words: "I found it uplifting and inspiring. So different to home. The thought of doing something like that at a UK conference is unthinkable" (Bassot, 2010).

In the same way, some of the sessions at the conference provided a different experience from those closer to home. My reflections on the first of the four Jiva sessions I attended at the conference again showed the stark contrast with similar sessions I had experienced in the UK and Europe: "Went to Jiva Session 1, which was great—in particular the links with Indian philosophy. Again we couldn't do anything like that in the UK. In any case, what would our philosophy be?" (Bassot, 2010).

By contrast other aspects of the whole experience felt very familiar. For example, our arrival at Bangalore airport, which I described as, "really quite like lots of other modern airports." My early diary entries described my first impressions as "globalization in action"; familiar brands could be seen everywhere and the impact of them could be felt and experienced. I noted that our shopping trip on the first day of our stay "could have been anywhere in the UK in one sense, with all the usual brands, KFC, Pizza Hut, Benetton, Sony etc." However, other aspects of the shopping trip, and later experiences stood out as being different, particularly in relation to the high level of customer service, which, although extremely welcome, showed "aspects of colonialism—very polite." This particular entry highlights an assumption on my part, as I mistook the politeness of traditional Indian culture as evidence of colonialism.

The phrase "familiarity breeds contempt" did not come to mind during the visit; rather the familiarities that were evident gave me a positive sense of security and confidence. When arriving at the conference, I was pleased and even relieved to find that the IT facilities were: "All very familiar and reassuring. Laptop and data projector just like home."

Rich and Poor

During my time in India, there were some clear contrasts between rich and poor, both in Bangalore and in more rural areas. My assumptions regarding poverty were not unfounded (although these would undoubtedly have been much more in evidence in other parts of India) and my diary entries at several points

describe this. For example, "The gap between the rich and the poor is huge here." Having decided to walk to the conference on the second day, I was struck by the contrast between rich and poor. "What a contrast—large modern houses with swimming pools on one side of the road and huts/slums with people cooking outside on the other."

Rural and Industrial

In Kerala, the contrast between rural and industrial was particularly evident in Kochi (one of the largest cities in Kerala). The peaceful coast with its authentic Chinese fishing nets sitting side by side with the bustling and growing center of Ernakulum (another large city in Kerala). My diary entry notes that there is: "A real mix of beautiful views over the water out to sea, large gas holders and lots of vegetation floating downstream." As we drove up to the tea plantations, again I wrote: "The contrasts really stand out here, for example, the beautiful scenery and the mobile phone towers, the cows and the football pitch, our ride on an elephant and my text message from Vodafone. But they blend together for me, rather than clashing."

However, the challenges expressed at the conference stayed in my mind, along with the gentle, and not so gentle, reminders of issues of social justice. I noted in my diary: "Technology has brought progress here. The challenge is can it bring prosperity for all? It should."

Constants

My diary entries also showed numbers of examples of things that had remained constant in Indian society and culture, sometimes for centuries.

Spirituality

The importance of religion in Indian life was very evident, although at times, the commercial side came to the fore. For example, after visiting the Bull Temple in Bangalore, I wrote "Felt more like a tourist attraction than a spiritual experience." However, especially in more rural parts, the sounds of chanting in the early morning and at other points during the day was evidence of devoted people seeking to live their lives in accordance with their beliefs and values. In particular, I found the closing of the conference to be a spiritual experience. The two children who had said prayers at the opening of the conference prayed again; these ended with a prayer for peace. Following this two doves were released from cages and came to rest for a short while on a large tree, before flying off into the distance. For me this symbolized how I felt at that moment, which I shared with the Indian woman standing next to me and expressed in my diary entry for that day. "I don't want to leave/I don't want this to end. I cried—a mixture of sadness, overwhelmed by the experience of the whole thing, and joy at the privilege of being here."

Work and Livelihood

Throughout my time in India, I was struck by the hardworking people I met and their need to earn a living to support their families. At the conference the discussions moved from *career* to *livelihood* and the need for consumers (particularly those from the West) to pay a reasonable price for goods to enable Indian people to move out of poverty. One particularly stark example was during our visit to the wildlife park, when everyone was asked to hire gaiters to protect their legs from insect bites. One member of our group said, "There's a lot of money to be made here," to which our guide responded in an understandably sharp tone that the charge was "not even 1 Euro."

Similarities

My diary entries also showed evidence of aspects of life that Indian people face that are similar to those faced by people in the UK.

Gender Inequality

On a visit to a tea plantation, we heard inspiring stories of the way the work had progressed over the years. In the early days of the plantation in the 1890s, it was found that women were very good at picking tea and men were good at the heavier work of planting the bushes and removing those plants that had become diseased. So both men and women were employed, which meant that a family could double its income. Couples then wanted to have children, so the employer provided crèches for all the children, where they employed older women who could no longer work outside to look after them. Women had maternity leave and healthcare benefits and I described this in my diary as "incredibly forward thinking." A large proportion of this tea plantation (95 %) is now owned by the workers who share the profits.

At the conference, meeting some women university lecturers from Goa (another Indian state) was also inspiring but in a very different way. They told fascinating stories of the way some women are treated. Their advice to all the women they counsel is to keep a separate bank account, to make sure that the family house is also in their name in a legal, binding agreement. They spoke passionately, with phrases such as "otherwise your husband can claim everything. If it doesn't work out, you will then not be on the street." They also talked about how some women are "made to stay at home and have to walk behind the man."

Elections

Visiting the world's largest democracy at the time of local elections in Kerala was an experience to remember. The loud hailers calling people to vote could be heard from early in the morning until late at night and all available surfaces were covered with candidate posters. There was a sense of excitement as the elections approached and the process appeared to be taken very seriously and seen as a privilege. Having experienced national elections in the UK earlier in the year, the contrast between this and the apathy of many in the UK was stark.

Relevance to Professional Practice and Multiple Cultures

Having kept a reflective diary, it is now important to evaluate what I gained from it and whether or not this concurs with Moon (2000) and Bolton's (2004) assertions that reflective diary writing prompts a deeper approach to reflection, and the findings of my students. In addition, it is important to consider the relevance of this to career counseling practice.

Overall diary writing came easily to me as, unsurprisingly, this was not my first experience of such an activity and I have a strong reflector learning style (Honey & Mumford, 2000). However, I was surprised by the emotional aspects of the experience, particularly in relation to certain diary entries, but also in the analysis that I undertook afterwards. Models such as Boud et al. (1985) and Gibbs (1998) that ask people to take the affective nature of learning into account now appeared to be particularly significant. In addition, writing about the feelings I was experiencing helped me to process them; in particular to continue to challenge myself regarding issues of equality and social justice. As a professional practitioner, it is important to acknowledge the part that feelings play in work with clients and to remember to work through them. Writing in a reflective diary can be very helpful in this regard as feelings (positive and negative) can thereby be externalized, enabling practitioners to move from an emotional response to a rational one (Mullins, 2010). In turn, this helps professionals work towards a higher level of counselor neutrality. It is clear that I would not have remembered some of the detail regarding my experiences without the diary. Re-reading it brought things back to my mind that I had completely forgotten, even things that had really impressed me at the time. I forgot them in the hustle and bustle of my everyday life, which I quickly reentered on my return home. Unless significant experiences are recorded in some way, whether they are seen as problematic (Osterman & Kottkamp, 2004) or positive (Ghaye & Ghaye, 2011), in fast paced professional life they will be forgotten and the learning from them will be lost.

My analysis of the diary gave me insights that I do not believe I would have had otherwise. This process helped me to "unpick" what I saw and experienced, which enabled me to gain a deeper understanding of life in India with its contrasts and constants. In particular, it highlighted the intense volume of new experiences over a short period of time. A particularly significant diary entry in this regard stated "There is so much to take in here, my mind at times feels fit to burst!" The writing itself helped me to slow down and take in more of what I was seeing and experiencing. I found I looked forward to writing in it each day and saw it as time invested not wasted. In busy professional lives it is important to take time out to reflect, to reassess priorities, and to regain focus.

Regarding the assumptions (Argyris, 1982) I made before the visit, certainly my initial anxieties were unfounded and I enjoyed every moment. I now understand much more of my good friend's positive feelings about her time in Bangladesh and feel I have greater empathy with her; this is evidence of Mezirow's (1978, 1981) perspective transformation and how some of my ways of thinking have changed. As a professional practitioner this would also be the case in relation to Indian clients I might see in a career counseling context, and international student counselors I work within my current role. Through the process of analyzing my assumptions and challenging them, my perspectives have been broadened and I am less likely to reach conclusions too quickly. This is a vital skill for career counselors who seek to practice in a nonjudgmental and impartial way.

In addition, the slow process of writing took my focus away from action, or single loop learning (Argyris & Schön, 1974; Kolb, 1984) to a deeper critical evaluation of my experiences via double loop learning (Argyris & Schön, 1974). I quickly learned not to take things, such as fresh running water, for granted, and to be grateful for courtesies shown, which often seem lacking at home. All professional practitioners should be motivated to improve their practice in an ongoing way (Kolb, 1984), but continuous improvement through action should not be the only focus. In order to practice in a culturally sensitive way, we need to challenge any assumptions we may be making in order to place the client and her or his worldview at the center. Many of my attitudes and values, particularly in relation to issues of social justice and in particular gender discrimination were reinforced, although the example of the foresight of the tea factory was surprising and inspiring.

New Concepts and Viewpoints: Starting a Reflective Diary

In order to enable culturally sensitive career counseling, people who are new to writing a reflective diary often value a starting point and the template in Box 25.2 is included here to offer this. The template incorporates many of the theoretical approaches discussed in this chapter.

Box 25.2 Template for a Reflective Diary
The Experience
- What happened?
- Describe the experience
- Describe the situation and the context
- What were the contributory factors?
Reflection
- What was I trying to achieve with the client?
- Why did I do what I did?
- Were there any cultural issues evident?
- What assumptions was I making about the client and my practice?
- What were the consequences for me and the client?
- How did I feel?
- How did the client feel and how could I tell?
- Were there any issues of equality and social justice that I needed to be aware of?
Theory
- How has this experience contributed to my professional knowledge?
- How does this fit with the models I have learned and use regularly?
- What new knowledge have I gained from this experience?

Preparation
- What will I do next time in similar situations?
- What will I now consider for next time?
- How has my thinking changed?
- What other strategies could I adopt to move my practice forward?

Conclusion

My lasting impressions of my time in India are that I gave a little and received much. Writing the diary proved to be a very worthwhile experience for me, although it is clear that this will not necessarily prove to be the case for everyone. However, for students of career counseling who are learning the skills needed for effective client-centered, nonjudgmental practice, writing in a reflective diary can cause people to slow down, examine their emerging practice at a deeper level, challenge their assumptions, and work towards a greater level of counselor neutrality and cultural sensitivity. It is clear that in busy professional lives there will never be enough time for reflection. For those who have not yet tried this kind of writing, setting aside a small, realistic, and achievable amount of time (say 15 minutes per week) to write in a reflective diary could be time invested in your own professional development. If you are someone who finds this helpful, this small investment of time can reap great rewards in relation to professional practice.

References

Argyris, C. (1982). *Reasoning, learning and action: Individual and organizational.* San Francisco, CA: Jossey-Bass.

Argyris, C., & Schön, D. (1974). *Theory in practice: Increasing professional effectiveness.* London, England: Jossey-Bass.

Arulmani, G. (2011). Striking the right note: The cultural preparedness approach to developing resonant career guidance programmes. *International Journal for Educational and Vocational Guidance, 11*(2), 79–93.

Bassot, B. (2010). *Reflective diary: India 2010*. Unpublished manuscript.

Bolton, G. (2004). *Reflective practice: Writing and professional development* (2nd ed.). London, England: Sage.

Boud, D., Keogh, R., & Walker, D. (1985). *Reflection: Turning experience into learning*. London, England: RoutledgeFalmer.

Boyd, E. M., & Fales, A. W. (1983). Reflective learning: Key to learning from experience. *Journal of Humanistic Psychology, 23*, 99–117.

Corey, G., Corey, M. S., & Callanan, P. (2007). *Issues and ethics in the helping professions* (7th ed.). Belmont, CA: Thomson Brooks/Cole.

Ellis, C., Adams, T. E., & Bochner, A. P. (2010). Autoethnography: An overview. *Forum Qualitative Sozialforschung* [*Forum: Qualitative Social Research*], *12*(1). Retrieved from http://nbn-resolving.de/urn:nbn:de:0114-fqs1101108

Ghaye, T., & Ghaye, K. (2011). *Teaching and learning through reflective practice: A practical guide for positive action*. New York, NY: Routledge.

Gibbs, G. (1998). *Learning by doing: A guide to teaching and learning methods*. Oxford, England: Further Education Unit, Oxford Polytechnic.

Honey, P., & Mumford, A. (2000). *The learning styles helper's guide*. Maidenhead, England: Author.

Kolb, D. (1984). *Experiential learning: Experience as the source of learning and development*. Englewood Cliffs, NJ: Prentice Hall.

Mezirow, J. (1978). *Education for perspective transformation: Women's re-entry programs in community colleges*. New York, NY: Teacher's College, Columbia University.

Mezirow, J. (1981). A critical theory of adult learning and education. *Adult Education, 32*, 13–24.

Moon, J. (2000). *Reflection in learning and professional development. Theory and practice*. London, England: Kogan Page.

Mullins, L. (2010). *Management and organisational behaviour*. Harlow, England: Financial Times, Prentice Hall.

Osterman, K. F., & Kottkamp, R. B. (2004). *Reflective practice for educators: Professional development to improve student learning*. Thousand Oaks, CA: Corwin Press.

Ratnam, A. (2011). Traditional occupations in a modern world: Implications for career guidance and livelihood planning. *International Journal for Educational and Vocational Guidance, 11*(2), 95–109.

Thompson, S., & Thompson, N. (2008). *The critically reflective practitioner*. Basingstoke, England: Palgrave Macmillan.

Online Careers Work: Colonist or Inhabitant?

26

Bill Law

Introduction

The chapter is addressed to professionals who, in a more or less formal way, set out to enable people in the management of their working lives. They are known as advisers, counselors, teachers, coordinators, coaches, and mentors. They are supported in some countries by managers, consultants, and trainers. In other countries, they work alone. In all cases, the activity is here called *careers work*, and its people, *career workers*. There is a difference between careers work and career management: Careers work is what career workers do; career management is what their clients and students do. Career management calls on a wider range of activity than career workers conventionally provide, and much of it is now online. The chapter, therefore, looks to professional educators—career workers and their colleagues—for the help that online life now needs.

Fuchs et al. (2010) set the scene. They analyzed the story so far, not in terms of what the Internet contains but, usefully, in three stages of activity:

Web 1.0 cognitive enquiring	Searching sources for offline use
Web 2.0 interactive communicating	Putting issues and seeking feedback
Web 3.0 cooperative changing	Sharing, probing, and challenging

All of these are a means of communication; and every such means has, sooner or later, been captured by powerful interests, whether in commerce or in politics. The custodians of the Internet claim to be exceptions to this rule: The web-2.0-to-3.0 journey is celebrated as leading to self-propelled independence, where the net's multiple connections can outflank all that corporations and governments might do to contain them. But US commentator Tim Wu (2010) wondered whether the *master switch* of the powerful is about to be thrown again, capturing and exploiting the Internet for dominant interests. Wu shows how inhabitants of the net can find more control not only of their own personal lives but of the shared terms in which their lives can be lived. But he also documents a history which shows that such autonomy is repeatedly thwarted if it undermines commercially and politically powerful interests. It is the interests of those whose hands are on a master switch which limits and controls access to the Internet. Wu raises a big question for what is to come—what we will one day call *Web 4.0*. This chapter examines the position professional educators, and especially career workers, adopt in response to these trends. How can the massively changing Internet most

B. Law (✉)
National Institute for Careers Education and Counseling, Cambridge, UK
e-mail: bill@hihohiho.com

G. Arulmani et al. (eds.), *Handbook of Career Development*, International and Cultural Psychology,
DOI 10.1007/978-1-4614-9460-7_26, © Springer Science+Business Media, LLC 2014

usefully feature in how people develop ready-for-anything flexibility in working life? The question is overdue, because the Internet can both help and hinder that process.

It is not assumed that all careers work is bound to invade and exploit the Internet. That would be colonizing. But there are dedicated careers-work sites which have captured and adapted online activity to their own ready-made purposes. In this chapter, how those sites are used is examined, and the question is raised about how career workers can usefully join-in with what is happening online, that is, how they can inhabit the net rather than colonize the net, as partners not invaders, not adapting the net to careers work, but adapting careers work to online life.

It is not possible to do any of this without understanding net dynamics, and they are not simply stated. Yet, it is necessary to understand careers work on the net as part of the gamut of online life.

Career Management on the Net

The Internet, which originated in military use, began by carrying more or less static pages. People could use it as if it were a library or a museum. That was Web 1.0. Web 2.0 permitted questioning and invited feedback, as if in a lecture theater or even a workshop. But *Facebook*, *YouTube*, *Second Life*, *Twitter*, *LinkedIn*, *Skype*, and *Xbox* games are Web 3.0 phenomena—not for a library or even a lecture theater. This is where clients and students meet their friends and find new ones, where plans are hatched, alliances forged, and action rehearsed. Internet users have become insiders and producers where they were once outsiders and consumers. And we have no idea how much all of this can be extended or contained by the coming of Web 4.0.

There is an immediate issue here for how people navigate online territory. It applies particularly to career workers who seek to colonize that territory by building routes to what they take to be important. The feature by which Web 3.0 outflanks such an invasion is its connectivity—any location can, in a mouse-click, be linked to

any other. This feature bypasses the content menus which are part of a good many dedicated careers-work sites. Indigenously navigated connectivity circumvents invasion, but it brings its own challenges. It is a double-edged sword: The exponentially expanding connectivity became impossible to search systematically. Impossible, that is, until search engines are programmed semantically to recognize word meanings. They might, for example, recognize that the search criterion *work* can also represent an interest in *career*, *occupation*, or *vocation*. At best, such semantically, rather than verbally, driven searches can start from any choice of words to recognize user intentions. But that reliance on semantics actually produces too many finds and in no particular order.

Dreyfus (2009) has shown how the problem of mass connectivity has become part of the solution, in two ways. Data-based systems, like the search engine Google, link user criteria to the sites to which people using a given criteria frequently go. The first page of finds can then list in descending order what has appealed to most such enquirers. Conversely, sites like Wikipedia call on user scrutiny of what they find by creating a forum where errors are noticed and corrected. And so, sheer mass, thought of as a problem, becomes a solution: The more sites, the more focused is Google; the more users, the more reliable is the wiki.

On both counts, menu-loading careers-work sites are losing control of whether and how they are used. A well-focused search engine may well carry enquirers to a nonexpert source. And an information-packed wiki, patrolled by virtually limitless monitoring, can be as trustworthy as an expert source. There is little hope for career workers becoming gatekeepers on those sources. They need another strategy, that of attending to the variability of what people find. This would involve a listening-and-questioning role.

Baym (2010) has pointed to online variability. There are varying degrees of talk-back interactivity. Some expect an immediate reply; some permit time for thought. Sites have varying concentrations of detail and social contact. Users may know each other or may not.

The material may be abiding or transient. Access is by increasingly portable devices. Baym does not mention further career-relevant features of variability. The content growth rate is exponential. It includes both verified information and gossipy opinion. It is put across in a mix of numbers, words, and images, variously animated. Users can come and go in seconds. There are frequent technological upgrades which digitally divide the well-off from the poor. Some sites require registration but not all protect privacy. Disclosure can be diverted to other uses, much of it as *spam*, enticing with bogus plausibility. The big picture is that websites are used for fun, shopping, indulging obsessions, carrying out research, and fomenting revolution. And none of these pursuits necessarily excludes any other.

On reducing costs and variable accessibility, the *Indian Hole-in-the-Wall* experiment has installed Internet connections in public outdoor areas close to urban slums and rural settlements. Camera monitoring shows children as young as six spontaneously learning to use them. There are no appeals here to theory or research, just a wish to reduce the digital divide (Judge, 2000).

Facer and Selwyn (2010) have collated evidence that young people tend to use 3.0 networking mainly for maintaining their social lives. However, they have also noticed what they call "backstage" resistance, where online exchanges criticize various aspects of schooling. Furthermore, Facer and Selwyn found professional educators to be cautious about the value of 3.0 sites. Educators do not encourage exploratory uses—they seek clearly bounded and familiar schooling activities. Facer and Selwyn are describing Western phenomena. Do we know what parallel enquiries among Indian, Malay, Singaporean, and Sri Lankan teachers might show?

An underlying reality may be that as students gain access to online devices, they do so at later stage than educators in fast-moving technological upgrading. Educators' familiarity will, then, become outdated. It is this that has persuaded some commentators to suggest that educators need to catch up with technological developments. But if teacher interest in technology is likely to be limited and shrinking, such a strategy in the long run will be futile. Facer and Selwyn (2010) have looked elsewhere for a professional response: They characterize the need as creativity, critical thinking, and learning-to-learn. That need, less urgent in the quiet library, is imperative in the noisy forum. Its support for user independence undermines any colonizing agenda. In this alternative thinking, the website still provides the content and technology remains the tool. But it is critical questioning that becomes the process.

Colonial Dynamics

Watts (1996) anticipated some of the features of colonization—showing how careers work can be exported into digital technologies, for example, in self-assessment profiles and writing CVs and also foreseeing individual control of those processes. The ensuing careers-work story is disappointingly unadventurous. That reticence may be explained, as much as anything, by the caution which Facer and Selwyn (2010) find among teachers in general. Bosley, Krechowiecka, and Moon (2005) noted a cautious tendency among UK career workers. Barnes and La Gro (2010) have argued for the need of a technological catch-up from careers work on the Internet. Hooley, Hutchinson, and Watts (2010) have spoken of careers work's own limited range of activities, neglecting the breadth of Web 3.0 possibilities. An underlying source of such caution may be identified in a report for the UK Commission for Employment and Skills by Bimrose and Barnes (2010a). It shows how the sheer range of digital formats can overwhelm career workers. Such studies find limited and static careers-work use of online resources: Diagnostic tools and databases are common, but there are fewer interactive processes such as conversational and student-generated material.

Hooley et al. (2010) also pointed to the way people use the Internet independently of career workers. And, in agreement with Facer and Selwyn (2010), they see a need more widely to engage with culture, education, and skills.

And student and client wider engagement with other-than-career-professional material is not much mentioned in any of these enquiries. Yet people use them. A growing number of sites present career experience in narrative terms (Law, 2010a). They resemble the sort of Web 3.0 talk-and-imagery on *YouTube*. There is an awkward compromise here: These sites mimic social networking. But they need education-professional support if they are to be usefully visible; and they need commercial sponsorship if they are to be financially sustainable. A consequence of these various needs to look good is that anecdotal accounts of labor market experience are presented as though they were generalizable labor market information. And there is a temptation to favor "inspirational" stories. It can mean that bad experiences of work-life are avoided. It can also mean that what are, after all, no more than anecdotes are not given any degree of scrutiny.

There is also careers-work blogging, *web-logging*, which is a call-and-response activity. Bloggers canvass facts, suggestions, and questions; people come back with reactions, feedback, and comments. The process can develop lengthy and discursive sequences of key-boarded discussion, in which everybody sees everybody's contribution. In surveying its careers-work use, Hooley (2011) argued that it has considerable unused potential. However, both blogging and classroom discussion can favor assertive and articulate people, especially when there is a commercial dynamic to self-promotion in a marketplace.

A UK-based survey by Richmond and Stephens (2010) showed how graduates make use of the Internet in managing careers. They found that social networking figures prominently, and blogging less frequently. And, although students are reported to use their own university's careers-service website, few use other careers-work sites. Some make direct contact with potential employing organizations. There are also social networking sites such as *LinkedIn* which offer a way for job-seekers to stay visible to potential employers and to learn from each other. They typically use a combination of listing and blogging formats. They also set up online groups with shared interests.

In summary, the evidence shows that professional online sites rely on familiar but limited techniques. They have not much ventured into Web 3.0. But their students and clients do—although they are not much invited to scrutinize sources and they tend to take things at face value. Larbalestier (2010) has pointed to risks which accrue where disclosure is a possibility. He particularly warns against the vigor with which the corporate world tracks Web 3.0 disclosures by potential recruits.

What the Net Can Do

Such professional concerns do not much trouble Internet enthusiasts. There is widespread enthusiasm for what the net can do, though not all of it is convincingly supported. Tapscott (1998) has ascribed the term *the net generation* to young people he claims to be liberated from authoritarians.

Some see the net in terms which are more directly useful to career concerns. For example, although Morzove (2010) is noted for his doubts concerning the usefulness of the Internet, he does argue that it can improve how people are heard, get educated, earn a living, and move up the social ladder. Some of what is argued is in detail. Shirky (2008, 2010) has pointed to the value of wiki-like online crowdsourcing for information. He also suggests that social networking's independence from organizational interests restores a more intimate form of social relations. He argues that the Internet is introducing people to an expanded consuming, producing, and sharing process. If he is right, it will reposition people in relation to working life in ways that print and cinema have already done. Naish (2010) has characterized that trend as the ability to rapidly gather and assemble data and coordinate group response. It is what appears to be an increase in intelligence, probably best understood as a selective improvement in those aspects of intelligence that contemporary life most calls upon (Flynn, 2007).

Learning from online gaming is also relevant to working life (Chatfield, 2010). Chatfield advocates the operational value of *Sims* and the *Call of Duty*. They require practice in managing tasks where commands of space, time, and logic are critical. Educators could usefully tap into how students navigate those challenges.

Bishop (2009) has been among the first to probe specifically for career relevance in online life. His ethnography shows trainee teachers using digital technologies to prepare for what they will later do with their students. He finds the Internet inviting a dialogue between, on the one hand, what people find online and, on the other, their own inner life. It is, he finds, a continuing soliloquy in which everything becomes a matter of interpretation and reinterpretation, achieving a deeper self-awareness for the offline management of career. Such reflection is necessary, for example, to transferring online learning into offline professionalism.

Most of the optimism concerning the Internet is based on Web 3.0 potential. It is easy to see all of this as "empowering." People can access more material, engage in more conversations, and—it is claimed—exercise more control. That sense of liberation may well be exhilarating for people who do not feel at ease with experts and professionals. The net offers their uneasiness more congenial ways of finding out what is going on and figuring out what to do about it. And where people change the way they learn, educators must change the way they help.

Mason (2012) has approached these issues from another angle, which is hopeful rather than optimistic. His account of the relationship between online life and career management collates evidence from a range of sociologists and economists, all setting out the situation of *graduates with no future*: young people whose accommodation of career management requirements for high-flying success has proven futile. Mason highlights *Occupy* movements which are sustained protests opposing the monetary maneuvering which brought about the 2008 global economic crisis. Occupy is a nonviolent, articulate, debating movement, opposed to self-protective corporate and policy interests. It has emerged, more or less simultaneously worldwide. Mason claims that it, and the more demonstrative *Arab Spring* movements, is unprecedented. They are born of an alignment of the interests of largely middle-class young people, with a *zeitgeist* awakened by political and economic failure, and drawing on information technology which makes globally coordinated action possible. Such movements compromise the position of careers work as an instrument of policy, serving corporate interests. Mason sees them as a significant means by which people assert their claim to a stake in their societies.

Any account of what the net can do must be layered and, however optimistic or hopeful, will at times be confusing. But in order to understand where the opportunities for positive development are, career workers need also to face bad news.

Collateral and Other Damage

There are relatively few reported cases of deliberately malicious and destructive activity on the net. But although commentators may not claim malice, they do worry about simplemindedness, displayed, for example, in a willingness to promote a passing whim as though it were a serious proposition. Indeed, the net is widely celebrated as if nothing is agreed or enduring. This is not good news for careers work, which sees itself as dispensing valid information and reliable diagnoses. But whatever we find online is quickly overlaid with updating and contradiction. Does it strengthen people's grasp on reality or weaken it?

A career-related reaction to confusion is the creation of niches. The reduced costs of dissemination make it possible for the net to reach any number of separate and different positions or niches. A niche is where people can meet whom they like, hear what they believe, and pursue what they want. But finding that what they seek means risking missing what they need. For while Shirky's (2008) "wise crowds" are useful as virtually limitless populations, they are less impressive in small groups. And managing careers online requires the skill to be able to separate what is reliable, from what is mistaken and self-indulgent, and sometimes malicious and predatory. They certainly need to know what it is safe to disclose to whom. But online protective barriers are dangerously permeable; and the best of them are easily breached by corporate interests which pay for *deep-net* searches of candidates' disclosures. This is what Larbalestier (2010) has warned against.

Savvy surfers are alert to risks of being misled or led into danger. But niches are themselves subtle-and-smiling forms of entrapment. They hide alternative perspectives: linking to "friends," saying what "I like," following "favorites," welcoming "people-like-us," and excluding the rest. Each niche celebrates its own beliefs, values, and expectations concerning what is worth doing and who is worth paying attention to. That would include what work is worth considering. It contradicts expansive and enlarging careers work. Sunstein (2009) has reported the limiting and narrowing effects, worrying about the way in which the net populates itself with more or less isolated enclaves, recycling habitual ways of looking rather than learning new ways of seeing. If these commentators are right, there could be disturbing implications for how online careers work falls short of maintaining the sort of expansiveness needed for achieving equal opportunities and social mobility.

Direct evidence of superficiality of net use by higher-education students comes from Hargittai, Fullerton, Menchen, Trevino, and Yates (2010). They find that habitual users are not sophisticated, they value the net mainly for its ease of use, they pay little heed to who owns and operates a site, and they do not probe for the credibility of sources. They have argued for an informed Internet citizenry and have claimed that such help is not commonly provided.

And there can be deeper, less obvious, and wholly unintentional damage. Brain plasticity adapts neurology to experience. The habitual use of tick-and-click websites may then diminish the abilities we do not use. The ability to read in depth (Wolf, 2008) and the ability to search for meaning in texts (Brabazon, 2002) can be casualties. And there are reports of benefits for maintaining concentration and grasping meaning afforded by the attentive reading of printed texts (Miedema, 2009). Such ideas do not support a rush from quiet library to noisy forum. They hold to a belief in the value of carefully presented language, carefully received. They resist the uses of language as though it were no more than a means of display. They worry about underlying habits of mind which limit understanding. They allow that there is more to any authorship than the meaning immediately assigned by its audience. These doubting voices are not from careers-work authors, but as we shall see, their observations raise careers-work concerns.

Carr (2010) has described in detail the way the Internet's diversionary links can modify behavior. An anecdotal report (Miller, 2010) has described the impact of online experience on mind-set: "countless spinning, dancing, blinking, multi-coloured and goodie-filled margins tempt us away to a scattered, skittering, browsing mind-set" (http://www.salon.com/books/laura_ miller/2010/05/09/the_shallows).

Carr has suggested that constant diversions favor short-term memory and scramble long-term memory. But long-term memory is the greater part of selfhood. And careers work assumes a more or less uninterrupted and meditative process of thinking which gets embedded so that it is reusable over time. Eye-tracking evidence supports Carr's worries (Nielsen & Pernice, 2010).

But before we leave the dangers of niches, we should note this: There are minority career interests which are worth voicing. Niches form what Anderson (2009) has called "the long tail," that is, a statistical display tapering into a line of minority positions, each attracting enough attention to get by. Career management has a long tail: Not everybody is attracted to competitive advancement, or wants to be defined by employability, or cares to be labeled by the assumptions built into a diagnostic technique. Engagement in work-life is more diversely motivated than that. It stretches, niche by niche, from the personal to the planetary: People consider family life and local communities; they have concerns about economic growth and the survival of species, indeed of the biosphere. It is not easy to colonize such diversity: The long tail of career concerns suggests that careers work must adapt to what goes on online, including reframing diagnoses and expanding labor market information.

We have seen how Selwyn (2010) and Hooley (2011) call for social, moral, and cultural responses to digital technologies. And if Sunstein (2009) and Carr (2010) are right, there is some dissonance with work-life. Work-life calls for reliability as well as flexibility; it is about consideration for others as well as self-fulfillment; it needs sustained engagement though there may be immediate rewards.

There is no simple unraveling of these issues. In a changing world, much depends on whether online careers work can engage the flexibility which demands a wider perspective than what is easy to find, looks familiar, and feels comfortable.

A Now-and-Future Net

No genuine educator wants to shackle students. But not all that is free is autonomous (Law, 1992). Freedom is liberation from constraint—like looking at an open door. Autonomy is knowing what to do about it—like seeing where to go. We can win freedom; but autonomy is learned. Upgrading their online devices may win some freedoms; autonomy comes by questioning what they find: Does this mean move now? Do I believe it? Is it enough to go on? Might I go with it? Would it work out well? Is that what I want? Might there be a better way? Then how sure can I be that I want to do this? We take it in our stride, in seconds. It's how we survived on the savannah and what we do every time we cross a busy street. It's also how we agree to routine arrangements with our mates. But dealing with action that can carry you any worthwhile distance poses more demanding questions: Do I

know anything about who's telling me this? Why are they saying it? Is it in their own interests? Is it in mine and the interests of people important to me? Can I check on it? By doing what? How sure can I be that it's trustworthy? These questions demand a lot of disentangling: of appearance and reality, of the plausible and the credible, of looking and learning, and of learning and doing. Plausibility entices, and sometimes it does not matter—smile and do it anyway. But, before anybody commits to a move of any significance, findings must stand up to scrutiny. It matters because there are not only inhabitants on the net, there are colonists. The colonist metaphor can represent extreme behavior. And there are on the net those who manipulate in their own interests, illustrated by Wu's (2010) fears concerning a history that might repeat itself. There are also predators who harm, as in grooming for sexual gratification. But these examples are extreme, and a boundary between less extreme versions of manipulation and predation is not easy to map. But we need careers work not to figure there.

We, therefore, need a clear agenda for developing professional online careers work. Lanier's (2010) work on the influences of digitization provides a framework. A test of its usefulness is the extent to which he covers the pros and cons of online life raised in this chapter. Table 26.1 sets out the framework. It draws, in the center, on Lanier's thinking. On the left is a parallel account of what an educator might notice about people's engagement online. On the right is a careers-work agenda based on Lanier's understanding of that engagement. The table sets out, top to bottom, three areas for development which suggest how online self relates to embodied identity, online connectedness links to wider realities, and online searching becomes reliable learning. Lanier implies that doing everything inside your comfort zone is living dangerously. But that does not mean that column 1 needs alarm—for most people, it reflects no more than party talk: "as simple as that"; so "just do it" because you should "follow your dream"; and "wishing can make it so"; for, like celebrities, we are all "worth it"; and whatever was once no better

Table 26.1 Online influences

The engagement	The thinking	The agenda
Taking appearance, and what is easily found, as reality	Digital images replace the whole with the partial (pp. 70ff)	Looking beyond appearance and realizing inner life
Valuing binary polarities, either "amazing" or "rubbish"	Binary systems are "on" or "off"; they do not show "maybe" (pp. 68ff)	Finding more aspects of life than at first sight seem obvious
Working with sharp-and-fixed branded self-images	Digital imagery misses the overlapping nuances of self (pp. 168ff)	Getting into contact with their own bodies
Acting without realizing other possibilities	Reliance wholly on online sources is dangerously limiting (pp. 69ff)	Imagining possible selves in unforeseen futures
Seeking reassuring confirmation of ready-made beliefs	Following "likes" substitutes the fashionable for the worthwhile (pp. 36ff)	Learning from the surprising and the disturbing
"Liking" and revisiting the familiar and undisturbing	Comfort zones lock-in self-perpetuating ways of seeing (pp. 2 ff)	Welcoming and exploring new ways of seeing
Comfortably settling for immediate "yes-no" ticks and clicks	On-off digital signals lose nuances of human interaction (pp. 9ff)	Engaging careful and sustained application of mind
Looking for immediate, spectacular, and celebrity-iconic contacts	Easy cut-and-paste "mash-ups" displace creativity (pp. 19ff)	Seeing that finding something is not the same as knowing what to do about it
Believing they know all that they need to know	The mass of online content feels like "everything" and "everybody" (pp. 26ff)	Grasping that whatever they now know they can find something more
Seeking simple answers from quick-fix sources	Online designs invite dependence (pp. 179ff)	Figuring out explanations and owning responsibility for their action

Note. Adapted from "You are not a gadget: A manifesto," by Lanier, 2010, London, UK: Allen Lane

than "cool" is now, at least, "brilliant." It is, of course, never as simple as that. But it's a curmudgeon, not an educator, who would want to spoil the party, as long as—deep down—nobody expects such talk to take anyone anywhere important. But, if they should, then they need to learn that there is more to life than the bright and breezy, and online devices are not just fun guns. We all have more than one voice on where to go, who to go with, and why to bother. It could be for fun, for keeping organized, for finding meaning—it could be for survival. In attending to students' voice, educators might usefully ask themselves which level of that multilateral talk they are hearing.

Living and Learning Online: Relevance Across Cultures

Curmudgeons cannot hold back technology, but career workers, with other educators, can enable people to make good use of it. An enquiry into the views of opinion leaders in career guidance (The Skills Commission, 2010) suggests that careers work needs to extend online perspectives beyond the conventional. The argument here is for a beyond-the-conventional curriculum program. It is not proposed as a satellite of careers guidance but as the exploratory, enabling, and developmental component in a broad-based careers-work program.

This section collates past and current evidence which shows how the demands of living and learning online require such reform. Among the evidence is Vygotsky's (1978) theory. His research anticipated the net, proposing what he called graphic learning tools—the net qualifies. The role of teachers is then to frame—he said scaffold—learning to support the climb into progressively enlarged learning zones. Vygotsky reaches beyond the enclosure that Sunstein (2009) fears and Lanier (2010) documents. Sociology also anticipates online cultures. Goffman's (1959) account of how we each take different roles in different social situations, some private others public, will stand as an account of online culture. And Riesman's (1961) analysis of the cultures of inherited tradition, inner life, and social expectation anticipates online tensions. He images people juggling with where they come from, who they are, and who they are with; and he shows how that can inform how they will act autonomously.

Selwyn's (2011) more recent sociology looks to the development of curriculum-based programs to address such cultural significance. His sociological doubts parallel Lanier's technological analysis: Both show that the feeling of being unique and connected is appearance, not reality. Both call for critical skepticism rather than a comfortable enthusiasm. This is compatible with emerging careers-work thinking. Garnett (2010) has listed enabling critical thinking as a career worker's most pressing task. He characterizes it as being concerned with how we find things out, communicate with one another, and gain knowledge and understanding. He asserts that these learning skills need to be taught. Garnett is speaking of what are called metacognitive skills. We need curriculum developed to foster metacognitive skills.

Ramsden (2010) has been concerned that critical thinking is hampered by aspects of conventional thinking. For example, vocational pressures on curriculum result in no better than compliance, where students settle for the subject-based reproduction of what assessment requires rather than creatively working across disciplinarily boundaries. Ramsden urges that students be helped to learn how to change what they find. This, he says, is education's greatest gift.

Mackey and Jacobson (2010) have gone into more detail, pointing out that there is more than one kind of literacy. They have developed a list, all career relevant: seeing what is going on, making contact, evaluating what is found, incorporating it into thinking, using it in planning, understanding it as a basis for action, and producing and sharing it as information. They show that regardless of how life and technology change, these abilities to adapt and engage can be learned and transferred from one situation to another. Such transfer of learning is essential for careers work.

These more recent accounts of curriculum development lack explanatory frames like Goffman's (1959), Riesman's (1961), and Vygotsky's (1978). But a survey by Mason and Rennie (2010) moves things on. They have redesigned the digitally based curriculum method, moving it away from holding existing learning on an established track, towards enabling more creative and flexible learning. It is a shift from cognitive content to a metacognitive process. It builds partnerships between teachers and students: Teachers are less concerned with managing the technology, more with engaging students with the sources.

Research focused on the practical use of the Internet points in detail to the need to develop metacognitive skills: not just acquiring knowledge but thinking about how it is acquired. A study into the careers-work uses of digital technology (Bimrose & Barnes, 2010b) shows that having acquired labor market information, people need help in making sense of it. This is more than carrying out searches; it reaches into a process of taking useful command of what is found. Kiliç-Çakmak (2010) has studied how students use the Internet; this research points to an underlying need for metacognitive abilities to be developed as part of life management, which includes career management. Kiliç-Çakmak goes further than others in giving examples of objectives and processes, suggesting complex and shared tasks. He describes a process: planning, monitoring, and managing the use of a range of information.

Any account of the contemporary need for students to think for themselves is bound to apply to career management. For example, Morgan, Williamson, Lee, and Facer's (2007) stage-by-stage account appears in a guide for the design of the future development of a life-relevant curriculum. An aim is to enable students to examine and voice what they find on the net. A progression is set out in four learning stages: initiating and eliciting; defining and responding; doing and making; leading to communicating, presenting, and evaluating.

It is important to note that educators have interests to protect. Weller (2011) has acknowledged that Internet-related reform is a challenge to education professionals. He sees connectedness as a key feature of the net, working across the boundaries of both professional disciplines and social containment. He argues that theory has not caught up with the sheer mass of online material. He adopts an account of intellectual applications about maintaining scholarship and protecting ownership.

However, educators also need less narrowly academic ways of engaging with students, if they are to gain students' interested attention in the life-relevant usefulness of learning. More exploratory examples of this expansive enabling would include what Goffman (1959), Riesman (1961), and Vygotsky (1978) seminally brought forward. And it is illustrated in detail by what Morgan et al. (2007), Mason and Rennie (2010), Ramsden (2010), and Kiliç-Çakmak (2010) variously have created. And Selwyn's (2011) argument encompasses all of these possibilities, seeking such freedom from rule-bound attitudes in developing curriculum. What is enabled in curriculum begins with not knowing, and Selwyn argues that students may not know enough to know how to use the net and that those most likely to be harmed are least likely to realize it. He sets out implications for family life and economic position, as well as for issues associated with gender, race, and social class. His core claim is that the field restricts development in these areas by misapplying technological solutions to educational and sociological problems.

All of these research and development voices show that online devices are no more than tools and what they find is no more than raw material. There must also be a process which transforms that material into useful outcomes. It is why The Skills Commission (2010) has argued for a reforming agenda. It would be professionally negligent for career workers to evade it.

What Educators Do Best

The colonizing metaphor embeds an argument: It is that in exploiting what the net can do for careers work, we risk losing sight of what educators can do for students. A feature of this thinking is the acknowledgement that in order to appreciate how career workers can do well, it helps to understand what they have done less well, such as the cautious holding onto what is familiar and feels manageable. In Table 26.1, Lanier's (2010) thinking provides a framework for developing that argument. Using that framework, Table 26.2 sets out where working with online sources can take careers work: relating an online self to an embodied identity, linking online life to offline realities, and moving from searching for answers to grasping their meaning.

Embodiment

Dreyfus (2009) chose *Second Life*, the popular online virtual world, as the occasion for closely questioning how far online experience represents humanity. It seems to come close, offering a total immersion in an alternative way of living. It accommodates its own characters, locations, encounters, and narratives. There are resonances with career management: Visitors can deal with products, markets, and academies. And they can earn income, in a currency with a dollar exchange rate. But Dreyfus argues that virtual reality conveys nothing of the risks, commitment, or shared meaning of human engagement. The net's ready-made menus, derived icons, and reinvented avatars cannot convey the texture of embodied, shared, and situated encounters where posture, style, expression, and proximity carry subtle and spontaneous communication. This is how we know each other, enter another culture, and become a part of the culture. Dreyfus suggests that the subtle, immediate, and wordless sensing of embodied communication—body

Table 26.2 Key questions for careers work and the Internet

The metaphor	Key questions
For embodiment	How can what is found online become part of inner life—internalizing and embodying as part of identity?
For reach	How far is it learning for living—equipping people for life in other settings, on other tasks, and with other people?
For grasp	Can the net's extent and variability offer a basis for action—supporting appropriate and fulfilling action that can be made to work?

language—completes communication. This analysis fatally undermines policy claims that much of what career workers do can be done online.

Reach

While the idea of embodiment raises issues for a person's authenticity, the idea of reach goes into how far online learning can take a person in offline life. Career learning is learning for living, and unlike so-called "academic" learning, learning for living is gathered in one location and used in another. If career learning is not in that sense transferable, then it is not working. But the evidence on getting this kind of online-offline transfer is not good. What is learned in any location is not readily recalled in any other (Radvansky, Krawietz, & Tamplinthe, 2011). However, Mackey and Jacobson (2010) have observed the transferability of process-based learning. And evidence collated by Meadows (1993) and Maclure and Davies (1991) is that the chances of transfer can be improved. It means, at source, encoded learning with markers signaling where in life it can be used. Students are reminded of life in their learning, so that they are reminded of learning in their life. A useful framework is provided by role thinking (Law, 2006), which can position a person in an offline location with other people, and taking on a task; they pose where, who, and what questions. And so the encoding process is interrogative: This is

what you have learned, now how can you use it in your life? Where might you be? Who might you be with? What might you be taking on? The answers to these questions can reach into life-wide, lifelong living. Drawing on them poses a challenge to how adventurously we use the word *career*. The concept is abstract, a social construct. It can, therefore, mean what we say it means. It can certainly be more inclusive than might at first seem obvious in online career management, say on LinkedIn career-coaching blogs or expert careers-work websites. It can accommodate greater connectivity than that both online and offline, life-wide and lifelong, for acceptance and reform.

Grasp

The idea of embodiment poses issue for the ways in which the nuances of offline life can be misrepresented. The idea of reach poses issues about the extent of its connectivity. The idea of *grasp* poses issues for how securely its learning is taken on board. Dreyfus (2009) saw the achievement of grasp as a stage-by-stage process. He set out a six-stage sequence ranging from *novice* to *mastery*. In his work as an educator, he reports that students value podcasts and online documents, but that they also seek the embodied presence of the teacher. However, his online material is no more than an extension of what professors do when they give a lecture or hold a seminar.

Morgan et al. (2007) have gone further, seeking to enable students to examine and voice what is found on the net. They also set out a learning process in four stages: eliciting, defining, making, and presenting. The stages are closely similar to a general career-learning framework recently reapplied to online learning (Law, 1996). As depicted in Table 26.3, it tracks how online searching becomes offline learning. The framing is substantially developed from a research-based account of constructivist learning first proposed for curriculum by Jean Piaget (1932). The thinking has received recent confirmation, notably from neurologists (Law, 2010b).

Table 26.3 Progressive learning

Stages	Experience	Questions
Sensing	Finding things out	Does what you find give you enough to go on?
Sifting	Sorting out what is found	Can you sort what you've found into a useful pattern?
Focusing	Checking out what is important	Do you find in that pattern anything needing further probing?
Understanding	Figuring out how it all happens	Does probing lead to seeing how things got this way and what to do about them?

It is a process, not of setting out information but of the questioning by which people learn for themselves. It is also a form of critical thinking, probing what affects life chances. The framing is generic; each stage can be posed in a number of ways and in any degree of detail. The stages are progressive, each step relying on a securely taken preceding step. And they are interactive; each subsequent question is shaped by the preceding answer. This is learning for action, articulating part of our hold on survival—whether on the savannah, on the street, or on the net. It is a questioning process, and in Dreyfus's (2009) view, a professor asks good questions, modeling how to question in order to learn for students, such that students learn to question for themselves. What the educator does is mirrored by the students. The process entails hesitations, restatements, and backtracking, because the educator is following the students as much as leading them, and both are learning. It needs mutual comprehension and reciprocated trust.

In Selwyn's (2011) terms, this is how people find sense and meaning in what they find online. He accepts that the process must be closely linked to communities, with families more involved in the education of their children. An alert career worker might also argue that communities need families who are interested in the education of other people's children, because, whatever a family may seek for its own, a community needs all of its children to be educated. There are implications here that curriculum is central to careers work, but that it must be reformed.

However, we are not yet there. A survey of British school-based work on information technology (Furber, 2012) has shown that students find the lessons boring and that teachers know less about technology than they do. The report shows that net-savvy students are disbelieving that a teacher would try to serve up practice based on word processors, spreadsheets, and databases. Those who argue about what educators should teach sometimes maintain that digital literacy means being able to work in programming code. The *British Educational Communications and Technology Agency* (BECTA) (2010) has disagreed, arguing instead for a rethinking of digital literacy. It urges that students instead should be able to locate technology in a social context. This means knowing how to act appropriately, to understand when and why to use it, and to be able to discern credible online sources. Enabling such metacognition is what, at their best, professional educators do. And it calls for a reversal of a content-driven program, where students ask questions and teachers know answers. In a process-driven program, students find the information and educators ask the questions—the method is Socratic; it nurtures a habit of questioning. Between student experience and teacher expertise, there is no single authority. And their partnership cannot be realized wholly online. The process needs the educator to know the students well enough to anticipate what line of questioning might be useful. It needs the sensitivity to anticipate what people might ask and need to ask. It also needs the right words. As Judge (2000) and Wolf (2008) each shows, progressively enlarging students' command of language is part of enabling their command of life. The gain is less in the answers and more in learning how to ask the questions. And that equips a person for life.

Postcolonial Careers Work: New Concepts and Viewpoints

The Internet, which originated for military uses, has developed into a postcolonial culture. In this chapter, few examples are found of extreme careers-work colonialism. That would be to cling to the colonialist myth: a belief in the possibility of a foreign past usefully shaping an indigenous future. But no half-awake colonialist ever expected to survive wholly on that extreme. And the careers-work responses reported here do not so much clinging as inclining. Dreyfus (2009) has occupied a middle-ish position, exporting into online work some features of an undisturbed offline repertoire but also inviting a rigorous scrutiny. Closer to the colonist is careers-work's online use of psychometric coefficients and data-based correlates (Hulse, 2010). It is a mouse-click exportation of a tick-box habit which may actually obstruct the questions that people now need to ask.

Newcomers to the net are welcome when they are ready to adapt, and if things go well, to join as neighbors. Habitual questions based on ready-made assumptions belong to another world. But there are questions to be asked, both inside the net's familiar enclaves and in being surprised by new encounters. They search for the reliable among the variable: What is being put about here? Who is pushing it? Why are they doing that? What interests do they have? Are these my interests? Or the interests of anyone who depends on me? So do I pay attention to this? And, if so, how can I act on it?

Able educators enjoy being challenged in that way. Dealing with awkward questions is what experience and training have taught professional educators to do. Mirroring what they do is what students most need to be able to carry away. And however clever Web 4.0 technology proves to be, they'll need it more than ever if arbitrary and powerful interests get their hands on Tim Wu's (2010) master switch. And they might.

References

Anderson, C. (2009). *The longer long tail: How endless choice is creating unlimited demand*. New York, NY: Hyperion.

Barnes, A., & La Gro, N. (2010). Using ICT: A step change in career guidance or a sop to the twittering classes. In H. L. Reid (Ed.), *Constructing the future: Career guidance for changing contexts?* (pp. 70–78). Stourbridge, England: Institute for Career Guidance.

Baym, N. (2010). *Personal connections in the digital age*. Malden, MA: Polity Press.

Bimrose, J., & Barnes, S.-A. (2010a). *Labour market information (LMI), information communications and technologies (ICT) and information, advice and guidance (IAG): The way forward?* Warwick, England: Institute for Employment Research.

Bimrose, J., & Barnes, S.-A. (2010b). *Careers information, advice and guidance: The digital revolution and repositioning of labour market information*. Warwick, England: Institute for Employment Research.

Bishop, J. (2009). Pre-service teacher discourses: Authoring selves through multimodal compositions. *Digital Culture & Education, 1*(1). Retrieved from http://www.digitalcultureandeducation.com/volume-1/bishop-2009/

Bosley, C., Krechowiecka, I., & Moon, S. (2005). *Review of literature on the use of information and communication technology in the context of careers education and Guidance*. Derby, England: Centre for Guidance Studies, University of Derby.

Brabazon, T. (2002). *Digital hemlock: Internet education and the poisoning of teaching*. London, England: University of New South Wales Press.

British Educational Communications and Technology Agency. (2010). *Digital literacy: Teaching critical thinking for our digital world*. Coventry, England: Author.

Carr, N. (2010). *The shallows: What the internet is doing to our brains*. New York, NY: W.W. Norton.

Chatfield, T. (2010). *Fun Inc: Why games are the 21st century's most serious business*. London, England: Virgin Books.

Dreyfus, H. (2009). *On the internet* (2nd ed.). London, England: Routledge.

Facer, K., & Selwyn, N. (2010). Social networking: Key messages from the research. In R. Sharpe, H. Beetham, & S. De Freitas (Eds.), *Rethinking learning for a digital age: How learners are shaping their own experiences* (pp. 31–42). London, England: Routledge.

Flynn, J. R. (2007). *What is intelligence?* London, England: Cambridge University Press.

Fuchs, C., Hofkirchner, W., Schafranek, M., Raffl, C., Sandoval, M., & Bichler, R. (2010). Theoretical foundations of the web: Cognition, communication, and co-operation. Towards an understanding of web 1.0, 2.0, 3.0'. *Future Internet, 2*, 41–59. Retrieved from http://www.mdpi.com/1999-5903/2/1/41/pdf

Furber, S. (Ed.). (2012). *Shut down or restart? The way forward for computing in UK Schools*. London, England: The Royal Society. Retrieved from http://royalsociety.org/education/policy/computing-in-schools/report/

Garnett, F. (2010). Contextualising digital literacies. In J. Gillen & D. Barton (Eds.), *Digital literacies* (pp. 22–30). Retrieved from http://www.tlrp.org/docs/DigitalLiteracies.pdf

Goffman, E. (1959). *The presentation of self in everyday life*. London, England: Pelican Books.

Hargittai, E., Fullerton, L., Menchen, E., Trevino K., & Yates, T. (2010). Trust online: Young adults evaluation of web content. *International Journal of Communication, 4*, 468–494. Retrieved from http://ijoc.org/ojs/index.php/ijoc/article/view/636

Hooley, T. (2011). Careers work in the blogosphere: Can careers blogging widen access to career support? In L. Barham & B. Irving (Eds.), *Constructing the future: Diversity, inclusion and social justice* (pp. 87–101). Stourbridge, England: Institute of Career Guidance.

Hooley, T., Hutchinson, J., & Watts, A. G. (2010). *Careering through the web*. Derby, England: International Centre for Guidance Studies. Retrieved from http://www.derby.ac.uk/ask-icegs-information-services/icegs-research-e-briefings/icegs-research-e-briefing-july-august-2010

Hulse, P. (2010, February). Focus on ICT: Matching programs fall into disrepute? *Careers Education and Guidance*. Retrieved from http://www.aceg.org.uk/wp-content/uploads/98578_Journal_Feb_2010.pdf

Judge, P. (2000, March). India: Hole-in-the-wall. *Businessweek Online Briefing*. Retrieved from http://www.greenstar.org/butterflies/Hole-in-the-Wall.htm

Kiliç-Çakmak, E. (2010). Learning strategies and motivational factors predicting information literacy self-efficacy of e-learners. *Australasian Journal of Educational Technology, 26*(2), 192–208.

Lanier, J. (2010). *You are not a gadget: A manifesto*. London, England: Allen Lane.

Larbalestier, M. (2010). The social web and careers work. *Career Development and Research*. Retrieved from: http://www.cew.wisc.edu/docs/The%20Social%20Web%20and%20Careers%20Work%20-%20Handout.pdf

Law, B. (1992). Autonomy and learning about work. In R. A. Young & A. Collin (Eds.), *Interpreting career: Hermeneutical studies of lives in context* (pp. 71–86). New York, NY: Praeger.

Law, B. (1996). A career-learning theory. In A. G. Watts, B. Law, J. Killeen, J. Kidd, & R. Hawthorn (Eds.), *Rethinking careers education and guidance: Theory, policy and practice* (pp. 46–72). London, England: Routledge.

Law, B. (2006). *LiRRiC: Life-role relevance in curriculum for effective and useful learning*. Retrieved from www.hihohiho.com/underpinning/cafqca.pdf

Law, B. (2010a). *Career-learning thinking for contemporary working life*. Retrieved from http://www.hihohiho.com/newthinking/crlrnupdate.pdf

Law, B. (2010b). *Career narratives*. Retrieved from http://www.hihohiho.com/storyboarding/sbwebsites.html

Mackey, T. P., & Jacobson, T. E. (2010). Reframing information literacy as a meta-literacy. *College and Research Journal*. Retrieved from: http://infolitlib20.blogspot.com/2010/03/reframing-information-literacy-as.html

Maclure, S., & Davies, P. (1991). *Learning to think: Thinking to learn*. London, England: Pergamon.

Mason, P. (2012). *Why it's kicking off everywhere: The new global revolutions*. London, England: Verso Books.

Mason, R., & Rennie, F. (2010). *Web based course design*. Retrieved from: http://wiki.alt.ac.uk/index.php/Web-based_course_design

Meadows, S. (1993). *The child as thinker: The development and acquisition of cognition in childhood*. London, England: Routledge.

Miedema, J. (2009). *Slow reading*. Duluth, MN: Litwin Books.

Miller, L. (2010, May). Yes, the internet is rotting your brain. *Salon*. Retrieved from: http://www.salon.com/books/laura_miller/2010/05/09/the_shallows

Morgan, J., Williamson, B., Lee, T., & Facer, K. (2007). *Enquiring minds*. Bristol, England: Future Lab.

Morzove, E. (2010, June). Losing our minds to the web. *Prospect*. Retrieved from http://www.prospectmagazine.co.uk/magazine/losing-our-minds-to-the-web/

Naish, J. (2010, July 12). Rise of the laptop revolutionaries. *New Statesman*, p. B1.

Nielsen, J., & Pernice, K. (2010). *Eye-tracking web usability*. Berkeley, CA: New Riders Press.

Piaget, J. (1932). *The moral judgment of the child*. London, England: Routledge & Kegan Paul.

Radvansky, G., Krawietz, S., & Tamplinthe, A. (2011). Walking through doorways causes forgetting: Further explorations. *Quarterly Journal of Experimental Psychology, 64*(8), 1632–1645.

Ramsden, P. (2010, August 5). No thinkable alternative: Producing graduates who are critical thinkers. *Times Higher Education*. Retrieved from http://www.timeshighereducation.co.uk/story.asp?sectioncode=26&storycode=412794&c

Richmond, K., & Stephens, L. (2010). *Social networking and careers: A survey investigating the use of social networking sites for career research, networking and profile among LSE students and graduates*. London, England: LSE Careers. Retrieved from http://www.slideshare.net/Richmonk10/lse-careers-social-networking-and-careers-survey-2010

Riesman, D. (1961). *The lonely crowd*. London, England: Yale University Press.

Selwyn, N. (2010). Looking beyond learning: Notes towards the critical study of educational technology. *Journal of Computer Assisted Learning, 26*(1), 65–73.

Selwyn, N. (2011). *Education and technology: Issues and debates*. London, England: Continuum.

Shirky, C. (2008). *Here comes everybody: The power of organising without organisations*. London, England: Penguin.

Shirky, C. (2010). *Cognitive surplus: Creativity and generosity in a connected age*. London, England: Penguin.

Sunstein, C. (2009). *On rumours*. London, England: Allen Lane.

Tapscott, D. (1998). *Growing up digital: The rise of the net generation*. New York, NY: McGraw Hill.

The Skills Commission. (2010). *Inspiration and aspiration: Realising our potential in the 21st Century*. London, England: The Skills Commission.

Vygotsky, L. (1978). *Mind in society: The development of higher psychological processes*. Cambridge, MA: Harvard University Press.

Watts, A. G. (1996). Computers in guidance. In A. G. Watts, B. Law, J. Killeen, J. Kidd, & R. Hawthorn (Eds.), *Rethinking careers education and guidance: Theory, policy and practice* (pp. 269–281). London, England: Routledge.

Weller, M. (2011). *The digital scholar: How technology is transforming scholarly practice*. New York, NY: Bloomsbury Academic.

Wolf, M. (2008). *Proust and the squid: The story and science of the reading brain*. London, England: Icon Books.

Wu, T. (2010). *The master switch*. New York, NY: Random House.

Career Helplines: A Resource for Career Development

27

Patricia Flederman and A.G. Watts

Global realities are stimulating a new international discourse about career guidance delivery systems relevant to both so-called developing and developed countries. In response to economic volatility and extensive unemployment alongside skill shortages, government policy in many countries is addressing choices and transitions between learning and work in a lifelong framework. The need for relevant, affordable career guidance for all is challenging traditional approaches. The traditional model of face-to-face counseling linked to psychometric testing is arguably inappropriate, but in any case unaffordable, when expanded to all citizens over a lifetime: innovative and more streamlined delivery mechanisms are needed. Not only expansion of services but transformation is required—a new paradigm and new approaches (OECD, 2004). This is especially the case for developing countries (ILO, 2006; Walters, Watts, & Flederman, 2009; Watts & Fretwell, 2004). Rapid technological changes over the last 10 years make the goal of career services for all more feasible by enabling affordable services accessed at a distance, increasingly through mobile devices. This has profound implications for career guidance delivery. Already the combination of telephone and Internet has changed service delivery in such fields as banking, medicine, and travel and has led to a cultural shift towards an expectation of any-place/any-time services. This shift is raising expectations with regard to career services as well (Watts & Dent, 2002). Today Web 2.0, which enables a telephone/cell phone helpline integration with the Internet, combined with social networking, user-generated content, and repurposable data, is changing the way career guidance practitioners and clients can learn, work, and communicate (Hooley, Hutchinson, & Watts, 2010).

With an integrated career guidance helpline, users can access career guidance as they choose, when they choose, through any channel they prefer, for example, combining Internet search and the telephone, cell phone, email, SMS, VOIP (such as Skype), chat, Facebook, and Twitter. They can do it from venues convenient to them, with little or no cost. The constraints of geography, time, travel costs, physical disability, and social isolation are mitigated. An integrated helpline clearly offers many advantages including flexibility, accessibility, convenience, and reaching out to a widened client base.

Counseling Effectiveness via the Telephone

A body of research in the UK, USA, New Zealand, and Australia has clearly established that personal and therapeutic counseling can be

P. Flederman (✉)
Claremont Consulting Incorporated, Western Cape, South Africa
e-mail: patricia.flederman@gmail.com

G. Arulmani et al. (eds.), *Handbook of Career Development*, International and Cultural Psychology, 481
DOI 10.1007/978-1-4614-9460-7_27, © Springer Science+Business Media, LLC 2014

carried out effectively via the telephone (King, Bambling, Reid, & Thomas, 2006; Reese, Conoley, & Brossart, 2002, 2006; Rosenfield, 1997; Rosenfield & Smillie, 1998). The evidence for counseling via computer-delivered support is also promising (Rochlen, Zack, & Speyer, 2004). King et al. (2006), evaluating a youth counseling service in Australia, found that online counseling had less session impact than telephone counseling but had distinct advantages for clients. Landlines and cell phones are known to be especially attractive to adolescents given their low cost, easy access, anonymity, control over the call, flexibility, safety, and user-friendliness. For this age cohort, self-determination and independence from parental involvement are additional attractions (Christogiorgos et al., 2010).

In a US study investigating client perceptions of counseling by telephone, Reese et al. (2006) found that more than half of those who had experienced both telephone and face-to-face counseling preferred telephone counseling. The telephone's appeal corroborated the literature, in which control, convenience, accessibility, privacy, low cost, and anonymity have been identified as advantages of telephone counseling for clients. Over half of the respondents (58 %) gave as their primary reasons for preferring telephone counseling: convenience; quicker, easier, and immediate access; and that it made them feel more comfortable, less intimidated, and able to speak more openly. Interestingly, two-thirds of the 58 % had annual incomes of $30,000 or below. This suggests that career guidance by telephone may have special appeal to lower-income people, for reasons that may go beyond savings on travel costs.

Over the last few years, the career guidance field in the UK in particular has assimilated telephone guidance into mainstream practice, with high levels of quality and customer satisfaction (Page, Newton, Hawthorn, Hunt, & Hillage, 2007). When telephone guidance is integrated with the Internet's vast information and advice resources, interactivity options, and social networking, new possibilities in the adviser–user relationship emerge. The user has more control over the information and the direction of her or his journey, using the adviser as needed. For example, the user can search the web, take a self-assessment test, and then choose to discuss the results with an adviser. This requires new skills from the careers adviser, who has to be proficient on many communication platforms—telephone, webchat, email, SMS, Skype, Facebook, Twitter, etc.—with the capacity to provide advice or counseling verbally and in writing, in real time as well as with a delay. It involves multitasking: searching for information while talking with the user or looking at the user's screen and discussing its content with the user.

Social Equity

Policymakers in most countries expect career guidance services to deliver on three main sets of policy goals, that is, those related to learning, the labor market, and social equity (OECD, 2004; Walters et al., 2009). Social equity relates to fair, just, and equitable opportunities and distribution of resources. Whereas social equality is about treating all people the same way, a social equity-driven service includes tailored strategies to mitigate the barriers and obstacles various groups face in accessing resources and services in order to ensure these can be accessed by all. Thus, not only does the telephone helpline broaden access, but it can differentially benefit the poor and disadvantaged by addressing barriers that especially affect them (Flederman, 2011). Eliminating the need to travel to a center also makes environmental sense.

While telephone and online services can extend access, there is also concern about the growing digital divide in both so-called developing and developed countries (Keevy, Steenekamp, & West, 2012). As helpline services innovate in the direction of social media and online sources, they need to focus on those who do not have access to the Internet or do not know how to use it effectively. However, mobile telephones are revolutionizing access to digital services. For example, far more people had cell phones (29 million) than personal computers (6 million) or landlines (5 million) in South Africa in 2010, and these cell phones were being used extensively to access the web (8 million people) (Hutton, 2011).

Examples of Practice

Early Examples

Telephone guidance is not new. Early examples in the USA date from the 1970s. In due course, other examples emerged in Canada, New Zealand, and the UK in particular (for an earlier review, see Watts & Dent, 2002). Most, however, were relatively small-scale in nature.

In 1998 a major development took place in the UK, with the establishment of Learndirect—a helpline that initially focused particularly on helping adults to find out about learning opportunities. This involved two large call centers in England, plus other arrangements in the rest of the UK, and was soon attracting massive volumes—over a million calls per year, covering a wide range of learning and career issues, requiring both information and guidance responses. This has been a significant model for other career helplines internationally.

Expansion

The last few years have seen a major broadening of interest in telephone helplines and online guidance services. Existing helplines in England, New Zealand, and Canada have continued to develop. In addition, many new career guidance helplines are now being launched in Europe and also in such countries as Australia and South Africa.

The Learndirect service in England has undergone significant model adaptation and rebranding. It became known as the Careers Advice Service and was then incorporated first into the Next Step service for adults and subsequently into a new all-age National Careers Service. The latter service also includes the previously separate Connexions Direct helpline

for young people aged 14–19. In the case of adults, referrals can be made to face-to-face services, either at the user's request or because the adviser has identified that the user may benefit from a face-to-face interaction.

New Zealand's Career Services (now Careers New Zealand) has run a free telephone career advice line since 2000. In-depth telephone guidance was added in 2009, following a successful pilot evaluation (Bean & England, 2009; England, van Holten, & Urbahn, 2008). The helpline is now integrated with webchat guidance, alongside self-help web-based tools and services and group and one-on-one face-to-face advice and guidance to a small number of targeted individuals. Capability-building services are provided to develop the skills of "career influencers" (such as teachers and parents). In December 2011, 28,400 people used the helpline, with 90 % reporting that they found the service useful. An independent 2011 outcome evaluation asked a sample of 1,389 clients if they felt the helpline had met their needs: 82 % said it had. In addition, 95 % reported that the service had made a difference to them or had supported a career or study decision being made (Careers New Zealand, 2012).

A more limited Labor Market and Career Information (LMCI) Hotline was established under the Provincial Government of Newfoundland and Labrador but has operated Canada-wide since the early 1990s. It has expanded from helping people make informed career decisions to also assisting callers (including individuals and employers) to utilize self-help web-based services.

Also in Canada, the Provincial Ministry of British Colombia launched the Employment Program of British Columbia (EPBC) in April 2012, primarily for job seekers. The main service delivery is via WorkBC Employment Service Centres (ESC)—job centers and complementary career learning services to help people prepare for, find, and maintain employment. Some centers offer facilitated online workshops and services alongside face-to-face workshops; they are also expected to use telephone/cell phone/email services where necessary to overcome access barriers, especially for people in remote areas. As well as face-to-face counseling, there are opportunities for text-based e-guidance through forums that include peer support and collaborative learning (Goddard, 2009). However, a helpline is not at this point a service design element.

Recently, a number of new helpline initiatives have emerged in Europe, all within a lifelong learning framework reflecting EU policy on lifelong guidance. France and Denmark both have new national helplines, while in Austria and Germany, progress is under way to launch such helplines. Some of the common core elements in such helplines are noted in Box 27.1 and include information resources, staff and management resources, business processes, and client relationship management (CRM) systems.

In 2009, a French law established the right of citizens to guidance as a means of helping lifelong learning to become a reality. This guarantee of career guidance for all is carried out through a multi-ministerial authority accountable directly to the Prime Minister's office, in cooperation with social partners, regions, and professional organizations. It is delivered via an integrated telephone helpline and website, in partnership with local face-to-face counseling services licensed by the government. By 2011, France had a telephone service on stream (with email and webchat services in the pipeline), with a target of 150,000 contacts in that year and 400,000 by 2013.[1]

In 2011, Denmark launched an integrated telephone helpline service, *E-vejledning* (E-guidance). This includes SMS, email, and online chat primarily aimed at youth and their parents, although accessible to all. In its first year, it had nearly 70,000 users, of whom 25 % were young people aged 18–23, 50 % were young people aged 14–17, 21 % were adults,

3 % were parents, and 2 % were "other." By the end of its first 2 years, 150,000 sessions had been conducted.

In Austria, building on existing regional networks to support adult education, the Ministry of Education, Arts and Culture in 2011 commissioned research to improve and develop tools for better access and implementation of a telephone and web-based helpline with a view to establishing a nationwide service. The service is to be especially addressed to groups facing particular barriers, such as those with low-skilled qualification levels, while also being integrated into guidance services for all adults.

In Germany, to facilitate access to guidance for continuing education, the Federal Ministry of Education and Research has commissioned a consortium to prepare a draft for a nationwide Educational Guidance Service Telephone and Internet Portal (Jenschke, Schober, & Frübing, 2011). Core elements of a career guidance helpline service have subsequently been developed, such as human resource training and knowledge management.

South Africa is the first middle-income country to create a national career development helpline. Launched in mid-2010, it operates within a paradigm of social equity and lifelong learning and is driven by the policy challenges of human capacity development in a context of high unemployment alongside skill shortages. Initiated and managed by the South African Qualifications Authority (SAQA), it is the only helpline internationally to be led and managed by an entity responsible for a National Qualifications Framework. It operates under the auspices of the Department of Higher Education and Training (DHET) and is viewed as a ministerial flagship project.

The development of the South African helpline followed investigations of the integrated multichannel helpline models in England and New Zealand. SAQA decided that their models were suitable for adaptation to the specific circumstances of South Africa. Envisaged as an *ecosystem*—a set of interrelationships between education, training, development, and work

---

[1] Information for countries covered has been collected from, and checked with, professional contacts in those countries.

(Isaacs, 2010)—the helpline is being established as the core of a career development system that includes partnership with other institutions such as colleges and the Department of Labor. Partnership agreements with these institutions provide a network of referral options from the helpline to 189 career guidance offices belonging to various institutions. Between its inception in mid-2010 and December 2012, 43,000 cases from telephone, email, and walk-ins have been logged, while the website and mobisite have had 216,000 and 73,400 visits, respectively. Weekly radio programs in ten languages reach an audience of 1.8 million people per week in rural areas.

These examples are not exhaustive. Other countries already offer or are developing career guidance helplines of various kinds. But the examples outlined here provide a useful evidence base for exploring some of the key issues facing such helplines.

Box 27.1. Some Elements of Career Development Helplines

Resources: Career and Labor Market Information
- Information on study, financing study, occupations, and the labor market
- Careers introduced through personal biographies and case studies
- Tools (e.g., interest questionnaires)
- Guides (e.g., how to prepare for a job interview)
- A research and updating system for formal and informal information sources
- Both information packaged for the public and an internal information resource for helpline advisors
- Production and packaging of information relevant, mediated for, and accessible to particular demographic groups

Resources: Staffing and Management
- Staffing: job profiles
- Clarity on career development and helpline competencies, which reflect a career development delivery model appropriate for helplines
- Preservice and in-service training and development systems
- Clear performance standards and performance monitoring systems
- Leadership in a continuous learning culture and quality performance management systems

Technology
- Telephony system
- Website (ideally integrated with the telephony system if appropriate)
- Internal searchable database or a paper-based library
- CRM software where possible or other technologically simpler ways to collect data on service delivery (e.g., tape recorder)
- Additional communication channels such as email, Facebook, and SMS as appropriate

Business Processes
- Steps involved in providing the service to be designed, mapped, documented, and shared for job clarity, as a monitoring tool, as a tool for service improvement, and to build institutional capacity
- Business processes to reflect operational policy guidelines and requirements, performance standards, criteria and indicators, and ethical policies
- Steps involved in implementing a quality performance management system documented
- Systems in place to review business processes, with participation by all

(continued)

Issues

Information Versus Guidance

In all countries reviewed, the government offers a service within a broad ethos of entitlement, with France the most explicit, that lifelong guidance is a citizens' right. But if a right, at what depth of guidance and information and at what cost per contact? The more in-depth, the more labor-intensive and therefore expensive it is likely to be (Watts & Dent, 2002).

A number of helplines, including those in England, France, and New Zealand, have created staff tiers to distinguish the functions of information/advice-giving and guidance/counseling. In well-established helplines, such as in England, these are linked to qualification levels and represent a structured progression route and the rudiments of a career path for guidance practitioners.

The service in England for some time had three tiers: Information Advisers (focusing on information), Learning Advisers (focusing on advice), and Lifelong Learning Advisers (focusing on guidance). These have subsequently been reduced to two in order to provide a more seamless service for the customer: a Frontline Adviser assists with qualifications and funding questions and—when appropriate—refers callers to the Career Coach at the second tier for career change and career coaching needs; the aim is to refer about one in ten calls to this second tier. The Career Coaches are more highly qualified, and around 30 % have a postgraduate certificate in telephone guidance.

Similarly, France is piloting a two-tier system with a first-level tele-counselor who provides information and can then refer the caller to a second level if a more highly qualified counselor is needed. While the first helpline tier is for all, the second tier specializes in particular target groups. In particular, a specialized service for employees (including temporary workers), and another one for youth and their parents, is managed under the title *Mon Orientation en ligne* by ONISEP (*Office National d'Information sur les Enseignements et les Professions*) and can be accessed via telephone, chat, or email. A separate youth service, operating on much the same basis but with a focus on international mobility and volunteer opportunities, is managed by CIDJ (*Centre d'Information et de Documentation Jeunesse*). There are plans to develop a further second-tier telephone service for unemployed people.

Centralized Versus Decentralized

In a centralized service, one central service site serves the whole country; in a decentralized service, calls are routed to helpline staff based in various local geographic locations. A key argument for a decentralized service is that locally based advisers are more likely to have local tacit knowledge and networks. Also, telecommuting from home or dispersed sites can offer flexible options for staff and service hours, expansion of work opportunities for physically disabled people, and cost savings on office rentals. The new British Columbia service is particularly decentralized, with centers tasked to find ways to reach those in remote areas with the assumption that they will provide cell phone and telephone access options.

However, such benefits must be weighed against the advantages of ongoing staff feedback and flexible training and development strategies that are more feasible in a central call center. Experience in England, for example, is that even the most motivated staff members benefit from ongoing interactions with other staff in order to maintain and improve their quality performance standards. Moreover, while decentralization can result in stronger customization of services, brand identity and the systems it supports can be weakened. It is simpler to assure consistency and economies of scale in a centralized service.

Some services have mixed models. In Denmark, for example, the service is staffed by 12 full-time counselors based in Copenhagen, plus 23 part-time counselors working from their home base.

Relationship to Face-to-Face Services

In New Zealand, the helpline is part of an integrated service structure, which also includes face-to-face and web-based services. All clients seeking career support are taken through a brief needs-assessment process to determine the appropriate service channel and level of service. This in principle enables maximum delivery efficiency and flexibility between the different channels. In England, the channels are part of the same National Careers Service but are managed through separate contracts: the local face-to-face centers are part of, or subcontractors to, 1 of 12 organizations contracted by the government to provide such face-to-face services and are therefore operationally separate from the helpline. In South Africa, the helpline has partnership agreements with other institutions, such as further education and training (FET) colleges and labor offices, enabling it to refer callers opting for face-to-face help to the career offices of these institutions; this includes agreements to build career development capacity at 40 FET colleges. Similarly, in France, the helpline has partnerships with local face-to-face counseling services licensed by the government under the label *Orientation pour Tous*. This complementary partnership approach capitalizes on the benefits of economy of scale and consistency of quality of a centralized integrated helpline service while offering sources of local information and networks through the local face-to-face service.

Age-Specific Versus All-Age

The issue of age-specific or all-age concerns the extent to which the service is for all or is targeted at a particular age group. New Zealand and South Africa are examples of all-age helplines. In Denmark, the service is all-age, but particularly focused on young people. In France, the first level is all-age; the second level covers all ages, though through separate, largely age-segmented helplines.

England started with two distinct services: a career helpline for adults aged 19 and over and a separate helpline (Connexions Direct) for those 14–19 (Watts & Dent, 2002). There are strong arguments against such a split, including lack of continuity and defining where the boundary should be placed (Watts, 2010). In England, the two services are now being brought together within the all-age National Careers Service, with some immediate convergence including a single telephone number being used for access to both helplines and with the possibility of fuller integration once the existing contracts have expired.

A more specific case of an age-specific service is the service in Australia which is for mature-age people aged 45 and over.

Marketing

If career development helplines are to be taken seriously as a public-policy tool as well as a citizen service, they have to be marketed. Watts and Dent (2008) compared the results of branding and marketing efforts in England and New Zealand and concluded that they have a strong effect on usage levels. They noted that the usage of the helpline in England had been significantly stimulated by marketing campaigns, including prime-time advertising on television. A review of the New Zealand all-age service (Watts, 2007) indicated that the level of take-up of its helpline had been under a quarter of that for the helpline in England, relative to population. This seems clearly related to the level of brand recognition among the general public: around 30 % in New Zealand in contrast to figures of over 80 % in England. Such differences in turn seemed linked to the size of marketing budgets: the marketing budget in England as a percentage of total turnover (its budget had been consistently set at one-third of total advice turnover) was nearly five times larger than that in New Zealand. More recently, a government embargo in England on advertising public services has resulted in a massive reduction in volumes of users (Careers Sector Stakeholders Alliance, 2012).

In the developing country context of South Africa, a challenge is to keep up with demand when it is stimulated. For example, when the Minister of Higher Education and Training has reminded the public of the contact details and encouraged people to use the helpline services (telephone, SMS, email, Facebook) or when the helpline's radio programs have been broadcast, a big spike in demand has followed. In addition, face-to-face group outreach services to more marginalized communities provide an essential bridge to service access. Providing an information stall at career exhibitions, especially in rural communities, not only informs people of the service but also communicates how it can help people who may find both career development and distance services unfamiliar.

There are two important goals behind marketing of helpline services. The first is that citizens should know about the service and be actively encouraged to use it. In addition, however, social marketing advertises socially beneficial messages in the interest of the citizen and therefore is an end in itself. For example, a career service might advertise a service by promoting the idea that career planning is valuable for the individual, which might have benefits even if the service itself is not used. An example of social marketing in the career development field was the "Yes" campaign in the Maldives, focused primarily on encouraging positive attitudes to career development linked to take-up of a skills program (Arulmani & Abdulla, 2007).

Targeting and Framing

Marketing is linked to targeting. If the aim is to target users from particular age groups or particular disadvantaged groups, for example, marketing can be focused on media used by such groups.

Similarly, marketing can influence the framing of the service: whether contacts are primarily concerned with learning opportunities, with work opportunities, or with career issues representing the interaction between the two. The title of the service can be influential here: the Learndirect helpline in England was initially focused strongly towards learning; whereas the Labor Market and Career Information Hotline in Canada is focused towards work. In addition, however, a specifically career-oriented marketing campaign in England played a significant role in deliberately moving from a mainly learning-oriented service to a more career-oriented service (Watts & Dent, 2008). In the case of Connexions Direct in England, the framing of the service was even broader, to include a wide range of personal as well as career issues: this has now been reduced to a more specific career frame as part of its integration into the new National Careers Service. Clarity on the framing of career guidance helplines is essential for public accountability, for managing public expectations, and for the maintenance of a viable strategic direction for the helpline.

Range and Balance of Channels

Hooley et al. (2010) have noted that technology can be used in three ways: to deliver information, to provide an automated interaction, and to provide a channel for communication. The first two are fully automated, with all costs invested in the creation and maintenance of the resource: there are no unit costs related to levels of usage. Where, however, technology is used as a channel for communication, whether by voice or in text form, each user involves a unit cost. The levels of cost are related in part to the length of the contact and in part to the salary levels of the staff member. Both of these mean that guidance tends to be more expensive than information.

Across all countries reviewed, there is a marked reframing of services to increasingly emphasize online self-help services. The service in Newfoundland and Labrador in Canada, for example, is seeking to move away from telephone guidance towards coaching callers to use self-help options.

In England, the annual volumes of users for the adult helpline have declined somewhat over time, being overtaken massively by the numbers of web sessions: between 2000 and 2006, the number of telephone calls fell from well over a million to just under 900,000, while the number of web sessions increased from under 200,000 to over 9 million, and both trends have continued since then (Watts & Dent, 2008). The same trend has been evident in New Zealand (Careers New Zealand, 2012). In the case of England, this has been linked to a change in the nature of the telephone calls: since requests for information (e.g., regarding places of study or addresses for bursaries) are now increasingly answered through the website, the telephone calls are tending to focus more on guidance—where the caller needs help, for example, in exploring their options, barriers, and action plans towards a career path—requiring a shift in the balance of staff to higher-trained staff capable of offering such guidance (Watts & Dent, 2008).

Web 2.0 provides the opportunity for an integrated helpline and Internet service with multichannel access at the convenience of the caller. In England, webchat is increasingly a first-choice channel for contact. Synergy between England's telephone service and web-browsing service is envisaged to expand, once funds are available, to include a collaborative browsing service in which a helpline adviser can initiate webchat with users browsing their website who seem to need help. The potential of the text-based dimension of e-guidance has been demonstrated by some contractors delivering the Employment Program in British Columbia, which has utilized the opportunities it offers—because it is asynchronous, with time delays for responses and a record of the interaction—for clients to review and reflect upon their recorded thoughts and dialogues (Goddard, 2009).

Even within the services where technology is used as a channel for communication, the balance between different subchannels may vary. In Denmark, the service has been framed as an e-guidance service rather than as a telephone service. Of the nearly 55,000 contacts received in its first 9 months of operation, 44 % were by online webchat, 31 % by telephone, 23 % by email, and 2 % by SMS; by 2012, the proportion by webchat had risen to 48 %. In 2012, counseling via social media was added using Facebook.

The key criterion for service balance is to create multiple access points that mitigate particular barriers various people face. The balance might look very different in different contexts.

Cost-Effectiveness

The balance between the helpline, referrals to face-to-face services, and the Internet is a question of resource investment and also of client choice. Clearer models, based on users' experiences of strengths and weaknesses of the different media and ways in which they can be effectively combined, can provide a stronger basis for planning coherent service delivery. Ongoing inspection of contact volume data can enable informed decisions about how many full-time and part-time staff to hire and what working hours to employ them for, in order to meet demand in a cost-effective way within acceptable response times (Watts & Dent, 2006).

Calls for greater public accountability require career guidance services, funded from the public purse, to demonstrate the ratio of money invested to client gain. Measuring productivity—comparing input costs to quantified outputs and outcomes—is important, though it can distort a service away from its central purposes and arguably needs to be complemented by qualitative measures to assess client impact or "client gain." An integrated multichannel helpline service has to clearly articulate the desired outcomes and their impact on individuals and society, making the case for responsible cost-effective investment in achieving this. New Zealand procures annual evaluations that provide quantifiable data using qualitative measures: this is useful not only for reporting purposes but also as a management tool for continuous improvement. England uses CRM (customer relationship management) software to integrate data-collection systems into its management operation, so that use of the data is translated rapidly into feedback, improvement systems, and plans; in addition, "mystery shoppers" (where evaluators call the service posing as clients in order to assess service quality), callback facilities, and external evaluations build systems of accountability into the service.

Quality

Establishing a set of quality criteria is essential to the delivery of the best possible service to clients, assessing value outcome with reference to resource input. A quality approach includes the nature of the inputs and delivery process but is driven by impact on the client.

In England, the National Careers Service helpline has created a quality management system built around the Matrix Standard, with formal and informal as well as internal and external data collection and feedback leading to continually updated strategic development plans. Included in this system is attention to an organizational culture of learning, improvement, and support as quality drivers. The Matrix Standard is outcome-based and serves both as a benchmark of the quality of the service and as a key service improvement tool. It has four elements: leadership and management, resources, service delivery, and continuous quality improvement. Each has a set of delivery standards: examples are that clients and staff influence the design and development of the service (leadership and management standard); that clients are provided with current, accurate, and quality-assured information which is inclusive (resources standard); that the service is defined so that clients are clear about what they might expect (service delivery standard); and that the organization evaluates feedback on the service to build upon its strengths and make improvements (continuous quality improvement standard).

The South African helpline has internal review systems to monitor for quality and promote helpline staff development. The first step was to establish an internal system for quality performance monitoring of written communication (emails) with clients using the criteria of accuracy, relevance, and sufficiency of information provided as well as a tone of encouragement and consistency of style. The resulting lessons are being translated into quality performance management systems for the telephone and other channels. CRM software is used to collect communication data, such as emails sent and records of telephone conversations, and to use this data for monitoring and learning purposes. However, technologically simpler methodologies can be used as well. The important issue is to collect specific data and to use it for correction, learning, and improvement. Client information security is a quality and ethical issue regardless of how the data are collected—via a CRM, a tape recorder, or a written record of a counseling session.

The core value of access (that drives the helplines) includes attention to the quality of communication whether by telephone or in written form. Plain language—a style of writing that is easy for the public to read, to understand, and to act upon after just one reading or hearing—is a highly relevant quality criterion for public access to career information. New Zealand's website linked to its helpline won the 2011 WriteMark New Zealand Plain English Award. Language criteria include short, straightforward sentences; familiar everyday language; and an active voice and tone. Both South Africa and England provide services in multiple languages, which introduces more complexity into quality monitoring when management languages may not cover all the service languages.

As Internet offerings become richer, more varied, and more interactive, there is a temptation to reduce more expensive interpersonal services in favor of fully automated services. However, a dash to automated services,

removing or minimizing the role of an interme-
diary, could undermine the quality of provision.
Career guidance developments on the web have
rushed ahead of research and career guidance
theory development (Hooley et al., 2010).
Research is needed as well as new theoretical
frameworks that address the optimal integration
of web options into quality career guidance
provision.

Staffing Requirements

In the general career guidance field, with rapid
changes in policy and practice, new staff
requirements have emerged including new forms
of training, certification, and job categories; but
the development of these new forms has lagged
behind the need for them (Bimrose, 2006). Lack
of formal training has led to ad hoc training on the
job and to inexperienced staffing.

New demands in an integrated helpline setting
can exacerbate this fragility. New Zealand tack-
led this issue at the pilot stage, with preservice
and in-service training, plus mentoring and close
supervision, even though the counselors were
considered highly experienced career advisers
(Bean & England, 2009). The service in England
has established a systematic approach to continuous staff improvement. In particular, it has
introduced the role of Quality Coaches: expert
practitioners to support other advisers on all
aspects of quality delivery, both through one-to-
one coaching and through cluster groups formed
to discuss and share best practice.

A national, integrated telephone helpline potentially widens the user base, bringing greater diversity than a smaller face-to-face clientele. Career
guidance counselors need not only specialized
telephone counseling skills but also sensitivity
and knowledge in helping a greater variety of
need and experience among callers. New Zealand
has specialist focus approaches providing options
that Maori and Pacific people might find more
culturally meaningful: these include a family-
based counseling option for a more traditional,
consensual approach to career decision-making.

Scripts can be used by call centers to ensure
consistency of service, but can lead to low staff
morale and high turnover, which tend to be
endemic to the call center sector as a whole. In
reviewing the low turnover in the career helpline
in England, Watts and Dent (2002) have
suggested that lack of scripts engendered a
more professional challenge and higher work
satisfaction for staff. The role of scripts and the
extent to which they should be used is an
important question for all career helplines. The
New Zealand service uses scripts as induction
and training tools for new helpline officers, who
are then able, as they gain confidence, to adapt
the process flow and content to suit their own and
clients' styles and preferences.

A further staffing, issue confronting helplines
is whether telephone guidance should be viewed
as a distinctive specialization within the
guidance field or as one among many areas of
application for generic staff (Watts & Dent,
2002). A related question is whether it is helpful
for advisers to have ongoing experience of face-
to-face guidance alongside their telephone work.
Further research is needed to assess how much
face-to-face involvement improves the quality of
helpline work and vice versa.

Adaptation: Sensitivity to Diverse Cultural Contexts

As is the case with many innovations, career
guidance models can fruitfully be adapted, but
blanket "borrowing" into other contexts is
unwise and rarely becomes embedded (Sultana,
2009). In this review, we have noted how
countries have adapted the idea of career
helplines with sensitivity to their context. South
Africa, for example, conducted a research study,
set up a career development stakeholder consultative group, conducted consultations with a
breadth of stakeholders, and invested in months
of dialogue with government officials before
launching its helpline project. It has continued
to adapt its model in response to evolving
stakeholder and client demands.

Introduction of a career development helpline is a complex management and leadership challenge because it represents innovation on many dimensions. The multichannel helpline model borrows from social service helpline methodologies, distance learning methodologies, lifelong learning models, and new thinking regarding career development practice and delivery. Technological innovation and the expansion of Internet and cell phone use and literacy are changing delivery options continuously in all countries.

While careful context-sensitive adaptation and redesign of the service before implementation is important, an ongoing learning approach is needed to develop the service. Sensitivity of approach to implementation is crucial. A model can appear a cultural misfit simply because it was carelessly implemented.

This review, with the exception of South Africa, has covered high-income Western countries in which individual client-counselor talking solutions as well as helplines are culturally familiar. As more countries adopt and adapt helplines and other distance career development methodologies, it is likely that those that do it best will be those with context sensitivity and an organizational learning approach.

Conclusions

New Concepts and Viewpoints: Charting New Directions

In this review, we have described a paradigm shift in career guidance policy and provision in Europe, Canada, New Zealand, Australia, and South Africa. The longer-established helplines have shown, through rigorous evaluation, that this approach can be extremely effective. The helpline in England in particular has exercised some influence on newer initiatives. Some of the more recently established helplines are calling their service "e-guidance." South Africa is demonstrating the potential of a national helpline service in a middle-income country to diversify channels for a highly diverse population and to find innovative approaches to address access barriers to career development help.

Relevance for Multiple Cultures: Sensitivity to the Universal and the Particular

It is likely that other countries will borrow from existing career helpline models as they respond to similar policy drivers (i.e., addressing skill shortages and social inclusion). While each country will need to adapt this distance model to its particular cultural, technological, and demographic contexts, a core universal requirement is the provision of a system to research, store, curate, and disseminate career information that is accurate, comprehensive, current, accessible, and useful to clients' particular circumstances. The universal principle of distance access to career services will be translated in each particular country that adopts a multichannel helpline deploying the optimal distance channels available in that country: telephone, cell phone, email, SMS, webchat, etc. It is likely that each country will need to keep adapting its delivery channels as new technology is mainstreamed.

As people become more Internet literate, the relative demand for self-help and mediated services will shift, requiring ongoing changes to delivery platforms. Research and theory need to be developed to explore and underpin effective career guidance through multichannel approaches in a wide variety of contexts and to ensure that ever-evolving technological options increase and enhance rather than narrow career development service delivery.

References

Arulmani, G., & Abdulla, A. (2007). Capturing the ripples: Addressing the sustainability of the impact of social marketing. *Social Marketing Quarterly, 13*, 84–107.

Bean, J., & England, G. (2009). *Career guidance by telephone: An emerging model of practice*. Wellington, New Zealand: Career Services.

Bimrose, J. (2006). *The changing context of career practice: Guidance, counselling or coaching? (CeGS Occasional Paper)*. Derby, UK: Centre for Guidance Studies, University of Derby.

Careers New Zealand. (2012). *Annual report for year ending 30 June 2012*. Wellington, New Zealand: Author.

Careers Sector Stakeholders Alliance. (2012). *National careers service: Strategic options for building a world class service*. London, UK: Author.

Christogiorgos, D., Vassilopoulou, V., Florou, A., Xydou, V., Douvou, M., Vgenopoulou, D., et al. (2010). Telephone counselling with adolescents and countertransference phenomena: Particularities and challenges. *British Journal of Guidance and Counselling, 38*(3), 313–325.

England, G., van Holten, A., & Urbahn, J. (2008). *Career guidance by telephone–A valuable tool for experienced consultants*. Wellington, New Zealand: Career Services.

Flederman, P. (2011). A career advice helpline: A case study from South Africa. *International Journal for Educational and Vocational Guidance, 11*(2), 111–123.

Goddard, T. (2009). *Considering online career interventions*. Retrieved from http://www.training-innovations.com/files/Considering-Online-Career-Interventions.pdf

Hooley, T., Hutchinson, J., & Watts, A. G. (2010). *Careering through the web: The potential of web 2.0 and 3.0 technologies for career development and career support services*. London, UK: UK Commission for Employment and Skills.

Hutton, J. (2011). *Mobile phones dominate in South Africa*. Retrieved from http://blog.nielsen.com/nielsenwire/global/mobile-phones-dominate-in-south-africa/

International Labour Office. (2006). *Career guidance: A resource handbook for low- and middle-economy countries*. Geneva, Switzerland: ILO.

Isaacs, S. (2010, October). *Creating a national NQF and career advice helpline*. Paper presented at the IAEVG-Jiva Conference, Bangalore, India.

Jenschke, B., Schober, K., & Frübing, J. (2011). *Career guidance in the life course: Structures and services in Germany*. Berlin: Nationales Forum Beratung in Bildung, Beruf und Beschäftigung e.V. (nfb).

Keevy, J., Steenekamp, S., & West, P. (2012). A qualitative approach to career development within the context of the South African National Qualifications Framework. *South African Journal of Higher Education, 25*(6).

King, R., Bambling, M., Reid, W., & Thomas, I. (2006). Telephone and online counseling: A naturalistic comparison of session outcome, session impact and therapeutic alliance. *Counseling and Psychotherapy Research, 6*(3), 175–181.

Organisation for Economic Co-operation and Development. (2004). *Career guidance and public policy: Bridging the gap*. Paris, France: Author.

Page, R., Newton, B., Hawthorn, R., Hunt, W., & Hillage, J. (2007). *An evaluation of the Ufl/Learndirect telephone guidance trial (RR833)*. London, UK: Department for Education and Skills.

Reese, R. J., Conoley, C. W., & Brossart, D. F. (2002). Effectiveness of telephone counseling: A field-based investigation. *Journal of Counseling Psychology, 49*(2), 233–242.

Reese, R. J., Conoley, C. W., & Brossart, D. F. (2006). The attractiveness of telephone counseling: An empirical investigation of client perceptions. *Journal of Counseling and Development, 84*(1), 54–60.

Rochlen, A. B., Zack, J. S., & Speyer, C. (2004). Online therapy: Review of relevant definitions, debates and current empirical support. *Journal of Clinical Psychology, 60*(3), 269–283.

Rosenfield, M. (1997). *Counselling by telephone*. London, UK: Sage.

Rosenfield, M., & Smillie, E. (1998). Group counselling by telephone. *British Journal of Guidance and Counselling, 26*(1), 11–19.

Sultana, R. G. (2009). *Career guidance policies: Global dynamics, local resonances*. Derby, UK: International Centre for Guidance Studies, University of Derby.

Walters, S., Watts, A. G., & Flederman, P. (2009). Navigating the national qualifications framework (NQF): The role of career guidance. *South African Journal of Higher Education, 23*(3), 561–574.

Watts, A. G. (2007). *Career services: A review in an international perspective*. Wellington, New Zealand: Career Services.

Watts, A. G. (2010). National all-age career guidance services: Evidence and issues. *British Journal of Guidance and Counselling, 38*(1), 31–44.

Watts, A. G., & Dent, G. (2002). 'Let your fingers do the walking': The use of telephone helplines in career information and guidance. *British Journal of Guidance and Counselling, 30*(1), 17–35.

Watts, A. G., & Dent, G. (2006). The 'P' word: Productivity in the delivery of career guidance services. *British Journal of Guidance and Counselling, 34*(2), 177–189.

Watts, A. G., & Dent, G. (2008). The evolution of a national distance guidance service: Trends and challenges. *British Journal of Guidance and Counselling, 36*(4), 455–465.

Watts, A. G., & Fretwell, D. (2004). *Public policies for career development: Case studies and emerging issues for designing career information and guidance systems in developing and transition economies*. Washington, DC: World Bank.

Part VI

Innovations in Career Counseling: Services for Special Groups

Overview

The apportioning of resources available within a community is governed by a delicate psychosocial process which has much to do with occupational role allocation. Work is a source of the person's sense of self-worth and feelings of connectedness with one's community. This section discusses the career development needs of special groups. Research in the last few decades has shown that children with learning disorders face multiple challenges during the school-to-work transition. Meeting many of these challenges requires skills that the child with disability needs time to acquire. One of the chapters in this section examines resources within the home, community, and institutions that could respond to children with disabilities as they grow into the occupational roles of adulthood. The social re-integration of those who are recovering from mental illnesses is closely connected with their re-integration into the world of work. Today, approaches to the care of persons with mental disorders have shifted from a hospital-based approach to care in the community. Writers in this section present information to understand mental illness better and describe frameworks for the assessment and delivery of career services to this highly neglected group. In the modern era, indigenous peoples all over the world have faced seismic changes in the culture and traditions of their ancient communities. The returns of economic development have reached only an elite few. Traditional livelihoods have been lost and only partially replaced by modern occupations. New approaches to career development include the revitalizing of close-to-nature vocations. Another chapter in this section discusses methods of guidance and counseling that would be relevant to young people from indigenous cultures and the relevance of the ancient ways of living of these cultures to contemporary career guidance. Older women are often at a double disadvantage in the labor market because of gender and age. Gender inequality persists as a pervasive feature of labor markets across the world. Drawing on research into women's career stories, implications for career theory and practice for this group are explored. In a global economy, we have an increasingly mobile workforce, yet the career development needs of immigrants (workers and students) are often addressed in a manner that is alien to their ways of thinking. Writers in this section highlight the challenges encountered by immigrants, repatriates, global careerists, and international students. Issues related to culture shock, transitions, credential recognition, language competency, relocation, and settlement are discussed with a focus on how career professionals can help.

In summary, this section highlights social equity as being pivotal to effective career guidance and counseling, because a key goal of practice is to help all individuals realize their full potential, irrespective of circumstances and constraints. Models and ideas are presented both from theoretical and applied perspectives that could sharpen the relevance of career counseling for a wide range of underserved groups.

Sonali Nag

General Introduction

Dyslexia, specific learning difficulties (SLD), and specific language impairment (SLI) are some common terms used by specialists to refer to the learning disorders. Diagnosis of these disorders is primarily based on learning difficulties experienced by the individual. Learning disorders may be accompanied by other conditions such as attention deficit disorder (ADD), speech sound disorder (SSD), and autism spectrum disorder (ASD). Literacy development, and how literacy attainments affect transition into the world of work, are aspects of learning of particular interest in this chapter. Here, we refer to literacy as the skills associated with basic and fluent levels of reading and writing. While most forms of learning disorders manifest in a degree of literacy difficulty, it is essential to be alert to the fact that difficulties with literacy also arise when there are sensory impairments, emotional and behavioral disorders, and, most importantly, low support for literacy learning. The most dramatic instances of low literacy support are print-starved environments or schools with disrupted instruction time. Research shows that in such low support environments, the lag in literacy attainments may be up to 2 years (Nag, 2007), and delays in skill development can mimic the deficit profile of a child with a learning disorder like dyslexia (Nag & Snowling, 2012). Literacy and learning difficulties that emerge from such environmental disadvantage and deprivation should most definitely not attract clinical labels, and attention to the career development needs of the learner from a deprived background is without question a pressing one (see, for example, Asian Development Outlook, 2012). This chapter will, however, only focus on groups that carry a specific diagnosis, and we will use the generic term of *learning difficulty* to refer to the several disorders that manifest in literacy learning difficulties. The full list of diagnostic categories is available from the World Health Organisation (ICD-10) and the American Psychological Association (DSM-V), and categories of interest to this chapter, along with more common names, have been listed in Table 28.1. Individuals who qualify for any of these diagnoses have *special educational needs* and will perhaps experience challenges when preparing to enter the world of work.

Tiers of formal as well as nonformal training mark the years before gaining employment. Apprenticeships, participation in courses, and presenting oneself to evaluation systems that gauge mastery and skill are all examples of such experiences. Formal courses could be of varying duration and there is usually an expectation of achieving a level of proficiency. A characteristic of the contemporary world of work is the ever growing demand for literacy skills both in the formal and nonformal settings. Eligibility criteria for entry-level jobs require

S. Nag (✉)
The Promise Foundation, Bangalore, India
e-mail: sonalinag@t-p-f.org

G. Arulmani et al. (eds.), *Handbook of Career Development*, International and Cultural Psychology,
DOI 10.1007/978-1-4614-9460-7_28, © Springer Science+Business Media, LLC 2014

Table 28.1 Common labels and labels in diagnostic manuals for literacy difficulties

	Reading with accuracy, speed, and comprehension		Spelling accuracy and speed			
Nature of literacy difficulty	No associated difficulty seen in arithmetic	With simultaneous difficulty in arithmetic	With a history of reading and spelling difficulties but currently difficulties with reading are resolved	With no indication of either current or earlier difficulty with any aspect of reading	Expressive writing	Reading and/or spelling and/or arithmetic
Common labels	SLD, dyslexia, or developmental dyslexia, may be linked with SLI	Dyslexia or an accompanying feature of SLD or SLI, and dyscalculia	Dyslexia (someone who has developed good compensatory strategies and is coping with day-to-day reading)	Specific spelling difficulties or developmental dysgraphia	Typically noted as an accompanying feature of dyslexia, SLD, or SLI	Dyslexia or an accompanying feature of SLD or SLI
Labels in ICD-10	Specific reading disorder	Mixed disorder of scholastic skills		Specific spelling disorder	Other developmental disorder of scholastic skills	Mixed disorder of scholastic skills
Labels in DSM-V	Reading disorder				Disorder of written expression	

ICD: International Classification of Diseases, DSM: Diagnostic and Statistical Manual, SLD: Specific Learning Difficulties, SLI: Specific Language Impairment

success in courses that are increasingly text-heavy, demanding more and more advanced skills with reading, writing, and the processing of textual information. These changes in the education and employment sectors inevitably influence the individual's preparations for the world of work.

Take the life story of RC who was first diagnosed with mild ADD and associated difficulties in reading comprehension at the age of 6. His education through open schooling, interleaved with short-term enrolment in mainstream schools, culminated in a low-average performance at the end of Grade 12. Assessment related to career development at this stage pointed to a high potential for careers in design. He, therefore, went on to a vocational course in animation and design. Persistent literacy difficulties with reading comprehension and symptoms of ADD, which were particularly manifest during group projects and other social aspects of the study program, however, led to RC dropping out of the vocational course. RC's well-connected extended family stepped in to organize work-skill training through various nonformal arrangements, attempting each time to capitalize on his interests and skills. He worked as a shop assistant, a tour guide for an adventure company, and a "spotter" for his ornithologist-uncle who was conducting a survey of local birds. At the time of this writing, RC, now a young adult, was continuing with this type of nonformal preparation for entry into the world of work. Two points are notable from a career counseling perspective: first, the manner in which RC's special educational needs affected his preparation for the world of work; and second, the creative solutions generated by his family and community to help him along. Surveys suggest that RC's educational history and interrupted career preparation is not uncommon among youth with disabilities (e.g., Kenya: Mugo, Oranga, & Singal, 2010; India and Pakistan: Singal, Bhatti, Januja, & Sood, 2012). It is also evident that the unconventional school and post-school history is the outcome of RC's learning-related disorder, and, in his own words, "a difficulty to settle down." But seen in its entirety, the career preparation of individuals like RC is also a story of perseverance and resilience (e.g., Aravind, Sailo, Arulmani, & Nag, 2011).

On many counts, the career development experiences of individuals with literacy learning difficulties can be similar to typically developing adolescents. But there are unique differences as well, and the challenges that have to be negotiated are often hidden. Three issues in particular have a direct bearing on understanding the career preparation of individuals with special educational needs. Knowing about the nature of the learning difficulty that a particular individual experiences with some degree of specificity is the first issue. If the difficulties are around reading comprehension and an inability to cope with higher-level textbooks, this has implications for whether an individual can move into higher education. If the difficulties are with reading speed, this has implications for whether the individual can take a timed exam. Such barriers to success in further education influence emotional well-being (Singal et al., 2012), and this brings us to the next issue which is to do with self-determination.

The degree of active engagement and foreplanning shown by the individual appears to define the nature of transition into the world of work. This is because there are deep differences in the quality of purpose that individuals with learning difficulties bring to the career preparation process, and it is this social-motivational aspect of the individual that can additionally determine the transition. A third issue relates to the roles of the home and community. Each may offer different solutions for making the transition from school to work smooth. These solutions are sometimes limited by the reduced expectations that others have of the individual's potential (Muuya, 2002; Nag, 2011), as well as the lack of preparedness of institutions to serve the special educational needs of individuals (e.g., see case study of a secondary school in Hong Kong: Hue, 2012). Growing evidence from the field of disability studies indicates that in the school years teachers may show a more facilitative approach to the individual's personal potentials, but in the world of work there may

be a startling absence of support (Mugo et al., 2010; Singal et al., 2012). In contexts where institutional support for individuals with special educational needs is weak, their transition into the world of work would require the family and social network to arrange for suitable opportunities.

In summary, a more comprehensive understanding of the career preparation of individuals with a learning difficulty comes from examining the influences on an individual's attainment profile and the broader psychosocial system. To illustrate this, we will review the case histories of 12 individuals with learning difficulties as they negotiate the transition out of school and through higher education. All 12 were first diagnosed with a learning disorder in school and, at the age of 17, were more than 2 years behind the reading and/or writing levels of their peers. Their diagnoses included dyslexia, SLI, developmental disorders, and vision-related difficulties. All had manifested literacy difficulties; some had co-occurring difficulties in the area of attention and social–emotional skills. The case histories we report here are based on clinical and school records, as well as detailed interviews. At the time of the interviews their ages ranged from 17 to 24 years. Table 28.2 provides a brief overview of their backgrounds.

Special Educational Needs

A host of cognitive, linguistic, and emotional-motivational processes influence the manifestation of special educational needs. If an individual is strong in the underlying processes that support literacy development, such as having a large vocabulary or being able to spell well, then these can emerge as protective factors against literacy failure. Conversely, difficulties with any one or more of these processes can place the person at risk for literacy-related difficulties. Skill liabilities may be at different levels of severity, with the presence of more than one risk factor cumulatively impacting literacy development. The origins of risk factors are often conceptualized as neuro-developmental in

Table 28.2 Profile of students interviewed including their age, clinical diagnosis, and career aspirations

Student[a]	Age	Diagnosis	Career aspiration
1	17	Moderate dyslexia	Not sure
2	21	Moderate dyslexia and co-occurring severe anxiety disorder	Join the Craft and Landscape Industry
3	18	Specific language impairment and dyslexia	Business Entrepreneur
4	22	Dyslexia, and history of severe emotional difficulties	Counselor
5	19	Severe dyslexia	Join the Sports Industry
6	17	Moderate dyslexia	Pilot
7	19	Severe dyslexia	Personnel Management
8	17	Literacy difficulties secondary to convergence insufficiency (a vision-related disorder)	Biophysical Engineering
9	24	Dyslexia and co-occurring attention deficit disorder	Join the Fashion Industry
10	22	Mild dyslexia	Join the Sports Industry
11	18	Severe dyslexia and co-occurring anxiety disorder	Business Entrepreneur
12	17	Dyslexia	Costume Designer

[a]*Note*: The serial numbers in this table will be referred to when excerpts of interviews with the particular student are reported in the rest of the chapter (e.g., S10, S6)

nature and the current thinking is that the best way to understand the complexity of learning difficulties is to view their origins as many-layered and multifactorial (Nag & Snowling, 2012; Pennington, 2006). In other words, a learning difficulty impacts literacy development, and the nature of the impact is shaped by an individual's profile of multiple strengths and multiple weaknesses.

A useful source for understanding an individual's special educational needs is to listen to parent observations and concerns. In a survey of 95 children with learning disorders attending a special needs clinic in Bangalore, a city in South India, we recorded parents' concerns about their children's delays in literacy attainments and more general difficulties in school. We were interested in developing a parent interview checklist using the language of the parents themselves (Nag & Lall, 2011), and report here a first thematic extraction of parental concerns (parent descriptions are given verbatim in parenthesis). In the area of literacy, parents spoke about difficulties with reading ("tends to jumble words," "needs a total explanation to understand," "can't get directly from school book") and writing ("makes mistakes when writing notes," "very short in written language"). Parents often noted that their child was better in oral skills than writing skills ("can say the

answer but cannot write well," "input very good, but output low"). In relation to coping in school, parents spoke about difficulties with managing time ("slow in writing," "finds writing boring," "takes time to do homework"), poor recall of materials ("weak to remember"), and a growing disenchantment with school ("reduced interest in all studies," "may not write in exam," "struggling to cope with school pressures," "giving up"). Clearly, special educational needs are varied and manifest with differing levels of complexity and severity.

Turning to the study of 12 case histories, all individuals had special educational needs in the post-school years (see Table 28.3 for a sample of their performance). They all spoke about continuing difficulties on literacy tasks and other pervasive challenges such as managing time and performing in the presence of others. One consistent area of difficulty was around written work, expressed by two students as follows:

S8: Whenever writing is involved I don't want to do it. [I] tell my friends to do it for me or type it and send an email… if I have to do something I can do it like on a laptop… [can correct] spellings and [there is no] handwriting. Only problem is that during some exam… like if writing and spelling used to get my grades… my grades would go low. So that is difficult. Yeah. Teachers don't understand what I write and stuff.

Table 28.3 Visible signs of literacy learning difficulties in secondary school and in higher educational settings

Signs of literacy difficulty	Test performance when individuals in our sample were 17 years old[a]
Errors in recognizing words during reading	Coerce read as *coarse*[12] and *course*[7]; reminisce read as *remances*[8] and *re-minensy*[7]; euphemism read as *emphasis*[7] and hierarchical read as *urasical*[12], *hierarcial*[5], *hierarchria*[7], and *hierarcal*[7]
Errors when spelling	*Wistle*[12, 5, 8] and *whisel*[9] for whistle; *assitance*[12], *acistance*[8], and *assistence*[7] for assistants; and *soverant*[12], *soverent*[5], *soweren*[7], and *soverign*[8] for sovereign
Low speed of reading	Speed ranged from 45 to 170 words per minute. At age 13–15 a range of 170–200 words per minute is expected and a skilled adult reader may read from 240 to 300 words per minute
Low comprehension of materials	A large number of words were misread[12, 7]; connections were not made between idea units in the text[12, 5]. Either the answer was guessed at or there was a mechanical retelling of an appropriate phrase or sentence from the passage[7]
Poor expressive writing	Sample:
	Match fixing, One of the worsth way of winning a game. Match fixing ruines the whole point of the game and become less fun and you won't have any interest in playing, Cause you all ready know that your going to win or loss. Match fixing should be a band from all game[7]
Low coping with school demands	"I always run out of time"[12]

[a]*Note*: Errors are shown in italics. All examples are for English. Subtle differences in error patterns in other languages can be expected, but crosslinguistic research suggests that the core difficulties listed in column one are present in more or less degree in most languages. The illustrated examples are from work done by Students 5, 7, 8, and 12 profiled in Table 28.2

S5: Basically I would say [the most difficult part is] coping with studies... meaning like passing [the exam]... my final exams that are coming up... uuhhh... instead of waiting till the last moment... slowly start studying uhh... which will help me... pick myself up now.

Difficulty with literacy skills persisting into high school and beyond is a trend corroborated by larger scale longitudinal studies (e.g., Shaywitz et al., 1999; Snowling, Muter, & Carroll, 2007), as well as in the personal reflections of persons with learning disorders (Webster, 2004). Taken together, the most visible areas of difficulties are poorer reading accuracy and comprehension, lower speed of writing more spelling errors, and significant difficulty with making a précis of material just read. Underlying cognitive difficulties that persist include lower phonological decoding skills (mapping sounds to symbols and manipulating sounds in words) and poorer verbal working memory (remembering details in just-heard information). Enduring emotional-motivational difficulties may include a continuing sense of uncertainty. These special educational needs bring subtle challenges in negotiating through the preparatory tasks for entry into the world of work.

It must be noted, however, that there are also experiences of success and unexpected achievements that help counter the downward spiral into anxiety and despair and allow individuals to meet the challenges of the transition years.

Transition from School to Work

We next turn to the processes linked with preparing for the world of work and the influences on this preparation. Many of the preparatory activities of the transition years between school and work may be seen as normative tasks; activities that most individuals need to attend to as part of a particular life stage. These tasks may be either formal or nonformal. Formalized opportunities are typically embedded in school, college, university, or industry-related systems, while less formal opportunities are casual, incidental, and serendipitous. Following the work day (work shadowing) of a family member or neighbor is an example of a nonformal activity, whereas attending a summer program conducted by an institute would be a formally organized activity. As seen later in this section, both forms of activities can have far-reaching influence.

The career preparation process leads towards a variety of outcomes linked with either immediate entry into the world of work or entry into intermediate courses for building skills and knowledge, specifically or generally, related to a career or livelihood. Each of these outcomes can be assessed for their potential to secure long-term integration into the world of work. Such a conception of the career preparation process sees the individual and the context in a two-way interaction, each reciprocally influencing the other. One model that attempts to capture this multiplicity of processes is the career preparation process model (henceforth, CPP model, Arulmani & Nag-Arulmani, 2004). An adapted version of this model is available as a framework for understanding the transitions made by individuals with special educational needs (Nag, 2011). Some of the key constructs within the CPP model which we will refer to in the next sections are the following: *social cognitive environment*, which refers to the work orientations and belief systems of an individual's social class; *self-efficacy*, which is related to an individual's belief in the personal ability to skillfully, and with control, negotiate a specific activity; and quality of *self-understanding*, which has to do with individuals' insights into their potentials and how their patterns of thinking may be influencing their choices. In the next section, we discuss three overlapping interactions as described by the CPP model, following which we suggest ideas for intervention based on the CPP model.

Privilege and a Sound Career Path

Access to social, economic, and cultural privileges offers advantages that are far-reaching. There is converging evidence, for example, from the fields of health, education, and emotional well-being, that better outcomes are associated with privilege and higher socio-economic status (SES) (for a review, see Bradley & Corwyn, 2002). Not surprisingly then, SES is also closely related to more successful career and livelihood development across the life-span (e.g., Arulmani, 2009; Asian Development Outlook, 2012; Bakshi, 2011; Nanjundaiah, 2011; Singal et al., 2012). The 12 case histories were of students from privileged homes whose parents were in socially prestigious positions within their communities and had annual family incomes that placed them in upper-middle class positions. Families belonging to this band of privilege have been found to have strong proficiency-related career beliefs (Arulmani, 2009; Arulmani & Nag, 2006). Accordingly, higher education rather than immediate employment is valued as the preferred path after school completion and some options (e.g., university degrees) are placed higher on the prestige ladder than others (e.g., vocational courses).

In line with the work orientations of socioeconomically privileged groups in India, the preferred pathway for all students in our study was further education, despite their difficulties with literacy learning. A closer look, however, showed an interesting split in the choices being made. Within our older sample, four students had chosen graduate/postgraduate level courses (psychological counseling, sports science, sports psychology, and engineering). All of these courses are known to be text-heavy, requiring advanced literacy skills and, therefore, exceptionally challenging for these students. The choices appeared to be motivated by prestige (e.g., "They [my family] said get into a good college," NT). Although the demands of the course on literacy and learning were a daily struggle for these students, we found them hopeful and resilient. All four told us that they anticipated the actual career to be less literacy-demanding and hence they intended to struggle through and complete the course. However, the other eight students in our study chose (or were planning to choose) vocational courses (e.g., craft design, fashion design, costume design, food and beverage management, civil aviation). While it is acknowledged that there are levels of prestige within vocational courses, recall that vocationally oriented courses, in comparison to university-based degree programs, are typically perceived to be lower down the prestige ladder in India and avoided by upper SES groups (Arulmani, 2009). A commitment to such courses by so many in the sample of 12 students suggests an important shift away from the dominant choices in this particular social cognitive environment. In our assessment, the shift was propelled by the experience of a learning difficulty. One student said:

> S2: When I think of career [the] first thing that comes into my mind is, do I have to speak to the public... new faces... I still... move away from that. This is a craft related design course... so we have soft materials which include textiles, hard materials, clay and ceramic, things like that. And hard materials which is wood... and metal. But what I'd really like to do is I would really like to overcome my fear.

Another student said:

> S6: Becoming a pilot... this involves a lot of technical skill and understanding of the different aspects of a plane. Since I have built various models and flown them, I think this skill could be of some use in the becoming [of] a pilot.

The presence of learning difficulties, it appears, can counter the influence of dominant preferences in an individual's social cognitive environment. Career options that may otherwise be left unexplored are more readily considered, and wider solution seeking appears to broaden out conventional school-to-work pathways. The expectations from the vocational courses by the students in our study were twofold. One was that the course would demand less of writing and reading and the other was that the course would draw upon their strengths rather than their literacy difficulties. We propose that it was the sharply experienced polarity of personal strengths and weaknesses that had brought about a more nuanced approach to career preparation among this group of students. While some may have started off seeking "an easy career," all were actively attempting to find meaningful options to further their personal aspirations. Anticipated ease in some foreseeable future perhaps offered the context within which the challenges in the short term were interpreted, as also the belief that personal strengths at some

point in time would overshadow learning weaknesses. It is perhaps beliefs such as these that allow for self-determination to thrive among individuals with learning difficulties. In this sample of socioeconomically privileged students, we repeatedly heard these beliefs expressed, even as the students attempted to balance ways for potential realization with career paths acceptable within their social cognitive environments.

Privilege Begets a Wider Range of Solutions

We next turn to examine the extent to which the family was an advocate for the individual with a learning difficulty. Family-initiated advocacy was on issues such as breaking stereotypes, promoting inclusivity, and actively raising the individual's aspirations. Thus, one student said:

> S4: My parents... because a lot of times, you know, before I started doing this course in my master's and even before undergraduation, I always thought, you know, I wanted to be into arts, like be a singer... and not that I am good or anything, I would just assume that, you know, that would be an easier career, it would be the best career, do something with music... But I think they made me understand the practicality of it as well... I was always interested in psychology from the beginning, even when I was in school I wanted to do it. But I always thought it would be so difficult and I won't be able to do it. It was always something like that you know. Yeah, they motivated me basically.

Looking further, different trajectories into the world of work may develop even among individuals with seemingly similar profiles of literacy learning difficulties. One important explanation for this is the extent of participation and advocacy emerging from the matrix of home–community–institutions to which particular individuals belong. A further explanation is that the many processes emanating from the various sources in the matrix are reciprocally influential, leading to more natural covariations. Such a perspective of interconnectedness for understanding the transition between school and work is in line with the causal explanations and risk models that have emerged for explaining the developmental outcomes following early difficulties (e.g., Anderson, 2007; Kumsta, Rutter, Stevens, & Sonuga-Barke, 2010). The individual's profile of strengths and weaknesses, a sense of well-being or crisis, and the resourcefulness of the broader ecology all interplay to make the transition what it is. We get a sense of these interwoven processes in the following narratives from the students in this study.

> *S4*: I have done a lot of internships. I have worked part time in... accent training places where they teach English... teach accent in the BPO sector... helped in workshops... It's been a great experience. It's been so much learning. Learning from my experience and learning from others as well.
>
> *S9*: Worked in a boutique... and event management... it gives you a great sense of understanding and it also assures you that... that uhhh... you are on the right track... that you are on par with everyone else around you. Uuhhhh... that you're capable of *doing* [emphasis added] you know... uuuhh... the job that everyone else does and you're no different from them... how everything which you now learnt have been put into practice... but umm... yes! It's all very, very good experience and necessary I believe.
>
> *S6*: In my school there are plenty of different activities that I am involved in, sports (football, volleyball, badminton, and athletics), music (I play two instruments as of now, Grade 6 drums and Grade 2 violin. I am hoping to finish my Grade 8 drums and Grade 4 violin this year). I also have sat for the Grade 5 music theory exam and passed the exam. I am also part of the school orchestra, and have performed in places around India with them... My parents on the most part encouraged me to take part in whatever I wanted to take part in and thus I have a large range of extracurricular activities.

While the narratives above suggest substantial planning, we also found that unanticipated opportunities shaped the transition. Such opportunities have variously been called *fortuitous events* (Bandura, 2001) and *planned happenstance* (Krumboltz, 2009). One student who went on to specialize in craft and landscape design recounted:

> *S2*: They were building this new site. So they had lot of plants which needed to be transported. Mainly the sapling, they need to be transported (like) to save them. So... I got the chance to do.

> [I] was transplanting a full grown coconut tree... So, [I] made a book on that..... There were these few houses where they asked me to design and (like) landscape their garden. So I did one. Well, I didn't really have the career in mind... I didn't really think about what I wanted to do... Yes, I think that exposure has helped me (like) think what I really wanted to do and I have had that interest.

The students in our study had access to wide-ranging materials, information, and resources. They also benefitted from the several formal and nonformal systems that could be drawn upon from their particular environment. Such multiplicity of opportunities and adaptive systems set these students apart and it may not be the same for all individuals with special educational needs in the same socioeconomic band. Further, their privileged circumstances are most certainly exceptional when compared to many families from a lower socioeconomic background who are vulnerable because of education systems that are neither inclusive nor equitable (Banerjee, Mehendale, & Nanjundaiah, 2011; Fletcher & Artiles, 2005; Hue, 2012; Singal, 2010). The few work-skill training options that are available for children from low-income families have been shown to inadequately prepare them for the contemporary world of work (Muuya, 2002; Nag, 2011) or prepare them for sectors that are "low wage, low productivity, resistant to new technology, vulnerable to shifting political winds..." (Anderson, 2007, p. 235). Thus, while privilege begets opportunity, the absence of privilege can interrupt a smooth entry into the world of work.

Challenges Emerging from Educational Systems

All students we met mentioned the pressures that they confronted daily. Four key themes emerged: an insensitive educational system, a struggle to overcome one's history of poor academic attainments, an accumulation of disadvantage especially when comparisons with peer group occurred, and an inability to assert oneself in the face of demands.

Poor Sensitivity of the System

Insensitivity to special educational needs and the absence of differentiated services for those with learning difficulties are major barriers to academic development in many countries (Hue, 2012; Muuya, 2002; Nag, 2011). The narratives of the students in this study reflected these challenges. They spoke of negative experiences with the evaluation system and distressing encounters with uninformed or uncaring teachers.

> S4: I felt that, you know, I wasn't understood there [school] for asking a doubt or if I wanted something to be repeated or, you know, if I couldn't complete on time. I was always told that, you know, you can't do it or, you know, I don't want to see your paper... A lot of times you are not accepted if you have something like this. I think understanding and acceptance (is needed). Understanding is an important factor. It would have made it a lot easier.
>
> S12: It was actually in my first year... [that] I got to know I was dyslexic... I had no support from [the] faculties [teachers]... I had no support... extra help... and that was most probably the most traumatizing time in my... like, the hardest period of time for me!
>
> S7: Why don't they know more about students like me?!

Poor Academic Record

All students were acutely aware of the fierce competition for different post-school courses. Many had a history of poor academic attainments. The challenge of not being able to do well when measured against normative systems was recurrent in their narratives. Clearly, within an environment that is narrowly focused on academics and literacy competencies, a poor academic record is a barrier to both personal and career development.

> S11: It was too much. I decided to leave school. Nobody agreed, but I decided.
>
> S9: I realized that subjects that require a lot of studying or mugging [rote learning] in particular were not for me.
>
> S4: All you do in school is education, everything else is secondary, and you can't do that well. It becomes really, you know, awkward in the school.
>
> S12: Even in arts colleges they see if you have got a diploma, passed your GCSE (school leaving exam).

It is important to note that some of the students had developed skillful strategies to sidestep the core deficits in their learning profiles. This certainly helped them cope well with a certain level of academic demand. Indeed, 5 of the 12 had also been among the highest achievers in their grade on some exams. We found that these occasional successes in academics were, however, often tempered by a belief that "the next course will be difficult."

Disadvantaged in Competitive Settings

Research findings with adolescents and young adults with learning difficulties in different cultural contexts suggest that one of the most persistent areas of difficulty is speed of performance and the slower pace of learning on literacy-related tasks (Nag & Snowling, 2012; Snowling et al., 2007). Ten students in the sample of 12 also mentioned slow speed as a substantial barrier to success. More importantly, this disadvantage had accumulated over time and across different contexts.

> S9: My other challenge is working fast and efficiently...everyone wants things quickly today. So I have to learn to do things well and as perfect as possible, but quickly.
>
> S4: I think my only challenge here would be I have to be a lot more hardworking than others. I find that a challenge. A lot more time...a lot more effort actually.

Unable to Be Assertive

A double disadvantage when negotiating through the transition years is not just the experience of failure because of a learning difficulty but also the experience of discomfort because of social–emotional pressures. Teachers of children with special educational needs have long recognized that the tendency to give up can become entrenched in some students (e.g., Hue, 2012). In this sample, socioemotional challenges were less often mentioned, but when they appeared, they were distressing and pervasive. Anxiety, panic attacks, mild-to-moderate levels of depression, withdrawn behavior, and an inability to assert were some of the experiences mentioned.

S9: I mean I would be the one who would fail... I mean, the one failure in the entire batch [of students], and that [would] turn out to be... and so... umm... discouraging... well I mean... especially a child with dyslexia it only cracks that person's uuhh... confidence level and uhh... I mean it took a lot. Every day I would come back home completely discouraged... to deal with that kind of stuff every single day... so it's a trial.

S2: I don't go out and talk to people. I just can't. I'm trying to work on that... when I think of career, first thing that comes in to my mind is do I have to speak to the public... new faces.

S1: Hmm... I don't know what to say to them. I just leave the place.

An insidious influence of socioemotional challenges was on the extent of engagement maintained by the individual with the career preparation process. The students in this study were aware that a foundational requirement for realizing their aptitudes and interests was literacy learning, and that this was also their biggest weakness. But, what may appear as disengagement may also be a much reduced career preparation self-efficacy, an issue discussed in the CPP model (Arulmani & Nag-Arulmani, 2004; Nag, 2011). Reduced self-efficacy for tasks such as developing a biodata and facing an interview has been shown to negatively impact career progression (Solberg & Good, 1994). What, therefore, emerges in the career preparation of the person with special educational needs is a precarious balance between a resilient, self-determined negotiation of the path between school and work, and a falling behind because of encountering seemingly insurmountable barriers. Consequently, it is not entirely surprising that choices made during the transition years could veer towards solutions suggested by others (the family, community, and institutions accessed), rather than the student's own reflection. This may potentially widen the gap between one's aspiration, interests and aptitudes, and the long-term career outcome.

Supporting the Career Preparation Process

Working Directly with Young People

We turn next to interventions that can help individuals with special educational needs during the transition years. Four interlinked areas in the preparation process are discussed.

Recognize the Individual's Interests and Aptitudes

The career preparation process is supported by the quality of self-understanding that an individual has, including insight into one's interests and aptitudes. It is this information that forms the basis for a long-term orientation to career development (Arulmani & Nag-Arulmani, 2004). Such self-understanding is all the more important for the young person with a learning difficulty. This is because the impact of a learning difficulty on activities related to one's interests and aptitudes may vary. The pursuit of some interests, for example, may be more literacy-demanding than others, and increasingly severe levels of literacy difficulties could become a barrier to success experiences. An important counseling target is, therefore, to examine and support insight into how an individual's interests, aptitudes, and learning profile interact with specific demands in a course, a career preparation activity, and job roles. An exercise that maps these different areas can support informed career decision making.

Recognize that Late Interventions Also Help

Children show dramatic improvement when they receive early intervention. But it is not unusual to find students showing spurts in skill development in response to interventions that they have received when older. These later gains have been recorded among youth with special educational needs that were caused by deprivation on account of institutional care in low-functioning orphanages and care homes (Beckett, Castle, Rutter, & Sonuga-Barke, 2010), poverty (Arulmani & Nag-Arulmani, 2001; but see Anderson, 2007), and sensory impairments such as low vision (Singal et al., 2012). It is important, therefore, that the career counselor asks specialist colleagues for updates on the changing learning profiles of their clients. A second, and arguably more dramatic, implication is that interventions, even if offered late in the student's life, can make a positive difference to skill development. Career counselors can become key agents who arrange interventions for young people with learning difficulties. The catch-up, even if uneven across cognitive domains, allows for better career preparation. Examples of skills that can be improved through interventions during the transition years include study skills such as note-making and timetabling; skills to manage written work through use of supports like mind maps, spell checkers, and note pads; and skills for managing noise and distractors so that one can remain focused on a task.

Recognize that Some Difficulties Will Persist

From this study as well as other research, it is known that some aspects of a learning difficulty will accompany the young person into adulthood and the world of work. Difficulties in the domain of phonological processing (skills in listening to sounds, manipulating sounds, and putting sounds together) are known to be particularly resistant to intervention, and even good quality remedial support in the early years may not completely reduce these difficulties (Snowling et al., 2007). This has implications for listening comprehension (e.g., understanding instructions) which in turn would affect the individual's learning of and performance on job tasks. Another area of difficulty that is more resistant to intervention is verbal working memory (capacity to hold a small amount of information actively in mind for immediate use, e.g., remembering a just-heard phone number before you start dialing). Apart from difficulties with reading comprehension, low working memory would make listening activities more difficult than when the activity is experiential or performance-based. This could affect career progress, especially if the entry-level courses as well as performance on job-related tasks are very language-based and/or text-heavy. But perhaps the most demanding are the written tasks typical of many post-school courses. The individuals in this study showed difficulties with writing speed, creative writing,

and the ability to summarize a recently read text irrespective of whether the clinical diagnosis was dyslexia, SLI, a sensory impairment, or comorbid conditions like ADD and severe anxiety. A useful way to understand persisting special educational needs is to visualize an individual's learning challenges on a hierarchy, with the more severe and broad-based difficulties (such as fluctuating attention and easy distractibility) being tier one, and specific and narrow-focused difficulties (such as learning spellings of new technical words like *photosynthesis* and *psychedelic*) being tier two. Elsewhere we have labeled these two tiers of difficulties as primary and secondary difficulties (Nag, 2011). Career counselors can use this framework to gain a better understanding of what aspects of the learning difficulties may more prominently shape the career preparation process.

Recognize and Support Self-Reflection

The development of "reflective self-consciousness" (Bandura, 2001, p. 10) is perhaps one of the most important targets of counseling. Many of the individuals in this study had grown introspective after high school and were showing greater forethought in their career planning. They had also grown in self-efficacy for some career preparation tasks. Others, while still anxious and uncertain, were reflective about the barriers to their personal growth and particularly their career development. In general, the multilayered systems of support around them appeared to have contributed to their career preparation by offering several solutions. It is, however, important to note that these multiple solutions could have easily overwhelmed the individual's self-determination. The active participation from multiple agencies can smother reflection among individuals and reduce their own say in the decision making. Even though in this study we did not find this to be the case (indeed, we found the opposite), career counselors would do well to be alert to the quality of self-determination being manifested by their clients. A useful question to ask is: "What propels the individual's engagement with a career preparation task?"

Working with Parents

Two key features appear to characterize the family that resourcefully supported the transition of the students in this study: first, the extent to which opportunities were generated by the family for their young, and second, the solution-focused nature of the social cognitive environment of the individual. These characteristics are not unlike the mechanisms of access and positive reactions proposed by Bradley and Corwyn (2002) to describe the associations repeatedly seen between SES and positive child development outcomes. A useful intervention for individuals with learning difficulties is to strengthen participation of the family and extended network in the career preparation process. Counseling sessions may be held with parents or significant others such as an influential uncle, aunt, an older sibling, or a grandparent. Box 28.1 is a worksheet that can be used for focused group discussions with parents of individuals with special educational needs. The worksheet is specific to the school-to-work transition years and is focused on increasing the family's awareness of the quality of their own participation in the individual's career preparation. The purpose of the worksheet is to begin focused discussions on (a) how to encourage self-

determination for the career chooser, and (b) how to ensure that the family participating in the career preparation process is doing so in an interactive fashion. The first two statements in the worksheet are related to creating access (what we arrange), the next pair refers to adaptive reactions when the individual is faced with challenges or failures (what we communicate), and the last set is about awareness of post-school options that are specific to the special needs of individuals with a learning difficulty (what we know).

Some insights from the use of this worksheet in our special needs center may help to clarify how this activity works. We found cultural differences in the way key words were interpreted by parents. A German mother interpreted *internship* within the institutionalized apprenticeship systems available in Germany, while an Indian mother, well aware that such institutionalized systems are not available locally, interpreted the same term as an informal arrangement. When the worksheet was given to the parent of a Grade 8 child, the main response was, "Isn't it too early to think about all this?" This comment was a useful starting point to talk of career choice as being a process and how an early beginning with career exploration was beneficial for future career-related decision making.

Box 28.1 Worksheet for discussion with parents

<table>
<tr><td colspan="4">When children leave school: How parents can help
A checklist for career counsellors</td></tr>
<tr><td colspan="4">Student's Name: Age: Education:</td></tr>
<tr><td colspan="4">One positive change in learning skills seen in student's profile:</td></tr>
<tr><td colspan="4">One current learning difficulty that is most challenging for student today:</td></tr>
<tr><td colspan="4">In this worksheet we have listed a series of areas in which parents can support their child's transition out of school and into the world of work Please look at each statement, keep your child in mind and note the following: N: I have not begun to do this as yet, S: I do this sometimes, O: I do this often. If your response is S or O please give an example in the space provided in the far right.</td></tr>
<tr><td></td><td></td><td></td><td>Examples</td></tr>
<tr><td>1. Arrange for internships through my family and friends</td><td>N   S   O</td><td></td><td></td></tr>
<tr><td>2. Arrange for discussions about work life with family and friends</td><td>N   S   O</td><td></td><td></td></tr>
<tr><td>3. Gave a solution to a failure that is because of a learning difficulty</td><td>N   S   O</td><td></td><td></td></tr>
<tr><td>4. Reacted positively when a crisis was faced because of the learning difficulty</td><td>N   S   O</td><td></td><td></td></tr>
<tr><td>5. Have found out about what others with special needs do when they leave school</td><td>N   S   O</td><td></td><td></td></tr>
<tr><td>6. Have found out about 3 provisions for special needs</td><td>N   S   O</td><td></td><td></td></tr>
</table>

Relevance Across Contexts: Sensitivity to the Universal and Particular

This chapter has focused on a small selection of options for preparing to enter the world of work: higher education, apprenticeships, and vocational education. There are other after-school pathways as well. A review of trends in the USA, for example, found that a large percentage of individuals with literacy learning difficulties chose to enter the world of work without further education after school (Greg, 2009). Most had dropped out of school or had been left without clear support because they belonged to populations that were least served by provisions: groups such as minority communities, socioeconomically less privileged homes, or those attempting to reenter higher education at a later stage in life. It is, therefore, particularly important for the career counselor to be alert when working with clients who show learning difficulties and who additionally belong to marginalized, disadvantaged, and less visible groups. For them, it will often be difficult to tease apart the relative contribution of the disadvantaged context to their learning weaknesses. But in terms of career counseling and livelihood planning, the specific targets are clear: The very presence of learning difficulties is a signal that the viability of recommending certain kinds of literacy-demanding courses will need to be realistically appraised. Importantly, if such courses do not offer reasonable adjustments and concessions to support the special educational needs of the client, then it may become necessary to consider an alternative.

Hence the points covered in this chapter have relevance across multiple contexts. We propose that the career counselor develops greater sensitivity to social cognitive environments. Other skills that are translatable into the particular realities of diverse cultures are those that examine the dynamic interplay between the individual's learning profile and the ways in which the social cognitive environment supports (or restricts) the transition years.

New Concepts and Viewpoints: Charting New Directions

Career guidance on the whole is presently not adequately attuned to students with special educational needs. Much theorizing about career-related constructs, both historically and currently (e.g., Brown, 2002; Holland, 1997), remains blind to the concerns and issues of disability, developmental disorders, and special educational needs. This is problematic since the learning disorders are a high-incidence disability (e.g., Hue, 2012; Mugo et al., 2010) where numbers affected are determined by local definitions of "difficulty" and "delays" (Nag & Snowling, 2012). New research is urgently needed to address the needs of a large number of young people who require specific forms of assistance as they navigate their world of education and prepare to enter the world of work. We list here skills for career counseling that point to potential new directions that the discipline of career guidance and counseling could consider, keeping in view the needs of individuals with special educational needs.

1. Skills to design late interventions that can build the individual's strengths and readiness for entry into the world of work.
2. Skills to ascertain which courses would draw upon the individual's weaknesses rather than strengths.
3. Skills to show parents the link between learning difficulties and a literacy-heavy course, and the long-term implications of poor performance on such courses, both on the individual's career development and self-esteem.
4. Skills to break through career beliefs related to the prestige of obtaining a degree.
5. Skills to identify and adapt career alternatives for individuals with special needs, especially ideas for person-centered, difficulty-mitigating career alternatives that draw on their strengths rather than weaknesses.
6. Skills to scaffold the family's acceptance of these career alternatives.

7. Skills to identify and facilitate access and use of provisions (e.g., concessions) and supports (e.g., support groups) available within the system that the individual and family would benefit from.
8. Skills for advocacy when a system does not recognize the individual's difficulties and special educational needs.
9. Skills for assessing individuals, especially skills to adapt standardized aptitude tests and interest inventories so that collected data is meaningful and sensitive to the special educational needs of the client.
10. Skills to identify the individual's potentials from hobbies and accomplishments beyond academics.
11. Skills to discern the influence of socioeconomic disadvantage on learning difficulties that can interfere with transition to work.
12. Skills to adapt career services for individuals with special educational needs from different socioeconomic groups.

Conclusion

Transition into the world of work is perhaps one of the most important achievements in the young person's life. For some, given their socioeconomic and opportunity background, reaching and crossing this milestone may be smooth. For others, it may require extra effort both on the part of the individual and his/her family. The career development needs of young people with special needs gain special significance against the background of the Biwako Millennium Framework for Persons with Disabilities which drew to an end in 2012 (Biwako Millennium Framework, 2003). Even after decades of intensive effort to actualize a rights-based society for people with disability (for example, United Nations Decade of Disabled Persons, 1983–1992), much additional action is required to ensure that those with special needs experience an inclusive and barrier-free entry into the world of work (Nag, 2011). Career counselors can make important contributions in realizing this aim by actively considering the career development needs of those with special needs.

A comment from a parent who turned introspective after participating in a discussion (based on the worksheet in Box 28.1) gives a fitting closure to this chapter on special educational needs, social cognitive environments, and the career preparation process. In her words, "It's a fine balance between how much I must do and how much I must let go. What is the right balance?" Career counselors and all others who wish to participate in the career preparation process of individuals with special needs will need to often revisit the question of how to maintain a fine balance between giving support and making space for self-determination to grow.

References

Anderson, J. (2007). Urban poverty reborn: A gender and generational analysis. *Journal of Developing Societies, 23*(1–2), 221–241.

Aravind, S., Sailo, E., Arulmani, G., & Nag, S. (2011, December). *I am learning so much more than I thought I would: A preliminary report of school to work challenges among individuals with special needs.* Poster presented at the International Conference on Language, Literacy and Cognitive Development, Bangalore, India.

Arulmani, G. (2009). The internationalization of career counselling: Bridging cultural processes and labour market demands. *Asian Journal of Counselling, 16*(2), 149–170.

Arulmani, G., & Nag, S. (2006). *Work orientations and responses to career choices: Indian regional survey (Monograph).* Bangalore, India: The Promise Foundation.

Arulmani, G., & Nag-Arulmani, S. (2001). The child in the community: Multiple dimensions to disadvantage. In G. Mohan Kumar, A. Umapathy, & S. Bhogle (Eds.), *Readings in child development.* Bangalore, India: Prasaranga.

Arulmani, G., & Nag-Arulmani, S. (2004). *Career counselling: A handbook.* New Delhi, India: Tata McGraw Hill.

Asian Development Outlook. (2012). *Confronting rising inequality in Asia.* Mandaluyong City, Philippines: Asian Development Bank.

Bakshi, A. J. (2011). Past adolescence, into and across adulthood: Career crises and major decisions. *International Journal of Educational and Vocational Guidance, 11*(2), 139–153.

Bandura, A. (2001). Social cognitive theory: An agentic perspective. *Annual Review of Psychology, 52*, 1–26.

Banerjee, R., Mehendale, A., & Nanjundaiah, M. (2011). *Understanding inclusive practices in school: Examples of schools from India.* Bangalore, India: Seva in Action.

Beckett, C., Castle, J., Rutter, M., & Sonuga-Barke, E. J. (2010). Institutional deprivation, specific cognitive functions, and scholastic achievement: English and Romanian adoptee (ERA) study findings. *Monographs of the Society for Research in Child Development, 75*(295), 125–142.

Bradley, R. H., & Corwyn, R. F. (2002). Socioeconomic status and child development. *Annual Review of Psychology, 53*, 371–399.

Brown, D. (2002). The role of work values and cultural values in occupational choice, satisfaction, and success: A theoretical statement. In D. Brown & Associates (Eds.), *Career choice and development* (4th ed., pp. 465–509). San Francisco: Jossey Bass.

Biwako millennium framework for action towards an inclusive, barrier-free and rights-based society for persons with disabilities in Asia and the Pacific, 2003–2012. UNESCAP, 2003.

Fletcher, T., & Artiles, A. (2005). Inclusive education and equity in Latin America. In D. Mitchell (Ed.), *Contextualizing inclusive education*. London, UK: Routledge.

Greg, N. (2009). *Adolescents and adults with learning disabilities and ADHD: Assessment and accommodation*. New York, NY: The Guilford Press.

Holland, J. L. (1997). *Making vocational choices: A theory of vocational personalities and work environments* (3rd ed.). Odessa, FL: Consulting Psychologists Press.

Hue, M.-T. (2012). Inclusion practices with special educational needs students in Hong Kong secondary school: Teachers' narratives from a school guidance perspective. *British Journal of Guidance and Counselling, 40*(2), 143–156.

Krumboltz, J. D. (2009). The happenstance learning theory. *Journal of Career Assessment, 17*(2), 135–154.

Kumsta, R., Rutter, M., Stevens, S., & Sonuga-Barke, E. J. (2010). Risk, causation, mediation, and moderation. *Monograph of the Society for Research in Child Development, 75*(295), 117–142.

Mugo, J., Oranga, J., & Singal, N. (2010). Testing youth transitions in Kenya: Are young people with disabilities falling through the cracks? (RECOUP Working Paper 14). Retrieved from http://recoup.educ.cam.ac.uk/publications/WP34_MUGO_ORANGA_SINGAL_Sep_2010.pdf

Muuya, J. (2002). The aims of special education schools and units in Kenya: A survey of head teachers. *European Journal of Special Needs Education, 17*(3), 229–239.

Nag, S. (2007). Early reading in Kannada: The pace of acquisition of orthographic knowledge and phonemic awareness. *Journal of Research in Reading, 30*(1), 7–22.

Nag, S. (2011). Re-thinking support: The hidden school-to-work challenges for individuals with special needs. *International Journal of Educational and Vocational Guidance, 11*(2), 125–137.

Nag, S., & Lall, R. (2011). *In their words. A survey of parental concerns expressed during in-take interviews at a Special Needs Center* (Unpublished report).

Nag, S., & Snowling, M. (2012). School underachievement and specific learning difficulties. In J. M. Rey (Ed.), *The International Association for Child and Adolescent Psychiatrists and Allied Professionals' e-textbook on child and adolescent mental health*. Retrieved from http://iacapap.org/wp-content/uploads/C.3-LEARNING-DISABILITIES-072012.pdf

Nanjundaiah, M. (2011). Enabling transition in mainstream schools: A case of government main higher primary school (GMHPS), Ramanagara, Karnataka. In R. Banerjee, A. Mehendale, & M. Nanjundaiah (Eds.), *Understanding inclusive practices in schools: Examples of schools in India*. Bangalore, India: Seva in Action.

Pennington, B. F. (2006). From single to multiple deficit models of developmental disorders. *Cognition, 101*, 385–413.

Shaywitz, S. E., Fletcher, J. M., Holahan, J. M., Shneider, A. E., Marchione, K. E., Stuebing, K. K., … Shaywitz, B. A. (1999). Persistence of dyslexia: The Connecticut longitudinal study at adolescence. *Pediatrics, 104*(6), 1351–1359.

Singal, N. (2010). Including children with special needs in the Indian education system: Negotiating a contested terrain. In R. Rose (Ed.), *Confronting obstacles to inclusion: International responses to developing inclusive education*. London, UK: Routledge.

Singal, N., Bhatti, F., Januja, S., & Sood, N. (2012). Increased expectations, unrealised gains: Educational outcomes for young people with disabilities in India and Pakistan. In C. Colclough (Ed.), *Education outcomes and poverty in the South: A reassessment*. London, UK: Routledge.

Snowling, M., Muter, V., & Carroll, J. M. (2007). Children at family risk of dyslexia: A follow-up in early adolescence. *Journal of Child Psychology and Psychiatry, 48*(6), 609–618.

Solberg, V. S., & Good, G. E. (1994). Career search self-efficacy: Ripe for applications and intervention programming. *Journal of Career Development, 21*(1), 63–71.

Webster, D. D. (2004). Giving voice to students with disabilities who have successfully transitioned to college. *Career Development for Exceptional Individuals, 27*(2), 151–175.

"I Don't Want to Make Candles!" Supporting the Career Development Needs of Those Recovering from Mental Illnesses

29

Gideon Arulmani and Srinivasa Murthy

Introduction

The following is an excerpt from an interaction with a 28-year-old young man who was pursuing a bachelor's degree in engineering when he was first affected by schizophrenia (Arulmani, 2006). His active symptoms had subsided and, as was the norm, he had been sent for "occupational rehabilitation." But within a week he refused to go to the rehabilitation center. Initially, this refusal was attributed to his illness, a relapse was feared, and the psychiatrists began to consider increasing his medication. Closer engagement with him led him to say, "Look, I had dreamed all my life of becoming an engineer. I was enrolled in a great college and then I fell ill. Okay, maybe that is fate. But this rehabilitation is worse! I am expected to go every day to the occupation center and make candles! Or if not that, paper envelopes! Look, I don't need rehabilitation. Everyone thinks I'm mad. I'm not mad. *I don't want to make candles.* I just want to complete my course and become an engineer." While at one level this statement may be touching and poignant, at another level, it is a vivid and stark representation of the disempowerment suffered by a person recovering from mental illness. Such disempowerment can incapacitate the individual personally, socially, and professionally.

The World Health Organization's (WHO, 2004) report on global mental health presented the following startling findings: Mental, neurological, and substance-use disorders (MNS) contribute to 13 % of the global burden of disease, exceeding both cardiovascular disease and cancer; the third leading contributor to the global disease burden is depression; and by 2020, 30 million will have attempted suicide. It is also known that despite being willing to work and having the appropriate educational qualifications, a large preponderance of those with psychiatric difficulties do not have long-term success in the labor market (e.g., McReynolds & Garske, 2003). Using data collected over 10 years from an inner London borough, Perkins and Rinaldi (2002) reported that those with long-term mental health problems suffered increasing rates of unemployment in the 1990s. Although during this period, employment for the general majority of the population increased, *un*employment rates of the mentally ill increased from 80 to 92 %. In a study by the Banyan Academy of Leadership in Mental Health (BALM) in India, mental illness was cited as one of the main reasons for not working and the average duration of illness was higher amongst nonworkers (BALM, 2012). These rates of unemployment are disproportionately high not only in comparison to the general population but also in comparison to other disabilities (World Bank, 2007). Surveys and reviews have consistently indicated that paid employment helps the person affected by mental illness to return to normal functioning, brings personal

G. Arulmani (✉)
The Promise Foundation, Bangalore, India
e-mail: garulmani@t-p-f.org

meaning back into his or her life, fosters pride, boosts self-esteem, and also teaches effective coping strategies (Dunn, Wewiorski, & Rogers, 2008). Of relevance to the discipline of career counseling is the finding that high unemployment rates amongst the mentally ill are related to the absence of effective vocational support and career guidance services (e.g., Resnick, Rosenheck, & Drebing, 2006).

Against this background, this chapter has two central objectives. The first is to provide information about mental illness with a view to helping the career guidance practitioner understand potential clients who have been affected by mental illness better. The second objective is to examine how career guidance and counseling can support those who are recovering from mental illness such that the all-important goal of *sustained* employment does not remain elusive for them. This chapter is also useful for mental health professionals who are otherwise not specialists in career guidance and counseling (e.g., psychiatrists). The content is valuable for building their sensitivity to and clarity about the career-related challenges faced by a person recovering from mental illness.

Understanding the Signs and Symptoms of Mental Illness

Our understanding and acceptance of mental illness has been strangely different from other ailments and a peculiar association has existed between mental illness and metaphysical/spiritual interpretations. Conceptions of "madness" in the Middle Ages in Europe were a mixture of the divine, diabolical, and magical. In fact, the term "lunatic" has its roots in Roman mythology: "moonstruck" by the goddess Luna. A deep-rooted belief emerged (and continues to persist in many cultures) that the mind and body of the mentally ill person has somehow been tampered with and tainted by "evil" forces. Today, of course, there is a deeper understanding of the risk factors, symptoms, and outcomes of this group of human ailments. Unfortunately

definitions of mental illnesses remain vague and noncommittal.

The behavior of the mentally ill person can be quite misunderstood. Therefore, we briefly describe the primary signs and symptoms of mental illness. Specific information about the symptoms of mental illnesses is presented in Table 29.1 as classified by the International Classification of Diseases, Version 10 (ICD-10) (WHO, 1992). It must, of course, be kept in mind that many of the symptoms described are not always signs of mental illness as many people who do not have a mental disorder experience them also. They can be considered as symptoms of mental illness only if they are associated with change in functioning and behavior and/or cause distress to self and/or to others.

Knowing the diagnostic category the person belongs to (i.e., does the person have schizophrenia, anxiety disorder, or phobia?) is not as important for the career counselor as understanding how the symptoms could impact the person's work life. We have, therefore, attempted in Table 29.1 to link key symptoms of specific mental illnesses with the manner in which they can affect the individual's work life. We now lay out a few points that could help the career counselor understand these symptoms and the implications they have for career counseling.

Symptom Intensity and the Notion of a Continuum

Earlier understandings of psychopathology categorized all mental illnesses into two broad categories: psychoses and neuroses. Psychoses (e.g., organic psychoses, schizophrenia, and mania) were described to be severe and debilitating mental illnesses. Neuroses (e.g., phobia, anxiety disorder) were described to be less debilitating and, therefore, less severe. Today, the classification of mental illness has moved away from dichotomous, mutually exclusive categorizations. The contemporary understanding is that symptoms lie along a continuum of severity and intensity (e.g., Johns & van Os, 2001). The key indicators that are still in use, however, are the

Table 29.1 The impact of the symptoms of mental disorders on work performance

Main classification	Example of specific disorders	Key symptoms	Negative effects on work performance
Schizophrenia: Perhaps the most severe psychotic illness; results in a devastating disorganization of personality	Classified as: simple, paranoid, hebephrenic, catatonic, and undifferentiated schizophrenia	Loss of ability to distinguish between what is real and not real; delusions; hallucinations; emotional dysregulation; poor personal care	Slowness in activities; low motivation; fluctuating concentration; emotional blunting; withdrawal from socializing; holding odd beliefs; displaying odd behavior
Mood disorders: Severe psychotic illnesses; related to the dysregulation of emotions	Mania	Elation of mood; overactivity; overconfidence; poor sleep; poor judgment	Recovery is mostly complete with no residual symptoms on remission; recurrent attacks can interfere with study/work/ family life. This could cause loss of employment
	Depression	Lasting sadness; slowness of activities; loss of interests; suicidal ideas; guilt; hopelessness	Recovery is mostly complete with no residual symptoms on remission; recurrent attacks can interfere with study/work/ family life; attention and motivation may be affected; feelings of helplessness/ hopelessness may affect work performance
	Bipolar affective disorder	Episodes of depression and mania at different times	Unpredictability of episodes can cause uncertainties at work and loss of work and social time during the episodes of illness
Neurotic disorders: Less severe; the person is in touch with reality	Phobias	Avoidance of specific situations; mental tension; anxiety; specific, unreasonable dread and fear	Restriction of life activities; can increase to a point at which the person may not even be able to leave home
	Anxiety disorder	General feelings of intense apprehension; palpitations; worrying	Poor concentration; lack of confidence; preoccupation with failure; easily fatigued; irritability; restlessness
	Obsessive-compulsive disorder	Recurrent absurd and intrusive thoughts; over-preoccupation with unnecessary details; compulsion to repeat an action meaninglessly; anxiety. Complete remission of symptoms is unusual	Uncertain and unable to make a decision easily; tendency to start and stop a task intermittently; tentativeness about performance; low assertiveness; hesitant and constantly in doubt
	Adjustment disorder	Inability to cope with a situational stressor or life event and manifested as: sadness, lack of enjoyment, crying spells, fighting, and recklessness	Functions are impaired in relation to the stress inducing situation; tendency to ignore important tasks; avoidance of friends, family, and colleagues
Disorders of adult personality: Personality disorders are not an illness. They refer to ingrained, long-standing, and chronic patterns of behavior that are disabling and	Paranoid	Tendency to distrust and be suspicious of others; excessive sensitivity; concern that other people have hidden motives; tend to become socially isolated	Overwhelming expectation that one will be exploited by others, hence experience difficulties in working with others; tend to

(continued)

Table 29.1 (continued)

Main classification	Example of specific disorders	Key symptoms	Negative effects on work performance
significantly different from how the average person in the culture perceives, thinks, and feels, particularly in relating to others			be detached and suspicious. Can also become hostile toward colleagues
	Schizoid	Lifelong pattern of indifference to others; emotional coldness; limited capacity to express feelings; preference for solitary activities	Low energy levels at study and work; unable to develop close deep relationships; tendency to avoid responsibilities
	Dissocial	Unconcern for feelings of others; disregard for social norms; inability to maintain relationships; insensitivity to guilt; low response to corrective action	Can be disruptive at work; tends to break rules; oppositional to authority; impaired interpersonal relationships; may vandalize property; may have repeated legal problems
	Histrionic	Excessive emotionality and self-dramatization; tendency to seek attention; easy suggestibility; excessive need for approval; overconcern with physical attractiveness; can exhibit inappropriately seductive behavior	Job performance is governed by need for appreciation; can be manipulative in order to achieve; excessive sensitivity to criticism could affect performance; pride could affect willingness to change; decisions could be made impulsively
	Anankastic	Excessive doubt; preoccupation with details; rigidity and stubbornness; over-preoccupation with details, rules, lists, order, or schedule; overly scrupulous; excessive preoccupation with efficiency; pedantic and rigorously observant of social conventions; experience of insistent and unwanted thoughts or compulsions	Feelings of excessive doubt, caution, and perfectionism can affect completion of job tasks and work can become a burden; has difficulties to work in a team; has a need for others to submit exactly to a personally preferred way of doing things; irrational unwillingness to allow others to function independently; tendency to withdraw and work alone if unable to get others to comply
	Anxious (avoidant)	Extremely sensitive to criticism; strong feelings of inadequacy; tendency to keep away from social interaction	Extreme sensitivity to negative evaluation can affect work performance; social anxiety can cause avoidable errors at work; anxiety may inhibit aspiration and initiative
	Dependent	Excessive dependence on others to meet emotional and physical needs; allowing others to make important decisions; unwillingness to make demands; helplessness when alone; limited capacity to take day-to-day decisions	Low assertiveness can affect job performance; low capacity to work alone; low confidence to make decisions can affect career progress

Note: This is not an exhaustive list. Interested readers are referred to the ICD-10 Classification of Mental and Behavioral Disorders: Clinical descriptions and guidelines (WHO, 1992) extent to which symptoms impair the individual's ability to distinguish between subjective experience and reality; the insight the individual has into the symptom; the individual's connectedness with reality. The terms *mild, moderate,* and *severe* are commonly used to describe different levels of mental health problems (National Institute for Health and Clinical Excellence, 2011). The term *common mental disorders* is also used based on the wider prevalence of certain illness (e.g., depression, generalized anxiety disorder, panic disorder, obsessive-compulsive disorder, posttraumatic stress disorder, and phobias).

To understand how symptom intensity affects the professional life of those suffering from mental disorders, let us take the example of the anxiety experienced by three individuals having to make a formal presentation to clients at work. The experience of anxiety for one person may be such that it motivates and pushes him or her to prepare well for the presentation. Anxiety may cause the other person to fumble through the presentation, but still complete it successfully. The third person's experience of anxiety for the same task may be so intense that it is debilitating, causing great distress, and detrimentally affecting performance. It is the third person who would be described as suffering from anxiety disorder. And it is when such a person makes an appearance in a career counseling center that attention must be paid to the manner in which the symptoms of anxiety disorder could affect his or her career development. This is discussed in greater detail later in the chapter.

Symptom Impact and Recovery

The symptoms of severe mental illnesses can be profoundly disabling and recovery can be painfully slow. It is most important for the career counselor to note that the impact of mental illness on the person's motivation, ability to persist with the tasks of daily life, and the ability to work can be significant. The onset of the symptoms could be acute and their intensity such that the individual loses control of self, of the manner of interacting with others, as well of professional

tasks and duties. The individual's behavior could be so bizarre, that it could affect others' perception of the individual. For example, when a person is symptomatic and suffering from paranoid delusions, a colleague could be viewed with suspicion and even be accused of hatching a conspiracy to spoil chances of promotion. The person at the receiving end of these accusations would, of course, not understand the deep psychological processes underlying the paranoid ideation. Hence, the relationship could suffer severe damage and, even after recovery, the colleague may continue to view the individual in the light of his or her behavior during the symptomatic period. Hence, while the symptoms themselves are debilitating, the social fallout of the manifestation of these symptoms could profoundly influence the affected person's reintegration into the world of work. Box 29.1 presents excerpts from case notes that illustrate the bewilderment and loss of trust experienced by colleagues and the shame and loss of confidence experienced by the affected person. Drawing the person back into the world of work requires the skills to manage the impact of the person's symptomatic behavior on the work context of which he or she was a part.

Residual Symptoms: A Waxing and Waning Course

Mental disorders are unlike chronic physical illness in their course and outcome. Diabetes and such illnesses, for example, can be well controlled if the prescribed regimen of medication and diet is followed. Treatments for most mental disorders are effective but for a substantial proportion of individuals, only partially so. With some mental disorders, symptoms are known to persist in a residual form after the acute phase of the illness is over. In the case of depression, for example, symptoms such as low mood, disturbed sleep, disturbed appetite, tiredness, and irritability have been found to persist subclinically, even a year after the acute phase (e.g., Mojtabai, 2001). Hallucinations and delusions that afflict persons with schizophrenia may not interfere significantly with their daily life after the acute phase, but can persist at a diminished level of intensity causing their behavior to be odd and strange. The same is the case with the less severe, common mental disorders as well. The case notes presented in Box 29.1 offer examples of residual symptoms and how they affect reintegration into work roles. Symptoms of mental disorder are reactive not only to internal biochemical changes but also to psychosocial factors. Hence, a vital point that the career counselor must note is that most symptoms will have a *waxing* and *waning* course. At the same time, there is clear research evidence that symptoms are much better controlled and recovery is stronger when the individual is connected to his or her community and to meaningful work roles (Bond & Campbell, 2004). The implications of this for career development are significant. When symptoms flare up, the individual may be so incapacitated that his or her work performance suffers. At the same time, abruptly dropping out of work would impair the possibility of reentry. Supporting the career development of those recovering from mental illness requires the career counselor to know how to support career development through the waxing and waning of symptoms.

Drug Side-Effects

The drugs available today have given people with mental illnesses better chances than ever before to live satisfying lives. At the same time, each of these drugs can cause side-effects. The type of side-effect and its intensity would vary across drugs and individuals. Sometimes, other drugs have to be taken to reduce the side-effects of the primary medications. Many of these side-effects affect the person's work performance. This in turn could set off a vicious spiral of frustration, irritation, and loss of motivation. The desire and need to get back to work could even cause the affected person to discontinue medication. These are critical issues that the career counselor must be aware of in order to support the individual's sustained reintegration into the world of work. The U.S. Department of Health and Human Services (2012) provides a comprehensive overview of the side-effects of mental health medications and is a useful resource.

When Does the Career Counselor Become Relevant?

The relevance of career counseling is closely related to whether the affected person can engage with the counselor. The discussions so far allow us to make the following observations regarding the symptoms of mental illness.

Quality of Symptom Manifestation

The quality of symptom manifestation could be at various levels. When yet to be treated, symptoms are florid and the individual is experiencing high levels of distress: the *acute phase* of the illness. At another level, treatment may have begun and symptoms may have started decreasing in intensity. The individual's distress may be lower and the individual's insight into and personal control over the illness may be increasing: the *treatment/recovery phase* of the illness. This is also a time, when the side-effects of medication could emerge.

Nature and Extent of Recovery

Recovery from mental illness is a slow process and the course of recovery could fluctuate. In many cases, residual symptoms could persist much after the acute phase. It is also to be expected that the illness has caused significant personality changes in the individual. The extent of recovery therefore cannot be easily predicted. At one end of the recovery continuum are those who may be so badly affected that they require continued custodial care and a sheltered environment. At the other end are those who have returned to earlier levels of functioning and can be gainfully employed. The majority, however, would lie at neither of these extremes. In most cases, symptoms wax and wane, in some situations slipping far back to almost the acute phase and in other situations making slow and steady progress toward normalcy.

The Point of Intervention: Three Key Markers

The earlier the person's reconnection with the regular routines of life, the stronger and quicker will be the recovery. Hence, creating opportunities for meaningful work is relevant at all stages of recovery from mental illness. This is true also for those whose recovery has not moved much beyond custodial care. On the other hand, it must be noted that when symptoms are flagrant and the affected person is in severe distress career counseling may not be effective or appropriate. For example, if the person is at a stage where his or her thoughts and actions are controlled by delusions and he or she is unyielding to counterargument, the person may not be ready for career counseling. Three key markers may be kept in mind when making an assessment of whether career counseling would be relevant and contribute to the recovery process:

- The individual's ability to distinguish between subjective experience and reality
- The quality of insight the individual has into his or her situation
- The quality of the individual's connectedness with reality

Box 29.1: Psychosocial Dynamics of Reintegration into Work Roles: Case Note Excerpts

I feel much better now. But how can I ever face my colleagues again? Memories of what I did keep coming back. And people tell me of what I don't remember. It seems I threw things around and ran out of the office. I also remember the voices telling me that I should escape. *32-Year-old male, Assistant Librarian in a college. Diagnosis: Paranoid Schizophrenia.*

I went back to my office. But I don't think it is going to work out. As soon as I entered the room went quiet. Then everyone came up and started speaking to me. It felt like a false friendliness. Very unnatural. Like they had been coached to treat me correctly or something. Then all through the day, I would catch people staring at me and look away when I looked up at them. Can't work like that. *39-Year-old female, Accountant in a company. Diagnosis: Bipolar Disorder.*

They are telling me that I stripped my clothes off and ran down the street. I only remember that vaguely. But if everyone else remembers, then how can I face them? When I heard that all my old fears started coming back. *42-Year-old male, Associate in a Law firm. Diagnosis: Mood Disorder (Mania).*

His outburst was major. Shouting and tore up files. He would not listen to anything I said. He was convinced that I was plotting to get him sacked. It is great he is back now. But still I feel he not his old self. As his friend I am never sure what will happen. *33-Year-old male, close workmate of a 32-year-old male. Diagnosis: Paranoid Schizophrenia.*

I cannot let him handle the machines anymore. When he went mad 6 months ago, he nearly killed his co-worker with the tool he was holding. I cannot take that chance again. Nor will the workers accept. Best I can do is give a watchman job to him. *Owner of a furniture manufacturing factory, in response to the counselor's attempt at reintegrating a highly skilled Product Engineer back into his workplace. Diagnosis: Mood Disorder (Mania).*

Note: Extracted from Unpublished Clinical Records (2000–2006) by G. Arulmani (2006), The Promise Foundation, Bangalore, India.

Understanding Disability That Is Caused by Mental Illness

Unlike other disabilities such as locomotor disability or blindness, disabilities that are caused by mental illness such as apathy, difficulty with concentration, amotivation, communication difficulties, and poor interpersonal skills are not visible. Hence, it may even be difficult for the lay person to accept that the person suffering or recovering from mental illness is disabled in any way. There are instances when disability benefits like bus passes have been denied because these individuals look physically strong (Chandrashekar, Kasthuri, Kumar, & Prashanth, 2010). This is further compounded by the stigma attached to mental illness and the discrimination that follows as a result (Murthy, 2005; Wig, 1997). It is important therefore that the career counselor orients himself or herself to contemporary understandings of disability.

What Is Disability?

Until about two decades ago, health and disability were viewed dichotomously: disability began where health ended. The disabled were segregated and the medical model was used to understand and support their needs. Since the 1970s, stronger emphasis has been laid on community and educational inclusion. The WHO (2002) has asserted, for example, that the objective is to understand the individual's functioning in society, irrespective of the person's impairments. Today, a comprehensive *biopsychosocial* model is used to understand and describe disability (e.g., The International Classification of Functioning, Disability and Health [ICF]) (WHO, 2001a, 2002), which may be physical, cognitive, mental, sensory, emotional, developmental, or some combination of these. The ICF does not make a distinction between the type and cause of disability, for instance, between "physical" and "mental" health. Disability is conceptualized on a continuum from minimal difficulties in functioning, to impacts that have major effects on a person's life. Within this conceptualization of disability, the ICF (WHO, 2002) categorizes difficulties in human functioning into three interconnected areas:

- Impairments: problems originating from body functions or alterations in body structure (e.g., loss of control over limbs due to paralysis).

- Activity limitations: difficulties in executing activities (e.g., difficulties in commuting to the workplace).
- Participation restrictions: difficulties with involvement in any area of regular life (e.g., facing discrimination in employment).

As per this framework, disability arises from complications faced in any or all of these three areas of functioning. The preamble to the Convention on the Rights of Persons with Disabilities (CRPD) (Committee on the Rights of Persons with Disabilities, 2006) highlights that, "disability results from the interaction between persons with impairments and attitudinal and environmental barriers that hinder their full and effective participation in society on an equal basis with others" (p. 1). Placing disability within an interactionist framework implies that disability is not an attribute of the person. It is the interaction between health conditions and contextual factors, namely environmental and personal factors, that results in disability.

Disabilities That the Mentally Ill Experience

Thara and Tharoor (2012) have identified four general areas in which disability that is caused by mental illness can manifest:

Activities of Daily Living
These include day-to-day adaptive activities such as cleaning, shopping, cooking, transporting oneself, maintaining a home, self-care, using public facilities, and other such routine, yet essential, activities.

Social Functioning: Relationships
This refers to the individual's capacity to interact appropriately and effectively with other individuals. Social functioning includes the ability to get along with others in one's environment. Impaired social functioning may be demonstrated by a history of altercations, evictions, fear of strangers, avoidance of social

occasions and interpersonal relationships, and social isolation.

Cognitive Functions: Attention and Concentration

The ability to manage concentration, task persistence, and pace may be affected. Particularly debilitating can be the decreased ability to sustain focused attention sufficiently long enough to permit the completion of tasks commonly found in work settings.

Work Life

Deterioration or decompensation in work or work-like situations refers to the repeated failure to adapt to stressful circumstances which cause the individual either to withdraw from the situation or to experience subjective distress and an exacerbation of symptoms. There could be an accompanying difficulty in maintaining activities of daily living, social relationships, and/or maintaining concentration and task persistence.

Stigma: Disabled by Society

Social stigma refers to the expression of strong disapproval and displeasure toward a person on the basis of some personal feature that differentiates him or her from other individuals in the group. Stigma attached to mental illness has been extensively studied and it is clear that it is a complex and deep-rooted combination of feelings, attitudes, and behaviors (Penn & Martin, 1998). The World Health Report on Mental Health (WHO, 2001b) unequivocally states that the "single most important barrier to overcome in the community, is the stigma and associated discrimination towards persons suffering from mental and behavioral disorders" (p. 108). Goffman (1963) has pointed out that mental illness hits directly at the person's identity and pushes him or her away from the realms of normalcy to be labeled and perceived as "abnormal." Stigma can become a part of the group's social structure and result in tangible barriers being placed before the affected person. For example, in many legal systems, people who have been diagnosed with a mental illness are not allowed to participate in the electoral process, hold certain offices, enjoy child custody rights, drive a car, hold certain occupational posts, and sign legal documents (e.g., Ratanlal, 2002). When the entire social structure directs stigma toward the affected individual, it is very likely that the individual would succumb and would judge self as wanting. Corrigan (2004) has described self-stigma as "a private shame that diminishes self-esteem and causes self-doubt regarding whether one can live independently, hold a job, earn a livelihood, and find a life mate" (p. 620).

More than the disabilities that result from mental illness, stigma causes prolonged periods of unemployment. This increases the affected person's difficulties to reenter the labor market which in turn leads to social decline. The best of career counseling efforts can fail if the dynamics between stigma and mental illness are not understood. As will be discussed further ahead, career counseling can make a significant contribution to arresting this stigma-induced decline.

Assessing Disability Related to Mental Illness

The meaning of recovery is hard to define for mental illness. Most persons who have suffered mental illness recover from the acute phase of their symptom manifestation with treatment and rehabilitation. To what extent they recover and how long they remain symptom-free varies from one individual to another and across mental disorders.

There is research to support that many mentally ill persons can return to a level of effective functioning socially, and at work, and contribute significantly to the life of the larger community. Some can remain free of symptoms, without medication. It is against this background that methods of assessing psychiatric disability have been designed. Being able to assess a client for the extent of disability caused by mental illness is a critical skill that the career counselor must develop.

Approach to the Assessment of Disability

Two approaches could be taken to plan career development interventions. One way is to base one's starting point on the diagnostic category to which the affected person has been allocated. This implies that one would plan an approach for persons with schizophrenia, a different one for those with anxiety disorder, another one for those diagnosed with a phobic disorder, and so on for each diagnostic category. As pointed out in the World Health Report (WHO, 2011), couched within such an approach is the assumption that each type of disorder has specific health, educational, rehabilitation, social, and support needs. In the second approach, the target is to obtain a clear view of the affected person's disabilities and impairments and develop career development plans based on this understanding. The next section introduces the reader to a well-known assessment schedule that follows a functions-based approach to the assessment of disability.

The International Classification of Functioning, Disability and Health

The ICF is the conceptual framework created by the WHO within which health and disability can be defined, measured, and understood (WHO, 2001a, 2001b). The ICF is particularly relevant when supporting the career development of those affected by mental illness because it helps the counselor understand the person's level of capacity: what he or she *can do* in a standard environment. It also provides a framework for understanding the client's present level of performance: what he or she *presently does in* the existing environment. The ICF therefore emphasizes *functioning*, rather than disability by shifting focus from a preoccupation with causes to the impact the illness or disability has on the individual. The ICF makes an observation that is critical when planning career development interventions for those recovering from mental

illness: A diagnosis, or the recognition of the presence of an illness, does not always predict work performance, the potential of returning to productive work, and the quality of reintegration into social roles. What is required when designing a career development program is data pertaining to the levels of functioning and disability. The ICF offers a systematic and internationally applicable method of collecting this crucial data. We will in the following paragraphs present information about the ICF that illustrate its relevance to the practice of career guidance for psychologically affected persons. However, these are only abbreviated illustrations and the interested reader is advised to go to the original ICF documents for a more complete picture (WHO, 2001a, 2002).

ICF Domains

The ICF classifies areas of life into three domains.

Body Function and Structures

This domain refers to the individual's *physiological* and *psychological* functions. The focus is not on causes but on the function itself. Fluctuating attention, for example, describes the quality of a psychological (cognitive) function that could be seen in schizophrenia, anxiety disorder, as well as phobic disorder. In this example, collecting more information about the individual's ability to pay attention would be the target for the counselor who is planning a program to reintegrate the affected person into the world of work. The ICF offers standardized formats through which functional abilities and impairments linked to eight body functions could be recorded in very specific detail.

Activities and Participation

Within this domain, the focus is on the individual's functioning as a whole person.

Activity is related to the performance of a task or action by the person. Activity Limitations are problems the person may have in executing certain tasks. Becoming unable to leave home because of overpowering anxiety is an example of an activity limitation.

Participation describes the person's quality of involvement in a life situation. Participation restrictions are difficulties the person may experience in connecting with and contributing to life situations in the manner that he or she did before the onset of the illness. Take, for example, an accountant who has rejoined duty after suffering an attack of schizophrenia. He may be reinstated to his original post, but his colleagues/employer may not be sure anymore of the accuracy of his calculations. Hence, he may not be allowed to *participate* as vigorously as before with crucial aspects of his earlier work roles.

The ICF classifies activity and participation domains into nine categories as shown in Table 29.2 ranging from basic to complex levels. For the career counselor, information derived from the ICF could provide invaluable information pertaining to the person's work-related functions.

Environmental Factors

The ICF recognizes that the physical, social, and attitudinal environment in which people live could be facilitative, or could become barriers. Hence, a significant emphasis is placed on the interface between the affected person's symptoms and contextual factors. Five categories of environmental factors are described in the ICF. Each category has a comprehensive listing of specific items. We provide illustrations below:

- Products and technology (e.g., architecture of buildings and access to a workplace).
- The natural environment and human-made changes to environment (e.g., the noise in the work location may be such that it exacerbates a disability).
- Support and relationships (e.g., the manner in which people in positions of authority, such as an employer, engage with the affected person).
- Attitudes (e.g., social attitudes toward the disability).
- Services, systems, and policies (e.g., sensitivity of labor policies to disabilities).

The ICF provides a 4-point-rating scheme by which each item could be examined for the extent to which it facilitates or creates a barrier. For example, a rating of 4 on the barrier side for labor and employment policies would mean that the affected person is living in an environment where no policy or legislation exists to help the person reintegrate into the world of work. Conversely, a rating of 4 on the facilitator side for the same item would mean that substantial support is available through legislation and policy for the person to reintegrate into the world of work. In this scheme, 0 indicates that the item is neither a barrier nor a facilitator. Information about environmental factors is of vital importance when planning a career development program for a mentally affected person. For example, it could be that the affected person's work location is a small, closed, windowless room. If one of the primary symptoms that this individual suffers is a fear of closed spaces, going back to work in a windowless room would only worsen his or her disability and cause severe participation restrictions.

ICF Qualifiers

The next construct in the ICF scheme is Qualifiers which allows the assessor to note the occurrence and seriousness of a problem across the three domains: body, activity, and participation along a 5-point scale (no, mild, moderate, severe, and complete impairment). These constructs are illustrated in Table 29.2 and explained briefly here.

The Performance Qualifier

This qualifier reflects the affected person's functioning in his or her "current" environment and indicates the extent to which the person's performance is restricted. It is a measure of "involvement in a life situation and the lived experience of the person" (WHO, 2001a, p. 12). Most important for career guidance and counseling is that the performance qualifier provides a measure of the struggle the affected person experiences in his or her attempt to reintegrate.

Table 29.2 Short list of the nine ICF activity and performance domains, scored for a person with anxiety disorder

Short list of activity and performance domains	PQ	CQ
Learning and applying knowledge		
Watching	0	0
Listening	0	0
Reading	1	0
Writing	1	0
Calculating (arithmetic)	1	0
Solving problems	1	0
General tasks and demands		
Undertaking a single task	0	0
Undertaking multiple tasks	2	1
Communication		
Receiving messages (spoken)	0	0
Receiving messages (nonverbal)	0	0
Speaking	1	4
Producing nonverbal messages	0	0
Holding a conversation	3	1
Mobility		
Lifting and carrying objects	0	0
Fine hand use (e.g., picking up, grasping)	1	1
Walking	0	0
Moving around using equipment (e.g., wheelchair)	0	0
Using transportation (e.g., car, bus, train, plane)	3	3
Driving (e.g., using bicycle, motorbike, car)	4	3
Self-care		
Washing oneself	0	0
Caring for body parts (e.g., grooming)	0	0
Toileting	0	0
Dressing	0	0
Eating	0	0
Drinking	0	0
Looking after one's health	0	0
Domestic life		

	PQ	CQ
Accessing goods and services (e.g., shopping)	2	1
Preparation of meals (e.g., cooking)	3	2
Doing housework (e.g., washing dishes)	3	2
Assisting others	3	2
Interpersonal interactions		
Basic interpersonal interactions	1	1
Complex interpersonal interactions	3	2
Relating with strangers	4	2
Formal relationships	3	2
Informal social relationships	2	1
Family relationships	2	1
Intimate relationships	3	2
Major life areas		
Informal education	0	0
School education	0	0
Higher education	0	0
Remunerative employment	4	2
Basic economic transactions	0	0
Economic self-sufficiency	4	2
Community, social, and civic life		
Community life	3	1
Recreation and leisure	3	1
Religion and spirituality	0	0
Human rights	0	0
Political life and citizenship	0	0

Note: PQ performance qualifier (performance restriction), *CQ* capacity qualifier (activity limitation)

Scoring key:

0 = No difficulty; has no problem

1 = Mild difficulty; problem present less than 25 % of the time; person can tolerate; happened rarely over the last 30 days

2 = Moderate difficulty; problem present less than 50 % of the time; interfering with day-to-day life; happens occasionally over the last 30 days

3 = Severe difficulty; problem present more than 50 % of the time; partially disrupting day-to-day life; happens frequently over the last 30 days

4 = Complete difficulty; problem present more than 95 % of the time; totally disrupting day-to-day life; happens every day over the last 30 days

The Capacity Qualifier

This is a description of the affected person's ability to perform on a task or execute an action. Accurate elicitation of information would reveal the affected person's "highest probable level of functioning in a given domain at a given moment" (WHO, 2001a, p. 13). Information obtained through this qualifier would help the career counselor understand the affected person's capacity relative to what would have been expected normally of that person before the onset of the mental illness condition.

The ICF provides a rating scale that ranges from 0 (*no difficulty*) to 4 (*complete difficulty*). The scoring scheme is detailed in Table 29.2. High scores on the performance qualifier indicate that performance restriction is high; that is, the environment is placing restrictions upon the person. On the other hand, high scores on the capacity qualifier indicate that the person's capacity itself has been affected and hence his or her activity potential is low.

The ICF provides a list of questions designed to elicit information related to the performance and capacity dimensions for each of the items. These are general questions and are to be adapted as necessary during the course of the interview. For example, ICF questions for Major Life Areas (subitem: remunerative employment) are as follows:

- Questions related to performance: In your present surroundings, how much of a problem do you actually have getting done all the work you need to do for your job? Does your work environment and the way in which your tools are set up make it harder for you to execute your work tasks? Is your capacity to do your job, without assistance, more or less than what you actually do in your present surroundings?
- Questions related to capacity: How much does your present state of health affect your ability to get done all the work you need to do for your job, without assistance? How does this compare with someone, just like yourself but without your health condition?

The Environmental Qualifier

The inclusion of environmental factors in the scheme makes it possible for the career counselor to better understand how contextual realities function as barriers and facilitators for both capacity and performance dimensions of actions and tasks related to work. Environmental factors include geographical features such as climate and terrain, characteristics of the work environment, social attitudes, institutions, and legal provisions. With such information in hand, practical plans could be made to support the functioning of the affected person at work.

The ICF is designed to measure disability emerging from all forms of illnesses and disorders. An example of using it to assess disability arising from mental illness is described in a later section. Similar approaches to the ICF have also been developed at the local level. In the following section we provide an example from India as an illustration of what the career counselor could search for in case a locally validated measure is required.

The Indian Disability Evaluation and Assessment Scale

Indian Disability Evaluation and Assessment Scale (IDEAS) is a tool developed by the Indian Psychiatric Society (2002) to measure disability related to psychiatric illnesses. It has been gazetted by the government and is the officially recommended instrument to measure psychiatric disability in India. Certification based on IDEAS qualifies a person for government benefits and schemes that have been made available for the mentally ill.

IDEAS has four themes: self-care, interpersonal activities (social relationships), communication and understanding, and work. As with the ICF, IDEAS also offers a framework to assess an individual keeping work and career development in mind. It could be used as a tool by the career counselor to plan the individual's reintegration into work. The work dimension addresses three areas: employment, housework, and education. Assessment of the individual's status on the work dimension includes employment seeking behavior and the ability to perform employment-related tasks completely, efficiently, and in proper time. At the level of performing housework, assessment includes the individual's ability to cook, care for others, belongings, and household items. The work dimension also includes the individual's engagement with the educational system and covers activities related to school/college performance such as regularity of attendance, ability to meet educational targets, reading and retention of material, ability to pay adequate attention, and prepare and succeed in examinations.

Links Between Career Counseling and Disability Assessment

Instruments such as the ICF and IDEAS, if executed with sensitivity, allow the career counselor to determine the "gap" between the affected person's capacity and performance and the extent to which the specific aspect of his or her environment is a facilitator or a barrier. An ICF assessment could reveal, for example, that capacity is less than performance. This would mean that the current environment is an enabling one, allowing and facilitating the affected person's performance. Most often the situation is the other way around: capacity is greater than performance. This indicates that barriers to performance exist in the affected person's environment blocking the manifestation of his or her capacities. Addressing this barrier, or preparing the person to deal with this barrier, would be a critical career development target.

The Clues Are in the Gaps: A Case Example

With a view to demonstrating the links between career counseling and disability assessment, we now draw the reader's attention to a more detailed examination of information presented in Table 29.2. The table presents the ICF Activity and Performance Domains and has been scored based on an interview with a person diagnosed

with anxiety disorder: a 39-year-old female accountant who referred herself for career counseling with the complaint that she was not able to do well at work and wanted to change her job (Arulmani, 2006). The person was interviewed using the ICF schedule. Let us briefly examine the ratings that were made for this individual and what these ratings mean for career counseling within the ICF scheme.

- *Speaking* emerges as an item of particular relevance where the capacity qualifier score is higher than the performance qualifier score. The interview with this person revealed that she had a significant stammer which considerably worsened when her anxiety increased. This difficulty was rated as a *complete difficulty* (score of 4) since it was present more than 95 % of the time, totally disrupting day-to-day life, particularly at work. On the performance qualifier side, the difficulty is only at the *mild* level (score of 1), since it restricted her performance less than 25 % of the time and that any performance restriction only occurred rarely. This implies that she ought to have been able to tolerate the disability. Yet, her disability (capacity qualifier) was high.

- The ratings for *holding a conversation* are also of relevance. Here, both the performance qualifiers and the capacity qualifiers are rated as *severe difficulty* (score of 3). The content of the interview revealed that this person's job role required her to make presentations to potential clients. This evoked a high level of anxiety in her and worsened her stammer as indicated by her high capacity qualifier score. On the performance side, her clients exhibited obvious signs of ridicule and displeasure. This aggravated her anxiety, increased her stammer, and so the vicious cycle spiraled, pulling her downwards. The final result was that on most occasions, she was not able to win confidence and lost clients. Here, although her immediate work environment (e.g., her employer, her colleagues) was supportive, persons external to her office were not as tolerant. Hence, her performance qualifier indicates performance restriction.

- Similar trends are seen for items under Interpersonal Interactions . While her difficulties at the level of *basic interpersonal interactions* are only at the *mild* level, discrepancies between performance and capacity become more complex. A particularly high discrepancy is seen in *relating with strangers* and *intimate relationships*.

- The culmination of these difficulties is seen in *remunerative employment*, where the rating is at the level of *severe difficulty*. This implies that her employment could be at risk.

Planning Career Development Based on a Functions-Oriented Assessment

The case example presented demonstrates how a functions-oriented assessment schedule could generate data, based on which a career development plan could be formulated. The person came to the career counselor with the complaint that she was not able to do well at work and wanted to change her job. The information gleaned and the ratings made point to developing a strategy that is focused primarily on the person and certain aspects of her work environment. The assessment indicates that although changing her job was what the client wanted, it was most likely that she would have encountered similar if not worse difficulties in another job as well. What she would benefit from is an intervention that would first of all address her anxiety and her difficulties with speech. Hence, the career counselor's target here was twofold. The first was to refer her to a specialist with the expertise to deal with her anxiety difficulties (e.g., a clinical psychologist) and/or a specialist with expertise to deal with stammering (e.g., speech therapist). The specific career counseling objective would be to mitigate the impact of her psychological difficulties on her work performance, rather than consider a change of job. The career counseling that she was provided is described briefly below:

- The career counselor, first of all, used the data obtained to point out to her that her immediate work environment (employer and colleagues) was exceptionally supportive. The job roles at which she was successful (e.g., solving problems, undertaking multiple tasks) were

delineated to highlight her *well-functioning* areas, rather than her difficulties.

- Her attention was drawn to the possibility that roles which required her to engage with people external to her company (e.g., potential clients) worsened her condition and thereby affected her work performance.

- The career counselor then worked with this person to list in detail, the specific components of her job role. Roles that were directly linked to her disability were identified. For example, client facing duties particularly when her clients were strangers emerged as a job role that significantly affected her work performance.

- Based on this information the career counselor prepared a referral note for her to present to the other therapist she was going to see.

- She was also encouraged to communicate with her employer, requesting to be relieved of duties that brought her disabilities to the fore. At the same time, she listed other duties she could take up instead.

- Follow-up after 6 months indicated that the approach had been successful. Her employer had taken her off duties that worsened her condition and replaced this with other duties. This in turn caused an immediate reduction in her anxiety, boosted her confidence, and her work improved remarkably. She had enrolled for therapy with a clinical psychologist and was gradually gaining control over her anxiety which in turn was improving her speech difficulties. Her final comment (with only a minimal stammer!) throws clear light on how career counseling helped her. She said, "I moved from a down cycle to an up cycle because career counseling showed me what I should *avoid* at work!"

This case example illustrates career counseling from the capacity qualifier side. There could be other instances where the career development plan may have to focus on the performance qualifier side, with greater emphasis being laid on environmental and contextual matters. Other individuals may require support both with their performance and their capacity. The point being made is that a careful assessment of activity and performance domains offers a strong, person-centered platform upon which to plan a career development program relevant to the needs of a person with psychological difficulties.

Integrating Disability Schedules with Career Services

We now list the skills that the counselor could develop in order to integrate information from disability schedules with career counseling.

- A critical skill is that of *elicitation*. Using tools such as the ICF, the career counselor is required to draw out as much information as possible with regard to the disability, along with its performance and capacity dimensions. The score given is not as important as the content of the interview and quality of responses that the counselor is able to elicit, keeping in mind the ultimate target of reintegration into work.
- Next is the skill of *delineation*. The plethora of difficulties elicited might seem overwhelming. The task before the career counselor now is to select from the information elicited, issues that belong in the realm of career counseling and those which need the expertise of other specialists.
- Another skill that the career counselor must acquire, particularly when working with the mentally ill, is the skill of *referral*. As illustrated in the case example described, the career counselor clearly identified targets that could be achieved through career counseling and referred the client to professionals for help with her other difficulties. It is essential that the career counselor working with those recovering from mental illness expands his or her referral network and develops professional relationships with other mental health professionals such as clinical psychologists, psychiatric social workers, psychiatrists, and psychiatric nurses.
- Another career counseling skill is that of *making links between* the difficulties that have been identified. In the case example

presented, the counselor made the links between: a desire for job change, anxiety, failure at certain job roles, and stammering. Identifying these linkages allowed the counselor to facilitate the breaking of the negative cycle that had gripped the client.

Supported Education and Supported Employment

One of the criticisms leveled against vocational rehabilitation models is that they excessively focus on prevocational skills and simulate work environments that have no real connection with career development (e.g., Hirsch, 1989). Some of the latest reviews of outcomes, for example, indicate that "sheltering" those with psychiatric disabilities is less effective than exposing them to the real world as quickly as possible (e.g., Cimera, Wehman, West, & Burgess, 2012). The challenge before the career counselor, therefore, is to move the person toward competitive and meaningful employment. We present below two salient themes emerging from the literature that have direct relevance to the practice of career counseling for the mentally ill.

Supported Education

Epidemiological surveys in different countries have shown that ailments related to the mind begin very early in life. Kessler et al. (2007) based on a comprehensive review of the literature stated, for example, that, "Half of all lifetime cases begin by age 14; three quarters have begun by age 24. Anxiety disorders often begin in late childhood, mood disorders in late adolescence, and substance abuse in the early 20s" (p. 2). This is exactly the period when the building blocks of the individual's career development, namely educational qualifications, are being laid. The onset of mental illness during late adolescence-young adulthood prevents many of these individuals from completing their education and obtaining qualifications to find suitable employment. Without appropriate education these individuals can be severely disadvantaged in pursuing employment goals. Furthermore, the rather mediocre success levels of vocational rehabilitation programs have been linked to the absence of postsecondary education and training amongst those recovering from mental illness (e.g., McQuilken et al., 2003).

Supported education which emerged in the early 1990s in the United States and Canada is an approach to educational programming that assists people with psychiatric disabilities in their pursuit of further education. Keeping in mind their psychological difficulties, supported education for these individuals is planned and paced according to their present level of functioning and the disabilities caused by the mental illness. Supported education programs are in vivo assistance extended to affected persons and are aimed at strengthening or restoring educational competencies while avoiding segregated classrooms (Mowbray, Collins, & Bybee, 1999). The avoidance of segregation is a key therapeutic point. Rather than sheltering the affected person from the competitiveness of a regular classroom, supported education exposes him or her to the real world. Hence, affected persons enroll for a course and then receive special attention in the form of supported education.

Evaluations of supported education programs have indicated that they have positive outcomes. Cook and Solomon (1993), for example, have reported that those who went through a supported education program to complete higher secondary education went on to enroll in college for further education. Hoffman and Mastrianni (1993) reported increases in competitive employment after the person went through supported education. Improvements in self-esteem and mastery have also been noted (Leonard & Bruer, 2007; Wolf & DiPietro, 1992).

Supported Employment

Supported employment emerged in the late 1980s as a response to the not-optimal outcomes of the sheltered workshop approach to rehabilitation.

Skills that were learned in sheltered workshops did not effectively translate into competitive employment and the majority became dependent on government subsidies (Hirsch, 1989). Hence, the notion of supported employment emerged as paid, competitive employment that, although requiring ongoing support, would occur in integrated work settings (Wehman & Kregel, 1995). This stands in contrast to traditional vocational rehabilitation programs which focus on skills training preparation, sheltered workshops, and transitional employment. Revell, West, and Cheng (1988) have provided a description of the components of supported employment programs which are: conduct community-based assessments to obtain a person-job match, design relevant skill training to facilitate job development, and offer placement services, and job site training. Supported employment also facilitates the identification and arrangement of natural supports both on and away from the work setting. The model recognizes that integral to the individual's employment success is the provision of support services such that the affected person achieves long-term stability in employment. At the same time, while support services are integral to this model, the interventions are designed to ensure that, over a period of time, a systematic reduction (fading) of on-site staff assistance is achieved. Supported employment stands in contrast to traditional vocational rehabilitation programs since it avoids a long period of preparatory work activities which are often disconnected from real-world requirements (Bond & Campbell, 2004).

Corrigan and McCracken (2005) refer to the traditional method of reintegration as "train-place." People recovering from psychiatric illness are first trained and, then when recovery has been achieved, they are placed in real-world jobs. The supported employment paradigm takes the "place-train" approach and focuses on ensuring reconnection with the real world of work as quickly as possible. Hence rapid placement of people with disabilities is the first target. This is followed by in vivo support, resources, and training designed to ensure that the person successfully retains his or her position in the world of work. The therapeutic objective here is that the recovering individual is brought as quickly as possible to face the realities of real-world employment. The individual is shielded from the ignominy of skills retraining which anticipates defeat rather than success, reflecting indeed the plea made by the young engineering student in the example cited at the beginning of the chapter: "I don't want to make candles!"

Bond, McGrew, and Fekette (1995) reported that 59 % of participants in a supported employment program successfully entered competitive employment in comparison with 29 % from a traditional vocational rehabilitation program. Another critical finding is that the pressures of reentering the world of work did not increase symptoms and the risk of rehospitalization amongst those who had taken up professional work roles through supported employment (e.g., Becker & Drake, 2003). Beyer (2007), using data from North Lanarkshire (UK), reported that employment rates improved and people were financially better off after obtaining a job through a supported employment program. Kregel (2012), reviewing a specific supported employment program in the United States (Work Incentives Planning and Assistance Program, WIPA), found that these individuals were more likely than others to have reached a position of employment security and could go off on welfare benefits. The Western literature is replete with such examples of the positive outcomes of supported employment.

Supported Education and Employment: Extensions Across Cultures and Contexts

This section presents ideas on how these techniques could be adapted for career counseling and extended across varied cultures and contexts.

Initiate Support Facilities

Given the successful outcomes that have been reported in research, an obvious career counseling function could be to initiate supported education/employment facilities in situations where they do not exist. However, a point we would like the reader to note is that the initiatives described are from the Western world. The career counselor who intends to facilitate the establishment of such services in other cultures would do well to keep the following in mind.

Educate Stakeholders

While the potential power of the supported education/employment is clear, it is also clear that a number of locally operating social and cultural factors could affect their implementation. Social stigma could be a significant barrier. The obvious point that emerges is that key persons must first be oriented and educated regarding the fundamental requirements of supported education/employment programs. This becomes an essential requirement in countries where there is no legislation or existing framework pertaining to the rehabilitation of the mentally disabled. It has been shown, for example, that relapse is significantly reduced when the family is included as part of the treatment team (e.g., Dixon, 2001; Richmond Fellowship Society, 2012). In similar manner, when institutions (e.g., schools, places of work) are first oriented, the success of the initiative is more likely. This orientation would include providing information about the nature of mental illness and then creating provisions specific to the supported education/employment framework. It is also essential that all parties involved are informed about any medications the client is taking and the impact side-effects could have on performance. MacDonald-Wilson, Rogers, Massaro, Lyass, and Crean (2002) have highlighted certain critical accommodations that would need to be made: flexible scheduling, job modification, facilitating communication on the job, modifying training methods, sensitizing personnel within the institution, modifying the physical environment, or allowing the individual to bring and use his or her special equipment. At the practical, day-to-day level, simple changes could make a world of a difference. This could include providing instructions in writing rather than verbally, creating schedules that allow for regular routines, reducing interruptions, and ensuring that the environment is not noisy.

Create Incentives

An interesting recommendation made by the BALM based on their field experience in India is to create incentives for potential employers. They suggest that jobs are created in organizations against clear-cut vacancies, and not merely to meet corporate social responsibilities. They further suggest that tax benefits are offered to companies that employ persons with mental health issues (BALM, 2012).

Reposition Career Development

The traditional understanding of healthy career development is that the individual stays in employment, performing in such a way that he or she is moving steadily from one level to another. The career counselor working with the mentally ill must acknowledge that this may not be possible for those who suffer from psychiatric ailments. One of the criticisms leveled against those with psychiatric ailments is that they do not stay on in employment. Keeping the person at the heart of the process, a new way of viewing employment would be to consider opportunities that allow for exits and reentries, aiming ultimately for the frequency of this fluctuation to reduce over time. This implies that the career counselor must strive to place clients in settings where they are likely to be successful without posing exceptional hardships on the employer (Caporoso & Kiselica, 2004).

Deploy Career Guidance and Counseling

The supported education/employment model offers a useful framework to deploy career guidance and counseling services. However, our review of the literature revealed that very little career guidance or counseling seems to be on offer for individuals with mental health difficulties. This is particularly so when they are planning to reenter education. Enrolling for education seems to be the primary motivation, rather than enrolling for education with a broader career development plan in place. We report here a significant study conducted by Getzel, Briel, and Kregel (2000), which articulates the link between career counseling and supported education/employment programs. Getzel et al. have identified some career development barriers that the mentally ill face despite being in supported education/employment programs:

- Lack of information about self: personal interests, aptitudes and talents, as well as of personal disabilities resulting from the illness
- Lack of needed information about available careers
- Lack of work-experience opportunities, networking skills, and job-seeking skills
- Poor knowledge about how to identify suitable educational/occupational possibilities
- Lack of orientation with regard to the manner in which requests for modifications and accommodations from an educational institution/employer can be made

Szymanski and Vancollins (2003) highlighted that poor preparedness severely compromises the person's career development after he or she has been placed in an educational/work role. Therefore, a vital contribution that career counseling could make is to help the individual understand his or her interests and talents, understand the world of work, identify possible career alternatives, and then plan for an education that would actually realize these possibilities. Here again, the career counselor must keep some of the characteristics specific to this client group in mind.

Adapt Standardized Assessment Procedures

If the career counselor uses inventories, tests, and other psychometric devices for assessing the individual, he or she must be aware that the standardized administration procedures required by these tests may not be applicable when working with the recovering mentally ill person. The entire purpose would be defeated if the counselor draws conclusions about a person's aptitudes based on a timed test if the individual's symptom profile affects his or her speed of performance. Similarly, relying on standardized norms to interpret test results may not yield accurate results given the fact that it is most likely that this client group does not any longer fall into the normative sample upon which the test was constructed. Arulmani (2014, see Chap. 34) has described a non-standardized, intraindividual approach that could be considered. In summary, tests that require timed administration are to be avoided and assessment should move at the test taker's pace. High emphasis is to be laid on the individual's hobbies and accomplishments, however small they may have been. Data is to be collected both from the individual and significant others (e.g., parents, siblings, friends). The individual's potential profile is to be constructed based on *intrapersonal* features, rather than on a comparison with a normative sample.

Help the Person Set Realistic Expectations

Lundin (2005), diagnosed at the age of 23 years with a schizoaffective disorder, looks back on his career development, and says in an editorial that he was invited to write, "Over the years of my illness I had been bedeviled by unrealistic career goals...becoming a diplomat, famous politician, a famous actor...With the administration of anti-psychotic medicine, I gradually settled on applying myself to an entry-level position with skills I had available" (p. 2). As this quotation indicates, the individual's expectation of recovery might be that he or she will continue from where he or she was before the onset of the illness. If it is the case that these capacities are presently still recovering, moving back to similar work tasks may accentuate the person's limitations and hence increase the chances of failure. It is important of course to be sensitive such that when bringing disabilities into the recovering individual's awareness he or she is not demotivated but rather becomes more mindful of potential pitfalls.

Facilitate Self-Mediated Job Matching

It has been pointed out that the placement of an individual in supported employment may be a decision made by the rehabilitation practitioner rather than the individual (Hirsch, 1989). It is vital that the career counselor teaches a client how to choose his or her job. This would facilitate the person's involvement in the process and cause him or her to take personal responsibility. This exercise would also include teaching the

individual that merely making a choice need not mean that one will obtain the job one desires. Learning to plan for career alternatives and being prepared to accept the closest match are all aspects of recovery that the career counselor is optimally positioned to facilitate.

Optimize the Person's Engagement with the Real World

Going back to school or to work is a significant step toward rejoining the mainstream of life. This goes beyond the teaching and learning that occurs in the classroom or the execution of tasks in the workplace. It allows the person to be absorbed into social activities that facilitate normalization. Opportunities to be engaged in sports, cultural activities, recreation, and leisure abound in educational/employment settings. For example, the simple activity of going to the canteen for a meal or a coffee *with everyone else* would itself begin to draw the person away from his or her "abnormal" persona. These opportunities could be missed if they are not actively facilitated and this is a role that could be sensitively played by the career counselor.

Promote the Person's Reclaiming of Identity

Goffman (1963) noted that stigmatization resulted in "spoiling" the individual's identity. Successfully enrolling for a supported education/employment program brings with it the prospect of affected persons reclaiming personal identity. The affected person could have acquired the identity of "sick person" or "strange" or "abnormal" person. Occupational identity emerges from the individual's occupational trajectory. Mental illness dramatically interrupts this trajectory. Enrolling into an educational program or regaining work roles implies that the person has actually moved from being a "psychologically ill patient" to a "learning and growing student" or a "contributing worker." Facilitating this insight is a career counseling function that would contribute significantly to the person's redefinition of self, the cornerstone of the new edifice of life that the person is attempting to reconstruct.

Be Prepared for Ongoing, Long-Term Follow-up

Caporoso and Kiselica (2004) have reminded us that the counselor who is interested in supporting the mentally ill must keep in mind that placing the person in a job does not signal the end of the career counseling. Central to long-term follow-up is the battle with stigma. While the broader systemic objective is to change the mindsets of the stigma holders, the career counseling objective is to empower the person recovering from mental illness to battle through the stigma. An important long-term requirement, after the client begins supported education/employment, is to keep him or her reminded of strengths and limitations and their potential impact on performance. This would include helping the client deal with symptoms, side-effects of medication, and conflicts that could arise at work or at home. Beginning a support group comprising individuals who are enrolled in supported education/employment is known to be an effective device for long-term follow-up (Caporoso & Kiselica, 2004). At one level, it reduces the burden on the career counselor. At another level, it creates a network of people with similar difficulties who could encourage and help each other.

New Concepts and Viewpoints: Charting New Directions

Most of the disabilities suffered by the mentally ill are in the cognitive and emotional realms of functioning. These disabilities cannot be easily understood by others, and hence the management of these disabilities requires considerations that are different from other illnesses. An important viewpoint for the future for career counseling is that the focus is not on what the person cannot do but instead on the person's functional attributes. This critical requirement was highlighted at an important seminar held in India entitled: Employment towards Empowerment for Persons with Mental Health Issues: Challenges and Prospects (BALM, 2012). In addition to the points made throughout this writing, we draw upon the salient recommendations of this seminar to highlight new concepts and viewpoints that have relevance for the career counseling of those recovering from mental illness.

- All papers presented at this seminar identified stigma as a major roadblock to finding work and sustained employment. Therefore, engaging in advocacy, sensitizing schools, communities, and employers to mental health issues emerged as a vital issue. If career counseling is to be effective, it is important that the career counselor also shows allegiance to the cause of effective employment for the mentally ill. If it is publicly seen that the career counselor is "standing beside" the mentally ill person, committed to his or her well-being at work, public perceptions could be impacted.

- Self-help groups composed of the mentally ill were found to be effective in sustaining their employment. This could be a lead taken by the career counselor, and clients and their families could be facilitated in networking to support and help each other.

- Emphasis on individual training processes was found to be more effective than en mass training. This finding seems to indicate that one-on-one career counseling designed to formulate individualized career development plans would be more effective. A wider canvas of career options should be brought into the scope of career counseling for the mentally ill, rather than the options that have an overtly rehabilitation or vocational type of focus.

- Of particular relevance to the career counselor is a job-matching data base. This would comprise a list of available persons with an indication of their aptitudes and interests on the one hand and a list of job openings on the other hand. Such a system is being increasingly recognized as important for the reintegration of the mentally ill into the workplace.

As of now, the career development of individuals affected by mental illness is a theme that is poorly represented in the career guidance literature. While a significant amount of work has been done in relation to the vocational rehabilitation of the mentally ill, these efforts have not been adequately informed by the theories and principles of career guidance and counseling. On the other hand is the fact that the discipline of career guidance and counseling does not seem to have exercised adequate effort to theorize, build models, and develop applications with specific reference to the mentally ill. With the emerging recognition of the importance of career guidance, it is critical that the discipline actively engages with this highly neglected client group.

Conclusion

Strong evidence from the literature has been presented in this writing to demonstrate that reintegration into the world of work and reengagement with meaningful employment contributes significantly to recovery of those affected by mental illness and to maintenance of these improvements in health. As is well known to the career counselor, career success is closely intertwined with the meaningfulness of the career to its practitioner. Frustration and dissatisfaction quickly become attending sentiments when a career is far removed from the individual's interests and inclinations. This is perhaps all the more true when working with the mentally affected. Models of vocational rehabilitation have made significant contributions to the reintegration of the mentally ill into the world of work. Yet, the young man's statement about candle making, which titles this writing, throws light on what can go wrong when career counseling is not integrated into vocational rehabilitation services. When confronted by the multiple and sometimes profound disabilities experienced by a mentally ill person, the career counselor may be overwhelmed and may feel that his or her skill-set is not adequate or even relevant. Nevertheless, the career counselor could become pivotal, making significant contributions to improving the mentally affected person's quality of work life. Not only is the career counselor well positioned to identify the "right candle" for the recovering mentally ill person, he or she can

contribute to the reinstatement of the person as a contributing member of society, rekindle the flame, and ensure that it burns bright and steady.

References

Arulmani, G. (2006). *Unpublished clinical records (2000 to 2006)*. Bangalore, India: The Promise Foundation.

Arulmani, G. (2014). Assessment of interest and aptitude: A methodologically-integrated approach. In G. Arulmani, A. J. Bakshi, F. T. L. Leong, & A. G. Watts (Eds.), *Handbook of career development*. New York, NY: Springer.

BALM. (2012, January). *Employment towards empowerment for persons with mental health issues: Challenges and prospects*. Paper presented at the meeting of the Banyan Academy of Leadership in Mental Health, Chennai, India.

Becker, D. R., & Drake, R. E. (2003). *A working life for people with severe mental illness*. New York, NY: Oxford University Press.

Beyer, S. (2007). *An evaluation of the outcomes of supported employment in North Lanarkshire*. North Lanarkshire, UK: Welsh Centre for Learning Disabilities, Cardiff University.

Bond, G. R., & Campbell, K. (2004). Evidence based practices for individuals with severe mental illness. *The Journal of Rehabilitation, 74*(2), 33–48.

Bond, G. R., McGrew, J. H., & Fekette, D. M. (1995). Assertive outreach for frequent users of psychiatric hospitals: A meta-analysis. *Journal of Mental Health Administration, 22*, 4–16.

Caporoso, R. A., & Kiselica, M. S. (2004). Career counseling with clients who have a severe mental illness. *The Career Development Quarterly, 52*(3), 235–242.

Chandrashekar, H., Kasthuri, P., Kumar, C. N., & Prashanth, N. R. (2010). Disabilities research in India. *Indian Journal of Psychiatry, 52*, 281–285.

Cimera, R., Wehman, P., West, M., & Burgess, S. (2012). Do sheltered workshops enhance employment outcomes for adults with autism spectrum disorder? *Autism, 16*(1), 87–94.

Committee on the Rights of Persons with Disabilities. (2006). *Convention on the rights of persons with disabilities*. Geneva, Switzerland: United Nations High Commission for Human Rights.

Cook, J. A., & Solomon, M. L. (1993). The community scholars program: An outcome study of supported education for students with severe mental illness. *Psychosocial Rehabilitation Journal, 16*, 83–97.

Corrigan, P. W. (2004). How stigma interferes with mental health care. *American Psychologist, 59*(7), 614–625.

Corrigan, P. W., & McCracken, S. G. (2005). Place first, then train: An alternative to the medical model of psychiatric rehabilitation. *Social Work, 50*(1), 31–46.

Dixon, J. (2001). A global perspective on social security programs for the unemployed. *International Social Work, 44*(4), 405–422.

Dunn, E. C., Wewiorski, N. J., & Rogers, E. S. (2008). The meaning and importance of employment to people in recovery from serious mental illness: Results of a qualitative study. *Psychiatric Rehabilitation Journal, 32*(1), 59–62.

Getzel, E. E., Briel, L. W., & Kregel, J. (2000). Comprehensive career planning: The VCU career connections. *Work, 14*, 41–49.

Goffman, E. (1963). *Stigma: Notes on the management of spoiled identity*. Englewood Cliffs, NJ: Prentice-Hall.

Hirsch, S. W. (1989). Meeting the vocational needs of individuals with psychiatric disabilities through supported employment. *The Journal of Rehabilitation, 55*(4), 26–29.

Hoffman, F. L., & Mastrianni, X. (1993). The role of supported education in the inpatient treatment of young adults: A two-site comparison. *Psychosocial Rehabilitation Journal, 16*, 109–119.

Indian Psychiatric Society. (2002). *Indian disability evaluation and assessment scale (IDEAS)*. India: The Rehabilitation Committee of the Indian Psychiatric Society.

Johns, L. C., & van Os, J. (2001). The continuity of psychotic experiences in the general population. *Clinical Psychology Review, 21*, 1125–1141.

Kessler, R. C., Amminger, G. P., Aguilar-Gaxiola, S., Alonso, J., Lee, S., & Üstün, T. B. (2007). Age of onset of mental disorders: A review of recent literature. *Current Opinion in Psychiatry, 20*(4), 359–364.

Kregel, J. (2012). Work incentives planning and assistance program (WIPA). *Journal of Vocational Rehabilitation, 36*, 3–12.

Leonard, E. J., & Bruer, R. A. (2007). Supported education strategies for people with severe mental illness: A review of evidence based practice. *International Journal of Psychosocial Rehabilitation, 11*(1), 97–109.

Lundin, R. K. (2005). Addressing the stigma of mental illness: Two approaches. *The Israel Journal of Psychiatry and Related Sciences, 42*(4), 219–220.

MacDonald-Wilson, K. L., Rogers, E. S., Massaro, J. M., Lyass, A., & Crean, T. (2002). An investigation of reasonable workplace accommodations for people with psychiatric disabilities: Quantitative findings from a multi-site study. *Community Mental Health Journal, 38*(1), 35–50.

McQuilken, M., Zahniser, J. H., Novak, J., Starks, R. D., Olmos, A., & Bond, G. R. (2003). The work project survey: Consumer perspectives on work. *Journal of Vocational Rehabilitation, 18*(1), 59–68.

Mcreynolds, C., & Garske, G. (2003). Psychiatric disabilities: Challenges and training issues for rehabilitation professionals. *The Journal of Rehabilitation, 69*(3), 24–36.

Mojtabai, R. (2001). Residual symptoms and impairment in major depression in the community. *American Journal of Psychiatry, 158*, 1645–1651.

Mowbray, C. T., Collins, M., & Bybee, D. (1999). Supported education for individuals with psychiatric disabilities: Long-term outcomes from an experimental study. *Social Work Research, 23*(2), 89–95.

National Institute for Health and Clinical Excellence. (2011). *Getting help and support for common mental health problems*. London, UK: Author.

Penn, D. L., & Martin, J. (1998). The stigma of severe mental illness: Some potential solutions for a recalcitrant problem. *Psychiatric Quarterly, 69*, 235–247.

Perkins, R., & Rinaldi, M. (2002). Unemployment rates among patients with long-term mental health problems: A decade of rising unemployment. *The Psychiatrist, 26*, 295–298.

Ratanlal, D. (2002). *The Indian Penal Code* (28th ed.). Nagpur, India: Wadhwa Publishers.

Resnick, S. G., Rosenheck, R. A., & Drebing, C. E. (2006). What makes vocational rehabilitation effective? Program characteristics versus employment outcomes. *Psychological Services, 3*(4), 239–248.

Revell, G., West, W., & Cheng, Y. (1988). Funding supported employment: Are there better ways? *Journal of Disability Policy Studies, 9*(1), 59–79.

Richmond Fellowship Society. (2012, January). *The efficacy of psychosocial rehabilitation programmes: The RFS experience*. Paper presented at the meeting of the Banyan Academy of Leadership in Mental Health, Chennai, India.

Srinivasa Murthy, R. (2005). Perspectives on the stigma of mental illness. In A. Okasha & C. N. Stefanis (Eds.), *Stigma of mental illness in the third world* (p. 112). Geneva, Switzerland: World Psychiatric Association.

Szymanski, E. M., & Vancollins, J. (2003). Career development of people with disabilities: Some new and not-so-new challenges. *Australian Journal of Career Development, 12*(1), 9–16.

Thara, R., & Tharoor, H. (2012). Disability and functioning. In B. S. Chavan, N. Gupta, P. Arun, A. Sidana, & S. Jadhav (Eds.), *Community mental health in India* (pp. 112–118). New Delhi, India: Jaypee Brothers Medical Publishers.

U.S. Department of Health and Human Services, National Institute of Mental Health. (2012). *Mental health medications*. Retrieved from http://www.nimh.nih.gov/health/publications/mental-health-medications/nimh-mental-health-medications.pdf

Wehman, P., & Kregel, J. (1995). At the crossroads: Supported employment a decade later. *Journal of the Association for Persons with Severe Handicaps, 20*(4), 286–299.

Wig, N. N. (1997). Stigma of mental illness (Editorial). *Indian Journal of Psychiatry, 39*(2), 187–189.

Wolf, J., & DiPietro, S. (1992). From patient to student: Supported education programs in southwest Connecticut. *Psychosocial Rehabilitation Journal, 15*, 61–68.

World Bank. (2007). *Persons with disabilities in India: From commitments to outcomes*. New Delhi, India: Author.

World Health Organization (WHO). (1992). *ICD-10 classification of mental and behavioural disorders:*

Clinical descriptions and guidelines. Geneva, Switzerland: WHO Press.

World Health Organization (WHO). (2001a). *The international classification of functioning, disability and health.* Geneva, Switzerland: WHO Press.

World Health Organization (WHO). (2001b). *World health report: Mental health, new understanding, new hope.* Geneva, Switzerland: WHO Press.

World Health Organization (WHO). (2002). *Towards a common language for functioning, disability and health.* Geneva, Switzerland: WHO Press.

World Health Organization (WHO). (2004). *The global burden of disease: 2004 update.* Geneva, Switzerland: WHO Press.

World Health Organization (WHO). (2011). *World report on disability 2011.* Geneva, Switzerland: WHO Press.

Career Counseling among Indigenous Peoples

30

Glenn C. Kharkongor and Sandra Albert

Introduction

Indigenous peoples are a widely diverse group, spread all over the globe. Representing only about 5 % of the world's population, they have remained outside the mainstream of scientific study. The body of research on indigenous peoples has historically fallen mainly in the purview of anthropology and sociology, and, in recent years, more in relation to development and human rights. In the discipline of psychology, there is now considerable interest in cross-cultural psychology, a segment of which is devoted to the study of indigenous peoples. There is some published research on career counseling among indigenous peoples in North America and Australasia. But from the countries of Asia, Africa, and South America, where the vast majority of indigenous peoples live, there are only occasional reports.

It is beyond the scope of this chapter to provide a comprehensive account of career guidance research and services among indigenous peoples worldwide, though an attempt has been made to cite studies that have wider application. This chapter will also draw from our familiarity with, and experiences in Meghalaya, a state in Northeast India. This region of the country is made up of eight states, together bordered by

Nepal, Bhutan, China, Myanmar, and Bangladesh and is largely populated by indigenous peoples. Meghalaya has a population of three million, 86 % of whom are tribal (Registrar General and Census Commissioner, 2011). Before we present Meghalaya as a case study, we begin with a brief examination of constructs related to the work, occupation, and career of indigenous peoples.

Overview of Indigenous Peoples

There are more than 370 million indigenous people living in about 70 countries all over the world. Most live in the geographical fringes of the planet, sparse communities inhabiting forests, hills and mountains, deserts, the circumpolar regions, and small islands. They reached their destinations through ancient migrations and, over the course of history, have yielded much of their spaces to more dominant societies. Isolation and strong self-identity enabled many of these communities to sustain their cultural uniqueness for many millennia, sometimes even in the absence of written forms of communication.

From antiquity to contemporary times, indigenous peoples have suffered from invasions, wars, colonization, and forced relocation and resettlement. In many ways, the diminution of the culture of indigenous groups is ongoing, and includes permanent loss of language, loss of

G.C. Kharkongor (✉)
Martin Luther Christian University, Shillong, India
e-mail: glenchristo@yahoo.com

G. Arulmani et al. (eds.), *Handbook of Career Development*, International and Cultural Psychology,
DOI 10.1007/978-1-4614-9460-7_30, © Springer Science+Business Media, LLC 2014

lands, encroachment of traditional territories, and disruption of traditional lifestyles.

> They frequently have inadequate access to clean water and other resources and may be pushed into fragile or degraded ecosystems. Compared to the general population of their countries, they have higher rates of infant and maternal mortality, less access to education and limited participation in the government and social systems that affect their lives. (United Nations Population Fund, n.d.)

The rights and development of indigenous peoples have been taken up by various United Nations (UN) bodies only in the last couple of decades and the United Nations Permanent Forum on Indigenous Issues was established in 2000.

Definition of Indigenous Peoples

An agreed-upon definition of indigenous peoples has proved elusive. In the 30-year history of indigenous issues at the United Nations (UN), and the longer history in the International Labour Organization (ILO), considerable thinking and debate have been devoted to the question of arriving at a definition of indigenous peoples, but no such definition has ever been adopted by any UN-system body. No single definition seems to capture the diversity of their cultures, histories, and current circumstances. However, all attempts to define the concept recognize the linkages between people, their land, and culture.

A widely used working definition of indigenous peoples proposed by the UN Working Group on Indigenous Populations argues that indigenous populations are:

> Those which, having a historical continuity with pre-invasion and pre-colonial societies that developed on their territories, consider themselves distinct from other sectors of the societies now prevailing in those territories, or parts of them. They form at present, nondominant sectors of society and are determined to preserve, develop and transmit to future generations their ancestral territories, and their ethnic identity, as the basis of their continued existence as peoples, in accordance with their own cultural patterns, social institutions and legal systems. (United Nations, 1986, p. 2)

For the World Bank's policy mission on projects that affect indigenous peoples, the term *Indigenous Peoples* is used in a generic sense to refer to a distinct, vulnerable, social, and cultural group possessing the following characteristics in varying degrees: (a) self-identification as members of a distinct indigenous cultural group and recognition of this identity by others; (b) collective attachment to geographically distinct habitats or ancestral territories in the project area and to the natural resources in these habitats and territories; (c) customary cultural, economic, social, or political institutions that are separate from those of the dominant society and culture; (d) an indigenous language, often different from the official language of the country or region (World Bank, 1991).

On September 13, 2007, the UN Declaration on the Rights of Indigenous Peoples was adopted by the General Assembly. This decision came as a result of more than 20 years of work by indigenous peoples and the United Nations system. According to the UN, the most fruitful approach is to identify rather than define indigenous peoples. This is based on the fundamental criterion of self-identification as underlined in a number of human rights documents.

The ILO Convention 169 (ILO, 1989) is the first attempt to formulate an international law designed to protect indigenous people's rights. The Convention does not define indigenous and tribal peoples. It takes a practical approach and only provides criteria for describing the peoples it aims to protect. Self-identification is considered as a fundamental criterion for the identification of indigenous and tribal peoples, along with the narrative criteria quoted below.

Practicing unique traditions, they retain social, cultural, economic, and political characteristics that are distinct from those of the dominant societies in which they live. Spread across the world from the Arctic to the South Pacific, they are the descendants, according to a common definition, of those who inhabited a country or a geographical region at the time when people of different cultures or ethnic origins arrived. The new arrivals later became dominant through conquest, occupation, settlement, or other means. Most indigenous peoples have retained distinct characteristics which are clearly different from those of other segments of the national populations. The UN-system has developed a modern understanding of this term based on the following:

- Self-identification as indigenous peoples at the individual level and accepted by the community as their member.
- Historical continuity with pre-colonial and/or pre-settler societies.
- Strong link to territories and surrounding natural resources.
- Distinct social, economic, or political systems.
- Distinct language, culture, and beliefs.
- From nondominant groups of society.
- Resolve to maintain and reproduce their ancestral environments and systems as distinctive peoples and communities.

Though the term *indigenous peoples* has become widely used, other terms also continue to be used. In some regions, there is a preference to use *tribes*, *first peoples/nations*, *aboriginals*, or *minority ethnic groups*. Some of these terms have been defined in the official documents of countries to the exclusion of other terms. The variability is considerable. The Bangladesh Government, for example, has stated that there are "no Indigenous Peoples in Bangladesh" (Ahmed, 2011). The Government of India, on the other hand, adopts the stand that all citizens of India are indigenous (ILO, n.d.). The Constitution of India uses the term *tribals* and the government has recognized tribals in the census as a separate demographic entity.

Indigenous Peoples in India

India has a population of 1.21 billion, of which 8.14 % are tribals (Registrar General and Census Commissioner, 2011). There are 624 tribes recognized (in a Schedule of the Constitution) by the government. The country has the largest indigenous and tribal population in Asia, about 98 million, more than one-fourth of the world total. Scheduled Tribes are found across the country, but are mainly concentrated in the north-central and north-eastern parts of India (often referred to as the tribal belts). The government of India avoids the term *indigenous* and uses the term *tribals* to refer to these communities and they are popularly known as *adivasis*, meaning original inhabitants.

Recognizing the need for the upliftment of the tribal people, on account of their deprivation and centuries of exclusion, they are accorded special status in the Indian Constitution. A legally recognized demographic group, they are referred to as *Scheduled Tribes* (STs). Scheduled Tribe status provides that seats are reserved for them in Parliament and state legislatures, jobs reserved in the civil services and government departments, and in admissions to government educational institutions. The Constitutional safeguards, policies, and welfare schemes for Scheduled Tribes are administered by the Ministry of Tribal Affairs.

There is considerable concern that the welfare and development schemes for STs in India have not yielded the desired outcomes. In the 12-year span between 1993–1994 and 2004–2005, the proportion of the population below the poverty line in India declined from 35.97 to 27.6 %. But among STs, it declined only marginally from 51.14 to 46.5 %. So, a major gap continues to exist between the tribal population and the national average. There are huge differences in literacy, health indices, and education enrollments (Xaxa, 2011).

Northeast India and Meghalaya

The Northeast region of India consists of eight states with a population of 45.58 million (Registrar General and Census Commissioner, 2011). This region was a corridor for early migrations between the Indian landmass and Southeast Asia, China, and Australasia. It is a genetic melting pot of Mongoloid, Australoid, and Caucasoid peoples and has been populated from the Middle Paleolithic Era, perhaps for 60,000 years (Reddy et al., 2007). The region is largely inhabited by indigenous peoples, totaling about 220 tribes.

These indigenous communities have lived continuously in this territory and have continuity with prehistoric societies. Each tribe has its own language, cultural traditions, social institutions, and legal system. Meghalaya, one of the states of Northeast India, has a population of about three million, 86 % of whom are tribals, mainly belonging to the Khasi and Garo tribes. Khasi belongs to the Austro-Asiatic group of languages, the oldest in India (Reddy et al., 2007). Both the Khasi and Garo tribes are matrilineal and matrilocal.

In this region, colonization, Westernization, the influence of Christianity, pressures of assimilation with mainstream India, rapid urbanization, and uneven economic development have caused seismic social upheavals. The benefits of economic development have reached only an elite few. The rates of unemployment, alcoholism, and HIV/AIDS are high, and the quality of school performance is low. All this has led to a high societal frustration. The interplay between external influences and surviving indigenous beliefs and practices has significant implications for psychosocial well-being and the development and delivery of counseling services.

Though most indigenous societies are in transition, many have retained a closeness to nature and occupations that are dependent on the natural environment. Traditional agricultural methods, such as shifting cultivation (called *jhum*, farming the forest), were first practiced in Northeast India about 7,000 years ago and are still being practiced (Jeeva, Laloo, & Mishra, 2006). Indeed, rice, tubers, citrus, and other fruits seem to have been domesticated in this region in the Neolithic period (Hazarika, 2006). The indigenous peoples of the rural areas retain their symbiosis with the forests and their produce in other occupations such as traditional medicine. The Meghalaya subtropical forests are considered one of the most species-rich in the eco-region (World Wildlife Fund, 2007). Many of the crafts, though in general decline, still offer livelihoods, such as bow and arrow making (for hunting, sport, and tourist souvenirs), blacksmithy, and basketry (Kurbah, 2010b).

Traditional occupations and livelihoods are being lost because of several factors: changing land ownership, mining, deforestation, and curbs on shifting cultivation (Karlsson, 2011). Modern occupations brought in by urbanization, education, and "development" have benefitted only a handful of the current generation of youth. The erosion of tribal customs and social institutions has weakened community safety nets. In this setting, not only is career counseling an imperative need, but also its appropriateness and suitability should be closely examined.

Indigenous Worldviews

In a treatise on cultural-preparedness, it is recommended that an evaluation be made of the belief system and attitudes of a particular culture to help determine the nature of interventions that will benefit them (Arulmani, 2011a). So, we shall consider first the concept of worldviews.

A worldview is considered to be the fundamental cognitive orientation of an individual or society encompassing the entirety of the individual or society's knowledge and point-of-view. The term is a calque of the German words *welt*, world, and *anschauung*, outlook (Merriam-Webster's online dictionary, n.d.). Additionally, it refers to the framework of ideas and beliefs through which an individual, group, or culture interprets the world and interacts with it. According to Lind (2011), a worldview is a more or less coherent understanding of the nature of reality, which permits its holders to interpret new information in the light of their preconceptions, operating at a community level.

In his treatise on indigenous worldviews, Ahukaramū (2002) describes three worldview systems: Eastern, Western, and Indigenous. According to him, the indigenous worldview is explainable by reference to the natural phenomena of the world. Hence, indigenous worldviews give rise to a unique set of values and behaviors which seek to foster this sense of oneness and unity with the world. The predominant themes in indigenous worldviews arise from the people's close relationship with the environment, nature, and the community. Within indigenous cultures, most have a high valuation of relationships. Awareness of self means understanding one's relationship with the physical environment, the spiritual world, and other people. Self-esteem derives from individual contributions to collective goals. Recognizing the continuing evolution of indigenous peoples, Peavy (1995) has categorized them into four groups. It is useful to keep this spectrum of indigenous individuals in mind, as career counselors will deal with a diverse range of indigenous clients. Though Peavy refers to Native Americans, the following descriptions have wide application.

- A "traditional" native supports and lives the traditional way of life through use of foods, medicines, social organization, ceremonies, and communication, and is happy with this way of life.
- An "assimilated" native supports and lives the modern, dominant society way of life through use of foods, social organization, and communication, and is happy with this way of life.
- A "transitional" native identity fluctuates between traditional and dominant society, and often exhibits dysfunctional ways of living. The transitional individual is not committed to either culture and may be unhappy, uncertain, or unaware of his or her own lifestyle. He or she is often abusive, substance-addicted, and manifests low self-esteem and lack of personal stability.
- A "bicultural" native person lives and supports the ways of living of both traditional and dominant societies. The bicultural person uses both traditional and dominant society foods, medicines, and social organization, and may engage in both clan and nuclear family patterns. In contrast to the other identities, the bicultural individual has reconciled cultural differences and is at peace with reconciliation.

If career counseling is to be at all effective, it must take these differing lifestyles and identities into account. Insensitive career counseling could propel indigenous young people towards career development that is assimilative or at risk of contributing to the creation of transitional, dysfunctional lifestyles. Though unintentional, career counselors could abet a kind of colonization of the native mind when they attribute higher importance to the academic, social, and vocational values and tasks preferred by the dominant, nonindigenous majority. If career counseling and development is to make sense to indigenous students, ways must be found for these youth to discover and use their own "cultural voices" in career exploration and to use their own life experiences as building blocks for a hopeful future. Their worldviews must be recognized (Madsen, 1990).

Career Knowledge, Perceptions, and Aspirations

Having highlighted that the understanding of worldviews is fundamental to conceptualizing an approach to the career counseling of indigenous young people, we now proceed to consider other pertinent aspects, especially the situation of career knowledge, perceptions, and aspirations of indigenous youth. We start with India and then take examples from other countries.

The Indian Situation

Whereas the overall Gross Enrollment Rate in higher education in India is about 20 %, among tribals it is only 6 % for men and 5 % for women. Among rural-poor tribal populations, it is as low as 1 % (Srivastava & Sinha, 2008). For the few that embark on a quest for higher education and a career, indigenous students start out with significant disadvantages. There are internal and external hurdles that impede their progress.

A government study in India made the following set of conclusions pertaining to tribal students in higher education. Among tribal students in universities and colleges in India, almost half lack sufficient knowledge about courses and hence cannot make informed choices. Teachers and friends are the most frequent sources of information about college courses, compared to the rest of the student population among whom parents are the main source of information. For admission to professional courses, fewer tribal students had taken coaching (a common strategy in India for admission to prestigious, but competitive, courses), though lack of financial support may be a factor. Once they are in college, teachers feel that tribal students are less motivated and perform less well. On the other hand, 79 % of employers felt tribal students are equally competent (Centre for Research, Planning and Action, 2007, p. 32).

In a national study using the Career Belief Patterns Scale, which examines the negativity of beliefs pertaining to career development, tribal students appeared to have less negativity and fatalism compared to other Indian students. This is despite the fact that, though, historically, tribal students did not have a caste system, with domination and assimilation into the mainstream Hindu society, tribal students were assigned low positions in the caste hierarchy, with consequent occupational assignments of low prestige (Arulmani & Nag-Arulmani, 2006).

Enforced conformity and stereotyping in schools by curricula and teachers is widely prevalent, though perhaps not intended. Indigenous students who attend "mainstream" schools are adversely affected by:

> School norms of attendance, discipline, homework, tests and exam and cognitively ethnocentric demands of concentration on and memorization of the content of the text by 'rote', all (of which) prove problematic for ST (scheduled tribe) children. School curricula fail to take account of tribal cultures as repositories of autonomous knowledge systems with their own epistemology, transmission, innovation and power. Scheduled tribes rarely feature in textbooks and when they do, it is usually in positions servile to upper caste characters; or as strange and backward exotica. (NCERT, 2005, p. 29)

Examples from Other Indigenous Groups

A study among aborigines in Australia found a major difference between indigenous and nonindigenous students in aspirational levels. Indigenous students were more likely to prefer vocational training to university study. They wanted to work in jobs that would result in helping their own people. Because of these differences, indigenous students were less likely than nonindigenous students to have a structured plan for their further education and careers. Indigenous students were more likely to be motivated to work for altruistic reasons rather than for financial rewards (Craven, Parente, & Marder, 2004). In Taiwan, substantial resources have been invested in upper-secondary vocational education for aborigines. Many indigenous students attend non-prestigious technological colleges and demonstrated unclear occupational aspirations along with low occupational self-efficacy. They preferred living in their homelands and wanted to benefit their people (Wua, 2012). Among Native American college students currently attending a tribal college, home/family commitment emerged as more salient than work participation. Correlational analysis indicated that the decision to attend college was associated with their perception of education being important to have a good life, their motivation to attend college to help their family and community, and their wish to escape the high unemployment rate on the reservation (Brown & Lavish, 2006).

All of these issues must have a significant effect on the tribal child's preparation for a career. Peavy (1998) has admirably brought all these issues into the career counseling context in a sociodynamic model, which is described later in the chapter. Our own experiences in Meghalaya brought to the fore these and several other concerns with regard to the career counseling of tribal youth in this region.

Career Counseling in Meghalaya: A Case Study

We now present career counseling in Meghalaya as a case study to better understand the career development of indigenous young people in this region and to consider approaches to the delivery of career counseling services.

Background

There are 6,612 primary (5,611 of which are government-run) and 783 secondary schools (561 of which are government-run) in the state of Meghalaya (Directorate of School Education, n.d.). In rural areas, only 43.17 % of children aged 15–18 years are in school and only 4.26 % of college-age youth are in higher education (Planning Department, Government of Meghalaya, 2008). One of the most significant challenges faced by the educational system in the state of Meghalaya is a high rate of school dropouts. The 2008–2009 Annual Report of the Department of Education of India shows that 75.9 % of students between Class I and X dropped out of school in 2006–2007 in Meghalaya; among students who continue in school, a majority fail in their examinations; in the 2009 Class X examinations, only 46.77 % passed (Ministry of Human Resource Development, 2009). In this educational milieu, career counseling is a major challenge. In a discussion with the Director of School Education of the state, she acknowledged that trained career counselors are not available for any of the government schools. A handful of private schools and colleges have appointed part-time counselors, usually teachers or psychologists, who offer career guidance in addition to their general teaching or counseling roles. Surveys have shown that the career preparedness and career planning confidence of students in Class X and XII in Meghalaya are appreciably lower than in the rest of India (Arulmani, 2011b).

Orientations to Career Development in Meghalaya: Some Research Findings

Among high school and college students in Shillong, the capital of Meghalaya, 87 % said they needed better information about careers; only 40 % of college students had decided on their choice of a career (Chen, 2011). The preferred career choices of indigenous students have been the subject of some surveys in Meghalaya. In a survey of Class XII students, professional courses like medicine and engineering held the greatest appeal, followed closely by business entrepreneurship. In another survey of Class X–XII students and parents, professional courses were again ranked highest, followed by business management (Quintesse Consultants, 2011).

Twice as many girl students as boys indicated an interest in starting a business (Kurbah, 2010a). An interesting finding, not incidental, is the higher preference for business entrepreneurship among girls compared to boys. The three major tribes of Meghalaya are all matrilineal and matrilocal and inheritance of ancestral property passes through the youngest daughter. Most small businesses such as a vegetable shop or tea stalls are run by a woman and her daughter, and many larger enterprises are headed by women as well. Gender differences in entrepreneurship and indeed the unique risk-taking behavior of Khasi women have been documented (Croson & Gneezy, 2009; Gneezy, Leonard, & List, 2009).

Traditional occupations still provide a livelihood for a significant number of people in the region. These occupations use skills that have evolved over long periods of time. But these skills and the knowledge systems remain largely informal, poorly protected, and inadequately documented and hence the practitioners of these occupations remain socially and culturally disadvantaged. The return on skill remains low, and markets remain small and unstable. However, engagement with these occupations provides supplementary income to farmers whose income is seasonal (Kurbah, 2010b). Traditional medicine as a livelihood is receiving renewed attention in Meghalaya. There are an estimated 10,000 practicing traditional healers in the state (Dkhar, 2011).

These studies point to indicators that are important for career counselors to take note of. The need to better disseminate information about career counseling is well known. The preferred career choices of indigenous youth are not very different from nontribal youth. There is still some interest in traditional occupations, but the economic viability of these livelihoods needs to be considered when career counseling is delivered.

Findings from a Focus Group Discussion with Career Counselors in Meghalaya

Career counseling by professionals trained in career counseling is a recent development in

Meghalaya. One example is the Jiva program (for an overview of the method, see Arulmani, 2010, 2011b). Jiva is an approach to career counseling and livelihood planning that has been developed specifically for the Indian context. Fifty-four teachers and youth workers have been trained in the Jiva method in Shillong since 2007. At the time of the writing of this chapter, 18 of these certified individuals were engaged in full-time or part-time career counseling.

An exploratory survey, followed by a focus group discussion, was conducted with ten of these Jiva-trained career counselors. A brief questionnaire was administered to ascertain their demographic, training, and practice profiles and to collate their experiences in career counseling. The session lasted about one and a half hours. All but one of the counselors were from the indigenous tribes (the nontribal counselor was from the Philippines, who is married to a tribal). All were based in Shillong and nine of them visited rural schools occasionally. Their experience as counselors ranged between 1 year 2 months and 4 years 3 months and each had provided counseling to between 100 and 800 students. Although their clientele was primarily indigenous, nine of them had counseled nonindigenous youth as well. The counselors reported that about 5–25 % of their clients were nontribal. Information collected during the focus group discussion was collated and subjected to thematic analysis. The findings are reported as follows.

Social Cognitive Factors: Career Beliefs

Social cognitions have been described to be habitual patterns of thinking present within societies and career beliefs are social cognitions that reflect attitudes and orientations to work, occupation, and career (Arulmani & Nag-Arulmani, 2004). The influence of social cognitions was clearly distinguishable among the tribal students. The counselors in this survey reported that indigenous students seemed less interested in a "career." In fact, there is no comparable word in Khasi (the language spoken by this group), for career. The counselors reported that tribal students are relaxed about life, less competitive about doing well in school, and less focused on or intense about having a career. Many feel that even after going to college, there is no guarantee of a job. Some are reluctant to travel outside their home region, because they would face discrimination in other parts of India, being ethnically different.

A commonly expressed desire is to help the family, and so they do not wish to travel too far to work. This is especially true of girls, who in matrilineal and matrilocal tribes have future family responsibilities, especially in the care of parents, older relatives, and ancestral property. Indigenous youth, especially those from the rural areas, believed in the dignity of labor and were not very concerned about the prestige of an occupation. Some youth were timid in making choices about newer careers such as in information technology, for fear that they may be seen as rising too far above their community and being considered as "proud." A critical observation was that the status of the career was more important for urban youth. Compared to rural youth, tribal students in urban areas were found to be more ambitious and expressed interest in the popular careers.

The Influence of Significant Others

There was little parental involvement in the career discussions and decisions among indigenous youth. Most parents were reluctant to attend career counseling sessions, "unless it is an order from the principal" as indicated by one of the participants in the study. Peer influences, such as from friends and siblings, were noted to be stronger. Role models seemed to have little influence on career planning. One counselor commented that in the very remote rural areas of the West Khasi Hills district, students come into contact only with teachers, pastors, and social workers, and these careers were often mentioned as top choices. More parental involvement and family discussions pertaining to career were noted among nontribal students.

The Influence of Gender

As per the counselors' observations, most young girls, even in rural areas, wanted to have some education. To complete Class X was a common goal, but only about a third were keen to finish

Class XII, as this meant going further away to a higher secondary school. This observation is borne out by the fact that in Meghalaya, more girls than boys are enrolled in school up to Class X, but thereafter, in Class XI, XII, and college, there are more male students than female (Directorate of Economics and Statistics, 2007). Girls would rather opt for a career where they can work within the state, to be close to home so as to be able to help the family.

Rural Versus Urban

The counselors' interactions with the students indicated that urban indigenous students were more focused on career development. They were better informed about careers and the aptitudes and preparation necessary to pursue their career aspirations, than their rural counterparts. They made independent decisions, but always after consultation with parents and peers. Among rural families, it is a common practice to select one child, usually the brightest, for higher studies. This child is exempted from farm work and household chores. The others would stay back and work on the farm. In peri-urban areas the educated child is even discouraged from contributing to farming chores. Counselors noted that the tendency of parents to give a different status to the educated child is potentially contributing to "low status" perception towards traditional occupations, especially in peri-urban areas. In such families education was perceived as a means to get a white collar job or one that involved "sitting in a chair in some office," so "Why study and then come back to the fields." Urban youth were more willing to study outside the state. Rural youth often said "I don't know" and wished to be told what to do. However, they were open to receiving new information and seemed to develop confidence when encouraged. Once they developed a focus, they worked hard towards career goals.

Indigenous Versus Nonindigenous

In comparison to nontribal youth, young people from tribal backgrounds were noted to be less motivated about careers. The counselors noted that they were less prepared and less self-aware.

On the other hand, they were relaxed about the future, unlike their nontribal counterparts who were more intense and competitive, thus prone to stress, anxiety, and suicides, phenomena that are well known among students in India.

Nontribal students appeared to be more informed about careers, more aware about the world of work, were more inclined to careers based in the sciences, and were willing to go beyond the boundaries of their home region to other parts of the country to pursue their education and careers. Nontribal students tended to study in *mixed* schools, whereas the indigenous students seemed to prefer schools where predominantly tribal students were enrolled. It was felt that tribal students who studied in mixed schools worked harder, because of the more competitive environment. More parental involvement and discussions on career were noted among nonindigenous families. Nontribal students were more likely to return for follow-up sessions.

Opening a discussion was noted to be more difficult with tribal students. As one of the counselors stated, "Just to break the ice takes a really long time." They preferred small-group discussions rather individual sessions and prescriptive rather than open-ended discussions. Locally contextualized and visual materials (rather than written text) were more effective for conveying abstract ideas.

Indigenous Occupations

The counselors agreed that there was interest in traditional occupations but the concern was whether a traditional occupation in current times would provide a means of livelihood that could be sustained. They felt that there was a "discriminatory" attitude against indigenous occupations and that positive presentations by counselors and the media could change such attitudes, citing the example of traditional medicine, which has gained new respectability because of recent documentation and media coverage of its usefulness. However, they confessed that counselors themselves needed additional training in the area of indigenous occupations. The counselors felt they had to undergo a mindset change, "barriers in my own mind," as there was considerable uncertainty and confusion about indigenous occupations. They said that they needed to have more information and be convinced first, "we ourselves should believe that this career is good and workable," to be in a position to guide clients.

Ethical Dilemmas

The counselors encountered a major difficulty in acceding to student requests to tell them what to do. Many students, especially tribal students, wanted help with choosing a subject stream after Class X, as students in the Indian system have to opt for studies in humanities, commerce, or science for Class XI and XII (higher secondary studies). The choice of stream determines to a large degree the range of course options for later university study. Most students wish to choose the sciences since it is the popular belief that this opens doors to prestigious and remunerative careers. Counselors felt reluctant to advise otherwise as this may "break their dreams" as stated by one of them. Some had already made seemingly inappropriate choices of stream and counselors reported that it was difficult to guide them further. Many tribal students are musically gifted, but career options in the fine arts are limited. So, counselors were often in a quandary as to whether they should encourage or discourage a career in music.

The focus group discussion also revealed that counselors worried that artificial class barriers would be created through participation in higher education leading to the possible abandonment of tribal, agrarian, and traditional occupations. Even if a rural youth is educated, he or she may not get a job, and now he or she was reluctant to go back to working in the fields. So, the counselors felt that traditional feelings of respect for labor were lost. On the other hand, there was concern about the sustainability and viability of the traditional way of life in today's times. They were also concerned about "commercial" counselors who advertise and advise students to join an institution in which the counselor works. As trained and knowledgeable career counselors, they were apprehensive about social workers, teachers, and other untrained persons entering the field of career counseling.

Needs and Recommendations

The counselors were unanimous in expressing the urgent importance of career counseling for indigenous students. However, they felt that the content of their training did not prepare them for certain needs that were special to tribal students: for example, the interest and aptitudes of tribal students in music and traditional occupations. There is a need to emphasize the importance and credibility of traditional occupations, as there is a perception that these occupations are less important than the newer careers. Half of the counselors had interacted with students who were interested in traditional occupations.

In the delivery of counseling services, they recommended a greater use of visual materials, and a preference for small groups, in addition to individual counseling. There are difficulties with translating concepts and contexts into the local dialects, raising questions about the validity of the testing process. The materials also need to be adapted to the context of rural worldviews. At a practical level, they reported that students needed specific information about financing their higher education, and which degrees offered better chances of employment.

Based on the themes that emerged from the focus group discussion, we have listed some tips and ideas in Box 30.1 that could be kept in mind by counselors who work with indigenous youth.

Box 30.1: Tips for Counseling Indigenous Youth

- Be familiar with indigenous worldviews.
- Incorporate family and community considerations in the decision-making process.
- Use a neighborhood setting, convenient for family members.
- Have individual and small-group sessions.
- Use narratives and storytelling.
- Use visual materials with cultural motifs.

(continued)

Box 30.1 (continued)

- Be knowledgeable about traditional occupations, challenges, and possible adaptations for current times.
- Discuss traditional occupations, especially the traditional and newly acknowledged values that undergird traditional occupations, and how traditional occupations can be made viable.

Discussion

Relevance for Multiple Cultures

One of the important features of humanitarian societies is their concern for the minorities living within their own communities. In the last few decades, there has been a growing interest in multicultural issues, one key factor being the increasing transborder flows of people, including legitimate professionals, illegal workers, political refugees, asylum seekers, and other types of migrants. As a result, many countries have experienced a dramatic shift in their demographic composition. Within psychology, the multiculturalism movement started in the 1970s, first in Canada and Australia, and then in the United States, followed by some European countries (Laungani, 2005).

Multicultural approaches to counseling have gained ground by understanding and using appropriate social and cultural cues, communication styles, and suitable group methods (e.g., Peavy, 2003). The cultural accommodation model (Leong & Lee, 2006) is an attempt to provide a theoretical framework within which to plan counseling interventions by selecting and applying culture-specific constructs when working with culturally diverse groups. Cultural approaches to counseling should incorporate awareness of traditional providers of health services, such as tribal healers who also administer "psychotherapy" as part of the maintenance of the continuum of physical and mental well-being (Albert & Kharkongor, 2010).

Focused approaches to the career counseling of indigenous peoples have begun to receive attention only in the last decade. The earliest documented efforts to provide a specialized approach in meeting the career guidance needs of indigenous peoples appear to be with the First Nation/Indians of North America and aboriginal peoples of Australia and New Zealand (Peavy, 1995). The work of Peavy (1992) deserves special mention as his ideas have particular relevance to career counseling services for indigenous people. Taking a meaning-making, sociodynamic, postmodern approach, Peavy brings in a hopeful, helpful, and respectful way of treating people as mindful, agentic beings who have the capacity and desire to construct meaningful lives. He introduced the idea of working with a person's life space instead of thinking of intrinsic traits and factors, and brought in local and cultural knowledge into the career counseling format. Peavy (1995) used the term *liminality* to describe the situation of individuals in transition, the socially dislocated, or those who are on the margins, and then made the case that to be at the limen is to be at the threshold of transformation and new positions in social life (Peavy, 1995). The efforts of other researchers and practitioners in a few countries have now begun to coalesce into a model for the career counseling of indigenous students. The need for grounding in cultural contexts is now widely accepted, and methods for such approaches are being developed in several indigenous communities. Several recommendations have emerged and these will now be considered.

New Concepts and Viewpoints

Many indigenous communities seem to lack information about career counseling services. For each indigenous community, the availability of services and communication of the availability may need to be strengthened in culturally resonant ways. Given the collectivist nature of indigenous communities, it is necessary to include the participation of the family and community in counseling. Counseling could take place in a variety of locations: school, community hall (where community members could be present), or at home (where family could participate). When conducted in a location where nonindigenous youth are also counseled, care should be given to including strong visual motifs and themes that recognize the presence of youth from indigenous communities. If possible, counselors should be available on a walk-in basis at a freely accessible helpdesk. Nongovernmental and youth organizations could be brought on board.

The materials and methods that are used should integrate themes from the community and the environment; it is important that topics, experiences, and role models are familiar to indigenous youth, and worthy of emulation (Wihak & Price, 2006). In Khasi society, it is claimed that oral communication is a more efficient tool for learning (Syiem, 2011). It has also been observed that twice as many tribal youth achieve qualifying scores in visual-spatial aptitude tests as nontribal youth (Asian Institute of Gaming and Animation, January 2013, personal communication). So activities and assessment that utilize oral and visual modes must be preferred over culture-bound tests and inventories that are in the written form. The use of the story and narrative approach are likely to be particularly effective. Storytelling can be a powerful medium to facilitate the rethinking of one's career identity in relation to social, political, and economic realities. It has the potential to help counselors and clients find ways to reclaim identities as members of a respected cultural group (Cahill, Wayne, Philpott, & Jeffrey, 2004). Storied counseling enables native clients to explore ways to navigate through a dominant culture (Peavy, 1992). In societies in which oral traditions are still a significant form of social discourse, the folklore may contain powerful suggestions for future life orientations. Adding cultural singing, drawings, and collage as culturally attuned methods has also been suggested (Maree, Ebersöhn, & Molepo, 2006).

An obvious advantage would be to use counselors from the local indigenous group. Among a few communities, trained career counselors are now working within their own

societies, for example, the Māori. Because Western career models, approaches, and theories continue to place individuals as the central actors in career processes, indigenous communities may be better served by counselors who are familiar with collectivist perspectives. In some languages, there is no equivalent term or concept for *career*. Counselors will have to skillfully draw from cultural themes to elaborate this concept. At the same time, sensitivity to individuals belonging to an indigenous community cannot be taken for granted just because the counselor belongs to the same community. In New Zealand there is a suggestion that a key challenge for Māori career practitioners is learning to view and work with Māori clients as distinctive rather than operating from a cultural stereotype and using stereotypically developed interventions, strategies, and techniques. The assumption that all Māori are the same and have an understanding of traditional Māori beliefs, values, and principles still prevails within the minds of some Māori career practitioners. There is, however, strong evidence that there is considerable diversity among Māori clients and a broader approach may be needed (Reid, 2010). Similar diversity may be present among other indigenous groups as well.

Irrespective of whether native or mainstream counselors administer career guidance to indigenous populations, a reorientation of their training is desirable. Such training must include indigenous worldviews and psychology, language, history, and culture. An understanding of social cognitive factors such as career and self-efficacy beliefs, perceptions of barriers, and skills in determining the effect of gender and significant others are critical in multicultural settings (Arulmani, 2005). Also of critical importance is the complex sense of self that individuals of marginalized societies tend to acquire. Colonization, conversion, and domination have diminished and contorted a traditional sense of identity (Sima & West, 2005). A skillful and empathic approach to promoting self-awareness in clients from marginalized societies has to be learned. Another framework that shows promise for work with indigenous groups is the concept of multicultural career counseling competencies (e.g., National Career Development Association, 2009). A critical point made within this framework is that the counselor needs to be aware of his or her own cultural biases. The potential of using this approach could be explored.

Career counseling theory and practice needs to build expertise in the area of traditional occupations. These forms of work have provided a sustainable existence for centuries and are well-integrated with the environment—in fact, they have served to mitigate climate change and loss of biodiversity. The ILO (2000), in one of its studies, examined the social and cultural settings in which traditional economic activities take place, and evaluated the impact of factors of change (mainly industrialization and urbanization and state policies) on the livelihoods of indigenous and tribal peoples. It recommended greater participatory arrangements with a sound policy framework to help sustain and revitalize the traditional occupations of indigenous and tribal peoples.

In the focus group discussion described in this chapter, counselors faced an ethical dilemma in advising their student clients about traditional occupations. Since they were not sure about the viability of traditional livelihoods as a career, they could not provide proper guidance on this question. Mainstream career counseling does not seem to have adequately considered the issues that surround traditional occupations and livelihoods. These are areas that need the urgent attention in the discipline of career guidance and counseling.

The importance of needs assessment has received only recent mention (Kavale, 2012). A careful approach to the conceptualization and evaluation of career guidance needs in a particular population group should be incorporated in the strategizing and planning of career counseling services. Effective counselor education and service delivery require coordination between governments, educational institutions, professional organizations, and indigenous communities for advocacy, policy formulation, budget allocations, training, and deployment. In many countries, these institutional arrangements are yet to be developed and, till then, the career

counseling services for indigenous youth will remain patchy.

The Future

The experience of the young career counselors in Meghalaya is a case study of the evolution and development of career guidance services in an indigenous society. We have presented their work as an example of approaches and services that could be undertaken to serve the career development needs of indigenous young people. The Meghalaya Association of Professional Counselors (MACP) was formed in 2011, and the association hosted the first national conference of the Indian Association for Career and Livelihood Planning in Shillong in the same year. This band of counselors and their colleagues across the state is a core group that provides awareness and services to schools and colleges and aims to influence policy and training. These efforts represent the motivation of civil society players. They also highlight the importance of creating structures and systems through which career counseling services can be formulated, monitored, and developed.

An essential step for the future is that existing and proposed government schemes are used as vehicles for career development programs. An example from the Meghalaya context is the Integrated Basin Development and Livelihood Program for the 12th Five-Year Plan (2012–2017) which has the objective of effective development and utilization of the State's natural resources for livelihood security and which aims to create livelihood opportunities for 400,000 families (Meghalaya Rural Development Society, n.d.). The MACP approached and presented career guidance to the relevant government department, and is today in negotiation to integrate career development services with this large government program. This is an example of identifying and then utilizing existing platforms for the delivery of career development services.

The importance of indigenous communities and their way of life is receiving renewed attention, not only from anthropologists and sociologists but also from political strategists, economists, and psychologists. To quote from a UNESCO document:

> Human societies all across the globe have developed rich sets of experiences and explanations relating to the environments they live in. These other knowledge systems are often referred to as traditional ecological knowledge or indigenous or local knowledge. They encompass the sophisticated arrays of information, understandings and interpretations that guide human societies around the globe in their innumerable interactions with the natural milieu: in agriculture and animal husbandry; hunting, fishing and gathering; struggles against disease and injury; naming and explanation of natural phenomena; and strategies to cope with fluctuating environments. (Nakashima, Prott, & Bridgewater, 2000, p. 11)

The time is ripe for the advancing field of career counseling to include indigenous peoples in its purview in a manner that resonates with their worldviews.

Acknowledgment Sandra Albert was supported by a Wellcome Trust capacity-strengthening grant awarded to the Public Health Foundation of India (PHFI) and a consortium of UK universities. We thank Ms. Darisuk Kharlyngdoh and Ms. Bobylin Nadon, Research Assistants, PHFI, and all the participants of the focus group discussion for their contributions.

References

Ahmed, H. S. (2011, June). Disregarding the Jumma (Featured Article). *Himal South Asian*. Retrieved from http://www.himalmag.com/component/content/article/4511-disregarding-the-jumma.html

Ahukaramū, C. R. (2002). *Indigenous worldviews: A comparative study*. Wellington, New Zealand: Ministry for Māori Development, Winston Churchill Memorial Trust.

Albert, S., & Kharkongor, G. C. (2010). Healing practices of the Khasi and Jaintia people of northeast India. In R. Moodley & H. Yusuf (Eds.), *Building bridges for wellness through counselling and psychotherapy* (pp. 348–359). Toronto, Canada: Centre for Diversity in Counselling and Psychotherapy.

Arulmani, G. (2005). *Career psychology and career counselling: Core concepts for a work in education curriculum*. Sevagram, India: National Council for Education, Training and Research, National Curriculum Framework.

Arulmani, G. (2010). *The Jiva approach to career guidance and counselling: An Indian model* (Project Report). Bangalore, India: The Promise Foundation.

Arulmani, G. (2011a). Striking the right note: The cultural preparedness approach to developing culture resonant career guidance programmes. *International Journal of Educational and Vocational Guidance, 11*(2), 79–93.

Arulmani, G. (2011b). *Career guidance and livelihood planning: Building resources for Meghalaya*. Bangalore, India: The Promise Foundation.

Arulmani, G., & Nag-Arulmani, S. (2004). *Career counselling: A handbook*. New Delhi, India: Tata McGraw-Hill.

Arulmani, G., & Nag-Arulmani, S. (2006). *Work orientations and responses to career choices: Indian regional survey (WORCC-IRS)*. Bangalore, India: The Promise Foundation.

Brown, C., & Lavish, L. A. (2006). Career assessment with Native Americans: Role salience and career decision-making self-efficacy. *Journal of Career Assessment, 14*(1), 116–129.

Cahill, M., Wayne, N., Philpott, D., & Jeffrey, G. (2004). From the roots up: Career counselling in first nations communities. In W. C. Nesbit (Ed.), *Cultural diversity and education: Interface issues* (pp. 129–138). Newfoundland, Canada: Memorial University.

Centre for Research, Planning and Action. (2007). *Career perception of SC/ST students in institutions of higher learning* (p. 132). New Delhi, India: Planning Commission, Government of India.

Chen, G. (2011, November). *Brief survey on career information and career development status of selected institutions and students in Shillong*. Paper presented at the first national conference of the Indian Association for Career and Livelihood Planning, Shillong, India.

Craven, R. G., Parente, A., & Marder, K. (2004). Indigenous students: The reality of their educational and career aspirations. In H. W. Marsh, J. Baumert, G. E. Richards, & E. U. Trautwein (Eds.), *Proceedings of the third international biennial SELF research conference* (pp. 97–108). Retrieved from http://www.voced.edu.au/search/apachesolr_search/sm.metadata.documentno=%22td/tnc%2086.270%22

Croson, R., & Gneezy, U. (2009). Gender differences in preferences. *Journal of Economic Literature, 47*(2), 1–27.

Directorate of Economics and Statistics. (2007). *Statistical handbook Meghalaya*. Shillong, India: Government of Meghalaya.

Directorate of School Education. (n.d.). *Number of schools (primary & upper primary) in Meghalaya*. Retrieved from www.megeducation.gov.in/dsel/statistics/stats.html

Dkhar, B. (2011, November). *Traditional medicine as livelihood*. Paper presented at the first national conference of the Indian Association for Career and Livelihood Planning, Shillong, India.

Gneezy, U., Leonard, K. L., & List, J. A. (2009). Gender differences in competition: Evidence from a matrilineal and a patriarchal society. *Econometrica, 77*(5), 1637–1664.

Hazarika, M. (2006). Neolithic culture of northeast India: A recent perspective on the origins of pottery and agriculture. *Journal of the Society of South Asian Archaeology.* doi: http://dx.doi.org/10.5334/aa.06104

International Labour Organization. (1989). *ILO Convention 169.* Geneva, Switzerland: International Labour Office.

International Labour Organization. (2000). *Traditional occupations of indigenous and tribal peoples: Emerging trends.* Geneva, Switzerland: Author.

International Labour Organization. (n.d.). *India.* Retrieved from http://www.ilo.org/indigenous/Activitiesbyregion/Asia/SouthAsia/India/lang–en/index.htm#P1_717

Jeeva, S. R. D. N., Laloo, R. C., & Mishra, B. P. (2006). Traditional agricultural practices in Meghalaya, North East India. *Indian Journal of Traditional Knowledge, 5*(1), 7–18.

Karlsson, B. G. (2011). *Unruly hills: Nature and nation in India's northeast.* New Delhi, India: Orient Black Swan.

Kavale, J. (2012). Needs and needs assessment in career guidance and counseling: Lack of scientific exploration and justification? *Indian Journal of Career and Livelihood Planning, 1*(1), 28–35.

Kurbah, S. (2010a). *A study on the determinants and prospects of entrepreneurship in the East Khasi hills district, Meghalaya* (Unpublished doctoral dissertation). Martin Luther Christian University, Shillong, India.

Kurbah, S. (2010b, October). *Traditional occupations in East Khasi Hill District, Meghalaya, India.* Poster presented at the IAEVG-JIVA International Conference, Bangalore, India.

Laungani, P. (2005). Building multicultural counselling bridges: The holy grail or a poisoned chalice? *Counselling Psychology Quarterly, 18*(4), 247–259.

Leong, F. T., & Lee, S.-H. (2006). A cultural accommodation model for cross-cultural psychotherapy: Illustrated with the case of Asian Americans. *Psychotherapy, 43*(4), 410–423.

Lind, M. (2011, January). The five worldviews that define American politics (Featured Article). *Salon Magazine.* Retrieved from http://www.salon.com/2011/01/12/lind_five_worldviews/

Madsen, E. (1990). The symbolism associated with dominant society schools in native American communities: An Alaskan example. *Canadian Journal of Native Education, 17,* 43–53.

Maree, K., Ebersöhn, L., & Molepo, M. (2006). Administering narrative career counselling in a diverse setting: Trimming the sails to the wind. *South African Journal of Education, 26*(1), 49–60.

Meghalaya Rural Development Society. (n.d.). *Integrated basin development and livelihood program for the 12th five-year plan (2012–2017).* Retrieved from http://mrds.nic.in/mrds_desc.htm

Ministry of Human Resource Development. (2009). *Annual report (2008–09) of the department of education of India.* New Delhi, India: Department of School Education and Literacy and Department of Higher Education, Government of India.

Nakashima, D., Prott, L., & Bridgewater, P. (2000). Tapping into the world's wisdom. *Sources: UNESCO, 125,* 11–12. Retrieved from http://unesdoc.unesco.org/images/0012/001202/120200e.pdf

National Career Development Association. (2009). *Minimum competencies for multicultural career counseling and development.* Broken Arrow, OK: Author.

NCERT. (2005). *National focus group on problems of scheduled caste and scheduled tribe children* (Position Paper, pp. 26–31). New Delhi, India: Author.

Peavy, R. V. (1992). A constructivist model of training for career counselors. *Journal of Career Development, 18* (3), 215–228.

Peavy, R. V. (1995). *Career counseling with native clients: Understanding the context.* Ottawa, Canada: Canadian Guidance and Counselling Foundation.

Peavy, R. V. (1998). *Socio dynamic counselling.* Victoria, BC: Trafford.

Peavy, R. V. (2003). Social and cultural context of intercultural counselling. *Canadian Journal of Counselling, 37*(3), 186–197.

Planning Department, Government of Meghalaya. (2008). *Meghalaya human development report.* Shillong, India: Government of Meghalaya.

Quintesse Consultants. (2011). *Vocational education in healthcare: Market survey for a skill development centre in Shillong.* Shillong, India: Author.

Reddy, M. B., Langstieh, B. T., Kumar, V., Nagaraja, T., Reddy, A. N. S., Meka, A., … Singh, L. (2007). Austro-Asiatic tribes of northeast India provide hitherto missing genetic link between south and southeast Asia. *PLoS One, 2*(11). Retrieved from http://www.plosone.org/article/info:doi/10.1371/journal.pone.0001141

Registrar General and Census Commissioner. (2011). *Census of India 2011: Provisional population totals.* New Delhi, India: Author.

Reid, L. A. (2010). *Understanding how cultural values influence career processes for Māori* (Unpublished doctoral dissertation). Auckland University of Technology, Auckland, New Zealand.

Sima, R. G., & West, W. (2005). Sharing healing secrets. In R. Moodley & W. West (Eds.), *Integrating traditional healing practices into counseling and psychotherapy* (pp. 316–325). Thousand Oaks, CA: Sage.

Srivastava, R. S., & Sinha, S. (2008). Inter-social groups disparities in access to higher education. In Secretary, University Grants Commission (Ed.), *Higher education in India: Issues related to expansion, inclusiveness, quality and finance* (pp. 103–110). New Delhi, India: University Grants Commission.

Syiem, E. (2011). *The oral discourse in Khasi folk narratives.* Guwahati, India: EBH.

United Nations. (1986). *Definition of indigenous people from the United Nations sub-commission on prevention of discrimination and protection of minorities and its study of the problem of discrimination against indigenous populations* (UN Doc. E./CN.4/Sub.2/1986/7/Add., para. 4, p. 379). New York, NY: United Nations Sub-Commission on Prevention of Discrimination and Protection of Minorities.

United Nations Population Fund. (n.d.). *Addressing the rights of indigenous peoples*. Retrieved from www.unfpa.org/rights/people.htm

Weltanschauung. (n.d.). In *Merriam-Webster's online dictionary* (11th ed.). Retrieved from http://www.merriam-webster.com/dictionary/weltanschauung

Wihak, C., & Price, R. E. (2006). *Counselling across cultures*: *Working with aboriginal clients*. Ottawa, Canada: National Consultation on Career Development (NATCON).

World Bank. (1991). *Operational directive: Indigenous peoples* (OP 4.10. World Bank Operation Manual). Washington, DC: Author.

World Wildlife Fund. (2007). *Meghalaya subtropical forests*. Retrieved from http://www.eoearth.org/article/Meghalaya_subtropical_forests

Wua, Y. L. (2012). Schooling experiences and career aspirations of indigenous vocational high school students: A case study in Taiwan. *Asia Pacific Journal of Education, 32*(1), 1–15.

Xaxa, V. (2011). *The status of tribal children in India*: *A historical perspective* (UNICEF Working Paper Series). New Delhi, India: UNICEF.

Older Women's Retrospective Narratives of Their Work and Learning Pathways

31

Jenny Bimrose, Mary McMahon, and Mark Watson

Introduction

To contribute to theory development that is relevant to women across countries and cultures, an international, qualitative research study has been undertaken into the retrospective career stories of older women (aged 45–65). Twelve women were interviewed in depth in each of three countries, Australia, England, and South Africa. The combination of developing, as well as developed, countries in the research has enriched the examination of the career development of older women in these contrasting economic contexts. Thirty-six in-depth interviews have provided stories of older women that have emerged from an exploration of their work and learning pathways. Based on these stories, in this chapter we review the broad context of women's position in labor markets internationally, briefly outline the qualitative research approach adopted for this research investigation, present emergent findings under three key themes (learning across the life-span, work influences, and social influences), and, in the light of these findings, consider the relevance of existing career theory for women.

Women's Labor Market Experiences

Despite some progress being made towards gender equality, women continue to suffer disadvantage in multiple areas of their lives (United Nations, 2010a). An exclusive focus on gender, however, restricts a true understanding of the depth and breadth of disadvantage suffered, because of the effect of the dynamic interaction of a number of factors associated with structural disadvantage that converge in individuals (or groups). Such factors include gender, race, socioeconomic status, and age (Bradley, 1996; Moore, 2009), with the negative impact of the convergence of multiple factors in individuals (or group) referred to as *intersectionality* (Begum, 1994). This concept is relevant to career theory and practice, since it highlights the multidimensional nature of the barriers to career development and progression that need to be navigated by particular clients.

Differences in the life chances, wealth, and health of women in developing countries compared with those in developed countries are well documented (United Nations, 2010b). The integration of skilled, female workers into the workforces of developing countries continues to be slow, even though it is recognized that the future economic competitiveness of these countries, internationally, will depend (at least in part) upon the success of this process:

> Generally speaking, in the developing world, women are still largely denied access to the formal labor market, do not have equal opportunities to qualify for higher employment and are

J. Bimrose (✉)
Institute for Employment Research, University of
Warwick, Coventry, UK
e-mail: Jenny.Bimrose@warwick.ac.uk

G. Arulmani et al. (eds.), *Handbook of Career Development*, International and Cultural Psychology,
DOI 10.1007/978-1-4614-9460-7_31, © Springer Science+Business Media, LLC 2014

consequently less likely to occupy administrative or managerial positions, lag significantly behind in terms of career development and earnings increases. (Jütting, Morrisson, Dayton-Johnson, & Drechsler, 2006, p. 7)

In comparison, the degree of integration of women into the workforces of developed countries tends to be greater, with higher representation of women in positions of power and influence: "Globally, one quarter of senior officials or managers are women, but in Western Asia, Southern Asia and Northern Africa, women hold less than 10 % of top-level positions" (United Nations, 2010b, p. 1).

The relative positions of women in these two economic contexts, therefore, differ significantly in certain respects. Yet other experiences are common. For example, from 1980 to 2008, the rate of female labor participation increased around the world, from 50.2 to 51.7 %, while the male rate decreased from 82.0 to 77.7 % (International Labour Office, 2010). The same source highlights how, despite this increased participation, nearly half (48.4 %) of the productive potential of the female population remains unutilized (compared to 22.3 % for men). Even in societies where gender role attitudes have become less traditional, little change has occurred in the gendered allocation of domestic duties, with women, on average, continuing to take the primary responsibility for domestic and care responsibilities (Thörnqvist, 2006).

One further example relates to part-time employment. Part-time employees work mainly in occupational sectors that are generally unskilled, low-status, low-paid, and characterized by lack of security. While men are overwhelmingly concentrated in full-time work, large numbers of women work part-time (see, for example, U.S. Bureau of Labor Statistics, 2006). A final example relates to occupational segregation, a feature of labor markets around the world. Both horizontal segregation (where women are employed in a narrow band of occupational sectors compared with men) and vertical segregation (where women are restricted in the levels to which they are able to progress) ensure that most women are typically employed in stereotypically

gendered occupational roles in which it proves consistently difficult to progress to the top senior positions. Characteristic of occupational segregation is the gender pay gap, with women earning less than men, even when employed in similar jobs (Bimrose, 2008). Overall, opportunities for full and productive employment remain relatively poor for women (e.g., McMahon, Bimrose, & Watson, 2010). Wide gaps remain in women's access to paid work in at least half of all regions of the world. Following significant job losses in 2008–2009 as a consequence of global recession, the growth in employment during the economic recovery in 2010, especially in the developing world, was lower for women than for men (United Nations, 2011).

These and other statistical trends relating to women's employment illustrate the distinctive and unequal nature of women's labor market experiences, irrespective of whether they live in developed or developing countries. Women's disproportionate share of domestic labor and care responsibilities, and their concentration both in part-time employment and in a relatively narrow band of occupational areas that are regarded as stereotypical female are key issues for career guidance theory and practice (Bimrose, 2008). The well-documented multidimensional, labor market disadvantage suffered by women across developed as well as developing countries poses legitimate questions about the nature and level of the career support required to help women realize their full potential. Moreover, it challenges the current common assumption that all clients can be accommodated through the use of generic, traditional career theory frameworks.

Career Theory for Women

Women's career choices are often multidimensional, vary over time, and are structured by context (Bimrose, 2008). Particular challenges are faced by older women as they make their transitions from education and training into and through the labor market. For example, women's unequal position in labor markets across the world results in impoverishment in old age, which is characterized by social exclusion and reduced quality of life (Smeaton & Vegeris, 2009).

A key goal of career guidance and counseling practice is to help all clients achieve their full potential, irrespective of circumstances and constraints. Traditional career theory fails to address the complex and relational nature of women's career development (August, 2010). Critiques of traditional career theory increasingly argue for alternative approaches that are holistic and, therefore, more sympathetic to the needs of women. A number of theoretical approaches that are more holistic in their conceptualization have been developed over recent decades specifically for women (e.g., Astin, 1984; Cook, Heppner, & O'Brien, 2002; Marshall, 1989). For example, Astin's (1984) primary intent was to construct a theory that would describe more adequately the career-choice process of women, as well as explain recent changes in women's career aspirations. She developed a model of career choice and work behavior that included personal (psychological) and social forces and their interaction. Her need-based socio-psychological model contains four important constructs: motivation, expectations, sex-role socialization, and structure of opportunity, thus combining psychological and sociological variables. Other theories have been promoted as having particular relevance to women, because they stress the complex and dynamic nature of individual career development (August, 2010; Farmer, 1997; Gottfredson, 1981, 1996; Hackett & Betz, 1981). An example here is Gottfredson's developmental theory of occupational aspirations (1981) which sets out to explain differences in aspirations by race, sex, and social class. It is different from psychological theories (Gottfredson, 1996, p. 181) since it proposes that career development is an attempt to implement, first, a social self and, second, a psychological self. It pays attention to the ways in which beliefs about the self and occupations develop and treats vocational choice largely as a process of eliminating options and narrowing choices. It also considers how individuals

compromise their goals in coming to terms with reality as they try to implement their aspirations.

Researching Older Women's Career Narratives

The tendency of psychologists using quantitative approaches to separate individuals from their context has been criticized as a particular weakness when studying women, because "who can deny on simply intuitive grounds that women's vocational behavior is a product of the interaction between individual and social contextual variables?" (Brooks & Forrest, 1994, p. 128). Hackett (1997), in agreement with this view, has argued that in studying women's careers there is a need to move beyond "simple correlational designs" (p. 184). In a research review of women's careers, O'Neil, Hopkins, and Bilimoria (2008) have recommended that future research needs to employ holistic approaches, as well as inform organizational practice. Further, they call for future research to give "voice to women's own career and life experiences with the intent of building integrated theory about these experiences" (p. 737). Harmon and Meara (1994) have also emphasized the value of qualitative research in enhancing understanding of policy and practice and have suggested that women have been neglected by empirical psychologists because the necessary inquiry "can result in messy science" (p. 362). Consequently, they argue that two separate traditions have developed within counseling psychology, one concerned with science, one with practice, and that "those who are interested in career counseling for women seem to be swimming against this tide in an attempt to integrate science and practice" (Harmon & Meara, 1994, p. 362). This view is endorsed by others (e.g., Lapour & Heppner, 2009).

In response to these calls, a qualitative research methodology was employed in the present study by an international, multidisciplinary, research team to investigate the career stories of older women in their country contexts, drawing on the disciplines of psychology as well as those of sociology and education. Qualitative research investigates real life in context and concerns itself with vivid, dense, and full descriptions of the phenomena studied in natural language (Polkinghorne, 1994, 2005). This approach requires flexibility and the ability not to prejudge issues. A growing body of opinion suggests that our current understanding of career development would be enriched by research approaches that go beyond the scientific positivist paradigms that have dominated traditional theories (O'Neil et al., 2008; Patton & McMahon, 2006; Savickas, 1993, 1997; Young & Valach, 2000). Not only is it argued that different approaches would increase our understanding per se, but also that research methods reflecting broader philosophical orientations would be more appropriate with previously neglected client groups such as women (Brooks & Forrest, 1994; Fassinger, 2005; Hackett, 1997; Lapour & Heppner, 2009; O'Neil et al., 2008; Rainey & Borders, 1997). The research study was conducted, therefore, within a qualitative paradigm, using grounded theory method which helped guide data collection and analysis through a systematic process while also permitting interpretivist concern for subjectivity and meaning (King & Horrocks, 2010). The overall aim was to investigate the career stories of older women (aged 45–65) across different country contexts.

Collecting Older Women's Career Stories

Interviewing is one of the most widely used methods of gathering qualitative data. As a technique, its primary purpose is to obtain descriptions of the real life world of the interviewee, with the intention of interpreting the meaning of the described phenomena (King & Horrocks, 2010). This method of data collection was particularly apposite for this study since it enabled immediate recording and provided in-depth accounts of the contexts in which the women participants are located, as well as the processes of career change and transition.

A semi-structured interview framework was used to guide data collection, comprising five sections that facilitated gathering information related to demographic information; present, past, and future work and learning experiences; previous work and learning transitions; learning from previous transitions; and moving forward. In particular, the five sections of the interview engaged participants in a reflective process that encouraged them to make recursive connections between their work and learning experiences; the personal, social, and environmental influences on those experiences; as well as their feelings about, and reactions to, their experiences. The interview framework was co-developed by the researchers through several iterations and, consistent with grounded theory method, the focus shifted to reflect insights gained as stories unfolded.

Adult women participants were recruited for the study across three nations, Australia, England, and South Africa, in ways that reflected researcher contexts. Purposive, convenience, and snowballing sampling techniques were employed (see Patton, 2002). Key criteria for inclusion were gender and age, since the aim of the study was to focus on the career development of older women. Data on socioeconomic status were not collected because of comparability issues across the three participating countries. In Australia, information was distributed to career counselors who then made the information and the researcher's contact details available to women in the specified age group. The women were invited to contact the researcher if they were interested in participating in the research project. None of the participants identified as being of Aboriginal or Torres Strait Islander descent. In England, participants were drawn from an online survey that had been carried out for research into the role of continuing education and vocational training across Europe. Respondents, who indicated that they would be willing to be interviewed, and who fitted the age and gender criteria for the research study, were contacted by email. Again, none self-identified as being members of minority ethnic groups. In South Africa, information was distributed to those women who responded to an invitation to

Table 31.1 Participants

	Australia	England	South Africa
Age			
45–50	1	3	9
51–55	2	5	1
56–50	2	1	1
61–65	7	3	1
Marital status			
Married	5	8	7
Single	7	3	4
Widowed	0	1	1
Educational level			
Subdegree	4	1	2
Degree	5	3	4
Post Grad. Diploma	2	1	0
Honors	0	0	1
Masters	0	6	2
Doctorate	1	1	3
Employment status			
Full-time	3	7	10
Part-time	3	0	0
Self-employed	2	2	0
Student	1	0	2
Unemployed	1	1	0
Retired	2	1	0
Vocation[a]	0	1	0

Note. [a]Refers to a Minister of Religion, who described her role as her "vocation"

participate that had been sent through a higher education institution's website. All 12 were Black, Xhosa-speaking women who also spoke English. This particular sampling decision was made around the political history of the country, focusing on participants who were more likely to have originated from a lower socioeconomic context, reflective of a developing country, yet had achieved progression into higher education. The key guiding principles in the recruitment of all participants were informed consent, and anonymous and voluntary participation. Each of the researchers met the ethical guidelines of their respective universities.

All participants were between 45 and 65 years of age. The lower age bracket is generally accepted as the benchmark in describing mature age workers, and it is an age after which it becomes difficult for adults to reenter the workforce once they have left it (Commonwealth of Australia, 2001). The upper age bracket was the age at which retirement was common in the three countries at the time of data collection. The recruitment procedure for the overall sample resulted in 12 Australian, 12 English, and 12 South African women participating in the study. Details of the sample are given in Table 31.1.

Making Sense of the Data

Grounded theory method aims to produce innovative theory that is grounded in data (Charmaz, 2007) and suited to prospective users (Fassinger, 2005; Glaser & Strauss, 1967; Lapour & Heppner, 2009). A key feature is that research design, data collection, and analysis are intertwined, allowing the focus to change and for hypotheses and key concepts to be generated as the data are collected (Bryman & Burgess, 1994; Charmaz, 2007). This approach also offers

Table 31.2 Code categories

Master codes	Subcodes
1. Learning across the life-span	(1a) Formal and informal
	(1b) Response to/reflection on learning
2. Transitions and responses	(2a) Unexpected/unanticipated chance events
	(2b) Response to circumstances/chance events
	(2c) Adaptability
3. Intrapersonal influences	(3a) Self
	(3b) Values
	(3c) Personality traits
	(3d) Age-related
	(3e) Role satisfaction (i) past (ii) present
4. Work influences	(4a) Employment description (past and present)
	(4b) Workplace dynamic (past and present)
	(4c) Unpaid activities outside the home
	(4d) Work–life balance/tension between roles
5. Financial influences	(5a) Current financial situation
	(5b) Future financial situation
6. Social Influences	(6a) Support networks
	(6b) Role models
	(6c) Life roles
7. Relocation	
8. Advice to others	
9. Future planning	

systematic and rigorous procedures for interpreting and analyzing rich qualitative data (Charmaz, 1995, 2007; King & Horrocks, 2010). Coding involves differentiation and combination of the data, together with reflection on this information (Miles & Huberman, 1994). Here, coding involved a rigorous three-stage, ten-phase process. Given the international dimension of this inquiry, both regular face-to-face meetings and remote methods (e.g., Skype, email) of communication were frequently used. Stage one of the analysis comprised five phases of code development using one transcript from each country, which culminated in a set of codes that were applied during stage two. Stage two comprised four phases related to the application of subsequent refinement of the master codes to a further three transcripts. In stage three, codes that had emerged from the initial phases of data analysis were applied to the remaining 30 interview

transcripts. From this process of analysis emerged nine master codes and 19 subcodes. These are presented in Table 31.2.

In essence, determining the codes adhered to criteria identified for grounded theory, whereby they were repeated across two or more interviews, were distinct from each other, and researchers made decisions about what to include and how to interpret the participants' comments (King & Horrocks, 2010). The following section focuses on selected findings from three of the major codes and ten subcodes. It is not feasible to report under each master code and subcodes, but codes have been selected to provide rich, detailed insights to the career narratives of participants, drawing material equally from the three participating countries. The three master codes are learning across the life-span, work influences, and social influences. Pseudonyms have been used to protect the identity of the participants.

Themes from Stories of Older Women

Learning Across the Life-Span

The importance of *learning across the life-span* emerged as a master code in all of the women's stories. Subcodes related to this master code included *formal* and *informal learning*. The term *informal learning* in this context describes the many forms of learning that occur independently of formal, instructor-led, accredited programs. It can be based on books, self-study programs, support materials, and often involves interactions with others, like work colleagues, community members, friends, and family. It can also take place across a variety of contexts, like home, work, or community organizations. A third subcode derived from the master code of learning across the life-span comprised the women's personal *responses to or reflections on learning*.

Formal Learning

Many of the women used *formal learning* to gain access to occupational areas and/or to redirect their lives. From Australia, Janice explained: "I did a [technical/scientific] certificate through the Technical College in [Australian city]... and that's 3 years training... I did a bit of a DipEd because when I finished [my technical/scientific qualification] they were very short of science teachers..."

The stories revealed that for some women, formal learning followed a traditional pathway of leaving school and then completing higher education or training before gaining employment. Stella, from England, described her pathway through something of a qualification maze to reach her occupational goal:

> Well, I have a degree from [name of University] in modern history and then I have postgraduate qualifications in social work; that was at [name of University] and [name of University]. It [formal qualification] was split in two. Because my first degree was not considered relevant, I had to do a year, a postgraduate diploma in social administration, and then the diploma in social work.

Other women had not continued with formal learning immediately after leaving school and their learning pathways were somewhat nontraditional. Examples from Australia illustrate this point. For example, Sandra completed her secondary education and commenced work. She completed a degree in her late 30s because "I needed to have a degree... to prove that I could have gone down that road if I'd chosen." By contrast, Megan had exited school at age 14 without a school certificate and reentered formal learning as an older adult, beginning by completing her school leaving qualification and continuing on to complete a degree and postgraduate studies part-time while supporting her family. As reflected by many of the stories, engagement and re-engagement with learning was evident. For example, Kay from Australia, who had postgraduate qualifications including a PhD, was considering retirement and "seriously exploring how you become a [bus] driver. I'd love to do that part-time. You know, something a bit different than head work."

From South Africa, Nozuku illustrates the length of time over which some of the women had engaged with formal learning:

> I have completed my B Tech (technical bachelor's degree) and I'm now doing my BA Hon. Since school I have been doing short courses some with (a correspondence college) on labor relations. I did the other one with (name of University), the advanced labor relations course for 6 months, yes. Then I moved on and registered in 1999 for my diploma for the first time in human resources management and I waited and moved on. Then there was that change and then there was a little bit of a break between 2003 and 2004 because of my work schedule and everything, but I restarted again and started my B Tech, completed that and started my labor relations honours in 2009.

Informal Learning

Also significant, the women's stories illustrate the critical importance of *informal learning* to their career development. An Australian participant, Janice, describes how she learned on the job when she went back to work after a break and kept her knowledge updated by observing more experienced colleagues:

Yes it was very much an informal way. I went back to work to a big school in [name of city] called [school] and … when I went back however I had to sort of, as I said learn again. Yeah, that was hard work because you really taught yourself. I mean you watched the one that was the head who'd been doing it for a while but you really learnt and it's always, they always change the textbooks, you've got to redo the experiments and all that sort of thing. Also it's just learning new equipment and then as the years progressed, the equipment got very sophisticated so you had to do data loggers and video microscopes and all that sort of thing. So it really even till now to this day is constantly learning…

Mary, an English participant, illustrates how essential engagement with informal learning has been in keeping her up to date with developments in her formal work role:

Well, I have to keep various things up to date of course. So, you know, I mean, I guess, I must do a safeguarding course virtually every 6 months because, you know, some such agency requires it. I spend a fair amount of time at the moment on updates for, you know, changes in [education sector] and so on, because, you know, to be effective as [occupational role] you really do have to fully understand the environment in which it is operating. So, I think that will be… those will be the sort of things I'd be thinking about. I'm certainly not seriously considering doing any other – anything with a major qualification or anything in that line, effectively it's the stuff I need to, in my view, discharge what I'm doing to the best of my ability.

Across continents, the importance of informal learning, including learning in non-accredited courses, was emphasized by the women's stories. Julie, from South Africa, tells how:

In terms of work it was moving to the [name of office] I thought there were a lot opportunities like, uhmm, travelling abroad, meeting people. It took me to a different level … it opened my eyes, I kind of learnt a lot from that and [names an individual] at some stage sent me for training before becoming a manager… Sometimes he had invested a lot in me in that area, took me for short courses, conferences… I attended a lot of things that I never thought I would find myself in.

Responses to or Reflections on Learning

The older women offered their *responses to or reflections on their learning experiences*, both formal and informal. For some, positive feelings

were associated with formal learning and strongly expressed. For example, the enthusiasm of Sandra, from Australia, shines through:

I loved it. I loved it. I love learning. I love the challenge of it. I love getting into something that I've got absolutely no idea about and finding out how it all works. It really inspires me and I guess that's why I keep going back, keep going back… so just learning, dabbling in different things and just seeing how that goes. I just like trying different things.

Similarly, the following quote from Jennie, in England, explains how one of the formal courses stood out from all others, even though it coincided with some very difficult personal circumstances:

It wasn't, it wasn't just what it was going to give me in terms of a career; it was the actual study itself was really interesting. It was really well taught, even though it was the busiest time of my life because it involved a lot of personal sacrifice and family sacrifice, you know, a lot of driving backwards and forwards, even though [name of child] had been ill and all of that, and I was ill. The whole course gave me an energy and enthusiasm that I hadn't received and hadn't felt in any other study I'd done. It was the best learning I'd ever had.

Lungsi, from South Africa, describes in some detail how her experiences of learning had changed her in a way that has personal, social, and cultural significance. She feels that as a result of her experiences of learning, she has become more assertive, more able to speak up for herself, and express her own point of view in a way that was previously not possible. This had a profound impact on the ways she interacted with others, particularly male members of her family:

I have learnt so much and I have changed as a person as well. Maybe I can start with myself, gaining some more confidence and how I deal with situations as an African woman. Sometimes you feel that you have to listen and succumb to other men like whether they impose things or what. But for me, I am starting with myself with whatever I do I put myself first and I always consider that it is important to focus on what you enjoy most rather than pleasing other people. That has changed because I haven't been like that. So through learning I have grown as a person. I have grown as an individual to say this is what I believe in, this is what defines me, this is who am I. So I am very proud of myself for doing that. And cognisance of the people around me as well, I do that in such a way that I respect them but I always... because for us, for other people it is kind of difficult. At home as well my husband couldn't understand that, and that until I kept on explaining to them that I am a changed person like this is how I believe that we should do things, and this is I respect you and if you can accommodate me and if we can move together in this change because this is what I have learnt and this is how I put it across and the way I think about things as well. The way I communicate things as well because, within my family as well as where I come from, men are always getting some status as well whenever you prepare rituals, whenever you prepare things. But there as well I exercise my rights as well. I know what is right. I know what is wrong, I don't usually keep quiet because previously I used to keep quiet and say 'okay they can do whatever'. But now I am so vocal to address things that I think that they are supposed to be addressing. So I communicate more compared to the previous period I have been and then I align myself with people of the same calibre, like friends as well.

Traditional career theory marginalizes the importance of informal learning and tends to assume that formal learning has the potential to deliver on its promises, while the evidence suggests that this is not always the case. For example, even where a formal qualification has been obtained, this may not be sufficient to achieve an occupational aspiration. The stories of these older women emphasize how learning per se contributes to career progression along a number of dimensions. Theory may also underestimate the role of learning experiences in altering participation in personal and cultural contexts. Each person empowered through learning impacts contexts through transformed participation.

Work Influences

Work influences also featured strongly as a master code. Subcodes to emerge under this code were *employment descriptions (past and present)*, *workplace dynamics (past and present)*, *unpaid activities outside the home*, and *work–life balance/tension between roles*.

Employment Descriptions (Past and Present)

Employment descriptions (past and present) highlight the nature of women's employment, with vertical segregation and part-time work as dominant influences. Lorraine, in Australia, talked about her work as a medical receptionist:

> I worked as a medical receptionist from about 1993 and that's the sort of work I had done. I had worked at various places but I'd been a medical receptionist from 1993. That was when our youngest started school. I think that was right, yeah. She was born '79, yes, she'd just started school. So I took that job on and I'd worked at various practices over that time. I did manage the reception at one particular practice and did a bit of full-time work there, but most of the work has been part-time work or casual work. That just seems to be the way the industry goes. There are not too many people that will put on a full-time medical receptionist and pay them full-time rates. I think that's – yeah, I think that's the nature of the industry. There's a lot of job sharing, a lot of women who have children and job sharing is just a big thing in that industry.

The employment descriptions of these older women also emphasize the fractured nature of many of the older women's career trajectories because of the dual impact of their caring roles and their husband's/partner's career progression. This was common across all three countries. In England, Debbie explained her career progression through no fewer than 26 jobs, as she brought up three children and followed her husband's career promotions:

> I did work at, for some 26 jobs since... I left school... and a lot of those have been very short-term and bits and pieces that were done in parallel with each other. But sort of ... So there's been a lot of employers there, mainly in the public service; I've worked for three universities, and I've worked at this one twice; and I've worked for a couple of local authorities, and, no, no, about five or six local authorities...

There were stories of success, among the employment descriptions, although these often related to stereotypically gendered occupational areas, like teaching. Lungsi, from South Africa, explained her swift promotion within a teaching post, related to her cultural background:

> I was a teacher before for thirteen years... high school... Fortunately for me within the first

2 years that I was employed as a teacher I managed to get through to a Head of Department post. And the period that was given for a person to be employed in a senior position was 5 years, but I think that the principal could see... he made recommendations that I should act if I can't be employed on that position. But fortunately the interviews were held and I was given the post of being Head of Department for African languages and guidance as well.

Workplace Dynamics (Past and Present)

Workplace dynamics, the second subcode within work influences, includes experiences of workplace discrimination, harassment, and bullying, which were particularly strong influences on the careers of some participants. Perhaps, this is unsurprising given what is already known about the mechanisms that operate as barriers to progression for women in work organizations (Bimrose, 2004). One of the Australian women (Megan) talked openly about her experiences of bullying:

> I've worked with workplace bullies and I find that is such a complex issue. There aren't easy ways to handle it and it doesn't matter how professional you are or how on the ball or what you know, it's really hard to work with those types of people. They work in such a way that you can't be heard by the people that need to be heard. That I find very difficult.

Another woman, Sam, from England, explained the discrimination she had faced as a woman in a nontraditional occupational job as an engineer in a large manufacturing company. She explained how she had moved from one part of the company to another, because she felt promotion was being blocked on the grounds of gender. However, this move within the company did not solve the problem. Eventually, she felt she had no alternative but to leave and seek employment elsewhere:

> I was a bit frustrated by what I would say was a bit of a glass ceiling in the organization, frankly. But as it turned out... the testosterone-fuelled environment that was the [the other part of the business] was quite objectionable to me... I wanted to move out completely.

Xoliswa, from South Africa, described a difficult situation where she had attempted to act as mediator:

And ya, we had problems, and last year there was another major, I don't know how to put it, a hurting thing to all of us... we had a restructuring of the department; our department had to be restructured. The reasons for the restructuring to me even today are unknown... I don't know how to put it but it is dealing with the ones you don't want, getting them out of the system, you know, out of the system, get rid of them, and the only way was to restructure the department... I was the one trying to calm people down, trying to have ways and means of trying to protect people not to lose jobs, because people's jobs were at stake... I was putting myself in the position of being victimized...

In the stories of the older women who had suffered workplace discrimination and harassment, what seems particularly surprising is the failure (possibly inability) of the victims of this behavior to recognize or label the processes to which they had been subjected. The failure to recognize systemic structural disadvantage poses something of an ethical dilemma for career practitioners. Where clients do not present or define such experiences as problematic, is it professionally defensible in a career guidance intervention to label behaviors that are simply described by the clients as impediments to their career progression as discriminatory, or as harassment, or even bullying? The argument has been made that failure on the part of practitioners to deal with this issue explicitly as part of career development support could constitute unethical practice, since it may lead to harm (or further harm) of the client (Bimrose, 2004). However, current theory remains blind to such issues, rendering them largely an invisible component of career interventions.

Unpaid Activities Outside the Home

The third subcode related to *unpaid activities outside the home*. It was striking that many of the women found time to commit to voluntary activities, some quite consciously engaging in activities that contributed to their career progression. For example, Lorraine from Australia explained:

> I've always done a lot of things – like I did (volunteer organization) there for a little while when the children – when I had like a break in the middle of the day, they were at kindy [kindergarten], I'd go

to Meals on Wheels. Or there'd be – I've done a lot of church work. I'd been a treasurer at the church. I'd been the administrator at the church. I was actually president of a women's Christian organization for 10 years in (state capital) before we came to (regional city). But now, currently I am on the board of the (volunteer organization) here in (regional city). I have done part-time work for (telephone counseling service). I'm a telephone counselor for (telephone counseling service) at the moment too. All those things are going to help me though in where I'm heading.

Similarly, Mary from England reported how she gives her expertise and time freely to a number of community organizations:

> I'm on the [name of organization] Council, Chair of Governors at [name] College. I chair the steering group for [name of organization and description] in [place]. I'm on the [name of organization] Joint Advisory Board for 14 to 19 education. I'm a board member of the [name] Group which is a [type of] partnership covering [regional areas]. What else is there? I do a fair amount... for the Church in terms of being Treasurer. I'm also on two [name of church] groups now, largely concerned with finance. Those, I think, are the main ones.

For the women in South Africa, unpaid activities often had a strong cultural and self-help overtone. Nozuko, for example, spoke about a women's club of which she is an active member:

> I'm a member of a women's club when I arrived in [city] we were women that originally come from [name of place] (previously an apartheid homeland) and we felt the need to form a social club that would help us, because whenever there is a bereavement or something at home people say the [name of place] is too far. We can't go. So we end up going ourselves in... so this club, if there is a bereavement in my family we hire a kombi and then we go together... When we come there is nothing, so this burial, this thing is a burial society, it is also a social club. We help each other it's like, you can go down, go home, and do your thing and then the group comes and joins and helps you in the catering and everything. We meet on a monthly basis, we raise funds, we do functions catering...

Work–Life Balance/Tension Between Roles

Under work influences, the subcode of *work–life balance and the tensions between roles* while trying to balance them emerged strongly from the stories of the women. Managing these different roles, responsibilities, and conflicting demands often proved to be challenging. Janice, in Australia, spoke about the flexibility and adaptability required to keep everything in balance with a young family and employment, without the support of her close family:

> That's right and just the whole juggling. You know what working mothers are like! I had no family in [City]. My family were in [City] for a while and then they moved up here because my sister needed more help with her family. So I didn't have any parents in [City] so it was always either friends helped me or you paid for somebody to come and care for the kids. That was very hard, that juggling.

These sentiments were echoed by women in England. Isabel identified the pressures associated with being the first woman in an employing organization to return to work soon after the birth of her baby:

> It was then particularly difficult. I was the first person actually to have a family in that ... current team that I was working in. I was certainly the first person to return to work and it just wasn't the done thing at the time. And I have worked fulltime ever since. So that's been quite difficult to balance that.

The juggling of work and family pressures are highlighted by Blanche, in South Africa, who reflected on the reaction of her children and the negative impact that had had on her:

> I suppose from a more personal perspective, earlier on in the career, is really that balancing act of being a mother and trying to grow a career. Um, I suppose my least satisfying moments have been at times where I have felt that the feedback that I get from children is 'oh, you were too busy working'. And in hindsight one understands that. But it isn't a good place to be in that regard.

Social Influences

The dominance of the master code of *social influences* and the relational nature of the women's careers are perhaps to be expected in view of extant theories (e.g., Astin, 1984; Cook et al., 2002). Subcodes to emerge under this code were *support networks*, *role models*, and *life roles*.

Support Networks

Social influences were highly significant within the gendered roles of the older women, like homemaker and caregiver roles, constraining individual choice. Many of the women made career decisions based on relational factors (such as the husband or partner's need to be geographically mobile for his career; caring responsibilities for children, elderly, or sick relatives). In these situations, *support networks*, the first subcode, became critically important. A powerful example comes from Australian, Fleur, who felt an acute sense of isolation as a result of being located to a remote cattle property with her husband, but who found one lifeline:

> I had one resource and that was the Royal Flying Doctor nurse. At the time that we lived on that property the Flying Doctor used to come once a month and do a clinic at our station. People from other stations around came with any medical problems they had. So I looked forward to that 1 day a month, just for contact with people. The Flying Doctor nurse that was on that plane at the time... was just absolutely brilliant. I don't know how I would have coped without her. I used to really pick her brain and just pour my heart out to her and she listened and often didn't really give a lot of advice but just helped me to understand where I was.

Support networks within a working environment also proved to be invaluable. An English woman, Alice, illustrated this point:

> Sometimes you can say, use somebody to bounce ideas off of them like that. And you can often find that you get a viewpoint, which is different to yours that you can actually use to inform your sort of thoughts and beliefs.

Consistent throughout many of the women's stories was the influence of support networks through the extended family. This influence could be seen as having a negative impact on the career transitions of the women, on the one hand, in that there were expectations on them to support and meet the needs of diverse family relations. On the other hand, some women's stories indicated that their extended family network had made it possible for them to realize their career aspirations. Minty, from South Africa, told a story of parental support that enabled her to make a career transition that involved further tertiary studies:

> My parents were so helpful. Remember my daughter was very young at that time... I would pick up her bag and take her to my mum's crèche and she would look after her. My father would help with the transport.

Role Models

The influence of *role models*, the second subcode, was also evident in the career progress of the older women. Sometimes, this confirmed gender stereotyping of "women's work." An example from Australia (Fleur) relates to the influence of her mother as a strong role model on her occupational aspirations from an early age:

> The only thing that I can say right from the beginning I wanted to be a hairdresser/beautician, because my mother was one and her mother before that and it was an interest that I just have always liked. I can honestly say that's the only thing that I really ever set my sights on.

Role models in the workplace also emerged as significant influences for the career development of women. For example, Stella (England) highlighted the positive influence of a female manager:

> I suppose in the social work setting the two heads of department that I had and one of them was my supervisor, I felt there was certainly, she was someone, although she was extreme, very different from me, the professionalism that she had taught me an awful lot about, you know, things, handling difficult situations, handling staff as well because, you know, I essentially ran the department myself. And so there was that sense of it was on a good foundation because of what had gone before, although we were very different personalities.

Role models were not, however, unequivocally positive influences. Noxolo, from South Africa, spoke about her mother as a role model, who was intolerant of career aspirations to which she was unable to relate.

> My mom I would say is one of those women. She is also a hard worker. She is just a nurse but she got divorced when apparently we were very young because I don't even have a picture of my father, but she managed to do everything for us

up to here. So, she didn't believe in quitters. So, she was saying, if you want something you should do it but sometimes I would say that there is, career wise, stuff that I wanted to do in life but since she was from the rural areas I don't know how to put it, 'no, you cannot do that, it is not for us, you have to be a nurse or you have to...' She used to say that if you want to do something you have to work hard for it. No one just get anything. She doesn't like people that are more dependent on other people, you have to be independent and you have to be strong to be where you want to be in life so whatever you have started you have to finish.

Life Roles

The final subcode related to social influences was *life roles*. All of the women were operating across various life theaters. Clare, from Australia, typifies this trend:

> I do a lot of work in the home, I mean I cook, clean, shop and do all those sorts of things that most women do although I do have a husband who does some. Certainly not equal but [my husband] does some and because I have two children who are studying full time I also spend a lot of time helping them to proof read... 'Can you look at this? Can I talk to you about this?'

This is also reflected in the story of Stella, from England:

> And then there's other things. I mean obviously there's the home to run here, and supporting my mother who's recently widowed. And my daughter - although she's independent, lives in [city], still seems to need quite a bit of... as they do, support.

In the sample of Black South African women, many women's stories reflected their sensitivity to partners' and family's more traditional perceptions of life roles. Lungsi's story is typical of the impact of this influence:

> It is the sense that African men are supposed to remain as head of the household and that can affect relationships and also their status within the family... I am a mother. I am an aunt, I am a sister as well to my two sisters. I am supporting them financially and emotionally and also in church I am playing a leadership role. I am part of the executive committee and offer my services to the church community members and also workshops to the

youth, so I am playing a bigger role there as a member of the church. And then also I am a sister in-law to my in-law family. With us you continue to be *ouma koti*, I am thinking of the right word to use but the bright - bright is not the right word, but it is similar because you become this daughter in-law continuously and playing that role whenever there are functions, when there are things that need to be done by my in-laws, I play that role as well.

On the one hand, a key theme that has emerged from the stories of older women in this study is one of struggle, self-sacrifice, inequality, disadvantage, and sometimes suffering, in the attempts of these women to achieve their career ambitions, or to realize their full potential in the workplace. On the other hand, there is evidence of tenacity, perseverance, resilience, determination, courage, ingenuity, and adaptability and not a picture of compliance. The findings from the research emphasize how career support for women needs to be differentiated and subtly nuanced, to accommodate their distinctly different labor market trajectories. Significantly, common across all 36 narratives has been the lack of formal career development support at key moments in their career development that might well have made a crucial difference as international literature indicates (e.g., Bakshi, 2011). Challenges that have emerged from the research in relation to the use of traditional career theory with older women are explored next.

New Concepts and Viewpoints: Charting New Directions

Research findings from this study support existing arguments for a holistic theoretical approach for this client group that is context-sensitive. They also confirm the well-documented trends of women's employment patterns in labor markets around the world, exemplifying the trends of labor market inequality. For example, care responsibilities placed constraints on the women's ability to be employed full-time or continuously, with part-time employment and/or interruptions in career histories to have children being a feature of the career trajectories of many of the women. Additionally, the majority of the women in the sample have been employed in traditionally female employment sectors (for example, teaching, social work, office work, and retail) with a minority of these women able to progress to a senior management position. Paradoxically, while labor market patterns and trends may be understood and described across countries and have marked implications for women's careers in all countries, most career theory and practice do not incorporate labor market information adequately.

Consistent with international research (e.g., Bakshi, 2011), the support and guidance received by the women during their career journeys had come almost exclusively from informal sources such as friends, colleagues, and family. Interestingly, this finding occurs at a time when the provision of career development services for adults is being widely promoted (Cedefop, 2011). It suggests that the introduction of such services may need to be accompanied by promotional and educational strategies if they are to attract a market that has not traditionally sought such services. Findings also indicate the need for an advocacy role in formal career guidance support for older women aligned to a social action and social justice approach to practice (Bimrose & McNair, 2011). Thus, the results suggest that career development practitioners may need to adopt a wider range of roles. Further, as suggested by Arthur and McMahon (2005), career guidance practitioners may also have to implement systemic interventions (e.g., in the contexts of workplaces or families) if they are to serve this client group effectively. An example would be where a career practitioner works with the whole family, rather than with just one member of that family. Such roles and interventions necessarily have implications for the training of career guidance practitioners who have traditionally been prepared for individual interventions (e.g., career counseling).

Relevance for Multiple Cultures: Sensitivity to the Universal and the Particular

In the context of the present book and its emphasis on the expansion of career guidance and counseling to countries and contexts beyond those in which it was originally conceived, the present chapter on women's career trajectories and the implications for career guidance theory, research, policy, and practice warrant consideration. The focus of the present study uncovers the individual careers of women from diverse backgrounds, yet concurrently identifies "universal" themes (these are learning across the lifespan, transitions and responses, intrapersonal influences, work influences, financial influences, social influences, relocation, advice to others, and future planning) which suggest that, over and above cultural contexts, there are core issues faced by women through their careers. Importantly, some of these themes are also supported by international labor market statistics. However, such "universal" themes by no means suggest that these themes can be automatically applied to, or predicted for, all women. Rather, the uniqueness of individual women in their personally perceived and experienced context and culture, with deep involvement in family and community, needs to be respected. In order to do this, the development of career guidance theory, research, policy, and practice related to women needs to encourage women to narrate and reflect on the stories of their career trajectories over time.

Conclusion

The career development stories of women require an understanding of the impact of the convergence of multiple influences upon which experiences of learning and work over their life-course have been constructed. The older women in this study have made their way through two or three decades of interactions with different labor markets in three countries—yet despite contrasting country contexts, many of their experiences are similar. Significantly, common across all 36 narratives has been the lack of career development support at key moments in their career development that might well have made a crucial difference. One strength of the present research is its international focus and the potential to internationalize career theory and practice for women. In this regard, the study has been extended to other countries (specifically, Argentina, Canada, China, Germany, Italy, and Portugal). Concomitantly, such understanding will contribute to theory building and the development of practices that have relevance across national boundaries.

References

Arthur, N., & McMahon, M. (2005). Multicultural career counseling: Theoretical applications of the systems theory framework. *The Career Development Quarterly, 53*, 208–222.

Astin, H. S. (1984). The meaning of work in women's lives: A sociopsychological model of career choice and work behavior. *The Counseling Psychologist, 12*(4), 117–126.

August, R. A. (2010). Women's later life career development: Looking through the lens of the kaleidoscope career model. *Journal of Career Development Online First*. Retrieved from http://jcd.sagepub.com/content/early/2010/05/13/0894845310362221.full.pdf

Bakshi, A. J. (2011). Past adolescence, into and across adulthood: Career crises and major decisions. *International Journal for Educational and Vocational Guidance, 11*, 139–153.

Begum, N. (1994). Mirror, mirror on the wall. In N. Begum, M. Hill, & A. Stevens (Eds.), *Reflections: The views of black disabled people on their lives and community care* (pp. 17–36). London, England: Central Council for Education and Training in Social Work.

Bimrose, J. (2004). Sexual harassment in the workplace: An ethical dilemma for career guidance practice? *British Journal of Guidance and Counselling, 32*(1), 109–121.

Bimrose, J. (2008). Guidance with women. In J. A. Athanasou & R. V. Esbroeck (Eds.), *International handbook of career guidance* (1st ed., pp. 375–404). Dordrecht, The Netherlands: Springer.

Bimrose, J., & McNair, S. (2011). Career support for migrants: Transformation or adaptation? *Journal of Vocational Behavior, 78*(3), 325–334.

Bradley, H. (1996). *Fractured identities: The changing patterns of inequality*. Cambridge, MA: Polity.

Brooks, L., & Forrest, L. (1994). Feminism and career counseling. In W. B. Walsh & S. H. Osipow (Eds.), *Career counseling for women* (pp. 87–134). Hillsdale, NJ: Lawrence Erlbaum.

Bryman, A., & Burgess, R. G. (1994). Reflections on qualitative data analysis. In A. Bryman & R. G. Burgess (Eds.), *Analyzing qualitative data* (pp. 216–227). London, England: Routledge.

Cedefop [European Centre for the Development of Vocational Training]. (2011). *Working and ageing: Guidance and counselling for mature learners*. Luxembourg, Luxembourg: Publications Office of the European Union. Retrieved from http://www.cedefop.europa.eu/EN/Files/3062_en.pdf

Charmaz, K. (1995). Grounded theory. In J. A. Smith, R. Harre, & L. V. Langenhove (Eds.), *Rethinking methods in psychology* (pp. 27–49). London, England: Sage.

Charmaz, K. (2007). *Grounded theory: A practical guide through qualitative analysis*. London, England: Sage.

Commonwealth of Australia. (2001). *National strategy for an ageing Australia: An older Australia, challenges and opportunities for all*. Retrieved from http://www.health.gov.au/internet/wcms/publishing.nsf/content/ageing-ofoa-agepolicy-nsaa-nsaa.htm/$file/nsaabook.pdf

Cook, E. P., Heppner, M. J., & O'Brien, K. M. (2002). Career development of women of color and white women: Assumptions, conceptualization, and interventions from an ecological perspective. *The Career Development Quarterly, 50*(4), 291–305.

Farmer, H. S. (1997). *Diversity & women's career development*. Thousand Oaks, CA: Sage.

Fassinger, R. E. (2005). Paradigms, praxis, problems, and promise: Grounded theory in counseling psychology research. *Journal of Counseling Psychology, 52*(2), 156–166.

Glaser, B. G., & Strauss, A. L. (1967). *The discovery of grounded theory: Strategies for qualitative research*. Chicago, IL: Aldine.

Gottfredson, L. S. (1981). Circumscription and compromise: A development theory of occupational aspirations. *Journal of Counseling Psychology Monograph, 28*(6), 545–579.

Gottfredson, L. S. (1996). Gottfredson's theory of circumscription and compromise. In D. Brown, L. Brooks, & Associates (Eds.), *Career, choice and development* (3rd ed., pp. 179–232). San Francisco, CA: Jossey Bass.

Hackett, G. (1997). Promise and problems in theory and research on women's career development: Comment on Lucas (1997), Richie et al. (1997), McCracken and Weitzman (1997), Rainey and Borders (1997), and Schaefers, Epperson, and Nauta (1997). *Journal of Counseling Psychology, 44*(2), 184–188.

Hackett, G., & Betz, G. (1981). A self-efficacy approach to the career development of women. *Journal of Vocational Behavior, 18*(3), 326–339.

Harmon, L. W., & Meara, N. M. (1994). Contemporary developments in women's careers counseling: Themes of the past, puzzles for the future. In W. B. Walsh &

S. H. Osipow (Eds.), *Career counseling for women* (pp. 355–368). Hillsdale, NJ: Lawrence Erlbaum.

International Labour Office. (2010). *Women in labour markets: Measuring progress and identifying challenges.* Retrieved from http://www.ilo.org/wcmsp5/groups/public/—ed_emp/—emp_elm/—trends/documents/publication/wcms_123835.pdf

Jütting, J. P., Morrisson, C., Dayton-Johnson, J., & Drechsler, D. (2006). *Measuring gender (in)equality: Introducing the gender, institutions and development data base (GID)* (Working Paper No. 247). Paris, France: OECD Development Centre. Retrieved from http://www.oecd.org/dataoecd/17/49/36228820.pdf

King, N., & Horrocks, C. (2010). *Interviews in qualitative research.* London, England: Sage.

Lapour, A. S., & Heppner, M. J. (2009). Social class privilege and adolescent women's perceived career options. *Journal of Counseling Psychology, 56*(4), 477–494.

Marshall, J. (1989). Re-visioning career concepts: A feminist perspective. In M. B. Arthur, D. T. Hall, & B. S. Lawrence (Eds.), *Handbook of career theory* (pp. 275–312). Cambridge, UK: Cambridge University Press.

McMahon, M., Bimrose, J., & Watson, M. (2010). Older women's careers development and social inclusion. *Australian Journal of Career Development, 19*(1), 63–70.

Miles, M. B., & Huberman, A. M. (1994). *Qualitative data analysis* (2nd ed.). Thousand Oaks, CA: Sage.

Moore, S. (2009). No matter what I did I would still end up in the same position: Age as a factor defining older women's experience of labor market participation. *Work Employment Society, 23*(4), 655–671.

O'Neil, D. A., Hopkins, M. M., & Bilimoria, D. (2008). Women's careers at the start of the 21st century: Patterns and paradoxes. *Journal of Business Ethics, 80*(4), 727–743.

Patton, M. Q. (2002). *Qualitative research & evaluation methods* (3rd ed.). Thousand Oaks, CA: Sage.

Patton, W., & McMahon, M. (2006). *Career development and systems theory: Connecting theory and practice* (2nd ed.). Rotterdam, The Netherlands: Sense.

Polkinghorne, D. E. (1994). Reaction to special section on qualitative research in counseling process and outcome. *Journal of Counseling Psychology, 41*(4), 510–512.

Polkinghorne, D. E. (2005). Language and meaning: Data collection in qualitative research and practice in adult literacy. *Journal of Counseling Psychology, 52*(2), 137–145.

Rainey, L. M., & Borders, L. D. (1997). Influential factors in career orientation and career aspiration of early adolescent girls. *Journal of Counseling Psychology, 44*(2), 160–172.

Savickas, M. L. (1993). Career counseling in the postmodern era. *Journal of Cognitive Psychotherapy, 7*(3), 205–215.

Savickas, M. L. (1997). Constructivist career counseling: Models and methods. *Advances in Personal Construct Psychology, 4*(2), 149–182.

Smeaton, D., & Vegeris, S. (2009). *Older people inside and outside the labor market: A review.* London, England: Policy Studies Institute. Retrieved from http://www.equalityhumanrights.com/uploaded_files/research/22._older_people_inside_and_outside_the_labor_market_a_review.pdf

Thörnqvist, C. (2006). Family-friendly labor market policies and careers in Sweden—And the lack of them. *British Journal of Guidance and Counselling, 34*(3), 309–326.

U.S. Bureau of Labor Statistics. (2006). *Charting the U.S. labor market in 2005.* Retrieved from http://www.bls.gov/cps/labor2005/home.htm

United Nations. (2010a). *Facts and figures on women worldwide.* Retrieved from http://www.unwomen.org/wp-content/uploads/2010/06/UNWomen_FactsAndFiguresOnWomen_20100702.pdf

United Nations. (2011). *The millennium development goals report 2011.* Retrieved from http://www.un.org/milleniumgoals/11-MDG%20Report_EN.pdf

United Nations. (2010b). *End poverty 2015: Millenium development goals* (DPI/2650 C). Retrieved from http://www.un.org/millenniumgoals/pdf/MDG_FS_3_EN.pdf

Young, R. A., & Valach, L. (2000). Reconceptualising career theory and research: An action-theoretical perspective. In A. Collin & R. A. Young (Eds.), *The future of career* (pp. 181–196). Cambridge, England: Cambridge University Press.

The Immigrant, Expatriate, and Repatriate Experience: How Career Professionals Can Smooth the Way?

Roberta A. Neault

Introduction

It has long been recognized that immigrants have unique counseling needs (Westwood & Ishiyama, 1991). However, in today's global economy it has become increasingly difficult to distinguish immigrants from expatriates and global careerists. Although in many ways that distinction may not matter, from a career counseling perspective, career planning, career decision-making, and career management strategies may be very different for a client who has migrated to a place he or she intends to make a permanent home (an immigrant), a client who has taken on a temporary international assignment (an expatriate), and a client who has made a career of moving to wherever the work may be (a global careerist).

Similarly, there are different types of repatriates. Some individuals return to their own countries after intentionally temporary experiences abroad (e.g., international students following graduation, employees in a multinational organization reassigned to their home office, or military families posted back home after international service). Others leave their international career paths when a shifting economy makes it impossible to sustain employment abroad, health problems require medical care at home, or family members need additional

support. Still others are wooed home after a targeted national campaign to repatriate skilled workers.

Some international workers also have family members migrating with them. Families may include trailing spouses (i.e., partners who migrate but do not work or whose careers take on secondary importance during an international placement), *third-culture kids* who may have been raised abroad and have little sense of cultural allegiance to the country whose passport they hold, or even parents and other relatives who are being supported by the international worker.

In this chapter, the literature examined relates to the career realities of immigrants, expatriates, and global careerists—while working away from home and also upon repatriation. Very little on this topic has been published in the counseling literature leaving counselors and career practitioners uninformed about the special needs of these unique populations. Perhaps because they are familiar with career services and community resources designed to support immigrants, counselors tend to consider *all* international students and workers as *immigrants*, overlooking the very different motivations and needs between immigrants, expatriates, and global careerists. An understanding of the unique career challenges of these different types of internationally mobile workers can, however, be drawn from other sources—primarily business and economics publications. Following a description of the groups and the challenges

R.A. Neault (✉)
Life Strategies Ltd., Aldergrove, BC, Canada
e-mail: Roberta@lifestrategies.ca

G. Arulmani et al. (eds.), *Handbook of Career Development*, International and Cultural Psychology,
DOI 10.1007/978-1-4614-9460-7_32, © Springer Science+Business Media, LLC 2014

they face, the chapter concludes with strategies designed to ensure that the support offered by career counselors and other career development practitioners is practical and relevant.

A Globally Mobile Workforce

Within recent decades, both counseling and human resource management literature has reported a new approach to careers—rather than an expectation of jobs for life, a new type of "boundaryless" career has emerged (Stahl, Miller, & Tung, 2002), resulting in a different type of psychological contract between individuals and their employers, a contract that lasts only as long as both parties' needs are being met. If career counselors are to adequately support the diverse clients they encounter, it is essential that they understand emerging career patterns. Not all "newcomers" or foreign workers are immigrants to a country—many are members of the expatriate workforce and some *global careerists* treat the world as their workplace (Neault, 2007). The following sections provide brief case examples of immigrants, expatriates (both *assigned* and *self-initiated*; Tornikoski, 2011), and global careerists, as well as a variety of repatriation experiences.

Immigrants: Growing New Roots

Some mobile workers have every intention of making their new country a permanent home. Jalwinder[1] is one such example. From the Punjab region in India, he has moved to a rural community in Western Canada to join two uncles who operate a large berry farm. After 2 years, Jalwinder briefly returned to India to get married and then relocated his new wife to Canada. She, too, works for the family business. Her brother, still in India, is also considering a move to Canada; he plans to bring their parents with him.

Countries like Canada have been settled by immigrant workers. Although the typical immigrants' countries of origin have changed over the years, immigration continues to be an important source of skilled workers in a wide range of occupations, from tradespeople to professional and technical workers. Many immigrants are entrepreneurs, building businesses that employ others, just as Jalwinder's uncles have done.

It is this group of mobile workers that career service providers are most used to serving. In some areas, specialized settlement services help newcomers transition to the local culture and customs. Immigrant services may also include access to translators, language classes, and support getting foreign credentials assessed and recognized. Some immigrants struggle to reestablish their pre-immigration careers, settling for survival jobs in their early years in the new country. Many parents make a choice to sacrifice their own careers and comfort, in order to focus on providing future opportunities for their children.

Unfortunately, however, it is not uncommon for other types of mobile workers (e.g., expatriates and global careerists) to be confused with immigrants. Also, immigrants' children and grandchildren, especially if members of visible minority groups, may be treated as if they too are immigrants, even if they hold a local passport and have lived their entire life within a single community. Clearly, the needs of a second or third generation citizen of a country are considerably different from the needs of someone who just arrived from abroad. Career practitioners, therefore, need to understand the variations within a global workforce and how to adjust their approach to meet the real needs of the diverse clients they serve. The following sections introduce two groups of global workers who, depending on where in the world they are working, may be confused with immigrants even though their needs are very different.

Expatriates: An International Experience

Expatriate workers can be defined as those who temporarily leave their countries of origin to

---

[1] Case examples in this chapter are composites to disguise identifying information and preserve confidentiality.

pursue short- or longer-term career opportunities abroad. Within this group, there are distinct subgroups (Altman & Baruch, 2011). Low-skilled migrant workers, at one extreme of the continuum, may be hired for jobs that are not attracting local workers. Jorge, for example, comes from Mexico every summer to pick apples in Washington State in the United States. He does not bring his family with him, has limited English skills, and lives in temporary housing on the farm. Even if his goal was to become a permanent citizen of the United States, his work permit will not allow that. His "home" is, and remains, in Mexico—he commutes annually to the United States for seasonal work. Eggerth and Flynn's (2012) research on the work adjustment of Latino workers similar to Jorge found that they are mostly focused on basic survival needs.

On the other end of the continuum is Helmut, an *assigned expatriate*. Helmut is an engineer, posted to China to manage a major bridge-building project for his German employer. Helmut's lifestyle is what would traditionally be considered that of an *expat*—his family has relocated with him and his friends are primarily members of the international expatriate community. Helmut and his wife live in a neighborhood populated primarily by expatriates, he is paid considerably more than his local counterparts, and his compensation package includes a return "home" every year for his entire family. Although German is his primary language, and all of the local workers speak Chinese, Helmut has found English to be the common language amongst his expat colleagues, so that is the language he has focused on studying. Helmut's children are attending an international boarding school a few hours away. Helmut has agreed to this one international placement, as he believes it will help advance his career once he returns home. He and his family are treating this temporary assignment as an adventure—although many expatriate postings are considerably longer, Helmut expects to be away for a maximum of 2 years.

Jessica is another type of expatriate worker, a *self-initiated expatriate*, teaching English in Japan. She took a contract directly after graduating from university, an "overseas experience" (OE) that is quite common for young adults from her homeland in New Zealand (NZ). Jessica welcomes this opportunity to develop her cultural competency; when not teaching English, she is learning all she can about Japan and studying the local language. Like Helmut, she sees this as a temporary experience. Unlike Helmut, however, she is not living a privileged lifestyle; instead, she is finding it a bit expensive to get by on what she is earning, especially when she is paying off student loans at home. Jessica's long-term boyfriend is still at university; they keep in touch by Skype and look forward to living together in NZ when Jessica returns from Japan next year.

Ironically, it seems easy to recognize Helmut and Jessica as expats when they are Caucasians working in Asia but they would likely be considered immigrants if they were working in Canada, the United States, or the UK. However, their career expectations and needs for support are, in reality, quite different from what an immigrant colleague's would be. Neither Helmut nor Jessica is planning to settle long term in their host countries. They are both there for a specific purpose; should their jobs end unexpectedly, they would likely return home rather than look for other work where they are. Although Jessica is interested in learning about Japan while she is there and Helmut is treating his international experience as an adventure, neither is making local friends nor working to build personal and professional networks within their local communities. In fact, they expect their career growth to continue back home, so that is where they are maintaining their professional connections. As most of their family and friends are at home, too, that is also where they focus most of their relational and emotional energy.

Global Careerists: The World Is Their Workplace

There is another group of expatriate workers quite different from Helmut and Jessica; these are global careerists who see the world as their workplace and may move across continents as opportunities arise (Neault, 2007; Tornikoski, 2011). Eduardo is one such example. Born in Argentina to German parents, he went to university in Spain and then worked in Italy for 3 years after graduation. It was there that he met his wife, Cora, from Australia. They both took contracts in New Zealand for a while to be closer to her family, but then Eduardo got the job of his dreams in Thailand and Cora became a *trailing spouse*, putting her own career on hold while they raised three young children. After 4 years in Thailand, Eduardo's family relocated to Argentina to help his aging parents; Eduardo worked in Argentina for the next 3 years and the children attended a local school to learn about their Argentine roots. Eduardo's company asked if he would move to India to set up a satellite office and he agreed. The children began attending an international school, which they continued to do until they graduated; in the meantime, Cora had returned to work and the family moved to Eastern Europe, Cambodia, and South Africa over the next 10 years.

Not surprisingly, children like Eduardo's and Cora's are called *third-culture kids*. Although the children were all born in Thailand, that is not where they consider home. However, neither does Australia (their Mom's birthplace) feel like home; although they were immersed in Argentine culture for a few years, they do not consider Argentina home either. They have more in common with peers from their international schools than their cousins in Argentina or Australia; they have been raised by global careerists to see the world as their home. This, of course, has implications for career counseling. In the career center in their international school, Eduardo and Cora's children are exposed to post-secondary institutions and job opportunities from all over the world. There is no assumption that they will remain in the city, or even the country, where they are currently attending school. This is quite different support than they would have received in the school that they attended in Argentina or if they were in a local school in North America, being considered immigrants rather than global citizens.

Aside from traditional international assignments, individuals and organizations are increasingly using such options as business travel, *commuter assignments* (where the family does not relocate), and *virtual assignments* where an individual may work on, or even manage, an international project through the use of information technology without ever leaving home (Collings, Scullion, & Morley, 2007). From a work visa perspective, this can raise a new set of challenges. For example, a teaching contract that I once had with an American university required me to complete standard work permit documentation that simply did not fit for online instructors. Questions like "What day do you land in the United States?" and "What day do you leave the United States?" were very challenging to answer; I was teaching online and, therefore, never physically left my office in Canada. However, as responses to each of those questions was required, it was not an option to leave any of them blank. Virtual mobility within the global workplace is another work option that career counselors need to understand.

Repatriates: Coming Home

Just as there are significant differences between immigrants, expatriates, and global careerists, so there are differences when individuals who have lived, worked, or studied abroad return to their home country. Jalwinder and his family made the choice to emigrate (i.e., leave India to make a new home in Canada). Should they at some point choose to repatriate to India, it would be very similar to a second immigration experience. They intended their move to be permanent; although they may return to India to visit family and friends and to introduce their children to their cultural roots, repatriating to India is not their goal—Canada has become their home.

Despite this loyalty to their new country, however, there is an increasing trend of *returnees*—especially to rapidly developing countries like India and China (Wadhwa, Saxenian, Freeman, & Gereffi, 2009). Jalwinder and his wife might take the business skills that they have learned on their uncle's farm, combine them with some formal education while they are in Canada, and return to India to establish a business there. However, this type of repatriation is quite different from the experience of expatriates such as Jessica and Helmut.

Jessica and Helmut have both viewed their host countries as only a temporary career stopover—they accepted short-term assignments with the expectation that they would return to their original countries within a few years and that their careers and lives would have benefitted from their international experiences. Statistically, however, 6 % of expatriates do not complete the full terms of their assignments (Brookfield Global Relocation Services, 2011); when assigned expatriates request an early return home, the reason is often related to family concerns. According to the Brookfield report, international assignees left their organizations at the same rate as regular employees (8 %). However, most of the assigned expatriates who left their companies did so mid-assignment (22 %), during their first year back home (28 %), or during their second year home (24 %). Only 26 % of those who eventually left remained with their employers 2 years after their return home. Unfortunately, however, only 14 % of the organizations in this study formally linked career management and retention to their repatriation strategies.

Some repatriates (e.g., international consultants, international bankers) find that their international experience is highly valued by employers when they return home. This tends to be especially true for individuals repatriating to a developing country with professional education and/or work experience from the West. An unexpected repatriation challenge, however, can occur when local culture and organization culture clash. For example, although an American or British expatriate working for an international consulting firm in Cambodia can do business without bribing, a Cambodian-born colleague, transferred to his home country after working for the firm in Australia, was expected by local business people to adhere to the local business culture. As his employer did not allow him to pay bribes, but local people would not do business

with him without one, ironically this highly skilled consultant found himself unable to do business effectively back in his home country as long as he remained working for the multinational firm.

Facing different challenges, many repatriates like Jessica and Helmut are surprised to find that their work abroad is not well understood by employers back home and, in fact, may be under-valued (Benson & Pattie, 2008; Bolino, 2007). When Jessica repatriated, she found that potential employers were interested in her "trip to Japan" but did not see her time there as "real work" and could not see its relevance to her work back in NZ. In supporting her transition, a career counselor helped Jessica to emphasize her skills and accomplishments on the first page of her resume, without any mention until Page 2 about where that experience had been acquired. Jessica also worked with her counselor to build a career portfolio of work samples that clearly illustrated the quality of the teaching aids and handouts that she had developed while working abroad. Helmut had expected a promotion upon his repatriation. Even within his own organization, however, being away for 2 years seemed to have had an "out of sight, out of mind" impact. He applied for several internal positions during his first year back and then, in frustration, sought out a career coach who encouraged him to consider another international posting where his rich experience in China would be highly valued. Helmut eventually accepted an offer from another firm who posted him back to China; he is an example of an assigned expatriate unintentionally joining the ranks of the global careerist.

James was a Canadian student who completed his law degree in Australia. With an exceptional undergraduate transcript, he had been accepted by prestigious Canadian law schools. However, he chose to attend law school in Australia, reasoning that the law was similar between Commonwealth countries and it would be good to have an international experience before returning to Canada to build his career. Much to his surprise upon his return, James' international education was less transferable than he had expected. He had to repeat more than half of his law degree in Canada and, even then, had trouble finding an organization that would hire him. Similarly, medical doctors, teachers, midwives, and many other Canadians educated abroad find they need to participate in bridging programs or professional upgrading to facilitate credential recognition before they can work in their professions back home.

James', Jessica's, and Helmut's repatriation experiences are surprisingly similar to the challenges that immigrant professionals have when attempting to reestablish their pre-immigration careers; their international experiences and, in James' case, education were not fully appreciated by employers in their home countries (Lamontagne, 2003). In all three cases, though, these challenges were unexpected; they were returning home, not trying to build careers in foreign countries. They did not have any of the barriers typically associated with immigrant professionals—they spoke the local language fluently, were returning to their own culture, and had preexisting personal and professional networks.

Some repatriates, of course, do find that their international experience helps to build their careers. Cathy, for example, was able to capitalize on her 3 years as a human resource management professional in South East Asia. Her employer in Western Canada valued her cultural knowledge and international contacts in her Canadian work role which involved recruiting and facilitating the orientation and inclusion of skilled immigrants. However, in several cases, as previously described, international experience seems to have the opposite impact—setting careers back rather than moving them forward.

There is another type of repatriate, briefly mentioned when discussing possibilities for Jalwinder's future. Some countries are addressing their current and anticipated skill shortages by actively encouraging their skilled workers who have emigrated, or are working temporarily abroad, to come home (European Commission, 2011). However, as New Zealand MP Nikki Kaye (2011) recently acknowledged, "there is no one policy that will bring more expats home. Only through a combination of

policies that improve wages, increase jobs, improve housing affordability and better schools will we see more New Zealanders coming home" (para. 9).

For some expatriates, their return home is at the end of their career, to retire. This group may have even less access to repatriation transition supports than repatriates who return to work. They may also have less access to retirement planning supports than those leaving their careers with local employers. If career counselors are committed to providing lifelong career guidance to diverse clients at all life stages, they need to more fully understand the specific needs of global workers, whether their moves are due to immigration, expatriation, or repatriation. Career counselors need to be equipped to provide appropriate services regardless of whether individuals' intentions are to stay in the current country, go to another country, or leave the workforce and retire. The following sections highlight some of the challenges encountered by immigrants, expatriates, repatriates, and global careerists, and strategies that career counselors can use to better meet their needs.

Career Challenges for Immigrants, Expatriates, Repatriates, and Global Careerists

Although the counseling literature tends to focus on the needs of immigrants or international students, there is much published in the business literature on the needs of expatriates, repatriates, and global careerists. Surveys on the career challenges of program participants and alumni from a Canadian-based international management cooperative program resulted in similar findings about the overarching challenges faced by mobile international workers (Neault, 2003). Although reported challenges can be clustered into cultural, relational, physical, educational, and career concerns, this section will focus primarily on career concerns.

Whether immigrating, reporting for an expatriate assignment, embarking on a self-initiated expatriate adventure, stringing together multiple international contracts in a global career, or repatriating, most international workers struggle with adjustment issues including culture shock. Although culture shock tends to be more expected when moving to a foreign place, *re-entry shock* can be just as jarring and uncomfortable when returning home after working or studying abroad.

Mobile workers may struggle with a wide range of relational issues as well. Even if competency in the local language is not required professionally, it can certainly help with day-to-day tasks like shopping, asking for directions, or accessing local services. Maintaining personal and professional relationships can also be a challenge—some international workers live within an *expat bubble*, forming very few local connections. Repatriation can be disappointing for many; returning home permanently may result in a very different level of connection with family and friends than being the center of attention on brief visits home. It is not uncommon for mobile workers to struggle with identity issues as they realize they are no longer the same as before their international move but also not fully acculturated to their host country's practices.

Many mobile workers and their families also experience health issues related to different levels of pollution, unfamiliar foods, and less than adequate sanitation. Even staying fit can be a challenge; people used to distance running outdoors in North America may struggle to find a similar fitness activity on the crowded streets of major international cities, with different air quality regulations. Maio and Kemp (2010), reporting a longitudinal study of immigrants to Canada, found that despite new immigrants arriving in better health than the average Canadian, this advantage does not persist. Instead poorer socioeconomic status, discrimination, and unequal access to community services negatively impacted immigrants' physical and mental health during their early years in Canada. Lebrun (2012) reported similar findings, especially for immigrants with limited local language proficiency—newer immigrants to Canada and the United States were less likely to access

health care than those who had been in their new country for 10 years or longer.

Recognition of education, foreign credentials, and work experiences can be challenging for mobile workers. In Canada, for example, immigration "points" are awarded at a federal (national) level; consideration is given to level of education and work experience. However, occupations are regulated at a provincial level; as a result, immigrants or self-initiated expatriates may be granted work visas to enter Canada but, upon arrival, not be eligible to work in their pre-immigration fields (Lamontagne, 2003; Neault, 2006). Although this tends to be less of an issue for assigned expatriates who continue working for the same employer, it may surface as an issue upon repatriation, particularly if recent professional education or new credentials were acquired abroad. This can also be an issue for trailing spouses who hope to reestablish their careers either internationally or upon their return home—many find that their credentials are not as mobile as they had expected or have expired during their absence from the labor market. These challenges are not unique to Canada; Walker (2007) reported remarkably similar issues in both Australia and New Zealand. For example, although language proficiency and professional qualifications are assessed pre-immigration to Australia, being granted immigrant status is no guarantee that foreign credentials will be recognized by professional regulatory bodies. Although the government situation in New Zealand is slightly less complicated (i.e., there are no state or provincial jurisdiction issues over credentialing such as are found in the United States, Canada, and Australia), immigrants still encounter challenges with credential recognition. However, the primary difference in New Zealand is that the two-step process (i.e., government assessment and credential recognition by the appropriate regulatory authority) occurs concurrently. This has, in turn, privileged applicants from countries like the United Kingdom and South Africa whose professional qualifications are recognized as equivalent to New Zealand standards.

A great deal of attention has been paid, in both the counseling and business literature, to the unemployment and underemployment of immigrants. Studies of immigrant professionals in Canada (Lau, 2010; Lee & Westwood, 1996; Novicevic, Zikic, & Fang, 2009), OECD countries (Stören, 2004), the United States (Waldinger, Bozorgmehr, Lim, & Finkel, 1998), and Israel (Remennick, 2003) show remarkably similar patterns. In the Israeli study, following the careers of 372 Russian engineers in the 1990s, 5 years after immigrating only 20 % were employed as engineers in their pre-immigration area of specialization, 17 % had retrained into a different specialization within engineering, 25 % were working in skilled positions in other fields, 28 % were employed in unskilled jobs, and 9 % were unemployed. For those who had made a successful professional transition, it had taken them on average 2.5 years to get their first "relevant" job. In the Norwegian study (Stören, 2004), and an American study (Sangganjanavanich, Lenz, & Cavazos, 2011), the unemployment challenges also applied to international students who chose to remain in the country after graduation (i.e., even if their professional education was local, immigrants had more challenges attaching to the workforce). Lau (2010) identified a pattern of career compromise for immigrant skilled workers, crediting openmindedness and human agency for their ultimate success.

Canadian Lamontagne's (2003) provocative title, "Seduction and Abandonment," captures the experience of many skilled immigrants who are actively encouraged to immigrate to a country based on their previous education and work experience, but then provided with insufficient supports to successfully find professional employment in their new home. He classified typical challenges into the broad categories of lack of experience and credential recognition, limited language proficiency, insufficient knowledge about local work practices and standards, discrimination, and limited knowledge about programs or services that could facilitate a successful transition. Many other researchers report similar challenges (Basran & Zong, 1998;

Canada Immigrants Job Issues, 2011; Reitz, 2001; Salaff, Greve, & Ping, 2002). Immigrants, especially those who are visible minorities (i.e., people who look or dress different from their local coworkers and neighbors), often share stories of discrimination; this tends to be exacerbated by language proficiency challenges, even for those fluent in the local language who speak it with a strong foreign accent.

In the business literature, the value of international work experience in moving one's career forward has been explored. Jokinen, Brewster, and Suutari (2008) found similarities between the *career capital* of self-initiated and assigned expatriates. In another study, van der Heijden, van Engen, and Paauwe (2009), not surprisingly, found that if expatriates perceived career support from their organizations, their performance was better and they expressed less intention to leave. An interesting finding of their study, however, was that there was no similar relationship between perceived career opportunities outside of their organizations and their intent to leave (i.e., an internal career development program rather than external economic realities seemed to have more of an impact). Shen and Hall (2009) also highlighted the impact of organizational career development initiatives on retention of valuable expatriate and repatriate talent.

Hutchings, French, and Hatcher (2008) identified significant gender differences amongst the career experiences of expatriates; although organizations reported treating men and women equally, that was not the perception of the female expatriates in the study. Several other researchers have reported on the unique career experiences of female expatriates, including their underrepresentation at the management level compared to women who remained working locally (Hartl, 2004) and the negative impact of an international family move on wives' employment status for the first year or two after the relocation (Spitze, 1984). Researchers have also reported on women experiencing an "expatriate glass ceiling" preventing them from getting the foreign experience they need to advance their careers (Insch, McIntyre, & Napier, 2008) and the impact of gender on the careers of immigrant women

(Rasouli, Dyke, & Mantler, 2008; Yakushko, 2006). Immigrant women, for example, tend to be the primary homemakers and may temporarily put their own careers on hold as they support a spouse to get reconnected to the workforce and help their children get settled into their new community and schools (Koert, Borgen, & Amundson, 2011). Being out of the workforce upon arrival may cause a second inequity—lack of access to workplace-based skills and language upgrading.

Finally, there is a significant body of literature describing the impact of repatriation on careers (Menzies & Lawrence, 2011; Stahl, Chua, Caligiuri, Cerdin, & Taniguchi, 2009; Tharenou & Caulfield, 2010). Bolino (2007) presented a model illustrating the complexity of expatriate assignments on subsequent career success, concluding this relationship "is not so straightforward" (p. 881). Similarly, Kraimer, Shaffer, and Bolino (2009) reported mixed results from their analysis of repatriates' career paths; although developmental expatriate assignments positively correlated with career advancement, the same was not true of building cultural competency, gaining management experience, or successfully completing an assignment abroad (i.e., none of these correlated with career advancement). The literature abounds with examples of employees frustrated by their repatriation experiences, including descriptions of reduced prestige and job responsibilities as well as loss of important local professional networks (McDonald & Arthur, 2003). Lazarova and Cerdin (2007) highlighted the increasing dependence on "individual career activism"; sadly, however, a recent Global Career Trends report (Brookfield Global Relocation Services, 2011) found few companies (14 %) with formal career management supports in place aimed at retaining their repatriates compared to slightly more (22 %) with a formal career management process for international assignments. The consensus in the literature is that international experiences have a mixed impact on career success; this is different from what many are led to believe before they accept their first international posting.

Strategic Interventions: How Career Counselors/Practitioners Can Help

Career counselors can play a significant role in supporting the careers of the various types of internationally mobile workers introduced in this chapter, including assigned expatriates and repatriates, many of whom have inadequate career support within their organizations. Although effective interventions need to be targeted to meet the unique needs of each individual client or family, this section presents holistic approaches extracted from the literature review. Recent career counseling literature presents relevant theoretical perspectives that can serve as useful foundations for most cross-cultural counseling interactions; Arthur and Collins' (2011) culture-infused approach to counseling, Leong's (2011) cultural accommodation model, Arulmani's (2009a, 2009b) cultural preparedness framework, and Pope's (2011) career counseling for under-served populations (CCUSP) are four such examples.

Arthur and Collins' (2011) culture-infused counseling is based on the premise that culture is relevant in career interventions with all clients, not just those in designated groups, and that counselors and career practitioners bring their own cultures to their work, which needs to be acknowledged and accounted for as well. They noted that our understanding of career and career issues is socially defined and that all career theories and models contain cultural assumptions. In a culture-infused approach, career goals and interventions are collaborative activities to ensure a reasonable cultural fit.

The cultural accommodation model attends to three domains of human identity: Universal (U), Group (G), and Individual (I) (Leong, 2011). This approach encourages counselors to begin by identifying cultural gaps or blind spots in the theories they use, then integrating relevant culture-specific constructs to fill those gaps, and testing the accommodated model or theory to determine its utility.

Arulmani (2009a, 2009b) similarly has advocated for incorporating culturally relevant content into case conceptualization and design of career interventions. He provided a compelling example of a career program in India, *Jiva*, which incorporates widely accepted and highly valued cultural constructs. Jiva, which means *life* in many Indian languages, was the theme for an international symposium on career development hosted in Bangalore, India, in 2011.

Pope (2011) extended the notion of culture to include groups who are traditionally under-served by career counselors. His model (CCUSP) offers 13 keys for effective practice with individuals from minority groups. Similar to Arthur and Collins (2011) and Arulmani (2009a, 2009b), Pope's 13 keys highlight the importance of acknowledging our own biases and, where necessary, playing an advocacy role to access appropriate supports and services for diverse clients, as well as knowing the unique issues encountered by members of specific cultural groups.

Set within an overall theoretically grounded counseling approach, the following ten strategies are intended to guide your work with internationally mobile clients and their families:

1. *Do not assume.* Recognize that not all newcomers you encounter will be immigrants; some may be migrant workers, expatriates, global careerists, trailing spouses, or third-culture kids. Also recognize that not all "locals" will have local experience; some of your clients may be repatriating, with all of their recent experience abroad.

2. *Listen carefully.* Your clients all have stories to tell; this is especially true for internationally mobile workers and their families. Take time to thoroughly assess each client's goals and needs. A one-size-fits-all approach does not work with this diverse group. For example, a trailing spouse who is choosing to use his or her partner's 2-year international posting as an opportunity to complete a Master's degree online will have very different needs for career counseling support than a trailing spouse who is struggling to reattach to a professional career in the new location.

3. *Address first things first.* Maslow (1943) identified a hierarchy of needs, which he presented as common to all individuals. As part of your initial assessment, confirm that survival needs have been met and, if not, address them first. However, also recognize that not all newcomers will require survival jobs or local language classes. Some will be closer to the self-actualization end of Maslow's hierarchy, looking for opportunities to fully contribute the skills they have to offer. In the career engagement model (Neault & Pickerell, 2011), underutilization is a contributing factor to disengagement. Sadly, many immigrants, migrant workers, trailing spouses, and repatriates are unable to find career challenges that are sufficient to facilitate engagement at work.

Your clients' cultural backgrounds will influence what each of them perceive as their top priority needs—for some, financial security, respect, or prestige may be much more important than Maslow's notion of self-actualization. Cerdin and Le Pargneux (2009) underscored "internationalism" as one of the most dominant career anchors for expatriates. This means that many expatriates highly value their international work experiences and identity as global citizens. Career counselors, therefore, need to take time to understand their clients' motivations before suggesting entry-level local jobs that may be completely misaligned with their clients' career values or goals.

4. *Customize interventions to the stage of migration.* Some of your clients may have never considered working abroad; you may be the first person to create awareness of the possibility of looking internationally for opportunities. Others may be in the contemplation stage of change (Prochaska & DiClemente, 1982)—your role may be to help them assess their global career competencies and/or readiness for an international experience. Other clients may have recently arrived or be in the process of leaving; they may need settlement or relocation

support. It is helpful to be aware of resources within your community that can provide relevant short-term assistance for those just arriving and to have access to relocation consultants to help those preparing to leave. As career counselors, it is reasonable to assume that most of the clients you see will be ready to work. As some, however, may be unaware of local regulations, providing information may be an important role for you at this stage. Repatriating clients may expect a seamless return to work; if they discover more barriers than anticipated, they may need your support to find ways to better explain their international work experience so that local employers can fully understand the transferability of their skills. They may also eventually make a decision to take another international placement; many global careerists find it very difficult to secure suitably challenging work back home.

5. *Be creative.* In the global workplace, the best career options may not be local for some of your clients. Third-culture kids may have rights to work in several countries; trailing spouses may find it more effective to complete a graduate degree online or work virtually for an employer in their home country. Repatriates may find that another international posting offers more opportunities than staying home. Even repatriates who have come home to retire may find that a temporary contract or part-time job helps with the transition process. Look beyond local opportunities for all of your clients—but especially those with international experience.

6. *Gather resources.* Your internationally mobile clients will benefit from different resources than those useful for clients who are only job-searching locally. If you have a resource center, consider adding some of Robin Pascoe's books; although now retired, she has written guides for expatriate women, repatriating spouses, raising global nomad children, and other practical books related to international careers and their impact on families. Her website, expatexpert.com, provides links to free YouTube lectures based on those books; the lectures address loss of identity, challenges of "moveable marriages," the question of "where is 'home' for a third-culture kid?," and many other topics relevant to expatriates and their families. If you provide links from your website, consider linking to government sites that describe local employment standards (helpful for the expatriates and immigrants you are serving) as well as blogs that serve the expatriate community (e.g., http://www.expat-blog.com/). Some financial institutions have extensive information online for their expat clients; you may want to link to HSBC's Expat Explorer as a starting place (http://expatexplorer.hsbc.com)—it provides survey results from over 3,000 expats in 2011.

7. *Facilitate mentorship opportunities.* Carraher, Sullivan, and Crocitto (2008) researched the impact of home- and host-country mentors on expatriate careers using information from surveys as well as company records. In total, 299 expatriates in 10 countries participated, reporting that both types of mentors (home- and host-country) were helpful in sharing knowledge about the organization and facilitating the expatriate's job performance and promotability. The authors were surprised to find, however, that home-country mentors had a negative impact on both the expatriate's identification with the organization and also his/her job satisfaction. Therefore, career practitioners may serve a useful role in organizing local mentors for newcomers, whether immigrants or expatriates.

8. *Support workplace-based career development programs.* Although there are benefits noted in the literature for organizations to offer career management support to their expatriate and repatriate workers (Brookfield Global Relocation Services, 2011; Stahl et al., 2002; Tornikoski, 2011), in most reported cases there is very little actually in place. Career counselors could partner with local employers

to offer career management and cross-cultural training at all stages of the expatriation/repatriation cycle. Services could be extended to spouses and families to meet the specific needs of trailing spouses and third-culture kids. For example, trailing spouses may need help to understand local job search strategies or to get recognition for foreign credentials to facilitate work in their fields. Third-culture kids may need support as they apply to international universities or contemplate career possibilities far beyond their current geographic location. Initiatives could also be offered to immigrant workers; Novicevic et al. (2009) explored the impact of training and human resource practices on employee career outcomes, analyzing data from the 2003 Canadian Workplace and Employee Survey. Although they found a generally positive correlation between training and development investments and career success indicators including wages and promotions, sadly this did not hold true for immigrant professionals, many of whom seem to remain stuck in entry level, lower paying roles despite investing substantial time and effort to move their careers forward. Within workplaces, therefore, career practitioners could help employers facilitate the career development and full engagement of the immigrants that they have become so dependent upon to fill skill shortages.

9. *Facilitate career management through professional associations.* Another venue to provide career management support is through professional associations. Associations are a natural point of connection for expatriates (self-initiated and assigned), immigrants, repatriates, and returnees (i.e., repatriates who have been wooed back to contribute their talents at home), as well as a logical source of mentors. Through partnering with professional associations, career counselors could present at networking events, offer individual and group coaching, or provide career management courses and workshops.

10. *Advocate.* Counselors and career practitioners have an ethical role to play in advocating for changes that will support their clients (Neault, 2009). Such advocacy may be at a policy level (e.g., supporting changes that facilitate foreign credential recognition as recommended by Lamontagne, 2003) or at the organizational level (e.g., creating and disseminating tools that support employers to fully integrate diverse workers—the Supporting Employers Embracing Diversity [SEED] toolkit is one such example, available at www.embracingdiversity.ca).

Skillbuilding for Career Counselors and Career Practitioners

"In a rapidly changing world, how can we be confident that the information about global careers that we share with our clients is accurate?" (Neault, 2003, p. 2). Today, after a decade, this question seems to have even more relevance. Although most educational programs for counselors do tend to focus on building multicultural competency and fostering an appreciation for diversity, few introduce the specific career development needs and realities of global careerists; fewer still distinguish between immigrants, expatriates, repatriates, and the various other groups that this chapter has addressed.

The four stages of learning model (Business Balls, n.d.) acknowledges that all learning begins from a place of unconscious incompetence (i.e., people don't know what they don't know). Blind spots are revealed through exposure to diverse perspectives, formal learning, and challenging work and life experiences. This not knowing, however, has implications as individuals seek out professional development and commit to continuous learning. Specialized courses and conference presentations on the topic of immigrant careers, for example, tend to draw immigrant professionals as participants—many of whom are working in the field serving other immigrant professionals. Presenters and instructors find themselves "preaching to the choir" (i.e., the information they are sharing is already familiar to their audience; they are not reaching those who know so little about the topic that they do not even realize that there is much to learn). As people progress through the four stages of learning, they move through conscious incompetence (a place of awareness about gaps in knowledge), then conscious competence (a place where new skills and attitudes may feel awkward and unfamiliar). Finally, learning and experiences are fully integrated into unconscious competence; at this stage, career counselors, without consciously thinking about it, are confidently supporting their clients who are engaged in global careers. To help move career counselors and practitioners from unconscious incompetence to conscious incompetence where they are aware of skill deficits and inspired to fill them, exposure to new ideas and approaches is key. Guest speakers, lunch and learn sessions, case conferencing, job shadowing, conferences, seminars, and formal courses can facilitate awareness of gaps and relevant skill development.

In a recent study on career practitioners' ability to explore self-employment as a career option with their clients, we found that the single best predictor that a counselor would have a career conversation about self-employment is self-employment coaching self-efficacy (i.e., the counselor or career practitioner's self-rated knowledge and skills to support clients to explore self-employment as a career option; Neault, Pickerell, & Saunders, 2012). It seems likely, therefore, that "international career coaching self-efficacy" would be a significant predictor that a counselor would engage clients in discussing the unique challenges faced by migrant international workers and their families. This specific type of self-efficacy can be intentionally developed once the counselor is aware that a unique body of knowledge exists, and that immigrants, expatriates, repatriates, and global careerists have needs that may be quite different from clients who are focusing exclusively on local career opportunities.

Specific training on the immigrant experience or international/global careers is available in a facilitated e-learning format through Life Strategies' LearnOnline (www.lifestrategies.ca); there may be similar courses available within other educational institutions. Attending conference presentations, inviting global careerists to share their experiences, and actively seeking out opportunities to mingle with people from different cultures at home and abroad are also good ways to learn more about individuals whose careers have extended beyond your national borders.

New Challenges and Viewpoints: Charting New Directions

Earlier in this chapter you were introduced to Jalwinder, an immigrant to Canada; James, a student who completed his degree abroad; Jorge, a migrant farm worker from Mexico; Jessica, a recent graduate from New Zealand engaged in her overseas experience in Japan; Helmut, a German engineer assigned to a project in China; Cathy, repatriating to Canada after working in Asia; and Eduardo (from Argentina) and his wife, Cora (from Australia), with their three third-culture kids. Wherever you are working in the field of career development you may meet clients like these who are attempting to manage their careers within an increasingly global workplace. Are you ready to engage in meaningful career conversations with a Jalwinder, Jorge, or Jessica? Would you be able to support Helmut's repatriation or his ultimate return to an international post because of his frustrating experiences when he returned home? Do you understand the complexity that Cora faces as she sets her own career aside to become a trailing spouse and to focus on parenting her global nomad children? Could you support her to reestablish her career, in a new country where she has no local ties and cannot speak the language? How might you help Eduardo and Cora's children narrow down their educational and career options, when they really see the whole world as a potential workplace?

Although this chapter presents an expanded perspective on the career issues encountered by internationally mobile workers, it is simply an introduction to a topic that could take a lengthy book to explore. In an increasingly global workplace, it is important for counselors and career practitioners to understand the different life-work experiences of immigrants, expatriates, global careerists, repatriates, and their families, including trailing spouses and third-culture kids. Some career service providers cluster everyone "from away" as immigrants. It is hoped that the literature review and case examples provided here serve to differentiate between these diverse groups of workers so that their needs can be more clearly identified and effectively met.

Relevance for Multiple Cultures: Sensitivity to the Universal and the Particular

Although there are similarities between the diverse groups of internationally mobile workers described in this chapter, there are significant between-group and within-group differences. Several theoretical models and frameworks were briefly presented to highlight the importance of cultural accommodation (Leong, 2011), taking a culture-infused approach (Arthur & Collins, 2011), cultural preparedness (Arulmani, 2009a, 2009b), and effectively providing career support to under-served marginalized populations (Pope, 2011). However, the research and resources cited are only a sampling of an extensive body of relevant literature within which one could become deeply immersed. Further research, specific to the role of career counselors, would provide helpful guidance on how to most effectively support the diverse needs of immigrants, expatriates, repatriates, global careerists, and their families as they migrate to wherever work needs to be done, all over the world. In the meantime, however, it is hoped that this chapter provides inspiration to learn more and do more to meet the unique needs of these fascinating groups of global workers.

References

Altman, Y., & Baruch, Y. (2011). Global self-initiated corporate expatriate careers: A new era in international assignments? *Personnel Review, 41*(2), 239–259.

Arthur, N., & Collins, S. (2011). Infusing culture in career counseling. *Journal of Employment Counseling, 48* (4), 147–149.

Arulmani, G. (2009a). Striking the right note: The cultural preparedness approach to developing resonant career guidance programmes. *International Journal of Educational and Vocational Guidance, 9*(1), 79–93. doi:10.1007/s10775-011-9199-y.

Arulmani, G. (2009b). Tradition and modernity: The cultural preparedness framework for counselling in India. In L. H. Gerstein, P. P. Heppner, S. Aegisdóttir, S. M. A. Leung, & K. L. Norsworthy (Eds.), *International handbook of cross-cultural counselling* (pp. 251–262). Thousand Oaks, CA: Sage.

Basran, G. S., & Zong, L. (1998). Devaluation of foreign credentials as perceived by visible minority professional immigrants. *Canadian Ethnic Studies, 30*(3), 7–23.

Benson, G. S., & Pattie, M. (2008). Is expatriation good for my career? The impact of expatriate assignments on perceived and actual career outcomes. *The International Journal of Human Resource Management, 19* (9), 1636–1653.

Bolino, M. C. (2007). Expatriate assignments and intra-organizational career success: Implications for individuals and organizations. *Journal of International Business Studies, 38*, 819–835.

Brookfield Global Relocation Services. (2011). *Global relocation trends: 2011 survey report.* Retrieved from www.brookfieldgrs.com/knowledge/grts_research/grts_media/2011_GRTS.pdf

Business Balls. (n.d.). *Conscious competence learning model.* Retrieved from http://www.businessballs.com/consciouscompetencelearningmodel.htm

Canada Immigrants Job Issues. (2011, December). *Racism in the Canadian job market: How widespread is discrimination against visible minorities in Canada's labour market?* Retrieved from http://www.canadaimmigrants.com/

Carraher, S. M., Sullivan, S. E., & Crocitto, M. M. (2008). Mentoring across global boundaries: An empirical examination of home-and host-country mentors on expatriate career outcomes. *Journal of International Business Studies, 39*, 1310–1326.

Cerdin, J. L., & Le Pargneux, M. (2009). Career and international assignment fit: Toward an integrative model of success. *Human Resource Management, 48* (1), 5–25.

Collings, D. G., Scullion, H., & Morley, M. J. (2007). Changing patterns of global staffing in the multinational enterprise: Challenges to the conventional expatriate assignment and emerging alternatives. *Journal of World Business, 42*(2), 198–213.

Eggerth, D. E., & Flynn, M. A. (2012). Applying the theory of work adjustment to Latino immigrant workers: An exploratory study. *Journal of Career Development, 39*(1), 76–98.

European Commission. (2011). *Managing immigration fairly and effectively.* Retrieved from http://ec.europa.eu/news/justice/110526_en.htm

Hartl, K. (2004). The expatriate career transition and women managers' experiences. *Women in Management Review, 19*(1), 40–51.

Hutchings, K., French, E., & Hatcher, T. (2008). Lament of the ignored expatriate: An examination of organisational and social network support for female expatriates in China. *Equal Opportunities International, 27*(4), 372–391. doi:10.1177/0894845311417129.

Insch, G. S., McIntyre, N., & Napier, N. K. (2008). The expatriate glass ceiling: The second layer of glass. *Journal of Business Ethics, 83*(1), 19–28. doi:10. 1007/s10551-007-9649-0.

Jokinen, T., Brewster, C., & Suutari, V. (2008). Career capital during international work experiences: Contrasting self-initiated expatriate experiences and assigned expatriation. *The International Journal of Human Resource Management, 19*(6), 979–998. doi:10.1080/09585190802051279.

Kaye, N. (2011). *Broadsides: Enticing expats home.* Retrieved from http://www.nzherald.co.nz/opinion/news/article.cfm?c_id=466&objectid=10766407

Koert, E., Borgen, W. A., & Amundson, N. E. (2011). Educated immigrant women workers doing well with change: Helping and hindering factors. *Career Development Quarterly, 59*(3), 194–207.

Kraimer, M. L., Shaffer, M. A., & Bolino, M. C. (2009). The influence of expatriate and repatriate experiences on career advancement and repatriate retention. *Human Resource Management, 48*(1), 27–47. doi:10. 1002/hrm.20265.

Lamontagne, F. (2003). Workers educated abroad: Seduction and abandonment. *Food for Thought, 10,* 1–4. Retrieved from www.clbc.ca/files/Reports/Communication_Strategy_No.10_Lamontagne.pdf

Lau, K. G. I. (2010). *Career compromise in immigrant professionals in Canada* (Master's thesis, Department of Adult Education and Counselling Psychology, University of Toronto, Toronto). Retrieved from https://tspace.library.utoronto.ca/handle/1807/25660

Lazarova, M. B., & Cerdin, J. L. (2007). Revisiting repatriation concerns: Organizational support versus career and contextual influences. *Journal of International Business Studies, 38,* 404–429. doi:10.1057/palgrave.jibs.8400273.

Lebrun, L. A. (2012). Effects on length of stay and language proficiency on health care experiences among immigrants in Canada and the United States. *Social Science & Medicine, 74*(7), 1062–1072. doi:10.1016/j.socscimed.2011.11.031.

Lee, G., & Westwood, M. J. (1996). Cross-cultural adjustment issues faced by immigrant professionals. *Journal of Employment Counseling, 33*(1), 29–42.

Leong, F. T. L. (2011). Cultural accommodation model of counseling. *Journal of Employment Counseling, 48* (4), 150–152.

Maio, F. G., & Kemp, E. G. (2010). The deterioration of health status among immigrants to Canada. *Global Public Health, 5*(5), 462–478. doi:10.1080/1744169092942480.

Maslow, A. H. (1943). A theory of human motivation. *Psychological Review, 50,* 370–396.

McDonald, S., & Arthur, N. (2003). Employees' perceptions of repatriation. *Canadian Journal of Career Development, 2*(1), 3–11. Retrieved from http://ceric.ca/cjcd/archives/v2-n1/article1.pdf

Menzies, J. L., & Lawrence, A. (2011). Do repatriate support practices influence repatriate experience, organizational commitment, turnover intentions, and perceptions of career success? In P. G. Benson (Ed.), *Emerging themes in international management of human resources* (pp. 189–212). Charlotte, NC: Information Age.

Neault, R. A. (2003). Managing global careers: Changes and challenges for the 21st century. *NATCON Papers.* Retrieved from http://www.contactpoint.ca/natcon-conat/2003/pdf/pdf-03-11.pdf

Neault, R. (2006). Ring roads and roundabouts: Navigating careers in the 21st century. *NATCON Papers.* Retrieved from www.natcon.org/archive/natcon/papers/natcon_papers_2006_e4.pdf

Neault, R. A. (2007). The immigrant/expatriate/repatriate experience: International work in a global economy. *VISTAS.* Retrieved from http://counselingoutfitters.com/vistas/vistas07/Neault.htm

Neault, R. (2009). The ethics of advocacy: A Canadian perspective. *The Bulletin.* Retrieved from http://www.contactpoint.ca/index.php?option=com_content&view=article&id=75&catid=38&Itemid=37

Neault, R. A., & Pickerell, D. A. (2011). Career engagement: Bridging career counseling and employee engagement. *Journal of Employment Counseling, 48* (4), 185–188.

Neault, R. A., Pickerell, D. A., & Saunders, C. M. (2012). *Look before you leap*: The role of self-employment coaching self-efficacy in facilitating client's success. *Canadian Journal of Career Development, 11*(1), 59–66.

Novicevic, M. M., Zikic, J., & Fang, T. (2009). Career success of immigrant professionals: Stock and flow of their career capital. *International Journal of Manpower, 30*(5), 472–488.

Pope, M. (2011). The career counseling with under-served populations model. *Journal of Employment Counseling, 48*(4), 153–155.

Prochaska, J. O., & DiClemente, C. C. (1982). Transtheoretical therapy: Toward a more integrative model of change. *Psychotherapy: Theory, Research and Practice, 19,* 276–288.

Rasouli, M., Dyke, L. S., & Mantler, J. (2008). A model of career adjustment for immigrant women in Canada. In L. Schweitzer (Ed.), *Proceedings of the 2008 annual conference of the Administrative Sciences Association of Canada* (pp. 49–73). Retrieved from http://ojs.acadiau.ca/index.php/ASAC/article/viewFile/896/781

Reitz, J. G. (2001). Immigrant success in the knowledge economy: Institutional change and the immigrant experience in Canada, 1970–1995. *Journal of Social Issues, 57*(3), 579–613.

Remennick, L. (2003). Career continuity among immigrant professionals: Russian engineers in Israel. *Journal of Ethnic and Migration Studies, 29*(4), 701–721. doi:10.1080/1369183032000123468.

Salaff, J., Greve, A., & Ping, L. (2002). Paths into the economy: Structural barriers and the job hunt for skilled PRC migrants in Canada. *International Journal of Human Resource Management, 13*(3), 450–464.

Sangganjanavanich, V. F., Lenz, A. S., & Cavazos, J., Jr. (2011). International students' employment search in the United States: A phenomenological study. *Journal of Employment Counseling, 48*(1), 17–26. doi:10.1002/j.2161-1920.2011.tb00107.x.

Shen, Y., & Hall, D. T. (2009). When expatriates explore other options: Retaining talent through greater job embeddedness and repatriation adjustment. *Human Resource Management, 48*(5), 793–816. doi:10.1002/hrm.20314.

Spitze, G. (1984). The effect of family migration on wives' employment: How long does it last? *Social Science Quarterly, 65*(1), 21–36.

Stahl, G. K., Chua, C. H., Caligiuri, P., Cerdin, J. L., & Taniguchi, M. (2009). Predictors of turnover intentions in learning-driven and demand-driven international assignments: The role of repatriation concerns, satisfaction with company support, and perceived career advancement opportunities. *Human Resource Management, 48*(1), 89–109. doi:10.1002/hrm.20268.

Stahl, G. K., Miller, E. L., & Tung, R. L. (2002). Toward the boundaryless career: A closer look at the expatriate career concept and the perceived implications of an international assignment. *Journal of World Business, 37*(3), 216–227. doi:10.1016/S1090-9516(02)00080-9.

Stören, L. A. (2004). Unemployment experiences during early career of immigrant and non-immigrant graduates. *Journal of Education and Work, 17*(1), 71–93. doi:10.1080/1363908042000174200.

Tharenou, P., & Caulfield, N. (2010). Will I stay or will I go? Explaining repatriation by self-initiated expatriates. *The Academy of Management Journal, 53*(5), 1009–1028.

Tornikoski, C. (2011). *Expatriate compensation: A total reward perspective* (Doctoral dissertation, University of Vaasa, Vaasa, Finland). Retrieved from http://www.uva.fi/materiaali/pdf/isbn_978-952-476-342-4.pdf

van der Heijden, J. A. V., van Engen, M. L., & Paauwe, J. (2009). Expatriate career support: Predicting expatriate turnover and performance. *The International Journal of Human Resource Management, 20*(4), 831–845. doi:10.1080/09585190902770745.

Wadhwa, V., Saxenian, A. L., Freeman, R. B., & Gereffi, G. (2009). *America's loss is the world's gain: America's new immigrant entrepreneurs: Part IV.* Retrieved from http://www.kauffman.org/uploadedFiles/americas_loss.pdf

Waldinger, R., Bozorgmehr, M., Lim, N., & Finkel, L. (1998). *In search of the glass ceiling: The career trajectories of immigrant and native-born engineers* (Working Paper No. 28). Retrieved from Lewis Center for Regional Policy Studies website: http://escholarship.org/uc/item/3pj3p5b3#page-1

Walker, J. (2007, Spring). International approaches to credential assessment. *Canadian Issues,* 21–25.

Westwood, M. J., & Ishiyama, F. I. (1991). Challenges in counseling immigrant clients: Understanding intercultural barriers to career adjustment. *Journal of Employment Counseling, 28*(4), 130–143.

Yakushko, O. (2006). Career concerns of immigrant women: Issues and implications for career counseling. In W. B. Walsh & M. J. Heppner (Eds.), *Handbook of career counseling for women* (2nd ed., pp. 387–426). Mahwah, NJ: Lawrence Erlbaum.

Should I Stay or Should I Go Home? Career Guidance with International Students

33

Nancy Arthur and Sarah Nunes

Introduction

International students have traditionally been viewed as temporary sojourners who live and learn in another country and then return home (Pedersen, 1991). The literature on international students has emphasized the initial stage of transition and adjustment issues associated with living in a new cultural context (Arthur, 2007, 2008). Literature addressing career guidance of international students is scarce, even though the decision to study in another country is inextricably linked to future career opportunities. It is important to consider the factors that influence international students' career decisions, the stability of their career choices, and what factors help them to persist in attaining their career goals (Singaravelu, White, & Bringaze, 2005).

The decision to study abroad may be motivated by a number of *push* and *pull* factors (Mazzarol & Soutar, 2002). There are numerous *push* factors operating within the home country that lead individuals to look for opportunities in other countries. Conditions in the home country that can lead international students to seek opportunities to study in another country include a lack of capacity at local universities; lack of employment opportunities; perceived

opportunities available at home with a foreign education; family pressure; and political, social, or economic conditions (Arthur, 2004). There are also numerous *pull* factors, or perceived benefits in a destination country, that influence the decision to become an international student, primarily centered on the perceived advantages of a foreign education (Mazzarol & Soutar, 2002). Additionally, the perceived quality of education, standard of living, lifestyle considerations such as personal safety (in some countries), and/or family reunification may be influential reasons for pursuing foreign education. Students may also seek to increase their understanding of foreign languages, economies, and technological applications (Gu, Schweisfurthb, & Daya, 2010). However, many students are seeking ways to enhance career opportunities (Brooks, Waters, & Pimlott-Wilson, 2012; Shih & Brown, 2000). Foreign education is often viewed as a commodity to enhance marketability and for future employment options. The decision to become an international student is intricately tied with perception of conditions in both the home country and the destination country. This point of reference is critical for understanding the career trajectories of international students from the time they begin pursuing education in another country to the time they are making career decisions after graduation.

This chapter focuses on the key influences impacting the career decision-making of international students, and, given these influences, the career guidance of international students.

N. Arthur (✉)
Werklund School of Education, University of Calgary, Calgary, AB, Canada
e-mail: narthur@ucalgary.ca

G. Arulmani et al. (eds.), *Handbook of Career Development*, International and Cultural Psychology, DOI 10.1007/978-1-4614-9460-7_33, © Springer Science+Business Media, LLC 2014

The term *international student* is used to replace the former term, *foreign student*, due to the pejorative association with the word *foreigner*. The home country refers to the country of origin or sending country and the host country refers to the receiving country or destination country where the international student enrolls in higher education. The focus of the chapter is on the career planning and decision-making needs of international students in higher-education-to-work transitions. First, the context for this discussion will be provided through reviewing the changing views about international students, ranging from student consumer to a valuable source of human capital in the global labor market. The discussion will then turn to career issues for students as they approach the end of their educational program and make the decision to return home or pursue employment and/or permanent immigration in the host country. Selected research on international students' transitions from higher education to work will clarify the reasons for pursuing employment and permanent immigration. Next, considerations for career guidance with international students will be discussed. Career practitioners who work with international students need to be prepared to explore the influences from both home and host cultures that impact the career planning and decision-making of international students.

Views Regarding International Students

There has been a substantial growth in the number of students who leave home to study in another country. It is estimated that the number of international students worldwide has risen from 0.8 million in 1975 to 3.7 million in 2009, which represents a more than fourfold increase (Centre for Educational Research and Innovation [CERI], 2011). The top two source countries for international students are China and India (United Nations Educational, Scientific & Cultural Organization [UNESCO], 2009). The main destinations preferred by international students are the United States, the United Kingdom,

Germany, France, and Australia (UNESCO, 2009). This pattern of mobility suggests that the majority of international students pursue education in more developed countries, many of which are dominated by an individualized worldview and knowledge-based economy. Malaysia, Singapore, and China are considered the emerging destinations for international students. This growth is positioned alongside increasing enrollment in tertiary education worldwide. The growth in international students also mirrors advances in the globalization of societies and economies.

Trends in International Student Mobility Patterns

The mobility of international students is demonstrated by three main trends. The first involves students from Asia entering the major academic systems of North America, Western Europe, and Australia. The second is within the European Union which boasts various programs to encourage student mobility. The Erasmus program in Europe was developed to encourage international student mobility in higher education between countries in the European Union and more than two million students have taken part in the program since 1987. However, the patterns of mobility are not evenly distributed between participating countries and factors such as quality of educational programs, program costs, country size, cost of living, climate, and language influence student enrollment patterns (Rodríguez González, Bustillo Mesanza, & Mariel, 2011). The third general geographic trend in international student mobility largely reflects a south to north phenomenon (UNESCO, 2009). However, as economies grow and economic power shifts between countries in the world, it is expected that patterns of international student mobility will also reflect patterns of mobility within Asian countries, with increasing interest in gaining educational opportunities within countries such as China and India.

Along with globalization, there has been a shift in the ways that international students have been positioned in the global market of international education and skilled labor. International students bring a multitude of benefits to educational institutions and the local economies (Arthur, 2004). First, international students are an integral part of internationalization mandates in higher education to incorporate global dimensions into institutional curriculum. Second, international students bring a wealth of expertise from their home countries which, if leveraged, can lead to a rich exchange of content knowledge between students. Third, international students provide opportunities for local students to increase their cross-cultural awareness, knowledge, and skills for interacting in a global society. Fourth, international students may provide sources of referral for future recruitment of international students.

Economic Contributions by International Students

The positive influences of international students extend well beyond the local campus environment and their contributions are often positioned as sources of financial gain for educational institutions and for the host country economies. For example, it is estimated that international students contribute more than $10 billion annually to the Canadian economy (Advisory Panel on Canada's International Education Strategy, 2012) and more than $17.6 billion to the economy of the United States (National Association of Foreign Student Advisers [NAFSA]: Association of International Educators, 2009). The total economy-wide contribution to the Gross Domestic Product (GDP) made by international students in Australia was estimated as $12.3 billion (Australian Council for Private Education and Training, 2009) and $14 billion to the UK economy (Department for Business, Innovation and Skills, 2011). The financial contributions of international students, through tuition revenues and spending in local economies, underscore the fierce competition between countries to maintain and increase their market share (Douglass & Edelstein, 2009). International student tuition

represents a major revenue stream in higher education. However, it is critical that increased efforts to recruit international students are matched with appropriate services to support their academic and employment success. Historically, American institutions viewed international students as temporary sojourners who studied abroad and then returned home (Pedersen, 1991). Conditions of immigration emphasized study permits with very strict conditions set around employment, so that international students were not able to enter the local employment market. In some countries, like Canada, trends over time have shown gradual relaxation of immigration stipulations to support international students in pursuing temporary status as foreign workers and/or permanent immigration. These trends are connected to marketing strategies for attracting international students and retaining them as permanent immigrants (Ziguras & Law, 2006).

Changing Immigration Policies

According to a report based on countries represented by the Organization for Economic Cooperation and Development (OECD), several countries have simplified their working visa and temporary residence procedures for international students and graduates (CERI, 2011). As a result, international students have increased opportunities to gain employment experience in the destination country while they are studying, as well as after graduation. Countries such as Australia, Canada, and New Zealand have revised their immigration point system in ways that advantage international students through taking into consideration time studying and/or working in local settings. For example, international students in Canada can now apply for a work permit that allows them to work up to 3 years after graduation in a noncontinuous manner (Citizenship Immigration Canada [CIC], 2008). This experience counts towards increased eligibility for an immigration application under the Canadian Experience Class (CIC, 2008). International students in Canada can then plan their experiences after graduation, taking into consideration the advantages of staying in Canada, returning home immediately, or taking time to gain valuable work experience in both countries. However, there continue to be issues surrounding the eligibility of international students for such programs due to issues of securing employment and navigating the bureaucracies of the immigration process. Immigration eligibility in Finland and Norway now takes into account the years that international students have lived and studied in their countries and France offers additional considerations for the naturalization of international students enrolled in advanced research programs (CERI, 2011).

Whereas several countries are facilitating longer-term international student study and employment visas, the United States, in light of the events of 9/11, has shifted the stance on international student study. The USA Patriot Act, created in October 2001, has resulted in a much more complicated and lengthy visa application and approval process for international students wishing to study in this country (Douglass & Edelstein, 2009; United States Government Printing Office, n.d.). International students with F-1 and M-1 student visas are permitted to remain in the United States for 6 and 3 months, respectively, following the completion of their course of studies (United States Citizenship and Immigration Services [USCIS], 2011). Foreign vocational students who have an M-1 nonimmigrant status visa may only accept employment if it is part of a practical training program after completion of their course of study. The student must receive an Employment Authorization Document (EAD) before working and can only work for a maximum of 6 months of practical training (USCIS, 2011).

These countries' examples are offered to show changes in the ways that international student mobility is positioned in relation to immigration policies. International students are now fundamentally connected to systems of higher education, systems of employment, and the labor market pool of many destination countries. International graduate students are highly

educated individuals. Their career decision-making about where to pursue employment and initiate their careers after graduation has significant social and economic implications for both the destination country and their home countries (Masumba, Jin, & Mjelde, 2011).

International Students as Preferred Migrants

International students are viewed as preferred migrants for several key reasons (Ziguras & Law, 2006). First, in most economically developed societies, population forecasts show a declining birth rate at the same time as the population is aging. Therefore, the trend to view international students more favorably than before is influenced by an impending skilled labor shortage of crisis proportions; there simply will not be enough skilled workers to fill existing job vacancies in many "developed" countries. The implication is that employers will be seeking young, skilled workers to fill vacated positions and there will not be enough people in the local population to do so. This situation leads to opportunities for international students to increase a country's pool of highly skilled workers. International students bring expertise regarding labor practices and customs from their home countries. Further, as a result of their education in the host country, they acquire valuable local experience. International students may be viewed as preferred immigrants because they have been educated at local institutions and may be more desirable to employers than immigrants with international credentials who lack local experience (Hawthorne, 2006). In these ways, the view about international students has shifted from considering them as consumers of international education to considering them as desirable human capital to support economic development of both home and destination countries (Guo, Schugurensky, Hall, Rocco, & Fenwick, 2010).

Permitting foreigners to stay in the host country has not been seamless for all countries. The US government, for instance, monitors the flow of international human capital through the H-1B visa levels that allow skilled foreign workers to enter the country for a limited period of time. This situation also applies to international students remaining in the United States after their student visas expire. Prior to 2002, it was relatively easy to obtain an H-1B visa. Since then, political pressures have reduced the allowable quota of noncitizens by two-thirds; this phenomenon is referred to by some as *brain blocking* (Gower, 2011). Those with an H-1B visa must be sponsored by a US company who files a Labor Condition Application (LCA) stating that the applicant will not be displacing a domestic person and that there are no current labor disputes involved in the hiring of a foreign worker. Those with H-1B visas are permitted to work in the United States for 6 years (Gower, 2011). However, it should be noted that immigration regulations and procedures change frequently and there are considerable differences between countries that receive international students. Readers are advised to check the most recent immigration regulations in specific countries to determine the current status of student visas and the rules concerning employment after graduation.

Brain Gain at Whose Expense?

The characterization of international students as temporary sojourners has shifted to account for changing immigration policies in some countries that encourage international students to pursue employment and permanent immigration to host countries. The narrative of desirable human capital emphasizes how international students are positioned as a commodity in our increasingly globalized economy. Host countries have a stake in keeping international students after graduation to address critical labor shortages and to take advantage of the knowledge of both home and host cultures that international students have acquired.

The implications of positioning international students as desirable immigrants and *brain gain* are rarely juxtaposed with a discussion about the implications for the home country. A second narrative of *brain drain* surfaces in light of the impact on home countries of international students. In essence, host countries tend to gain the intellectual and economic benefits of international education; in turn, home countries may stand to lose highly educated international students when they pursue employment and permanent immigration. As previously noted, the inflow of international students has been primarily from east to west. The inflow of international students towards developed countries positions lower-income countries to lose intellectual and financial capital (Adnett, 2010). A pattern is evident in the growth of international education in favor of more economically advantaged countries, whereas the costs associated with foreign education are disproportionately managed by poorer countries. It is speculative that a parallel pattern exponentially occurs when increasing numbers of international students from poorer countries are recruited as candidates for education, employment, and permanent immigration, which will increase patterns of global income inequality. The extent to which future alliances and business partnerships can be mutually and equitably beneficial is an additional narrative that deserves attention in the discussion about the growth of international education and student mobility. What is at stake is whether or not such trends prove to enhance the economies of both sending and receiving countries, or whether such patterns result in fewer benefits for sending countries who have more to lose when international students do not return home.

To Stay or Go Home? A Critical Career Question for International Students

The discussion in the previous section highlighted that in some destination countries, like Canada, international students have increasing opportunities to be employed during their academic program, to work for a period of time after graduation before returning home, or to pursue employment and permanent immigration. These increasing opportunities suggest that many international students face a critical career question upon graduation: Should I stay or should I go home? Close to 70 % of international students studying in the United States reported that they would like to remain in this country permanently after graduation (Spencer-Rodgers, 2000). In a recent study of international graduate students at a large US university, 22 % of the respondents stated preference to begin their careers in their home country, 51 % preferred staying in the United States, and 27 % were not sure (Masumba et al., 2011). This implies that a large number of graduate students have clear preferences about their career pathways in either the home or destination countries, whereas many others may be in the process of considering such a decision. Career guidance may be a useful intervention to help international students to explore their future options and decision-making.

One way of estimating the numbers of international students who stay in the destination country is through examining changes in their immigration status, to a status other than student, and the number of students who do not renew their study permits in the same year, known as *the stay rate* (CERI, 2011). The stay rate in countries, with available data, averages 25 % with a range of 17–33 %, with Canada showing the highest rate (CERI, 2011). These numbers may be interpreted with caution due to available data; however, they may actually underestimate the total number of international students who stay in destination countries. For example, international students studying in the European Union may be able to move between countries without a residence permit and their mobility may not show up in estimates of the stay rate (CERI, 2011). Regardless, these statistics underscore three notable points: (a) there are increasing numbers of students who are pursuing opportunities to stay in destination countries; (b) there are barriers that impact the actual numbers of students who successfully stay in destination countries to work after graduation; and (c) the majority of international students leave the destination country and eventually return home. The decision to stay or to go home is important for considering the career guidance needs of international students.

Returning Home

Many students are primarily motivated to study abroad as a means to improve their educational attainment and employment opportunities upon returning home. Other students may prolong their international experiences through travelling or enrolling in school in another country. There is not just one pattern or career pathway, as many students will find ways to continue their global experiences. However, most international students eventually return to their home country. The reentry transition does not begin with the physical relocation home, rather it begins with resolving the ending of the foreign education experience and the life established in the destination country (Arthur, 2003; Martin & Harrell, 1996). Many such ex-students may experience a sense of loss about leaving the destination country, including the physical conditions in the country, lifestyles, relationships, and perceived opportunities. They must also resolve the psychological process of adapting to the home culture. Ex-students may have mixed feelings about returning home, such as excitement to reunite with family and friends, but may realize that their involvements in aspects of lifestyles and/or relationships found in the destination country are no longer sustainable.

Reentry Transition Issues

Several reentry transition issues have been associated with the career guidance needs of international ex-students (Arthur, 2007). A main issue pertains to the perceived relevancy of the international learning experience for skills and attributes needed for career success in the home context (Campbell, 2010). In addition to loss of contact with the host culture, international ex-students may face value conflicts regarding contrasting cultural norms and lifestyle expectations or gender role expectations. Their experiences may also vary with the transferability of educational and language expertise, and how such experience enhances job search and occupational mobility in their field of study. Although students may have prepared for the initial adjustment issues of living and learning in a foreign country, they are often ill-prepared for the reverse culture shock that they might experience when returning home (Arthur, 2003; Gaw, 2000; Leung, 2007). Reverse culture shock may depend on the length of time spent in the host country, the extent of integration into the host country culture, and the extent to which the host and home cultures differ. International ex-students may not expect to face adjustment issues when they return home to a "familiar" culture. For example, they may not be aware of how much they have changed as a result of the interactions and acculturation process of living and learning in the destination country. Fundamental values, political perspectives, and lifestyle choices may have shifted considerably while living aboard. The degree to which people in the home environment are willing to accommodate them may determine the degree of interpersonal conflict experienced. There may be expectations that they return to their home country and settle into usual roles and routines.

International ex-students may experience dissonance about returning home that is centered on career concerns. Although foreign education is often a vehicle for enhancing opportunities in employment market at home, that is not always the case. International ex-students may feel considerable pressure to secure employment in their chosen field and to improve their economic and social standing. Some international ex-students may also feel pressured when they compare their employment success to peers who have already secured employment in the home country. A major concern is how well the curriculum and foreign credentials will transfer to local employment conditions. Students who have been away from their home countries for several years may lack occupational information and employment contacts. It is critical that international students continue to network, maintain connections, and build new connections to support reentry into the employment market in their home country. They need to prepare how to represent their experiences in ways that demonstrate the value of their international education to employers. These examples illustrate that it is not just a decision to return home; the transition of returning home is associated with a broader picture of influences in both the destination and home countries.

Pursuing Employment and Permanent Immigration

In deciding to return home or remain in the host country, international students face a critical decision that has implications for career and lifestyle opportunities, as well as personal identity and familial relations. How international students cope with this cross-cultural transition is not well understood. There is limited research that describes the experiences of international students who are in the final stage of their educational programs and most of the available studies focus on preparation for reentry to the home culture (Christofi & Thompson, 2007; Gaw, 2000; Leung, 2007). Only recently has research surfaced that explores the experiences of international students who are embarking on the transition from higher education to seeking employment in the host country (e.g., Arthur & Flynn, 2011; Popadiuk & Arthur, 2012; Sangganjanavanich, Lenz, & Cavazos, 2011).

Research in the Canadian Context
We (Arthur & Flynn, 2011, 2012) conducted a study that examined the transition and employment experiences of international students who remain in Canada after completing their educational programs. The key findings of this research, outlined in subsequent paragraphs, provide some foundational knowledge about international students' transitions to a host country and what factors influence their decisions to pursue employment and permanent immigration. Although the findings are based on data from a Canadian university, the suggested themes offer a starting point for exploring career-related influences with international students in other settings. The study consisted of two phases. Phase one investigated the experiences of international students as they considered the career decision to pursue employment and permanent immigration to Canada. Phase two assessed the

impact of employer, academic, and personal influences on the same group of participants (i.e., international ex-students pursuing employment or immigration to Canada) after they had completed their academic programs. There were 19 international students involved in this research. Students were undergraduate and graduate international students at a large Canadian university. We used a semi-structured interview to assess the influences on international students' career decisions, the stability of their career choices, and what factors help them to persist in attaining their academic and career goals.

The Decision to Stay in the Host Country

International students, in the final years of their academic programs, were motivated to pursue employment/immigration to Canada for four key reasons. First and foremost was enhanced quality of life. This included such things as a cleaner environment, slower pace of life, more freedom than in home country, other immigrants' satisfaction here, and friendliness. Second was career-related incentives—students noted that their academic degrees were highly valued, Canada is a financially stable country, and others (from their home countries) had obtained jobs. The third reason was an enhanced work environment. This aspect included being paid for working overtime, the existence of employee protection laws, and stories of negative experiences back home. The final reason related to safety and political stability. Students spoke of the safe environment and democracy of the Canadian government. International students' decisions to remain in Canada after graduation were largely independent choices but were influenced by both parents and partners. Barriers encountered by these international students in the process of deciding to stay in Canada related to culture, language in particular. Students noted several concerns or fears about staying in Canada, the number one fear was not getting a job or losing one's job. Students were also fearful of cultural barriers (both generally and in the workplace) and of missing their families back home.

Transition Experiences and Expectations

On completion of their academic programs, the same participants, now international ex-students, were asked about their transition experiences and expectations. General transition difficulties included the necessity of finding or retaining a job, a lack of daily structure compared to student life (for job applicants), and an uncertainty about (or discomfort in) the Canadian work environment.

A mere 25 % of ex-students had secured a job since graduating. Most ex-students believed that a lack of experience was the most difficult aspect of the job search. As well, not having Canadian citizenship or permanent residency status, and a lack of connections or network made this process difficult. For those who had secured a job, the most difficult aspect of the new workplace was language barriers; instability in funding in the nonprofit sector, the workplace culture, and insecurity about skills or lack of skills were also problematic. Ex-students believed diversified, well-advertised career fairs, and having a network would have been useful during the job search. Also, having Canadian experience or an internship would have been helpful.

Perspectives on Immigration

The two major influences on deciding to immigrate were career/education and lifestyle/familial. Within the career/education realm, ex-students identified attractive career opportunities in this country and recognized and valued other ex-students' career-related successes. In addition, ex-students were influenced by the substantial educational investment they had made in Canada and were encouraged by supportive faculty. A major influence in the lifestyle/familial realm was the high quality of life offered in Canada compared to participants' home countries. Further, some ex-students noted the possibility of achieving a work–life balance as critical in their decision, while others noted the possibility of sponsoring one's family as crucial. Most international ex-students felt as though the decision to remain in Canada and to eventually immigrate was a good decision and this decision was strengthened by their experiences to date. Ex-students' expectations about better job prospects were unmet while their expectations about an enhanced quality of life in Canada were met.

Ex-students believed that Canadian employers should refrain from discriminating against them due to their international status, lack of citizenship, or language barriers. Ex-students hoped that those employed in career services will help them build networks and meet prospective employers. Ex-students advised future (or incoming) international students to educate themselves about Canadian culture, Canadians, and the Canadian work environment. As well, ex-students advised incoming international students to research potential job opportunities and create a network prior to degree completion.

In summary, this Canadian-based research indicates that international students were prompted to consider remaining in Canada due to the enhanced employment opportunities and high standard of living in this country. Relationship support to stay in the country was a key factor for their career decision-making. This finding is echoed in the Popadiuk and Arthur (2012) study in which relationships in both the home and host cultures were key influences on the motivation to pursue employment and permanent immigration. The endorsement of parents and other family members in the home country was a strong consideration in planning life and career after graduation. International students viewed the relationships that they formed in the host country with new friends and partners, their academic mentors, and other international students as important influences in helping them to successfully transition from university to employment.

Similar to our findings, international students in a study based in the United States experienced a number of employment and cultural barriers in their job search (Sangganjanavanich et al., 2011) such as language proficiency, networking, interview expectations, and variations in whether or not employers actually valued their unique international experience. There is considerable pressure for international students to secure employment and they may experience strong feelings of fear about their capacity to succeed with their job search. In all three studies, contact with international ex-students who are further ahead in the job search and transition from university to employment was identified as important for role modeling, job search information, and sustaining a positive expectancy of success.

The overarching goal for increasing international student immigration is their potential contribution to the host country's economic and cultural prosperity (Advisory Panel on Canada's International Education Strategy, 2012). The achievement of this mandate is dependent on (a) positioning international students to acquire suitable employment and (b) ensuring students' success in the workplace and broader industry. Given this, host country governments, institutions, and institutional student services must align their agendas to ensure international students meet (and exceed) their career aspirations. Developing targeted, accessible resources for international students is crucial to this goal. Career guidance is an integral institutional resource that is continually advancing as new research findings emerge. The role of career guidance in international students' development in host countries will be explored in the following section.

Career Guidance with International Students: Best Practices

Trends in international student migration endorse the claim that there is an increasing scope of roles and responsibilities for providing support programming to international students (Yang, Wong, Hwang, & Heppner, 2002). This challenge includes the ways that guidance services are designed and delivered within institutions of higher education. This section of the chapter outlines practice considerations for professionals who assist international students with career planning, decision-making, and job search. The discussion is organized around four key themes, namely theories and models of practice, clarification of values, awareness and accessibility of services, and job search connections and skills. The recommended practices for career guidance within each of these domains are discussed. Career guidance occurs within the systems and structures of educational institutions and there are implications for expanding institutional responsibilities for supporting international students.

Theories and Models of Practice

Career practitioners are challenged to consider how well the theories and models they use in their work with international students address both individual and systemic influences on career development. A number of concerns have been raised regarding the cultural validity of career development theories and the strengths and limitations of Western frameworks for application in global contexts (e.g., Flores, 2009; Leong & Gupta, 2008). There are concerns about the degree to which the underlying assumptions of career development theories and models of career counseling are congruent with the worldviews of international students from diverse countries and cultures. For example, an emphasis on individual choice in career planning and decision-making represents an urban, white, Western bias; utility of such theories and models may be limited for students from cultures where family values or community goals are paramount for their plans. International students from more collectivistic cultures may highly value career goals that honor their families' wishes or see their roles in light of making an important contribution to their local communities (Arthur & Popadiuk, 2010; Reynolds & Constantine, 2007).

A key point is that career practitioners need to find ways to establish a strong relationship with international students in which the cultural meanings of career issues can be explored. Career practitioners are invited to consider how their personal values may intersect with the decision-making styles of international students who seek their services. Beyond linear or cognitive frameworks for decision-making, they may need to incorporate cultural beliefs about intuition, fate and destiny, spirituality, and/or

emotional reasoning, depending on the worldview of clients (Hong & Domokos-Cheng Ham, 2000). This implies that career practitioners have taken the time to be reflective about their personal values, models that guide their practice, and have developed competencies for assessing the worldviews of their clients. A number of models have been developed which specifically incorporate cultural diversity into career assessment and intervention planning (e.g., Arthur & Collins, 2011; Fouad & Bingham, 1995; Leong & Hartung, 1997; Leung, 1995). For example, Arthur and Collins (2011) have argued that practitioners need to be reflective about culture and how it influences views of people's career development and the issues that are addressed in planning and decision-making. They exhort that culture needs to be infused into practices with all clients to strengthen the working alliance and negotiate relevant goals and interventions.

Beyond considering the cultural validity of specific theories and models of career counseling, career practitioners need to be knowledgeable about the nature of international student transitions and common issues that may surface during various phases of their student and post-student experience (Arthur, 2007). As previously noted, there has been more emphasis placed on the initial stage of cross-cultural transition when students arrive in the destination country than attention paid to their career-related needs while studying or in the transition from higher education to employment. Through the experience of learning in a new cultural context, some international students discover that their choice of academic program is not what they expected and they require assistance to determine what to do next. It is also possible that through exposure to new ideas in the destination country, international students may find that their interests shift from their original plans. The level of academic rigor may be either under- or overestimated, requiring students to gain additional support for academic skills. Teaching and learning methodology may be different than what was instructed in their home countries, and students may find it difficult to adjust to local expectations. The extent to which international perspectives are welcomed in the classroom and community may be integral for students' experiences of academic and social integration. International students' capacity to resolve perceived intercultural stressors during the acculturation process has been linked to academic learning performance (Hwang, Wang, & Sodanine, 2011) and both career aspirations and career outcome expectations (Reynolds & Constantine, 2007; Zhou & Santos, 2007). As students come to an end of their international education program, they may face critical decisions about the direction of their career trajectory.

Clarification of Values

The experience of cross-cultural transitions can result in profound learning about self, about the host country, and prompt reflection about life at home. Consequently, exploration of values is a critical aspect of career guidance for international students. Through exposure to new cultural norms, students may experience a sense of dissonance or feel conflicted about their priorities. Exploring values can help international students to explore how their values are related to career decisions, what values are most salient, and incorporate values into their career decision-making (Arthur & Popadiuk, 2010). Career guidance practitioners can facilitate international students in exploring changes in their cultural identities and selecting career options that are congruent with their values. Working from a constructivist approach can be useful in supporting international students to examine the cultural meanings of their experiences and to incorporate new understandings into their current career issues. Career practitioners can guide international students to gain better appreciation of the ways that their cultures influence their present and future career options (Arthur & Collins, 2011). However, this implies that career practitioners are aware of their personal values, the values that are embedded in their professional ways of working, and are flexible about supporting contrasting points of view.

It is important for career practitioners to take into account cultural influences on career-related concerns, including the degree to which a student has maintained home country values or acculturated to the cultural norms of the host country. When students are embarking on the journey to employment and permanent immigration, they are making a decision that concerns not only their future life in the host country but also their life in terms of relationships and connections in the home country. Some international students will have unwavering support from their families to pursue permanent immigration, in recognition of a better quality of life afforded in the host country. Other students will feel pressured to return home to fulfill family, employer, or other community responsibilities. It is important for career planning and decision-making to include exploration of the impact of a decision to remain in the host country for relationships at home. Decisions made in one cultural context can have profound implications for the roles and relationships within another cultural context.

Awareness and Accessibility of Services

Efforts are needed to increase service utilization by international students who are unfamiliar with career guidance services. Perhaps one of the biggest barriers for the provision of career guidance may be the lack of knowledge about the purpose of such services, and how international students might benefit from accessing those services. Terms such as *career*, *career development*, *career counseling*, *career guidance*, and *career planning* are culturally constructed terms with varied meanings, transferability, and relevance across cultures.

It is important that career practitioners establish a positive profile in the international student community and provide information about the benefits of seeking services. Bringing about international students' awareness of career services is the first step in the effective delivery of these services. This may be best accomplished as members of an interdisciplinary team of student support services with strong connections to the academic community. Professors and academic advisors must be informed about the services offered at university career centers. Information on career center location, hours of operation, available assessments, workshops, and other resources must be made readily available to professors and academic advisors to distribute to international students. Moreover, practitioners working in career centers should be well connected with university counseling centers (and other psychological services) for the purposes of cross-referrals.

Accessibility is a second concern for international students. International students who are unfamiliar with career guidance or who do not understand the full breadth of this service may be reluctant to seek services. They may view these services as inaccessible or irrelevant. In addition, international students often equate career services with work experience and/or job placement (Shen & Herr, 2004). It is important that student support services highlight the full scope of available services, that is, in job search *and* in career planning and decision-making. An issue related to accessibility is that of relevance. Career practitioners must reach international students through means that make sense to them. In other words, they must design career interventions that are culturally relevant and meaningful for students from diverse countries and cultural backgrounds. The choice of theoretical approaches and models of practice used with international students directly relates to the issue of relevance. For example, Arthur and Popadiuk (2010) have suggested the use of a cultural formulation approach along with a relational theoretical perspective such that the interconnections of gender, social class, and ethnicity can be examined with international student clients.

Another suggested direction for increasing access and relevance of career-based information to international students is the use of the Internet and social media. Although some students may be reluctant to seek services face-to-face, most students are familiar with accessing information through the Internet. Information and educational programming can be delivered through websites specifically designed with topics that are relevant for the international student population, such as job search, tips for networking, common experiences in the reentry transition, and visa and immigration considerations. Career practitioners are invited to consider their level of interest and technological savvy for delivering guidance services in a variety of formats. As a starting point, there are resources available to help practitioners to consider practical and ethical considerations of service provision via the Internet (e.g., Osborn, Dikel, Sampson, & Harris-Bowlsbey, 2011).

Job Search Connections and Skills

Guidance services in higher education may offer general services for the entire student population yet neglect some of the specific needs of international students. All students should be aware of the need to engage in their job search well before the end of their academic program. International students need to be encouraged to start their preparation for career plans after graduation early and as an ongoing consideration during international studies. Although this chapter was positioned around the decision to stay or return home, some international students may wish to continue education, or their positive international experiences may foster interest in a global career that involves working between countries. The growth in multinational companies may provide students with increasing opportunities to pursue terms of employment that offer additional international experiences.

International students who are planning to return home may be encouraged to maintain or establish new employment connections to support their transition into the home country workforce. Job search workshops for students returning home may incorporate content related to the reentry process and help students to develop anticipatory coping skills for managing reverse culture shock (Gaw, 2000). Career practitioners can educate international students regarding some of the issues that commonly surface during reentry transitions and help them to identify their specific issues and possible coping strategies. Preparation for reentry is a key time to revisit career plans and decision-making to help manage anticipated adjustment issues and to encourage students about ways to be proactive about implementing their career plans upon returning home. Some institutions in higher education have invested resources to support students with their job search in their main source countries. This interface pays off in terms of supporting student employment, and leveraging the reputation of the host institution for future networking and referral.

It is also important that guidance personnel are knowledgeable about the ways to help international students pursue employment in the host country. This might include developing resources, such as a database of companies interested in hiring individuals with international experience. Workshops can be organized as well to discuss techniques students can use to market the skills they have obtained through their international education. Programming directed at helping international students secure employment can include content on cultural norms for job search and interviewing skills (Behrens, 2009), how to develop and implement networking skills, and provide linkages for students to gain paid or unpaid experiences in the host culture. Interventions such as workshops and sharing of experiences in a group format may help international students navigate expectations for job search and workplace behavior, particularly when students are pursuing employment in cultural contexts that may have considerably different norms and expectations for networking, interviews, and employee behavior than their home country (Arthur, 2007; Sangganjanavanich et al., 2011).

The importance of cultivating relationships in the host country has been shown to be pivotal for supporting successful transitions to employment after graduation (Nunes & Arthur, 2013; Popadiuk & Arthur, 2012). These relationships help to establish the foundation for students' professional networks in the host country. International students report that their academic supervisors are key mentors for helping them to make important connections related to educational and employment opportunities. Students report that participating in internships or co-op placements in their fields of study would be useful in helping them to establish professional networks (Nunes & Arthur, 2013).

Relationships with local students take on greater importance as international students live away from their families of origin and friendships in the host culture take on new importance for feeling established with a sense of belonging. International students also benefit from role modeling from other international ex-students who are further along in the job search, employment, or immigration process. These relationships are powerful opportunities for learning, for instilling hope, and for sharing information about the transition journey from student to employment.

Regardless of the choice to stay or return home, students need to be able to represent their international experience in meaningful ways to employers. This entails translating general international experience into specific skills that are valued by employers. Career practitioners can help international students to understand the job search process and help students to better understand how they can translate their experience into marketable skills. There will inevitably be a range of reactions from employers regarding the value of international experience. The onus remains with international students to show how their international experience and multicultural knowledge are relevant for employment contexts. Finally, career practitioners can advocate for funding and services directed towards international students and advocate for the resources to develop a stronger interface between career services in higher education and future employers.

Institutional Responsibilities

The choice to remain in a foreign country after completing one's studies is an exciting prospect yet is a decision accompanied by inherent risk. It appears as though international students are willing to embrace the risks associated with remaining in a host country (like Canada) following their degree completion to forward important career, lifestyle, and familial objectives. The challenges, faced by many international students, must be addressed through shifts in institutional ideologies related to the recruitment and retention of international (ex)students and through the student services these institutions offer. It is the responsibility of the institutions that recruit international students as well as the host country governments to ensure that students looking to remain in their country receive a fair chance of obtaining sustainable employment. Several recommendations are outlined to guide institutions in their efforts to support international students.

Universities, through their international student centers and academic departments, can educate host country employers about what international students can offer as potential employees. Brochures, websites, or presentations may be used to highlight, for instance, students' multilingual skills, knowledge of foreign economies and market trends, or their familiarity and comfort working with individuals from diverse cultural groups. Furthermore, an emphasis must be placed on the long-term benefits of hiring an individual with multinational experience. Such benefits include establishing and strengthening global relationships and enhancing business communication through students' global perspectives and multilingualism. As well, employers should have a standard means of evaluating students at the end of their work terms and internships. This will provide students with constructive, practical feedback to prepare them for the job acquisition process. International students offer unique resources based from their international knowledge (Sangganjanavanich et al., 2011); however, not all employers have an appreciation for how such experience might be utilized.

Extending beyond their individual counseling services, university career centers might help to establish a strong and stable relationship between students and host country employers. Career practitioners must have an adequate understanding of employers' perspectives on hiring new graduates educated in a particular host country who have international credentials. Comparing employers' agendas and concerns with international students' specific career ambitions would assist career practitioners in helping to adequately prepare international students for the host country workforce. The bottom line is that sufficient resources have to be allocated by the administration of educational institutions beyond recruitment to adequately support the guidance needs of international students.

Supporting International Students' Career Development: Sensitivity to the Universal and the Particular

The international student population is not homogeneous; rather, the population comprises students from many different countries and cultures. Moreover, it should not be assumed that students from the same country share a uniform belief system; there are many subcultures with social, religious, and political beliefs that influence socialization within countries. Although the content in this chapter has emphasized common issues and approaches, it is imperative that career guidance also addresses the unique value systems and particular perspectives and needs of international students. Career practitioners must be willing to adapt their models of practice to incorporate the value systems of individual students. For example, decision-making in a collective culture may not resonate with theories and models of decision-making that emphasize individual choice and autonomy. There can be gender issues associated with career expectations and cultural norms regarding the career pathways expected of adult male and female children. Family expectations and obligations may be highly influential in the choice of academic major and for commitments after graduation. Career practitioners are encouraged to see the strengths in the beliefs, values, and adherence to diverse ways of decision-making (Arthur & Popadiuk,

2010). It is also important to take into account international students' degree of acculturation to the host culture and their priorities in career exploration and decision-making.

The career-related needs of students may vary according to the stage of their academic program and whether they are pursuing undergraduate or graduate education. Although many individuals return to school later in adulthood, direct-entry students in undergraduate programs are typically younger and at earlier stages of their career development. Exploration and change of academic interests are not uncommon when students are exposed to new curricula and fields of study. However, as mentioned, many students feel considerable pressure about pursuing particular academic programs and career pathways. In contrast, most graduate students tend to be older, they have invested more time and resources into their education, and they are looking for ways to use their specialist skills as they launch their careers after graduation.

When some students move to another country for their education, they may shift from conditions of relative affluence to different standards of living in the destination country. Disparities in the economic conditions between and within countries may mean that some students are burdened by the financial costs of their international studies, while others are economically advantaged. The demographic distribution of the destination country's population may also have implications for whether or not international students live in areas with a high or low degree of ethnic diversity. Some international students may experience shifting from a dominant to non-dominant ethnic or minority identity for the first time in their lives. Experiences of racism and discrimination can have serious and adverse effects on cross-cultural transitions and the degree to which students feel like the new country and culture could ever become their new home. These examples illustrate the plurality found within the international student population and the importance of career practitioners attending to individual student experiences.

The discussion in this chapter is intended to encourage readers to consider how they balance the universal and the particular with regard to supporting international students in their career development. It is likely that most international students will experience transition demands that are related to their career development. After all, the decision to become an international student begins a journey that undoubtedly has a profound impact on their educational and personal experiences. However, the ways in which that journey unfolds is highly individual and nuanced with the particular circumstances of international students in navigating home and host cultures. Career guidance practitioners are reminded that general background knowledge can guide their understanding of transition experiences; however, they need to be mindful about assessing the unique circumstances and individual needs of international students.

Charting New Directions in Career Guidance with International Students

In this chapter we have attempted to show some changes in the ways that international students are positioned in the global education and labor markets. Many students pursue international education with the belief that their academic credentials and experience will provide unique skills and give them an advantage for future employment (Brooks et al., 2012). The promise of career advantage in the global marketplace needs to be substantiated by research about international students' actual experiences of navigating the transition from higher education to employment in their home countries, to employment in the host countries, and in pursuing career pathways that may involve mobility between several countries.

There is surprisingly little research on international students' career guidance needs for the reentry transition of returning home. Although some of the common issues suggested are connected to job search and transfer of international learning, there is a gap in research about the actual experiences of international students who return home and their subsequent career development. Research with international student alumni would help to uncover perceived barriers and successes and help to inform campus programming designed to help students prepare for the reentry transition.

The examples of research cited in this chapter suggest that even though immigration policies have changed in several countries to support the migration of international students, there are layers of complexity involved in their career planning and decision-making. Additional research is needed to uncover how international students navigate a myriad of systemic, cultural, and personal challenges for pursuing employment in the host country and permanent immigration. The results of existing research suggest the need for expanding the scope of support services offered through institutions of higher education from the predominant focus on early adjustment, to facilitating their career development within a fuller cycle of cross-cultural transition. Stronger linkages between educational institutions and employers appear to be key partnerships for enabling international students to implement their career plans.

As noted in the introduction of this chapter, there are growing numbers of students pursuing experiences of living and learning in other countries. At the same time, there is a burgeoning growth of international education that is delivered through distributed learning methods, including distance delivery. The increased use of technology via the Internet, along with pedagogical advances in curricular design, implies that it is not always necessary to leave home to access higher education programs from other countries. It is undetermined how such advances may impact the physical migration of international students pursuing higher education. However, it seems likely that there will be increased options for students to be selective about the location and format of their international studies.

In reflecting about guidance services for international students, readers are encouraged to consider the format of programs and services designed to support international students. The content of this chapter emphasizes that services need to be linked to the full cycle of transition experienced by international learners, including support to prepare students for the next phase of returning home or pursuing career opportunities in the destination country and host culture. However, the ways in which guidance services are organized may contribute to the likelihood that international students will actually access them. Services may include individual appointment and face-to-face appointment for individuals who request this level of support, but there is a plethora of information and education that may be delivered more efficiently through other means: for example, postings of topics via the international student services' list serve, content delivered through interactive platforms on the Internet or webinars, and the use of social media tools. Introducing international students to career-related information and modes of service delivery can help them to self-select if they require more intensive personal assistance. Although some of the guidance needs of international students are going to be similar to the needs of local students, there are confounding issues of cultural learning that warrant the development of services specifically designed for international students.

Lastly, career practitioners who work with international students need to consider their competencies for working with students who come from many different countries and cultures. Although the literature on multicultural counseling has emphasized the need for intercultural competence, there are few sources that advance this topic in the literature on career guidance with international students (Arthur, 2007; Sangganjanavanich et al., 2011). There are several frameworks of multicultural counseling (e.g., Arredondo et al., 1996; Collins & Arthur, 2010) that can be used as foundational knowledge from which to identify areas for competency development. These frameworks elaborate on competencies in the domains of self-awareness, knowledge of other cultures, and skills for enhancing the working alliance. Guidance practitioners can utilize the frameworks to consider their strengths areas for competency development. Guidance practices with international students inevitably require working across cultures and developing competencies to support the application of relevant assessment and intervention frameworks.

Conclusion

The practices outlined in this section identify several directions through which practitioners can respond to the career guidance needs of international students. Helping students to explore their evolving value systems, in light of their cultural identities and goals, is an important practice. Increasing students' awareness of and access to career counseling, information, and educational services is a second important mandate. The theories and models of practice selected must be encompassing of students' unique values and practitioners are encouraged to consider their multicultural counseling competencies for supporting the diverse population of international students. As emphasized in the discussion, international students may have different guidance needs, depending upon the phase of their transition, as career issues may surface or change during their time as an international learner. Preparation for the transition from higher education to employment must incorporate students' decision-making about their career pathways to return home, to work in the host country after graduation, or plans for pursuing education or employment in different countries. For those students pursuing employment and permanent immigration in the host country, infrastructure and resources must be established to help students connect with employers and navigate this pinnacle transition.

One of the key directions for addressing the career priorities of international students is outreach to employers. As noted in the example provided from the Canadian research, many international students view employment as the key for their future success. Although many international ex-students find suitable employment and move forward with their career plans, there are several barriers that remain to be addressed. First, many employers are unfamiliar with the strengths that international students would bring to their organizations. Hiring practices may still show biases in favor of local students and international students may be marginalized to the position of being hired *only if* no other suitable candidates can be found. Similar to the plight of other types of immigrants, international students may face stereotypes and obstacles for the recognition of their experience and credentials acquired in another country (Chen, 2008). The premise that international students should have an advantage over other immigrants because of local educational experiences does not eliminate a legacy of discrimination against people whose cultures and customs may contrast the practices of employers in the dominant culture.

The extent to which immigration policies are successful for retaining international students may depend on the ease of integration into the destination country. It is prudent to remember that as economies shift throughout the world, there will also be increasing opportunities for employment mobility. Changing policies need to be matched by guidance practices that support international students during different phases of the transition process, as they pursue their short- and longer-term career goals. Further research is needed to better understand how international students overcome barriers and make successful transitions to employment in either the destination or home countries. International students' career plans and decisions are inevitably bounded by market conditions and fluctuations in local and global economies. After all, the decision to stay or to go home is not a decision made at a single point in time. If, after several months or years of living in the destination country, international students ascertain that their career goals are not being met and opportunities surface in other countries, they may make the decision not to stay.

References

Adnett, N. (2010). The growth of international students and economic development: Friends or foes? *Journal of Education Policy, 25*, 625–637.

Advisory Panel on Canada's International Education Strategy. (2012). *International education: A key driver of Canada's prosperity.* Ottawa, ON: Foreign Affairs and International Trade Canada. Retrieved from http://www.international.gc.ca/education/report-rapport/strategy-strategie/index.aspx?view=d

Arredondo, P., Toporek, R., Brown, S., Sanchez, J., Locke, D. C., Sanchez, J., et al. (1996). Operationalization of the multicultural counseling competencies. *Journal of Multicultural Counseling & Development, 24*(1), 42–78.

Arthur, N. (2003). Preparing international students for the re-entry transition. *Canadian Journal of Counselling, 37*(3), 173–185.

Arthur, N. (2004). *Counselling international students: Clients from around the world.* New York, NY: Springer.

Arthur, N. (2007). Career planning and decision-making needs of international students. In M. Pope & H. Singaravelu (Eds.), *A handbook for counseling international students in the United States* (pp. 37–56). Alexandria, VA: American Counseling Association.

Arthur, N. (2008). Counseling international students. In P. Pedersen, J. G. Draguns, W. J. Lonner, & J. E. Trimble (Eds.), *Counseling across cultures* (6th ed., pp. 275–290). Thousand Oaks, CA: Sage.

Arthur, N., & Collins, S. (2011). Infusing culture in career counselling. *Journal of Employment Counseling, 48*, 147–149.

Arthur, N., & Flynn, S. (2011). Career development influences of international students who pursue permanent immigration to Canada. *International Journal of Education and Vocational Guidance, 11*(3), 221–237. doi:10.1007/s10775-011-9212-5.

Arthur, N., & Flynn, S. (2012). International students' views of transition to employment and immigration. *Canadian Journal of Career Development, 12*(1), 28–37.

Arthur, N., & Popadiuk, N. (2010). A cultural formulation approach to counseling international students. *Journal of Career Development, 37*(1), 423–440. doi:10.1177/0894845309345845.

Australian Council for Private Education and Training. (2009). *The Australian education sector and the economic contribution of international students.* Australia: Access Economics Pty. Retrieved from http://globalhighered.files.wordpress.com/2009/04/theaustralianeducationsectorandtheeconomiccontributionofinternationalstudents-2461.pdf

Behrens, D. (2009). Interview practice U.S. style: A workshop for international students. *Journal of Employment Counselling, 46*, 182–184.

Brooks, R., Waters, J., & Pimlott-Wilson, H. (2012). International education and the employability of UK students. *British Educational Research Journal, 38*, 281–298. doi:10.1080/01411926.2010.544710.

Campbell, A. (2010). Developing generic skills and attributes of international students: The (ir)relevance of the Australian university experience. *Journal of Higher Education Policy & Management, 32*(5), 487–497. doi:10.1080/1360080X.2010.511121.

Centre for Educational Research and Innovation. (2011). *Education at a glance 2011: Highlights.* Paris: Organization for Economic Cooperation and Development. Retrieved from http://www.oecd-ilibrary.org/education/education-at-a-glance-2011_eag_highlights-2011-en

Chen, C. P. (2008). Career guidance with immigrants. In J. Athanasou & R. Van Esbroeck (Eds.), *International handbook of career guidance* (pp. 419–442). New York, NY: Springer.

Christofi, V., & Thompson, C. L. (2007). You cannot go home again: A phenomenological investigation of returning to the sojourn country after studying abroad. *Journal of Counseling & Development, 85*, 53–63. doi:10.1002/j.1556-6678.2007.tb00444.x.

Citizenship Immigration Canada (CIC). (2008). *Canadian experience class.* Retrieved from http://www.cic.gc.ca/english/immigrate/cec/index.asp

Collins, S., & Arthur, N. (2010). Culture-infused counselling: A fresh look at a classic framework of multicultural counselling competencies. *Counseling Psychology Quarterly, 23*(2), 203–216. doi:10.1080/09515071003798204.

Department for Business, Innovation and Skills. (2011). *Estimating the value to the UK of education exports.* Retrieved from http://www.bis.gov.uk/assets/biscore/higher-education/docs/e/11-980-estimating-value-of-education-exports.pdf

Douglass, J. A., & Edelstein, R. (2009). *The global competition for talent: The rapidly changing market for international students and the need for a strategic approach in the US* (Research & Occasional Paper Series: CSHE.8.09). Berkeley, CA: University of California, Center for Higher Studies in Education. Retrieved from http://escholarship.org/uc/item/0qw462x1

Flores, L. Y. (2009). Empowering life choices: Career counseling in the contexts of race and class. In N. Gysbers, M. Heppner, & J. Johnston (Eds.), *Career counseling: Contexts, processes and techniques* (pp. 49–74). Alexandria, VA: American Counseling Association.

Fouad, N. A., & Bingham, R. P. (1995). Career counseling with racial-ethnic minorities. In W. B. Walsh & S. H. Osipow (Eds.), *Handbook of vocational psychology* (2nd ed., pp. 331–366). Hillsdale, NJ: Lawrence Erlbaum.

Gaw, K. F. (2000). Reverse culture shock in students returning from overseas. *International Journal of Intercultural Relations, 24*(1), 83–104.

Gower, J. L. (2011). As dumb as we wannabe: U.S. H1-B visa policy and the "Brain Blocking" of Asian technology professionals. *Selected Works.* Retrieved from http://works.bepress.com/jeffrey_gower/1/

Gu, Q., Schweisfurthb, M., & Daya, C. (2010). Learning and growing in a 'foreign' context: Intercultural experiences of international students. *British Association for International and Comparative Education, 40*(1), 7–23. doi:10.1080/03057920903115983.

Guo, S., Schugurensky, D., Hall, B., Rocco, T., & Fenwick, T. (2010). Connected understanding: Internationalization of adult education in Canada and beyond. *The Canadian Journal for the Study of Adult Education, 23*(1), 73–89.

Hawthorne, L. (2006). *Labour market outcomes for migrant professionals: Canada and Australia compared—Executive summary.* Retrieved from http://www.cic.gc.ca/english/resources/research/2006-canada-australia.asp

Hong, G., & Domokos-Cheng Ham, M. (2000). *Psychotherapy and counseling with Asian American clients.* London, UK: Sage.

Hwang, K., Wang, M., & Sodanine, S. (2011). The effects of stressors, living support, and adjustment on learning performance of international students in the Taiwan. *Social Behavior & Personality: An International Journal, 39*(3), 333–344. doi:10.2224/sbp.2011.39.3.333.

Leong, F. T. L., & Gupta, A. (2008). Theories in cross-cultural contexts. In J. Athanasou & R. Van Esbroeck (Eds.), *International handbook of career guidance* (pp. 227–248). New York, NY: Springer.

Leong, F. T. L., & Hartung, P. J. (1997). Career assessment with culturally different clients: Proposing an integrative-sequential conceptual framework for cross-cultural career counseling research and practice. *Journal of Career Assessment, 5*, 183–201. doi:10.1177/106907279700500205.

Leung, S. A. (1995). Career development and counseling: A multicultural perspective. In J. G. Ponterotto, J. M. Casas, L. A. Suzuki, & C. M. Alexander (Eds.), *Handbook of multicultural counseling* (pp. 549–566). Thousand Oaks, CA: Sage.

Leung, S. A. (2007). Returning home and issues related to reverse culture shock. In H. Singaravelu & M. Pope (Eds.), *A handbook for counseling international students in the United States* (pp. 137–154). Alexandria, VA: American Counseling Association.

Martin, J. N., & Harrell, T. (1996). Reentry training for intercultural sojourners. In D. Landis & R. S. Bhagat (Eds.), *Handbook of intercultural training* (2nd ed., pp. 307–326). Thousand Oaks, CA: Sage.

Masumba, M., Jin, Y., & Mjelde, J. (2011). Factors influencing career location preferences of international graduate students in the United States. *Education Economics, 19*(5), 501–517. doi:10.1080/09645290903102902.

Mazzarol, T., & Soutar, G. N. (2002). "Push-pull" factors influencing international student destination choice. *The International Journal of Educational Management, 16*(2), 82–90. doi:10.1108/09513540210418403.

NAFSA: Association of International Education. (2009). *Foreign students spent nearly $18 billion in the United States during 2008–2009 academic year.* Retrieved from http://www.nafsa.org/PressRoom/PressRelease.aspx?id=17188

Nunes, S., & Arthur, N. (2013). International students' experiences of integrating into the workforce. *Journal of Employment Counseling, 50*, 34–45.

Osborn, D., Dikel, M., Sampson, J., Jr., & Harris-Bowlsbey, J. (2011). *The Internet: A tool for career planning* (3rd ed.). Broken Arrow, OK: National Career Development Association.

Pedersen, P. (1991). Counseling international students. *The Counseling Psychologist, 19*, 10–58.

Popadiuk, N., & Arthur, N. (2012). *Key relationships for international students' university-to-employment transitions.* Manuscript submitted for publication.

Reynolds, A., & Constantine, M. (2007). Cultural adjustment difficulties and career development of international college students. *Journal of Career Assessment, 15*(3), 338–350. doi:10.1177/1069072707301203.

Rodríguez González, C., Bustillo Mesanza, R., & Mariel, P. (2011). The determinants of international student mobility flows: An empirical study on the Erasmus programme. *Higher Education, 62*(4), 413–430. doi:10.1007/s10734-010-9396-5.

Sangganjanavanich, V. F., Lenz, A. S., & Cavazos, J., Jr. (2011). International students' employment search in the United States: A phenomenological study. *Journal of Employment Counseling, 48*, 17–26. doi:10.1002/j.2161-1920.2011.tb00107.x.

Shen, Y., & Herr, E. L. (2004). Career placement concerns of international graduate students: A qualitative study. *Journal of Career Development, 31*(1), 15–29. doi:10.1177/089484530403100102.

Shih, S., & Brown, C. (2000). Taiwanese international students: Acculturation level and vocational identity. *Journal of Career Development, 27*(1), 35–47. doi:10.1177/089484530002700103.

Singaravelu, H., White, L., & Bringaze, T. (2005). Factors influencing international students' career choice: A comparative study. *Journal of Career Development, 32*(1), 46–59. doi:10.1177/0894845305277043.

Spencer-Rodgers, J. (2000). The vocational situation and country of orientation of international students. *Journal of Multicultural Counseling and Development, 28*(1), 32–49. Retrieved from http://onlinelibrary.wiley.com

UNESCO. (2009). *Trends in global higher education: Tracking an academic revolution.* Retrieved from http://unesdoc.unesco.org/images/0018/001831/183168e.pdf

United States Citizenship and Immigration Services. (2011). *Foreign students.* Retrieved from http://www.uscis.gov/sitemap

United States Government Printing Office. (n.d.). *USA Patriot Act of 2001.* Washington, DC: U.S. Government Printing Office.

Yang, E., Wong, S. C., Hwang, M. H., & Heppner, M. J. (2002). Widening our global view: The development of career counseling services for international students. *Journal of Career Development, 28*(3), 203–213. doi:10.1177/089484530202800305.

Zhou, D., & Santos, A. (2007). Career decision-making difficulties of British and Chinese international university students. *British Journal of Guidance & Counselling, 35* (2), 219–235. doi:10.1080/03069880701256684.

Ziguras, C., & Law, S.-F. (2006). Recruiting international students as skilled immigrants: The global 'skills race' as viewed from Australia and Malaysia. *Globalisation, Societies and Education, 4*(1), 59–76. doi:10.1080/14767720600555087.

Career Services: New Directions for Assessment and Evaluation

Overview

This section examines innovations in assessment and evaluation of career guidance models, strategies, services, programs, and interventions. Paradigmatic positions influence approaches to career assessment and today, career counselors would benefit from frameworks that would allow them to integrate quantitative and qualitative, traditional and contemporary methods and techniques. One of the writers in this section examines vocational interests and aptitudes against the background of social organization, culture, and socioeconomic factors and present a methodologically integrated approach to assessment. The notion of potential, a blend of interests and aptitudes, is proposed as a relatively more stable construct around which career guidance services could be developed. The relationship between career assessment and career counseling has been challenged by recent developments in narrative career counseling. Writers in this section describe an approach that demonstrates the complementarity of quantitative career assessment and storytelling. One of the motivations that undergird career guidance and counseling is to help people optimize the quality of their working experience within the broader context of their lives. However, the concept of quality of working life has remained poorly defined and difficult to assess, although it would seem to be central to the process of choice, development, and change in work and career settings. Writers in this section review the development of the concept of quality of working life and its relevance to career guidance and counseling. The section moves on to examine the issues that surround evaluation and assessment of outcomes. Career guidance centers are rapidly mushrooming, particularly in emerging economies, in response to the urgently expressed need for support with career decision-making. The quality of these centers needs to be evaluated and monitored on an ongoing basis. Based on their research, writers present themes that could be used to develop frameworks and tools to assess the effectiveness of career guidance centers. A prominent call emerging from contemporary discussions on career development and public policy is: "Prove it works." The many issues related to outcome-focused, evidence-based practice are discussed. Methods and systems that could be put in place to develop more powerful accountability arguments supporting the effectiveness of career development services are presented.

In summary, this section presents ideas pertaining to two key issues: career assessment and the assessment of career services. Both of these are controversial topics and writings in this section present a wide range of arguments that address these debates.

Gideon Arulmani

Introduction

A significant proportion of the engagement between the client and the career counselor in many forms of counseling is devoted to gathering information about the individual that would promote self-awareness to aid the career decision-making process. While the methods employed to collect this information would rely on the paradigmatic persuasions of the career counselor, assessment (i.e., the collecting, structuring, and interpreting of information about the client in some form or the other) lies at the heart of most systems of career guidance and counseling. In this chapter, I examine the conceptual relationships between two key constructs related to assessment for career guidance: vocational interests and aptitudes. I also discuss the polarized debate related to the measurement of these constructs. A system of career guidance and counseling developed in India is presented to illustrate a *methodologically integrated approach* to career assessment. Two Indian studies are discussed, the first of which investigates the relative stability of interests and aptitudes and introduces for further consideration, the notion of *potential* as a blend of interests and aptitudes. The second study describes an assessment technique that integrates a more qualitative approach

along with a quantitative approach and examines the effectiveness of such an approach for career guidance and counseling. The prevailing views about the stability of interests and the relative merits of interest-based or aptitude-based career guidance are questioned in the light of data emerging from the Indian context. The impact of socioeconomic change and the involvement of sociocultural factors such as collectivist social organization are presented as a matrix within which to understand and interpret constructs such as vocational interests and aptitudes.

Theoretical Positions and Assessment Stances

The purpose and methods of assessment and measurement have been the subject of controversy. The field has polarized into the psychometric (quantitative) and the non-psychometric (qualitative) positions, and the stance taken toward assessment is often a reflection of the career counselor's theoretical and philosophic position. The trait-factor theory was conceivably the earliest approach to career assessment and emerged in response to the need for accurately matching people to specific occupations. Resting on the assumption that individuals possess a unique combination of traits which can be accurately measured and quantified, assessment methods emerging from the trait-factor position are usually quantitative and psychometric in their stance and attempt to generate objective and

G. Arulmani (✉)
The Promise Foundation, Bangalore, India
e-mail: garulmani@t-p-f.org

G. Arulmani et al. (eds.), *Handbook of Career Development*, International and Cultural Psychology,
DOI 10.1007/978-1-4614-9460-7_34, © Springer Science+Business Media, LLC 2014

reliable data, which a career counselor can use to find an effective "fit" between the Person (P) and his or her Environment (E). This theoretical position continues to have significant influence, and an important aspect of career counseling will always rest on data that is gathered through psychological tests. Career development, however, is a dynamic process that changes and evolves, and an individual's engagement with the world of work goes much beyond profiles emerging from psychometric testing. Hence, an exclusive reliance on the methods of the trait-factor approach has rightfully come into question. More recent theoretical positions have pointed in other directions. Three of these are of particular relevance to this chapter.

Sampson and colleagues have presented the cognitive information processing (CIP) approach to career development and services (e.g., Sampson, Reardon, Peterson, & Lenz, 2004). Of specific importance is the argument made by CIP that thoughts, emotions, and metacognitions influence the process of career decision making. Similar constructs have been presented by Arulmani and Nag-Arulmani (2004), when they describe social cognitive environments and career beliefs.

Patton and McMahon have extended systems theory to the discipline of career guidance (e.g., Patton & McMahon, 1999) and present their systems theory framework (STF) "as an overarching framework within which all concepts of career development described in the plethora of career theories can be usefully positioned and utilized in theory and practice" (Patton & McMahon, 2006, p. 153). Of importance to contemporary conceptualizations of career is that STF locates the individual "within myriad social influences" and emphasizes "the centrality of the individual actively construing the meaning of his or her life within multiple content and process influences" (Patton, 2008, p. 144).

Viewing career from a contextualist perspective, career construction theory brings for discussion the possibility that development is "driven by adaptation to an environment rather than by the maturation of inner structures" and that "individuals construct their careers by imposing

meaning on their vocational behavior and occupational experiences" (Savickas, 2005, p. 43). Of significance is the theory's focus on neither the P nor the E of the person–environment formulation but on the dash (–) between the two (Savickas, 2005). By this, the theory implies that the subjective definition of career is the integration of experiences into a cohesive whole such that a meaningful story emerges, based on the individual's active engagement with meaning making rather than the unveiling of preexisting facts.

A common thread that seems to run through these more recent perspectives is a questioning of the relevance of the trait-factor approach to contemporary career guidance. These approaches view the role of the counselor not as an "expert" but rather as a co-constructor partnering with the client, through a process of dialogue. This has further led to a shift in the understandings of the role played by assessment in career counseling, so much so that formal assessment in career guidance is said to "reflect old science" (Bradley, 1994, p. 224). It must be noted, however, that some of these new theoretical positions have their roots in sociocultural processes that characterize the West. They seem to rest on the assumption that the individual has the cultural freedom and the economic resources to be able to volitionally engage in career construction (also see Sultana, 2014, Chap. 18). The possibility of such self-mediated actions occurring spontaneously in non-Western collectivist contexts needs to be examined more closely. This will be discussed throughout this chapter.

Irrespective of the theoretical position taken, it may continue to be assumed that interactions between career counselor and client aim at generating material, information, and data that is then used to take the counseling further forward. Hence, understanding what is to be assessed or what kind of data needs to be collected continues to be a question worthy of being addressed. And this too has been the subject of debate. Intelligence, interest, aptitude, social cognitions, career thoughts, and personality are all constructs that have been variously considered to be relevant to promote effective career decision making. Clarity regarding which of these constructs best contribute to further career counseling objectives is also poor. Tests and methods have been developed to assess individuals/clients in one or many of these areas, and this has further spawned an industry to translate and adapt tests for new contexts. Against the background of globalization and the multicultural nature of contemporary career counseling contexts, questions have been raised with regard to test adaptation and test translation. The issue of bias has been highlighted with concern, particularly the possibility that when testing devices are transported to new contexts, the underlying constructs they assess may not remain equivalent (Duarte & Rossier, 2008). If this is true for testing methods and devices, it could also be true for theoretical positions and paradigms. Most of the research pertaining to these questions has been conducted in the West and hence is influenced by the cultural and economic realities of these contexts. In this chapter, these critical questions are discussed drawing upon experience and research from non-Western contexts such as India and other Asian and African countries.

The Importance of an Undergirding Theoretical Framework

Effective career guidance and counseling require the coming together of multiple units of information. It is essential that each of these information units contributes meaningfully and substantially to the process of career guidance and counseling. A career counseling system that is undergirded by a culturally and economically relevant theoretical reference point can facilitate this integration of information. At the intrapersonal level, such a framework could inform assessment techniques and methods and facilitate the development of a congruent and internally consistent picture of the contours of the individual's personal profile. A commonly encountered situation, particularly in contexts where the scientific

practice of career counseling is in its infancy, is one where information about the individual is collected through tools and devices that are each based on different theoretical persuasions. It is common in India, for example, to see on a career report, information from a battery of tests such as the Strong Interest Inventory for data pertaining to interests, the Differential Aptitude Test (DAT) for information about aptitudes, and the Cattell's 16 Personality Factors Questionnaire for data about personality. While they may be independently useful, it would be difficult to reconcile the information that is gathered into a coherent description of the individual's personal profile since each of these instruments originate from different theoretical frames of reference.

Theoretical consistency is also required in reference to the individual and the world of work. The usefulness of a device that generates information about the individual but does not find a close corollary in an occupational classification system would be limited. Effective career counseling requires the *concurrent* analysis of two sets of data: information about the person and information about the world of work. If this is to be achieved, the career counseling system must rest on a theoretically validated framework that uses comparable constructs, terminology, and methods for assessment and classification. The absence of such a theoretical platform would affect the extent to which information about the person and information about the world of work could inform each other and thereby lead the individual toward effective career decision making. Ideally, the primary motivation behind the deployment of a method would be to address the client's felt need rather than being a medium that applies a certain theory's tenets. As will be discussed later in the chapter, a blending of methods (e.g., cross-sectional with longitudinal, quantitative with qualitative, questionnaires with interviews) would perhaps yield the better result.

Promoting Self-Understanding: The Central Objective of Assessment

It may be argued that assessment is meant to promote the individual's insights into self and thereby support career decision making and facilitate the client's engagement with the world of work. If this is a central objective, then the question that surfaces is as follows: What should be assessed that will foster effective career decision making? Historically, a variety of factors have been the target of measurement to promote self-awareness. In their overview of this history, Swanson and D'Achiardi (2005) have pointed to three main constructs that have been typically understood to be pivotal to career choice: interests, needs/values, and abilities. In the following sections, the constructs of interests, abilities, and aptitudes are examined in greater detail.

Interests

Defining Interests

The construct of interest has been central to some of the most well-known contemporary approaches to career guidance and counseling. Summarizing the history of interest assessment, Hansen (2005) has highlighted three major components of interests: personality, motivation, and self-concept. She describes interests to be "a preference for activities expressed as likes or dislikes" (p. 281). Our definition of interest is similar: Interests are activities that draw a person's attention, things that a person is curious about, matters a person wants to pursue further, activities that a person considers worthwhile, and activities a person enjoys. Indeed, interests are like the steam in a locomotive: Interests motivate and drive a person to preferentially seek out and engage with certain kinds of activities over others.

Determinants of Interests

Having defined interests, a further question that arises pertains to the determinants of interests.

Although theorists do not overtly deny the role that inheritance and genetics might play in determining an individual's interests, the overwhelming opinion is that interests are the result of socialization and learning and are, therefore, subject to the individual's experiences and exposure (see Hansen, 2005). It is highly unlikely, therefore, that someone who has never seen the sea would develop interests in activities related to fishing, deep sea diving, or surfing.

Stability of Interests

A feature that is of crucial relevance to this discussion is the *stability* of interests. Hansen (2005) in her review underscored several notable points: "If interests are not stable (in other words, if interests are a state rather than a trait), interest inventories have no chance of predicting occupational or educational choices even over short time spans" (p. 284). Reviewing the work of E. K. Strong (the doyen of interest assessment) and decades of research since his early work, she makes the statement that "we know that interests are very stable over time. In fact interests may be the most stable of all psychological constructs" (Hansen, 2005, p. 284). Based on the same review, Hansen also reports that it has been consistently found that the individual's age at the time of testing reflects the stability of his or her interests: The younger the individual, the less stable interests are. The duration between Time 1 and Time 2 assessments affects measures of the stability of interests: The longer the interval between the first and second measurements, the less stable the interest. Similar evidence from a wide range of research (e.g., Campbell & Holland, 1972; Lubinski, Benbow, & Ryan, 1995; Pendergrass, Hansen, Neuman, & Nutter, 2003; Swanson & Hansen, 1988) has led to the acceptance that "by age 20 interests are stable even over periods of 5–10 years, and by age 25 interests are very stable" (Hansen, 2005, p. 285). Low, Yoon, Roberts, and Rounds (2005) extended these findings in a meta-analytic review of 66 longitudinal studies of vocational interests from early adolescence (age 12) to middle adulthood (age 40). They found that interest scores attained stability during early adolescence. This stability increased during late adolescence-early adulthood and then remained stable for the next two decades. It must be noted that the studies in this meta-analysis comprised samples only from the USA and Canada (J. Rounds, personal communication, May 24, 2013). In a follow-up to this meta-analysis, Low and Rounds (2006) proposed five forms of stability: rank-order stability, profile stability, mean-level stability, structural stability, and congruence (or interest-fit) stability. They also highlight that the "existence of one form of stability does not rule out the possibilities of other types of change" (Low & Rounds, 2006, p. 29).

It is important to note that the nature of interests has been studied mainly from two perspectives: *situational* and *dispositional*. Situational interests are characterized by emotional states evoked by experience and exposure and hence are transitory and influenced by the attributes of an activity (Hidi, Renninger, & Krapp, 1992). This has been contrasted with dispositional interests, which are assumed to reflect the individual's "psychological disposition associated with his or her preferences for activities and actions" (Low et al., 2005, p. 2). Dispositional interests are rooted in the features of the person's personality, and as Strong (1943) put it, are groupings of likes and dislikes that lead to enduring and consistent patterns of behavior. Sufficient evidence has accrued leading to the conclusion in the literature that (dispositional) interests have stability across age and time. Indeed, it is based upon the *consistency* of interests that entire schools of career guidance and counseling have been founded and successfully practiced (e.g., Holland, 1959). I will, however, present later in this chapter findings from India that are somewhat at variance with the assertion that interests are stable over time.

Aptitudes

Defining Abilities and Aptitudes

In common parlance, the terms *ability* and *aptitude* are often used synonymously. However, in the psychological literature, a distinction is drawn between the two. Ability is described as the capacity to perform a particular act or task, either physical or mental (Snow, 1994), and is considered to be an attribute of the individual revealed by differences in the levels of task difficulty, on a defined class of tasks that he or she performs successfully (Carroll, 1993). Gottfredson's (2003) description is incisive: "Abilities are what people can do, not their style of doing it. Abilities are not the bodies of knowledge that people amass but their aptness in amassing them" (p. 117). The modern understanding of the nature and constitution of abilities has been informed by the conceptualizations of J. P. Guildford and J. Carroll and are often cited in relation to ability testing for career guidance. Guildford's (1967) structure of intellect model outlined 120 distinctive cognitive abilities organized in three dimensions: type of content, type of operation performed, and the product resulting from the operation of each ability. Carroll (1993) presented a hierarchical model of ability. Based on comprehensive factor-analytic studies of 467 data sets spanning several decades, in this model abilities are organized in strata along a three-level hierarchical structure. The highest and broadest has been called stratum III which comprises general cognitive abilities referred to as the *g* factor of intelligence and reflected as the individual's Intelligence Quotient (IQ). Abilities seen at stratum II become more specific and much more narrowly and specifically defined in stratum I. Strata II and I are seen to comprise 8 and 68 ability areas, respectively (Carroll, 1993).

Aptitudes have been described to be potential abilities (Snow, 1992). They reflect how *likely* an individual is to be successful in the performance of a certain task. Our description of aptitude is similar: Aptitudes reflect what one would be naturally good at, the person's talents and capabilities, and the strength of likelihood for achievement in a particular area. If interests are the steam in a locomotive, aptitudes could represent the engine: the actual ability to move toward and be successful in the execution of a specific set of tasks.

Determinants of Abilities and Aptitudes

Here again, theorists and researchers have not presented conclusive evidence to support either the nature or nurture position with regard to what determines abilities and aptitudes. Snow (1994) has indicated that abilities could be learned, or if innate, they could have some kind of neurological/genetic basis. This writing takes the position that abilities lie along a continuum with heritability and learning lying at either ends. There are certain careers (e.g., professional sport) that are grounded upon a specific physiological substrate (e.g., a certain kind of muscle structure, certain levels of stamina, and capacity for endurance). Such abilities could fall closer to the heritability end of the continuum and may perhaps be less influenced by socialization and learning. At the same time if an individual with a high capacity for professional sport is part of a culture that does not value this ability, it would be difficult for the capacity to find its fulfillment. By contrast, other careers (e.g., office secretary) would require skills that could be sharpened through learning (e.g., telephone management, dealing with customer's queries). The argument being developed in this chapter rests on the understanding that wherever it is along the continuum that an ability lies, learning and socialization are required to bring it to fruition.

Stability of Abilities and Aptitudes

The consensus in the literature seems to be that abilities tend to reach a high level of stability by early adolescence (e.g., Carroll, 1993; Dixon, Kramer, & Baltes, 1985). Keeping the hierarchical model of abilities in mind, Gottfredson (2003) argued that while change and development continue to be possible, this is more likely only at the narrow and specific ability levels than at the broader levels. In other words, abilities that fall in strata II and III are less changeable than the specific abilities represented at stratum I. Gottfredson, therefore, recommended that effective career counseling would help clients choose careers based on the broader abilities, since these abilities are less likely to change,

and then fine-tune personal suitability by developing the more changeable stratum I abilities.

The Controversy

In the foregoing section, the two main pillars of assessment for career guidance and counseling—interests, on the one hand, and abilities and aptitudes, on the other—have been described. Historically, the formalization of vocational guidance in the 1900s was largely in response to the pressing demand from the rapidly industrializing labor market to appropriately match workers with jobs. The need at this time was to assess abilities and ascertain a person–job fit as accurately as possible. In the beginning, perhaps the very purpose of career guidance was to obtain correct measurements of ability and aptitude. Methods of assessment grew increasingly sophisticated and gave rise to a wide range of assessment devices such as the General Aptitude Test Battery (GATB) (U.S. Department of Labor, 1970) and the DAT (Bennett, Seashore, & Wesman, 1990). The scope of assessment was broadened to include vocational interests as a part of assessment for career development (e.g., Holland, 1959; Strong, 1935). This critical inclusion formed a comprehensive whole as it were, since it drew the wishes and desires of the career decision maker more firmly into the career decision-making process. Indeed, Strong (1943) himself said, "Counseling that considers both abilities and interests is distinctly superior to that based on either alone, for it is in a position to establish both what the person can do and what she or he wants to do" (p. 19). Yet, by the 1960s the value placed on the assessment of abilities and aptitudes declined and faded from favor. Remarking on this in her review of the literature, Gottfredson (2003) asked, "Why did the field no longer pay much attention to one of the twin pillars in person-job match? Why did the career literature say so little about abilities and their role in counseling?" (p. 115). She went on to answer her question by pointing to developments in political stances particularly since "civil rights and women's movements had made counseling psychologists reluctant to tell counselees they could not become whatever they wished to be" (p. 116). It is perhaps difficult in a culture that celebrates the individual to tell someone that they have "lower abilities" for something. Commenting on lower levels of interest for a certain set of activities is perhaps easier because it does not place the individual at a lower status or capability level. In addition, philosophic paradigm shifts that occurred in the world of education caused trait-factor theories to fall into disfavor. A corollary was a decline in the importance placed upon psychometric testing, based on the perception that it was reductionist in its approach, since the issues surrounding standardization, development of meaningful norms that had equivalence across cultures, remained hard to resolve. Against such a background, opinions pertaining to the assessment of abilities grew antagonistic, and the use of ability testing seems to have become limited in Western forms of career counseling. As argued above, career guidance based on interests only completes half the picture. The rest of this chapter will present information to support the argument that the assessment of abilities and aptitudes is at least as important as the assessment of interests in the practice of effective career guidance and counseling. Indeed "the relationship among abilities, interests and achievements maybe likened to a motorboat with a motor and a rudder. The motor (abilities) determines how fast the boat can go, the rudder (interests) determines which way the boat goes" (Strong, 1943, p. 10).

A Methodologically Integrated Approach to Career Guidance and Counseling

A methodologically integrated approach to career guidance and counseling has been developed for the Indian/Asian cultural and economic context based on the cultural preparation process model (Arulmani, 2010, 2011a; also see

Arulmani, 2014, Chap. 6). Accordingly, career guidance and counseling are embedded into the culture of the audience, namely, Indian career choosers, their families, and communities. These career development programs are implemented at various levels ranging from large-group workshops to individualized one-on-one sessions. Arulmani's (2010) report has provided a detailed description of this approach. Described here are some of the elements of this method that have relevance to this chapter.

Key Principles

In Indian thought, work is pictured not as a job to earn a living but as an extension of one's life. Keeping this deeply embedded cultural orientation in mind, this program has been named *Jiva* which means *life* in almost all Indian languages. The approach rests on the central idea that work and occupation are interwoven into the individual's life as a whole. The method is based on five principles which are drawn from culturally embedded symbols and beliefs in the Indian conceptualization of the individual's engagement with life. Workshops based on these principles take career choosers through four career development activities: building self-awareness, understanding the world of work, developing career alternatives, and career path planning. Assessment is a part of the self-awareness component of the program and will be described in detail in the following sections.

Multiple Potentials Framework

Within this system, assessment devices are based on the multiple potentials framework (Arulmani & Nag-Arulmani, 2004), which is an adaptation of Gardner's (1983) theory of multiple intelligences. The multiple potentials framework comprises five factors: linguistic (L), analytical–logical (AL), spatial (S), personal (P), and physical–mechanical (PM) (see Arulmani & Nag-Arulmani, 2004 and http://www.jivacareer.org/project/page/multiple-potentials-framework.

html for a detailed description of the components of the multiple potentials framework).

Approach to Assessment

A multipronged approach is taken to assess interests and aptitudes, which blends quantitative along with more qualitative methods. Qualitative sources of information include interviews, the counselee's academic history, hobbies and accomplishments, and parent/teacher opinions. Quantitative methods include psychometric devices such as the Multiple Potentials Interest Inventory (MPII) and the Multiple Potentials Test-5 (MPT-5). These two quantitative measures are now briefly described, and one of the qualitative methods, the Strengths and Accomplishments Questionnaire (SAQ), will be introduced next.

Multiple Potentials Interest Inventory

This is an interest inventory that taps the five factors of the multiple potentials framework described above. It has been standardized for the Indian context on a randomly drawn, stratified sample of close to 9,000 Indian adolescents–young adults in the age range of 14–21 years (Arulmani, 2005a). The MPII was constructed from an item pool of about 250 items per potential through a process of item and factor analyses. Items reflect occupational tasks associated with a particular potential. For example, the item "present information to people in a written form" is linked to the linguistic potential. Similarly, the item "use data to make predictions" is linked to the analytical–logical potential, "design things from ideas" to the spatial potential, "understand people's feelings and behavior" to the personal potential, and "be involved in physically demanding work" to the physical–mechanical potential. With 12 such items for each potential, the scale comprises a total of 60 items. Participants rate each activity for how much they would like to engage in it as a part of their work life. Response choices are anchored to 5 scale points where 1 indicates the lowest and 5, the highest level of interest. The maximum

obtainable score per potential is 60, and respondents' scores are summed separately for each potential. The score obtained on each potential yields an interest profile across the five factors.

The validity of the MPII was examined by testing the correlations between respondents' ratings and external criteria: ratings by parents/teachers of respondents (i.e., criterion-related concurrent validity). Parents/teachers provided their estimate of respondents' interest levels across the MPII factors based on their everyday interactions with the respondents. Positive, statistically significant correlations ranging from .62 to .81 have been consistently obtained between external criterion estimates and respondents' interest scores, across the five potential areas and across samples from different age bands, socioeconomic status (SES) groups, and geographical locations, indicating that the MPII has an acceptably high validity. Tests of split-half reliability have shown high and significant Pearson's r ranging between .74 and .83 for all the potential areas. This also indicates that the scale has high internal consistency. The test–retest reliability of the MPII has been examined for different age groups, gender, and SES level. The 3-month reliability coefficients ranged between .72 and .91. However, reliability coefficients dropped to much lower values when the interval between test and retest was increased. This decrease is discussed in greater detail below.

Multiple Potentials Test-5

This is an aptitude test battery that taps the five factors described by the multiple potentials framework described. It has been standardized for the Indian context on a randomly drawn, stratified sample of about 8,700 Indian adolescents–young adults in the age range of 15–21 years (Arulmani, 2005b). Based on the multiple potentials framework, this is a timed test that comprises 30 items per factor. These items were selected from an item pool of about 90 items per potential area through a process of potential and item analyses. Items have been designed to tap subdomains of each potential area and include paper pencil as well as performance formats. Each item carries a score of 1 and the maximum obtainable score per potential area is 30. Norms for the MPT-5 have been developed by SES and gender, and an individual's score can be interpreted across the semantic labels of low, low-average, average, high-average, and high-aptitude levels.

The validity of the MPT-5 was examined by testing the correlations between respondents' ratings and external criteria such as academic performance and ratings by parents/teachers of respondents (i.e., criterion-related concurrent validity). For the latter, parents/teachers provided estimates of aptitude levels across the MPT-5 factors based on their knowledge of respondents' capabilities. Positive, statistically significant correlations ranging from .64 to .71 have been consistently obtained between the external criterion estimates and respondents' aptitude scores across the five potential areas and across different samples, indicating that the MPT-5 has an acceptably high validity. The 12-month test–retest reliability of the MPT-5 across different age groups, gender, and SES groups was moderate to high with reliability coefficients ranging from .62 to .81.

It must be noted that this assessment is embedded in a system of career counseling where students engage in a number of activities related to understanding what interests and aptitudes are, before they answer the MPII and the MPT-5. Hence, they take the tests only after they have comprehended the notion of interests and aptitudes.

The Profile Approach

An intraindividual approach is taken and emphasis is laid on the individual's *profile* across the five potential areas. This refers to the relative ranking of the scores obtained by the individual on the subtests for each of the five potential areas. Hence (taking 1 as the highest and 5 as the lowest rank), the interest scores obtained on the MPII may yield a ranking of the five potential areas in one client as L = 3, AL = 4, S = 5, P = 1, and PM = 2, while in another client the rankings may emerge as follows: L = 1, AL = 5, S = 3, P = 4, and PM = 2. In the first client, P (personal) would be identified as

the area for which the individual has the highest interest. The same intraindividual, profile approach is used with the MPT-5 aptitude test battery.

Occupational List

In keeping with the earlier assertion that an effective career guidance program must be undergirded by the same theoretical framework both for self-awareness activities and for occupational classification, this system uses the multiple potentials framework to classify occupations (Nagesh, Kumar, & Arulmani, 2010). This is an occupational list drawn from the International Standard Classification of Occupations (International Labour Organization, 2008). It comprises a total of 164 careers with viable educational and career pathways in India, classified into one of the five factors of the multiple potentials framework.

Data from the MPII and MPT-5 will now be used to discuss the question: What should we assess to best promote the individual's awareness of self?

Study 1: The Relationship Between Interests, Aptitudes, and Potentials

The Sample and Intervention

The career counseling program in this study was designed for students in grades 10 and 12 (approximately 15 and 17 years of age, respectively). It was an 8-hour one-to-one interaction delivered over one day, which comprised a wide range of career development activities addressing self-understanding, understanding the world of work, generating career alternatives, and planning career paths and career preparation. A comprehensive assessment of interests and aptitudes using the MPII and the MPT-5 was a part of this program.

Students who attended this career counseling program in grade 10 had the option of voluntarily returning for further counseling when in grade

12. During the period of this study, a total of 201 students were seen at grade 10. Of these, 130 students voluntarily returned to our center for follow-up counseling at grade 12. The sample for this study comprises this opportunistic sample, and the data are their responses in grades 10 (T1) and 12 (T2) on the MPII and MPT-5. All students were from upper-middle-class backgrounds, and their average age at T1 and T2 was 15.24 (SD = 0.61) and 17.29 (SD = 0.62) years, respectively. Fifty-two percent of the group was female. This sample represented individuals from eight states of India and five religious groups. All students were fluent in English, the language in which the workshop and assessment were conducted. The duration of time that elapsed between T1 and T2 ranged between 24 and 26 months.

Findings and Interpretations

The Relationship Between Interests and Aptitudes

While the associations between aptitude and career/interest and career have been studied, not much research attention has been directed toward understanding the association between aptitudes and interests. The first set of findings I report is with regard to this association.

No statistically significant correlations were found between interest and aptitude scores at T1 on any of the five factors. Thus, at grade 10 we did not find that having a high interest score on one of the factors meant that the person would also have a corresponding high aptitude score on the same factor. These findings seem to point to the possibility that in the sociocultural and socioeconomic context from which this sample was drawn, interests and aptitudes may not be as strongly associated as expected. A critical question that emerges, therefore, is which of these two important constructs, interest and aptitude, should one consider in order to best promote the individual's self-understanding for career decision making? Counseling based on any one alone could move the counselee in different directions. For example, the interest profile on the MPII that one of the students in this sample obtained was as

follows: L = 1, AL = 3, S = 5, P = 2, and PM = 4. The same student's aptitude profile on the MPT-5 painted quite a different picture: L = 3, AL = 2, S = 1, P = 5, and PM = 4. The reader is reminded here that 1 is taken as the highest and 5 as the lowest rank. If counseling were to be based on *interests* and followed the MPII, examples of the kind of careers this student would have been encouraged to explore are journalism (linguistic), social work, and psychology (personal). If counseling were, however, to be based on *aptitudes* and followed the MPT-5, examples of careers for exploration could have been architecture and commercial art (spatial) and software development (analytical–logical). Each set of career options is worlds apart from each other! How then does one make the decision as to whether counseling should be based on interests or aptitudes? Our findings about the apparent lack of association between interests and aptitudes could imply that they each contribute *independently* to understanding the individual's suitability for the world of work. It could also mean that relying on the assessment of interests *or* aptitudes to the exclusion of the other would yield only a part of the information required. It could well be that a *combination* of information about interests and aptitudes would contribute to a deeper and more stable understanding of the individual's profile.

Reviewing the literature, Ackerman and Haggestad (1997) showed the overlapping between interests and aptitudes. They cite, for example, studies that showed that literacy interests are associated with verbal ability and other studies that found that a positive correlation exists between verbal ability and Holland's artistic and investigative interests and so on. However, there do not seem to be many studies that have investigated interest–aptitude relationships within the *same* construct, based on the same theoretical reference point. Take the spatial construct (one of the five in the multiple potentials framework) as an example. It would be useful for a career counselor to know what an individual's abilities as well as what his or her interests are for spatial activities. For example, if an aptitude test shows that a person's ability to transform observations into two-/three-dimensional images/figures is

Table 34.1 Change in scores on MPII (Interest) and MPT-5 (Aptitude) across T1 and T2 for each of the five factors ($N = 130$)

Potential areas	Range of change in scores from T1 to T2[a]		% of individuals whose ranking changed from T1 to T2, irrespective of direction of change		% of individuals for whom scores decreased at T2		Pearson's r for scores on potential at T1 and T2[b]
	I	A	I	A	I	A	
L	−57 to 60	−20 to 10	57	25	47	5	.448**
AL	−57 to 47	−40 to 3	62	29	45	2	.721**
S	−60 to 60	−16 to 30	59	33	31	3	.676**
P	−58 to 65	−23 to 3	53	25	33	2	.514**
PM	−53 to 53	−20 to 6	46	33	66	1	.596**

Note: L linguistic, AL analytical–logical, S spatial, P personal, PM physical–mechanical, I interest, A aptitude
**$p < .001$ level
[a]A minus score means T1 score was higher than T2 score and a plus score means T2 score was more than T1 score
[b]Average of MPII and MPT-5 scores at each time point is the potential score for that time point

high and an interest inventory shows that his or her interest to work with colors and designs is high, this would point to the possibility that both ability and interest are high for spatial activities. The finding may also be that while ability is high, interests for activities in the area are low or vice versa. Such information about the same construct would allow career guidance to be much more effective. I move now to the second set of findings to further explore the relationship between interest and aptitude.

Stability of Interests and Aptitudes

This set of findings is with reference to an issue that has been extensively researched and apparently put to rest in the Western literature, namely, the stability of interests (also see Bakshi, 2014, Chap. 4). Firstly, an examination of the T1 and T2 scores (Table 34.1) indicates that the range of scores is remarkably higher for interests than for aptitudes. Secondly, the findings indicate that when compared with aptitude rankings, a greater percentage of individuals' interest rankings changed from T1 to T2 for all the five potential areas. Finally, the percentage of individuals whose scores decreased from T1 to T2 is greater in all five areas for interests than aptitudes. Excerpts from interviews with members of the sample whose interests showed a marked decline at T2 (Box 34.1), throw further light on these findings.

The (predominantly Western) reports in the literature presented in earlier sections in this chapter have led to the seemingly firm conclusion that interests are stable over time. The findings from this study seem to be contrary: Over time, and for the middle-to-late adolescent age band, interests seem more liable to change than aptitudes and hence may not be as stable as reported in the literature. It further seems from this data that aptitudes are more stable than interests. We postulate that three main reasons could underlie the apparent changeability of interests in the Indian context as represented by this sample. The first is already explained in the literature and relates to the age of the participants. The second is a cultural explanation. In collectivist cultures, the mediation of others (parents, family, community) in the decision-making process is much stronger than the wishes of the individual, and this could influence the manifestation of the individual's interests. As indicated by some of the quotations (Box 34.1), it seems the ease with which one can act on one's interests emerges only later in the individual's life. The third reason is related to the profound economic changes that have swept across collectivist cultures over the last two decades. Taken together, this raises questions about not only the validity and reliability but also the adequacy of using interest as the primary construct to inform career guidance and counseling. This is especially with reference to societies that are collectivist in structure and economies that are experiencing rapid growth and change. These points will be addressed in greater detail in the final section of this chapter.

> **Box 34.1. Excerpts from Interviews with 12th Grade Students Whose Interest Scores Reduced over Time**
>
> Question asked: *Your Interest Profile has changed significantly from the first time you answered the questionnaire and the second time. How do you explain this change?*
>
> - I was a kid then. Now I am older. Lots of experiences and chances to check out. That made me change. Now I am more sure. But still what I like can change all through my life right?! *Female, 17 years old.*
> - I had met an airforce pilot when I answered those questions on the paper. Was so totally impressed and wanted to be like that. Then I realised airforce is killing people. I don't want make my life out of shooting others from the air. No way. Civil aviation is just flying from one place to another. Lost interest when I found out this. *Male, 17 years old.*
> - Hey! Gimme a chance to grow up! I was just in Class 10 then. *Female, 17 years old.*
> - At that time you are not really thinking. Just doing what others think is cool. It's been 2 years right? And what I liked also changed. That's why I'm back here today. But still, I don't want to fix my options for my whole life. *Male, 17 years old.*

Note: The interval between T1 and T2 in all the cases reported is 24–26 months.

Proponents of aptitude-based counseling have pointed out that costly failures could result when a student is not informed that he or she may have a low ability to do well in a course in which he or she is interested (Gregoire & Nils, 2008). Gottfredson (2003) states:

> Effective career exploration has to address the obstacles as well as possibilities that counselees face in career development. No option is a good one unless it is truly feasible—or can be made so. Noncompetitive ability levels for a preferred occupation are clearly an obstacle (p. 15).

Her *reality-based career exploration* is designed such that the career choosers identify a list of "best bet" careers to explore in detail based on a consideration of their strata II and III abilities (Gottfredson, 1985). This offers an effective method for career guidance from the abilities angle. However, this does not answer the objections raised by the proponents of interest-based career guidance, particularly the view that data for ability-based counseling must perforce rely on psychometric devices. As stated earlier, counseling could be more effective if it is based on information about *both* interests and aptitudes. But at a practical level, how does this work? Does this mean that two sets (interests and aptitudes) of scores are to be generated? How would one then deal with contradictions between the scores?

Interests and Aptitudes Are Both Important

Two observations from Study 1 stand out: Interests change over time and high interest may not signify high ability. This corroborates our observations across more than 150,000 adolescents and young adults in India and other Asian and African countries over nearly two decades. These observations and experiences have shown us that as the person's career development progresses, personal experiences and external influences could reinforce current interests or could cause a swing of interests to some other point of focus (Arulmani & Nag-Arulmani, 2005). Sensitive and person-centered career counseling ought not to chain the young person to a group of interests for which he or she declared an attraction at a certain stage in life. Also, career success is often mediated by intense competition. Merely being interested and motivated, however strong this motivation, is not assurance enough that the individual will develop an adequately high level of ability to succeed in the face of competition.

It is here that a vital point emerges. An interest inventory can help to delineate a person's interests, while an aptitude test would help identify capabilities and talents. Closer examination might reveal that some of the interests identified do not complement the individual's aptitude profile. Similarly, it is also possible that the individual may not have a high interest for careers connected to some of his or her aptitudes. The all-important task before the career counselor, therefore, is to help the career chooser uncover the point of overlap between a person's interests and aptitudes.

Defining Potential

Discovering the connection between interests and aptitudes can help delineate career areas in which the individual is not only interested but for which he or she possesses talents. We refer to this point of overlap between interest and aptitude as *potential*: a blend or a combination of specific interests and specific aptitudes. The integrated approach to career counseling described in the earlier sections generates data for both interests and aptitudes using several devices and methods linked to the multiple potentials framework. Based on a system of weightages, interest and aptitude data is then blended to construct the individual's potential profile. This is discussed in greater detail in sections ahead.

The Stability of Potential

At this point, I would like to go back to the findings of the study described above and draw the reader's attention to the last column in Table 34.1. This column presents the correlation coefficients between the scores on what I have termed as "potential" (i.e., the average of interest and aptitude percentage scores) at T1 and T2. The correlations between scores on potential at T1 and T2 range from modest to moderately high and are all statistically significant. In other words, the scores recorded by this sample on potential, showed (greater) stability over time.

Data such as this, along with anecdotal evidence and field experience, have consistently pointed us to the strong possibility that the

potential profile is a relatively more stable reference point within which the individual's career exploration may be framed. Indeed, between interest and aptitudes, it is the combination, namely, the potential as we have called it, that seems to matter. We offer this construct as worthy of further investigation.

Alternative Methods and Techniques for Assessment

Criteria for the Usefulness of Psychometric Devices

One way of identifying the individual's potential profile is to use standardized psychometric devices such as interest inventories and aptitude tests and then use a statistically validated system of weightages to combine this data. Tests provide useful cross-sectional information. However, the accuracy of data obtained from psychometric instruments rests on a number of assumptions. Writing from the Indian context, Arulmani and Nag-Arulmani (2004) have highlighted that psychometric devices are useful only when the items are culture, age, and gender appropriate; administered by a qualified person; scored accurately; and interpreted on the basis of contextually validated norms. It is vital that the test-taker is able to give the test his or her "best shot." Anxiety, fatigue, skepticism, playfulness, and succumbing to socially acceptable responses, can all affect test performance.

Relevance

The cultural and statistical suitability of a test is central to the debate about the relevance of psychological tests. If, for example, a test developed in the USA is used on an Indian clientele, without being culturally contextualized and statistically re-standardized for use with Indians, the test-taker's performance on that test is not likely to be an accurate reflection of his or her profile. As famous as it is in the Western context, a trial of Holland's Vocational Preference Inventory indicated that its relevance to the Indian situation was limited (Leong, Austin, Sekaran, & Komarraju, 1998). When examined in the Chinese context, it was found that Holland's six interest types tended to group together in configurations that reflected the cultural orientations and occupational or educational sensitivities characteristic of a particular cultural context (Law, Wong, & Leong, 2001). Examples such as this are plentiful (see Leung, 2008). Despite this, the wholesale import of tests is an uncomfortably recurring occurrence in not just India, but many other countries as well (e.g., Hong Kong: Leung, 2002).

Translation and Adaptation

Commenting on the adaptation and translation of tests developed in one culture for use in another culture, Hambleton (2005) highlighted that test adaptation goes far beyond merely creating literal translations of test content and requires translators to find concepts, words, and expressions in the recipient language that are psychologically and linguistically equivalent to the language in which the test was originally developed. Here, culture is a powerful mediating variable. It is quite possible that a certain concept or construct is unfamiliar, considered strange, or perhaps even unacceptable in the culture for which a translation is being undertaken. Hence, Duarte and Rossier (2008), in their excellent review of testing and assessment in an international context, express uncertainty about the very nature of test adaptation when they state, "Test adaptation does not run in straight lines. Evaluative information on culture and context is much more complex than creating guidelines for cross-cultural normative assessment" (p. 489). A further concern is that although many psychological tests are constructed using samples composed primarily of Anglo-Americans, normative data for the use of these devices with other racial, ethnic groups is rarely developed (Hansen, 2005). For a country like India, this would be a gigantic task. If a given test were to be adapted for India, translations and norms would be required for at least 22 linguistic groups! Further,

psychological testing today has become corporatized and is big business. A trend that can be noticed over the recent past is the loosening of the rigor with which training and licensing are provided, particularly when large psychological testing businesses move into countries where career counseling is in its infancy. Hence, while we endorse the use of psychometric devices, we view the transport of psychological tools across cultural boundaries and the licensing of testers without adequate training in psychology, statistics, and the device itself, with deep concern.

Two points emerge from the foregoing discussion on psychometric tests. Firstly, they are useful and can offer vital information if they are culturally and statistically relevant to the context in which they are used and administered and interpreted by adequately trained personnel. Secondly, the construction and development of sound psychometric devices is a complex and expensive exercise that may not be easy to accomplish in situations where career counseling services are in their infancy. Yet, the need for rigorous assessment methods that could inform career guidance and counseling is an urgent and pressing one. It is against this background that we have experimented with alternative methods and techniques of assessment which are now described.

The Strengths and Accomplishments Questionnaire (SAQ)

Description

As stated, there are new paradigms that highlight the importance of career guidance being a co-constructive activity between counselor and client. The SAQ is an attempt to create a method that can allow this kind of a partnership between client and counselor. This is a method that uses the multiple potentials framework to dip into the participant's everyday life focusing on his or her *accomplishments*. It requires the participant to look back over a period of 3–4 years to identify accomplishments. It is qualitative to the extent

Box 34.2. Linguistic section of the Strengths and Accomplishments Questionnaire (SAQ)

Question number	Areas of accomplishment	I am involved in this activity at the personal level	I have participated in events and competitions in school	I have won prizes at school OR my work was selected for school publications	I have participated in events and competitions outside school	I have won prizes outside school (in a public forum) OR my work was selected for publication outside school
1	Writing (essays, articles)	✓	✓			
2	Writing (poetry, short stories)	✓	✓	✓		
3	Public speaking (debating, elocution, giving speeches)	✓	✓	✓	✓	
4	Drama and acting	✓	✓			

that it allows the assessor to construct a questionnaire as per the accomplishments for which the student is most likely to have had opportunities given his or her culture, SES, schooling, and cultural background. It attempts to be contextualized to the extent that it draws upon the person's lived experience rather than expecting the individual to respond to items that may or may not be relevant to his or her situation. It is co-constructive to the extent that it requires the counselor to engage in a dialogue with the client and capture aspects of his or her life that are relevant to career development. At the same time, it includes quantification through the use of a rating scale. As an illustration, Box 34.2 provides an extract from the linguistic section of the SAQ. In this approach, the career counselor is free to identify "areas of accomplishment" (column 2 in Box 34.2) that have the highest likelihood of occurrence given the student's (or test-taker's) sphere of experience and opportunities within the multiple potentials framework.

Administration

The SAQ is typically introduced after students have engaged in a number of activities related to what aptitudes are and the difference between interests and aptitudes. The counselor explains the meaning of the word *accomplishment* as any activity in which the person has had some level of success that has been noticed by others (e.g., being a class leader, organizing an outing, repairing something). Participants are to read each item and fill in the table by indicating their level of achievement.

Scoring

The first row in Box 34.2 shows the scoring scheme which in fact follows the principle of a rating scale. The rating scale runs from 1 to 5 with a rating of 1 for the first level of involvement (I am involved in this activity at the personal level) and the rating of 5 for the highest level of accomplishment (I have won prizes outside school...). Respondents are required to study the items, think back over the last 3–4 years, and place a tick mark to indicate their level of accomplishment for each of the activities. A participant could fill in one or more cells. Here again, the assessor is free to work out a rating scale as per the realities of the context. For example, terminology used for rating labels would change if the client is a school dropout, a college student, or someone older who is considering a career shift. Scoring is cumulative and the maximum obtainable score is 15 per item $(1 + 2 + 3 + 4 + 5)$, because the device allows entries under more than one level of involvement. In the example given, the respondent obtains a score 22 out of a possible maximum of 60 for the linguistic factor.

Study 2: Comparing the Outcomes of the SAQ and the MPT-5

The obvious question that emerges at this point is: Does the SAQ work? Study 2 compared the outcomes of the SAQ with the MPT-5 which is a psychometric device designed to assess aptitudes (described earlier). The comparison was against the external criterion of independent ratings by trained teachers who were also the career counselors of the participants.

The Sample and the Intervention

The data presented in this section is drawn from the responses of 42 grade 10 and 11 students from a school that offered the integrated career counseling program described above. The program comprised eight modules of 2 hours each and was delivered in a group workshop format, covering a wide range of career development activities including comprehensive assessment of interests and aptitudes. The sample comprised students from middle, to upper-middle class backgrounds falling in the age range of 14–16 years with a mean age of 14.98 (SD = 0.6) years. Females composed 57 % of the group and 76 % were in grade 10 with the rest in grade 11. All students were fluent in English, the language in which the workshop and assessment were conducted.

Collection of Data

All students were administered the MPT-5 and the SAQ. Teacher ratings of students were taken as the external criterion against which the MPT-5 and the SAQ were compared. Two of these teachers knew the students for a minimum of 4 years and one knew them for 10 years (from preschool onwards). They were currently teaching the participating students and were trained in and had 4 years of experience in the career counseling approach described in this chapter. It was assumed that the ratings of these teachers would be an accurate indication of students' aptitude profiles. The teachers were required to rate each student using the multiple potentials framework where a rating of 1 indicated a *low* aptitude for that factor and a rating of 5 indicated a *high* aptitude for that factor. The teachers were blind to each other's ratings, and the average of their ratings was taken as the external criterion against which the MPT-5 and SAQ were compared.

Findings and Interpretations

The objective was to check how close the ranking from both the aptitude test (MPT-5) and the accomplishments questionnaire (SAQ) was to the ranking based on teacher ratings. If the relative rankings for each pair (MPT-5 and teacher rating, SAQ and teacher rating) were the same, then the difference score would be 0, but if the rankings were different, then the difference score could lie between 1 and 4 (here we ignore the direction of difference). Recall that the rankings were for the five potential areas (L, AL, S, P, PM). Next, we ran a series of repeated measures t-tests to examine whether the difference scores for each pair of sources were similar or not. As shown in Table 34.2, the difference scores were not statistically significant for all five areas, confirming that the ranking emerging from MPT-5 scores and ranking emerging from the SAQ scores were both as close (or distant) to teacher ratings. This may be taken as one line of evidence to argue that *either* forms of testing can yield valuable overlapping information. This finding also

Table 34.2 Comparison of the difference in mean of ranking of teacher ratings against MPT-5 (Aptitude Test) and SAQ (Accomplishments Questionnaire) ($N = 42$)

Potential areas	Difference in Mean (SD) ranking of teacher ratings with		
	SAQ ranks	MPT-5 ranks	t-test (df 41)
Linguistic	.595 (1.75)	−.381 (1.52)	−0.531 (ns)
Analytical–logical	.595 (1.75)	.310 (1.66)	−0.176 (ns)
Spatial	−.381 (1.62)	.238 (1.55)	−0.552 (ns)
Personal	.119 (1.87)	.095 (1.66)	−1.855 (ns)
Physical–mechanical	−.929 (1.86)	−.262 (1.76)	−0.919 (ns)

Note: ns not significant, $p > .05$

suggests that the guidance that stems out of the MPT-5, a standardized, quantitatively oriented aptitude test, would perhaps be similar to the guidance that would stem out of the more qualitatively oriented SAQ. The study provides preliminary evidence of the scope, validity, and reliability of the SAQ. The field is in need of similar research to better understand the role of assessment devices like the SAQ which are closely attuned to an individual's everyday life.

Relevance for Multiple Cultures: Sensitivity to the Universal and Particular

This chapter has been written primarily from the Indian context. However, the questions raised have relevance across multiple cultures. A significant point made in this chapter is that interests are likely to be unstable for longer durations of time in the story of the individual's career development. The possible reasons and their relevance across cultures are discussed below.

Stability of Interests Across Age

The existing literature clearly asserts that interests are likely to be unstable at younger ages. This could be one of the explanations for the findings obtained in the studies reported in this chapter, since the samples were composed of adolescents in the age range of 15–17 years.

However, as discussed above, the Western literature does assert that interests stabilize by early adulthood (e.g., Hansen, 2005). Research pertaining to interest stability for this age group is based on studies conducted in Western schools. Reflecting on the environment in American classrooms, Low and Rounds (2006) pointed out that "classroom instruction is typically divorced from social contexts" and "there is little internal or external press towards crystallization of adolescents' interests" (p. 27). It is possible that the stability and predictability of the educational and social environments of these samples allow for the early stabilization of interest orientations.

Culture as a Mediating Variable

Commenting on the evolution of work, Arulmani and Nag-Arulmani (2004) have observed that the protestant work ethic brought the individual and his or her productivity onto center stage in the West. The accent in these cultures is on the individual's desires and interests. Conversely, work behaviors in collectivist cultures are relatively more strongly influenced by cultural expectations that require the role of the individual be subsumed under the collective. The individual's expression of interests during adolescence (or indeed through early and middle adulthood), therefore, may not be related "purely" just to him or her. They could reflect a blend of the expectations of the collective. This way of life has been practiced with success, for thousands of years in collectivist cultures where the wisdom of the elders guided the young. Over the last few decades however, the influence of the collective has become increasingly blurred. The forces of social change, particularly Westernization and globalization, have been such that individuals in collectivist cultures are beginning to assert personal desires at later stages in their lives, after they have gained greater independence from the collective. This has not been systematically documented, but sometimes individuals who have made career decisions based on family/community expectations seem to reach a career development crisis in their late 30s–40s expressing dissatisfaction with their existing careers and wishing for career shifts (Arulmani, 2006). This could be (and warrants further research) because individuals in this age bracket can allow their "personal" interests to be manifested only in adulthood, after they have complied with the wishes of their parents and the collective. Having said this, it is also highlighted that this argument does not answer questions pertaining to whether interests are in fact stable across the entire life span. Ideas from the life span literature, particularly evidence related to the construct of plasticity, indicate that interests are likely to vary and change with the individual's own development (see Bakshi, 2014, Chap. 4). This requires further investigation.

New Concepts and Viewpoints: Charting New Directions

The Development of Vocational Interests

Mention was made earlier of differentiations between situational and dispositional/individual interests. Models of interest development have been presented in the literature, for example, the four-phase model of interest development (Hidi & Renninger, 2006), the model of domain learning (Alexander, 2004), and the person-object theory of interest (e.g., Krapp, 2002). These formulations draw upon the broader constructs of affect, cognition, and learning. Career guidance could further investigate these ideas to gain a better understanding of the development, nature, and stability of vocational interests.

Economic Change and Social Organization

Over the last two decades, economic change, historically unparalleled in its nature and scale, has swept across the world. The impact this has had on employment and career development has been markedly different across developed and developing economies (e.g., Arulmani, 2011b). The practice of outsourcing work to cheaper locations and the recent economic down turn have together contributed to a massive loss of jobs in developed economies. Driven by the allure of lower costs of production, the destinations of outsourcing have been developing economies. This has resulted in an unprecedented increase in occupational opportunities in developing economies. It has been observed that in contexts that were deficient of occupational opportunities and where rates of unemployment were high, getting a job that pays well gains higher priority than personal interests, talents, and satisfaction (Arulmani, 2011a; Upadhya & Vasavi, 2006). Among the group that this writing has commented on (Indian adolescents–early adults), interests have shown the tendency to shift from long-term educational pathways such as bachelor's or master's degrees to short-term job-oriented courses. For example, it has become common in Bangalore, India, which is a large hub for business process outsourced jobs (e.g., call centers), for students to drop out of a college-based degree course, undergo a short training, and take up a job in the call center industry (Arulmani, 2006; Upadhya & Vasavi, 2006). Here, it seems that opportunity can mold or perhaps even override interest. It is possible that interests change when economic and financial prosperity allow greater freedom for self-expression. This has also been indicated in the literature (e.g., Lent, Brown, & Hackett, 2002). The point that emerges therefore is that interests can remain prone to variation much later into the individual's life in such economies.

Taken together, social organization and economic change seem to raise important questions with regard to the development and stability of interests. The received wisdom is that interests stabilize with age. As discussed, where social organization is characterized by collectivist systems, interests may be "imposed" on the individual by the collective. More often than not, the individual's interests, particularly during adolescence and early adulthood, through the process of enculturation are molded by social expectations (see Arulmani, 2014, Chap. 6). At the same time, against the background of the profound economic changes that have swept across collectivist cultures over the last two decades, the primary experience of workers in emerging economies is the burgeoning of occupational opportunities on a scale that has never before been seen. This sudden and unprecedented increase in the availability of lucrative job opportunities could trigger the wish for career shifts reflecting a change of interests. Socially molded interests could therefore be overridden through the processes of acculturation (see Arulmani, 2014, Chap. 6). Hence, measurements of interests in such contexts, using Western paradigms, may not yield accurate results. Indeed the points made in this chapter question the presumption that interests can be dispositional. This is an area that requires reinvestigation keeping economic, social, and cultural factors in mind.

Blending Interest and Aptitude to Understand Potential

Adolescence is a time of intense change in the individual, and given the nature of this developmental stage, it is likely that interests at this time are volatile and reactive to external experiences. Adolescence is also a time when the most critical educational (and thereby career) decisions are made. Therefore, the question that emerges here

is that if interests are indeed unstable at this stage of life, can they be used as the basis upon which to provide advice at this critical juncture in the individual's career development? The primary proposition upon which this writing rests is that interests and aptitudes are *both* essential aspects of self-discovery. As we have seen above, some career guidance systems are oriented toward interests, while others are driven by tests of abilities and aptitudes. The position we have taken is that the analysis of interests and aptitudes for self-understanding is not an either-or question. The task before the counselor is to help the young person discover interests as well as aptitudes. Comprehensive career counseling would offer methods whereby interests and aptitudes, both, could be assessed and compared with each other. Independent of whether vocational interests are dispositional and hence stable, in a competitive, performance-oriented work context, the requirement remains of the individual having to perform at levels that would contribute to career progress. Hence, the matter of aptitude remains an issue that the career counselor must reckon with. The notion of potential, a blend of interest and aptitude, has been proposed in this writing as a construct that could be explored further.

Conclusion

This chapter draws to a close with a final point. The outcomes of assessment are sometimes accorded (by both the counselor and the client) a status of infallibility. This is a danger that must be guarded against. An assessment device, whatever its form, is merely a tool used to gather information. It is vital that career counseling is not reduced to a variety of test taking and assessment exercises and that the career aspirant is not limited by the results of these exercises. Career counseling ought to go beyond—placing the individual and not the test at the center of the process of career development.

References

Ackerman, P. L., & Haggestad, E. D. (1997). Intelligence, personality and interests: Evidence of overlapping traits. *Psychological Bulletin, 121*, 219–245.

Alexander, P. A. (2004). A model of domain learning: Reinterpreting expertise as a multidimensional, multistage process. In D. Y. Dai & R. J. Sternberg (Eds.), *Motivation, emotion, and cognition: Integrative perspectives on intellectual functioning and development* (pp. 273–298). Mahwah, NJ: Lawrence Erlbaum.

Arulmani, G. (2005a). *Development and validation of the Multiple Potentials Interest Inventory (MPII)*. Bangalore, India: The Promise Foundation.

Arulmani, G. (2005b). *Development and validation of the Multiple Potentials Test-5 (MPT-5)*. Bangalore, India: The Promise Foundation.

Arulmani, G. (2006). *Unpublished clinical records (2000 to 2006)*. Bangalore, India: The Promise Foundation.

Arulmani, G. (2010). *The Jiva approach to career guidance and counselling: An Indian model (Project Report)*. Bangalore, India: The Promise Foundation.

Arulmani, G. (2011a). Striking the right note: The cultural preparedness approach to developing resonant career guidance programmes. *International Journal for Educational and Vocational Guidance, 11*(2), 79–93.

Arulmani, G. (2011b, December). *Political, economic and social changes and the changing role of career guidance and career guidance policies*. Paper presented at the sixth international symposium on career development and public policy, Budapest, Hungary.

Arulmani, G. (2014). The cultural preparation process model and career development. In G. Arulmani, A. J. Bakshi, F. T. L. Leong, & A. G. Watts (Eds.), *Handbook of career development*. New York, NY: Springer.

Arulmani, G., & Nag-Arulmani, S. (2004). *Career counselling: A handbook*. New Delhi, India: Tata McGraw-Hill.

Arulmani, G., & Nag-Arulmani, S. (2005). *Work awareness and responses to career choices: Indian regional survey (WORCC-IRS)*. Bangalore, India: The Promise Foundation.

Bakshi, A. J. (2014). Life span theory and career theories: Rapprochement or estrangement? In G. Arulmani, A. J. Bakshi, F. T. L. Leong, & A. G. Watts (Eds.), *Handbook of career development*. New York, NY: Springer.

Bennett, G. K., Seashore, H. G., & Wesman, A. G. (1990). *Differential aptitude tests* (5th ed.). San Antonio, TX: Psychological Corporation.

Bradley, R. W. (1994). Tests and counseling: How did we ever become partners? *Measurement and Evaluation in Counseling and Development, 26*, 224–226.

Campbell, D. P., & Holland, J. L. (1972). A merger in vocational interest research: Applying Holland's theory to Strong's data. *Journal of Vocational Behavior, 2*, 353–376.

Carroll, J. B. (1993). *Human cognitive abilities: A survey of factor-analytic studies*. New York, NY: Cambridge University Press.

Dixon, R. A., Kramer, D. A., & Baltes, P. B. (1985). Intelligence: A life-span developmental perspective. In B. B. Wolman (Ed.), *Handbook of intelligence: Theories, measurements and applications* (pp. 301–350). New York, NY: Wiley.

Duarte, M. E., & Rossier, J. (2008). Testing and assessment in an international context: Cross and multicultural issues. In J. A. Athanasou & R. V. Esbroeck (Eds.), *International handbook of career guidance* (pp. 489–510). New York, NY: Springer.

Gardner, H. (1983). *Frames of mind: The theory of multiple intelligences*. New York, NY: Basic Books.

Gottfredson, L. S. (1985). *A system for reality-based career exploration: Methods and materials*. Baltimore, MD: Johns Hopkins University, Center for Social Organization of Schools.

Gottfredson, L. S. (2003). The challenge and promise of cognitive career assessment. *Journal of Career Assessment, 20*(10), 1–21.

Gregoire, J., & Nils, F. (2008). Cognitive measurement in career guidance. In J. A. Athanasou & R. V. Esbroeck (Eds.), *International handbook of career guidance*. New York, NY: Springer.

Guildford, J. P. (1967). *The nature of human intelligence*. New York, NY: McGraw Hill.

Hambleton, R. (2005). Issues, designs and technical guidelines for adapting tests into multiple languages and cultures. In R. Hambleton, P. Merenda, & C. Spielberger (Eds.), *Adapting educational and psychological tests for cross-cultural assessment* (pp. 3–38). Mahwah, NJ: Erlbaum.

Hansen, J.-I. C. (2005). Assessment of interests. In S. D. Brown & R. W. Lent (Eds.), *Career development and counseling: Putting theory and research to work*. Hoboken, NJ: Wiley.

Hidi, S., & Renninger, K. A. (2006). The four-phase model of interest development. *Educational Psychologist, 41*(2), 111–127.

Hidi, S., Renninger, K. A., & Krapp, A. (1992). The present state of interest research. In K. A. Renninger, S. Hidi & A. Krapp (Eds.), *The role of interest in learning and development* (pp. 3–25). Hillsdale, USA: Erlbaum.

Holland, J. L. (1959). A theory of vocational choice. *Journal of Counseling Psychology, 6*, 35–45.

International Labour Organization. (2008). *International standard classification of occupations, 2008 (ISCO-08)*. Geneva, Switzerland: Author.

Krapp, A. (2002). Structural and dynamic aspects of interest development: Theoretical considerations from an ontogenetic perspective. *Learning and Instruction, 12*, 382–409.

Law, K. S., Wong, C. S., & Leong, F. (2001). The cultural validity of Holland's model and its implications for human resource management: The case study of Hong Kong. *International Journal of Human Resource Management, 12*, 484–496.

Lent, R. W., Brown, S. D., & Hackett, G. (2002). Social cognitive career theory. In Duane Brown and associates (Eds.), *Career choice and development* (pp. 255–311). San Francisco, CA: Jossey-Bass.

Leong, F. T. L., Austin, J. T., Sekaran, U., & Komarraju, M. (1998). An evaluation of the cross-cultural validity of Holland's theory: Career choice by workers in India. *Journal of Vocational Behaviour, 52*, 441–455.

Leung, S. A. (2002). Career counselling in Hong Kong: Meeting the social challenges. *Career Development Quarterly, 50*(3), 237–245.

Leung, S. A. (2008). The big five career theories. In J. A. Athanasou & R. V. Esbroeck (Eds.), *International handbook of career guidance* (pp. 115–132). New York, NY: Springer.

Low, K. S. D., & Rounds, J. (2006). Interest change and continuity from early adolescence to middle adulthood. *International Journal for Educational and Vocational Guidance, 7*(1), 23–36.

Low, K. S. D., Yoon, M., Roberts, B. W., & Rounds, J. (2005). The stability of vocational interests from early adolescence to middle adulthood: A quantitative review of longitudinal studies. *Psychological Bulletin, 131*, 713–737.

Lubinski, D., Benbow, C. P., & Ryan, J. (1995). Stability of vocational interests among the intellectually gifted from adolescence to adulthood: A 15-year longitudinal study. *Journal of Applied Psychology, 80*, 196–200.

Nagesh, R., Kumar, S., & Arulmani, G. (2010). Development of an occupational list for India. *Newsletter of the International Association for Educational and Vocational Guidance, 66*, 2.

Patton, W. (2008). Recent developments in career theories: The influences of constructivism and convergence. In J. A. Athanasou & R. V. Esbroeck (Eds.), *International handbook of career guidance* (pp. 133–156). New York, NY: Springer.

Patton, W., & McMahon, M. (1999). *Career development and systems theory: A new relationship*. Pacific Grove, CA: Brooks/Cole.

Patton, W., & McMahon, M. (2006). The system theory framework of career development and counseling: Connecting theory and practice. *International Journal for the Advancement of Counselling, 28*, 153–166. doi:10.1007/s10447-005-9010-1.

Pendergrass, L. A., Hansen, J.-I. C., Neuman, J. L., & Nutter, K. J. (2003). Examination of the concurrent validity of the scores from CISS for student-athlete college major selection: A brief report. *Measurement and Evaluation in Counseling and Development, 35*, 212–218.

Sampson, J. P., Jr., Reardon, R. C., Peterson, G. W., & Lenz, J. G. (2004). *Career counseling and services: A cognitive information processing approach*. Pacific Grove, CA: Brooks/Cole.

Savickas, M. L. (2005). The theory and practice of career construction. In S. D. Brown & R. W. Lent (Eds.), *Career development and counseling: Putting theory and research to work* (pp. 42–70). Hoboken, NJ: Wiley.

Snow, R. E. (1992). Aptitude theory: Yesterday, today and tomorrow. *Educational Psychologist, 27*(1), 5–32.

Snow, R. E. (1994). Abilities and aptitude. In R. J. Sternberg (Ed.), *Encyclopedia of human intelligence* (pp. 3–5). New York, NY: Macmillan.

Strong, E. K. (1935). Permanence of vocational interests. *Journal of Educational Psychology, 25*, 336–344.

Strong, E. K. (1943). *Vocational interests of men and women*. Palo Alto, CA: Stanford University Press.

Sultana, R. (2014). Career guidance for social justice in neoliberal times. In G. Arulmani, A. J. Bakshi, F. T. L. Leong, & A. G. Watts (Eds.), *Handbook of career development*. New York, NY: Springer.

Swanson, J. L., & D'Achiardi, C. (2005). Beyond interests, needs/values and abilities: Assessing other important career constructs over the life span. In S. D. Brown & R. W. Lent. (Eds.), *Career development and counseling: Putting theory and research to work* (pp. 353–381). Hoboken, NJ: Wiley.

Swanson, J. L., & Hansen, J.-I. C. (1988). Stability of vocational interests over four-year, eight-year and twelve-year intervals. *Journal of Vocational Behavior, 33*, 185–202.

U.S. Department of Labor. (1970). *Manual for the USES General Aptitude Test Battery (Section 3: development)*. Washington, DC: Department of Labor, Manpower Administration.

Upadhya, C., & Vasavi, A. R. (2006). *Work, culture, and sociality in the Indian IT industry: A sociological study*. Bangalore, India: School of Social Sciences, National Institute of Advanced Studies.

Making Meaning of Quantitative Assessment in Career Counseling through a Storytelling Approach

35

Mark Watson and Mary McMahon

Introduction

With the move towards narrative career counseling gathering momentum, its uneasy relationship with the dominant traditions of quantitative career assessment has become apparent. The traditional quantitative career counseling and assessment paradigm has lent itself more easily to practical applications, whereas the emergent narrative career counseling and qualitative assessment paradigm has remained largely theoretical rather than practical. Thus, narrative career counseling may have intuitive appeal, but career practitioners have found difficulty in its practical application (Reid, 2006). In a sense, the limited range of practical suggestions about how to apply narrative career counseling approaches has reinforced the dominant and more applied quantitative career tradition.

An unfortunate consequence of this situation is that an unhelpful divide has emerged that has positioned many career practitioners in dichotomized approaches to career counseling and assessment. Within this divide, how to include career assessment into career counseling has been differentially viewed. The predominant tradition of quantitative career assessment has remained more linear and directive in its approach; in

contrast, qualitative approaches to career counseling and career assessment favor agency and acknowledgment of context. However, McMahon and Patton (2002) have suggested that career practitioners need to adopt "a plurality of practices" (p. 7) that bridges the two dominant philosophical positions of logical positivism and constructivism. Such a suggestion challenges the career counseling and assessment fields to find ways of converging what have previously been recognized as diverging career counseling and assessment approaches (Sampson, 2009). More specifically, we need to consider the challenge of how quantitative career assessment and qualitative approaches to career counseling and assessment can be used to complement each other.

Addressing this challenge would help provide career counselors using narrative approaches with the opportunity to more easily use applied and established forms of career assessment. The challenge itself is not new; indeed, it is deeply embedded within the discipline of career psychology's approach to career counseling which has predominantly involved administering career assessment instruments in combination with a brief interview. This limits our understanding of a client's career development, in that such an approach runs the risk of providing "an incomplete and unbalanced picture of the person and of his [sic] prospects" (Super, 1957, p. 305). More recently, Savickas (2000) returned to this theme and argued that career counselors should translate quantitative career assessment into a more qualitative career process that allows

M. Watson (✉)
Department of Psychology, Nelson Mandela Metropolitan University, Port Elizabeth, South Africa
e-mail: mark.watson@nmmu.ac.za

G. Arulmani et al. (eds.), *Handbook of Career Development*, International and Cultural Psychology,
DOI 10.1007/978-1-4614-9460-7_35, © Springer Science+Business Media, LLC 2014

clients to consider their career decisions more contextually and holistically.

Thus, the challenge to find some common ground between quantitative and qualitative perspectives of career counseling and assessment draws our attention to the issue of process in career counseling and assessment and, more specifically, the issue of how to introduce and conduct career assessment in a meaningful way in the career counseling process. This chapter considers how quantitative career assessment could be reconceptualized less as a set of scores that defines clients as a psychometric identity and more as a means to achieve the goal of allowing clients to "open up avenues of movement, promote empowerment, support transitions," and to "assist the client gain eligibility for more participation" in their career developmental process (Peavy, 1998, p. 180). This goal is reflective of the constructivist philosophy that provides a foundational underpinning of narrative career counseling.

This chapter describes the use of an *Integrative Structured Interview* (ISI) process within a storytelling approach to career counseling that demonstrates the complementarity of quantitative career assessment and storytelling. First, the storytelling approach will be described. Second, broad guidelines for qualitatively incorporating quantitative career assessment into career counseling will be presented. Subsequently, the ISI process will be presented to illustrate how quantitative career assessment may be storied. The ISI process is demonstrated through two case studies using internationally applied quantitative career assessment instruments, specifically Holland's (1985) Self-Directed Search (SDS) interest questionnaire and Super's Work Values Inventory-Revised (SWVI-R; Zytowski, 2006). In concluding the chapter, new directions in the use of quantitative career assessment in career counseling are offered. In addition, the relevance of storying quantitative career assessment in diverse cultural contexts is considered.

The Storytelling Approach

A number of approaches to narrative career counseling have been proposed, one of which is the storytelling approach (McMahon & Watson, 2010, 2011a, 2011b). Theoretically founded in the systems theory framework (STF; Patton & McMahon, 2006) of career development, the storytelling approach applies systemic thinking to career counseling. Consistent with other narrative approaches, individual clients are central to the career counseling process. Moreover, the storytelling approach takes a "client in context" view of career counseling and encourages clients to be active agents in telling multiple stories from a range of settings within their contexts. Through the telling of multiple stories, career counselors and clients work together to identify the themes and patterns that facilitate connectedness between stories and enable meaning making to occur. Thus meaning making, connectedness, and agency are core constructs of the storytelling approach. Unlike other narrative career counseling approaches, the storytelling approach also incorporates learning and reflection as central constructs. By facilitating connectedness and meaning making processes, narrative career counselors using the storytelling approach also facilitate a learning process in which knowledge, skills, attitudes, values, beliefs, and emotions are constructed and transformed from the experiences described in clients' stories (McMahon & Watson, 2012a). Essentially, the storytelling approach to career counseling is a reflective process in which clients examine their thoughts, feelings, and responses about their career situations in order to find a sense of direction and construct a future career story.

Broad Guidelines for Storying Career Assessment

Broad guidelines have been proposed for qualitatively incorporating assessment into career counseling processes (McMahon & Patton, 2002, 2006). McMahon and Patton (2002) have offered nine such guidelines. These guidelines may be grouped according to their focus, specifically personalizing the process for the client, introducing assessment into the career counseling process, and the conduct of the career assessment process (see Table 35.1). As

Table 35.1 Incorporating career assessment into career counseling

Focus	Guidelines (see McMahon & Patton, 2002, 2006)	Examples from practice
Personalize the process for the client	Individualize the process for the client	I notice that you have mentioned your values in relation to lifestyle and your preference to work with other people and I'm wondering if it would be useful for you to complete . . .
	Map the qualitative assessment onto the story previously told by the client	
	Make the qualitative assessment fit for the client, not the client fit the assessment	
Introducing career assessment into the career counseling process	Broach the subject of using a qualitative assessment device tentatively, respectfully, and informatively	Some of my clients have found it helpful to complete. . . . And I'm wondering if you would too
	Acknowledge that it is the client's prerogative to engage in the activity	Essentially, this assessment provides a way of finding out more about your values which may help us to understand more about why you are unhappy in your present work and what might satisfy you more in the future. It will take about 20 minutes to complete . . .
		Do you think it is something you would like to do during our time together?
The conduct of the career	Work with and support the client through the process of the assessment using counseling skills	*Work with and support the client*
		Now to get started, you . . .
		At this point, it might be useful to . . .
		Let's think about what these results mean and how they could apply in your life
		Using counseling skills
		Open question: What does this score mean to you?
		Reflection of feeling: You seem to be puzzled by that score
		Paraphrase: From what you've just said, it seems that having good social networks at work and in your leisure time are very important to you
Assessment process	Debrief/process the activity	What have you learned about yourself?
		How might you apply what you have learned?
	Invite feedback on qualitative assessment processes	What was the process of completing that assessment like for you?
		Would you recommend that process to a friend?
	Be creative and flexible in the career assessment process	With your artistic background, I'm wondering if it would be useful for you to sketch some of those images you have just described
		What would someone who knows you well say about your scores on this assessment?

illustrated by the examples in Table 35.1, the guidelines regarding *personalizing the process for the client* suggest that career assessment is not automatic but rather its inclusion in career counseling emanates out of the story the client has previously told. Thus, clients are offered a rationale in terms of their own story to engage in a career assessment process. Further, in *introducing assessment to the career counseling process*, McMahon and Patton suggest that this is done tentatively, respectfully, and informatively, and the client is empowered in terms of decisions to participate or not.

McMahon and Patton's (2002) guidelines for *the conduct of the career assessment process* reflect the importance of developing good counseling skills in order to guide and support clients through the assessment process. In order to maximize the learning from the assessment process, McMahon and Patton specifically advocate debriefing so that clients find meaningful ways of applying the knowledge gained from assessment. Clients are encouraged to provide feedback about the assessment process in order to (a) value them as active, collaborative participants in the assessment and counseling process whose opinions are valued, and (b) also position counselors as learners who are open to feedback on their practice. Thus, a collaborative, less expert-driven relationship is advocated. Finally, McMahon and Patton encourage career counselors to be creative and flexible in the career assessment process. As illustrated in Table 35.1, we offer examples to demonstrate how McMahon and Patton's guidelines may be implemented in practice.

The Integrative Structured Interview Process

While broad guidelines have been proposed to qualitatively embed career assessment in career counseling, no such guidance has been offered about using a qualitative process with quantitative career assessment. Recently, however, McMahon and Watson (2012b) outlined a specific qualitative interview process, the ISI process, for facilitating clients in crafting stories from their quantitative career assessment results.

The ISI (McMahon & Watson, 2012b) incorporates the core constructs of narrative career counseling, generally, and the storytelling approach, specifically. Further, the ISI mirrors McMahon and Patton's (2002) guidelines in that the career counselor has a facilitative role and clients become actively involved, as well as supported, in the telling of their stories. The ISI personalizes clients' career assessment scores by posing a series of story crafting questions specific to a particular career assessment instrument that engages them in a narrative process in which they contextually explore their scores. In essence, the ISI offers a structured process in which clients tell stories about their career assessment results in relation to their life contexts, work contexts, and personal reflection. The ISI also provides clients with an opportunity to craft an integrative future story using their career assessment results and their past and present experience.

In facilitating the telling of stories, the ISI demonstrates the core constructs of the storytelling approach to career counseling, that is, connectedness, meaning making, learning, reflection, and agency (McMahon & Watson, 2012b). Connectedness refers to the recursive relationship between clients and their contextual influences, the relationship between clients and counselors, and also the relationships between clients and their career stories. An essential feature of narrative career counseling is its acknowledgement of clients in context. Narrative career counselors collaborate with clients to consider their situations within the broader context of their lives such as families, workplaces, and other roles and settings that are important to the client. In doing so, themes and patterns are identified that permeate across roles and settings, enabling clients to make connections between their present career situation and aspects of their context that may previously have been disconnected. Such themes and patterns and the connections clients make help them to ascribe new meaning to their stories and experiences. For example, a client may realize that what they value in a work role is also reflected in their voluntary participation in a community organization and in their family. Similarly, a client may come to realize that their need to be challenged at work is also apparent in their interest in the challenge presented in their hobby of mountain climbing. Thus, clients demonstrate personal agency in career counseling by taking an active role as they come to reflect on their situations, make meaning of them, and apply their consequent learning to the construction of their future story. In addition, through their engagement in the narrative career counseling process, clients are expected to be active agents in the telling of their stories and in the construction of future stories. Importantly, an effective client-counselor relationship is a critical element of narrative career counseling.

Structure of the ISI Process

Reflecting the core constructs of the storytelling approach, the ISI process represents a series of story crafting questions tailored to the quantitative career assessment instrument being used. For instance, McMahon and Watson (2012b) provide an example of the ISI process tailored for the qualitative use of Holland's (1985) SDS. In its generic form, the ISI process is structured according to six main sections within which a series of story crafting questions related to the quantitative career assessment instrument are posed. Following a brief introduction of the assessment results by the career counselor to the client, the career counselor then proceeds to work through these six sections of the ISI process which will now be described.

1. Crafting a story about the quantitative scores
   This section of the ISI process introduces clients to their quantitative scores and invites them to develop a personal explanation of them. In this way, clients become familiar with the instrument and begin to construct meaning around their scores.

2. Crafting a story about the relative value of the quantitative scores
   This section of the ISI process encourages clients to consider their scores holistically. Thus differences between scores and relative values of scores are considered. Dependent on the quantitative career assessment instrument, this might involve exploring how the client understands the prioritizing of the scores in relation to each other in the assessment results.

3. Crafting a story about the quantitative scores in life contexts
   This section of the ISI process begins a process of contextualizing the quantitative career assessment results and is the first of three such sections. This particular section invites clients to consider the meaning of their scores in the context of their lives including the roles they play and the relationships they have.

4. Crafting a story about the quantitative scores in work contexts
   This section of the ISI process is the second to contextualize the quantitative career assessment results. In this section, clients are provided with the opportunity to explore their quantitative career assessment results in relation to their past, present, and future work situations. This may include paid employment and unpaid work such as volunteer work and work in the home.

5. Crafting a story about the quantitative scores through personal reflection
   This section of the ISI process is the third to contextualize the quantitative career assessment results. In this section, clients are encouraged to reflect on the ISI process so far and to consider their personal qualities, strengths, and weaknesses that they have identified as part of contextualizing their scores in different life and work contexts. Importantly, this section prepares clients for the concluding section of the ISI process.

6. Crafting an integrative future story using the quantitative scores and past and present experience
   In this summative section of the ISI process, clients are encouraged to begin the construction of a future career story by applying the meaning they have made of the contextualized career stories they have told based on their quantitative career assessment scores. The storytelling constructs of connectedness, reflection, meaning making, learning, and agency are evident throughout the ISI process.

The ISI process was first applied to the SDS (Holland, 1985) because of the latter's widespread international use as a quantitative career assessment instrument. This application has been described in the literature (McMahon & Watson, 2012b). In this chapter, the ISI process is applied to both Holland's (1985) SDS interest questionnaire and to the SWVI-R (Zytowski, 2006) through the case studies of Zinzi and Michael, respectively.

Application of the ISI to Holland's SDS

The application of the ISI process to Holland's (1985) SDS interest questionnaire is demonstrated through the case study of Zinzi. The SDS will be briefly described before the presentation of the case study.

The SDS (Holland, 1985) is one of the most widely used quantitative career assessment instruments in the world despite criticism that it is less well suited for some client groups such as women or people from cultures other than white, Western. The SDS is based on Holland's (1997) theory which proposes that an ideal career choice represents a good match between an individual's personality type and a corresponding work environment. Holland defines this ideal match in terms of his concept of congruence and he believes that such a match will maximally benefit and reward individuals in terms of their career development. The SDS provides an assessment of the six personality types proposed by Holland's theory. Commonly referred to as Holland's RIASEC model, this acronym refers to the six personality types of realistic, investigative, artistic, social, enterprising, and conventional. Essentially the SDS provides an individual with a three letter code. Similarly, occupations may be described in terms of three letter codes and there are several occupational dictionaries that list such codes. Thus, individuals may "match" their personality typology with those of occupations.

The matching processes suggested by quantitative career assessment instruments such as the SDS have resulted in perceptions of career counseling being "test and tell" processes that are directed by "expert" career counselors. In such processes, clients are viewed as having limited and passive roles to play. Further, Lamprecht (2002, p. 124) has suggested that a quantitative career assessment process reduces the story of clients to "psychometric selves." Similarly, Sampson (2009) has argued that we need to consider that our clients have multilayered stories that go beyond standardized assessment. The ISI process (McMahon & Watson, 2012b) offers a mechanism for addressing the concerns expressed by Lamprecht and Sampson through incorporating quantitative career assessment into rich and multilayered stories narrated by clients. This will now be illustrated through the case study of Zinzi.

The Case of Zinzi

Zinzi (a pseudonym) was a black African woman in her early 30s from a rural area. She was a single mother with an 8-year-old child. As a teenager, she had been offered a scholarship to attend a boarding school where she had completed her secondary education and obtained a university entrance pass. Despite having hoped to study further, her mother became ill and she had to return home to look after her. Subsequent to her mother's death, she had remained at home to look after her younger siblings who were now independent. Zinzi had obtained work in a local supermarket although she was not happy with the repetitive nature of this work. Her extended family had recently indicated their willingness to provide financial support for Zinzi to finally further her studies and had strongly encouraged her to study nursing. While Zinzi was excited about the opportunity to study that had been presented to her, she felt very uncertain about following her extended family's advice that nursing would be a suitable career for her. Someone from the legal advice office where Zinzi did voluntary work suggested that she could seek free career advice from the university at which she hoped to enroll.

The case study presents brief excerpts of Zinzi's interview with a career counselor after she had completed the SDS (see Box 35.1). Zinzi agreed to participate in the ISI process after an

Box 35.1. Zinzi's ISI Process

Crafting a story about the code letters
1. What is your three-letter code?
   EIS
2. How would you explain each of these letters?
   Well in my community the S is very important, especially for women. You know, as a woman I am expected to care for my family and the women in my community all support each other in different ways. I've been a volunteer in the legal advice office of our local community and our role is to help people. But the legal advice office also helps to explain the I because I like to think and work things out and the volunteer work I do there needs that. The E is easy to understand because I have always wanted to be independent. In my job at the supermarket, I sometimes get an opportunity to be in charge of other staff and it's that type of thing that I like rather than being on the cash register which is so boring.
3. How would you explain the order of your three-letter code?
   I can see why the S is there. This could be because of the community I live in and what is expected of women and the work I have done helping my mother and my volunteer work. I am interested in people but I don't like the really hands on stuff like I had to do when my mother was sick. I just don't want to do that for a job. That is why the E and the I are higher.

Crafting a story about the code order
4. If you were to locate your letters on a scale from 1 to 10 where 1 was least important and 10 was most important, where would you locate the first letter, the second letter, and the third letter?
   I would give a score of 8 to the E and I but I would only give a 4 to the S.

5. How do you interpret the location of your letters on the scale? For example, are they close together, evenly spaced, or far apart?
   Well I guess it is what I just said, the E and the I are close together but they are quite far away from the S. S is important in my community but it is not as important for my career.

Crafting a story about the code letters in life contexts
6. In what ways is the first letter of your code evident in your life?
   E is there in my work at the supermarket and in my voluntary work at the legal advice office. I like being at the legal advice office more than I like the caring jobs I've had to do in my family. I get to think at the legal advice office than I do at the supermarket so I like being there more.
7. In what ways is the second letter of your code evident in your life?
   It's a bit like what I said about the legal advice office. You know, we assist people get ready to go to the labor court. I enjoy this because I had to go to the court house to look up documents to support some people's claims. I liked watching how the lawyers worked out how to argue for the people.
8. In what ways is the third letter of your code evident in your life?
   I think it's a community thing like I said. As a black woman S is important in our family and community; you know we have to be there for our family and our friends and I am. But when I think about my work and what I want in the future it's not that important.
9. What relationships do you see between your three letters and various facets of your life, such as your work, learning, and other life roles?

(continued)

Box 35.1. (continued)

Crafting a story about the code letters through personal reflection

10. What personal qualities have you identified in your reflection so far that are most important to you?

   Well I don't want you to think that people aren't important to me. After all I have taken my responsibilities very seriously to look after my family. But I have always had in my mind that I could have gone to university and I haven't given up on that yet. In my community it's very important to listen to the advice of elders and my extended family but I think I have a better idea of what is right for me.

Crafting a story about the code letters in work contexts

11. If in general the dominant letters for your profession is EIS, what proportion of your work would reflect that letter? What work responsibilities do you have that accord with that letter? What letters would describe the other major responsibilities of your work role?

   Well, my E and I are pretty equal and I think the work I do in the legal advice office fits those letters. There's a bit of E in my work at the supermarket when I get some responsibility. But my other work at home is more like S.

12. Of all your work responsibilities, which do you find most satisfying or rewarding, and which are least satisfying and least rewarding, and how do you relate these to your three-letter code?

   Oh, that's easy. It's the legal office that I get the most out of. It's just really nice to be a volunteer there. What I like least is my home and family responsibilities that I have to do and the routine of my work at the

supermarket. You know, there are more different things to do at the legal office.

Crafting an integrative future story using the SDS code and past and present experience

13. Based on your reflection in the previous questions, what could you look for in future work opportunities in order to achieve greater work satisfaction?

   Well, I like to think about how I can help people and work things out for them. At home helping just involves doing things. You know I like looking up the documents and finding things out. So if I could do that more often I'd be happy.

invitation from the career counselor to consider her personality in relation to her present work experience and her future career path. It is not possible within the confines of this chapter to describe the whole interview, that is, to describe Zinzi's responses to all the ISI questions.

As evidenced in this final dialogue, by the end of the ISI process, Zinzi felt that she had a clearer picture of the systemic influences that had more narrowly understood her interests and prescribed nursing as a career for her. Despite going against the wishes of her extended family to study nursing, Zinzi decided to talk to the lawyers at the legal advice center about their work as she was beginning to feel that studying law was what she would like to do. She decided to ask them to support her decision to study law because of the potential contribution she could make to her extended community.

Application of the ISI to Super's SWVI-R

The application of the ISI process applied to SWVI-R (Zytowski, 2006) is demonstrated through the case study of Michael. As demonstrated in the case study of Zinzi, the ISI offers a six part structure each of which contains questions related to the specific career assessment instrument being used. Thus, in applying the ISI process to the SWVI-R, the sections remain constant but the questions become tailored to the results of the assessment instrument in order to provide a framework for the storying process. The SWVI-R will be briefly described before the presentation of the case study.

The SWVI-R (Zytowski, 2006) is a revision of Donald Super's (1970) Work Values Inventory and is widely regarded as a valuable measure in career counseling because of its relationship to job satisfaction and its potential to assist clients discriminate from among career options. The SWVI-R provides scores on the relative importance of 12 work values that have been identified as critical in career development and the career choice process. The inventory consists of six items for each of 12 scales, specifically: achievement, coworkers, creativity, income, independence, lifestyle, mental challenge, prestige, security, supervision, variety, and work environment. Items are responded to on a five-point Likert scale with responses as follows: 1 (*Not Important at all*), 2 (*Somewhat Important*), 3 (*Important*), 4 (*Very Important*), and 5 (*Crucial*). Scores per scale can range from a minimum of 6 to a maximum of 30, with these raw scores converted to normed scores. The results are provided to the client in a ranked order derived from the percentile scores. The *Technical Manual* (Zytowski, 2006) for the SWVI-R estimates the reading level of the inventory as approximately at the sixth grade.

Zytowski (2006) states that the SWVI-R provides clients with an opportunity to clarify what is important to them in the career they seek. Part of such an exploration process could involve clients considering their quantitative value assessment in relation to other quantitative assessment such as interest assessment which could result in "a career objective that is held with greater confidence than by interests or work values alone" (Zytowski, 2006, p. 17). For example, a client whose values reflect a high score on coworkers may also score highly on the social

dimension of Holland's (1985) SDS. Alternatively, the SWVI-R could provide clients with an opportunity to refine career options (as evidenced in the case study of Michael presented later in this chapter) that have resulted from other quantitative career assessment instruments. The application of the ISI process to the SWVI-R (see Table 35.2) will now be considered through the case study of Michael.

The Case of Michael

Michael was a second year university student who came to career counseling because he was disillusioned with his program of study in engineering after returning from a summer holiday work experience in which he felt dissatisfied. Because he had always wanted to be an engineer, Michael felt very confused that his work experience had not been fulfilling and he was not sure whether to continue with engineering. His parents suggested that he seek career counseling to "sort himself out" before he "went much further" with his course. The case study presents brief excerpts of Michael's interview with the career counselor after he had completed the SWVI-R. Michael agreed to participate in the ISI process after an invitation from the career counselor to consider his career values scores in relation to his present work experience and his future career path (see Box 35.2). It was not possible within the confines of this chapter to describe the whole interview, that is, to describe Michael's responses to all the ISI questions.

As evidenced in this final dialogue, by the end of the ISI process Michael had an understanding of both why he did not enjoy his work experience of engineering and also the elements that he could look for in his future career that he would find satisfying. He decided to speak with his parents about withdrawing from his engineering studies. With his career counselor, Michael identified sources of career information which he could use that would further his career exploration and assist in his career decision making.

The ISI excerpts illustrate the manner in which a set of scores can be storied in a narrative process that actively involves clients in contextualizing and making meaning of their

Table 35.2 Integrative structured interview process for the SWVI-R

Integrative Structured Interview Process for the SWVI-R Using Story Crafting Questions
The following questions invite participants to craft stories around their Super's Work Values Inventory—Revised (SWVI-R) scores in a structured interview process
Crafting a story about the work value scores
1. What are your highest ranked work values?
2. How would you explain each of these work values?
3. What are your lowest ranked work values?
4. How would you explain each of them?
Crafting a story about the rank order of the work value scores
5. How would you explain the overall rank order of your work values?
6. If you were to locate each of your 12 work values on a scale from 1 to 10 where 1 was *least important* and 10 was *most important*, where would you locate them? (Note: The counselor could use a flip chart, whiteboard, or a prepared scale)
7. How do you interpret the ranking of your work values on this scale? For example, are they close together, evenly spaced, or far apart?
Crafting a story about the work value scores in life contexts
8. In what ways are your highest work values evident in your life?
9. In what ways are your lowest work values evident in your life?
10. What relationships do you see between your highest and lowest work values and various facets of your life?
Crafting a story about the work value scores in work contexts
11. Of all your work responsibilities, which do you find most satisfying or rewarding, and which are least satisfying and least rewarding, and how do you relate these to your rank-ordered work values?
Crafting a story about work values through personal reflection
12. What work values have you identified in your reflection so far that are most important to you?
13. What work values have you identified in your reflection so far that are least important to you?
14. What other work values that are not listed are you aware of that you would like to consider in your career planning?
Crafting an integrative future story using the SWVI-R scores and past and present experience
15. Based on your reflection in the previous questions, what could you look for in future work opportunities in order to achieve greater work satisfaction?

© McMahon and Watson (2012a, 2012b)

quantitative career assessment. Specifically, Zinzi and Michael were active agents in the career counseling process and they were afforded the opportunity to contribute as experts in their lives as they reflected on their quantitative career assessment scores. By contrast, the career counselor did not act as an expert but adopted a facilitative role that encouraged and supported Zinzi and Michael's participation in the ISI process. Consistent with narrative career counseling in general, and the storytelling approach specifically, the constructs of connectedness, meaning making, agency, reflection, and learning underpinned the ISI process. The ISI process creates a reflective space for clients in which the emphasis is not on the content of the quantitative career assessment instruments as such, but rather on the processes of relationship building, listening, and facilitating, and the core constructs of the storytelling approach.

General Principles for Using Quantitative Career Assessment Qualitatively

Importantly, the design of the ISI offers clues to the development of further processes that may be applied to other quantitative career assessment instruments. First, the ISI process suggests general principles for using quantitative career assessment qualitatively and, secondly, it identifies key elements of the ISI process. In

Box 35.2. Michael's ISI Process

Crafting a story about the work value scores

1. What are your highest work values?
   It was creativity and independence.

2. How would you explain each of these work values?
   I like to think for myself and work things out. I don't really like things being prescribed for me. And I'm really creative. I won a couple of junior art competitions last year. I just like thinking up my own projects and going for broke and see what happens.

3. What are your lowest work values?
   My lowest scores were for supervision and prestige.

4. How would you explain each of them?
   I think I'd rather enjoy what I do. You know, in school I sometimes won awards and praise from my teachers and parents but I never felt that I was performing for them or for the recognition of others. I mean, it's nice but I just like to feel good about what I do. I guess that is why supervision is low as well; I think it is more important to go for self-recognition than the recognition of others.

Crafting a story about the rank order of the work value scores

5. How would you explain the overall rank order of your work values?
   I'm not sure what you mean here. (The counselor then explains that she is referring to Michael's ranked 12 work value scales). *Oh, ok, well I guess that I am pretty comfortable with the high and low values. They sound like me. I guess I wondered why lifestyle was just in the medium band. I mean, I don't have to live in luxury but I don't want to struggle either. I think I would have expected*

it to be higher. And some of the others in the middle, I don't know, I guess I haven't ever thought about them much.

6. If you were to locate each of your 12 work values on a scale from 1 to 10 where 1 was least important and 10 was most important, where would you locate them? (Note: The counselor could use a flip chart, whiteboard, or a prepared scale)

7. How do you interpret the ranking of your work values on this scale? For example, are they close together, evenly spaced, or far apart?

Crafting a story about the work value scores in life contexts

8. In what ways are your highest work values evident in your life?
   I've always loved art and drawing and anything where I can just let my imagination go. I even don't mind writing. I always take a book on holidays with me and do sketches. I've got a few completed books now and I like to look through them. If ever I'm worried or have nothing to do, I just take out my art things.

9. In what ways are your lowest work values evident in your life?
   I guess my parents always told us to do our best and if we do then we should be happy with that. It was always more about ourselves than what other people thought. You know, even when I won the art prizes and I went and got an award, I really liked knowing that I had done a good piece of work that I could be proud of.

10. What relationships do you see between your highest and lowest work values and various facets of your life?
    My parents have encouraged us to do things for ourselves and not depend on others or wait to be told what to do. So

(continued)

Box 35.2. (continued)

I guess that's why independence and supervision are on opposite ends of my report. Also I think being creative means I have to think for myself—I mean nobody tells me what to draw. So art is pretty independent really.

Crafting a story about the work value scores in work contexts

11. Of all your work responsibilities, which do you find most satisfying or rewarding, and which are least satisfying and least rewarding, and how do you relate these to your rank-ordered work values?

    I guess that the job I had in my work experience over summer didn't give me much of a chance to be creative. As far as I could tell, even the qualified engineers were bound by rules and protocols in their designs. I found that frustrating and sometimes it took some of the challenge out of what was possible and mental challenge was fourth down in my report. I did enjoy the people I worked with. They were quite nice so that was satisfying. It was more that the work itself wasn't satisfying. You know, on the weekends I work at a sports shop and I like dealing with the customers and trying to satisfy them. One of my jobs now is doing the window display for the next week and I really enjoy working out how to make it look good and what will go into the display and thinking about how it will attract people into the shop. So I guess that's a bit creative and I work on my own.

Crafting a story about work values through personal reflection

12. What work values have you identified in your reflection so far that are most important to you?

13. What work values have you identified in your reflection so far that are least important to you?

14. What other work values that are not listed are you aware of that you would like to consider in your career planning?

    I'm not sure really but when I was at school other kids used to talk with me about their problems and they trusted me to help them. I was a monitor for a junior class and I enjoyed helping the kids settle into school life. I don't know what to call it but doing something for others is satisfying.

Crafting an integrative future story using the SWVI-R scores and past and present experience

15. Based on your reflection in the previous questions, what could you look for in future work opportunities in order to achieve greater work satisfaction?

    I don't know. I went into engineering because I thought it would let me be creative but I really don't think it will anymore. And even though the people were nice, they didn't seem to have as much control over their own decisions as I thought. Just thinking about what we've said, I think I need more freedom and even though engineering is important I think I'd like to make a more meaningful contribution to people's lives. I also think money and lifestyle aren't everything. I guess that's why they're not at the top of my report.

order to making meaning of quantitative assessment in career counseling through a storytelling approach, some general principles may be elicited from McMahon and Patton's guidelines and the ISI process. Fundamental to facilitating qualitative exploration of quantitative career assessment are three central elements: (a) the career counseling relationship, (b) the narrative career counseling process, and (c) familiarity with the quantitative career assessment instrument and its core constructs. These elements are recursively related.

The creation of a collaborative working relationship with the client requires that the career counselor believes in the ability of clients to be actively engaged in the construction of their careers as well as a willingness on the part of the career counselor to facilitate clients' engagement in the narrative career counseling process. In essence, clients are given a voice in the narrative career counseling process and the role of the career counselor is defined more as a facilitator of a process of meaning making rather than as an expert interpreting test results. The interpretation of results becomes more a process of clients making sense of their results in the context of their life experiences rather than a decontextualized counselor-driven process based on theory and psychometric properties. In sum, a qualitative exploration of quantitative career assessment results represents a mutual learning process.

New Concepts and Viewpoints: Charting New Directions

The debate about how to use quantitative career assessment in career counseling, especially in narrative career counseling, is not new (e.g., De Bruin & De Bruin, 2006; Sampson, 2009; Savickas, 2000; Super, 1957). To date, however, few practical suggestions have been offered about how this persistent issue may be addressed. In this regard, the ISI process charts a new direction in offering a seamless approach to effectively merge quantitative career assessment with narrative career counseling. This the ISI process enables through its six-part structure which is adaptable for a wide variety of quantitative career assessment instruments as illustrated in this chapter.

Relevance for Multiple Cultures: Sensitivity to the Universal and the Particular

Quantitative career assessment has been criticized for failing to consider sufficiently the context within which individuals make their career decisions. There has also been persistent concern that the interpretation of quantitative scores by career counselors is largely decontextualized (Lamprecht, 2002). Concomitantly, narrative approaches to career counseling call for a more holistic view of the client's life in the career choice process. Given other concerns about the psychometric properties of quantitative career assessment in multicultural contexts, there is a need to reconsider how quantitative career assessment can be used in culturally sensitive ways. The use of the ISI process as illustrated in this chapter with a traditional client, that is a white, Western, young male, and also with a nontraditional client, that is a female, non-Western adult, demonstrates how quantitative assessment can be qualitatively interpreted. The ISI process can be considered as both universal and particular in its application. While the assumption that quantitative career assessment instruments have universal application has been challenged, the ISI process offers a means of developing meaningful "client particular" interpretations located within their specific cultural contexts.

On the one hand, this process can be used within any cultural context, while, on the other hand it provides the career counselor with an opportunity to explore the particular context of a career client.

Conclusion

The present chapter suggests that the binary between quantitative career assessment and narrative career counseling does not have to be so. Indeed, it supports claims about the complementarity of quantitative assessment and qualitative processes (e.g., Savickas, 1993; Whiston & Rahardja, 2005) in which strengths and limitations of each counterbalance those of the other. The ISI process is an attempt to meet some of the challenges facing narrative career counseling such as the lack of models of this approach and also the need to integrate narrative and storytelling approaches with traditional career assessment practices. Importantly, the ISI also illustrates a way of meeting the challenge of how to story the scores provided by quantitative career assessment.

References

De Bruin, K., & De Bruin, G. P. (2006). Career assessment. In G. B. Stead & M. B. Watson (Eds.), *Career psychology in the South African context* (2nd ed., pp. 129–136). Pretoria, South Africa: Van Schaik.

Holland, J. L. (1985). *The self-directed search: A guide to educational and vocational planning*. Odessa, FL: Psychological Assessment Resources.

Holland, J. L. (1997). *Making vocational choices: A theory of vocational personalities and work environments* (3rd ed.). Odessa, FL: Psychological Assessment Resources.

Lamprecht, J. C. (2002). Career assessment skills. In K. Maree & L. Ebersöhn (Eds.), *Lifeskills and career counselling* (pp. 119–127). Sandown, South Africa: Heinemann.

McMahon, M., & Patton, W. (2002). Using qualitative assessment in career counselling. *International Journal for Educational and Vocational Guidance, 2*(1), 51–66.

McMahon, M., & Patton, W. (2006). Qualitative career assessment. In M. McMahon & W. Patton (Eds.), *Career counselling: Constructivist approaches* (pp. 163–175). London, UK: Routledge.

McMahon, M., & Watson, M. (2010). Story telling: Moving from thin stories to thick and rich stories. In K. Maree (Ed.), *Career counselling: Methods that work* (pp. 53–63). Cape Town, South Africa: Juta.

McMahon, M., & Watson, M. (Eds.). (2011a). *Career counseling and constructivism: Elaboration of constructs*. New York, NY: Nova Science.

McMahon, M., & Watson, M. (2011b). Career counselling: What's the story? In M. McMahon & M. Watson (Eds.), *Career counselling and constructivism: Elaboration of constructs* (pp. 13–24). New York, NY: Nova Science.

McMahon, M., & Watson, M. (2012a). Story crafting: Strategies for facilitating narrative career counselling. *International Journal for Educational and Vocational Guidance*. doi:10.1007/s10775-012-9228-5.

McMahon, M., & Watson, M. (2012b). Telling stories of career assessment. *Journal of Career Assessment*. doi:10.1177/1069072712448999.

Patton, W., & McMahon, M. (2006). *Career development and systems theory: Connecting theory and practice* (2nd ed.). Rotterdam, The Netherlands: Sense.

Peavy, R. V. (1998). *Sociodynamic counselling: A constructivist perspective*. Victoria, Canada: Trafford.

Reid, H. L. (2006). Usefulness and truthfulness: Outlining the limitations and upholding the benefits of constructivist approaches for career counselling. In M. McMahon & W. Patton (Eds.), *Career counselling: Constructivist approaches* (pp. 17–29). Abingdon, UK: Routledge.

Sampson, J. P., Jr. (2009). Modern and postmodern career theories: The unnecessary divorce. *The Career Development Quarterly, 58*, 91–96.

Savickas, M. L. (1993). Career counseling in the postmodern era. *Journal of Cognitive Psychotherapy: An International Quarterly, 7*, 205–215.

Savickas, M. L. (2000). Renovating the psychology of careers for the twenty-first century. In A. S. Collin & R. Young (Eds.), *The future of career* (pp. 53–68). Cambridge, UK: Cambridge University Press.

Super, D. E. (1957). *The psychology of careers*. New York, NY: Harper & Row.

Super, D. E. (1970). *Manual, Work Values Inventory*. Chicago, IL: Riverside.

Whiston, S. C., & Rahardja, D. (2005). Qualitative career assessment: An overview and analysis. *Journal of Career Assessment, 13*, 371–380.

Zytowski, D. G. (2006). *Super's work value inventory revised. Technical manual*. Adel, IA: Kuder. Retrieved from http://www.kuder.com/downloads/SWV-Tech-Manual.pdf

The Assessment of Quality of Working Life in Career Guidance and Counseling

36

Simon Easton and Darren Van Laar

Introduction

It has been suggested that effective career guidance interventions can help people "to become more motivated learners/workers, stay in the workforce longer, have reduced levels of workplace stress, and be less marginalized in society. These services contribute to social and economic outcomes related to increased employment opportunities, improved quality of life, social inclusion, and a more vibrant, dynamic economy" (Lalande, Hiebert, Magnusson, Bezanson, & Borgen, 2006, p. 1). The reference to quality of life in this description of the benefits of career guidance and counseling draws attention to a category of outcomes for which there have hitherto been very few, if any, valid and reliable assessment measures.

In this chapter, we will briefly review the career guidance and counseling context in which the evaluation of a client's quality of life can be considered, before endeavoring to define in more detail just what is meant by the term quality of working life (QoWL). We then describe a measure which might assist career guidance counselors in their initial assessment of clients, as well as in the evaluation of the outcomes of interventions. An example of the

use of such a measure to assess the experience of a group of individuals in the work setting is presented, wherein a cohort of graduates were assessed with a view to better understand their QoWL using the work-related quality of life scale (WRQoL). We then discuss the possible role of such a measure in work with individuals, both as regards its contribution towards formulation as a basis for interventions and in relation to its use as a pre- and post-assessment measure in the career guidance and counseling setting. Lastly, we consider the need for further research into possible adaptations according to the cultural environment of the individual being offered career guidance and counseling.

Assessment of Outcomes of Career Guidance and Counseling

While attention has previously been given to the assessment of the potential benefits of career guidance and counseling, there have been calls for more evidence to support the value and impact of career development services (Roest & Magnusson, 2004). Although there is evidence to support the claim that career advisors and their managers do believe it is appropriate to evaluate the results of the career guidance services they provide, it would appear that few actually formally evaluate the outcomes of their interventions (Baudouin et al., 2007).

Career guidance can be defined in terms of its aims and assessed in terms of its outcomes. Thus,

S. Easton (✉)
Department of Psychology, University of Portsmouth, Portsmouth, UK
e-mail: simon.easton@port.ac.uk

Flynn (1994) stated that career counseling can be seen as an endeavor to help an individual make improved career decisions. The assessment of the effectiveness of career guidance and counseling has been examined in some detail by Oliver and Spokane (1988), who recommended that investigators choose from several major classes of career counseling outcomes, and suggested that, although career decision-making is important, it should be considered alongside other "adjustment variables" such as career maturity, self-esteem, anxiety, need for achievement, and the evaluation of the counseling itself (e.g., ratings of satisfaction or effectiveness).

Watts and Dent (2006), in their broader view of the outcomes of career guidance, proposed that four major areas should be considered: client satisfaction, learning outcomes, behavioral outcomes, and economic and social outcomes. However, Watts and Dent observed that, in practice, "career guidance services tend to count activities, rather than to measure these against outcomes" (p. 177). In all fairness, Watts and Dent did argue that assessment of career guidance and counseling can be difficult in practice, because some of the outcomes may only be observed after a significant amount of time has elapsed, and follow-up assessments can be difficult. They have further suggested that evidence relating to some outcomes is complex and costly to collect and have expressed the opinion that there can be a risk that a focus on the individual interests of the client can be undermined by organizational and other pressures.

Some measures of career counseling and guidance do exist but often only address some, rather than all, of the relevant outcomes. In their review of possible measures, Kidd and Killeen (1992) proposed four categories of career outcomes:

1. Measures of career maturity (attitudes, knowledge, and competences related to developmental stage)
2. Knowledge and competence tests (e.g., rational decision skills or job-seeking skills)
3. Standardized self-report measures of states and attitudes (e.g., measures of career indecisiveness)

4. Self-report measures of behaviors (e.g., frequency of information-seeking and range of sources employed)

The gulf between identifying what could be measured and what can realistically be assessed remains wide, however, with Watts and Dent (2006) emphasizing that, in practice, the assessment of all potentially relevant aspects may simply be impractical and too time consuming. So how might this broader assessment of the effectiveness of career guidance and counseling be undertaken? The measure of guidance impact (MGI) (Christophers, Stoney, Lines, & Kendall, 1993) has been promoted as a useful and brief self-report measure. However, the MGI evaluates four learning areas (decision-making, opportunity awareness, transitional skills, and self-awareness), rather than the effect of the use of those skills. The focus on such specific outcomes may be relevant to an overall assessment of the intervention, but it could be argued that such an assessment would need to be matched with other measures which evaluate the degree to which these skills are usefully applied to the benefit of the client, if it is to be shown that higher scores on the MGI really reflect useful and meaningful change. Another popular assessment procedure might be that of client satisfaction with career guidance and counseling. It is relatively easy to measure and appears to have some credibility but can be criticized as measuring the extent to which clients liked the process of the intervention, rather than assessing whether the intervention was actually helpful.

New Directions in the Assessment Career Guidance and Counseling Outcomes: Quality of Working Life

It is argued here that one way of measuring the effectiveness of career counseling and guidance is to see if clients experience an improvement in their perception of the key factors that affect their working lives, that is, the quality of their working lives, after they have experienced career guidance or counseling. The adoption of such outcome criteria would involve assessment of QoWL prior to the intervention, so that reassessment after the intervention could allow evaluation of direction and/or amount of change. A reliable measure would be required, however. An initial assessment of QoWL could also identify areas of dissatisfaction in the factors influencing someone's job and allow consideration of options such as adapting the current job, challenging expectations and assumptions, or identifying jobs or roles that might better meet the individual's needs and better match their preferences.

The suggestion that consideration of the concept underpinning QoWL might offer something to the process of career counseling and guidance is, of course, not wholly new. Rose, Beh, Uli, and Idris (2006), for example, reported findings that indicated that, for the majority in their sample, the most important determinant of QoWL was career achievement, followed by career satisfaction and work-life balance. Just as some of those writing about career counseling and guidance have considered the relevance of the concept of QoWL, so those writing about the concept of QoWL itself have recognized the relevance of career counseling and guidance. Walton (1975), for example, concluded that the opportunity for personal growth and development was a key dimension of QoWL. Indirectly and directly, reference has been made in the literature to the relevance of various concepts in QoWL which would seem to draw heavily upon themes central to career counseling and guidance. For example, the focus on needs in QoWL has been reflected in the career guidance and counseling literature, with Kerr (1985) writing about the relationship between career goals and Maslow's (1943) hierarchy of needs model. Lau and Bruce (1998) suggested that the QoWL construct should encompass training and career advancement opportunities, and Mirvis and Lawler (1984) placed particular emphasis on the relevance of opportunities for career advancement in their model of QoWL.

Quality of Working Life: Models and Theoretical Descriptions

The term "quality of work life" has been referred to in academic literature for over 50 years (e.g., Mayo, 1960) and represents an endeavor to address the specific aspects of the broader concept of quality of life that relate to work. The concept of QoWL has tended to include aspects such as job satisfaction and stress at work (SAW) and may thus be particularly relevant to the evaluation of career guidance and counseling interventions.

Various models of QoWL have subsequently been proposed, each drawing upon different combinations of a wide range of factors, which tend to be developed from theory, and only rarely from the findings of empirical research. For example, Hackman and Oldham (1974) proposed that an individual's psychological growth needs must be met if employees are to experience high QoWL. Sirgy, Efraty, Siegel, and Lee (2001) proposed that higher levels of QoWL reflected satisfaction of key needs such as those based on job requirements, the working environment, and organizational commitment. Martel and Dupuis (2006) in their review of the QoWL literature have identified four main models: the transfer model (or spillover effect), the compensation model, the segmentation model, and the accommodation model. Each model can be interpreted as having implications for career counseling and guidance.

The transfer model or spillover effect (Kavanagh & Halpern, 1977) is seen as emphasizing the positive links between work and nonwork areas of life (Schmitt & Bedeian, 1982). This model draws upon evidence that job satisfaction affects and is affected by an individual's nonwork experience (George & Brief, 1990). This model draws attention to the direct and indirect influences of work aspects (e.g., relocation of offices) on home life (e.g., birth of a child) and vice versa. Staines (1980) and Rousseau (1978), however, have emphasized that, while it may be the case that specific spheres of work life are positively correlated with specific aspects outside work, the transfer model may not apply to all spheres and all kinds of jobs, as it appears that jobs with relatively extreme characteristics (such as high levels of solitude and/or physical demand) may fit better with the compensation model.

Thus, the *compensation model* (Schmitt & Mellon, 1980) places emphasis on the way in which an individual might seek outside work that which is absent in the work setting, wherein, for example, a tedious job might be held by someone who actively seeks excitement through their hobbies and interests. The underlying assumption in the compensation model is that if someone is not fully satisfied at work, they will strive to compensate through stimulating activities outside work (Schmitt & Mellon, 1980). Staines (1980) provided some support for the compensation model in certain circumstances in demonstrating that certain spheres of work life tend to correlate negatively with specific nonwork spheres. However, the compensation model has been criticized by some on the basis that, taken to its logical conclusion, this model would predict an inverse relation between job satisfaction and nonwork satisfaction (Martel & Dupuis, 2006).

The *segmentation model* (George & Brief, 1990), by way of contrast, proposes that work and home life do not substantially affect each other. Thus, Martin and Schermerhorn (1983) proposed that a clear separation of job and life dimensions could foster satisfaction, while a spillover could adversely affect overall life satisfaction. Martin and Schermerhorn emphasized what they saw as the importance of boundaries between these work and nonwork aspects in the maintenance of required balance. Edwards and Rothbard (2000) have provided evidence in support of the claim that spillover can adversely affect psychological well-being.

A more active variation of investment from work to home, and vice versa, to balance demands in each sphere is envisaged in the *accommodation model* (Lambert, 1990). The accommodation model is based on the premise that an individual can choose to reduce their investment in one sphere of activity to allow them to meet the demands elsewhere (Lambert, 1990). By way of example, it can be argued that this approach to balancing work and home life can be seen among mothers of young children, as they may seek to reduce working hours to allow more time at home with their children.

Such models have implications for the way in which an individual's QoWL can be affected by factors other than work and thus imply that such factors would need to be taken into account by career counselors as they seek to help people identify changes that would be relevant and appropriate to each individual.

The Work-Related Quality of Life Scale

The relevance of the concept of QoWL to career counseling and guidance may hitherto have been limited because both the concept of QoWL and its measurement have been poorly operationalized. Recent developments, however, may lead researchers and practitioners to reconsider the possibility that attention to an individual's QoWL and the subcomponents comprising it might usefully contribute to the identification of any career guidance or counseling themes. Information about QoWL could also offer information relevant to possible solutions and provide the basis of an assessment of the effectiveness of interventions. Unfortunately, agreement about the definition of QoWL has, for many years, eluded researchers and theoreticians, and a broader conceptualization of someone's experience of working has therefore tended to be set aside in favor of simpler and narrower concepts, such as job satisfaction.

Psychologists at the University of Portsmouth in the UK have worked with a range of organizations to develop a valid and reliable measure of QoWL—the WRQoL scale. The scale has been developed through a number of large-scale studies within the UK National Health Service (NHS). On the basis of analysis of data from 953 employees from UK NHS trusts, a 23-item five-point scale (see Table 36.1)

Table 36.1 The 23-item work-related quality of life (WRQoL) scale

Question number	WRQoL factor	WRQoL question text
1.	JCS	I have a clear set of goals and aims to enable me to do my job
2.	CAW	I feel able to voice opinions and influence changes in my area of work
3.	JCS	I have the opportunity to use my abilities at work
4.	GWB	I feel well at the moment
5.	HWI	My employer provides adequate facilities and flexibility for me to fit work around my family life
6.	HWI	My current working hours/patterns suit my personal circumstances
7.	SAW	I often feel under pressure at work*
8.	JCS	When I have done a good job it is acknowledged by my line manager
9.	GWB	Recently, I have been feeling unhappy and depressed*
10.	GWB	I am satisfied with my life
11.	JCS	I am encouraged to develop new skills
12.	CAW	I am involved in decisions that affect me in my own area of work
13.	WCS	My employer provides me with what I need to do my job effectively
14.	HWI	My line manager actively promotes flexible working hours/patterns
15.	GWB	In most ways my life is close to ideal
16.	WCS	I work in a safe environment
17.	GWB	Generally things work out well for me
18.	JCS	I am satisfied with the career opportunities available for me here
19.	SAW	I often feel excessive levels of stress at work*
20.	JCS	I am satisfied with the training I receive in order to perform my present job
21.	GWB	Recently, I have been feeling reasonably happy all things considered
22.	WCS	The working conditions are satisfactory
23.	CAW	I am involved in decisions that affect members of the public in my own area of work

GWB general well-being, *HWI* home-work interface, *JCS* job career satisfaction, *CAW* control at work, *WCS* working conditions, *SAW* stress at work
Note. All items are scored on a 5-point Likert scale from 1 = *strongly disagree* to 5 = *strongly agree*, with starred items (*) reverse scored

Table 36.2 Subscale and overall reliability scores for the WRQoL scale

Factor	Cronbach's alpha
Job and career satisfaction (JCS)	.86
General well-being (GWB)	.89
Home-work interface (HWI)	.82
Stress at work (SAW)	.81
Control at work (CAW)	.81
Working conditions (WCS)	.75
Overall scale (23 items)	.91

representing six factors was developed by Van Laar, Edwards, and Easton (2007). The WRQoL scale has good subscale reliabilities (see Table 36.2) and good convergent and discriminant validity, and test-retest reliability. Further details of the validity and reliability of the WRQoL, including the marking and scoring scheme, along with relevant norms, can be found in the WRQoL user manual (Easton & Van Laar, 2012) and at www.qowl.co.uk

The WRQoL scale has been widely used across the world and, although developed in English, has been translated into seven languages: Chinese, Farsi, French, Portuguese, Spanish, Turkish, and Welsh. International applications include Chinese nurses (Wen-Liang et al., 2006), Canadian academics (McGinn & Skorobohacz, 2011), Indian teachers (Parameswari & Kadhiravan, 2012), and Turkish general employees (Duyan, Aytaç, Akyıldız, & Van Laar, 2013). For further details and access to the translated questionnaires and the WRQoL manual, please contact the authors. The WRQoL scale has been used at organization level, work group level, and at an individual level to determine the key factors that contribute to a high QoWL. The WRQoL scale consists of six factors which cover the main elements affecting an individual's QoWL and are thus relevant to the evaluation of the individual's contentment with their job—something of keen interest to career counselors. In a recent survey of 3,792 participants from nine UK universities by the authors, a multiple regression procedure used to predict answers to the question *I am satisfied with the overall quality of my working life* from the six WRQoL factors accounted for 68.8 % of the variance ($R^2 = .688$), demonstrating a very high level of construct validity.

WRQoL Factors and Their Relevance to Guidance and Counseling

Factor one: *job and career satisfaction (JCS)*. This factor contains six items, has a subscale reliability of .86, and contains items relating to satisfaction with the job and career opportunities: for example, *I am satisfied with the career opportunities available for me here* (Item 18). The JCS factor appears to measure the level to which the workplace provides a person with the best things at work, the things that make them feel good, such as sense of achievement, high self-esteem, and fulfillment of potential. This factor has been shown to have excellent convergent validity with other measures of job satisfaction, such as with the Warr job satisfaction scale ($r = .87$) (Easton & Van Laar, 2012; Mullarkey, Wall, Warr, Clegg, & Stride, 1999).

The JCS factor assesses the degree to which an individual's workplace offers the opportunity to experience satisfaction in the workplace. These ideas mirror the work of Herzberg in his hygiene theory (1966) and Maslow (1954) in his description of a hierarchy of needs. Souza-Poza and Souza-Poza (2000) have proposed that the key determinants of job satisfaction include an employee's interest in their work, clearly defined career opportunities, good relationships with

colleagues, high incomes, and independent working. The JCS factor would therefore seem to have a most direct and obvious relevance to assessment in career guidance and counseling and the factor that may well be among those most affected by career or role change.

Factor two: *general well-being (GWB)*. This factor contains six questions and has a subscale reliability of .89. The items contributing to this factor are broadly related to the general feeling of happiness and life satisfaction the individual experiences: for example, *Generally things work out well for me* (Item 17). GWB assesses the extent to which someone feels good or content within themselves. Thus, an individual's sense of GWB may be more or less independent of their work situation but may both influence and be influenced by his or her work, nevertheless. The GWB factor includes questions about psychological well-being and general physical health. The GWB subscale of the WRQoL has high convergent validity with measures of GWB, such as the General Health Questionnaire 12 ($r = .57$) (Easton & Van Laar, 2012; Goldberg, 1978).

When people experience physical or mental ill health, their performance at work can be affected, and their sense of psychological well-being can be reduced. Thus, higher GWB scores might be expected to correlate with absence of psychological distress, with fulfilling relationships, and with the ability to adapt to change and cope with adversity at work (see Seymour & Grove, 2005). When the WRQoL is used to assess career guidance and counseling interventions, the GWB scale would be expected to reflect the indirect impact on the individual of the positive or negative changes affecting their work. A low GWB score might suggest further investigation of this aspect in the career and guidance counseling context as part of the assessment process.

Factor three: *home-work interface (HWI)*. This factor is based on three items related to issues of accommodating family and work commitments: for example, *My current working hours/patterns suit my personal circumstances* (Item 6). Within the WRQoL scale, the HWI factor has a subscale reliability of .82 and addresses work-life balance and the extent to which an employer is perceived to support the employee's home life. The concepts addressed in the HWI factor have also been referred to as work-family conflict in the wider literature. Work-family conflict has been shown by Bruch, Allen, and Spector (2002) to be related to decreased job satisfaction, whereas, for example, work by White and Beswick (2003) indicates that flexible hour policies are associated with increases in work performance and job satisfaction. Dorsey, Jarjoura, and Rutecki (2003) have highlighted the increasing importance placed on balancing home and work demands by people making career choices and decisions.

From the perspective of career guidance and counseling, more detailed exploration of this factor with the individual may be warranted where higher levels of dissatisfaction on the HWI subscale are detected at initial assessment. The HWI factor may be the most important aspect of their working lives for some individuals and so require positioning at the very center of career planning processes.

Factor four: stress at work (SAW). This factor is represented by two items related to demands, for example, *I often feel under pressure at work* (Item 7), and reflects the extent to which an individual perceives they have excessive pressures and/or feel undue levels of SAW. This factor has a subscale reliability of .81. Workplace stress is considered one of the top five job-related health problems in the USA (Kinman, 1996). Freeborn (2001) underlined the relationship between SAW in research which indicated that individuals who see their work demands as reasonable tend to report higher levels of job satisfaction. A high stress subscale score at a pre-assessment may well be a symptom of the dissatisfaction clients may be experiencing at pre-assessment during any evaluation, and a demonstrable reduction in SAW may well be a key outcome measure from a successful intervention.

Factor five: control at work (CAW). Three items loaded on the CAW factor has a subscale reliability of .81. The items for this subscale are primarily related to the individual being able to have control over what happens at work: for example, *I am involved in decisions that affect me in my own area of work* (Item 12). Feelings of being in control of a situation have appeared as a key concept in many stress research studies undertaken in Western cultures (Freeborn, 2001; Jex & Spector, 1996; Parkes, 1991; Spector, 1988), and evidence from Spector (1986) indicates that there is also a significant positive association between personal control and job satisfaction. Spector (2002) has also shown that greater CAW can be an important factor in an employee's health and well-being. Perceived CAW is an issue for which career and counseling advisors can provide effective support. Counseling on how to influence decisions of managers and coworkers can be provided.

Factor six: working conditions (WCS). The WCS factor, which has a subscale reliability of .79, is based on three questions related to the physical working environment. For example, Item 22 asks respondents to assess their agreement with the statement: *The WCS are satisfactory.* The WCS factor can be seen as assessing the extent to which an employee is satisfied with their security at work as well as the available resources and their WCS. While the JCS factor assesses the degree to which their workplace provides individuals with the best things at work, the WCS factor reflects the degree to which the workplace meets someone's basic requirements and their dissatisfaction with physical work environment.

Where WCS play a key role in someone's dissatisfaction with their experience of work, the WRQoL may assist the career counselor in the development of a clearer understanding of the relevance of the various factors for each individual. Leigh, Kravitz, Schembri, Samuels, and Mobley (2002) and Deshpande and Deshpande (2011), for example, on the basis of studies of physicians, reported that attention to the quality of the conditions in which employees work can play a key part in career satisfaction.

It needs to be kept in mind that the WRQoL assesses the aspects of someone's experience of work that have been identified as usually being of the greatest importance and influence. There may be factors that are not assessed by the WRQoL that play a key role for any one individual, or for a group of individuals. Thus, any such measure requires careful interpretation by the assessor within the context of an individual or group of individuals. When exploring the experience of a group of workers, therefore, the WRQoL can be used to provide a snapshot of their overall QoWL, as well as offering an indication of what will tend to be the most important underlying factors.

Use of the WRQoL in a Survey of Career Destinations of Psychology Graduates

The WRQoL offers the opportunity to compare the experiences of groups of workers and can thereby contribute to the development of an understanding of the relationship between QoWL and career satisfaction. Thus, Van Laar and Udell (2008) used the WRQoL to survey a sample of British Psychological Society (BPS) members who obtained a BPS-accredited psychology degree in the year 2000. Of the 939 surveys originally sent out, 430 useable questionnaires were retained for the analysis (a response rate of 49.9 %).

The results indicated that, compared to a QoWL benchmark sample, the BPS year 2000 sample reported a generally higher overall QoWL. In addition, BPS year 2000 respondents showed higher levels of QoWL when compared with a general sample on all WRQoL factors except HWI. The WRQoL findings were considered in more detail in a full survey report, wherein the authors sought to help graduates identify costs and benefits of the various professional routes open to them in psychology. The survey provided a wealth of information for career advisors dealing with psychology students. For example, one key finding was that of the ten occupational sectors entered into by psychology graduates 7 years after graduating (clinical, occupational, forensic, counseling, educational, university, teaching, nonuniversity research, other psychology, other sectors), none

differed significantly from any other in their perceived QoWL.

The BPS report contextualizes QoWL in indicating that respondents tended to value their job satisfaction and personal development more highly than financial reward, and 48 % reported that they did not get their main fulfillment from work (although 38 % said they did). In a related question, the majority of respondents said they "worked to live" (67 %) rather than "lived to work" (14 %). This reinforces the relevance of QoWL for career guidance counselors and highlights the relevance of ascertaining how important a job or the wider experience of employment is to the individual and even how far these aspects are linked to the sense of self; a person who "lives to work" is likely to have very different expectations and requirements from a career compared to someone who "works to live." Careful interpretation of these results by those offering career guidance to those leaving university with a degree in psychology needs, of course, to be undertaken in the context of the sample and other factors which may have been affecting the group at that time.

As ever, such results reflect the average responses for a group and can mask individual variation or even distinct variations within minority groups. However, such findings might lead to a wider focus in career guidance, wherein greater emphasis is placed on the parallel development of nonwork interests or commitments. While the WRQoL addresses some key factors, further investigation might be warranted as advisors seek to better understand the balance between personal development and financial reward, for example, in so far that it might relate to career paths and options.

Use of the WRQoL for Staff Groups in Organizations

The WRQoL has been used in many staff surveys, and informal feedback has consistently indicated that organizations have found the results helpful in their endeavors to better understand their employees' experience of their work environment and as they seek to identify aspects warranting further investigation and/or consideration. As previously stated, some caution is appropriate when interpreting survey findings, and although WRQoL surveys have been undertaken across the world and in several languages, it is possible that it will be necessary to produce a range of local (national/culturally specific) norm datasets to be able to validly interpret the WRQoL scale scores of a newly assessed group or individual. For example, researchers from Turkey found that, in the Turkish WRQoL translation, respondents' scores on items relating to stress (e.g., *I often feel under pressure at work*) and GWB (e.g., *Recently, I have been feeling unhappy and depressed*) were much lower compared to the UK benchmark rates. After considering this disparity in some depth, the Turkish researcher proposed that the translation was correct and that it was possible that Turkish individuals were much less likely to *admit* they had such problems in a questionnaire. Analysis of further results from research across the world should provide opportunities for further consideration of the cultural relevance of the WRQoL scale and confirm the worth of having culturally specific norms.

The current WRQoL scale and associated norms (Easton & Van Laar, 2012) have been developed with a view to providing organizations with information on the quality of working lives of their staff and the key underlying contributors to that experience. Within any sample, however, the various unique individual experiences can be lost, and there is a risk that the overall survey result for a group will fail to fully reflect the specific experiences of individuals. While descriptive statistics can be provided for a group as a whole, in the context of career counseling, any intervention aimed at enhancing QoWL must be assessed and the WRQoL scores considered, at the level of the individual. Indeed, it is possible that the assessment of individuals using the WRQoL scale would be of particular value in the career guidance and counseling setting, where it could help not only to assess outcomes but would also serve to guide

discussion of the identification of appropriate interventions for that individual.

Use of the WRQoL for Individuals

Hitherto, the WRQoL has been used for surveys of groups of workers, and benchmark samples have allowed organizations to compare their staff survey results with staff from other organizations. Thus, within the UK university sector, the WRQoL benchmark is based on an all-staff sample from ten universities, and norm tables based on this data are used to benchmark findings and conclusions for organizations in general (Edwards, Van Laar, Easton, & Kinman, 2009). The WRQoL results for different groups or subgroups can also be compared within an organization. For example, the WRQoL subscale scores of managers can be compared with other groups of workers. In addition, the WRQoL subscale scores of managers in one work location within an organization could be compared with managers at another site.

The more detailed analysis of survey data in the light of comparisons with a benchmark allows identification of areas of good practice, as well as draws attention to aspects of their QoWL which may warrant attention. Survey results provide an averaged snapshot and may conceal wide variation in the views of respondents within any one group. As a result, there is a danger that while interpretation of the results may have value in relation to the group, the results may fail to adequately relate to individuals. Similarly, any intervention will be targeted at the average member of the group— and average people do not exist. If the WRQoL is to be used to inform the process of career guidance and counseling, while information on groups may be valuable, access to the results of individuals would be most helpful.

At this stage, some caution needs to be maintained if the group norms are used in an endeavor to provide a benchmark context for any one individual set of results. It may be that current benchmarks will be wholly adequate as a basis for the interpretation of individual profiles, but further research is required to fully address this issue. At present, informal, exploratory use of the WRQoL with individuals indicates a high level of face validity, and the existing norms appear similarly to offer a benchmark context for interpretation of subscale scores in a manner that individuals find helpful.

Thus, examination of the various subscale scores for any one individual may be particularly helpful and informative in the career guidance and counseling setting: An individual may have relatively low scores on the HWI and CAW scales, for example, and therefore, attending to these aspects will be crucial in the counseling process. Also, it may be that a desire for autonomy would be important for one individual, while another may place particular importance on the home-work balance. The WRQoL may therefore help draw out and understand the relevance of the factors underpinning the broader career guidance- and counseling-related needs of clients.

The use of the WRQoL scale with individuals allows career advisors to quickly interpret the questionnaire responses and generate a personal profile which can be compared with an appropriate benchmark group. The individual assessment pack (Easton & Van Laar, 2012) contains an illustrative graphic that provides a straightforward and readily accessible summary of results for discussion and can serve to contribute to developing an understanding of someone's present situation and help identify possible aims. In due course, reassessment using the WRQoL scale can contribute to monitoring of the effects of interventions and evaluation of outcomes at the individual level. Interviewees can be invited to predict their levels of satisfaction on the various factors, such that disparities between the assessment results and their predictions can be explored. As with all psychometric devices, discussion must take into account the limitations of the measure and avoid placing undue weight on the results.

If used in follow-up assessments, it might be that repeat use of the WRQoL would usefully contribute to the process of reflection on the specific outcomes of interventions—did a low HWI score change? Does the new job or role foster a higher CAW subscale score where that score was low before?

Relevance for Multiple Cultures: Sensitivity to the Universal and the Particular

Since the concept of QoWL has largely been developed within the Western literature (e.g., Martel & Dupuis, 2006), concerns have been raised as to the relevance of such models to other countries. In the absence of extensive comparative studies of QoWL across cultures, other theoretical models can be considered. Thus, for example, in the Haire, Ghiselli, and Porter (1966) exploration of Maslow's (1954) model of hierarchy of needs, the findings for USA-based managers very closely matched the expected pattern; however, other nationality groups investigated showed a variety of patterns, wherein, for example, self-actualization was achieved in the absence of complete satisfaction of lower-order needs.

Hofstede (1980) proposed four factors which, he concluded, could explain approximately half of the differences in responses in work-related value patterns among various cultures. The four key dimensions were power distance (acceptance or rejection of hierarchies of power), individualism (contrasted with collectivism and referring to the assumed focus of commitment), masculinity (wherein the focus of cultures can be seen as on material success/assertiveness, e.g., as opposed to interpersonal relationships and caring for the weak), and uncertainty avoidance (e.g., the degree to which a culture can be associated with tendencies towards avoidance of the unpredictable versus acceptance of personal risk) (Hofstede, 1984). As these dimensions appear to vary among cultures, Hofstede proposed that attempts to increase what he saw as quality of work life may be unsuccessful if these culture-specific differences are not taken into account. Thus, individuals with low uncertainty avoidance will tend to seek clear rules and structure in the work setting. Hofstede (1980) reported that Greeks had a low uncertainty avoidance score, which would suggest that they may be reluctant to make decisions and prefer more highly structured work. Imposition of organizational structures which fail to meet these needs could therefore lead to stress and distress and/or to reduced levels of performance and job satisfaction.

Hofstede's earlier work (1972) had indicated that occupational differences may also lead to differences in work values. Thus, it was proposed that there may well be an emphasis on the content of jobs among professionals and managers which might be distinct from the focus on the social context common among clerks and technicians. Schwartz (2004), however, has challenged Hofstede's model and identified an alternative set of seven culture level value types:

1. Conservatism (incorporating the degree to which a culture or society places importance on the maintenance of the status quo)
2. Intellectual autonomy (incorporating the degree to which individuals are seen as entitled to pursue their own intellectual interests and desires)
3. Affective autonomy (e.g., how much a society values and accepts the pursuit of hedonism and personal interests and desires)
4. Hierarchy (the degree to which a society or culture legitimizes hierarchical structures and roles)
5. Mastery (this refers to the emphasis placed by societies on concepts such as mastery of the social environment and focus on promoting competition between individuals)
6. Egalitarian commitment (acceptance or rejection of self-interest)
7. Harmony (the level of emphasis placed on the value of harmony with nature)

While there is a degree of commonality between the culture level value types put forward by Schwartz and Hofstede, Schwartz appears to have identified elements of culture that are not fully considered in Hofstede's conceptualization of values (for more, see Ng, Lee & Soutar, 2007; Steenkamp, 2001). Individualism-collectivism has been perhaps the most widely studied of these dimensions, largely because of its apparent impact in relation to various psychological differences across cultures (Hofstede, 2001;

Matsumoto & Triandis, 2001; Triandis, 1995). Thus, in more collectivist cultures people will tend to be more interdependent with those around them (e.g., family, work colleagues) and give greater priority to shared goals. In individualist cultures, on the other hand, competitiveness can be relatively high, and there can be a greater emphasis on self-reliance and independence from others. The WRQoL has been developed in the UK setting and is being used in many other cultures. In due course, it is anticipated that the WRQoL may need to be adapted to better reflect the relevance of the kinds of cultural differences identified by Hofstede (1972), Schwartz (2004), and others.

Conclusion

"With the current emphasis on evidence-based practice and outcome-focused intervention, it is important to be able to demonstrate the value of career services in a manner that service providers find meaningful and funders find useful" (Baudouin et al., 2007, p. 146). The WRQoL appears to offer a reliable and valid assessment of the core factors underpinning QoWL in the settings and contexts in which it has been developed. The WRQoL offers potential for use with individuals as part of annual appraisals, occupational health assessments, and other work-related contexts. In particular, it would appear that it may have something to offer in the career guidance and counseling setting, in relation to both assessment of needs prior to intervention and assessment of outcomes.

The WRQoL scale has been translated into various languages and has, as of October 2012, been requested to be used by 290 researchers from 49 countries. The countries with the most requests are India (85), USA (37), UK (36), Philippines (16), Canada (13), and Malaysia (11). Such research provides the opportunity for benchmarks to be developed which may reflect differences between cultures. Research in different cultures may also allow the WRQoL to be adapted to ensure that it is culture free, or it may be the case that culture-specific versions would be required in due course.

In the interim, the use of a measure such as the WRQoL scale may be helpful as the emphasis on the development of evidence-based interventions in career guidance and counseling gains momentum.

References

Baudouin, R., Bezanson, L., Borgen, B., Goyer, L., Hiebert, B., Lalande, V., ... Turcotte, M. (2007). Demonstrating value: A draft framework for evaluating the effectiveness of career development interventions. *Canadian Journal of Counseling, 41*, 146–157.

Bruch, C. S., Allen, T. D., & Spector, P. E. (2002). The relation between work-family conflict and job satisfaction: A finer-grained analysis. *Journal of Vocational Behavior, 60*, 336–353.

Christophers, U., Stoney, S., Lines, A., & Kendall, L. (1993). *Measure of guidance impact (MGI)*. Windsor, England: NFER.

Deshpande, S. P., & Deshpande, S. S. (2011). Career satisfaction of surgical specialties. *Annals of Surgery, 253*(5), 1011–1016.

Dorsey, E. R., Jarjoura, D., & Rutecki, G. W. (2003). Influence of controllable lifestyle on recent trends in specialty choice by US medical students. *Journal of the American Medical Association, 290*(9), 1173–1178.

Duyan, E. C., Aytaç, S., Akyıldız, N., & Van Laar, D. (2013). Measuring work related quality of life and affective well-being in Turkey. *Mediterranean Journal of Social Sciences, 4*, 105–116.

Easton, S., & Van Laar, D. L. (2012). *User manual of the work-related quality of life scale (WRQoL)*. Portsmouth, England: University of Portsmouth.

Edwards, J. R., & Rothbard, N. (2000). Mechanisms linking work and family: Clarifying the relationship between work and family constructs. *Academy of Management Review, 25*, 178–200.

Edwards, J. A., Van Laar, D. L., Easton, S., & Kinman, G. (2009). The work-related quality of life (WRQoL) scale for higher education employees. *Quality in Higher Education, 15*(3), 207–219.

Flynn, R. J. (1994). Evaluating the effectiveness of career counselling: Recent evidence and recommended strategies. *Canadian Journal of Counselling/Revue Canadienne de counseling, 28*(4), 270–280.

Freeborn, D. K. (2001). Satisfaction, commitment, and psychological well-being among HMO physicians. *Western Journal of Medicine, 174*(1), 13–18.

George, J. M., & Brief, A. P. (1990). The economic instrumentality of work: An examination of the moderating effects of financial requirements and sex on the pay-life satisfaction relationship. *Journal of Vocational Behavior, 37*(3), 357–368.

Goldberg, D. (1978). General health questionnaire. In J. Weinman & S. C. Wright (Eds.), *Measures in health psychology: A user's portfolio*. Windsor, England: NFER-NELSON.

Hackman, J., & Oldham, G. (1974). *The job diagnostic survey*. New Haven, CT: Yale University.

Haire, H., Ghiselli, E. E., & Porter, L. W. (1966). *Managerial thinking: An international study*. New York, NY: Wiley.

Herzberg, F. (1966). *Work and the nature of man*. Cleveland, OH: World Press.

Hofstede, G. (1972). The colors of collars. *Columbia Journal of World Business, 7*(5), 72–80.

Hofstede, G. (1980). *Culture's consequences: International differences in work-related values*. Beverly Hills, CA: Sage.

Hofstede, G. (1984). The cultural relativity of the quality of life concept. *Academy of Management Review, 9*(3), 389–398.

Hofstede, G. (2001). *Culture's consequences: Comparing values, behaviors, institutions and organizations across nations* (2nd ed.). Thousand Oaks, CA: Sage.

Jex, S. M., & Spector, P. E. (1996). The impact of negative affectivity on stressor-strain relations: A replication and extension. *Work & Stress, 10*, 36–45.

Kavanagh, M. J., & Halpern, M. (1977). The impact of job level and sex differences on the relationship between life and job satisfaction. *Academy of Management Journal, 20*(1), 66–73.

Kerr, B. A. (1985). Smart girls, gifted women: Special guidance concerns. *Roeper Review, 8*(1), 30–33.

Kidd, J. M., & Killeen, J. (1992). Are the effects of careers guidance worth having? Changes in practice and outcomes. *Journal of Occupational & Organizational Psychology, 65*(3), 219–234.

Kinman, G. (1996). *Occupational stress and health among lecturers working in further and higher education*. London, England: National Association of Teachers in Further and Higher Education.

Lalande, V., Hiebert, B., Magnusson, K., Bezanson, L., & Borgen, B. (2006). Measuring the impact of career services: Current and desired practices. In R. Neault, N. Arthur, & L. Edwards (Eds.), *Natcon papers 2006*. Ottawa, Canada: Canada Career Consortium.

Lambert, S. J. (1990). Processes linking work and family: A critical review and research agenda. *Human Relations, 43*(3), 239–257.

Lau, R. S. M., & Bruce, E. M. (1998). A win-win paradigm for quality of work life and business performance. *Human Resource Development Quarterly, 9*(3), 211–226.

Leigh, J. P., Kravitz, R. L., Schembri, M., Samuels, S. J., & Mobley, S. (2002). Physician career satisfaction across specialties. *Archives of Internal Medicine, 162*(14), 1577–1584.

Martel, J. P., & Dupuis, G. (2006). Quality of work-life: Theoretical and methodological problems, and presentation of a new model and measuring instrument. *Social Indicators Research, 77*, 333–368.

Martin, T. N., & Schermerhorn, J. R. (1983). Work and nonwork influences on health. *Academy of Management Review, 8*, 650–659.

Maslow, A. H. (1943). A theory of human motivation. *Psychological Review, 50*(4), 370–396.

Maslow, A. H. (1954). *Motivation and personality.* New York, NY: Harper.

Matsumoto, D., & Triandis, H. C. (2001). Individualism and collectivism: Past, present, and future. In D. Matsumoto (Ed.), *Handbook of culture and psychology* (pp. 35–50). New York, NY: Oxford University Press.

Mayo, E. (1960). *The human problems of an industrial civilisation.* New York, NY: Viking Press.

McGinn, M. K., & Skorobohacz, C. (2011, June). Academic service and quality of working life in Canada. *Proceedings of the consortium of higher education researchers*, Reykjavík, Iceland.

Mirvis, P. H., & Lawler, E. E. (1984). Accounting for the quality of work life. *Journal of Occupational Behaviour, 5*, 197–212.

Mullarkey, S., Wall, T., Warr, P., Clegg, C., & Stride, C. (1999). *Measures of job satisfaction, mental health and job-related well-being.* Sheffield, England: Institute of Work Psychology.

Ng, S. I., Lee, J. A., & Soutar, G. N. (2007). Are Hofstede's and Schwartz's value frameworks congruent? *International Marketing Review, 24*(4), 164–180.

Oliver, L. W., & Spokane, A. R. (1988). Career-intervention outcome: What contributes to client gain? *Journal of Counseling Psychology, 35*, 447–462.

Parameswari, J., & Kadhiravan, S. (2012). Influence of personality on quality of work life of teachers. *International Journal of Research in Commerce, IT & Management, 2*(5), 79–82.

Parkes, K. R. (1991). Locus of control as moderator: An explanation for additive versus interactive findings in the demand-discretion model of work stress. *British Journal of Psychology, 82*, 291–312.

Roest, A., & Magnusson, K. (2004, February). *Annotated bibliography of current research on the efficacy of career development interventions and programs.* Paper presented at the meeting of the Canadian Research Working Group for Evidence-Based Practice in Career Development, Ottawa, Canada.

Rose, R. C., Beh, L., Uli, J., & Idris, K. (2006). Quality of work life: Implications of career dimensions. *Journal of Social Sciences, 2*(2), 61–67.

Rousseau, D. M. (1978). Relationship of work to nonwork. *Journal of Applied Psychology, 63*, 513–517.

Schmitt, N., & Bedeian, A. G. (1982). A comparison of LISREL and two-stage least squares analysis of a hypothesized life-job satisfaction reciprocal relationship. *The Journal of Applied Psychology, 67*, 806–817.

Schmitt, N., & Mellon, P. M. (1980). Life and job satisfaction: Is the job central? *Journal of Vocational Behavior, 16*(1), 51–57.

Schwartz, S. H. (2004). Mapping and interpreting cultural differences around the world. In H. Vinken, J. Soeters, & P. Ester (Eds.), *Comparing cultures: Dimensions of culture in a comparative perspective* (pp. 43–73). Leiden, The Netherlands: Brill.

Seymour, L., & Grove, B. (2005). *Workplace interventions for people with common mental health problems: Evidence review and recommendations.* London, England: British Occupational Health Research Foundation.

Sirgy, M. J., Efraty, D., Siegel, P., & Lee, D. (2001). A new measure of quality of work life (QoWL) based on need satisfaction and spillover theories. *Social Indicators Research, 55*, 241–302.

Souza-Poza, A., & Souza-Poza, A. A. (2000). Well-being at work: A cross-sectional study of the levels and determinants of job satisfaction. *Journal of Socio-Economics, 29*, 517–538.

Spector, P. E. (1986). Perceived control by employees: Meta-analysis of studies concerning autonomy and participation at work. *Human Relations, 39*, 1005–1016.

Spector, P. E. (1988). Development of the work locus of control scale. *Journal of Occupational Psychology, 61*, 335–340.

Spector, P. E. (2002). Employee control and occupational stress. *Current Directions in Psychological Science, 11*(4), 133–136.

Staines, G. L. (1980). Spillover versus compensation: A review of the literature on the relationship between work and nonwork. *Human Relations, 33*, 111–129.

Steenkamp, J.-B. E. M. (2001). The role of national culture in international marketing research. *International Marketing Review, 18*(1), 30.

Triandis, H. C. (1995). *New directions in social psychology: Individualism and collectivism.* Boulder, CO: Westview Press.

Van Laar, D. L., Edwards, J., & Easton, S. (2007). The work-related quality of life (scale for healthcare workers). *Journal of Advanced Nursing, 60*(3), 325–333.

Van Laar, D. L., & Udell, J. (2008). *Graduate 2000* (Unpublished research report). Leicester, England: British Psychological Society.

Walton, R. E. (1975). Criteria for quality of working life. In L. E. Davis & A. B. Cherns (Eds.), *The quality of working life* (pp. 9–104). New York, NY: The Free Press.

Watts, A. G., & Dent, G. (2006). The 'P' word: Productivity in the delivery of career guidance services. *British Journal of Guidance & Counselling, 34*(2), 177–189.

Wen-Liang, C., Sze-Yuan, C., Su-Chuan, Y., Hsien-Hwa, K., Jih-Sheng, J., & Hsien-Wen, K. (2006). Factors affecting musculoskeletal disorders among hospital nurses. *Mid-Taiwan Journal of Medicine, 11*(4), 252–260.

White, J., & Beswick, J. (2003). *Working long hours.* Sheffield, England: Health and Safety Laboratory.

Nirmala Almeida, Aziel Marques, and Gideon Arulmani

Introduction

Giant strides in technology in the 21st century, together with the forces of globalization, have led to significant changes in the world of work. Methods and systems of education need to adapt to these changes if societies and the individuals within them are to be productive. Today, we are already witnessing, particularly in emerging economies and the developing world, a lack of congruence between the competencies and skills imparted by the education system and what is expected in the work place. Surveys in India have found, for example, that barely 17 % of individuals who had successfully obtained a bachelor's degree in engineering were employable (e.g., Aspiring Minds, 2011). Reducing this incongruence is imperative.

The Organization for Economic Cooperation and Development (OECD, 2004) has defined career guidance as follows:

> Career guidance refers to services and activities intended to assist individuals, of any age and at any point throughout their lives, to make educational, training and occupational choices and to manage their careers. Such services may be found in schools, universities and colleges, in training institutions, in public employment services, in the workplace, in the voluntary or community sector

and in the private sector. The activities may take place on an individual or group basis, and may be face-to-face or at a distance (including help lines and web-based services). They include career information provision (in print, ICT-based and other forms), assessment and self-assessment tools, counseling interviews, career education programmes (to help individuals develop their self-awareness, opportunity awareness, and career management skills), taster programmes (to sample options before choosing them), work search programmes, and transition services. (p. 10)

Career guidance refers to professional assistance and support rendered with the objective of helping individuals (a) explore and understand themselves (capabilities, skills, aptitudes, interests, personality traits, health condition) and the related/relevant contexts in their life (family background, religious community, caste affiliation, socioeconomic level); (b) explore and understand the educational and vocational pathways available with respect to job opportunities, economic conditions, and job market requirements; (c) integrate information obtained from the analysis of self and the analyses of education and careers; (d) make and implement relevant educational and vocational plans, such that one is empowered to fulfill one's dreams and aspirations and also contribute meaningfully to the community at large.

Career guidance could become a powerful means of bridging the gap between education and the world of work. The development of career guidance services is important for several reasons. In the absence of formal systems for

N. Almeida (✉)
Department of Human Development, Nirmala Niketan College of Home Science, University of Mumbai, Mumbai, India
e-mail: nirmala.almeida@gmail.com

G. Arulmani et al. (eds.), *Handbook of Career Development*, International and Cultural Psychology,
DOI 10.1007/978-1-4614-9460-7_37, © Springer Science+Business Media, LLC 2014

guidance, career choosers turn to a wide variety of sources for support: peers, parents, family members, or teachers (Arulmani & Nag-Arulmani, 2004). After career entry, there are many career-related decisions and turning points; once again, it appears that dependence is on informal sources of support (Bakshi, 2011). The nature of guidance received from these sources is often influenced by their own expectations, aspirations, and an inadequate knowledge base. Some youth enter occupations by trial and error which then results in frustration, rapid shift in jobs, and unstable career development (Ali & Graham, 2003). Further, industrialization and technological advancements have increased the number of options available and thus the selection of a career can be daunting. Moreover, careers are chosen and re-chosen today, and career reconsideration is increasing in prominence as a construct (Porfeli & Lee, 2012). Finally, if countries are to continue to progress economically and technologically in the 21st century, then the suitability of candidates for jobs must be addressed. For these and similar reasons, timely and judicious career guidance is important. This brings focus to bear on the quality of career guidance services that are provided through career guidance centers. This chapter will focus on the evaluation of the quality of career guidance centers.

Challenges Faced in the Provision of Career Guidance Services

Variations in the Quality of Career Guidance Services

The type and quality of career guidance services vary across contexts. Based on its survey, the OECD (2004) made the following observations:

> There is little regular and systematic evaluation of the quality of career guidance provisions in most countries. Service standards for provision do not exist or are present in some sectors but not in others. Quality frameworks, where they exist,

tend to be voluntary rather than mandatory and operate as guidelines. Users of career guidance services have a key role to play in the design and evaluation of services. (p. 8)

In countries where services are still in the initial stages of their development, counseling and guidance services are affected by a shortage of qualified professionals. Those who do provide career guidance in these contexts are often not trained for the same, and in many of these countries, no certification is required for the practice of career guidance (Arulmani, 2007). Institutions that do have trained and qualified counselors expect them to perform other duties as well, such as teaching, administrative, or clerical work. Their primary role as counselor often does not receive the support of administrators and teachers (Poduval & Almeida, 1993). Finally, a common lacuna across countries is that career guidance services are often not audited.

Need for the Evaluation of Career Guidance Centers

The need of career guidance services in emerging economies, such as India, is a pressing one. This has led to a rapid increase in the number of career guidance centers. The type and quality of services offered by these centers are not known, and hence, it becomes imperative to evaluate centers and practitioners to understand their functioning as well as to set parameters for best practice. The challenge is to collect data that will help us understand which delivery strategies are the most effective in relation to individuals and target groups. This data, importantly, is also the basis for making decisions about future program improvements and directions. In other types of countries also, there is a need to have clear indicators for measuring the quality of career guidance centers. Watt (1998) has spelt out the many reasons why it is necessary to measure the quality of career guidance services: to justify the service for political reasons, to show that the service is worthwhile for funding purposes, to assess implementation of planned objectives, to measure client progress, to record what is happening for the purpose of documentation, to promote organizational development through strategic planning, and to assess good practice for policy development. However, as already pointed out, systematic evaluation of the quality of career guidance services, in many countries, is the exception rather than the rule.

Challenges in Evaluating the Effectiveness of Career Guidance Centers and Services

Several challenges are faced by those attempting to evaluate career guidance services. A major challenge is the phobia of accountability. The need to account for quality is perceived as threatening and this frequently leads to an avoidance of evaluation. Those who do subject their services to scrutiny believe that accountability is a one-time event and not an ongoing requirement which is closely connected to the success of their own center. Some fail to realize that accountability is an ethical responsibility that reflects the center's professional commitment at multiple levels (e.g., national, state, local, and individual).

From a research design point of view, obtaining a matched group that has not participated in guidance as a comparison group has been identified as a hurdle (Killeen & White, 2000). Quality assurance becomes difficult in small countries. Inspections and sanctions are less easy to manage because they are not bureaucratized (Sultana, 2006). In developing countries, career counseling is a new field, and hence, more time and energy is invested in developing career counseling programs, rather than in evaluating them. Finally, in quite a few countries, there is no national policy regarding the metrics and indices that schools, organizations, and private practitioners could use to evaluate the quality and impact of their career guidance services.

A further point to be considered is the objectivity with which assessment is executed. A common difficulty encountered is that practitioners are more oriented to service delivery than to rigorous research methods. Hence, data that is made available, more often than not, is vulnerable to being criticized as being of poor quality. It is essential, if evaluations and assessments are to make useful and sound contributions, that there is compliance with methodological requirements. These requirements need not be extended to the day-to-day service delivery of a career guidance center. However, attempts could be made to ensure that at periodic intervals, a systematic "research project" is set up within a career guidance practice that aims at executing an evaluation of effectiveness that is scientifically reliable and valid.

Exploring Concepts and Constructs Related to the Quality of Career Guidance Centers

The chapter is written from the Indian context where, in response to the current, urgent need for career development support, career guidance centers are mushrooming quite rapidly. In such contexts, sensitizing practitioners and centers to the quality of career guidance services rendered becomes essential. It is these factors that served as the impetus for the Marques and Almeida (2010) study reported in this chapter.

Objectives of the Study

The objectives of the study were (a) to formulate guidelines for evaluating the quality of career guidance centers drawing upon the perspectives of experts and suitable literature; (b) to ascertain from career guidance personnel, the structure and the functioning of their centers; (c) to obtain feedback from clients regarding the structure and the functioning of the career guidance centers, whose services they had utilized; (d) to evaluate the quality of the career guidance centers (based on the guidelines formulated through the first objective); and (e) to provide suggestions for enhancing the quality of career guidance centers. We present in this writing, some of the key concepts and constructs that emerged from this exercise with reference to quality markers that distinguish effective career guidance centers.

Sample

Experts are likely to be especially skillful judges of relevant services. Thus, experts in the field of career guidance were included in the study to lay down the guidelines that career guidance centers could follow to ensure quality. This group will be referred to as *experts*. Personnel serving in career guidance centers would be aware of the reasons for delivering a specific type of service, and hence, their inclusion in the evaluation process was considered essential. This group will be referred to as *personnel*. Finally, a high-quality service would be one that which fulfills the needs and expectations of the client. Hence, clients were an integral part of the research. This group will be referred to as *clients*.

The sample consisted of six experts, eight personnel drawn from eight centers in Mumbai (the business capital of India), and 19 clients who had availed of career guidance services at these eight centers. The inclusion criteria were specified as follows: (a) experts who had a minimum of 10 years of experience in career guidance and who had made a special contribution to the field, (b) career guidance centers that had been in operation for a minimum period of 2 years, (c) personnel who had provided career guidance in the center for a minimum period of 2 years, (d) clients who had availed of the services of one of the eight selected career guidance personnel in the past 3 years. The participants were selected using purposive sampling. Most of the experts had over 15 years of experience in career guidance. One was a reputed international expert in the field. The career guidance centers had been operating, on an average, for 10 years. The career guidance personnel (six females, two males) had experience in their center that ranged from 6 to 32 years. The clients (12 females and seven males) were between the

ages of 15 and 21 years and two to three clients were drawn from each center for the study.

Research Design and Data Collection

The study employed a multi-agent, multi-method evaluative research design and the data was analyzed both quantitatively (descriptive statistics) and qualitatively. The interview was the main method for collecting the data. Only in one case, the expert e-mailed the responses, as personal contact was difficult. The observation method was also employed. Center records were also examined. Data verification was possible using these methods.

Tools

Interview Schedule for Experts
Marques and Almeida (2010) developed this schedule after reviewing the available literature, in particular, the guidelines for guidance services set up by the United Nations Educational, Scientific and Cultural Organization (UNESCO, 2002), the International Association for Educational and Vocational Guidance (IAEVG, 1996), and tools developed in Mumbai, India (i.e., the interview schedule developed by Doctor and Almeida [2005] for their research on assessing the quality of school counseling services and the interview schedule developed by Kanitkar and Almeida [2000] for their research on assessing child guidance clinics. The interview schedule for experts consisted of 76 open-ended items tapping various domains).

Interview Schedule for Career Guidance Personnel
Marques and Almeida (2010) constructed this interview schedule after reviewing the relevant literature, in particular, the questionnaire developed by Luk-Fong and Lung (2003) for their research on evaluation of guidance and counseling services in schools. The final interview schedule for career guidance personnel consisted of 87 items, almost all of which were

open ended in nature. The various domains tapped in the interview schedule were similar to those included in the interview schedule for experts.

Interview Schedule for Clients

The development of this schedule was led by a review of the relevant literature. It consisted of 52 open-ended and 35 closed-ended items. The various domains tapped were similar to those included in the schedule for experts and personnel. The closed-ended items were in the form of a 4-point rating scale, where 1 was the lowest rating and 4, the highest rating. The theoretical range of the scale was 35–140. Higher scores were indicative of a better quality of services provided.

Quality Markers of Career Guidance Centers: Themes and Criteria

The data collected was rich and varied. We present in this section the themes that emerged recurrently, with high frequency and consistency across the opinions of the experts, career guidance personnel, and the clients in the Marques and Almeida study.

Philosophy and Model of Career Guidance

The importance of the career guidance center being grounded upon a clearly defined philosophy and its ability to articulate and follow a model of career guidance and counseling emerged consistently as an important theme. The experts expressed unequivocally the importance of the center articulating a vision statement, chalking out goals, and adopting a suitable and culturally relevant model to undergird its service delivery. It is likely that personnel who work in centers that have a clear philosophy are able to deliver a better service, and clients who utilize the services of such centers experience better outcomes.

Personnel and Qualifications

Qualifications and Professional Development

The issue of qualifications is a critical one in contexts where courses in career guidance are few and far between, while simultaneously, the need for career guidance is high. The experts emphasized that career guidance should be provided by those with a minimum of a Master's degree in psychology/counseling, preferably with a degree/diploma in career counseling. The experts and personnel felt that on-the-job/in-service training is provided by an effective career guidance center in order to cater to professional development requirements. This could include in-house training, case discussions, and supervisions, as well as opportunities to attend conferences and training programs.

Training Ground

The experts strongly felt that the center should be a training ground for interns, as novices in the field required opportunities for supervision and guidance. In addition, organizing seminars and workshops were the suggested areas of training. At the same time, the experts cautioned that the personnel should provide good quality training and accept only a manageable number of interns.

Ethical Code

All the experts strongly emphasized that a well-functioning center would have a clearly articulated ethical guideline that would guide the functioning of the center, to which all members of the center were committed. Personnel should adhere to the ethical codes of the profession, such as competence (updating information, sharpening skills and proficiencies), client welfare (respecting clients, maintaining privacy and confidentiality), and conduct (punctual, organized, available, and facilitative).

Services

The following specific themes related to service delivery emerged as potentially linked to the effectiveness of career guidance centers.

Self-Inventory

Services and tools that help the client undertake a self-inventory to improve their understanding of themselves emerged as a salient theme. The role that could be played by standardized tests emerged as a highlight. Markers of quality with regard to testing would be reflected in (a) ensuring privacy and confidentiality, organizing test materials, and following the test manual faithfully; (b) ensuring that the test report included the client profile, interpretation of the test results, a description of implications of these findings for career choice, and recommendations for a plan of action; and (c) ensuring that test results are communicated in simple language, both orally and in writing. Both the experts and the career guidance personnel indicated that the relevance of tests was qualified by client-related factors (e.g., age and dominant language) and test-related factors (e.g., reliability, validity, existence of normative data, and cultural appropriateness).

Career Information

In the view of the experts, an effective career guidance center would be fully equipped with all forms of career information: career definitions, career paths, growth trends within careers, and such information. This would also include institution-related information: names and addresses of institutions, recognition, affiliation, courses and subjects offered, admission procedures, facilities available, and so on. The personnel indicated that this information ought to be available in multiple media: print and electronic media as well as the oral presentation of this information when necessary.

Career Planning

Career planning could become limited to knowing about current trends in employment and orienting clients to these trends. The experts in this study pointed out that in addition to being aware of labor market dynamics, an effective career guidance center trains its personnel to be sensitive to clients' backgrounds: religion, socioeconomic status, cultural persuasions, family type, career beliefs, and how these and similar factors could influence the individual's career planning. The need for a collaborative partnership between client and counselor was emphasized. An interesting subtheme that emerged from client interviews indicated that clients often felt that the career guidance personnel played a directive role and provided either too few or an unlimited number of career options. The importance of including the client in career planning process as well as identifying the optimal number of career options, therefore, emerged as a key feature of an effective career guidance service.

Networking

An important point highlighted by the experts was that career guidance is not an isolated activity of matching the individual with careers. They were of the opinion that networking was relevant, as the resources available in a career guidance center could be limited and clients needed to be directed to other sources for assistance. Therefore, the career guidance center must network and develop relationships with government organizations to identify policies, scholarships, schemes, and programs that would be relevant to clients' career development needs and also with nongovernmental organizations to identify relevant services. The career guidance center must also build links with the corporate sector and other potential employers to develop opportunities for work experience, internships, and placement services that clients could benefit from.

Referral

Linked to networking was the theme of referral. The experts pointed out that an effective career guidance center would cultivate a wide referral network. This would include specialists and service providers from other disciplines for specialized inputs. It would also include tie-ups with other guidance centers that had a location advantage for the client. Personnel also emphasized the importance of referral skills particularly when clients needed specialized services or when there was an "overflow" of appointments at a given center. From the client point of view, referral decisions were most effective when they were communicated in writing with a clear referral note to the organization to which the client was being referred.

Follow-up

The experts highlighted that a well-functioning career guidance center would be committed to follow-up whereby ongoing support would be offered to clients even after guidance sessions were completed.

Information Technology

The experts advocated the incorporation of information technology at three levels. At one level, the value of using computers and relevant software to manage client records was highlighted. A well-functioning center would be able to access clients' reports easily and efficiently. At another level, the use of software to make career information and institutional information data bases available to clients was underlined. An effective center would be able to offer clients access to search databases for information related to their career choices. Finally, the importance of using the Internet to link clients to wider networks and websites was flagged as being important. An effective guidance center would be equipped with information about relevant websites and other Internet-based resources.

Outreach

The experts felt that an effective guidance center would conduct outreach activities, such as creating awareness in schools, colleges, and the community, using methods such as exhibitions, fairs, lectures, seminars, and workshops.

Clientele

Lifelong Approach

The experts, personnel, as well as clients were of the opinion that effective career guidance centers would be able to address career development needs across the life span. While it could be offered earlier, the relevance of career guidance would become sharper from the high school years since the most important educational decisions are made at this stage. They also felt that young adults could be supported in their ongoing career development, middle-aged adults in exploring career changes, and older adults in planning their post-employment plans.

Diversity

Another theme that emerged in relation to the clientele theme was that an effective career guidance center would be committed to client diversity and maintain equality across clients, regardless of their socioeconomic status and cultural or religious background. A further critical point identified was sensitivity to the collectivist nature of Indian families. The importance of including significant others, parents, community leaders, and religious heads (as relevant), was highlighted.

Fees

Experts, personnel, and clients felt that the fees charged for career guidance services rendered should be based on the socioeconomic strata of the clients. They believed that considerations should be made for clients who have difficulty in affording fees. An effective center would have provisions to serve financially disadvantaged clients through concessions, payment in installments, and free-of-cost services as necessary.

Record Keeping

An efficient center would have systems in place for record keeping. The experts and personnel indicated that the kind of records the center should maintain were case records, center activity records, financial records, stock registers, staff files, statistics on cases, feedback about the services from the stakeholders, appointments and phone calls, monthly and annual reports, and minutes of meetings.

Monitoring and Evaluation

The experts felt that a quality marker for a career guidance center is its commitment to ongoing monitoring and evaluation of the tools used for guidance as well as the methods of career guidance. It also emerged that in an effective career guidance center, systems would be in place to monitor psychosocial factors such as attitudes and career beliefs, pre-and post-career guidance. The experts further indicated that an effective career guidance center would include, in its overall strategy, time and resources to regularly conduct controlled evaluation studies to measure the outcomes of its interventions. All experts strongly advocated conducting an ongoing evaluation of the center to review the services, improve professional output, and provide good quality services. They felt that personnel, client, and expert feedback was essential and that evaluation should be conducted half yearly/yearly.

Access

Access to the career guidance center and its services was a critical theme that was pointed to by the experts, personnel, and clients.

Location and Visibility
It was consistently highlighted that the center should be highly visible and easily accessible. Clients preferred centers that they were able to reach by public transport. Effectiveness of centers could be influenced by such factors as easy-to-find address and signboards that aid the client in locating the center.

Timings and Appointments
It was highlighted that an effective center would be more attuned to clients' availability rather than standard "office timings", since most self-referred clients would be able to visit the center after school/work timings. Therefore, an effective center is open on weekends and holidays and at timings when most other offices would have closed. Flexibility in timings was repeatedly highlighted by clients as a positive feature of the career guidance centers. The convenience of the client and promptness were endorsed by the experts, personnel, and clients when scheduling appointments.

These were the key themes that emerged in relation to the efficient functioning of career guidance centers. A summary of domains and criteria is provided in Table 37.1.

Relevance for Multiple Cultures

Themes that emerged from the exercise reported above could be of value to construct devices to evaluate the effectiveness of career guidance centers. However, modifications will have to be made, depending on the specific context in which these themes are operationalized. Illustrations are provided below on how themes that have universal appeal need to be adapted to match indigenous realities.

Having a philosophy and vision statement for the center and chalking out the objectives of career guidance emerged as a salient theme and is perhaps relevant across a wide range of contexts. However, cultural frameworks would need to be considered in drafting these objectives, as guidance does not operate in a vacuum. To expand career guidance services, outreach is important. Here again, the target group for outreach would vary across cultures and contexts. Developing countries, for example, are increasingly recognizing the importance of career guidance. In such economic contexts, outreach may need to focus on reaching out especially to financially disadvantaged individuals to, first of all, help them view career guidance as

Table 37.1 Efficient functioning of career guidance centers: domains and criteria

Domains	Criteria
Philosophy	Vision statement and goals, objectives, model for career guidance services
Personnel and qualifications	Qualifications and professional development: master's degree in psychology/counseling, on-the-job/in-service training, conferences and training programs
	Training ground: internships, supervision and guidance, seminars and workshops
Ethical code	Professional competence, client welfare, personal conduct
Services	Self-inventory: test usage, orientation, precautions for test administration and interpretation, communication of test results and test reports
	Career information: career definitions, options, scope, trends; institutional information: names and addresses, recognition, courses offered, admission procedure, facilities
	Career planning: knowledge of labor market dynamics; sensitivity to clients' backgrounds: religion, socio-economic status, cultural persuasions, family type, career beliefs
	Networking: relevant institutions (educational, occupational, government agencies, corporates)
	Referral: wide network, interdisciplinary, tie-ups with other centers, collaboration with agencies
	Follow-up: ongoing support at relevant intervals
	Information technology: manage client records, career information and institutional information data bases, Internet to link clients to wider networks and websites
	Outreach: awareness programs in schools/colleges, participation in career exhibitions/fairs
Clientele	Lifelong approach: services relevant across the life span
	Diversity: socioeconomic, religion, special needs
	Fees: rationale for fixing fees; provisions to serve financially disadvantaged clients: concessions, payment in installments, free of cost services as necessary
Record keeping	Types of records maintained, storage (files, electronic), time period
Monitoring and evaluation	Systems for ongoing monitoring, commitment to conduct evaluation at regular intervals. Sources: experts, clients, personnel. Methods: questionnaire, interview
Access	Location and visibility: easy access, public transport, signboards
	Timings and appointments: clients' availability, weekends and holidays, flexibility in timings

relevant to their needs. It is also a reality in these countries that the relevance of career guidance services is not perceived by potential clients (e.g., Arulmani & Abdulla, 2007). The theme of awareness building that emerged in this study could be appropriate across a wide range of developing countries and could serve to attract individuals to a service that may not necessarily be a high priority for them. By contrast, awareness building for young people from affluent backgrounds, fresh immigrants, those who have been retrenched, newly qualified individuals, would each have a different focus.

Clientele was another theme that emerged from this study and effectiveness was linked to embracing client diversity with regard to aspects such as age, religion, socioeconomic status, and disability. With globalization, diversity in the work place has become a reality. Hence, this domain could have universal relevance. Diversity in different countries, however, may be manifested in different ways. Ethnicity, language, religious persuasion or affiliation, and geographical location are examples of the features of diversity which would need to be taken into account when evaluating the effectiveness of career guidance centers. The theme of personnel and qualifications, including aspects such as recruitment, selection, qualification, qualities, and updating of skills, has universal relevance. But here again, aspects peculiar to the context should be kept in mind. In countries where there is an acute shortage of trained personnel, emphasis on postgraduates in psychology and counseling may not be fruitful. At the same time the risk of perpetuating a cycle of poor quality services and therefore poor usage of services must be kept in mind. Clear and rigorous, yet context-relevant guidelines must be established regarding how a person may qualify himself/herself. This could also be established through high-quality on-the-job training.

Regarding the services theme, the following were included as subdomains: self-inventory, career information, career planning, networking, referral, follow-up, information technology, and outreach. All these are vital for the effective delivery of services. However, depending on the context, other aspects in each subdomain may need to be introduced. For example, the use of culture-relevant psychological tests would need to be emphasized. Involving the family and respecting their role in career decisions, helping clients overcome their resistance to taking up nontraditional occupations could be important. Hence, it is essential to ensure that the location-specific goals of counseling point to the adaptations to be made when assessing the effectiveness of career guidance.

Arulmani (2011) in his review of reports from 25 countries pertaining to political, economic, and social changes and the changing role of career guidance and career guidance policies has pointed out that these changes have thrown up new kinds of client groups that require to be served in a special manner. Examples of such groups are: individuals with needs for requalification, those who have lost traditional occupations, career development needs associated with migration, career crisis faced by older workers as well as the newly qualified but unemployed, and individuals with special educational needs. Arulmani also urges that in the process of addressing the needs of special groups, career guidance centers must not lose sight of serving the "main group," that is, individuals who do not qualify for any special requirements. The assessment of effectiveness would need to take such factors into consideration.

In this chapter, themes and concepts that could be used to assess the effectiveness of career guidance centers have been described. Although this data was generated in India, many of the themes that have emerged have universal

relevance. But as illustrated in this section, when constructing a method to assess effectiveness, it is essential that themes such as these are adapted to suit local realities.

New Concepts and Viewpoints

Operationalization

The themes that have been described in this chapter offer a conceptual framework for the construction of devices to evaluate the quality of career guidance centers. These devices could be questionnaires, semi-structured interview schedules, or checklists. Table 37.2 provides an illustration for *Types of constructs assessed* which is part of Test Usage in the Self-Inventory domain (theme: services). Examples are provided of items for questionnaires, a semi-structured interview schedule, and a checklist. It must be noted, of course, that not all themes would lend themselves to being assessed equally well by all devices. It might be best to use a checklist when the frequency of use is to be evaluated, a rating scale when the importance attributed to a certain activity is to be assessed, or a semi-structured interview when questioning needs to be more open ended. Evaluations usually require a summative numerical value to be computed as indicative of the quality of service delivered. In this case, scores and weightages may be assigned to items using standard psychometric procedures. Should there be a need for the development of standardized assessment devices, factor analytic procedures would first need to be used to identify and validate the factors and constructs the device is tapping. Norms could also be developed to compare the performance of a given center against a normative standard.

Making Evaluation a Positive Experience

In the Marques and Almeida (2010) study, resistance was shown by quite a few center personnel to participate in the study. Perhaps they felt threatened about disclosing private information

Table 37.2 Operationalization of the types of constructs assessed item (test usage subtheme of the self-inventory domain)

Item	Questionnaire: multiple choice format	Questionnaire: rating scale	Semi-structured interview	Checklist
Types of constructs assessed	Which one of the following is most frequently tested in your center?	Given below is a list of constructs commonly assessed in a career guidance center. Use a rating scale where 1 indicates *lowest frequency* and 4 indicates *highest frequency* to rate the frequency at which the listed constructs are assessed in your center	Tell us about the constructs most often assessed in your center	Given below is a list of constructs commonly assessed in a career guidance center. Tick all the constructs that are assessed in your center
	a. Interests	a. Interests		a. Interests
	b. Aptitudes	b. Aptitudes		b. Aptitudes
	c. Personality	c. Personality		c. Personality
	d. Social cognitive influences	d. Social cognitive influences		d. Social cognitive influences

to outsiders. The challenge thus is to make evaluation a favorable experience for counselors, administrators, and clients, while at the same time, catering to the requirements of policy planners and program funders. Greene (1994) has suggested that the more narrative, participatory approach of qualitative evaluation can foster greater understanding, solidarity, and contextualization of a career counseling program. In his paper, Schulz (1995) has described an approach used by an external team to evaluate seven small career counseling programs. The evaluations were funded mainly by the sponsor of the counseling centers, and a quantitative/qualitative evaluation process with a strength-challenge approach to counselor feedback was used. The evaluation team realized that all stakeholders in the career counseling centers were apprehensive about being evaluated by outsiders and about future funding being affected. Therefore, a collaborative approach was adopted, in which evaluators requested input from the counseling centers and invited evaluatees' reactions to the observations of the evaluation team. The team found that helping clients, counselors, and administrators become comfortable talking about themselves and their career counseling was valuable in getting a better picture of what counselors were doing and what clients were

receiving. The evaluation team shared their own experiences, talking about heroes or heroines who had influenced them. They posed questions such as: "Tell us about significant people in your life who would be good to have as colleagues at your center." Since the collaborative approach was found to be most effective, the following recommendations were made: (a) take time to build rapport with the career counselors before beginning the review, (b) inform all the stakeholders beforehand that they will be involved in reviewing the evaluation report before release, (c) obtain staff and administration input into the review process, (d) external reviewers should provide both formative and summative evaluation and include case studies/anecdotal information in the evaluation report, and (e) in-person follow-up of the review should be conducted.

Conclusion

Conducting an evaluation is not without challenges; nevertheless, it is vital. A sound evaluation tool and a collaborative approach could yield rich dividends. Most important for the evaluator to note is that when the person(s) being evaluated fears censure, then the outcomes of the evaluation are not likely to go very much beyond an administrative routine, where maintaining discipline and accountability is the objective. However, when the purpose of evaluation is to improve performance and the approach taken is collaborative, then evaluation could truly contribute to enhancing the quality of services provided through a career guidance center.

References

Ali, L., & Graham, B. (2003). *The counseling approach to career counseling*. New York, NY: Brunner-Routledge.

Arulmani, G. (2007). Counselling psychology in India: At the confluence of two traditions. *Applied Psychology: An International Review, 56*(1), 69–89.

Arulmani, G. (2011, December). *Political, economic and social changes and the changing role of career guidance and career guidance policies*. Paper presented at the Sixth International Symposium on Career Development and Public Policy, Budapest, Hungary.

Arulmani, G., & Abdulla, A. (2007). Capturing the ripples: Addressing the sustainability of the impact of social marketing. *Social Marketing Quarterly, 13* (4), 84–107.

Arulmani, G., & Nag-Arulmani, S. (2004). *Career counseling: A handbook*. New Delhi, India: Tata McGraw-Hill.

Aspiring Minds' Analytics Team. (2011). *National employability report: Engineering graduates annual report 2011*. Haryana, India: Aspiring Minds.

Bakshi, A. J. (2011). Past adolescence, into and across adulthood: Career crises and major decisions. *International Journal for Educational and Vocational Guidance, 11*(2), 139–154.

Doctor, R., & Almeida, N. (2005). *Assessment of the quality of counseling services provided in selected schools in Mumbai* (Unpublished Master's thesis). College of Home Science, Nirmala Niketan, University of Mumbai, Mumbai, India.

Greene, J. C. (1994). Qualitative program evaluation: Promise and practice. In N. K. Denzin & Y. S. Lincoln (Eds.), *Handbook of qualitative research* (pp. 530–544). Newbury Park, CA: Sage.

International Association for Educational and Vocational Guidance. (1996). IAEVG ethical standards. *Educational and Vocational Guidance Bulletin, 58*, 1–19.

Kanitkar, K., & Almeida, N. (2000). *Assessment of child guidance clinics in Mumbai* (Unpublished Master's thesis). College of Home Science, Nirmala Niketan, University of Mumbai, Mumbai, India.

Killeen, J., & White, M. (2000). *The impact of careers guidance on adult employed people* (Research Report RR226). Sheffield, England: DfEE.

Luk-Fong, Y. Y., & Lung, C. L. (2003). The initial development of an instrument for the evaluation of guidance and counseling services in schools. *School Psychology International, 24*(3), 292–312.

Marques, A., & Almeida, N. (2010). *Evaluation of the quality of career guidance centers in Mumbai* (Unpublished Master's thesis). College of Home Science, Nirmala Niketan, University of Mumbai, Mumbai, India.

Organization for Economic Cooperation and Development. (2004). *Career guidance: A handbook for policy makers*. Retrieved from http://www.oecd.org/education/country-studies/34060761.pdf

Poduval, S., & Almeida, N. (1993). *A comparison of the expectations and reality experiences of Bombay school counselors regarding their functions* (Unpublished Master's thesis). College of Home Science, Nirmala Niketan, University of Mumbai, Mumbai, India.

Porfeli, E. J., & Lee, B. (2012). Career development during childhood and adolescence. *New Directions for Youth Development, 134*, 11–22.

Schulz, W. E. (1995). *Evaluating career counseling centers: A collaborative approach*. Retrieved from http://www.eric.ed.gov/

Sultana, R. G. (2006). *Challenges for career guidance in small states*. Msida, Malta: EMCER.

United Nations Educational, Scientific and Cultural Organization. (2002). *Handbook on career counseling: A practical manual for developing, implementing and assessing career counseling services in higher education settings*. Retrieved from http://unesdoc.unesco.org/images/0012/001257/125740e.pdf

Watt, G. (1998). *Supporting employability: Guides to good practice in employment counseling and guidance*. Luxembourg, Luxembourg: Office for Official Publications of the European Commission.

Demonstrating the Impact of Career Guidance

38

Bryan Hiebert, Karen Schober, and Lester Oakes

Practitioners who deliver career guidance are being confronted by the challenge to "prove it works." In the history of career guidance, this challenge is a relatively new one. There has been seminal work published pertaining to the evaluation of career guidance services (e.g., Killeen, White, & Watts, 1992; Watts, 1999). However, until recently, the field has not widely embraced the need to address this issue, even though how we respond to it is critical for the health and survival of our work. In this chapter, we examine the journey to date and discuss what needs to happen next to meet this challenge.

Ever since career guidance has been a recognized field of endeavor, the focus has been primarily on the development of theories and associated practices, loosely based on the client-centered practices of counseling psychology. As professionalization grew and professional associations were created, additional focus developed around practitioner ethics and competencies. These developments were driven by practitioners themselves, to raise the quality of service delivery and safeguard the rights of clients. Little heed was paid to the interests of the funders of guidance services. Indeed, the International Association for Educational and Vocational Guidance (IAEVG), formed in Paris in 1951, focused solely on practitioners and their client interface for most of the first 50 years of its existence. Only late in the last century has IAEVG become involved in discussions around demonstrating the value of career guidance services.

To date, career guidance has been concentrated predominantly in countries that enjoyed substantial economic prosperity from the 1950s to the 1980s. In most of these countries, career guidance, particularly for young people, was funded largely by national, state, or local governments. In the 1980s, many Western governments began to seek assurances that public money spent on public services was being well used, which resulted in service providers needing to account for their actions. Initially this involved rudimentary methodology such as counting numbers of transactions, attempting to show that each year the amount of service was increasing, trying to demonstrate that demand for services was greater than their ability to deliver, and then presenting a case for increased funding. Others extended their data reporting to include information on client satisfaction with services. Such information often was collected through questionnaires provided to clients at the conclusion of their sessions. However, as economic conditions tightened, governments came under increasing funding pressures. Value for money spent became a more common concern, along with the challenge to "prove it works." Evidence to support the impact and efficiency of career guidance was required to ensure ongoing funding.

B. Hiebert (✉)
University of Calgary, Calgary, AB, Canada
e-mail: hiebert@ucalgary.ca

G. Arulmani et al. (eds.), *Handbook of Career Development*, International and Cultural Psychology,
DOI 10.1007/978-1-4614-9460-7_38, © Springer Science+Business Media, LLC 2014

Although the focus on *prove it works* is increasingly important in many countries, controversy remains. For publicly funded career guidance services to prosper, practitioners need to be able to show added value in relation to wider government policy goals in areas such as education, employment, social inclusion, and economic development. However, practitioners, clients, researchers, and policymakers can have differing views about what constitutes success in career guidance. Success is much easier to determine in a simple commercial market where value needs only to be in the eye of the purchaser, who personally buys goods or services, and is the direct recipient of the benefit. However, most career guidance in Western countries is delivered to citizens who are not the buyers of the service, as the service is purchased, either directly or indirectly, by public funds. In this case, the ongoing challenge is to deliver a service that adds public value (from a policy perspective) and also adds value through the eyes of individual recipients (clients).

IAEVG has played a prominent role in the discussions described (see Jenschke, 2012). It has been actively involved in the establishment of the International Centre for Career Development and Public Policy (ICCDPP) which works directly at the policy-practice interface. IAEVG has been a strong participant in the six international symposia convened by the ICCDPP to discuss issues such as "prove it works" and has disseminated proceedings of those symposia to its members. IAEVG has been represented on the board of ICCDPP since its inception and IAEVG also plays an active role within the European Lifelong Guidance Policy Network (ELGPN). In addition, IAEVG has been strongly represented in the Canadian Research Working Group on Evidence-based Practice in Career Development (CRWG). It is no surprise then, that outcome-focused, evidence-based practice, and demonstrating the value of career guidance services, have been an important part of IAEVG's strategic planning. Thus, members of the IAEVG executive committee (i.e., the authors of this chapter) are in a unique position to comment on the matter of demonstrating the value and impact of career guidance services.

Background

At the International Symposium on Career Development and Public Policy held in 2001, an interesting observation emerged. Policymakers indicated that their main concern was providing quality services to clients, but one of the obstacles they faced was that practitioners and researchers did not see the connection between their policies and client welfare. At the same time, practitioners and researchers indicated that their main concern also was providing quality services to clients, but policy often seemed to interfere with their ability to do that. Each group claimed that their primary concern was the client's best interest and they saw the other group as interfering with their efforts. During the meeting, policymakers, practitioners, and researchers realized that they were working towards common goals and that they likely would be more successful in reaching those goals if they worked together.

In 2003, a National Symposium on Career Development, Lifelong Learning and Workforce Development was held in Canada where policymakers issued a challenge to the career development community: "Show us the evidence. You have not made the case for the impact of career development services." In response to this challenge, an informal consortium of researchers from seven Canadian universities and one private foundation formed the Canadian Research Working Group on Evidence-based Practice in Career Development. At about the same time, the Organization for Economic Cooperation and Development (OECD) was conducting a major review of career guidance policy in its member states, and later, the European Union (EU) and the World Bank conducted similar reviews in some of their member states. Collectively, these initiatives created a high priority interest in demonstrating the value of career services. As a result, "Prove It Works" became one of the most important themes addressed at subsequent international symposia held in 2006, 2007, 2009, and 2011. As the initiatives mentioned above began to unfold, several observations emerged:

1. Policymakers and agency administrators wanted solid, research-based foundations for policies on the cost-effectiveness of guidance services, the benefit to citizens, the effectiveness and efficiency of services in the educational system and the labor market, and the role of guidance services in promoting social inclusion.
2. Providers of career guidance services (public, semipublic, and private agencies) wanted to improve their services, enhance their competitiveness, and gain public or private funding for their services.
3. Career guidance practitioners wanted to improve professional performance, develop effective methods and techniques, improve the outcomes and impacts of their intervention, and increase client satisfaction.
4. Users and clients wanted information about good quality service, successful individual career decisions and outcomes, and consumer protection.

Speaking from a practitioner perspective, providers of career services need to know more about outcomes and the impacts of their services not only to improve the quality of service, but also to inform policymakers and funders who provide resources for the delivery of career services. Policymakers need an evidence base to support their efforts to improve national or regional career guidance systems and to justify the expenditures of tax payer money on career guidance services. Although abundant research has been conducted in the field of career development, most of it deals with factors such as influences on career choice, career decision-making processes, and career satisfaction. Very little research has been done that permits making a causal link between career services and the impacts of those services on the lives of clients or on broader societal or economic factors. Projects currently underway in Canada

and Europe illustrate some of the initial attempts to address this situation.

Evidence-Based Practice: The Canadian Experience

To address the "show us the evidence" challenge, one of the first tasks that the CRWG undertook was to survey practitioners and managers to determine the current state of practice regarding the evaluation of career services. The results indicated that while all sectors said that evaluation was important, very little evaluation of the impact of career services was being done. Furthermore, practitioners reported that many indicators of client change were undocumented and unreported because they were considered not relevant by the funders. In response to those findings, the CRWG developed an evaluation framework that was comprehensive enough to cover the main factors that needed to be addressed, but simple enough to understand that service providers, policymakers, and funders would use it.

A Framework for Evaluating Career Services

Two trends that are becoming increasingly more prominent in human services settings (e.g., mental health, school guidance, career services, health services) are outcome-focused intervention and evidence-based practice. The foundational goal in outcome-focused intervention centers around demonstrating how clients (or students or learners) change as a result of the interventions (or programs or lessons) they receive. The foundational goal in evidence-based practice is to understand what sorts of interventions, delivered under what circumstances, work best with what kinds of people, striving to achieve what sorts of goals. When these two trends are addressed adequately, as they are in the CRWG framework, it is possible for practitioners (teachers, counselors, youth workers, career advisors, etc.) to provide convincing evidence that links client change to the intervention they received (see Baudouin et al., 2007).

To gather this sort of evidence, the CRWG adopted a simple Input → Process → Outcome framework. The framework is illustrated in Fig. 38.1 and described briefly below. A more detailed description and examples from the field are available on the CRWG website: http://www.crwg-gdrc.ca/crwg/index.php/resources/evaluation. The framework has been used extensively to evaluate career development interventions, but it also is appropriate in other types of counseling, mental health, physical health, educational, and other human services settings (Hiebert & Charles, 2008; Hiebert, Domene, & Buchanan, 2011). For ease of reading, we use the term *client* when referring to people who are receiving services, but we could also have used terms like: *learner, student,* or *patient.* Similarly, we use the term *practitioner* to refer to people who are providing services, but we could also have used terms like, *counselor, teacher, youth worker, career advisor, nurse,* or *physician.* Thus, although we use the terms *client* and *practitioner,* we encourage readers to substitute the appropriate terms that make sense in the countries and settings in which they are working.

The CRWG framework centers on the needs and goals of clients. In planning an appropriate intervention, it is important to examine the context in which clients live, including factors such as ethnicity, culture, significant others, structure of opportunity, past learning history, and previous work history. A client's context can have limiting or facilitating influences on the types of interventions that are possible, on the success of interventions undertaken, and also on what outcome expectations are reasonable. In the process of examining client context, it usually is possible to identify the types of needs a client would like to see addressed and to set explicit goals that practitioner and client can work on together. The CRWG approach to intervention and evaluation is based on practitioners and clients working together in collaboration where goals, outcome expectations, and indicators of success are negotiated and mutually agreed on by practitioners and clients, and where appropriate, by third party stakeholders and funders. Once the goals are set, planning the intervention (How will

we accomplish the goals?) and the evaluation (How will we tell that the goals are being accomplished?) can begin.

Constructing an intervention plan and an evaluation plan begins by identifying the types of changes that a client will experience as a result of the intervention, developing a method for documenting what changes take place (i.e., the indicators of change), and then planning the processes that are needed in order for the goals to be achieved (Wiggins & McTighe, 2005). Going on a road trip provides a useful metaphor. A journey begins by identifying a destination. Once the destination is clear, then the route can be planned. Sometimes, people enjoy just going for a drive or a walk in the country with no particular destination in mind. In those cases, enjoying the process is the main goal. However, if the main goal involves a definite outcome (destination), then the planning process must begin by being clear about the outcome and the indicators (evidence) that will be used to determine progress towards the outcomes (see Wiggins & McTighe, 2005).

In the CRWG framework, client change refers to the competencies that clients acquire as a result of an intervention. Consistent with much of the literature on professional competencies (see Canadian Standards and Guidelines for Career Development Practitioners [S&Gs], 2004; Career Industry Council of Australia [CICA], 2006; Council for the Accreditation of Counseling and Related Educational Programs [CACREP], 2001; Hiebert, 2008; Repetto, 2008), competencies are composed of the knowledge (K) that clients gain, the skills (S) they acquire, and the attitudes and other personal attributes (A) they develop, that can be connected directly to the intervention the client is following. The KSAs are important for they can be connected directly to the program or intervention and also because they are precursors (Killeen et al., 1992) of the ultimate goal of the intervention. The outcomes also refer to the impact of the KSAs on the client's life, or on social or economic factors. Thus a client may learn how to do an effective job search, acquire the skills needed to put that knowledge into practice, and as a result be more motivated and more

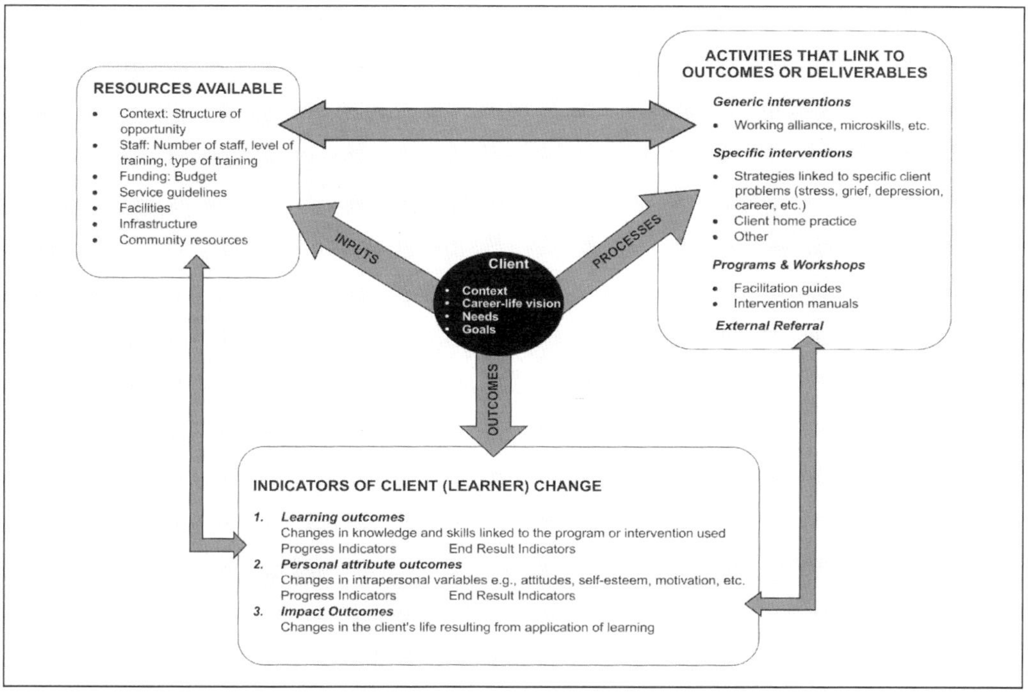

Fig. 38.1 Intervention planning and evaluation framework

confident about finding a job. But the ultimate impact is for the client to find employment. To demonstrate the value of career services, it is important to have evidence documenting what a client has learned during an intervention and also evidence of the ultimate impact of that learning.

In the CRWG framework, processes refer to the activities that clients and counselors engage in for the purpose of achieving the outcomes. These include generic process that normally would be used with all clients (e.g., relationship building, collaborating) and also specific processes that are linked directly to a client's goals (e.g., job search, interviewing skills, anger management). In the CRWG framework, a distinction is made between outcomes and outputs. Outcomes refer to changes that clients experience, while outputs refer to the products or artifacts produced during an intervention. Thus, a resume, portfolio, cover letter, list of job leads, etc., that are created as part of a job search program are outputs. They are not outcomes because they do not indicate client change.

In the CRWG framework, inputs refer to the resources that are needed to engage in the processes designed to produce the outcomes. Resources are important for they influence what outcomes can be reasonably expected. It also is the case that if new programs (processes) are introduced, additional resources might be needed in order for the new programs to be successful.

Any comprehensive plan for evaluating the effectiveness of career services needs to incorporate systematic methods for documenting all three components of the framework depicted in Fig. 38.1. In order to get an accurate picture of which interventions work best, with which clients, under which circumstances, it is necessary to examine the client outcomes, the processes used to obtain those outcomes, and the resources (inputs) needed to enact the processes.

Total Quality Service

Total quality service (TQS) refers to an ongoing process focused on customer satisfaction, incorporating the establishment of benchmarks for customer service, measuring performance against the benchmarks, and recognizing and rewarding exemplary behavior by service providers (Stamatis, 1995). In the career guidance field, the primary focus for TQS usually involves variables such as access to services, wait times, office decor, and client record keeping procedures (Bezanson & Plant, 2010). TQS variables are important when evaluating career services. They have an effect on the general operation of an agency. We know that a client who gets rude treatment from a receptionist or encounters a dismissive attitude by a group facilitator, likely will receive a less-than-best outcome even from a very good program. A list of quality service factors might include items such as client satisfaction, client relationship with the agency (clients return for service, clients are self-reliant), stakeholder satisfaction, employer satisfaction (this could be also an impact outcome if job stability was a goal), level of service utilization, number of clients seen, types of client problems addressed, number of visits made by a client, wait time for receiving services, number of applicants for services, agency reputation, ability to fund-raise. Even though these factors sometimes are thought of as outcomes, they are not indicators of client change, per se, therefore, the CRWG suggests that they be regarded as separate from intervention planning and outcome evaluation. We suggest also that agencies and funders include client change as an important factor when thinking of *total quality service*. Ultimately, reducing client wait list time or increasing the number of clients seen is not useful if the services are not resulting in client change.

Data Sources

We are aware that in many circles Randomized Controlled Trials (RCTs) are considered the gold standard for research studies (Dozois, 2011). However, several authors (e.g., Hiebert et al., 2011; Horan, 1980; Posavac, 2011) have described some of the problems associated with using RCTs as the sole basis for determining intervention efficacy. For many practitioners there is a conceptual problem because, in practice, virtually no clients are assigned to an intervention on a random basis. The intervention is purposively

chosen, based on the unique constellation of client needs and goals. Further, in many research reports incorporating RCTs, the intervention is not described in sufficient detail to permit replication. Thus, it is difficult for practitioners to incorporate research findings in their practice. Moreover, there usually are few data provided to indicate how closely an intervention guide was followed by either experimenters or research participants. Thus, for many (perhaps most) studies, the articles become reports of what happens when participants are assigned to a research condition or intervention, and not evidence for the effectiveness of an intervention per se. RCTs are useful and we would not advocate abandoning RCTs as a methodology, but we resist using RCTs as the *sole basis* for determining intervention efficacy and we also resist using a traditional hierarchical way of ranking research studies, which inevitably places RCTs at the top of the list and designates all other research approaches as less suitable for making evidence-based practice decisions. Instead, we agree with Glasziou, Vandenbroucke, and Chalmers (2004) that different kinds of questions require different kinds of methodological approaches.

Dozois (2011) has reminded us that if we want more evidence-based practice we need more practice-based evidence. Consistent with this directive, the CRWG approach to demonstrating the value of career services centers on the belief that service providers and agency managers are the best people to evaluate the impact of the services they provide. This is contrasted with the approach used by many funders that hire an external evaluator who has not been associated with the service to inspect the service and pass judgment on it. Instead of that practice, the CRWG framework embraces a *local clinical scientist* (Stricker & Trierweiler, 1995; Trierweiler, Stricker, & Peterson, 2010), sometimes referred to as *professional practitioner* (Hiebert & Magnusson, 2014), approach. In this approach, practitioners adopt a scientific manner in their work, documenting the client changes they observe, documenting the processes that were used to produce client change, and looking for patterns connecting the processes with the outcomes.

Using this procedure, a practitioner's client base becomes the data source for demonstrating client change and larger personal or societal impact. This approach is gaining traction in the fields of career counseling, counseling psychology, and clinical psychology, and holds great promise for practitioners interested in "proving it works." It is well documented that most practitioners do not read research and do not incorporate research findings into their interactions with clients, likely because they do not find the research relevant to the work they are doing and because the research findings are not usually published in sources that practitioners read (Domene, Buchanan, Hiebert, & Buhr, in press; Methei, 2006; Sexton, 1996). We believe that using individualized indicators of success and building them into service delivery, increases the relevance of the data for both counselor and client, helps to integrate research and practice, and can have a positive influence on the day-by-day professional work of practitioners (Hiebert et al., 2012).

Two field tests illustrate the CRWG framework in action. The *Applied Career Transitions Program* was an online program designed to assist university graduates to integrate into the workforce. It was field tested with 29 participants who had recently graduated from university with a bachelor's degree and were having difficulty finding work. The program was located within the Career Services Department of the university and participants elected to complete this program rather than wait for face-to-face sessions with a career practitioner. Due to difficulties with the practitioners delivering the program, no other demographic data are available. The program was individually paced and supported by up to four appointments with a career coach, depending on the needs of individual participants. Typically, it took participants 4–6 weeks to complete the program. The program included components such as understanding the processes involved in moving forward in one's career; developing a clear career vision; self-assessment of past work, education, and life experiences; and job finding skills.

To evaluate the effectiveness of the program, a survey instrument was created that indexed survey items to the KSAs of the modules in the program. In the survey, participants were asked "Given what you know now about career planning, for each item mentioned below rate yourself before you started the program and rate yourself now. Please use a two-step process: (a) decide whether your level of mastery was acceptable or not acceptable. Then, (b) decide on the appropriate number: If your level is unacceptable, is it *really unacceptable* $= 0$, or *not really acceptable, but almost there* $= 1$? If it is acceptable, is it *minimally acceptable* (but still OK otherwise it would be 0 or 1) $= 2$, *exceptional* $= 4$, or *somewhere between minimally acceptable and exceptional* $= 3$?"

At the beginning of the program, 50 % of participants rated their level of competence as unacceptable and unlikely to be effective. At the conclusion of the program, 86 % of the ratings were in the acceptable range and the ratings of *exceptional* increased from 2 to 44 % (learning outcomes). By the end of the program, 27 of the 29 participants had found work, and for half of those, the work was a good match for their ideal career vision (impact outcomes). Two-thirds of the participants attributed their success mostly to participation in the program, with the remaining one-third indicating that the changes they experienced resulted from a combination of what they learned in the program and other factors operating in their lives, such as luck, family support, or a sudden increase in the number of jobs available.

As part of the data gathering process, we tracked the degree of participant engagement with the program and also the fidelity with which the career coaches followed the agenda for their interactions with participants. This tracking made it possible for us to say that the career coaches followed the game plan, the participants were engaged in the program, as a result participants acquired new knowledge, developed new skills, experienced an increase in positive attitudes that facilitated integration into the workforce, and attributed their success mostly to the program they had just completed. Some people in the social sciences community hold steadfastly to the belief that in order to claim a causal relationship, a control group must be used. We have presented an argument earlier in this chapter that there are alternate ways to demonstrate a causal relationship. The case described here is frequently used in educational contexts: There are data to show that the facilitator and learner are both engaged in the program; data documenting shifts in knowledge, skills, and personal attributes associated with the elements of the program; and the learners attribute the changes they experienced to the program they just completed. We think this indicates a strong connection between the intervention and the outcomes. Furthermore, the job placement rate was more than 90 % and for half of the participants, the job they found was a good match for their career vision. We think that data such as these provide a strong argument for proving it works and that the evidence gathering process is readily incorporated into the service delivery, making evaluation an integral part of practitioner–client interactions.

A recent research project addressing the *Impact of Labor Market Information* (*LMI*) *on Career Decision-making and Job Search* (Hiebert et al., 2012) provides a further example of the usefulness of the CRWG approach. The project was designed to address two questions: (a) To what extent is independent self-help sufficient for clients to use LMI effectively? (b) To what extent does assistance by a service provider enhance the effective use of LMI? An action research approach was used to address these questions. The service providers were career and employment counselors, working in their usual career services centers, with clients who were part of their typical client case loads. Every client who fit the selection criteria described as follows was invited to participate in the study.

A standard Initial Employability Assessment protocol was developed to identify clients who had needs pertaining to either career decision-making or job search. The protocol included items pertaining to job readiness (e.g., financial needs, personal needs, motivation, ability to keep a job), career decision-making (e.g., client self-knowledge [abilities, interests, values, personal characteristics], knowledge of career options,

ability to research options), and job search (e.g., clarity of client's career vision, possession of appropriate job search tools [resume, references, professional pitch, ability to find job leads]). If clients demonstrated needs in the area of career decision-making or job search, they were invited to participate in the study, and if they agreed to participate, they were assigned randomly to either an independent or an assisted delivery condition.

In both delivery conditions, participants received LMI packages, tailored to their particular area of need, and containing lists of possible resources, instructions for accessing the information, and tips for interpreting and applying the information to a client's personal situation. Clients in the independent delivery condition worked by themselves. Clients in the assisted delivery condition received two short (20 min) advisory interviews designed to offer support and answer any questions. The advising sessions were quite minimal because we wanted to isolate the use of LMI as a viable approach, independent of other interventions such as psychoeducational workshops or career counseling. All clients remained in the program for 3 weeks, at which time they completed the final assessment forms.

Complete data were obtained from 151 participants, 74 males and 77 females. Most of the participants ($n = 118$) had not previously participated in employment services programs. At the beginning of the study, 115 participants were not employed, 22 were working part time and 13 were working full time. Of those who were working full- or part time, 6 (17 %) said their work was a good fit for them, 11 said it was alright for them, and 18 said it was a poor fit for them. The age of participants ranged from 19 to 62 years, with a mean age of 44 years. One-third of participants indicated that they did not have a high school graduation certificate and about half of the participants had completed some sort of specialized education or training at a university, college, or technical institute. Participants had a varied employment history. In the past 5 years, 30 of them had been in 5 or more jobs and only 24 had been in the same job for the past 5 years. Furthermore, in the past 5 years, only 28 % of the sample had been in steady employment for the past 5 years and 20 % of participants had been unemployed for more than half of that time.

The dependent measures used in this project came from researcher developed questionnaires, indexed to the expected outcomes of the intervention, and utilizing the CRWG framework summarized earlier in this chapter. The intervention outcomes were mapped onto a 14-item questionnaire where the items fell into three categories: changes in client knowledge about LMI, changes in client skills for using LMI, and changes in client personal attributes that might result from participation in the interventions. Thus, there were four dependent measures: the total score on the 14-item questionnaire, and three subscale scores: knowledge, skills, and personal attributes.

Comparing before intervention with after intervention self-assessments, clients in all four treatment combinations experienced substantial positive change. Regardless of whether clients were seeking help with job search or career decision-making, and regardless of whether clients used the LMI packages independently or with assistance, they demonstrated substantial increases in their general ability to access and use LMI (the total score on the 14-item questionnaire), their knowledge about how to use LMI (the knowledge subscale score), their skills for using LMI and taking action (the skills subscale score), and personal attributes such as optimism and confidence (the personal attributes subscale score). Of particular note were items that suggested increased ability to self-manage careers: for example, having a clear understanding of what they needed to do to move forward in their career; knowledge of print and online resources to help them research career and employment options; a clear vision of what they wanted in their career futures; the ability to access career resources that could help them implement their career vision; confidence in their ability to manage future career transitions; and confidence in their ability to research career, employment, and training options that are available.

These results were clinically meaningful in that after intervention scores were on average twice as high as the before intervention scores. There was a statistically significant main effect for time ($p < .01$), suggesting that the after intervention average scores were higher than the before intervention scores for the total score and all three subscale scores. Furthermore, the delivery condition-by-time interaction effect also was significant ($p < .01$), indicating that clients who received assistance demonstrated greater gains than those working independently. As a further indication of the efficacy of the interventions, 80 % of the clients attributed changes they experienced to the program and not other factors operating in their lives. The impact of the learning outcomes (i.e., the knowledge, skills, and personal attributes that the participants gained) is reflected in the changes in employment status and quality of work. There was a 50 % increase in the number of people who were working at the end of the study, compared to the beginning, and the number of people who thought their job was a good fit for them increased by a factor of 4.

Several factors contributed to the positive gain experienced by clients in this project. The role of a structured client needs assessment interview process was essential. In order for interventions to be successful, it is important to make sure that the intervention addresses the needs that prompted a client to seek assistance. Often, agencies develop programs that they think will be appropriate for the clients they serve and then clients are forced into the existing programs that an agency offers. We think that the reverse order is more appropriate, that is, first, client needs must be identified, and then programs developed to address the needs that clients express. The interventions used in this research comprised websites, print materials, self-exploration checklists, and other publically available resources. The resources for each intervention were selected to be a good match for the identified need, either career decision-making or job search, which in Canada are two frequently occurring categories of client need. The interventions were developed, keeping in mind the kind of client characteristics and client needs that the intervention was intended to address and the sorts of client outcomes that could be expected to occur as a result of the intervention. Next, an assessment protocol was developed to identify clients who would be suitable for the intervention, and checklists were developed to track the extent to which the intervention was implemented as intended, and the degree to which clients were engaged in the intervention process. The client outcomes could then be assessed in a manner that made it possible to link the client changes to the intervention process. This project demonstrates a clear link between the processes that practitioners and clients engaged in and the outcomes that clients experienced.

Further evidence of the impact of this program came from follow-up interviews with practitioners and managers. Of the 16 practitioners and 5 managers who participated in the follow-up interviews, 90 % indicated that participation in this project had changed the way they interacted with clients, and 70 % indicated that they had begun using the research materials in their interactions with all of the clients they saw. They indicated also that the data collection process was instrumental in helping them track the progress of their clients and as a result, they had more confidence in the value of the services they provided. The full reports of the field test results and the impact on practice are available on the CRWG website, http://www.crwg-gdrc. ca/crwg/index.php/research-projects/lmi. Select Phase 2 Report for the field test results and Impact Report for the impact on practitioner practices.

Demonstrating Impact for Policy Development: The European Approach

In Europe, a somewhat different approach has been taken for demonstrating the impact of career guidance that is more policy-driven rather than research-oriented. In order to understand the European approach, some background information is presented on the process followed

and the goals behind the process. Subsequently, a description of the European Quality Assurance and Evidence Base Framework (QAE) is provided. Although many of the specific policies will need to be revised to fit different countries, the process followed in Europe is very generalizable to other countries. We provide this example because it provides an alternate way for others to design their own approach to developing a quality evidence base for career guidance.

The 27 sovereign countries in the European Union (EU) aim to equalize living and working conditions for all citizens in the EU by agreeing on common social and economic goals and strategies. In the *Lisbon 2010 Strategy* (adopted in 2000), the goal was that by 2010 Europe should be the most competitive and dynamic knowledge-based economy in the world, capable of sustainable economic growth, with more and better jobs, and greater social cohesion. Lifelong learning and a common European employment strategy were seen as centrally important to achieving the objectives of the *Lisbon 2010 Strategy*. Access to high quality career and LMI, career guidance and counseling services, and the assessment and recognition of formal and nonformal learning, were seen as important factors in achieving these objectives (Watts, Sultana, & McCarthy, 2010).

After adopting the *Lisbon 2010 Strategy*, career guidance issues were on the policy agenda of the EU and the European Commission (EC), the executive body of the EU. Additionally, the Review of Guidance Systems and Policies referred to earlier in this chapter (see Cedefop, 2011; OECD, 2004; Sultana & Watts, 2007; Sultana & Zelloth, 2003; Watts et al., 2010) spawned several initiatives. For example, a *Lifelong Guidance Expert Group* was mandated to draft guidelines for further guidance policy development at national and EU levels. From 2002 to 2007 the Expert Group produced a number of reference tools (Cedefop, 2005), such as *Common Aims and Principles of Lifelong Guidance Provision, Common Reference Points for Quality Assurance Systems for Guidance Provision in Europe* and *Key Features of a Systems*

Model for Lifelong Guidance for European Countries. The Expert Group also worked with the OECD, to create a *Career Guidance Handbook for Policy Makers* (OECD & EC, 2004), which highlights the importance of developing a reliable evidence base for assessing the outcomes and impact of guidance interventions. The *Handbook* contains suggestions for policy development to support the creation of a common evidence base and provides practical tools for helping to make that happen.

As a first step in developing a common set of indicators for career guidance, the Expert Group investigated existing practices in the EU member states for assessing the impact of career guidance services (den Boer, 2005). The results indicated that in most member states few data were collected pertaining to guidance outcomes. A number of Public Employment Services (PESs) reported collecting data, but their focus was on broader concerns than just career guidance, for example, number of labor market integrations, duration of unemployment, amount of money spent for guidance, and qualification measures undertaken to improve the chances for labor market integration.

Based on these findings, the Expert Group ultimately agreed on five reference points for defining quality assurance benchmarks in career guidance: (a) citizen and user involvement, (b) practitioner competence, (c) service improvement, (d) outcome and impact, and (e) coherence and coverage. One unique aspect of this framework is that quality assurance is seen as necessitating the involvement of guidance providers, policymakers, and users of guidance services. These five reference points were the foundation for creating tools that practitioners and policymakers could use for self-assessment and self-development of quality assurance systems for guidance services and products within and across sectors at national, regional, and local levels (Cedefop, 2005, p. 18).

The common reference points were approved by the European Ministers of Education in the *Maastricht Communiqué* (Cedefop, 2004). This approval gave guidance more importance on the European agenda and member states were actively encouraged to use these tools to support lifelong guidance systems and to demonstrate their outcomes and impact not only for individuals but also for the economic and social well-being of society as a whole (Cedefop, 2004, p. 2). Given the emphasis on collaboration in the European approach, the support from the European Ministers of Education, and the translation of the tools into various European languages, it was expected that implementation at a national level would be high. However, it seems that despite the collaborative approach, there was a lack of national ownership of the common reference tools and the implementation was lower than expected. This underscores the need for lobbying and promotion of these large-scale initiatives at a national and local level, in order to obtain a high level of implementation.

ELGPN: Towards a Common Framework for Quality Assurance and Evidence-Based Policy

Through the experiences just described, it became clear that the development and implementation of a common European Framework for Quality Assurance and Evidence Base needed to be driven by the member states. Thus, in 2007, the ELGPN was established to focus on the development and implementation of national-level quality assurance and evidence-base guidance policies (ELGPN, 2010, p. 12). Findings from an initial survey indicated that in a number of European countries considerable progress had been made to obtain evidence for career guidance outcomes and impacts (ELGPN, 2010, p. 53). For example: (a) Denmark collects data from 50,000 students every year. Results to date indicate positive correlations between guidance intervention and indicators such as educational enrolment and retention. (b) Scotland has a comprehensive all-age guidance approach and gathers evidence on a range of individual and societal outcomes including economic benefit, which showed a cost-benefit ratio for investment in career guidance of 1:5, that is, every 1.00 Pound spent yielded a 5.00 Pounds return on investment. (c) In Hungary, findings from a Sheltered Employment Program indicated that the cost-benefit ratio was 1:477, that is, an investment of 1€ on guidance produced a social return of 477€. (d) The German PES provides an evidence base on the overall outcome of guidance services, including placement services, financial assistance for clients, labor market integration, duration of unemployment, cost-benefit ratio, and customer satisfaction.

The type of data described in the preceding paragraph are interesting, however, they are somewhat arbitrary and not comparable across countries. To create a system for coherent policy development across countries, ELGPN members used the five reference points developed earlier to develop a common European QAE. The reference points were reconceptualized as quality elements, with special emphasis on the outcomes and impacts of guidance services and the cost-benefit to the individual and to society.

The ELGPN QAE Matrix, contains both qualitative and quantitative indicators, depending on the nature of the indicator and on the guidance sector in question. Both types of measures were used in order to assess the broad range of factors influencing the success of guidance services. For example, if the success of guidance services is measured exclusively by factors such as school drop-out rates or the number of graduates, important factors which influence those metrics, and are addressed by guidance services, may be overlooked. The goal was to achieve a balance between professional needs to track a broad range of factors and the demands for quantitative evidence which policymakers and service managers need in order to justify the investment of tax-payer money into lifelong career guidance services. Figure 38.2 provides a sample of the types of criteria and indicators that have been identified. The complete chart is included in the ELGPN Work Report, Annex D (ELGPN, 2012, p. 98).

The draft QAE Framework was piloted in a number of member states in early 2012 and revised to incorporate feedback from the pilot. The final QAE Framework has become part of the *ELGPN Resource-Kit* designed to provide a guide for Policy Makers in the European Member States to review their national guidance systems. In order to assist countries in the self-assessment of the criteria in the QAE and the integration of the QAE with their existing QA systems, an assessment tool was developed that depicts for each quality element a continuum of possible achievements from the lowest to the highest standard. Figure 38.3 provides a snapshot of part of the quality continuum associated with each element.

The *ELGPN Resource Kit* was presented to the national governments at the European Career Guidance Conference in October 2012 (ELGPN, 2012) and will be implemented by the member states during the working period 2013–2014. To assist this implementation, *Policy Review Clusters* will be formed, consisting of groups of countries with similar structures or interests. The Policy Review Clusters will permit countries to support each other in the development of guidance policies by facilitating the exchange of ideas and experiences and finding solutions to common problems. It is hoped that this approach will assist countries in improving national policies for career guidance and obtaining reliable data to "prove it works." We have described the process followed by the ELGPN so that readers from other countries can adapt the process to their own particular situations. The process of developing a QAE Framework illustrates how countries can work together to provide evidence for the positive impact of guidance services. Career guidance policies can have a meaningful role to play in achieving the objectives of the EU 2020 Strategy and the Education and Training 2020 objectives and also in non-European countries that want to raise the profile of career guidance and demonstrate the impact of career guidance services. The most important success factor is a supporting network of countries, regions, or institutions with a shared

Quality Element	Criteria	Indicator	Examples of Possible Data	Policy Review Comments
1. Practitioner competence	1.1. Recognized qualifications relevant to careers sector 1.2. Engaged in Continuing Professional Development 1.3. Membership level of Careers Professional Association(s)			
2. Citizen/user involvement	2.1. Ease of access to relevant services and products 2.2. Client satisfaction with services provided, including level of awareness in differing sectors e.g., schools, VET, HE, Adult Education, Employment settings and Social Inclusion initiatives. 2.3. Participation of users in planning and programming of Service's activities and action plan. 2.4. Participation of users in self and external evaluation of the Service.		For details see ELGPN 2012 p. 98.	
3. Service provision and improvement	3.1. Learning and applying career management skills (CMS) 3.2. Quality management system (QMS; national, sector, or provider based) 3.3. Appropriate ICT tools and software 3.4. Up-to-date knowledge in and expertise of education and labour markets 3.5. Profile and characteristics of service user groups *(clearly defined to target groups)*			

Quality Element	Criteria	Indicator	Examples of Data	Policy Review
4. Cost-benefits to governments	4.1. Immediate, medium and long-term savings to public purse from specific forms of interventions *(This can be adapted to focus on a range of differing guidance interventions including cost benefit to employers and governments)*	**Percentage of users progressing into employment, education/ training, unemployed,** including evidence of follow up **Duration and rate of progression into learning and/or work** e.g., *duration of time spent on unemployment register or prolonged staying on rates in education.* **Keeping track of the progress of individual advisees** to the next stage of their employment, career path or of the education and training process e.g., *# of individuals no longer claiming benefits as a direct result of specific intervention* e.g., *# of reduced drop-out rates from schooling,* e.g., *transfer rates from NEETS into education, training and/or employment.*	• Destination measures • NEET monitoring system • Balance Score Card • Longitudinal studies • Control Group studies • Register of clients • Breakdown of intervention measures • Costs or cost savings linked to telephone or web-based approaches • Pre- and post- treatment assessments	

	4.2. Savings on expenditure:
	
	- national telephone helpline service
	
	- national web portal for careers service
	
	- face-to-face delivery
		• Annual expenditure costs on:
		  – e.g., *national telephone helpline service*
		  – e.g., *national web portal for careers service*
		  – e.g., *face-to-face delivery*
			• Audit report
			• Business accounts	

5. Cost-benefits to individuals	5.1. Increase in household income	**Reduced dependency on welfare benefits through employment** e.g., *higher earnings/ salary information captured by careers practitioners*	• Annual performance and reporting plans	

Fig. 38.2 ELGPN quality assurance and evidence base framework (QAE)—selected indicators

Quality element 1: Practitioner competence		
Ad hoc arrangements not framed by policy	>>>>>>	Highly regulated 'register' or 'license to practice' arrangements
Quality element 2: Citizen/user involvement		
Fragmented and/or 'one-off' user satisfaction surveys	>>>>>>	Highly organized quality assurance and evidence-based systems that involve users actively in the design and development of services
Quality element 3: Service provision and improvement		
Absence of a career management skills framework, linked to access to services by key priority groups	>>>>>>	Total quality management system in place that also captures data on career management skills, levels of investments and added-value returns
Quality element 4: Cost-benefits to governments		
No information held on cost-benefits to governments	>>>>>>	Immediate, medium and long-term calculated savings to the public purse in the form of economic and/or social returns on investment (SROI)
Quality element 5: Cost-benefits to individuals		
Limited information on added-value returns as a result of individuals participating in careers services	>>>>>>	Evidence of ongoing longitudinal tracking and studies that measure the impact of differing careers interventions in differing settings

Source: ELGPN, 2012, p. 52

Fig. 38.3 Continuum of quality elements of a National Lifelong Guidance System. *Source*: ELGPN, 2012, p. 52

interest and vision so that knowledge and experience can be pooled to the benefit of all partners.

Relevance for Multiple Cultures

In this chapter, we have provided examples of differing approaches for demonstrating the value of career guidance services. We have identified various places where we think the ideas illustrated in the examples can easily be adapted to countries and cultures that are different from those in the example. The main tenet underlying the professional practitioner approach (i.e., practitioners should be systematic in their interactions with clients and look for connections between what they do, what their clients do, and the client changes that seem to be associated with counselor and client behaviors) is readily transported across country boarders. Similarly, the focus on practitioners using their clients as part of the evidence base to demonstrate the impact of career guidance services is applicable in most, perhaps even all, service settings. The general evaluation framework provided by the CRWG has been used successfully in career services, counseling services, educational settings, family and social service settings, and health settings, in a variety of countries in Africa, the Middle East, Europe, North America, and South America.

One of the key elements in the CRWG approach is collaboration between evaluators, funders, administrators, and practitioners. This type of collaboration also has been central to the European approach to policy development and resource creation. It underscores the importance of making sure that all parties who have a stake in the provision of career services and the outcomes associated with career services are represented also have a voice in the creation of policies, tools, and delivery mechanisms associated with career guidance services. The work of the ELGPN provides a good example of the steps that other countries might consider when developing their own "prove it works" initiatives. The Internet sources provided in these examples offer details about what factors are essential to address and detailed descriptions of how to go about making sure those factors are addressed adequately. In our experience, when some of these items are overlooked, problems usually result, but when attention is given to these details, the probability for success is great.

Future Directions and Conclusions

The initiatives described in this chapter represent important steps towards providing a trustworthy data base that supports the efficacy and impact of career guidance services. Comprehensive service evaluation needs to move beyond collecting easy-to-measure variables such as client volumes; client presenting problems; number of sessions; staff credentials, competencies, resources; adherence to mandate; and cost-effectiveness. Evaluation needs to include also service delivery variables, client outcome variables, and the types of data that will serve as indicators of success, all of which need to be negotiated between practitioners, funders, and policymakers. In some settings, funders might identify personal attributes (client motivation, improved job satisfaction, increased self-confidence) or knowledge, or skills, as accountability indicators. However, it is more likely that funders and policymakers will identify impact outcomes (e.g., employment status, enrolment in training, reduced number of sick days, increased productivity) or inputs (e.g., client flow, accessibility, timeliness of paper work) as the variables of interest. Therefore, service providers will need to identify the knowledge, skills, personal attributes that will produce the impacts and negotiate with funders and policymakers that these are important accountability indicators.

To demonstrate the value of career guidance services, and in the process "prove it works," we need to develop a culture of evaluation where the identification of outcomes is an integral part of providing services. This will involve broadening the conceptualization of professional identity to include both providing services and evaluating the impact of those services: where measuring and reporting outcomes is integrated into practice, reporting outcomes is a policy priority, and outcome assessment is a prominent part of counselor education. This needs to be a priority in all sectors.

In times of unprecedented economic turmoil and uncertainty which we currently face, the "prove it works" issue becomes magnified, as state spending comes under increasing scrutiny. In such circumstances, decisions are often driven by the need to achieve immediate savings and arguments based on long-term benefits can fall on deaf ears. By its very nature, career guidance does not operate in isolation, and the challenge of demonstrating a link between the interventions that we offer and the impact of those interventions on clients' lives, and on wider government goals, is an ongoing one. Part of that challenge is to establish strong working relationships with policymakers so that debate can take place and reasonable consensus can be reached on what are reasonable expectations for the outcomes and impacts of career guidance services.

There is a role for professional associations such as IAEVG to provide a practitioner perspective within the ICCDPP and the ELGPN and at the same time emphasize with its practitioner membership the importance of being able to demonstrate the impact of career services to a dispassionate and often skeptical audience. There also is potential to better coordinate and focus career guidance research and evaluation to ensure that such work is undertaken in a way that supports the push for meaningful evidence of the impact of career guidance services. If our messages regarding value are not being heard, then we need to rapidly adopt new strategies for getting our messages across and/or change the messages. The answer is definitely not just to shout the same messages louder!

References

Baudouin, R., Bezanson, L., Borgen, B., Goyer, L., Hiebert, B., Lalande, V., ... Turcotte, M. (2007). Demonstrating value: A draft framework for evaluating the effectiveness of career development interventions. *Canadian Journal of Counselling, 41,* 146–157.

Bezanson, L., & Plant, P. (2010). *Quality standards in career development services: A Canadian "snapshot" and an international perspective.* Ottawa, ON: Canadian Career Development Foundation. Retrieved from http://www.iccdpp.org/PolicyResearch/Ensuringquality/tabid/155/articleType/ArticleView/articleId/180/Default.aspx

Canadian Standards and Guidelines for Career Development Practitioners [S&Gs]. (2004). *The history of the S&Gs.* Ottawa, ON: Author. Retrieved from http://career-dev-guidelines.org/career_dev/index.php/a-living-document/history-of-the-initiative

Career Industry Council of Australia [CICA]. (2006). *Professional standards for Australian career development practitioners.* Hawthorne, VC: Author. Retrieved from http://www.cica.org.au/practitioners/standards

Cedefop. (2005). *Improving lifelong guidance policies and systems using common European reference tools.* Luxembourg: Office for Official Publications of the European Communities. Retrieved from http://www.cedefop.europa.eu/etv/upload/Projects_Networks/Guidance/expertgroup/Thematic%20Projects/Reference_tools_EN.pdf

Cedefop. (2011). *Lifelong guidance across Europe: Reviewing policy progress and future prospects* (Working Paper 11). Luxembourg: Publications Office of the European Union. Retrieved from http://www.cedefop.europa.eu/EN/Files/6111_en.pdf

Cedefop [European Centre for the Development of Vocational Training]. (2004). *Maastricht communiqué on the future priorities of enhanced European cooperation in vocational education and training (VET).* Retrieved from http://www.cedefop.europa.eu/EN/Files/communique_maastricht_priorities_vet.pdf

Council for the Accreditation of Counseling and Related Educational Programs [CACREP]. (2001). *CACREP accreditation manual.* Alexandria, VA: Author. Retrieved from http://www.cacrep.org/2001standards.html

den Boer, P. (2005). *Indicators and benchmarks for lifelong guidance: Draft final report.* Thessaloniki, Greece: Cedefop. Retrieved from http://libserver.cedefop.europa.eu/F/IRGFHGGQRLDMXCM6Y5G485TUUBUQTPTTU1T7QF4SE79IJEV5LA-11388?func=full-set-set&set_number=000105&set_entry=000009&format=999

Domene, J. F., Buchanan, M. J., Hiebert, B., & Buhr, E. (in press). The present and future of counselling and counselling psychology research in Canada: A call to action. In A. Sinacore & F. Ginsberg (Eds.), *Canadian counselling psychology in the 21st century*. Montreal, PQ: McGill-Queen's University Press.

Dozois, D. J. (2011). Training in professional psychology: The content and process of learning. *Psynopsis, 33*(4), 7.

ELGPN [European Lifelong Guidance Policy Network]. (2010). *Lifelong guidance policies: Work in progress* (A Report on the work of the European Lifelong Guidance Policy Network 2008–2010). Jyväskylä, Finland: Author. Retrieved from http://ktl.jyu.fi/img/portal/8465/ELGPN_report_2009-10.pdf?cs=1284966063

ELGPN [European Lifelong Guidance Policy Network]. (2012). *Lifelong guidance policy development: A European resource kit*. Retrieved from http://ktl.jyu.fi/img/portal/23229/ELGPN_resource_kit_2011-12_web.pdf?cs=1350649791

Glasziou, P., Vandenbroucke, J. P., & Chalmers, I. (2004). Assessing the quality of research. *British Medical Journal, 328*, 39–41.

Hiebert, B. (2008). International competencies for educational and vocational guidance practitioners: Implications for professional practice. *International Journal for Educational and Vocational Guidance, 8*, 176–181.

Hiebert, B., Bezanson, L., O'Reilly, E., Hopkins, S., Magnusson, K., & McCaffrey, A. (2012). *Assessing the impact of labour market information: Final report on results of phase two (field tests), phase three (follow up interviews), and phase four (impact on practice)* (Research report presented to Human Resources and Skills Development Canada). Ottawa, ON: Canadian Career Development Foundation (CCDF). Retrieved from http://www.crwg-gdrc.ca/crwg/index.php/research-projects/lmi

Hiebert, B., & Charles, G. (2008). *Accountability and outcomes in health and human services: Changing perspectives for changing times*. Calgary, AB: Canadian Outcomes Research Institute. Retrieved from http://homepages.ucalgary.ca/~hiebert/research/files/CORI_Issue1_web.pdf

Hiebert, B., Domene, J. F., & Buchanan, M. (2011). The power of multiple methods and evidence sources: Raising the profile of Canadian counselling psychology research. *Canadian Psychology, 52*, 265–275.

Hiebert, B., & Magnusson, K. (2014). The subversive power of evidence: Demonstrating the value of career development services. In B. Shepard & P. Mani (Eds.), *Canadian career practitioners handbook*. Toronto, ON: Counselling and Educational Research Institute of Canada.

Horan, J. J. (1980). Experimentation in counselling and psychotherapy. Part I: New myths about old realities. *Educational Researcher, 9*(11), 5–10. doi:10.3102/0013189X009011005.

Jenschke, B. (2012). *History of IAEVG 1951–2011: Chronicle, policies and achievements of the global guidance community*. Berlin, DE: Bielefeld. Retrieved from http://www.iaevg.org

Killeen, J., White, M., & Watts, A. G. (1992). *The economic value of careers guidance*. London, UK: Policy Studies Institute.

Methei, R. J. (2006). What can clients tell us about seeking counselling and their experience of it? *International Journal for the Advancement of Counselling, 27*, 541–553. doi:10.1007/s10447-005-8490-3.

OECD [Organization for Economic Cooperation and Development]. (2004). *Career guidance and public policy: Bridging the gap*. Paris: Author.

OECD [Organization for Economic Cooperation and Development] & EC [European Commission]. (2004). *Career guidance handbook for policy makers*. Paris: Author. Retrieved from http://www.oecd.org/dataoecd/53/53/34060761.pdf

Posavac, E. J. (2011). *Program evaluation: Methods and case studies* (8th ed.). Boston, MA: Prentice Hall.

Repetto, E. (2008). International competencies for educational and vocational guidance practitioners: An IAEVG trans-national study. *International Journal for Educational and Vocational Guidance, 9*, 135–195. doi:10.1007/s10775-008-9144-x.

Sexton, T. L. (1996). The relevance of counseling outcome research: Current trends and practical implications. *Journal of Counseling & Development, 74*, 590–600.

Stamatis, D. H. (1995). *Total quality service: Principles, practices, and implementation*. Boca Raton, FL: CRC Press.

Stricker, G., & Trierweiler, S. J. (1995). The local clinical scientist: A bridge between science and practice. *American Psychologist, 50*, 995–1002.

Sultana, R. G., & Watts, A. G. (2007). *Career guidance in the Mediterranean region: Comparative analyses*. Luxembourg: Publications Office of the European Union.

Sultana, R. G., & Zelloth, H. (2003). *Review of career guidance policies in 11 acceding and candidate countries: Synthesis report*. Luxembourg: Publications Office of the European Union. Retrieved from http://www.etf.europa.eu/pubmgmt.nsf/(getAttachment)/43062485065B0E82C1257020002FEB25/$File/ENL-Career%20guidance-0703_EN.pdf

Trierweiler, S. J., Stricker, G., & Peterson, R. L. (2010). The research and evaluation competency: The local clinical scientist-review, current status, future directions. In M. B. Kenkel & R. L. Peterson (Eds.), *Competency-based education for professional psychology* (pp. 125–141). Washington, DC: American Psychological Association.

Watts, A. G. (1999). The economic and social benefits of career guidance. *Educational and Vocational Guidance Bulletin, 63*, 12–19.

Watts, A. G., Sultana, R. G., & McCarthy, J. (2010). The involvement of the European Union in career guidance policy: A brief history. *International Journal for Educational and Vocational Guidance, 10*, 89–107.

Wiggins, G., & McTighe, J. (2005). *Understanding by design*. Alexandria, VA: Association for Supervision and Curriculum Development (ASCD).

Overview

The quality of counselor training and the formulation of counselor competencies and standards lie at the heart of building capacity for the effective delivery of career development services within a specific context. Developments and innovations in career services are enabled and strengthened through high quality counselor education benchmarked by well-articulated counselor competencies and standards. This theme presents new developments in counselor training, examples of counselor competencies and standards across countries, and illustrations of international competencies. Training and credentialing mechanisms to acknowledge and validate practitioners who possess the required competencies are discussed. Today, it is important for counselors to view their roles as expanding beyond providing direct services to students. Their roles include working with school staff members and other stakeholder groups to provide a comprehensive, institution-wide approach to guidance and counseling services. Chapters in this section provide an outline for staff in-service training from international perspectives.

In summary, this final section of the handbook brings focus to bear on career practitioner training. Career guidance contexts are becoming increasingly multicultural and there is a call for training career practitioners whose skills and knowledge are relevant across cultures. This section explains, with illustrations, the concept of standards and competency-based training and also points to new directions for training and capacity building.

Bryan Hiebert and Roberta Neault

Training programs for career practitioners have increased substantially over the past decade and wide variation exists in the content and quality of these programs. For example, Niles and Karajic (2008) mentioned the differences in the type of training for career development facilitators, compared to career coaches and career counselors. They also highlighted the changing nature of work, which requires training programs to be constantly updated in order to ensure that trainees are equipped to meet the changing realities of the workforce. Furthermore, many programs have a limited and restricted view of what constitutes comprehensive career services, and, therefore, trainees in those programs end up with a skill set that has not adequately prepared them to deal with the complexity of career development in the 21st century.

In response to the variation in content and quality, many initiatives have been undertaken, or are in progress, to establish procedures for reviewing and validating the knowledge, skills, and personal attributes that are required to offer quality career guidance services (Sultana, 2009). However, to date these initiatives are characterized by wide differences in terminology and approaches, and in many cases the results are country specific or specific to particular training providers. There is utility in examining some of the more prominent approaches, with a view to identifying some of the issues that practitioners and policymakers need to be mindful of, and to assist the various stakeholders in making informed decisions regarding how to proceed with validating and acknowledging the practitioners who possess an appropriate level of competence for delivering career services.

Background

In recent years there has been an increasing emphasis in many countries on providing quality career services to clients and this has been a frequently occurring theme in many international symposia (see http://www.iccdpp.org/Symposia/tabid/78/Default.aspx). The discussions at international symposia have revealed several issues that are important to address when examining the factors involved in providing quality career services to clients. We highlight three issues in this chapter: language, approach to determining the scope of practice, and the nature of services being offered.

Language

Niles and Karajic (2008) discussed the importance of developing a common language in order to facilitate the globalization of training practices and provide greater international career mobility for career practitioners. Many writers

B. Hiebert (✉)
University of Calgary, Calgary AB, Canada
e-mail: hiebert@ucalgary.ca

G. Arulmani et al. (eds.), *Handbook of Career Development*, International and Cultural Psychology, DOI 10.1007/978-1-4614-9460-7_39, © Springer Science+Business Media, LLC 2014

(e.g., Arthur, 2008; Evangelista, 2011; Hiebert, 2008, 2009; Niles & Karajic, 2008) have attempted to describe the factors that should be included in the qualification standards for career practitioners. However, the lack of a common language often interferes with achieving a common understanding of the characteristics that are required to ensure that quality career services are provided by competent career practitioners.

At the most general level, there usually is agreement that competent practitioners are those who are qualified, or have the expertise, to offer quality services. However, the factors that contribute to being a competent practitioner are described in quite different ways. For example, in North America (see Canadian Standards and Guidelines for Career Development Practitioners [S&Gs], 2004, 2011; Council for the Accreditation of Counseling and Related Educational Programs [CACREP], 2001) competent practitioners are thought to possess certain competencies, and competencies are usually defined as involving three components: knowledge, skills, and personal attributes (or attitudes, or certain affective characteristics). A similar approach was taken by the International Association for Educational and Vocational Guidance (IAEVG) in developing the International Competencies for Educational and Vocational Guidance Practitioners (see Hiebert, 2008, 2009; Repetto, 2008) and the Career Industry Council of Australia (CICA) when developing the Professional Standards for Australian Career Development Practitioners (CICA, 2006).

In European countries, however, the term *competence* (or *competences* as the plural) is used instead of *competency* (or *competencies* as a plural) (see Sultana, 2009). The rationale for the difference in terminology seems to be that competent practitioners need to demonstrate competence in the various aspects of their job, and these many competences can be grouped together to form a competence framework. The nature of the competences is not explicit, but there is acknowledgement that competence involves both having the ability to do something, and also performing at a high level compared to some predetermined standard. The distinction is not merely semantic, for although the European Centre for the Development of Vocational Training (CEDEFOP, 2007) advises authors to simply substitute the words *competence* (and *competences*) for *competency* (and *competencies*), others point out that the terms *competency* and *competence* have different meanings and should not be used interchangeably (see Evangelista, 2011; Sultana, 2009). Perhaps Evangelista (2011) put it most clearly when he suggested that competencies are the antecedents of performance, while competence refers to the ability to provide a good performance without reference to what causes the performance to be good.

In most countries, career services are delivered by people with a variety of professional backgrounds, working in a wide range of settings, and having a broad range of professional preparation. In some countries, a competency-based approach to establishing professional standards is taken, focused on identifying what practitioners do, rather than the training they have taken. In other countries, there is criticism of a competency-based approach to education and training based on the belief that focusing on training outcomes places exaggerated emphasis on skills and not enough emphasis on knowledge and comprehension, thereby detracting from a learner-oriented instructional approach (see Psifidou, 2010a, for a review). It also is the case that a competency-based approach places additional responsibility on instructors who must be clear about the student learning outcomes they are trying to achieve (Psifidou, 2010b). However, most of the debate has taken place in the context of Technical and Vocational Education and Training (TVET), not the preparation of career practitioners. Furthermore, the controversy around competency-based approaches is largely focused on education and training concerns, not on the creation of professional standards. From our perspective, the debate around the utility of competency-based approaches is only marginally related to the main theme in this chapter. The concerns seem to us to provide an example of how any idea, narrowly interpreted, applied in a different context, and taken to an extreme, can end up being less than optimally useful. It underscores the need for readers to filter the fine points and the contexts of the work they consult when embarking on initiatives intended to create standards for practice or competency frameworks.

Niles and Karajic (2008) pointed out, quite correctly in our opinion that language often serves as a barrier to international cooperation and collaboration. They proposed standard definitions of key terms in the hope that it would begin a dialogue that ultimately will result in greater compatibility between training programs and greater internationalization of training opportunities. Attempting to resolve language issues surrounding counselor competencies and standards is beyond the scope of this chapter; however, we think it is important that readers are aware of the key language differences, take steps to make informed decisions about the nomenclature they use to describe their attempts to develop and/or promote systems for acknowledging competent practitioners, and take care to be consistent in the way they use terms like *competent*, *competence* (*competences*), and *competency* (*competencies*). Our preference in this chapter is to use the term *competency* to refer to the knowledge, skills, and attitudes (KSAs) that practitioners need in order to provide quality services to clients and to leave it to agencies or national professional organizations to define what types, and what levels, of KSAs practitioners need in order to have the competence to provide quality services in the jurisdictions they represent. Also, we use broad and encompassing terms, such as *career practitioners* or *providers of career services*, as a generic way to refer to a range of service providers, some of whom may be career counselors, career guidance practitioners, career advisors, or employment consultants. When we use a specific term such as *career guidance practitioners*, we are referring to that specific occupational group as distinct from others.

Approaches to Determining Scope of Practice

After reviewing the available literature, we can say with confidence that there are two main approaches used to define and validate the characteristics of competent practitioners in the career guidance field. One approach focuses on the KSAs that practitioners need, regardless of their professional affiliation (we call this an inclusive approach); the other focuses on the KSAs that are unique to those providing career guidance services and are not required for practitioners from other fields (we call this an excluding approach). The key decision when developing a qualifications standards framework is whether the framework should focus on the competencies required to deliver quality career services regardless of the primary professional affiliation of the person providing services, or focus on the competencies that are unique to career practitioners and not likely to be part of the competency set of other professional groups.

Inclusive Approaches to Describing Competent Career Guidance Practitioners

Career services are sometimes provided by practitioners whose main function, or only function, is to provide career guidance. However, career services also are provided by practitioners, from many different professions, who do career guidance as part of their jobs. The list includes social workers, psychologists, teachers, counselors, librarians, child-care workers, family therapists, and others in the helping professions. Therefore, many of the competencies that are required to deliver quality career services are likely also to be required to deliver quality services in other areas, not necessarily related to career guidance. For example, good communication skills are necessary for career practitioners, but also necessary for counselors, social workers, psychologists, and many other fields of practice in human services. In a similar way, being aware of one's own strengths and limitations, demonstrating ethical behavior, ability to integrate theory into practice, and likely

692 B. Hiebert and R. Neault

many more, will be part of the KSAs required for competent practice in a variety of different professional fields. Furthermore, many of these shared competencies have a knowledge component (knowing what to do), a skill component (being able to do it), and also an attitudinal component (a belief, or commitment, or feeling that it is important to do it). However, there are some competencies that career practitioners need that are not as relevant for other areas of professional practice. For example, labor market information is needed for career practitioners, but may not be needed, or at least is not as important, in the practice of family therapy. Similarly, knowledge of lifelong career development processes and work search strategies are likely to be more important for career practitioners than for other groups of helping professionals.

Excluding Approaches to Describing Competent Career Guidance Practitioners

In his review of existing frameworks for defining competent career practitioners, Evangelista (2011) criticized some existing frameworks because they include factors that are common to many professionals and, therefore, tend to focus attention on elements external to the career services sector. He suggested that a better way is to ignore factors such as communication skills or ICT skills and instead focus on features that are specific and prominent for the job being examined (i.e., providers of career services). We have called this an excluding approach because, in focusing on the factors that are specific and prominent for career practitioners, other professional groups are excluded even though they might possess some (but not all) of the KSAs needed to be competent career practitioners. The excluding approach may be useful in that it identifies the elements that are unique to providers of career services and not likely to be possessed by those working in other settings. However, it also is the case that many of the elements that are shared with other professional groups are centrally important for identifying competent career practitioners. Evangelista does acknowledge that in many countries career guidance is delivered by people

as only a part of their work mandate, and that it is not a good idea to develop a framework that excludes these people (i.e., where career guidance is not their main function); however, he goes on to criticize initiatives that make an attempt to be more inclusive in their approach.

Summary

When defining the competencies needed to deliver quality career services, a central question that needs to be addressed is: Do we include competencies that career professionals share with other professional groups or focus only on competencies that are unique to career professionals? If the shared competencies are not included, it could create the impression that competencies such as communication or ICT skills are not needed by career practitioners, which clearly is not the case. Thus, in many (perhaps most) competency frameworks, the focus is on being comprehensive, identifying KSAs needed to deliver quality services, including those KSAs that are shared with other professional groups for whom delivering career services is only a part of their work roles, and acknowledging that some of those competencies are shared with professional groups not involved in providing career services (see Canadian Standards and Guidelines for Career Development Practitioners [S&Gs], 2011; CICA, 2006; Hiebert, 2009; Repetto, 2008).

Nature of Service

People seek career services for a variety of different reasons and, therefore, comprehensive career services require many different types of services to meet the different needs of different clients. As Borgen and Hiebert (2002) pointed out, for some clients, information and advice is all that is needed. Service providers draw from their backgrounds the information that is relevant for a client's particular problem; the client processes the information and takes action. Other clients need career guidance, which is a broader scope of service tailored to the person's concerns or goals and designed to give people full opportunity for personal development and satisfaction from work. Also, there are clients who need career counseling that facilitates exploring and clarifying their thoughts, feelings, and actions in order to arrive at answers that are best for them. Advising is most appropriate for people who are seeking information, know how to use it, and are open to the advice they receive. Guidance can help people consider their suitability for different career and educational opportunities, explore alternatives they may not have considered previously, and engage in appropriate decision-making about their future career-life path. Counseling is required in situations where people need to explore their views and attitudes related to career and educational opportunities, their personal level of readiness to pursue various options, their cultural and societal contexts, and the need to include others who may be important in the decision-making process for that person.

In many countries today, advising is readily available. Guidance services often are available in basic education, but frequently are not available for those outside the schooling system. Counseling services are more rare, especially outside the school system, even in the so-called more developed countries (Borgen & Hiebert, 2002). An integrated and holistic approach is needed that provides advising and guidance to those who need it and offers counseling to those who need additional help to understand the potential options that are available to them (Van Esbroeck, 1997). The approach would begin with a client needs assessment to determine the most appropriate type of service, followed by service directed at meeting the client's needs. Van Esbroeck (1997) argued that such an approach has the potential to resolve many of the problems associated with fragmented services and would help to implement a learner-oriented and worker-oriented way of operating that is more capable of meeting individual and societal needs across the life span.

The current emphasis on lifelong learning in many countries also has implications for career development practice. As Van Esbroeck (2002) pointed out, lifelong learning brings with it a need for lifelong guidance. The nature of lifelong guidance will vary from one country to another,

but most certainly it will involve in most countries a wider variety of services being made available, to people across a broader range of personal and employment situations, and across a more extensive age range. The services would best be provided in a one-stop shop format to avoid fragmentation and promote a wholistic approach (i.e., focusing on the whole person needs of individuals). (Please note that the spelling of wholistic is deliberate, intended to emphasize a focus on the whole person needs of clients, see Hiebert, 2009.) By implication, it will require service providers at all organizational levels to have a more comprehensive set of competencies in order to provide the services and to create an infrastructure that would facilitate the delivery of this broader range of services.

Summary

People talk as if career guidance is an intervention, rather than the object of an intervention, and practitioners (as well as clients) often confuse the terms *career advice*, *career guidance*, and *career counseling* (Niles & Karajic, 2008). Furthermore, career practitioners are involved in a variety of roles including direct service to individual clients, services to businesses, and services to schools, to name but a few. They also are involved in providing a wide range of services, to clients who have a broad range of needs. The best way to conceptualize the situation is not likely to be as different points along a continuum of services, from least intense to most intense. These services are likely best depicted as a Venn diagram where there are intersecting circles of services and the KSAs needed to provide those services (see Fig. 39.1).

The main point here is that different clients have different needs, and, therefore, require different types of service, not more or less of the same type of service. The different types of service are best offered by different types of service providers, with different types of training. In a contemporary context, career development refers to the lifelong process of managing learning, work, and transitions in order to move toward a personally determined and evolving preferred future (Canadian Standards and Guidelines for

Figure 39.1 Conceptualizing the competencies for different types of service

Career Development Practitioners [S&Gs], 2004). It is the case that some people naturally develop the ability to manage their careers in a meaningful way. However, many more need assistance, different types of assistance from different types of service providers, across their life spans. As the rate of economic, occupational, and social change continues to grow, this will become increasingly true for a greater number of people in many countries. In order for that assistance to be available, policymakers, professional associations, and service providers need some basic training in the KSAs that are required to assist clients in developing meaningful lifelong learning plans that are interconnected with their career paths.

Sample Professional Standards and Credentialing Programs

To date, there have been many initiatives focused on developing professional standards initiatives and credentialing programs for career development practitioners. Some of them are local (e.g., state or provincial certification systems), some are national (e.g., Canadian Standards and Guidelines for Career Development Practitioners [S&Gs], 2004, 2011; CICA, 2006), and some global (e.g., Global Career Development Facilitator [GCDF], Educational and Vocational Guidance Practitioner [EVGP]). Although most of these initiatives share some common features, there are differences between each of them, which can make career mobility for career practitioners somewhat challenging. A comprehensive review of all of these initiatives is beyond the scope of this chapter; however, some examples will help to illustrate the main concepts described earlier.

The Global Career Development Facilitator

The GCDF credentialing process began almost 30 years ago in the United States when the National Occupational Information Coordinating Committee (NOICC) piloted the Work in America initiative (Brawley, 2009). Later, NOICC and the Career Development Training Institute (CDTI) facilitated a needs assessment survey of career and workforce development employees. The results, combined with input from several professional associations in the USA, informed the development of the original Career Development Facilitator (CDF) credential and the training curriculum to support the credential. The CDF credential was initially developed in 1997 through a collaborative arrangement between the Center for Credentialing and Education, Inc. (CCE), the National Career Development Association (NCDA), and NOICC. The GCDF was established in 1999 to recognize the similarities and differences between career and employment practices in different parts of the world (Clawson & Shafer, 2002).

The GCDF involves at least 120 hours of professional training, covering 12 core competency areas: helping skills, labor market information and resources, assessment, diverse populations, ethical and legal issues, career development models, employability skills, training clients and peers, program management and implementation, promotion and public relations, technology, and consultation (See http://cce-global.org/GCDF/CoreComp). Although the GCDF does not state it explicitly, some of the core areas (e.g., helping skills, diverse populations, technology) contain competencies shared among all helping professionals, while other core areas (e.g., labor market information and resources, career development models, employability skills) are unique to those offering career services (Furbish, Neault, & Pickerell, 2009).

The GCDF is administered by the CCE, an affiliate of the National Board for Certified Counselors (NBCC), and each participating country has a designated contact person or organization. At the time of writing, there are 14 country-specific designations: Bulgaria, Canada, China, Cyprus, Germany, Greece, Japan, Macedonia, New Zealand, Romania, South Korea, Turkey, Taiwan, and the United States (see http://cce-global.org/GCDF). Aside from obvious language differences, country-specific content includes information about government policies, local workplace culture, regional resources (web-based or print), relevant ethnic or cultural considerations (e.g., regional restrictions on the types of work specific individuals can do), local labor market information, and effective work search strategies. Within some countries (e.g., Canada, the United States) there are different associations or training institutions offering slightly different programs leading to the GCDF. Curricula must be pre-approved through a comprehensive review process, which is facilitated by the CCE, ensuring that the 12 core competencies as well as country-specific content are adequately covered. A combination of education and relevant work experience is also required in order to receive the GCDF credential.

Students who successfully complete an approved GCDF program, and have the required education and relevant work experience, can apply for the credential through their country-specific administrator. To maintain the GCDF credential, facilitators must engage in and document ongoing professional development; at least 75 contact hours within the 5-year time period is required for recertification. The 75 contact hours can come from a variety of sources: formal educational programs, professional workshops, participation in approved conferences, and relevant employer training, to name a few.

The Educational and Vocational Guidance Professional

In 1999, the General Assembly of the IAEVG approved an initiative to identify the competencies practitioners need in order to perform their jobs effectively and propose recommendations for training programs that would provide practitioners with these competencies. The process to develop the *International Competencies for Educational and Vocational Guidance Practitioners* spanned 10 years (see Van Esbroeck, 2008), with the IAEVG General Assembly approving the competency framework in 2005, and the EVGP certificate being made available in 2007.

The international competencies that form the basis of the EVGP were developed empirically, through an extensive research process, coordinated by a research team based in Spain, which identified the competencies required for delivering quality educational and vocational guidance services and the training available to practitioners. The final validation study involved administering a survey that had been developed in seven languages (English, French, Finnish, German, Greek, Italian, and Spanish) and involved over 700 participants from 41 countries. (See Repetto (2008) for a detailed description of the research that went into the development of the EVGP.)

The EVGP competency framework utilizes a functional approach, based on what practitioners do (i.e., the KSAs required to deliver quality services) rather than the training they should take. There are two major categories of competencies: core competencies and specialized competencies. The core competencies are required by all practitioners, and involve: ethical behavior; advocacy; cultural awareness; integrating theory and research into practice; designing, implementing, and evaluating programs; awareness of own capacity; communicating effectively; knowing updated information; social and cross-cultural sensitiveness; team building; and knowledge of the lifelong career development process. An example of how the KSAs feed into competencies is provided in Fig. 39.2.

In addition to the core competencies there are 11 areas of specialization that pertain to specific work settings: assessment, educational, guidance, career development, counseling, information management, consultation and coordination, research and evaluation, program/service management, community capacity building, and

Figure 39.2 An illustration of how competency areas are composed of KSAs

Competency Area	Function	Competency
Communicate effectively with colleagues and clients	Communicate Effectively	Work with climate and context to enhance communication Use a framework for verbal communication Use a framework for written communication Use effective listening skills Clarify and provide feedback Establish and maintain collaborative work relationships
	Develop Productive Interactions with Clients	• Foster client self-reliance and self-management • Deal with reluctant clients

placement. To receive the EVGP applicants need to document their proficiency with all core competencies and at least one area of specialization. There also are minimum requirements for education and relevant work experience, as well as a declaration of adherence to the IAEVG Ethical Standards (see http://www.iaevg.org/ for further details).

The EVGP is designed to be of interest to three potential groups of users: practitioners, trainers, and professional associations. Practitioners wanting to document their competencies can apply individually to the Center for Credentialing in Education (CCE), which administers the EVGP, providing the appropriate supporting information. The application process can be conducted in any of the four official languages of the IAEVG: English, French, German, or Spanish. Trainers who want pre-approval of their curriculum can apply to the IAEVG Administrative Centre, providing appropriate documentation, to have their training program pre-approved as meeting the requirements for the EVGP. Instructions for this process are available on the IAEVG website (http://www.iaevg.org). Professional associations who wish to adapt the international competencies to their own unique contexts can work with the IAEVG Administrative Centre to use the requirements for the EVGP as a foundation for developing their own credentialing system. Promotion of the EVGP has been minimal and, therefore, user rates are low. However, expressions of interest have been received from Germany, India, Greece, and Venezuela, as well as government training organizations and professional associations in Canada. With this interest, it is expected that the EVGP will continue to grow in popularity as an international designation.

Applying for EVGP Pre-approval of Training: A Canadian Case Example

The LearnOnline Division of Life Strategies Ltd. (see http://www.lifestrategies.ca) offers a comprehensive range of e-learning courses, primarily focused on the professional development of career practitioners and counselors. Many of their courses and certificates are offered in partnership with educational institutions, employers, and professional associations. Where feasible, they have aligned their courses to external standards (e.g., S&Gs, GCDF-Canada, Job Developer's Institute) or applied for pre-approved Continuing Education credits through professional associations (e.g., Canadian Counselling and Psychotherapy Association, Vocational Rehabilitation Association). The online nature of the training means that students may access the courses from anywhere in the world that provides internet service. Since 2004, more than 1,000 students have enrolled in the program; most have been from Canada but international students have registered from countries including South Africa, the United Arab Emirates, Australia, Ireland, and the United States. Therefore, international recognition via the EVGP credential was particularly appealing.

Due to the complexity of the LearnOnline suite of courses and programs (more than 30 courses in total), aligning with the EVGP requirements required some consultation. The first step was to review the EVGP competencies to determine overlap with the content of the LearnOnline courses. Next, several courses (e.g., Administering and Interpreting Career Assessments, Career Coaching Skills, Helping Skills to Facilitate Career Development, and Program Management) were selected that seemed, in combination, to address the core competencies and one area of specialization. After extensive review and consultation, in 2010 a seven course (130 hours) package was pre-approved as meeting the requirements of the EVGP. This permitted students who had already completed some or all of the relevant LearnOnline courses to use those courses to qualify for the EVGP credential. It also permitted students who had completed the LearnOnline Career Management Professional Program to qualify for additional specializations within the EVGP credential.

As with most situations where an existing program is mapped to a new credential, the fit described above was somewhat awkward. Therefore, a second, more streamlined option was developed and ultimately approved, later in 2010. The more streamlined option is a 6-week, 60-hour e-course, Foundations for Practice in Educational and Vocational Guidance, which was customized to cover all EVGP core competencies and also the Career Development Specialization. The Foundations course can be further customized for intact work groups or members of professional associations in different parts of the world. Although currently only offered in English, partnerships with professional associations or training institutions could result in translation and localization of the readings, discussion questions, and activities, and through a train-the-trainer process, local trainers could be equipped to offer the course independently or within a partnership agreement (e.g., site hosting by Life Strategies Ltd. but instructed by a local trainer). Additional resources (e.g., PowerPoint, Facilitator's Guide) could also be developed to support offering the course in a classroom-based setting.

Advantages and Challenges Associated with Developing Professional Standards

There are some challenges associated with aligning existing training to any external credential, especially an international one, or customizing specialized training to match exact requirements. These challenges include course development or revision costs, application fees, time invested to organize an application package, clearly communicating course content, understanding different learning systems and requirements, and working across international borders. However, the benefits far outweigh the challenges. For independent training providers or those aligned to a specific college or university, benchmarking to competencies endorsed by an external professional body can establish or enhance credibility, providing quality assurance to potential students. In turn, international students can better leverage their credential. For example, currently a student from Dubai could take the EVGP Foundations course from a Canadian institution, thereby earning a professional credential that will be recognized across many countries on every continent. The LearnOnline Division of Life Strategies noted some additional benefits associated with aligning its courses to external credentials such as the EVGP, including staying current with what are considered to be core competencies in the career guidance sector and contributing to the ongoing professionalization of career and employment service providers. The example of Life Strategies provides one illustration of how involvement with professional standards initiatives helps to promote professionalism in the career services sector.

Although the GCDF and EVGP seem to be the most well-known international models at the time of writing, other models have been developed to guide the work of career practitioners in various parts of the worlds. For example, the JIVA principles of career development (The Promise Foundation, 2009) are based on Indian philosophy. Principle 1: The Jiva Spiral highlights the importance of taking "a nonlinear approach to career development." Principle 2: The Jiva Tick Mark promotes exercising objectivity and evaluating pros and cons before making decisions. Principle 3: Green and Blue focuses on different types of environmental sustainability. Principle 4: The Changing and the Unchanged addresses the "paradox of change and constancy." Finally, Principle 5: Give, in Order to Get promotes lifelong learning and ongoing skill development and working toward a collective good.

It is interesting to note that some approaches which in the literature appear to be unique to a non-Western country, when investigated further, have their roots in Western practices. For example, in South Africa, Diale and Fritz (2007) adapted Cajete's (2000) model highlighting the importance of storytelling, rituals, and mentoring, in the learning and development of indigenous people. In Singapore, Torres-Rivera, Nash, Sew, and Ibraim (2008) used an American model as their foundation for describing the developing school counseling profession. Clearly, international models need applicability across cultures. Through conferences and publications, ideas can be shared and adapted for local use, just as the JIVA model served as a foundation for a vibrant international IAEVG conference in Bangalore, India, in 2010.

Discussion

We have outlined some of the main issues that need to be addressed in any professional standards initiative and described in more detail two different examples. At the time of writing, there are several national and international systems in place. In Australia, Canada, and the United States, national competency frameworks have been developed. The GCDF and the EVGP are two international initiatives. In Europe, there is some interest in developing a system for EU countries (see Evangelista, 2011) and some countries are also exploring their own systems. With so many systems already developed, there is little need for individual countries or professional associations to begin from scratch to develop their own system. Most of the competency frameworks that exist are in the public domain and therefore it is possible to incorporate work already completed and tailor it as necessary to new situations.

Relevance for Multiple Cultures

Training programs exist in other countries, and there is lots of literature describing the history of guidance and counseling in different countries (e.g., Chang, 2002; Pope, Musa, Singaravelu,

Bringaze, & Russell, 2002; Tatsuno, 2002). Also, there is growing interest in establishing professional associations for career guidance, as witnessed by recent developments in India (in 2010) and South Africa (in 2011). An inaugural meeting of the Asia Pacific Career Development Association took place during the NCDA Conference held in Atlanta, Georgia, in July 2012. At this meeting the intent was to adopt bylaws, elect officers, and officially commence the association. However, in spite of growing interest in forming professional associations, and abundant descriptive information on the practice of career guidance and counseling in many countries, there are only a few examples (and those are from the so-called developed countries) of initiatives focused on creating standards for practice or formal ways to acknowledge the professional competence of those who deliver career services.

For those wishing to develop professional standards for practice, it is useful to draw upon work that has already been completed in other countries. Most areas of competency likely will be quite similar across countries; however, the content of a competency area likely will be different from one country to another. For example, all countries likely will have a competency area related to knowledge of government regulations; however, the specific relevant government regulations likely will be different for different countries. In a similar vein, most countries likely will have a competency area dealing with the involvement of third party stakeholders. In collectivist cultures, career counselors will need to have competencies in addressing and integrating the role of the family in career decision-making. Thus, the structure of a competency framework might be quite transportable from the existing frameworks that already have been developed. However the specific components within the competency areas likely will need to be tailored to the particular country in question.

Charting New Directions

Our focus in this chapter has been on using an inclusive approach to creating competency frameworks. We think that it is important to develop a system that can embrace all career service providers: those whose main work roles involve career guidance as well as those who do career guidance as only a part of their main work roles. Thus, even though good communication skills, for example, are part of the knowledge and skill sets for many occupational groups, they are important also for career practitioners and therefore should be included in a competency framework. We think also that because different clients have different needs, agencies that provide comprehensive services will need a variety of different service providers to meet the broad range of client needs. The different types of services are best conceptualized as somewhat overlapping circles, not different points on a single continuum. The different services may be best provided by a range of practitioners having a range of competencies. Certainly all service providers regardless of their work roles will require some basic set of competencies (e.g., good communication skills, knowledge of career development theories, knowledge of the labor market, and awareness of the boundaries of their own expertise and that of their colleagues). However, career librarians will need specialized training in information management, beyond that required of placement officers or teachers doing career education. Similarly, practitioners doing mainly group career guidance will need specialized competencies that are not necessarily part of the competency set for those who do primarily individual career counseling. Some practitioners may have extensive training and be able to fulfill many different roles, while the training of others may be narrower, equipping them for only one or two areas of specialization. We suggest that it is most useful to avoid thinking in a hierarchical manner, for someone who specializes in information management or labor market analysis is equally as important to providing comprehensive services as a career guidance workshop facilitator or a career counselor. Thus, we advocate embracing the notion that different clients have different needs and therefore require different types of services, offered by people with different sets of competencies, obtained through different types of training, not more or less of the same type of training.

To summarize, when creating a competency framework we think it is important to adopt a philosophical position that includes all the competencies needed to provide comprehensive career guidance services. Many services can be adequately met by providers with only some of the competencies; therefore, not all service providers need all the competencies. There is a basic set of entry level competencies that will be required by all practitioners regardless of their areas of specialization, and some competencies will require more extensive or more intense training than others. However, it is important to build a comprehensive framework that can cover all of the areas of practice involved in providing comprehensive career guidance services.

On a related note, and keeping in mind that career services are provided by people from different professional backgrounds and different types of education and training, it will be important to establish a system for prior learning assessment and recognition (PLAR). Including some form of PLAR acknowledges that people become competent through a variety of pathways, including formal education, job shadowing, on-the-job training, and life experience. Therefore, some sort of PLAR assessment process needs to be part of any competency framework. It will be important also to build a system that requires practitioners to demonstrate their competence rather than merely document the training they have taken. This can be done in many ways, ranging from submitting videotapes of practitioner's work with clients, to supervisor confirmation that a practitioner has been observed demonstrating particular competencies at a satisfactory level of proficiency.

In addition to helping define the career guidance sector more explicitly, competency frameworks can be used in other creative ways. For example, one school board in Canada used the S&Gs to create an employee training program for in-service career counselors. The in-service program was instrumental in fostering a common vocabulary among career counselors, promoting sharing of knowledge and peer coaching, and creating an increased degree of uniformity in the quality of services being provided in different schools within the school district. Other Canadian school jurisdictions used the S&Gs to establish training benchmarks, determine gaps in their training programs for practitioners, and develop new curriculum to fill the gaps. In one university initiative, the S&Gs were used to develop a competency-based graduate-level counselor training program (see Collins & Hiebert, 2002). These types of field tests helped to increase practitioners' level of competence and also to develop curriculum for in-service and professional development. Other field tests involved professional associations and agencies delivering career services. Although these examples are drawn from a Canadian context, the nature of the challenges, benefits, and uses is quite applicable to career guidance professionals working in other countries.

At this point we want to insert one caution. The field of career guidance is evolving in response to the rapidly changing social, economic, and societal contexts in which people live today. Therefore, the competency frameworks for career guidance also need to be living documents, changing and developing to remain relevant to current societal conditions. For example, the Canadian Standards and Guidelines for Career Development Practitioners (S&Gs) were introduced in 2002, revised in 2004, and remained relatively unchanged for 7 years. However, recently, revisions have been made to the S&Gs to reflect more appropriately the current contexts in which career services are offered. There were three primary areas of focus for the revisions: updating the core competencies to better reflect the competencies needed to address (a) diversity and (b) the use of technology, and (c) clarifying the Career Counseling Area of Specialization to better address the differing work domains of career practitioners and career counselors. In the revised framework, career counselors are conceptualized as occupying the intersection between counselors broadly defined and career development practitioners. As such, career counselors are recognized to require all the *core* competencies of both a counselor and a career development practitioner, but perhaps not all of the *specialized* competencies of either profession. This is a relationship that fits well with a Canadian context, but other countries may have different issues to address and may go about resolving the issues in different ways.

Creating, validating, and maintaining professional standards is a demanding task but one that is important to engage in so that the degree of professionalization among practitioners who deliver career guidance services can continue to grow. Far too often there is acknowledgement of the importance of keeping the competency frameworks current and relevant, but the effort involved in creating the first edition is so great that it interferes with a process of regularly revisiting the competency framework to make sure it is still current and relevant. Thus it is important in the beginning to conceptualize a timeframe and a process for revisiting the competency framework and making sure it reflects the reality that practitioners face in the workplace. We suggest that every 3–5 years is a workable interval for reviewing competency frameworks and modifying them as necessary to reflect the current realities faced by service providers and service recipients. When this is done, the competency frameworks will continue to be a useful benchmark against which to measure the KSAs that practitioners need in order to be competent to provide quality services to clients.

Conclusions

In this chapter, we have outlined some of the main issues that need to be addressed in any professional standards initiative and described in more detail two different examples. At the time of writing, national competency frameworks have been developed in Australia, Canada, and the United States. The GCDF and the EVGP are two international initiatives. There is interest in developing a common system for EU countries (see Evangelista, 2011); however, some countries (e.g., Germany) are also developing the foundation to create their own systems (Fruebing, 2011). We encourage countries and professional associations who wish to develop their own system of professional standards to begin by consulting the work that has already been completed and adapting the existing frameworks to their own geographic, cultural, or professional contexts.

The complex and ever changing society in which people live today presents people with a wide variety of differing demands. Over time, some people develop the capability to deal with the multitude of demands they face; however, others require assistance in order to be able to clarify their personal and work-related priorities and create realistic and achievable career-life goals. When seeking assistance, it is reasonable for the general public to expect to be able to access educational and vocational guidance services from competent and recognized guidance professionals (Van Esbroeck, 2008). Competency frameworks are one way to specify the capabilities that are needed to produce competent career guidance professionals. Using a competency framework will help to define more clearly the various role descriptions involved in delivering quality career services, thereby offering some protection to the public, while at the same time raising the profile of the professionals involved in delivering career guidance services.

For practitioners who wish to self-assess their career guidance competencies, a sample checklist is provided in Appendix A, adapted from the self-assessment checklist used in the EVGP application process.

Appendix A: Sample Career Guidance Self-Assessment Checklist

For each competency listed below, please assess the degree to which you know, understand and are able to perform each competency. Please use a two-step process.

(A). decide on whether your knowledge, understanding, or ability to perform is acceptable or unacceptable, then

(B). assign the appropriate rating using the 5-point scale below:

(0) Negligible
(1) Inadequate, but almost OK
(2) Competent, but barely so
(3) Significant, between minimally competent and outstanding
(4) Outstanding.

Graphically, the scale looks like this: $\rightarrow$ $\rightarrow$ $\rightarrow$ $\rightarrow$ $\rightarrow$ $\rightarrow$ $\rightarrow$ $\rightarrow$

Core Competencies		Unacceptable		Acceptable		
		0	1	2	3	4
C1	Demonstrate appropriate ethical behavior and professional conduct in the fulfillment of roles and responsibilities	□	□	□	□	□
C2	Demonstrate advocacy and leadership in advancing clients learning, career development, and personal concerns	□	□	□	□	□
C3	Demonstrate awareness and appreciation of clients' cultural differences to interact effectively with all populations	□	□	□	□	□
C4	Integrate theory and research into practice in guidance, career development, counseling, and consultation	□	□	□	□	□
C5	Skills to design, implement, and evaluate guidance and counselling programs and interventions	□	□	□	□	□
C6	Demonstrate awareness of his/her own capacity and limitations	□	□	□	□	□
C7	Ability to communicate effectively with colleagues or clients, using the appropriate level of language	□	□	□	□	□

(continued)

C8	Knowledge of updated information on educational, training, employment trends, labor market, and social issues	□	□	□	□	□
C9	Social- and cross-cultural sensitiveness	□	□	□	□	□
C10	Skills to cooperate effectively in a team of professionals	□	□	□	□	□
C11	Demonstrate knowledge of lifelong career development process	□	□	□	□	□

Specialized Competencies

1.	Assessment					
1.1	Accurately and thoroughly conceptualize and diagnose clients' needs based on different assessment tools and techniques	□	□	□	□	□
1.2	Use the data derived from assessment appropriately and according to the situation	□	□	□	□	□
1.3	Identify situations requiring referral to specialized services	□	□	□	□	□
1.4	Facilitate effective referral by means of initiating contacts between referral sources and individuals	□	□	□	□	□
1.5	Maintain up-to-date listings of referral sources	□	□	□	□	□
1.6	Conduct a needs assessment of the clients' contexts	□	□	□	□	□
2.	Educational Guidance					
2.1	Demonstrate concern for students' potential and the skills to facilitate its achievement	□	□	□	□	□
2.2	Guide individuals and groups of students to develop educational plans	□	□	□	□	□
2.3	Assist students in their decision-making process	□	□	□	□	□
2.4	Assist students to improve their self-awareness	□	□	□	□	□
2.5	Assist students in their course selection	□	□	□	□	□
2.6	Assist students to overcome learning difficulties	□	□	□	□	□
2.7	Motivate and help students to take part in international exchange programs	□	□	□	□	□
2.8	Consult with parents on their children's educational progress and development	□	□	□	□	□
2.9	Assist teachers to improve teaching methodologies	□	□	□	□	□
2.10	Assist teachers to implement guidance within the curriculum	□	□	□	□	□
3.	Career Development					
3.1	Knowledge of career developmental issues and the dynamics of vocational behavior	□	□	□	□	□
3.2	Demonstrate knowledge of pertinent legal factors and their implications for career development	□	□	□	□	□
3.3	Plan, design, and implement lifelong career development programs and interventions	□	□	□	□	□
3.4	Knowledge of decision-making and transition models to prepare and plan for transitional stages: School to work transition, Career shifts, Retirement, Job dismissing, Downsizing.	□	□	□	□	□

(continued)

3.5	Identify influencing factors (family, friends, educational and financial opportunities) and biased attitudes (that stereotype others by gender, race, age, and culture) in career decision-making	☐	☐	☐	☐	☐
3.6	Assist individuals in setting goals, identifying strategies to reach them, and continually reassess their goals, values, interest, and career decisions	☐	☐	☐	☐	☐
3.7	Knowledge of state and local referral services or agencies for job, financial, social, and personal issues	☐	☐	☐	☐	☐
3.8	Knowledge of career planning materials and computer-based career information systems, the Internet, and other online resources	☐	☐	☐	☐	☐
3.9	Skills to use these career development resources and techniques appropriately	☐	☐	☐	☐	☐
3.10	Skills to use career development resources designed to meet the needs of specific groups (migrants, ethnic groups. and at-risk populations)	☐	☐	☐	☐	☐
3.11	Help clients to build their career and life project	☐	☐	☐	☐	☐
4.	Counseling					
4.1	Understand the main factors related to the personal development of clients and the dynamics of their individual behavior	☐	☐	☐	☐	☐
4.2	Demonstrate empathy, respect, and a constructive relationship with the client	☐	☐	☐	☐	☐
4.3	Use individual counseling techniques	☐	☐	☐	☐	☐
4.4	Use group counseling techniques	☐	☐	☐	☐	☐
4.5	Address the needs of at-risk students	☐	☐	☐	☐	☐
4.6	Assist clients in:	☐	☐	☐	☐	☐
	4.6.1. Prevention of personal problems	☐	☐	☐	☐	☐
	4.6.2. Personality development	☐	☐	☐	☐	☐
	4.6.3. Personal problem solving	☐	☐	☐	☐	☐
	4.6.4. Decision making	☐	☐	☐	☐	☐
	4.6.5. Sexual identity	☐	☐	☐	☐	☐
	4.6.6. Social skills	☐	☐	☐	☐	☐
	4.6.7. Health education					
	4.6.8. Use of leisure time					
4.7	Help clients to develop a personal life plan	☐	☐	☐	☐	☐
4.8	Detection and referral of cases to other specialized services	☐	☐	☐	☐	☐
5.	Information Management					
5.1	Knowledge of legislation, pertaining to education, training, and work at local, national, and international level	☐	☐	☐	☐	☐
5.2	Knowledge of equivalence of degrees and professional qualifications obtained in different countries	☐	☐	☐	☐	☐
5.3	Collect, organize, disseminate, and provide up-to-date career, educational, and personal/social information on:					

(continued)

	5.3.1. Education and training		☐	☐	☐	☐	☐
	5.3.2. Occupational information		☐	☐	☐	☐	☐
	5.3.3. Employment opportunities		☐	☐	☐	☐	☐
	5.3.4. Others (Health, Leisure…)						
5.4	Use Information Technologies to provide educational and occupational information (Data-bases, Computer-based educational and career guidance programs, and the Internet)		☐	☐	☐	☐	☐
5.5	Assist clients to access and use educational and occupational information in a meaningful way		☐	☐	☐	☐	☐
6.	Consultation and Coordination						
6.1	Consult with parents, teachers, tutors, social workers, administrators, and other agents to enhance their work with students		☐	☐	☐	☐	☐
6.2	Demonstrate interpersonal skills needed to create and maintain consultation relationships, goals, and desired behavior change		☐	☐	☐	☐	☐
6.3	Demonstrate skills in working with organizations (universities, business, municipalities, and other institutions)		☐	☐	☐	☐	☐
6.4	Interpret and explain concepts and new information effectively		☐	☐	☐	☐	☐
6.5	Coordinate school and community personnel to bring together resources for students		☐	☐	☐	☐	☐
6.6	Use an effective referral process for assisting students and others to use special programs, services, and networks		☐	☐	☐	☐	☐
6.7	Skills to coordinate and stimulate the student's creativity to build their own programs (studies and work)		☐	☐	☐	☐	☐
6.8	Skills to build up a good image as a professional		☐	☐	☐	☐	☐
7.	Research and Evaluation						
7.1	Knowledge of research methodologies, data gathering, and analysis techniques.		☐	☐	☐	☐	☐
7.2	Promote research projects in relation to guidance and counseling		☐	☐	☐	☐	☐
7.3	Use presentation methods to report the outcomes of the research		☐	☐	☐	☐	☐
7.4	Interpret the results of this research		☐	☐	☐	☐	☐
7.5	Integrate the results of this research into the guidance and counseling practice		☐	☐	☐	☐	☐
7.6	Evaluate guidance programs and interventions, applying up-to date techniques and program evaluation models		☐	☐	☐	☐	☐
7.7	Keep up-to date with current research findings		☐	☐	☐	☐	☐
8.	Program/Service Management						
8.1	Identify target populations		☐	☐	☐	☐	☐
8.2	Conduct needs assessment		☐	☐	☐	☐	☐
8.3	Inventory resources relevant to program planning and implementation		☐	☐	☐	☐	☐
8.4	Knowledge about relevant current literature, trends, and issues		☐	☐	☐	☐	☐

(continued)

8.5	Promote community awareness of the programs and services	☐	☐	☐	☐	☐
8.6	Manage (design, implement, supervise) programs and interventions	☐	☐	☐	☐	☐
8.7	Evaluate effectiveness of the interventions	☐	☐	☐	☐	☐
8.8	Use results to effect program enhancement by recommending institutional/agency improvements	☐	☐	☐	☐	☐
8.9	Skills to organize and manage the educational, counseling, guidance, and placement services	☐	☐	☐	☐	☐
8.10	Manage and supervise personnel	☐	☐	☐	☐	☐
8.11	Promote staff development	☐	☐	☐	☐	☐
9.	Community Capacity Building					
9.1	Skills to develop relationships with key community partners	☐	☐	☐	☐	☐
9.2	Conduct analysis of human and material resources	☐	☐	☐	☐	☐
9.3	Conduct needs assessment of the community	☐	☐	☐	☐	☐
9.4	Work with the community to effectively use these resources to meet their needs	☐	☐	☐	☐	☐
9.5	Work with community to develop, implement, and evaluate action plans to address economic, social, educational, and employment goals	☐	☐	☐	☐	☐
9.6	Work with local, national, and international resource networks for educational and vocational guidance (e.g. IAEVG)	☐	☐	☐	☐	☐
10.	Placement					
10.1	Coach clients in work search strategies	☐	☐	☐	☐	☐
10.2	Use of the Internet in the job search process	☐	☐	☐	☐	☐
10.3	Present work opportunities to clients and facilitate their appropriate job selection	☐	☐	☐	☐	☐
10.4	Liaise with employers and with education and training providers to obtain information on the opportunities they offer	☐	☐	☐	☐	☐
10.5	Consult with policymakers	☐	☐	☐	☐	☐
10.6	Follow-up on placement suggestions	☐	☐	☐	☐	☐
10.7	Match individuals to particular vacancies in employment, education, or training	☐	☐	☐	☐	☐
10.8	Support clients with employment maintenance	☐	☐	☐	☐	☐

References

Arthur, N. (2008). Qualification standards for career practitioners. In J. A. Athanasou & R. Van Esbroeck (Eds.), *International handbook of career guidance* (pp. 303–323). Dordrecht, The Netherlands: Springer. doi: 10.1007/978-1-4020-6230-8_15

Borgen, W. A., & Hiebert, B. (2002). Understanding the context of technical and vocational education and training. In B. Hiebert & W. A. Borgen (Eds.), *Technical and vocational education and training in the twenty-first century: New roles and challenges for guidance and counselling* (pp. 13–26). Paris, France: United Nations Educational Scientific and Cultural Organization.

Brawley, K. T. (2009, November). *Solution for success: Working ahead, moving forward.* Paper presented at the IAEVG Conference, Wellington, New Zealand.

Cajete, G. (2000). *Native science: Natural laws of interdependence.* Santa Fe, NM: Clear Light.

Canadian Standards and Guidelines for Career Development Practitioners [S&Gs]. (2004). *The history of the*

S&Gs. Ottawa, ON, Canada: Author. Retrieved from http://career-dev-guidelines.org/career_dev/index.php/a-living-document/history-of-the-initiative

Canadian Standards and Guidelines for Career Development Practitioners [S&Gs]. (2011). *Defining the competencies career development practitioners need in order to practice effectively and ethically*. Ottawa, ON, Canada: Author. Retrieved from http://career-dev-guidelines.org/career_dev/

CEDEFOP [European Centre for the Development of Vocational Training]. (2007). *Presentation of CEDEFOP manuscripts for publication in English*. Thessaloniki, Greece: Author. Retrieved from http://www.cedefop.europa.eu/EN/Files/3020-att4-1-style_manual.pdf#

Chang, D. H. F. (2002). The, past, present and future of career counselling in Taiwan. *Career Development Quarterly, 50*, 218–225.

CICA [Career Industry Council of Australia]. (2006). *Professional standards for Australian career development practitioners*. Hawthorne, VIC, Australia: Author. Retrieved from http://www.cica.org.au/practitioners/standards

Clawson, T., & Shafer, S. P. (2002, Winter). Expansion of the global career development facilitator (GCDF) credential in Japan. *The GCDF Connection: The Global Career Development Facilitator Newsletter*. Retrieved from http://www.cce-global.org/Downloads/Archive/gcdfnewsletterwinter02.pdf

Collins, S., & Hiebert, B. (2002). Developing a competency framework for career counsellor training. In H. Suzin (Ed.), *Natcon papers 2002*. Toronto, ON, Canada: Career Centre, University of Toronto. Retrieved from http://www.contactpoint.ca/resources/natcon-conat/2002/foreword.shtml

Council for the Accreditation of Counseling and Related Educational Programs [CACREP]. (2001). *CACREP accreditation manual*. Alexandria, VA: Author. Retrieved from http://www.cacrep.org/2001standards.html

Diale, B., & Fritz, E. (2007). Indigenous knowledge and learning development. In N. Duncan, B. Bowman, A. Naidoo, J. Pillay, & V. Roos (Eds.), *Community psychology: Analysis, context and action*. Cape Town, South Africa: UCT Press.

Evangelista, L. (2011). *Study on existing frameworks to validate competence of career guidance practitioners*. Brussels, Belgium: European Commission. Retrieved from http://www.improveguidance.eu/sites/default/files/Issues-08082011.pdf

Fruebing, J. (2011, October). *Developing quality in career guidance: The German approach*. Paper presented at the IAEVG Conference, Cape Town, South Africa. Retrieved from http://www.apollo.co.za/pace/conference/

Furbish, D., Neault, R. A., & Pickerell, D. (2009). The global career development facilitator credential: An international perspective. *Journal of Employment Counseling, 46*, 187–189.

Hiebert, B. (2008). International competencies for educational and vocational guidance practitioners: Implications for professional practice. *International Journal for Educational and Vocational Guidance, 8*, 176–181.

Hiebert, B. (2009). Raising the profile of career guidance: Educational and vocational guidance practitioner. *International Journal for Educational and Vocational Guidance, 9*, 3–14. doi:10.1007/s10775-008-9152-x.

Niles, S. G., & Karajic, A. (2008). Training career practitioners in the 21st century. In J. A. Athanasou & R. Van Esbroeck (Eds.), *International handbook of career guidance* (pp. 355–372). Dordrecht, The Netherlands: Springer. doi: 10.1007/978-1-4020-6230-8_18

Pope, M., Musa, M., Singaravelu, H., Bringaze, T., & Russell, M. (2002). From colonialism to ultranationalism: History and development of career counselling in Malaysia. *Career Development Quarterly, 50*, 264–276.

Psifidou, I. (2010a). *Bridging knowledge with skills and competences in school curricula: Evidence from policies and practices in nine European countries* (Background paper for the CEDEFOP Second Annual Workshop on Curriculum Innovation and Reform, Thessaloniki, Greece, January 2011). Retrieved from http://events.cedefop.europa.eu/curriculum-innovation-2011/images/stories/files/Irene%20Psifidou_WCCES_June%202010a.pdf

Psifidou, I. (2010b). *Empowering teachers to focus on the learner: The role of learning outcomes in curricula* (Background paper for the CEDEFOP Second Annual Workshop on Curriculum Innovation and Reform, Thessaloniki, Greece, January 2011). Retrieved from http://events.cedefop.europa.eu/curriculum-innovation-2011/images/stories/files/Irene%20Psifidou_WCCES_June%202010b.pdf

Repetto, E. (2008). International competencies for educational and vocational guidance practitioners: An IAEVG trans-national study. *International Journal for Educational and Vocational Guidance, 9*, 135–195. doi:10.1007/s10775-008-9144-x.

Sultana, R. G. (2009). Competence and competence frameworks in career guidance: Complex and contested concepts. *International Journal for Educational and Vocational Guidance, 9*, 15–30. doi:10.1007/s10775-008-9148-6.

Tatsuno, R. (2002). Career counselling in Japan: Today and the future. *Career Development Quarterly, 50*, 211–217.

The Promise Foundation. (2009). *The Jiva framework for career counselling*. Retrieved from http://www.jivacareer.org/project/page/jiva-framework.html

Torres-Rivera, E., Nash, S., Sew, C. W. B., & Ibraim, S. B. (2008). Training school counselors in Singapore: First impressions of a multicultural challenge. *Journal of Counseling and Development, 86*, 219–223.

Van Esbroeck, R. (1997). A holistic model for career guidance. *Revista de Orientación y Psicopedagogia, 8*(13), 5–13.

Van Esbroeck, R. (2002). Career guidance and counselling for lifelong learning in a global economy. In B. Hiebert & W. A. Borgen (Eds.), *Technical and vocational education and training in the twenty-first century: New roles and challenges for guidance and counselling* (pp. 49–66). Paris, France: UNESCO.

Van Esbroeck, R. (2008). Editorial. *International Journal for Educational and Vocational Guidance, 8,* 133–134. doi:10.1007/s10775-008-9145-9.

William Borgen and Bryan Hiebert

Introduction

The context in which career development is conducted today is radically different than it was in 1911 when Frank Parsons began his work with youth in the United States. A leading indicator of this shift in context is the fact that we live in a time of unprecedented social, economic, and technological change. One occupation for life is no longer the norm in many countries. Instead, in a sense, we are preparing students for jobs that do not yet exist, using technologies that have not yet been invented, in order to solve problems that have not yet been defined (Arzuaga, de Tezanos, & Arzuaga, n.d.). How are young people in North America reacting to this changing world? Studies done with Canadian adolescents (Borgen & Hiebert, 2006; Hiebert, Kemeny, & Kurchak, 1998; Magnusson & Bernes, 2002; Posterski & Bibby, 1988) have found that the most frequent and intense worry of adolescents is "What do I do after high school?" This is a career–life planning concern and the aspirations of these students are not realistic (see Fig. 40.1). For example, in Canada, 80 % of grade 10 students plan to attend university, or some other formal post-secondary

education, and their parents expect that also (Collins & Hiebert, 1995). This expectation is impossible to meet, because there is not enough space in post-secondary institutions to accommodate that many students. Furthermore, only 30–40 % of students expect to leave high school and go directly into the labor force. In reality, about one-third of students attend some form of formal post-secondary education and two-thirds move from high school directly into the labor force. Of those who do attend post-secondary education, only about half of them complete the programs they begin. The rest change majors or drop out, moving directly into the labor force. The number one reason that students report for changing programs or dropping out is "lack of fit," that is, they do not see the relevance of the programs they are taking (Lambert, Zeman, Allen, & Bussiere, 2004). The question arises: How well is the majority being served?

The International Research Seminar, the research arm of the International Association for Counselling (IAC), facilitated two foundational multinational studies that focused on issues identified by adolescents from different countries, along with the coping strategies they used to address these issues, who they sought for help, and the characteristics of effective helpers from an adolescent point of view (Gibson-Cline, 1996, 2000). The first study involved more than 5,000 young people from 13 countries between 13 and 15 years of age (Gibson-Cline, 1996). These young people were from Australia, Brazil, China, Greece, India, Israel, Kuwait, Netherlands, Philippines, Russia, Turkey,

W. Borgen (✉)
Department of Educational and Counselling Psychology,
and Special Education, University of British Columbia,
Vancouver, BC, Canada
e-mail: william.borgen@ubc.ca

G. Arulmani et al. (eds.), *Handbook of Career Development*, International and Cultural Psychology,
DOI 10.1007/978-1-4614-9460-7_40, © Springer Science+Business Media, LLC 2014

What is Career-Life Planning?

Career planning and life planning are inseparably linked. We refer to career development as the lifelong process of managing learning, work, and transitions in order to move toward a personally determined and evolving preferred future. Thus, an individual's career vision is an integral part of his or her life vision. The guiding question in career-life planning is: "What sort of a person do I want to become?" When there is clarity on the answer to that question, a person can plan their educational and informal learning experiences, their volunteer and paid work experiences, their choice of leisure activities, choice of friends and acquaintances around becoming the type of person they want to become.

Fig. 40.1 A contemporary conceptualization of career–life planning

the United States, and Venezuela. The second study (Gibson-Cline, 2000) again involved over 5,000 young people. Their ages ranged from 18 to 20 years and they were from Brazil, China, Canada, England, Ethiopia, Greece, India, Israel, Japan, the Philippines, the United States, and Venezuela.

The research explored differences between male and female adolescents from advantaged, non-advantaged, and poverty subgroups. At the time the research was conducted, the research team agreed that the important variables related to socioeconomic status (SES) that existed for all participating countries included education and career expectations, type and location of residences and employment, and income. For each country, participants who were above the mean on these variables were placed in the *advantaged* group while participants who were below the mean on these variables were placed in the *non-advantaged* group. Participants in the *poverty* group were not only below the means of their countries, but did not always meet their basic needs. This categorization system permitted comparison across countries, in the absence of internationally validated standardized scales related to SES (Gibson-Cline, 2000, pp. 9–10).

The predominating concerns reported by young people centered around schooling, identity and self-concept, family issues, and employment. Students in the advantaged groups expressed worries about time pressures, academic achievement, and the need for high grades.

Non-advantaged students were concerned that their jobs interfered with their ability to learn at school. Those living in poverty were less concerned about schooling and more concerned with meeting basic needs, helping family members with issues and problems, and personal challenges related to gaining employment, self-identity, and schooling. Identity and self-concept were concerns for both advantaged and non-advantaged students. Specific issues were related to career choice, gender roles, educational choices, and becoming financially independent. Similar to the results regarding schooling, those living in poverty raised identity and self-concept issues less frequently and were more concerned with meeting basic needs and with family issues. Family issues were most prevalent for adolescents living in poverty. Family issues also were more prominent for young women, even though the specific nature of the issue varied across cultures (i.e., India—arranged marriages; Brazil—extended family responsibility; England—divorce and familial dysfunction). Furthermore, family issues decreased in importance as SES increased. Employment and family issues were often intertwined. Employment issues were prevalent for both genders. Adolescents from advantaged and non-advantaged groups tended to focus on concerns related to attaining desired educational experiences and occupations. Employment concerns were more frequent among those living in poverty, especially in the area of gaining some type of employment. It is interesting to note that, generally speaking, young people did not talk about major problems like AIDS and drugs as personal concerns. These problems were viewed as social issues.

The most frequently used coping strategy by all socioeconomic groups and both genders was individual goal-oriented problem solving, which included assessing the situation and planning for action. Other coping strategies were disengagement and resignation regarding problems encountered, avoiding addressing a problem, distancing themselves from their problems physically or mentally, or complete resignation and giving up (a non-goal-oriented approach). In these studies, adolescents in the advantaged group used this non-goal-oriented approach more often than their peers. Other strategies also reported were trying harder and seeking assistance (reported by young women more often than young men).

Young people in these studies sought help with their personal concerns outside the family three times more often than inside. Friends were the number one source of help for all groups. Advantaged young people sought professional help more often than their other age peers. Adolescents from both advantaged and non-advantaged groups looked for helpers who were good listeners, trustworthy, and honest. They also wanted helpers who had knowledge about the issues being discussed, and who were similar to them, or who had had experiences similar to theirs. As the seriousness of the problems increased, the focus on advice and guidance decreased and the focus on support and counseling increased.

The results of these two studies suggest that young people have concerns about a range of life issues which they are trying to deal with as best they can. Some people have learned to be flexible and are able to adjust to the constantly changing world in which they live, but many are having difficulty. The Gibson-Cline studies also illustrate that the role of guidance and counseling in helping young people adapt to new and changing environments is critical, not just in the area of careers, but in all facets of living. It is clear that, given the escalating rates of economic and social change evident in most parts of the world, the need for lifelong guidance and life-wide guidance is more important today than it ever has been in the past. In the guidance field, there is a need to attract the young and the brightest to see professional guidance as a challenging but very rewarding career path that helps others understand, and deal successfully with, their constantly changing world.

Van Esbroeck (2002) has argued that lifelong guidance and counseling are needed to support lifelong learning in a global economy. He has suggested that to support and sustain focus in a lifelong learning process, adequate lifelong career guidance and counseling will be needed (i.e., that guidance and counseling must be continuously accessible to accompany people on their journey though life). Furthermore, he advocates adopting a holistic approach, based on the realization that people's learning experiences and career choices do not occur in isolation from other aspects of people's lives (i.e., the personal, social, economic, and cultural realities that people face). We adopt the term *life-wide guidance* to refer to such a holistic approach. Life-wide guidance takes place across the full range of life activities (personal, social, professional, etc.) and at any stage in a person's life.

Context

The accelerating rate of unpredictable change in the nature of occupations and in the social and cultural contexts in which people live has had a major influence on how occupational/vocational/career development is viewed. Over the past decade, our work with the IAC (Borgen) and International Association for Educational and Vocational Guidance (IAEVG, Hiebert) has brought us face-to-face with a broad range of ways that people consider occupational and career options and the challenging contexts in which they are required to make career and life decisions. For example, conferences and other professional development initiatives in Greece, India, Kenya, New Zealand, Oman, Switzerland, Jamaica, Bhutan, Argentina, and Australia have illustrated that even though these countries vary considerably in their economic development, all were challenged to address the career-related needs of young people and adults within the context of rapidly evolving economic, cultural, and social conditions. The differences across these countries have often been related to the infrastructures and resources available. In North America and Europe, professional services developed over time when traditional methods of assistance from family and community members became unavailable due to migration of people away from their traditional home centers. In developing countries, this process has been occurring more recently and this has created a vacuum in assistance available to people. Also, generally speaking there is increased awareness in countries that do not have a tradition of professional career-related guidance and counseling services, that, in addition to the scarcity of resources and policies needed to create professional services, approaches centered on Western European and North American models are limited in their effectiveness for addressing issues in broader cultural contexts. That said, there also is recognition of the importance of the need to enact far-reaching culturally relevant changes in the education and other community-based systems, including the development of guidance and counseling programs; especially mobilizing those initiatives that take into account the current context of rapid economic, social, and cultural change to better position young people to make effective career/life decisions. Seeing as when these services were created in North America and Europe, the aim was to assist individuals and also to reduce strife and violence in the broader society that is bred by the frustration of people not being able to meet their basic career-related needs.

Changing Assumptions in Career–Life Planning

In planning a new approach to anything, it is important to be aware of key assumptions underlying traditional approaches. In the fields of vocational guidance and vocational psychology, key traditional assumptions include the following (Borgen & Hiebert, 2006):

- There are individual attributes or traits that draw people to certain occupations and these are pivotal to effective occupational, vocational, and career-related decision-making.
- Occupations that match the vocational interest of individuals are accessible to them.
- The qualifications required to be successful in an occupation are stable enough that assessment instruments for matching individual traits with occupational requirements are valid over time: There is little need to update the assessment results.
- Once desired occupations are secured, individuals have the capability to stay involved in them.

These assumptions led to a greater interest in occupational entry than in the ongoing adjustment of individuals to the workforce. They also spawned the belief that if things did not work out, it was as a result of a bad match or some type of problematic situation located within the individual. However, these assumptions are being questioned in research and theory development that considers the influence of labor market and social forces on the career-related choices of individuals.

Countries in Asia, Africa, the Middle East, South America, North America, and Europe are experiencing rapidly changing economic, social, and cultural influences that suggest that a revised set of assumptions regarding occupational, vocational, and career decision-making processes is warranted (Borgen & Hiebert, 2006). The new assumptions include:

- Several factors influence choice of occupations or career paths, including individual attributes or traits; family perspectives; rapidly evolving societal influences such as poverty, addiction, conflict, displacement, and discrimination; along with internationalization, and rapid change in labor market opportunities.
- These factors are differentially important within and across cultural contexts, and in economically developed and developing nations.
- Occupations of choice may not be accessible.

For Hoyt (1991), jobs consist of activities for which a person gets paid, either with cash or by barter. Occupations consist of a cluster of jobs related on some theme. A person can change jobs without changing occupations. Work consists of the activities in which a person engages, that require conscious effort and produce benefits to self and/or others. Work consists of the things a person derives satisfaction from, regardless of whether they are paid work or volunteer work. Work is not tied to paid employment, but to meaningful and satisfying activities. Some of the paid and volunteer activities a person undertakes are drudgery, that is, they are things in which a person finds little or no satisfaction and little sense of personal fulfillment. Career is the sum total of activities in which a person engages, that require conscious effort, and produce benefits to self and/or others, that is, the things from which a person derives satisfaction and a sense of fulfillment. In other words, career is the sum total of the work (paid and unpaid) that people engage in over their lifetime. Hoyt suggests that an important part of career planning involves seeking a job that is work, that is, something that is meaningful and personally satisfying and for which a person gets paid. Everyone has a career, even elementary school students.

Fig. 40.2 The relationship between common career-related terms

- Many tasks and processes related to occupations are unstable.
- People need the skills and attitudes required to successfully manage rapid and unpredictable changes that characterize many occupations and career trajectories.

The following example illustrates the overarching influence of cultural contexts on career–life decisions. In 2003 and 2008, we were invited by UNESCO to offer a training program for school and college personnel that would utilize career guidance and counseling concepts in Technical and Vocational Education and Training (TVET) Programs in Nigeria. Through offering this program, we became aware that one of the challenges faced in implementing a TVET program in that country was the expectation of parents for their children to enter professional rather than technical programs. This cultural norm was a major barrier to the success of TVET programs.

Lifelong Career Planning

In the last 20 years, the word *career* (rather than *vocational*) has been used more regularly within the context of counseling and guidance. This has expanded the focus to occupational and then to life decision-making over time. In this context, actualizing a vocational desire could happen within or outside of the context of paid employment (Hoyt, 1991) and through non-job-related activities such as hobbies or other life activities. This perspective has helped people take a longer life view and perhaps made them better able to cope with an unstable and rapidly changing workforce.

The work of several North American career theorists and researchers reflects the evolution of the concept of career since the mid-20th century. Super characterized career development as evolving over the life-span of an individual, with the multiple roles in which people are engaged all contributing to a person's career self-concept. When people are successful and satisfied with their careers, their view of self (self-concept) includes a sense of self-as-worker (career self-concept) (Super, 1963, 1987). Later, Hoyt (1991) differentiated between job, work, occupation, and career in terms of their activities, their influence over time, and the amount of personal satisfaction involved (see Fig. 40.2). Others began to recognize the influence of changing economic and social circumstances in career development and introduced concepts such as *positive uncertainty* (Gelatt, 1989) and *planned happenstance* (Mitchell, Levin, & Krumboltz, 1999). Positive uncertainty refers to a philosophy characterized by a realization that the future will be uncertain, accepting that reality, and looking for the opportunities that will arise when the future is uncertain and unpredictable. Planned happenstance involves positioning oneself to be able to take advantage of unexpected opportunities as they arise, so that many events, that seem to be accidental, are in fact the result of people doing things that put them in the right place at the right time. These developments illustrate that the concept of career is changing and suggest that a new focus for career planning is needed.

The High 5 + 1: A New Message for Young People

Taking all of the above into account, the question arises: How can practitioners convey these concepts to young people who are in the early stages of planning their careers? In the early 1990s, a think tank of leading Canadians in the career development field was convened to grapple with the answers to this question. The result was the High 5 + 1 key messages for youth regarding career–life planning. It provides an illustration of a career development approach that takes a lifelong career planning perspective that incorporates the contemporary perspectives we described (cf. Redekopp, Day, & Robb, 1995). This perspective also has been well received when presented in other countries where we have worked. This suggests that studies related to its use in a broader range of cultural settings may be warranted. It is summarized as follows:

1. *Change is constant.* From the evidence presented earlier in this chapter, it is apparent that in all countries, society is changing and the rate of change is accelerating. In some respects, the only thing that is not changing is the fact that everything is changing. Thus, workers need to be flexible and adaptable in order to be able to adjust to the rapid change that is taking place. It is important also to realize that people can influence the nature of change. Many events that seem to be accidents could have a large element of planned happenstance embedded in them. However, in order to influence the direction of change, it is necessary to take some risks

and be willing to engage in things where the outcome is uncertain. There also is a need to reflect on one's experience and to learn from it. A colleague once remarked that some people seem to have 10 years of experience, while others have 1 year of experience ten times. The first group learns from their experiences, while the second group repeats the same mistakes time and time again. Thus, while change is inevitable, constructive growth is optional. However, the bottom line message is that in a constantly changing world, people must be flexible and adaptable and realize that it is possible for them to influence the nature of the change.

2. *Focus on the journey.* Since change is happening so rapidly, the job we are preparing for today may not exist when the training is complete. Thinking of an occupational destination is a thing of the past. Not only can we influence the direction of the journey, we also can influence the nature of the journey. The degree of enjoyment in the journey is largely a function of a person's state of mind. When occupational destinations are uncertain, it is important to enjoy the journey.

3. *Follow your heart.* Passion drives the soul. People tend to strive for, and be motivated by, things in which they are interested. Many people who find their jobs a drudgery develop a new zest for living when they change jobs to something that is more in line with their passions. When the job market is strong, workers frequently make dramatic change in their mid-40s to pursue a dream job that they "always wanted to do." Students who are doing poorly in school often suddenly begin to succeed when they encounter a teacher who recognizes and helps them to follow their passion in a subject area. It is important for teachers, parents, and others involved with students, to help young people begin the process of integrating their developing career-related passions with short-term and longer-term career opportunities.

4. *Keep learning.* Lifelong learning is a priority in many countries and governments are

encouraging people to participate in lifelong learning opportunities. It is also true that people continue developing across their life-spans. The question is whether or not people are able to act intentionally to influence the direction of their development or leave it to chance. It is a matter not only of *if* people will keep learning but also of *what* they will continue to learn. It is important to help students understand that people continue to learn and change vocationally over their lifetimes and to be planful with their continuing learning.

5. *Access your allies.* It continues to be the case that personal contacts are the richest source of job leads. In some countries, job search trainers report that as many as 80 % of all jobs are filled through informal networks. Thus, it is important to view parents, relatives, neighbors, and others in one's personal network as sources of career education and potential job leads. It is important also to be allies for others and experience the richness that results from expanding personal networks. Personal networks are what keep our thinking straight (or not), keep us motivated, and help us grow.

6. *Believe in yourself.* Belief in self is one of the most important personal characteristics—it pervades everything that we do. If people do not believe in themselves, it will be hard to get others to believe in them. Everyone has many positive characteristics. Building a belief in self is largely a matter of focusing on the positives, rather than dwelling on the negatives. It is important to help students focus on their personal and vocationally related strengths, and highlight examples of success, in the face of the tendency to focus on deficits in times of change and uncertainty. At the bottom line, if you do not believe in yourself, others likely will not believe in you either.

Lifelong Guidance and Counseling

An area of great importance when considering guidance and counseling across the life-span is the concept of Education for All (EFA), across the life-span. EFA is a global movement led by UNESCO, aiming to meet the learning needs of all children and youth. It focuses on the importance of access to and viable participation in educational opportunities across ages, cultures, gender, socioeconomic levels, and abilities. For this to happen, lifelong learning must become a fundamental right to all (people of all ages and not just children and youth), in exactly the same way as basic education is a fundamental right to all. Achieving that goal requires going beyond resource availability, to address participation rates and education and training outcomes, especially where marginalized people are concerned. A meaningful lifelong learning program needs to tap into people's intrinsic motivation, so that it becomes self-driven by the creative imagination of the learner (Esbin, 2002) and offered in a context and time frame that fits the realities of the learner, especially when the learner belongs to a marginalized segment of society (Grierson, Schnurr, & Young, 2002).

Contemporary concepts of career guidance and counseling such as the High 5 + 1, developed in North America, suggest that in advocating the importance of EFA across the life-span, it is important to remember to avoid making the connection between education and job so ironclad that we cut people off from the wide range of opportunities and resources that may be available to them. EFA needs to be seen as giving people the equipment to make a journey on their own. By tying education too closely to a single job, we end up narrowing and restricting the purposes and benefits of education, and we may be setting up people for what they perceive as failure when, due to changes in labor market opportunities, the job they trained for is not available. When this situation occurs, it is important that people are able to review the skills and competencies resulting from their education and have the ability to consider the range of other occupations that may be open to them. This flexibility and adaptability is more likely to result from a lifelong learning context characterized by a holistic approach that prepares people for a range of possible job alternatives. If this happens rather than becoming overly tied to a single occupation, they may be more open to considering other possibilities. This will also likely reduce the time that they are without work. The main purpose of a lifelong learning focus is not to overcome problems, but to help individuals develop in a manner that allows them to respond effectively to changes and new developments (Van Esbroeck, 2002).

To be truly effective, lifelong learning requires lifelong career guidance and counseling services. This is clearly not the case at present. Even in countries that have a tradition of professional guidance and counseling service, career guidance and counseling are most often available for young people and those who are unemployed. In countries without this tradition, they may not be available at all or may be offered unevenly even to young people (Van Esbroeck, 2002). The consequences can often be seen in personal challenges and frustrations experienced by individuals and which sometimes also results in periods of social unrest. Lifelong guidance and counseling services will help ensure that a broader range of people will be able to recognize opportunities for themselves in a range of educational and training experiences, and be planful in orchestrating their lifelong learning experiences. It will also help them be welcomed as full participants in the educational programs they enter and be better able to utilize the education they receive. In order for this to happen, policymakers and practitioners need to work together to help motivate all citizens to participate in the process of lifelong learning and view as viable a wide range of educational and training opportunities, and the career paths resulting from them.

Roles for Service Providers

As indicated in the two multination studies reviewed at the beginning of this chapter, people seek assistance with career–life planning issues from a range of individuals known to them for a variety of reasons. It seems obvious that they select sources of help that they believe will meet their individual needs. In creating

professional services to augment traditional sources of assistance, it is important to keep these two foci—range of services and individualized services—in mind.

Advising

Some people need advice to address an immediate problem, often regarding where to find relevant information or how to use information. Advising involves providing general, "non-personalized" information regarding a particular topic; for example, describing different styles of résumés to a client, helping clients access career information, or making them aware of other career services that are available. This knowledge does not need a theoretical foundation in order to be credible. The integrity of the information is largely dependent on the reliability of the provider's knowledge and experience. For example, if someone requests information about entrance requirements for a college or university program, or training requirements for an occupation, they are provided with advice about what is expected.

Guidance

In other instances, people need guidance, which is more personalized service that is tailored to a client's unique needs and often is psycho-educational in nature. Guidance is broader in scope than advising and requires a service provider to first gather information about a client, often through an interview or other kind of assessment, and then to focus the services on meeting a client's particular needs. A practitioner explaining to clients how the results of an interest assessment might influence their occupational choices would be providing guidance, as would a teacher who provides psycho-educational instruction on appropriate job interviewing skills. The tailoring process in guidance increases the likelihood that services obtained are congruent with a client's unique needs and are offered within a holistic context.

Fig. 40.3 The overlapping functions of advising, guidance, and counseling

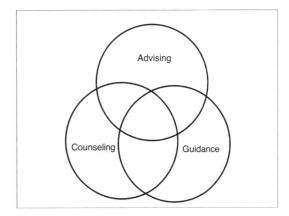

Counseling

Other clients need counseling, which is a more intense service designed to help clients explore, examine, and clarify their thoughts, feelings, beliefs, values, and behaviors to arrive at plans for action. Counseling typically addresses broader issues such as exploring how personal values impact career direction and work-adjustment, or examining the integration of work roles with other life roles that may or may not be directly related to work. The counseling process helps people consider the utility of different insights, feelings, and information, and the applicability of different possible actions regarding the issue. As Peruniak (2010) has suggested, career counselors help "those people who seek to sort out and act on the multifaceted roles or potential roles in their lives" (p. viii).

Different people, with different needs, require different types of services, from professionals with different types of education and training. Advising is most appropriate for people who are seeking information, know how to use the information when they find it, and are open to the advice they receive. Guidance can help people to consider their suitability for different career and educational opportunities, explore alternatives they may not have considered previously, and engage in appropriate decision-making about their future career–life path. Counseling is required in situations where people need to explore their attitudes related to career–life planning, their personal readiness to entertain various options, the cultural and societal contexts in which they operate, or the need to include others who may be important in the decision-making process for that person. In order to be able to meet the broad range of client needs, different types of services need to be offered, and agencies need practitioners that collectively have a broad range of competencies, keeping in mind that it is not necessary for each practitioner to be able to address all client needs. This situation is best visualized, not as a single continuum of services from less intensive to more intensive, but, as Fig. 40.3 illustrates, overlapping circles signifying services that are different in nature, designed to meet different client needs (see Borgen & Hiebert, 2002, 2006; Hiebert & Borgen, 2002 for elaboration of the multiple roles needed for comprehensive career services).

General Professional Development for Capacity Building in Career Development

In more developed and less developed countries alike, people's careers unfold over time. Careers are not the result of a single choice made at a single point in their lives. People's careers are the result of a series of events, some of them deliberate choices, some of them more circumstantial. Thus, a new metaphor is needed to depict how people's careers develop.

One particularly compelling metaphor is to talk about people's career paths. Career development is then seen as a journey along a path where

Fig. 40.4 Road map for
guidance and counseling
planning

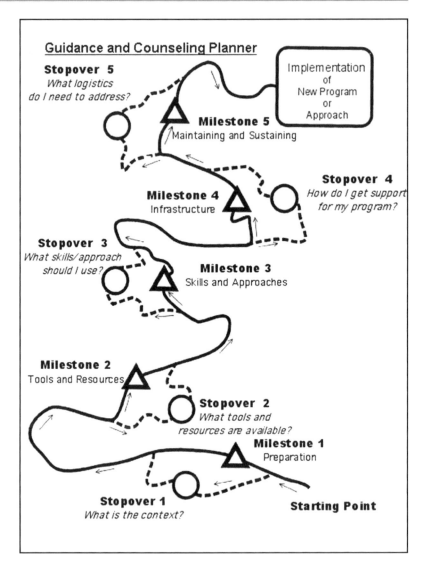

there may be several branching paths, milestone events along the way, and stopover points where a traveler gains new knowledge or skills. The general direction of the journey may be clear, but often the specific spot in the journey is not certain. Figure 40.4, adapted from a program titled "Starting Points" (Westwood, Amundson, & Borgen, 1994), illustrates this process. This figure has been used successfully in career development presentations and programs in Bahrain, Bhutan, Canada, Denmark, Hungary, India, Nigeria, the Philippines, and Sweden.

We see planning for the journey as having five main components or milestones: (a) preparation,

(b) tools and resources, (c) skills and approaches, (d) infrastructure, and (e) maintaining and sustaining the journey. At each milestone, the traveler may need to have a stopover, to provide time to stop and take stock, in some cases, to address certain barriers, in other cases to obtain information or skills in order to continue the journey. For example, to make sure the traveler is well-prepared, careful consideration should be paid to the context of the journey (i.e., the terrain, direction of the path, others involved with the journey, etc.). In obtaining the necessary tools and resources to make the journey successful, the traveler will need to know what tools and resources (e.g., road maps, places to eat, accommodation, alternative routes to a destination) are available for the type of journey being undertaken. In considering the career journey, accessing information needed to make informed decisions, and utilizing people in your network of contacts (including professional help, if available) to help you assess your career-related strengths and areas for improvements are both worthwhile stopover activities to consider as you move forward. In deciding what special skills might be required for the journey and how the journey should be approached, the traveler will need to have a process for determining which specific skills or approaches are best suited for the journey. The example in Fig. 40.4 represents the process used in the workshop we describe.

At any given milestone, some travelers may already possess the necessary knowledge, skills, and support required to continue successfully. However, others may need to stop over and gain additional knowledge, skills, and resources. In the career–life planning field there are abundant resources available, and many of these resources can be used at several different places in the planning process. Therefore, it is not appropriate to map a particular resource onto a specific place in the road map. However, the underlying message is that there are certain milestones that indicate progress and, at each milestone, some people may need to stop and access more resources in order to continue. For example, people who have a clear and explicit vision for their life and for the place of their career in their life may have the necessary requirements to reach Milestone 1 and progress onwards, towards Milestone 2. However, people who do not have a clear sense of what kind of person they want to become and the role of their career in their life may need a Stopover to access some standardized assessment inventories, or some self-assessment tools in order to gain the clarity needed to proceed towards Milestone 2. The appropriate resources could include inventories to clarify values, interests, and abilities. They may need also to clarify the external sources of influence in their career plans, such as peer pressure, parent expectations, family

obligations, and time constraints. A large part of reaching Milestone 1 is to have a clear sense of the context in which the career–life planning process is taking place. In a similar vein, people who have a well-developed awareness of labor market information (LMI) may pass Milestone 2 successfully and be ready to proceed to Milestone 3. However, others may need a Stopover to obtain coaching or instruction on what resources are available to assist them in their career–life planning. These resources could include inventories of values, interests, or abilities, or computerized programs such as Career Cruising or Kuder Journey: Career Assessment, Education and Career Planning. At Stopover 3, some people may find it useful to do some informational interviewing, to find out from people currently working in a particular field what skills and personal attributes are important to be successfully employed in that field. At Stopover 4, some people will need to find out what financial resources are available to support any further training they might need to take or they may need a third-party intervener to assist with getting family members to agree with the person's emerging career path. At Milestone 5, people typically will be employed, and their attention will need to be focused on job maintenance. This may involve for some people a stopover to develop interpersonal skills, mentoring to understand the nuances involved in being successful in the chosen field of employment. Thus, the resources needed will vary from one person to another, depending on the client's needs, and the constellation of client skills. These components are summarized in other documents (e.g., Hiebert, Borgen, & Schober, 2011) and elaborated in the following section of this chapter. They are introduced now so that readers may have an idea of what lies ahead and begin to think about career/life planning in a new way.

Introducing Guidance and Counseling Approaches to Service Providers

From our experience, a multilayered approach is most efficient in introducing guidance and counseling approaches that may be unfamiliar to people working in educational or community agency settings. A useful beginning point is to create an orientation workshop designed to use individual and group consultation to facilitate the use of advising, guidance, and counseling processes for helping adolescents and adults to consider a broad range of educational and career alternatives, and to make more informed decisions about those alternatives.

It is most effective if the orientation workshop is part of a larger initiative involving all potential stakeholders who are in a position to promote the use of counseling and guidance processes to assist young people and adults in making informed decisions that regard all legal potential career paths as legitimate and valued alternatives. A combination of individual and group consultations will need to be used with key individuals (e.g., ministry officials, community leaders, and people from relevant NGOs, policymakers, and service providers) to help them consider expanded and enhanced approaches for using guidance and counseling to assist young people and adults in considering a broader range of career-related alternatives. In-service training may be needed to help those already offering career guidance and counseling services to understand the new approach (i.e., the philosophical underpinnings, theoretical foundations, knowledge base, and expanded skillsets needed to operate effectively in the new approach). This encompassing approach has been effective in orienting professionals to similar programs in Canada (e.g., Borgen, 2000) and shows promise for success in other countries as well.

An Example from the Field

In 2003, we were invited by UNESCO to develop a training program for teachers, counselors, and administrators in public school and post-secondary education systems in Nigeria. This was conceived as an initial step towards implementing the expanded perspective on career–life planning underlying the career path metaphor, with a particular focus on the effective implementation of newly developed TVET programs.

In many countries, particularly in Europe, technical and vocational occupations have a long tradition and are well accepted. However, in other countries without this tradition such as Nigeria, there is a perceived bias that favors obtaining a university education and pursuing a career path in the so-called professions while jobs in the technical field and jobs labeled "vocational" go unfilled, or are filled by workers from other countries. TVET is often seen as a fallback plan rather than a first choice, even though in most countries, the number of jobs in TVET areas exceeds those in the professions.

In response to UNESCO's request, we developed a Career Guidance Orientation Workshop, a five-day interactive workshop, designed to help teachers and counselors work more effectively within their school and college communities. The primary components of this workshop are described below. The main goals of the workshop are to provide (a) a summary of foundational career development theory and contemporary approaches for implementing career guidance programs in educational settings, and (b) knowledge and skill practice in appropriate ways to teach others basic concepts that promote considering a broader range of educational and career alternatives and to make more informed decisions about those alternatives. Career development is portrayed as being centered on helping people create a vision for their life and then situating their education, training, and job search pursuits in a way that is consistent with their life-vision. Participants engage in an experiential learning approach to exploring their own career development as a means for understanding how to engage students in career exploration and career decision-making. Emphasis is placed on cultivating attitudes that are important for adopting a broad perspective on career–life planning, implementing the concepts and approaches covered in the workshop, and evaluating the effectiveness of these new approaches. Versions of this workshop have now been delivered in several countries (Nigeria,

Bahrain, and Bhutan) and the results have been uniformly positive. An example from our experiences in Nigeria is summarized below.

Workshop Objectives

Process Objectives
This aspect of the workshop focuses on making sure that the way in which the workshop is conducted provides a good example of the processes participants might use in their own follow-up activities. An experiential learning approach (rather than a seminar or lecture experience) is used, consisting of a mixture of oral presentations, individual reflection by participants, small-group discussions to help participants personalize the concepts, dyad or triad skill practice, and large-group discussions to generate ideas and promote participant engagement in the workshop. The focus on process permits the participants to operationalize career development concepts in a manner that addresses their own cultural uniqueness and the social and economic factors that operate in their countries.

Learning Outcome Objectives
The focus here is on the competencies (knowledge, skills, and personal attributes) that participants learn from participating in the workshop. These included the following: (a) developing an understanding of basic career development theory (i.e., that career development is a process, unfolding across time, not a destination towards which one is working in the future; what factors contribute to people's career development; the difference between advice, guidance, and counseling; and how each plays an equally important, but different, role in helping people be planful with their career paths); (b) learning the basic principles involved in group process and the principles involved in successfully facilitating groups; (c) developing basic facilitator skills used in career–life planning and the skills involved in teaching others how to do career–life planning; and (d) developing a framework for demonstrating the value of career–life planning and becoming aware of tools that can be used to demonstrate the value of career–life planning in TVET. (*Note*: Space limitations prevent us from providing a more detailed description of workshop; however, the complete workshop package is available from either of the authors upon request.)

Results

The results presented here are from one offering of the workshop in Nigeria. In this case, there were 28 participants, ranging in age from 35 to 60 years (4 were in their 30s, 14 were in their 40s, 9 were in their 50s, and 1 was 60). The participants came from a broad range of work settings: administrators, vocational counselors, lecturers, and coordinators from the national ministry. Their formal education spanned the range from master's degrees in guidance and counseling; to master's degrees in nonsocial science areas; to bachelor's degrees in physical sciences, guidance and counseling, engineering, or religious studies. Two participants had bachelor's degrees in guidance and counseling and six had master's degrees in guidance and counseling. The participants with degrees in guidance and counseling had some rudimentary awareness of career development concepts, but those with degrees in other areas had little awareness of career development theory or the factors affecting career choice. This diversity provided a broad cross section of perspectives on the workshop content. Generally speaking, participants were open to trying out new ideas, translating the new ideas into practice, and adapting them to their local context.

To evaluate the workshop we used an innovative approach developed by the Canadian Research Working Group (CRWG) on Evidence-Based Practice in Career Development. The approach has been described previously (Baudouin et al., 2007) and sample tools and resources are available on the CRWG web site http://www.crwg-gdrc.ca/index.html; therefore, it is summarized only briefly here. In evaluating participant learning we used a decision-making approach, in contrast to a judgment-making approach. First, a respondent

Post-Pre Assessment is different from traditional Pre-Post Assessment. In Pre-Post Assessment, the same evaluation instrument is administered at the beginning and again at the end of a program or workshop and participant ratings are subject to the shifting measuring stick based on their more complete understanding of the concept involved. In Post-Pre Assessment, the evaluation instrument is administered only at the end of a program or workshop. Participants are asked: "Knowing what you know now about X (e.g., career guidance), think back to your level of competence at the beginning of this workshop and rate yourself. Then think about where you are now and rate yourself." Post-Pre Assessment avoids the shifting measuring stick by asking participants to use the same measuring stick, "knowing what you know now about X…" See Hiebert (2012) for more detailed descriptions.

Fig. 40.5 Post–Pre Assessment: an approach to self-assessment

assesses the adequacy of the competency under consideration (*adequate* or *not adequate*). Second, a respondent assesses the level of competence within the first decision (*Really quite poor, Almost OK, Just barely OK, Really very good*, or *somewhere in between* [better than minimally acceptable, but not yet excellent]). The resulting scale differs from a typical Likert scale in that there is no midpoint, participants are forced to "get off the fence" by declaring whether the level of competence is adequate or not adequate, and the order of the responses is different, that is, is it *barely adequate* (=2), or *really very good* (=4), or *somewhere in between* (=3). For a complete explanation, see Hiebert (2012) or www.crwg-gdrc.ca/crwg/index.php/resources/evaluation.

We coupled the decision-making approach with a form of retrospective assessment called Post–Pre Assessment. One difficulty with using self-assessments to determine changes in skill or knowledge resulting from workshops or counseling interventions is that people do not know what they do not know. Thus, if people are asked to rate their communication skills (for example) at the beginning and the end of a workshop on interpersonal communication, they often think their communication skills are reasonably good and they rate themselves highly at the beginning. However, during the course, they develop greater understanding of interpersonal communication, and when they rate themselves at the end of the course the ratings are lower than they were at the beginning, even though they have learned a lot and have a more adequate level of skills. This is because their measuring stick has changed, as they developed greater knowledge about interpersonal communication. Post–Pre Assessment addresses this problem by asking participants only at the end of a course or program to use their current level of knowledge to assess their pre-course and post-course level of competence (see Fig. 40.5).

The evaluation results provide a convincing indication of the effectiveness of the workshop and are representative of the results that usually are obtained when this workshop is offered. The data not only demonstrate the effectiveness of the workshop, but also are an example of the rich data that can be obtained from this evaluation approach. About half of the participants indicated that prior to the workshop they had had an inadequate understanding of basic career development theory, knowledge of practical tools and approaches for facilitating career development, and knowledge of the factors that contribute to positive career development and the importance of career–life planning in TVET. All participants (100 %) indicated that their level of competence after the workshop was acceptable in all of the areas covered. Only 2 % of participants indicated that they had an excellent level of competence on one or more of the main learning objectives prior to the workshop, compared with 74 % at the completion of the workshop. The mean scores of the *Before Workshop* ratings on all items in the evaluation instrument were in the *Unacceptable* range, while the *After Workshop* ratings on all items had mean scores greater than *Minimally Acceptable*. Taken all together, the self-assessments indicated that participants experienced gains in competence as a result of their participation in this workshop.

Informal observations during the workshop clearly illustrated a substantial shift in the way participants thought about career, career development, career guidance, and career counseling. There was some variation in how useful participants found each of the workshop activities, which would be expected given the range of educational experiences and the variety of work roles of the participants. However, 88 % of participants gave ratings of 3 or 4 (on a scale ranging from 0 to 4) for the usefulness of *all* workshop activities. The usefulness of the workshop in general and the quality of the facilitation both had a mean score of 4. These types of positive ratings likely are the result of a good match between the content of the workshop, the style of facilitation, and the participants' willingness to explore new ways of thinking.

The responses to the open-ended questions on the evaluation form corroborated the questionnaire results and attested to the impact of the workshop on participants. Participants commented on the open and accepting relationship among workshop participants, plus the "cordial relationship between workshop members and facilitators," on the clear presentations that resulted in a more clear understanding of career concepts, and the many practical and interactive activities that helped to put theory into practice. Several participants commented on the broad impact of the workshop, using comments such as "The workshop is inspiring, which has equipped participants in all fields to operate in their various work places," and "The workshop has actually changed my total way of life. I was always casting my mind to my past way of life whenever the workshop was going on and thinking how I could be more effective in my future endeavors." Thus, there is triangulation between different data sources: quantitative data pertaining to the workshop objectives, quantitative data regarding the usefulness of the workshop activities, and testimonial responses attesting to the positive impact of the workshop on the ways in which participants think about career development, as well as career guidance and counseling. Our intention in sharing these results is not to make a statement about our role

as workshop facilitators, but instead to illustrate the importance of staff development in preparing educators to infuse career development into their school systems and the impact of a somewhat different approach to evaluating the impact of staff training.

To summarize, the results reported in this section come from one offering of the Orientation to Career Guidance workshop that was prepared for UNESCO to help educators infuse career development into the curriculum. The workshop has been offered many times in several countries, with results similar to the ones reported above. Thus, we can say with confidence that the approach has been successful in helping participants revise the ways in which they conceptualized career development and the skills they could use to put their new ideas into practice. The workshop ended with participants developing a detailed and specific action plan for how they would implement the workshop content in their daily work-related activities. However, it was beyond the mandate of the facilitators to conduct any follow-up; therefore, it has not been possible to obtain data on the extent to which the action plans have in fact been followed.

The term *workshop* is often used in many ways and can encompass a variety of approaches, ranging from mostly didactic to a series of activities that seem rather unrelated to any central theme. In the workshop reported here, as well as the other instances where the workshop has been conducted, the workshop was run as a group experience and an attempt was made from the outset to develop collective buy-in to the goals and procedures in the workshop. This resulted in two related but different types of learning. First, participants grasped the major concepts of guidance and career–life planning (i.e., they were able to personalize those concepts and translate them into concrete action plans). Second, participants learned the impact of a different way of teaching that was different from approaches many had experienced in the past. They noted that the interactive presentation style was congruent with the types of message being taught. This is an important observation because using a didactic approach to teach school students about career–life planning is usually not very effective. Therefore, it is important that staff training experiences in the area of career development provide a good example of the way in which career development should be approached. In order for participants to fully grasp the concepts and personalize them, an interactive facilitation style is necessary, allowing time for reflection and application, as well as guided follow-up. If participants are to be successful in working with their colleagues and students, they will need to adopt a similarly interactive process.

Relevance for Multiple Cultures: Sensitivity to the Universal and the Particular

With the large-scale globalization of business, decisions are made by a board of directors in one county, that impact the labor market conditions in other countries, and they are often made by people who have minimal understanding of the cultural and interpersonal conditions in the countries affected. How are we as policymakers, researchers, educators, counselors, guidance practitioners, and parents preparing young people to deal with these types of situations? In this chapter, we have described a guidance orientation workshop designed to help educators develop a contemporary approach for addressing career-related issues with school students. This workshop has demonstrated success in developing countries and also in countries where career development is more firmly established.

In closing we want to mention one overarching concern that needs to be addressed in order for the approach described in this chapter to be successful. In the countries where we have worked, one major barrier expressed by participants was lack of infrastructure and resources for implementing career guidance programs. Many schools do not have a career resource center, thus it is difficult to get students actively engaged in the sort of exploration that helps them develop a meaningful vision for their life. Given that reality, internet resources can be used for many of the exploration activities; however, it will most often be necessary to augment these with county-specific labor market information. In a similar vein, most participants in our workshops made explicit plans for follow-up action. However, often there was no formal mechanism to sustain follow-up activity. A formal follow-up process would help to ensure the implementation of the concepts that participants learned and maximize the benefit from the workshop. In all workshops conducted to date there were informal commitments to follow up, keep in touch, and share ongoing ideas. However, the follow-up role would be fulfilled more effectively if it were formally coordinated locally. This is an area where a professional association could provide leadership, providing participants with a forum to discuss their action plans, document what was working, identify barriers encountered, describing strategies for dealing with barriers, and documenting what infrastructure support was needed to implement career guidance and counseling services within the educational system. Additionally, state or national ministries could facilitate such action.

Charting New Directions

People today live in a complex and changing world where the need for adaptability and flexibility is paramount. Some people are able to develop a meaningful life direction and work towards realizing their vision. However, many more have difficulty doing that and are often left floundering in a system they do not understand and in which they have difficulty coping. In this chapter, we have described some of the most prominent components of that changing world, and put forward the argument that the nature of work and life requires that people are purposeful in their lifelong learning endeavors, and have lifelong guidance and counseling to support them in their quest to become meaningful and contributing members of the society in which they live. We also have outlined a broadened orientation for approaching career–life planning and described a way that has shown promise in initiating a process to help prepare practitioners to function effectively within their own changing contexts.

Acknowledgment Portions of this chapter were presented to the IAEVG-JIVA International Career Conference 2010, October, Bangalore, India.

References

Arzuaga, G., de Tezanos, M., & Arzuaga, F. (n.d.). *Glumbert: Shift happens.* Retrieved from http://www.glumbert.com/media/shift

Baudouin, R., Bezanson, L., Borgen, B., Goyer, L., Hiebert, B., Lalande, V., et al. (2007). Demonstrating value: A draft framework for evaluating the effectiveness of career development interventions. *Canadian Journal of Counselling, 41*, 146–157.

Borgen, W. A. (2000). Developing partnerships to meet client's needs within changing government organizations: A consultative process. Joint special edition of the *Career Development Quarterly, 48*, 357–369, and the *Journal of Employment Counseling, 37*, 128–142.

Borgen, W. A., & Hiebert, B. (2002). Understanding the context of technical and vocational education and training. In B. Hiebert & W. A. Borgen (Eds.), *Technical and vocational education and training in the twenty-first century: New roles and challenges for guidance and counselling* (pp. 13–26). Paris, France: United Nations Educational Scientific and Cultural Organization.

Borgen, W. A., & Hiebert, B. (2006). Youth counselling and career guidance: What adolescents and young adults are telling us. *International Journal for the Advancement of Counselling, 28*, 389–400.

Collins, S., & Hiebert, B. (1995). Coping with the future: Challenging traditional beliefs about what adolescents need. In M. Van Norman (Ed.), *Natcon 21: National consultation on vocational counselling papers* (pp. 91–99). Toronto, Canada: OISE Press.

Esbin, H. (2002). Basic education and TVET. In B. Hiebert & W. A. Borgen (Eds.), *Technical and vocational education and training in the twenty-first century: New roles and challenges for guidance and counselling* (pp. 67–84). Paris, France: UNESCO.

Gelatt, H. B. (1989). Positive uncertainty: A new decision-making framework for counseling. *Journal of Counseling Psychology, 36*(2), 252–256.

Gibson-Cline, J. (1996). *Adolescence: From crisis to coping.* London, England: Routledge.

Gibson-Cline, J. (2000). *Youth and coping in twelve nations.* London, England: Routledge.

Grierson, J., Schnurr, J., & Young, C. (2002). Reaching marginalized people: Linking TVET to opportunity in the world of work. In B. Hiebert & W. A. Borgen (Eds.), *Technical and vocational education and training in the twenty-first century: New roles and challenges for guidance and counselling* (pp. 85–102). Paris, France: UNESCO.

Hiebert, B. (2012). Post-pre assessment: An innovative way for documenting client change. *Guidance perspectives around the world (GPAWS).* Retrieved from http://www. iaevg.org/crc/resources.cfm?subcat=200,202&lang=en

Hiebert, B., & Borgen, W. A. (2002). Where to from here? Guidance and counselling connecting with TVET. In B. Hiebert & W. A. Borgen (Eds.), *Technical and vocational education and training in the twenty-first century: New roles and challenges for guidance and counselling* (pp. 131–147). Paris, France: United Nations Educational Scientific and Cultural Organization.

Hiebert, B., Borgen, W. A., & Schober, K. (2011). *Career development: The role of guidance and counselling in fostering an increased range of educational and career alternatives* (A Briefing Note for Policy makers developed for the United Nations Education, Cultural, and Scientific Organization). Available in TVETipedia. Retrieved from http://www.unevoc.unesco.org/tviki_front.php

Hiebert, B., Kemeny, K., & Kurchak, W. (1998). Guidance-related needs of junior high school students. *Guidance and Counselling, 14*(1), 3–9.

Hoyt, K. B. (1991). The concept of work: Bedrock for career development. *Future Choices, 2*(3), 23–29.

Lambert, M., Zeman, K., Allen, M., & Bussiere, P. (2004). *Who pursues postsecondary education, who leaves and why: Results from the youth in transition survey* (Statistics Canada, Education, Skills and Learning Research Papers, Catalogue No. 81-595-MIE2004026). Retrieved from http://www.statcan.ca/bsolc/english/bsolc?catno=81-595-M2004026

Magnusson, K., & Bernes, K. (2002). Comprehensive career needs survey: An overview. *The Alberta Counsellor, 27*(2), 12–17.

Mitchell, K. E., Levin, A. S., & Krumboltz, J. D. (1999). Planned happenstance: Constructing unexpected career opportunities. *Journal of Counseling & Development, 77*, 115–124.

Peruniak, J. S. (2010). *A quality of life approach to career development.* Toronto, Canada: University of Toronto Press.

Posterski, D., & Bibby, R. (1988). *Canada's youth: "Ready for today": A comprehensive survey of 15–24 year olds.* Ottawa, Canada: The Canadian Youth Foundation.

Redekopp, D. E., Day, B., & Robb, M. (1995). The "High Five" of career development. In B. Hiebert (Ed.), *Exemplary career development programs and practices: The best from Canada.* Greensboro, Canada: ERIC/CASS.

Super, D. E. (1963). Self-concepts in vocational development. In D. E. Super (Ed.), *Career development: Self-concept theory* (pp. 1–16). New York, NY: College Entrance Examination Board.

Super, D. E. (1987). Career and life development. In D. Brown & L. Brooks (Eds.), *Career choice and development.* San Francisco, CA: Jossey-Bass.

Van Esbroeck, R. (2002). Career guidance and counselling for lifelong learning in a global economy. In B. Hiebert & W. Borgen (Eds.), *Technical and vocational education and training in the twenty-first century: New roles and challenges for* *guidance and counselling* (pp. 49–66). Paris, France: UNESCO.

Westwood, M. W., Amundson, N. E., & Borgen, W. A. (1994). *Starting points: Finding your route to employment*. Ottawa, Canada: Human Resources Development Canada.

Training Career Practitioners: Opportunities and Challenges

Spencer G. Niles

Today, one would be hardpressed to identify a counseling setting in which knowledge and expertise related to career intervention would not be relevant. Children, adolescents, and adults experience career development challenges on an almost daily basis. For example, whether they realize it or not, children are challenged to learn about themselves and the world-of-work in ways that are not influenced by bias and discrimination related to gender, race/ethnicity, heterosexism, socioeconomic status, and so on (Gottfredson, 2002). Adolescents must develop clear and accurate pictures of who they are and what educational and career options exist for them. They must also learn how to access the options they choose to pursue (Niles & Harris-Bowlsbey, 2013). In collectivistic contexts, they must engage in decision making from the orienation of the relevant group (Hartung, Speight, & Lewis, 1996). Adults must cope with unstable employment situations while they also live their lives within a multiple life role context (Herr, 2003). They must learn skills and acquire knowledge that will allow them to remain viable to current and prospective employers as lifelong learning becomes a requirement not simply a preference (Herr, Cramer, & Niles, 2004). In countries experiencing an economic downturn, adults must also deal with the stress associated with actual or potential unemployment, which impacts every employment sector thereby making job security nearly nonexistent in many countries (European Centre for the Development of Vocational Training [CEDEFOP], 2011). The world-of-work is not what it used to be; therefore, the work performed by career practitioners must continually evolve to keep pace with the emerging career development challenges people experience (Niles & Karajic, 2008).

In this chapter, I discuss the need for effective career practitioner training to address individual and societal needs in the current context, factors influencing career practitioner training, and future (hoped-for) trends related to career practitioner training.

Effective Career Practitioner Training to Address Individual and Societal Needs

The need for currency in career intervention and in career practitioner training is both an individual and a societal need. It is individual in the sense that when persons receive effective career interventions they tend to make more positive educational and career decisions, which, in turn, increases the probability that they will lead more satisfying and productive lives. At the societal level, the need for effective career interventions and competent career practitioners is evident when one considers the fact that positive correlations exist between events such as increase in

S.G. Niles (✉)
The College of William & Mary, Williamsburg, VA, USA
e-mail: sgniles@wm.edu

G. Arulmani et al. (eds.), *Handbook of Career Development*, International and Cultural Psychology,
DOI 10.1007/978-1-4614-9460-7_41, © Springer Science+Business Media, LLC 2014

unemployment rates and the occurrence of partner abuse, substance abuse, depression, and suicide (Herr et al., 2004). The ripple effects of employment situations gone awry are dramatic, substantial, and, unfortunately, negative. Such concommitant issues result in substantial societal and economic costs globally and nationally. Thus, it is no surprise that there is increased attention globally to the importance of the services that competent career practitioners provide relative to their capacity to help others cope with the career challenges they encounter (CEDEFOP, 2011).

To engage their clients competently, career practitioners must be trained effectively to provide services that include career assessment, career counseling, career and/or educational planning, job-search skill training, and career coaching. Likewise, those involved in training career practitioners must be knowledgeable of the factors influencing career development and the challenges these factors present to individuals attempting to manage their careers effectively. Training experiences provided to current and future career practitioners must constantly be updated and adjusted so that trainees have relevant knowledge, awareness, and skills to provide effective career interventions. That said, training experiences for career practitioners occur in a broader context that contains its own challenges that must be addressed for training to occur.

Factors Influencing Career Practitioner Training

Those engaged in training career practitioners encounter challenges as they seek to design and deliver training for competent career practice in the 21st century. Summarizing papers presented at a symposium of the International Association for Educational and Vocational Guidance (IAEVG) that was devoted to the topic of training career practitioners, Niles, Engels, and Lenz (2009) identified three main challenges for the profession that have important implications for career practitioner preparation. I have added a fourth challenge to this list:

1. The need for stronger public policies addressing career development.
2. The need for greater competency standardization.
3. The need to create innovative training programs.
4. The need to demonstrate evidence-based practices.

The Need for Public Policies Addressing Career Development

Public policies set the context for the existence of career services and can influence the type and level of training opportunities that exist for career practitioners. Across nations, provinces, states, and municipalities, career policies and regulations (or the lack thereof) influence the delivery of career services, stipulate the nature of career service delivery requirements, and determine which segments of the population receive career services. These factors, in turn, influence career practitioner training. In many countries, public policies supporting career development constitute mandates for services and reflect a dedicated sense of priority toward workforce development. For example, the Australian government's career development policies demonstrate national respect for, and commitment to, worker career preparation, adaptability, and workforce sustainability. In contrast, public policies in the United States tend to focus on macroeconomic workforce employment and training issues, with attention to workers primarily limited to employment rather than career development. Often, as is the case in the United States, a general lack of understanding regarding the specific services career practitioners offer limits the capacity to develop strong career development policies and regulations. When stakeholders (e.g., consumers, legislators) experience confusion regarding career services, the profession as a whole is weakened. This issue is not limited to the United States. For example, Buyukgoze, Guneri, and Koydemir (2007) have noted the confusion that exists among the public and school personnel (e.g., teachers, administrators) in Turkey regarding the roles and functions of school counselors (the primary providers of career services to students in grades PK-12). Although there are efforts underway to provide a more unified voice within the field regarding the need for public policies supporting career development (see www.iccdpp.org for resources related to international symposia reports on international career development and public policy initiatives), it is clear that there is much more work to be done in the public policy and career development arena.

This is an issue for the training of career practitioners because it is reasonable to suggest that the impetus for creating public policies that support career development services is most likely to emerge from those who care the most (and have the most understanding) about delivering quality career services to the greatest number of people. Although there are many consumers, potential consumers, and other advocates for career services who must be included in the public policy process, career practitioners represent the group that is best positioned to identify the type of services needed and the populations most in need of services (Niles & Herr, in press). When the need for quality career services is recognized through public policy and legislation, then it is often the case that career practitioner training programs are created to provide the practitioner pipeline to effective career services. When career practitioners can clearly communicate their value and demonstrate their effectiveness, then policies supporting career services and career practitioner training often follow. The converse is also true. Thus, advocacy is a vital role for career practitioners and an essential component of career practitioner training. When this occurs within the private sector, the collection and dissemination of qualitative and/or quantitative outcome data demonstrating treatment efficacy are important to communicate to policymakers as also the motives and purposes of career services.

Not only is advocacy a key activity in the pipeline leading to the recognition of the importance of career services and, therefore, the need for career practitioner training programs, the importance of career practitioners engaging in advocacy has implications for the specific competencies that must be included in career practitioner training. Engaging in effective professional advocacy requires career practitioners to develop and then demonstrate core skills essential to the advocacy process. Typically, however, career practitioner training programs have focused solely on individual and, to a lesser degree, group career interventions as the preferred modes of service delivery. Nassar-McMillan and Niles (2009) surveyed more than 70 syllabi for career counselor training in the United States and found very few that contained any reference to advocacy as a course topic. Although, for many reasons, the emphasis on individual and group level interventions in career practitioner training makes sense, it does not justify the lack of training in core public policy advocacy competencies. So what are the competencies career practitioners must be trained in to be able to engage in effective advocacy?

To engage in advocacy effectively, career practitioners must be able to identify cultural, social, and economic factors influencing the client or student; help the client or student identify the external barriers that are affecting his or her development; train students or clients in self-advocacy skills; help students or clients identify indicators of systemic oppression (e.g., sexist and/or racist hiring practices; exclusion of a particular group from the workforce, such as persons with disabilities, heterosexism); and, help clients or students develop and implement self-advocacy action plans (Lewis, Arnold, House, & Toporek, 2003). Practitioners must also learn competencies related to helping students or clients access required services. Often, these competencies take the form of environmental interventions that practitioners must perform on behalf of their clients or students (e.g., when a business does not provide appropriate accommodations for persons who are physically disabled or if a client is denied employment benefits to which they are entitled). In some instances, practitioners must engage in community collaboration to eradicate environmental barriers to student or client career development.

For example, career practitioners might need to collaborate with civic and/or business groups to raise community awareness as to how environmental barriers (e.g., structural barriers that limit mobility of persons with disabilities) restrict work opportunities for some persons. Nag (2011) has described the importance of understanding the challenges confronting students with special needs from a home-community-institution context in order to foster such students' successful transition from school-to-work. Additionally, there may be the need for practitioners to engage in the political process to help elected officials become aware of the need for career services and the importance of public policies to support those services. These competencies include those that involve being able to collect useful data to demonstrate accountability and effectiveness.

Clearly, those engaged in the training of career practitioners must consider advocacy competencies as critical to the work of career practitioners. In many cases, being able to use these skills effectively can make the difference between whether career services are available or not. When career practitioners are not trained to engage in advocacy, then many factors that inhibit career development go unaddressed (e.g., discrimination in the workplace, bias in providing access to quality educational opportunities). When career services are not supported by public policies, there *often* are no career services provided and career practitioner training opportunities evaporate. It is possible for small-scale efforts (directed at providing career services and related practitioner training) to be initiated successfully without supportive public policies but such initiatives are rare and large-scale implementation becomes a struggle. To reiterate, this means that career services do not become widely available and many or most remain underserved or not served.

The Need for Greater Competency Standardization

Many European countries have recently sought to strengthen the competencies of career practitioners by providing more standardized career practitioner training (CEDEFOP, 2011). For example, Austria and Denmark have introduced legislation regulating the training of career guidance practitioners. In Denmark, career guidance practitioners are required to complete a diploma program in educational and vocational guidance (or document equivalent competencies through prior learning). A professional training program at the bachelor's level has also been established in Denmark (CEDEFOP, 2010). Likewise, in Austria, the Federal Ministry of Education regulates the pre- and in-service training of career guidance practitioners (CEDEFOP, 2011). Other countries have emphasized enhancing the quality of in-service training for guidance practitioners. For instance, in Bulgaria, career guidance practitioners in educational settings have received government organized training opportunities since 2006. In Greece, educators at Panteion University provided 200 hours of career guidance training to 740 participants in 2007–2008.

Competency documents such as those promulgated by the Canadian Counseling Association (2003), the IAEVG (2003), and the National Career Development Association in the United States (NCDA, 2007), constitute fundamental bases for career development practitioner training and have direct implications for preparation of curricula and training programs. Accreditation standards, such as those of the Council for Accreditation of Counseling and Related Educational Programs (CACREP, 2001) in the United States, serve to guide preparation requirements and, thus, influence the future of the counseling profession generally, as well as career counseling specialty programs specifically, by providing a "stamp of approval" for accredited counseling programs engaged in training career counselors.

Of course, one of the many challenges regarding competency identification across national contexts relates to clarifying which competencies should be part of all career practitioner training and which competencies are more unique to specific contexts. For example, the US model of Master Career Counselors (MCCs) possessing at least a master's degree plus relevant experience in career counseling may not apply to settings accustomed to less rigorous and less extensive training programs. Despite this limitation, there is still the possibility of identifying core competencies in all national contexts (e.g., the need for career counselors to be conversant in basic career intervention skills and assessment approaches).

The 2001 CACREP standards for master's degree level training in career counseling represent a sort of "gold standard" in relation to career counselor training in the United States. This specialization for career counseling focuses on preparing students to work as career counselors who will demonstrate the professional knowledge, skills, and practices necessary to help a person develop a life-career plan, with a focus on the definition of the worker role and how that role interacts with other life roles (CACREP, 2001). More specifically, in addition to training in general counseling competencies, students in a CACREP-accredited career counselor preparation program must receive coursework in areas such as: foundations of career counseling (history, trends, roles, theories, ethical issues, and public policies related to career development); career counseling skills, practices, and interventions including the capacity to help others cope with career transitions (planned and unplanned; diversity and advocacy—understanding the effects of racism, discrimination, power, privilege, and oppression in one's own life and career and those of the client); career assessment (the capacity to administer, score, interpret, and report career assessment results as well as the ability to assess conditions of the work environment); research/evaluation (understanding how to critically evaluate research relevant to career counseling, how to conduct program evaluation for career counseling and career programs, and how to evaluate outcomes in career counseling); managing and implementing career programs (understanding organizational and leadership theories; having the capacity to engage in policy analysis, planning, and job forecasting; being able to market career programs effectively); and information resources (understanding education, training, and employment trends; as well as labor market information and resources that provide information about job tasks, functions, salaries, requirements, and future outlooks related to broad occupational fields and individual occupations).

Coursework addressing these career counseling competency areas, along with related general counseling competencies, is typically delivered over a 2-year period at the postbaccalaureate level. These competencies are comprehensive and extensive; unfortunately, however, there has been a general lack of support within the profession relative to the adoption of master's level training programs in career counseling. Such programs require extensive time and, often, financial commitments on the part of students. The lack of support for more advanced and formalized career counselor training programs is disappointing as it limits the professionalization of career counseling both within the United States and across the world. When the profession does not value advanced training, then it should not be surprising when policymakers and legislators do not recognize the value of it. This is a major challenge to the career development profession internationally. Until it is addressed globally, the career development profession will largely be viewed as a paraprofessional entity.

Competency statements not requiring advanced training have also been developed. In 2003, IAEVG developed a set of international competencies for entry-level career practitioners. These competencies reflect those developed by NCDA (1997) in the United States. There are, however, some important distinctions between the two sets of competencies. The IAEVG competencies address the important area of community capacity building, thereby noting the importance of collaboration between community partners to assess human capital and community needs, as well as developing plans to address the economic, social, educational, and employment goals of the community. The NCDA competencies contain sections related to diversity and technology, both critical competency areas for all career practitioners. Thus, collectively, the two competency statements provide a comprehensive overview of the knowledge, skills, and awareness career practitioners need in the 21st century regardless of national context. It is not likely that we can find one set of common competencies that address the needs of each national context (without focusing on an extremely minimal set of competencies). Thus, the NCDA or the IAEVG competency statements serve as useful starting points for countries developing their own competency statements. These statements also provide a common ground for creating innovative training programs that can help ensure that trainees receive at least minimal training in essential skills for effective career intervention practice.

United States was one of the first countries in which an important training program at the para-professional level was first developed. Specifically, more than two decades ago the National Occupational Information Coordinating Committee (NOICC) through its Career Development Training Institute (CDTI) initiated the Career Development Facilitator (CDF) training program. A major emphasis in the initial CDTI effort was to develop a curriculum and train instructors who would in turn develop programs to train CDFs. Today, CDF instructors are delivering training programs in postsecondary settings, community settings, and state agencies. The programs are delivered in intensive 3-week and semester-long programs. Career Development Training may carry college credit, continuing education credit, and/or certificates of completion.

The NCDA was an early partner with the NOICC and the Center for Credentialing and Education, Inc. (CCE—headquartered in North Carolina, USA) in developing and implementing the CDF concept. Groups worked with CCE to develop requirements for the Global CDF credential, originally referred to as the CDF certification. These organizations (based in the United States) include the NCDA, the National Employment Counseling Association (NECA), and the National Association of Workforce Development Professionals (NAWDP). Collectively, they endorsed the CDF credentialing requirements. The Global Career Development Facilitator (GCDF) certification is provided through CCE

(see http://www.cce-global.org). GCDFs must have a combination of education and work experience as specified in the credential guidelines: (a) graduate degree plus an estimated 1 year of career development work experience; (b) bachelor's degree plus an estimated 2 years of career development work experience; (c) 2 years of college plus an estimated 3 years of career development work experience; or (d) a high school diploma/General Educational Development Test (GED) plus an estimated 4 years of career development work experience. In addition to the education and work experience, persons who want to become GCDFs must complete an approved CDF curriculum that includes 120 hours of classroom training and field experience. GCDFs are bound by a code of ethics.

Creating Innovative Training Programs

Curricula-driven formal university-based programs constitute a primary source for career counselor preparation. Other formal and informal career practitioner training occurs in a variety of distance education programs, apprenticeships, on-the-job training, mentoring, credit for experience, and similar approaches, ranging from informal and formal worksite teams to corporate/agency/institution human resource development programs and activities. There is substantial variation across the world in the professional training opportunities that are available for career practitioners. A balance must be struck between making training opportunities accessible and providing training opportunities that foster the development of competent practitioners.

Turcotte and Michaud (2007) have described important developments in Quebec, Canada, in which four universities offer a complete educational training program for career counselors. What is unique about this initiative is the fact that these four university-based training programs are coordinated by the College of Career Counselors, which serves as the organization regulating the career counseling profession in Quebec. This college worked collaboratively with the four universities to develop training competencies for career counselors (e.g., knowledge of occupational information resources, listening skills, and Internet-based career guidance systems). The competency statement provides the organizing framework for the four university-based training programs. Thus, this Canadian example provides an excellent instance in which training programs work collaboratively with a regulatory body to provide consistent training curricula addressing important areas of career counseling competence.

Neault (2007) has been concerned with accessibility of training curricula to current and prospective career practitioners. She has noted the usefulness of providing high quality and current training using the Internet as the vehicle for delivering training experiences. Using an electronic format provides training access to those working full-time and/or those living in remote areas. Neault and her associates have developed modularized learning formats that address training competencies such as those articulated by the IAEVG and those required for the GCDF certificate. Students are able to enroll in a single course for professional development or they may enroll in an entire certificate program (usually ten or more courses) to expand their professional credentials.

Sometimes, students complete their training in more general areas of counseling or psychology and then realize their interest in working within the career counseling field. To address the needs of these students, faculty at the University of Sao Paulo (Brazil) have developed a highly specialized program for their psychology graduates who wish to receive training in career interventions. Gatti, Silva, Uvaldo, and Ribeiro (2007) have described how they have integrated the use of the university's career service with a 2-year training program to provide career counseling experience and academic content to prepare career practitioners.

Amundson (2007) has described a career practitioner training model that uses an *active engagement* approach and focuses on infusing experiential components into career counselor training. Obviously, simply discussing career development is insufficient in training competent practitioners. Trainees require exposure to carefully sequenced behavioral rehearsal experiences. In constructing such experiences, Amundson emphasizes the importance of providing a proper training atmosphere. Specifically, he notes the importance of using a training space that is free from distractions and creating a sense of security and safety among trainees. Regarding the latter, a *strength challenge* training orientation is recommended. By first focusing on trainee strengths and providing opportunities for trainees to demonstrate their strengths, it is then easier for trainees to challenge themselves with new skills. Amundson also clarifies that learning to be an effective career practitioner is more than simply learning skills and techniques; it also involves the capacity to engage in critical self-reflection. Providing critical reflection activities from the onset of training provides the foundation for engaging regularly in reflective exercises. For example, encouraging novice trainees to consider such basic questions as to whether the typical structure of a career intervention session (i.e., two participants sitting in a room talking to one another for a set period of time) makes the most sense in all situations encourages trainees to reflect upon important factors such as time structure, social conventions, cultural differences, communication styles, and participant engagement levels. Bigeon (2007) has pointed to the importance of addressing media influence in the career development process. She encourages trainees to be aware of how media portrayals of workers create impressions that will move clients toward or away from specific occupational options. Clients often bring such stereotypes with them into the career intervention process. Being aware of this fact sensitizes career practitioners to the need to educate clients regarding the myths and realities pertaining to various occupations.

A subtheme in this category relates to the historical emphasis within training programs to prepare practitioners to provide individual services to students and clients. Although individual counseling has been and will continue to be the core means of providing career counseling, many forms of career services can be delivered more efficiently in other formats. Career practitioner-to-client ratios are often quite large. For example, in the United States, each school counselor (the primary providers of career services to students in elementary and secondary school settings) has a case load of 476 students on average (American School Counselor Association, 2007). It is naïve at best to assume that such counselor-to-student ratios offer an optimistic scenario for addressing the career concerns of all students. Given that financial resources for employing additional career practitioners are typically not available, school counselors must place greater emphasis on small group interventions, classroom guidance, web-based services, and peer facilitator services to more creatively meet the needs of their students. Regarding the latter, Reardon and Lenz (2007) have used a variety of techniques including individual counseling, group counseling, peer-to-peer supervision, and self-directed learning plans to prepare career advisors who serve students in the career center at Florida State University.

Developing effective and readily available resources that can be used in training career practitioners should also result in more career services being provided to more clients (Rondon, 2007). For example, two major national counseling-related professional associations in the United States (NCDA and the Association for Counselor Education and Supervision or ACES) created a Commission on Career Development to address the need to revitalize career courses. Efforts at revitalizing career courses have been accelerated via many means, most notably by developing outstanding compilations of best practices and techniques for engaging activities for training career counselors (Minor & Pope, 2006) and challenging case studies (Niles, Goodman, & Pope, in press) with poignant and highly relevant general and specific materials for use and adaptation in career courses. The Commission uses materials such as these to help meet the goal of revising career courses and disseminating training materials to faculty teaching career development courses. The Commission also sponsors conference presentations that emphasize innovative strategies for career

practitioner training. The NCDA-ACES Commission represents an important step toward elevating the training experiences that career practitioners receive. It also serves as a model that should be replicated by other professional associations (e.g., IAEVG). More professional engagement in dialogue around innovative training methods should translate into stronger career practitioner training programs.

The Need to Demonstrate Evidence-Based Practices

Strengthening training and practice requires both trainers and practitioners to rely upon evidence-based practice whenever possible. Functioning without such evidence relegates the work of both trainers and practitioners to an over-reliance upon "face validity" (i.e., the sense that a particular practice simply seems like it should be effective) in their work. This, in turn, stunts the capacity of the profession to be regarded as a legimate service, especially when primary, secondary, and postsecondary school budgets are constrained and resources for community services are dwindling. Bimrose, Barnes, and Hughes (2008) have noted that most policymakers rely on a very limited evidence-base when evaluating career services and deciding whether to continue the funding for such services. Plant (2009) has also noted that what evidence there is supporting the efficacy of specific interventions tends to be fragmented and is not sufficiently comprehensive for the purposes of impacting public policy. A case-in-point supporting Plant's view exists in the United States. On the one hand, the sheer number of career development researchers within the United States is huge and they produce a significant amount of research (quantitative and qualitative) related to career intervention. On the other hand, these research efforts tend to reflect attempts at theory validation, rely heavily upon samples of convenience (e.g., university students), and do not address policy concerns relative to issues such as the return on investment for service provision.

Another issue relative to the bulk of what evidence does exist supporting specific career interventions is that this research tends to focus on short-term, time-limited interventions. Rarely do researchers conduct longitudinal studies that could address the impact of services relative to outcomes such as graduation from a secondary school, transition to postsecondary education, graduation from postsecondary education, the successful acquisition of satisfying employment, and so on. Often this is because researchers are academics concerned with promotion and tenure considerations that require a more rapid turnaround of research projects to publication than what occurs with longitudinal research. Additionally, practitioners in school and community settings seldom have the financial resources and/or the administrative support to engage in longitudinal research to determine the long-term results of the services they provide. There are, however, some notable exceptions to these limitations. For example, in England, Bimrose et al. (2008) conducted a longitudinal study in which they examined the impact of career services by tracking the career trajectories of research participants over a 5-year period. This study highlighted how important it is to be clear about *what* is being measured to ascertain the impact of career services on career development (outcome and process measures) and *how* these are being measured, as also the need for more sophisticated research designs appropriate for return-on-investment studies. Studies such as the one conducted by the Ministry of Education, Science and Culture in Iceland (CEDEFOP, 2009), which found that effective career guidance results in greater school retention rates provide the sort of evidence necessary to solidify the need for career practitioners and, by extension, the need for effective career practitioner training programs. More specifically, to strengthen the evidence base supporting career services across the life span researchers need to:

1. Address research questions that are relevant to stakeholders including potential clients, employers, policymakers, and legislators.
2. Be rigorous in using research study designs that pose important return-on-investment questions and examine these questions by using psychometrically sound measures and appropriate statistical methods.
3. Engage in more longitudinal research.
4. Disseminate their research results extensivley so that policymakers and the general public become aware of the value-added impact of career services.

A significant issue related to developing an evidence base related to career interventions relates to the lack of uniformity regarding career-related language. Career development interventions are shaped, in part, by how terms are defined. Many would contend that within the area of career development interventions, there are frequent misuses of terminology among career practitioners as well as clients. For example, it is not uncommon for professional career counselors to use the terms *career* and *work* interchangeably. It is also not unusual to hear professionals talk about "doing career development" as if career development were an intervention rather than the object of an intervention. Similarly, career practitioners often confuse the terms *career guidance* and *career counseling*. This lack of precision confuses practitioners, students, clients, and policymakers, and therefore, is a barrier to advancing the efficacy of, and legislative support for, career development interventions. When language lacks precision, the implication is that terminology does not matter. Words have power, however, in that career practitioners are "engaged in a verbal profession in which words and symbols frequently become the content of the interactions they have with clients" (Herr, 1997, p. 241). Thus, the need exists for greater clarity and specificity with regard to the key terms related to career development interventions. A glossary of career-related terms is currently being developed by the European Lifelong Guidance and Policy Network. Such uniformity is urgently needed to enhance the credibility of the profession and provide a common ground for training career practitioners as well as devising, implementing, and evaluating career development interventions. In this chapter, I define key terms as follows.

Career

Rather than limiting the definition of career to work, Niles and Harris-Bowlsbey (2013) advocate viewing *career* as a lifestyle concept. Super's (1976) view of career as the course of events constituting a life, and Herr et al.'s (2004) notion of career as the total constellation of roles played over the course of a lifetime provide more wholistic definitions of *career*. Broader definitions highlight the multiple life roles people play and acknowledge differences across people regarding life-role salience generally and provide flexibility regarding the areas in one's life where work is located. For example, broad definitions of career apply to those locating work in the life role of homemaker or in volunteer activities.

Career Development

Career development refers to the lifelong psychological and behavioral processes as well as contextual influences shaping one's career over the life span. As such, career development involves the person's creation of a career pattern, decision-making style, integration of life roles, values expression, and life-role self-concepts (Niles & Harris-Bowlsbey, 2013).

Career Development Interventions

Career development interventions, defined broadly, involve any activities that empower people to cope effectively with career development tasks (Spokane, 1991). For example, activities that help people develop self-awareness, develop occupational awareness, learn decision-making skills, acquire job-search skills, adjust to occupational choices after they have been implemented, and cope with job stress can each be labeled as career development interventions. Specifically, these activities include individual and group career counseling, career development programs, career education, computer-assisted career development programs, and computer information delivery systems, as well as other forms of delivering career information to clients.

Career Counseling

Career counseling involves a formal relationship in which a professional counselor assists a client, or group of clients, to cope more effectively with career concerns (e.g., making a career choice, coping with career transitions, coping with job-related stress, or job searching). Typically, career counselors seek to establish rapport with their clients, assess their clients' career concerns, establish goals for the career counseling relationship, intervene in ways that help clients cope more effectively with career concerns, evaluate clients' progress, and, depending on clients' progress, either offer additional interventions or terminate career counseling (Niles & Harris-Bowlsbey, 2013).

Career Guidance

Career guidance can be defined as services intended to assist individuals make educational, training, and occupational choices and to manage their careers across the life span. Such services include career information provision, assessment and self-assessment tools, counseling interviews, career education programs that help individuals develop their self-awareness, opportunity awareness, and/or career management skills, experiential activities (e.g., internships, externships), and transition services (OECD, 2004).

Career Development Programs

Career development programs can be defined as "a systematic program of counselor-coordinated information and experiences designed to facilitate individual career development" (Herr et al., 2004, p. 43). These programs typically contain goals, objectives, activities, and methods for evaluating the effectiveness of the activities in achieving the goals.

Whether the broader career development community adopts these terms or alternative definitions, progressing toward greater uniformity will have important and positive implications for current and future career practitioners. When common definitions become infused into career practitioner training programs, trainers and trainees will be clearer about who is being trained to perform which practices for which prospective recipients of career services. Career intervention process and outcome studies will also become more useful and generalizable to more stakeholders when these common definitions are integrated into research studies.

New Concepts and Viewpoints: Charting New Directions

There is reason for concern for those engaged in providing career services and those involved in training career practitioners. On the one hand, the need for career services has perhaps never been greater. Because career interventions emerged from the changing demographics and economic needs of the 20th century, it is clear today that career interventions will need to change to respond to evolving career challenges in the 21st century. Indeed, the rapid changes occurring in the world-of-work influenced by technological developments, the emergence of an interdependent (and weak) global economy, and an increasingly diverse workforce provide ample evidence that career development interventions need to be revised to meet the career development tasks confronting people currently. The evidence includes the fact that people, both young and old, are struggling to cope more effectively with these tasks. Thus, although the need for trained career practitioners is great, on the other hand, career practitioners and career intervention theorists must accelerate their efforts toward developing evidence-based practices that are relevant to the present context. The lack of evidence supporting the functions that career practitioners perform weakens the profession and will not inspire policymakers to support funding for more practitioners and related training programs.

Research results also indicate that when an individual's career situations go awry, the effects are far-reaching and often negative, for both the person and society (Niles & Harris-Bowlsbey, 2013). Daily news stories cite statistics regarding high levels of global unemployment, corporate downsizing, and a jobless economic recovery.

These statistics provide examples of the fact that the social contract between employer and employee is gone. Other evidence that the nature of work is changing is found in the number of companies now offering day care and parental leave, increases in the number of families requiring dual earners, and increases in the number of people working at home. These themes reflect the strong intertwining of work and family roles. Thus, career theories, career interventions, career development practitioners, and those engaged in training career practitioners must respond to these evolutionary shifts occurring in the nature of work. Career interventions must be embedded in assumptions that reflect the shifts workers experience in work (e.g., that adults change occupations many times over the course of their lives, that lifelong learning is essential to maintaining one's marketability, that life roles interact, that rapid changes in the world-of-work are a constant, and that everyone must become skilled at interacting with diverse coworkers). Herr (2003) has contended that the demand for career assistance will expand due to rising unemployment rates and an increase in part-time work. It is also reasonable to suggest that career development interventions in the 21st century will need to become more sophisticated to address effectively the complexities contained within the career concerns many experience. If these two predictions are accurate, then the global trend toward training paraprofessional career practitioners is important but insufficient to meet the growing needs for career practitioners who are trained to address career issues from a more holistic perspective. Training programs such as the GCDF model prepare practitioners to fulfill a particular and limited niche within career practice. The rarity of advanced degree career training programs and the related funding to hire such practitioners makes an implicit argument that career practice is not a true profession. It is not unreasonable, therefore, for policymakers to view career practitioners similarly, resulting in a lack of training programs and funding for career services.

Additionally, career theorists cannot remain content to conduct research studies that simply address the validation of their respective theories. Such studies in the current funding context are short-sighted relative to the longevity of the profession. Policymakers care little about theory validation if it does not address relevant social concerns such as helping students become more successful learners and helping them transition to gainful employment successfully, or assisting an adult in identifying new strengths that enable a career shift. Thus, the need exists for career development researchers to commit to integrating such questions into their work.

Career practitioners must also be cognizant of the need to demonstrate the efficacy of their work. It is not sufficient to simply assume others will appreciate the good work that career practitioners perform. Career practitioners must also gather data to demonstrate that their work is good in the sense that the outcomes of their interventions result in a positive impact upon the individual and society.

Those involved in career practitioner training must integrate best practices in their training, equip their trainees to not only provide individual and group-based interventions but also instill in their trainees the importance of gathering and dessiminating data to support the efficacy of their work (i.e., evidence-based practice), and engaging in advocacy to effectively communicate the importance of career services to stakeholders.

Relevance for Multiple Cultures: Sensitivity to the Universal and the Particular

In this chapter, challenges, trends, practices, and opportunities for training career practitioners have been reviewed. Clearly, each of these must be contextualized in particular cultural settings. Collaborative learning, ideally, involves understanding trends that have emerged and appreciating the cultural influences that led to the emergence of specific trends and practices. Such is the case with training career practitioners. For example, even in nations as similar as Canada and the United States, significant variations exist

in training career practitioners. The strong valuing of First Nation persons in Canada, the openness to more socialistic government policies (e.g., in healthcare), a valuing of a bilingual society, and a continued openness to immigration represent some key ways in which Canada differs from the United States. Thus, it is not surprising that the provision of career development programming to indigenous persons, the availability of government funding for the provision of career services, and access to career services in multiple languages all are more common in Canada than they are in the United States.

Context also influences priorities related to training requirements of career practitioners. In more affluent societies, graduate level training is more commonly accepted as a route to achieving professional credentials. For example, the master's level training specialty in career counseling advocated by CACREP may stand as an example for preferred career counselor training in the United States but less extensive training programs in another part of the world may be equally legitimate for preparing career practitioners in that particular context. The popularity of the GCDF training outside the United States represents a specific example of a training alternative to the CACREP option. As indigenous career development theories and interventions continue to emerge globally, context-specific models provide useful fodder for global conversations regarding what is universal and what is particular relative to career development processes. Such conversations are needed as the field of career development continues to evolve in ways that empowers career practitioners around the world to more effectively meet the needs of their clients.

References

American School Counselor Association. (2007). *The role of the school counselor*. Alexandria, VA: Author. Retrieved from http://www.schoolcounselor.org/content.asp?contentid=240

Amundson, N. (2007, September). *A model of career training in international contexts*. Paper presented at the symposium of the International Association for Educational and Vocational Guidance, Padova, Italy.

Bigeon, C. (2007, September). *Interdisciplinary interaction: A key to the vocational guidance counselors and researchers*. Paper presented at the symposium of the International Association for Educational and Vocational Guidance, Padova, Italy.

Bimrose, J., Barnes, S.-A., & Hughes, D. (2008). *Adult career progression and advancement: A five-year study of the effectiveness of guidance*. England: Warwick Institute for Employment Research.

Buyukgoze, A., Guneri, O. Y., & Koydemir, S. (2007, September). *Career development of Turkish school counselors: A qualitative investigation*. Paper presented at the symposium of the International Association for Educational and Vocational Guidance, Padova, Italy.

Canadian Counseling Association. (2003). *2003 CCPA accreditation procedures and standards for counsellor education programs at the master's level*. Ottawa, ON: Author. Retrieved from http://www.ccacc.ca/en/accreditationmanual/

CEDEFOP. (2009). *Continuity, consolidation and change: Towards a European era of vocational education and training*. Luxembourg: Publications Office of the European Union.

CEDEFOP. (2010). *A bridge to the future: European policy for vocational education and training 2002–10*. Luxembourg: Publications Office of the European Union.

CEDEFOP. (2011). *Lifelong guidance across Europe: Reviewing policy progress and future prospects*. Luxembourg: Publications Office of the European Union.

Council for the Accreditation of Counseling and Related Educational Programs. (2001). *2001 CACREP accreditation standards*. Retrieved from http://www.cacrep.org/2001Standards.html

Gatti, M., Silva, F. F., Uvaldo, M. C., & Ribeiro, M. A. (2007, September). *The role of a specific approach in vocational psychology training: The formation process at USP/Brazil*. Paper presented at the symposium of the International Association for Educational and Vocational Guidance, Padova, Italy.

Gottfredson, L. S. (2002). Gottfredson's theory of circumscription, compromise, and self-creation. In D. Brown et al. (Eds.), *Career choice and development* (4th ed., pp. 85–148). San Francisco, CA: Jossey-Bass.

Hartung, P. J., Speight, J. D., & Lewis, D. M. (1996). Individualism-collectivism and the vocational behavior of majority culture college students. *Career Development Quarterly, 45*, 87–96.

Herr, E. L. (1997). Super's life-span, life-space approach and its outlook for refinement. *Career Development Quarterly, 45*, 238–246.

Herr, E. L. (2003). The future of career counseling as an instrument of public policy. *Career Development Quarterly, 52*, 8–17.

Herr, E. L., Cramer, S. H., & Niles, S. G. (2004). *Career guidance and counseling through the lifespan: Systemic approaches* (6th ed.). Boston, MA: Allyn & Bacon.

International Association for Educational and Vocational Guidance. (2003). *International competencies for educational and vocational guidance practitioners*. Retrieved from http://www.iaevg.org/iaevg/nav.cfm?lang=2&menu=1&submenu=5

Lewis, J., Arnold, M. S., House, R., & Toporek, R. (2003). *Advocacy competencies*. Retrieved from http://www.counseling.org/resources/competencies/advocacy_competencies.pdf

Minor, C., & Pope, M. (2006). *Experiential activities for teaching career counseling classes and for facilitating career groups*. Tulsa, OK: National Career Development Association.

Nag, S. (2011). Re-thinking support: The hidden school-to-work challenges for individuals with special needs. *International Journal for Educational and Vocational Guidance, 11*, 125–137.

Nassar-McMillan, S., & Niles, S. G. (2009, June). *Social justice and public policy in training career practitioners*. Paper presented at the annual meeting of the International Association for Educational and Vocational Guidance Conference, Jyvaskyla, Finland.

National Career Development Association. (1997). *Career counseling competencies*. Retrieved from http://www.ncda.org/

National Career Development Association. (2007). *Code of ethics*. Retrieved from http://ncda.org/aws/NCDA/asset_manager/get_file/3395/code_of_ethicsmay-2007.pdf

Neault, R. (2007, September). *Learning online: Accessible professional development for career practitioners, human resource professionals, and vocational counselors*. Paper presented at the symposium of the International Association for Educational and Vocational, Padua, Italy.

Niles, S. G., Engels, D. W., & Lenz, J. (2009). Training career practitioners: International perspectives. *Career Development Quarterly, 57*, 358–366.

Niles, S. G., Goodman, J., & Pope, M. (in press). *The career counseling casebook: A resource for practitioners, students and counselor educators* (2nd ed.). Broken Arrow, OK: National Career Development Association.

Niles, S. G., & Harris-Bowlsbey, J. (2013). *Career development interventions in the 21st century* (4th ed.). Columbus, OH: Merrill Prentice-Hall.

Niles, S. G., & Herr, E. L. (in press). Public policy and the psychology of work. In D. Blustein (Ed.), *The psychology of working*. New York, NY: Oxford University Press.

Niles, S. G., & Karajic, A. (2008). Training career practitioners in the 21st century. In J. A. Athanasou & R. V. Esbroeck (Eds.), *International handbook of career guidance* (pp. 355–374). New York, NY: Springer.

Organisation for Economic Cooperation and Development. (2004). *Career guidance and public policy: Bridging the gap*. Retrieved from www.oecd.org

Plant, P. (2009). *Quality assurance/evidence-base for policy and systems development: Reflection note.* Helsinki, Finland: European Lifelong Guidance and Policy Network.

Reardon, R. C., & Lenz, J. G. (2007, September). *Translating theory to practice: An effective model for preparing career counselors-in-training.* Paper presented at the symposium of the International Association for Educational and Vocational Guidance, Padova, Italy.

Rondon, M. E. (2007, September). *Social pertinence of graduate studies in guidance at the Universidad Central de Venezuela.* Paper presented at the symposium for the International Association for Educational and Vocational Guidance, Padova, Italy.

Spokane, A. R. (1991). *Career interventions.* Upper Saddle River, NJ: Prentice-Hall.

Super, D. E. (1976). *Career education and the meaning of work.* Washington, DC: Office of Education.

Turcotte, M., & Michaud, G. (2007, September). *Training of career guidance researchers and practitioners.* Paper presented at the symposium for the International Association for Educational and Vocational Guidance, Padova, Italy.

Author Index

A

Abdulla, A., 90, 98, 232, 245, 260, 266, 488, 667
Ablett, J., 242
Abraham, K.M., 151
Achenbach, T.M., 176
Achtenhagen, F., 279
Ackerman, P.L., 57, 260, 618
Adam, S., 151, 310
Adams, M., 155
Adams, T.E., 458
Adnett, N., 591
Aguayo, D., 153
Aguilar-Gaxiola, S., 529
Ahadzie, W., 265
Ahmed, H.S., 541
Ahukaramū, C.R., 542
Akerman, R., 405
Akkok, F., 274
Akyıldız, N., 649
Albert, S., 8, 431, 539–552
Alexander, K.P., 186–188
Alexander, P.A., 626
Ali, L., 660
Ali, S.R., 152, 154
Allen, M., 709
Allen, T.D., 651
Allik, J., 89
Alloway, N., 261
Allport, G.W., 124–125
Almeida, D.M., 127
Almeida, N., 659–670
Almerigi, J.B., 176
Alonso, J., 529
Altman, Y., 573
Alvarez, A.A., 155
Amminger, G.P., 529
Amundson, N.E., 22, 30–32, 163, 328, 579, 718, 733
Anand, P., 155
Andersen, S.H., 252
Anderson, C., 470
Anderson, J., 504, 506
Andoh, P., 261
Ang, R.P., 161
Antràs, P., 242
Appadurai, A., 319
Aravind, S., 499

Arbib, M.A., 90
Arendt, H., 81
Argyris, C., 454, 455, 462
Argyropoulou, K., 90
Arkin, R.M., 75
Arneson, R., 337
Arnett, J.J., 151
Arnold, M.S., 729
Arora, S., 298
Arredondo, P., 602
Arthur, M.B., 17, 18, 61, 204, 309
Arthur, N., 39, 159, 234, 329, 331, 568, 579, 580, 584, 587–604, 690
Artiles, A., 504
Arulmani, G., 1–10, 13, 17, 23, 81–101, 105–116, 153, 185, 186, 193, 225–237, 241–253, 256, 259, 260, 262, 264, 266, 291, 296, 298, 302, 311, 319, 351, 384, 392, 405, 428, 431–450, 457, 488, 499, 502, 503, 506, 513–535, 542, 544–546, 550, 579, 580, 584, 609–627, 659–670
Arum, R., 348
Arviso-One Feather, V., 406
Arzuaga, F., 709
Arzuaga, G., 709
Ashton, D., 220
Astin, H.S., 557, 565
Atkins, L., 264
August, R.A., 557
Austin, J.T., 56, 92, 622
Aytaç, S., 649

B

Baars, S., 405
Backus, F., 155
Badawi, A.A., 276
Badroodien, A., 366
Bainbridge, A., 416, 428
Bakshi, A.J., 1–10, 43–64, 121–145, 173–199, 291, 292, 296, 300, 302, 303, 351, 379, 386, 502, 567, 568, 619, 626, 660
Ball, B., 204
Ball, J., 149
Ball, S., 264
Baltes, A., 293
Baltes, P.B., 44–52, 60, 62, 64, 175–177, 293, 614
Bambling, M., 482

Bandura, A., 62, 150, 166, 185, 258, 442, 504, 507
Banerjee, R., 504
Banga, R., 228
Banks, M., 204
Bansel, P., 329
Barbaranelli, C., 258
Barham, L., 313, 331
Barling, J., 155, 161
Barnard, A.J., 82
Barnes, A., 467
Barnes, S.-A., 204, 205, 217, 226, 230, 467, 473, 734
Barrat, V., 152
Barrick, M.R., 130
Bartrum, D.A., 162
Baruch, Y., 573
Bascom, W.R., 437
Baskin, B., 299
Basran, G.S., 578
Bassot, B., 328, 453–463
Bates, I., 204
Batterham, J., 260–263
Baudouin, R., 645, 655, 674, 721
Bauman, Z., 151, 322, 327, 329
Baym, N., 466, 467
Beale, E., 229
Bean, J., 483, 491
Beck, A.T., 442
Beck, U., 151
Beck, V., 264
Becker, D.R., 339, 342, 344, 348, 349
Becker, R., 531
Beckett, C., 506
Bedeian, A.G., 647
Bee, H., 297
Begum, N., 555
Beh, L., 647
Behrens, D., 599
Beier, M.E., 57, 260
Bell, D., 256
Bellah, R.N., 89
Bellwood, P., 83
Bemak, F., 251
Benbow, C.P., 612
Benet-Martinez, V., 70
Benjamin, K., 152
Bennell, P., 265, 400
Bennett, G.K., 614
Benson, G.S., 575
Benson, P.L., 175–178, 180–182, 197, 198
Bentley, K., 287
Ben-Zur, H., 161
Berger, R., 152
Berglund, M.L., 176
Bernard, H., 166
Bernes, K., 709
Berry, J., 437
Berry, J.W., 67–69, 73–75, 87
Berthet, T., 323
Beswick, J., 651

Bettelheim, B., 434, 441
Bettinger, E.P., 352
Betz, G., 557
Betz, N.E., 53, 58, 159, 162
Beyer, S., 531
Bezanson, L., 645, 676
Bhadha, B.R., 152
Bhatti, F., 498
Bialik, C., 294
Bibby, R., 709
Bichler, R., 465
Biddle, B.J., 93
Bierman, K., 137
Biermann, F., 249
Biesta, G., 211, 213, 217
Bigeon, C., 733
Biggeri, M., 319
Bilimoria, D., 557
Bimrose, J., 31, 188, 203–221, 226, 228, 230, 231, 467, 473, 491, 555–569, 734, 735
Bingham, R.P., 596
Birman, D., 152
Bishop, J., 469
Bissell, W.N., 99, 242, 392
Bisson, P., 241, 244, 247
Björklund, A., 352
Blanchflower, D., 256
Bledsoe, M., 159
Bloch, D.P., 23
Block, J., 127–130
Blossfeld, H.-P., 339
Blustein, D.L., 15, 16, 18, 22, 23, 31, 34, 35, 37, 149, 153–155, 227, 241
Boas, I., 249
Bochner, A.P., 458
Bogardus, E.S., 77
Bogin, B., 51
Bolino, M.C., 575, 579
Bolton, G., 456, 462
Bonar, E.E., 151
Bond, G.R., 518, 530
Bonnett, H.R., 16, 17, 23
Borbély-Pecze, T.B., 317
Borden, L.M., 173, 181, 183
Borders, L.D., 558
Bordin, E.S., 34
Borgen, B., 645, 655, 674, 721
Borgen, W.A., 579, 692, 709–725
Borhans, L., 230
Bortei-Doku, E., 261, 262, 264
Bosch, G., 271
Bosley, C., 467
Botchie, G., 265
Bouchart, D., 405
Boud, D., 454, 455, 462
Boudon, R., 341
Bowen, G.L., 155
Bowers-Brown, T., 263
Boyatzis, R., 204

Boyd, E.M., 453
Bozorgmehr, M., 578
Brabazon, T., 470
Bradley, H., 555
Bradley, R.H., 502, 508
Bradley, R.W., 610
Brady, D., 403
Brandtstädter, J., 127, 176
Braude, L., 93
Braungart-Rieker, J.M., 156
Braver, S., 155
Brawley, K.T., 694
Breakwell, G., 204
Breen, R., 339, 340, 342, 346, 349
Brewster, A.B., 155
Brewster, C., 578
Bridgewater, P., 552
Brief, A.P., 647, 648
Briel, L.W., 532
Bright, J.E.H., 14, 18, 19, 21, 29, 37, 205
Bringaze, T., 587, 698
Briscoe, J.P., 228
Brislin, R.W., 77
Britzman, D., 426
Broda, C., 151
Bronfenbrenner, U., 35, 176
Bronk, K.C, 180
Brooks, L., 557, 558
Brooks, R., 587, 601
Brooks-Gunn, J., 176, 179, 183, 189, 197
Brossart, D.F., 482
Brown, A., 188, 203–221
Brown, C., 544
Brown, D., 13, 14, 21, 23, 31, 32, 36, 248, 509
Brown, D.K., 295
Brown, M.T., 69–72, 78
Brown, P., 220, 221, 255, 256
Brown, R., 245
Brown, S., 602
Brown, S.D., 58–60, 62, 63, 150, 158, 587, 626
Browne, L., 69
Bruce, E.M., 647
Bruch, C.S., 651
Bruchac, J., 436
Bruer, R.A., 530
Bryant, B.K., 153, 160
Bryman, A., 559
Brynin, M., 215
Buchanan, M.J., 674, 677
Bucher, A., 145
Buchmann, C., 344, 351
Buhler, P., 246
Buhr, E., 677
Buhrmester, M.D., 135, 136
Büning, N., 255
Burdett, R., 245
Burgess, R.G., 559
Burgess, S., 529
Buriel, R., 150

Burlingame, G., 166
Burritt, R., 313
Bussiere, P., 709
Bustillo Mesanza, R., 588
Butler, S., 14, 24
Buyukgoze, A., 728
Byars-Winston, A., 260
Bybee, D., 530
Bynner, J., 204
Bysshe, S., 287
Byun, S.-Y., 351

C
Cahill, M., 550
Cairns, B.D., 46
Cairns, R.B., 46
Cajete, G., 698
Caligiuri, P., 579
Callanan, P., 455
Campbell, A., 592
Campbell, D.P., 612
Campbell, J., 435
Campbell, K., 518, 530
Canton, N., 297
Cantrell, S., 255
Caplan, G., 162
Caporoso, R.A., 532, 534
Caprara, G., 258
Care, E., 16, 17, 23
Carlson, A., 416
Carlson, C., 149
Carr, N., 470, 471
Carraher, S.M., 581
Carroll, D., 152
Carroll, J.B., 613, 614
Carroll, J.M., 501
Carver, C.S., 161
Caslione, J.A., 121, 144
Caspi, A., 125, 127–129, 143
Castle, J., 506
Catalano, R.F., 176, 183, 184
Catraio, C., 155
Caulfield, N., 579
Cavazos, J. Jr., 578, 593
Cerdin, J.L., 579, 580
Chambers, R., 379, 404
Chan, D., 75
Chanda, N., 226
Chandrashekar, H., 520
Chang, D.H.F., 698
Chang, E.C., 161
Chang, L.C., 75
Chang-Schneider, C., 135
Chapeland, V., 155
Charest, J., 271
Charles, G., 674
Charmaz, K., 559, 560
Chatfield, T., 469

Chaves, A.P., 155, 159
Chen, C.P., 31, 603
Chen, G., 545
Chen, S., 99
Cheng, Y., 530
Chetty, C., 38
Cheung, F.M., 70, 76
Cheung, S.F., 76
Childe, G., 83
Chinmayananda, 138–143
Chong, W.H., 161
Christofi, V., 593
Christogiorgos, D., 482
Christophers, U., 646
Christopher-Sisk, E.K., 149
Chronister, K.M., 154
Chua, C.H., 579
Chung, R.C.-Y., 251
Cimera, R., 529
Cinamon, R.G., 153, 161
Clarke, S., 416
Clawson, T., 694
Clegg, C., 650
Clough, B., 211
Cochran, L., 30, 163
Cochrane, A.L., 72
Coenjaerts, C., 360
Cohen, D., 96
Cohen, G.A., 337
Cohen, P., 402, 406
Cohen, R., 325
Colley, H., 264, 319, 323, 328, 417
Collin, A., 14, 17, 18, 23, 37, 204
Collings, D.G., 574
Collins, D., 389
Collins, J., 407
Collins, M., 530
Collins, S., 331, 579, 580, 584, 596, 597, 602,
    700, 709
Coltrane, S., 152
Connell, R., 402, 406
Conoley, C.W., 482
Constantine, M., 596, 597
Conway, G.R., 379, 404
Cook, E.P., 31, 35, 557, 565
Cook, J.A., 530
Cooley, C.H., 130, 132, 133, 185
Coon, H.M., 89
Coppola, M., 161
Corey, G., 445
Corey, M.S., 445
Corrigan, P.W., 521, 530
Corwyn, R.F., 502, 508
Costa, P.T. Jr., 123, 128, 243, 292
Courlander, H., 437
Court, D., 247
Coutinho, M.T.N., 31, 155, 227, 241
Cramer, S.H., 725
Craven, R.G., 544

Crawford, M., 402
Crean, T., 531
Creed, P.A., 162
Cribb, A., 325, 330
Crick, N.R., 149
Crocitto, M.M., 581
Croity-Belz, S., 155
Croson, R., 545
Crutsinger, M., 85
Cruza-Guet, M.C., 55, 56

D
D'Achiardi, C., 612
Dæhlen, M., 203, 206, 207, 211, 214, 217–220
Dalley-Trim, L., 261
Dam, U.C., 31, 227, 241
Damon, W., 175–177, 180
Dan, O., 153
Dasen, P.R., 67, 68
Dauwalder, J.-P., 21, 31, 150, 157, 159, 162, 328, 413,
    415, 418, 425
David, D., 81
Davies, B., 329
Davies, P., 475
Davis, D., 260
Dawis, R.V., 52–54
Day, B., 714
Daya, C., 587
Dayton-Johnson, J., 556
De Bruin, G.P., 643
De Bruin, K., 643
de Fillipis, A., 155
De Grip, A., 230
de Tezanos, M., 709
Deardorff, A., 295
Dechézelles, S., 323
DeFries, J.C., 125
den Boer, P., 681
Denner, J., 186
Denniston, R., 403
Dent, G., 481, 483, 486–489, 491, 646
Derrida, J., 324
Deshpande, S.P., 651
Deshpande, S.S., 651
DeVries, R., 149
Diale, B., 698
Dick, E., 244
DiClemente, C.C., 580
Diemer, M.A., 152–154
Dikel, M., 598
Diment, K., 264
DiPietro, S., 530
Dippo, D., 426
DiPrete, T.A., 344
Dixon, J., 531
Dixon, R.A., 614
Dkhar, B., 545
Dobbs, R., 249
Doctor, R., 662

Doh, D., 261
Dollmann, J., 347
Domene, J.F., 14, 18, 21, 674, 677
Domokos-Cheng Ham, M., 596
Donkin, L., 407
Doren, B., 151
Dorsey, E.R., 651
Douglass, J.A., 589, 590
Douvou, M., 482
Dowling, E.M., 176, 178
Dozois, D.J., 676
Drake, R.E., 531
Drebing, C.E., 514
Drechsler, D., 556
Dreyfus, H., 466, 474–477
Drosos, N., 90
Drummond, D., 229, 230, 232
Duarte, M.E., 21, 30, 31, 150, 157, 159, 162, 328,
    415, 418, 425, 611, 622
Dullabh, A., 24
Dun, O., 249
Dunham, P., 82
Dunn, E.C., 514
Dunn, R., 352
Dunning, J., 255
Dunston, K., 154
Dupuis, G., 647, 648, 654
Duran, G., 69
Durkheim, E., 85
Duyan, E.C., 649
Dweck, C.S., 136
Dworkin, R., 337
Dyer, F., 301
Dyke, L.S., 579

E
Earl, J., 205
Easton, S., 153, 193, 351, 645–656
Eaton, D., 407
Ebersöhn, L., 550
Ebner, C., 293
Eccles, J., 175, 177, 178
Eckstein, D.G., 13
Edelstein, R., 589, 590
Eden, L., 241
Eduarda Duarte, M., 413, 415, 418, 425
Edwards, J.A., 653
Edwards, J.R., 648, 649
Edwards, R., 426
Efraty, D., 647
Egan, G., 414, 418
Eggerth, D.E., 573
Eizmendi, G., 247
Elder, G.H. Jr., 129
Elias, P., 216
Ellis, A., 442
Ellis, C., 458
Elmer, N., 204
Emery, G., 442

Engels, D.W., 728
England, G., 483, 491
Enriquez, V.G., 68, 74
Erikson, E.H., 123
Erikson, R., 341, 342, 347, 349, 350
Ernst, C., 360
Esbin, H., 715
Estrada, Y., 260
Evangelista, L., 690, 692, 698, 700
Eversole, R., 404

F
Facer, K., 467, 473–475
Fales, A.W., 453
Fang, C., 247
Fang, T., 578
Farh, J.-L., 56
Farmer, H.S., 557
Farver, J.A.M., 152
Fassinger, R.E., 558, 559
Feenstra, C.R., 242, 243
Fehr, E., 338
Feirman, D., 166
Fekette, D.M., 531
Felsman, D.E., 155
Fenwick, T., 590
Ferber, T., 176
Fernet, C., 156
Ferrari, L., 149–166, 185
Ferrari, M., 136
Ferrari, T.M., 184, 186, 188
Ferry, T.R., 158
Field, J., 214
Fielding, A.J., 419
Finkel, L., 578
Fisher, W.R., 434
Fitoussi, J.P., 311
Fitzgerald, L.F., 204
Fitzpatrick, M.E., 152, 164
Flederman, P., 296, 371, 481–492
Fletcher, T., 501, 504
Flint, K., 264
Florentino, A.R., 158
Flores, L.Y., 153, 596
Flores, P., 166
Florou, A., 482
Flynn, J.R., 469
Flynn, M.A., 573
Flynn, R.J., 646
Flynn, S., 593
Fogo, W.R., 151
Follero-Pugh, F., 227
Ford, A., 418
Ford, D., 32, 34
Ford, M., 32, 34
Forrest, L., 557, 558
Fortuny, M., 360
Fouad, N.A., 152, 158, 164, 596
Foucault, M., 403

Fouin, R., 323
Foxcroft, C., 24
Fraser, N., 321, 323
Frautschy DeMuth, R.L., 228
Frazer, J.G., 431
Freeborn, D.K., 651
Freeman, R.B., 85, 574
Freire, P., 322
French, E., 578
Frese, M., 51
Fretwell, D.H., 272, 274, 275, 287, 317, 399, 481
Freud, S., 130
Freund, A.M., 51, 293
Friedlander, M.L., 155
Friedman, S.M., 158
Friedman, T.L., 227, 228
Friel, M., 404
Fritz, E., 698
Frosh, S., 428
Frübing, J., 484
Fruebing, J., 284, 700
Fuchs, C., 465
Fuller, A., 207, 219, 264
Fullerton, L., 470
Furber, S., 476
Furbish, D., 694

G
Gabbard, S.M., 152
Gadd, C.J., 86
Galab, S., 405
Galambos, N.L., 160
Galinsky, E., 160, 161
Gallagher, L.A., 153–155
Gandhi, A., 115
Gandhi, M.K., 4, 105–116
Gangl, M., 6, 351
Ganz, W., 295
Garcia, M., 155
Garcia, P.R.J.M., 158
Gardner, H., 50, 615
Garnett, F., 473
Garrett-Peltier, H., 250
Garske, G., 513
Gasskov, V., 272
Gati, I., 204
Gatti, M., 733
Gauthier, L., 156, 158
Gaw, K.F., 593, 598
Gebel, M., 336
Geertz, C., 82
Gelatt, H.B., 309, 403, 713
Gemenne, F., 249
George, J.M., 647, 648
Gereffi, G., 574
Gestsdóttir, S., 176, 177, 180, 195
Getzel, E.E., 532
Gewirtz, S., 321, 325, 330
Ghali, A.A., 325

Ghaye, K., 454, 462
Ghaye, T., 454, 462
Ghiselli, E.E., 654
Gibbs, G., 454, 462
Gibson, R., 293
Gibson-Cline, J., 709–711
Giddens, A., 84, 413
Ginevra, M.C., 4, 10, 149–166, 185
Glaser, B.G., 559
Glasscock, J., 149
Glenn, J.C., 151, 539–552
Gneezy, U., 545
Goddard, T., 484, 489
Goffman, E., 472–474, 521, 533
Goldberg, D., 650
Goldthorpe, J.H., 342, 348, 349
Goleman, D., 204
Gonthier, F., 321
Good, G.E., 506
Goodall, J., 81
Goodman, D.M., 325
Goodman, J., 734
Gootman, J.A., 175, 177, 178
Gordon, T.J., 124–125, 151
Gore, A., 310
Gottfredson, L.S., 309, 557, 613, 614, 620, 727
Gottlieb, G., 130, 179
Gowdy, J.M., 82
Gower, J.L., 591
Goyer, L., 645, 655, 674, 721
Grabosky, T.K., 251
Graham, B., 660
Graham, M.D., 14, 18, 21
Gramsci, A., 320
Granvold, D.K., 32
Gration, G., 275, 278
Gravino, K.L., 149
Green, A., 256
Green, K., 398
Green, S.J.D., 324
Greene, J.C., 669
Greene, K.M., 174, 187, 188
Greene, L., 166
Greenhalgh, P., 401
Greg, N., 509
Gregoire, J., 620
Gregory, R., 256
Greve, A., 578
Grierson, J., 715
Griffin, A., 186
Griffin, J.P., 98
Grønning, T., 203, 207, 211, 214, 217–220
Grossman, J.M., 155
Grove, B., 650
Grubb, W.N., 225, 237, 279
Grusec, J.E., 86
Gu, Q., 587
Guay, F., 156, 158
Guerra, A.L., 156

Guichard, J., 15, 21, 30, 150, 157, 159, 162, 328, 401, 406, 413–416, 418, 421, 423, 424, 429
Guildford, J.P., 613
Guindon, M., 299
Gulati, A., 242
Gummere, R.M., 315
Guneri, O.Y., 728
Gunz, H., 18
Guo, S., 590
Gupta, A., 71, 78, 596
Gupta, M., 293
Gustafsson, M., 366
Gutman, L.M., 405
Gysbers, N., 293

H
Haag, S., 164
Habermas, J., 402
Hackett, G., 62, 63, 150, 164, 557, 558, 626
Hackman, J., 647
Haggestad, E.D., 618
Hahn, H., 416
Haijke, H., 230
Haire, H., 654
Hall, B., 590
Hall, D.T., 61, 204, 228, 578
Hall, R., 313
Halpern, M., 647
Halpern, R., 184–186, 188
Hambleton, R., 622
Hamill, A.C., 151
Hamilton, M.A., 186, 187
Hamilton, S.F., 175, 176, 186, 187
Hanh, T.N., 137
Hannum, E., 351
Hansen, J.-I.C., 57, 58, 612, 622, 625
Hansen, L.S., 23, 234
Hansen, T., 328
Hanson, H.G., 242, 243
Hardin, E.E., 74, 75
Hargittai, E., 470
Harmon, L.W., 557
Harrell, T., 592
Harris-Bowlsbey, J., 166, 598, 727, 736, 737
Harsdorff, M., 249
Harter, S., 130, 133, 134, 185
Hartl, K., 578
Hartung, P.J., 60, 157, 160, 161, 596, 727
Harvey, L., 267
Hastings, P.D., 86
Hatcher, T., 578
Hawkins, J.D., 176, 183, 184
Hawthorn, R., 318, 482
Hawthorne, L., 590
Hazarika, M., 542
Hecken, A.E., 348, 349
Heckman, J.J., 336, 348
Heerwagen, J., 228
Heinonen, K., 161

Heintz, J., 250
Helpman, E., 242
Henderson, J.A., 329
Heppner, M.J., 31, 35, 154, 557–559, 565, 595
Herman, K., 153
Hermans, H.J.M., 130, 134, 135
Herr, E.L., 317, 319, 598, 727–729, 735–737
Hershenson, D.B., 35
Herskovits, M.J., 86
Herzberg, F., 650
Hesketh, A., 255
Hesse, M.B., 90
Hidi, S., 613, 626
Hiebert, B., 9, 645, 655, 671–685, 689–725
Hillage, J., 482
Hill-Fotouhi, C., 152
Hillmert, S., 348
Hirsch, B.J., 186–188, 195
Hirsch, S.W., 529, 530, 533
Hirschi, A., 159
Ho, Y.F., 68, 74
Hobbes, T., 322
Hobsbawm, E., 398
Hodkinson, H., 258, 319, 323
Hodkinson, P., 258, 319, 323
Hoebel, E.A., 82
Hoeckel, K., 257
Hoelson, C., 17, 24, 38, 39, 632
Hoffman, F.L., 530
Hofkirchner, W., 465
Hofstede, G., 89, 654, 655
Hoggett, P., 416
Holland, J.L., 20, 21, 36, 54, 56, 127, 129, 309, 414, 435, 509, 612–614, 632, 635, 636, 639
Honey, P., 454, 462
Hong, G., 596
Hong, K.L., 38, 56, 69, 75, 243, 499, 622
Honneth, A., 325
Hooley, T., 467, 468, 471, 481, 488, 491
Hopkins, M.M., 557
Hopkins, S., 677, 678, 722
Hoppe-Rooney, T.L., 173, 181–183, 197
Hopps, J., 154
Horan, J.J., 676
Horrocks, C., 558, 560
Hoskisson, R.E., 241
Hou, Z., 17
House, R., 729
Howard, C., 260
Howard, K.A.S., 156–158
Hoxte, H., 275
Hoyt, K.B., 713
Hsien-Hwa, K., 649
Hsien-Wen, K., 649
Huan, V.S., 161
Huang, J.L., 71, 78
Huberman, A.M., 560
Hue, M.-T., 499, 504, 505, 509
Huebner, A.J., 173, 182, 189

Hughes, D., 31, 204, 212, 217, 230, 275, 278, 317, 556, 564, 734, 735
Hulot, N., 310
Hulse, P., 477
Hunt, C., 423
Hunt, W., 482
Hursh, D.W., 329
Hutchings, K., 578
Hutchinson, J., 287, 467, 481, 488, 491
Hutton, J., 483
Hwang, K., 597
Hwang, M.H., 595
Hynes, K., 185–188, 195

I
Ibraim, S.B., 698
Ichou, M., 345–347
Idris, K., 647
Immerwahr, J., 84
Irani, B., 183
Irby, M., 176
Irving, B.A., 313, 322, 323, 331
Isaacs, S., 485
Ishiyama, F.I., 571
Issac, B., 407

J
Jackson, M., 347, 349, 350
Jacob, M., 348
Jacobsen, M., 329
Jacobson, T.E., 473, 475
Jain, A., 253, 297
James, D., 264
James, W., 130–132, 134
Jamieson, L., 204
Jansen, M., 285
Jäntti, M., 352
Januja, S., 498, 499, 502, 506
Jarjoura, D., 651
Jarvis, P., 272, 277
Jeeva, S.R.D.N., 542
Jeffrey, G., 550
Jenschke, B., 284, 403, 484, 672
Jex, S.M., 651
Jih-Sheng, J., 649
Jin, Y., 590, 592
Johns, L.C., 514
Jóhnson, G., 405
Johnson, P., 151
Johnston, B., 258
Jokinen, T., 578
Jones, G.B., 153
Jonsson, J.O., 341, 342, 347, 349, 350
Jordan, T.E., 160
Jordan, W.J., 153
Joyce, A., 166
Juang, L.P., 155
Judge, P., 467, 476
Jung, C.G., 448
Jütting, J.P., 556

K
Kadhiravan, S., 649
Kagan, J., 47, 48
Kahyarra, G., 255, 265
Kampschroer, K., 228
Kanitkar, K., 662
Kantamneni, N., 164
Kao, G., 405
Karajic, A., 689–691, 693, 727
Karjalainen, M., 285
Karlsson, B.G., 542
Karmel, T., 256
Kasthuri, P., 520
Kavale, J., 551
Kavanagh, M.J., 647
Kawasaki, T., 34
Kawlra, A., 407
Kaye, N., 576
Keep, E., 256, 258
Keevy, J., 482
Keith, J.G., 173, 181–183, 197
Keller, B.K., 152, 163
Keller, S., 342
Kelly, K., 228
Kemeny, K., 709
Kemmelmeier, M., 89
Kemp, E.G., 577
Kempen, H.J.G., 135
Kendall, L., 646
Kenny, M.E., 155, 159
Keogh, R., 454, 455, 462
Kerr, B.A., 647
Kessler, R.C., 529
Ketterson, T.U., 155
Khapova, S.N., 61
Kharkongor, G.C., 8, 431, 539–552
Kidd, J.M., 318, 648
Kidd, K.K., 51
Kiesler, D.J., 69, 123, 130, 131
Kiliç-Çakmak, E., 473, 474
Kim, H., 153
Kim, K.-K., 351
Kim, U., 68, 69, 73, 74
Kim, Y., 152
King, N., 558, 560
King, R., 482
King, Z., 212
Kinman, G., 651, 653
Kirkham, P., 401
Kirkland, R., 241, 244
Kirkwood, W.G., 436
Kirpal, S., 203, 206, 207, 211, 214, 217–220
Kirshner, B., 182
Kiselica, M.S., 532, 534
Kitayama, S., 259
Kitazawa, K., 245
Klein, D., 186
Klein, K.L., 159
Klein, M., 340, 341
Kluckhohn, C., 71

Knappert, J., 438
Knasel, E.G., 59, 62, 328
Kobos, J.C., 166
Koert, E., 579
Kogan, I., 336
Kolb, D., 454, 462
Kolby, K., 229, 230, 232
Komarraju, M., 56, 92, 622
Koshy, S., 297
Kotler, P., 121, 144
Kottkamp, R.B., 454, 462
Kowal, A., 149
Koydemir, S., 728
Kraimer, M.L., 579
Kramer, D.A., 614
Kramer, L., 149
Krapp, A., 613, 626
Kraus, S.W., 151
Kravitz, R.L., 651
Krawietz, S., 475
Krebs, D.L., 323
Krechowiecka, I., 467
Kregel, J., 530–532
Kremen, A.M., 128
Kress, H., 149
Krishna, S., 248
Krishnamurti, J., 6, 137, 379–381, 390, 394
Krull, J.L., 149
Krumboltz, J.D., 13, 19, 34, 90, 153, 159, 185, 205,
        309, 403, 504, 713
Kuhn, T.S., 43, 44, 74, 136, 145
Kuijpers, M., 262
Kumar, C.N., 520
Kumar, K., 111
Kumar, S., 225–237, 245, 384, 617
Kumar, V., 541, 542
Kumsta, R., 504
Kurbah, S., 542, 545
Kurchak, W., 709
Kush, K., 163

L
La Gro, N., 467
Lahti, J., 161
Lalande, V., 645, 655, 674, 721
Laloo, R.C., 542
Lambert, M., 709
Lambert, S.J., 648
Lamontagne, F., 576–578, 582
Lamprecht, J.C., 636, 643
Langstieh, B.T., 541, 542
Lanier, J., 471, 472, 474
Lapan, R.T., 158
Lapour, A.S., 154, 557–559
Larbalestier, M., 468, 470
Lareau, A., 405
Larsen, L.J., 152
Larson, R.W., 179, 180

Lau, C.M., 241
Lau, K.G.I., 578
Lau, R.S.M., 647
Lauder, H., 220, 221, 256
Laungani, P., 549
Lavish, L.A., 544
Law, B., 309, 310, 318, 434, 436, 465–477
Law, J., 318
Law, K.S., 56, 622
Law, S.-F., 589, 590
Lawler, E.E., 647
Lawlor, L., 325
Lawrence, A., 579
Lawrence, B.S., 204
Lazarova, M.B., 579
Le Pargneux, M., 580
Lea, S., 155
Leach, M.M., 67
Lebrun, L.A., 577
Lee, B., 186, 187, 660
Lee, D., 647
Lee, G., 578
Lee, J.A., 655
Lee, R., 69
Lee, S., 529
Lee, S.-H., 71, 78, 549
Lee, T., 473–475
Lee, Y.H., 151
Lees-Maffei, G., 401
Leffert, N., 178
Lefranc, A., 337, 352
Leibtag, E., 151
Leidy, M.S., 155
Leigh, J.P., 651
Leith, J.E., 151
Leitner, H., 329
Lemme, B., 292, 295
Lemola, S., 161
Lent, R.W., 14–16, 31, 58–63, 149, 150, 156,
        164, 626
Lenz, A.S., 578, 593, 595, 599, 600, 602
Lenz, J.G., 23, 610, 728, 734
Leonard, E.J., 530
Leonard, K.L., 545
Leong, F.T L., 1–10, 56, 57, 67–78, 92, 97, 121, 145,
        405, 549, 579, 584, 596, 622
Lerner, J.V., 176, 177, 179, 180, 195
Lerner, R.M., 33, 34, 130, 174–180, 187, 195
Leung, K., 75, 76
Leung, S.A., 129, 593, 596, 622
Leung, S.-M.A., 13, 17
Leventhal, C.R., 246
Levesley, T., 260–263, 268
Levin, A.S., 19, 204, 309, 403, 713
Levinas, E., 324, 325
Lewin, C., 417
Lewin, K., 71
Lewis, D.M., 727

Lewis, J., 729
Lewis, M., 152
Lewis, S.Z., 152
Lickliter, R., 130, 179
Liebel, M., 398
Lieuw-Kie-Song, M., 249
Lilly, R.L., 69
Lim, N., 578
Lim, V.K.G., 151, 158
Lin, C.A., 155
Lind, M., 542
Lindenberger, U., 44, 46, 175, 293
Lindstrom, L., 151, 155
Lines, A., 646
Linn, S.G., 158
Linton, R., 86
Lipsey, R., 407
List, J.A., 545
Liu, J.H., 82
Liu, W.M., 154
Lloyd, D., 227
Locke, D.C., 602
Loehlin, J.C., 125, 128
Lofquist, L.H., 52, 53
Loiselle, M., 229, 230, 232
Lonczak, H.S., 176, 183, 184
London, M., 205
Long, B.T., 352
Lonner, W.J., 77
Loo, G.L., 151, 158
Low, K.S.D., 612, 613
Lubinski, D., 612
Luchetta, E.J., 55
Luijkx, R., 339, 340
Luk-Fong, Y.Y., 662
Lundan, S., 255
Lundin, R.K., 533
Lung, C.L., 662
Lyass, A., 531
Lynge, F., 312

M
MacDonald-Wilson, K.L., 531
MacIntyre, A., 324
Mackey, T.P., 473, 475
Maclure, S., 475
Macrae, S., 264
Madden, T., 152
Madsen, E., 543
Magnusson, K., 645, 676, 709, 722
Maguire, M., 264
Maio, F.G., 577
Malik, B., 313, 323
Manfredi, T., 251
Mann, A., 278
Mannering, K., 296, 301
Mantler, J., 579
Manzi, A.J., 149
Marder, K., 544

Mare, R.D., 341, 344
Maree, K., 550
Marginson, S., 351
Mariel, P., 588
Maringanti, A., 329
Markus, H.R., 259
Marlowe, F.W., 82
Marques, A., 9, 659–670
Marris, L., 226, 231
Marsella, A.J., 67
Marshall, B., 255
Marshall, C., 331
Marshall, J., 557
Marshall, K.G., 153, 154
Marshall, S.K., 14, 18, 21
Marshman, S., 329
Martel, J.P., 647, 648, 654
Martin, J., 521
Martin, J.N., 592
Martin, T.N., 648
Martinez, C.R., 152
Marx, K., 326, 327
Maslow, A.H., 580, 650
Mason, A., 226
Mason, P., 469
Mason, R., 473, 474
Massaro, J.M., 531
Mastrianni, X., 530
Masumba, M., 590, 592
Matsumoto, D., 655
Matthews, K.A., 161
Mayer, M., 357–374
Mayo, E., 647
Mayo, P., 321
Mazkoory, P., 183
Mazzarol, T., 587
McAdams, D.P., 123, 130
McCaffrey, A., 677, 678, 722
McCash, P., 17
McClain, M.C., 323
McClarty, K.L., 135
McCormick, R.M., 22
McCracken, S.G., 530
McCrae, R.R., 123, 292
McDaniel, A., 344
McDonald, S., 579
McDowell, D.J., 149
McDowell, L., 402
McGinn, M.K., 649
McGrath, S., 366
McGrew, J.H., 531
McGrew, W.C., 81
McIlveen, P., 135
McLaughlin, M., 182
McLean, H.B., 22
McLeroy, K.R., 162
McMahon, M., 3, 4, 8, 9, 13–24, 29–39, 135, 145,
        331, 555–569, 610, 631–644
McNair, S., 568

McQuilken, M., 530
Mcreynolds, C., 513
McTighe, J., 674
McWhirter, E.H., 154, 162, 323
Meadows, S., 475
Meara, N.M., 557
Medel-Añonuevo, C., 403, 405
Meer, J., 257
Mehendale, A., 504
Mehta, K., 152
Meijers, F., 262
Meka, A., 541, 542
Mekinda, M.A., 186, 188, 189
Mellon, P.M., 648
Memmo, M., 181
Menchen, E., 470
Mendelson, M.B., 161
Mendoza-Denton, R., 124, 126
Menon, J., 180
Menzies, J.L., 579
Merrill, R., 413, 416, 421, 422
Merton, R.K., 93
Methei, R.J., 677
Metheny, J., 151, 155
Mezirow, J., 455
Michaud, G., 225, 231, 732
Miedema, J., 470
Miles, M.B., 560
Miller, E., 98
Miller, E.L., 572, 581
Miller, L., 470
Miller, M.A., 155
Miner, R., 229, 230, 232
Mines, R., 152
Minor, C., 734
Mirvis, P.H., 647
Mischel, W., 125–127, 130
Mishra, B.P., 542
Mitchell, A.M., 153, 204, 309, 713
Mitchell, K.E., 19
Mitchell, M., 293
Mjelde, J., 590, 592
Mkhize, N., 13, 14, 17, 22
Mlotkowski, P., 256
Mobley, S., 651
Mohan, A., 242
Mojtabai, R., 517
Molden, D.C., 136
Molepo, M., 550
Monbiot, G., 315
Monk, C., 416
Monk, G., 264
Moon, J., 456, 462
Moon, S., 467
Moore, C., 82
Moore, E., 293
Moore, R., 287
Moore, S., 555
Morduch, J., 389

More, A.J., 436
Morgan, G., 402
Morgan, J., 473–475
Morley, M.J., 574
Morrisson, C., 556
Morton, P., 407
Morzove, E., 468
Moshenberg, D., 152
Mount, M.K., 130
Mowbray, C.T., 530
Mpofu, E., 13, 14
Mroczek, D.K., 127, 129, 130
Muchinsky, P., 301
Mugo, J., 498, 499, 509
Mullarkey, S., 650
Mullener, W., 13
Müller, W., 6, 335–353
Mullins, L., 455, 462
Mumford, A., 454, 462
Munck, R., 247
Munka, L.M., 17
Mureithi, G., 264
Murphy, K.A., 155
Murray, A., 229, 231
Murray, H.A., 71
Murray, M., 348
Musa, M., 698
Musch, E., 323
Muter, V., 501, 505, 507
Muuya, J., 499, 504, 505

N
Nadeem, S., 85
Nag, S., 90, 91, 497–510, 730
Nagaraja, T., 541, 542
Nag-Arulmani, S., 87, 88, 90, 108, 110, 113, 185, 231, 232, 234–237, 245, 248, 256, 259, 260, 262, 264, 266, 291, 292, 302, 311, 502, 506, 544, 546, 610, 615, 620, 621, 625, 660
Nagesh, R., 617
Naish, J., 468
Nakashima, D., 552
Nanjundaiah, M., 502, 504
Narang, S.K., 152
Narasimhan, L., 247
Nash, S., 698
Nassar-McMillan, S., 729
Nayak, A., 402, 406
Naylor, F.D., 185
Neault, R.A., 8, 9, 571–584, 689–705
Needham, S., 261, 262, 264
Neugebauer, M., 344
Neuman, J.L., 612
Neumann, H., 22
Neville, H.A., 69
Newton, B., 482
Ng, S.I., 655
Nichols, C.W., 34
Nielsen, J., 470

Niles, S.G., 9, 166, 689–691, 693, 727–738
Nils, F., 620
Nisargadatta, M., 136–138, 143
Nixon, D., 402
Noelke, C., 336
North, C.E., 322
Nota, L., 4, 15, 21, 30, 31, 149–166, 185, 328, 413, 415, 418, 425
Novak, J., 530
Novicevic, M.M., 578, 582
Nunes, S., 8, 587–604
Nussbaum, M., 319, 321
Nutter, K.J., 612
Nykaenen, S., 285
Nyoni, A., 38

O
O'Brien, K.M., 31, 35, 158, 557
O'Donoghue, J.L., 182
Oesch, D., 256
Offer, M., 231
Ojeda, L., 153
Okun, A.M., 338
Oldfield, B., 264
Oldham, G., 647
O'Leary, C.J., 229
Oliver, L.W., 646
Olmos, A., 530
O'Neil, D.A., 557, 558
Ong, A., 152
Onnismaa, J., 285
Oppenheim, J., 249
Oranga, J., 498
O'Reilly, E., 677, 678
Oreopoulos, P., 352
Orton, M., 230
Osborn, D., 598
Oser, F.K., 145
Osipow, S.H., 21, 31, 74, 204
Osterman, K.F., 454, 462
Overtoom, C., 229
Ow, R., 71, 78
Owens, T.J., 155
Oyserman, D., 89

P
Paa, H.K., 162
Paauwe, J., 578
Paccoud, A., 245
Pace, F., 159
Page, R., 482
Palladino, D.E., 155
Palmer, S., 163
Papier, J., 261, 262, 264
Parameswari, J., 649
Paranjpe, A.C., 136, 142, 143, 145
Parente, A., 544
Parke, R.D., 149, 150, 152
Parkes, K.R., 651

Parnham, P., 407
Parsons, F., 15, 16, 30, 36, 225, 314, 315, 414, 709
Parsons, P., 153
Parsons, T., 336
Paseluikho, M., 172
Pastorelli, C., 258
Paton, K., 257, 258
Pattie, M., 575
Patton, M.Q., 29–39, 558
Patton, W., 4, 14, 17, 18, 21, 22, 24, 29–31, 33–36, 38, 135, 145, 162, 558, 610, 631–634
Payne, J., 257
Pearce, M., 4, 13, 15, 17, 24, 67–77, 97, 121, 145, 405
Peavy, R.V., 309, 543, 544, 549, 550
Pedersen, P., 587, 589
Peiperl, M., 18
Pek, J.C.X., 75
Pelham, B., 135
Pendergrass, L.A., 612
Penn, D.L., 521
Pennington, B.F., 500
Perkins, D.F., 181, 182
Perkins, R., 513
Perlmutter, M., 48
Pernice, K., 470
Perry, J.C., 16, 23, 187, 323
Peruniak, J.S., 717
Pesonene, A.-K., 161
Peterson, A., 366
Peterson, C., 252
Peterson, G.W., 23, 159, 610
Peterson, R.L., 676
Pfeffer, F., 339
Phelps, E., 145
Phillips, S.D., 149
Philpott, D., 550
Phinney, J.S., 152
Piaget, J., 45, 46, 133, 329, 475
Pickerell, D.A., 580, 583, 694
Pickett, T., 154
Pickren, W., 67
Pilgrim, M., 360
Pillay, P., 6, 357–374
Pimlott-Wilson, H., 587
Ping, L., 578
Pistolesi, N., 337, 352
Pittman, K., 176
Plank, S.B., 153
Plant, P., 6, 87, 250, 309–315, 676, 734
Plomin, R., 125, 128
Poduval, S., 660
Poeylioe, L., 285
Polkinghorne, D.E., 558
Pollak, R., 339, 340, 343, 344, 348
Pollin, R., 250
Poortinga, Y.H., 67
Popadiuk, N., 593, 595–600
Pope, M.L., 160, 580, 584, 698, 734
Porfeli, E.J., 14, 15, 24, 156, 159–162, 186, 187, 660

Porter, L.W., 654
Portillo, S., 152
Posavac, E.J., 676
Posterski, D., 709
Pransky, G., 152
Prashanth, N.R., 520
Presser, H.B., 227
Price, R.E., 550
Pringle, H., 83
Prochaska, J.O., 580
Prott, L., 552
Proyer, R.T., 145
Pryor, R.G.L., 14, 18, 19, 21, 29, 37, 205
Psifidou, I., 690
Purcell, K., 216
Pye, E., 405

Q
Quigley, N.R., 205

R
Radvansky, G., 475
Raffl, C., 465
Rahardja, D., 644
Raikes, H.A., 153
Raikkonen, K., 161
Rainey, L.M., 558
Rajagopalan, R., 400, 402, 407
Ramachandran, K., 7, 431–450
Ramioul, M., 215, 221
Ramos, F., 245
Ramsden, P., 473, 474
Randers, J., 310
Raskin, J.D., 18
Rasouli, M., 579
Ratanlal, D., 521
Ratnam, A., 397–408, 458
Rauner, F., 271, 272
Ravallion, M., 99
Rawls, J., 322, 324, 336, 337
Realo, A., 89
Reardon, R.C., 23, 159, 323, 610, 734
Reddy, A.N.S., 541, 542
Reddy, M.B., 541, 542
Redekopp, D.E., 714
Redfield, R., 86
Reese, L.E., 98, 448
Reese, R.J., 482
Rehfuss, M.C., 164
Rei, D., 360
Reid, H.L., 7, 413–429, 631
Reid, L.A., 550
Reid, W., 482
Reitz, J.G., 578
Remennick, L., 578
Renne, E.P., 407
Rennie, F., 473, 474
Renninger, K.A., 613, 626
Repetto, E., 674, 690, 692, 695

Resnick, S.G., 514
Restubog, S.L.D., 158, 159
Reuveny, R., 249
Revathi, E., 405
Revell, G., 530
Reynolds, A., 596, 597
Reynolds, P., 153
Rhee, K., 204
Ribeiro, M.A., 733
Rice, P., 294
Richardson, M.S., 16
Richmond, A., 299, 302
Richmond, K., 468
Richmond, L.J., 23
Richwine, M.H., 55
Riesman, D., 474
Rifkin, J., 310
Rinaldi, M., 513
Robb, M., 714
Roberts, B.W., 612
Roberts, K., 21, 37, 213, 320, 321
Rocco, T., 590
Rochlen, A.B., 482
Rode, P., 245
Rodríguez González, C., 588
Roehlkepartain, E.C., 176, 180, 181, 197
Roemer, J.E., 337, 338, 343, 352
Roeser, R.W., 145
Roest, A., 645
Rogers, C., 309
Rogers, E.S., 514, 531
Rogers-Sirin, L., 155
Rogler, L.H., 77
Rojewski, J.W., 153
Rolfe, H., 287
Rondon, M.E., 734
Rose, R.C., 647
Rosenfield, M., 482
Rosenheck, R.A., 514
Rossier, J., 611, 622
Roth, J.L., 176, 179, 183, 189, 197
Rothbard, N., 648
Rounds, J., 612, 613, 625
Rousseau, D.M., 309, 647
Rowold, J., 20
Roy, T., 398
Ruch, W., 145
Rudmin, F.W., 86
Rudolphi, F., 347
Ruitenberg, C., 324, 325
Rumbaut, R.G., 152
Rush, A.J., 442
Ruskin, J., 109, 111
Russell, M., 698
Rutecki, G.W., 651
Rutherford, S., 389
Ruthven, O., 389
Rutter, M., 504, 506
Ryan, C.W., 39

Ryan, J., 612
Ryan, J.A.M., 176
Ryan, N.E., 158, 162
Ryff, C.D., 151

S
Safaye, B.N., 293–294
Sailo, E., 499
Saito, R.N., 176, 181, 198
Saka, N., 204
Salaff, J., 578
Saletore, R.N., 438
Sam, D.L., 87
Sampson, J.P. Jr., 23, 159, 166, 323, 598, 610, 631,
    636, 643
Samuels, S.J., 651
Sanbonmatsu, L., 352
Sanchez, J., 602
Sandefur, J., 264
Sandil, R., 152
Sandino, L., 401
Sandoval, M., 465
Sangganjanavanich, V.F., 578, 593, 595, 599,
    600, 602
Śaṅkarācārya, A., 136, 142, 143
Sankh, S., 242
Sanna, L.J., 161
Santiago-Rivera, A., 71, 76
Santos, A., 597
Sarmela, M., 87
Saunders, C.M., 159
Saunders, D.E., 583
Savard, R., 225, 231
Savickas, M.L., 14–16, 18, 20, 21, 24, 29–31, 34, 55,
    58–62, 135, 150, 156, 157, 159, 162, 164, 195,
    213, 217, 328, 413–415, 418, 420, 421,
    423–425, 429, 558, 610, 631, 643, 644
Saxena, R., 247, 248
Saxenian, A.L., 574
Scales, P.C., 175, 176, 178
Scarlett, W.G., 145
Scarpetta, S., 251
Scarr, S., 51, 337
Scarre, C., 82, 83
Schafranek, M., 465
Schaltegger, S., 313
Scharber, H., 250
Scharmer, C.O., 314
Scheier, M.F., 161
Schell, D., 227
Schembri, M., 651
Schermerhorn, J.R., 648
Schilling, J., 205
Schindler, S., 340, 342–344, 346–349
Schmidt, K., 338
Schmidt-Kallert, E., 244
Schmitt, A., 51
Schmutte, P.S., 151
Schnurr, J., 715

Schober, K., 9, 284, 484, 671–685, 719
Schofield, T.J., 152
Schön, D., 454, 455, 462
Schoon, I., 153
Schugurensky, D., 590
Schulenberg, J.E., 33
Schultheiss, D.E.P., 149
Schultz, D., 296
Schulz, W.E., 669
Schwalje, W., 255
Schwartz, S.H., 655
Schweisfurthb, M., 587
Schweitzer, R., 13
Schwentker, B., 247
Scoones, I., 397, 404
Scrase, T.J., 227, 243, 405, 407
Scrine, C., 405
Scuderi, L., 228
Scullion, H., 574
Sears, H.A., 160
Seashore, H.G., 614
Secibovic, R., 286
Segall, M.H., 67
Sehgal, R., 227
Sekaran, U., 56, 92, 622
Selwyn, N., 467, 471, 474
Selz, M., 344, 345
Sen, A., 219, 311, 321, 394
Senécal, C., 156
Sennett, R., 327, 328
Serrat, O., 379, 386
Sesma, A. Jr., 175, 176
Sethi, R., 403
Sew, C.W.B., 698
Sexton, T.L., 677
Seymour, L., 650
Sgaramella, T.M., 161
Shafer, S.P., 694
Shaffer, M.A., 579
Shah, I., 436, 437
Shamash, J., 267
Shanahan, M.J., 129
Sharf, R.S., 20
Sharma, S., 293, 294
Shashidhar, P., 295
Shavit, Y., 336, 339, 348
Shaw, B.F., 442
Shen, Y., 578, 598
Shepherd, C., 377, 383, 405
Shepherd, J., 285
Shepphard, E.S., 329
Shiban, A.P., 17
Shih, S., 587
Shiner, R.L., 125, 127–129, 143
Shirky, C., 468
Shoda, Y., 125–127
Shoesmith, K., 267
Shweder, R.A., 68
Sibley, C.G., 82

Sidiropoulou-Dimakakou, D., 90
Sidler, N., 145
Siegel, P., 647
Silbereisen, R.K., 175, 177–179, 187
Silva, F.F., 733
Sima, R.G., 550
Simms, L., 439
Simon, H., 319
Simon, V., 323
Singal, N., 498, 499, 502, 504, 506
Singaravelu, H., 587, 698
Singh, L., 541, 542
Sinha, D., 68, 73, 97
Sinha, S., 543
Sirgy, M.J., 647
Sirin, S.R., 155
Skorobohacz, C., 649
Small, S., 181
Smart, R., 252
Smeaton, D., 557
Smillie, E., 482
Smith, A., 310
Smith, D., 255
Smith, D.P., 431
Smith, E., 271, 272
Smith, L.B., 130, 176
Smith, P.L., 158
Smither, J.W., 205
Snow, R.E., 613, 614
Snowling, M., 497, 500, 501, 505, 507, 509
Sodanine, S., 597
Solanki, A.B., 111, 114
Solberg, V.S.H., 156, 158, 506
Soleck, G., 154
Solmonson, L.L., 13
Solomon, B., 228
Solomon, M.L., 530
Sonnet, A., 251
Sonuga-Barke, E.J., 504, 506
Sood, N., 498
Soresi, S., 4, 149–166
Soutar, G.N., 587, 655
Souza-Poza, A., 650
Souza-Poza, A.A., 650
Sparkes, A.C., 258, 319, 323
Sparreboom, T., 228
Speake, J., 436
Spector, P.E., 651
Speight, J.D., 727
Speight, S.L., 166
Spencer-Rodgers, J., 592
Speyer, C., 482
Spiro, A. III, 127, 129, 130
Spitze, G., 578
Spitzer, S., 149
Spokane, A.R., 55, 56, 646, 736
Spungin, P., 268
Srinivasa Murthy, R., 513–535
Srivastava, R.S., 543

Staff, J., 174, 187, 188
Stahl, G.K., 572, 579, 581
Staines, G.L., 647, 648
Stamatis, D.H., 675
Stanley, L., 413
Starks, R.D., 530
Staudinger, U.M., 44, 46, 175, 293
Stead, G.B., 16, 17, 23, 30, 31
Steenekamp, S., 482
Steenkamp, J.-B.E.M., 655
Stein, C.H., 151
Steinberg, L., 174, 175
Steindel, C., 295
Stephens, L., 468
Stephenson, E., 241, 247
Stern, N., 310
Stern, R., 295
Sternberg, R.J., 136
Stevens, S., 504
Steward, J.C., 158
Stiglitz, J.E., 311, 359
Stixrud, J., 336
Stocké, V., 342
Stokes, H., 260
Stoney, S., 646
Storck, E., 154
Stören, L.A., 578
Strauss, A.L., 559
Streumer, J., 100, 296
Stricker, G., 676
Stride, C., 403, 471, 650
Strong, E.K., 613–615
Suarez-Orozco, C., 152
Suarez-Orozco, M., 152
Su-Chuan, Y., 649
Sullivan, S.E., 122, 123, 581
Sultana, R.G., 204, 272, 274–278, 287, 317–331, 491, 610, 661, 680, 689, 690
Sunstein, C., 470–472
Sunwolf, J.D., 432, 436, 441, 445
Super, D.E., 20, 31, 33, 58–60, 252, 292, 309, 312, 414, 631, 643, 713
Suresh, V., 295, 378
Sutherland, P., 431
Suutari, V., 578
Swaminathan, M.S., 390
Swann, W.B. Jr., 135, 136
Swanson, J.L., 612
Sweet, R., 273, 274, 278, 281
Sydney, E., 296
Syiem, E., 550
Sze-Yuan, C., 649
Sziarto, K., 329
Szymanski, E.M., 35, 532

T
Tamplinthe, A., 475
Taniguchi, M., 579
Tapscott, D., 468

Tatsuno, R., 698
Taylor, D., 439
Taylor, K.M., 159
te Velde, D.W., 251
Teal, F., 264
Tedder, M., 264
Templer, A.J., 228
Tendulkar, D.G., 115
Teranishi, R.T., 152
Terkel, S., 327
Terzaki, M., 90
Thackrey, J.L., 152
Thapar, R., 92, 93
Thara, R., 520
Tharenou, P., 579
Tharoor, H., 520
Thelen, E., 130, 176
Theokas, C., 176, 178, 179
Thomas, I., 482
Thompson, C.L., 593
Thompson, F., 249
Thompson, N., 455
Thompson, R.A., 153
Thompson, S., 455
Thorndike, R.M., 77
Thörnqvist, C., 556
Tienda, M., 405
Tilgher, A., 92, 93
Tipton, L.C., 158
Tiwari, R., 300, 301
Toffler, A., 229
Tolstoy, L., 109
Tomasello, M., 82, 83
Tomlin, J.H., 39
Tomlinson, J., 87
Toporek, R., 602, 729
Tornikoski, C., 572, 574, 581
Torres, R.M., 229
Torres-Rivera, E., 698
Tractenberg, L., 100, 296
Trannoy, A., 337, 352
Treiman, D.J., 336
Trevino, K., 470
Triandis, H.C., 73, 76, 77, 655
Trierweiler, S.J., 676
Tsukamoto, M., 249
Tung, R.L., 572
Turcotte, M., 645, 655, 674, 732
Turkel, H., 149
Turner, S., 158
Tymon, W.G., 205

U
Udell, J., 652
Uli, J., 647
Unwin, L., 207, 219, 264
Upadhya, C., 85, 226, 228, 295, 300, 626
Urbahn, J., 483
Urzua, S., 336

Usinger, J., 151
Üstün, T.B., 529
Uttal, D.H., 48
Uvaldo, M.C., 733

V
Valach, L., 14, 18, 558
Vallentyne, P., 338
Valles, R., 180
Vallet, L.-A., 344–347
Valsiner, J., 49
van de Vijver, F.J.R., 70
van de Walle, G., 85
van der Heijden, J.A.V., 578
van der Hoeven, R., 227
Van Deursen, P., 285
van Engen, M.L., 578
Van Esbroeck, R., 31, 693, 695, 701, 711, 716
van Holten, A., 483
Van Laar, D.L., 9, 153, 193, 351, 645–656
van Os, J., 514
van Vianen, A.E.M., 21, 30, 31, 150, 157, 159, 162, 328, 413, 415, 418, 425
van Zolingen, S., 100
Vancollins, J., 532
Vandello, J.A., 96
Vargas-Silva, C., 247
Vasavi, A.R., 85, 226, 228, 295, 300, 626
Vassilopoulou, V., 482
Vaupel, J.W., 247
Vegeris, S., 557
Vembu, R., 295
Vera, E.M., 98, 166, 448
Vgenopoulou, D., 482
Vignoli, E., 155, 156
Viguerie, S.P., 247
Viljamaa, H., 285
Villarruel, F.A., 173, 181–183, 197
Vittal, I., 242
Vokey, D., 324, 325
von Bertalanffy, L., 31
von Eye, A., 176, 178–180, 195
Vondracek, F.W., 33–35, 157, 160
Vygotsky, L., 472, 474

W
Wadhwa, V., 574
Wahlsten, D., 130, 179
Walbridge, M.M., 155
Waldinger, R., 578
Walker, D., 454
Walker, J., 577
Walker, K., 261
Walker, M., 320, 330
Walker, R., 405
Wall, T., 650
Wallace, E.W., 187
Walling, S., 325
Walsh, W.B., 15, 16, 23

Walters, S., 481, 482
Walton, R.E., 647
Wane, N., 431
Wang, C., 161
Wang, M., 597
Ward, C., 76
Warr, P., 650
Waters, J., 587
Watson, M., 4, 8, 9, 13–15, 17, 22, 24, 29–39, 135, 145, 331, 555–569, 631–644
Watt, G., 660
Watts, A.G., 1–10, 96, 272–277, 280, 287, 296, 309, 310, 317–319, 328, 371, 399, 406, 417, 467, 481–492, 646, 671, 680
Wayne, N., 550
Weber, M., 84, 89, 145, 309
Webster, D.D., 501
Wegner, L., 256
Wehman, P., 529, 530
Weinberg, R.A., 337
Weinstein, D.E., 151
Weise, B.S., 51
Weller, M., 474
Wendel, M.L., 162
Wen-Liang, C., 649
Wesman, A.G., 614
West, A., 256
West, L., 413–429, 432
West, M., 529
West, P., 482
West, W., 530, 550
Westen, D., 89
Westwood, M.J., 571, 578
Westwood, M.W., 718
Wewiorski, N.J., 514
Whiston, S.C., 152, 158, 159, 163, 644
White, J., 651
White, L., 587
White, M., 661, 671
Whiteman, H., 406
Wierenga, A., 260
Wig, N.N., 520
Wiggins, G., 674
Wiggins, J.S., 122–124
Wihak, C., 550
Wilderom, C.P.M., 61
Wilkenfeld, S.H., 205
Williams, S., 255
Williamson, B., 473
Willis, P., 317
Wilton, N., 216
Winnicott, D., 416, 425
Winslade, J., 416
Winters, A., 262

Wolf, J., 530
Wolf, M., 470, 476
Wolfe, J.B., 162
Wong, C.S., 622
Wong, S.C., 595
Wong, Y., 149
Woods, J.F., 229
Worthington, R.L., 185
Wright, M., 241
Wu, C.C., 153
Wu, T., 471, 477
Wu, X., 351
Wua, Y.L., 544
Wyn, J., 260

X
Xaxa, V., 541
Xue, C., 87
Xydou, V., 482

Y
Yakushko, O., 152, 579
Yang, E., 595
Yang, K.-S., 68, 69, 73–76, 121, 136, 174
Yankelovich, D., 84
Yates, T., 470
Yeo, L.S., 161
Yip, K.-B., 336
Yoon, M., 612
Young, C., 715
Young, I.M., 323
Young, R.A., 14, 18–21, 149, 204, 558
Yuen, M., 13, 17, 30, 31, 38

Z
Zacher, H., 51
Zack, J.S., 482
Zahniser, J.H., 530
Zaidman-Zait, A., 14, 18, 21
Zalapa, J., 260
Zane, C., 151
Zavalloni, M., 342
Zelloth, H., 5, 110, 145, 271–288, 680
Zeman, K., 709
Zhang, N., 17
Zhang, Z., 351
Zhou, D., 597
Ziguras, C., 589, 590
Zikic, J., 578
Zolingen, S., 100, 296
Zong, L., 578
Zuroff, D.C., 124–126
Zvonkovic, A.M., 153
Zytowski, D.G., 632, 636, 638, 639

Subject Index

A

Abilities and aptitudes
  accomplishments, 616
  definition, 613
  determinants, 614
  hierarchical model of ability, 613
  intelligence, 613
  modifiability of traits, 609
  source traits, 123
  stability of, 614
  structure of intellect model, 613
  surface traits, 123
  vocational traits, 610
Advocacy
  career guidance, 568
  demonstrate efficacy, 729
  family initiated, 503
  indigenous peoples, 551
  mentally ill, 534
  social justice, 319
  special educational needs, 503
  women, 568
  youth development, 175
Aspirations
  aspirational levels, 544
  capacity to aspire, 319
  ethnicity, 405
  occupational aspirations, 544, 557, 563, 566
Assessment
  instruments
    Career Decision Self-Efficacy Scale, 159
    Chinese Personality Assessment Inventory (CPAI), 76
    Holland's Self-Directed Search (SDS), 632
    Holland's Vocational Preference Inventory (VPI), 92
    How much confidence do I have in myself?, 163
    Indian Disability Evaluation and Assessment Scale (IDEAS), 526–527
    The International Classification of Functioning, Disability and Health (ICF), 8, 520, 522
    Minnesota Multiphasic Personality Inventory (MMPI), 124
    Multiple Potentials Interest Inventory (MPII), 616
    Multiple Potentials Test-5 (MPT-5), 616–617
    parent interview checklist for children with special needs, 500
    Rorschach Inkblot test, 122
    story telling approach, 39
    strengths and accomplishments questionnaire (SAQ), 616, 622–624
    super's work values inventory-revised (SWVI-R), 9, 632, 639, 640
    thematic apperception test (TAT), 122
    Wiggin's Interpersonal Adjective Scales (IAS), 123
    Work-Related Quality of Life Scale (WRQoL), 6, 645, 648–650
  purpose
    career constructs, 74, 75
    client feedback, 634
    context, 611
    learning and reflection, 632
    meaning making, 640
    political stances, 615
    recursive relationship, 634
    relevance, 233
    theoretical positions, 609–611
    translation and adaptation, 622
    transporting of a measure, 520
    usefulness of psychometric devices, 621–622
    validity and specificity, 69, 77
    what should be assessed, 612
  special groups
    assessment of disability, 522
    culture-bound tests, 550 (*see also* Indigenous peoples)
    functions oriented assessment, 528–529 (*see also* Mental illness)
  techniques
    alternative techniques, 621–624
    methodologically integrated approaches, 609–627
    multicultural contexts, 643
    multi-pronged approach, 616
    non-psychometric, 609
    plurality of practices, 631
    post–pre assessment, 722
    profile approach, 617

G. Arulmani et al. (eds.), *Handbook of Career Development*, International and Cultural Psychology,
DOI 10.1007/978-1-4614-9460-7, © Springer Science+Business Media, LLC 2014

psychometric qualitative-quantitative
      blending, 609
quantitative retrospective standardized
      procedures, 625
story crafting questions, 634, 635
storying career assessment, 632–634
student assessment, 350

C

Career guidance
   challenges and gaps, 372–373
   culturally relevant practices
      culture-infused approach to counseling, 579
      culture-relevant, 668
      differing needs, 298
      ethnicity, 667
      needs of young people, 260, 266, 267
      Rishi valley grassroots action model, 389–392
   descriptions
      definition, 271
      distinguishing features, 137
      terminological pluralism, 276
   environment
      current growth paradigm, 400–401
      environmental protection, 99
      green accounting, 313
      green investments, 249
      green jobs, 250, 374
      green occupations, 230
      mutual responsibility, 312
      stewardship, 312
      sustainability, 5–6, 97
   ethics
      ethical dilemma, 548, 551, 564
      ethical traditions, 325–326
      work ethic, 90, 250
   functions
      access to next steps, 666
      age-specific *versus* all-age, 487
      career advising, 716
      career alternatives, 298
      career development activities, 615
      career exploration skills, 278
      career fair, 19, 267, 372
      career-life planning, 22, 709, 710, 712–714, 716,
         717, 719–724
      career management, 61, 219, 220, 281, 466–467,
         469, 470, 473–475, 575, 579
      career management skills, 100, 218, 277, 279, 281,
         285, 287, 319, 659, 683, 736
      career management strategies, 38, 571
      career orientation, 163, 219, 284, 405
      career pathways, 211, 214, 220, 261, 267, 368,
         592, 600, 601, 603, 617
      career planning, 72, 163, 166, 229, 301, 318, 367,
         403, 488, 507, 545, 546, 571, 588, 595–598,
         602, 642, 651, 664, 667, 668, 703, 710,
         713–714, 719
      career resource center, 724
      career selection, 115

career self-management skills, 272
   counseling, 717
   equalizing educational opportunity, 348–350
      (*see also* Social justice)
   exposure to world of work, 186, 189
   information *versus* guidance, 486
   interest-aptitude blending, 9, 260, 609, 616, 627
   internship placement, 197
   job performance, 69, 205, 220, 581
   job/vocational satisfaction, 51, 55–57, 69, 92, 129,
      165, 264, 302, 405, 581, 639, 647, 648,
      650–652, 655, 684
   preventive career education, 162
   quality of life, 647–648
   self-development, 293
   self-exploration, 231
   societal mainstream options, 287
   types of career services, 414
   types of services, 717
   work adjustment, 52–53
   work decisions, 23
   work experience, 267
   work with communities, 197
impact of
   distance career development, 492
   economic growth, 5, 241–242, 247, 357–359, 363,
      365–367, 369, 393, 398
   models of delivery, 371
models
   after school matters, 188
   applied career transitions program, 677
   career counseling for under-served populations
      (CCUSP), 579
   DOTS model, 309
   green guidance, 309–315
   the high 5 + 1, 714–715
   Integrative Structured Interview Process (ISI),
      634–640
   ISI to Holland's SDS, 636–638
   ISI to super's SWVI-R, 638–640
   Jiva approach to career and livelihood
      planning, 546
   life design approach, 146, 150, 162
   lifelong career guidance, 576, 682, 711, 716
   lifelong career planning, 713–715
   lifelong guidance and counseling, 715–716
   my system of career influences (MSCI), 38
   The Partners Program, 163
paradigm
   lifelong guidance perspective, 272
   pedagogical paradigm, 277
   psychological paradigm, 61, 277, 280, 287
perception
   bias toward general/academic education, 280
   career guidance services, 264
   expectations, 161, 259
   individualistic connotations, 276
   social vice, 276
provision
   absence of formal systems, 659

access to information and guidance, 291
career guidance provision, 221, 272, 284, 285, 287, 491, 660
career services for all, 481 (*see also* Social justice)
marketing, 487–488
targeting and framing, 488
techniques
auto/biographical narrative methods, 413
career biography, 414
career choice passport, 284
career education for children, 163, 164
career management on the net, 466–467
career programming, 188
career stories, 21, 30, 39, 62, 218, 555, 557–559, 634, 635
career storytelling approach, 632
cell-phone helpline, 481–484, 491
face-to-face services, 483, 487, 489
helplines, 371, 481–492
mentors, 178, 186, 188, 189, 195, 301, 403, 465, 581, 582, 595, 599
narrative approach, 413–429
reality-based career exploration, 620
reflexive play, 416
story as counseling technique, 441–448
telephone guidance, 482, 483, 486, 489, 491
test and tell, 36, 145, 636
testing to tasting, 281
web-based information sources, 221
web chat, 482–484, 489, 492
web-logging, 468
web-/text-based guidance, 484, 489
workplace-based career development, 581
Career practitioner
acknowledging and validating career coach, 9
career development practitioners, 30, 568, 572, 674, 690, 692, 693, 700, 730, 737
categories of status, 727
competent career practitioners, 692, 727, 728
Educational and Vocational Guidance Practitioner (EVGP), 9, 225, 695, 696
ethics, 731
Gandhian career counselor, 114
Global Career Development Facilitator, 9, 694, 732
identity, 579
Lifelong Learning Advisers, 486
livelihood counselor, 6, 394
new settings/roles, 173
paraprofessional, 737
part-time counselors, 486, 545
roles, 729, 731
training
accreditation standards, 730
advantages and challenges, 697–698
certificate/certification/credentials, 695, 696
client needs assessment, 679, 693
competencies, 9
critically reflective practice, 453–463
criticism of competency-based approach, 690

entry-level career practitioners, 731
excluding approaches, 692
general professional development, 717–719
inclusive approaches, 691–692
influences on, 728
internationalization of training, 691
Kolb's experiential learning cycle, 454
staff training, 723, 724
standards, 690, 694–695, 698
variation in content and quality, 660
working with communities, 197
Career shift
career reconsideration, 187
career trajectories, 217
career transition, unplanned, 731
globalization, 626
linear sequence, 296
mid-career, 217
multiple career options, 298
multiple career transitions, 253
multiple-trial careers, 252
needs, changes in, 296–297
one right career, 5, 292
over-qualification, 213
progression, 53, 58, 203, 206, 207, 213, 214, 216, 218, 219, 506, 555, 563, 564
re-schooling, 403
reskilling, 203, 206, 214, 217
second career, 5, 291–304
stress and burnout, 300
transition skills, 300, 301
vocational identities, revision, 187, 189
work conditions, changes in, 296
Community
common language, 573, 689
community youth development and PYD, 181–182
definition of determining scope of practice, 691
key features of a community development, 182
nature of service, 689, 692–693
scope of practice, 689
Context
context-resonant, 29–39
contextual perspectives, 23
diverse environmental-societal system, 31, 35, 37, 38
exploration, 155–157, 162
geographic location, 31
heterogeneity of populations, 29
historical and sociocultural individual in context, 33, 416
native cultural contexts, 67, 76
recipient context, 10
rural, 31
urban, 38, 382
Crafts
art and craft, porosity, 401–402
craftspeople, 397–398
employment potential, 398
handicraft, 398
hand made products, 398

Crafts (*cont.*)
  kinds of crafts, 399
  as meaningful work, 402
  as modern career option, 399–400
  modernization of the artisan, 407–408
  need for crafts, 404–405
  theoretical training, 402
  validating traditional knowledge, 402–403
  work codes, 406
Cultural relevance
  cultural gaps, 69
  cultural validity, 4, 67, 70
  indigenization, 13, 17, 68, 73, 121, 145
Culture
  constructs
    acculturation, 75, 85–88, 92, 95–97, 99, 100, 152,
      593, 597, 601, 627
    compensation, 45, 51–52
    cultural learning, 81–82
    cultural products, 51
    definition of, 51
    emulation learning, 82
    enculturation, 85–88, 90, 92–94, 96, 97, 99, 627
    imitative learning, 82
    symbolic representation, 82
  diversity
    combined etic–emic approach, 70
    cultural differentiator, 75
    cultural dissimilarities, 76
    culturally diverse, 70, 77, 197, 402, 549
    cultural relativism, 75, 145
    cultural specificity, 69, 70
    dissonance, 85, 95, 471, 593, 597
    diverse client groups, 17
    diverse communities, 24
    imposed etic, 70, 75, 136
    uniformity myth, 69
    universal laws, 68
  shock, 8, 77, 251, 577, 593
    reverse culture, 593, 598
  tradition
    culture-bound knowledge systems, 68
    traditional knowledge, 98, 400, 402, 403, 406, 407

D
Decent work
  deficits, 184
  livelihood options, 400
  unemployment, 402
  vocational careers, 266
Decision making
  career decision making, 9, 15, 22, 30–32, 34, 57, 114,
    153, 156–159, 204, 205, 212, 217, 226, 231, 248,
    258, 260, 393, 415, 491, 506, 571, 587, 595, 597,
    610–612, 614, 618, 639, 646, 673, 678, 679, 698,
    703, 712, 720
  career indecision, 156, 163
  decidedness, 155–158
  Gandhian, 114, 115
  hybrid models, 258–260, 266
  instrumental rationality, 257–258

locus of control, 30
  pragmatic rationality, 258
  structuralist theories, 258
  volition, will, 22
Definitions and terms
  career, 3, 736
    advisor, 674
    counseling, 414, 736
    development, 16, 736
    development interventions, 736
    development programs, 736–737
    guidance, 16, 276, 414, 736
  career-related terms, 735
  client, 674
  context resonant definitions, 36
  counseling, 276
  counselor, 674
  disability, 520
  etymological meaning, 327
  guidance, 276
  knowledge base, 68
  lack of consensus, 16
  learner, 674
  practitioner, 674
  vocational guidance, 16, 276
  youth, 174
  youth worker, 674
Demographic shift
  aging workforce, 217
  dependency ratios, 246
  fertility rates, 246
  labor force composition, 228 (*see also* Labor market)
  life expectancy, 246
  longer working lives, 247
  retirement age, 247
  shrinking workforce, 246–247
  world population, 246
  young workforce, 247–248
Diagnostic and statistical manual of mental disorders
    (DSM-V), 497, 498
Digital communication
  boundaryless career, 572
  connectivity, 466
  cost, 7
  cultural adaptation, 491
  de-linearisation, 100
  de-synchronisation, 100
  digital literacy, 476
  effectiveness, 481–482
  email, 7, 481, 482, 484
  helplines, 7, 481–492
  inclusion and outreach, 488, 665
  IT infrastructure, 294
  multichannel, 484, 489, 492
  portable devices, 467
  SMS, 7, 482, 484
  social equity, 7, 482–483
  VOIP, 7, 481
Disability
  biopsychosocial model, 520
  Biwako Millennium Framework, 510

career counseling and disability assessment, 527
   (*see also* Assessment, special groups)
Convention on the Rights of Persons with Disabilities
   (CRPD), 520
disability studies, 499
interactionist framework, 520
medical model, 520
physical disability, 481
what is disability, 520
Disadvantage and privilege
affluence, 403
circumstances, 152
disadvantage, 8, 21, 35, 90, 162, 174, 193, 225, 235,
   265, 336, 338, 339, 347, 352, 399, 400, 405, 406,
   482, 488, 497, 504, 507, 509, 510, 543, 555, 556,
   564, 567
disadvantaged youth, 399, 400, 405
educational inequality, 335–352
high SES families, 153
internalized inferiorities, 155
learning performances, 342
lower SES adolescents, 153, 154
lower-SES youth, 154
low socioeconomic status, 151
marginalized communities, 235
minority groups, 16
poverty, 153, 165
privilege, 22, 24, 46, 91, 141, 142, 154, 155, 162, 175,
   185, 190, 193, 235, 264, 274, 319, 321, 325–328,
   339, 344, 351, 461, 502–504, 509, 573, 577, 731
rural adolescent, 31
vulnerable groups, 373

E
Education, career development
choices of subject groups, 291
continuous learning, 252, 300
craft-centered education, 113
education of the hand, 112–113
episodic learning, 214, 215
essential skills, 300
formal-informal qualification, 205, 206, 212, 213,
   215, 563
integral education, 108
learning through life experiences, 207
literary education, 112
mathematics, 364, 365
Nai Talim, 106, 111–114
post-school education, 366–367
science, 367
short-term training, 413
word based education, 112
work and education, 111
work-based learning, 108, 271
Emerging economies
career guidance, 241–245
characteristics, 241
collectivist cultures, 259, 260
cost of labor, 242

definition, 241
domestic markets, 242
employment boom, 242
external factors, 390
labor market, 241–253
new middle class, 247
outsourcing of jobs, 5
per capita incomes, 242, 247
rural–urban migration, 377
young workforce, 247–248
Employability
career guidance, 221
employability skills, 229
generic skills, 229
initial employability assessment protocol, 678
mid career, 203–221
unemployment, 213
vocational skills, 255–268
Employment
influences on
   age, 212, 374
   corporate downsizing, 737
   critical influencers, 72
   disability, 530
   educational attainment, 592
   education and job, 373, 715
   low skill and low cost rationale, 243
   mental illness, 513, 521
   quality of education, 364–365
   race, 264
stability
   at-risk occupations, 299–300
   job security, 228, 727
   precariousness, 151
   precarization, 227–228
   retrenchment, 100
   stable unstable, 5, 213, 217, 727
types
   entrepreneurial skills development, 369
   family based employment, 406
   flexible employment, 251 (*see also* Labor Market)
   low-quality jobs, 251
   low-skilled work, 215–216, 221
   mass employment, 401
   new possibilities, 227–228
   non-standard work, 227
   part-time work, 227, 563
Environment
attitude to
   ashramas, 311
   eco-education, 310
   individualistic thinking, 310
   inuit values, 312
   moral challenge, 310
   sufficient economy, 312
impact of career on
   consumption, 310
   ecological credit, 99
   economy and ecology, 313–314

gross national happiness, 312
impact of career paths
market-oriented thinking, 310
public interest, 310
resource constraints, 249
Equity
access to resources, 415
career services for all, 7
discrimination, 368
disparities, primary and secondary, 343, 344, 346, 347, 350
distributional inequality, 336
equity targets, 366
exploitation, 115, 338
fair equilibrium, 324
income, 358, 359
inequalities, genesis of, 335
inequality, forms and degrees of, 335
meritocracy, 317
social equity, 7, 311, 368, 482–484
social inclusion, 408
wealth, 328
Ethnicity
aspirations, 405
cultural validity, 69, 70
decision making, 258
indigenous psychology, 74
international students, 598
motivational factors, 34
parent–child relationship, 150, 155
prejudice, 77, 319
social class, 154, 258, 598
social justice, 318
value interactions, 150
Ethnocentrism
attraction–selection–attrition cycle, 71
colonial education, 111
cultural distance, 77
cultural encapsulation, 77
cultural imperialism, 87
cultural stereotypes, 77
ethnocentric, 75–78, 87, 544
hegemony, 87
monoculturalism, 71
nationality, 211
Evidence-based practice
career guidance centers
evaluation, 659–670
quality markers, 659–670
career outcomes, 582
career services framework for evaluation, 681
contextual change hypothesis, 181
culture level value types, 655
demonstrating efficacy, 734–737
evidence base, 75, 655, 672–674, 676, 721, 728, 734–735, 737, 738
evidence based interventions, 656
goals and aims, 655, 734–735
measure of guidance impact (MGI), 646

practice-based evidence, 676
prove it works, 671, 672
PYD efficacy of, 181
quality of working life, 645–656
results of career guidance services, 672
success indicators, 582
youth action hypothesis, 181
youth career development programs, efficacy of, 188–189

G
GDP. See Gross Domestic Product (GDP)
Gender
benevolent sexism, 75
disadvantages, 556
expanding women's rights, 107
female labor participation, 556
gender-sensitive interventions, 407
general ambivalent sexism, 75
modernization, 97
occupational role, 61, 93, 556
patriarchal gender roles, 75
pay gap, 556
role attitudes, 556
sexist values, 75
stereotypes/barriers, 185
upliftment of women, 105
village girl, 384–386
women, 8, 16, 56, 58, 75, 184, 205, 264–265, 286, 339, 343, 344, 361, 366, 407, 461, 545, 555, 556, 558, 565, 578, 710, 711
workplace-specific sexism, 75
Globalization
accelerated change, 227
business process outsourcing (BPO), 85, 242, 300
economic growth, 5, 85, 99, 241, 242, 251, 310, 311, 313, 314, 393
economic liberalization, 241
economic trends, 5, 94, 295
global workforce, 8, 84, 85, 572
international trade, 84–85, 404
job creation, 247, 311, 368–370, 373
jobless growth, 100, 310, 314
job mobility, 215, 217
migration of jobs, 100
new international division of labor, 84, 85
Global trends
de-industrialization, 400, 403, 405
Eastward shift, 241
global economic crisis, 184, 252, 469 (see also Globalization)
modernity, first, 75, 150, 329, 402
modernity, second, 75, 150–151, 329, 402
natural phenomena, 94, 542
political changes, 94
recession, 213, 251, 299, 361, 556
sectoral change, 226 (see also Labor market)
silver economy, 247
slow down, 5, 244, 428, 456, 462, 463

urbanization, 89, 111, 121, 195, 244, 249, 542, 551
Gross domestic product (GDP), 6, 85, 241, 338, 357, 358, 361, 364, 589
Gross national income (GNI), 357–360

H
Human development
  adolescence, 4, 45, 46, 51, 55, 57, 61, 63, 123, 128, 129, 133, 134, 150, 175, 176, 291–294, 303, 529, 612–614, 625, 627
  adulthood, 4, 45–51, 53–55, 57, 59–62, 128–130, 132, 134, 151, 173–176, 180, 182, 197, 292–294, 300, 301, 303, 507, 529, 601, 612, 613, 625–627
  bidirectionality, 60, 181
  biocultural co-construction, 45, 51–52, 64
  career maturity, 59, 74, 75, 646
  career readiness, 184, 188, 189, 193, 198
  childhood, 46, 47, 49, 51, 61, 111, 128, 131–134, 149, 150, 161, 174, 175, 198, 294, 364, 368, 405, 406, 416, 419–421, 424, 425, 529
  developmental tasks, 20, 58, 59, 98, 133, 151, 296, 414
  evolving personhood, 184, 187
  life course, 46, 57, 58, 61, 179, 205, 209, 214, 215, 219, 258, 568
  life-role salience, 736
  life trajectories, 180, 198
  middle adulthood, 61, 62, 134, 292–294, 301, 612, 625
  older women, 8, 461
  plasticity, 47, 48, 50, 52, 54, 58, 60, 62–64, 130, 133, 176, 293, 470, 626 (*see also* Personality)
  reciprocal interaction, 3, 100, 296
  retirement, 53, 58, 62, 216, 231, 233, 247, 252, 296, 301, 414, 559, 561, 576
  young adults, 45, 61, 110, 150, 179, 293, 296, 301, 377, 379, 381–384, 498, 505, 529, 573, 616, 620, 665
Human development index (HDI), 6, 311, 358–360

I
IAEVG. *See* International Association for Educational and Vocational Guidance (IAEVG)
Indigenous peoples, 8, 17, 539–552, 698
Industrial revolution, 1, 2, 83, 84, 93, 96
Interest–aptitude relationship, 618–619
Interests
  definition, 16, 74, 612
  determinants, 59, 612
  dispositional, 613, 626, 627
  four-phase model, 626
  impact of economic change and social organization, 8, 90, 609, 626–627
  model of domain learning, 626
  person-object theory, 626
  RIASEC typology, 20
  situational, 59, 613, 626
  stability, 8, 57, 63, 294, 609, 612–614, 619, 621, 625–627
  vocational interests, 8, 55–57, 62, 63, 90, 609, 612, 614, 626–627, 712

vocational preferences, 20, 55, 621
International Association for Educational and Vocational Guidance (IAEVG), 225, 313, 317, 323, 453, 457, 662, 671, 672, 685, 690, 695–696, 698, 705, 711, 728, 730–734
International classification of diseases (ICD-10), 497, 498, 514, 516
International development context, 357–360
Internationalization, 13, 16, 17, 67, 144, 589, 691, 712
Internet
  bogus plausibility, 467
  content growth, 467
  memory
    long-term, 470
    short-term, 470
  net dynamics, 466
  non-expert source, 466
  online, 7, 465–470, 474, 482, 696, 703
  reach, 473, 481
  stages of activity, 465
  talk-back interactivity, 466
  uses of, 7, 358, 467, 470, 473, 477
  virtual mobility, 574
  virtual workspaces, 100, 227
  virtual world, 296, 474

L
Labor market
  career guidance outcomes, 681
  climate change, impact on, 249
  composition, 228
  concept, 226–227
  cost of labor, 242
  economic shifts, 228
  employer–employee relations, 228
  entry, 184, 368
  external shocks, 249, 251
  flexible labor market, 327
  geographical change, 226
  integration of workers, 217
  interconnectedness, 251
  labor market information (LMI), 5, 221, 225, 226, 229–237, 267, 277, 280, 281, 369, 372, 468, 471, 473, 485, 568, 678–680, 692, 694, 719, 724, 731
  mobility, 203, 205
  new sectors, 214, 242, 250, 253
  outsourcing, impact on, 227, 242–244
  polarization, 256
  rural sector, 245
  sector dynamics, 249
  success in, 209, 228–229, 368, 513
  traditional occupations, 227, 244–246, 249, 399, 401, 403, 458
  uncertainty, 251, 252
  unskilled labor, 244
  women's labor market experiences, 555–556
  women's/position, 8, 555
Labor Market Information System (LMIS)
  data types, 229
  information and intelligence, 229, 230
  labour market information hotline, 488

Labor Market Information System (LMIS) (*cont.*)
    LMI in career guidance, 5, 226–237
    locally available sources, 232–233
    occupational information, 372, 694
    presentation, 235
    provision, 233, 235
    research, 232
    self-access, 235
Livelihood
    caste, 382, 400, 403, 407
    counselor, 6, 394
    definition, 379
    economic cycle, 383
    enhancement, 386, 387
    family profession, 382
    Green Revolution, 390
    income, 383
    landless farmers, 390
    versus lifestyle, 379–381
    local communities, 388, 389
    models, 379, 385–387, 389–393, 397, 402, 405
    planning, 6, 9, 249, 386–389, 392–394, 397–408
    right livelihood, 379–381, 394
    rural livelihoods, 386–394
    sustainable livelihoods, 366, 379, 386, 396, 399,
        404, 408
    transition, 383, 403
    tribal communities, 390

M
Mental illness, 7, 8, 513–535, 650
Migration
    career counseling for employment experiences,
        589, 593
    environmental immigrants, expatriates, types gender
        differences, 249, 251
    immigration, 5, 151, 247, 248, 253, 572, 574, 576,
        578, 588–595, 597–599, 602, 603
    indigenous peoples, 8, 539, 541
    internal migration, 244
    international migration, 247
    liminality, 549 (*see also* Indigenous peoples)
    low-skilled migrant workers, 212, 215–216
    migration experiences, 8, 574
    pre-migration stressors, 251
    refugees, 75, 152, 249
    relocation, 8, 226, 539
    repatriate, 8, 571–584
    rural-urban, 6, 264, 377, 394
    stage of migration, 580
    survival, 295, 394, 405
    third culture kids, 571, 574, 581–584
    trailing spouse, 571, 574, 577, 580–584
    upward mobility, 154
Multiculturalism
    cultural group, 71
    cultural informants, 77
    homogeneity, 71
    multicultural career counseling competencies, 550
    multicultural movement, 70–71
    prevailing and countervailing forces, 70–71
    psychological reactance, 71

N
Non Western concepts
    Advaita, 4, 107, 136, 137, 142, 144, 145
    ashrama, 6, 107, 311, 312
    Bhagawad Geeta, 106, 138–141
    Dharma, 99, 100, 107
    distinguishing features, 84, 137, 139, 272
    Dvaita, 107
    Gunas, 139–143
    Jiva, 235, 453, 457, 458, 460, 546, 580, 615, 698
    Karma, 98, 107
    Kiasu, 75, 76
    Mahabharatha, 106
    Moksha, 107, 108
    Nishkama, 99
    personality theory, departure from, 123, 143–144
    Rig Veda, 10
    Samsara, 98
    spiritual goals, 143, 145
    transcendence, 137, 138, 141, 142, 145
    Varna system, 92
    Vishishtadvaita, 107

O
Occupational classification
    caste and varna, 92, 93, 107, 108
    International Standard Classification of
        Occupations, 617
    occupational classification system, 611
    occupational list, 617
Occupations
    occupational prestige, 2, 5, 92, 110, 116, 154
    rural occupations, 2, 245, 393
    traditional occupations, threats to, 400
Opportunity
    education, 6, 258, 335–350, 352, 588, 693, 715,
        717, 730
    equal, 115, 206, 234–235, 336, 338, 343, 416,
        470, 555
    inequality of, 338, 339, 345, 346
    school-career, 153–154
    social distribution of, 336
    socioeconomic background, 153–154, 504
Outcome-focused intervention
    characteristics of, 673
    needs and goals of clients, 674
    outcome measures, 651
    outcome of the 5Cs, 180
    outcomes/impact of career guidance, 275, 281, 318,
        645–646, 671–685
    PYD outcomes of, 175–184, 189–195
    total quality service, 675–676
    youth programs outcomes of, 175, 183–184

P
Parents
    agents of socialization, 152
    autonomous/autonomy, 156–158, 406
    children's career achievements, 150
    father–child relationship, 152
    fathers' professions, 157
    maternal support, 158

parent–child conflict, 152
parents' role, 150–151, 163
parent training programs, 163
rural, 377–394, 547
shared perceptions, 160
special needs, 508–510
Personal agency
career self-management, 205, 272
economic independence, 317, 379, 384
effort, 220
self-reflective evaluation, 204
Personality
Advaita, 4
career assessment, 36, 636
Cognitive-Affective Processing System (CAPS),
126–128
development, 130, 145, 703
dimension of interest, 274
explanatory position, 128, 1125
five-factor model (FFM), 76, 123
Guna, 139–143
Indian position, points of departure, 143–144
multiple frames of reference, 121–145
paradigms, 122
plasticity, 133
realist position, 125
vocational personality, 20, 21, 54–57, 62, 129, 144
Positive development
building blocks, 177, 529, 543
definition, 121, 174, 178
positive developmental trajectory, 175, 177
Protestant Reformation, 1, 2, 83–84, 89, 93, 96
Public policy
for career development, 9, 121, 155, 215, 216, 219,
221, 273, 317, 319, 487, 728–731
career progression, 215, 216, 219, 221
craft, 406
educational policy, 280
evidence base, 673, 680–682
evidence-based policy, 318, 681–684
green guidance, 5, 250, 309–315
indigenous peoples, 540, 541
quality of career guidance, 668
research oriented, 680
social justice, 99, 317, 319
unemployment, 319, 357, 361, 367, 370
vocational training, 214, 216, 219, 220, 266
women, 8
youth development, 173–199

R
Related disciplines
applied psychology, 15
career psychology, 3, 13–24, 631
cross-cultural psychology, 67, 68, 71–73, 76–78,
121, 539
cultural psychology, 68, 77, 78
developmental psychology, 16, 17, 33, 44, 46, 47,
54, 175
economics, 21
indigenous psychology, 68–70, 73–75, 78

sociology, 16, 17, 21, 37, 85, 88, 121, 322, 323, 397,
406, 473, 558
vocational psychology, 4, 15, 16, 23, 33, 67–78, 323,
405, 712
Research, approach to
attraction–selection–attrition cycle, 71
bottom-up, 74, 77, 386
culturally-relative approach, 75
culturally-valid research, 70
dual approach, 70
false consensus effect, 71
grounded theory method, 558, 559
indigenization of psychological research, 68
indigenous psychological research, 74
mixed methods research, 70, 198
multi-agent, multi-method evaluative research
design, 662
randomized controlled trials (RCTs), 676
retrospective career stories, 555
retrospective narratives, 555–569
semi-structured interview framework, 558
top-down, 77
Role models
advocacy, 319, 568, 580
career guidance, 566–567
influence of, 566
international students, 595
learning through work, 205, 206, 208
parents, 546
social influence, 565
in stories, 435
vicarious learning, 442–445
work place, 211, 216, 659, 667, 723
youth development, 186, 189, 191–193, 195, 197

S
Self
agentic construct, 185
attributes, 133
cognitive and social construction, 133
continuity of, 132
extending the boundaries of, 185
hierarchy, 131, 132, 137, 139
I–me distinction, 132, 134
multiplicity, 131, 133–135
mutability, 134, 139–142, 144, 145
renewal, 133
salience, 131, 133, 134
selectiveness, 131–132
self-esteem, 85, 131–132, 134, 161, 178, 179, 187,
190, 196, 218, 252, 297, 327, 329, 509, 514, 521,
530, 543, 646, 650
self-knowledge, 58, 204
social self, 131, 132, 557
Self-efficacy
boys, 158
career self-efficacy, 154, 156, 158
college self-efficacy, 153
decision making, 158
educational self-efficacy, 63
family support, 156

Self-efficacy (*cont.*)
  girls, 158
  outcome expectations, 63, 149, 158, 163
  parental encouragement, 158, 159
  performance accomplishments, 150
  search self-efficacy, 156
  self-efficacy beliefs, 63, 150, 156–160, 162–164, 185
  social cognitive model, 149 (*see also* Theories,
    models and constructs)
  socioeconomic status, 153, 154
  verbal persuasion, 150
  vicarious experience, 150, 443
Skill
  development strategy, 365
  gaps, 255
  literacy, 113, 243, 266
  occupation-specific skills, 187, 189, 195
  re-qualification, 100, 668
  reskilling, 203, 206, 214, 217
  shortages, 361
  skilled work, 108, 206
  substantive skills, 187–188
  transferable skills, 187–188, 190, 206, 211, 216, 243
  upskilling, 203, 206, 214, 217
  work and skill as capital, 109–110
Social class
  class-based stereotypes, 154
  ethnicity, 154, 155
  middle-class, 16–17
  new middle class, 247, 248
  psychological approach, 154
  socioeconomic status and, 4, 153, 263–264
  sociological perspective, 154
  upper class, 349, 350
  worldview model, 154
Social influences
  barriers to career development, 492, 555
  contextual family factors, 153
  expectations, 566
  family, 37, 185, 566–568
  family, modern idea of, 157
  friends, 568
  process family variables, 4, 153, 166
  sibling subsystems, 150
  social experiences, 149
Socialization
  acculturation, 85–87, 94
  determinants of interests, 612
  enculturation, 85–86, 94
  global socialization process, 85
  international students, 600
  need-based socio-psychological model, 557
  parenting, 152
  role allocation, 88
  social justice, 329, 351
  value attributions, 90–92, 94, 96, 97
  vocational training, 558
  youth development, 186

Social justice
  affordable career guidance, 481
  Arab spring, 321, 469
  capabilities approach, 321, 323
  career guidance and social justice, 317, 324, 330
  collective bargaining, 228
  context-bound social justice, 322
  labor market exclusion, 251
  levels of engagement, 319–320
  literacies of lower castes, 113
  neoliberalism, 329, 330
  Occupy Wall Street, 400–401
  personal fulfillment, 313, 328, 713
  politics of responsibilization, 328
  power hierarchies, 92
  private and public goals, 317
  promoting social justice, 323, 335
  self-interest, 321, 322
  stance, 322
  theory of justice, 326, 330
  types of justice, 324
Social media
  career helplines, 482, 489
  international students, 598, 602
  social networking, 468, 481, 482
Social system/organization
  caste system, 92, 93, 105, 111, 544
  centrally planned economies, 212
  collectivism, 22, 69, 89, 94, 99, 260, 654
  collectivistic cultures, 97, 161, 185, 259, 260, 596
    (*see also* Indigenous peoples)
  individualism, 22, 89, 97, 260, 329, 654
  individualism-collectivism continuum, 88, 89, 94
  norms, 2, 75, 85, 87, 90, 181, 248, 516, 592, 597,
    599, 600
  self-exploration, 163, 184–186, 189, 198, 231
  social practices, 61, 68
Socioeconomic status (SES)
  career beliefs, 546
  persistence, 91, 158
  precariousness, 151
  vocational careers, 266
Special groups
  indigenous peoples
    assessment, 668
    career guidance for, 7, 8, 668
    collectivist societies, 89, 90
    continuing evolution of, 543
    definition of, 540–541
    higher education, 543, 545, 548
    indigenous *vs.* nonindigenous, 547
    influence of gender, 546–547
    Meghalaya, 539, 541, 542, 544–549, 551
    occupations, 547–548
    preferred career choices, 545
    rural *vs.* urban, 547
    scheduled tribes (STs), 541, 544
    significant others (parents, community, peers), 546

social cognitive factors, 546, 550
teaching–learning approach, 112, 436, 438, 448,
    492, 533, 596, 720
technology, 544, 546
terminology, 361, 370
work motivations, 161, 544, 551
worldview, 542–543
international students
    careers service for, 468
    ethnicity, 598
    gender role expectations, 592
    institutional responsibilities, 596, 599–600
    push and pull factors, 587
    reentry transition, 592–593, 598, 601, 602
    relevance of international learning experience, 592
    reverse culture shock, 593, 598
    theories and models of practice, 595–597, 603
    value conflicts, 592
mentally ill
    awareness and advocacy, 534, 695
    career counseling, relevance of, 518, 647, 665, 667
    common mental disorders, 517, 518
    culture as a mediating variable, 625–626
    diagnostic category, 514, 522
    drug side effects, 518
    functions oriented assessment, 528–529
    ICF domains, qualifiers, 522–525 (*see also*
        Assessment, techniques)
    identity, 533
    Indian Disability Evaluation and Assessment Scale
        (IDEAS), 526–527
    International Classification of Functioning,
        Disability and Health (ICF), 520, 522
    long term follow up, 534
    rehabilitation models, 529
    stigma, 521
    supported education, 529–534
    supported employment, 529–534
    symptom, 513–519, 521, 523, 531, 532, 534
special educational needs
    accompanying conditions, 497
    areas of difficulty career preparation process, 502,
        506–508
    clinical labels, 497
    Dyslexia, 497–500, 506, 507
    educational systems, 504
    factors affecting career development, 721
    family participation, 508
    instruction time, 497
    interconnectedness perspective, 503
    interests and aptitudes, 506
    late interventions, 506–507
    learning disorders, 497, 499–501, 509
    privilege, 503–504 (*see also* Disadvantage and
        privilege)
    quality of purpose, 499
    self-determination, 482, 503, 507, 510
    social cognitive environment, 497–510

Spirituality
    career theory, 23, 105–108, 460–461
    Eastern perspectives, 122, 136, 137
    Indian spirituality, 107–108
    international students, 596
    practical spirituality, 105

T
Technology
    accelerated change, 227
    automation, 113, 227, 403
    for career guidance, 485
    career progress, 507, 516, 566, 627
    dependence on, 227
    green guidance, 250, 311
    hegemony, 403
    helplines, 7, 485, 490, 492
    indigenous youth, 546
    industrialization, 113, 114, 660
    information technology, 229, 242, 294, 300, 441, 442,
        458, 469, 476, 546, 574, 665, 667, 668
    internet, 7, 371, 459, 467, 469, 473, 477, 481, 489,
        490, 492, 598, 602, 665, 667, 704
    traditional occupations, 227, 295, 406, 668
    youth development, 369
Theories, models and constructs
    career beliefs, 546
    career construction theory, 14, 18, 20–21, 24, 29,
        60–62, 135, 610
    career-life planning model, 22
    career preparation process model, 502
    chaos theory of careers, 14, 19–20, 29, 37
    circumplex, 56, 123
    circumscription and compromise, 309
    cognitive information processing, 610
    compensation, 50–51
    congruence, 56, 57
    consistency, 611
    constructivism, 14, 18, 20, 30, 32–35
    constructivist career theory, 35
    contextual action theory, 14, 18–19, 21
    continuity and discontinuity, 134–136
    cultural accommodation model, 549, 579
    cultural preparation process model, 4, 94–96, 98
    cultural products, 45, 51, 52
    developmental change, 45, 47, 60, 62
    developmental systems theory, 34, 176
    developmental view, 293
    dialogical self theory, 130, 134, 135
    differentiation, 32, 57, 133, 626
    empirical Paradigm, 123–124
    five-factor model (FFM), 76, 123
    gain-loss dynamic, 45, 47, 49, 50, 54, 63, 64
    general system theory, 31
    Holland's theory of vocational personalities,
        54–57, 129
    indigenous models of career development, 67–78
    interpersonal paradigm, 123

Theories (*cont.*)
  life space, 58–60, 549
  life-span theory, 44–52, 60, 64, 176, 309
  logical positivism, 14, 32, 631
  materialism, 154
  models of indigenous psychology, 74–76
  motivational systems theory, 34
  multidimensionality, 48
  multidirectional, 17, 33, 37, 60, 62
  multifunctionality, 48
  multiple potentials framework, 615–618, 621–624
  multivariate paradigm, 123
  ontogenetic, 45, 49
  paradoxical theory, 32
  personality theory
    Block, Caspi and Shiner, 127–129, 143
    Charles H. Cooley, 132
    Gordon W. Allport, 124–125
    Susan Harter, 130, 133–134
    Walter Mischel, 125–127
    William James, 130–132, 134
  person-by-environment models, 69
  person-environment fit theory, 20, 309
  personological paradigm, 123
  planned happenstance, 19, 204, 309, 403, 504, 713, 714
  positioning in time and space, 135
  positive youth development, 174, 175
  psychodynamic perspectives, 416
  quality of work life
    accommodation model, 647, 648
    segmentation model, 647, 648
    transfer model or spillover effect, 647, 648
  relational theory of working, 15, 18, 22–23
  selective adaptation, 45, 49
  selective optimization with compensation (SOC) theory, 49–51
  social cognitive career theory, 62–63, 156
  social cognitive environment, 90, 185, 502, 503, 508–510, 610
  social cognitive theory, 34, 62
  social constructionism, 14, 18, 20, 34
  social constructionist career theory, 22
  sociodynamic approach, 30
  super's life-span, life-space approach, 58–60
  systems theory framework (STF), 14, 21–22, 29, 35–38, 610, 632
  theory of career construction, 60–62
  theory of multiple intelligences, 615
  theory of work adjustment, 52–53
  trait and factor theories, 32
Theory, approach to
  convergence of theory, 16, 21, 31, 34–35
  disciplinary isolation, 16–18
  importance of theory, 135–136
  metatheory, 20, 34
  what is a theory, 13
Tradition and modernity
  craft(s), 401–404
  traditional culture, 75, 97
  traditionality-modernity, 75

Training and qualification
  accessibility of training curricula, 733
  active engagement approach, 733
  additional training, 547
  advanced training, 731
  competencies, 9–10, 729, 730
  complementarity of learning, 219
  ethnicity, 258, 667, 727
  inner logic, 206
  innovative training programs, 728, 732–734
  learning through work, 206, 208
  main challenges, 728
  self-initiated learning, 206
  staffing requirements, 491
  teacher connections, 157

U
Unemployment
  underemployment, 151, 152, 245, 578
  youth, 251–252, 256, 348, 357, 360–364, 373, 374, 399

V
Values
  bread labor, 109
  capital and labor, 109
  charkha, spinning, 110
  dignity of labor, 109
  economic self-reliance, 329
  effort, 110
  environmental work ethic, 250
  manual work, 110
  productive work, 106
  purpose of work, 90
  Sarvodaya, 105
  Satyagraha, 105
  self-dependence, 110
  self reliance, 329
  self-supporting, 112, 114
  Swadeshi, 114
  Swaraj, 114, 115
  truth, 109, 110
  work ethic, 90
  work-related value patterns, 654
Vocational education and training (VET)
  apprenticeship, 261
  arguments for, 273
  benefits, 257, 258, 272
  career-management skills in TVET, 285–286
  cultural differences, 261
  definition, 271
  delivery agents, 280
  dualism, 271
  entrepreneurship, 277, 286
  forced allocation, 278
  gender influence, 2645–265
  image of TVET, 275, 278
  interests and aptitudes for, 260, 265
  labor market demands, 257, 277
  non-kinship based apprenticeships, 406–407 (*see also* Crafts)
  occupational prestige hierarchies, 5, 92

outcomes, 257, 287
parental influence, 262–264
policy implications, 266–267
segmentation, 278
skills, 271, 272, 275, 277–279, 281, 285–286
traditional craft occupations, 277
transition responsibility, 279
TVET and career guidance, 271–288
types of, 256, 271
work-based learning, 271
Vocational guidance, 1, 9, 15, 16, 96, 162, 193, 225, 276,
    298, 313, 317, 324, 453, 662, 671, 690, 694–696,
    701, 705, 711, 712, 728, 730

W

Women's career development
    career theory for women, 555–557
    employment descriptions, 563–564
    intersectionality, 555
    learning across the lifespan, 568
    life roles, 565, 567
    older women, 555
    segregation (horizontal/vertical), 556
    structure of opportunity, 557
    traditionally female employment sectors, 568
    universal themes, 568
    unpaid activities, 560, 563–565
    work-life balance, 560, 563, 565
    workplace dynamics, 563, 564
Work
    career, 87–88, 731
    history of
        agriculture, 82, 83
        artisanal production, 398
        automaticity, 93
        de-industrialization, 400, 405
        delineation of career from work, 2
        division of labor, 85, 93
        domesticate, domestication, 82
        guild(s), 1, 93, 256, 261
        homo faber, 81
        industrialization, 1, 89, 96, 105, 106, 111,
            113, 114
        mass production, 398, 401
        mechanization, 227, 398
        modes of production, 401
        neolithic revolution, 82, 83
        occupational categories, 83
        occupational mobility, 92, 317, 407

pre-agricultural societies, 89
pre-industrial features, 2
specializations, 83, 92
suitability, 1, 5, 88, 99, 369
technological advances, 94
tool(s), 81, 526
work and family roles, 737
holistic development, 111
instrument of service, 110
power, 109, 111
socialization, 85–86
transformations
    changing nature of work, 83
    new work processes, 1, 206
    work environment, 5–6, 54–57, 69, 129, 187, 188,
        197, 253, 295–297, 300–302, 406, 526–529,
        594, 595, 636, 639, 651, 731
Worker
    artisans, 84, 407
    at-risk workers, 299–300
    discouraged workers, 184, 360
    global auction, 220, 221
    global careerists, 571–574, 576–584
    globally mobile workforce, 572
    global professional elite, 227
    international worker, 571, 576, 577, 583
    mid-career workers, 5, 203, 205, 207, 208, 210,
        215–220
    viable employees, 248

Y

Youth development
    alienation, 179
    asset model, 175–176
    career role models, 186
    common good, 180–181
    community services, participation in, 183
    competence, 179, 183
    deficit model, 175–176
    developmental-asset framework, 178
    education, persisting in, 188
    heterogeneity of youth, 198
    initiative, development of, 179–180
    intentional change, 181
    main approaches, 181
    NEET, 184
    negative view of youth, 175
    purpose, 180–181
    social capital, 186